GENERAL PSYCHOLOGY

GENERAL PSYCHOLOGY

Modeling Behavior and Experience

by William N. Dember and James J. Jenkins

13–350843–9

Full citations for illustrations and quotations appear in the Credits, starting on page 764.

Design by John J. Dunleavy

Illustrations by Felix Cooper

Prentice-Hall International, Inc., London
Prentice-Hall of Australia, Pty., Ltd., Sydney
Prentice-Hall of Canada, Ltd., Toronto
Prentice-Hall of India Pvt. Ltd., New Delhi
Prentice-Hall of Japan, Inc., Tokyo

Current printing (last digit)

10   9   8   7   6   5   4   3   2

To David Dember and his grandson, Greg,

and Mrs. Frances Jenkins Cosby

Preface

It is becoming increasingly evident that man's recent technological feats far outstrip his ability to make wise and satisfying use of them, that man's problems are more self-created than they are imposed on him by the hostile forces of nature. In search of help to cope with these problems, we more and more turn to those who presume to know something about man's behavior, in particular to the social and behavioral scientists. And they, in turn, seek solutions in the accumulated knowledge of their disciplines; where that is lacking, they attempt to gather the information that is not yet on hand.

What kind of knowledge does one need in order to tackle the problems of humanity? At times, no more than specific pieces of information. But the history of physical science and technology clearly reveals that knowledge is most powerful, most useful, and most interesting when it is abstracted from particulars, simplified, and organized into those coherent conceptual structures called scientific models or theories. We have only this analogy with physical science to go on; however, it seems a safe bet that what has been true in that domain will also hold for the behavioral and social sciences. What we need are ever better theories of behavior if our attempts at problem-solving are to have more than fleeting effectiveness and are to do more good than harm.

Granted that, where will these powerful theories come from? Quite clearly they will be created by individual human beings who find it exciting to use their intellectual resources in that endeavor. Chances are good that many of tomorrow's psychological theorists will come from the ranks of today's psychology students (in contrast with the past, when typically the innovators came to psychology from backgrounds in other disciplines).

In writing this book, in addition to providing a comprehensive overview of the field for the general student and the potential professional alike, we wanted to have an opportunity to influence the thinking of some of those future theorists, and that of their colleagues-to-be on whose research efforts the theorists' creations will be so closely dependent. Needless to say, we wanted that influence to be a salutary one, and that to us meant several things, most importantly these: (1) that our readers come to understand the centrality of theoretical models; (2) that they appreciate the close tie between theory and empirical data; (3) that they see psychology as an enterprise conducted by usually well-meaning but often fallible people, an enterprise to which the readers are welcome to contribute; (4) that they appreciate the diversity inherent in psychology and be tolerant of different approaches and points of view, including the one which holds that scientific psychology may not provide the solution to mankind's ills; (5) that they learn the language and methods of scientific psychology and a base of knowledge on which to build further, more advanced study. Of course, these guidelines apply, if with different emphases, to the future "consumer" of psychology as well as to the future "producer."

The increasing popularity of the behavioral sciences as a career choice and the increasing assistance they have received from research-supporting agencies have been a mixed blessing. As more and more information is acquired and communicated, it becomes harder for anyone to keep up with the ensuing "publication explosion." This is particularly depressing for writers of textbooks, who feel compelled to be both scholarly and interesting. A book that is too cluttered with references to all the latest and often conflicting work on a given topic is not much fun to read, especially for the beginning student. Selectivity is called for. On the other hand, we are often uncomfortably aware that in being selective we run the risk of being incomplete and perhaps misleading. To counteract the latter, we offer two antidotes: (1) the level-headed instructor in whose course this book is being read and (2) our own unique built-in conscience, in the form of a most unusual student's workbook prepared by Richard Kammann to accompany this text. The workbook, among other virtues, contains Dr. Kammann's wise commentary, satirical observation, and sometimes scathing criticism on each chapter in a "dialogue" between him and our readers. He has made our task easier through that device, and we would like here to acknowledge our gratitude to him. We urge our readers to join in his dialogue.

Many others, of course, have given us considerable assistance at various stages in the preparation of this book. We are especially grateful to Ronald Nelson for his painless and unerring editorial advice, and to his staff members in the Project Planning department of Prentice-Hall, Miss Helen Maertens and John Dunleavy, who helped transform our manuscript into this book. Finally, we would like to thank the several secretaries who worked on the manuscript, especially Mrs. Wilma Schmedding, Mrs. Jean Heckenmueller Blackburn, and Mrs. Barbara Aiduk in Cincinnati and Miss Kathleen Casey in Minneapolis. They have endured a great deal.

Contents

GENERAL PSYCHOLOGY

Introduction

One of the problems with a textbook is that there is no correct place to start. Everything that the authors want to talk about is better discussed after the reader knows everything else. The only satisfactory form for a textbook, then, is probably something like James Joyce's *Finnegans Wake,* a book that begins in the middle of a sentence and ends with the first part of that opening sentence. Presumably the reader is invited to return to the beginning and start again.

With this problem in mind, we have decided to jump ahead and give you at the outset some items that ordinarily would be illustrations later in the book. These examples have been chosen because they are close to your experience, because they are usually interesting to students, or because they are truly dramatic. Then, having given you this teaser, we plan to take you on the long journey through the book, introducing you to scientific psychology, and finishing with a chapter on the use of psychological information and techniques. The last chapter leads again into the material used here in the introduction. We hope that you will take it as an invitation to return to the beginning and traverse the pages once more. The second trip through the subject matter will earn you richer rewards than the first because you will know where you are going and will be able to bring a more knowledgeable and critical attitude to the task.

Here are a dozen instances of situations that involve the material of this book. Some of them are quite general and appeal to knowledge that might be gained in the study of any science. Others are specific to psychology and, generally, these examples cast a psychologist in the leading role. We suspect that you will not have any difficulty telling which are which. By the end of the book you will have a fair knowledge of the answers to most of the questions raised here.

I

Everyone has seen a good deal of excited reporting about the relation between smoking and cancer and between smoking and circulatory diseases. "Authorities" take various positions about what we know concerning the effects of smoking on health. Some authorities say there is no question about proving the causal relationship: Smoking causes these diseases. Other authorities say the case is not proved, that there is no "real" evidence that smoking causes cancer, or heart disease, or anything else.

Surprisingly enough, these authorities do not necessarily disagree about the "facts." They both agree, for example, that the death rate from lung cancer is higher for smokers than for nonsmokers. For one man this is proof of causality. Another man, however, launches an extensive rebuttal. He points out that smokers and nonsmokers are different in a thousand different ways. They live in different places; they work at different occupations; they come from different backgrounds; they eat different foods; and so on for a long list. (Notice that all these are facts too.) He argues that any one of these differences may be *the* important difference that "really" affects the rate of disease and death. Finally, he says that smoking may just be a consequence of the kind of person one is; perhaps nervous people smoke and nervous people have cancer and heart attacks and the like. Smoking may not be the causal agent at all. It is just a result of some other cause that also happens to produce disease.

These men are clearly not debating the facts. They are debating what the facts mean, how they are to be interpreted. Can you really have trouble knowing what a fact means? If you do wonder what a fact means, is there some way or set of ways to find out? What are these techniques and how do they work? Are there always systematic ways for moving from facts to interpretations? Can these methods always be applied? Do they always work?

II

A famous physiologist who had won a Nobel Prize for his studies of digestion in dogs noticed a curious thing in his laboratory. If the attendant who ordinarily fed the dogs came into the room when he was studying a dog's stomach, he observed that the dog began to secrete gastric juices, just as if it had been given some food. The physiologist called this *psychic secretion* and noted that it affected the whole digestive system, starting the flow of saliva in the mouth as well as the secretion of acids in the stomach.

The advice of his friends and colleagues in physiology was to forget the whole mysterious business. He was assured that he had nothing to gain and everything to lose by getting associated with something so unscientific, so insubstantial, and so unphysiological as "psychic secretions." From the point of view of mechanistic physiology, there was every reason to avoid these intangible sources that supposedly produced tangible secretions. The "mind," the "life force," and the emergent spirit had all been swept out of physiology, and they were not to be allowed to sneak back via psychic secretions. His friends thought that his observations were probably in error in some way. And even if there were such secretions, the whole matter would be cleared up when the nervous system was completely explored.

After a good deal of soul-searching, the physiologist made the painful decision to desert the work that had brought him fame and turn to the pursuit of the nature and origins of psychic secretions. He embarked on a career of studies that was to last for 30 years and provide support for theories of learning unformulated at that time. Thus, Ivan Pavlov committed himself to his classic research on the conditioned reflex.

How does a scientist decide what to study? Can he be sure that a field will be productive or nonproductive or that even a particular question can be answered? Where do psychologists get their ideas? How do they know which ones are good?

III

Dr. Celeste McCollough, a psychologist at Oberlin College, was concerned with the unusual adaptations that the visual system is capable of making when a person wears wedge prisms. Wedge prisms are "funny glasses" that make the world look as if it is shifted about five or ten degrees to the side. They also make little rainbows around lights and edges. Dr. McCollough was particularly interested in the fact that *after* wearing such glasses, people told her that they still saw color fringes around vertical lines such as door posts and edges of furniture.

After some experimentation she found that she could produce a similar effect in the laboratory in a few minutes' time. She had students look at black vertical lines on a bright blue background for 10 or 20 seconds then look at black horizontal lines on an orange background for the same length of time, then back to the first display, then the second, and so on. After a few minutes she showed her subjects horizontal and vertical lines on a neutral background. The subjects saw orange tints around the vertical lines and blue tints around the horizontal lines. Curiously, when they tilted their heads 45 degrees to the side, the colors disappeared, but when they put their heads all the way over on the side, the color fringes came back; only now the tints around the vertical lines were blue and the tints around the horizontal lines were orange. When they returned their heads to the upright, the first set of fringes returned. Even more remarkably, the effect lasted for hours!

The psychologist postulated that the eye was far from a passive receiver of spots of light. She hypothesized that "edge detectors" in the eye were interconnected with the color-sensing system, and she guessed that these detectors could be differentially adapted ("washed out") by exposure to one color. The facts have been substantiated by many experimenters and many related phenomena have been described, but the debate about the nature of the visual system is far from settled.

Why should this be a matter of debate? Can't you just look at the physiology of the eye and find out? What do you learn from strange experiments like this? Is it possible to study the machinery of the visual system from the outside, so to speak?

IV

An unusual figure walked into a makeshift bull ring. He was dressed in ordinary clothes instead of the colorful garb of the matador. In his hand he carried a traditional cape but instead of a sword, he had a small box. The bull sighted him and, being properly incensed, charged furiously toward him, head down and horns threatening. When the bull was in midcharge, the man pressed a button on the box, triggering an electrical signal that was transmitted by radio waves to a small apparatus affixed to the bull's skull. This apparatus, in turn, sent a tiny electrical signal to an electrode implanted deep in the bull's brain. The bull broke his stride, stopped, raised his head, and looked about. The man pressed another button and the bull turned and walked slowly away.

In a laboratory at a large midwestern university, a physiological psychologist demonstrated a device that controlled the behavior of an opossum. The opossum had 12 electrodes mounted in its brain. Each could deliver a slight amount of electricity to a specific point in the brain stem as the experimenter pressed his controls. On one signal the animal attacked a rat that up to now had been playing unnoticed in the cage. Impulses in another location led the opossum to shake and crunch the rat in its formidable jaws. At another signal the opossum became "curious" and started looking out the glass of its box and peering around corners. Still another signal and the opossum began courtship behavior toward a stuffed toy that was lying in the cage.

How are these almost magical feats possible? Dr. J.M.R. Delgado who performed the feat in the bull ring and Dr. W.W. Roberts who has tirelessly explored the structure of the opossum's brain are both studying the architecture of the brain and its relation to behavioral patterns through brain stimulation. How do they do such work? Do their findings have meaning for human beings? Will we at some time soon have a detailed atlas of the brain mapping psychological functions?

V

A powerful new airplane is being built. Although many of the functions are automatic, there are "overseeing" functions that are left to human beings exclusively. At some point, the human pilot or engineer is expected to digest some information and make a decision, especially when some aspect of routine functioning goes awry. After the engineers have decided how much information is to be made available to the human agent and what he will be able to do about it, a team of anthropologists and psychologists comes in to recommend the design of the displays to give the agent the information and the design of the controls so that he can actually make use of them.

This kind of planning, at least with respect to the design of workplaces and tools, is an old notion that goes back at least to the turn of the century. It has been forgotten many times, however. In particular, when a new piece of machinery is first being attempted, it is common to worry about the primary task of getting the machine to work while the designers let the human-control aspect of the task wait till last. Thus, when the first airplanes were built, it was common to make people adapt to the machine as it stood, however awkward that might be. It was only when such awkwardness began to be costly in equipment and lives that the airplane was considered as a workplace as well as a flying machine.

One classic kind of accident was the following: A plane would come in to land at an airport. The wing flaps would be lowered (increasing the "lift" that lets the plane stay airborne at slow speeds) and the landing gear would be lowered. If at this point the pilot decided not to land (judging that he was overshooting the field or seeing traffic on the strip), the normal procedure would be to pull up the gear (thus decreasing drag) and circle around the field for another attempt. The most common mistake was to pull up the flaps instead of the landing gear, thus decreasing the lift (instead of the drag) and usually dropping the plane flat on the strip in a crash landing. Studies showed that the controls for the flaps and the landing gear were identical in shape and "feel," were in about the same place, and were both located down beside the seat out of sight of the pilot! In short, this kind of accident was engineered into the plane even though the accident was classified as "pilot error."

A host of other examples of the same nature can be found in virtually every situation that involves a man-machine interaction. Displays and controls are just two aspects of the important considerations of the total working environment of the human being. How bright should a radarscope be? What size and shape should the scanner be? What kinds of figures should be used on a dial for displaying altitude? What is the best arrangement for dials that must be continuously monitored? Which way should the stick move to change a dial reading? Should the room be hot or cold? Should the air be moving or still? Where could you look for the answers to these questions? How could you find out?

VI

At state and county fairs it has become fashionable to have "acting animals" in some of the displays, either for advertising or for entertainment. A few seasons ago an act went around that was developed by a husband-and-wife team of applied animal psychologists, the Keller Brelands. They jokingly called the routine their "packaged pig act."

The performance went this way: There was a stage like a small living room. A sequence began when a pig entered the door of the room. He moved rapidly and purposefully about, first turning on the radio and then picking up the items of clothing that had been left lying about and putting them into a hamper. He even ran a vacuum cleaner. When everything was neat and clean, he went over to a feeding machine and unerringly selected the sponsor's brand of pig feed while rejecting the competitor's. Obviously, "Smart pigs prefer. . . ."

In other displays there were pigeons playing ping pong, chickens picking out tunes on a toy piano, or rats riding in elevators driven by other rats pulling strings and turning wheels. In each of these cases, there was no deception. The animals really did the things described. How they were brought to do these things, however, is another matter and one that ought to be well worth our attention.

How do you get an animal who cannot understand your instructions to do these complicated acts? How do you keep him at the task after it has once been learned? Do these demonstrations with animals have any implications for training human beings or are they just tricks of animal trainers? Are there some general principles of training that we can use for all species?

VII

A businessman was preparing to take his family to a new position in Germany where he expected to remain for several years. In getting ready for the trip, he and his wife and their college-age daughter studied German faithfully for six months. Their two younger children (ages 8 and 14) played a little at studying German but, in fact, did not do much with it.

The family moved to Hamburg and became involved with the German community. The businessman had daily contact with other businessmen. His wife tried to get to know people in their neighborhood and at the market.

The children went to German-speaking schools. The results were quite surprising. The businessman found that no one understood his German at all. Most of his business acquaintances spoke English and preferred to talk with him in English rather than struggle with his German. His wife tried hard to use her German and finally gave up and enrolled in a night school where she worked intensively on learning to speak the language acceptably. The college-age daughter had much the same experience though her two years of college German were some help. The 14-year-old was very unhappy and did poorly in school because of the language handicap, so they moved her to an English-speaking school. To everyone's delight, the 8-year-old fitted into the German community smoothly. He rapidly picked up German and, though he seemed not to know many words, he managed to express himself and spoke in a manner that Germans understood. In three months he was the chief interpreter for the family and the only one who was really at home in the new language.

Why should this have happened? Are children more capable of learning than adults? Is language learning different from other learning? Are boys better at language than girls? Why are languages so hard to learn in school when two- and three-year-olds learn their own languages so easily?

VIII

At the end of World War II, a group of scientists and engineers met to consider priorities for research in the face of the large numbers of injured men who would be coming home to try to find places in society. It was agreed to give high priority to a machine that could read to blinded soldiers. The task seemed feasible, the technology appeared to be adequate, and the accomplishment of the goal obviously had great social importance.

A group of engineers made a device that produced different sounds as the "reader" pushed a stylus over the lines of a printed page. The sound for each letter was different from the sound of every other letter. "Reading" seemed to be a simple learning problem from that point on. All that was needed was a training program to build up speed in interpreting the sounds that the device made. The psychologists who came in to help with the training found that the reading was painfully slow and remained slow even after extensive practice. (They also discovered that the idea of a reading machine was an old one. Some people had been practicing since World War I with reading devices invented in England and still had not attained even a minimal tolerable reading speed.) Increasing differentiation of the stimuli did not help. In spite of psychological theory to the contrary, the highly different stimuli were worse than the simple stimuli.

Eventually the research group reached the conclusion that natural speech sounds are processed by the auditory system in some special way and much more rapidly than it can handle any arbitrary set of sounds that the engineers invented. They then set out to find out what speech sounds are like so they could mimic them with their machines. To everyone's surprise, they found that instances of the "same" speech sound in different settings (for example, the *b* in *beep* and the *b* in *boop*) are very different physically even though the ear hears them as identical. After 20 years of research, it is now possible to describe the way many of the speech sounds are made in their various contexts and to say how to mimic them. With a fair-sized computer, it is now possible to have a reading machine that reads in English by rules that let the computer synthesize the needed noises.

What kind of apparatus is there in the ear or the brain that processes language? Why can we hear and identify speech sounds at a rate at which we cannot even discriminate other sounds? What was the matter with the psychologists' theories of perception and learning that led to such failures when arbitrary sounds were used?

IX

Many computer scientists and not a few other scientists spend a lot of time trying to get computers to play games—a quite human-like activity. About 10 years ago, A. L. Samuel built a computer program that played checkers rather well. Samuel tried a variety of ways of modifying the machine and finally developed an efficient program that not only played checkers but also had the unusual and enormous advantage of "self-improvement;" that is, it learned from its own mistakes. This is another way of saying that it altered its program in significant ways when it did poorly.

After a "training period" in which the computer played against run-of-the-mill human players and against championship games taken from books about checkers, the computer (or, more exactly, the computer program) was matched against a live checkers' champion. To the surprise of the popular press, the machine won. Reflecting on the game, the human champion said: "It is very interesting to me to note that the computer had to make several star moves in order to get the win, and that I had several opportunities to draw otherwise. That is why I kept the game going. The machine, therefore, played a perfect ending without one misstep. In the matter of the end game, I have not had such competition from any human being since 1954, when I lost my last game" (from Feigenbaum and Feldman, 1963, p. 104).

This poses some interesting problems—and undoubtedly arouses some fears that computers will take over the Earth. If we ignore the latter possibility, it is clear that computers represent a powerful step forward in the complexity of robots that we can now design and build. Further, they offer opportunities for testing our ideas about how people learn, change, and instruct themselves.

Is it fair to say that computers think? When the computer learns, is it like human learning? Can we learn something about the nature of the human system by studying the systems that make computers operate? If a computer could play a game like a person, would you say that it was a model of a human being? How could you find out if it was a good model?

X

A young man who was finishing high school looked forward to attending the state university. He and his parents felt that it would be worth the financial sacrifice if he made it through to his college degree. They thought that professional school would be even better but did not believe that they could afford it. Besides that, they were not sure he would succeed. He went to the counseling office of his high school and talked to the school psychologist.

His counselor looked at his grades and his class standing in high school. Then she took out the results of his college entrance examinations. Consulting a chart that the school counseling office had prepared, she told him that his chances of achieving a college degree at the state university were about 60 out of 100, and the chances that he would finish his first year with at least a C average were 80 out of 100.

His prospects in professional schools did not look quite that good, she said, and it was unlikely that he would be accepted by the local medical school. She pointed out, however, that his college grades would be the best predictor of success in professional school. She advised him, therefore, to see how he got along in college before he made a final decision about further education. She went on to talk about financial aids that were available, and together they made plans for applications to several colleges and several aid programs.

Did the counselor just "make up" these predictions? How could she tell what his chances were in college if he had never tried college work? What do college tests tell anyway? Are they really measures of intelligence or just ways to cut some people out of college? Can you really tell what a person is able to do or what he ought to do?

XI

A businessman told a clinical psychologist that he was worried about his uncle. He went on to say that his uncle seemed to be acting strangely and he wondered if he was mentally ill.

When questioned further, he said that his uncle was a moderately successful small farmer who had led a quiet and undistinguished life. Recently, however, he had been talking about taking the family savings and buying a business or converting the entire farm into a resort with a roadhouse and a pizza parlor in the hayloft. He was sure that the young people in the area needed a place to go for entertainment and that tourists would flock in. He was convinced that he would double his money in no time. He had talked to the local banker about a large loan. The week before he had gone into the nearest city and bought five suits, two top coats, and three hats. He had also enquired at the Cadillac agency about getting their most expensive model.

A friend of the family brought an additional complaint over the weekend. He reported that the uncle had behaved in a strange fashion toward his 14-year-old daughter, acting as if he were courting her and actually making a "pass" at her when no one else was around.

Everyone agreed that his general behavior was optimistic, enthusiastic, happy, nervous, and excited. He was convinced that economic affairs were going his way and that his plans were bound to succeed. He had trouble sleeping at night because he had so many good ideas that they kept him awake. Besides, he wanted to be sure that he got them all written down. His family was worried that he would spend all the family's money, and they thought something was wrong with him. After the psychologist had talked with the family members, he advised them to ask their uncle to have a psychiatric examination. If he refused, it seemed wisest to compel him to be examined under the legal procedures of the state.

Because the uncle refused help, he was taken into custody by the county sheriff for an examination. To everyone's relief and surprise, he seemed glad to have the issue settled in this fashion. He confided to his nephew, "I was afraid that there was something wrong with me but I just couldn't go in by myself. Now it is all in someone else's hands." The diagnosis was hypo-mania.

After a hospitalization of several months, he was released on drug therapy. He was instructed to take his pills regularly and return at intervals for further examinations. In addition, his family was asked to watch him for either a recurrence of his expansive, manic ideas or a growing depression. In either case, they were urged to persuade him to see a psychologist or psychiatrist for an evaluation.

Clearly, having someone examined and committed is a serious step. How can you tell he is not just a poor businessman who happens to be optimistic? What are the signs of abnormal behavior? Why do people act in these strange ways? What kinds of help are available? Is it possible to "cure" a person with mental disturbance?

XII

A little girl entered a special clinic room that had been prepared for Dr. Ivar Lovaas, a psychologist doing experimental therapy. She was a pitiful sight. Her face was beaten black and blue. Her right eye was nearly swollen shut. She was crying in a sort of dry scream. Her hands were encased in gloves to keep her from scratching herself, and her arms were restrained at her sides. Normally when her hands were released, she began to hit and tear at her face. Her bruises were self-inflicted. She was a severe example of a rare diagnostic category, an autistic child. She was retarded in the development of language; she did not notice people any more than she noticed pieces of furniture; in sum, she was shut off from the world and dramatically self-destructive.

The psychologist directed that her hands be released. Almost at once she slapped herself in the face, hard and apparently painfully. At the psychologist's signal, the floor was suddenly electrically charged, giving the little girl a severe electric shock of several thousand volts. The girl gasped and screamed. A few moments later, she hit herself again. Instantly she was shocked again. After those two dramatic "punishments" the little girl never hit herself again.

The treatment is wildly unorthodox. The little girl is a terrible case. It is a question of whether she will be tied to a bed 24 hours a day or given this radically different treatment. Surprisingly enough, punishing her for punishing herself worked. She stopped her self-destructive behavior. (Her therapy from this point on took a different form.)

How does the psychologist know that this is going to work? Is there any way he can evaluate the worth of this radical therapy? What kind of theory is he working with and how will he go on from here? Can he continue to control the little girl's behavior in such a way that he also solves her other problems?

These are a dozen instances chosen from a list that could be made as long as you like. These are the worthwhile examples, the puzzlers, and the items of general interest that intrigue most of us in and out of psychology. Of course, this book is not supposed to be a juicy set of stories or an entertaining set of case histories. Further, it is not a book that will emphasize the applied, clinical, or counseling portions of psychological research.

This book does present experimental psychology in such a way as to give you an honest view of the field. We do not believe that any useful purpose is served by textbooks that ignore facts or strain interpretations to make everything fit some neat and tidy picture of what psychology should be. Psychology today is *not* all of one piece and it would be a disservice to you to tell you that it is. It is many different things from one topic to the next and from one investigator to the next, even in the same area. It is an exciting field in ferment and revolution with different points of view contesting to be established as the more correct and the more likely to lead to fruitful work. While avoiding the tyranny and distortion of a single point of view, we have also tried to avoid the opposite tactic of reporting everything in sight. What we have tried to do is to capture the major theories and models that are in active contention in as clear a fashion as possible to let you see some of the action and conflict and to bring you to an understanding of the important issues in modern psychology.

We emphasize experimental psychology because we think that the science of psychology rests on experimental bases. We firmly believe that further experimentation provides the best path to more complete understanding of the nature of man. Both authors are experimentalists, and we hope that you will find here some of the excitement and the thrill of experimental work on some of the most important problems that face man as he probes ever more deeply for the understanding of his own experience and his own behavior.

PART ONE

Psychology and the Scientific Approach to Knowledge

CHAPTER ONE   To be fully understood, contemporary psychology must be viewed as part of the larger scientific enterprise. The scientific approach to knowledge has as its goal the creation of abstract models that are meant to capture the essence of observed objects or events. In this chapter we consider the appropriateness of model-making for psychology, the nature of scientific models, their origin, and the ways in which they are evaluated. We briefly discuss the relation between the often-used terms "model" and "theory," as well as the intricate relation between models and theories on the one hand and empirical data on the other. The model-building and -testing character of psychology is a theme that repeatedly recurs throughout the remaining chapters of this book.

Contemporary psychology is committed to the scientific approach to knowledge. Critics may charge that the commitment is misguided on the grounds that the kind of knowledge the psychologist is pursuing will elude the scientific approach and that alternative approaches might prove more fruitful. Be that as it may, any attempt to characterize the goals, methods, and achievements of modern psychology accurately must treat it as a scientific endeavor. Indeed, as part of the larger enterprise of science, psychology cannot be fully understood without some notion of the purpose and nature of science itself. In formulating such a notion, it will be useful first to consider what is common to all approaches to knowledge.

It seems fairly obvious that the search for knowledge derives from a strong and abiding curiosity about some aspect of the searcher's experience. The theologian, who speculates on the nature of God, is motivated by the same kinds of concerns that move the physicist to try to understand the nature of matter. The poet, who in his verses seeks to capture the essence of Man, shares with the psychologist the common goal of comprehending human behavior.

To characterize the "scientific approach" is to specify its differences from other paths to knowledge. In the discussion that follows, those other approaches—art, literature, theology, and so on—will serve as a general comparison group against which to highlight the unique features of science. We will gloss over the considerable differences between, say, theology and art, in order to show how they contrast grossly with their scientific competitor. For want of a more exact term, we will call these nonscientific approaches "humanistic."

The Form of the Goal

The scientist and the humanist may share the impulse toward understanding although their goals may not necessarily resemble each other. To employ a crude analogy, the poet and the scientist may be equally "hungry," but their specific appetites may be highly disparate: One may be delighted with chocolate-covered ants, while the other demands a full-course steak dinner, and indeed would be repelled by the ant-eater's meal.

What specifically can we say about the form of the scientist's goal? What is he trying to accomplish? Ultimately, his aim is to create a "map" of some segment of the world—a world that, he assumes, exists outside his own private, subjective experience. By "map," here, we mean something somewhat different from standard, everyday usage. Familiar maps are drawn so as to preserve the major geometrical features of the geographical area they are meant to represent. For example, suppose someone painted a broad black stripe around the State of Pennsylvania and photographed the entire state from a suitable height; the resulting picture would reveal a black-bordered figure that would fit exactly over the outline of a well-made map of the State of Pennsylvania. That is, the map and the photo would be geometrically congruent. Indeed, if the standard-size map were expanded until it were state-size, or if Pennsylvania were shrunk until it were map-size, the borders of map and state would also be congruent. Thus, maps reproduce certain geometrical features of the world, but in much reduced scale.

Of course, in the process of reduction many details are lost, and the map in that sense is only a crude approximation to the real thing. For this reason, a yachtsman would not try to sail along the coast of California using a road map of the state as a navigational guide. The road map simply does not contain the finely detailed information necessary to a successful sailing venture. The driver of a car, however, does not need to get from his road map the same type or degree of detail that the sailor needs. The task of the automobile driver is simply to follow the road itself, and he consults the map, not to regulate every turn of the steering wheel, but rather to determine which turn to make at an intersection.

A map not only leaves out details, it also fails to preserve complete topographical congruence with the geographical world. For example, a typical map, being two-dimensional, cannot give a three-dimensional representation of hills and valleys. This aspect of the terrain is suggested through the use of symbols—perhaps a cluster of inverted *v*'s. Persons versed in map-reading know how to interpret such conventional symbols; inverted *v*'s do look something like mountain tops, but the symbols need not even remotely resemble the objects symbolized.

Thus, the standard map combines geometrical congruence and symbolic convention. But if symbolic representation is feasible at all, it should be possible to dispense with geometrical congruence. One could construct a "map" of the State of Pennsylvania that is composed entirely of symbolic elements. The average user might not appreciate such a map, but he could in principle learn to read it.

It is a map in this last sense—one whose elements *represent* but do not necessarily *resemble* elements of the real world—that the scientist is trying to construct. It addition, the scientist, like the cartographer, is interested not only in elements but also in the relations among them. Thus, a "map" of Ohio that consists merely of a list of the cities within that state would not be nearly as useful for most purposes as one that contains information about their locations relative to one another. Similarly, the modern mapper of matter, the atomic physicist, wants not only to establish the identity of the elementary particles but also to determine the interrelations among them.

In general, then, the scientist's goal is to learn enough about a selected portion of the real world to be able to make a symbolic map of that world, a goal that the psychologist shares with his fellow-scientists. Moreover, it is in his map-making role that the psychologist is least likely to be understood by the layman and most likely to be derided by the humanist. For the latter especially, to try to capture the essence of man in a set of symbolic elements and relations among these elements—to make a map of man—is to do violence to his very nature. To treat man as though he were mappable—if only in principle—is to thoroughly dehumanize him.

For these critics, the scientific approach to man is crude, blundering, insensitive, and superficial, of necessity dealing only with those aspects of human behavior that are both obvious and trivial. The beauty and mystery of man, the uniqueness of each human being—the important things to wonder about and try to understand—are beyond the fringe of science.

In Defense of the Goal

The humanist's criticism of a scientific psychology seems to have two components, one *pragmatic*, the other *aesthetic*. The pragmatic critics assert that the mapping goal is unrealistic and pretentious, that it cannot be achieved because the infinite complexity of human behavior does not lend itself to the approach that works for the much simpler and more orderly world of the physical sciences. Any psychological map would undoubtedly fall far short of adequate representation of the behavioral world. Such a map, in short, is bound to be so much oversimplified that it cannot work. Those whose criticism we call aesthetic focus on the obvious discrepancy in appearance between map and man. People are so interesting, while abstract symbols and formulas are so dull and lifeless.

How can the psychologist respond to these concerns? The pragmatic criticism calls for a pragmatic answer: The best way to determine whether or not something will work is to try it. There is no *a priori* reason why the scientific approach, with its map-making goal, is doomed to failure. It may not succeed. But to discontinue the attempt on grounds that a scientific psychology is unlikely to work would constitute a gross capitulation to the fear of failure that sometimes tempts us all. In more positive terms, it is the very difficulty of the task and the low probability of its successful completion that motivates many psychologists.

Moreover, psychologists are encouraged in their endeavor by the obvious successes of some of the other scientific disciplines, such as physics, chemistry, astronomy, and biology. These fields, after all, have tackled problems that at the beginning seemed formidable indeed.

Imagine a world suddenly devoid of books, documents, information of any sort, laboratories, instruments, educators, scientists—a world populated by intelligent, but uneducated and culturally primitive human beings. Could such a group dare even to dream of the possibility of sending a rocket (whatever that might be) to the moon (whatever that is), or of understanding the weather, or the tides, or what glass is, or why grass is green? How could they, and their offspring, hope *ever* to generate what we know now as atomic physics, meteorology, biochemistry, neurophysiology?

Viewed in the light of the intellectual miracle of modern science, the hope of a science of psychology does not seem irrational, even granting the vastly greater complexity of man's mind than that of the physical world. However, it would be naive to expect this goal to be achieved, to any satisfactory degree, in a short time through a few dramatic breakthroughs. Considering that the first formal psychological laboratory was founded as recently as 1879 (by Wilhelm Wundt in Leipzig, Germany), the accomplishments of scientific psychology are quite impressive.

In summary, the argument against the pragmatic criticism is threefold. First, in deciding whether, and to what extent, a science of psychology is possible, let those make the attempt who want to do so. Furthermore, the goal may not be nearly so unrealistic as it appears. Finally, even in the relatively few years of its formal existence as a scientific discipline, psychology has already made progress toward its goal of mapping the world of behavior.

The aesthetic criticism challenges the treatment of man as an object of scientific investigation because the method is irrelevant to, and perhaps destructive of, man's special, distinctive properties. A graph, it might be argued, cannot capture the qualities of human thought and feeling. These

Figure 1.1 Wilhelm Wundt. (The Bettmann Archive.)

must be left to the craft of the artist. Is this necessarily so?

Consider some analogies. It does not rob a sunset of its beauty to know how the colors are generated. Knowledge of the physics of sound and of the structure of the ear does not preclude enjoyment of a Beethoven symphony. A poem need not lose its aesthetic value under analysis by a literary critic; on the contrary, analysis may enhance its appeal.

Clearly, understanding and appreciation are not necessarily incompatible. A sunset, a painting, a poem, even a person, all can be both enjoyed and understood. Certainly no one could argue that only one approach to an object is permissible—for example, dealing with a sunset only through the science of physics. Similarly, the attempt to construct a scientific psychology does not require casting out all other approaches to man, nor does the effort to uncover the motives of a person's behavior demand relinquishing the privilege, and at times the duty, of evaluating and judging that behavior. In short, the aesthetic criticism, like the pragmatic one, turns out not to be entirely wrong, but to be beside the point. The critics of the goal of scientific psychology view the issue from too narrow a perspective.

Maps, Models, and Plans

We have used the word "map" extensively in trying to describe the goal of science and, therefore, of scientific psychology. "Map" is only one of the terms used in this context, however, and is probably less familiar than "law," "theory," or "model." In using this word "map" in this unconventional way, we hoped to minimize any special and perhaps distracting connotations that might have accrued to the standard vocabulary of the philosophy of science. It would be useful now to introduce and explore the meanings of one of those terms—*model*. This word popularly calls to mind two kinds of image, a small-scale copy (as of an airplane) and a fashion mannequin. Some of the attributes of each apply to the nature of a scientific model.

A model airplane (or automobile, railroad, building, and so on) is a replica in miniature of the real thing (the *original object*). Depending on the skill and intent of its constructor, a model may incorporate many or few details of the object it represents, just as a map may vary in crudity or refinement of representation. Thus, a model airplane may or may not fly; if it does fly, it may or may not utilize the same method of propulsion as the original, and so on. Complete duplication of parts between model and original would undoubtedly be impressive, though for most purposes is not at all necessary. Frequently, and especially when there is some practical use intended, a model will suffice if it captures the essence of the original, even if this means leaving out features in the original that are irrelevant to the present purpose. For example, to test the aerodynamic properties of a new jet, a wind-tunnel model might need to replicate, in miniature, only the external form and texture of the plane's surface.

To construct a model, one first decides which attributes of the original to copy and which to ignore. The next step, ordinarily, is to make measurements of the relevant parts of the original and draw up a set of specifications including not only these measurements, scaled down, but also the interrelations among the parts. These data are often transformed into plans, diagrams, and layouts that are designed to be maximally informative. Given good plans, and adequate skills, tools, and materials, the model-builder can then translate the information given in the plans back into a tangible replica—a model—of the original object.

But it should be apparent that the last step—actually building the model—might for many purposes be superfluous, since the tangible model contains no more information about the original object than does the plan. In short, the plan is itself a model. Whether a tangible replica can be built from a plan does not bear on the adequacy of the plan as a representation of the essence of the original object; it bears, rather, on the technical skills of the builder, his ability to follow the plan, the availability of suitable material, and similar matters.

To pursue this last point a bit further, we could start with a tangible model and work from it, through a plan, to the construction of a full-scale object. This sequence is often followed by architects and designers. For example, a new community might be first laid out in model form; once the designer has achieved a pleasing and functional arrangement of miniature houses, schools, playgrounds, roads, and so on, he can then create an abstract plan from the model. The plan, in turn, will form the basis for the construction of the real community.

One further point will reveal the centrality of the plan: A plan can be devised without prior reference to either an original object or a model. Thus, the plan can precede either the original or the copy.

To relate this last point to the nature of the scientific enterprise, recall our earlier assertion that the goal of the scientist is to "map" some selected part of the real world. But *making* the map, or plan, is not crucial to the goal. Rather, the goal requires no more than *finding* a plan that adequately fits the domain of interest. It often is easier to borrow someone else's plan than to construct one. Thus, whereas Isaac Newton created the calculus as a necessary step in modeling the motions of physical bodies, Albert Einstein recognized the appropriateness of an already developed "tensor algebra" for expressing his general theory of relativity.

Adapting existing plans, rather than constructing new ones, is the typical strategy in psychology. For example, the eminent psychological theorist Clark Hull made heavy use of the calculus as a mathematical system for expressing the nature of the learning process. The acquisition of a habit, in Hull's model, takes the form of the graph in Figure 1.2; with the axes of that graph relabeled, it might serve to express the build-up of voltage in a condenser. Some of the more recently formulated schemes for modeling the learning process make use of less conventional mathematical systems (see, for example, Bush and Mosteller, 1955; Estes, 1958, 1960).

What we have been calling a "plan" is indeed so central to the scientific enterprise, and the making of tangible models so peripheral, that we do not need to distinguish between plans and models. For convenience we can refer to both as models, as in the phrase "mathematical models."

We can learn more about scientific models by turning our attention now to fashion models. Clearly, these creatures are not replicas, full-scale or miniature, of some "real object." A fashion model serves as a framework, an elaborate "hanger," on which to display clothing, say, a dress. It is the model's function to reveal the qualities of the dress. A model is chosen, from among competing candidates, primarily on the basis of goodness of fit—fit in the sense not only of measurements, but also of more subtle characteristics, such as hair color and posture.

A scientific model serves much the same function and is selected on much the same criterion—that is, the goodness of fit between model and events. Sometimes there are several models which are equally good on that criterion; then a choice might be made on such grounds as "elegance." On the other hand, just as fashion models are at times in short supply, on some occasions there may be no really adequate scientific model available to fit a set of

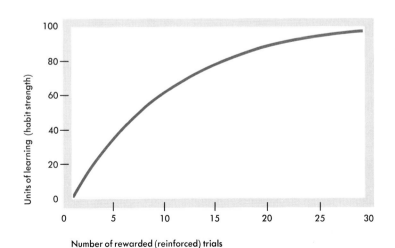

Figure 1.2 Hull's model of the learning process showing how strength of learning grows with increasing number of rewarded training trials. (Modified from Hull, 1943.)

events. Or, just as a certain fashion model might be especially popular, there may be a scientific model which is in vogue. That model might be selected, by virtue of its success elsewhere, to do a job for which it is not perfectly suited. For example, the general type of model employed by Hull to represent the process whereby rats learn to make a simple response, such as pressing a lever, has been applied to behavioral events as complex as the learning of language by human beings. In those instances when model and events do not quite fit, the events may be tailored to fit the model. There is the obvious danger here of overly distorting reality in one's eagerness to use or keep a partly inadequate model.

Figure 1.3 Clark Hull.

But how can an objective scientist change reality? Isn't he stuck with the facts at hand and constrained to deal with them just as they are? Of course he is, but the tailoring we refer to is not a matter simply of denying facts. By judiciously ignoring certain kinds of data—data that we might ultimately like to see incorporated into the general theoretical framework that the model represents—and by looking only at selected aspects of the remaining facts, we might effect a reasonable fit between reality and model.

What makes such compromise strategies acceptable is that they are plainly temporary. The intent, and hope, is that through continued efforts of this sort—through an unending process of such "successive approximations"— more and more of the data will be incorporated. Indeed, behavior is so vast and complex that anyone who attempted to model it without recourse to a strategy of successive approximations would surely be overwhelmed. Even the grand theorists, such as Freud, who take as their domain the broadest possible range of human behavior, employ this strategy, though perhaps with less patience, greater ambition, freer use of analogy, and bigger "bites" of the behavioral world than their more cautious colleagues.

MODELS OF WHAT?
PHENOTYPE AND GENOTYPE

Scientists can be selective about the data to be fit because of the nature of the original object being represented. Most frequently the object of a scientific model is, unlike that of a model airplane, not itself directly observable. The model is constructed to represent some hypothetical object or process which can be known only indirectly, through its effects on observable events. The genetic model of biology, for example, makes reference to a set of hypothetical entities called "genes." Gregor Mendel, who devised the initial version of the model (in the 1860s), never saw a gene; what he could see was the characteristics of certain plants and the way in which these characteristics were influenced by breeding. From these observable facts, Mendel drew the inference that inheritance must be controlled by certain agents (which were later called genes) with certain properties (such as dominance and sex-linkage). Subsequent experimentation yielded data that suggested other properties of these hypothetical genes, such as their location on the chromosomes.

Mendelian genetics provides not only an illustration of the hypothetical nature of the original object to which the genetic model relates, but also useful terminology. The observable characteristics of a plant constitute its *phenotype;* the hypothetical genetic determinants of that phenotype constitute its *genotype*. Thus, two plants can share a phenotypic property, such as leaf shape, but have different genetic bases, or genotypes. The genotypic difference between them might show up in their offspring.

For a psychological example of phenotypes and genotypes, consider the following question, which might be an item on a poll of political attitudes: "Are you in favor of the President's proposal to give federal money to pay elementary-school teachers' salaries?" Several people answer "no" to this item. Phenotypically they are identical. All made the same response. But does the identity of their responses imply an identity of attitudes? Is there genotypic identity? Actually, a few quite distinct attitude structures would yield the same negative response. For example, person A might say "no" because he is opposed to any federal expenditure of money on the local level. Person B might say "no" because he is opposed to federal spending on nonessentials so long as the national debt exists at a high level. C does not object on either of the above grounds, but he is afraid that federal support of teachers' salaries will mean federal control of what is taught; he, too, says "no." D is eager to see teachers' salaries increased, and is not unhappy about federal intervention, but he says "no" because the particular proposal in question does not go far enough in the desired direction; D is holding out for more support than the proposal recommends. E really has no opinion on this particular question; he just happens to be a very negative individual.

Surely, then, these five persons, all of whom said "no" to the question, are very different from each other at one level (genotypic), though the same at another (phenotypic). And clearly, if we knew the genotype, we would be much farther along toward understanding these individuals—and predicting their future behavior—than if we only have phenotypic information. Knowing the genotype, in the present context, means having a genotypic model.

To achieve a genotypic model, of course, requires access to information at the phenotypic level. In the case of political attitudes, it would be useful to have the individuals' answers to a whole set of questions. The genotypic attitude structures could then be drawn from the *patterns* of responses.

In a very general way the same considerations apply to all psychological model-building. The model that is sought is one that will "go beneath the surface," that will explain instances of overt behavior by revealing their "underlying" determinants. Such a model would enable the integration of whole sets of otherwise isolated bits of behavior, just as knowing the geno-typic attitude structure enables understanding and successful prediction of an individual's responses to the several items of a questionnaire, or just as knowing genotypic eye-color of parents enables prediction of the distribution of eye-color of their offspring.

To say this in a somewhat different fashion, we might refer to the distinction between *description* and *explanation*. That person A said "no" to question 1, "no" to 2, "yes" to 3, "no" to 4, and so on may be an adequate description of his behavior ("may be," because for some purposes it might be useful to know how vigorously he responded, how quickly, with what concomitant changes in respiration rate, pulse, and sweating). To explain why he gave that particular pattern of responses, rather than some other, and to predict how he might respond to other questions or generally behave in other situations (as in a voting booth), we need to go beyond description. To do so we attempt to reconstruct a system that would generate the observed response pattern. In short, we seek a model, *not of what has been observed, but of what cannot be directly observed.*

Pursuing this thought a bit further, we can now understand why scientific models are not perfect analogs of, say, model airplanes. Scientific models seek to go beneath the surface, beyond the mere description of phenotypic events, in order to explain the occurrence of those and other events. A scientific model, then, has no specific original object to which it relates in a simple one-to-one fashion. The "object" of a scientific model is, therefore, entirely hypothetical.

TESTING A MODEL

The heart of science is self-evaluation, self-criticism, and a continual striving for perfection. Scientific models are not accepted merely because they seem intuitively right, or because they are aesthetically pleasing, or because they are the creation of some authority. Their acceptance—and even that is expected to be temporary—is contingent upon their sturdiness under the onslaught of repeated empirical tests. Only after a model has survived the "goodness-of-fit test" are its other assets taken into account. How, then, can a psychological model be tested in the absence of an observable object against which to compare it?

The strategy in principle, if not always in practice, is simple. If a model is properly constructed, its elements can be manipulated so as to *derive predictions*, or hypotheses, about observable behavior. The test of the model takes the form of comparing these logical derivations with the relevant real behaviors. So long as major discrepancies do not arise between what is predicted from the model and what is observed, then the model remains acceptable.

To return to the political attitude example, if we construct a genotypic model from a person's responses to a set of questions, we might be able to predict how that individual would respond to a set of new but related questions. If our predictions are indeed logically derived, or deduced, from a valid model, then they will be borne out in the individual's behavior.

A model, then, is tested not directly, but inferentially through comparison between the hypotheses it can generate and relevant behavioral observations. With that basic notion established we can now explore more fully some additional features of model-testing.

When predicted and obtained results are compared, either (1) the prediction is verified—the observed behavior matches the behavior predicted from the model, or (2) the prediction is not verified—the behavior that occurs is different from that predicted from the model. The implications for the validity of the model of each of these outcomes are not as obvious as they seem. If the prediction is verified, can we not assert that the model is proved?

The generally accepted view on this issue is that a model can only be disconfirmed (and then only under certain circumstances, to be discussed below), but never proved. The argument runs as follows: To say that a model is "proved" is to imply that it alone is the correct model, that no other model is true. Such an assertion could be made only if all possible alternative models were known, tested, and found inadequate. By itself, the verification of the predictions from a given model does not rule out the possibility that some other model might be equally successful in predicting that same set of behaviors. Verification does not constitute proof, then, unless it is accompanied by disconfirmation of all possible competing models. In the absence of the latter condition, we must be content with the weaker, but still satisfying conclusion that our model "looks pretty good, so far."

And when the predictions from the model do not match the observed behavior? Is the model disproven? Must it then be rejected? Even in this case, the outcome is not so simple. In order to test a model, we need access to relevant data. As it turns out, there is of necessity a gap between model and data, a gap into which "error" can creep and thereby distort the data. Thus, when data and predictions do not match, either, or both, may be wrong.

Consider where data came from, in particular, data relevant to the testing of a psychological model. The data are sifted, squeezed, filtered, milked, or, to be less metaphorical, derived from observations on the behavior of subjects, who are living organisms. Such sets of observations are called *protocols*. The protocols may exist in the form of sound tapes, photographs, motion-picture records (or some combination of sound and pictures); they may take the form of a verbatim or near-verbatim written record of the subjects' verbalizations, or a written description of the subjects' nonverbal behavior, as prepared by an observer; or instead of being comprehensive, they may be made according to check lists or other short cuts that preselect what gets recorded. An extreme form of short-cutting is the attitude questionnaire, which forces a subject's behavior into two possible categories, "yes" and "no." Similar instances of the use of reduced protocols can be found in all areas of psychological research. For example, a dog's progress in being trained to respond to a signal may be indexed by the number of drops of saliva collected from its salivary gland each time the signal is presented.

In short, protocols may vary considerably in richness of detail as well as in the extent to which they objectively reflect the behavior under observation. The most desirable protocols are those that are the richest and the most objective. And yet neither the original behavior nor the protocol that describes it constitutes usable data for comparison with predictions from a model. Reduction and transformation of the material in a rich protocol are required to yield a manageable amount of relevant information—what we have been calling "data." The reduction and transformation are perhaps analogous to what goes on when a truckload of earth is put through refining processes to produce a small vial of uranium. To attain the usable product, we must get rid of the superfluous material in which it is embedded. No one would claim, of course, that a vial of uranium is identical with a truckload of earth. If our need is for uranium we would not be upset by the observation that the end-product of our refining process is different from its origin. Similarly, behavioral data are identical neither with behavioral protocols nor with behavior itself. The data are derived from protocols through a variety of techniques involving categorizing, coding, counting, measuring, and so on, and through a liberal use of the technique of throwing away huge gobs of superfluous (for the purpose) behavior. To arrive at usable data—typically, *numbers* or their equivalents—we must be willing to be ruthless with our protocols. This refining process undoubtedly leaves slag heaps of discarded behavior that are mountainous compared with the small vials of data that remain.

Consider the following protocols, which take the form of stories written by United States soldiers. The soldiers had been instructed to look at a picture and then make up an "imaginative story" about the picture, indicating such things as who the people in the picture are, what they are feeling, what led up to the situation depicted, what the outcome will be. In the experiment in which they were serving as subjects, each soldier wrote several such stories.

> A woman is on a picnic with her family. She is looking at some birds in the sky and thinking how good it is to get away from the city. They will have their picnic and then go back to their house.

> The girl is watching some airplanes. She is afraid they are going to drop bombs on the city. She runs for the shelter. The planes drop their bombs and a lot of people are killed, but the girl is not hurt.

The soldiers were participating in the first maneuver in which military personnel were brought up close (within 1000 yards) to an atomic explosion. One such group (an *experimental* group) composed their stories immediately after the shock wave had passed, standing outside their trenches, writing in little booklets propped on their gun stocks. One of the protocols reproduced above is typical of those written under such circumstances. The other is like those written by soldiers who were members of a group (a *control* group) far removed from the scene of the atomic explosion. The point of the experiment—which was part of a much larger study of soldiers' reactions to an atomic explosion—was to see if the intense fear which would be expected to occur in the experimental subjects could be picked up by the story-writing technique, fear, incidentally, which the soldiers denied experiencing on direct questioning.

How do you "pick up" evidence of intense fear in a story? Without going into all the fine details of procedure, and their rationale, we might simply note that psychologists specifically trained for the task (such people are usually referred to in the technical jargon of psychology as "judges") read each protocol and decided which, if any, of several categories of response were present in each. The categories, listed in Table 1.1 on p. 28, were selected for use in the scoring system primarily because they had worked in previous research of a similar nature (see Atkinson, 1958). To prevent biased decisions, the judges were kept ignorant of which group, experimental or control, a given story belonged to.

Each story was read by one of the judges, who was thoroughly familiar with the meaning of the various rating categories; the appearance of a phrase or sentence fitting any of the categories was noted. Then the number of categories represented in a given story was determined; when this procedure had been followed for each of the stories written by a particular soldier, the numbers assigned to each story were added, yielding a total "fear score" for that soldier.

The greater fear expected for the experimental group would be revealed by higher "fear scores" obtained by the members of that group than those obtained by the control subjects. The data whereby that expectation, or *hypothesis,* could be tested were the sets of scores associated with the members of the two groups. The soldiers in the experimental condition did indeed have higher fear scores than those in the control condition.

The point to note for our purposes is how imaginative stories were transformed into data by imposing a "scoring system" on them. Further, it should be apparent that the transformation from protocol to fear score leaves a considerable amount of behavior by the wayside—some that at least gets reflected in the score and some that is entirely unrepresented because it is irrelevant to the scoring system. For example, a given protocol may reveal, through the imposition of some other scoring system devised to test a very different hypothesis, a high degree of some other motivation, perhaps a

Threat Imagery	Brief Definition	Example
	An external condition poses a threat to physical welfare.	"The house is on fire and the people are running to escape injury."

If threat imagery is present in the story, then the following categories can be scored.

Need	Someone wants something that would remove threat.	"They want to get out of the burning house."
Instrumental Activity	Someone does something, or thinks of something, that might remove threat.	"She runs into the bomb shelter."
Anticipation of Pain	Statement of fear or anxiety, or thoughts about painful outcome.	"She is worried."
Anticipation of Relief	Statement of thoughts of relief or escape from threat.	"The soldiers think they will be safe."
Negative Affective State	Statement of present experience of pain.	"They suffered painful wounds."
Positive Affective State	Statement of present experience of relief from threat.	"She was happy when she was rescued from the fire."

Table 1.1 Response categories used in the scoring of fear stories. (Modified from Table 1, Walker and Atkinson, 1958.)

strong motive to affiliate with other people. Indeed, that protocol might indicate a great deal about the writer besides his motives, including such attributes as his intelligence, imaginativeness, and educational level. But when the protocol is assigned a fear score, say six points, all of these other potential types of information are lost. What might seem even worse, two very different protocols, written by two very different individuals, might be assigned the same fear score, and all the obvious differences between them relegated to what we have called the slag heap.

In general, any behavior has multiple meanings. Only certain of these meanings are relevant to some given scientific purpose and the other potential meanings must be ignored. Completeness, richness, complexity, all are sacrificed for data to test some hypothesis. And hypothesis-testing, of course, is the only route through which model-testing can proceed.

Having gone through our example of the fear stories in detail, we can turn to two important questions: (1) Why is the refining process indispensable? (2) What does it have to do with the interpretation of a failure to confirm a model-derived hypothesis? The answer to these questions will also clarify why a gap between model and data is inevitable.

First, why can't we simply make the behavioral observations called for by our model and check them against the predictions from the model? Perhaps the major reason for the necessity of the less direct approach—employing refined protocols to yield data—is that most models generate simple, abstract, and frequently mathematical predictions. Even the crudest of models makes predictions in a form that is less rich than the behaviors with which the predictions are to be compared. Thus, our fear model might indicate, grossly, that the experimental group will show more fear in their stories than will the control group. Even so crude a prediction, however, cannot be checked convincingly and objectively by having someone simply read all the stories and then decide whether the predicted results obtained. As observers and processors of behavior, we do not always make such judgments accurately. We cannot see and hear all that occurs, and what we do observe is often distorted by our own needs and expectations. We do not have the memory capacity to store all the information that can temporarily be received, and we cannot, with sufficient precision, make the quantitative judgments that often are required for hypothesis-testing. As the hypotheses under investigation become more and more refined, precise, abstract, and mathematical, the information-processing demands on the observer-judge correspondingly become increased. Thus, props are needed to shore up the shaky foundations of the human observer of behavior. These props take the form of protocols and schemes for transforming those protocols into data (for example, scoring systems), as you have seen in the fear example.

By now it should be apparent that these indispensable props—what we have called the "refining process"—intervene between model and data. One must rely on them in order to get to the data, so that the hypotheses derived from the model can be tested. Yet the data that enter the hypohesis-testing process are in some part a function of the nature of the props. That is, the data are not solely a reflection of behavioral reality; they are a joint product of that reality and the devices (the type of protocol taken, the particular scoring system used, the skill and reliability of the users of the scoring system, and so on) employed to tap that reality.

There is, then, a "gap" between model and data. The gap is bridged with recording devices, scoring systems, and judges, all imposing their own characteristics and their own defects on the data. It is a gap, as we have noted, into which error can easily creep.

When data and prediction do not match, where is the defect? Is the prediction wrong and hence also the model from which it was logically derived? Or is the model right, so that the prediction should have been verified, but was not because of too much error in the methodological bridge between prediction and data? Practicing scientists, of course, need some guidelines for resolving the dilemma that arises when prediction fails. The convention that seems to prevail is this: The more credible the model, the more one suspects the inadequacy of the methodology, when predictions from the model are disconfirmed. The usual next step, then, following disconfirmation, would be to try to improve the method. Indeed, many scientists profitably devote their careers to working on the development of good methodology.

If methodology is considered adequate, then of course failure to confirm an hypothesis reflects on the model. In this case, the scientist would either discard the model or modify it in such a way as to make it compatible with the data. Sometimes a slight adjustment in one term of a model is all that is necessary to restore compatibility between predictions and data. Economy would dictate the strategy of modification. But when data are so deviant that they are devastating to the model, the wisest strategy is to throw out the model and start afresh.

Whatever the case, failure to confirm implies that some action must be taken, either modifying the methodology or revising, adjusting, or perhaps discarding the model. When the appropriate changes have been made, testing of the model continues; once it can handle the old data, its ability to generate further testable hypotheses must be explored.

Model and Theory

We need to introduce formally one additional major concept, that of *theory*. Recall that, in describing the goal of science, we started with "maps" and then switched to "models." The major intent in making the switch was to elaborate on the scientist's goal in ways that were naturally suggested by the word "model." In addition, "model" is one of those jargon words that are firmly entrenched in the present scientific vocabulary.

Similarly, discussion of scientific psychology could hardly proceed without the term "theory" (later in the book we will be talking about Hullian learning theory, psychoanalytic theory, the theory of evolution, dissonance theory). Clearly, we cannot avoid using the word. Moreover, in the process of introducing the term "theory," we might gain a few additional insights into the details of the scientific enterprise.

One note of caution is in order. There are no universally accepted conventions concerning the meanings or applications of the words "model" and "theory." Indeed, "model" and "theory" are often used as synonyms. For example, Clark Hull's venture into understanding the learning process is sometimes referred to as "Hull's learning theory," sometimes as "the Hullian model." If there are different connotations intended in such usage, they are not easy to specify. What follows, then, reflects to a considerable extent the authors' own arbitrary version of what is meant by "scientific theory," and how the terms "theory" and "model" might be related.

One useful distinction between model and theory relates to size or comprehensiveness. "Theory" connotes an attempt to map a large piece of the real world, while "model" suggests a less ambitious, less inclusive endeavor. A further implication of this difference is that a theory tends to be bigger and more complex than a model: The theory contains more concepts, axioms, relations, and definitions coordinating the elements of the theory to those of the real world.

It is standard practice to refer to the totality of some scientific map of the real world as a theory, and to refer to independent segments of the map as models. For example, "psychoanalytic theory" refers to everything of a formal nature that Freud and his collaborators postulated about the human personality. But that effort can be broken down into separate, though interrelated, smaller units. Thus that part of the theory which refers to personality development is labeled the "genetic model"; that part which deals with levels of awareness (conscious, preconscious, unconscious) and their characteristics is called the "topographical model"; that part in which Freud describes the various "institutions" of the mind (id, ego, superego) is called the "structural model."

A similar analysis can be made of other psychological theories. Hullian theory, for example, contains several subparts that, although bound together in the theory, can be examined in isolation. The core of the theory is a model of the learning process, but the theory also contains a motivational model and a rudimentary perceptual model. Of course, in the total theory, these subparts and their constituent elements (habits, drives, stimulus traces) are interlocked. However, for purposes of analysis of the theory and especially for purposes of criticism and revision, the separate models can be examined and handled independently. Thus, certain data may suggest a revision in the motivational model, while bearing no implication about the validity of the other models within the theory. As a crude analogy, you might think of a theory as a radio set, and the several models within it as tubes, condensers, and resistors. In the intact, functioning radio all these component parts work together, but for purposes of trouble-shooting, they can be pulled out and tested in isolation.

There is some reason to feel uneasy about calling the subparts of Freudian or Hullian theory models; if so, it is largely because they lack the formal precision that the term "model" connotes. Ideally, a model might be expressed as a set of mathematical functions, or at least as a set of formal statements that have no more words and sentences than are exactly needed, and no ambiguity in meaning. By contrast, theory connotes a somewhat looser structure, one that is held together by elements less precise and unambiguous than those permitted in a model. In general, then, we expect a model to be more precise, less wordy, less ambiguous, and less fuzzy than a theory.

You might wonder how a theory that is composed of models can be any fuzzier than the models themselves, or at least any fuzzier than the fuzziest of its subparts. The explanation is that "theory" suggests a structure containing pieces in addition to the formal models that it incorporates. At any rate, however it comes about, the ambiguity in a theory is not entirely to be deplored. A certain amount of looseness or vagueness does give flexibility to a theory, thereby increasing the generality of its application and lending it resiliency in the fact of contradictory evidence.

Figure 1.4 Sigmund Freud. (The Bettmann Archive.)

The theorist, of course, continually strives to eliminate ambiguity from his product; if he does not, someone else will. Should he be completely successful in this venture, and should the theory successfully meet every empirical test, then the scientist's goal would be reached. Should the goal be reached (and you can be assured that for many generations it will not be achieved in psychology, if indeed in any of the sciences), the rejoicing will be vigorous, but also short-lived. Remember, scientists are people, and science is their game. When the goal is reached, the game is over.

SOME CRITERIA OF A GOOD THEORY

The major criterion of what constitutes a good theory is the ability to withstand the test of data. This requirement implies not merely that data fail to disconfirm the theory, but also that the theory is *vulnerable* to disconfirmation. A theory so constructed that it cannot lose—because it cannot be adequately tested—is not worthy of attention.

Critics of psychoanalytic theory, for example, often level this charge of invulnerability against it, asserting that the theory has been so stated as to be virtually closed to empirical test. Thus some proponents of the theory argue that it can be meaningfully tested only within the confines of the psychoanalytic treatment session. Attempts to test the theory in the laboratory, with evidence from social anthropology, by reference to literature and art, through any source of data other than that associated with psychoanalytic therapy are, according to this view, inappropriate. This argument might be defensible were it not accompanied by the further assertion that the psychoanalytic treatment session must remain private if it is to remain true to its nature. Invasion of this privacy through taping, photographing, observing, and so on, destroys the nature of the session, and data obtained through such means become as irrelevant as those collected in the laboratory.

You can see that the point of the argument, whether intended as such or not, is that psychoanalytic theory cannot be tested. And you can see why— were this really the case—it would be considered "poor theory," or worse, "no theory at all" by the scientifically oriented critic. Of course, this is not the only view held by those interested in psychoanalysis as a scientific theory. In fact, there have been various attempts, often ingenious, at testing the theory (see Chapter Seventeen).

Vulnerability to empirical test, then, is an essential characteristic of a scientific theory. *Fruitfulness* and *elegance*, the other frequently cited criteria of "goodness," are important, but not crucial.

A fruitful theory generates a multitude of predictions; from a sterile theory, few predictions emerge. The value of fruitfulness seems to lie not so much in the logic of the scientific approach as in the motives of the researcher. Science is a game, a serious one, but a game, nevertheless. A large part of the game lies in the testing of hypotheses. The more hypotheses available for testing, the more likely it is that the game will continue and that all who are qualified can continue to participate in it. Fruitful theories keep scientists occupied.

It often happens that there are fads in scientific endeavor. An old, success-ful theory will be displaced by a novel one, not because the latter is necessarily "better," but because it is new, challenging, intriguing, fun. Recently, for example, biologists' imaginations have been captured by a new model of genetic transmission, the "genetic code," and the journal *Science* is suddenly replete with articles on DNA. Hull's learning theory had a similar effect on American psychologists, and it is only recently that other, competing theories have begun to supplant it.

Such fads are not entirely due to whimsy and irrationality. Once a theory has been mined of its potential predictions, there really is little to be gained, either for scientific progress or the entertainment of the scientist, in persever-ing indefinitely on that theory. It may even be that a theory which has been dropped in this fashion will eventually re-emerge with renewed vigor and perhaps in a more sophisticated form, after attention has turned to, and then away from, some of its competitors.

Elegance is another of the desirable, though not essential, characteristics of a good theory. Like fruitfulness, its precise definition is hard to come by, and for the same reason. That is, the relative elegance of a theory is partly a function of its own structure, and partly a matter of judgment and even of emotional response. In general, the elegant theory is one that does the maximum amount of work (maps the biggest piece of reality) with the minimum of concepts. The elegant theory is, thus, simultaneously *powerful* and *simple*. The exact application of this notion, however, in the evaluation of theories is not so easy, for there is no mechanical way of assessing either a theory's power or the simplicity of its structure.

An elegant theory is very much like an elegant building or an elegant woman. It evokes a response that is a mixture of the intellectual and the emotional. Thus, it would not be unusual to hear a newly presented model or theory referred to as "beautiful" by those who are sufficiently sophisticated in the science to appreciate its elegance.

At the opposite extreme, much of the aversion that some theories elicit results from their lack of elegance. Such theories are overstuffed with concepts, too complicated, too fancy. Psychoanalytic theory frequently elicits this kind of negative reaction, even from those who support its basic postulates. This group has set itself the task of "cleaning up" the theory by eliminating superfluous concepts and tightening its internal logic. However, those who attempt to simplify the theory—any theory—should be on guard against concomitant loss in power. After all, of the two components of elegance—simplicity and power—the latter is primary. A powerful, but overly complex theory is certainly to be preferred to a weak, but simple one.

THEORY AND DATA

Clearly, there is an intimate relation between theory and data. Three points can be made about this relation.

First, we have continually emphasized that the viability of a theory lies in its ability to generate hypotheses that are consistent with obtained data. An untestable theory is no theory at all, and a theory that yields unverified hypotheses needs to be modified or replaced. Quite obviously, then, although the goal of science is good theory, that goal cannot be reached without reference to data.

Second, theories rarely are developed in a dataless vacuum. Although it is conceivable that a theory might be created purely out of the imagination of the theorist, the occurrence is most unlikely. Far more likely is a sequence of events that begins with a set of observations that arouse someone's curiosity. Further observations are made, perhaps with increased refinement, until a set of data is put together that demands explanation. Either an existing theory is found that can account for the data, or a new theory is created for the purpose. At this point, theory-testing begins through the generation of hypotheses from the theory to be checked against new data.

Frequently, the words *deduction* and *induction* are used in reference to the two roles that data play in relation to theory, deduction to the theory-testing role and induction to the role of data in theory-creation. These words are appropriate to use in that context if we remember that the total process of theory development is not nearly so mechanical and impersonal as the words imply. Data do not automatically present themselves for comparison with a theoretical hypothesis. Obtaining the proper data is a creative act on the part of the scientist. Similarly, data do not assemble themselves into a neat package, from which an abstract theory suddenly emerges. The creative scientist is crucial in both the deductive and inductive phases of theory development.

Finally, data themselves cannot exist in a theoryless vacuum. There are no data, in the technical sense, without at least some rudimentary theory. As we have suggested earlier, data are abstracted from protocols; the process of abstraction is dependent on theoretical notions about what is relevant in the protocols and what kinds of transformations, from protocol to data, are permissible. Indeed, without belaboring or even defending the point, theory, often only implicit, enters into the decisions, often implicit, about what protocols are worth collecting in the first place.

In a most general sense, then, theory and data are in continual interaction. The "breakthroughs" in a science occur when new theory emerges from the standard mass of partially formulated theory and incomplete, ambiguous data. How well that new theory fares, after the initial rejoicing in its emergence, depends partly upon its formal properties—its validity, fruitfulness, elegance—and partly on the vigor with which potentially competing theories are pursued. Sometimes a particular theory is so successful and so appealing that it dominates a field and as a result inhibits the collection of the very data that might topple it. In these instances, the science suffers, for a one-theory science is as inimical to scientific development as a one-party political system is to democratic government.

Where does psychology stand in its development as a scientific discipline? As you will see in later chapters, there is a host of data; there are some neat little models and a few larger theoretical structures; and there are decades of empirical and theoretical work to be done, and with it all the concomitant promise of plenty of fun.

SUMMARY

Man's curiosity about the events in the world around him, and in himself, finds expression in the many formal and informal approaches to the acquisition of knowledge that can be identified. For simplicity, we refer to two broad classes of approach to knowledge, the humanistic and the scientific. Contemporary psychology follows the scientific path and can be fully understood only as a part of the larger scientific enterprise.

In essence, the goal of a scientific discipline is to create abstract maps, or *models,* of some segment of the world. The elements of scientific models represent, but need not resemble, the observable events in that segment of the world which is the province of a particular scientific discipline. Psychological models certainly bear little resemblance to the behavior of human beings. For that reason, the appropriateness of a scientific psychology has been questioned, as well as its usefulness. Does a scientific approach to man deprive him of his humanity? No, at least no more so than an understanding of the physics of light destroys the beauty of a rainbow. Can a scientific psychology work? There is good reason to believe that it might, but the only way to find out is to try it.

Like fashion models, scientific models are chosen so as to *fit* the events in question and to provide an *elegant framework* on which to display them. Sometimes models may not quite fit some aspects of the relevant events. In that case, the events may be "tailored" to fit the model, or perhaps the misfit may simply be ignored. That is, given an otherwise useful model, the scientist may choose to omit from consideration data that fail to fit the model. But this is only a temporary strategy, based on the expectation that through a process of successive approximations increasingly better and more comprehensive models will be created.

The scientist can be selective about data, moreover, because of the particular nature of scientific models. These models are not designed to represent observable, or *phenotypic*, events, but rather are meant to reflect those unobservable, *genotypic* processes and relations that are assumed to "lie beneath" surface appearance. That is, a scientific model relates to events that are entirely hypothetical.

The scientific approach is characterized by self-evaluation. Models are rejected if they grossly fail to fit the data. But since model and data cannot be directly compared, a model is evaluated indirectly, by deriving *predictions* from the model and comparing these predictions with empirical data. If the predictions closely match the data, the model is supported—though not "proven," since some other model might work just as well. If the predictions are not verified, then the model is *disconfirmed*, but only if it can be shown that the poor fit is not the result of imperfect methodology, apparatus, measurement techniques, and so on.

Models are often distinguished from *theories*. If there is utility to the distinction, it probably lies in the notion that a theory is a "bigger" structure than a model; indeed a theory may incorporate several models as subparts. These constituent models can then be tested separately, allowing disconfirmation of parts without requiring that the theory be discarded *in toto*.

Good theories have three major characteristics. They are open to the possibility of disconfirmation; that is, they are *vulnerable*. They generate many testable predictions; that is, they are *fruitful* (and thereby help keep the researcher busy). They do the most "work" (of prediction and explanation) with the simplest structure; that is, they are *elegant*.

Theory and data in science are intimately related in at least three ways. First, to be retained a theory must make predictions (or *deductions*) that fit relevant data. Second, theories typically are developed in order to account for, or explain, existing data; the *induction* of theory from data requires considerable creativeness on the part of the scientist and is not a simple, mechanical process (neither is the "deduction" of testable predictions, for that matter). Third, there can be no pure data, independent of some theoretical framework. Data are abstracted from observable events with the aid of theoretically based measuring instruments. Moreover, what events are considered interesting and what data are abstracted from them depend on the scientist's theoretical frame of reference.

SUGGESTED READINGS

Asch, S.E. *Social psychology.* Englewood Cliffs, N.J.: Prentice-Hall, 1952, pp. 9–11.

Barzun, J. *Science: the glorious entertainment.* New York: Harper & Row, 1964.

Broadbent, D.E. A mechanical model for human attention and immediate memory. *Psychological Review,* 1957, 64, 205–215.

Brown, R. Models of attitude change. In *New directions in psychology.* New York: Holt, Rinehart & Winston, 1962, pp. 3–85.

Chapanis, A. Men, machines, and models. *American Psychologist,* 1961, 16, 113–131.

Freud, S. *New introductory lectures on psychoanalysis.* New York: Norton, 1965, pp. 57–80.

Miller, G.A. *Mathematics and psychology.* New York: Wiley, 1964.

Miller, G.A., E. Galanter, and K.N. Pribram. *Plans and the structure of behavior.* New York: Holt, Rinehart & Winston, 1960.

Psychological Research

CHAPTER TWO　　Psychological research has many origins, ranging from attempts to follow up in systematic fashion informal personal observations, hunches, or unexpected findings, to the hypothesis-testing that is sometimes thought of as the only legitimate basis of research. In the design of psychological research, it is especially important to be wary of several sources of ambiguity that bear on the interpretation of the results. A major problem is to specify the exact nature of the variables that are presumed to influence the behavior being investigated. The solution to that problem lies in the use of the proper control conditions against which to contrast the effects of the intended experimental manipulations. Some of the unwanted sources of error that can affect the behavior of research subjects are described in this chapter, not only for their relevance to the design and evaluation of psychological research, but also for what they reveal about the nature of the subjects who participate in such research.

Origins of Research

If model- or theory-building is the goal of scientific psychology, then the indispensable route to that goal is research. Models are constructed to fit the data that are accumulated through research, and models are evaluated largely by the closeness with which the hypotheses they generate are matched by empirical data. Theory and data, as we argued in Chapter One, continually interact in the development of a science.

The data that contribute to the growth of a scientific discipline are obtained in various ways, depending both on the subject matter of the science and on its stage of development. For example, the data of astronomy come from observations of the heavenly bodies. Good astronomical data of 2000 years ago seem crude today. Current findings, dependent on advanced technology and advanced theory, were not possible 2000 years ago. But astronomy could not have achieved its present sophistication without the primitive data of the early astronomers.

The moral here, which points to tolerance and open-mindedness, is especially relevant to psychology. In their eagerness for psychology to reach the status of the well-developed scientific disciplines, psychologists sometimes forget the value of methods that are appropriate to the early states of a science; in their haste, they reach out prematurely for the sophisticated methodology of their older siblings in physics, chemistry, biology, and so on. The simple truth is that psychological research in the present century cannot and need not mimic in every detail the research of the other sciences. This is a "fact of life" tied to the present stage of development of psychology; it is, after all, an infant among the sciences. This condition is also related to the content of psychology, for psychology faces methodological problems that are unique and independent of its level of maturity.

It is the main purpose of this chapter to examine the origins and nature of psychological research, both what it has in common with the other sciences and, especially, what its unique features are. As you will see, many problems in conducting psychological research are simultaneously exasperating (if you are in a hurry for the truth) and fascinating (if you enjoy trying to solve difficult problems). Furthermore, and this should be stressed, some of the impediments to research in psychology have more than nuisance value in that they highlight characteristics of man and animals that are themselves worthy of investigation. We will discuss this last point in the second part of this chapter.

In formal discussions of "the scientific method," the impression is frequently given that every piece of research originates in an hypothesis derived from a theory. The reality is that research, like any other human activity, has a diversity of origins. Sometimes it does proceed from the dictates of a formal theory. More often, especially in a "young" science, research has less formal roots. Some examples may make the variety more vivid. We start with an instance taken from the experience of one of your authors, an example of the category of research origins that might be labeled: *"Gee, that's interesting; let's take a closer look and see if it's real."*

"GEE, THAT'S INTERESTING"

Several years ago, when I was choosing new eyeglass frames, I noticed that each time I tried on an empty frame—that is, one devoid of corrective lenses—my already blurred view of the world seemed to get even more blurry. My near-sightedness, or myopia, as severe as it was, appeared to be increased while I was wearing the empty frames.

Later, I experienced the same thing, and remembering how striking the phenomenon was the first time, I began to wonder seriously why empty glasses frames should decrease my already poor visual acuity. But before I devoted too much time to such speculation, I decided it would be worthwhile to verify my observation. First, I wanted to know whether other myopes responded similarly to empty glasses frames. Second, I wished to obtain *objective* data in preference to the type of impressionistic evidence, or "phenomenal report," that I myself had provided. That is, I wanted to measure acuity instead of simply asking people how the world looked while they were wearing empty frames. Accordingly, I designed and ran some experiments in which visual acuity was measured in myopic people with and without glasses frames. Though the details of the experiment need not concern us here, the results in general confirmed my original observation: Acuity was impaired by empty glasses frames.

Now, with confidence in the original observation, I went on to speculate about how such an effect might be mediated. Having found what seemed a reasonable explanation, involving the concept of "classical conditioning" (to be treated in Chapter Nine), I am now seeking ways of testing that explanation. When I find them, some new experiments will undoubtedly be generated.

The latter phase of the research will be of the more familiar hypothesis-testing variety. The early phase, however, illustrates a type—the careful and objective checking of a personal and informal observation—that frequently precedes and indeed sets the stage for the later variety through which hypotheses are tested and the theory evaluated which led to the hypotheses.

The point, then, is that research is often conducted with the intent simply of establishing the validity of certain observations. Whether this information has any theoretical value depends, of course, on what the scientist can make of it. Indeed, the theoretical and practical significance of the results of research of the "Gee, that's interesting" type is often not appreciated immediately.

Lest the "Gee, that's interesting" origin of research seem entirely atheoretical and fortuitous, you should keep in mind that every observation, scientific or otherwise, takes place in a context that partly determines the occurrence and nature of the observation. The context is provided by the observer's total personality—crudely, his past experience, training, intelligence, interests, motives, expectations, and so on. Thus, apparently accidental scientific discoveries are not fortuitous. Although they are not the result of self-conscious attempts at hypothesis-testing, they are the work of individuals whose intellects and interests predispose them to see significance in events that would ordinarily go unnoticed. And certainly, once the observation has been made, what the observer makes of it and what he does next are heavily influenced by his theoretical inclinations and his scientific habits.

Here we run into a real dilemma. To *make* an observation that is offbeat, unusual, innovative, a scientist must have an "open mind." If his interests, his ideas, and his ways of seeing the world are too conventional or too much bound by prevailing theory, then he runs the risk of missing the events that will lead to theoretical breakthroughs. This is the danger of a scientist's knowing too much about his field and thereby being restricted by prevailing theory. On the other hand, to *make something of* an interesting observation requires a high degree of theoretical sophistication as well as sufficient acquaintance with the history of the field to recognize and communicate the novelty of the contribution. Thus, the innovator must walk a fine line between open-mindedness and scholarship.

HUNCHES

Frequently in the course of listening to or reading a report of research, one is suddenly struck by an idea that seems at once valid and compelling. The idea may involve a reinterpretation of someone else's data, or it may take the form: "I bet that if I tried his procedure with schizophrenic subjects, I would find . . ." Very often such hunches come, not from exposure to research data, but from everyday experiences.

For example, the story is told that the identification of the Zeigarnik effect—the tendency to remember incompleted tasks better than completed ones—had its origin in a hunch that occurred to Madame Bluma Zeigarnik as a result of her experience with a waiter who had an especially impressive memory. Zeigarnik was struck by the waiter's ability to recall accurately the several dozen orders he handled during the course of a meal. In questioning him about this feat, she discovered one factor that seemed especially significant: As soon as he had served an order—for example, as soon as he had handed Madame Zeigarnik her schnitzel—he immediately and completely forgot it. At any one time, then, his memory contained only those orders that had not yet been filled, thus considerably reducing the potential confusion from items that no longer needed to be remembered.

From this experience, Zeigarnik got the hunch that completed and incompleted tasks are differentially retained in memory. She speculated that an incompleted task sets up a "tension system" that facilitates memory for it; but once the task is finished, the tension dissipates, and along with it goes the memory. This type of speculation fit well within the theoretical framework that prevailed in the group of psychologists with whom Zeigarnik worked (a group led by Kurt Lewin, a German-born psychologist who emigrated to the United States in the 1930s and subsequently had considerable impact on both developmental and social psychology) and easily lent itself to experimental tests in the laboratory.

The elements that led to the laboratory research on memory for completed and incompleted tasks are very much like those of the "Gee, that's interesting" category: (1) a compelling personal experience and (2) a desire to convert the experience into a laboratory analog. The difference is that in the glasses-frames example, the reality of the phenomenon—do glasses frames really decrease acuity?—was the main point at issue. In the other case, experimentally establishing the reality of a phenomenon—can people store in memory as much information as the waiter did?—was of secondary importance to the theoretical hunch.

An especially fertile source of theoretical hunches is the "clinical situation," wherein a clinical psychologist or a psychiatrist is exposed intensively to details and patterns of human behavior that are ordinarily not revealed in everyday life. In the course of his diagnostic and therapeutic work, the clinician continually generates hypotheses to help him account for the behavior he is observing. These hypotheses typically are drawn from an already existing theoretical framework, implicit or explicit; but even the best of the personality theories has gaps. The astute clinician, drawing on experience with a variety of patients, sometimes has hunches or "insights" that may serve to fill some of these gaps. These clinical insights, if formalized and properly communicated, can ultimately be translated into scientific language and incorporated into existing theory or form the basis of a new theory. The original, informal hunches may become empirically testable, and hence lead to rigorous scientific research.

The example *par excellence* here, of course, is the work of Sigmund Freud, the creator of psychoanalytic theory. Freud's theorizing originated in hunches, derived largely from clinical encounters with neurotic patients, but also from his constant probing of his own experience. In addition to the contribution of his own unusual intellect and his intense motivation to understand and help his patients, Freud was aided in his theoretical creativeness by the inadequacy of psychiatric or psychological theory on which he could draw for his clinical practice. That is, if he was to do what he had to do—successfully treat his patients—Freud had to create the theory and the techniques necessary to the task.

The richest source of insight and ideas about human personality probably still lies in the clinical situation, broadly defined to include any setting in which a highly trained professional comes into intimate contact with the thoughts, feelings, experiences, and behavior of other human beings, and tries not only to understand these particular human beings, but also has the desire and capacity to transform particulars into generalities.

SERENDIPITY

When a fruitful observation has been the unexpected, unplanned, but felicitous by-product of research done for "other reasons," it is ascribed to serendipity. What distinguishes serendipitous observations from the "Gee, that's interesting" type is that the former emerge from formal research endeavors, frequently of the hypothesis-testing type, whereas the latter occur within the context of the casual, personal experiences of the scientist as informed, but informal spectator of the world outside as well as inside the laboratory. Whether this difference makes a difference is open to question. Thus, if serendipitous observations are more interesting, more fruitful, more frequent, and more widespread than the other type, the implication would be that the scientist should be actively and continually engaged in formal research activity, even if what he is currently doing seems, to him and others, uninteresting or unprofitable. For it may be that only in this way will the truly interesting and important observations occur that are especially crucial in the early development of scientific discipline.

Serendipitous findings are rarely described as such in the professional journals. Rather, the articles tend to follow a rather rigid style that presupposes only one origin for research, hypothesis-testing. To conform to this style, a writer often presents his research results as though they emerged from hypotheses deduced from theory, whereas in reality the hypotheses were developed, after the fact, to account for the results. This is a little game scientists play with one another, and knowing this, the sophisticated reader of journal articles approaches them with a skeptical eye. There is danger in such a practice, however, to the extent that the naive reader, and especially the neophyte scientist, believes every word he reads. The danger is that the novice will get a seriously distorted picture of the scientific process, and as a result may become less open to serendipitous experiences.

Fortunately, to counteract this influence, many psychologists, secure in their reputations, have given realistic descriptions of the origins of their own work. These accounts, which reveal a very high frequency of serendipitous observations and subsequent follow-ups, are often to be found in published versions of scientific talks.

An example at this point may be instructive. Consider the discovery by James Olds and Peter Milner of reward centers in the brain. This finding was perhaps the single most exciting contribution to knowledge of psychophysiology in the past several decades. How this important discovery happened to be made is revealed by Olds in a talk at the University of Nebraska in 1955.

> In the fall of 1953, we were looking for more information about the reticular activating system. We used electrodes permanently implanted in the brain of a healthy, behaving rat. We discovered, quite to our surprise, that an electrical stimulus applied to the brain in the region of the anterior commissure has an effect tantamount to primary reward.
>
> Our systematic aim at the time was to stimulate the reticular formation in a maze to find whether such stimulation might increase attention and learning. We were constrained to find first whether the animal might approach or avoid the point of stimulation. Avoidance was considered a distinct possibility, and it had to be studied because if the animal were to avoid places where the electrical stimulus was applied, this would inhibit his maze performance and he would appear to learn slowly. Thus avoidance of the stimulus would obscure the main effects of the experiment. Quite by accident, an electrode was implanted in the region of the anterior commissure.
>
> The result was quite amazing. When the animal was stimulated at a specific place in an open field, he sometimes moved away but he returned and sniffed around that area. More stimulations at that place caused him to spend more of his time there.
>
> Later we found that this same animal could be "pulled" to any spot in the maze by giving a small electrical stimulus *after* each response in the right direction. This was akin to playing the "hot and cold" game with a child.

Each correct response brought electrical pulses which seemed to indicate to the animal that it was on the right track.

Still later, the same animal was placed on an elevated T maze. As there was an initial right turn preference, he was forced to the left and stimulated at the end of the left arm. After three such trials, he proceeded to make 10 consecutive runs to the left for electrical stimulation alone, with decreasing running times. Then the stimulus was stopped on the left, and 6 runs were forced to the right with electrical stimulation in the right arm. After this, the animal made 10 runs to electrical stimulation in the right arm. Up to this point, no food had been used in the maze at all.

Afterwards, the animal was starved for 24 hours. Food was put in both arms of the T maze. The animal was given two forced runs to each arm. He was stimulated in the left arm. After this, he made 10 runs to the left, *stopping at the point of stimulation and never going on to the food.* (Olds, 1955, pp. 83–84.)

It is clear from the passage quoted above, and from the rest of the talk, that in their original experiment, Olds and Milner *intended* to locate their stimulating electrodes in a portion of the rat's brain called the reticular activating system. They had sound theoretical reasons for doing so; but, by a combination of technical ineptitude and very good luck, the electrode placement was inaccurate. Instead of stimulating the reticular activating system, they were stimulating within the limbic system, wherein the reward, or so-called "pleasure," centers happen to lie. Theirs was very much the luck of the farmer who digs a well seeking water and hits an oil field, or more nearly, that of the gold prospector who, misreading a map, digs in the wrong place and finds a vein of silver. This is serendipity at its best.

Such fortune, however, is not a product of luck alone. Neither the oil field nor the silver mine would be found if someone had not taken the trouble to dig. Furthermore, the lucky farmer and treasure hunter at least need the sense to recognize the value of their unexpected discoveries. Similarly, Olds and Milner capitalized on their error in electrode placement both by seeing the potential significance of the behavior they had observed and by following up their initial lucky finding with subsequent systematic work.

Figure 2.1 James Olds. (University of Michigan Information Services.)

The serendipitous sequence, thus, seems to be: work, luck, recognition, work. All steps in the sequence are obviously necessary, though the one that separates the creative scientist from his pedestrian colleagues is clearly the third one. To turn error into discovery requires both the flexibility to see one thing when you are looking for another and to give up one line of investigation when a more promising lead presents itself. This latter asset of the innovator is nicely summarized by B.F. Skinner, in the course of an autobiographical tour of his highly productive scientific career, as "a first principle not formally recognized by scientific methodologists: When you run onto something interesting, drop everything else and study it" (Skinner, 1956).

REPLICATION

When an important empirical finding is reported in the professional physics journals, other experimental physicists rush to their laboratories—at least such is the impression given—to see if they can repeat, or "replicate," the finding. Replication is a corollary of the public nature of scientific research; a "fact" does not enter the archives of scientific information until its replicability is documented. The insistence on replication has two bases: (1) Sometimes a result is a fluke; that is, its determinants are unknown, and not the ones dictated by theory. Such a result has the appearance of the one predicted and seems therefore to confirm some hypothesis, but its appearance is misleading because it occurred for reasons unrelated to the hypothesis. Although the probability is low that a good match will occur by chance between prediction and result, even very unlikely events do occur once in a while, and the scientist, recognizing this, remains on guard against overevaluating the results of a single experiment. (2) The second basis for a concern with replication, especially by investigators working in different laboratories, is that successful replication provides assurance of the reliability and sturdiness of a finding. For a replication attempt to be successful, all the essential conditions of the original experiment must be reproduced; for the conditions to be reproduced, they must be identified and communicated. Ability to identify the crucial conditions of an experiment and to communicate them to other scientists implies a high degree of control over that piece of the world encompassed by the experiment. Replicability, then, is a sign of scientific power.

Given the significance of replication in the scientific process, you might expect that in psychology, as in the other sciences, a desire to replicate the findings of other investigators (as well as one's own findings) would constitute a major origin of psychological research. Unfortunately, although the virtues of replication are recognized in principle, replication research in practice has little prestige. The laurels, and the financial support, go to the innovators. Replication is tacitly, if not openly, left to the "unimaginative," the "pedestrian," the "second-rate" researcher. Reports of replication experiments do find some outlet in the professional journals, but even then they are put "in the back of the bus."

It is especially ironic that replication research should carry such low prestige in psychology, for the field needs it. As you will see later in this chapter, psychological experiments are extremely hard to design properly and even more difficult to carry out clearly and precisely. A whole host of sources of error are available to contaminate the most carefully planned and executed study. And yet, despite their acute awareness of the tenuousness of their research results, many psychologists fail to adopt the obvious safeguard of replication.

Even the replication attempt that fails may be valuable, for it is often a source of insight into the identity of the variables that are really operating in an experimental situation. Thus, a researcher may try conscientiously to repeat someone else's experiment, as reported in a journal article, but fail. An examination of the fine details of the two experiments may reveal a difference in procedure—perhaps something so "trivial" as whether the experimental subjects were male or female, white rats or black rats, first-born or later-born children, or whether the experimenter wore a beard, and so on —that accounts for the discrepant results. Further research can then show whether that difference was responsible; if so, an important variable will have been discovered. In this sense, failure to replicate, if pursued, may generate serendipitous findings. Thus, even the lowly replication study is a potential source of new information. Recognition of this prospect should further enhance the value of the replication attempt.

Figure 2.2 B.F. Skinner. (Compliments of B.F. Skinner, © Boris of Boston.)

HYPOTHESIS-TESTING

We have been stressing the many informal origins of psychological research for two reasons: because informality (in origin, if not in conduct) is, and must be, the rule in the early stages of scientific development, and because we wanted to counteract the myth that hypothesis-testing is the main and most important function of psychological research. In this regard the psychologist David Bakan provides us with an apt simile. He writes:

> What I wish to point out, however, is that by the time the investigatory enterprise has reached the stage of testing hypotheses, most of the important work, if there has been any, has already been done. One is tempted to think that psychologists are often like children playing cowboys. When children play cowboys they emulate them in everything but their main work, which is taking care of cows. The main work of the scientist is thinking and making discoveries of what was not thought of beforehand. Psychologists often attempt to "play scientist" by avoiding the main work. (Bakan, 1965, p. 189.)

Bakan is also trying to counteract a myth, and to do him justice it should be noted that preceding the passage above, he says:

> Again, I must qualify. There is nothing intrinsically wrong with testing hypotheses. It is an important part of the total investigatory enterprise.

Our position is the same as Bakan's. Hypothesis-testing is an important part, but only a part, of the work of the scientist.

Design of Psychological Research: Some Basic Considerations

How do psychologists plan and execute research? That question is what we turn our attention to now, especially to problems that are dictated by the peculiar nature of the subject matter of psychology and related disciplines.

CORRELATIONAL VS. EXPERIMENTAL RESEARCH

At the outset, we should make a distinction between two types of research design: "correlational" and "experimental." We can illustrate the difference between them, and the major implication of this difference, by a familiar example from medicine mentioned in the Introduction—the attempt to establish a causal relation between smoking and diseases such as cancer. Considerable controversy has arisen over the assertion that such a relation has been empirically established. Why should the results of extensive research, carefully done by reputable scientists, be controversial? How can these results be questioned?

Aside from the attitude of those who have a vested interest in casting doubt on the validity of the relation (though even the most cynical manufacturer of cigarettes would scarcely fail to react responsibly to evidence that he could wholeheartedly accept), there is reason to doubt the evidence —or rather the conclusion drawn from the evidence—that *smoking bears a causal relation to cancer*. The basis for doubt lies in the nature of the design of the research from which the evidence was gleaned: The design was correlational, not experimental. And, as you will see, results obtained in studies using correlational designs are subject to an ambiguity of interpretation considerably greater than the normal uncertainty inherent in any research attempt.

The cancer studies in particular and correlational designs in general yield ambiguous results because they do not allow unequivocal assignment of a direction to the relations obtained. Thus, suppose it is established that the incidence of lung cancer is greatest among those people who are heavy smokers, next highest among light smokers, and least among nonsmokers. Can we draw the inference that smoking "causes" cancer? Or, recognizing the philosophical problems inherent in trying to assert any causal relations, can we even claim that smoking *per se* contributes to the occurrence of lung cancer?

Consider these two possible conclusions from the data. (1) Heavy smokers are more likely to contract lung cancer than are light smokers or nonsmokers. (2) Smoking is directly involved in the etiology of lung cancer. Are they equivalent? The first statement is an actuarial one. It simply says that a person identified as a heavy smoker is a more likely candidate for lung cancer than is a person identified as a nonsmoker. The statement attributes no etiological significance to smoking; smoking just provides a way of labeling people that enables us to predict the likelihood of their eventually being labeled as lung cancer patients. The second statement points the finger at smoking as an activity that is likely to contribute to a person's contracting lung cancer.

The difference between these two conclusions may at first seem trivial and obscure. Its significance, however, becomes quite apparent when we make the following interpretation of the first statement: Perhaps people who are susceptible to lung cancer are also, for whatever physiological or psychological reasons, more inclined than others to smoke heavily. The "causal relation" implied in this interpretation is that some factor, X, makes people simultaneously cancer-susceptible and smoking-prone. Rather than contributing to the etiology of cancer, smoking may be simply indicating an underlying condition that will ultimately lead to cancer. Further, the cancer may have occurred even if a person, with factor X, had never had the opportunity to smoke.

Correlational studies are invariably subject to this ambiguity of interpretation. In general, then, if A and B are found to be highly correlated, so that knowledge of the value of A enables one to predict the value of B, the correlation by itself does not permit the attribution of a causal direction to the relation.

How might we get around the ambiguity inherent in correlational designs? How might we redo the cancer-smoking study to yield unequivocal results? The ideal procedure would employ the following design: Several "conditions" are established, and each person (subject) to participate in the experiment is randomly assigned to a condition; each condition is defined in terms of number of cigarettes per day that a subject *must* smoke.

Suppose we set up four conditions, defined as zero, one, two, and four packs per day. The subjects' smoking is regulated entirely by the condition to which they are assigned, and they have no choice in the matter. The remainder of the experiment can then proceed as in the original cancer studies. The subjects' health would be evaluated at appropriate times, and data relative to the incidence of various diseases would be collected. If the hypothesis is correct—that smoking is causally related to cancer—then the incidence of cancer should increase from the zero- through four-pack-per-day conditions. Were the data to come out that way, no one could claim that they did so because people who are cancer-prone also have a greater than normal need to smoke.

The key to the design called experimental is *random* assignment of subjects to conditions. By random assignment we insure against the influence on the results of some extraneous variable that is tied to or correlated with the variable under investigation. By contrast with experimental designs, correlational designs allow subjects, in a sense, to assign themselves to conditions. Thus, in the cancer studies as they have been done, only people who are four-pack-a-day smokers—*by their own "choice"*—get into a four-pack-a-day condition. Whatever the factors are that contribute to a person's being a heavy smoker surely also must make him different from the typical non-smoker in other ways. Hence the ambiguity of interpretation in correlational designs, and hence the virtue of experimental designs. In the latter case, if assignment to conditions is truly random, then prevailing differences among individual subjects cannot *systematically* confound the results. Put another way, the experimenter has under his control all the variables that can influence the results. Whether he can exactly identify these variables is another question, as we will shortly see. Thus, experimental designs do not yield entirely unambiguous results, merely results that are less ambiguous than those associated with correlational designs.

To make a formal definition, (a) In an experimental design subjects are randomly assigned to conditions. (b) In a correlational design subjects enter conditions by virtue of prevailing individual differences.

Given the preferability of experimental designs, why are they not universally employed? The reason is a practical one. It is not always possible to assign subjects randomly to conditions; or, rather, it is easy to assign them to conditions, but not always possible to impose the conditions. Who would agree to smoke four packs of cigarettes a day for "science"? How many heavy smokers would give up smoking entirely if they happened to be assigned to a zero-pack-a-day group? In such studies, for such reasons, the preferred design simply cannot be put into effect, and the researcher must be satisfied with a correlational design and its attendant ambiguity.

Practical impediments of this sort are not confined to medical research. They appear in any research involving human subjects, including, obviously, much psychological research.

AMBIGUITY IN EXPERIMENTAL RESEARCH

Even when it is feasible to employ experimental designs, there still remains considerable ambiguity in the interpretation of results. The successful researcher is alert to this problem, and designs his experiments so as to minimize the inevitable ambiguity.

Where does the ambiguity come from? To help answer this question, let's look at two new terms—*dependent variable* and *independent variable*. Crudely, the dependent variable in psychological research relates to that aspect of behavior which the scientist is trying, through experiment, to manipulate, influence, modify, and thereby ultimately to understand. The independent variable relates to those conditions, preferably manipulated or established by the experimenter, through which the behavior in question is to be influenced. In the terminology of cause-and-effect relations, the independent variable would be equated with cause and the dependent variable with effect.

In the smoking and cancer studies, the intent is to show the influence of the amount of smoking (independent variable) on the incidence of cancer (dependent variable). In the Zeigarnik experiments, whether tasks are completed is the independent variable, memory for these tasks the dependent variable.

As short-hand expressions, these terms facilitate communication, and thus can be useful in scientific discourse. What is more important for the present purpose is that they highlight both the obvious ambiguity of correlational designs and the more subtle sources of ambiguity in experimental designs. We already have said that the problem with correlational designs lies in the difficulty they pose for specifying the direction of an obtained relation: Does smoking cause cancer or does susceptibility to cancer increase smoking? We now have another way of defining the problem. The ambiguity of correlational designs lies in our inability to specify which is the dependent and which the independent variable.

With experimental designs some of the confusion is eliminated. Thus, you *can* tell which is the dependent and which the independent variable in a smoking-and-cancer study with random assignment of subjects to conditions. No one could argue, with such a design, that the amount of smoking might be the dependent variable. Since that level of ambiguity does not plague us, what ambiguity does remain in interpreting results obtained through an experimental design?

In brief, the problem lies in the difficulty of *specifying exactly the identity of the independent variable*. We can point to the independent variable; we can label it; we can distinguish it with ease from the dependent variable. But we cannot always say with assurance what it really is. The rare ingenious experimenter designs his research so that his way of specifying the identity of the independent variable is convincing.

In the rest of this chapter we will try to spell out the meaning of these abstract and perhaps puzzling remarks. At the core of our explanation is the concept of *control*.

The fundamental rule of research design is that every experiment must have a *control group*. That is, if a certain manipulation is performed on one group of subjects (the "experimental group"), then their behavior must be compared with that of an unmanipulated group (the "control group"). If the two groups behave differently, the manipulation can be considered effective.

Thus, the effectiveness of some independent variable is assessed by comparing the experimental and control groups on some dependent variable. Manipulation, then, means imposing on the experimental group some value of the independent variable greater than zero; for the unmanipulated, or control, group the value of the independent variable is left at zero. Should it be unfeasible to achieve a value of zero, the experimental group would be the one receiving the higher value of the independent variable, or, to cover the most general case, the one receiving the nonnormal value of the independent variable. To assess the effect of some treatment, both a treated and a nontreated group are needed.

For example, if you wanted to find out what effect, if any, alcohol has on driving skill, your experimental design would undoubtedly call for at least two groups: (1) an experimental group, who are given a certain amount of alcohol, and (2) a control group, given no alcohol. You might want more than one experimental group to assess the effects of different amounts of alcohol, but that would not alter the basic logic of the design. Although moving from the simple two-group (one experimental, one control) to a multigroup design poses no problem, moving in the other direction produces serious consequences. You simply could not do the experiment with only one group whose driving skill is investigated while they are under the influence of alcohol. Two groups are the minimum requirement for an acceptable experimental design.

But is a control group really essential, since anyone doing research on driving skill certainly knows how sober people drive? If the behavior of a group given alcohol departs from normal, then the effectiveness of the manipulation would be quite apparent.

This kind of argument is frequently encountered in the context of applied research. Thus, it would not be unusual to hear from a psychiatrist engaged in research on the effectiveness of a certain type of psychotherapy: "I don't need a control group [of untreated patients], because I can tell when people are mentally ill and when they are well, and if these [treated] patients improve, I will know it."

Naïveté about proper research design may lie behind such arguments, or our hypothetical psychiatrist may be saying, in effect, that he carries around with him an image of the appropriate control group, that a real control group need not be employed because the group already implicitly exists. Thus, even in an apparently single-group experiment, the logic is preserved of the experimental-group–control-group design. But if the necessity of the dual-group design is acknowledged, why not go all the way and obtain data on an explicit, real control group? Real data are certainly more convincing than the researcher's putative ability to divine the appearance of these data were they to be obtained.

Experiments that rely on implicit control groups, then, may do no violence to the logic of experimental design, but they do considerably weaken the experimenter's persuasiveness. And, as we shall see shortly, good design demands even more than the existence of a real control group. In essence, the problem facing the researcher is not whether to have a control group, but *what to control for*. Now we are ready for some interesting examples.

THE HAWTHORNE EFFECT

In 1924 at the Hawthorne Works of the Western Electric Co. in Chicago, an inquiry was initiated into conditions that might increase worker productivity. In particular, an attempt was made to investigate the effect on performance of lighting conditions within the factory. The basic hypothesis was that working efficiency could be improved by determining, through experiment, optimal conditions of illumination quality and intensity.

What followed from this modest beginning was an eight-year research program that had unanticipated but profound effects on the problem of human relations in industry and, pertinent to our purpose, highlighted a major problem in the design of research with human subjects. Both of these consequences emerged from the rather distressing result that the level of illumination seemed to have no appreciable effect on productivity.

The engineers conducting the original illumination experiments were well versed in the logic of experimental design. In particular, they were careful to employ both control and experimental groups. Over a series of studies, carried out with increasing concern for careful design, the basic plan was to vary illumination over a wide range in the experimental condition and to keep illumination as constant as possible in the control condition.

In one of the studies, illumination was increased for the experimental group over a range from about 24 to 70 foot-candles, while illumination for the control group was maintained at a fairly constant, lower level. As illumination was increased in the experimental condition, "very appreciable production increases" were noted. But comparable increases in production were also disconcertingly observed in the control group.

In a subsequent study, illumination was systematically decreased in the experimental condition from 10 to 3 foot-candles, while the control group enjoyed a constant level of 10 foot-candles. Now, even more disconcertingly, as the illumination was *decreased* in the experimental condition, "the efficiencies of both the test and control groups increased slowly but steadily." Only when illumination reached 3 foot-candles (about the same as dim moonlight) did production rate decrease.

Surely, something strange was taking place. The experimental group became more productive with both increases and decreases in illumination, and furthermore the "untreated" control group also showed increases in production rate.

Fortunately, the experimenters did not give up in despair. Instead, their curiosity was aroused by these unexpected (and serendipitous) results. From this point on, the story becomes too complicated to summarize briefly. At least one conclusion, however, seems justified from the several years of research that constituted the Hawthorne studies: The production increases resulted from enhanced worker morale, which in turn resulted from the workers' *participating in the experiment* and thereby feeling that the company cared about them. This feeling was aroused about equally among experimental and control subjects.

Since our interest here is not in the problem of employee morale, but rather in the design of psychological research, let us focus on the latter implication of the Hawthorne studies. It happened that the workers in the control group were aware of their participation in the study. Suppose, instead, that they have been kept ignorant of this fact, that the illumination experiments were so designed that the relevant manipulations were imposed on the experimental group with their knowledge whereas the control group was both unmanipulated and *uninformed*. Suppose further that observations of the performance of both groups began under normal lighting, after which illumination was increased in the experimental condition. What might have happened? Production rate would have gone up in the experimental group and remained unchanged in the control group. Conclusion? Obviously, the higher level of illumination yields the greater production. Implication? Install brighter lights in the factory.

Fortunately, if fortuitously, the first Hawthorne experiment was conducted with control subjects who knew that they were participants. Therefore, the implication is not "install brighter lights . . .," but rather "control subjects should be treated exactly the same as experimental subjects except for the variable to be manipulated—and this includes, where appropriate, knowledge that they are participants in an experiment if the experimental subjects are so informed." In honor of the results that led to this implication, prospective researchers are admonished to "control for the Hawthorne effect." How to heed that warning is sometimes the most challenging part of the task of designing psychological research.

Although the Hawthorne effect relates to a specific problem in doing psychological research, it is illustrative of a generic characteristic of such research: The independent variable is not always what the experimenter thinks it is.

Closely related to the Hawthorne effect is a phenomenon long known to physicians and medical researchers that has considerable relevance to psychological research. This is the placebo effect. In the medical context, the effect might appear when a physician gives a patient medication to ameliorate unpleasant symptoms. Shortly after taking the medication the patient reports feeling better; the symptoms are gone, and the physician's task is done. But we might ask, did the specific medication affect the patient, through its pharmacological properties, or did the patient improve because he expected the medication to help him?

The possibility of a psychological component to the effectiveness of medication is not so far-fetched as it might first seem. Such an effect can be simply demonstrated: Give some patients the "real" medication and give others a pharmacologically inert substance—a placebo—and compare outcomes. For example, we might randomly assign patients complaining of a headache to either an "aspirin" condition or a placebo condition (telling the latter that they are getting aspirin); we could then compare the numbers of those in each condition who report feeling better. Under some circumstances the numbers of such reports in both conditions might be the same, or at least a sizable proportion of the placebo subjects will indicate improvement.

The placebo effect, as it has been called, is sufficiently widespread that it must be controlled for in medical research. Thus, to assess the purely pharmacological effectiveness of a new drug it is necessary to determine its effectiveness as a placebo. In more general terms, the effectiveness of any treatment (from drugs through psychotherapy) must be compared with that of a suitable placebo.

Of course, there may be times when it does not matter why a particular treatment works. For immediate, pragmatic reasons, the only thing that matters is the total therapeutic impact of some procedure, even if that total is comprised entirely of placebo effect. Indeed, the physician may see fit to capitalize on the placebo effect, and administer only placebos when there is reason to withold the appropriate medication. It often happens that certain well-publicized medications gradually lose their initial effectiveness, not through any physiological adaptation, but apparently because of a loss of appeal like that which plagues even the best comedians, singers, and politicians. Not entirely facetiously, physicians have been admonished to "use the new drugs while they still retain their effectiveness."

Although the placebo effect was first noted in medical practice, its implication for the design of any research involving human subjects is apparent. The moral is that people sometimes respond to what they think you are doing to them, and not necessarily to what *you* think you are doing to them; or, as we noted, in summarizing the implication of the Hawthorne effect, the independent variable is not always what the experimenter thinks it is.

One obvious way to control for the placebo effect is to establish a placebo control group, especially when subjects cannot be prevented from knowing that some experimental manipulation is being imposed on them. Although they may not know the intended nature of the manipulation, they will undoubtedly attempt to impose meaning on their experience as subjects, and in so doing they may distort the "true" or pure effect of the independent variable. Whatever the design, however, it certainly seems advisable in most types of research to keep subjects uninformed of what is being done to them. In drug research, uninformed subjects are said to be "blind."

But now an interesting complication is introduced. If it is so important to keep subjects blind about the experimental condition they are undergoing, how about the experimenter? Might he unintentionally influence the outcome of his research through knowledge of how his subjects ought to behave? In the next section we will consider the answer to those questions as they apply to psychological research. But we can point out that the answer has been anticipated by medical researchers, who insist that where feasible both subjects and experimenters be kept uninformed; this is the so-called "double-blind" procedure. In a drug study, for instance, one group of subjects would receive the drug, one group a placebo, and the experimenter would not know, either while conducting the experiment or while translating his protocols into data, which group any given subject belonged to. (The double-blind procedure, incidentally, was followed in the nationwide studies that evaluated the effect of the Salk polio vaccine.)

Why should the experimenter be kept uninformed? The answer is given most convincingly in a series of experiments done by Robert Rosenthal under the rubric of "the experimenter effect."

THE EXPERIMENTER EFFECT

What is now referred to as the experimenter effect has been known to psychologists for several decades (though its lesson was ignored) in the form of the story of Clever Hans. Hans was a horse, owned by a teacher of mathematics in Germany, Herr Von Osten; Hans's intellectual feats were widely publicized in the press in the first decade of the present century.

Herr Von Osten believed lower animals to be much more intelligent than they appeared. What they lacked was a means of communicating their knowledge. Accordingly, Herr Von Osten set out to train Hans to tap one of his forelegs according to a code that he was taught. For example, each letter of the alphabet was assigned a number; Herr Von Osten "taught" this code to Hans by naming a letter and then helping him to move his leg the appropriate number of times. Eventually, Hans was able to tap his leg, in response to a letter, without the trainer's help.

After about two years of intensive training, Hans appeared able to spell out words and sentences in response to questions, to solve arithmetic problems, and so on. Claims of his remarkable abilities attracted the attention of scientists; unlike other owners of performing animals, Herr Von Osten welcomed examination of Hans by the scientific community. A commission of psychologists and zoologists that was formed to look into the matter concluded that Hans's performance was not merely the result of trickery or deceit on the part of his owner. However, dissatisfied with the implication that the demonstration of Herr Von Osten's honesty vindicated his assertion of Hans's intellectual prowess, the psychologists Oskar Pfungst and Carl Stumpf pursued the investigation further. In fairly short order, they were able to show that Hans was clever, indeed, but not in the way Herr Von Osten believed he was.

What Pfungst and Stumpf discovered was that Hans was extremely sensitive to almost imperceptible movements unintentionally made by his owner, or by those observing his performance. For example, when Hans was about to complete the number of taps required for a correct answer, his examiner might slightly nod his head, or relax his facial muscles. Hans picked up these cues and stopped tapping. Thus, the horse's behavior was being controlled through a very subtle form of communication of which his trainer or examiner was unaware.

Most psychologists in the course of their own training learn the story of Clever Hans, but few seem to have taken its implications to heart until the recent reports by Robert Rosenthal of analogous results in research on human subjects as well. Indeed, Rosenthal's discovery of the experimenter effect was serendipitous, and only after his initial discovery did Rosenthal himself see the relation between his work and the story of Clever Hans.

Rosenthal made the discovery in the course of analyzing the data for his doctoral dissertation, in which he was trying to test the hypothesis that people "project" their own impulses and feelings onto others. Thus, for example, a person who is himself extremely, though perhaps unconsciously, hostile will see more hostility in other people than is actually present. The projection hypothesis provides the basic rationale for use of the kind of psychological test known as the "projective test," and indeed in that context it is not a hypothesis but a working assumption. Despite its crucial role in personality theory and in clinical psychology, which relies heavily on projective tests, the projection hypothesis has received disappointingly little empirical verification.

To study projection in the laboratory, Rosenthal established the following situation. One group of subjects was shown a set of 14 photographs of people's faces (Set A). The subjects were asked to rate each face according to whether the person depicted had just been informed of success or failure on some important task. The ratings were made on a scale from −10 to +10, representing a range from extreme failure to extreme success.

After these ratings were obtained, the group was administered a test purporting to measure intelligence; they were told that the purpose of this study was to see if there is any relation between intelligence and empathy. Half the subjects were made to feel that they had done very well on the "intelligence" test, and half were treated in such a way as to experience failure. Following the "success" or "failure" experiences the subjects were asked to rate a second set (Set B) of faces just as they had the first. In addition to the success and failure groups there was a control group that made both sets of ratings but was not administered the intervening test.

Rosenthal predicted that from Set A to Set B the ratings of the success group would shift in the positive direction, the ratings of the failure group would shift in the negative direction, while the control group's ratings would remain about the same. The prediction was not confirmed.

Figure 2.3 Robert Rosenthal. (Harvard University News Office.)

In an attempt to salvage something from his own failure experience, Rosenthal made several additional analyses of his data (the experiment was actually far more complicated than it is described here). Out of that process emerged one peculiar result: *Prior* to any intended differential treatment, the "success" subjects gave lower (that is, more negative) ratings than did the subjects in either the "failure" or the control group. Given that initial difference, the projection hypothesis could have been at least partially confirmed if only the control group did not change from Set A to Set B and the success group moved in the direction of neutral ratings.

In short, the difference between the Set A ratings of the success group and those of the other groups considerably enhanced the likelihood of confirming the projection hypothesis even if the projection effect were itself negligible. But where did that initial difference come from? As in any good research design, subjects had been randomly assigned to the three groups, so there was no reason to suspect that the groups had been biased through some impropriety in subject assignment. Of course, the initial difference could have been one of those improbable events that do after all sometimes occur by chance.

Instead of ignoring the difference, or attributing it to "chance," Rosenthal chose to take it seriously and speculate on its origin. He was struck by the idea that he himself, the experimenter, might in some way have influenced the subjects to make their ratings so as to "help" him confirm the hypothesis and thereby assure the acceptability of his dissertation. Perhaps he was subtly communicating to his subjects, as Herr Von Osten had done with Clever Hans, how he wanted them to behave. This notion was so intriguing that, after completing his dissertation, Rosenthal dropped projective tests and picked up the experimenter effect. He conducted a lengthy series of experiments demonstrating in a thoroughly convincing fashion the operation of the experimenter effect. Rosenthal's general strategy involved implanting in a group of experimenters expectations about how their subjects ought to behave, either through rather direct communication or more subtle means.

One example of the latter is a study in which each experimenter would be shown what purported to be the data from his first few subjects; data from subsequent subjects then tended to conform to the values of the false, early returns. This is a particularly significant study in that experimenters, impatient to see how their research is coming out, frequently are tempted to peek at the results obtained from their first few subjects. Rosenthal's work raises the question of how many hypotheses have been confirmed as an artifact of the early-returns phenomenon.

Another example of the more subtle communication of expectations to experimenters, and an example of the generality of the experimenter effect, is a study involving rats and psychology students enrolled in a laboratory course. When the student-experimenters got the rats they were to use in a lab exercise, they discovered that some cages were labeled "maze-bright" and other cages were labeled "maze-dull." Being good psychology students, they knew that the psychologist Robert Tryon had developed through selective breeding of rats a strain of efficient maze learners and a strain of inefficient learners. Each experimenter was led to believe, then, that his rat was either smart or stupid, depending on the label on the cage. The rats, of course, had actually been obtained from the local animal colony and randomly assigned to cages. But their behavior reflected their false labels. Those identified as bright learned their task faster than those rats labeled dull. Somehow the experimenters' expectations had influenced the rats' behavior. This finding was later replicated and extended in a more elaborate experiment (Rosenthal, 1966).

Rosenthal's experiments have a way of suggesting analogies to important situations in everyday life. Consider, for instance, the school situation in which a child, as he enters a class, is labeled "bright" or "dull," "good" or "troublesome," and so on, through test scores, previous grades, teacher scuttlebutt, or what have you. Sure enough, the child fulfills the prophecy implied in the label. But how much of this consistency of behavior is intrinsic to the child's make-up and how much is the result of teachers' influences? One experiment (Rosenthal and Jacobson, 1966) has demonstrated convincingly that teachers' expectations can markedly influence students' performance. All the children in each of several elementary-school classrooms were given an IQ test. Then, a randomly selected group of these students were falsely identified to their teachers as having an unusually good potential for intellectual growth. When retested eight months later, these children showed a much larger gain in average IQ score than did control students. The most pronounced effect was obtained on first- and second-graders. Whether false labeling can depress IQ scores has not yet been demonstrated experimentally, though if rats can be retarded by a biased experimenter, it seems reasonable to believe that a similar effect might be exerted on children by their teachers.

To go a step further, to what extent can a child's impression of himself as, for example, bright or stupid, worthy or unworthy, influence his behavior so as to conform to the impression? Labeling, by others and by himself, may be a powerful determinant of a child's behavior, in and out of the classroom. The relevance of this point to the issue of racial segregation should be readily apparent.

The experimenter effect, then, has implications both for experimental design and for our understanding of human and animal behavior. With respect to the latter, think how subtle the communication must be that mediates the experimenter effect. In a manner analogous to Herr Von Osten's slight gestures, the experimenters in Rosenthal's studies must somehow have conveyed to their subjects how they should respond. The communication is indeed subtle, for neither experimenter nor subject is aware of it, and Rosenthal himself, through careful analysis of films of the interaction between experimenters and subjects, has not yet been able satisfactorily to put his finger on the experimenter-produced cues to which the subjects so graciously respond.

ORDER EFFECTS

Hawthorne, placebo, and experimenter effects are especially intriguing instances of the problems to be faced in the design of psychological research. We close this discussion with a topic that may be anticlimactic, but is nevertheless of equal significance to the other types of effect that require control.

It is often desirable to collect data from a given subject on more than one occasion. For example, what is the effect on IQ of nursery school experience? The "obvious" strategy might be to measure IQ in a group of children before their attendance at nursery school and again afterwards. Any effect of nursery school attendance should be revealed in a change in IQ score.

But, you should immediately ask, what about possible Hawthorne, placebo, and experimenter effects? Might not they account for any obtained change in scores? Yes, they might, so we deal with the possibility of such effects by not letting the children, their parents, or teachers, or even the psychologist who administers the IQ tests know that an experiment is being conducted. This precaution should take care of all three types of effect. Assuming that we are successful in accomplishing that end, are we now ready to attribute IQ change to the nursery school experience?

Again you may object, arguing that after a year's nursery school experience the children are also a year older, and perhaps that alone would be enough to account for the change (let us assume that a change was observed and that it represented an increase in IQ). That would be a reasonable expectation except that IQ scores are so computed as to reflect both performance and chronological age; that is, five-year-olds are smarter than four-year-olds, but their average IQ scores are the same (100, as you will see in Chapter Fourteen). The argument, however, is on the right track. Not only has a school year elapsed between administrations of the IQ test—which we will agree is not relevant to the IQ increase—but the children have also taken the IQ test twice. More directly to the point, if it is not already obvious, when the children were given the test the second time, they had already been through it, or an equivalent test, before. Thus, IQ scores on the second administration might have been influenced by either or both the nursery school experience and the prior experience with an IQ test. Perhaps having taken the test once they are more "test-wise" for the second testing session.

In more general terms, then, when behavior at time-two is compared with behavior of the same subjects at time-one, the second set of behaviors may have been influenced by the first or by the conditions imposed on the subjects in eliciting or observing the first set of behaviors. This condition is referred to as an *order* effect. As with the other problems of this sort that we have discussed, order effects have significance on two grounds. First, they must be controlled for in the design of psychological research. Second, they imply something about the nature of man and animal. Just as experimenter effects emphasize the kinds of subtle communication that can take place between organisms, so order effects highlight another unique feature of the objects of psychological investigation: *living organisms are modified by what they experience.* The modification may be slight or great, brief or of long duration, but modification through experience is the rule. So universal and so important is this property of organisms that it has captured a large share, perhaps a disproportionately large share, of the attention of psychological theorists; it falls under the general rubric of "learning," a topic that we will return to in later chapters.

Order effects intrude themselves into a variety of contexts. In a television commercial of a few years back, people were asked to compare the harshness of two brands of cigarette. Brand A, the sponsor's brand, would invariably come out the winner, with the alternative brands consistently being judged the harsher. The judge's instructions were to take a puff of Brand A and blow the smoke through his nose, and then do the same for Brand B.

If you think of this as though it were a real experiment, you should immediately note the possibility of the influence of an order effect—Brand A was always smoked first. You might be able to generate some plausible hypotheses about why the second of two experiences in which cigarette smoke is blown over the delicate membranes of the nose might be judged the harsher. The naive judge would be likely to identify the source of the harsher experience as the cigarette that accompanied it. Thus, Brand B would be called harsher, whereas in reality the second *experience* was the harsher.

As our last example here, consider the following experiment. The hypothesis to be tested is that highly anxious people will perform less well on a complex task than will people low in anxiety, but will perform as well on a simple task. To test this hypothesis, subjects categorized as high- or low-anxious on the basis of a questionnaire are given two tasks to perform, the first a complex task (the Stroop test, as illustrated in Plate 1), the second a simple task. Sure enough, the data conform to the hypothesis. But do they confirm it?

Quite obviously not, because of the possibility of an order effect; the complex task was always given first, the simple second. As in all the previous examples, such a design produces uncertainty about the identity of the independent variable. Is it task complexity or order of administration of tasks? This question, incidentally, while clearly demanded by the logic of research design, is also reasonable to ask on psychological grounds. That is, a good case could be developed for the "order effect" interpretation on the following basis: high-anxious subjects, on entering a new situation and given a task to perform, do not work as effectively as their ability would allow; however, if the task turns out to be relatively easy, and their initial apprehension is allayed by a warm, or at least accepting, experimenter, then by the time the second task is given them, they no longer function like highly anxious people. Put another way, the anxiety of a high-anxious subject may not be chronic; rather it may be high only initially and then decline, if testing conditions permit.

Order effects can be controlled for, usually in a rather straightforward fashion. For example, if it is really necessary to use a given subject in more than one condition, then the order in which the conditions are imposed can be varied. When there are but two conditions, half the subjects would be assigned to condition A first and condition B second, while the other half would be assigned to the opposite order. When the number of conditions exceeds two, further complexities in design may arise, sometimes requiring highly sophisticated and elaborate solutions.

SUMMARY

The data which theories are devised to handle and by which the validity of theories is assessed come from many sources. As psychology has developed, the source of its data has increasingly been systematic research efforts. But even systematic research can take many forms, and there is need in psychology for all of these: attempts to establish the reality of personal observations or hunches; following up unexpected, or *serendipitous,* findings from previous research; replication of earlier research to assess its sturdiness, or reliability; the testing of predictions, or hypotheses, derived from formal models.

A distinction can be made between two broad classes of research design: *correlational* and *experimental.* The weakness of correlational designs (for example, in research relating incidence of cancer to amount of smoking) is that they do not allow an unequivocal specification of a direction to whatever relations are uncovered: Is it excessive smoking that leads to cancer, or do cancer-prone people smoke more than others? In experimental designs, subjects are randomly assigned to the various conditions of the experiment, or, technically, to various values of the *independent variable;* their behavior, the *dependent variable*, can then unambiguously be interpreted as stemming from the independent variable. Unfortunately, experimental designs are not always feasible.

Moreover, some ambiguity of interpretation remains even in the results obtained from experimental designs. Although the independent variable can be "pointed at," its exact identity may be uncertain. The incorporation of control conditions or *control groups* into research design is a device for decreasing the ambiguity about the exact identity of the independent variable.

There are several ways in which unintended sources of influence on the subject's behavior can be introduced into an experiment, and these must be controlled for, or eliminated, if they are not to contaminate the data. The *Hawthorne* effect refers to the possibility that subjects' performance may be influenced simply because they know they are serving as subjects in an experiment. The *placebo* effect, long known in medical research and practice, refers to the potential influence on subjects' behavior of the expectations about the effects of the manipulation being imposed on them, or what they believe is being imposed on them. The *experimenter* effect occurs when the experimenter's expectations about how the subjects ought to behave are unintentionally communicated to the subjects, who then act in accord with the experimenter's expectations rather than in response to the presumed independent variable. *Order* effects, which reflect the fact that living organisms are modified by their experience, occur when subjects are exposed to two or more experimental conditions; their behavior in subsequent conditions is affected by what happened to them in previous conditions. To deal appropriately with these kinds of effects, so as to allow unequivocal interpretation of experimental data, is a major challenge to the psychological researcher.

SUGGESTED READINGS

Bachrach, A.J. *Psychological research: an introduction*. New York: Random House, 1962.

Bakan, D. The mystery-mastery complex in contemporary psychology. *American Psychologist*, 1965, 20, 186–191.

Orne, M. On the social psychology of the psychological experiment: with particular reference to demand characteristics and their implications. *American Psychologist*, 1962, 17, 776–783.

Pfungst, O. *Clever Hans* (edited by R. Rosenthal). New York: Holt, Rinehart & Winston, 1965.

Rosenberg, M.J. When dissonance fails: on eliminating evaluation apprehension from attitude measurement. *Journal of Personality and Social Psychology*, 1965, 1, 28–42.

Rosenthal, R. On the social psychology of the psychological experiment. *American Scientist*, 1963, 51, 268–283.

Shapiro, A.K. A contribution to a history of the placebo effect. *Behavioral Science*, 1960, 5, 109–135.

Skinner, B.F. A case history in scientific method. *American Psychologist*, 1956, 11, 221–233.

Measurement in Psychology

C H A P T E R   T H R E E   Now that we have seen something of the aims of science and the important characteristics of psychological research, we must turn to the topic of measurement, which is a vital part of almost all scientific activity. We will discuss the general role of measurement in science; how hard it is to achieve and how much it means. We will discuss the four general uses of numbers and what they imply. Taking one of the oldest areas of psychology, psychophysics, we will illustrate the fact that psychological assumptions determine the kind of measures one makes and what one can say about them. Our discussion will then turn to psychological traits and to the assumptions necessary for their measurement. You will be introduced to the common statistics that we use in the measurement of individuals and to various kinds of scores in which these measures are reported. Then we will explore the meaning of a measure of relationship (the correlation coefficient) and conclude with a discussion of reliability and validity of psychological measures. Throughout the chapter the emphasis will be on the relation between logic and quantification, and our aim will be to help you to become sensitive to that relationship.

The history of every science is marked by a struggle for precision. Part of the effort is devoted to the physical tools of the science, especially in the development of new instruments to extend the senses of man; another important part is devoted to advances in measurement and the development of quantified concepts and models. It is usually true that as a science advances it becomes increasingly mathematical.

Origins of Measurement

The power of effective quantification, and the accompanying development of mathematical models, has been dramatically demonstrated over and over again, but no example is more powerful than the one that marks the birth of modern physics.

One day a young man who was a student at the University of Pisa visited the cathedral of that famous town. The services must have been boring for instead of listening attentively he watched the swinging of a great hanging lamp. He soon noticed that when the lamp swung through a wide arc, the time it took to perform one swing seemed to be the same as when it swung through a narrow arc. He did not use his pocketwatch to check this observation for the simple reason that such a timepiece had not as yet been invented; but he did think to use his pulse beat. The observation turned out to be correct, and a mere youth had discovered a scientific law governing all pendulum motion: the time required by a pendulum to perform a swing is independent of the amplitude of the swing. Not long afterward this law was used to design the serviceable clock which the young man lacked. More important, the discovery suggested a new concept of scientific activity which defines modern science and at the same time endows it with its "magical" power. . . . The secret of the success of modern science was the selection of a new goal for scientific activity. This new goal, set by Galileo and pursued by his successors, is that of obtaining *quantitative descriptions* of scientific phenomena *independently of any physical explanations.* . . .

The principle Galileo followed next was to measure what is measurable and to render measurable what is not yet so. His problem then became that of isolating those aspects of natural phenomena which are basic and capable of measurement. . . . By analyzing and reflecting on natural phenomena he decided to concentrate on such concepts as space, time, weight, velocity, acceleration, inertia, force and momentum. Later scientists added power, energy and other concepts. In the selection of these particular properties and concepts Galileo again showed genius, for the ones he chose are not immediately discernible as the most important nor are they readily measurable. Some, such as inertia, are not even obviously possessed by matter; their existence had to be inferred from observations. Others, such as momentum, had to be created. Yet these concepts did prove to be most significant in the rationalization and conquest of nature. (Kline, 1953, pp. 184–187.)

Galileo wrenched physics from its position in philosophy and made it a scientific pursuit in the modern sense. This effort required not one, but two revolutions in thought. First, it required seeing *measurement,* or quantification, as an adequate goal in itself. Second, and coordinately, it required selecting *appropriate dimensions* for physical science. Neither of these tasks appears particularly formidable to the modern thinker, but these were problems of overwhelming difficulty in Galileo's time. The physical sciences, as they were then pursued, consisted of logical speculations and logical constructions about *categories* of objects and things, not measurement along dimensions.

Of course, quantification in itself is of no value since there is no virtue in merely piling up numbers. The things being quantified and the dimensions being considered must be relevant to the problems being considered. The dimensions Galileo chose are to us commonplace, natural choices, but there was nothing "natural" about them at that time. Although weight and distance were commonly being measured with high accuracy in Galileo's day, time was hardly measurable at all. Crude systems for "keeping time" existed, but precise timing, which was to play a key role in the study of motion, was nonexistent. Instruments for measuring time had to be *created* in order for the work of physics to go forward.

It is interesting to note that time cannot be measured in the same way that weight and distance can be. For *weight* one can begin with any arbitrary value, find matching units with a pan balance, and go on to build a scale. With *length* one can always pick a value, such as a stick of a given length, match that length with another stick, or lay out the distance on the ground and go on to build a scale. But with *time* there is no easy way to create intervals, there is nothing that can be put in a balance or carried around in a standard form. We have to build a machine to "make the units" of time. Galileo's discovery of the law of the pendulum represents a kind of "boot-strapping" technique that psychologists often try to emulate. He used an imprecise instrument, his pulse, to discover a much more precise instrument, the pendulum. This kind of refinement (using a crude method to discover a more precise methodology that can then be put to use in more advanced work) is one to which psychologists return again and again.

Until the nineteenth century, psychology was as philosophical and specula-tive as physics had been in pre-Galilean days. Scientific psychology had many different roots but all of them had one common aspect: They were all concerned with measurement. In one major line of research, Galileo's dimen-sions and modes of measurement were adopted to describe stimuli, and investigators simply asked what the sensory impressions were like for various values of the physical dimensions. This research, called *psychophysics*, was important in securing recognition for psychology as a science. It broke down the old common-sense notion that the mind, being immaterial, could not be measured, and it justified its measurements by discovering some interesting properties of human sensory processes.

The general model of human sensibilities that arose from this work is represented in the *Weber-Fechner Law*. This law, discovered by a physiol-ogist, Ernst Heinrich Weber, and extended by a philosopher, Gustav Theodor Fechner, can be given a very general expression that holds over many domains of human experience. To put it in its simplest form, as a physical stimulus increases logarithmically (that is, by powers, such as, 10, 100, 1000, 10,000, and so on), the sensation quality of that stimulus as it is perceived by an observer increases arithmetically (1, 2, 3, 4, and so on). This relationship has a number of interesting consequences: Suppose that when you are holding a 10-ounce weight, you can just barely detect the addition of an ounce to that weight. The law tells us that if you pick up a 100-ounce weight, an additional 10 ounces will be needed to be barely detectable. According to this law, the sensory systems are delicate instruments that are finely tuned to detect minute changes at minimal levels but are "buffered" to be able to cope with massive changes at higher levels. The general characteristics of this model are given in Figure 3.1, which shows human sensitivity to noise in terms of physical energy and sensory impression.

Psychophysical investigators, then, borrowed their description of the external world from physics. In their experiments, as they varied the physical world along its relevant dimensions, they asked observers to report changes in what they felt or saw or heard, that is, changes in their *sensations*. The resulting laws of psychophysics were couched in terms of the relation between the physical set of changes in the world and the changing *states of consciousness* of the observer.

INDIVIDUAL DIFFERENCES

It became apparent that no one simple set of quantitative procedures would be sufficient in psychology. Problems outside of psychophysics required different approaches. One of the first concerns of the infant science was the problem of individual differences. The best-known early appreciation of the existence of this problem came from the field of astronomy. In 1796, N. Maskelyne, the head of the Greenwich Observatory, discharged a young assistant, D. Kinnebrook, because the latter persisted in recording the transit of stars about half a second later than his master. Transits were measured in what was believed to be a simple and straightforward manner: A telescope was placed in a given position, and an observer watched as a star approached a cross hair in the telescope. Just before the star crossed the hair, the observer looked at his chronometer and began counting beats of the clock. He then estimated to the nearest fraction of a beat when the star crossed the hair line. Given this system, it seemed that Kinnebrook's failure to improve his work must be due to sheer negligence and carelessness.

Some years later, a German astronomer, Friedrich Wilhelm Bessel, was intrigued by this incident. He could not understand why a bright young man would ruin his career in such a manner. As he investigated the facts of the matter, he made an astonishing discovery: Experienced, mature astronomers such as himself had disagreements of even greater magnitude than the one for which Kinnebrook had been fired. Bessel traveled to various observatories and did joint observations with many astronomers in an effort to calibrate each man for his particular "error." For each observer he developed a "personal equation" for use in standardizing his results with those of other astronomers. The phenomenon of individual differences in reaction time led to the notion that there are personal equations to be added to the general laws of psychology.

HOW MANY MEASURES?

Corrections and personal constants raised additional problems. How many different kinds of values were needed for an individual? Would one personal

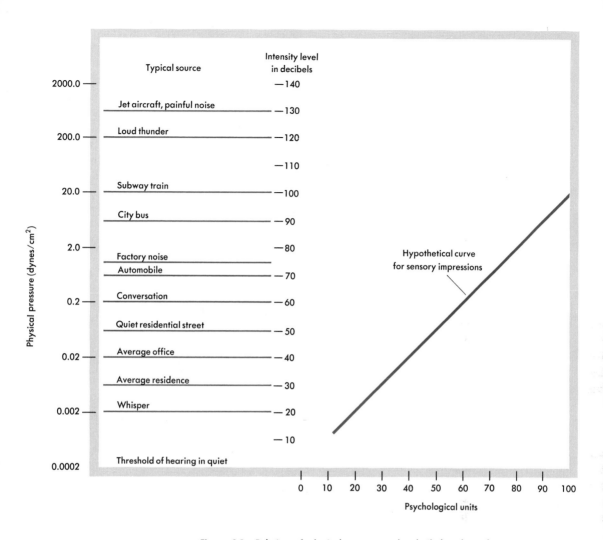

Figure 3.1 Relation of physical energy to the decibel scale and to sensory impression.

equation do for all reaction time or did it take a different correction for visual reaction, auditory reaction, reaction to touch, taste, and smell? Did the equations need to be changed with age? Were they different for men and women? Were equations needed for sensitivity, discrimination, attention, memory, imagery, and judgment? What were the appropriate (and sufficient) dimensions on which human beings were to be measured and how were such measures to be made? These difficult questions were forced on psychology both by evidence from the laboratory and by the interests of society, which wanted to know whether all children should be taught in the same way, whether the mentally ill should be given differential treatments, and other like matters.

On the surface it appears that these questions ought not to be difficult to answer. Like Galileo, "by analyzing and reflecting on natural phenomena" we ought to be able to decide on the relevant dimensions appropriate for our science. Then we would only have to discover how to measure them. Having done both of these feats, we could explore relationships among the dimensions and cast them into mathematical expressions. So far, however, although we have achieved remarkable practical successes with certain individual measurements, we have failed to discover "the basic dimensions" of human behavior.

The problem is not at all simple. With considerable justification we might start with the dimensions of consciousness, such as kinds of awareness, groupings of sensory experience, discriminations, choices, and decisions to act. But, equally, we could argue that we should begin with the emotions, that love and hate are the wellsprings of action. One psychologist proposes that we ought to deal with central personality variables because large blocks of behavior are attributable to general traits such as "introversion" or "extroversion." Another suggests that the most important dimensions are skills and abilities since they determine what a person can do and thus govern all the choices that he can make. There is no end to the debate. In short, although we have great agreement that we ought to move toward quantification, we have little agreement about the basic dimensions in psychology.

Quantification at the present time varies radically from one psychological area to another. Some psychologists in specialized experimental areas use elegant mathematical models; other psychologists in equally specialized clinical areas use none. Most measures of abilities and aptitudes assume simple quantitative models that add all test items equally, assuming some sort of cumulation of the trait being measured. But many uses to which the test scores are put give up quantification and use intuition and educated judgment. Over all areas of psychology, however, there is a general awareness of the importance of modern statistics and a realization that descriptions of events, the conduct of experiments and the final scientific evaluation of any claim to knowledge depend on some form of quantification.

This book can only give the briefest introduction to quantification, measurement, and statistics in psychology. We aim to do only two things here. First, we will try to give you some insight into the interaction between psychological thought and quantification, that is, the degree to which a given view in psychology demands particular kinds of quantification and the extent to which particular kinds of mathematics suggest particular psychologies. Second, we will briefly introduce you to some of the common statistics that are employed in this book and in the literature of the social sciences generally so that you can understand what you read in these areas. This latter aim includes the development of practical knowledge concerning test scores and measures so that you can make meaningful interpretations of information given to you about yourself and others.

Numbers for Measurement

Let us first consider certain ways in which we can use numbers, starting with ways based on simple assumptions and working up to those based on complex ones. We will take as our general problem the assignment of numbers to people as an aid in describing them. We will begin with a list of English language terms for human description compiled by Gordon W. Allport and Henry S. Odbert as part of a study of personality characteristics. These investigators searched the dictionary and discovered a remarkable abundance of terms for saying something about people, ranging over all domains of human experience and covering all the simple characteristics that we normally talk about. The list starts with "abandoned" and ends with "zoöphilous" 17,953 items later. Surely, such an extensive listing, culled from actual human usage, must be rich enough to provide all that we need for personality description.

NUMBERS AS NAMES

The nominal use of numbers simply means that numbers are used as *names*. We can take each of the descriptive words and assign a number to it. Then when we want to describe a person we can just say that his major characteristics are 105, 273, 5567, 13,980 and 17,001. These numbers do not measure or quantify anything; they only identify a particular classification or a label. Similarly, we could take a large population and assign numbers to the individuals (such as social security numbers, soldiers' serial numbers, payroll code numbers) and then list the numbers under the adjectives that describe the people best. Then if we want to know what "contentiousness" looks like, we can simply look up the set of people whose numbers are under that adjective.

Notice that this use of numbers is for convenience. We could just as well use letters, laundry marks, or special names. We tend to use numbers for labels because it is convenient. But you must remember that the numbers serve *only* as labels and have only the properties that we explicitly code into them by arbitrary rules, such as "All license plate numbers beginning in 8 belong to county A" or "All football players who have numbers beginning with 1 are quarterbacks." It would be silly to add such numbers together or multiply or divide them to try to discover something. The most that we can do with such numbers is to count *how many* of a given sort there are or how many are assigned to the same person. In our proposed study of the Allport-Odbert traits, we could ask if all the terms are used equally often (by counting the number of times each trait number is used), or we could ask how many numbers were assigned to each person, and so on. The important thing to remember is that these are classifications rather than measurements.

The second use of numbers *orders* the objects to which the numbers are attached. We saw above that the use of numbers as names works by wholly arbitrary rules. Under *ordinal* rules, however, we must agree that the numbers correspond with some meaningful arrangement of our knowledge about people or categories.

Suppose that we are interested in how "sociable" people are. If we know the students in a class well, we can line them up in order of sociability. Then we can assign the number 1 to the most sociable, number 2 to the second most sociable, 3 to the next person, 4 to the next, and so on until the last person gets the figure equal to the total number of people in the group. Now each person has a number and the number is more than a name; it tells where a person stands in the group in terms of our judgments about his sociability.

Examples of ordinal numbers are common. Most high schools arrange a roster of the graduating students in rank order of achievement in high school. Thus, you may know that you ranked Xth in a group of N many, for example, 35th in a class of 157. This means that you can tell how many people did better than you (34) and how many did worse (122). The number 35 tells your ordinal position.

You know, of course, that the differences between ranks may not be uniformly the same. For example, if we line everybody up by height, the people who are very tall or very short are likely to differ greatly one from another, but the people in the middle will be very much alike; indeed, it may be hard to detect the differences among them. Thus, the individuals at the extremes reflect great differences from one rank to the next and the ranks in the middle may reflect almost no change.

Ordering, or ranking, is a powerful step forward over simple classification. If we only have a list of terms, we can assign or not assign each term, classifying a person as being in or out of a given category. This is a form of typology and represents the crudest possible approach to human measurement. Once we have the notion of orders and ranks, however, we can assign degrees of a given term instead of resorting to an all-or-none, present-or-absent classification. Thus, ordering, even though it may not appear particularly impressive, is an important advance in quantification.

NUMBERS WITH CONSTANT INTERVALS

Ranks do not provide wholly satisfactory measurements because the differences between them do not represent equal differences in what is being measured. If possible, we would like not only an ordinal scale but also a scale in which the difference between adjacent numbers is uniform throughout.

If we can order a group of traits or qualities at all, it seems as though there should be some simple way to get at the underlying "real" scale. But this next step is a very difficult one to take and depends on our willingness to make strong assumptions about the "real nature" of the psychological variables we are measuring. For example, suppose that we have a random sample of 100 people and we have ordered everyone on "sociability." If we are willing to assume that each person is just one psychological unit different in sociability from the person next in order, we could assign the ordinal numbers themselves, 1, 2, 3, 4, . . . , to use as interval measures. But if we assume that the differences between people get larger as we go down the order, we might want to give our subjects numbers that had increasing differences like 1, 2, 4, 7, 11, 16, ... If on the other hand we assume that differences get smaller, we might want to assign numbers like 1, 11, 20, 28, 35, 41, 46. . . . Similarly, if we assume that the differences start large, grow small and then become large again, we might choose a series like 0, 10, 18, 24, . . . 49, 49.5, 50, 50.5, 51, . . . 76, 82, 90, 100, which reflects that fact. (We will return to this problem later when you know a little more about number systems.)

A familiar example of an interval scale is the ordinary mercury thermometer. A thermometer assigns numbers (degrees) to temperatures and with it we can compare temperatures in terms of how many degrees lie between them. Thus, we may say that today it is 29 degrees warmer than it was yesterday, or that the average temperature in Minneapolis is five degrees colder than the average temperature in Chicago, and so on. Comparisons are made in terms of distances on the scale in number of degrees. This scale works because there is a more or less constant increment of heat (physically measured) with constant applications of energy (physically measured) and because mercury expands about the same amount with each increase in energy. The thermometer fails at both extremes when the mercury freezes or boils and the interval relaton is lost. Two very important qualifications must also be noted: Psychological response to temperature is not additive in this simple fashion, and we are sharply restricted even in what we can say about physical temperature.

The psychological point is obvious. A change of temperature of 10 degrees may not be noticeable (say from 65 to 75 degrees) or it may be acutely noticeable (say from 85 to 95 degrees). Also, whether we experience a temperature as comfortable or uncomfortable depends on wind, humidity, previous experience, and other factors. With a good breeze, warm temperatures are more bearable, but with the same air movement very hot and very cold temperatures become more *un*bearable. Psychological temperature is a complex function of many variables of which actual physical temperature is only one.

More relevant to our discussion is the set of restrictions on what we can say about temperature scales. It is clear that we cannot make meaningful *ratio statements*, for example. If it is zero today and it is going to be "twice

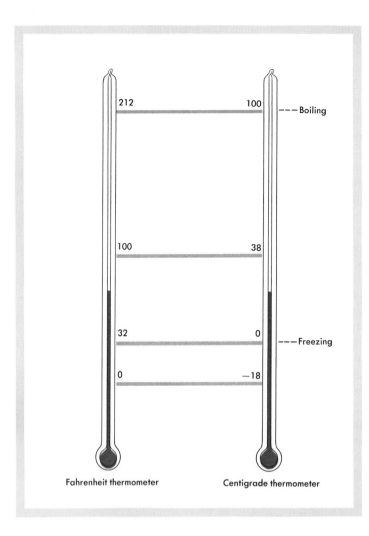

212   100   ---Boiling

100   38

32   0   ---Freezing

0   —18

Fahrenheit thermometer   Centigrade thermometer

Figure 3.2 Examples of interval scales. Notice that any interval on the F scale can be converted into the appropriate interval on the C scale by multiplying by 5/9. Also notice that ratios do not have comparable meanings in the two scales.

as cold" tomorrow, it is obvious that multiplying the temperature by two is meaningless. Similarly, 40 degrees cannot be considered half as warm as 80 degrees or twice as hot as 20 degrees. A comparison of the Fahrenheit scale with the Centigrade scale in Figure 3.2 shows that ridiculous results would be obtained if we tried to make the same statements concerning ratio comparisons on the two scales, yet each is valid as an interval scale. In brief, with an interval scale it is meaningful to talk about increases and decreases, to describe averages and to talk about ranges from low to high, but it is *not* meaningful to make ratios of the numbers.

To take another example from the adjective list, it might be possible for us to develop a scale of *neatness* in which we agree on the order of numbers.

Then if we can use panels of judges, we may be able to get good agreement about what constitutes an increase of one unit in neatness. We may even be lucky enough to get agreement on this all along the scale so we can say that X is 10 units "neater" than Y and have this mean about the same difference at any point along our scale. We will *not* be able to say that X is twice as neat as Y, however, because we do not know what zero neatness is like or how far we are away from that hypothetical zero point when we give a value to either X or Y. Scales like this may be quite useful, however, in many tasks, such as describing people, measuring improvement or deficit, evaluating a trait so that we can ask if it is related to another trait, and establishing critical levels for jobs.

NUMBERS WITH MEANINGFUL RATIOS

Let us now consider a scale that has everything. It orders events along a dimension or continuum; it has solved the problem of equal intervals between the numbers; and it has a meaningful zero point, where none of whatever the scale is measuring exists. With such a scale, and only with such a scale, it is possible to make ratio comparisons, such as A is twice B, C is only one hundredth of D, M is 1000 times greater than N, and so forth.

The only ratio scales with which most of us are acquainted are found in physics. For example, we know what we mean by zero weight; we can operate a pan balance in order to make equal units; and we can cumulate units along a single dimension to match any desired amount of weight that we choose. Because this is true, we can say "X is 20 times as heavy as Y." We know this means that if we took the weight of Y as a unit, we would need to make 20 just like it to put in the balance to equal the weight of X. As we said earlier, *weight* and *length* form such scales and, since the invention of the clock, *time* may be considered as such a scale. But other ratio scales are difficult to achieve.

If you have studied physics, you know that it is possible to get a ratio scale of temperature, the Kelvin scale, which has an absolute zero (the complete absence of any heat) at —273 degrees on the Centigrade scale. This is a true ratio scale. But the Kelvin scale was not "discovered" or observed; *it was derived from a rather complete theory concerning the nature of heat.* Consequently, it is not at all the simple affair that balancing weights and measuring lengths turned out to be. It is virtually certain that psychology is in the position that physics once was with respect to heat and other difficult dimensions. Effective ratio scales will have to be developed from a considerable background of theory, and they will prove their usefulness in theoretical domains rather than in the day-to-day concerns for which less powerful scales may suffice.

In order to help you understand how the psychologist works with numbers, let us take a few facts and try out some assumptions to see what kinds of scales we get. Consider the classic question of the relation of a stimulus to its sensation. As we pointed out above, research 100 years ago established that there is a general law of discrimination, according to which actual differences between stimuli are not directly observed although the *ratio* seems to be observed. Thus, in any set of objects some constant fraction of increase (in the length of a line, the heaviness of a weight, or the brightness of a light) is necessary in order for each object to be clearly distinguished from the one preceding it and from the one following it. A set of such stimuli placed in order looks like a series in compound interest. Suppose that the constant fraction of increase is one-tenth (not an unreasonable figure; smell and loudness increase at about this value). If we begin arbitrarily with 10 physical units, the series would look like this:

Basic stimulus	10 physical units
First discriminable stimulus	11 physical units
Second stimulus, discriminable from the first	12.1 physical units
Third stimulus, discriminable from the second	13.31 physical units
Fourth stimulus, discriminable from the third	14.64 physical units
Fifth stimulus, discriminable from the fourth	16.10 physical units
Sixth stimulus, discriminable from the fifth	17.71 physical units
. . . . Twentieth stimulus	67.27 physical units
. . . . Fiftieth stimulus	1174.00 physical units
. . . . One hundredth stimulus	137,700 physical units

What can we say about this series other than declaring that each stimulus is just discriminable from the one before it and the one after it? Are we justified in saying that this is a psychological scale of some sort? Clearly this is *at least* an ordinal scale. We have in fact shown that the stimuli *are* ordered; the operations of constructing the scale guarantee that it increases along some continuum.

Given that our scale is ordered, can we assert that it is also an interval scale? That depends on what we are willing to assume. Fechner assumed that the appropriate unit was the *just noticeable difference*, or *jnd*. He further assumed that these jnd's cumulated directly as one proceeded along a dimension. From his point of view, the physical scale that we have constructed does have equal intervals *psychologically* speaking. This scale, then, is based on the assumption that equal detectability means equal psychological units. If that assumption is accepted, then we have a *psychological interval scale*. Many psychological scales measuring everything from *goodness of handwriting* to *attitudes toward war* have been built on this basic assumption.

If we have a procedure for establishing an interval scale, do we also have a means to make it a ratio scale? Perhaps so. We might argue that the point where a stimulus can just be detected (its absolute threshold) is, in fact, the psychological zero point. If we use physical energies below this value to test the responses of subjects, we will elicit uniformly negative reports. If this dividing mark *is* the zero point, and if we set up a scale from that point according to the equal-unit procedure, then we can qualify the scale as a *psychological ratio scale*.

It is apparent that we have stretched a rather long string of assumptions and part-truths to get to this point. But there are many weak points: Careful research convincingly shows that the Weber-Fechner Law does not hold well at extreme values of physical energy; absolute thresholds are unreliable and turn out to depend on background conditions, instructions to the subject, the order in which stimuli are presented; and jnd's may not really cumulate. We need to find independent evidence that supports the kind of scale we have just built.

In order to test our scale, we find that we have to make still other assumptions. For example, suppose we know that a response learned to one stimulus will transfer in reduced amount to "similar" stimuli. Is the phenomenon dependent only on the psychological distance of one stimulus from the other? If we assume so, *and* if psychological similarity is measured on the scale that we built above, then we ought to be able to show two things: Symmetrical transfer on both sides of one stimulus and equal transfer for given psychological units at different places on the scale.

Symmetrical Transfer. Going back to our example of a scale above, let us teach subjects to respond to the third stimulus in the series and observe how well it transfers to other stimuli. It should transfer equally to the fifth stimulus in the series as it does to the first. The argument, of course, is that the fifth and first stimuli are equal psychological distances from the original stimulus (two psychological units) even though they are different distances away in physical units (2.31 units versus 2.79 units).

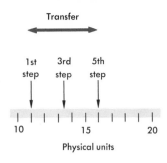

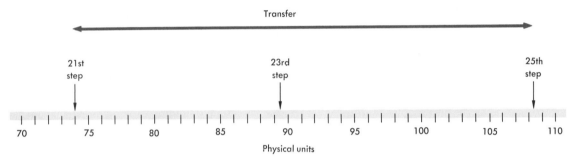

Figure 3.3 Comparable transfer for comparable psychological intervals rather than physical intervals—a test of the psychological scale.

Equality of Transfer. If we find that a response transfers over a given psychological range (perhaps two psychological units to each side of the original stimulus), we expect that range to be the same no matter where we choose the original stimulus on the scale. If training on the third stimulus transfers to the first and fifth stimulus we expect training on the 23rd stimulus to transfer to the 21st and the 25th in the same amounts even though the physical changes involved are very different. Figure 3.3 shows the expected results.

Although this kind of experimentation is much more complicated than we can indicate here, the results can be interpreted as showing that transfer is symmetrical and that transfer is governed by the number of jnd's involved rather than the magnitude of physical change. Such results give support to Fechner's notions of the psychological scale. Note that this support depends on an entire network of assumptions and beliefs about psychological phenomena and experimental situations. We will see that such interdependence is true of virtually all confirmations and disconfirmations of theoretical constructions, whether scales or deductive theories. It is in this fashion that the whole scientific enterprise proceeds.

Another line of research seems to yield strong evidence confirming Fechner's notions of psychological scales. B.H.C. Matthews (1931) measured the rate at which a single nerve fiber produced electrical signals when he added increasing weight to a frog muscle. He noted that the signals increased arithmetically (1, 2, 3, 4. . . .) with a geometrical (logarithmic) increase (2, 4, 8, 16, 32. . . .) in the weight. H.K. Hartline and C.H. Graham (1932) found the same general effect with the rate of firing of an optic nerve fiber as the intensity of light shining in the eye increased logarithmically. These are encouraging findings, but a note of caution must be observed: Although this evidence looks at first like dramatic proof of the adequacy of Fechner's form of psychological scaling, remember that these studies, too, require assumptions. It seems reasonable to accept the idea that *sensation* is equivalent to the number of times a nerve fiber fires, but it is by no means established that the nervous system employs such a simple "rate code" or that measures of single fibers are appropriate to gross psychological processes.

Let us propose a direct *psychological* test of a full ratio scale and see how it survives the test. Having determined absolute threshold and measured up 100 psychological units, we can present the appropriate stimulus to a subject and ask him to note this stimulus and then pick one that is half as great. To use our earlier example, we might ask him to observe a stimulus with physical intensity of 137,700 units and expect him to select the stimulus of 1174 units as being half as great (that is, we would give him the 100th psychological step and expect him to pick the 50th). Imagine our surprise if he were to pick a physical stimulus with an intensity of 68,000 units, which corresponds roughly to the 93rd psychological step. Yet, that is what he tends to do in many cases. Clearly, we need to rethink our work.

POWER FUNCTIONS

S.S. Stevens (1936), who proposed and executed many direct tests of the Fechner scales, argued from a wealth of data that the psychophysical scale was better represented as a *power law*. He showed that the psychological ratios corresponded in a direct fashion to the physical ratios rather than to scales built from equally detectable psychological units. This, then, was an attack on the assumptions made by the first scale builders that each jnd was equal to each other jnd. Stevens's argument is that the jnd tells us what we can reliably detect in the way of change at each level but that the psychological feeling of that change is a very different thing. Thus, he says that although a person might be able to *detect* a change of 1 ounce when holding a 10-ounce weight and to *detect* a change of 10 ounces when holding a 100-ounce weight, no subject would think that the addition of 1 ounce and the addition of 10 ounces *feels* the same, nor would a subject ever confuse one with the other.

Stevens and his coworkers (1957) have explored a number of different senses and have obtained sets of power laws that seem to be convincingly stable whether a subject is asked to find stimuli that are half (or twice) as bright, half (or twice) as heavy, and so on, or to do *magnitude estimation* (assigning arbitrary numbers to stimuli under the instructions to keep the

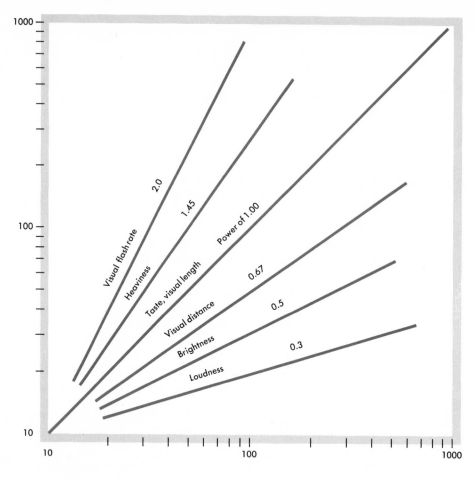

Psychological units

Physical units

10   100   1000

1000

100

10

2.0

Visual flash rate

1.45

Heaviness

Power of 1.00

Taste, visual length

0.67

Visual distance

0.5

Brightness

0.3

Loudness

Figure 3.4 Above, examples of power-law functions. Notice that both axes are in logarithms. Straight lines on the graph indicate that the psychological units are some particular power function of the physical units. Thus, as brightness increases, the sensation increases by only the .5 power. When visual flash rate increases, the sensation of the rate increases very rapidly—as the square of the actual rate. (After Stevens, 1957.) Left, Stanley S. Stevens.

ratios equivalent: "If the next stimulus is twice as big, give it a number twice as big; if it is three times as big, give it a number three times as big; if it is half as big, give it a number half as big, and so on").

Power laws allow for great variation in psychological scales over various kinds of physical stimuli, as Figure 3.4 shows. If the power is 1.0, it means that the psychological scale increases right along with the physical scale. When the physical stimulus changes from 1 to 50 to 100, the psychological scale goes from 1 to 50 to 100. If the power is 0.5, it means that the psychological scale changes slowly, increasing as the square root of the physical scale. When the physical stimulus goes from 1 to 50 to 100, the psychological values go from 1 to 7 to 10. If the power is 2.0, it means the psychological scale changes rapidly, increasing as the square of the physical stimulus. When the physical scale goes from 1 to 50 to 100, the psychological values go from 1 to 2500 to 10,000.

Power functions differ markedly for the different senses (just as Weber fractions did, though they do not correspond). Some sensory modalities have very small powers associated with them (*loudness*, which is a function of physical intensity to the .3 power), and other sensory modes have very large powers associated with them (like *painful shock*, which is a function of the physical intensity to the 1.6 power). In general, it appears that the senses that are highly "buffered" (those that range from sensitive detection to the withstanding of enormous magnitudes) have low powers and those that serve warning purposes have high powers that act to magnify the effect of the physical change.

When we look for confirmation of the power scales, we find encouraging interrelations between modalities. For instance, if we know the power scales for brightness and for loudness, we can accurately predict what a subject will do when he is told to make one noise as much louder than another as one light is brighter than another. This amounts to saying, "Find a ratio in this domain and apply it in the other domain." Although this may sound confusing, people can do such tasks with high accuracy. This is good evidence for Stevens's contention that the psychological ratios can be applied to any physical dimension and transferred from one to another.

SIGNAL-DETECTION THEORY

Recently another group of psychologists has attacked another assumption of Fechner's psychophysics. These psychologists, who are interested in the detection of signals under difficult conditions (locating airplanes on radarscopes or finding submarines by sonar), maintain that an absolute threshold is really undefinable. Without an absolute threshold, of course, there is no zero point in a Fechner scale and therefore no meaningful ratios can be computed no matter what the intervals are like.

The argument is essentially that no one can define the proper set of conditions for the measurement of the absolute zero point. Suppose we are interested in loudness. Clearly, the noise in the experimental room limits what a subject can detect at very low signal values. If we build a so-called "soundproof" room, there is still some noise and there are echoes of the noise produced by the subject himself. If we put the subject in an *anechoic* chamber (where the walls are especially absorbent and the reduction of outside noise is almost complete), we will discover that we have not solved the problem, for a new source of noise becomes apparent: the sounds generated within the subject himself by the beating of his heart, the blood pulsing through his ears, and the squeaks and creaks that his muscles and joints make when they move. In short, if we insist on being really precise, we must admit that we cannot escape from the interfering presence of "noise."

A second problem will become evident to us as we conduct these experiments: Some subjects are ready to report a signal on very little evidence. They make many errors which are called *false positives*, that is, they report hearing a signal even when we know there is no signal there. In contrast, other subjects are conservative and, unless they are absolutely sure that there is a signal, they report that no signal is present, even when we know there is one. Such reports are called *false negatives*. The solution to this problem is to get all subjects to report perfectly just what happened (that they really heard or did not hear the signal). But, of course, a subject is not at all confident about what "really" did happen. The instructions given to him amount to asking him to do the job we as psychologists are trying to do, that is, to report exactly where his absolute threshold is; and he is no more able to do that than we are.

In an effort to cope with these two problems, John A. Swets, Wilson P. Tanner, Jr., and Theodore G. Birdsall (1961) evolved a whole new approach to the measurement of sensory functions. The approach developed from the general theory of signal detectability originated by electrical engineers in the early 1950s. Although the theory and its elaborations are much too rich and complex to be developed here, the essential ideas have an elegance and simplicity that you can grasp quickly.

Let us take a simple example, detection of a radio signal by listening. (The same arguments can be applied to detection of appropriate signals by seeing, feeling, smelling, and tasting.) Suppose you are listening for a signal on a transistor radio. You are allowed to listen for a few seconds each hour. The signal will not be a long broadcast; it will only be a short pulse of a tone. Perhaps you are a scientist waiting to launch a rocket or a spy waiting for a signal to pick up a message. Because of cost or distance or because your superiors do not want anyone else to interpret your signal, it is made very short and simple. How can we make sure the signal is loud enough for you to hear it and yet as weak as possible so we can save money or avoid other people hearing it?

If the radio were absolutely silent, we could use a very tiny signal because any signal at all would stand out. But the radio is not silent, of course. It

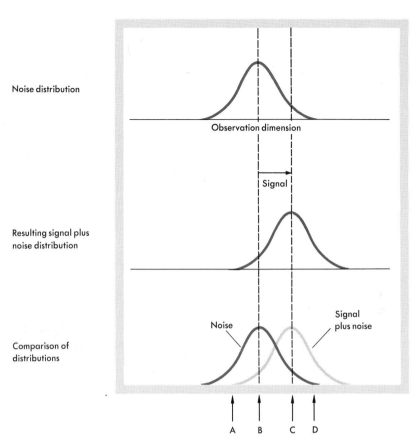

Noise distribution

Observation dimension

Signal

Resulting signal plus
noise distribution

Noise

Signal
plus noise

Comparison of
distributions

A   B   C   D

Figure 3.5 An illustration of the way signal-detection theory looks at the observation dimension. Point A is clearly noise; B is called noise but might be signal; C is called signal but might be noise; D is clearly signal.

produces all sorts of noise, static, hums, hisses, faint sounds from interfering stations, clicks from other electrical equipment, and the like. Since you are not interested in any of these, we will call them all *noise*. Sometimes there is a lot of noise, sometimes there is just a little. Most of the time you listen you will hear some average amount of noise. Because of this variation in the strength of the noise, we will use the bell-shaped curve shown in Figure 3.5 to represent the amount of noise you are likely to hear at any given time.

Now, when a signal is transmitted to you, it does not replace the noise; it merely adds some more energy on top of it. Thus, we can think of the result of the signal as coming to your ears as "signal plus noise." If we assume the signal adds some constant amount to what you hear, then the "signal plus noise" distribution can be drawn as in Figure 3.5. If we like, we can combine both distributions on the same graph. Now, if we look at various sound-level values that might be present, we can show how you might work as an observer when you are listening and reporting to us either "signal" or "noise."

Suppose you listen briefly and you hear only weak sounds (point A on the Observation Value in Figure 3.5). You can say with great confidence that there was *no* signal. This is a *true negative* report. Later, you listen again and hear a very strong sound (point D). Now you can say with great confidence that there *was* a signal. This is a *true positive* report. If you listen again and hear a moderate amount of sound, like points B and C, it will be harder for you to decide what you heard. You may just be hearing loud noise, or you may be hearing low noise plus the signal. You might guess that what you hear is "just noise" at point B and you are likely to guess that it is "the signal" at point C. Though you will be correct most of the time in each of these decisions, you will be wrong part of the time, of course. Sometimes when you said "noise" at B, there really was a signal present. (You made a *false negative* response.) Part of the time you said "signal" at C, there was only noise present. (You made a *false positive* response.)

Now that you understand the situation, how does it help us deal with the psychological question of talking about the detectability of the signal? We can choose some signal to be presented to you and "run the theoretical situation backwards" to see how the distributions of "noise" and "signal plus noise" must look. We persuade you to listen over and over again for a few seconds each time. Half the time there is a signal and half the time there is not. We find out how often you give true positives, true negatives, false positives, and false negatives. If, for example, you give 85 per cent true positives and 85 per cent true negatives with only 15 per cent false positives and 15 per cent false negatives, we know that the two curves must look like those in Figure 3.6. We have now identified your subjective "cutting point" *and* we have a measure of how much the signal is different from the noise.

We can further check the relation of the signal and the noise by getting you to change your "cutting point." We might say, "It is terribly important to identify all signals and it is all right if you make false positives. If you think there was a signal, be sure to say so. Only report 'no signal' when you are positive there was not one there." Or we might say: "We will pay you a dollar every time you say 'signal' when there is really a signal there and fine you ten cents for reporting a signal if there isn't one there." Both these instructions should move your cutting point to the left. Under these instructions you might give 98 per cent true positives, 51 per cent true negatives, 49 per cent false positives, and 2 per cent false negatives. As you can see in Figure 3.6, however, this would still describe the same relation between the signal and the noise as shown by the relation between the curves. It would, of course, be possible to check this further by changing your cutting point again, this time to the conservative side, by reversing the instructions or the payoff for detection.

If signal-detection theory holds, we can specify the discriminability of the

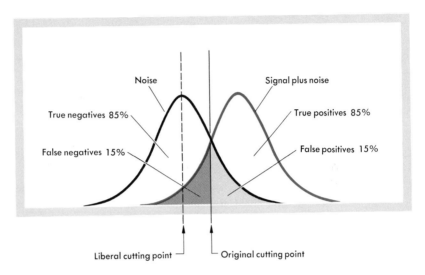

		Subject says	
		"Noise"	"Signal"
Condition	Signal	15	85
	Noise	85	15

Figure 3.6 Graphic representation of the noise and signal-plus-noise distributions for a particular subject's performance.

signal by relating the "signal plus noise" distribution to the "noise" distribution. When the distance between the two distributions is small, the stimulus is not very detectable. When the distance between the two distributions is large, the stimulus is highly, or even perfectly, detectable. Once we have a set of such curves we can tell how accurate the typical subject is likely to be for any given value of the signal. And, for the first time, we can evaluate the individual subject's characteristics as a "detector" both in terms of accuracy and in terms of his tendency to be "liberal" or "conservative" in reporting signals. Beyond that we can study the effect of variables, such as instructions and payoffs, on the likelihood of detecting a stimulus. Thus, by giving up the notion of an absolute threshold (and the absolute zero point), we have found an interesting technology that both measures the sensitivity of human beings as detectors of signals and provides a general answer to the question of the subject's bias in reporting.

Signal-detection theory can be extended to problems in identification, memory, physiological measurements, communication, and test construction. Of course, the theory can be applied only by making a host of critical assumptions concerning the nature of the observation dimension, the shape of the noise and signal-plus-noise distributions, the effects of instructions, and so on. In many settings, however, the assumptions seem both appropriate and productive. A burst of research articles give evidence that this most recent addition to psychophysical thought furnishes a powerful new tool for tackling some classic problems.

WHICH IS RIGHT?

At this point you are surely tempted to ask which one of these approaches is "really true" and which ones are false. It would be very satisfying to say that one model is correct and that it yields the right kind of information for all purposes. But the last phrase, "for all purposes," is exactly what stops us. Each model does some things very well and captures part of "the truth," but no one model represents all that we want to know.

If we are interested in comparing the discriminability of a set of stimuli for some task, then we will want data of the sort that Fechner recommended (*"Throw the switch under the brightest light"*). If we want to know how people will feel about the comparison of intensities of stimuli or how they judge their relations, we had better use Stevens' approach (*"As the light gets brighter, move the stick forward proportionately"*). If we are worried about the detection of a signal at all, we will want to study the problem in terms of the work of Swets, Tanner, and Birdsall (*"Press the button when you see the 'blip' on the radarscope"*).

The most appropriate questions to ask are not those concerning the absolute truth of a formulation but rather: What does the model do? And what is it good for? It is sufficient for our purposes here to show that these different views of psychophysical measurement are rational constructions that mirror different aspects of the original question concerning the relation of the psychological world to the physical world. Which model is useful and (for the moment) "true" depends on the task before us and on the assumptions that we can make concerning the relation of the human being to that task.

The most important lesson for you to learn from psychophysics right now is that all measurement is set in a network of theory and assumption and that all tests of the adequacy of measurement are similarly set. This is true of science in general but it is conspicuously true of psychology. Appreciation of this lesson is basic to understanding much scientific controversy.

Trait Measurement

In psychophysical measurement we are free to vary the stimulus material and we can specify just the kind of response we want. Even so, there are conflicting views of psychophysics. You can imagine, therefore, that the measurement of human traits is a more formidable problem. First, we must take people as they are; we cannot arbitrarily manipulate them. Second, there are traits galore in the form of lists of attributes, but we do not know which are important. Third, we do not know what makes observers think that someone qualifies as an instance of a trait. Nor do we know exactly what a person with a given trait is supposed to do in a particular situation.

Our problem is doubly ambiguous. Two observers see a person do quite different acts (one sees him argue in class, the other watches him play football), but they may agree that he is "aggressive." On the other hand, one observer may see the same act performed by two different people, say, pushing a little old lady, and conclude that one pusher is aggressive and the other is concerned for her safety.

As a first move we can design a standard behavior situation. Clearly, if we can define the situation tightly enough, we will be able to squeeze some of the ambiguity out of the behavior we are observing. A standardized behavior situation is most commonly called a *test*. We hope that tests involve responses that can be readily interpreted as being related to the trait we are trying to study.

Tests can be divided into two gross classes depending on whether the responses are *structured* or *unstructured*.

With a structured test such as a multiple-choice achievement examination, a typical intelligence test, or an interest test, both the stimuli and the responses are commonly held constant. The subject is merely permitted to choose from the responses available to answer some specific question. Although this procedure clearly indicates the test-taker's behavior and lets us identify each response, it may be meaningless if none of the responses we furnish is one the subject wants to select or if he wants to select all the answers but we only let him take one. Such tests put a heavy burden on the test constructor and demand both careful preparation of alternative answers and subsequent study to ensure that like responses do in fact indicate like qualities.

In an unstructured test like the Rorschach or Thematic Apperception Test (see pp. 598–599), the stimulus is held constant (people see the same ink blots or the same pictures), but the response is allowed to vary within wide limits, on the assumption that the responses the subjects make reflect something about their personalities. The problem is that interpretation is likely to be very difficult since almost every response is unique. As a result, such tests put a heavy burden on the interpreter and require great practice and skill on the part of the psychologist to overcome the ambiguity of the responses.

For the present, we will assume only that tests furnish us with *scores*, that is, that we can look at the way the person behaves on the test and *count* something that will be a measure of a particular ability or trait of the test taker. If we give a mathematics achievement test, we can count the number of problems correctly solved or we can count the number of minutes it takes the person to finish the test. If we are trying to measure "achievement motivation," we can ask the subjects to write a story for us and then have judges count the number of sentences about success or successful people as a measure of the motive. If we are interested in a personality test we may ask people to sort statements about themselves into true and false categories. ("I am worried most of the time." "The top of my head feels tender.") Then we can count the number of sentences that are sorted the same way neurotic or psychotic patients sort them. In ways like these, we can give scores to the people we examine. Then we face the question: How do we decide what kind of a measure that score is?

First, we must make some assumptions and select some kind of model. A common assumption is that trait measures are additive. The more items you get right on a mathematics test, the more mathematics you know; similarly, the more you talk about people achieving success, the more achievement-oriented you are, or the more items you answer like neurotic patients, the more neurotic you are. Notice that this is an assumption, not a fact. If an examination only covers one fact in mathematics but asks 400 questions about it, getting all 400 items right may mean no more than getting one of the items right. If a student is asked to write a story about a picture, he may elect to write a story about achievement. In doing so, he may include many achievement-oriented sentences but the important thing might be the initial decision to write that kind of story, not the number of sentences. If neurotic patients are asked about matters that are true of all human beings, a person may agree with all their answers and merely be claiming membership in the human race, not giving testimony about his neuroticism. We must remember, therefore, that the common procedure of adding items together to get a trait measure depends on many assumptions, each of which must be investigated sooner or later.

If we are willing to assume an additive model, we are merely saying that the scores are ordered; the bigger the number, the more of the trait. In short, we have an ordinal scale. We can check on our assumptions by asking if the scores that we have given to people order them the way judges or teachers or friends line them up with respect to the trait we are testing. Or we can ask if the people at one end of our scale are noticeably different from the people at the other, that is, whether they pass their mathematics course while the others fail, whether they go on to work hard for success while others of equal ability do not, or whether they are hospitalized or go into psychotherapy while the others do not. If our scale passes this type of evaluation, we can conclude that it is measuring the kind of thing that we want to measure and that it is really cumulative.

The next thing we might want to know is whether it is an interval scale, whether differences between scores have the same meaning at different points on the scale. We cannot solve this difficult question without making some broad assumptions. In this kind of scale, we must make an assumption about the distribution of the trait. Do we think the trait is "all or none"?

Do most people have a lot of the trait and a few people have a little? Do most people have a little of the trait and a few have a lot or none at all? If we can make a rational argument that the trait has a particular distribution in our subjects, we can make our scores fit that particular distribution (with a little simple mathematical juggling). Then we can talk about the new units as being equal. Our problem is that these assumptions are usually made in ignorance. This does not mean that our task is hopeless; it just means that we will want to gather a lot of extra data on our scale before we will bet a lot on the fact of equal intervals.

A common assumption is that psychological traits are distributed *normally*. (The reference is not to the opposite of "abnormally," but to a mathematical distribution that, when plotted on a graph, is known as the *normal curve*, or the *Gaussian curve* after the great mathematician, Karl Frederich Gauss. It is also sometimes called the *random-error curve* or the *chance distribution*.) The curve in Figure 3.7 (p. 88) represents the assumption that most people have a medium amount of each trait and that a few people have a lot of it and a few people have a little of it. It is usually described as "bell-shaped" and symmetrical. A few examples will give some notion of the many places this distribution applies. If we measure the height of all 20-year-old men, they fall into a normal distribution. If we flip 100 pennies a thousand different times and write down the number of heads on each trial, we will find an approximately normal distribution ranging from zero to 100, with a mean at 50. If we have 500 different people try to measure the length of a line to the nearest hundredth of an inch, the results will fit a normal distribution.

The assumption of a normal distribution for psychological traits is reasonable on psychological and common-sense grounds. First, we believe that most traits are matters of degree, not matters of classification into types, so we want some kind of continuous distribution for a model. Second, we believe that most traits are so distributed that the extremes are rare. For instance, we expect to find a few people who are very aggressive and a few who are very submissive, but we expect to find most people somewhere in the middle—they are aggressive some times and to some degree and submissive some times and to some degree. Similarly, a few people are very sociable and outgoing and a few are very shy and retiring, but most people are both to some degree depending on the situation and the circumstances. Thus, we should select a distribution that will put most people in the middle rather than at the ends. Finally, we think that psychological traits have multiple causes; that is, they result from the interaction of many genetic and environmental factors. It is, therefore, reasonable on statistical grounds to argue that the normal curve is the appropriate distribution.

It is also true that the normal distribution has a number of convenient and useful mathematical properties. For example, if we take a distribution of any shape—flat, humped, or even U-shaped—and draw repeated samples from it, the averages of those samples form a normal distribution. Further,

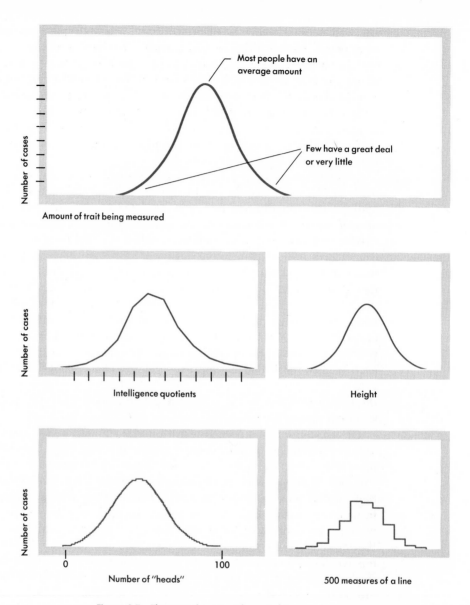

Figure 3.7 The normal curve with examples.

the distribution has been studied, tabled, and applied for about 200 years and is understood in greater depth than any other similar-looking distributions that we might choose. For all of these reasons (only part of which are psychological), we usually make the assumption that traits are normally distributed. Once we have made the assumption, we can transform our scale until the numbers fit a normal curve (in case they do not happen to do so already) and then we can act as if we know what the "real" units are and as if all the units are equal. In short we can act as if we have an interval scale.

The consequences of this assumption are far-reaching. We can apply all the usual statistical techniques to our numbers because the techniques only require dealing with an interval scale. This is very convenient for us and gives us access to powerful methods of summarizing our data and dealing with it.

Simple Statistics on the Normal Curve

Once we have made the assumption that our data correspond to the normal curve and have adjusted our numbers as needed, we can describe our data in a compact and simple way. We can always, of course, draw a picture of the data. Such pictures (as shown in Figure 3.8) are called frequency polygons or histograms depending on their form. However, we can do the same job with the normal curve and just two statistics: *a measure of central*

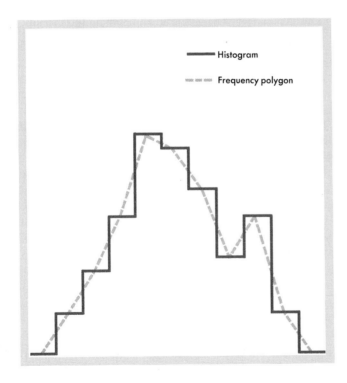

Figure 3.8 Histogram and frequency polygon for the same data.

Number of cases

Amount of measure

tendency and a *measure of dispersion*. We will consider these two measures separately.

Measures of Central Tendency. These measures tell where the curve is located in general; that is, they locate the center of the distribution along the measurement dimension or baseline. There are three common measures of central tendency: the mode, the median, and the mean.

The *mode*, abbreviated as *Mo*, is the score achieved by more people than any other. It is the highest point on the frequency polygon or the highest bar on the histogram. It can be applied to any scale from the *nominal* scale on up in that it merely says, "There are more people in this classification than any other." A distribution can have only one mean and one median, but it is possible for it to have several modes if several categories are equally popular.

The *median* (*Mdn*) is simply the midpoint of all scores—half fall above, half fall below. It is the middle rank. If there are eleven scores ordered in a distribution, the sixth one is the median; five cases are above it and five cases are below it. If you have ten scores, the median is midway between the fifth and sixth scores. It reflects only the ordinal nature of the scale.

The *mean (M)* is simply the arithmetical average. To find the mean you add together all the scores and divide by the number of scores. We symbolize this with the formula: $M = \dfrac{\Sigma X}{N}$. The symbol Σ means "the sum of" and "ΣX" means "the sum of all the X's." X is the symbol for each score. N is the symbol for the number of scores involved. For most sets of test scores, the mean is the most useful measure of central tendency. It is also the measure that is ordinarily most likely to be stable from one sample of subjects to another.

In a symmetrical, bell-shaped distribution, the mean, median, and mode will fall at the same point. If the distribution is not symmetrical, the mean, median, and mode will diverge as shown in the examples in Figure 3.9. Such diverging curves are said to be *skewed*. A curve is called *positively skewed* if it is pulled out toward the right side or high end and *negatively skewed* if it is pulled out toward the left side or low end.

For some purposes we may prefer to use the median or mode when talking about skewed distributions. If we are talking about the "average income" per family in a small town where a millionaire happens to live, it is clear that the mean is greatly raised by the millionaire's income, but the median and mode are not influenced by the size of this one extreme value. If it is important to know a score or value that applies to many people, the mode alone is justified as a measure. If, for example, we were manufacturing equipment (hammer handles, say, or work benches) and could make only one size, the mode might well be the best choice. The largest number of people for whom the equipment will be precisely adapted will be found at the mode. In many matters of size, preference, taste, and fashion, the mode is important.

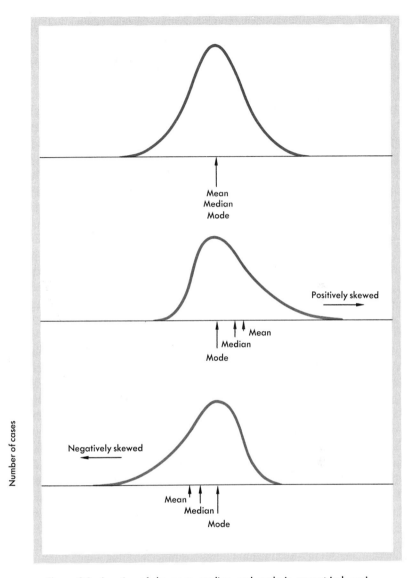

Figure 3.9 Location of the mean, median, and mode in symmetrical, positively-skewed and negatively-skewed distributions.

Measures of Dispersion. Once the distribution is pinned down to the base line by some measure of central tendency, other issues arise: How much does the distribution vary around the point? Is it flat or peaked? Wide or narrow? Such questions are answered by one of the measures of dispersion. There are many such measures, but we shall discuss only two here: the *range*—the easiest measure to calculate—and the *standard deviation*—the most useful measure.

The *range* is simply the distance from the lowest score to the highest score in the distribution. If the scores run from 20 to 80, the range is 60. The range is a very crude measure and is subject to wide variation from one group of subjects to another because it depends on only two values, the top and bottom scores. It gives us the gross limits of dispersion but tells us little else.

The *standard deviation (SD)* appears complex, but it contains a great deal of useful information about dispersion. It is customary to dazzle students by defining the standard deviation as "the square root of the average squared deviation of each score from the mean" or, even worse, as the "root mean square." You can understand these mysterious definitions by carefully reading the following directions for calculating the SD: First, find the distance along the base line between each score and the mean, symbolized as $(X-M)$; square this figure $(X-M)^2$; add all such squares together, $\Sigma (X-M)^2$; to find the average squared distance divide by the number of scores (N). This *mean squared deviation* is the *variance* of the distribution, and the square root of the variance is the standard deviation. Algebraically, the procedure is expressed as:

$$SD = \sqrt{\frac{\Sigma (X-M)^2}{N}}$$

The standard deviation and the mean together describe the normal curve. If you know that a distribution is normal and what its mean and standard deviation are, it is possible to draw a picture of the distribution and interpret the scores on it. Tables for this purpose can be found in most statistics books. A very abbreviated table is given here as an example.

Table 3.1 Relation of standard deviation and normal curve.

Standard Deviations Above or Below the Median	Height of the Curve Having One Unit of Area	Percentage of Cases Between This Point and the Mean	Percentage of Cases Having Lower Scores
+3 SD	.004	50	100
+2 SD	.054	48	98
+1 SD	.242	34	84
0	.399	0	50
−1 SD	.242	34	16
−2 SD	.054	48	2
−3 SD	.004	50	0

As the descriptive statistics above suggest, there are many ways of reporting scores or measurements. Some are more useful for one purpose, some for another. Because psychologists are so frequently concerned with the problem of making sense out of scores—as on school tests, army examinations, job placement tests, or supervisors' ratings—we will take time here to examine some of the most common forms of expressing measures.

Raw Scores. Raw scores are simply the numbers originally assigned to performance. Ordinarily they must be supplemented with other information to be psychologically meaningful. A raw score of 67 on a school test does not tell whether it is an A or an F. It could be the top score in the class or the bottom score. We need to ask: What are the mean and standard deviation of the distribution? Or, what is the rank in the group?

Rank. A rank tells you where you stand in a distribution. If you know the size and quality of the group, your rank is a very valuable score indeed. It is not, of course, comparable from a group of one size to a group of another size. Being fifth in a group of 100 is likely to indicate a better performance than being fifth in a group of 10.

Centile Rank. The centile rank, or percentile rank, like the median, is a method of cutting the total distribution into zones. The first centile point is the point at or below which one per cent of the distribution falls. The second centile point is the point at or below which two per cent of the distribution falls. Similarly, the 95th centile point is the point at or below which 95 per cent of the distribution falls. This method of presenting scores is widely used in standardized tests of achievement and in vocational guidance tests. Centiles have a marked advantage over ranks in that they can be interpreted more immediately. They do not depend on the actual number of people being scored but rather on the *proportion* falling above and below the given score. If a person is better than 80 per cent of his group, he is at the 80th centile whether his group contains 10, 100, or 1000 people. Of course, the larger the group the more stable and precise the centile rank will be.

Standard Score (SS). We saw above that you could get a great deal of information for interpreting a score if you had the mean and standard deviation of the distribution and knew that it was normal. *The standard score contains all this relevant information in itself.* It is calculated by finding the difference between the person's score and the mean, $(X - M)$, and dividing by the standard deviation (SD). The formula is:

$$SS = \frac{X - M}{SD}$$

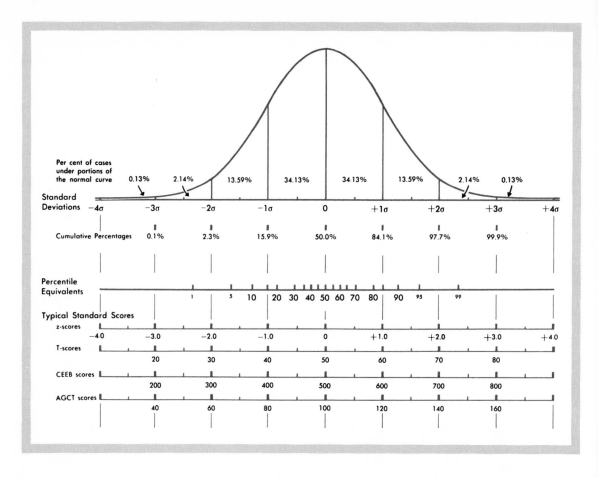

Figure 3.10 Normal curve with standard scores and percentiles. (Adapted from Seashore, 1955.)

giving a score that tells how many standard deviations away from the mean the individual's score is. Figure 3.10 shows a normal curve with standard scores. A standard score of zero means that the individual is at the mean or average. A standard score of plus one indicates that he is one standard deviation above the mean and is, therefore, at the 84th centile of the distribution. A standard score of minus two indicates that the person scored two standard deviations below the mean and is, therefore, at the second centile.

The economy of the standard score is easy to see. With this method, each person interpreting scores does not need to sit down with a score, a mean, a standard deviation, and a table of the normal curve. If he has one complete picture of a normal curve like Figure 3.10, he can use it for all interpretations of standard scores, no matter what kinds of tests or initial raw scores are involved. Standard scores have been widely adopted by schools, the armed forces, college testing agencies, and such organizations. In order to avoid the use of fractions, decimals, and positive and negative signs, various constants have been added to the mean and various units have been used to stand for each standard deviation. In World War II the Army employed 100 as the mean and 20 as the standard deviation. Thus, 120 on any test meant a score one standard deviation above the mean and 80 meant a score one standard deviation below the mean. Some of the common standard scores are given in Figure 3.10. In order to translate scores from one standard score system to another, we only have to convert to simple standard scores and then connect into the new system by multiplying by the standard deviation unit and adding the arbitrary mean value.

When psychological scores are to be averaged or summed, it is customary to assume that standard scores are comparable and can be treated this way. A little simple experimenting will convince you that it makes a good deal of difference whether you add raw scores, centile ranks, or standard scores in combining two tests. You need to be quite clear about your objectives in averaging or adding scores before following any one procedure.

In *all* interpretations of scores, the reference group, or *norm group*, must be kept clearly in mind. *Scores are useful and comparable only when norm groups are relevant and comparable.* If a person is interested in interpreting a college entrance examination, it is most useful to know how he compares with college freshmen or, even better, successful college freshmen. A blanket comparison with, say, all high school seniors in the state or, even worse, high school juniors, may be flattering to the ego but is hardly useful or relevant to the prediction problem at hand. Similarly, if you are going to work as a clerk it is important to know how you compare in clerical skills with employed clerical workers and of little interest how you compare with college students or auto mechanics. The importance of good normative data to the successful interpretation of psychological measures can scarcely be overemphasized.

MEASURES OF RELATIONSHIP

There is one final question to be answered about psychological measurement: What do the scores relate to? We know at this point how to relate a measure to the distribution of the group and how to interpret a position in that distribution, but we still lack a precise tool for showing either (1) whether the measure relates to something else that we care about or (2) whether it measures the same thing as other tests. As human beings and applied psychologists, we are concerned with many practical problems of the first kind. If a person scores high on "Test X" as compared to college sophomores, does this indicate that he will get high grades in college, be popular with girls, make a lot of money, or be a good pilot? We need some measure that can describe how closely some "outside" measure like these covaries with the test measure. As psychologists we are concerned with

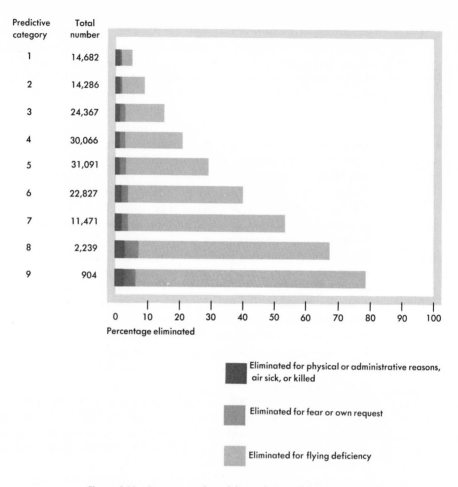

Figure 3.11 Percentage of candidates eliminated from primary pilot training as related to scores on the selection battery. (Adapted from Army Air Forces Staff, Psychological Section, 1945.)

many scientific, descriptive problems of the second type. Can we describe a whole set of behaviors simply by measuring one or two of them? Can we demonstrate that two tests which "look different" really do measure the same thing?

Certain obvious measures suggest themselves. We can take the people who do well on college entrance tests and the people who do badly, send them all to college, and at the end of the year compare the average grades of the two groups, or compare the number in each group still in school, or count the number in each group who make the honor roll. The Army Air Force actually did such a study on flight-training (separating the cadets into nine groups instead of just two) with the very encouraging results shown in Figure 3.11. This is a sound procedure but it is difficult to express concisely.

Further, in finely graded data (such as we might have in comparing two measures), it sacrifices too much accuracy. In brief, this method is both clear and good, but it is crude.

A more refined method was invented by Sir Francis Galton in the nineteenth century. He called it the *coefficient of co-relationship* and today we call it *correlation*. It is a measure of the extent to which two variables change together or, more formally, *covary*. For example, suppose that for each of a group of 100 freshmen we have two scores, a college entrance examination and a grade-point average for the freshman year. Such a set of 200 paired numbers is given in Figure 3.12. Ordering on either one of the sets of numbers reduces the chaos somewhat, but it is still difficult to determine the exact relationship (if any) between the examination score and the grade-point average. Note, however, that we could take all the students with examination scores above 70 and make a frequency distribution of their average grades. Then we could take those between 60 and 70 and similarly distribute them; then those between 50 and 60, then 40 to 50, and so on. It immediately becomes clear that some relationship exists. The students who scored high on the test have *on the average* higher grades than students scoring at the mean and considerably higher grades than students scoring below the mean. We can see that we would do considerably better than chance prediction if we found out where a given student fell on the examination and then predicted that he would earn the average grade obtained by the students falling in that same zone.

But this method still sacrifices accuracy unnecessarily. Surely the students who scored 69 on the examination will tend to have higher averages than those who scored 61—yet here they are grouped in the same class. The answer that suggests itself is to subdivide the distribution even further. We

Figure 3.12 Determining the relation between pairs of scores.

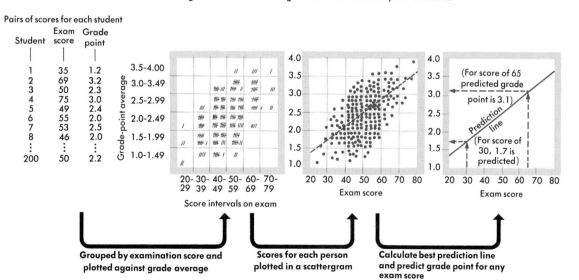

Pairs of scores for each student

Student	Exam score	Grade point
1	35	1.2
2	69	3.2
3	50	2.3
4	75	3.0
5	49	2.4
6	55	2.0
7	53	2.5
8	46	2.0
⋮	⋮	⋮
200	50	2.2

Grouped by examination score and plotted against grade average

Scores for each person plotted in a scattergram

Calculate best prediction line and predict grade point for any exam score can carry this approach to its ultimate conclusion and plot each individual separately on a *scattergram,* or *bivariate* (two-variable) *correlation surface.* Each point on the scattergram represents the pair of scores belonging to a single person, an examination score and a grade average. Clearly a general prediction line can be fitted to the data. For every examination score there is a predicted grade average. Inspection of the scattergram will show how much variation will be found around the predicted values.

With a little simple algebra and geometry it is possible to describe very exactly and concisely this whole process in a single index number called the *correlation coefficient.* This number expresses the relation between the two sets of scores, the slope of the prediction line and the amount of error around the line. For our purposes you need not be able to compute this statistic, but you should develop some understanding of its meaning.

The correlation coefficient (which we symbolize as r) ranges from +1.00 (a perfect positive relationship), through zero (no relationship at all), to −1.00 (a perfect negative relationship). The predictive power of a correlation is determined by its size, as the several illustrations in Figure 3.13 show. Large correlation coefficients approaching either plus one or minus one yield predictions over most of the range with little error. As the correlation moves toward zero the predictions move in toward the mean value of the predicted variable. In effect, as the prediction becomes less certain we "hedge our bets" by predicting closer and closer to the average. Finally, at zero correlation the only reasonable prediction *is* the average of the predicted variable, and all the variation can be taken as prediction error.

You may find it of some interest to make predictions for yourself with your own test scores. If you express the scores in terms of ordinary standard scores, the prediction equation is very simple:

> Predicted Standard Score = Standard Score on Test multiplied by the Correlation Coefficient.
>
> In symbols:
>
> $$SS \text{ (predicted)} = r \times SS \text{ (predictor)}$$

In most psychology classes, the midterm examination correlates about .70 with the final examination. Suppose that you were one standard deviation above the mean on the midquarter, you would then expect to be about .7 of a standard deviation above the mean on the final. Notice that this does not mean that is exactly where you *will* be; it just says that is the best prediction to make for you. Similarly, if you were two standard deviations above the mean on the first examination you would expect to be 1.4 standard deviation above the mean on the final. Note that if you were *at* the mean on the first test (that is, zero standard deviation from the mean), you can expect to be at the mean on the final. Also note that if you are below the mean on the first test, your most likely final score is also below the mean but not as far

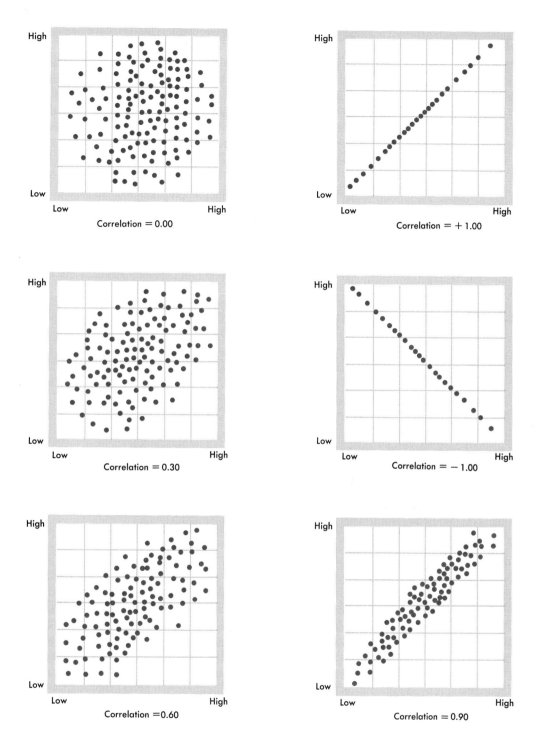

Figure 3.13 Examples of scattergrams for various values of the correlation coefficient.

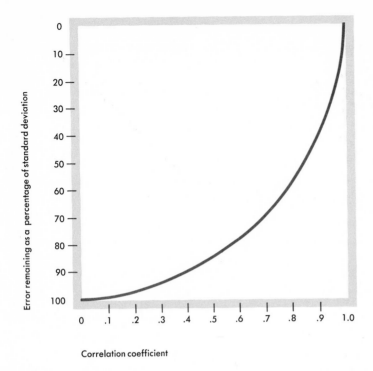

Error remaining as a percentage of standard deviation

Correlation coefficient

Figure 3.14 Relation of the correlation coefficient to the error remaining in the predicted values.

below it (for example, —3 SD on the first test predicts —2.1 SD on the final, though this may not be much consolation).

For good individual prediction a high correlation coefficient is required—a rough rule of thumb says greater than .80. However, for tasks involving large groups (college admission, army screening, and the like) even moderate (.50) or low (.20) correlations may prove to be important and useful. If we have lots of decisions to make, even a little information about chances of success will prove to be valuable in the long run.

One curious property of the correlation coefficient is that it does not *directly* reflect the amount of error in prediction. A correlation of 1.00 predicts perfectly of course, and a correlation of zero adds nothing to our prediction, but a correlation of .50 is not halfway in between. It is poorer than we might have expected it to be. If, however, we ask what proportion of the variation is "accounted for" by the prediction, we can find a simple relation. The *variance* that is successfully predicted is proportional to the square of the correlation coefficient. This means that a correlation of .20 accounts for only 4 per cent of the variance we would like to predict, a correlation of .40 accounts for 16 per cent, one of .60 for 36 per cent, one of .80 for 64 per cent, and so on. As Figure 3.14 shows, the prediction power of the correlation coefficient increases rapidly as it approaches perfect predictability—or to look at it the other way, falls off rapidly as it departs from perfect predictability. In this sense the difference between a correlation of

.20 and one of .30 is much less than the difference between correlations of .80 and .90.

Be careful not to think of correlation as if it meant causation when anyone says "X accounts for so much of Y." As we pointed out in Chapter Two, correlation does *not* imply causation. It simply reports the degree of covariation. A few simple examples will help you remember this.

If we tested all the children in an entire grade school on reading speed and then correlated reading speed with height, we would get a correlation of about .70 or .80. Yet, obviously, neither of these variables *causes* the other. They are related because they both *covary* with age. Children get to be taller *and* they get to be better readers as they grow older. Note further that you cannot say that age *causes* either of these effects, even though it correlates highly with both.

As a second example, consider what the correlation would be between the population of New York City and the population of London, year by year for the last 50 years. Each city would increase each year. Clearly the correlation would be positive and very high. It is equally clear that the increase in the population of New York City has no *causal* effect on the population of London or vice versa. We have simply illustrated the well-known fact that most cities of the world are steadily increasing in population.

Reliability and Validity

With some understanding of the concept of correlation we can now discuss two other very important aspects of measurement: reliability and validity. In all psychological measurement, questions of reliability and validity must be raised.

RELIABILITY

Reliability can be defined as the *accuracy* with which a test (or any other instrument) measures whatever it measures. In psychology we talk about two kinds of reliability: (1) *stability* over time and (2) *internal consistency*, or homogeneity.

If we are measuring a trait which is assumed to be stable over time (color vision, clerical aptitude, general intelligence), the stability coefficient can be obtained quite easily. We give the test to a group of people, wait a few days, weeks, or months, and give the same test to the same people again. Scores from the two administrations of the test are correlated. If the correlation is high (that is, if the people come out in about the same order), the test is said to have high stability or a *high test-retest reliability*. If the test-retest correlation is low, either the test does not measure consistently or the people have changed during the interval.

The second kind of reliability is of special concern if (1) the trait being tested is changeable or (2) if the investigator wants to know whether the items on the test are all measuring the same kind of thing. Measures for gauging internal consistency depend on the data from a single administration of the test. In some methods half of the items are correlated with the other half, in other methods more complex statistics are employed. All aim at discovering how much the fragments of the test—the items—covary with one another. The question in other words is: How well do the parts of this test measure the same thing (whatever it may be) and how much of it do they measure?

The two kinds of reliability are quite different, cannot be substituted for each other, and should not be confused. Some tests may have *both* high stability and high internal consistency. Such tests are presumably accurate, homogeneous measures of relatively enduring traits. A good vocabulary test, for example, probably ought to have both of these characteristics. We expect that splitting the test in half ought to yield two subtests that will correlate highly with each other and we expect further that persons who are high in measured vocabulary at one time will be high in measured vocabulary at another time.

Some tests may have high stability but low internal consistency. Such tests, we assume, sample enduring characteristics but a heterogeneous collection of them. The way a person responds to a given item may not change with time, but that item does not necessarily predict how he will respond to any other item in the test. Many tests of vocational interests have these characteristics, since they are composed of collections of activities that a person may like or not like individually in a consistent fashion. Just because lawyers, say, like a certain set of activities does not mean that these items intercorrelate.

Finally, some tests have low stability and high internal consistency. Such tests may measure "dynamic" traits (which change markedly from time to time), even though at any one time they may be measured with great precision. We commonly assume that some of the personality traits are of this sort. People can be "up" or happy one day and "down" or unhappy a few days later. The change is attributed to a change in the person, not to measurement error in the test. Some motor measurements, like "steadiness," also show this pattern; they can be reliably measured at any one time but change from one day to the next in response to complex determiners.

A test that is low in both internal consistency and stability would presumably be of little use to anyone.

VALIDITY

Validity can be most simply defined as the *extent* to which a test measures what it is *supposed* to measure. Three different kinds of validity are important in appraising a test or measuring instrument: (1) *content validity,* (2) *criterion validity,* and (3) *construct validity.*

Content validity is arrived at by sampling items from some defined body of information. If experts in mathematics agree about the proper content of a college algebra course and if we devise a good way to sample that content, the resulting test will be said to have content validity. If we want to construct a vocabulary test, we can select a certain collegiate dictionary as the universe of content and then sample words from it according to some explicit plan. The test, by definition, has content validity. Most achievement tests rely on this kind of validity. They sample from "standard texts" of modern history, American literature, and so on. Notice that this validity is not represented as a number; it is based on a defense of its logic of definition and selection.

Criterion validity refers to the extent to which a test correlates with and predicts some "outside" criterion. Correlating scores on a clerical-ability test with ratings of success on a clerical job is an example of this kind of validity. If a test is given at one time and the criterion data collected later (for example, testing job applicants and then evaluating them after they have worked for six months), the validity is called *predictive*. If the testing is correlated against a current criterion (for example, testing employed persons who are currently rated from "good" to "poor" by their supervisors), the validity is called *concurrent*. Any particular test has many predictive and concurrent validities; a specific clerical test might correlate .40 (predictive) with success in company X as file clerk, .60 (concurrent) with success in company Y as a bookkeeper, .70 (predictive) with success as key-punch operator in company Z, and zero with ratings of success in department store sales clerking. It is important to know the exact conditions under which validity data were obtained.

Construct validity is the most difficult of the validities to explain and it is also difficult to report concisely. It is very much like the question of understanding the genotype from many varying phenotypes. Roughly speaking, one proceeds as follows: "Here is a test which is supposed to be largely a test of 'anxiety' (or any other abstract trait). There is no explicit criterion for 'anxiety.' However, there are some situations in which 'anxiety' might manifest itself and there are some other instruments that ought to measure at least a little bit of 'anxiety.' Now, if the people who are high on this test really do have a lot of 'anxiety' *and* if 'anxiety' is the kind of trait we think it is, then the people who are high on the test will behave in a particular way in these situations and will make certain kinds of scores on the other tests."

We then pick situations that ought to make anxious people show their anxious behavior (waiting in the Dean's office, being given a painful shot, being asked to deliver important papers, and so on), and we look for evidence of their anxiety (sweaty palms, pacing the floor, trembling, talking too loudly or too softly). We expect high scorers on our test to show more of these "nervous" signs than low scorers if the test really measures anxiety. Similarly, we can argue that anxious people ought to have more neurotic symptoms than nonanxious people, and that they ought to work harder at simple tasks like finding and crossing out all *a*'s in a page of type. Here we would give appropriate tests (a list of neurotic symptoms with instructions to "check the things that bother you" and a test in which the person is asked to cross out some letter in a page of mixed letters) and expect to find positive correlations with the anxiety test we are developing.

As you can see, this approach leads to a set of predictions about the way the test will relate to other situations, behaviors, and tests. If all the predictions are right, this provides evidence that our test really measures anxiety *and* evidence that anxiety is the kind of trait we thought it was. If the predictions (or some of them) are incorrect, then either the test does not measure anxiety, *or* anxiety does not manifest itself the way we thought it did, *or* both.

RELATION OF RELIABILITY AND VALIDITY

A final comment on the relation between reliability and validity seems warranted. All of the validities are constrained or limited by reliability. If the original measurement is not accurate, it cannot be validly related to anything. If it is highly accurate, it may or may not be validly related to some criterion.

Concern with internal consistency versus stability will vary with the particular validity an investigator has in mind and the particular use to be made of the instrument. If a test is supposed to measure some enduring trait or supposed to predict a long-range criterion, high stability will be required. If it is to measure a transient state or changing relationship, stability cannot be expected and internal consistency or moment-to-moment equivalence may be employed as an index of accuracy. Overall, it is perhaps best to remember that tests and measurements do not just spring into being fully formed. They are constructed to serve some purpose, broad or narrow, pure or applied. Adequate validities and reliabilities must be determined in the light of the use to which the test is to be put. Reason, not arbitrary rules, should govern.

SUMMARY

Science often moves ahead by precision of measurement and quantification. But bringing quantification to a new science poses enormous difficulties. Early psychology tried to prove itself scientific by showing that sensations could be measured and found that a set of interesting relations to physical variables resulted. Before psychologists could be carried away with their success, however, astronomy put before them the puzzle of the personal equation and the unsolved riddle of how many dimensions are needed to account for individual differences.

Numbers play different roles depending on how well we understand scientific dimensions and on what assumptions we can make. Numbers are used as names (nominal scale), as ordered series (ordinal scale), as series with each point at a fixed distance from the next (interval scale), and as true number systems with a zero point (ratio scale).

Psychophysical measurement illustrates the fact that different scales can be constructed for the same kinds of problems with different assumptions and different operations. Fechner's scale of just-noticeable-differences assumes that equally noticed differences make equal psychological units. Stevens's power law assumes that physical ratios produce consistent psychological ratios. Signal-detection theorists, who make still different assumptions, study signals in noise and draw conclusions concerning the subject as a signal receiver. Each of these approaches captures some important aspect of psychophysical functioning.

Trait measurement is even more dependent on assumptions than psychophysics. Because we assume most traits are normally distributed, we can use efficient ways to describe people and to report data.

Descriptive statistics compress information into just a few numbers. Measures of central tendency and measures of dispersion are sufficient to describe whole sets of data when we can assume the normal distribution. There are three common measures of central tendency: the mode, or most popular score; the median, or middle score; and the mean, or average score. Two common measures of dispersion are: the range, or the extreme limits of the scores; and the standard deviation, which together with the mean was found to have high descriptive power. The formula for the mean is: $M = \frac{\Sigma X}{N}$. The formula for the standard deviation is: $SD = \sqrt{\frac{\Sigma (X-M)^2}{N}}$.

Common methods of reporting scores are: raw scores, ranks, centile ranks, and standard scores. Centile ranks are most readily interpretable but standard scores are probably the most generally useful. For interpreting any kind of scores, thorough knowledge of the norm group is of great importance.

The correlation coefficient serves as a measure of how much two variables covary, or change together. The correlation coefficient is important in both description and prediction. Correlation, however, does not in any sense imply causation.

Reliability is the accuracy with which a test measures whatever it measures. Two kinds of reliability are distinguished: stability over time and internal consistency. Validity is the extent to which a test measures what it is supposed to measure. Three kinds of validity are: content validity, criterion validity, and construct validity. The first is a matter of definition and procedure, the second a matter of correlation with "outside" measures, and the last a matter of a network of correlations and logical relationships.

A test can be reliable without being valid, but cannot be valid without being reliable. Judgments concerning appropriate measures of reliability and validity depend on the nature of a test and the uses to which it will be put.

Measurement and quantification rest on logical constructions, not on the arbitrary use of numbers. The purpose of quantification and the assumptions that one is willing to make should determine how psychological scales and measures are developed. Quantification is fruitful only in the context of a rationale for measurement and psychological justification of the assumptions.

SUGGESTED READINGS

Amos, J.R., F.L. Brown, and O.G. Mink. *Statistical concepts: a basic program.* New York: Harper & Row, 1965.

Hays, W.L. *Basic statistics.* Belmont, Cal.: Brooks-Cole, 1967.

Huff, D. *How to lie with statistics.* New York: Norton, 1954.

Tyler, L.E. *Tests and measurements.* Englewood Cliffs, N.J.: Prentice-Hall, 1963.

Contemporary Psychology:
Its Multiple Roots and Many Routes

CHAPTER FOUR   Contemporary psychology is highly diverse both in subject matter covered and method of approach. This diversity can be understood by reference to psychology's many historical antecedents, including philosophy, physiology, biology, psychiatry, and other disciplines. Psychologists also follow many different paths in their theoretical and experimental efforts. These several "roots" of modern psychology and its many "routes" to the fulfillment of its goal are sketched in the present chapter—a chapter that also serves to provide a rationale for the organization of the rest of the book.

One of the most important insights into "human nature" which psychology can offer is that every behavioral act has multiple determinants and, as a result, has a multitude of possible meanings or interpretations. By "multiple determinants" we imply that a large number of variables interact to yield the behavior in question; thus, we do not expect to find a single "cause" for each act, but rather a large set of causes.

Just as single behavioral acts are multiply determined, so too are the institutions that are created through such acts. Psychology, as an institution, thus has multiple origins (or historical roots) and many ways of expressing those origins; there are many routes for reaching its goals. Hence, the title of this chapter, which deals with the major origins of contemporary psychology and with the variety of strategies followed by psychologists as they try to understand behavior.

The Major Roots of Psychology

If, as we argued in Chapter One, curiosity is the basic motive behind the scientific enterprise, then in some sense science is as old as mankind, and the science of psychology as old as man's curiosity about his own behavior and that of other living beings. As a formal discipline, of course, psychology comes very late in the history of mankind; as an experimental science, it is only about 100 years old. Even if we take a broad view of what constitutes psychology and include, for example, the speculations of the ancient Greek philosophers, we are still left with a time span of only about 2500 years—a very small fragment of the estimated million-and-three-quarters or more years that human-like creatures have inhabited the Earth.

What, then, are the immediate roots of modern psychology, broadly defined, and how has their influence been felt? In this section, we will discuss the four disciplines that have had the most impact on the development of psychology: philosophy, physiology, psychiatry, and biology.

PHILOSOPHY

Clearly, and one can say this about all but the most exotic of modern scientific disciplines, the oldest and most important source of contemporary psychology lies in the field of philosophy. Indeed, it is only within the past 75 or 80 years that university courses in psychology have been taught in departments of psychology; earlier, psychology was administratively the province of philosophy departments.

Many of the questions that psychologists ask—and others ask of psychologists—are questions that have always intrigued philosophers. For example: What is the origin of mental content, and how do people come to differ among themselves in intelligence and other talents and aptitudes? What is the relation between "mind" and "body"? Does man have freedom to choose among alternative behaviors (that is, "free will"), or are all his acts determined by factors over which he can exercise no control? What are the essential differences between man and the other animals? Can there be mental activities (such as wishes and ideas) that are not conscious, that a person is unaware of in himself?

You might keep an eye out in subsequent chapters for the residue in contemporary psychology of these and other philosophical issues. We shall examine here only the first of them, with the intent of illustrating how one philosophical question has been transformed into a psychological problem and thereby has itself somewhat transformed psychology.

On both theoretical and practical grounds, psychologists are concerned about the origin of behavior differences among individuals. This issue has arisen in many forms over the years and various solutions have been offered. Crudely, the solutions can be reduced to two categories: *native endowment* and *experience*.

In modern terminology, native endowment refers to a person's genetic composition, transmitted from his parents. This pool of genes determines not only such obvious bodily attributes as skin, hair and eye color, facial appearance, and height, but also presumably such basic psychological attributes as intelligence and perhaps temperament. The belief that intellect is transmitted genetically depends on two assumptions: (1) that intellectual functioning, like all behavioral events, is mediated by the nervous system, and (2) that the fine structure of the nervous system, like its gross structure, is genetically determined. More simply, whatever makes one person more capable than another lies in slight differences in the structure (biochemical as well as anatomical) of their respective nervous systems; these subtle structural differences, in turn, are assumed to be built in, or given (that is, native), in the sense that they originate and unfold according to the "commands" issued by a set of stable, virtually immutable genes.

The alternative to genetic endowment as the source of individual differences—experience—refers to all the events in a person's life that are capable of changing his psychological functioning. The relevant "events" may range from simple stimuli such as lights and sounds to highly complex social interactions. The basic assumption of the experiential (or *empiricist,* as it is often called) approach is that intellectual (and other) functions can be markedly influenced by the constant stream of events that impinge on a developing human being. As with native endowment, it is assumed that the impact of these experiences is mediated by the nervous system. But empiricists hold that the system is sufficiently similar in all persons, yet sufficiently plastic, so that fine differences in quantity and quality of experience can have a significant developmental effect.

In summary, at their extremes, the nativist position emphasizes stable genetic differences and their inevitable unfolding while the empiricist approach accentuates the importance of differential environmental impact. Of course, there is no compelling reason to expect either position to have an exclusive hold on the truth, although a great deal of controversy and research have been generated by that expectation. The modern view, which will be fully developed in Chapter Fourteen, is that differences among individuals, in intellectual functioning as well as in other areas, emerge from both sources, and from both sources *in interaction* with each other. We can leave the elaboration of that point for Chapter Fourteen and look now, instead, at some of the philosophical roots of the controversy between nativism and empiricism.

Actually, a purely nativist or empiricist position is hard to find. There are those, however, who put major emphasis on one or the other of the two proposed sources of individual variation.

Plato (ca. 427–347 B.C.) seems an

Figure 4.1 Plato. (Brown Brothers.)

extreme nativist, at least in certain of his works. He asserts that there are some fundamental ideas that cannot be taught, in the sense of being imparted *de novo* from the outside; teaching, rather, is a procedure for drawing out and making evident knowledge that is innately, though latently, present. By this same token, learning is essentially reminiscence.

In one of his dialogs, *Meno,* Plato tries to demonstrate the validity of this strange contention through what may be the first recorded psychological experiment. Arguing that the universal truths of mathematics are possessed by all of us, even the untutored, Plato's spokesman, Socrates, proceeds to "prove" his point by showing how Meno's uneducated slave boy really "knows" the Pythagorean Theorem that the square of the hypotenuse of a right triangle equals the sum of the squares of the other two sides. Through lengthy and judicious questioning, usually requiring but a simple "yes" or "no" answer, Socrates gets the slave boy to accept the validity of the theorem, and then concludes in the following fashion:

> SOCRATES: Well; what think you, Meno? Has this boy, in his answers, given any other opinion than his own?
>
> MENO: None other: he has given his own opinion only.
>
> SOCRATES: And yet, but a little before, as we both observed, he had no knowledge of the matter proposed, and knew not how to give a right answer.
>
> MENO: True.
>
> SOCRATES: But those very opinions, which you acknowledge to be his own, were in him all the time: were they not?
>
> MENO: They were.
>
> SOCRATES: In a man therefore, who is ignorant, there are true opinions concerning those very things of which he is ignorant.
>
> MENO: It appears there are.
>
> SOCRATES: Those opinions then are stirred up afresh in the mind of that boy, as fancies are in dreaming. And if he should frequently be questioned of these things, and by many different persons, you may be assured he will at length know them with as much certainty as any man.
>
> MENO: Indeed, it seems so.
>
> SOCRATES: Will he not then know them without being taught them, having only been asked questions, and recovering of himself from within himself his lost knowledge?
>
> MENO: He will.
>
> SOCRATES: But our recovery of knowledge from within ourselves, is not this what we call reminiscence?
>
> MENO: Without doubt.
>
> SOCRATES: And this knowledge, which he now has, must he not at some time or other have acquired it, or else have always been possessed of it?
>
> MENO: Certainly.

The notion of innate ideas is a recurrent one in the history of philosophy, taking various forms, but never straying too far from the position that experience cannot impose order on an initially unstructured, unformed mental substrate. Thus, for Plato, experience, in the guise of education, is effective only to the extent that there already exists a matrix of latent ideas to be uncovered and transformed into conscious knowledge. The slave boy comes, through Socratic tutoring, to "know" the Pythagorean Theorem just as a seed, through proper nurturing, becomes a plant. Indeed, without the seed the best soil and the best care would yield no plant. Similarly, without some pre-existing mental structure on which to act, experience would have no impact.

Of course, the seed that is not nurtured will also not grow, and innate ideas will remain latent if they are not helped to develop through the proper experience. In the dialog *The Republic*, Plato presents some of his opinions about the optimal set of experiences for the intellectual and moral development of the future leaders (the Guardians) of his ideal State. In the course of that discussion, Plato offers one especially interesting insight: Those best endowed by nature suffer the most from inadequate or improper education, and not simply because they have the farthest to fall. Rather, these persons with the greatest potential for positive development are also the ones most susceptible to influence in the opposite direction.

Plato, then, actually stresses both innate endowment and experience as determinants of intellectual development. Perhaps the most extreme of the nativist philosophers is Gottfried Leibnitz (1646–1716). Although he is perhaps best known for his contribution to mathematics (both he and Isaac Newton, working independently of each other, developed similar versions of the calculus), Leibnitz was also spokesman for the opposition to the extreme empiricism of his contemporary, John Locke. In his reaction against Locke's position, which we will review below, Leibnitz proposed a philosophy intended to encompass all of nature.

The main concept of Leibnitz's system is the *monad*, the elementary constituent of all being, simple or complex, physical, mental, or spiritual. According to Leibnitz, the monad, along with its other characteristics, is continually active and developing. Its development proceeds according to its own inner laws and is not susceptible to external influence. This notion of "development from within" applies as well to the human mind as to what ordinarily would be considered purely material entities (indeed, for Leibnitz mind and body are not distinct categories, but rather represent different, though parallel, aspects of the same underlying substance).

Translating Leibnitz into modern terminology—and undoubtedly doing some violence in the process to his complex and subtle ideas—we would say that his system stresses the inner determinants of human development, as opposed to the external influences emphasized by the empiricists; further, the mind is a continually active entity, not impelled by chance external events, but rather "pulled" by the long-term goal of its own ultimate perfection. The most highly developed monad of all is God; the human intellect strives to attain, though it cannot reach, that degree of perfection.

For a fuller appreciation of the relevance of the Leibnitzian philosophy for contemporary psychology, we need to make a closer comparison with the empiricist position of the British philosopher, John Locke (1632–1704). Locke's philosophy grew out of an attempt to answer the question: How can one obtain valid information about the physical world? In the terminology of philosophy, this is the problem of *epistemology*. This same general epistemological concern also lay behind Plato's inquiries in the *Meno* as well as in others of his dialogs, though Plato was more concerned about abstract concepts, such as justice and beauty, than physical events. Locke also addressed himself to highly abstract concepts, but his approach called first for an attempt to understand the way one gets to know about such basic physical attributes as color, size, shape, and motion.

Figure 4.2 Gottfried Wilhelm Leibnitz. (The Bettmann Archive.)

Locke's answer, in brief, was built on the assumption that all knowledge originates in sensory experience. In his well-known metaphor, Locke described man's intellect as being initially a *tabula rasa,* a blank tablet on which sensory experience made its marks. All knowledge, Locke believed, no matter how complex or abstract, derived from primitive sensory encounters with the physical world; there were certainly no innate ideas of the sorts postulated by Plato and Leibnitz and other nativist philosophers.

Figure 4.3 John Locke. (The Bettmann Archive.)

Close examination of Locke's work, however, reveals that it is as difficult to maintain a pure empiricist approach as it is to be an extreme nativist. Although Locke asserts that all knowledge originates in experience—which certainly sounds like pure empiricism—he mentions two sources of experience. The one relates to sensory events stimulated by environmental influence, the other to the "operations" which the intellect performs on these sensory events. This second source of experience—its own operations—the intellect can "reflect on," just as it does on the ideas mediated by the sensory system. Knowledge, then, derives from two kinds of experiential events: sensations and the mental operations performed on these sensations.

But where do the operations originate? Here Locke is noncommittal, but surely by his neglect of the question he must imply that these necessary intellectual operations are built-in. Thus, even Locke's empiricism is tainted with a modicum of nativism, strengthening the impression that different positions on the nativism-empiricism issue represent differences in emphasis and not in kind.

To some, however, a difference only in emphasis on this issue can still be of great importance, for it can have ramifications that go well beyond the immediate problem; indeed, it can color one's whole view of human nature and the nature of what constitutes good psychological theory. For example, in his book *Becoming*, the psychologist Gordon Allport offers the following way of comparing current psychological theories, with Leibnitz and Locke serving as representatives, if not originators, of two quite disparate theoretical approaches:

> Virtually all modern psychological theories seem oriented toward one of two polar conceptions, which, at the risk of some historical oversimplification, I shall call the Lockean and Leibnitzian traditions respectively. It is not the total philosophy of Locke or of Leibnitz that is here in question. Rather it is their views on one aspect of man's mind—its essentially passive nature (Locke) or its active nature (Leibnitz)—that I wish to contrast. The same polarity, as I say, is found in current theories of growth and change in human personality. . . .
>
> John Locke, we all recall, assumed the mind of the individual to be a *tabula rasa* at birth. And the intellect itself was a passive thing acquiring content and structure only through the impact of sensation and the crisscross of associations, much as a pan of sweet dough acquires tracings through the impress of a cookie cutter. Locke insisted that there can be nothing in the intellect that was not first in the senses. . . .
>
> To Leibnitz the intellect was perpetually active in its own right, addicted to rational problem-solving, and bent on manipulating sensory data according to its own inherent nature. For Locke the organism was reactive when stimulated; for Leibnitz it was self-propelled. . . .
>
> The Lockean point of view, as I have said, has been and is still dominant in Anglo-American psychology. Its representatives are found in associationism of all types, including environmentalism, behaviorism, stimulus-response (familiarly abbreviated as S-R) psychology, and all other stimulus oriented psychologies, in animal and genetic psychology, in positivism and operationism, in mathematical models—in short, in most of what today is cherished in our laboratories as truly "scientific" psychology.
>
> Lockean empiricism . . . [assumes] that what is earlier is more fundamental than what is late in development. The early impress upon the wax of the mind is important. First impressions, to be sure, may later be compounded and crisscrossed, but the original simple ideas are still the elements of later mental life. This type of geneticism has taken a firm hold upon American psychology. In keeping with the doctrine of *tabula rasa,* American geneticism holds that what is important is childhood learning, childhood fixations, childhood conditioning. . . .

The Leibnitzian tradition, by contrast, maintains that the person is not a collection of acts, nor simply the locus of acts; the person is the *source* of acts. And activity itself is not conceived as agitation resulting from pushes by internal or external stimulation. It is purposive. To understand what a person is, it is necessary always to refer to what he may be in the future, for every state of the person is pointed in the direction of future possibilities. (Allport, 1955, pp. 7–12.)

This one example, then—the nativism-empiricism controversy—should be suggestive of how contemporary psychology has been influenced by philosophy in two major ways. First, philosophical issues enter psychology as problems for scientific investigation (for instance, discovering the role of experience in intellectual development). Second, philosophical approaches (such as the Lockean versus the Leibnitzian) enter as basic and usually implicit assumptions that impart their flavor to psychological theories.

Of course, one example does not suffice to make the complete case. In a more extensive discussion of the impact of philosophy on psychology, we could cite many more philosophical issues and approaches (the "mind-body" problem, the problem of "free-will," and so on) and point out their residue in modern psychology. But there are other roots of contemporary psychology that need to be discussed; for more on the debt of psychology to philosophy, consult the suggested readings at the end of this chapter.

PHYSIOLOGY

To the extent that philosophy is the "mother of the sciences," a contribution to psychology from any of the other sciences is ultimately a contribution from philosophy. Since psychology was the last of the sciences to break away from philosophy, however, there was considerable time for other scientific fields to develop separate identities and hence to have separate influences on the later-developing discipline of psychology. Physiology was one of these.

In brief, physiology is concerned with the functioning of the various organ systems of the body—for instance, respiratory, circulatory, digestive, reproductive—and with their role in the maintenance of life processes. Of special relevance to psychology is the *nervous system,* which includes the brain, spinal cord, nerves, and sense organs; this system serves to regulate and integrate the functioning of the various other systems through control of the *effector organs,* that is, the muscles and glands.

The branch of physiology concerned with nervous system functioning has had the most direct and obvious influence on the development of psychology. Indeed, one area of research now primarily in the province of psychology— the study of sensory and perceptual processes—stemmed from the work of nineteenth-century physiologists. Any survey of the chief figures in this group would certainly include Thomas Young (1773–1829) who, among many other contributions, identified the lens of the eye as the structure through which the process of accommodation (fine focusing) is mediated. Young also de-

Figure 4.4 Thomas Young. (The Bettmann Archive.)

veloped a theory of color perception, known now as the Young-Helmholtz theory, that still stands virtually intact.

Another of the nineteenth-century physiologists who shaped the course of sensory psychology was Johannes Müller (1801–1858). In his *Handbook of Physiology* Müller formulated his famous doctrine of the specific energies of nerves, an heroic attempt to relate sensory experience to both neural events and to events in the physical world—in short, an attempt simultaneously to solve two of the knottiest philosophical issues, the problem of the relationship of mind and body and the problem of how we gain knowledge of the physical world. Very simply, Müller asserted that we experience only the state of our own nerves; that this experience often happens to be informative about the external, physical world is a fortunate byproduct of the peculiar sensitivities of our sense organs, which are selectively "tuned" to different types of physical energy.

Whatever the philosophical merits of Müller's doctrine, it is a serious attempt to bring to bear on philosophical issues data obtained from empirical research. In this respect, Müller's work anticipates that of his successors in physiology, psychology, physics, and other scientific fields. Thus, gradually, philosophical questions with empirical referents have been translated into scientific questions. It is through just such a translation, of course, that scientific psychology achieved its independence from philosophy. And, indeed, in a somewhat similar fashion sensory psychology became a separate discipline from physiology. That is, through a kind of specialization of labor, any statements that made reference to experience (and later to *behavior*) became the property of psychologists, while physiologists concentrated on their specialty, the study of organ systems. Müller's role in the evolution of modern psychology was to turn the problem of experience into a physiological problem, and hence make it available for later investigation by scientific psychology. Of course, such separations among disciplines are neither complete nor permanent; you will see later in this chapter how physiology and psychology are presently reuniting in the specialty of psychophysiology. This kind of unification, however, is much more "mature" than the primitive fusion of the two disciplines that prevailed in Müller's time.

Figure 4.5 Johannes Müller. (The Bettmann Archive.)

The nineteenth-century physiologist who had the most widespread effect on psychology was Hermann von Helmholtz (1821–1894). His contributions include, but go well beyond, the modification of Young's color theory that bears their joint names. Among many other scientific ventures (which include an early statement of the law of the conservation of energy, the cornerstone of modern physics), Helmholtz created a theory of tone perception that, with some recent amendments, has yet to be bested. Through his own research, and through his compilation of the work of others in his *Physiological Optics,* he set into motion research and speculation about visual phenomena that still pulsate in psychology laboratories. Indeed, there is virtually no problem that is no problem of current interest in the area of sensation and perception which was untouched by Helmholtz.

As though all that were not enough, Helmholtz also further opened the study of reaction time, initiated early in the nineteenth century, as we noted in Chapter Three, by the astronomer Friedrich Bessel. Whereas Bessel's interest was primarily in documenting the existence of reliable individual differences in speed of reaction time—of considerable practical importance to astronomers of that era —Helmholtz used reaction time in a remarkably successful attempt to measure the velocity of nerve conduction. He did so by locating a tactile stimulus at varying distances from the spinal cord—along the leg, for example—and noting the resulting change in reaction time to this stimulus. The value he calculated, about 25 to 40 meters per second, is quite accurate according to modern measures taken directly from electrical recordings from sensory nerves. Helmholtz's value is certainly closer to the mark than those hypothesized by other

Figure 4.6 Hermann von Helmholtz. (Culver Pictures, Inc.)

Figure 4.7 Franz Joseph Gall. (The Bettmann Archive.)

scientists of his day, one of whom, for example, proposed that the nerve impulse traveled at the speed of light.

The physiologists mentioned so far, Young, Müller, and Helmholtz, tended to concentrate their investigations on the functioning of the sense organs and the sensory nerves. Other physiologists and anatomists were at the same time beginning to explore the brain and some of its functions. During the nineteenth century one of the major questions about the brain was whether it worked as a homogeneous unit (by analogy with the supposedly unitary soul) or whether it was differentiated into parts that performed different functions.

One of the early proponents of the latter point of view—which in current terminology argues for "localization of function"—was the anatomist Franz Joseph Gall (1758–1828). Gall is probably best known in the history of psychology as the originator of *phrenology*—crudely, the attempt to formulate relations between conformations of the skull ("bumps on the head") and personality characteristics. The phrenology movement, which had considerable popularity outside of scientific circles, lasted for over a hundred years. It began with Gall's observation as a young boy that certain of his classmates had exceptionally good memories (Gall's was poor) and that these same boys also seemed to have unusually bulging eyeballs. Gall was apparently so impressed by his observation that it later set him to notice similar relations between physical and psychological attributes of his fellow medical students.

Eventually, Gall's casual observations were replaced by systematic, empirical investigations, in an attempt to support and extend his hunch with scientifically respectable data. For example, Gall visited prisons in order to study the heads of a group of pickpockets, and he came to the conclusion that the particular bump they shared indicated excessive "acquisitiveness." In general Gall's strategy was to select people with some outstanding psychological characteristic and then search for a concomitant bump on the skull. You will recognize this as a correlational approach to research design, as described in Chapter Two. It is certainly akin to the style of a good deal of contemporary psychological research, especially in psychopathology.

Out of his extensive investigations, Gall was able to formulate what he

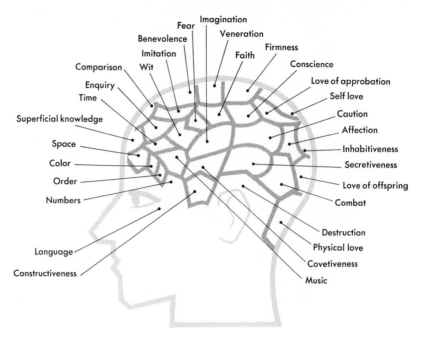

Figure 4.8 A phrenological chart.

believed to be valid generalizations relating bumps on the head to psychological traits, propensities, talents, and so on. These relations were expressed in the form of maps or charts of the head, where each delimited region was assigned a particular psychological function, as illustrated in Figure 4.8. Any unusual development in a particular region of the head could then be interpreted to indicate an extreme value on the trait associated with that region. In short, to know a person one need only to know the topography of his skull. No wonder the *promise* of phrenology was so eagerly greeted and treated as though it were a gift.

Why should such simple relations be expected to hold between skull shape and "personality"? The answer lies in a set of assumptions made by Gall:

1. Each psychological characteristic is localized in a particular portion of the brain, these brain regions being identically patterned for all people.

2. Within a given person's brain, the size of a particular region is directly related to its importance in his personality.

3. The shape of the skull conforms to the shape of the brain which is encased within it.

Of particular interest to us is the first assumption. This idea, revolutionary in its time, led to a line of inquiry in neuroanatomy and psychophysiology that is still being pursued. As we noted earlier, the prevailing view about the brain, even as late as the nineteenth century, was that it operated essentially as a unit. Of course, there was some dissent from the orthodox view other than that offered by Gall. Nevertheless, Gall's bold assumption of localization—and localization of such fineness and precision as his phrenology demanded—engendered strong opposition from the scientific community.

The major opposition, however, was to phrenology, and unfortunately that hostility generalized to the excellent anatomical studies of the brain that Gall carried out at the same time. Indeed, Gall's skill and care in dissecting the brain led him to discoveries of fine structure that had gone unnoticed by his less proficient colleagues. Gall published his anatomical findings, along with the results of his phrenological studies, in a monograph with the imposing title (translated from the French): "Anatomy and physiology of the nervous system in general, and of the brain in particular, with observations on the possibility of identifying several intellectual and moral traits in man and animals through the shape of their heads." Even though the merits of his anatomical work were recognized, Gall himself was rejected for membership in the French Academy of Sciences, undoubtedly because of his sponsorship of phrenology.

Gall's own career aside, however, his work clearly had considerable effect on the pursuit of knowledge about the relation between brain and behavior. Following Gall's lead, others took up the localization banner. For example, in 1860 the French physician Paul Broca discovered (by lucky accident) what is now accepted as a "speech center" in the brain—a small, delimited region of the cerebral cortex that controls linguistic behavior. Over the next several decades similar identifications were made of localized cortical functions. Nowadays, in fact, localization is taken for granted, and the controversial problem is to account for the unity, or integrity, of functioning that obviously also characterizes the activity of the brain. Although we seem to have come full circle, the present version of the problem is different from the one posed a century-and-a-half ago in at least this respect: The functional unity of the brain can no longer be explained simply by asserting that the brain is a homogeneous unit; the unity is superimposed on a highly differentiated structure.

In addition to its effect through studies of sensory-processes and brain functioning, physiology has contributed to present-day psychology in one other way that deserves special mention; that is, through the work of those like Walter Cannon (1871–1945) and Claude Bernard (1813–1878) on the physiological mechanisms that control the "internal environment." For example, a certain level of sugar must be maintained in the blood for optimal bodily functioning. When the amount of sugar begins to decline, perhaps because a person has been physically active, or has gone without food for some time, a system is called into play that releases sugar into the blood and, at least temporarily, restores the proper level. Analogous regulatory mechanisms exist to serve other bodily requirements. These remarkable, automatic devices are called *homeostatic* mechanisms; the general process of maintaining physiological balance through such mechanisms is called *homeostasis*.

Now to the extent that the homeostatic devices are automatic, internally aroused, and have only internal effects—that is, to the extent that they are isolated from a person's ongoing behavior—they would seem of only limited interest to the psychologist. This certainly has been true of the specific details about specific homeostatic mechanisms. But the *concept* of homeostasis has had a profound effect on psychological theory, particularly on theories of motivation. Indeed, homeostasis served as the model for the motivational system incorporated by Clark Hull into his highly influential behavior theory, which has dominated American psychology in the recent decades of the present century.

Hull's theory, which is representative of a general type, starts with a hypothetical organism in a state of physiological balance, or equilibrium. This is an organism without needs—until something happens, perhaps just a normal metabolic process operating over time, which produces a significant departure from physiological equilibrium. Assume, for example, that blood sugar level begins to decline. The appropriate homeostatic mechanism is activated and balance is restored. But the restoration is only temporary, because a system cannot act indefinitely without depleting itself: It demands external support. The body's source of sugar, of course, is obtained through food.

Thus, the maintenance of proper bodily functioning is dependent on more than the operation of the internal homeostatic mechanisms that Cannon described. Certain *behaviors* are also required, for example, searching for, locating, and ingesting food. Where do these behaviors originate? How are they initiated and controlled? Hull's answers to these questions take the following form:

When physiological imbalance is large enough, an organism is in a state of need. Needs, in turn, give rise to psychologically relevant states called *primary drives*. Drives have two aspects: (1) They serve as general arousers or activators of behavior; in this respect, then, all drives are alike. (2) Through what is called their "stimulus" or "cue" value, they activate behaviors that are specific to the drive that is dominant at the moment; thus, although hunger and thirst both raise an animal's general level of activity, each drive also has a distinctive set of behaviors associated with it, eating and drinking, respectively.

Certain behaviors elicited by a drive will be ineffective in reducing the need and its associated drive, while other behaviors will better fit the realities of the external environment. The latter will enable an organism to obtain what is needed (or to escape from injury), to restore physiological balance, and to reduce the drive.

Drive-reduction, through need-reduction, plays a special, central role in Hull's theory. It is through drive-reduction that *learning* takes place: Whenever a particular behavior occurs in a particular environmental setting and is immediately followed by drive-reduction, the tendency is strengthened to engage in that behavior, in that setting, when the drive is again aroused. Drive reduction is synonymous with "reward" in Hull's theory, and reward is necessary for learning to occur.

The theory also asserts that the tendency to engage in behaviors that are not followed by reward will be weakened. Thus, through the differential strengthening and weakening of various behaviors, by virtue of reward and nonreward, an organism's behavioral repertory is in a continual state of flux. In this fashion, reward acts to transform what began as an *innate hierarchy* of behaviors into a *learned hierarchy*, allowing the organism to adapt to changing environmental circumstances. Of course, if there were no environmental variability—if, for instance, food were always in the same place—then plasticity would have no adaptive value. But the world in which most organisms live *is* a changing one, and behavioral plasticity is a great asset in the struggle for survival.

We might conceive of the innate behavioral repertory as an extension of the organism's homeostatic system in at least two respects: (1) The behaviors are dormant until aroused by a specific physiological need; (2) the successful functioning of the behavioral repertory results in restoration of physiological balance. The main points of difference between the system of homeostatic devices and the behavioral repertory are these: There is far more potential variability in the behavioral repertory than in the homeostatic system; if the initial behavior in the hierarchy does not work, then the next one will be "tried" and so on, until the need is reduced; the hierarchical ordering of behaviors within the repertory is subject to modification as a consequence of the success or failure of specific behaviors; that is, the repertory is characterized not only by variability but also by modifiability, or what we have been calling "plasticity."

It is clear that Hull's theory, particularly in his motivational concepts, is erected on the foundation laid down by Bernard and Cannon. For Hull and his numerous followers, there is no motive, in animal or man, that does not originate, directly or indirectly, in some physiological need. And "need," moreover, is defined in the narrow sense of the kind of systems that Bernard and Cannon investigated.

One of the most interesting theoretical controversies of the past several years has arisen from a dissatisfaction on the part of some psychologists with the orthodox view of motivation, as represented by Hullian as well as by Freudian theory. For dissident psychologists, the Hullian approach, by staying so close to the homeostatic model, is excessively narrow in the behaviors it can account for; it is forced to exclude from consideration, or seriously distort, certain facts of behavior that seem to demand a broader view of motivation. The behaviors in question, the competing theories, and the evidence supporting these theories will be treated in detail in Chapter Sixteen.

The contribution of physiology to psychology is considerable and is only hinted at above. In universities, physiology is typically considered one of the basic medical sciences. Somewhat less clear in its role within the medical curriculum, but of unquestioned significance in the development of contemporary psychology is the discipline of psychiatry. Indeed, so close is the contact, both conceptual and professional, between psychiatry and clinical psychology that laymen are often hard-pressed to see the differences between them. Of course, one can easily distinguish between the two fields on at least one simple basis: Psychiatrists have a medical degree (the M.D.), whereas clinical psychologists hold nonmedical advanced degrees, typically the Ph.D. Beyond that obvious distinction, the lines are blurred. Nevertheless, we can still ask what role psychiatry has played historically in molding contemporary psychology.

It has been the province of psychiatry to diagnose, manage, and treat psychopathology in all its myriad forms. As with medical practice in general, psychiatric practice has been a mixture of art, personal experience, superstition, tradition, empirical rules (that is, rules that seem to work, but for no known theoretical reason), and some theory. As psychiatry has matured, it has come more and more to seek and rely on an underpinning of theory—and incidentally to seek ways of testing and modifying the theoretical basis underlying its clinical practices.

In the present century the major theoretical developments within psychiatry have emerged from the observations, techniques, speculations, and theories of Sigmund Freud (1856–1939) and his followers. With some exceptions, psychiatric theory today is virtually synonymous with Freud's psychoanalytic theory, or modifications thereof. The exceptions, while of interest to the psychiatrist, need not concern us here, since none has had an effect on psychology comparable to that of Freudian theory. Both because of the great complexity of psychoanalytic theory and because of its many ramifications in contemporary psychology, at this point we will allude only to some of the most obvious ways in which its influence has been felt. The theory itself is treated in more detail in Chapters Seventeen and Eighteen.

We might start by looking at psychoanalytic assumptions about "human nature." Freud's view of man was derived in large part from his medical training, with its heavy emphasis on the anatomy and physiology of the human body. In this respect, Freud saw man in much the same way that Hull did—that is, as a biological organism, subject to the same primitive physiological needs as other animals. Freud's term for these needs was *trieben* usually translated as "instinctual drives," and in his view it is from this set of instinctual drives that man's total personality develops.

But man's development occurs in a social context. Because of his helplessness at birth and for several years thereafter, man is dependent for survival on other human beings, his parents initially, and later other family members and members of the larger social group of which the family is a unit. It is these other people who both gratify and frustrate his instinctual drives. Through its control over drive satisfaction, "society" plays a significant role in personality development, both grossly and in fine detail. To the extent that families have common ways of dealing with infants' needs, human beings develop in a grossly similar fashion; but because of fine differences among familial styles in handling infants (both between and even within families, and between and within cultures), personality differences emerge.

Psychoanalytic theory views human personality as the joint product of biology and culture—but it relentlessly reminds us of our biological heritage. This refusal to play down man's animal nature is one of the theory's major strengths, but it also has been a barrier to the theory's general acceptance. At any rate, although psychoanalytic theory may not have introduced this conception of man into psychology, it certainly shares this view with most theories of personality of any significance within contemporary psychology.

A pair of concepts related to the psychoanalytic view of man constitute a unique Freudian contribution: the concepts of *unconscious impulses* and *defenses* against them. The newborn infant, according to Freud, is largely a collection of instinctual drives. He lacks organized awareness both of his own drives and of external reality, but through the repeated collision between his drives and the demands of social and physical reality, the infant gradually develops a structure (the ego) that mediates between drive and reality. The ego consists of perceptual, cognitive, and motor systems that enable a person to relate adaptively to the external world; it emerges out of the matrix of blind, unconscious drives through such events as delay in drive-gratification, frustration, and punishment, as well as through the recurring association of certain events (such as perception of the mother's face) with drive-satisfaction.

There is a second product of the encounters between drives and social reality. Certain drives (destructive, incestuous, and so on) with their associated ideas and fantasies are unacceptable to society; sooner or later their expression is disallowed; they are taboo. A young child may be severely punished, or at least threatened, by his parents for attempting to act on these unacceptable impulses, and by implication even for having these drives. Under threat of punishment and loss of love, the unacceptable impulses and ideas are kept from, or removed from, conscious awareness. In a word, they are *repressed*. But being tied to basic biological drives, the repressed impulses and ideas continue to strive for some outlet. Hence, they must be continually guarded against by the *defense mechanism* of repression, as well as by other defenses (to be discussed in Chapter Seventeen).

Defense, however, whether military or psychic, is expensive and rarely is perfect. For the individual, the maintenance of strong defenses against unacceptable impulses consumes considerable "energy," but if as Freud assumes, there is a fixed quantity of such energy available to each person (the quantity may vary among persons), and if its use for defensive purposes is excessive, then too little remains free for use in other functions. Here, then, is a potential route to one type of psychopathology. On the other hand, inadequate defenses mean a continual flooding of consciousness with primitive impulses and ideation—another route to psychopathology. In contrast, the psychologically healthy person has adequate defenses, but is not overinvested in their maintenance.

Psychopathology aside, there are ways in which the repressed material can find expression. A major outlet is dreams. Indeed, one of Freud's earliest contributions was his assertion and documentation (with clinical and anecdotal evidence) of the notion that what seem to be trivial bits of behavior, such as dreams, slips of the tongue, lapses of memory, and so on, are really of great psychological significance. That is, they represent the expression, though in disguised and therefore relatively safe form, of unconscious impulses and conflicts. But if these trivia have meaning, then surely all behavior must be meaningful. No behavior just "happens"; there are no behavioral "accidents"; nothing psychological occurs "by chance."

Freud's view of human nature thus rests on at least three fundamental assumptions: (1) Personality development is the product of the interaction between man's biological needs and the demands of society; (2) conflict between these two forces may result in certain impulses being kept out of, or expelled from, conscious awareness; (3) all behavior is meaningful, reflecting the expression of both conscious and unconscious impulses. Within contemporary psychology there is little quarrel with the assumption that all behavior is meaningful, that it can be explained, in principle at least, according to some theoretical structure; Freud's insistence on this assumption certainly has facilitated its acceptance by psychologists of various theoretical persuasions. Considerably more controversial are Freud's views concerning personality development and his concept of unconscious impulses, ideas, and conflicts, though even these have been extensively incorporated into current psychological thinking.

Having looked at Freud's contributions to psychology at the level of assumptions about "human nature," we might next note a few of the specific types of psychological research that his work has stimulated. One line of investigation being pursued with great vigor, and with exciting results, is the study of dreaming. Interest in the dream, as an object of scientific research, is a clear legacy of Freud's own pioneering speculations and theory. Recent work on dreaming will be considered in fuller detail in Chapter Fifteen, but we can anticipate here one finding that speaks to the essence of Freud's dream theory.

Dreams, according to the theory, are of great value to the psychoanalyst in his attempt to learn about the unconscious in general, and about a particular person's unconscious conflicts. Freud called the dream "the royal road to the unconscious." That is what the dream does for the analyst, but what does it do for the dreamer? Here Freud made a bold assumption, that dreams are a biological necessity, that their function is to preserve sleep.

The dream is purported to be a relatively safe outlet for the expression of unconscious impulses. If it were not for the dream, which allows at least partial discharge of these impulses, though in distorted form, either these impulses would remain suppressed and tension would build up to a dangerous level, or else the forbidden impulses would enter awareness undisguised, and the person would be terrified and unable to sleep. The dream, then, serves both to keep the tension low and the person asleep.

The notion that dreams are both biologically and psychologically essential is certainly novel, but also rather difficult to accept. And yet recent research indicates that preventing people from dreaming, by a technique to be described in Chapter Fifteen, has a profound effect on their emotional state. Furthermore, each person seems to need a fairly constant amount of dreaming; if he is deprived of dream time on one or more nights, he will "make up" the deficit by extra dreaming on subsequent nights.

A second area of active psychological research, closely related conceptually to dream research and similarly stimulated by Freudian theory, can be categorized under the label *subliminal perception*. In keeping with the psychoanalytic assumption of unconscious impulses and ideas that influence behavior in disguised and subtle ways, the hypothesis has been proposed that certain stimuli of external origin might also affect behavior without entering awareness. These are stimuli that would be anxiety-provoking if the person were to become aware of them, because they would arouse unacceptable impulses. Such stimuli might be most successfully warded off, by way of the defense mechanism of repression, if they are of sufficiently weak intensity, or of sufficiently brief duration, or if by virtue of other physical properties they do not intrude on attention. That is, lying just barely above the threshold of awareness, they can be pushed below threshold (made "subliminal") through the efforts of repression.

Although the concept of an effective though subliminal stimulus may seem paradoxical, or even nonsensical, it need not be if you keep in mind the following interpretation: Subliminal means only that a stimulus fails to enter awareness; but we have no compelling reason to insist that awareness is prerequisite for a stimulus to have some behavioral impact. The issue is one that must be settled empirically; many researchers, psychologists as well as psychiatrists, have turned their attention to this difficult problem, with results that in sum lend credence to the subliminal-perception hypothesis.

The research on subliminal perception is one instance of a broad class of psychological investigation originating in psychoanalytic theory. The broad class consists of all those studies concerned with the effects of drives, emotions, conflicts, and defenses, not only on perception, but also on memory, learning, problem-solving, speech, creativity, and so on.

Biology is concerned with living beings, with their origin, with the processes that characterize "life," with the structure of living organisms and their elementary constituents, with classification of the huge number of different types of organism, with the relations among organisms and between organisms and their environment (thus including, in the case of animals, the "behavior" of organisms). Obviously, there is a great deal of overlap in interest between biology and physiology and between biology and psychology. The barriers separating these fields are somewhat artificial and arbitrary, and in their most advanced forms they merge into one. Nevertheless, it is possible on historical and institutional grounds to maintain distinctions among these disciplines and to consider the influence of one on another.

The work of the biologist Charles Darwin (1809–1882) profoundly affected the development of psychology and imparted to it some of its present flavor. In particular, it was Darwin, more than anyone else, who directed psychologists toward the study of animal behavior, through the impact of his theory of evolution. Darwin's theory, published in 1859, was devised to account for the large variety of distinct species in the plant and animal kingdoms.

His solution took the following form. All present species share a common primitive ancestry. New species emerged by virtue of two selection processes, which operated on spontaneously occurring variants within a given species. These two processes are: (1) *natural selection,* which occurs through the mechanism of the survival of the fittest, and (2) *sexual selection,* which relates to whatever factors (such as appearance or aggressiveness) make a given organism likely to reproduce. The two selection processes are related in at least two respects. First, survival of the fittest means, in effect, survival long enough to reproduce; second, certain characteristics of an organism may decrease its survival potential while enhancing its sexual attractiveness, and vice versa.

Spontaneously occurring variants are obviously essential if the processes of selection are to have an opportunity to operate. In terms of our modern knowledge of genetics, any variants relevant to the formation of species must be the products of genetic change, or *mutation.* Once mutants have occurred within a population, the formation of a new species is greatly enhanced if they are geographically isolated from members of the original genotype.

To relate Darwin's theory to the development of psychology, we must make explicit a revolutionary assumption that the theory made, the assumption of the *biological continuity* among the species, including man. No longer was man to be considered, as most theological systems asserted, a product of special creation, qualitatively distinct from all other living beings. Instead, man is but one point in a complex network of evolutionary development, or to use a popular metaphor, one twig on the evolutionary tree.

Once biological continuity was accepted, the next obvious step was to postulate *psychological* continuity between man and the other animals, with the expectation of finding in "lower" animals humanoid behaviors, skills, feelings, and so on, and in man psychological remnants of his animal ancestry. One consequence of this assumption was the search for evidence of continuity by way of a comparative study of animal and human behavior. Thus emerged the field known as *comparative psychology.* Darwin himself participated in this endeavor through his work on the comparative study of emotion, as described in his book *Expression of the Emotions in Man and Animals,* published in 1872.

Figure 4.9 Charles Darwin, 1840, a portrait by George Richmond. (New York Public Library.)

In the latter decades of the nineteenth century evidence was accumulated to support the assumption of psychological continuity. The prototype of this enterprise was the work of George Romanes (1848–1894), whose *Animal Intelligence,* published in 1882, the year of Darwin's death, contained carefully selected accounts of animal behavior purporting to reveal humanlike traits. The excerpt below is illustrative of the type of evidence offered by Romanes, in this instance for the existence of highly developed emotions in a dog.

> The terrier used to be very fond of catching flies upon the windowpanes, and if ridiculed when unsuccessful was evidently much annoyed. On one occasion, in order to see what he would do, I purposely laughed immoderately every time he failed. It so happened that he did so several times in succession—partly, I believe, in consequence of my laughing—and eventually he became so distressed that he positively *pretended* to catch the fly, going through all the appropriate actions with his lips and tongue, and afterwards rubbing the ground with his neck as if to kill the victim: he then looked up at me with a triumphant air of success. So well was the whole process simulated that I should have been quite deceived, had I not seen that the fly was still upon the window. Accordingly I drew his attention to this fact, as well as to the absence of anything upon the floor; and when he saw that his hypocrisy had been detected he slunk away under some furniture, evidently very much ashamed of himself. (Romanes, 1882, p. 444.)

One unintended effect of Romanes's book was to make biologists and animal psychologists wary of his approach to the topic. Two criticisms were offered. First, the evidence cited was largely *anecdotal,* rather than being derived from experiment, and was therefore subject to the same flaws as all data obtained without proper controls. Romanes himself was aware of this defect. Second, Romanes was accused by his critics of not being parsimonious enough in his explanations of the behavior described. They argued that it was not necessary to resort to such concepts as reasoning and emotion. Animal behavior, they claimed, could be accounted for in simpler terms, or at least such an attempt should be seriously made before turning to more complex explanations.

To put it another way, Romanes was considered guilty of *anthropomorphizing,* that is, of attributing human-like traits to animals. Of course, that is exactly what Romanes wanted to do, in the interests of documenting the Darwinian assumption of continuity. The guilt, if any, lay not so much in his anthropomorphizing, as in his doing so unnecessarily.

To guard against this temptation, Lloyd Morgan (1852–1936), another student of animal behavior, proposed the following rule in his book, *Introduction to Comparative Psychology,* published in 1894, the year of Romanes's death:

> In no case may we interpret an action as the outcome of the exercise of a higher psychical faculty, if it can be interpreted as the outcome of the exercise of one which stands lower in the psychological scale.

It is interesting to note that Morgan's canon has been applied not only to animal behavior but to that of human beings as well. Indeed, certain psychological theories have been developed for the very purpose of eliminating the taint of anthropomorphism from explanations of human behavior!

Interest in animal behavior, of course, did not await Darwin's theory. Aristotle (384–322 B.C.) devoted considerable attention to this topic, as did other philosophers and scientists in the ensuing centuries. But in contrast to the researchers of the late nineteenth century, at least part of the motivation of pre-Darwinian investigators was to demonstrate the *discontinuity* between man and the lower animals by emphasizing man's presumably unique attributes, such as his ability to reason, to use language, to laugh, to build culture, and so on.

Present-day biologists who investigate animal behavior, *ethologists,* differ from comparative psychologists in at least three ways: (1) Ethologists prefer to study animals in their natural habitats rather than in the laboratory; (2) they are interested in behaviors that may be unique to a given species, whereas comparative psychologists emphasize behaviors that are common among species; (3) they adhere closely to Morgan's canon, as revealed in their general reluctance to speculate about unobservable psychological processes occurring in their subjects, while they pay careful attention to the observable environmental and internal (such as hormonal) circumstances that trigger and direct certain behaviors.

In recent years the two approaches to the study of animal behavior have been to some extent converging. Psychologists such as Frank Beach and Daniel Lehrman, impressed by the ethologists' methods and results, are beginning to incorporate into their own work naturalistic observation and a concern for species-specific behaviors. At the same time, ethologists are increasing their use of experimental manipulations, examining the ways in which species-specific (and therefore presumably fixed, or "instinctual") behavior patterns can be modified, and constructing models to account for "animal behavior" in general. Two European ethologists, Niko Tinbergen and Konrad Lorenz, are especially prominent in this latter endeavor.

A very recent way in which biology is beginning to make contact with psychology is through the relatively new but fast-growing field of molecular biology. In particular, the molecular biologists have discovered a complex protein (deoxyribonucleic acid, or DNA) that seems to store genetic information, or the genetic code. This information is transmitted to all cells in the body by another protein molecule, ribonucleic acid, or RNA. Some theorists have speculated that RNA may also serve as the mechanism for storing information acquired by the organism through experience; that is, RNA molecules may mediate learning and memory.

Empirical support for this notion is starting to accumulate; it has been reported, for example, that when RNA is extracted from the brains of trained rats and injected into naive rats, these latter animals behave more like the trained rats than do control animals (Jacobson, Babich, Bubash, and Goren, 1966). Such a finding, should it be borne out in subsequent research, would constitute a major breakthrough in psychology's hitherto futile attempt to uncover the specific bodily mechanisms through which learning and memory are effected.

From the four disciplines cited thus far—philosophy, physiology, psychiatry, biology—psychology derives much of its present character. Even those four broad fields, of course, do not fully account for the many facets of contemporary psychology. Significant influence has come, for example, from anthropology and sociology, from education, physics, mathematics, and so on. But to continue listing influential fields would quickly lead to a state of diminishing returns. One final point should be made, however, in closing this section. Psychology is of such broad scope and in sufficiently early stages of development that there is still room within it for contributions from many sources, academic or otherwise, formal or informal. Its receptivity to ideas from beyond its own borders and from novices within the field is one attribute of psychology that makes it so attractive to students seeking a career in an area in which they can hope to make important contributions to knowledge.

The Multiple Strategies of Psychology

For the most part it is fairly easy to see how psychology's heritage from other disciplines has dictated the substantive issues with which contemporary psychologists concern themselves. What may not be so clear is that psychology is characterized not only by a diversity of interests and issues, but also by a wide variety of approaches to, or strategies for dealing with, these many problems. The burden of this brief section is to offer a rationale for what may otherwise appear to be a hodgepodge of routes, as in the title of this chapter, that psychologists follow in pursuit of their common goal. In providing such a rationale, we will also reveal the basis for the organization of the remaining chapters of this book.

FOCUS ON BEHAVIOR

Although theory is the goal of scientific psychology, the motivation to achieve that goal is provided by behavioral phenomena that demand explanation. For example, the construction of psychoanalytic theory was initiated in Freud's early concern about the behavioral symptoms exhibited by his neurotic patients. The theory of evolution had a similar beginning in Darwin's curiosity about the origin of the many species of plants and animals he encountered on a sea voyage, as reported in *The Voyage of the Beagle*. Theories, big or small, typically start in a casual way and are nourished by repeated inputs of new data.

Quite obviously, then, psychological theory needs to be fed by observations of behavior, behavior that is sufficiently intriguing to hold the continued interest of the theorist. Many psychologists thus contribute to the development of their field by focusing their attention on specific behaviors of particular concern to them. The primary objectives of this approach are to describe those behaviors as accurately as possible and to discover, often through experiment, the conditions that influence them. Potential relevance to psychological theory may be lurking in the back of the scientist's mind, but while he is following this approach, his eye is on the behavior, not on the theory.

Often, of course, a person's interests may change, and the psychologist who started with a behavioral focus may find himself gradually becoming enmeshed in the theoretical implications of the behavior. For example, a psychologist with an initial interest in the phenomenon of suicide may eventually become enraptured by the psychoanalytic concept of the superego (employed in certain attempts at explanation of suicidal behavior); he may then abruptly switch approaches, drop his investigation of suicidal behavior *per se,* and concentrate on the theoretical nuances of the concept of the superego and its relation to other concepts within psychoanalytic theory.

Whatever the professional life-history of any particular psychologist, it is clear that a considerable proportion of the total scientific endeavor in psychology is devoted to the fundamental task of discovering, describing, and exploring interesting behavioral phenomena.

FOCUS ON PROCESSES

We can illustrate what we mean by focus on processes as follows: Consider any piece of behavior, say, an automobile driver's stopping his car at a red light, or to be somewhat more technical, "engaging in those behaviors that bring his car to a stop"—that is, removing his foot from the accelerator and depressing the brake pedal. What processes might we postulate to be operative in the performance of that behavioral act? Without pretending that the ensuing is inclusive, we could point to such items as these:

Information-Reception. Obviously, if the person's behavior is controlled by an external stimulus, the red light, then he must be sensitive to the presence of—that is, *detect*—that stimulus. Furthermore, since he depresses the brake when the light is red, but behaves differently when it turns green, he must be able to *discriminate* between those colors. What are the processes that are implied by the terms detection and discrimination?

You are quite well aware, of course, that detecting traffic signals and discriminating between green and red involve processes operative within the visual system. You also know that analogous processes take place in other *sense modalities*, such as the systems called "auditory" (hearing), "olfactory" (smelling), and "tactual" (touching). Indeed, human beings are endowed with an extensive set of separate systems that make them sensitive to physical signals of many types—lights, sounds, odors, tastes, and so on. These systems provide channels of communication between a person and his environment (including the person's body itself). Through these channels, information is transmitted from the environment, and hence *about* the environment, to the person. Speaking broadly, we might refer to a set of processes that subserve the function of information-reception. Any attempt at a full understanding of a person's behavior must include an understanding of these crucial processes.

Information-Processing. To an automobile driver a red light emanating from a traffic signal is more than just another stimulus to which his visual system is sensitive. That red light has special significance, or *meaning*. It means "stop," and in that respect differs from all other red lights. Moreover, it means stop (depress the brake) only to the driver of the car, not to the passengers (though many passengers will find their right feet reaching for the brake if the driver's response is a little slower than theirs might be).

Thus, a red light means "stop" only if it is associated with a traffic signal and ordinarily means "do something to make this car stop" only to the automobile driver. The meaning of the stimulus is determined by the context in which it occurs. To illustrate further, consider the driver of an ambulance on an emergency run to a hospital. To that driver, a red traffic light means, not "stop," but "slow down a little, sound the siren, and get through the intersection as quickly as possible." Here the simple change in context profoundly affects the behavioral implications of the red light.

These brief remarks should be sufficient to suggest the vital role of *information-processing*. People respond not just to the simple physical properties of stimuli, but also to the ways in which these stimuli are categorized—that is, to their meanings.

Arousal. Automobile drivers differ in the degree to which they are alert to incoming information, both at a given moment and perhaps chronically. After traveling for several hours at top speed on a superhighway, the typical driver is probably more drowsy than when he started out. Similarly, the driver leaving for home from a New Year's Eve party, with several ounces of alcohol in his blood, is probably much less alert than when he arrived at the party.

You need not be told of the importance for good driving of the driver's state of alertness. The very sleepy or intoxicated driver might fail to see a pedestrian in his path. On approaching a red light, he might not even notice it, at least not soon enough to stop on time. Clearly, then, the driver's behavior at the traffic light depends not only on his information-receiving-and-processing systems, but also on his level of *arousal*. At a low arousal level, information reception and processing may be disrupted; a similar effect may also occur at the "output" end of the behavioral sequence: The red light may be detected and assigned a proper meaning, but the driver may not depress the brake quickly enough, because the efficiency of his movements is retarded. Finally, a drunken driver may not stop simply because he does not want to.

Motivation. It is frightening to contemplate the extent to which one's own safety depends on others' motives. While driving you probably rarely reflect on the motives of the other drivers. You may be suspicious of their skills, or their alertness, or their sobriety, but it is unlikely that each time a car approaches you wonder whether its driver *wants* to keep from colliding with you.

Our faith in other drivers' intentions is, of course, reasonable. But just because the vast majority of drivers want to avoid accidents (at least as far as they are aware), and because we all take this for granted, the role of motivation in driving is not negated. Thus, again, a complete account of the behavior of the automobile driver in our original example would incorporate information about his motives. And this would surely be the case for any behavior under scrutiny. So it is that psychologists, with applied or theoretical interests, pay a considerable amount of attention to motivational processes.

Learning and Memory. How does it happen that the alert, motivated, "informed" driver so readily and almost automatically stops his car at a red light? Clearly, the behavior in question was acquired, or *learned,* during the period when the driver was being trained. Theoretical consideration of driving or of any skilled behavior must include the role of learning in the acquisition and maintenance of that behavior. Indeed, learning and the retention of what has been learned—or memory—are so pervasive in all forms of behavior that many psychological theories have learning and retention as their core concepts.

Some critics have asserted that psychology, especially American psychological theory, is overly concerned with the learning process, to the exclusion of other, equally important processes. Whatever the merits of that claim, however, it is apparent that the concept of learning must enter into the explanation of almost all behavioral phenomena, even many that superficially seem to be instances of purely innate behaviors.

To grasp more firmly the importance of learning, you should note that learning enters not only directly into the determination of a given behavioral act, but also indirectly through its effects on other processes that control the behavior. Thus, the driver's motivation to drive safely is itself undoubtedly acquired through the learning process. In a similar vein, learning affects the way in which stimulus inputs are categorized, as when a neophyte learns the rule that a red light associated with traffic signals means "stop." It is quite likely that through learning, people become better able to detect the presence of significant stimuli, as for example when an experienced driver becomes adept at noticing out of the corner of his eye a child about to run in front of his car. Even arousal level may be determined in part by learning factors.

Because of its obvious importance, the learning process is of primary concern to many psychologists, and their interest is not tied to particular behaviors. That is why it is so easy for the learning theorist to move so freely from investigation of college students learning lists of words to rats learning to turn right in a T-maze. With a focus on process, behavioral particulars become peripheral. Thus, to the question about why he is interested in studying learning in rats, the researcher answers: "I'm not studying learning *in rats;* I'm studying *learning.*" The spirit behind that answer pertains equally well to any of the processes referred to in this section.

Ideation. Unfortunately, stopping at a red light does not exemplify very well the full range of ideational processes, which typically are not prominent in that kind of behavioral setting. Later in the text we will use the term "ideation" to include those processes ordinarily called "reasoning" and "problem-solving." But in the act in question there rarely is need for recourse to these forms of ideation—except perhaps when the brakes fail. Similarly, it is highly unlikely that a person who is alert enough to be driving safely is engaging in that type of ideation referred to as dreaming. However, between the extremes of problem-solving and dreaming there are forms of ideational activity that are pertinent to our example. The red light might, for instance, set off a chain of associations, beginning with thoughts about policemen, turning to soldiers and the current war, shifting to ideas about morality, religion, God, and so on.

This kind of ideational activity usually accompanies, or runs parallel with, overt behavioral acts, but does not directly influence the latter. To explain adequately the behavior of stopping at the red light we need not refer to these ideational events, at least in the same sense that we must refer to information-reception and -processing, motivation, arousal, learning, retention, and so on.

Sometimes, however, ideational activity interacts with ongoing overt behaviors, and then it becomes relevant to a full explanation of those behaviors. For example, the chain of ideas initiated by the red light might be so compelling that, distracted by his ideation, the driver momentarily neglects to execute the proper act of depressing the brake. Indeed, the ideational chain might take such a direction that strong guilt feelings and perhaps a consequent desire for punishment are aroused, and the driver fails to stop in time and has an "accident."

It should be mentioned that modern psychologists tend to be wary of such terms as "ideas," "thoughts," "images," and so on, taking the position that overt behaviors are the only proper subject matter of psychology. In this book, we will accept the reality and importance of ideational processes, while recognizing the difficulties inherent in trying to uncover their properties.

FOCUS ON DEVELOPMENT

Earlier, when we touched on the Darwinian influence on psychology, we noted that out of the assumption of continuity among species there arose an interest in the comparative study of behavior and of the processes that underlie behavior. Within the framework of this kind of interest, one may, for example, want to see how the learning process develops from simple, primitive organisms (paramecia, worms) to highly complex ones (rats, cats, monkeys, men). Indeed, there may be no single general learning process, but rather different types of processes that subserve behavior change in different levels of development. Such a finding would be of considerable interest not only in its own right; it would cast serious doubt on the strategy of studying learning in but one or two species, as many investigators of the learning process currently do.

One virtue of phylogenetic comparison, then, is that it may obviate the possible error of attributing to some process properties that are manifested in only a few species. Another virtue is that by comparative study, one may obtain a better perspective on the nature of the processes under consideration. For example, it is helpful in understanding the fine details of problem-solving in human beings to know how representatives of other species cope with similar problems. If nothing else, the observation that even the lowly rat shows evidence of processes that might appropriately be labeled "reasoning" might change the ancient conception of man as "the animal that can reason." On the other hand, evidence showing limitations in ideational power exhibited by the higher, subhuman primates provides an empirical base against which the marvel of human thought can better be appreciated.

Development that can be traced phylogenetically—that is, from lower to higher species—has its analog in the changes that occur within a given species over time, or *ontogenetic* (frequently shortened to "genetic") development. As with phylogenetic comparisons, there is considerable interest and profit in studying the ontogenesis of the various psychological processes. For example, recent genetic investigations of visual perception reveal that human infants are considerably better able to make discriminations than had previously been suspected. Although psychologists have been especially concerned with the ontogenesis of human behavior, they have paid some attention to the lower animals, as in the dramatic findings of Harry Harlow on the role of mothering in the emotional, social, and sexual development of monkeys (see Chapter Fifteen for further details).

In this book we will include developmental material in our discussion of particular processes. Thus, studies of the genetic development of form discrimination will be cited in the section on information reception and processing; material on emotional development will similarly be presented within the chapter devoted to emotional processes—and so on for the several other topics to be covered in the succeeding chapters.

FOCUS ON THE PHYSIOLOGICAL SUBSTRATE

Since we have already documented the influence of physiology on psychology, we need only touch on it lightly here. For the most part, our earlier discussion dealt with substantive issues—on how so many of the present concerns of psychology had their origin in the work of physiologists. But the two fields make contact at the level of approach as well as content. In the opinion of many psychologists, it is of fundamental importance for understanding psychological processes and the behaviors they subserve to know their physiological correlates.

Those who hold this opinion look to physiology, especially neurophysiology, for explanations of psychological events. This reductionist approach implies that events in one realm (psychology) must, to be understood, be "reduced to" a set of corresponding, presumably more basic, events (physiology). A good analogy might lie in the argument that the ultimate account of chemical events must be sought within the field of atomic physics. For another example of the reductionist approach, consider the view that social institutions—the province of sociology—can be understood only by recourse to what is known about the behavior of individual human beings.

A total commitment to a reductionist strategy would demand something like the following chain of dependencies among various disciplines:

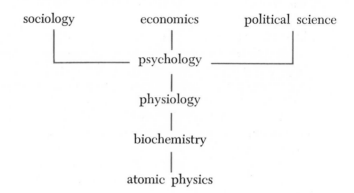

Not all scientists accept the reductionist strategy. Some say it is "nice but not necessary." Some might argue that reductionism is not even possible: that events at one level cannot entirely find their explanation in events at a "lower" level, that there are *emergent* properties of, say, psychological processes, that could not be deduced from even total knowledge of physiological processes, just as water has properties that are not inherent in its constituents, oxygen and hydrogen.

While awaiting the outcome of this debate between the reductionists and their opponents, we might be wise to take the intermediate position that though reductionist attempts may not be essential, they can be useful and certainly are interesting. If, for example, in our search for understanding of the learning process, certain information from neurophysiology or biochemistry would seem to be pertinent and illuminating, let us by all means consider it. That is the approach we will follow here. Evidence and concepts from physiology will be brought into our discussion whenever they promise to be useful and interesting, just as we will introduce developmental material.

FOCUS ON SYNTHESIS

Throughout its brief history, science has achieved its greatest successes while pursuing a strategy of breaking down complex events into smaller, simpler components, or elements, in short, in following the strategy of *analysis*. This is the approach of the physiologist who treats the body as a set of subsystems (circulatory, digestive, nervous, and so on) and it motivates the psychologist to analyze the separate processes he believes make up a total behavioral act.

Granting the utility of an analytic approach, we can also demand from the scientist some attempt at *synthesis*—putting the pieces back together. The human body, after all, is not simply an arbitrary collection of unrelated subsystems; the systems are intimately interrelated; they interact in such a way as to yield a unified, integrated organism. Similarly, a person's behavior has a quality of unity, integration, or wholeness that is not satisfactorily captured by reference to a set of basic processes, such as perception, emotion, motivation, and learning. Many critics of scientific psychology are undoubtedly reacting to the obvious artificiality that permeates the analytic approach. With justification, they want to see Humpty Dumpty put together again.

In sympathy with this desire, some psychologists have made attempts at synthesis, usually under the guise of creating a theory of personality. Freud was the most ambitious of the personality theorists. A careful examination of his work, incidentally, reveals the great extent to which he called on information related to the processes of interest to the experimental psychologist.

Freud's has not been the only attempt at theoretical synthesis in the history of psychology. Similar attempts have come from diverse sources—for example, from the Gestalt psychologists with their emphasis on perception; from the Hullians and from the followers of Ivan Pavlov, with their emphasis on learning; from certain social psychologists who emphasize behavior in groups and the behavior of groups. Given the appropriateness of the goal of synthesis—which in the language used in Chapter One is no more than the goal of a comprehensive psychological theory, incorporating and integrating smaller models—any introduction to psychology should certainly consider some of these attempts. In this text, as in most others, such a discussion will appear following the chapters that deal with the results of analysis, that is, with the various processes that psychologists have teased out of the complexity of the behavioral world, and from which the synthetic product will eventually be reconstituted.

SUMMARY

Psychology, as a formal discipline, is only about 100 years old, but its historical roots go back many centuries. Its beginnings are in philosophy. For example, the controversy in philosophy between the *nativists* and *empiricists* over the origin and validity of knowledge (that is, the problem of *epistemology*) still reverberates within psychology, transformed into the broad question of the source of the many behavioral differences that are apparent among people. Indeed, it has been argued that contemporary psychological theories are heavily influenced by assumptions about human nature that can be characterized as either *Leibnitzian* or *Lockean,* after the seventeenth-century philosophers, Leibnitz and Locke. The former are theories that stress psychological development "from within," whereas the latter assume the individual's development to be entirely reactive to whatever environmental events happen to impinge on him.

Contemporary psychology has roots in several other fields, prominent among them *physiology, psychiatry,* and *biology.* From physiology comes psychology's concern with topics such as sensory functioning, reaction time, brain-behavior relations, and the regulation of the "internal environment" through homeostatic mechanisms. The concept of homeostasis, as borrowed from physiology and applied to adaptive behavior in general, has had a profound influence on the nature of psychological models of motivation and learning.

From psychiatry, especially Freud's psychoanalytic psychiatry, have come many current psychological concepts and assumptions about human nature. Freud stressed the significance of interaction between instinctual, biological drives and the demands of society in the formation of personality. He also introduced the concepts of unconscious impulses and ideas ("residing" in the *id*) and of the devices, chiefly unconscious (that is, the *defense mechanisms*), used by the *ego* for controlling them. Further, Freud argued that all behavior is meaningful and that even such apparently trivial events as *dreams* can be explained and, when properly explained, can help in understanding the dreamer in particular and man in general. Scientific research on dreaming stems directly from Freud's speculations, as does the recent experimentation on *subliminal perception*.

Psychologists' interest in animal behavior can be seen as directly flowing from the theory of organic evolution developed by the biologist Charles Darwin. In essence, if man is biologically related to the other animal species, then there should also be evidence of continuity between man and the "lower" animals in psychological, or behavioral, functioning. The search for evidence of such continuity became the province of the *comparative psychologist*. Overemphasis by some researchers on human-like qualities in animals led to the caution against unwarranted *anthropomorphizing;* to guard against this tendency, Lloyd Morgan proposed that explanations of behavior should not be based on concepts that are "higher" on some psychological scale if concepts at a "lower" level will suffice. Whereas the comparative psychologist emphasizes behavioral similarities among species, his counterpart in biology, the *ethologist,* focuses on species-specific behaviors. These two approaches to the study of animal behavior are, however, beginning to converge, and richer theories of animal and human behavior may emerge from that fusion.

The influences of psychology from other fields are not just historical. For example, recent findings by microbiologists on the role of the protein molecules, DNA and RNA, in genetic transmission have suggested to psychologists the possibility of a molecular basis of learning and memory.

Just as psychology has many roots, so too does it follow many routes to its goal. Some psychologists emphasize in their research particular behaviors, whereas others attend to the processes assumed to underlie these behaviors. We have classified these processes as involving: *information-reception, information-processing* (which imparts *meaning* to stimuli), *arousal, motivation, learning* and *memory,* and *ideation,* or thinking. The behaviors of interest, or the underlying processes, may be studied from the point of view of how they develop, *phylogenetically* (from lower to higher species) and *ontogenetically* (as the members of a given species mature). In similar vein, considerable attention is being paid to the physiological subtrates of behavior. Finally, there are those psychologists who attempt, through synthesizing efforts, to reverse the analytic strategy characteristic of scientific research and put the psychological pieces back together.

SUGGESTED READINGS

Allport, G.W. *Becoming.* New Haven: Yale Univ. Press, 1955.

Boring, E.G. *A history of experimental psychology.* New York: Appleton-Century-Crofts, 1950.

Freud, S. *A general introduction to psychoanalysis.* Garden City, N.Y.: Doubleday (Perma Books), 1953.

Hull, C.L. *Principles of behavior.* New York: Appleton-Century-Crofts, 1943, pp. 57–83.

Lorenz, K. *King Solomon's ring.* New York: Thomas Y. Crowell, 1952.

Schwartz, M. Physiological psychology: or can a science over 95 afford to be "grubo"? *Psychological Bulletin,* 1967, 67, 228–230.

Scott, J.P. *Animal behavior.* Chicago: Univ. of Chicago Press, 1958.

Silverstein, A. The "grubo" psychology: or can a science over 95 be happy without reductionism? *Psychological Bulletin,* 1966, 66, 207–211.

Tinbergen, N. *The herring gull's world.* Garden City, N.Y.: Doubleday (Anchor Books), 1967.

PART TWO

The Visual System:
Physics, Anatomy, and Physiology

C H A P T E R F I V E　　Through his several sensory systems, a person gains information about his environment. In this and in the succeeding two chapters the visual system is described in detail; this description is meant to serve as a prototype of the kinds of knowledge that one would need for a comprehensive understanding of all the sensory systems. We start in this chapter with a consideration of (a) the nature of the visual stimulus—light; (b) the structures and functions of the components of the visual receptor organ—the eye; and (c) the nature of the "message" that is transmitted over neural structures from the eye to the brain—the electrical impulses that constitute the "code" into which all stimulation is translated.

The Visual Stimulus: Light

The visual system is sensitive to a narrow band of electromagnetic radiation called light. Although the physical theory of light is highly complex, for our present purpose we can make use of the concept of light as a *wave*. For the place of light in the electromagnetic spectrum see Figure 5.1 (p. 144).

Light waves have two important parameters, *length* and *amplitude,* as illustrated in Figure 5.2 (p. 145). For some purposes it is convenient to transform wavelength into frequency, which is the number of wave units, or cycles, contained within a given time period, say one second. Frequency is the inverse of length, since the shorter the wavelength, the greater the number of wave cycles that can be packed into a unit of time. The simple inverse relation between wavelength and frequency holds, however, only when light is traveling through a vacuum; when light passes through a physical medium (such as water) its frequency remains constant, but its length changes. The change in length accompanies a change in velocity, but frequency is unaffected.

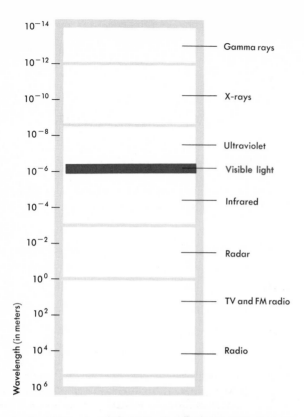

10^{-14}	
10^{-12}	Gamma rays
10^{-10}	X-rays
10^{-8}	
	Ultraviolet
10^{-6}	Visible light
10^{-4}	Infrared
10^{-2}	
	Radar
10^{0}	
10^{2}	TV and FM radio
10^{4}	Radio
10^{6}	

Figure 5.1 The place of visible light in the broad range of electromagnetic radiation. Note that 10^0 = one meter (or 39.37 inches).

For example, the velocity of light waves in air (approximately the same as the velocity in a vacuum) is about 3×10^{10} centimeters per second. When light is traveling through glass, its velocity is reduced to about 1.91×10^{10} centimeters per second. For wave frequency to be preserved, wavelength must decrease in proportion to the drop in velocity—in the present example, a decrease of a little more than one third. The ratio of the new wavelength to the original would be the ratio of the new velocity to the original, or 1.91/3.00. Thus, if the original wavelength were 600 units, the transformed length would be about $600 \times (1.91/3.00)$, or about 382 units.

An analogy here might help clarify the relations among frequency, length, and velocity. Consider a platoon of soldiers, marching on a paved road at a fixed cadence ("hup-two-three-four, . . .") and at a steady velocity. The cadence, expressed as number of steps per minute, is analogous to wave frequency. Now imagine these soldiers on a muddy road, where marching is difficult and their velocity slows down; it will take them longer to move a given distance here than on a good road. Their slowing down can come about in either of two ways: (1) They can take the same size steps as before but decrease their cadence; or (2) they can maintain the original cadence (take the same number of steps in a given time period) but shorten their steps. The second alternative is the analog of what happens to light as it moves from a vacuum, or from air, into a more resistant medium such as water or glass.

The wavelength of light is symbolized by the Greek letter λ (lambda) and is measured in units called *millimicrons*, symbolized mμ. A millimicron is one-thousandth (1/1000) the length of a micron, which in turn is one thousandth the length of a millimeter. Thus, a millimicron is .001 × .001, or .000001 (one millionth) the length of a millimeter. To put the discussion into more familiar units, one millimeter is about .04 inches. When we talk of wavelengths of light, we talk of very small units indeed.

The *visible spectrum* is that band of wavelengths, within the entire electromagnetic spectrum, to which some visual system is sensitive. For normal

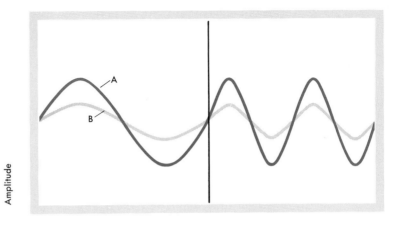

Amplitude

Time

Figure 5.2 How waves may differ in frequency or amplitude: Left panel, low frequency; right panel, high frequency. Curve A, high amplitude; curve B, low. High frequency is equivalent to short wavelength.

human beings, the visible spectrum ranges from about 430 mμ at the "short" end to about 780 mμ at the "long" end. Some animal species are sensitive to a different range of the spectrum. The honeybee, for example, responds to wavelengths as short as 300 mμ, in the ultraviolet band, but loses sensitivity at about 650 mμ. In terms of human phenomenology, the honeybee is "red-blind."

Wavelength not only determines the limits of the visible spectrum but also contributes to the quality of visual experiences. All other things equal, what we call the color (more technically, the *hue*) of light is a function of its wavelength. The relation between experienced hue and wavelength for normal human beings is given in Plate 2. To pick off some easily labeled regions within the visible spectrum, the band extending from about 430 to 470 mμ is associated with what we call "violet"; from about 470 to 480 mμ is the "blue" portion; from about 480 to 500 mμ are the "blue-greens"; from about 500 to 550 mμ is the "green" band; from about 550 to 580 mμ are the "yellow-greens"; from about 580 to 600 is "yellow"; from about 600 to 650 mμ is the "orange" region; from about 660 to 780 are the "reds." Wavelengths greater than about 780 mμ are called infrared; they are not visible to human beings.

The eight subbands listed above are quite crude, because people are capable of making very fine distinctions, or discriminations, with respect to hue. For most people, a few crude categories suffice, but an artist, for example, needs and uses a richer repertory of color names.

Wavelength, then, is the major determinant in the physical stimulus of the experience of hue. *Wave amplitude* contributes primarily to the experience called *brightness:* The greater the amplitude, the greater the brightness. This is not to say that wave amplitude, or its crude equivalent "light intensity," is the sole determinant of brightness; wavelength also affects apparent brightness, as do several other variables.

Under ordinary circumstances, we are not exposed to light of a single wavelength or even of a very narrow band of wavelengths. Instead, light typically comes as a *mixture* of wavelengths. Sunlight, for example, is a mixture of all the wavelengths in the visible spectrum. Such a complete mixture gives rise to an experience we usually call "white."

Of course, the visual world is not typically a world of disembodied colors. Rather, except under special circumstances it is a world of *objects.* So we must be concerned with the question of how objects get their hue. Surely, from what has preceded, we must answer "from the wavelength(s) of light with which they stimulate the eye." But where does that light come from, and why that particular mixture of wavelengths? Unless the object in question is a radiant source, such as a flame or its equivalent (for instance, the heated filament of an incandescent lamp), the light by which it stimulates the eye is borrowed from such a source. That is, visible objects that are not themselves light sources *reflect* some of the light by which they are illuminated, as for example the moon becomes visible by reflecting the light of the sun.

Not all the light striking an object is necessarily reflected; some may be *absorbed.* The most familiar technique for manipulating the mixture of wavelengths reflected by an object is to coat its surface with a pigment (paint, dye, and so on). Pigments work by absorbing certain wavelengths and reflecting others. It is those reflected wavelengths that impart a particular hue to the pigment-coated object. Of course, in order to be reflected, a given wavelength must be present in the light striking the object. Thus, how an object stimulates the eye is a joint function of the wavelengths impinging on the object and on its reflecting characteristics.

How can the wavelength composition of the light illuminating an object (or directly striking the eye) be regulated? Three basic techniques are available.

1. As Sir Isaac Newton (1642–1727) reported as long ago as 1704, white light, as from the sun, is a mixture of all wavelengths in the visible spectrum. These several components of white light can be separated, as illustrated in Plate 3, by passing the light through a prism which differentially bends, or *refracts,* light of different wavelengths. As you can see from Plate 3, the longer wavelengths are the less bendable, or *refrangible.*

Since refraction has the effect of spreading out the components of a beam of white light, it becomes possible to pick off one desired band from the spectrum by masking all other wavelengths. An instrument for doing so with considerable precision—as narrow as 10 mμ—is called a *monochromator* (from *mono,* meaning single, and *chroma,* referring to hue). Monochromators have an internal light source, and to spread the light they use prisms or an analogous, but more sophisticated device known as a *diffraction grating*. The physical theory of diffraction gratings need not concern us here; it is sufficient to note that they take advantage of the fact that in passing over a straight edge, a beam of light, by virtue of its wave nature, spreads and does so differentially as a function of wavelength. (Incidentally, because of diffraction, it is impossible to bring light to a perfect focus, even with a perfect lens; there will always be some light distributed in concentric rings around the point of maximum concentration of energy. Thus, diffraction sets a limit to the precision of the image of fine details of objects on the photosensitive surface of the eye. As an additional aside, note that the short wavelengths are the most susceptible to diffraction; consequently, under stimulation by blue light, visual acuity is considerably impaired relative to acuity under monochromatic stimulation by light of longer wavelengths, such as green or red. If poor acuity is desired, as in a burlesque theater, then blue light is the obvious choice of illuminant.)

2. Surfaces that either absorb or reflect all the incident light are called *opaque*. Certain materials, such as glass, which allow light to pass through them are called *transparent*. Transparent objects may absorb and reflect some of the light that strikes them; to the extent that they do not transmit all of the incident light they act as *filters*.

Some filters are so composed that they act with equal effectiveness on all wavelengths; these are called *neutral density filters*. When interposed between a light source and a surface, say the eye, they merely decrease the intensity of the light striking that surface by a fixed proportion.

Filters can also be constructed so as to be differentially effective on different bands of the spectrum, allowing only certain wavelengths to be transmitted. The best *color filters*, however, do not have the precision of a monochromator. For many purposes color filters are adequate, but for other purposes, as in research on color vision, very narrow bands of wavelength are called for, in which case a monochromator would be used.

3. Artificial sources of light, such as incandescent lamps, ordinarily do not yield truly white light. They are biased in one portion of the spectrum. When bias is desired, this characteristic of artificial light sources can be exploited. For example, if light with a predominant yellow component is desired, then a sodium lamp would be an excellent source, since it yields light heavily saturated in the yellow band.

There is considerably more that can be said about light, but the foregoing information is enough foundation for the following discussion on the visual receptor itself, the eye. Indeed, in that context the model of light as a wave, with all its attendant complexities, can be set aside, and light can be treated as a body that travels in straight lines, or "rays." Such a conception of light forms the basis of a model known as *geometrical optics,* which is concerned with the simple interactions between light and such objects as mirrors and lenses. Since the eye in many respects resembles an optical system, it is convenient, especially for purposes of exposition, to apply the concepts of geometrical optics to the description of the way in which light reaches the photosensitive surface of the eye.

The Visual Receptor: The Eye

In attempts to convey the structure and function of the eye, people often use a camera as an analogy. Thus, both have a device (the *pupil* of the eye, the diaphragm of the camera) for controlling the amount of light entering what is otherwise a light-tight "box"; both have a *lens* for focusing the light onto a photosensitive surface (the *retina* of the eye, the film of a camera). The analogy is useful so long as we recognize its limitations, for in many ways the eye is not like a camera.

The major structural components of the eye are shown in Figure 5.3. One crucial feature of the visual receptor system that is not represented in the figure is binocularity: The intact visual system has two eyes, whose functions are coordinated. Another feature that cannot easily be represented in a diagram is its dynamic nature: The eyeball is not static, but is continually moving, even when apparently closely fixated on a stationary object. These tiny, but measureable, involuntary eye movements, called *nystagmic* movements, assure that the image of an object is not fixed in one spot on the retina, as a static diagram might imply. With these deficiencies in the diagram in mind, we can consider the major structures of the eye, and their contribution to visual functioning.

ILLUMINATION CONTROL

The pupil of the eye, like the diaphragm of a camera, regulates the amount of light striking a photosensitive surface. In a camera, what constitutes the right amount of light depends on the length of exposure (the longer the exposure the less light that is needed) and on the speed of the film employed (the faster the film, the less light that is needed). In the eye, there is no clear analog of exposure duration, since under ordinary viewing conditions, exposure duration is effectively infinite. The closest analog of film speed is the adaptation state of the retina. After being in bright light, the sensitivity of the retina is relatively low, and the retina is said to be *light-adapted;* after a period in the dark, or in very dim light, the retina is relatively highly sensitive, and is said to be *dark-adapted* (this topic is discussed below). The effective intensity of stimulation in the eye is thus a joint product of the absolute intensity of the illumination and the adaptation state of the retina.

The pupil, which is a circular opening in the pigmented iris, regulates the amount of light (technically, total light flux) entering the eye per unit of time. If illumination is intense, the pupil constricts, reducing the size of the

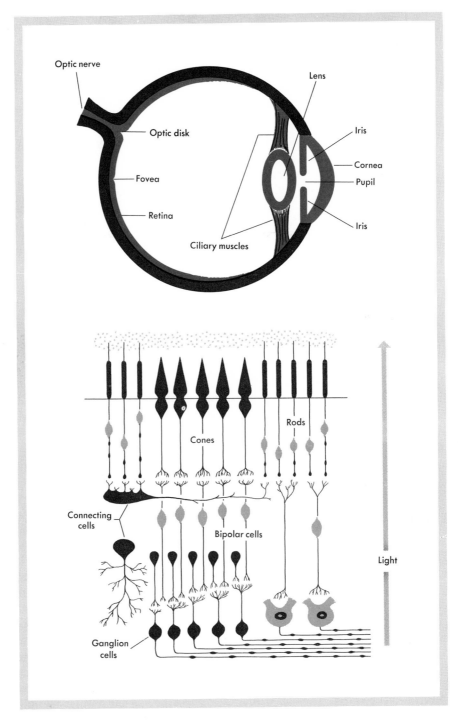

Figure 5.3 Sketch of right eyeball, top view; simplified schematic illustration of the nerve-cell network in a vertebrate retina. (Network adapted from Detwiler, 1941.)

aperture through which the light can pass, and hence decreasing the amount of light striking the retina. This device is only partially effective, however, since there is a limit to how small the pupillary aperture can be.

If the intensity of illumination is low, the pupil dilates, increasing aperture size and thereby allowing more light to stimulate the retina. Again, there is a limit to the extent of pupillary dilatation, so that inadequate stimulus intensity cannot entirely be compensated for by increases in pupil size.

The response of the pupil is reflexive, in the sense that it occurs automatically whenever the stimulating conditions are appropriate. Furthermore, the pupillary reflex is one of many such behavioral subsystems that can be described as a *negative-feedback* system. That is, the response is initiated by an event that can be called an *error* (in this case, a discrepancy between optimal and actual illumination level), and the response itself is error-reducing (retinal illumination is either decreased or increased). Like other mechanisms that operate according to a negative-feedback principle, the pupillary reflex follows an oscillating path. Instead of quickly reaching and fixing on an appropriate aperture size, the pupil goes through a sequence of overshooting and undershooting maneuvers, gradually homing in on the desired value.

Pupillary constriction and dilatation are regulated by the *autonomic nervous system*. Constriction is effected by a muscle, called a *sphincter,* that is controlled by the *parasympathetic* branch of the autonomic nervous system; dilatation is effected by the *dilater* muscle, which is innervated by the *sympathetic* branch of that system. The autonomic nervous system is largely involved in the control of *smooth muscle* activity, such as that involved in digestion, in cardiovascular activity, in urogenital functioning, as well as in the control of the endocrine glands. The two branches of the autonomic system are largely, though not entirely, antagonistic: Essentially, the sympathetic branch arouses activity while the parasympathetic one modulates or dampens activity. The sympathetic system dominates during periods of excitation, the parasympathetic during periods of relaxation.

Since the autonomic system in general is rather diffuse in its effects, events primarily directed at one site controlled by the system may have repercussions in other areas. For this reason, the pupil may respond to events unrelated to retinal illumination. For example, pupillary dilatation is observed in response to painful stimulation, or indeed to any event that activates the sympathetic system. Thus, dilatation occurs when a person looks at pictures, or objects, that are attractive to him (Hess, 1965), as, for example, when a woman looks at a picture of a baby. Incidentally, most people tend to prefer a photograph of a person showing dilated pupils rather than one showing constricted pupils. It is as though dilated pupils convey the message: "I am looking at you and find you attractive, so my pupils are dilated; if I find you attractive, I must be pretty nice myself." The photographs in Figure 5.4

Figure 5.4 Picture of woman's face with large and small pupils, simulating states of high and low arousal. (Camera Clix.)

are like those used in the research by Hess. Which one do you like?

The pupillary responses of the two eyes are coordinated, so that if stimulation is applied just to one eye, initiating a pupillary reflex, the pupil of the other eye will also respond. The two pupils, therefore, are ordinarily of the same size. Discrepancy in the sizes of the two pupils, called *anisocoria,* is indicative of a pathological condition.

The pupillary response influences visual function not only through illumination control, but also in another important way. When the pupil is constricted, light reaches the retina only through the central portions of the focusing devices—that is, the cornea and the lens. The central portions of these structures are relatively free of the optical imperfections, or *aberrations,* that are present in the peripheral portions. These aberrations act to blur the image cast on the retina by light passing through them. Thus, pupillary constriction cuts out those light rays that would otherwise cast a somewhat blurred image on the retina and, hence, constriction serves to enhance acuity. An obvious implication of this fact is that acuity is best under conditions of highly intense illumination—when pupil size is smallest. Conversely, events that elicit pupillary dilatation decrease acuity, thus making it difficult to see clearly objects with emotional significance.

Movement of the eyeball is effected by a set of six *extraocular* muscles; these are striped muscles and so are under the *somatic,* rather than the autonomic, nervous system.

If we consider the two eyes in relation to each other, we note three types of movement: *convergence, divergence,* and *conjugate* movement. Convergence occurs when fixation is directed at a close object, and the two eyes rotate toward each other, as diagramed in Figure 5.5. Divergence is the opposite of that response, occurring when the eyes shift from fixation on a close object to fixation on a far object. In conjugate movements, which are superimposed on convergence and divergence, the two eyes move, either laterally or vertically, in concert. For example, if fixation shifts from one object to another, as a person *scans* the visual field, then the two eyes will move in the same direction and to the same extent, as they will also in order to maintain fixation on, or pursue, a moving object.

Convergence, divergence, and conjugate movements serve to position the image of a visual target on the retina. The image is usually placed in the center of the retina, the *foveal* region, which, for reasons to be expounded later, assures maximal acuity. Ordinarily, this positioning is involuntary, or reflexive, though the reflexive tendency can be overcome, with difficulty, through voluntary effort.

There is a category of entirely involuntary eye-movements that, moreover, are so small as to require special apparatus to be detected and measured. These movements prompted our earlier caution that the eyeball is never perfectly stationary, as implied in diagrams, but is, rather, continually in motion.

The basic technique for measuring these small, involuntary eye-movements utilizes a tiny mirror mounted on a contact lens, which in turn is fitted tightly over the outer surface of the eye. Whenever the eye moves, the mirror moves, and so long as body and head movements are restricted, the movements of the mirror give an accurate indication of eye-movements. To pick up and amplify movements of the mirror requires simply that a beam of light be reflected from the mirror to some recording device, such as a movie camera.

When eye-movements are traced by this method, several types are noted, even when the eye is presumably carefully fixating on a particular point. For example, there are *slow drifts,* which gradually take the eye off exact fixation; these in turn seem to be compensated for by a type of jerky motion, called *saccades,* which tend to return the eye to its original fixation. In addition, there are continual, low-amplitude, high-frequency motions, called *tremors,* or nystagmic movements. These latter movements especially justify the assertion that the eye is never stationary.

If we think of the eye as a camera, we may be tempted to wonder what

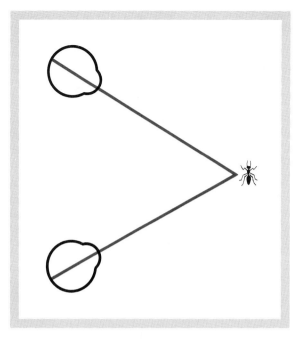

Figure 5.5 Convergence of the two eyes on a near object.

effect these continual tremors have on visual acuity. Just as a photograph is blurred if the camera moves while the film is exposed, so, we might expect, the retinal image will be blurred by the nystagmic movements. And if the retinal image is blurred, then acuity would be impaired.

Following this line of argument, we might anticipate that acuity would be enhanced if there were some way to eliminate these nystagmic movements. But how can this be done? An obvious solution in principle, but one that is unfeasible in practice, would be to immobilize the eyeballs by cementing or pinning them in place or by so heavily weighting them that their movements were dampened virtually to zero. Fortunately, an unlikely, but nonetheless quite feasible solution is also available to us.

We can come to the solution by asking a different question. Instead of trying to eliminate the nystagmic eye movements, we ask how to eliminate their consequences—that is, how to prevent eye movements from continually displacing the retinal image. It turns out that the technique for recording eye movements can serve also, with some modification, to eliminate, or at least greatly reduce, their effects on the stability of the retinal image. The procedure for creating a *stopped,* or *stabilized, retinal image,* as in Figure 5.6 (p. 154), makes use of the contact-lens-mounted mirror. The visual stimulus to be stabilized on the retina is reflected from the mirror, passes through an optical system, and ultimately is presented to the eye on which the mirror is mounted. In this fashion, the eye effectively becomes its own source of stimulation. When the optical system is properly designed, every time the eye moves, the image it is transmitting to its own retina moves also—and *just enough to compensate exactly for the eye movement.* Thus, the stimulus, say a straight line, stays fixed in the same retinal position despite small eye-movements.

The effect of stabilizing the position of the retinal image is quite dramatic. Acuity is essentially unaffected. But very shortly after a stabilized image is presented, it disappears; it may reappear sporadically, perhaps as a result of imperfect stabilization (as through slight slippage of the contact lens), but for the most part, though physically present, the stabilized image is phenomenally absent. Thus, it appears that the involuntary, nystagmic movements of the eye serve to maintain the perception of visual stimuli, and that

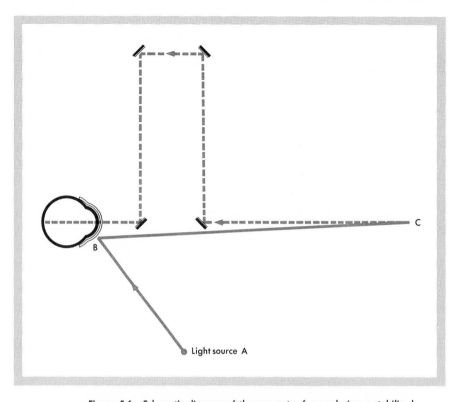

Figure 5.6 Schematic diagram of the apparatus for producing a stabilized image on the retina. Light from the source at A is reflected from a tiny mirror, B, attached to a contact lens, onto the screen at C. The light from C reaches the subject's eye through the path indicated by the dashed lines. Whenever the eye moves through a given angle, the light at C moves through twice that angle. The length of the optical path from C to the eye is selected so as to compensate exactly for this difference in extent of angular movement. Thus the image which reaches the retina remains fixed in location, despite normal eye-movements. (Adapted from Riggs, Ratliff, Cornsweet, and Cornsweet, 1953.)

unchanging visual stimulation rapidly becomes ineffective. A potential physiological basis for the significance of *stimulus change* will be suggested later in the chapter.

IMAGE FORMATION

The formation of a clear retinal image is the province of two structures, the *cornea* and the *lens*. Light rays from an object first pass through the cornea and are thereby *refracted*, or bent, over a large angle. The cornea does the gross focusing. Fine focusing is accomplished by the lens, which like a camera lens, deals with the problem imposed by variations in the distance between an object of interest and the retina. The lens makes it possible to maintain in clear focus objects ranging in distance from optical "infinity" (about 20 feet) to a few inches (approximately 4 to 8) from the eye.

A camera lens accomplishes its task through slight changes in its distance from the film. The lens of the eye works somewhat differently. As first demonstrated by Thomas Young in 1800, the lens remains fixed in position, but changes in shape. To bring close objects into focus, the lens bulges more than it does for objects at a greater distance. The *accommodation* of the lens (that is, its flattening and bulging) is controlled by the *ciliary* muscles, which are smooth muscles innervated by the autonomic nervous system, and largely so by the parasympathetic branch.

Accommodation is a reflexive response. When fixation shifts from a far to a near object, the lens automatically changes shape to maintain the image of the object in good focus on the retina. Thus, reflexive positioning of the image on the foveal portion of the retina, reflexive constriction and dilatation of the pupil, and reflexive accommodation of the lens, all contribute to a single end—maximizing visual acuity. How acuity is measured, and the nature of some common defects in acuity are topics to be taken up in the next chapter.

THE RETINA

The structures considered so far function together to place a clearly focused image of a visual object on the photosensitive surface at the back of the eyeball, that is, the *retina*. It is now appropriate to consider the makeup of the retina itself and the relation between retinal structure and visual function.

Rods and Cones. The human retina is composed of a mosaic of elements; various sources of evidence suggest two types of these retinal elements in the human eye, called *rods* and *cones*. The central portion of the retina, the *fovea,* seems to be composed almost entirely of cones, with rods predominating in the periphery. It is estimated that altogether there are about seven million cones and perhaps as many as 150 million rods in the entire retina. Line drawings of typical rods and cones are given in Figure 5.7 as shown on page 156.

Rods and cones have a diameter ranging from about 1 to 2.5 μ in thickness; about 34,000 cones are densely packed in the most central region of the fovea, which is about 500 to 600 μ in diameter. The fine grain resulting from a high density of very small elements enhances the resolving power of a photosensitive surface such as the retina, and hence increases visual acuity. Thus, the fovea, which is the portion of the retina with the finest grain, should be the area associated with the best acuity, and that indeed is the case.

Duplicity Theory and Supporting Evidence. The original evidence in support of the distinction between rods and cones was indirect, in the form of *psychophysical* data, that is, data relating sensory functioning to physical variables. Until recently, rods and cones were no more than hypothetical concepts within a model called *duplicity theory.* With the development of the electron microscope, however, it became possible to examine the retinal elements more directly. Two morphologically distinct types of elements are evident in electron micrographs; it was a simple inferential step to identify these elements with the hypothetical rods and cones of duplicity theory. Here, incidentally, is an excellent example of the convergence of concepts inferred from behavioral data with anatomical or physiological evidence. Indeed, the idea of looking for rods and cones through the electron microscope might

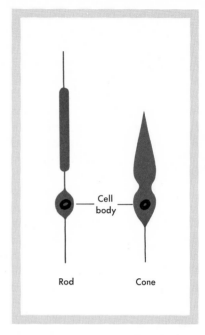

Figure 5.7 Schematic drawing of a typical rod and cone from the human eye. Some cones are much more similar in structure to rods than the one illustrated.

never have occurred to anyone had their existence not been inferred already from available psychophysical data.

One type of psychophysical data that led to the formulation of duplicity theory involves the relation between visual sensitivity and length of time the eye has been unstimulated, or kept in the dark. In general, the longer the eye remains unstimulated, the more sensitive to light it becomes, a relation that is accounted for by a process called *dark-adaptation.* We will consider dark-adaptation in greater detail shortly. Here, we want to point out one feature of the typical *dark-adaptation curve* that bears on duplicity theory. Note that the curve shown in Figure 5.8 is not smooth; it has a break in it, indicated by the arrow. That break suggests the conjunction of two separate curves, each of which tracks the temporal course of dark-adaptation in a separate system. The usual interpretation of these data is to identify the first limb of the curve (labeled A in the figure) with the operation of the cone system; the second limb (labeled B) is identified with the rod system. For about the first 12 minutes of dark-adaptation, the cone system detects weak visual stimuli, but thereafter the rod system, which is potentially the more sensitive to low-intensity illumination, takes over.

Other types of psychophysical evidence also support the notion of two receptor systems within the retina. For example, sensitivity to low-intensity stimuli is greater in the periphery of the retina, where the rods predominate, than in the cone-dominated fovea, whereas both acuity and hue discrimination are sharper in the fovea than in the periphery. These data suggest not only the existence of two systems, but also something about the details of their operation. Thus, the foveal receptor system is specialized for both acuity and color discrimination; the periphery is served by a system that is specialized for detection of low-intensity illumination but only crudely sensitive to fine differences in pattern and color. In effect, human vision is mediated by two distinct, though overlapping, receptor systems, each with its own special contribution to the visual process.

Possible Bases for Rod-Cone Differences. One way of accounting for rod-cone differences in sensitivity to light is to postulate differences in sensitivity between individual receptor elements, whereby the average rod is more sensitive than the average cone. This difference might in turn be attributable to differences in the quality and quantity of the photosensitive pigments characteristic of the two types. Thus, the pigment associated with

Figure 5.8 The general form of the dark-adaptation curve, showing the rod-cone break (at about 12 minutes).

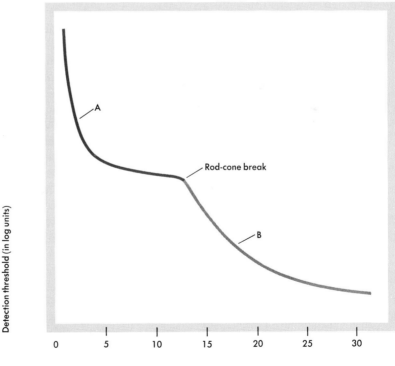

the rods, *rhodopsin,* may simply be more sensitive to light than is the cone pigment. Instead, or in addition, each rod may contain a greater amount of photosensitive pigment than does each cone, and thereby gain in sensitivity. There is, indeed, evidence supporting this latter assumption.

Differences of this sort may account for the sensitivity difference between groups of rods and cones, but they leave unanswered the question of why the cone system is superior for pattern and color discrimination. To deal simultaneously with both sets of characteristics—what we might call sensitivity and precision—seems to require a different, or perhaps a supplementary postulate, of the sort illustrated in Figure 5.9 and discussed immediately below.

In essence, individual cones remain distinct from one another because they have separate neural fibers, each transmitting electrical impulses from a single receptor element to the brain; by contrast, individual rods lose their identity because their neural fibers converge on a common path to the brain. By sharing a neural path, however, the rods can transmit to the brain a signal of greater magnitude than can any individual receptor element. Thus, by summating the electrical effects of weak points of light, the rod system gains in gross sensitivity, while losing precision. Conversely, the cone system retains precision at the expense of sensitivity, through the one-to-one relation between receptor elements and neural paths.

Light- and Dark-Adaptation. As we have indicated, the receptor elements of the retina are sensitive to light by virtue of certain light-sensitive pigments. The entire complex sequence of biochemical events initiated when light strikes the pigmented tip of a rod or cone need not concern us here. It is sufficient to note that in the presence of light a photosensitive pigment breaks down into several components, and that these components reconstitute themselves into the original substance in the absence of light. The initial decomposition of the pigment is assumed to trigger an electrical impulse in the neural fiber, or *neuron,* associated with each rod and cone. Later in this chapter we will trace in some detail the nature and fate of that electrical impulse. In the meantime, you might note that the eye, from cornea to photosensitive pigment, can be thought of as an elaborate device for translating radiant energy into electrical activity. In general, each of the several sense receptors can be considered as a mechanism for transforming energy of a particular sort into electrical activity.

Since light-initiated breakdown of pigments is an essential step in the visual process, it is obvious that stimulation by light results in a change in the state of the eye itself. What might this change imply for visual sensitivity? By analogy with the effect of light on other photosensitive materials (for instance, photographic emulsions), it is reasonable to expect that the greater the intensity and the longer the duration of stimulation, the greater the amount of pigment that will be depleted. Further, since there is a finite amount of pigment, then the greater the amount depleted, the less there is

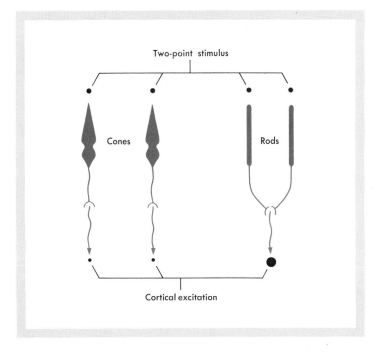

Two-point stimulus

Cones

Rods

Cortical excitation

Figure 5.9 A schematic diagram of one hypothetical difference between the rod and cone systems. The two elements on the left, representing cones, when separately stimulated, send separate messages to the cortex. The two elements on the right, representing rods, when separately stimulated, send a single, joint message to the cortex. The cones preserve the duality of the original stimulus situation, but each separate message is weak. The rods transform two stimulus events into a single, strong message. The actual neural mechanisms of summation and transmission are much more complicated than this figure suggests.

available for breakdown under subsequent stimulation. Finally, if sensitivity is proportionate to the amount of available pigment, then we can expect that the more the eye has been stimulated, the less sensitive it will be for some time thereafter. Thus, one consequence of stimulation is a temporary decrease in sensitivity—temporary, because in the absence of stimulation, the photosensitive pigment is reconstituted.

The temporary effects on sensitivity of stimulation and lack of stimulation are referred to, respectively, as *light-* and *dark-adaptation.* Between the light- and dark-adapted states, there is a considerable difference in sensitivity: In order to be detected in the light-adapted state compared to the dark-adapted state, a visual stimulus must be about 10,000 times as intense.

Some theorists have attempted to go beyond the empirical fact of marked sensitivity changes during dark- and light-adaptation by constructing quantitative models of the processes, photochemical and perhaps neural, that are manifested in the psychophysical facts. One of the earliest and most ambitious of these models was developed by Selig Hecht (1934). The basic assumption in Hecht's model is that there is a direct relation between loss in visual sensitivity and amount of pigment depleted, or *bleached,* during light-adaptation. For example, in order for sensitivity to be reduced to half its normal value, half the photosensitive pigment must be bleached away.

The Hecht model was generally accepted until doubt was cast on it from two sources. First, it was calculated that under the amount of illumination necessary to decrease visual sensitivity to half its value after prolonged dark-adaptation, each rod would be stimulated by one quantum of light, on the average, every 100 seconds. At this rate, after three years of continual illumination, each rod would be stimulated by a million light quanta. That may seem a considerable number of quanta, until you realize that each rod contains more than two million rhodopsin molecules. If, as is generally assumed, a quantum of light is absorbed by, and hence bleaches, one molecule of rhodopsin, then it would take more than three years to bleach half the rhodopsin in the entire rod system.

Second, it became possible to measure the density of rhodopsin present in the living eye at any moment by use of an instrument called a retinal densitometer (Rushton and Campbell, 1954). A comparison of the measured density of rhodopsin present in the dark-adapted and light-adapted states made it possible to calculate the percentage of rhodopsin bleached. For example, in the case considered by Hecht, in which sensitivity is decreased by one-half, rhodopsin density should also be reduced by half. However, virtually no decrease in density was found except under extreme intensities of illumination. It became apparent, as a result of these direct measurements, that the very great decrease in visual sensitivity during light-adaptation is accompanied by only a slight depletion of photosensitive pigment.

In an attempt to improve on Hecht's model so as to be able to incorporate these newer findings, the biologist George Wald has hypothesized that each rod is composed of a number of separate "compartments," each containing a large store of rhodopsin. Any compartment, on absorbing one quantum of light, can initiate electrical discharge in the neural fiber attached to its rod. Additional quanta striking that compartment will be absorbed, but will generate further electrical discharge only if the previously bleached pigment has regenerated. That is, a compartment can contribute to the electrical activity of the visual system only if its entire supply of pigment is intact. For the rod to be effective, after one molecule of rhodopsin has been bleached in one compartment, a second compartment must be stimulated, and so on.

In this model, a rod's potential for initiating an electrical impulse is determined by how many of its compartments are "fresh" rather than by how much rhodopsin remains unbleached. Thus, half of a rod's compartments may be rendered ineffective while only a minute fraction of its total rhodopsin supply has been depleted (Wald, 1954).

Finer details of Wald's model need not be of concern here. It is worth noting, however, that Wald's "compartments" seem to have turned up in electron-microscopic studies of retinal cells. They can be identified with membranes, stacked one upon another. These membranes are estimated to be about as thick as twice the diameter of a rhodopsin molecule.

Negative Afterimages. The stimulation leading to adaptation need not be applied uniformly to the entire retinal surface; it can be restricted to a circumscribed retinal locus. In this way, localized adaptation can be produced;

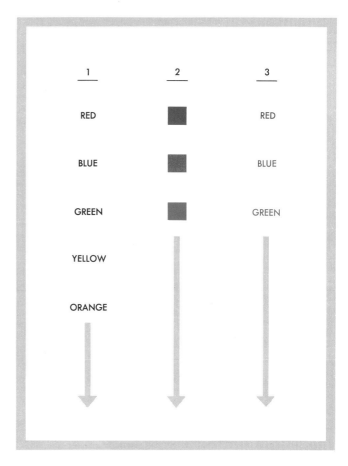

Plate 1 The kinds of materials used in the Stroop test. The subject reads the names of colors printed in black ink, as in column 1. He names the colors, as in column 2. He names the color in which the color names are printed, as in column 3—a task that usually takes longer to perform than either 1 or 2. In actual use, the three tasks are presented separately.

Plate 2 The visible spectrum.

700 mμ   600 mμ   500 mμ   400 mμ

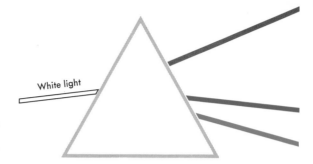

Plate 3 How the component wavelengths of white light are dispersed by a prism through differential refraction.

Plate 4 With the page well illuminated look carefully at the center of the figure for about one minute and then shift your gaze to a blank sheet of white paper or to a blank wall.

Plate 6 Simultaneous contrast, a type of color induction. The color in the circles is physically the same, but the circles appear different because of the color induced in them through contrast with their respective backgrounds.

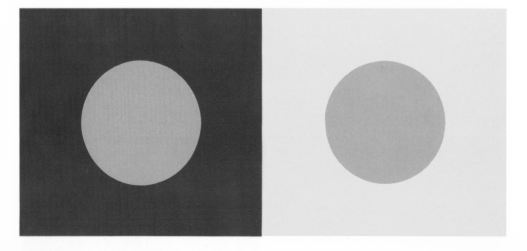

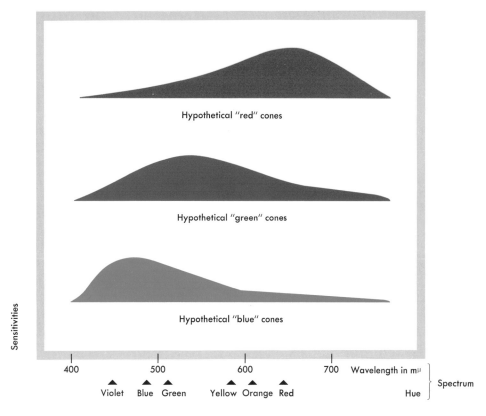

Sensitivities

Hypothetical "red" cones

Hypothetical "green" cones

Hypothetical "blue" cones

| 400 | 500 | 600 | 700 | Wavelength in mμ |

Violet   Blue   Green   Yellow   Orange   Red   Hue

} Spectrum

Plate 5 Color sensitivity, according to the Young-Helmholtz theory, depends on three hypothetical cone classes, each maximally sensitive to different wavelengths.

Plate 7 If the mantid hidden in this scene by "protective coloration" were to move, it would be readily seen. (Wards Natural Science Establishment, Inc.)

Plate 8 Two views of the same scene. In the upper photo, the presence of haze enhances the effect of aerial perspective. In the lower, the air is clear, and the mountains seem considerably closer. (David Muench.)

the result is a *negative afterimage*—"negative" because the image has an apparent brightness and/or hue opposite to what the adapting, or "inducing," stimulus has. For example, if the inducing stimulus is a black figure on a white background, then the afterimage will appear as a white figure on a black background. Similarly, as you will find on following the instructions in Plate 4, if the inducing figure is red, then the negative afterimage will be the hue (blue-green) that is the complement of red. (Complementary hues are those pairs which, when additively mixed, yield gray; further details are given in Chapter Six.) As you will also have noticed, negative afterimages are short-lived; following a series of disappearances and reappearances, they ultimately disappear completely, presumably as the adapted region returns to its normal state.

When light strikes the photosensitive pigments in the retinal receptors, the ensuing chemical reaction which we have referred to as pigment breakdown or bleaching, triggers an electrical impulse in the neural fiber that leads from each rod and cone ultimately to the brain. We now want to consider that phase of the visual process that begins with the neural impulse. But before discussing the nature of the neural impulse, and the manner and route of its transmission through the nervous system, we need to take up three interesting issues concerning retinal structure.

The Orientation of Retinal Receptors and the Optic Disc. First, how are the rods and cones oriented with respect to the incoming light rays? Contrary to what you might expect, the rods and cones have their backs turned to the light. That is, instead of pointing their business ends toward the outside world, they are oriented in the opposite direction. As a result, the light rays must pass through a tangle of neural fibers before they strike the photosensitive tips of the receptor cells. It is indeed remarkable that our vision is as precise as it is in the face of that kind of apparently inefficient arrangement.

Second, how do the neural fibers exit from the eye? If the receptor cells had their appended fibers in back, there would be no problem. Given the arrangement that does prevail, however, the neural fibers take up retinal space that might otherwise be occupied by photosensitive cells. As shown in Figure 5.3, the fibers leave the retina in a single bundle (the *optic nerve*) in a small region called the *optic disc* about 1.5 millimeters in diameter.

The phenomenal counterpart of the anatomical optic disc is called the *blind spot*. The optic disc is located above the fovea and toward the nasal (close to the nose) rather than the temporal (outside) region of the retina. Because visual optics inverts and reverses the retinal image of an object, as depicted in Figure 5.10, the optic disc receives light rays from objects in the lower, temporal portion of the external environment; the locus of the blind spot is thus the inverse of the locus of the optic disc. Although small visual stimuli disappear, as might be expected, if located entirely within

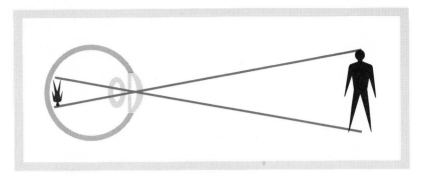

Figure 5.10 Inversion (if this were a side view of the eye) and reversal (if this were a top view) of the retinal image.

the optic disc, there are ordinarily no corresponding gaps in large stimuli that extend beyond the border of the optic disc; despite the blind spot, the normal visual field has no apparent holes in it. When a small portion of an extended visual stimulus falls in the optic disc, the resulting gap in effective retinal stimulation is somehow "filled in," as though the visual system is capable of supplying small pieces of missing information. It is not known how this filling-in process occurs.

Neural Structures between Retinal Receptors and the Optic Nerve. Third, what is the connection between the optic nerve and the retinal receptors? The neural fibers that exit at the optic disc to form the optic nerve do not come directly from the rods and cones. Instead the fibers appended to the latter are functionally connected to *bipolar* neurons; the bipolars in turn connect with neurons called *ganglion* cells. Further structural complexity is added by a set of *horizontal* cells that interconnect the rods and cones and another set of connecting cells, the *amacrines,* that spread bipolar activity over several ganglion cells and that may also feed bipolar activity back to the rods and cones. Thus, between the retinal receptors and the optic nerve there is a very elaborate neural network with a complexity that rivals that of the brain itself. Indeed, embryologically the retina is an outgrowth of the brain; it is no wonder, then, that a considerable amount of neural interaction takes place at the retinal level, and that the "message" transmitted over the optic nerve is already markedly transformed from its original status as a pattern of light distributed on the retinal surface.

The optic nerve, which is the bundle of neural fibers that leaves the eye at the optic disc, is the channel through which information is transmitted to the brain about retinal stimulation, and hence ultimately about the physical world giving rise to that stimulation. How is the information conveyed that is carried by the optic nerve?

The Neuron and the Neural Impulse

We have repeatedly referred to the electrical impulse that is initiated by the breakdown of photosensitive pigments in the retinal receptors; now we will consider the nature of neural transmission in more detail. Since neural impulses are the basic units of all behavior and experience, what follows is pertinent not only to the visual system, but also to all psychological events. In essence, if not in detail, the transmission of information along neural pathways is assumed to follow the same principles regardless of locus or function.

NEURAL FORM AND FUNCTION

A nerve, such as the optic nerve, is a bundle or cable of individual, insulated fibers called *neurons*. A neuron is a single cell, which shares with all cells certain general morphological (structural) and physiological (functional) properties. The neuron differs from other cells, however, in several respects. For example, the neuron comprises not only a *cell body*, which regulates metabolism, but also at least two (typically several) protoplasmic *processes*, or *fibers*.

The cytoplasm of the neural cell body contains material, called *Nissl granules*, not found in other cells; these Nissl granules are composed mainly of a protein, ribonucleic acid (RNA). The function of the Nissl granules is still unknown, though there is speculation that they participate in the complex process of neural conduction of electrical impulses. In addition, RNA has been suggested as a device for encoding and retaining the long-term effects of experience—that is, as a participant in memory storage.

Dendrites and Axons. It is the protoplasmic processes, or fibers, that give neural cells their distinctive appearance and also contribute to their distinctive function, the conduction of electrical impulses. These fibers are usually classified into two types, *dendrites* and *axons*, a somewhat ambiguous classification based on a combination of structural and functional characteristics. Where structure is concerned, the following criteria generally apply:

1. Neural cells typically have only one axon, but may have many dendrites.
2. Dendrites ordinarily are shorter than axons and usually have multiple branches, whereas axons branch very little and then typically only at their terminations.
3. Dendrites contain Nissl granules, but axons do not.
4. Where axons leave the cell body, there is a characteristic elevation, called the axon hillock.

5. Axons, unlike dendrites, may be covered by a white fatty substance, called the myelin sheath; this covering begins shortly after the axon leaves the cell body. The myelin sheath acts as an insulator and probably serves to facilitate the electrical conductivity of the enclosed fiber.

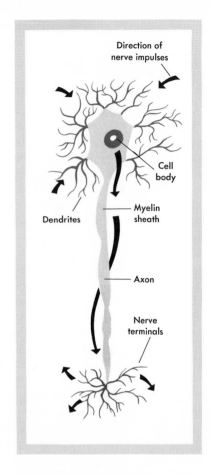

Figure 5.11 The neuron, or nerve cell, is the structural and functional unit of the nervous system.

The differentiating structural characteristics of dendrites and axons do not provide perfect criteria for distinguishing between the two fiber types, since they do allow of exceptions, and do not always mirror functional differences. For example, certain nerve cells in the spinal cord, called *unipolar*, have a single fiber emerging from the cell body; this fiber then branches into two separate processes. The two processes of the unipolar cell are structurally like axons, but they serve different functions. One of the two fibers reaches toward a receptor cell on the body surface; the other enters the central nervous system. Functionally, the former acts like dendrites in that it conducts impulses toward the cell body, whereas the latter conducts impulses away from the cell body, as do axons. This functional difference is conventionally accepted as the overriding criterion for distinguishing between dendrites and axons when structural and functional properties conflict (Crosby, Humphrey, and Lauer, 1962).

All-or-None Versus Graded Activity. There is one additional functional distinction between dendrites and axons that some writers (for example, Altman, 1966) consider significant. The type of electrical activity generated by axons follows the *all-or-none law*. According to that law, if a neural impulse occurs at all in an axon, its magnitude is always maximal for a given state of the neuron. To put it differently, if a neuron does propagate a neural impulse, the magnitude of that impulse is related only to the state of the neuron, and in particular is not related to any properties of the event that triggered the impulse. By analogy, the amount of light emitted from a lamp is not related to the force exerted on the switch that allowed electricity to flow to the lamp.

Not all of the electrical activity in neural cells, however, is of the all-or-none discharge type (often called "spike potentials"). There is, in addition, *graded* activity, in which voltage change may increase in a continuous, gradual fashion. Such changes in electrical potential occur in dendrites, as well as cell bodies and at the ends of neurons, where the interactions take place that make a *system* of the billions of neurons that populate the body.

The Synapse. Neural interactions occur at synaptic junctions, or *synapses.* At a synapse two neurons come into such close contact (though still preserving their separate identities) that the "message-carrying" electrochemical activity in one neuron can affect the electrochemical state of the other. In *synaptic transmission* an electrical impulse travels the length of a given neural fiber and then initiates a similar impulse in another neuron across a synaptic junction.

THE NEURAL IMPULSE

To discuss synaptic transmission further, we must first consider in more detail the nature of the neural impulse. Although the neural impulse is electrical, it is not like an electric current passing through a conductor such as a copper wire. The electrical activity of a neuronal message is very much slower than that of an electric current and quite different in form. By way of an approximate analogy, the neural impulse is somewhat like the flame that travels along a firecracker fuse. At any moment in time, only a small segment of the fuse is burning, but the location of that segment changes continuously in time. By contrast, an electric current occurs throughout the entire conductor, simultaneously and virtually instantaneously; moreover, an electric current stops flowing if the generating force that initiated it is removed. Once a fuse is lit, it does not matter, of course, if the igniting flame goes out. Similarly, the propagation of a neural impulse is not dependent on the continued action of the initiating event.

A neuron, like a fuse, is a medium for the transmission of energy. It works this way: Some form of energy is applied to one end of the neuron. If the stimulating energy is adequately intense, it will induce a localized electrical discharge; the first discharge will then serve as a "stimulus" for the immediately adjacent portion of the neuron, causing it to discharge, and so on. It is this electrical discharge passing along the neuron (the neural impulse) that serves as the message conveyed by the neuron.

What is the content of the message? Nothing more than a report that the neuron has been stimulated by some type and amount of energy sufficient to initiate a neural impulse. That may seem to be an impoverished message, and yet it is the functional unit on which all behavior and experience are constructed.

The Quantitative Information in Neural Impulses. To speak of the neural impulse as an "impoverished" message is to emphasize the kinds of information it does not, by itself, convey. First, there is nothing in the impulse itself that relates to the type, or quality, of the stimulating event. To the extent that the neural impulse can be triggered by a variety of forms of energy—electrical, chemical, mechanical, and so on—then the occurrence of an impulse implies nothing about the particular quality of the initiating event. Second, a single impulse carries no information about the *intensity* of the stimulus, other than that it was of sufficient magnitude to be effective. In accord with the all-or-none law, stimuli of greater-than-adequate intensity trigger individual impulses no different from those associated with stimuli of barely adequate intensity. We might say that so long as a stimulus is above the *threshold* intensity needed to arouse the neural impulse, then it does not matter—so far as that impulse is concerned—how far above threshold the stimulus intensity is. It would be easy to imagine a system in which some attribute of the individual impulse, such as its magnitude, varied along with variation in stimulus intensity. But neural fibers do not act that way.

The all-or-none law of neural discharge does not demand that all neural impulses be identical. The law merely asserts that the significant properties of an impulse are related in only a trivial manner to attributes of the stimulus —that is, if the stimulus is adequate, the neuron will "fire." Such attributes of the neural impulse as its speed and magnitude are free to vary among neurons as a function of such parameters as neural diameter (in general, the "fatter" the fiber, the faster the impulse), metabolic state, and so on. Indeed, variation may occur over time within a given neuron, resulting from momentary shifts in its own status.

The all-or-none law applies only to individual neural impulses, not to the total activity of a neuron or to the pattern of impulses in a group of neurons. Thus, while a single impulse may convey minimal information about the stimulus, additional information may be contained in sequences of impulses traveling over one neuron and in spatial and temporal patterns of impulses carried by groups of neurons.

For example, as stimulus intensity increases, there may be a concomitant increase in both the *rate* of firing of a given neuron and in the number of neurons firing. Hence, information about stimulus intensity may be conveyed through such measures as number of impulses or amount of electrical activity delivered to some point in the system per unit of time.

Qualitative Information and "Specific Nerve Energies." A satisfactory solution to the problem of how neural impulses might carry *qualitative* information is not yet available. This was one of the problems that vexed the nineteenth-century physiologist Johannes Müller, whose doctrine of the specific energies of nerves was mentioned in Chapter Four. Müller offered two hypothetical means whereby information about stimulus quality might be conveyed. (1) The nerves serving the various sense modalities transmit qualitatively different forms of energy—Müller's "specific energies." (2) The various nerves terminate in different places in the brain, and it is this difference which imparts qualitative uniqueness to the various sense modalities.

In Müller's time, about 130 years ago, very little was known about nerve structure and function. For example, the notion of the neuron as the structural unit—called the *neuron doctrine*—was not to be developed until several decades later. Moreover, there was then no means for making the electrical measurements necessary for determining the nature of the neural impulse. It is now quite clear that qualitative differences *do not* exist among the messages transmitted by nerves serving the various sense modalities. In Müller's terms, to hypothesize "specific nerve energies" will not solve the problem.

Müller's second alternative—locus of termination in the brain—is compatible with modern knowledge, at least as far as differences among modalities are concerned. Each sensory system is represented in, or technically, "projected onto," a different region of the cerebral cortex, or in some cases more than one region. However, it is hard to see how the same argument can be applied to qualitative differences within a modality. For example, what is the basis in neural activity of the qualitative difference between two hues or between two odors? It is likely that answers to questions of this type will eventually be phrased in terms of spatial and temporal patterns of neural activity more complex even than those that carry information about stimulus intensity.

Other Features of the Neural Impulses. To return briefly to the neural impulse, we might consider some of its other features, besides its all-or-none character. Figure 5.12 is a schematic drawing of the electrical activity measured from the inner surface of a neuron, "downstream" from the point of stimulation. The drawing is a graphic representation of voltage change (sometimes called "potential change") occurring at a point over a time span of about 20 milliseconds. Note that the neural impulse comprises several segments. The major voltage change, segment A in the figure, is the so-called *spike potential* which follows the all-or-none law. But the spike is preceded and followed by smaller, less abrupt voltage changes. Segment B in the illustration represents a potential change in the same direction as that of the spike—that is, a decrease in negativity. (The normal, "resting potential" of a typical unstimulated neuron is slightly negative, on the order of about -50 to -100 millivolts.) Note that after the spike discharge has occurred, the neuron temporarily has greater-than-normal negative voltage—segment C in the figure—and only gradually returns to its resting state. During the period of increased negative potential it is more difficult than normal to elicit a spike discharge; the neuron is said to be in a *refractory* phase. The

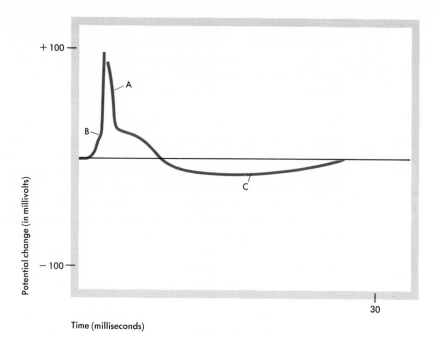

+ 100 —

— 100 —

Potential change (in millivolts)

A

B

C

30

Time (milliseconds)

Figure 5.12 Schematic drawing of a neural impulse; time and voltage scales are approximate. The base line, or resting potential, is typically between —50 and —100 millivolts. The spike (segment A) is a voltage change in the positive direction. The spike is preceded by a slight decrease in negativity (B) and then followed by an increase in negativity (C).

existence of this refractory phase sets a limit on how frequently a given neuron may fire.

Consideration of some of these fine details of the neural impulse reveals the very marked difference between a neuron and a fuse. The latter can only fire once, and then it is permanently burned out. A neuron, having fired, is indeed temporarily less excitable than normal (though even then it can be aroused by a sufficiently intense stimulus), but in short order it returns to its prespike level of excitability.

The Electrochemical Bases of the Neural Impulse. The mechanism underlying the neural impulse is fairly well understood, and can be described at two levels, electrical and chemical. Think of the neuron as a membranous tube, the outer surface of which is positively charged relative to the negatively charged inner surface. As long as nothing disturbs the electrical balance between inner and outer surfaces of the neural membrane, no electrical activity is recorded. When an adequate stimulus is applied to a portion of the outer surface, however, the balance is upset. Now the positive charge on the outer surface no longer equals the negative charge on the inner surface. A local potential difference exists, and current begins to flow between the two surfaces, ultimately restoring the balance between positive and negative charges at the point of initial disturbance. But restoration of balance at one point is accomplished at the cost of loss of balance in adjacent regions. This process is repeated down the length of the neural fiber, until eventually the neuron returns to its original resting state.

The electrical events sketched above have a chemical basis. The local current flow initiated by stimulation is effected by a flow of charged *ions* through the semipermeable neural membrane. The specifics of the chemical process need not concern us here; it is sufficient to note that because of the chemical substrate of neural discharge, and by virtue of the particular chemicals involved, the activity of the nervous system is highly sensitive to the chemical composition of the blood and other fluids that constitute the neural environment. This sensitivity explains the powerful neurophysiological, as well as experiential and behavioral, effects of such substances as alcohol and other "psycho-active" drugs—LSD, amphetamine, meprobamate, and so on.

Finally, the transmission of the neural message across the synaptic gap, once believed to be entirely an electrical phenomenon, is most likely chemically mediated. Recent evidence (see Morgan, 1965) strongly suggests that the arrival of the spike potential at the tip of the axon stimulates the emission of chemical substances, or *neurohumors*. These substances are transported across the synaptic gap and serve to initiate electrical activity in the dendrites, or cell body, of the adjacent neuron. By contrast with the all-or-none impulse transmission along an axon, synaptic transmission is graded.

Synaptic transmission is crucial to the integrated functioning of the nervous system, and again it is no wonder that certain chemicals and drugs, even in minute quantities, can have profound behavioral effects. It is only in recent years, however, that information has been obtained on the specific type and locus of effect of specific chemical substances. Some chemicals, for example, affect the ease of synaptic transmission but have no impact on neural transmission itself; some act only at the juncture between axon tip and muscle (called the myoneural junction); some substances are restricted in their effect to very specific centers within the brain. The study of such relations between chemical and neural-behavioral events has become the province of one of the many newly developed cross-disciplinary fields, which until a better name is forthcoming, is often referred to as "psycho-neuro-pharmacology." From this field, whatever its name, will undoubtedly come some of the major breakthroughs of the next several decades in our understanding and control of behavior.

The above remarks about neural structure and functioning apply generally to any sense modality, and indeed to any subsystem of behavioral significance. They were introduced, you will recall, as part of our description of the structures subserving vision. Before continuing with a description of the neural "pathways" in the visual system, we need to look into two further concepts of general significance—*inhibition* and *response-to-change*. These concepts have been most extensively employed in reference to vision, but undoubtedly will prove useful for understanding the other senses.

Discussions of neural activity usually stress its *excitatory* function. Thus, light strikes the retina; a photochemical reaction occurs which initiates an electrical discharge in the neural fibers appended to the retinal receptors; spike potentials travel down the neurons that make up the optic nerve; chemical substances are emitted at the axon tips and carry the neural message across the synaptic gap, thus exciting the dendrites of adjacent neurons; spike potentials are aroused in these postsynaptic neurons . . . and so on until the sensory message arrives at its various destinations in the cerebral cortex, where it perhaps initiates activity in motor neurons, ultimately resulting in some behavioral act. But this is only part of the story. Omitted is any mention of the *inhibitory* function of neural activity and of the existence of fibers that are activated by the *termination* of stimulation. In regard to the latter point, there is good evidence that both the termination and the onset of stimulation—that is, stimulus change in either direction—can arouse activity in some neurons, whereas other neurons are responsive either to onset only or to termination only. The first class are called *on-off* fibers, the second are *on* fibers, and the third, *off* fibers.

Retinal Inhibition. A convincing demonstration of inhibitory phenomena at the retinal level was first offered by Floyd Ratliff, and Haldan Hartline (1959). Through the development of exceedingly precise techniques of dissection, they were able to record the electrical activity in a single neural cell in a living organism. These recordings were taken from the optic nerve of the horseshoe crab, *Limulus*. The *Limulus* eye, like that of many other species, such as the bee, for example, is structurally different from the mammalian eye; it is called a compound eye and is composed of a set of tightly packed segments, called ommatidia.

The basic strategy was to record the electrical activity from a single neuron, and by probing the *Limulus* eye with a point of light to discover the ommatidium which excited that neuron. Then they found that, as the point of light was moved so as to stimulate adjacent ommatidia, the electrical activity in the neuron under investigation was suppressed, the amount of suppression, or inhibition, being inversely related to the distance between the interacting ommatidia.

Inhibition in Cortical Neurons. Although Ratliff and Hartline worked with the crab retina, other researchers have found analogous inhibitory effects in higher species, such as cats and monkeys, that have visual structures much like man's. Recordings have even been made within the cerebral cortex itself. For example, recording wires of very fine diameter, called *microelectrodes,* have been implanted in single neural cells in the visual cortex of the cat. When a small spot of light is moved systematically over the retina, it becomes possible to map those points which, when stimulated, affect the electrical activity in the cortical neuron being monitored. Typically, each neuron is affected by an area, or field, rather than just by a single point of stimulation, giving rise to the term *retinal receptive fields* of cortical neurons.

In conducting such mapping studies, various researchers (for example, Granit, 1947; Hubel and Weisel, 1962) have found not only retinal receptive fields that are excitatory in function, but also fields that are inhibitory. Photic stimulation on these latter areas inhibits the excitability of specific cortical neurons. Moreover, these excitatory and inhibitory fields tend to be organized in a fairly limited number of spatial configurations. According to Hubel and Wiesel, a typical configuration might be a set of excitatory points surrounded by inhibitory points, as shown in Figure 5.13. Electrical activity in the central excitatory field is dampened if the surrounding inhibitory fields are stimulated. We might therefore anticipate occasions in which increasing the size of a small spot of light will lead, not to an increase in its apparent brightness, but rather to a decrease. Additional findings about inhibitory and excitatory fields, and their more subtle implications, are available in references listed at the end of this chapter. We will make further use of the concept of neural inhibition in Chapter Six, and close the present discussion of that topic by raising a question to which there is as yet no answer.

Is inhibition an essential property of the visual system, or is it simply an interesting, but unnecessary characteristic, perhaps an evolutionary accident? It makes sense to ask this question in the light of recent attempts to

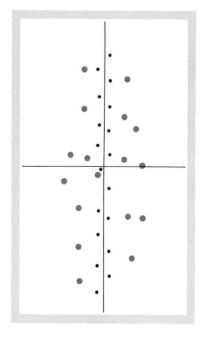

Figure 5.13 Example of a retinal receptive field of a cortical neuron. The small, black spots represent points on the retina that activate the neuron when stimulated by light. The large, colored spots are inhibitory retinal points for that neuron. Note how this particular arrangement makes their field maximally responsive to a vertical line.

construct machines that perform some of the functions of the human eye. For example, devices have been built that can "read" printed letters or numbers with considerable accuracy. These machines utilize such components as photoelectric cells and TV-like scanning units as "receptors"; the receptors feed their outputs to electronic computers that are programed to interpret them. Up till now, these vision machines, or "perceptrons," as one of them is called, operate entirely through messages of an excitatory nature; they do not have inhibitory outputs. The question raised above, then, asks whether such vision simulators can ever match the incredibly complex and precise performance of real visual systems without incorporating the inhibitory elements that appear to play an important role in the functioning of the latter.

This same question, phrased perhaps in more general terms, will become pertinent some time in the distant future when attempts are made to restore vision to certain blind people by replacing their nonfunctioning eyes with artificial ones. These artificial eyes may take the form of miniaturized perceptrons which feed their output, not to computers, but directly to the person's brain. The general question then to be considered will be: How much of what is characteristic of the human visual receptor system must be incorporated into the design and construction of artificial receptors in order to adequately simulate human visual capacity? Or, in the language developed in Chapter One, in how much detail must the model match the original object to be a "good" model?

Neural Pathways in the Visual System

Meanwhile, back in the retina, complex spatial-temporal patterns of neural impulses are coursing through the neurons that make up the optic nerve. Our final concern in this chapter is with the route these impulses follow in their trip to the visual cortex of the brain. The route, of course, consists of neural pathways, and it can be traced with a fair degree of confidence.

THE OPTIC CHIASMA

Figure 5.14 shows, in schematic form, the route of the neural impulses between the retina and the first major "interchange," the *optic chiasma*. In the human visual system, though not in that of some other species, such as fish, the optic chiasma marks the place where certain neural fibers cross from one side of the head to the other. Note in the figure that fibers from the temporal half of each eye remain uncrossed, whereas fibers from the nasal half do cross at the chiasma. Thus, fibers from the right half of the left eye cross at the chiasma and join the uncrossed fibers from the right half of the right eye; similarly, fibers from the left half of the right eye cross and merge with the uncrossed fibers from the left half of the left eye. In this manner, each eye is represented on each side of the brain.

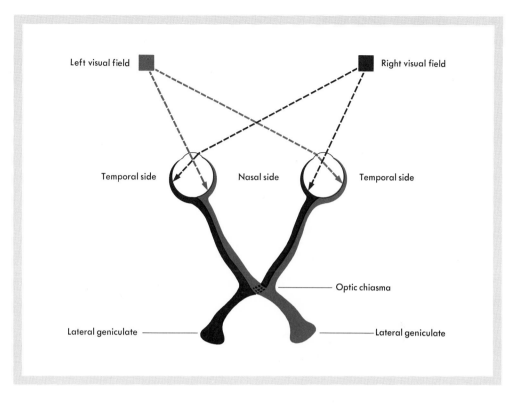

Left visual field

Right visual field

Temporal side

Nasal side

Temporal side

Optic chiasma

Lateral geniculate

Lateral geniculate

Figure 5.14 Schematic drawing of optic nerves and chiasma. Note how fibers from the temporal half of each eye remain uncrossed, whereas fibers from the nasal half cross to the opposite side of the brain.

Since the right half of each retina—the *right hemiretina*—is stimulated by objects to the left of fixation, should a penetrating injury (as from a bullet) enter the right side of a person's head and sever the optic nerve postchiasmically, then he would retain sight in both eyes, though he would be blind to objects to the left of fixation. Destruction of the optic nerve prechiasmically on the right side of the head would result in total blindness of the right eye. You can verify these statements by reference to Figure 5.14. Incidentally, the exact location of penetrating wounds to the head can sometimes be ascertained by reference to the type of visual defect that ensues.

Major "Relay Stations." Beyond the optic chiasma, the visual neural pathway has two major components. The majority of the fibers continue on to a brain center called the *lateral geniculate body,* located about as indicated in Figure 5.15. Some fibers, however, leave the main optic tract and make synaptic connections in two adjacent centers, the *superior colliculus* and the *pretectal region.* It is likely that the cells of the superior colliculus participate in the regulation of the pupillary response, with fibers entering

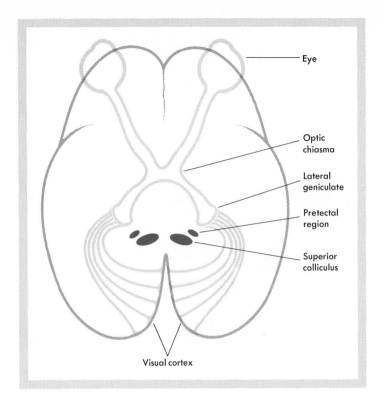

Eye

Optic chiasma

Lateral geniculate

Pretectal region

Superior colliculus

Visual cortex

Figure 5.15 The underside of the cerebral cortex, showing the major waystations of the neural messages between eye and visual cortex.

the superior colliculus from the optic tract providing information about level of retinal illumination. The pretectal region probably is involved in the control of eye movements.

The Lateral Geniculate Body. Information about visual images, their shape, locus, color, and so on, is carried over the main path of the optic tract to the lateral geniculate body, the neural organization of which is quite remarkable. Within the top, or "dorsal," part of this body there is a collection of cell bodies, or a "nucleus"—specifically, the *dorsal nucleus*—that are arranged in six distinct layers. Fibers from the nasal hemiretina (the crossed fibers) all fall in the same three layers, while all of the uncrossed fibers are located in the other three layers. Thus, while both eyes are represented in each of the two lateral geniculate bodies (one on each side of the head), the fibers within a given layer all come from one eye or the other, but not both. Further, there is evidence that cells in the layers of the dorsal nucleus are differentially responsive to different wavelengths of light striking the retina (De Valois, 1960).

The Striate Cortex. The final portion of the visual pathway goes from the lateral geniculate body to the "striate region" in the optic lobe of the cerebral cortex. Axons leave the lateral geniculate in a group, called the *geniculo-*

striate bundle, and reach the striate region of the occipital lobe through a route which carries them first forward, then downward, then backward, as sketched in Figure 5.15.

The remarkable organization characteristic of the lateral geniculate body is also achieved in the striate cortex. The retina is mapped with great precision on the cortex, so great in fact that topographic relations on the retina generally hold also on the cortex. Thus, if point B on the retina falls between points A and C, the cortical representation of B is very likely to be located between that of A and C.

In the human being, the striate, or visual, cortex (Figure 5.16) is essential to vision. If the entire striate lobe on both hemispheres of the brain is destroyed in man, the result is total blindness, from which there is no recovery. In lower animals rudimentary visual functioning (for instance, the ability to discriminate light from dark) may remain intact even after complete removal of the total striate cortex, though pattern discrimination and other more complex functions may be lost. It is likely that in these subhuman species, some of the functions of the visual cortex can be taken over by such precortical centers as the lateral geniculate body. Man's possession of his uniquely powerful cerebral cortex also renders him highly vulnerable, should this organ be extensively damaged.

FROM ELECTRICAL ACTIVITY TO EXPERIENCE

In this chapter we have tried to give an account of how a pattern of electromagnetic radiation strikes the photosensitive retinal cells, and is transformed into a pattern of electrical activity that is eventually "displayed" in a specialized "visual area" of the cerebral cortex. The question that naturally arises at this point is: How does the electrical display in the visual cortex get further transformed into the events that we call visual experience? That is, while the neurophysiological and neuroanatomical bases of visual experience

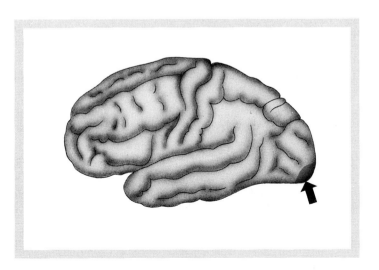

Figure 5.16 A sideview of one hemisphere of the cerebral cortex. The colored area at the back of the brain shows the approximate location of the area where visual neurons are projected from the lateral geniculate bodies.

can now be described in impressive detail (with a degree of complexity only hinted at here), the problem of the relation between these physical events and those we categorize as "mental," "experiential," or "phenomenal" remains to plague us. This is the age-old *mind-body problem,* and it may indeed never be satisfactorily settled, at least so long as we insist on what seems the reasonable assumption that physical and experiential events exist in separate domains.

SUMMARY

The visual stimulus, light, can be conceived of as a wave, with a wavelength that places it within a narrow band of the broad electromagnetic spectrum. The *visible spectrum* ranges from waves of about 430 millimicrons (mμ) in length at the short ("blue") end to about 780 at the long ("red") end. Wavelength and amplitude are major contributors to the visual attributes of *hue* and *brightness,* respectively. Sunlight is a mixture of all the visible wavelengths and appears "white." As light of a single wavelength is mixed with greater amounts of white light, it becomes increasingly less *saturated* in appearance.

The light that strikes the eye comes either directly from a radiant source or is reflected from objects illuminated by a radiant source. Objects do not necessarily reflect all the light incident on them; some may be *absorbed.* Various materials, such as *pigments,* differ in the amount and wavelength, or spectral composition, of light they absorb (and hence reflect). Objects that allow no light to pass through them are *opaque,* whereas those that transmit some light are *transparent.* The latter serve as *filters. Neutral density filters* simply reduce by a fixed proportion the amount of light of all wavelengths that is transmitted. *Color filters* selectively reduce transmission of certain wavelengths. By interposing appropriate material between a light source and the eye, one can control the amount and spectral composition of the light that stimulates the eye.

In many, but not all respects the eye is like a camera. The amount of light that strikes the eye's photosensitive surface (the *retina*) is regulated by reflexive *constriction* and *dilatation* of the diameter of the eye's *pupil,* which is under the control of the *autonomic nervous system.* Gross and fine focusing of the light so as to produce a clear image on the retina is accomplished by the *cornea* and *lens,* respectively. The lens works by changing its shape, bulging to bring close objects into focus. This *accommodation* of the lens is regulated by the *ciliary* muscles, which are under the control of the autonomic nervous system.

The positioning of the image of a stationary or a moving object on the retina is accomplished by the *extraocular* muscles, controlled by the *somatic nervous system.* The two eyes move in relation to one another through *convergent, divergent,* and *conjugate* movements. Ordinarily, the image of the object being fixated is reflexively placed on the *fovea,* the central part of the retina, wherein visual acuity is best.

The two eyes are continually in motion; measurement of these small, involuntary movements reveals several types, among them low-amplitude, high-frequency *tremors,* or *nystagmic* movements. The various involuntary eye-movements result in a continually moving retinal image. Through special optical arrangements the retinal image can be stopped, or *stabilized,* despite eye-movements. Rather than improving vision, stabilizing the retinal image results in the phenomenal disappearance of the object being viewed.

Several lines of evidence suggest two kinds of photosensitive elements in the retina, *rods* and *cones,* with cones dominant in the fovea and rods in the peripheral portions of the retina. The cone system is specialized for acuity and color discrimination, whereas the rod system is primarily responsible for the eye's remarkable sensitivity to very small quantities of light.

When the eye is stimulated by light, photosensitive pigments in the rods and cones break down, initiating an electrical impulse that signals stimulation. But stimulation also leaves the eye temporarily *light-adapted*—that is, less sensitive to subsequent stimulation. After a period of nonstimulation, the eye becomes *dark-adapted* and is then maximally sensitive to light. A model of light- and dark-adaptation devised by Hecht has prevailed until recently, when data from direct measurements of amount of photosensitive pigments present in the retina after stimulation cast serious doubts on Hecht's basic assumptions. An alternative model proposed by Wald not only is compatible with the newer data, but also seems to fit with electron-microscopic evidence on the structure of rods and cones. Dark- or light-adaptation of restricted portions of the retina results in short-lived *negative afterimages.*

The rods and cones are pointed away from the incoming light; neural fibers appended to them leave the retina in a bundle, the *optic nerve,* in a small area, the *optic disc,* located above the fovea and towards the nasal side of the retina. The optic disc, being devoid of rods and cones, is insensitive to light, yielding a *blind spot* for small stimuli in the lower, temporal parts of the external environment.

The optic nerve, like all nerves, is a cable-like collection of individual fibers called *neurons.* Neurons are cells specialized for the transmission of electrical impulses. A typical neuron consists of a cell body plus two or more protoplasmic processes, or fibers. Functionally, *dendrites* are fibers that conduct impulses toward the cell body, whereas *axons* conduct impulses away from the cell body. Dendrites and axons can also be distinguished on the basis of several structural criteria. Electrical impulses associated with axons follow an *all-or-none* principle: If an impulse occurs, it does so at maximal voltage (for that neural fiber) without regard to the intensity of the triggering event, so long as the latter is above a minimum, or *threshold,* intensity. Electrical activity in dendrites and cell bodies may be graded, reflecting continuous changes in the magnitude of the triggering events.

The billions of structurally separate neurons interact at *synapses* to form a highly complex transmission system. The neural impulse is the basic unit of neural transmission. Neural impulses are qualitatively the same throughout the nervous system, contrary to one interpretation of the *doctrine of specific nerve energies* proposed by Müller. Information about quantitative and qualitative features of stimulation must be carried by such higher-order relations as are contained in rates and temporal patterns of neural firing in large populations of neurons, as well as by the place in the brain where a train of neural impulses terminates.

The main features of the neural impulse have been well described, including the *spike potential* itself, as well as a number of rapid changes in the neuron's ability to fire preceding and following the occurrence of the spike. For some time after a spike discharge the neuron is in a *refractory* state, during which the threshold for further spikes is raised. A series of chemical events mediates the neural impulses as well as the transmission of impulses across the synaptic gap, leaving the nervous system in general quite vulnerable to chemical influences.

Some neurons in the visual system (the "off-fibers") are activated not by the onset of illumination but by its termination. Furthermore, activity in some neurons is *inhibited* by activity in adjacent neurons. By the use of microelectrodes for recording electrical activity in single neurons—for example, in the visual cortex of the brain—it has become possible to map areas of the retina that affect the activity in a given neuron—the so-called *retinal receptive fields*. Using this technique, investigators such as Hubel have discovered a few basic patterns into which excitatory and inhibitory fields are organized in the visual system.

The major way-stations of a neural impulse originating in the retina are the *optic chiasma*, the *lateral geniculate body*, the *superior colliculus* and *pretectal* region, and finally the *striate region* of the *optic lobe* of the *cerebral cortex*. Whereas considerable processing of information occurs at the level of the lateral geniculate body, and some vision remains in animals without the visual cortex, in man, at least, the visual cortex is essential for visual functioning. But how the electrical activity in the visual cortex is translated into *visual experience* remains a mystery.

SUGGESTED READINGS

Hochberg, J.E. *Perception*. Englewood Cliffs, N.J.: Prentice-Hall, 1964, Chapter 3.

Hubel, D.H. The visual cortex of the brain. *Scientific American*, 1963, 209, 54–62.

Morgan, C.T. *Physiological psychology*. New York: McGraw-Hill, 1965, Chapters 3 and 6.

Riggs, L.A. Light as a stimulus for vision. In *Vision and visual perception* (edited by C.H. Graham). New York: Wiley, 1965, Chapter 1.

Basic Visual Discriminations

C H A P T E R   S I X   The preceding chapter was devoted mainly to a description of the structural and physiological features of the visual system. In addition, we mentioned certain visual phenomena, such as color, acuity, and brightness. But we still need to provide a fuller account of those and other simple visual phenomena as well as an introduction to the many—and more complex—items that constitute the broad field of visual perception. Now, in the present chapter, we will extend our earlier remarks about brightness and color, prefacing our treatment of brightness discrimination with discussions of the threshold and psychophysical methods. Then, after examining the evidence and theories of color vision, we will turn to the topics of acuity and flicker (that is, the discrimination between continuous and discontinuous stimulation). In the next chapter we consider some of the more complex phenomena involved in the perception of objects organized in two- and three-dimensional space.

Brightness

The most primitive visual function is *brightness discrimination,* which is a differential response to differences in quantity of illumination. This function is "primitive" in two respects: (1) It is present phylogenetically before more elaborate visual functions (for example, color discrimination) make their appearance. (2) It is the visual function that is least vulnerable to severe brain damage, as is illustrated by the continuing ability of decorticate rats (rats with all cerebral cortex surgically removed) to discriminate brightness although they lose their capacity for other normal visual discriminations.

Brightness discrimination is a broad category, encompassing behaviors ranging from the crude ability to notice gross differences in illumination (for example, night and day) to refined sensitivity to very minute changes or differences in light intensity. The research on brightness discrimination has been largely concerned with the latter end of the range—with the variables that influence sensitivity to just noticeable, or *threshold,* differences. As we noted in Chapter Three, measurement of thresholds falls in the province of a field called *psychophysics.* This field originated in the intense desire of a nineteenth-century philosopher-scientist, Gustav Fechner (1801–1887), to solve the *mind-body problem*—that is, the problem of the relation between mental events, such as sensations, and physical events, such as variations in the intensity of light. Fechner convinced himself that a satisfactory solution to the mind-body problem would be at hand were it possible to discover a mathematical function that described the relation between the two types of events, the *psychological* and the *physical* (hence psychophysics).

Suppose physical and psychological measurements can be related by a simple mathematical expression (such as the Weber-Fechner Law, $S = k \log I$, which means that sensation magnitude is proportional to the logarithm of stimulus intensity). Then, Fechner argued, physics and psychology must be concerned with merely different manifestations of the same basic unitary reality, and the apparent duality of mind and body must be illusory. Such a conclusion was indeed just what Fechner the philosopher was seeking. To bolster this conclusion, Fechner the psychophysicist turned to empirical investigation, and in the service of this endeavor helped develop the psychophysical methods that were necessary for measuring the threshold.

PSYCHOPHYSICAL METHODS

Of course, it is not necessary to subscribe to Fechner's metaphysics in order to be interested in psychophysical relations. Origin aside, psychophysics is concerned with the ways in which the psychological outputs (such as sensation magnitudes) of a sensory system are related to various kinds of physical inputs. When such relations have been empirically established it may be possible to construct models of the system that mediates between inputs and outputs. Thus, psychophysics provides one route to constructing a theory about the operation of the various sensory systems.

In terms of the research task, the problem of establishing psychophysical relations is to manipulate some dimension, or dimensions, of physical stimulation and measure the observer's responses "to" that stimulation. We put the word "to" in quotation marks in order to indicate that the subject's response may be determined by variables other than those associated with the stimulus itself. For example, the kinds of instructions given to the psychophysical observer contribute to the nature of his responses. This point must be emphasized for two reasons: (1) In the typical psychophysical experiment, the stimuli are so weak and uninteresting that by themselves—unaccompanied by special instructions, training, and other pressures—they would ordinarily elicit no measurable, behavioral response. (2) In the history of psychophysical investigation, the tendency has developed to equate the observer's responses with his sensory capacity; insufficient weight has been given to the contribution made to the psychophysical response by variables such as instructions, the observer's expectancies about the target stimuli, his willingness to make errors of different types, and so on.

Recently, psychologists have developed models that enable us to make a separate assessment of the contribution of these "nonsensory" variables; with these effects eliminated from the responses by mathematical analysis, it becomes possible to obtain pure measures of sensory functioning. These models fall in the general category called *signal-detection theory*, which was discussed in Chapter Three. Here we will concentrate on the classical, and still useful, psychophysical model based on the concept of the threshold, going into greater detail on psychophysical methodology than was provided in our earlier treatment of this topic.

Let us start with a simple example. Suppose the problem is to determine the smallest increment (ΔI) in light intensity that can just be detected, with the prevailing, or background, intensity (I) set at a value of 100 units. Note that although the absolute values of intensity we are dealing with might be quite high, it is *increments* of intensity which are to be varied; these increments constitute the miniscule events of interest to classical psychophysics.

To attune the observer to these miniscule events, we might give him the following instructions: "On the center of the screen in front of you, a very small, weak, and brief spot of light can be presented. The spot, when presented, will always be in the same location and will come on briefly right after this tone is sounded. Your task is to say 'yes' if you saw the spot and 'no' if you did not see it."

The observer's responses, like the stimulus inputs, are quite restricted, in this case to "yes" and "no." For purposes of mechanization, we can even dispense with these verbal responses and have the observer push one of two buttons to indicate his answer. The psychophysical situation involves minimal inputs and severely limited outputs. Not unreasonably, psychophysics has been tagged "the study of impoverished perception." But whether, in terms of its ultimate value, such research deserves the same description remains to be seen.

How, in the experiment sketched above, do we go about determining the value of the jnd, or the threshold (we use jnd and threshold synonymously)? Of several methods available, we will describe two that are commonly employed.

The Method of Limits. First, consider the *method of limits*. The basic procedure here is to start with a value of the target stimulus (the little spot of light in the present example) that is far removed from the expected threshold value—say, far below it. We present that value and note the observer's response. If, as anticipated, he says "no," then we add a small, predetermined increment to the stimulus, and so on until the observer says "yes." Somewhere in the small interval between the last "no" and the first "yes" is the value of the threshold.

In the example above, where the background intensity is 100 units, we might start with a target stimulus of 101 units and move up in steps of one unit. If the observer first says "yes" when the target value is 111 units, the threshold increment, ΔI, is estimated to be midway between 10 and 11 units. But one measurement is probably not enough to obtain a reliable estimate of ΔI. We would, in practice, take several such measurements. Our final estimate of the threshold value would be derived from this large set of measurements, typically by taking their average.

It turns out that a serious bias is introduced if we follow only the procedure described above, starting below the threshold and successively adding increments in intensity until the response shifts from "no" to "yes." This constitutes an *ascending method of limits*.

A *descending method* can also be employed, starting with a target well above threshold and decreasing the intensity in small steps until the response switches from "yes" to "no." If we use both methods, we usually find that the ascending method yields a higher estimate of the threshold than does the descending method. It seems reasonable to assume that the best estimate of the threshold value lies midway between the estimates obtained from the ascending and descending methods.

If we were to run a descending method, and from it estimated the threshold at 9.5 units, then the final threshold estimate would be the average of the two estimates—10.5 and 9.5—or 10.0 units. Note that this value, if expressed as a ratio of the background intensity, provides an estimate of the *Weber fraction* for visual brightness, as alluded to in Chapter Three. Thus, if the background intensity, I, = 100 units, and the threshold value, ΔI, = 10 units, the Weber fraction, $\Delta I/I$, = 10/100, or 0.1.

The bias associated with the direction of measurement (ascending or descending) is only one of several sources of error in the method of limits. It might matter, for example, how far from the threshold value the starting point lies, and whether the number of steps between them is constant from one measurement series to the next. Such factors tend to establish *expectancies* on the part of observers of the sort: "I've said 'no' seven times in a row; it's about time to say 'yes.'" There are ways of getting around potential sources of bias, such as randomly varying the value of the starting point. A more drastic solution is to move to other psychophysical methods that presumably are less subject to bias. The chief alternative to the method of limits has been the *constant-stimulus method*.

The Constant-stimulus Method. In the constant-stimulus method several values of the target stimulus are preselected for presentation by the experimenter. The values are so chosen that response to them is expected to range from near zero per cent to near 100 per cent. If the values are properly chosen, they will necessarily encompass the threshold stimulus.

Suppose we employed five values of target stimulus, 105, 110, 115, 120, and 125. These values, when contrasted with the background intensity of

100 units, correspond to increments—symbolized here by the letter *d*—of 5, 10, 15, 20, and 25 units. The virtue of the constant-stimulus method is that the *d* values need not be presented in series. Instead, they can be mixed randomly so that the observer cannot anticipate which value is coming next. Hopefully, in this way the biasing effects of expectancies are minimized. But how does one estimate the threshold from data collected by this method? What indeed do the data look like?

Again, assume the observer says "yes" if he detects the target, "no" if he does not. Suppose each target value is presented 100 times. If the system were perfectly reliable, then the observer would always give the same response to the same target value, and the data would resemble those plotted in Figure 6.1, where the percentage of "yes" responses is given on the ordinate (the *Y* axis) and the target value on the abscissa (the *X* axis). Note the step-wise shift, at the *d*-value of 15, from zero per cent to 100 per cent "yes." Of course, the system is not perfectly reliable, and so the obtained data do not correspond to this hypothetical ideal case. A more typical instance of the form of real psychophysical data collected by the constant-stimulus method is shown in Figure 6.2. Here, as *d* increases there is a smooth, rather than a step-wise increase in the "yes" percentage. The five data points can be neatly connected by fitting to them a continuous S-shaped, or *ogival*, curve.

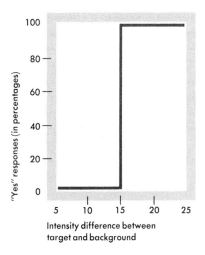

Figure 6.1 Probability of a "yes" response as a function of target intensity, when there is no variability in the threshold.

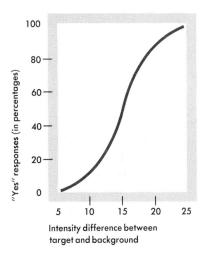

Figure 6.2 The S-shaped relation between probability of a "yes" response and target intensity, a relation that implies variability in the threshold.

There remains the problem of estimating "the threshold" from such data. One solution lies in a model designed to account for the variability that characterizes psychophysical performance. Somewhat different solutions have been offered, based on somewhat different models of the source of variability, but the classical model will best serve the present purpose.

The classical model very simply attributes performance variability to random fluctuations over time in the typical sensitivity of the sensory system. Because of these moment-to-moment changes in sensitivity, the same physical stimulus may be detectable at one moment but not at another. There is thus no single, fixed threshold value—that is, no single target intensity which is just barely detectable. Instead, there is a set of momentary threshold values corresponding to the moment-to-moment sensitivity fluctuations. If it were possible to measure each of the momentary threshold values, their frequency distribution would take the form of the normal curve, as described in Chapter Three.

The normal-curve model depicted in Figure 6.3 assumes a typical, or central, value for the threshold. If the threshold were assessed a large number of times, this central value would be the most likely to be obtained; other threshold estimates would also occur among the data, but the further these estimates depart from the central value, the less likely they are to occur. Even unlikely events do happen, however, so it is possible to obtain a highly deviant threshold estimate at any given moment. The way to insure against grossly misjudging the central value in a normal distribution because of such deviation is to take several sample measures. If the sample is large enough, then the average sample value will very closely approximate the central value of the total distribution.

The particular "average" we are referring to here is called the *arithmetic mean,* symbolized as M. The "total distribution" is technically called the *population,* and the "typical," or "central," value of the population is the *population mean,* symbolized as $\overline{M}$. To rephrase the point above in these terms, if the sample size is large enough, then M (the mean of the sample of threshold estimates) $= \overline{M}$ (the population, or "true" mean). How large a sample is "large enough" depends on how much variability there is in the population distribution around $\overline{M}$. Obviously, if there were no variability at all, then any sample threshold estimate would correspond exactly with the "true" threshold, and only a single sample would be required. As variability around $\overline{M}$ increases, the number of required sample estimates increases if we expect M closely to approximate $\overline{M}$. The principle of "diminishing returns" does operate here, however, and once the size of a sample has reached about 30, there is less and less gain in precision from further increasing the number of measures in the sample.

With the above model as a basis we can begin to answer the question of how to estimate "the threshold" from constant-stimulus data. For convenience, refer to Figure 6.3, in which numerical values have been arbitrarily assigned to the abscissa to match the hypothetical values in our standard example.

Suppose we present an observer with the target stimulus of intensity 125. Referring to Figure 6.3 we note that there is virtually no moment in which the threshold is that *high* or *higher.* Virtually every time a target stimulus of value 125 is presented it will fall above the threshold and elicit a "yes" re-

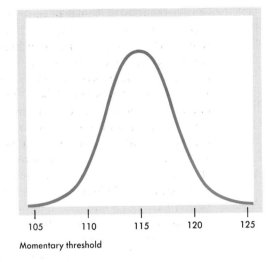

Figure 6.3 A normal distribution of momentary threshold values.

105   110   115   120   125

Momentary threshold

Frequency

sponse: The percentage of detection for that target is close to 100. We can capture that expectation graphically by locating a point in Figure 6.4 at the intersection of the stimulus value, 125, and the value of detection, 100.

Continuing in this same vein, suppose a target stimulus of intensity 105 were presented. Referring to Figure 6.3, we note that at virtually no moment is the threshold that *low or lower*. Hence an observer will almost never report detection of a target of such low intensity; the percentage of detection for that target is close to zero, which we indicate by an appropriate point on the graph in Figure 6.4. The same logic applies to target values of intermediate intensity. Thus, a target of value 120 will be above threshold more often than not, while a target of value 110 will produce just the opposite result. The percentage of time that either is above threshold is equal to the proportion of the total area of the normal curve that falls to the left of the stimulus value in question. We could specify those proportions (one for 120 and one for 110) if we knew, or could assume, the value of an important parameter of the curve that is shown in Figure 6.3—the *standard deviation* of the distribution.

As indicated in Chapter Three (p. 92), the standard deviation, symbolized by the Greek letter sigma (σ), is a measure of the amount of variability of the members of a distribution around their own mean value. The mathematical properties of the normal curve are such that between the mean and one sigma unit above (or below) it there is exactly 34 per cent of the total area of the curve. Indeed, the relation between the area under the curve and the distance in sigma units from the mean can be specified for any number of sigma units.

In our example, where for convenience we set the mean of the normally distributed momentary threshold values at 115, we need know only σ (and have access to the proper table) to be able to specify the percentage of area to the left of the stimulus value for any target stimulus. For the sake of simplicity, let us assume that σ is 5 in our example. A stimulus value of 120 is one σ unit above the mean of 115. Hence, between that stimulus and the mean lies 34 per cent of area under the normal curve. We need to add to that figure how much more area is to the left of the mean to find the total percentage of area to the left of the stimulus of value 120. Happily, the mean of a normal distribution splits the distribution exactly in half, so 50 per cent

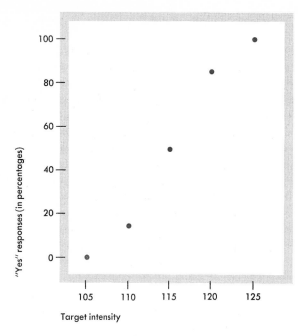

"Yes" responses (in percentages)

Target intensity

Figure 6.4 The "data points" generated from Figure 6.3, assuming a value of 5 for the standard deviation.

of the area falls to the left of the mean. We come to the conclusion in this case that on 84 $(34 + 50)$ per cent of those occasions on which the threshold is measured, a stimulus of intensity value 120 will be detectable. The "data" point can then be plotted in Figure 6.4. The detectability of stimulus 110 can be similarly calculated; assuming again that $\sigma = 5$, it will be detected 16 $(50 - 34)$ per cent of the time.

It should be obvious that a stimulus with an intensity equal to that of the population mean, 115, will be detectable on 50 per cent of its presentations. With that point in place, we have transformed our hypothetical distribution of momentary thresholds into a graph showing the relation between target intensity and detectability. From the model, we have generated a prediction about the exact form of the behavioral data. And the model tells us what to do with obtained data if we wish to extract from it an estimate of the "true" threshold. We must simply find the stimulus which is detectable 50 per cent of the time.

To find the target stimulus that yields a 50 per cent rate of detection, we must connect with a continuous curve the individual data points. If we accept the classical model of threshold variability outlined above, that curve will be ogival in form. With the form of the curve fixed and the data points given, there are two remaining steps. First, to determine the one ogive that "best fits" the data points requires a mathematical process of curve fitting, the details of which need not concern us here. Once that particular curve is drawn, the last step is simply to draw a line perpendicular to the ordinate, between the 50 per cent value and the ogival curve; then a perpendicular line is drawn from the point of intersection to the abscissa. These last two steps are illustrated in Figure 6.5. Note especially that the threshold value so estimated may not correspond to that of any target stimulus actually presented to the observer. The stimuli employed have to encompass the threshold value, but need not include it specifically.

In many discussions of psychophysical methods, the threshold is defined arbitrarily as the stimulus that is detected 50 per cent of the time, but the question of why 50 per cent is left open. The burden of the discussion above is to provide a rationale for the accepted definition. It should be clear that the criterion of 50 per cent detection identifies the stimulus which matches the mean of a distribution of hypothetical momentary threshold values. In

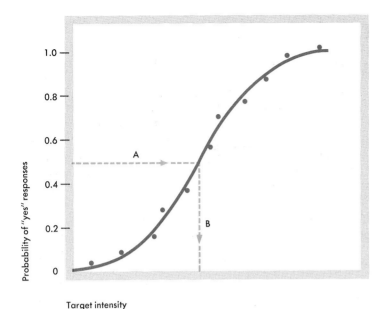

Figure 6.5 Estimation of the threshold from a normal ogive. A line, A, is drawn perpendicular to the ordinate at the 50 per cent point. Where the line A meets the ogive, a second line, B, is drawn perpendicular to the abscissa. The point where the line B meets the abscissa is the estimated value of the threshold stimulus.

that regard the definition is still arbitrary, but also meaningful: It follows from an explicit model, based on a conception of the nature of threshold variability.

Yes-No and Forced-Choice Indicators. We ought to raise one final issue concerning psychophysical methodology before turning to other matters. In our example, the observer said "yes" and "no" to indicate whether he had or had not detected the target. But how can we be sure that detection really occurred when the observer said "yes," or that the target was really not seen when the response was "no"? If an observer wants to appear very sensitive, he might say "yes" even when the target is not detected; on the other hand, a very cautious observer might say "yes" only if he were absolutely certain of what he saw. Clearly, if it is visual sensitivity we are after, these other influences on the observer's responses might introduce serious distortions in the data. In short, the yes-no response may not be a valid indicator of detection.

There is a solution to the problem posed by the observer's saying "yes" promiscuously. Such *false-positive* responses can be drastically reduced by the introduction of *blank trials,* that is, occasions which are just like normal trials except that the target is physically absent. When observers are instructed that such blank trials will be interspersed among normal trials, they tend to become cautious and cut down on the number of false-positive responses—as shown in the small number of "yes" answers to blank trials.

Decreasing false positives in this manner, however, may have the unwanted side effect of increasing the number of *false negatives,* occasions on which detection "really" occurred but the observer was reluctant to say "yes" for fear of false positives. Thus, introducing blank trials may solve one problem, but create another.

Signal-detection theory, mentioned earlier, has found a way to capitalize on these types of errors. By manipulating their relative frequency of occurrence through the use of instructions and of differential rewards and punishments (payoffs) for making false positives and false negatives, the experimenter can, through an explicit model contained within the theory, assess the various response biases and remove their effects from the data. What is left is a pure measure of the observer's sensory capacity, uncontaminated by response bias.

Prior to the development of signal-detection theory by Wilson Tanner, John Swets, and others (see Swets, 1964, and Green and Swets, 1966), another solution to the problem posed by the yes-no indicator was offered in the form of the *forced-choice* technique. Through a forced-choice indicator, the observer is made to demonstrate actual detection by the accuracy of some response contingent on detection. For example, he may be asked to indicate the location of the target, or he might have to specify when it occurred. Typically, he is given a small number of choices from which to select his response, say four, so as not to make the task too difficult. But with few alternatives, the correct answer will occur, with a predictable frequency, "by chance," even in the absence of detection. If there are four alternatives, one of which is correct, then simply by random guessing, the observer could hit the correct alternative on an average of one in four trials.

To overcome this problem, the practice is followed of transforming the raw data (percentage correct) by a so-called correction-for-guessing formula. If p is the raw, or obtained, percentage correct, and pc the percentage correct expected from chance guessing alone, then the true percentage correct, P, is obtained from the equation:

$$P = \frac{p - pc}{100 - pc} \times 100$$

If there are four alternatives, then $pc = 25$. If, in a forced-choice situation, the observer is correct on 75 per cent of the trials, then his true percentage correct, P, would be

$$\frac{75 - 25}{100 - 25} \times 100, \text{ or } \frac{50}{75} \times 100, \text{ or } 66.67$$

If he were correct on every trial, suggesting that he really was detecting the target, and not simply being lucky some of the time, then, by the formula, P would equal

$$\frac{100 - 25}{75} \times 100, \text{ or } 100$$

At the opposite extreme, if he were correct on only 25 per cent of the trials, suggesting nothing but lucky guesses, the formula would show P to be equal to zero. Thus, the formula not only corrects for guessing, it does so differentially, depending on how much of a contribution chance guessing seems intuitively to be making to the observer's performance.

The forced-choice indicator lends itself naturally for use in conjunction with the constant-stimulus method. In extensive testing, H.R. Blackwell (1953) found that the combination did in fact yield psychophysical data that were both more reliable and valid than similar data obtained with the yes-no indicator. However, those results were obtained before signal-detection theory had been developed.

From recent work, it now seems that the forced-choice and yes-no indicators yield essentially the same conclusions about sensitivity if the data are processed through the signal-detection model. In any event, we seem to have reached the point, a century after Fechner initiated his program, where the psychophysical researcher has at his disposal a variety of methods for gathering data and some alternative models to employ in drawing inferences from his data. The section that follows presents briefly some of the results of visual psychophysical investigations, along with some suggestion of their potential implications for models of the visual system. It is an interesting exercise for the theorist—though beyond the scope of this text—to see what degree of convergence there is between models of visual functioning suggested by psychophysical data and models arrived at through inference from psychophysiological data of the sort alluded to in the previous chapter.

VARIABLES AFFECTING THE CONTRAST THRESHOLD

As Weber's Law indicates, the value of the threshold, ΔI, is a direct function of the amount of background intensity, I. Thus, ΔI *per se* is not a very informative value concerning visual sensitivity; it can serve as a meaningful dependent variable only if I is fixed. However, we can determine a threshold measure that is relatively independent of the value of I by expressing ΔI as a fraction of I, or $\Delta I/I$. That ratio you will recognize as the Weber fraction, or as it is sometimes called, the *contrast threshold*. The generality of $\Delta I/I$ derives, of course, from Weber's Law, which specifies that the ratio is constant over all values of I. (If $\Delta I = kI$, then $\Delta I/I = k$, for all values of I.) In what follows, then, when we speak of "the threshold" we mean $\Delta I/I$, or the contrast threshold.

Background Intensity. There are several physical variables which markedly affect the contrast threshold. Strangely enough, one of these happens to be I. Weber's Law, it turns out, does not hold perfectly over the entire range of background intensities; the law is valid only in the middle range. At the very low end of the I range, $\Delta I/I$ is higher than would be expected from

Weber's Law, whereas at the very high end of the I range, it is lower than expected, as illustrated in Figure 6.6. Apparently the visual system is capable of its finest brightness discriminations at the highest levels of stimulation.

Other physical variables that affect the contrast threshold include the following properties of the target stimulus.

Target Size. In general, the larger the target, the lower the threshold. This relation, which has been extensively studied, has been variously labeled and mathematically described. For example, *Ricco's Law* specifies an inverse linear relation between threshold and target area, as shown in Figure 6.7. The linear relation holds, however, only over a limited range of target areas. For example, there must come a point when further increases in target area have no impact on the threshold, otherwise we could imagine a target so large that it would be detectable even if it was no more intense than its background. Somewhere before this point of no returns from adding to the target area there is a point of diminishing returns, where adding to the target area begins to have less and less effect on the threshold. Exactly where these inflection points are need not concern us here.

The general relation between target area and threshold, though, does have interesting implications for the functioning of the visual system. It has suggested to some theorists the notion of *spatial summation of excitation.* According to models that employ this concept (see Graham, Brown, and Mote, 1939; Kristofferson, 1954), the electrical activity generated by the stimulation of a single point on the retina reaches some central "display" area, most likely in the occipital lobe of the cerebral cortex. At that display area, the excitation delivered by many such retinal points summates, and gives rise to an *excitation distribution*. It is some parameter of this distribution that determines the detectability of the target which gave rise to it. The most likely parameter, according to a model developed by A.B. Kristoffer-

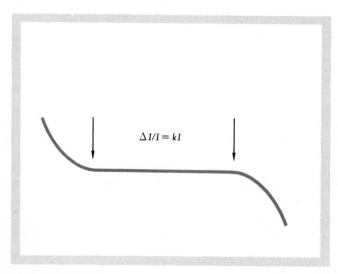

Figure 6.6 The relation between $\Delta I/I$ and I, showing how Weber's Law ($\Delta I/I = kI$) holds only in the middle range of intensity values (between the arrows).

$\Delta I/I = kI$

$\Delta I/I$

Background intensity (I)

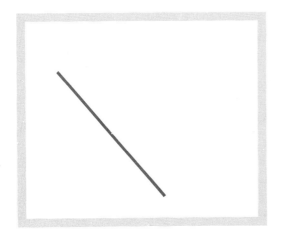

$\Delta I/I$

Target area

Figure 6.7 The relation between $\Delta I/I$ and target area according to Ricco's Law; as area increases, threshold decreases. The linear relation illustrated here holds for only a limited range of values of target area.

son, is the *peak* value of the distribution—that is, the excitation value at the point of *maximal* excitation, called $E_{\max}$.

In assessing the expected detectability of visual targets, we must take into account all those variables that influence the value of $E_{\max}$. One of these, obviously, is target intensity. Another is target area, for the larger the target, the more opportunity there is for spatial summation of excitation to occur. Thus, a dim but large target might generate the same value of $E_{\max}$ as does a bright but small target. In this sense, area and intensity are interchangeable: Loss of one can be compensated for by addition to the other.

The reciprocal relation between area and intensity is not unlimited, as has already been indicated, suggesting that excitation points that are far from the point of $E_{\max}$ contribute less to $E_{\max}$ than do points which are close to it. This feature of the Kristofferson model makes it possible to venture some predictions about the effect of target shape on the contrast threshold.

Target Shape. The shape of a visual target is determined by the spatial distribution of its elements. Two targets may be equal in area, but quite different in shape, as, for example, are a square of 16 square inches and a 2-x-8-inch rectangle.

The Kristofferson model of spatial summation asserts that the amount which an element contributes to the value of $E_{\max}$ decreases the farther that element is from the center of the target. For example, in the case of the square and rectangle of equal area, it can be inferred that the $E_{\max}$ associated with the square will be greater than that associated with the rectangle. The basis for this inference is that the square is a more compact target than the rectangle: Its elements are closer to their own center than are the elements of the rectangle, so they should generate the greater peak value of cortical excitation. Since similar comparisons can be made among other target shapes of equal area, it is possible to predict the relative detectability of targets from a knowledge of their shape. In an extensive test of such predictions, the model was impressively verified (Kristofferson, 1954).

To a considerable extent, target area and shape do determine detectability in conformity with the Kristofferson model. But certain discrepancies between predicted and obtained threshold values suggest the operation of even more subtle shape-related variables. For example, long, thin rectangles are more detectable than expected, while cross-shaped targets have higher thresholds than they should according to the model. These small, but systematic prediction errors may very well derive from inhibitory effects of the sort alluded to in Chapter Five. Thus, a long, thin rectangle may fall entirely on excitatory receptive fields, missing the adjacent inhibitory fields that wider targets would stimulate. Similarly, cross-shaped targets are most likely to fall on both excitatory and inhibitory fields, thereby somewhat reducing their detectability. Whatever the ultimate validity of the above suggestion, it does nicely illustrate the potential convergence of inferences drawn from psychophysical and psychophysiological data.

Target Duration. In general, the greater the duration of a visual target, the lower its threshold. As with target area, this relation if graphed is not linear throughout the entire range of the independent variable (duration), since no amount of additional duration can compensate for target intensities below a required minimum value. There is, however, a linear portion of the curve relating detectability and duration, and it probably reflects the fact that the initial event in the visual process is photochemical. You know, for example, that when taking a photograph, you can decrease exposure time if you compensate by using a wider *f*-stop, or diaphragm opening (thereby letting in more light). In photochemical processes outside the eye, in which time and intensity are inversely related, the relation is called the Bunsen-Roscoe Law. The analogous psychophysical relation—in which target duration and threshold are inversely related—is referred to as Bloch's Law. Though the reciprocal relation between target duration and threshold is probably largely accounted for by photochemical events, some kind of temporal integration of neural excitation may also be involved. It is likely that the integration of excitation over time occurs within the brain much as spatial summation, or integration, takes place. That is, the brain may temporarily store excitation and allow additions to the store if they enter soon enough. Or, to put it another way, all excitation may be treated as simultaneous if it enters the visual system within a brief time period (perhaps 100 milliseconds). Here again is a possible point where psychophysical and psychophysiological models may converge.

Target Wavelength. As we indicated in Chapter Five, the visual system is sensitive only to a small band of electromagnetic radiation, extending from wavelengths of about 430 to 780 mμ. Within that band the visual system is also differentially sensitive, as is reflected in different values of contrast threshold that have been experimentally determined for different wave-

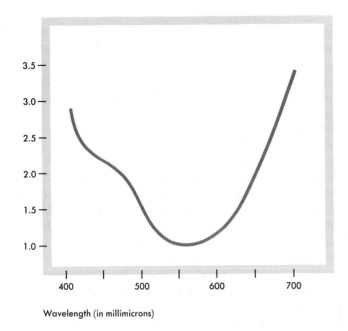

Log relative threshold

Wavelength (in millimicrons)

Figure 6.8 The relation between threshold and target wavelength.

lengths. Note that we are referring here to simple detection of the presence of a target; in experiments on this matter an observer is not required to respond to the hue of the target, just as he is not asked, in the experiments above, to respond to size, shape, or duration. Indeed, detection may occur at intensity values of the target which are below those needed to arouse the experience of hue.

The data, then, come from a situation in which the target stimulus is presented against an achromatic background, and the observer is expected to indicate whether the target occurred. From data obtained in this way, a value of $\Delta I/I$ can be obtained for each of a large number of wavelength values. The smaller the value of $\Delta I/I$ the more sensitive is the visual system to that wavelength. In Figure 6.8, data of this sort are plotted to show the relation between target threshold, on the ordinate, and target wavelength, on the abscissa. Clearly, the visual system is maximally sensitive to wavelengths in the middle of the visible spectrum. Under conditions of high background intensity, when detection is mediated by the cone system (known as *photopic vision*), peak sensitivity falls at about 555 mμ. When the data are collected under conditions of low background intensity or when the target is peripheral rather than foveal, that is, when the rod system prevails (under *scotopic vision*), maximal sensitivity is shifted somewhat toward the blue-green end of the spectrum, falling at about 510 mμ. This change in sensitivity from photopic to scotopic conditions is referred to as the *Purkinje shift*, after the scientist who first investigated it.

Instead of plotting threshold values on the ordinate, we can plot the reciprocal of the threshold ($\frac{1}{\Delta I/I}$, or $I/\Delta I$). These reciprocals are a measure of the effectiveness of light of a given wavelength in exciting the visual system. When target intensity is held constant, the effectiveness—or technically, the *luminosity*—of low-intensity stimulation varies according to target wavelength. The *luminosity function*—the graph showing the relation between luminosity and wavelength—is simply the inverse of the type of curve illustrated in Figure 6.8.

The luminosity function derived from threshold data is essentially the same as that derived from experiments on above-threshold luminosity. That is, if relative luminosity is estimated from assessments of the *apparent brightness* of chromatic stimuli that are of an intensity well above threshold, the resulting luminosity function matches the one obtained from threshold measurements. Thus, when the rod system dominates, the brightest stimulus is one of about 510 mμ, and the brightness trails off on either side.

The Purkinje shift also prevails under these conditions, as you can observe if you pay attention to the relative brightness of yellow-greens and blue-greens as twilight approaches. Here, then, is one case of close congruence between threshold data and data obtained from stimuli of greater intensity. This congruence lends credence to the idea that threshold data have general application beyond the highly restricted stimulus-and-response conditions under which they are collected.

Color

Luminosity or brightness functions, whether derived from threshold or suprathreshold data, clearly depend on the mechanisms that subserve color vision, but they do not bear directly on the experience of color, or hue. For documentation we need only to point to luminosity functions, obtained from threshold data, in which the attribute of hue is not a part either of the observer's task or indeed of his experience; furthermore, the typical luminosity function can be obtained from animals with limited or no ability to discriminate among stimuli or different wavelengths on the basis of hue alone.

Under the natural conditions in which people live outside the laboratory, the hue, not the brightness of chromatic stimuli, is the interesting attribute. In this section, then, which concentrates on hue, we will refer to brightness only as it bears on the mechanisms underlying hue discrimination.

Color-vision theory has been dominated for over a century by a model proposed first by Thomas Young early in the nineteenth century and elaborated by Helmholtz a few decades later—the Young-Helmholtz Theory. But several alternative models have also been available, chief among them the opponent-process theory, first formulated by Ewald Hering in the late nineteenth century and recently developed by Leo Hurvich and Dorothea Jameson (1957).

Color theories based on psychophysical data have attempted to deal primarily with two broad classes of phenomena: (1) color mixture and (2) defective color vision. In general, the theories have been created to account for data on color mixture, and once formulated, their ability to explain color-vision defects has been used as one test of their adequacy. We turn first to some of the facts of color mixture.

COLOR MIXTURE

It is important at the outset to clarify a possible ambiguity in terminology. The phrase color mixture refers to two different procedures. In one, *pigments* of different hue are mixed, and the hue of the resultant mixture is the subject of interest. This type of operation—which is well known to school children and artists—is technically called *subtractive* mixture. In the other procedure, *lights* of different hue are mixed and the hue of the resultant light is what is of interest. This second type is called *additive* mixture. It is the facts of additive mixture with which color theory is directly concerned, for, as you will see below, subtractive mixture is just a special case of additive mixture.

In Chapter Five the point was made that a pigment "works" by absorbing light of certain wavelengths and reflecting all others; the hue associated with the pigment is determined by the wavelength(s) it reflects. When two pigments are mixed, each component of the mixture continues to absorb and reflect wavelengths in its characteristic fashion. But some of the wavelengths reflected by pigment A will be absorbed by B, and vice versa. Thus, it is only the wavelengths that are not "captured" by either pigment that get reflected and impart a hue to the mixture. Each pigment thus subtracts some of the wavelengths that would have been reflected by the other acting in isolation: hence, "subtractive mixture." The appearance of the mixture is determined, however, by the way in which the reflected wavelengths interact, and that interaction follows the principles of additive mixture.

Research on additive color mixture has a long history; data are extensive, and from the mass of information certain principles have emerged. We can state some of these principles in fairly simple terms, but with the warning that exceptions do obtain and that some principles, though relatively simple, require highly complex mathematical formulation. In short, what follows is by no means the whole story of color mixture and color theory. We begin with the additive mixture of two wavelengths.

In general, *if two lights close together in wavelength* (λ) *are mixed, the resulting hue matches that of a light of intermediate wavelength.* However, although a good hue match can be obtained, the saturation of the mixture is somewhat less than that of the pure, intermediate wavelength. Furthermore, as the λ values of the two lights get increasingly farther apart, the difference between the saturation of the mixture and the saturation of the light of a single wavelength increases. Finally, a difference in λ is reached when the mixture is apparently completely unsaturated, and hence also without hue. That is, the mixture becomes achromatic, and retains only the attribute of brightness.

Two wavelengths that, when mixed, yield an unsaturated, achromatic result (that is, appear "white") are called complementary, and the hues associated with these wavelengths are called *complementary colors*. The minimum wavelength difference for complementary pairs is slightly less than 100 mμ, and some complementary pairs may be separated by as much as about 150 mμ. Two examples of such pairs are: yellow (about 575 mμ) and blue (about 475 mμ); orange (about 609 mμ) and blue-green (about 494 mμ). There is no complement of light in the band between about 496 and 570 mμ. To get white from a mixture containing a light within that band, the "second" hue must be one of the purples. But purple is not a *spectral* hue; that is, it cannot be generated by presenting light of a single wavelength. What we call purple derives from the mixture of red and blue. Thus, although lights in the 496-to-570 mμ band (the "greens" and "greenish-yellows") do have a complementary hue (purple), that hue is a mixture of values, rather than light of a single wavelength.

To create the experience of whiteness, then, it is necessary *at most* to present three lights of properly chosen wavelengths—one each from the low, middle, and high portions of the spectrum. These three lights, known as *primaries*, have hues in the "blue," "green," and "red" regions, though there is considerable leeway possible in their exact wavelength and corresponding hue. In one of the major investigations of color mixture (Wright, 1928–29) the three primaries employed had values of 460, 530, and 650 mμ. However, for reasons of practical convenience (certain wavelengths are easier to produce from available light sources than are others), somewhat different primary values were accepted in 1931 as standard by an international commission on illumination, the Commission Internationale de l'Eclairage, abbreviated as CIE. These standard CIE primaries have values of 435.8, 546.1, and 700 mμ.

Three turns out to be a sort of "magic number" in research and theory in color vision. Not only is three the largest number of primaries that must be mixed to yield white, but three is the number of primaries that, mixed in suitable proportions, make it possible to match any hue in the spectrum. In some instances, however, one of the three primaries must be added to the mixture in a "negative" manner. Thus, in an equation indicating that the hue associated with a given wavelength (λ_X) can be matched (symbolized as $\Rightarrow$) by the hue arising from the addition of three primary wavelengths ($\lambda_B + \lambda_G + \lambda_R$), one of the primaries may take a negative value. Conceptually, this means subtracting that wavelength from the mixture. Of course, in practice it is impossible literally to subtract a wavelength that is not already present. There is, fortunately, an operationally feasible solution, and that is to add that wavelength to the one being matched by the mixture. Thus, if the equation reads $\lambda_B + \lambda_G - \lambda_R \Rightarrow \lambda_X$, its operational counterpart would be $\lambda_B + \lambda_G \Rightarrow \lambda_X + \lambda_R$.

If negative values are allowed in the color-mixture equation, then surely zero values are also possible. That is, in many instances the mixture of only two primaries will match the hue of some wavelength. These instances, you will recognize, are those mentioned earlier in which the mixture of two close values of λ yields a hue which matches that of the intermediate wavelength.

In general, then, color-mixture data can be encompassed by an equation involving three primaries, though there may be special cases in which one of the primaries takes either a negative or a zero value. Many attempts have been made to give precise mathematical expression to that general idea. Some of these attempts take the form of geometrical models that incorporate the facts of color mixture in a geometrically simple—though conceptually complex—manner. The best known of these models, developed by the CIE, is the CIE *chromaticity diagram*. With this diagram, one can determine the proportion of each of three primaries that must be present in a mixture to match the hue and saturation of any chromatic stimulus. (Details of this model can be found in the references suggested at the end of the chapter.) For our purposes, the significant feature of the CIE diagram is that it is based on three dimensions, one for each of the primary hues. It is a simple conceptual step to assert that the mechanism the model represents must also have three primary components. Thus, the data of color mixture and the model by which they are neatly ordered argue for a three-component receptor system. That description, indeed, identifies the Young-Helmholtz theory.

In essence, with fine details omitted, three-component models postulate the existence of three classes of color receptors (blue, green, and red) among the cones. Each class of receptors is distinctively sensitive to the various wavelengths in the visible spectrum, as is shown by a curve that plots sensitivity against wavelength. What differentiates among the three classes is the shape of the entire curve, not any single point on it. Plate 5 depicts three such sensitivity curves, one for each of the hypothetical cone classes, the B, the G, and the R. Note especially that, although each cone class is maximally sensitive to wavelengths in the band associated with its name, it is also sensitive to a wide range of other wavelengths.

As we indicated, the three cone classes are hypothetical; their existence is inferred from color-mixture data. But once again, inferences about mechanisms derived from behavioral data converge with those from more direct observation, for in recent biochemical investigations by Paul Brown and George Wald (1964) the three cone classes seem to have been uncovered. There is evidence of three types of photosensitive pigment within the cone system with the proper distributions of spectral sensitivity, very much in the manner that Young postulated over 150 years ago.

The three-component theory of color vision was devised to account for color-matching data obtained from human beings with normal color vision, or *trichromats*. The theory has had only limited success, however, in explaining certain types of defective color vision, though this drawback also pertains to competing theories.

The several varieties of defective color vision are usually organized into three categories: (1) anomalous trichromatism; (2) dichromatism; and (3) monochromatism. People who fall in the second category can be divided into three major subtypes: *protanopes* (the "red-blind"), *deuteranopes* (the "green-blind") and, much more rarely, *tritanopes* (the "blue-blind"). For more exact specifications of these various defects we must refer to certain standard laboratory procedures.

For example, an instrument known as an anomaloscope allows easy identification of anomalous trichromats as well as of protanopes and deuteranopes. The person being tested views a circular field split into two semicircles. One half-field is illuminated with yellow light, the other with a variable mixture of red and green. For an observer with normal color vision, it is possible to regulate the ratio of red to green so as to make a good match to the hue, brightness, and saturation of the yellow half-field. When the match is perfect, the two half-fields merge into a single, uniform circular field. Among normal observers there is very little variation in the ratio of red to green that yields such a good match. Anomalous trichromats also require both red and green to match yellow, but the particular ratio of red to green is greatly divergent from that of the average person. Moreover, among anomalous trichromats the ratio varies considerably. For protanopes and deuteranopes a satisfactory match to yellow can be made with *any* mixture of red and green, including pure red or pure green. For the protanope (the "red blind"), however, the red must be of high intensity if it is to match the yellow perfectly.

Dichromatism shows up in other laboratory tests. For example, unlike normal or anomalous trichromats, dichromats will accept a match between white light and light from a single wavelength. For protanopes and deuteranopes this wavelength, called the *neutral point,* is in the neighborhood of 500 mμ, while for tritanopes the neutral point lies around 570 mμ. Similarly, dichromats can match any hue with a mixture of only two primaries, one from the "short" and the other from the "long" end of the spectrum.

In general, dichromats behave as though widely separated bands of wavelengths were equivalent. Thus, protanopes and deuteranopes fail to distinguish between red and green, while tritanopes respond much the same to blue and yellow. Aside from their particular defect, dichromats function with essentially normal color vision. A tempting, though unfortunately oversimplified, way of characterizing dichromats is to say that they are simply lacking or grossly deficient in one of the three component cone-types of the Young-Helmholtz theory—that is, protanopes lack the red receptor, deuteranopes the green, and tritanopes the blue. The color experiences of, for example, the protanope should therefore be limited to those that are available to the normal person from the mixture of green and blue. Some doubt is cast on that conception by data collected from those rare people with normal vision in one eye and either protanopic or deuteranopic vision in the other. In either case, certain experiences are attributable to the defective eye that are theoretically impossible (Müller, 1924, as cited by Judd, 1951).

The third type of color defective person, the monochromat, is the only totally color-blind person. For him the world lacks differentiated hues; it is like black-and-white TV for the normal person. All the rules of color mixture collapse into their most trivial terms: Any hue can be matched by a light of any wavelength simply by properly adjusting the relative intensities.

Most monochromats simply lack a functional cone system. To judge from other defects unrelated to color, such as acuity, the typical monochromat seems to have only the rod system. There are some monochromats, however, with apparently well-functioning cones, aside from their inability to mediate color vision. In any event, the existence of monochromatic color vision does not enable us to differentiate among the various competing color theories.

OPPONENT-PROCESS THEORY

In the Young-Helmholtz type of theory, which postulates three classes of color-sensitive retinal receptors, it is the relative amount of neural activity generated by each of the three receptor classes that determines color experience. Nothing further is said in the theory about the neural interactions among the three subsystems. In effect, the crucial "decisions" about color are made in the retina. The neural apparatus simply transmits those decisions to higher brain centers for display and evaluation.

As we saw in Chapter Five, however, there are inhibitory as well as excitatory neural interactions in the visual system. It is not unlikely, then, that similar inhibitory effects also occur among neural impulses from color-sensitive receptors. The chief competitor to the Young-Helmholtz type of theory, the *opponent-process* theory of Hurvich and Jameson, involves such direct inhibitory interactions between pairs of color-sensitive subsystems.

In particular, the model proposes that impulses delivered by yellow-sensitive and blue-sensitive receptors and by green-sensitive and red-sensitive receptors are mutually inhibitory, and that, in addition to and independently of their chromatic responses, the cones also deliver impulses that relate only to brightness. One version of the model is shown in Figure 6.9. This version assumes three photosensitive pigments, given the neutral symbols, α, β, and γ (alpha, beta, and gamma); this much is consistent with the Young-Helmholtz theory and with the recent evidence reported by Wald. Note, for example, that in the model presented in Figure 6.9, a "red" neural response

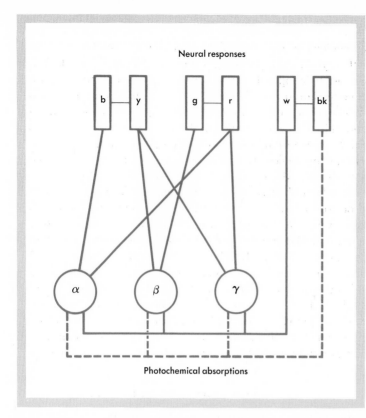

Neural responses

Photochemical absorptions

Figure 6.9 The Hurvich-Jameson opponent-process model of color vision. Three photochemical pigments (α, β, and γ) and four types of neural response (blue, yellow, green, and red) are postulated. Blue and yellow are paired, as are green and red; when both members of a pair are activated, their outputs cancel one another. In addition to their chromatic effects, the three pigments have achromatic effects. Each arouses a white neural response, but it also arouses a black response (dashed line in figure) which inhibits, or "opposes" a white response. See text for further discussion.

(shorthand for "a neural response that by itself would lead to a yellow sensation") is generated through the combined activity of pigment types α and γ, whereas a "green" neural response results simply from stimulation of pigment β. In this fashion four types of chromatic neural response (blue, yellow, green, and red) are possible from the stimulation of various combinations of three types of photopigments.

Furthermore, these four chromatic neural responses are paired, blue-yellow and red-green, and, as mentioned, the two members of each pair are mutually inhibitory. If all three pigments are stimulated, no chromatic neural response will be forthcoming since activity in both the blue-yellow and the red-green pairs will be canceled.

A third pair, black-white, completes the set. Incidentally, in this scheme, black is an active sensation, not simply the result of lack of stimulation. The latter, according to Hurvich and Jameson, gives rise to a grayish sensation; their "black" which occurs as the result of inhibition (the black which is the complement of white) is "blacker than black."

Members of a pair mutually inhibit one another in the following way. If, for example, neural response "yellow" is elicited, the chromatic sensation it would normally yield can be canceled if an equal degree of neural "blue" is simultaneously elicited, and vice-versa.

The pairing in this fashion of blue and yellow and red and green encompasses more than the fact that they are complementary. The two members of each pair are tied together in other ways, for example, in the types of known color defects, especially dichromacy (thus, there are no defects, such as red-yellow blindness or blue-green blindness, that might be expected to occur if the three primary subsystems were entirely independent of one another). Hurvich and Jameson cite other behavioral evidence, both qualitative and quantitative, to support the general model. And very recently, confirming evidence has been emerging from physiological investigations (DeValois and Abramov, 1966). It appears, then, that the prevailing theory of color vision for some time to come will, like Hurvich and Jameson's, be "three-component" at the retinal level and "opponent-process" at the neural level. This surely would represent a remarkably satisfying and productive resolution of what has been a conflict among models.

COLOR INDUCTION

Color experience is not determined exclusively by the spectral distribution of immediate, local stimulation. Color may be "induced" in an area by the aftereffects of preceding stimulation as well as through the effects of present, but spatially displaced stimulation. The former, the *negative afterimage,* is already familiar to you through our discussion of "localized adaptation" in Chapter Five. In essence, if an area is stimulated by light of a particular wavelength, for some time after that light is removed the area will respond as though stimulated by the complement of the original stimulation.

A similar effect—the appearance of hue in an area stimulated by achromatic illumination—can be obtained from simultaneously present, adjacent stimulation, as illustrated in Plate 6. Here the apparent color is again the complement of the inducing color. This type of induction is often referred to as an instance of *simultaneous contrast;* it occurs with achromatic as well as with chromatic stimuli.

Negative afterimages, at least in the simple form reported here, are relatively easy to account for by either a three-component or an opponent-process model. For the latter, the argument would be that the negative afterimage results not only from pigment depletion during stimulation (and hence reduced sensitivity to the inducing wavelength until the pigment is reconstituted), but also from neural interaction. Thus, during stimulation by an inducing blue light, the "yellow" neural apparatus is inhibited; this inhibition is released upon cessation of stimulation, and the yellow apparatus "rebounds," giving off neural impulses as though it were actively being stimulated. This account of negative afterimages, which postulates both a photochemical and a neural component, is likely to be more valid than the classical explanation of the Young-Helmholtz model based solely on pigment depletion. Moreover, the results of research (Brindley, 1963) suggest that the photochemical basis of the negative afterimage is more complex than originally assumed. Apparently, in addition to simple pigment depletion, light stimulation produces certain photochemical by-products that yield their own sensory effect; furthermore, these chemicals spread, or diffuse, beyond their original locus, and thereby generate certain spatial characteristics or afterimages that are otherwise inexplicable.

Simultaneous contrast poses a more difficult problem for both the Young-Helmholtz and the Hurvich-Jameson approaches. One explanation under the Young-Helmholtz model transforms the phenomenon into a case of negative afterimages. It is argued that the eye, in the course of its continual movements, brings the retinal area receiving achromatic stimulation over the area occupied by the inducing color. In this way, the presumably "unstimulated" area really does receive chromatic stimulation; then, when fixation reverts to the achromatic area, the negative afterimage of the inadvertent chromatic stimulation appears. An alternative, or a supplementary, explanation involves the spreading photochemical by-product postulated by Brindley. Both explanations, however, might be questioned on grounds that simultaneous contrast makes its appearance much too quickly to be mediated solely by the rather slow-acting effects of eye-movements and chemical diffusion.

According to the Hurvich and Jameson model, activity in one member of a pair will affect activity in elements of the "opponent" member, even if the latter are spatially removed from the area of direct stimulation. Exactly how this happens is not specified, although reference is made to spatial summation of excitation, as described earlier in this chapter, as a relevant example of interactions that take place "at a distance."

A clue to the second step in this type of explanation of color induction by simultaneous contrast is given in another phenomenon. If a person is stimulated by a completely homogeneous chromatic visual field, a so-called *Ganzfeld*, within a few minutes the color fades and the person soon reports a colorless, foggy, gray experience (Cohen, 1958). Apparently, continual stimulation by a given color reduces the responsiveness of that color system; why this reduced responsiveness is manifested so dramatically (as complete disappearance of color) only in the Ganzfeld situation is another question. But note that as responsiveness to one color system decreases, so might suppression of the system with which it is paired. Thus, continued stimulation by blue leads both to a decrease in responsiveness of the blue system and to an increase in activity in the yellow system. We need only add the assumption that these effects spread outside the area of direct stimulation to account for color induction by simultaneous contrast. Again, however, the major barrier to the acceptance of this account is that it would seem to require more time for the postulated processes to occur than is compatible with the rapid occurrence of the phenomenon itself. We are left, then, with some uncertainty about whether either a Young-Helmholtz or an opponent-process model can cope with all details of the phenomenon of simultaneous contrast.

There are other interesting instances of color induction that at this point are theoretically neutral. An especially fascinating case is the induction of color from black and white figures. Certain patterns of black and white, distributed properly over time, yield what have been referred to as "subjective colors." Exactly how the experience of color can be induced from achromatic stimulation is not well understood. If you remember that "white" stimuli contain chromatic components, however, then some of the mystery is removed. The remaining problem is to account for the significance of the particular temporal sequences and rates of black-white stimulation that lead to color induction. It is quite likely that such an account will refer to differences among the color subsystems in latency and rate of firing, as well as interactions that are both excitatory and inhibitory.

Acuity

This chapter has been devoted so far to two important attributes of visual experience, brightness and color. The visual system is capable, of course, of many other types of simple discriminations, as well as of more complex integrations of visual inputs. One such basic discrimination, acuity, has already been discussed in Chapter Five. We continue that discussion here, with an emphasis on the methods of measuring acuity and on the nature of defects in acuity.

MEASUREMENT OF VISUAL ACUITY

The measurement of visual acuity is important both for research and for evaluations of the vision of individuals. One widely used procedure for making clinical assessments of acuity for distant objects is the well-known *Snellen chart,* or variations thereof. A person being examined is placed 20 feet from a chart containing rows of letters that decrease in size from the top to the bottom of the chart. The task is to read correctly as many letters as possible. That row where accuracy of performance falls below a fixed criterion defines the level of the person's acuity. His performance can then be compared with that of a large number of other people on whom the Snellen chart was *standardized.*

Thus, if "normal" performance is defined as the row with the smallest-size letters that the average person in the standardization group can read from a distance of 20 feet, then an individual has "normal acuity" if his limit of accurate performance is also reached at that row. His acuity level is designated 20/20, meaning he can read at 20 feet neither better nor worse than the average person; better and worse refer to the row (the letter size) where reading accuracy breaks down.

If a person's limit is reached at a row that the average person can just read from a distance of, say, 50 feet, then his acuity is labeled 20/50.

Figure 6.10 Typical targets used in laboratory investigations of visual acuity. The limit of acuity is reached when the subject sees a target as uniform, rather than differentiated into separate light and dark elements.

Similarly, if the best he can do from 20 feet is what the average person can just read from 200 feet, then his acuity is assessed at 20/200. In general, the larger the denominator of the ratio, the poorer the person's acuity for distant objects—that is, the more *myopic* he is.

Some people, of course, are better than average. For example, a person might be able to read at 20 feet a letter size that is too small for the average subject to make out until he moved up to, say, 15 feet. The acuity of such a person, who can be called *hyperacute,* would be 20/15; he might be farsighted, but not necessarily so. A test for farsightedness, *hyperopia,* would assess ability to read material at very close distances, say about 12 inches, for a farsighted person would have difficulty reading material that close.

From the Snellen chart alone, then, we can only tell if a person is normal, myopic, or hyperacute (at 20 feet), not if he is hyperopic. In short, nearsightedness and farsightedness are not at opposite ends of the same dimension. Testing for one does not necessarily yield information about the other. This limitation is especially important to note, since mass screening of acuity, as is often conducted in elementary schools, typically employs only the Snellen chart, and hence assesses only myopia. But the child who looks "normal" or even hyperacute on that test may still be hyperopic, a condition that could seriously impede his school work; although he would have no trouble reading the blackboard, he might have difficulty in reading textbooks and doing other close work.

For purposes of research on acuity, the Snellen chart does not provide sufficiently precise measures; therefore, techniques using other kinds of stimuli have been developed. One is the *Landolt ring,* which is in effect a circle with a gap. The gap can be variously positioned by rotating the ring, and the subject's task is simply to locate the gap. To find the limits of acuity, gap size can be varied, as can the subject's distance from the stimulus. Or, if the purpose of the research is to find the effect on acuity of some variable such as level of illumination, gap size and distance can be held constant; in this case the dependent variable would be the probability of correctly locating the gap. Other types of acuity target devised primarily for research purposes are illustrated in Figure 6.10.

In an oft-quoted passage the psychologist William James (1842–1910) described the phenomenal world of the infant as a "blooming, buzzing confusion" (James, 1890). No doubt it is, relative to the fairly well-organized world of the normal adult, but experiments by R.L. Fantz, J.M. Ordy, and M.S. Udelf (1962) suggest much less perceptual chaos than James imagined. These experiments reveal that infants are quite alert to differences in visual patterns and exhibit a visual acuity only slightly inferior to that of the average adult.

Their technique is perhaps as interesting as are the results it yielded. The technique relies on the fact that even very young infants have preferences in visual patterns (Figure 6.11). The experimenter presents pairs of visual stimuli from above to an infant lying awake in his crib, as illustrated in Figure 6.12 (p. 206). If lighting and other conditions are right, the experimenter can determine which stimulus the infant is looking at by observing its reflection on the infant's cornea. It is thus possible to measure how much time the infant spends looking at each member of a pair. Since each stimulus is presented half the time on the right and half on the left (thus controlling for the infant's possible preference for stimulus position), differences in looking time can serve as a measure of preference. Preference, of course, implies discrimination. Thus, by showing a preference, through differences in looking time, the infant also reveals his ability to discriminate between two visual stimuli. (What inference about discrimination could be made if no preference were exhibited?)

Some of the patterns that were used are shown in Figure 6.11. In general, infants prefer to look at the more complex stimuli. One clear-cut preference is for a striped pattern over a uniformly gray field (not illustrated in Figure

Figure 6.11 Interest in form was proved by infants' reactions to various pairs of patterns presented together. (The small and large squares were used alternately.) The more complex pairs received the most attention, and within each of these pairs differential interest was based on pattern differences. (Adapted from Fantz, 1961.)

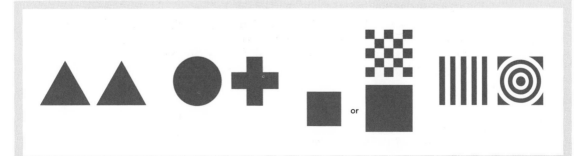

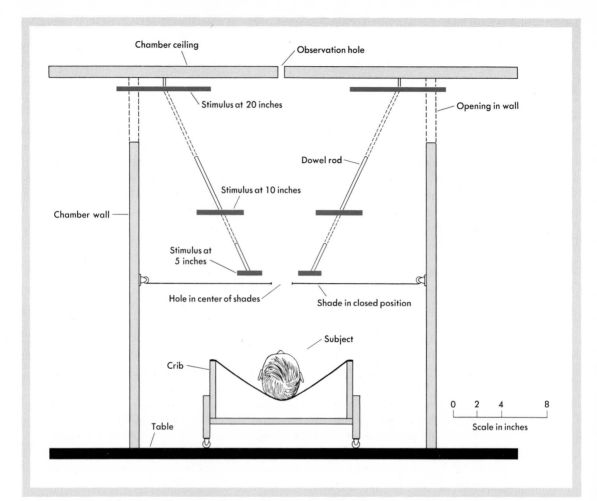

Figure 6.12 Schematic cross section through the middle of the testing chamber, with the stimulus objects used at the three test distances superimposed on the same drawing. The drawing is to scale except for the quarter-inch observation hole. (Adapted from Fantz, Ordy, and Udelf, 1962.)

6.11). Herein lies the key to measuring visual acuity in infants. Suppose the stripes were made increasingly fine. Eventually the limits of acuity would be reached; at that point, the physically striped pattern would be phenomenally uniform, or *homogeneous*, and so would no longer be preferred to a physically homogeneous stimulus.

According to this reasoning, the experimenters estimated acuity in infants. Neonates could discriminate from gray a pattern consisting of black and white stripes one-eighth inch in width at a distance of ten inches. This corresponds to Snellen chart acuity of about 20/200 or better. By the age of six months, lines as narrow as one-sixty-fourth inch could be seen, corresponding to acuity of about 20/70. These figures reveal considerably better acuity in infants than had previously been suggested by results obtained with different methods.

The well-functioning lens can make rapid adjustments to near and far fixation, and a person with such a lens can see clearly both near and far objects. Many people, however, do not have good acuity for all object distances. There is considerable controversy over the etiology of the two basic types of defective acuity, myopia and hyperopia. The conventional view is that myopia and hyperopia represent opposite forms of a common structural abnormality. According to this hypothesis, the myope's eyeball is abnormally long, whereas the hyperope's is too short. It is argued that the myopic eye brings the image to a focus in front of the retina. In effect, the cornea and lens of the myope are too powerful, and the lens is unable to relax sufficiently and assume the normal flattened shape that allows the proper placing of far objects on the retinal surface. The hyperopic eye, by contrast, does not have sufficient focusing, or *dioptric*, power to compensate for its too-short eyeball by bringing the image from a point "behind" the retina to its proper location on the retinal surface.

Developmentally, myopia is a defect that initially appears around age six, whereas hyperopia is usually associated with older people. In the type of hyperopia that can be directly attributed to aging—*presbyopia*—an anatomical explanation seems quite tenable. Because the lens does become less flexible as it gets older, it may become less capable of the change in shape required to bring near objects into focus.

The anatomical account of myopia, however, is not as readily acceptable as it may seem. Certain optometric theorists are especially skeptical of the "long-eyeball" explanation, claiming that there is no supportive anatomical evidence. Moreover, they assert that the eyeball is one of the few structures that is virtually fully developed in a young child. According to their view, myopia is not the result of a structural anomaly, but rather is a developmental phenomenon—a product of the interaction between a child and his visual environment. In short, myopia is learned.

In particular, these theorists point to reading and other close work, which play an increasingly prominent role in a child's life at about the time he starts school. After a few years of excessive attention to close objects, under poor lighting and with bad posture, the young child becomes myopic as a mode of adjustment (or perhaps "maladjustment") to his visual world, a world that from an evolutionary point of view is quite unnatural.

The controversy between the structural and functional views of myopia is waged most intensely around the issue of treatment. The conventional prescription for myopia is to fit a person with lenses providing a *minus,* or *negative,* correction to compensate for his refractive error. If a nearsighted person is imposing excessive refractive power on the light rays coming from distant objects, then lenses are placed before his eyes which subtract that amount of refractive power (hence "minus," or "negative" lenses).

One of the problems with the use of negative corrective lenses is that such treatment may be only temporarily effective. Frequently, a correction that was adequate when first applied gradually becomes insufficient, and stronger lenses must be prescribed. Those who consider myopia a functional, rather than a structural, defect are not surprised by adaptation to corrective lenses; indeed, they view it as evidence for their hypothesis. Moreover, they argue that the use of corrective lenses not only represents an attack on symptoms rather than on underlying causes, but is also a practice that in the long run exacerbates the problem.

The alternative approach to treatment of myopia is to deal with the underlying mechanism, rather than with surface symptoms. On the assumption that if myopia is learned, it can be unlearned, optometrists who accept the functional approach have developed techniques of "visual re-education." These techniques involve various procedures and devices for training myopic patients to recognize objects at a distance; beyond this, treatment is directed at the whole body, not just the eyes, in an attempt to help myopic children to use their bodies in a freer, more expansive way than is typical of them, to improve their balance and especially their posture—in short, to correct their total style of visual-motor adjustment.

Unfortunately, in light of the great practical as well as theoretical significance of the issue, there are no good data, other than clinical impressions, to substantiate the functional point of view. Until such time as convincing empirical support is forthcoming, this approach will probably retain its present off-beat flavor. If sufficient controversy is engendered, however, collection of the necessary evidence may be accelerated to the benefit of the theorist, the practitioner, and perhaps even the myope.

Flicker

Acuity is the ability to detect spatial discontinuities in stimulation (for example, detecting that a stimulus is composed of tightly packed, alternating black and white lines rather than a uniform homogeneous gray field); *flicker* involves responses to *temporal* discontinuity. If a visual stimulus is fluctuating in intensity (in the extreme, going on and off), the changes that occur over time may or may not be reflected in visual experience. If the temporal discontinuity is detected—if the fluctuating stimulus can be discriminated from one that is continuously illuminated—the experience is called flicker. If the discontinuity is not detected, the experience is one of *fusion.*

The primary determinant of whether flicker or fusion prevails is the rate at which the fluctuations occur. It should be intuitively obvious that the faster the rate, the less likely it is that flicker will be detected. Indeed, there ought to be some point of transition between flicker and fusion, a sort of threshold (with the statistical properties of other thresholds) that might be measured and related to various independent variables. This particular threshold is known, by convention, as the *critical flicker frequency,* or the CFF, and it represents the rate, or frequency in cycles per second, at which flicker merges into fusion. By analogy with acuity, we may think of the CFF as an indicator of the temporal resolving power of the visual system.

Depending on testing conditions, the CFF may range from about 10 to 100 cycles per second (cps). Under viewing conditions that are fairly typical of those outside the laboratory, the CFF is in the neighborhood of 40. That is, a light going on and off at a rate faster than about 40 cps will appear fused. Ordinary incandescent lamps are powered by current alternating at a rate of 60 cps; although the filament of the lamp does not cease glowing during the "off" moment of a cycle, there is a slight dimming. In effect then, incandescent lamps provide a flickering source of illumination, and yet we are not aware of it. Were the alternating current rate somewhat less than 60 cps, however, we might very well experience the resulting flicker.

Target Locus, Size, and Luminance. Investigation of the CFF has a long history, and one that is marked by more than the ordinary amount of conflicting data. Simple relations between CFF and other, single variables seem the exception, rather than the rule. For example, one cannot make an unqualified assertion about where on the retina (fovea or periphery) CFF is higher (remember: the higher the CFF, the more refined the system). Rather, the data require a generalization of this sort: CFF is higher in the fovea than in the periphery when the target area is small, but the reverse is true for large targets (about 2° in diameter or larger). Apparently, the cones individually are more efficient than the rods at the task of temporal discrimination, just as they are for spatial discrimination; however, through its greater capacity for the spatial summation of excitation, the rod system can be more effective than the cones in integrating the information in a large target. Essentially, in the periphery a larger target becomes a brighter target. And it turns out, again with some qualifications, that the brighter the "on" part of a flickering light, the higher the CFF. Indeed, for a wide range of target luminance values, the relation between CFF and luminance is linear—a relation known as the Ferry-Porter law.

Cycle Form. Among the many other physical variables related to CFF, the *light-time fraction* is one of the most interesting. This variable represents the duration of the "on" portion of a light-dark cycle relative to the duration of the entire cycle. The ratio need not equal .5; that is, light-time and dark-time need not be equal. In general, the smaller the light-time ratio the higher the value of the CFF, though this is unequivocally so only if the average luminance of the target is held constant. This latter qualification is necessary since decreasing the duration of the light-time means decreasing the amount of light entering the eye within a target cycle, and, according to the Ferry-Porter law, decreasing target luminance should lead to a decrease in CFF. One way to compensate for the decrease in average target luminance that results from decreased light-time is to increase the luminance of the light portion of the cycle. When that is done, targets with smaller light-time ratios have the higher CFF values, but again with a qualification. At some point, the light-time ratio begins to get too small, as evidenced by a decrease in the CFF. In short, there is an optimal light-time ratio, somewhere in the range between about .40 and .25, depending on other variables such as target area.

The fact that the light-time fraction can get too small for optimal functioning, even with average luminance held constant, has elicited some speculation about possible neural factors in the determination of the CFF. One suggestion (Bartley and Nelson, 1961) points to the role of the "off" response that can be recorded in some neural fibers, as noted in Chapter Five. According to this argument, the "off" response is an important element in the discrimination of temporal discontinuity. Very short light flashes, however, fail to yield measurable "off" responses, so small light-time fractions will not yield high values of CFF. At the opposite extreme, where the light-time fraction is large, there is a very brief dark interval between successive light flashes in a train of light-dark cycles. Under these circumstances, the "off" responses that would ordinarily occur, upon termination of long light flashes, are inhibited by the strong "on" response to the next flash. Hence, the optimal light-time fraction falls between the extreme values. Why it happens to be somewhat below a value of .5 is yet to be explained.

Target Duration. Ordinarily, investigators of flicker utilize as target stimuli lengthy trains of light-dark cycles. Indeed, the longer the train, the higher the CFF usually is, at least for train lengths up to one second.

The limiting case of a flickering target is one with only two cycles, or two light pulses separated by a dark phase. The observer's task is to discriminate the two-pulse target from a comparison stimulus consisting of a single pulse of equal total duration. For such a discrimination to be made the two pulses must be separated by a dark phase on the order of .035 seconds long. This value is considerably greater than the duration of the dark phase in the typical flicker experiment employing lengthy target trains. For example, if the CFF has a value of 40 cps, then each cycle has a duration of 1/40, or .025 seconds; if the light-time fraction is .5, the dark phase of each cycle is thus half of that, or .012 sec.

Clearly, the resolution of temporal fluctuations is poor for two-pulse targets. Why this should be so has been the object of some speculation. According to one account, a longer train provides what amounts to a larger sample of events on which the observer can base his decision; as in all such situations where statistical considerations apply, the larger the sample, the more accurate the decision. It is possible that other factors are also relevant, involving complex interactions among the excitatory and inhibitory events triggered by a flickering stimulus. Perhaps a satisfactory explanation can be built along the lines followed by Bartley and Nelson in their attempt to deal with the problem of the light-time fraction, as sketched above.

INDIVIDUAL DIFFERENCES

Many theorists have seen in the CFF a measure of the efficiency of the visual system, and perhaps of the brain in general, in processing information. This is obviously true in a trivial sense, for a CFF of zero would imply a system with no capacity for temporal discrimination. It is true also in the nontrivial, but still restricted, sense that variation in CFF implies variation in capacity to make discriminations of temporal discontinuity, which is prerequisite to the transmission of certain kinds of basic messages through the visual channel. It is not necessary, though it may be true, that the CFF has any general significance. For example, is the person with the higher value of the CFF under standard testing conditions *in general* a more efficient information-processer than the person with the lower value of the CFF? Does his ability to make fine temporal discriminations imply anything more general about him, in the same way that a person's unusual ability to discriminate among tones might mark him as a potentially good musician?

There are those who, conceiving of refined temporal resolving power as a fundamental asset of a nervous system, speculate that differences among individuals in the value of the CFF should be reflected in other important behavioral differences. For example, attempts have been made to correlate CFF and intelligence, as measured by standard IQ tests. Such attempts so far have not proven fruitful, perhaps because of inadequacies in the purported measures of intelligence. In somewhat less direct approaches to the problem, it has been shown that CFF declines with age (Medina, 1957) and that it is affected by temperature in both lower animals and in human beings. A host of other variables have been investigated with some promising results, though at present CFF does not seem quite the key to individual differences in efficiency of brain functioning that it once promised to be.

It is interesting to note, in this regard, that some investigators are now seeking "the key" in a more direct measure of the brain's response to brief visual stimulation, the *evoked potential*. The evoked potential is an electrical response of the cortex to sensory stimulation that can be recorded with electrodes placed on the scalp. To obtain the recording requires highly sophisticated instrumentation, including an electronic computer for isolating

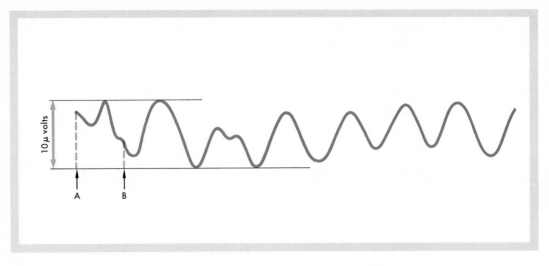

Electrical potential (in microvolts)

10 μ volts

A   B

Time (in milliseconds)

Figure 6.13 An evoked response from the occipital lobe of a human subject to a bright, 10-microsecond light flash. The arrow at A indicates the onset of the flash; B is a point 80 milliseconds later. The vertical line shows the length of a 10-microvolt deflection. The regular waves that start after about 200 milliseconds continue for a second or more and occur at a frequency of about 10 per second—the frequency of the alpha rhythm of the EEG. The graph is based on the average response to 100 light flashes. An upward deflection of the curve represents a positive change in voltage. (Adapted from data courtesy of Dr. Marvin Schwartz.)

very weak signals (the evoked potential in this case) from the electrical "noise" in which they are embedded. The evoked potential, an example of which is given in Figure 6.13, has several characteristic components. It has been claimed (Chalke and Ertl, 1965) that differences among individuals in the latency of one of these components are correlated with IQ differences. The validity of that claim awaits the test of further research.

SUMMARY

Brightness discrimination is the most primitive visual function. One approach to the experimental study of brightness is to investigate the relation between simple physical variables and simple responses to them—that is, *psychophysical relations*. The philosopher-psychologist Fechner saw in the field of *psychophysics* the solution to the age-old *mind-body* problem, and developed many of our current methods for obtaining psychophysical data. Although a "new psychophysics," *signal-detection theory*, is beginning to supplant the classical version, there is still merit in the older methods, which are designed to yield an estimate of the *threshold*.

In one of the classical psychophysical methods, the *method of limits*, small changes are made in the intensity of a target stimulus until the observer indicates that the detectability of the stimulus has changed. In an *ascending* series the target stimulus is initially undetectable (below threshold) and the intensity changes are increments; in a *descending* series small units of intensity are subtracted from an initially above-threshold stimulus until detection fails to occur. The transition point between detection and nondetection defines the threshold. Operationally, that point is found by taking the average of a number of measurements from both ascending and descending series. That threshold value (ΔI), expressed as a ratio of the intensity of the background intensity (I) on which the target was presented, defines the *Weber fraction*, $\Delta I/I$.

To eliminate some of the biases that observers bring to the limits task, the *constant-stimulus method* was developed. Several values of target-stimulus intensity are selected so as to straddle the threshold value. Each intensity value is presented a large number of times and a detection probability is found for each. When detection probability is plotted against target-stimulus intensity, the resulting curve typically is S-shaped, or *ogival*. The threshold value is estimated as that intensity value which is associated with a detection probability of .50. The rationale for that procedure is contained in the assumption that "the threshold" is not a fixed value, but rather is one that fluctuates from moment to moment around an average value; this threshold fluctuation, in turn, is assumed to be the result of momentary changes in the sensitivity of the observer's visual system.

To determine whether an observer has detected a target stimulus, he might be asked to say "yes" for detection and "no" for a nondetection. But if the observer wants to appear especially sensitive, he may say "yes" even when he truly did not detect a stimulus. To minimize that tendency, blank trials can be introduced—that is, trials on which no target is presented. But knowing that blank trials will occur may make the observer excessively cautious: He may say "no" to any target presentations that are not clearly detectable. In general, the "yes-no" kind of detection indicator is highly vulnerable to the observer's relative willingness to make either of two kinds of error: (a) *false positives*—saying "yes" in the absence of the target, and (b) *false negatives*—saying "no" when a target was presented.

Signal-detection theory permits a separate assessment of the observer's response biases and his sensitivity. Within the classical approach to psychophysics, the problems associated with the yes-no indicator are dealt with by substituting for it a *forced-choice* technique, whereby the observer has to "prove" that detection has occurred by identifying some attribute of the target that is unrelated to its intensity, such as its spatial location, or the time period during which it occurred.

The value of the Weber fraction, or the contrast threshold, $\Delta I/I$, is related to several variables, among them I itself (since Weber's Law—$\Delta I = kI$—does not hold at high and low values of I). In general, the *larger* the target, the lower its contrast threshold, suggesting some kind of *temporal summation* of excitation. Target wavelength is complexly related to detectability; in general, the visual system is most sensitive to wavelengths in the middle portion of the visible spectrum. The point of peak sensitivity shifts (the Purkinje shift) from about 555 mμ when background intensity is high to about 510 mμ at low values of background intensity.

The classical Young-Helmholtz theory of color vision was devised primarily to account for the facts of additive color mixture, as efficiently summarized in the *CIE chromaticity diagram*. In essence, the theory postulates three kinds of color receptors, each maximally sensitive to wavelengths from different portions of the spectrum. Though it works reasonably well for color mixture data from normal people, the theory has some difficulty in accounting for certain types of *defective* color vision. Thus, to assert that people with color defects are simply lacking one or another of the three kinds of color receptors does not fit all the data.

Color defectives are classified into three major types: (a) *anomalous* trichromats, people who are quantitatively different from normals, but not qualitatively so; (b) *dichromats* (who may be "red-blind"—*protanopes*; "green-blind"—*deuteranopes*; or, very rarely, "blue-blind"—*tritanopes*); and (c) *monochomats,* the true color-blind—that is, people for whom the visual world is entirely without hue.

Of the several alternatives to the Young-Helmholtz theory, a model first proposed by Hering, and recently modified by Hurvich and Jameson, seems the most promising. This *opponent-process* theory postulates three types of photosensitive pigments in the retina (like Young-Helmholtz), but the neural responses associated with them are so combined as to yield four chromatic types—red, green, yellow, and blue. In addition, red and green, and yellow and blue are paired, with the members of each of the two resulting pairs being mutually inhibitory (for example, a "red" neural response inhibits a "green" neural response). Finally, a third achromatic pair, black-white, is also postulated. Recent psychophysical and neurophysiological evidence seems supportive of this type of model.

Other color phenomena that must be dealt with by a complete color theory are *negative afterimages,* color induction by *simultaneous contrast,* and *subjective color,* generated by moving patterns of black and white elements.

Visual acuity is another of the basic discriminations that have been extensively studied. Various methods for measuring acuity have been devised. The well-known *Snellen chart,* consisting of rows of letters of decreasing size, enables screening people for the normality of their acuity for distant objects. Those performing below normal on this test are labeled *myopic,* or nearsighted. Farsightedness, or *hyperopia,* is tested with reading material that is close to the person. Laboratory research on acuity demands measurement finer than that provided by the Snellen chart; for this purpose such stimuli as the *Landolt ring*—a circle with a gap in it—have been employed. Still other methods have been developed for testing the acuity of young infants, based on the fact that they will prefer to fixate a patterned over a homogeneous stimulus. Research using such materials reveals a degree of hitherto unsuspected acuity in infants.

Myopia and hyperopia have traditionally been considered to result from abnormality in the structure of the eye. The myope's eyeball, according to this hypothesis, is too long, whereas the hyperope's is too short. However, some theorists argue that these defects are learned rather than structural. Moreover, it is argued, the typical prescription of *minus lenses* to compensate for the excessive focusing, or *dioptric,* power of the myope's lens serves to exacerbate rather than alleviate the problem. Unfortunately, there are virtually no data that allow a test of the competing hypotheses.

Flicker refers to the *temporal* resolving power of the visual system. The *critical flicker frequency,* or CFF, is the rate at which a light that is going on and off stops being seen as flickering and begins to be seen as continuous, or *fused.* Under normal conditions the CFF is about 40 cycles per second. Several variables interact to determine the CFF, among them the size and intensity of the target, whether it is presented to the center or the periphery of the retina, the *light-time fraction* (the ratio of "on" time to total cycle duration), and the duration of the presentation of the flickering target. There are reliable individual differences in the value of the CFF, but attempts to relate these to other differences, such as in intelligence, have not proven successful. The latest candidate for a simple visual indicator of efficiency in brain functioning is an electrical measurement taken from the brain in response to visual stimulation—the *evoked potential*. It remains to be seen whether early promising results with this measure will have the same fate as those with the CFF.

SUGGESTED READINGS

Fantz, R.L. The origin of form perception. *Scientific American,* 1961, 204, 66–72.

Galanter, E. Contemporary psychophysics. In *New directions in psychology.* New York: Holt, Rinehart & Winston, 1962, pp. 87–156.

Gregory, R.L. *Eye and brain.* New York: McGraw-Hill, 1966, Chapters 6 and 8.

Hurvich, L.M., and Dorothea Jameson. *The perception of brightness and darkness.* Boston: Allyn & Bacon, 1966.

Teevan, R.C., and R.C. Birney (eds.). *Color vision.* Princeton: Van Nostrand, 1961.

Perceptual Organization

The psychological events we have referred to in the last two chapters have traditionally been called "sensory." These sensations (particular colors and brightnesses, individual lines, flashes of light, and so on) may be the elements of which everyday experience is composed, but they do not, by themselves and in isolation, simply add together to form that experience. Rather, they are integrated in the brain into complex, organized events. It is these higher-order "perceptual" events that are the components of ordinary experience. And it is these perceptual phenomena, exemplified by visual experience, that we examine in the present chapter. In particular, we consider first the organization of the perceptual world into figures that stand out from their backgrounds. Next, we take up the rules that govern the manner in which several perceptual figures become organized in two-dimensional space—rules formulated for the most part by a group of theorists called Gestalt psychologists. We also investigate various instances in which perceptual events influence one another, as in the case of well-known optical illusions. Finally, we take up the topic of perception of objects in three-dimensional space—the condition that typically prevails in everyday experience.

Contour Formation and Figure-Ground Segregation

The visual perceptual world is organized at its simplest level into figures that "stand out from," or are segregated from, their backgrounds. A blob of ink on a white sheet is an example of a visual figure; geometrical forms, such as circles, triangles, and squares, constitute another class of figures; line drawings, sketches, silhouettes, paintings, and photographs of real objects, such as faces, animal and human bodies, flowers, trees, buildings, and so on, make up yet another set of figures. Finally, visual figures appear to us when we look out into the real world—that is, when we look up from books, magazines, newspapers, and TV and movie screens. Whatever we look at, if there is something to be seen, we see it as figure, or figures, against background. This fact of perceptual life is so much with us that it seems superfluous to mention it—but so is gravitational attraction, and that concept has proven useful in physical theory. We begin our discussion of perceptual organization, then, with what seems to be the unit of organized experience, the figure.

What constitutes a figure? The main and most likely the indispensable ingredient is *contour,* or *border.* Several lines of evidence support this assertion, some of them already mentioned. In a perfectly homogeneous field (by definition, a field with no contours), highly saturated colors rapidly fade into an achromatic fog. More directly relevant is the perceptual fate of a figure with a blurred border. Such a figure can be created by projecting an image out of focus or, more simply, by casting a shadow with relatively diffuse light. If a large figure with a blurred border is carefully fixated, very shortly the figure will disappear, apparently fusing with its background.

The disappearance of figures with blurred borders is reminiscent of two already familiar instances of disappearance—stabilized images and afterimages. In all these cases we might argue that the stimulation provided by the figures is inadequate to elicit activity in receptors that are responsive to *change.* This explanation is, as we saw, quite clear for stabilized images and afterimages. With respect to figures with blurred borders, the argument might go in the following way.

Change Receptors. Suppose you are looking at a sharply focused figure, say, a black rectangle on a white background. Normal involuntary eye-movements, as well as eye-movements that are specifically attracted by the borders of the rectangle, will carry the eye back and forth over the figure's edges. When these edges are sharp, there will be many abrupt transitions between black and white inputs. These transitions trigger activity in change receptors (the "on," "off," and "on-off" units referred to in Chapter Five). Presumably, such activity is essential for maintaining the perception of the borders. But if the rectangle you are viewing has blurred borders, then, in effect, the transition from black to white is gradual rather than abrupt. Hence, eye-movements, in interaction with the available stimulation, do not provide an adequate amount of change-receptor activity. The absence of enough such activity is tantamount to the absence of a border. The interesting consequence is not just that the border disappears (because of insufficient change activity), but that the entire figure vanishes—no border, no figure.

A simple, but convincing demonstration adds weight to the foregoing interpretation of why figures with blurred borders disappear. We might reasonably attribute the disappearance of the entire figure simply to adaptation of the retinal receptors on which the figure falls. Thus, continual fixation of a black figure on a white background might lead to localized dark-adaptation in the area of the figure; furthermore, while that area is becoming more sensitive, the surrounding area, stimulated by the white background, is becoming light-adapted and hence less sensitive. Soon an equilibrium state is reached, so that there is, in effect, no figure: The retinal response is uniform, rather than differentiated as is the physical stimulus field.

This interpretation places no special emphasis on the border. Although it may have other weaknesses, its major flaw is quickly revealed by a simple maneuver. After fixating on the blurred figure, and watching it disappear, move the figure slightly but abruptly. For example, if the figure is being projected onto a screen or a wall, lightly tap or jiggle the projector. The entire figure will reappear. Notice that most of the figure still lies over the original area of stimulation, but it is the complete figure which reappears, not just the part that has been moved onto an area previously unstimulated by the figure. The perceptual fate of the figure follows the status of its border.

Embedded Figures. Another way of destroying a figure by interfering with the integrity of its border is to embed it in a more complex design that incorporates its contours. An example is given in Figure 7.1. Its own contours now are serving other functions, and the simpler figure loses its identity. However, given proper instructions and the ability to screen out the embedding context, a person can discover the hidden figure; in this sense the simple figure is not eliminated, but rather fails to emerge because it is relatively ineffective in the competition for attention.

The importance of the "ability to screen out the embedding context" has a firm basis in empirical research. It has been established most notably in the extensive work of Herman Witkin and his collaborators (Witkin, Dyk, Fat-

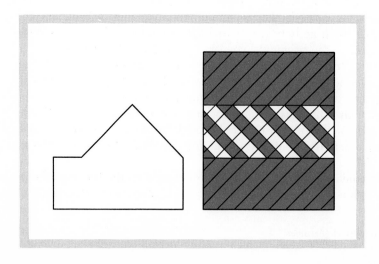

Figure 7.1 Example of an embedded figure. The simple figure on the left is contained in the more complex one on the right. (Adapted from Witkin, 1959.)

Figure 7.2 A reversible figure. One cross stands out as "figure" for a while and the other serves as background; then the two crosses switch roles—with no comparable change in the physical stimuli.

erson, Goodenough, and Karp, 1962) that there are reliable and general individual differences in such an ability. For example, some people can quickly find an embedded figure, once shown it in isolation, while for others this task is difficult, if not impossible. The same people who can easily overcome the contextual effect in the embedded-figures task also perform well in other situations requiring a similar analytic ability. In one such situation an observer sits in a dark room and must set a luminous rod upright, or vertical. The rod is surrounded by a luminous frame, which is tilted. Some people, in this *rod-and-frame test*, are heavily influenced by the orientation of the frame, and will accept as upright a setting of the rod that leaves it parallel to the sides of the frame, but far off the actual vertical, failing to use the cues to verticality provided by the orientation of their own bodies. The analytic-approach to tasks of this sort is referred to as *field-independence*, the opposite style as *field-dependence*. (A fuller account of this personality characteristic is given in Chapter Eighteen. Incidentally, our present digression from the topic of contour formation illustrates how readily one can move in psychology from a basic process like figure formation to a consideration of problems that seem far removed in complexity and perhaps of far greater intrinsic interest than their simple starting point.)

To return to our starting point, we have seen that, in their formation, figures are highly vulnerable to disrupting effects; if their contours are weakened by blurring, for example, or pre-empted by embedding them in a more complex design, figures either disappear or simply do not even appear. Another manifestation of the same principle is found in a phenomenon called *reversible figures*.

PERCEPTUAL FLUCTUATIONS

Reversible Figures. Reversible figures may take several forms. Perhaps the simplest is shown in Figure 7.2. Here, you will see, one figure stands out from its background, but after a period of continual viewing, ground becomes figure, and the original figure recedes into the background. This fluctuation proceeds in a fairly cyclical fashion.

A similar case of reversible figures is shown in Figure 7.3. Here, one first sees the silhouette of a vase, but soon the colored area that constitutes the vase becomes background, and two profiles, facing each other, emerge as figure. Again, the fluctuation between vase and faces continues in a regular, periodic manner. Indeed, once a reversal has first occurred, it is difficult to prevent further fluctuations through any sort of self-instruction.

Figure 7.3 A classical illustration of figure-ground reversal. It is possible to see either the color region as figure, a vase, and the white as ground, or the white portion as figure, two profiles, and the color as ground. The two possible organizations tend to alternate repeatedly with continued inspection.

Reversible Perspective. Somewhat more complex instances of figure reversal involve more than just figure-ground interchange. One of the best known of these, the *Necker cube*, was first described by the geologist Louis Necker in 1832; an example is given in Figure 7.4. Notice, on examining the cube, that it undergoes periodic shifts in apparent orientation. A similar type of reversal is provided by the staircase, depicted in Figure 7.5.

All of the examples we have cited are characterized by a perceptual fluctuation that has no counterpart in the physical stimulus. Clearly, the fluctuation is a function of changes that occur in the visual system itself. These changes, in turn, come about as a function of exposure, though not necessarily a lengthy one, to a given stimulus pattern. Thus, the primary basis for reversible figures must lie in some kind of adaptation process within the visual system, undoubtedly one that occurs at a fairly high level —perhaps cortical—in the system. The exact nature of the adaptation, as well as its locus, is still not well understood.

Individual Differences. Figure reversal is a common experience of virtually everyone who is exposed to the kinds of stimulus patterns shown. There are reliable differences, however, in the rate at which people report the fluctuations. If reversal is a product of some type of cortical adaptation, or perhaps inhibition, then individual differences in reversal rate may reflect an important quantitative difference among individuals in the functioning of their nervous systems. As with other such attempts to use individual differences in basic parameters of visual functioning as indexes of cortical efficiency, research on reversal rate has met with some success. For example, it has been found that people suffering from diffuse (that is, gross and unlocalized) brain damage exhibit slower reversal rates of the Necker cube than do normal control subjects (Levine and Spivack, 1962). But in somewhat similar studies, results purporting to show perceptual differences between brain-damaged and control persons turned out to be better interpreted as differences in the way various groups understood the experimenter's instructions. The same problem of interpretation may pertain to the experiments on the rate of Necker cube reversal.

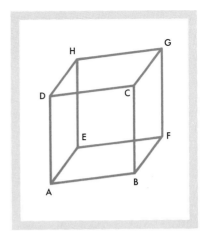

Figure 7.4 Another ambiguous figure. The cube may be seen in either of two ways: the nearest surface is either the quadrilateral A,B,C,D, or E,F,G,H. The two replace each other with continued inspection.

THE ORIGIN
OF CONTOURS

So far we have focused on the crucial role of contour in figure formation and maintenance. We have not yet asked about the origin of contours themselves. Here again, the question may seem trivial, since the answer must be self-evident. Surely, contours arise (given enough time and no disrupting influences) wherever there is an abrupt change in visual stimulation. That is, perceptual contours are the phenomenal counterpart of sharp physical discontinuities. These discontinuities may occur with respect to any of the three basic attributes of luminous energy: intensity, wavelength, and saturation.

Figure 7.5 Another reversible figure. The apparent orientation of the staircase fluctuates, with continual exposure, between two alternatives. It may be seen either as though viewed from above or from below.

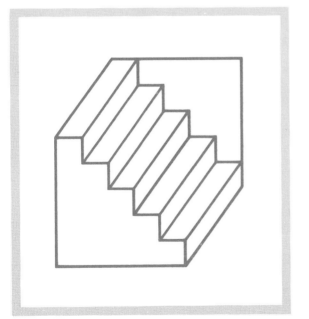

Mach Bands. There would seem little more to say here about the origin of contours if it were not for a phenomenon that does not quite fit the above specification. Under certain stimulus conditions that are not characterized by sharp discontinuities, perceptual contours are nevertheless evident. Such contours are known as *Mach bands,* or *Mach rings* (depending on their shape), named in honor of a nineteenth-century physicist-philosopher-psychologist, Ernst Mach (1838–1916), who discovered and investigated them.

It is difficult to illustrate Mach bands photographically; Figure 7.6 is an imperfect attempt at such an illustration. There is no corresponding physical line for the black line in the figure. That is, if you were to carefully probe the stimulus with a meter that measured light intensity, no abrupt drop in luminous intensity would be noted as the probe passed over the place where the line appears. However, this does not mean that the apparent line is unrelated to physical stimulation. On the contrary, Mach bands appear only under certain, specifiable conditions. In essence, the Mach band is the product of the spatial *distribution* of light, rather than of a narrowly localized segment of light. If light is distributed over a surface in a manner depicted graphically in Figure 7.7, then Mach bands will appear at the points indicated, where the rate of change in illumination intensity undergoes an abrupt change.

When the perceptual output (in this case Mach bands) departs from a single, one-to-one correspondence with stimulus input (there is no line in the physical stimulus), it is quite obvious that the mediating mechanism (the visual system) is imposing its own properties on the relation between input and output. This is really true, though less obvious, even when there is no distortion, for without the mediating mechanism there would be no output at all. But special cases are especially instructive, and Mach bands have in this sense posed an interesting problem for the theorist. The most ambitious and successful attempt to account for Mach bands in terms of modern knowledge about the neurophysiology of the visual system has been made by Floyd Ratliff (1965), who bases his explanation on the notion of excitatory and inhibitory interactions. (The details of this account are far too intricate for us to present here, but they can be found, along with a fascinating biographical sketch of Ernst Mach, in Ratliff's book, *Mach Bands.*)

THE ONTOGENETIC DEVELOPMENT
OF FIGURE-GROUND SEGREGATION

Since, as we have said, the perceptual world is built on figures, you might expect figure-ground segregation to be a primitive visual function, in the same sense in which we called brightness discrimination primitive in Chapter Six. Although conclusive evidence on a point like this is rather hard to come by, there is a strong suggestion of the ontogenetic primitiveness of figure-ground segregation in the work of a German psychologist, M. von Senden. In his book, translated under the title *Space and Sight*, von Senden has compiled reports on the perceptual functioning of people who, having been born blind by virtue of cataracts of the lens, had their sight restored through surgical operation. These were people, then, who had had no visual experiences up until the time they recovered from their operations and the bandages were removed. It seems safe to assume that whatever visual capabilities they manifested were developmentally primitive in the sense

Figure 7.6 Model for producing visual Mach bands. A cardboard disk is constructed in which a white star shape is drawn on a black background. On the left, the stationary disk is seen mounted on a wheel ready to be rotated. On the right is the rapidly rotating disk. (Teitelbaum, 1967.)

of being uninfluenced by any opportunities for visual perceptual learning. They were, in effect, visual infants, but mature reporters of their newly acquired visual experience. Even though the evidence presented by von Senden is anecdotal, rather than an account of carefully controlled experiments, at least one conclusion seems justified. These patients were aware of the presence of visual figures: They were capable of figure-ground segregation.

That this function is intact in visually naive persons is all the more interesting in view of their inability to do much more with visual stimulation. They could not, for example, discriminate among simple shapes as easily and as readily as normal adults; nor could they recognize visual figures as being the same as ones they had previously seen. Some of the patients were able to accomplish tasks of this latter sort, but only after a lengthy and difficult period of visual learning. In terms used by one of the foremost of contemporary psychological theorists, Donald O. Hebb, who found support in von Senden's book for some of his own concepts, newly sighted patients are capable of perceiving "figural unity" but not "figural identity" (Hebb, 1949). For "figural unity" read "figure-ground segregation."

Figure 7.7 One way to provide a distribution of light that yields Mach bands; the graph shows how illumination level (L_m) varies over a surface that is lighted according to the method sketched. The "Mach bands" that appear on this surface are exaggerated by painting for illustrative purposes. (Ratliff, 1965.)

Other, more direct evidence for the primitiveness of figure-ground segregation is implicit in the work, referred to in Chapter Six, by Fantz and others on visual fixation in human infants. We cited that research for its relevance to the problem of acuity, but it quite clearly also bears on the issue at hand. It seems a reasonable inference

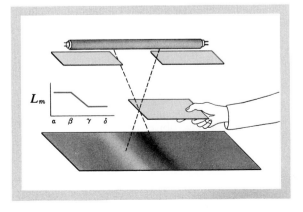

that biased fixation, of the sort that very young infants exhibit, implies a capacity for discrimination that must be based, at the very least, on figure-ground segregation.

Organization of Figures in Two-Dimensional Space

The typical visual field contains a collection of separate figures. Considered strictly as physical stimuli, the items in such a collection have no pattern, but as perceptual units the figures exist as elements of an organized whole. The individual figures contribute to the total pattern and also derive some of their own properties from the pattern of which they are a part. This notion forms the basic tenet of one of the major perceptual theories, Gestalt psychology. (The German word *Gestalt* translates in this context as "configuration" or "pattern.")

THE GESTALT THEORY
OF PERCEPTUAL ORGANIZATION

Gestalt theory was formulated by a small group of psychologists working together in Germany in the early decades of the present century and then in the United States after the rise of Naziism in the 1930s. The leader of this group was Max Wertheimer, and his chief students and collaborators were Kurt Koffka and Wolfgang Köhler. The Gestaltists were in revolt against the approach to perceptual theory, and to psychology in general, that had dominated both Europe and the United States since the foundation of Wundt's laboratory in 1879. That traditional approach, known as Structuralism, had many defects, according to the Gestaltists; its major error lay in its acceptance and promulgation of what was referred to as the *mosaic hypothesis*.

Criticism of Structuralism. In the passages that follow, Köhler characterizes the mosaic hypothesis:

> The most fundamental assumption of Introspectionism [a synonym for Structuralism] is therefore this: true sensory facts are local phenomena which depend upon local stimulation, but not at all upon stimulating conditions in their environment.
> . . . first, local sensation depends upon local stimulation. It does not depend upon other processes in the nervous system, not even upon those which issue from adjacent parts of the same organ. The only assumption which can explain this independence of local sensation is conduction of processes along insulated pathways from one point of the sense organ to one point in the brain, where activity is accompanied by sensory experience.
> What happens at the end of a one-way street depends upon the events which happened at its entrance at an earlier moment. According to the [Structuralist] picture of sensory functioning, objective experience must be composed of purely local sensory facts, the characteristics of which are

strictly determined by corresponding peripheral stimuli. For the sake of the maintenance of order, processes in individual pathways and in corresponding cells of the brain have been separated from one another and from the surrounding tissue. It follows that no processes in other parts of the nervous system can alter sensory experience. . . . Thus sensory experience is a mere mosaic, an entirely additive aggregation of facts; and this mosaic is just as rigid as is its physiological basis. (Köhler, 1959, pp. 56–57, 58, 67–68.)

Köhler, as the spokesman for Gestalt theory, goes on to argue that the Structuralist deals with apparent exceptions to the mosaic hypothesis by invoking the concept of association, or learning. That is, the originally isolated sensory events can be made to interact, but only through arbitrary, fortuitous association. Perceptual *organization*, then, becomes a product of learning, rather than an intrinsic, given property of experience.

Field Effects. The Gestaltist alternative to the mosaic hypothesis, and its supplementary principle of association, is that organization is intrinsic to the perceptual system. Interaction among elements—as, for example, in color induction by contrast—is the rule, rather than the exception. This built-in organization in perceptual experience has its counterpart in the nervous system, which is also characterized by interactions among parts. The insulated, point-to-point conduction of neural events described by classical neurophysiology does indeed occur, but an additional principle applies—namely, that neural events which are both spatially and temporally separated can nevertheless influence each other. The brain acts not only like a telephone switchboard, with no "cross-talk" occurring among lines, but also like a dynamic physical *field*, in which "action at a distance" is an intrinsic feature. Just as no mechanical links, such as ropes or chains, are necessary for the moon to affect the tides on Earth, so no *direct* neural connections are required for events localized in one part of the brain to influence events in another part.

In summary, the Gestalt position is two-fold: (1) organization (that is, interaction among units) is intrinsic to perceptual experience, and specifically is not always the product of learning; (2) activity in the brain that accompanies perceptual experience must also be characterized by built-in "field effects." The latter point enters Gestalt theory as an inference from the former, and its validity is not crucial to the validity of the Gestaltist description of perceptual experience. Indeed, Köhler's attack on Structuralism serves as a warning not to let one's preconceptions about neurophysiology so bias one's psychological observations that they become distorted. Rather, the psychological facts should serve as a guide to what the neurophysiological processes must be like.

Thus, it is not crucial whether the "brain field" that Köhler postulated is the best way to describe the neurophysiological underpinning of perceptual experience. Other brain models may very well do as good a job and fit better with current neurophysiological knowledge. But the Gestaltists' psychological contribution remains: They have provided a myriad of examples of perceptual organization, and have induced from them a few simple comprehensive principles. Some of these examples, and the principles they exemplify, are given in the next several figures.

The Gestalt Principles of Organization

In a collection of figures, for which there is no other competing basis of organization, grouping will occur as a function of the closeness, or proximity of units. This principle is illustrated in Figure 7.8.

Although proximity is a powerful basis of figural organization and seems to occur immediately upon presentation of a stimulus, there is evidence that organization takes time to develop. This evidence comes from experiments in which a pattern that could be organized into rows or columns by virtue of proximity is briefly presented to a group of subjects. The subjects are asked, as part of another task, to reproduce what they see by placing marbles in a matrix of depressions (like a Chinese Checkers board). Many subjects at first fail to perceive the pattern inherent in the stimulus; their placement of the marbles suggests that the elements are uniformly spaced over the field. On repeated trials, the exposure duration is gradually increased (as in an ascending method of limits). Some persons who at first saw a homogeneous pattern where there might have been a differentiated one switch to the latter when exposure duration is lengthened sufficiently. A few, however,

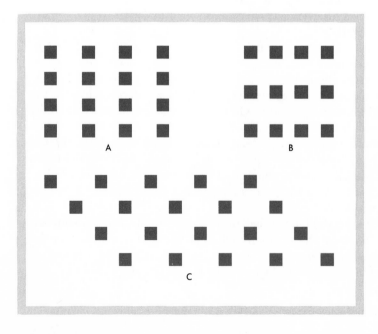

Figure 7.8 The influence of proximity on figural organization. (A) Proximity leads to an organization into columns. (B) The figure is organized into rows. (C) Diagonal lines are perceived. Note that the diagonals may run either from top left to bottom right, or from top right to bottom left. Proximity favors neither of the two possibilities though the top-left-to-bottom-right orientation seems to predominate.

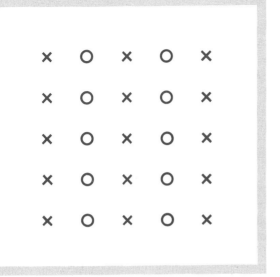

Figure 7.9 Perceptual organization through similarity in the shape of elements.

never perceive the differentiated pattern even at very long exposure durations (Krech and Calvin, 1953).

Of further interest is the rather high correlation between intelligence and ease in recognizing the differentiated pattern; that is, those persons with relatively high scores on the vocabulary subscale of the Wechsler intelligence test (which asks for definitions of words of increasing difficulty) tend to pick up the perceptual pattern relatively quickly.

SIMILARITY

If there is no competing basis of organization, the elements of a collection will tend to be perceptually grouped according to their similarity. This principle is illustrated in Figure 7.9. It would not be surprising to find that organization through similarity takes time to develop, as it does in the case of proximity, but such data are yet to be reported.

COMMON FATE

The principle of common fate cannot be illustrated without stimulus elements that move. You might imagine, however, a collection of dots that are apparently randomly scattered over a surface, as in the left-hand panel of Figure 7.10. Now, pick out a subset of those dots that would form a common figure if there was some basis for their perceptual organization, such as similarity (we have effectively ruled out proximity by the way in which the dots have been located). For example, we can make the letter M emerge, as in the right-hand panel of Figure 7.10, simply by darkening certain of the dots. We could obtain the same result—the emergence of the letter M—if those same dots, instead of being darkened, were all moved together. While in motion, the dots would form a coherent pattern, by virtue of a type of similarity—that is, their common motion, or more generally (to use the Gestalt phrase) their common fate.

It is common fate that destroys the effectiveness of the protective coloration certain animals enjoy. So long as an animal remains motionless, it is very difficult for potential predators to detect it (Plate 7)—an obvious advantage in the struggle for survival. This indeed may be the basis for the reflexive freezing that many species resort to when in danger, and it is

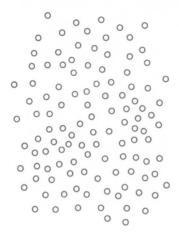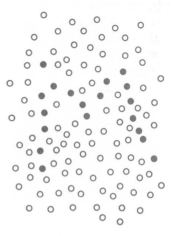

Figure 7.10 The letter "M" emerges from the random assortment of circles in the panel on the left when certain of them are blackened; figural emergence would also occur if those same circles, unblackened, were suddenly moved, all together in the same direction ("common fate").

certainly the basis for the voluntary freezing that well-camouflaged soldiers are trained to perfect if they wish to go unnoticed by the enemy.

GOOD CONTINUATION

A collection of elements may be so arranged that as a viewer scans the array, the elements seem to be properly located with respect to one another, just as the successive notes of a melody seem to fit together. When such "good continuation" prevails in spatially distributed visual elements, it is as though the pattern were generated by the smooth movement of a single element over each of the positions occupied by the separate figures that make up the actual pattern. An example is given in Figure 7.11(A). By means of good continuation, an organized pattern can be created in the absence of any of the other principles of organization.

There may be occasions, of course, when two or more of the various principles will conflict. For example, good continuation may conflict with similarity, or with proximity, as illustrated in Figure 7.11(B). In these cases, one of the principles may dominate, or continued observation may result in a shift in organization from one to another principle, much like the fluctuating patterns that characterize instances of reversible figures. One rule does seem to apply to these cases of conflicting bases of organization. Only one pattern can occur at a time. If multiple patterns do emerge from a given configuration, their appearance is serial rather than simultaneous.

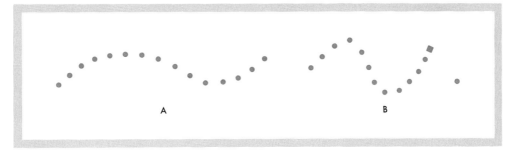

Figure 7.11 (A) An illustration of the principle of "good continuation."
(B) How good continuation might prevail over similarity in perceptual
organization; the square element "belongs" to the wave-shaped figure,
whereas the circular element to the right is perceptually isolated.

CLOSURE

A basic tenet of Gestalt theory is that figures, and patterns composed of
figures, will be perceived if conditions allow. Indeed, "organization" not
only *describes* what typically happens when a person is presented with
sensory stimulation, but in Gestalt theory it is also a motivating force: Perception *will* be organized, or patterned, if it possibly can be. One deterrent
to organization is gaps, or missing elements, in a potentially integrated
pattern. Just as it is difficult to extract the meaning from a sentence if some
of the words in the sentence are deleted or not understood, so too it's difficult to perceive a pattern if parts of it are missing.

For example, a strong contour, as we have seen, is conducive to the formation and maintenance of a good figure. Contours may be weakened in a
variety of ways, as we have also seen. One simple way to weaken a contour
is to break up its continuity by removing pieces of it. Figure 7.12 shows
several stages in the degradation of a simple, familiar contour. Even though
it is apparent that greatly degraded contours lose some of their effectiveness
as bases for figure-formation, nevertheless you can still perceive a circular
figure, perhaps even from the weakest contour illustrated. Gestalt theory
has raised this observation to the status of a major principle of organization
—and by implication a major attribute of the functioning of the brain. Gaps
in stimulation are filled in by the perceptual mechanism in the service of
creating good figures and organized patterns. This principle is called
closure.

THE GENERALITY
OF THE ORGANIZING TENDENCY

To the Gestaltist, as we have mentioned, perceptual organization not only
does occur, but in some sense it must occur. Closure, as well as perceptual
organization according to the other Gestalt principles, is an obvious instance

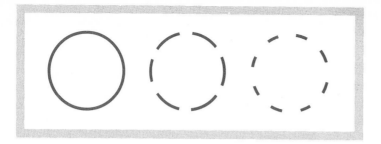

Figure 7.12 Successively degraded circles. Even the figure with the least original contour remaining retains its circular appearance; an example of the "closure principle" in perceptual organization.

of a much more general and pervasive tendency. Just as perceptual gaps must be filled in, so too must gaps at higher levels of functioning. Recall the tension that persists until the last blank space in a crossword puzzle is filled, and the pleasure that accompanies the solution of any puzzle or intellectual problem that was undertaken "for its own sake." What is a problem, after all, but a set of symbolic elements that are almost but not quite satisfactorily organized? And what is the solution of a problem if not the missing element that enables us to integrate the components of the problem?

A similar view can be applied to the analysis of wit and humor. A good joke consists also of two parts: (1) a set of elements that make sense, but not quite enough sense, and (2) a set (the "punch line") that completes the sense of the first part or imparts additional meaning to the first part that was only vaguely hinted at, or implicit in it. Many theorists have tried their hand at an analysis of humor—which certainly is a profound and pervasive attribute of "human nature"—among them Sigmund Freud and Arthur Koestler. Freud's approach has some Gestalt flavor, but he also gives great weight to the content of jokes, puns, and so on, while perhaps playing down their abstract, formal properties. That is, Freud emphasizes the joke as a vehicle for the somewhat disguised, and hence relatively safe, expression of repressed impulses, especially the sexual and aggressive ones. Koestler, in his book *Insight and Outlook*, focuses more on the structure of humorous behavior, in closer conformity with the Gestalt approach. The following example was first used by Freud and later employed by Koestler:

> A man about town showed his devotion to a young actress by lavish gifts. Being a respectable girl, she took the first opportunity of discouraging his attentions by telling him that her heart already belonged to another man. "I never aspired as high as that," was his polite answer.

The sexual connotation of the joke is obvious, but that hardly accounts for its success. One can, however, see in the "polite answer" a multitude of meanings that bring out, and to some extent ridicule, the implications of the girl's reference to "her heart." Of course, the punch line is even more successful than it might have been through the double meaning of the word "high." It has both a direct anatomical reference and a metaphorical one. He might have said, "It's not your heart I'm after," which would have been funny, though perhaps too blatant. But in using the word "high," he combined a more subtle reference to anatomy with a complex message that is simultaneously cynical, hostile, and face-saving ("It's not love I'm after, but something that you—hypocritically at that—consider baser, and besides for the latter I really don't need you, though you can't blame me for trying."). The punch line, in the form of the playboy's retort, at once closes one gap and opens and closes several others, all with great economy. In a "flash," to use Koestler's term, a host of temporarily unconnected elements, and groups of elements, are neatly packaged, and thereby disposed of.

Geometric Illusions

The so-called geometric or optical illusions have long been of interest to the perceptual theorist. To the Gestaltist they provide further, compelling instances of the operation of "field effects": Elements are perceived in relation to the totality of stimulation and not simply as a function of the local stimulation that is their immediate source. Of course, in Gestalt theory, field effects characterize all perception, including the vast number of percepts which might be called "veridical" rather than illusory—that is, those wherein a person's perceptual response to a stimulus corresponds closely to impersonal measures of the stimulus. The geometric illusions are of special interest only because they dramatize what is less obviously true of perception in general. In this regard, the analogy is often made between illusions and abnormalities of behavior. It is often argued that the latter concern the personality theorist (as contrasted with the clinician, who has a practical interest in them), because through exaggeration and magnification they reveal what may be hidden in the mundane behaviors of the normal person.

In his classic work *Principles of Gestalt Psychology*, Kurt Koffka (1935) poses the question, "Why do things look as they do?" One answer, which he rejects, is attributed to the naive layman (as well as to the Structuralist). That answer, in effect, runs, "Because they are what they are." But, Koffka carefully demonstrates, things do not always look the way "they are," and the geometric illusions are a good case in point. Koffka's own answer, by the way, is stated in a manner that may seem trivial at first, but it gets at the heart of Gestalt theory: "Because of the field organization to which the proximal stimulus distribution gives rise" (Koffka, 1935, p. 98).

FIELD EFFECTS OR LEARNING?
THE MÜLLER-LYER ILLUSION

The Gestalt interpretation of illusions is not the only one available, of course. Some of the standard examples of illusions are amenable to a type of interpretation that is consistent with the Structuralist emphasis on learning. A very good case in point is provided by one of the best known of the optical illusions, the Müller-Lyer illusion, as shown in Figure 7.13. "Objectively"—that is, as measured by a ruler—the two vertical lines are equal in length; perceptually, the one labeled B is the longer. This distortion in perceived length is clearly attributable to some effect associated with the short, diagonal lines appended to the vertical lines, since in their absence there is no illusion. But is the effect the product of "field forces" or of learning? If the latter, how might learning enter into the illusory effect?

One early argument was that the Müller-Lyer illusion occurs because we see the two vertical lines as being at different distances from us. Since they are casting retinal images of the same size, then the one that seems farther away (B) must also be longer,

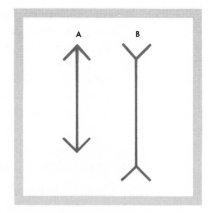

Figure 7.13 The Müller-Lyer illusion. Line B seems longer than line A despite their physical equality.

as indicated in Figure 7.14. If it must be longer, we see it as longer. But why should line B seem farther away than A? Here is where the diagonals make their contribution.

Look at Figure 7.15. You see a drawing of two books. Obviously, the one on the left depicts a book opened up with its pages facing you. The one on the right has its spine close to you; its front and back covers are visible, but the pages are not. The edges of the book covers on the left are closer to you than the spine, while the opposite is true of the book on the right. If the two books, as total objects, are about the same distance from you, then the spine of the one on the left is farther away than the spine of the book on the right. Since the two spines cast the same length retinal images, however, the one on the left must be the longer.

Clearly, the "books" in Figure 7.15 are merely elaborations of the line elements of the Müller-Lyer pair of Figure 7.13. This example does not prove that every instance of the Müller-Lyer illusion is the result of its being

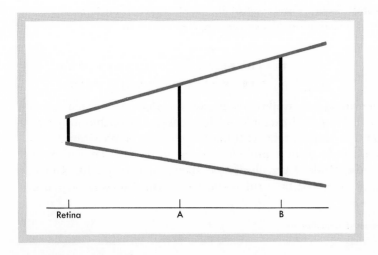

Retina   A   B

Figure 7.14 To cast equal-sized images on the retina, lines at different distances from the retina must be unequal in length; the farther the line (compare A and B) the longer it must be for the retinal image to stay the same.

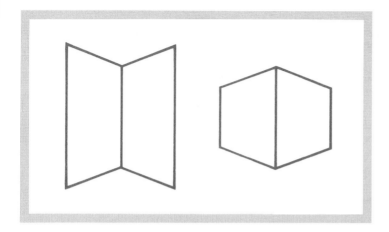

Figure 7.15 How the oblique lines in the Müller-Lyer figure may contribute to differences in the perceived distance of the "shaft" and hence to differences in perceived length.

seen as a fragment of a larger scene, the details of which would reinforce a difference in the apparent distance of the two lines in question and hence also in their apparent length. It does, however, suggest how learning, and the expectations acquired through learning, *might* generate the illusory effect that the Gestalt theorist would attribute to simple, built-in field effects.

Cross-Cultural Differences. There is, moreover, some very interesting evidence in support of a learning interpretation that comes from a cross-cultural comparison of susceptibility to illusions. In this study (Segall, Campbell, and Herskovits, 1966), illusory figures of several types were shown to people from a variety of cultures, including citizens of the United States. Predictions were made about the relation between susceptibility to certain illusions and the type of physical environment characteristic of these various cultures. Western cultures, for example, are replete with man-made structures which are composed of right-angled components. By contrast, there are cultures in which the environment is relatively free of such structures. People growing up in the "carpentered environment" typical of Western culture, the argument goes, develop habits of perceptual inference whereby they can perceive two-dimensional drawings of acute or obtuse angles as right angles with their legs extending into the third dimension. Such an inference is less likely among people for whom it has less validity by virtue of the relative paucity of right-angled structures in their environments.

With the above rationale, Segall and his colleagues measured susceptibility to the Müller-Lyer illusion (as well as to other illusory figures) in people who lived in more or less carpentered environments. Included were samples of people from 12 African locations and one in the Philippines. Also tested were some white South Africans living in Johannesburg and a large group of college students (see Segall, *et al.,* Chapter 5, for further details of the samples and how they were chosen for study). The researchers attempted to sample various degrees of carpentered environments, in addition to a

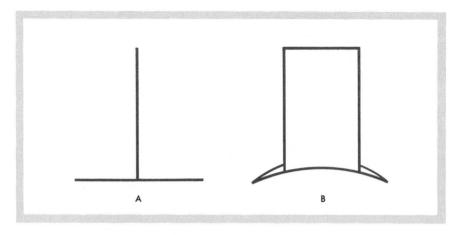

Figure 7.16 (A) The vertical-horizontal illusion. The vertical line seems longer than the horizontal, though the two lines are equal in length. (B) The top-hat illusion, a variant of the vertical-horizontal illusion. The stove pipe portion of the hat seems longer than the brim, though they are physically equal.

variable (extent of open vistas) relevant to predictions about illusory figures other than the Müller-Lyer figure. At the extreme "noncarpentered" end of the dimension fell the African Bushmen, described by the experimenters as occupying houses that are circular in configuration and living "in an environment in which rectangular objects are virtually nonexistent." In all cases, the non-Western environments are characterized as less carpentered than that of the Western subjects.

The data on the extent of the illusory effect were collected with great care, far exceeding that associated with previous pioneering efforts of this sort (for example, Rivers, 1901, 1905). Again, details of procedure and data analysis can be found in the fascinating book by Segall and his collaborators. The results can be briefly summarized here, however: Extensive cultural differences were found and they were, with some minor but puzzling exceptions, as predicted. For example, the Bushmen were among the groups least susceptible to the Müller-Lyer illusion, whereas the American subjects (residents of Evanston, Illinois, both children and adults, and Northwestern University students) were the most susceptible. Because of data obtained on other illusory figures, such as the vertical-horizontal illusion (see Figure 7.16(A)), for which both American and Bushmen adult subjects showed average susceptibility, we can reject the hypothesis that differences on the Müller-Lyer illusion result from differences in rapport between experimenter and subject, subjects' intelligence, understanding of instructions, and so on. Considered *in toto,* the results quite convincingly support the position that learning plays a major role in determining susceptibility to many illusory effects. Furthermore—and this may be the most important contribution of the study—susceptibility to illusions is not a general trait, but rather is specific both to the type of illusory figure and to the kind of environment in which the subjects lived.

OTHER COMMON GEOMETRIC ILLUSIONS

The Vertical-Horizontal Illusion. A host of illusory figures has been devised; many of them, however, are merely elaborations of certain basic geometric illusions. For example, the top hat illusion is depicted in Figure 7.16(B). Note how much longer the stove pipe portion looks than the brim. This illusion is undoubtedly built on the simpler, but equally compelling vertical-horizontal illusion shown in Figure 7.16(A). In general, vertical lines appear longer than horizontal lines, although the effect is enhanced if the vertical line bisects the horizontal.

Illusory Curvature. The Müller-Lyer and vertical-horizontal illusions are characterized by a distortion in the apparent length of lines. In some illusory figures, parallel lines seem to converge or diverge, and in others straight lines appear curved. The version of the latter depicted in Figure 7.17 is usually attributed to Hering and is based on a type originally created by Zollner. The effect here is one of apparent curvature. In Zollner's illusion *per se*, shown in Figure 7.18, the cross-hatchings impart an impression of divergence and convergence to the objectively parallel vertical lines. For the illusions shown in Figures 7.17 and 7.18, an explanation similar to the one applied to the Müller-Lyer figure is pertinent—that is, in viewing these two-dimensional figures, a person may get an impression of depth. If so, segments of the straight lines may seem to be at different distances from the observer. As a result, the lines may "need" to appear curved, or otherwise distorted if the dimensions of the retinal images they cast are to be reconciled with their apparent differences in distance. Indeed, it is quite easy to

Figure 7.17 An illusion illustrating shape distortion. The two horizontal lines are straight and parallel, but appear bowed in opposite directions.

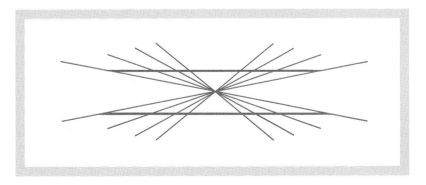

Figure 7.18 One version of Zollner's illusion. The vertical lines are parallel but seem tilted.

generate an illusion based on apparent differences in distance, as is illustrated in Figure 7.19. The vertical "poles," which are objectively equal in length, seem to be quite different—those that appear to be farther away also appear to be longer.

Illusory Size Differences. A third class of illusory effect involves apparent size. For a classic example, attributed to Wundt, see Figure 7.20, p. 238. Although the two figures are exactly congruent, the lower one appears considerably larger than the upper one. In this case, there seems to be no concomitant difference in apparent distance (that is, the bottom figure does not seem closer to the observer than the upper one). This may be one of those illusions that cannot be explained by concepts of learning and expectancies.

In general, the geometric illusions pose an interesting problem for the perceptual theorist. They nicely illustrate the divergent views of the two competing approaches, the assumption of inherent organization of Gestalt theory and the invocation of learning of Structuralism to account for perceptual organization. But theory aside, awareness of the possibility of illusions also has practical impact. Judgments or actions based on superficial appearances may be quite misinformed, for appearances can be misleading. In this same vein, of course, knowledge about illusions can be used to create desired effects, as in the advice given to stout women not to wear clothing decorated with horizontal stripes.

As with many other fundamental perceptual phenomena, there has been considerable investigation of illusions from a developmental point of view, beyond the cross-cultural study of Segall. Such research, besides its intrinsic interest, has potential bearing on the theoretical issue of whether particular illusions results from Gestalt-like field effects or from expectancies built on learning. If an illusion were attributable primarily to learning, we might expect that the illusory effect would increase with age, though perhaps leveling off as soon as enough time has passed for the necessary learning to occur. On the other hand, if the illusory effect were "built-in," simply reflecting in perception the field effects that characterize brain functioning, then we might expect no developmental changes in susceptibility to illusions.

Interestingly enough, the data support neither position. There is one class of illusory figures that have their maximal effects at the youngest ages. Included in this class are the Müller-Lyer and vertical-horizontal illusions.

There is another class of illusions that show increasing effectiveness with increasing age, but these illusions seem to depend on ideational structures that could only develop through experience. The size-weight illusion is one of these. A person is shown two boxes, one much larger than the other, but they are otherwise identical (including their weight). If the person then lifts the boxes, the larger box will seem lighter than the smaller box. Obviously, an expectancy that the larger of two otherwise identically appearing objects will also be the heavier underlies this illusion. Until that expectancy has had the opportunity to develop fully, as a result of extensive experience with the sizes and weights of objects, the size-weight illusion will be weak. Thus, it is not surprising that some illusions will increase in strength with age. But to find a large set of illusions following the opposite developmental trend is quite surprising to both the nativism of Gestalt theory

Figure 7.19 Though the two lamp posts are equal in length, the one on the left seems shorter than the one on the right since linear perspective cues make it also seem closer.

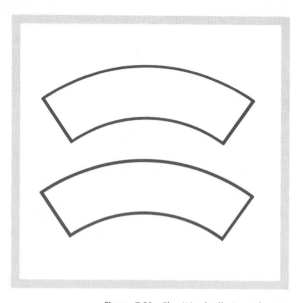

Figure 7.20 The Wundt illusion. The two figures are perfectly congruent, but the upper appears to be smaller than the lower.

and the empiricism of perceptual theories that stress learning.

There are, however, two prominent theories of development that find the results just mentioned supportive rather than embarrassing, one developed by Heinz Werner and the other by the Swiss psychologist Jean Piaget. Indeed, it was in their laboratories that a good deal of the developmental data on illusions was collected. Although the models of Werner and Piaget are quite different in many respects, they both call for a decrease in susceptibility to illusions of the first class and other field-effects as a person develops more mature modes of perceptual and intellectual functioning. And they both can handle illusions of the second class that are mediated by well-developed ideational processes.

There has been relatively little research on the response of lower animals to the various geometric illusions. What has been done, however, suggests that susceptibility to illusions is not just a human weakness. For example, in one experiment (Révész, 1924), chickens were trained to peck for food from the objectively smaller of two visual figures. They were then presented with two forms like the ones shown in Figure 7.20; their preference was for the upper of the two identical forms, as though the chicks categorized it as the smaller, just as human subjects would.

Context Effects

The geometric illusions are a subclass of a broader class of perceptual phenomena called context effects. In general, context effects are the influences of concurrent psychological events on the perception of a particular stimulus. We can broaden the application of this definition if "concurrent events" include (a) the residues of preceding stimulation and (b) occurrences in systems other than the one containing the affected, or target, stimulus. Thus, we can go well beyond the restricted notion in Gestalt theory of "field effects" and assert that the perception of a stimulus element is potentially influenced by a wide variety of factors besides the very obvious one of local stimulation.

We have already discussed in some detail two subclasses of context effects, the geometric illusions and the so-called principles of organization. A thorough discussion of all other types of context effect, as broadly defined above, is beyond our present interest, but we can offer representative examples of the range of effects that psychologists have uncovered and investigated. In this regard, we can set up four logical categories of context effect. For a visual target stimulus, the context can be provided by (a) other visual stimulation currently present; (b) current stimulation in other sense modalities; (c) the presently active aftereffects, or residues, of previous visual stimulation; and (d) the aftereffects of previous nonvisual stimulation. Since a sufficient number of examples has already been given for effects of type (a) and convincing evidence for the reality of effects of type (d) is not available, we will offer examples here only from categories (b) and (c).

Good data relevant to category (b) are scarce, but there have been reports of *cross-modal* interactions, especially in experiments by Russian investigators (as reviewed by the American psychologist Ivan London, 1954). For example, it is claimed that foveal sensitivity to white light is enhanced by auditory stimulation of moderate intensity. This type of cross-modal effect may reflect direct interactions between two sensory systems, or the auditory stimulation may have an indirect effect, by raising the general level of alertness of the observer (Dember, 1960, p. 221). The latter interpretation has sound behavioral support as well as a firm basis in neurophysiological evidence.

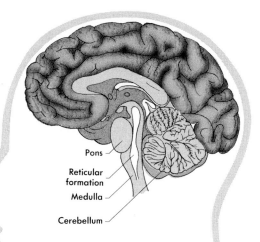

Figure 7.21 The "inside" of one hemisphere of the brain, showing the location of the reticular system. (French, 1957).

Pons
Reticular formation
Medulla
Cerebellum

The Role of Arousal. In the brain stem, as depicted in Figure 7.21, there is a system, called the *ascending reticular system* (ARS), which serves as an "arousal center." When the ARS is activated, it sends neural impulses to the cerebral cortex; one effect of these impulses seems to be to enhance cortical efficiency. The ARS itself is activated, partly from "above" (that is, from the cortex) and partly by way of branches, or "collaterals," from the various sensory systems. Thus, the picture of the visual pathways presented in Chapter Five is incomplete, for it ignores these collaterals to the ARS. Furthermore, the chain of events triggered by visual stimulation is more complex than what we previously described: While specific sensory information is finding its way back to the visual cortex, generalized input is being fed into the ARS, which in turn is priming the cortex to receive the sensory information. Thus, visual stimulation, in part, prepares for its own reception. But then, there is no reason to believe that the generalized input to the ARS is specifically relayed to the visual cortex. Rather, it is most likely that input to the ARS from any sensory system has the ultimate effect of enhancing sensitivity in all cortical sensory centers. Thus, auditory stimulation might very well be expected to increase visual sensitivity, through the mediation of the ARS.

The Russian investigators cited by London report cross-modal effects that are more difficult to explain, in that specific rather than general interactions are obtained. For example, it is claimed that concurrent auditory stimulation leads to an increase in sensitivity to light of a blue-green hue, but *decreases* sensitivity to orange-red. Such a differential effect, should it be valid, does not lend itself to explanation based on a generalized arousal of the visual system. Instead, specific auditory-visual interactions are called for.

Synesthesia. It is worth noting, in this regard, the phenomenon of auditory-visual *synesthesia*. For some people, stimulation of the auditory system with musical tones is accompanied by vivid visual experiences, typically in the form of flights of colors. This type of *fusion* of two otherwise discrete sense modalities is reportedly facilitated by certain drugs, though objective evidence on this point is hard to come by. In general, synesthesia is considered by theorists such as Werner to be a primitive mode of functioning, characteristic of the immature, the culturally primitive, and the person suffering from severe psychopathology, such as schizophrenia. But since all of us, no matter how psychologically mature, sophisticated, and mentally "healthy," are constructed on that same primitive base, we may at times *regress* to primitive modes. Thus, under the right conditions, a diluted form of synesthesia (of the sort reported by the Russian experimenters) may occur, showing up as an increase or decrease in sensitivity to various hues under auditory stimulation.

Indeed, there may be continual "cross-talk" among the sensory systems, although in the course of development this type of interchange may be suppressed. The separate senses that we take for granted may, in short, be partly the product of learning. Imagine, for example, a young girl with an especially sensitive auditory system, who at a very early age complains that certain noises (as of a vacuum cleaner) "hurt." Her parents, knowing that noise at the intensity levels in question may be annoying, but not "painful" in the same way that a bump on the head is, or a pinched finger, tell her insistently that "noise doesn't hurt." Eventually, she gets the message, and perhaps eventually noise no longer hurts her; but maybe it really did hurt before she was taught to separate hearing and pain.

The example given here of auditory-visual interaction is only one of several that have been reported. Further instances are cited in the article by London (1954) referred to earlier. Examples of more exotic types of cross-modal fusions, such as the various synesthesias, can be found in Werner's *The Comparative Psychology of Mental Development*. But whether these tenuous phenomena can be produced and studied objectively in the laboratory still remains to be seen.

FIGURAL AFTEREFFECTS

Context effects of category (c)—that is, from residues of previous stimulation within the modality in question—can be classified according to their approximate duration. There are short-term effects, mediated by some readily reversible physiological change; there are effects of longer duration, again mediated by physiological changes that are reversible, but slowly so; and there seem to be effects that may last indefinitely, and these undoubtedly result from relatively stable, perhaps permanent modifications in the organization of the nervous system—in short, from "learning." We have already encountered one example of short-term effects, the negative afterimage. The exact duration of negative afterimages is hard to trace because the image fades, in part by virtue of its being stabilized on the retina. It seems unlikely, however, that negative afterimages last much longer than about 15 to 30 minutes.

Another instance of category (c) effects is the *figural aftereffect*. This phenomenon was first studied by J.J. Gibson (1933) and was later the topic of a thorough empirical and theoretical investigation by the Gestaltist Wolfgang Köhler and his collaborators (see Köhler and Wallach, 1944). Figural aftereffects, to be described below, may be of short duration, but under certain circumstances they can extend over long periods of time, perhaps weeks or months. In this respect they seem to fit the class of intermediate duration; they probably involve changes in the brain, rather than peripheral changes, but the brain changes are different from those that are believed to subserve learning.

To produce a figural aftereffect, we might instruct a subject to stare at the X in the left panel of Figure 7.22, so as to bring the dark bar onto a fixed retinal locus. In the terminology of the literature on figural aftereffects, the bar in this example is called the *inspection figure*, or *I-figure*. After a sufficiently long exposure to the I-figure, the observer then looks at the X next to the *test figure*, or *T-figure* shown in the right panel of Figure 7.22. Note that if the fixation points (the X's) are superimposed, the two lower squares of the I-figure surround the region of the dark bar. When asked to compare the apparent distance between the two lower squares and that

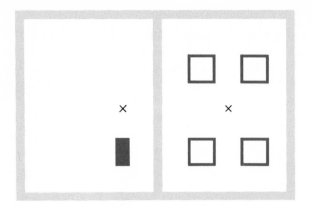

Figure 7.22 How to produce a figural aftereffect. After steady fixation for one or two minutes on the X in the left panel, fixation on the X in the right panel will reveal the aftereffect. The area occupied by the colored bar in the left panel (the inspection figure) is presumably "satiated"; this satiation perceptually spreads the lower boxes in the right panel (the test figure).

between the two upper squares, the observer will most likely say that the lower squares seem farther apart. It is this type of *spatial displacement* of parts of a T-figure that operationally defines a figural aftereffect. The example given here is only one of a large variety of figural aftereffects that can be produced with various combinations of I- and T-figures. All such aftereffects share the property of spatial displacement of T-figure contours.

The Köhler and Wallach Satiation Model. On the basis of their research and their Gestaltist conception of the functioning of the brain as a medium for field effects, Köhler and Wallach devised a model to account for figural aftereffects. In essence, the model asserts that the phenomenal distance between two contours is determined by the time it takes an electrical current to flow through the brain region between the cortical representations of the contours. The longer the duration of current flow, the farther apart the contours seem. When a particular brain region is stimulated, as during inspection of the I-figure, that region becomes *satiated*. As a result of satiation, current flow through that brain region is impeded. Hence, when the T-figure is observed, the time it takes for current to flow between the contours of the lower squares is greater than the time required for the current to flow through the unsatiated brain region that lies between the contours of the upper squares. Phenomenally, the lower squares are pushed apart.

Within the framework of this basic model, Köhler and Wallach were able to devise a considerable number of imaginative experiments. In addition, Köhler was led to make certain neurophysiological observations he might not otherwise have considered. In general, the behavioral and neurophysiological data have been favorable to the model. Despite this success, or perhaps because of it, alternative models have been proposed (see, for example, Osgood and Heyer, 1952), based on a more conventional neurophysiology.

Individual Differences. At this point, the theoretical issues related to figural aftereffects are blurred, but the phenomenon itself remains a salient characteristic of perceptual functioning. Moreover, as with many other perceptual phenomena, the attempt is being made to relate individual differences in strength of the figural aftereffect to other variables of practical interest, such as general intellectual functioning. For example, it is argued (Spitz, 1963) that the mentally retarded—people with IQ scores of less than 70—have brain processes that are slower and less amenable to both short- and long-term modification than those of more intelligent people. This presumed difference in modifiability shows up, it is claimed, in a variety of ways, including differences in ease of inducing figural aftereffects, and in the dissipation of such effects once they have been induced. As with the investigation of the correlates of individual differences in other perceptual phenomena that we have mentioned (for example, CFF, reversible figures), here, too, there is so far more promise to the hypothesis than payoff, largely because of the considerable methodological barriers that stand in the way of collecting data that can be interpreted unambiguously.

Whether we categorize long-lasting figural aftereffects as the products of learning or as some other temporary modification in brain functioning depends on our definition of learning—a topic to be discussed in later chapters. But even without a clear-cut definition of learning, we can say that certain long-term products of stimulation (products that provide the context in which present stimulation is perceived) seem to fit intuitive notions of learned effects. For example, people who are born blind but have their vision restored by surgery cannot identify visual figures; they can only tell that "something is there." They cannot easily discriminate between geometric figures of different shape, such as squares and triangles; they cannot recognize a figure seen previously; and they cannot recognize "familiar" people by vision alone. However, these basic visual skills, which normal adults take for granted, are gradually acquired. Extrapolating from these results, theorists such as D.O. Hebb (1949) argue that the same kind of *perceptual learning* takes place in all people, most extensively during infancy.

There is indeed almost no visual function, simple or complex, that is not subject to the influence of learning. Even the Gestaltist, with his emphasis on built-in organization, does not deny the possibility of a learned overlay on innate structures. Of course, some theorists demand an explanation based on learning for all perceptual phenomena beyond the level of the most primitive sensations. Somewhere between the extreme nativist and the extreme empiricist the truth probably lies.

Movement Perception

Historically, the phenomenon that gave the initial impetus to the Gestalt school of psychology was movement perception. At first glance, movement would seem to be an unlikely topic on which to challenge the prevailing position that experience is a function of local stimulation. Ordinarily, the perception of movement demands a moving stimulus, and real movement would seem to be a prerequisite for perceived movement.

There are, however, instances of apparent movement that are not the products of real movement. One of these, stroboscopic motion, became the prototype of all those perceptual phenomena that call for an explanation in terms of field effects.

Stroboscopic motion is familiar from advertising displays, movie marquees, and the like, in which individual lights go on and off in succession, yielding the impression that a single light is moving over the display surface. It is also the basis of the motion picture: a rapid sequence of still frames in which particular elements are spatially displaced from frame to frame, yielding the impression of movement.

Reduced to its simplest elements, the phenomenon can be generated by two lights. Light A goes on and off; light B goes on and off. If the temporal and spatial relations between A and B are just right, then A will seem to move from its location to that of B. For example, the duration of each light might be 50 milliseconds; if the time interval between lights is less than about 25 milliseconds, they seem to come on simultaneously; when the interval is as long as 1000 milliseconds—one second—they appear to be turned on successively, but there is no apparent movement; with intervals in the range between 25 and 400 milliseconds, apparent movement occurs, until at some value within that range, A will seem to move smoothly across the space to B. As the time interval is further increased beyond 400 milliseconds, at a certain value *movement* itself is seen, even though no particular object appears to move. This impression of abstract movement is referred to as the *phi phenomenon;* it represents an extreme lack of correspondence between local stimulation and perceptual experience.

The Gestalt Theory Approach to Perceived Movement. The Gestalt account of phi and other types of apparent movement—and by implication of "real" movement, too—is based on the notion of field effects in the brain, as developed by Köhler. Without going into the details of how such field effects might operate, we can summarize the Gestalt account this way: Apparent movement and real movement, being mediated by the same neural mechanism, are necessarily indistinguishable. But on this point there is now convincing contradictory evidence. Even though apparent movement can be as compelling as real movement, the two are different in several respects.

Differences between Real Movement and Apparent Movement. For example, a line in real movement has a different effect on a visual target, say, a light, that lies in its path than does a line in illusory movement (Kolers,

1964). A line that is really moving increasingly inhibits detection of the target light the closer it gets to the target, but a line that only appears to be moving towards a light has an approximately constant effect on detection of the light regardless of its "distance" from the target. Other differences led Kolers to conclude that the neural mechanisms related to real and illusory movement are not identical. But whether the differences are qualitative or merely quantitative remains to be determined. Thus, it may turn out that apparent movement occurs through field effects, whereas real movement involves the complex excitatory and inhibitory interactions among discrete neural impulses which are alluded to towards the end of Chapter Five.

The Perception of Objects in Depth

There are several sources of information about the distance of an object from an observer; some of the so-called "cues" to distance convey no more than the relative distance of two or more objects, while some provide the basis for a fairly accurate judgment of absolute distance.

The impression that objects are at different distances from an observer, or that one part of an object is farther away than another part, implies a three-dimensional phenomenal space. The impression of depth relates not to any particular stimuli but to the whole visual experience itself. In general, the richer the distance cues, the more compelling this impression of depth. Attempts to understand "depth perception," therefore, usually take the form of an investigation of the various distance cues.

The distance cues themselves can be divided into two sets: (1) those that are available to one eye and (2) those that require the simultaneous operation of both eyes. The former set is usually referred to as *monocular*, the latter as *binocular* cues. Monocular cues remain monocular even when presented to both eyes; as far as these cues are concerned two eyes are no better than one. On the other hand, the binocular cues are effective only if both eyes can be properly stimulated.

MONOCULAR CUES

An artist is restricted to monocular cues when he tries to capture a scene on canvas. He has to translate a three-dimensional stimulus array into one with only two dimensions, and he must do so without recourse to the binocular cues. Photographers, too, are limited, for the creation of the experience of depth, to the set of monocular cues. Only with the aid of special devices such as stereoscopes, as we will see later, can reproductions of reality incorporate the binocular cues. Despite this restriction, however, an artist can often quite successfully convey in his paintings the impression of

Figure 7.23 Perceptual depth effects from monocular cues.

depth. The monocular cues, it turns out, are really quite powerful. A brief account of the major ones is given below.

RELATIVE ANGULAR SIZE

The farther an object is from an observer, the smaller is its angular size, or the retinal image cast by that object. If two objects of approximately equal size cast retinal images of unequal size, they must lie at different distances from the observer. This relation, which is a fundamental principle of geometric optics, provides the basis for a powerful cue to distance.

For relative retinal size to serve as a distance cue, however, two conditions must prevail: (1) The observer must have some "access" to the relation, though not necessarily conscious knowledge of the relation or the ability to state it verbally; in some manner, even crudely, however, the relation must be psychologically operative. (2) The observer must "know" that the objects are approximately equal in size.

Since relative angular size can, indeed, be a very effective distance cue, at least for adults, both conditions are quite obviously met. How the first relation becomes psychologically operative is not entirely clear. There is no good evidence on which to decide whether it is entirely induced through experience or whether it is partially built into the nervous system and refined through experience. Theorists such as Helmholtz have argued for an empiricist explanation, but evidence to support the argument is yet to appear.

As for the second condition—the appreciation of the equality of objective, or *distal*, size—learning, clearly, must play a dominant role. We assume equality of distal size associated with images of different angular size primarily because we know the objects themselves are identical in size. Thus, if two images on your retina produce a perception of "two automobiles," and one image is larger than the other, then you will perceive the two objects (the autos) at different distances if distal object sizes are assumed equal.

Note that the cue in question is by no means infallible. To the extent that you erroneously categorize objects as being of about the same distal size, then their apparent relative distances will also be in error. For example, one automobile may be a toy, the other a limousine. If, because of authenticity of design and a clever display, the toy auto seems to be a full-scale one, then you will perceive it as being much farther away than it really is. It is possible, in this fashion, to generate some very compelling illusory effects, as a group of psychologists, called Transactionalists, have convincingly demonstrated and described in their articles and books (see, for an example of this work, Ittelson and Kilpatrick, 1951).

Of course, we need not turn to laboratory demonstrations for examples of illusory perception of depth. It occurs whenever the perception of depth is induced from a flat surface, such as the page of a book, or an artist's canvas, or a TV screen, through the manipulation of the distal sizes of visual figures. Look, for example, at Figure 7.23. The depth effect is quite pronounced—though objectively, of course, all the stimulation reaching your eyes is coming from the same distance.

Figure 7.24 Henri Matisse, *Lady in Blue* (1937). A modern painting in which the artist has ignored linear perspective. (Collection of Mrs. John Wintersteen; photo, Philadelphia Museum of Art.)

Artists, interestingly enough, have not always made use of relative retinal angle to achieve the impression of depth in their paintings. Not until the fifteenth century was *perspective*, as the cue is often called, introduced into the painter's repertoire of techniques. Some contemporary artists have ignored or distorted perspective, giving their paintings an aura of primitivism (an example of one such painting is given in Figure 7.24), and suggesting indirectly that perhaps for primitive persons, such as young children, the world looks that way.

Figure 7.25 Illustrations of texture gradients. In the picture on the left, note how the field of grain seems to grow smaller and more densely packed from bottom to top, providing a cue to distance. Perspective is absent in the picture of the ocean on the right, leaving the texture gradient as the only distance cue. (H. Armstrong Roberts.)

GRADIENT OF RETINAL
TEXTURE DENSITY

The surfaces on which objects are located, whether natural terrain, such as a grassy field, or a man-made setting, such as a brick-paved courtyard, are seldom entirely uniform. Rather, surfaces are ordinarily characterized by some sort of texture. The texture, in turn, is composed of an array of similar elements (for instance, individual blades of grass or individual waves). Two such textured surfaces are depicted in Figure 7.25. The more closely packed these individual elements are, the greater their density is. If these elements are projected onto the retina, we can speak of *retinal texture density*. Geometrical optics plays the same role here that it does in relation to relative retinal angle as a cue to distance: The farther away from an observer a "row" of such elements is, the greater their density will be on the retina. Indeed, retinal texture density increases in direct relation to the distance between observer and any arbitrary segment of the stimulus surface. This regular increase in retinal texture density is referred to as a *gradient*. Clearly, another potential distance cue lies in the gradient of retinal texture density.

The psychologist James J. Gibson is responsible for much of the research on the effectiveness of this cue. His work is admirably summarized in his book *The Perception of the Visual World* (Gibson, 1950) and need not be reviewed here. The effectiveness of this cue is well documented in the illustrations given in Figure 7.26.

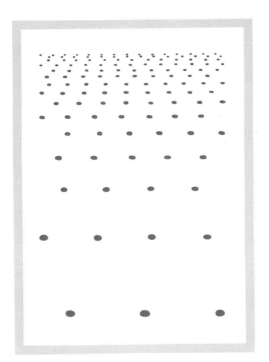
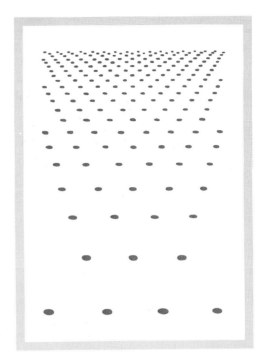

Figure 7.26 How gradients of texture density can create a strong perceived depth effect. (Gibson, 1950.)

INTERPOSITION

If an opaque object, A, falls between an observer and another object, B, then A will wholly or partly block out the retinal image that B would otherwise cast. To the extent that partial blocking occurs, we have a cue to the relative distance of two objects, and we ordinarily use it. Examples of *interposition* as a distance cue are given in Figure 7.27. As with angular size, interposition can be manipulated not only to yield the impression of depth (as in any two-dimensional representation, such as those in Figure 7.27) but also to reverse apparent distance relations. Thus, we can make the closer of two objects seem the farther, as in Figure 7.28. Clearly, any of the cues to distance can be employed so as to create illusory, or *nonveridical*, effects. This conclusion is a special case of the general rule that knowledge of the conditions that control behavior enables us, at least in principle, to elicit that behavior through the simulation of the proper conditions.

Figure 7.27 Examples of perceived depth through interposition of contours. (Gibson, 1950.)

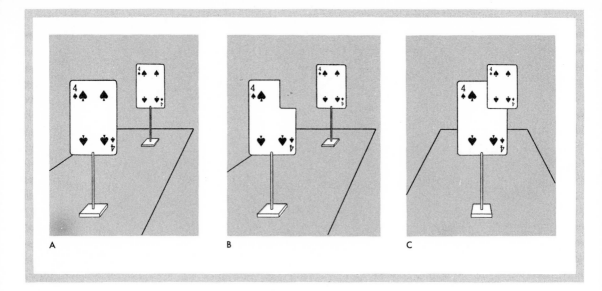

Figure 7.28 How interposition can override both size and familiarity cues in the perception of distance. The playing cards and their stands are viewed monocularly and are the only objects illuminated. In panel A, the two cards seem to be about equal in size, and the right-hand card is seen as the farther away. The same is true of the arrangement in panel B, where a piece of the left-hand card has been cut out. In C, however, with the right-hand card "filling" the opening, and with its stand obscured, the right-hand card appears nearer, though much smaller than the left-hand card.

SHADING

Often, when light strikes a solid object, the object's surface is not uniformly illuminated. The resulting pattern of light and shadow, as illustrated in Figure 7.29, can serve as a depth cue. Shading, in the hands of a skilled artist, can add considerable reality to the appearance of figures in a painting that otherwise offer little opportunity for depth cues.

AERIAL PERSPECTIVE

Should the air between observer and object (say, a building) not be clear—an increasingly chronic condition in most urban regions—then the light which is reflected from that object will undergo a wide variety of transformations, such as scattering and filtering, that change its original character. Under these circumstances, objects at a considerable distance from an observer look hazy and may have a purple tint. The farther away the object, the greater the effect, typically called aerial perspective. Here, then, is one more potential distance cue (see Plate 8), and another one that is often used to advantage by artists. Incidentally, if a person has come to expect the aerial perspective effect to prevail, its absence can lead to a considerable

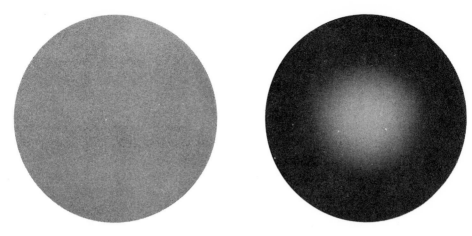

Figure 7.29 Examples of perceived depth through shading.

error in judging the apparent distance of objects. For this reason, in the clear air of mountainous areas, the peaks seem much closer than they are; as a result, people are often misled into thinking that a distant mountain is perhaps only an hour's walk away, when in fact it is several days away.

MOTION PARALLAX

The five distance cues mentioned so far can all be illustrated on a two-dimensional surface, so that the figures or elements making up the surface are motionless relative to one another. Our final monocular cue, motion parallax, requires a dynamic display in order to be illustrated.

Imagine yourself in the thoroughly familiar situation of looking out of the window of a moving automobile. Close by the road are some fence posts; at a much greater distance are some trees, laid out in a line parallel to the road. Do you notice a difference in the apparent motion of the fence posts as compared with the trees? If your imagination is working well, you will get the impression that the fence posts are moving past you at a much faster rate than the trees are. Indeed, the trees may even seem to be moving with you, rather than in the direction opposite to that of your movement. Should your imagination not be serving you well, a simple alternative is available. Hold up your two index fingers in front of your face, both at about eye level, with your left index finger closer than your right. Now, move your head from left to right. The closer finger, the left one, will seem to move in the opposite direction (from your right to left), while the farther finger, the right one, remains apparently stationary.

This disparity in the apparent motion of objects at different distances as an observer moves past them is known as motion parallax. This cue to distance can be simulated, though not on a static textbook page. If the objects to be made to seem at different distances are in reality at the same distance

—as they are on a surface such as a book page—then it is necessary to move the objects at different velocities over the surface. Thus, if objects belonging to set A (fence posts) are moving across the surface at a faster rate than are the objects belonging to set B (trees), then set A will seem closer to the observer than will set B. For a good example, you need only look as far as the nearest TV or movie screen.

Although the dynamic nature of motion parallax makes it difficult to illustrate, it points up a truth about visual perception that is often forgotten in the mass of static illustrations that are easy to provide on the page of a book: Perceiving persons are, except under the most artificial of circumstances, moving persons. The significant inputs to their visual systems are not unrelated, discrete, still "frames"—as though they were viewing a randomly ordered sequence of slides. Rather, a moving person sees a highly interrelated series of stimuli, in which succeeding phases are transformations of preceding phases. Indeed, "the visual stimulus" may not be any single event or even a collection of successive events, but the *relations* among events. Thus, the cue called motion parallax is really a relation among the velocities of sets of visual elements. In other, more complex cases, the effective input may be an even higher-order relation among events. (A very promising attempt to build a model of perceptual functioning through elaborating on that last point has been made by James J. Gibson and is presented in his book *The Senses Considered as Perceptual Systems.*)

Motion parallax is evidently an important depth cue in experiments employing an apparatus called the *visual cliff*. This apparatus was devised as a means of investigating the question of the innateness of depth perception. In essence, the visual cliff provides an animal, or a human infant, with two alternative areas onto which it can move. Both areas are at the same, safe distance below a platform on which the subject is first placed. One area, by virtue of the way it is "decorated" seems, however, to be closer to the platform than does the other. The latter is made to appear quite deep, relative to the platform, as though the subject would experience a considerable drop were he to try to descend onto it from the platform. The illustration in Figure 7.30 clarifies this description.

In general, experiments have shown in a variety of species (chickens, rats, cats, goats, human infants) that the apparently deep side is avoided. The subjects, however, will fairly readily descend onto the apparently shallow side. Moreover, this result obtains in subjects that have had virtually no visual experience up to the time of testing. One conclusion drawn by Richard Walk and Eleanor Gibson (1961), who initiated this line of investigation, is that preference for the apparently shallow side will be manifested as soon as a subject is able to locomote over the apparatus. One cue has come to the fore as essential to achieve the depth effect on the visual cliff: motion parallax (Palen, 1965). Such potential cues as relative size of the elements of the patterns on the two sides seem to be dispensable, but motion parallax seems crucial. Should this conclusion prove valid, the mechanism would

Figure 7.30 The visual cliff, used for studying depth perception. Subjects typically climb off the central platform onto the side that appears less deep. (Gibson and Walk, 1960.)

appear to be a fortunate outcome of evolution. Unlike the other monocular distance cues, with motion parallax the perceiver does not have to identify the visual elements. The cue is available to a visually naive organism, requiring for its effectiveness only the apprehension of a difference in the velocity of visual elements.

BINOCULAR CUES

The one powerful cue to depth that requires stimulation of both eyes is called *binocular disparity*, or *retinal disparity*. Because the two eyes are separated from each other horizontally by several inches, each eye receives a slightly different view of any solid object on which both are fixated: The two retinal images are somewhat *disparate*. Figure 7.31 illustrates the basis of this disparity in geometric optics.

We might conceive of several potential outcomes of retinal disparity. For example, since the two eyes send different messages to the brain, the result might be a confused or jumbled percept. But it is also possible that the two messages enter the relevant brain center successively, rather than

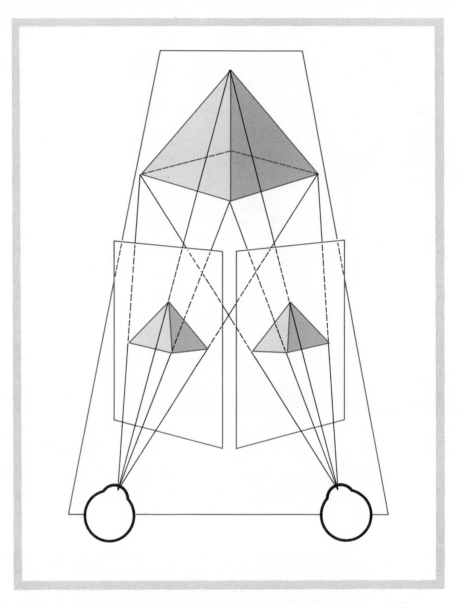

Figure 7.31 How the two eyes receive somewhat disparate images of the same solid object. (Adapted from Gibson, 1950.)

simultaneously, so that first the "right-eye view" and then the "left-eye view" is transmitted; no more confusion would be generated than if one eye were to be alternately presented with two disparate scenes. Alternatively, one of the two channels (the right or left eye) might be suppressed, with the result that only one message reaches the brain. Finally, the two messages could simultaneously reach the brain, which interprets their disparity properly (as a normal condition of binocular viewing); instead of confusion the end result would be an apprehension of the object's solidity.

The demonstration that binocular disparity is, indeed, a powerful cue to depth was first made by the British scientist Sir Charles Wheatstone (1838). In his report, Wheatstone described a device, the stereoscope, whereby he could exert control over the stimulation reaching each eye. By manipulating the amount and kind of disparity, Wheatstone was able to simulate on a flat surface the conditions that normally prevail when the two eyes are viewing a solid object. In short, by means of two-dimensional stimuli (stereograms) presented in the stereoscope, Wheatstone could elicit a compelling impression of depth, or *stereopsis.*

Since a three-dimensional percept is more informative than the two-dimensional input reaching either retina, where does the additional information come from? For after all, solid objects as well as a pattern of lines on the flat surface of a stereogram can cast only two-dimensional images on the retina.

The answer here, as in the case of motion parallax, is that the additional information is contained in the *relation* between the disparate images on the two retinas. To carry this point one step further, when the thing that is apprehended is the relative depth of two perceived objects, then the basis of that experience lies in a higher-order relation—a relation on a relation, that is, the disparity among the elements in the two retinal images of object A is greater than the disparity that characterizes object B.

The exact details about how information on disparity is processed are still unknown. For example, it is not clear whether the disparate images are processed simultaneously or successively, or whether there is an inhibitory interaction between the two retinas. Indeed, though about 130 years have elapsed since Wheatstone's original contribution to this problem, it is only within the past few years that any significant developments have taken place.

Julesz Figures. One major innovation has been introduced by Béla Julesz (1964). Prior to the work of Julesz, the stimulus patterns used on stereograms had been either line drawings or photographs of geometric forms or other familiar objects. It had been implicitly assumed that the stereoptic effect could come only from such patterns. Julesz has shown, however, that stereopsis is possible with stereograms that consist of meaningless, unfamiliar, randomly determined black-and-white "patterns" such as the ones given in Figure 7.32.

The Julesz stereograms were constructed in the following way. One stereogram was generated by a computer programmed to produce a random array of black-and-white elements of a specified density. The second stereogram was copied from the first, except that in a block in the center, each element was displaced laterally by a prescribed amount. With the right

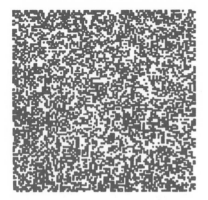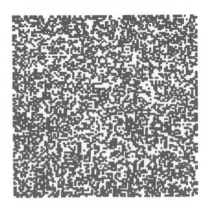

Figure 7.32 Stereograms, composed of randomly arranged black and white elements, used for studying depth perception. The elements in the central portion of one stereogram are laterally displaced to form the central portion of the other stereogram, thereby introducing retinal disparity. When the two stereograms are viewed stereoscopically, the central portion appears in front of the background. (Julesz, 1964.)

amount of displacement, the two stereograms yield a strong depth effect when viewed in a stereoscope or by an equivalent device. The block of elements that are thus disparately displayed on the two retinas is seen either in front of or behind the rest of the pattern, depending on which stereogram is placed before which eye.

In further research, Fender and Julesz (1967) showed that the amount of displacement can be altered without loss of stereopsis, in the following manner. First a good depth effect is obtained; then while the observer is viewing the stereograms, the extent of displacement is gradually increased (this is most readily done with patterns shown from a movie projector). The process seems to involve a type of short-term memory whereby the limits of stereopsis are pushed well beyond those imposed by the structure of the retina and the facts of geometrical optics. The system can be pushed only so far, however; at some point, disparity becomes so great that stereopsis is lost. When that happens, stereopsis can only be regained by returning to the optimal amount of disparity, then once again the normal limits can be exceeded by the gradual "stretching" maneuver.

Research such as that of Julesz, and of others whose work is indicated in the suggested readings at the end of the chapter, has both increased our knowledge of depth perception and reminded us further of how little we actually understand about some of the most basic phenomena of our experience and behavior. What, naively, could seem simpler than seeing distant objects as distant and solid objects as solid? But, as you are by now aware, there is a considerable gap between the facts of objective reality and the facts of experience. It is that gap which psychology, with its perceptual and other models, is trying to fill.

The Size-Distance Relation

One of the monocular distance cues mentioned above is the relative size of the retinal image associated with a given object. Since the size of an object is usually fixed, decreasing retinal size implies increasing distance. By the same token, this relation has implications for perceived object size: If two objects are perceived to be equidistant from the observer, the one that casts the larger retinal image will appear to be objectively the larger.

If one variable is fixed (say, perceived object size), then the other two variables (perceived distance and retinal size) are closely related. A good illustration of these relations is provided by the apparent size of an afterimage. Fixate for about one minute on a well-illuminated figure. Then, with an afterimage visible, look at a near-by surface and note the apparent size of the "stimulus" that the afterimage becomes when projected onto that surface. Shift your fixation to a farther surface, and the apparent size of the projected stimulus will grow. Here the retinal size is fixed, and apparent size increases with an increase in the apparent distance of the "object" that presumably is casting the retinal image. The phenomenon is referred to as *Emmert's Law*.

The Moon Illusion. There is one very familiar experience that seems to defy Emmert's Law. When the full moon is on the horizon it seems much larger than when it is at the zenith (so does the sun, though the phenomenon has come to be known as the *moon illusion*). Speculation about the basis of the moon illusion has been offered since the time of Ptolemy. Of all the explanations so far suggested, the one that has received the best empirical support (see Kaufman and Rock, 1962) points to the significance of the terrain that lies between the observer and the horizon moon, but is absent in the case of the zenith moon. What effect does the terrain have? Taking Emmert's Law seriously, we might argue as follows.

Since both moons cast essentially the same-size retinal images, the one that looks larger must be the one that is seen as farther away. The horizon moon does look the larger; therefore, the intervening terrain must act to make the horizon moon look farther away. So far so good. But it just happens that the horizon moon not only looks larger, it also seems closer, exactly contrary to what is expected from Emmert's Law. How this paradox will ultimately be resolved is not the least bit obvious.

The Constancies

Another of the many combinations of variables that interact to relate perceived size and perceived distance demands attention: A and B are identical objects located at different distances from the observer. However, the retinal size cast by A is smaller than that cast by B; but, for reasons unrelated to retinal size, A is also perceived to be farther away than B. Object A will then appear to be about the same size as object B. Thus, the apparent size of an object remains fairly constant, despite marked changes in the size of the retinal image cast by that object, but only if the distance of the object is veridically perceived. This rather complex statement defines what is referred to by psychologists as *size constancy*.

You can easily demonstrate just how compelling a phenomenon size constancy is. First look around a room where several people are seated. Then fix your attention on the apparent sizes of their heads. All the heads look about the same size, in accord with the constancy principle. But now, using the thumb and forefinger of one hand, bracket a head belonging to one of the people close to you; then do the same for a distant head, keeping your hand at the same distance from your face in both cases. The distant head, viewed in this fashion, shrinks considerably. You are seeing it with distance cues blocked out, and respond primarily to retinal size alone.

Size constancy does not hold under all circumstances, even though distance cues may still be available. When the object being viewed is at a great distance (as when you are looking at the street below from the top of a tall building), then its apparent size "regresses" to its retinal size. Automobiles look like toys, and people become ant-sized. The surprise people experience at this change in apparent size upon first viewing the world from a considerable height attests to the strength and universality of size constancy under ordinary viewing conditions.

As objects undergo various changes in their relations to observers, the objects themselves remain fixed. Objects do not become smaller as they move farther away, nor do they change their real shape as their orientations change. Thus, a circular dinner plate objectively remains circular as you look at it first from above and then at an angle, or as it is rotated in front of you. However, as these object-viewer relations change, there are corresponding changes in the retinal image cast by the object. We have already noted the decrease in retinal size as the distance of an object increases. There is a corresponding modification in the shape of the retinal image as the orientation of an object changes. The circular plate if not viewed "head on" will cast an oval, not a circular, retinal image.

Just as perceived size remains fairly constant—if distance is not too great and if adequate cues to distance are available—so does perceived shape, despite changes in the shape of the retinal image, so long as adequate cues to the object's orientation are present. The plate on the table looks circular even when it is not viewed from the ceiling; the tilted book still looks rectangular, as do windows and doors seen from an angle. This *shape constancy* —like size constancy, as well as constancies of other characteristics such as brightness and color (an apple may continue to look "red" when illuminated by blue light)—helps to preserve the stability of the perceived world in the face of the numerous transformations of the stimulation impinging on the receptor surfaces of a moving organism. Thus, the perceptual apparatus, at least in a mature person, is able to abstract out of raw stimulation those relations that are functional for adaptation. The system is by no means perfect, and it can often be fooled; but try to imagine living in a perceptual world in which objects are continually changing in size, shape, brightness, and color, disappearing and reappearing in part or in whole, as they move behind one another, or as you momentarily close your eyes. Such a chaotic world might be fun to visit, as the saying goes about New York City, but who would want to live there?

SUMMARY

Figure-ground segregation is a basic feature of perceptual organization. Crucial to the establishment and maintenance of a figure is its contour. Figures with blurred contours, if steadily fixated, tend to disappear; embedding a simple figure in a more complex one that preempts its contours makes the simple figure very difficult to perceive. People differ reliably in their ability to locate embedded figures, and this difference relates to what seems to be a general trait, called *field-dependence*.

The contours of certain figures may be interpreted so as to yield more than one percept; continual viewing of such stimuli typically leads to a cyclic fluctuation in what is perceived. These *reversible figures* dramatically illustrate the lack of any simple correspondence between perception and physical stimulation. The rate at which figure fluctuation occurs is believed to reflect efficiency of brain functioning, though the data on this point are equivocal.

Contours arise where there is an abrupt change in one of the attributes of visual stimulation, such as intensity. But here, too, the physical-perceptual relation is not simple, since contours will be perceived where they do not physically exist; these induced contours, called *Mach bands* or *rings,* are a function of the total distribution of light over an extended area of the visual field.

The perceptual experience of people born blind, but with vision restored through surgery, suggests that figure-ground segregation is a primitive visual function. Further support for this position comes from evidence of well-developed visual-form discrimination exhibited by very young infants.

In contrast to prevailing models of perception, especially the one labeled Structuralist, Gestalt theory emphasized the innate organization or patterning of perceptual elements and rejected the centrality of learning in perceptual organization. Because of the strong self-organizing tendencies found in perceptual patterns, one of the chief spokesmen for the Gestalt approach, Köhler, inferred that the brain acts more like a dynamic physical *field* than like a machine based on simple direct linkages among parts.

As illustrations of "field effects" in perception, the Gestaltists pointed to the so-called *principles of organization,* among them: *proximity, similarity, common fate, good continuation,* and *closure.* Recent evidence shows that at least in the case of proximity, the organization evident under normal viewing conditions takes time to develop and that the speed with which this occurs is related to intelligence. The principle of closure seems to have generality beyond the perceptual process, extending to such cognitive functioning as problem-solving and humor.

Additional instances of the influence of the total pattern on the perception of parts are found in the several *optical,* or *geometric illusions.* Both cross-cultural and ontogenetic comparisons suggest, contrary to the Gestalt hypothesis, that at least some illusions are the products of learning. Some illusory effects decrease with age, whereas some increase. The developmental theories of Werner and of Piaget can incorporate these paradoxical findings.

Perception is pervaded by *context effects.* On logical grounds context can take the form of: (a) concurrent stimulation within the same sensory system as the affected or target stimulus; (b) concurrent events in systems other than that of the target stimulus; (c) the residues of previous stimulation within a system; (d) the residues of previous events in other systems. The Gestalt principles of organization and the geometric illusions are illustrative of (a); *cross-modal* interactions, such as between auditory stimulation and visual sensitivity, have been reported, though their interpretation as evidence for pure type (b) effects is made ambiguous by the possible mediating role of the *reticular activating system; negative afterimages* and *figural aftereffects,* as well as all instances of *perceptual learning,* are representative of context effects of type (c); evidence is lacking for effects of type (d).

That perception and stimulation are not always in perfect correspondence is well illustrated by the various types of *apparent movement* (in the absence of physical movement) such as *stroboscopic movement.* The *phi phenomenon,* whereby movement *per se* is perceived although no object appears to move, is an extreme example of the dissociation that can prevail between perception and physical stimulation. Whether the perception of physical movement and instances of apparent movement are mediated by the same brain mechanism, as the Gestaltists assume, has recently been questioned.

The perception of objects in depth is carried by two classes of visual cues, monocular and binocular. Monocular cues (those available to one eye) include: *relative angular size, texture-density gradients, interposition, shading aerial perspective,* and *motion parallax.* Motion parallax (relative rate of movement of near and far elements as the observer moves past them) seems to be the only indispensable cue on the *visual cliff,* an apparatus that has revealed depth discrimination in visually naive subjects of many species.

The binocular cue, *retinal disparity,* results from the fact that the two eyes are laterally separated and hence receive somewhat disparate images of the same, solid object. The effectiveness of this cue was clearly demonstrated over a century and a half ago by Wheatstone by means of the *stereoscope.* Recent work by Julesz shows that *stereopsis,* the impression of depth through retinal disparity, can be created by stereoscopic stimuli, *stereograms,* consisting of randomly arranged black and white elements so long as the elements on each of the two stereograms (one presented to the left eye, the other to the right) are in proper spatial relation to one another.

The perceived size of an object is a function of its perceived distance if the size of its retinal image is fixed (*Emmert's Law*). An apparent exception to Emmert's Law is the moon illusion, wherein the moon on the horizon seems both much larger than the zenith moon and also closer.

Even though the retinal image of an object decreases as it gets farther from an observer, its perceived size remains fairly constant (*size constancy*). Analogous constancy principles apply to the shape, color, and brightness of familiar objects, though the constancies break down under extreme conditions, as size constancy does when the distance between observer and object is very great. The constancies serve a highly adaptive function, imposing stability on what otherwise could be a chaotic perceptual world.

SUGGESTED READINGS

Dember, W.N. *Visual perception: the nineteenth century.* New York: Wiley, 1964a.

Hochberg, J.E. *Perception.* Englewood Cliffs, N. J.: Prentice-Hall, 1964.

Kaufman, L., and I. Rock. The moon illusion. *Scientific American,* 1962, 207, 120–130.

Köhler, W. *Gestalt psychology.* New York: Mentor, 1959.

Vernon, M.D. *The psychology of perception.* Baltimore: Penguin, 1962.

Other Sensory Modalities

CHAPTER EIGHT A person's contact with the external world, as well as with his own body, is mediated by several sensory modalities in addition to vision. We will not attempt to treat each of these in the great detail afforded the visual system in the preceding chapters; rather, in this chapter each of these modalities is described briefly according to the scheme elaborated in the chapters on vision. That is, for each we will discuss: (a) the nature of the adequate stimulus, (b) the structure of the receptor organ and attendant neural apparatus, and (c) the basic discriminations performed. The modalities to be considered are those that mediate hearing, smell, taste, touch, pain, warmth, cold, position of the limbs (kinesthesis), and orientation and movement of the head and body (vestibular sensitivity).

Hearing

Hearing ("audition") and vision, at least for the human being, are the sense modalities chiefly responsible for transmitting information about distant objects and events. For many animal species the sense of smell plays a similar role; though smell is by no means trivial for human beings, its significance does not match that of audition. Think of only one major function of hearing—the reception of speech sounds—and you can appreciate its relative importance. Besides their importance the visual and auditory systems share other properties. One obvious similarity is the nature of the physical stimulus, which for both modalities can be described according to a wave model.

Sound waves originate in vibratory motion. For example, when the string of a guitar is plucked, it undergoes periodic vibration; that motion, in turn, induces an alternate compression and expansion of the molecules in the surrounding air (or any other elastic medium). Those pressure changes travel as a wave through the air and constitute the basic auditory, or "acoustic," stimulus to which the auditory receptor (the ear) responds. Acoustic stimuli that are adequate to affect the auditory system are thereby translated into "sounds." For convenience we can refer to "sound waves," keeping in mind that an acoustic stimulus does not literally become a sound until it appropriately affects an observer's ear.

The Speed of Sound. By comparison with the speed of light (186,300 miles per second) sound waves travel rather slowly—at a velocity of about 1100 feet per second through air. This difference between light and sound is readily apparent over relatively short distances, for example, when an outfielder sees the ball start toward him before he hears the crack of the bat.

The Basic Parameters of Sound Waves. Like light waves, sound waves have two independent parameters, *amplitude* and *length;* for sound waves, length is conventionally transformed into *frequency,* defined as the number of wave-cycles per second (c.p.s.). Amplitude reflects the intensity of the acoustic stimulus—intensity as understood in a general, nontechnical sense. Since the intensity of a sound wave decreases with increasing distance from its source, researchers usually determine the intensity of a particular acoustic stimulus as close as possible to the ear of the research subject (indeed, as close as possible to his *eardrum,* which initiates the transformation of sound waves into electrical impulses that are transmitted to the brain).

As with luminous intensity, measurement of the intensity of an acoustic stimulus is enmeshed in a complex network of physical and mathematical concepts and physical measuring instruments, far too elaborate to go into for purposes of this chapter. We can note, however, that acoustic intensity is measured, typically, either in pressure units (for example, in dynes per square centimeter) or in units of power (for example, in watts). Conveniently, power is proportional to the square of the pressure when the sound wave is traveling through air. Symbolically, if a stands for pressure, P for power, and c is a constant of proportionality, then $P = ca^2$.

Sound-Wave Mixture. Separate acoustic waves interact with each other algebraically—that is, if two sound sources generate waves that travel through the same medium, the acoustic stimulus takes the form of a single, complex resultant wave; the amplitude of the resultant wave at any moment is the algebraic sum of the momentary amplitudes of the two waves presented separately.

When several acoustic stimuli are mixed, the resultant wave is far more complex than the simple *sinusoidal* form taken by each of its constituents. But by a mathematical technique called Fourier analysis the sinusoidal components of a complex wave can be recovered, as they can also by instruments called "wave analyzers." Indeed, the auditory system itself performs a type of wave analysis; to a considerable extent, though not with the precision of a mathematical analysis, a complex wave is "heard" for what it is—a mixture of simple waves.

THE AUDITORY RECEPTOR

The translation of acoustic waves into sounds is done by the auditory receptor system—loosely, by "the ear." Like the eye, the ear is a complex organ, with many interrelated subparts. It is conventional to refer to three gross divisions: the *outer, middle,* and *inner* ear. These are shown in Figure 8.1.

The Outer Ear. The *pinna* of the outer ear is more than decorative; not only in animals such as dogs, but also in men it serves to "capture" sound waves. These waves are carried through the external *meatus* to the *tympanic* membrane (the "eardrum") where the first step occurs in their translation into auditory signals. The eardrum, very simply, vibrates in response to the periodic air pressure changes that constitute the sound wave. Clearly, an intact, healthy eardrum is essential to hearing; a damaged or otherwise imperfect eardrum will not faithfully respond to the full range of sound-wave frequencies, resulting in impaired hearing.

The Middle Ear. The vibrations of the eardrum are transmitted to the middle ear by a set of three small bones (or *ossicles*). Attached to the apex of the cone-shaped tympanic membrane is the first of these bones, the *malleus;* the malleus, in turn, is connected by ligaments to the *incus,* which is similarly joined to the *stapes.* The stapes, so-called because of its stirrup-like shape (*stapes* is Latin for stirrup), is the final link between the eardrum and another membrane, the *oval* window, where the middle and *inner* ears meet.

Two important muscles serve the ossicles. The *tensor tympani,* when contracted, so moves the malleus that tension is applied to the eardrum; the *stapedius* muscle, when contracted, dampens the movement of the stapes, thereby protecting the inner ear from excessive activity induced by sounds of unusually high intensity. Contraction of the stapedius muscle is a reflexive response (the "acoustic" reflex) to loud sounds, and is somewhat analogous to the reflexive constriction of the pupil of the eye to high-intensity illumination.

The adaptive significance of the acoustic reflex is that the *cochlea* of the

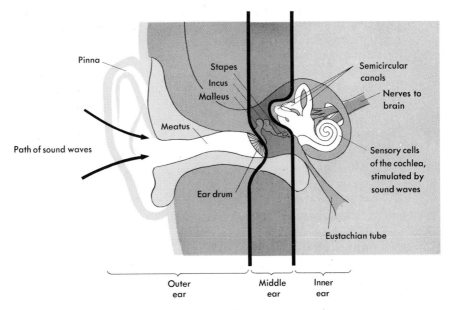

Figure 8.1 Schematic drawing of the ear.

inner ear, where mechanical vibrations are transformed into electrical impulses, can be damaged by repeated, highly intense sounds. Such damage, which decreases the sensitivity of the auditory system, is a typical result of contemporary urban living, with its pneumatic drills, jet engines, elevated trains, and even hi-fi sets; its effect is seen in comparisons of *audiograms* (auditory threshold as a function of tonal frequency) of the young and the not-so-young. In general, sensitivity to tones at the high-frequency end of the scale declines with age; this change is considered to be a function primarily of amount of exposure to high-pitched, loud sounds, rather than of age *per se*. The acoustic reflex serves to reduce the extent of this normal deterioration of the cochlea.

The Inner Ear. The inner ear is composed not only of the cochlea, but also of the receptor organs for the orientation sense, to which we will turn later in this chapter. As indicated in Figure 8.1, the cochlea is a coiled structure. Within the bony cochlea are three fluid-filled canals, separated from one another by two membranes (*Reissner's* membrane and the *basilar* membrane). A schematic drawing of the cochlea, as it would look uncoiled, is given in Figure 8.2 (p. 267), showing its major internal components.

Without dwelling on the intricacies of cochlear structure and function, we can point out its major features, following a model developed and tested by Georg von Békésy (1959): The vibration of the stapes, and hence also the oval window, initiates a pressure wave within the cochlear canals. This pressure wave moves from the oval window toward the round window (see Figure 8.2). The pressure wave takes the form of a traveling bulge along the basilar membrane, the extent of the bulge generally increasing as it goes, since the basilar membrane grows wider and less stiff from its origin at the oval window to its termination near the round window. At some point along the basilar membrane the bulge reaches a maximum, since by its very occurrence the bulging of the membrane dissipates the energy by which it was initiated. The exact location of the maximum is a function of the frequency of the acoustic stimulus; the lower the frequency of the sound wave, the farther along the basilar membrane the maximum bulging occurs. This last feature is what enables the basilar membrane to serve as a frequency analyzer.

But how does the location of the maximum bulge of the basilar membrane (which defines the frequency of the acoustic stimulus) get translated into the language of the brain—that is, neural impulses? Again simplifying some rather complex anatomical detail, we need only note here that the basilar membrane lies close to a structure, the *organ of Corti*, that contains, among other elements, *hair cells*. These hair cells, when touched by the bulging basilar membrane, stimulate the nerve endings of the auditory nerve that lie just below them. Which hair cells are affected, and hence which neurons are stimulated, depends on the location of the bulge on the basilar membrane.

Electrical Activity in the Cochlea and the Auditory Nerve. How do the hair cells of the organ of Corti stimulate the endings of the auditory nerve? When the hair cells are activated, a change in electrical potential (voltage) occurs; this is a relatively slow, graded change, characteristic of receptor cells, not an all-or-none spike. It is this so-called "receptor potential" that generates spike activity in the adjacent fibers of the auditory nerve. Measurement of the receptor potential indicates that the hair cells very closely recreate electrically the form of the pressure fluctuations that constitute the sound wave. In this sense the hair cells of the cochlea act like a high-fidelity microphone, which transforms mechanical vibrations into voltage changes; the electrical output of the hair cells is, therefore, often referred to as the *cochlear microphonic.*

The auditory nerve transmits the pattern of spike discharges through various way-stations to the cerebral cortex. Recording of this electrical activity in the auditory nerve reveals a remarkable correspondence between the frequency of the neural spikes and the frequency of the acoustic stimulus, up to about 4000 c.p.s. Beyond that, no systematic relation is found between input and output frequency.

Discovery of the relation between the firing pattern in the auditory nerve and frequency of the acoustic stimulus had two important ramifications. First, how could the auditory nerve possibly fire at the required rate? There is good evidence that the minimum refractory period of a single neuron in

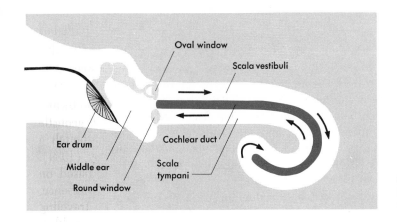

Figure 8.2 Schematic drawing of the cochlea as it would look uncoiled.

the auditory nerve is about one millisecond. Clearly, then, the maximum firing rate of a single auditory neuron is about 1000 times per second. But how are the measured firing rates from 1000 to 4000 obtained? The answer came in the form of a speculative model proposed by Wever and Bray (1937), referred to as the "volley theory." In essence, the model asserts that the neurons composing the auditory nerve fire in staggered groups. Thus, while one group is refractory, another group will fire, and so on until the first group has regained its firing ability. In this manner, the *nerve* can produce higher rates of firing than any single neuron is capable of.

Second, firing rates, or *periodicity*, as it is sometimes called, might serve to convey information to the brain about the frequency of the auditory stimulus, but only for acoustic frequencies up to 4000 c.p.s.; beyond that value, some other principle must operate. Considerations of parsimony should lead auditory theorists to allow that other principle, whatever it might be, to serve for both low- and high-frequency tones.

As already mentioned, a likely candidate for such a principle has been offered by von Békésy: Acoustic frequency is translated into a spatial parameter—the locus on the basilar membrane of the maximum bulge. Indeed, von Békésy's model is but one of a class of auditory theories that have been termed "place theories." Helmholtz (1862) offered one such theory when he speculated that each segment of the basilar membrane *resonates* to a different acoustic frequency. Thus, the wider portions would resonate maximally to low frequencies and the narrower portions to high frequencies (just as the bars of a xylophone, when struck, emit increasingly high pitched tones as bar length decreases).

Place theories also have limitations. In particular, place theories do not seem able to account for frequency discriminations at the low end of the scale. Thus, the traveling wave model proposed by von Békésy—the most sophisticated of the place theories—works well for high-frequency tones; for low-frequency stimuli, however, the bulge in the basilar membrane is not discretely localized. Rather, all low-frequency tones produce essentially the same "flat" bulge, with no distinctive peak that could serve to identify tonal frequency.

If you consider where periodicity theory breaks down (for high-frequency stimuli) and where place theory is inadequate (for low-frequency stimuli), an elegant, if not utterly parsimonious solution should become apparent to the problem of how information is transmitted neurally about acoustic frequency: simply combine the periodicity and place models, using the former to handle low-frequency stimuli and the latter for the rest of the acoustic range. Such a combination model has been generally accepted, though a unitary model, based on place, is still being urged by von Békésy (1959).

Von Békésy's confidence in the validity of a place model is based on psychophysical research that he has done on the sense of touch. In essence, a vibratory stimulus is applied to the skin of the forearm so that a traveling wave is set up that is analogous to the one postulated to occur in the cochlea. At vibration frequencies that produce the analog of a "flat bulge" on the skin, trained subjects are still able to discriminate between the apparent locations of stimuli of different frequency. By analogy, then, one could argue that auditory-frequency discrimination might also be possible despite the seemingly undifferentiated effects produced on the basilar membrane by different acoustic stimuli within the low-frequency range.

To account for this paradoxical ability of sensory discrimination to exceed the limits imposed by the effective stimulus (in this case, the locus of the maximum bulge on the basilar membrane), von Békésy (1967) invokes the concept of inhibition that has been found so useful in accounting for certain visual phenomena. He argues that the interaction of excitatory and inhibitory effects may so "sharpen" the neural resultant of stimulation that two apparently identical stimuli may produce different sensations. In somewhat more general terms, the argument seems to be that it is not simply the location of the maximal bulge that is involved in the discrimination of acoustic frequency, but the entire spatial and temporal pattern of excitatory and inhibitory events associated with a given acoustic stimulus.

The Auditory Pathway. The auditory nerve originates in the cochlea; the pathway between the cochlea and the cerebral cortex is highly complex, and perhaps not yet thoroughly established. Simplifying grossly, we can identify the following major relay stations: The *medulla* contains two relevant nuclei (centers of rich synaptic connections), called the *cochlear nuclei.* These nuclei, one on top of the medulla (the dorsal nucleus) and the other on its underside (the ventral nucleus), are the terminal points of neurons coming from the cochlea via two branches of the auditory nerve. Within the cochlear nuclei, neurons of the auditory nerve synapse with neurons that travel to several other relay stations on the way to the cortex, the last of which is the *medial geniculate body* of the *thalamus.* From the medial geniculate body auditory neurons move up to the cerebral cortex.

The pathway sketched above is the direct route that sensory information (in the form of neural impulses) takes from receptor (the cochlea) to cortex. There are also side-tracks, or "collaterals," running to the *reticular*

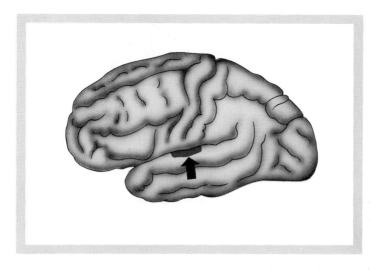

Figure 8.3 The lateral surface of the cerebral cortex showing (colored portion) approximate location of the auditory projection area.

formation. These collaterals form a nonsensory pathway, the function of which seems to be to stimulate the reticular formation, just as do collaterals from the visual system and other sense modalities; you may recall that the reticular system, when activated, serves to arouse or heighten the level of activity in the cerebral cortex itself.

The projection of auditory neurons onto the cerebral cortex is a complex matter, since there is no single region of the cortex that can be called "the auditory projection area." Again simplifying somewhat, we can identify an area in the *temporal lobe* of the cerebral cortex as the primary auditory projection area, located as shown in Figure 8.3. In addition, through various techniques, such as electrical recording from the brain during auditory stimulation and behavioral studies following removal (ablation) of parts of the brain, researchers have found other auditory areas. One conclusion that emerges from this brief sketch of the auditory pathway is that its structural complexity affords considerable opportunity for the auditory system to interact with other systems, both sensory and nonsensory.

SOME ATTRIBUTES OF SOUND

For normal human beings the *audible range* of wave frequencies is from about 20 to 20,000 c.p.s. Acoustic stimuli below 20 c.p.s. are detectable, if sufficiently intense, but phenomenally they are "felt" rather than "heard." Sounds of a frequency above the upper human limit can be heard by other animals, such as dogs—hence the effectiveness of dog whistles that are inaudible to people.

Loudness and Pitch. Wave amplitude and frequency affect, primarily, the *loudness* and *pitch* of sounds: the greater the amplitude the louder the sound, and the higher the frequency the higher the pitch. But just as the brightness of a light is a function of wavelength as well as wave amplitude, so too is auditory loudness influenced by both wave amplitude and frequency. This dependence of loudness on frequency clearly indicates that the auditory receptor is differentially sensitive to wave frequency. A graphic display of the relation between auditory threshold and wave frequency is given in Figure 8.4. Note that maximum sensitivity lies in the range from 1000 to 10,000 c.p.s.

Timbre. Other attributes of sounds, besides loudness and pitch, have been identified. *Timbre* is one of these. A trombone and a saxophone playing the same note, say middle C, with equal loudness, sound different. Furthermore, that difference is not specific to any particular notes; rather, it is characteristic of the instruments themselves. Each instrument, or sound source, is thus associated with a quality of sound, called timbre. Though the exact basis of timbre remains controversial, it undoubtedly is related to the physical nature of the source and the resulting pattern of *harmonic* frequencies emitted along with the *fundamental* frequency that defines a given note.

What are fundamental and harmonic frequencies? The fundamental frequency is the lowest value of wave frequency emitted when a sound source is activated. For example, when the string of a guitar is plucked, it vibrates. The vibration frequency is determined by physical properties of the string, such as the degree of tension imposed on it and its length (the greater the length, the lower the frequency of vibration). A given string will vibrate

Figure 8.4 Audibility curve showing threshold intensity as a function of frequency. (Modified from Wever, 1949.)

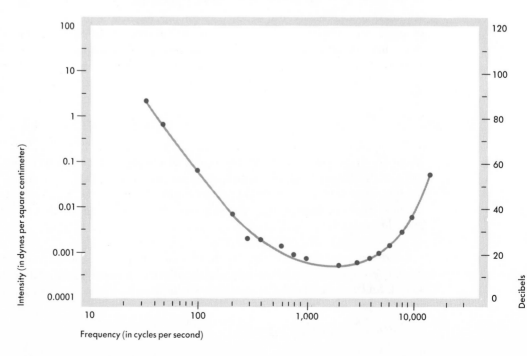

Intensity (in dynes per square centimeter)

Frequency (in cycles per second)

Decibels

at some minimum frequency—the fundamental—but vibrations may also occur at higher frequency values; these latter are called harmonic frequencies. Harmonics are always whole number multiples of the fundamental (that is, 2, 3, 4, 5, . . . N times the fundamental frequency). It is possible for certain harmonics to be more intense than the fundamental.

The fundamental frequency determines the pitch of the resulting sound, or musical "tone." Middle C, for example, is associated with a fundamental frequency of about 261 c.p.s. The pattern of harmonics that accompany the fundamental is responsible for the timbre of the instrument. A simple model was proposed by Helmholtz (1862), in which timbre was determined by the most intense harmonic frequency. Though this model works fairly well, it is not perfect, and alternative models have been developed (see Corso, 1967, pp. 287–289 for details).

Whatever its exact physical correlate, timbre clearly adds to the esthetic value of tones. Pure tones (fundamentals devoid of harmonics) can be generated by electronic devices; they are not nearly as pleasant to hear as tones of the same pitch produced by conventional musical instruments. Whether this difference has a physiological basis or is the product of our auditory experience (in which pure tones are extremely rare events) is an open question.

Other Tonal Attributes. Additional attributes of tones include *chroma, volume, brightness,* and *density.* Chroma (or "tonality") relates to the greater similarity between the same musical notes one or more octaves apart than between adjacent notes within the same musical octave. For example, two notes called "C" sound more alike than a C and its neighboring D, even though in frequency the C and D are the more similar pair. The phrase "absolute pitch" refers to a person's potential ability to identify exactly the chroma of a given note, along with the easier task of locating the note in its proper octave—an ability that purportedly is confined to a small segment of the general population (see Licklider, 1951, p. 1004, for further discussion).

Volume, brightness, and density, as clear, reliable, and independent attributes of tones, are less well established than those already discussed, both conceptually and empirically. The following quotation, from a noted psychoacoustician, typifies attempts at verbal specification of the meaning of these suggested attributes: "The tones of a tuba sound bigger than those of a piccolo, and a bugle blast appears to be hard and compact and to have a luster that is lacking in the more diffuse sound of an organ" (Licklider, 1951, p. 1004). Attempts to confirm the psychological reality of these suggested attributes have met with some success, at least for volume and density (for example, Stevens, 1934). Thus, trained subjects can reliably judge two tones to be equal in volume (or in density) even though the tones differ in pitch and loudness. It is clear, moreover, that no single physical parameter of sound waves forms the basis of these attributes (as frequency determines pitch). They are presumably the resultant of the interactions among the basic parameters. For example, for two tones differing in pitch to be judged equal in volume, the higher-pitched tone must be more intense than the lower (Thomas, 1949).

The auditory system is remarkably sensitive. The absolute threshold, in pressure units, of a 1000 c.p.s. tone is about .0002 dynes per square centimeter. To put that value in a meaningful frame of reference, it is about the pressure that would be exerted on the eardrum (beyond that imposed by the surrounding air) by dropping on it half the front leg of a mosquito (thanks to R. J. Senter for this image). Or, to indicate further the extreme sensitivity of the auditory system, it has been calculated that if our ears were just a little bit more sensitive, we would hear the "Brownian movement" of air molecules. Clearly, that degree of sensitivity would be more of a nuisance than it would be a help.

Figure 8.5 Decibel level and pressure in pounds per square foot of some familiar sounds.

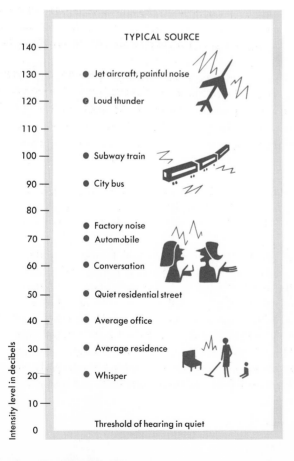

<table>
<tr><td>140 —</td><td></td></tr>
<tr><td></td><td colspan="2">TYPICAL SOURCE</td></tr>
<tr><td>130 —</td><td>● Jet aircraft, painful noise</td></tr>
<tr><td>120 —</td><td>● Loud thunder</td></tr>
<tr><td>110 —</td><td></td></tr>
<tr><td>100 —</td><td>● Subway train</td></tr>
<tr><td>90 —</td><td>● City bus</td></tr>
<tr><td>80 —</td><td></td></tr>
<tr><td>70 —</td><td>● Factory noise
● Automobile</td></tr>
<tr><td>60 —</td><td>● Conversation</td></tr>
<tr><td>50 —</td><td>● Quiet residential street</td></tr>
<tr><td>40 —</td><td>● Average office</td></tr>
<tr><td>30 —</td><td>● Average residence</td></tr>
<tr><td>20 —</td><td>● Whisper</td></tr>
<tr><td>10 —</td><td></td></tr>
<tr><td>0</td><td>Threshold of hearing in quiet</td></tr>
</table>

Intensity level in decibels

The Measurement of Loudness. It is convenient, for purposes of both research and application, to have a standard scale of auditory loudness. Such a scale has been developed, the *decibel scale*. In practice, we refer to a sound as being of so many decibels; the loudness in decibels of some common sounds is given in Figure 8.5.

The decibel scale is essentially a ratio scale; that is, the loudness of a given sound is expressed as a ratio of the loudness of a standard sound. By convention, the standard is taken as the absolute threshold, in pressure units, of a tone of 1000 c.p.s., given above as .0002 dynes per square centimeter. For mathematical convenience, those ratios are converted by a logarithmic transformation. An intensity of .002 dynes per square centimeter is 10 times that of the standard, or one log unit greater than the standard (that is, $\log_{10} 10 = 1$). A sound with an intensity of .02 dynes per square centimeter is 100 times, or two log units, as intense as the standard ($\log_{10} 100 = 2$). With that mathematical basis and Fechner's Law as its psychological rationale (see Chapters Three and Six), the loudness scale simply identifies a *bel* as the loudness unit that is associated with each log unit of acoustic intensity. Thus, the sound with an intensity of .002 dynes per square centimeter has a loudness of 1 bel. For finer degrees of loudness, the *decibel* (abbreviated, db) is introduced, arbitrarily defined as 0.1 bel: that is, 10 db = 1 bel.

As mentioned, the decible scale is based on the logic of Fechner's Law; its validity as a loudness scale therefore rests on the validity of Fechner's Law for hearing. To remind you, Fechner's Law asserts that $S = k \log I$ (the intensity of sensory experience is proportional to the log of the intensity of the physical stimulus). If the law is valid, then you need only to know the value of the physical intensity of a stimulus and the value of k for the appropriate sense modality in order to compute the intensity (loudness, brightness, and so on) of the corresponding sensory experience. If Fechner's Law does not hold for loudness, the decibel scale is simply an indirect way of referring to the physical intensity of sounds.

It is now fairly well agreed that Fechner's Law is not entirely valid; hence the decibel scale is not a true loudness scale, though it remains as a useful device for expressing the physical intensity of a sound relative to the absolute threshold of sound, and that is its conventional role in auditory research. Alternative loudness scales have been proposed, primarily by S. S. Stevens and his collaborators. These scales are based on Stevens's techniques of direct measurement of sensory intensity, of the sort described in Chapter Three. The *sone* scale of loudness is the best known of these. Its relation to the decibel scale is shown in Figure 8.6. Note that loudness in sones at first grows slowly as intensity in decibels increases, but then, at about 50 db, perceived loudness increases more rapidly than does acoustic intensity. Clearly, though loudness and intensity are directly and positively related, their relation is far from linear. If the sone scale validly measures loudness, then the decibel scale obviously does not.

Figure 8.6 The relation between the sone scale of loudness and the decibel scale of sound intensity for a tone of 1000 c.p.s. (Adapted from Licklider, 1951.)

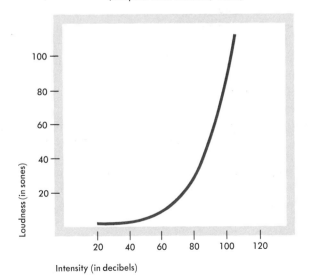

Loudness (in sones)

Intensity (in decibels)

SOUND LOCALIZATION

Aside from the several intrinsic attributes of sound, such as pitch, loudness, timbre, and so on, sounds also typically have a localizable source, or directionality. Even young infants respond to the directionality of a sound by turning their heads toward it. Sometimes the position of a sound source is ambiguous, as when you hear the siren of a fire engine and cannot tell whether it is coming from in front of or behind you. What are the cues to localization? How accurate can localization be, and under what conditions is it disrupted?

Localization Cues: Laterality. When a sound source is, for example, to the right of a person, two obvious effects on the acoustic stimulus can be noted: The sound wave will strike the right ear before it reaches the left ear, and the intensity of the sound in the right ear will be greater than that in the left (because the head occludes some of the sound wave arriving at the left ear). Clearly, then, differences between the two ears in time of arrival and intensity of the acoustic stimulus are potential cues to the lateral direction, or *laterality*, of a sound. Laboratory investigations of sound localization, where the two cues can be studied independently through the use of earphones, show that a difference in the intensity of sound reaching the two ears (*interaural intensity difference*) is an effective localization cue for high-frequency stimuli (greater than 1000 c.p.s.). It turns out that when earphones are not in use low-frequency sounds bend around the head, and thereby retain much of their original intensity. An interaural intensity difference as little as one decibel can be adequate to affect the apparent location of the sound source. As the intensity difference increases, the apparent location moves farther in the direction of the ear receiving the more intense input (referring again to the situation where earphones are being used). Experiments in which time of arrival is varied between the two ears indicate that it too can be an effective cue to laterality, but not for tones greater than about 2000 c.p.s. in frequency. Note that interaural intensity difference works best for high-frequency tones; thus, the two cues complement one another.

An interaural arrival time difference (or *interaural asynchrony*) of about 30 to 40 microseconds is enough to produce a shift in the apparent locus of a sound source, when the acoustic stimuli are brief pulses or *clicks*. Somewhat greater asynchrony is required for relatively long, low-frequency tones. Again, the greater the asynchrony, the farther the apparent location of the source moves in the direction of the leading ear; however, if the asynchrony gets too great (on the order of a few milliseconds), then the listener hears two separate stimuli (one coming from the left and one from the right) rather than one stimulus located off center.

Localization: Elevation. Sound sources can also be defined according to their height, or *elevation*, with the hearer's head as the point of reference. Imagine yourself standing perfectly still, with a sound source located directly in front of you. Let it then move in orbit around your head, along a path that keeps the sound source at a point equidistant between your two ears. What cues to its elevation might be available, analogous to the cues that arise from the lateral displacement of a sound source (with the resulting asymmetry in interaural stimulation)? So long as differences in elevation do not introduce interaural differences in some aspect of the acoustic stimulus, such as its intensity or arrival time, then there can be no such cues. The situation described above is one where differences in elevation are uninformative: no matter how high or low the sound source is, if it is located at a point equidistant from the two ears, it will fail to stimulate them differentially. If we think of "elevation" as being continuously variable along a 360° path around the head, we can well understand why it might be very difficult to tell, from auditory cues alone, whether a fire engine is in front of, or behind us.

The example above refers to the special case where the sound source is located along the perimeter of a plane that lies perpendicular to a line between the two ears. In general, unless the head is moved so as to turn elevation into lateral localization, the elevation of sound sources is not reliably perceived without supporting visual cues. Indeed, visual cues typically will resolve any ambiguity about the location of a sound source. The sound will appear to emanate from the most likely place. Hence the effectiveness of a proficient ventriloquist: If his lips are immobile and his dummy's movements are well executed, the dummy will seem to be the source of the sound. Similarly, when we watch TV, even though all the sounds physically emanate from the same source—the speaker(s) of the TV set—they seem nevertheless to be coming from the appropriate parts of the visual display.

BINAURAL STIMULATION

The dependence of the auditory system on interaural disparity for sound localization points up the significance of ears coming in pairs. Just as we cannot do justice to the full range of visual phenomena by reference to "the eye," so too is it inadequate for discussing audition to speak of "the ear."

Stereophonic Presentation. One of the recent technological developments that exploits the fact of binaurality is the stereophonic audio system. In essence, stereo recreates the natural acoustic situation that a person encounters when listening to a widespread sound source, such as an orchestra. In monaural recordings, a single microphone picks up the acoustic output of the entire orchestra; this recording is then played back to the hearer from a single source—the loudspeaker. What emanates from the loudspeaker is thus different from the original acoustic stimulus in that it lacks whatever contribution binaurality makes to the auditory experience. In stereo, two microphones are employed, laterally separated from one another by the width of the average head. Each microphone therefore picks up a right- or left-ear acoustic pattern. The dual recording is then played back through two loudspeakers, one "aimed" at the left ear and the other at the right, thereby simulating the natural situation more closely than does a monaural audio system.

Dichotic Listening. Ordinarily, the left and right ears receive stimuli that are the same in "content," though perhaps differing quantitatively, for example, in intensity and arrival time. Sometimes, however, two powerful sound sources are simultaneously operative, and located in such a way that one stimulates primarily the left ear and the other the right. This might happen at a party when you are standing between two people, each of whom is talking to you. How are such simultaneous but different auditory messages responded to?

Experiments have been done simulating the "party" situation, employing what is technically known as *dichotic stimulation.* One perhaps obvious conclusion from such research is that dichotic listening is inefficient: Two messages so presented cannot be attended to simultaneously. Typically, one message is ignored, or inhibited, and only the other is heard. All other things equal, the message that is heard is the one entering whichever is the dominant ear. However, people can readily switch attention from one ear to the other if given a signal in advance instructing them to do so. Switching might also occur in midstream if a particularly salient item appears in the inhibited message, such as the listener's name.

An especially interesting variant of the dichotic presentation experiment was initiated by the British psychologist D.E. Broadbent (1954). Two sets of items are recorded, say, two lists of three numbers each. List A—for example, the numbers 5, 2, 8—is presented to the left ear; list B—3, 6, 4—to the right ear. Furthermore, the items from the two lists are paired, so that 5 and 3 occur simultaneously, as do 2 and 6, and 8 and 4. When asked what he heard, the typical subject reports, "5, 2, 8 . . . 3, 6, 4," at least so long as the rate of presentation is sufficiently rapid. That is, the items are clustered by ear instead of by order of presentation. Moreover, the clustering-by-ear effect is most pronounced when the two sound sources are maximally separated (Bryden, 1962).

Thus, though the two ears cooperate under many circumstances to yield a single, integrated auditory experience, under the special conditions of dichotic stimulation they seem to function as independent channels. In this respect the auditory system acts very much like the visual system when the two eyes are presented with images that are too disparate to be fused into a single, three-dimensional percept. That is, only one eye's image is seen at a time, and the other eye is temporarily suppressed, or inhibited. As we noted in Chapter Seven, the two possible images tend to alternate, leading to *binocular rivalry.* However, what we might call "binaural rivalry" does not seem to occur. It remains to be determined whether this difference between the two sense modalities reflects a fundamental difference in associated neural mechanisms or whether it is due simply to a difference in the kinds of stimulation employed in the various experiments that have so far been conducted.

As we have seen, the auditory receptor is a remarkably sensitive device composed of several delicate structures. Damage to, or defects in, any of these components of the auditory system would be expected to lead to hearing deficits. Such deficits, of course, are fairly common, ranging from partial hearing loss, perhaps restricted to a particular frequency band, to complete deafness. Those who specialize in the clinical evaluation of hearing ability (*audiologists*) usually refer to two gross categories of hearing deficits, deficits resulting from malfunction of the receptor organ and those due to neural impairment. The former, called *conduction* deficits, might be related to defects in any of the structures that translate the acoustic stimulus into neural impulses. The eardrum, the ossicles, and the basilar membrane are the major potential sources of conduction deficits.

As one way of assessing where damage is, audiologists can take advantage of the fact that sound waves can be conducted not only through air but also through a solid medium such as the bones of the head. If a vibratory stimulus of appropriate frequency is applied directly to the head, it is heard as a sound both by people with normal hearing and also by those with conduction deficits (but with otherwise normal neural apparatus). Thus, if a person who cannot hear sounds transmitted through the air can "hear" a vibratory stimulus applied to his head, then the audiologist knows that he must be suffering from a conduction deficit. This conclusion can be an important one, since some forms of conduction deficit can be treated, usually surgically, whereas at present deafness due to neural malfunctioning cannot be. Partial deafness ("hearing loss") of whatever etiology that can be characterized as simply an elevated threshold is, of course, treatable through the use of a device (a "hearing aid") that amplifies sound waves.

The Chemical Senses

Smell (*olfaction*) and taste (*gustation*) are jointly referred to as "chemical" senses because the adequate stimulus for each is chemical in nature. For smell, the stimulus is gaseous, whereas for taste the stimulus is liquid. The two modalities are often categorized together for a second reason: There seems to be considerable interaction between them, even to the extent that what people believe to be a taste sensation often turns out to be dependent almost entirely on smell. Thus, to a person who is made *anosmic* (unable to smell) the tastes of coffee and tea are virtually indistinguishable.

Despite the practical significance of smell, not only for animals but also for human beings (as attested to by the enormous sums of money spent on perfumes and deodorants), the olfactory system is not as well understood as vision or audition. In particular, there is still no consensus on the exact nature of the olfactory stimulus other than that it involves gaseous substances; similarly, and partly because of our ignorance about the stimulus, we cannot fully describe the olfactory receptor and the exact manner in which it translates stimulus properties into neural signals. We know so little about the olfactory system largely because experimenters find great difficulty in precisely controlling olfactory stimuli and in precisely presenting them to the receptor organ—the former problem arising from the physics of gases and the latter from the relative inaccessibility of the olfactory receptor surface.

In the absence of good psychophysical data, it would seem futile to construct olfactory models. But enough is known of a gross, qualitative sort about smell to have motivated considerable speculation about the olfactory system. Typically, it has been the aim of models in this domain to specify the nature of both the olfactory stimulus and the receptor organ with enough detail and precision to answer the simple question: "Why do certain substances smell alike and others different?"

Olfactory Models. About two decades ago Lloyd Beck and Walter Miles (1947) developed a promising and highly novel model. In essence they proposed that odorous substances act as filters of infrared radiation passing between opposite surfaces of the olfactory receptor. The exact absorptive property of each substance depends on its molecular structure; the wavelengths that are not absorbed determine the odor of a given substance. Substances with highly similar absorptive properties in the infrared band of the electromagnetic spectrum are expected to have similar odors. Like its several predecessors, however, the Beck and Miles model proved short-lived as instances accumulated of substances that have similar molecular structure but do not smell the same.

In a recent and equally innovative model, it is the three-dimensional "shape" of the gaseous molecule that determines its characteristic odor. According to this so-called "stereochemical" model (Amoore, 1963), the odor-sensitive tissues of the olfactory receptor contain variously shaped "holes." In order to pass through a hole of a given shape, a molecule must itself have a particular shape. In effect, this is a key-and-lock model; thus, all those molecular "keys" that fit the same type of lock will smell the same, and will smell different from molecules of different shape.

As presumptive evidence for the validity of the model, Amoore has been able to demonstrate that groups of substances that do have similar odors also share highly similar molecular shapes even though they might be quite different chemically. Some instances are illustrated in Figure 8.7. The shapes depicted are themselves "models"—in this case molecular models developed by physical chemists. A rather nice property of these molecular models is that their shape is exactly determined; that is, one and only one three-dimensional, or stereo, model will fit a given molecular type. Once a model has been found that fits the molecules of a given substance, its shape is fixed. This permits fairly rigorous testing of Amoore's hypothesis—"fairly" because there remains some ambiguity about what constitutes "similar" shapes and considerable uncertainty about the similarity of various odors. The latter, of course, is a familiar problem to psychologists; measuring degree of similarity in any class of stimulus is fraught with difficulty, especially so for odors.

Despite the problems in testing its validity, Amoore's model has so far been quite successful. Note, however, that only one-half of the model has been subjected to test—the key half. The existence of the variously shaped holes, or locks, remains hypothetical.

The Olfactory Receptor and Neural Apparatus. We smell, of course, with our noses. Beyond that, what do we know about the olfactory receptor? It is, of course, contained deep within the nasal cavity and is composed of

Figure 8.7 Models of the molecular structure of three types of odorants (top). Hypothetical apertures in the olfactory receptor cells into which each type of molecule would fit (bottom). (Amoore, Johnston, and Rubin, 1964.)

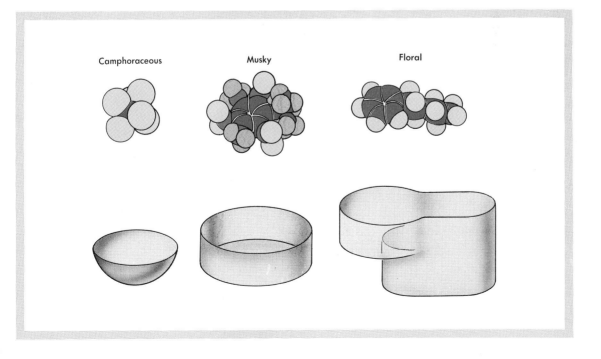

Camphoraceous   Musky   Floral

mucous membrane covering an area of about **240** square millimeters; the effective surface area is greatly magnified, however, by *cilia,* or hairs located at the ends of the primary receptor cells, as illustrated schematically in Figure 8.8. From each receptor cell an axon extends directly into the *olfactory bulb* of the brain (see Figure 8.9), where synaptic connections are made with the dendrites of neurons that travel thence to the cerebral cortex via the *lateral olfactory tract.*

It is undoubtedly the cilia of the receptor cells on which the olfactory stimulus (whatever that really is) makes its impact. Since these cilia are surrounded by mucus, it seems likely that odorous gases must be soluble in liquid (Morgan, 1965, p. 125). If this is so, then the similarity between taste and smell, already alluded to, is further strengthened.

Granted that the cilia of the olfactory cells are the site of contact with the olfactory stimulus, there still remains the question of how that contact is mediated. Should Amoore's model of the olfactory stimulus prove valid, then we might expect the cilia to house the variously shaped apertures that screen the variously shaped odor molecules. Perhaps electronmicroscopic investigation will reveal something like those apertures, just as the "compartments" of Wald's model of photochemical bleaching can be identified

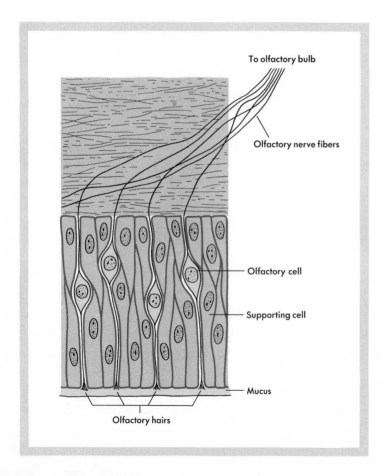

Figure 8.8 Schematic drawing of olfactory receptor cells. (Amoore, Johnston, and Rubin, 1964.)

To olfactory bulb

Olfactory nerve fibers

Olfactory cell

Supporting cell

Mucus

Olfactory hairs

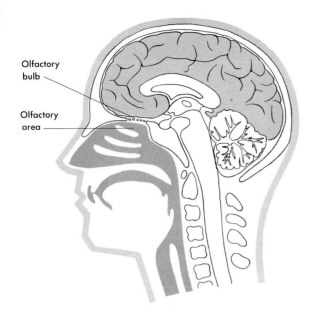

Olfactory
bulb

Olfactory
area

Figure 8.9 Schematic drawing showing the location of the olfactory bulb of the brain. (Amoore, Johnston, and Rubin, 1964.)

with the "membranes" that appear in electronmicrographs of rods and cones (see Chapter Six).

Olfactory Quality. As we have already suggested, the task for any model of a sensory system, or subsystem, is to account for what the system does—for example, the fineness of the discriminations it can make. In the case of odor, the basic function that needs first to be investigated, and explained, is the rather gross, qualitative partitioning of olfactory stimuli into groups on the basis of which ones smell alike and which smell different from one another. It is primarily that issue to which Amoore's stereochemical model is directed.

Obviously, people can distinguish among a large number of odors, or groups of odors, just as they can discriminate among a great many colors or tones. The central issue, then, is not so much one of fineness of discrimination; rather, it is to determine whether a relatively small number of basic, or *primary,* olfactory qualities can account for the much larger number of distinguishable odors. Is there, in the olfactory system, anything analogous to the three primary colors in vision? If so, what are the olfactory "primaries"?

Various schemes have been proposed for identifying a minimal number of primaries that would account for the large number of distinguishable odors—most of which presumably are the resultant of primary mixtures. And various lists of primaries have been offered. Amoore took the unusual approach of starting with his stereochemical model of the olfactory stimulus as a rationale for selecting what are intended as psychological elements. In essence, he argued that the primary odors should arise from molecular structures that are rigid and inflexible—in effect, molecular structures that could fit only one receptor site. Having found a number of such odorous compounds (or "odorants"), he then determined the most common verbal descriptions given by subjects to these odorants. In that simple, but appealing, way he arrived at a list of seven primary odors: camphoraceous, musky, floral, minty, ethereal (as in ether), pungent, and putrid. For the field of psychology, where three usually turns out to be the "magic number," seven primaries seems somewhat extravagant. And yet in Amoore's particular model these seven primaries make good sense, and it is hard to find a better justification than that.

The notion of primary odors implies complex odors composed of two or more of these primaries. In principle, then, any odor can be analyzed into its primary constituents; conversely, any complex odor ought to be capable of synthesis from the set of primaries. It is this last point which lends considerable practical utility to models like Amoore's. They hold open the possibility of synthesizing specific odors by reference to a rational scheme, rather than through the much slower and inefficient alternative procedure of trial-and-error.

There is theoretical utility also in an explicit scheme for specifying the primary components of a complex odor. It permits interesting tests of the validity of the formal model with which the scheme is associated. Amoore, for example, was able accurately to predict the odor of a newly synthesized compound by, so to speak, putting its molecular structure through his model. The compound, methyl-4-carbomethoxypimelate by name, has a structure that would enable it to fit into three receptor sites, associated with the primary odors, ethereal, floral, and minty. These three odors, in turn, when combined yield a complex odor that is labeled by people as "fruity." Hence, methyl-4-carbomethoxypimelate should smell fruity; as it turns out, subjects describe its odor as fruity, or "grape-like." Moreover, this newly synthesized compound can be slightly varied structurally and transformed into what is called its "4-methyl homologue." The latter has a molecular structure that would allow it easily to enter the ethereal site, but it would be partially blocked from both the floral and minty sites. Its odor should be dominated by the ethereal component, and that is how subjects describe it.

Pheromones. One special class of odorants has been of especial interest recently to biologists and animal psychologists. These are odorous substances secreted by an animal from special glands and left as an "odor trail" wherever the animal goes. Such substances are called *pheromones;* they are known to be secreted by a wide variety of species, ranging from ants to gerbils. Analogous to pheromones in function, if not exactly like them physiologically, are odorous substances, such as urine, excreted by animals and left at various places in the territory over which they travel. One function of pheromones and similar odorants is to "mark off" an animal's territory. The odor, which in order to work this way must be characteristic of an individual animal, serves as a sign to potential competitors that the territory so marked has already been "claimed."

Another function of such odorants is that of a trail-marker. That is, by tracking its own odor trail an animal can determine where it has and has not been. Thus, it has recently been found that rats leave an odor trail on the floor of a maze over which they have been moving. This odor trail serves as a clue for an interesting behavior pattern in the rat that has long been studied under the rubric *spontaneous alternation.* In essence, alternation refers to the tendency of animals not to re-enter a part of the environment after having recently entered it.

Generally, the alternation tendency is investigated in a simple piece of apparatus—a T-maze, so called for obvious reasons (see Figure 8.10). If an animal enters the right-hand "arm" of the T-maze, is removed from the apparatus and then put back in the stem for a second trial, the chances are that it will not re-enter the right-hand arm; that is, it will "alternate" rather than repeat maze arms.

It has been found by Robert Douglas (1966) that the alternation tendency is decreased if the typical paper flooring of the maze is changed between trials. Further research makes it quite clear that part of the alternation tendency is attributable to animals' avoidance of the maze arm containing their odor trail. However, the odor trail need not be specific to a given animal. At least in the case of male rats, the odor trail of other males (though not females) is avoided as strongly as the odor trail left by a given rat itself (Brill, 1967). What adaptive function is served by odor-trail avoidance is unfortunately still not known. Odor, of course, does play a significant role in sexual behavior. There is good evidence that animals can discriminate between odors associated with males and females of their species and even between females in and not in heat (Le Magnen, 1952). It is possible that odor-trail avoidance, as manifested in T-maze alternation, has a sexual function. But alternation behavior probably serves other functions as well— perhaps helping the animal more efficiently to explore its environment. We say this because animals will alternate in the absence of odor cues. In particular, it has been well documented (Douglas, 1966; Sherrick and Dember, 1966) that rats alternate the direction in which they have just been moving; this behavior probably involves the vestibular system, the sense modality that mediates bodily orientation.

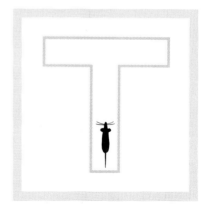

Figure 8.10 A T-maze used for studying alternation behavior in rats and other small animals.

TASTE

The sense of taste is somewhat better understood than smell, largely because there is less mystery about the exact nature of the taste ("gustatory") stimulus and also in part because the taste receptor is readily accessible for ex-

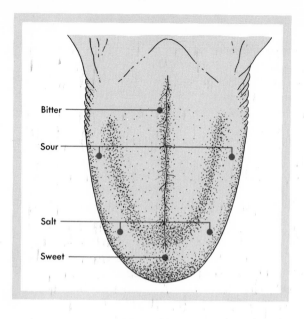

Figure 8.11 Diagrammatic representation of the distribution of taste receptors over the surface of the tongue.

Bitter

Sour

Salt

Sweet

perimental investigation. As we noted earlier, the taste stimulus takes the form of a rather dilute chemical solution of any substance that is readily ionized, such as salts, acids, sugars, and so on. Receptor cells for taste are located within small groups of supporting epithelial cells called *taste buds,* distributed within the ridges, or papillae, on the surface of the tongue.

Each taste cell is served by a neuron; electrical activity in the neuron is triggered when the taste cell is stimulated by chemical solutions that enter through openings in the taste bud. Penetration of the taste bud and subsequent stimulation of the taste cell is a relatively slow process (on the order of seconds) compared with the much more rapidly acting stimulation of the auditory and visual receptor elements.

Taste Primaries. There is unusually good agreement about the number and identity of the primary taste sensations and corresponding stimulus and receptor types. The number here is four: sweet, sour, salty, bitter. Each of the four primary sensations is elicited by a particular class of chemical stimuli and each is mediated by a type of taste cell that is maximally (though not exclusively; see below) sensitive to one stimulus class. Moreover, the four types of receptor cell tend to be distributed differentially over the tongue's surface; for example, bitter substances can be tasted only if applied to the back of the tongue. A "map" of taste cells is given in Figure 8.11.

Few natural substances have a taste that can be described simply in terms of one of the primaries. Most foods, for example, have complex tastes, though one quality may dominate. It is usually possible, however, to simulate the taste of a natural substance by an appropriate mixture of the four types of simple chemical solutions. That possibility, of course, is implied in the concept of sensory primaries.

Receptor Specificity. From the sensory data, of the sort mentioned above, it would seem that there is a one-to-one relation between stimulus type and type of receptor cell—that, for example, salt solutions stimulated only cells of type A and furthermore, cells of type A responded only when stimulated by salt solutions. But such a simple relation does not hold for the other sense modalities (recall that cones which are maximally responsive to "green" light also respond to light from other parts of the spectrum), nor does it hold for taste. Here, too, the situation is complex. Thus, electrical recordings from single taste neurons (see Pfaffman, 1965) and from individual taste cells (Kimura and Beidler, 1956) reveal that a given receptor unit may respond to more than one type of stimulus, perhaps both to salt and to sugar solutions.

How, then, is taste quality signaled? The answer must be in terms of *patterns* of neural activity. Thus, Pfaffman argues that though a given cell may respond to more than one stimulus type, it nevertheless is maximally responsive to one type. It is this differential responsiveness that carries the qualitative message. Consider, for example, two taste cells, A and B. Both respond (with neural impulses) to both salt and acid solutions, say to NaCl (sodium chloride) and to HCl (hydrochloric acid). However, A responds consistently more vigorously to the salt than to the acid solution, whereas B responds more to the acid than to the salt solution. When the tongue is stimulated by NaCl, the pattern of neural activity from A and B will be such that the amount of activity from A (measured perhaps in number of neural spikes per second) will exceed that from B; when the stimulating substance is HCl, a higher frequency of spikes is recorded from B than from A. Of course, the brain mechanism that receives these messages does not "know" the data we have just described. What it can do, however, and all that it needs to do, is to follow this rule: "If frequency of firing in A exceeds that in B, interpret to mean that the stimulus was salty; if B exceeds A, stimulus was sour." Other patterns of relative firing rates in groups of neurons can be assigned similar interpretations.

Exactly what makes a given cell differentially responsive to different chemical solutions is not known. One possible explanation lies in differences in the permeability of the cell membrane to different kinds of ions. That is, the cell membrane could act as a filter, allowing certain kinds of ions through and blocking others.

The Neural Pathway. The pathway for neural impulses originating in the taste receptors is quite complex. Neural fibers appended to the taste cells travel along three of a total of 12 nerves serving the head—the *cranial nerves.* The three nerves conveying "taste impulses" are identified, by convention in Roman numerals, as the Vth, VIIth, and IXth cranial nerves. Fibers from these nerves terminate in the *medulla* and the *pons* at the level of the *hindbrain* (see Figure 7.21 in Chapter Seven). From there, neurons travel in a short bundle, or "tract"—the *solitary tract*—to the *solitary nucleus.* A second tract, the *medial lemniscus,* carries taste impulses to the major sensory relay station of the *forebrain,* the *thalamus.* Specifically, taste fibers make synaptic connections in the *posteroventral nucleus* of the thalamus, where they are closely intermixed with neurons that serve the sense of touch for the facial area. Taste neurons then travel along with those for touch to the *somatosensory* area of the cerebral cortex, as indicated in Figure 8.12.

Considering the many similarities already noted between the gustatory and olfactory systems, as well as the frequent confusion between taste and smell experiences, it is interesting that those two modalities are projected onto different cortical areas. In terms of cortical locus, taste has more affinity with touch than it does with smell. From the point of view of embryology, however, this may not be surprising, since taste and touch receptors have a common embryological origin (see Morgan, 1965, p. 119).

Taste Preference and Physiological State. The primary adaptive function of taste would seem to be to enable the individual to monitor the types of substances ingested. From the point of view of adaptation, it would be ideal if all potentially harmful substances tasted bad and all good-tasting substances were healthful. Of course, the process of natural selection has not created ideal organisms, and no biological mechanism is perfect, taste included. In general, however, there does seem to be a relation between the "tastiness" of substances and their biological utility, a relation that in part must be innate and in part acquired. Fairly young children, for example, will typically reject foods that are extremely bitter or salty, but there are also unfortunate instances of infants eating formula inadvertently prepared with salt instead of sugar—and dying as a result. Apparently taste is not as well-developed in newborn infants as is vision or hearing.

Granting a crude relation between the palatability and healthfulness of substances, we can ask further whether momentary states of biological need are reflected in a preference for the needed commodity. Suppose, for example, that a person or animal has been deprived of salt and has a physiological need for it. Will preference for salty substances be increased until the salt deficit has been made up? Considerable research has been done in order to answer that and related questions. In one line of investigation, for instance, the adrenal glands were surgically removed from rats; in animals without

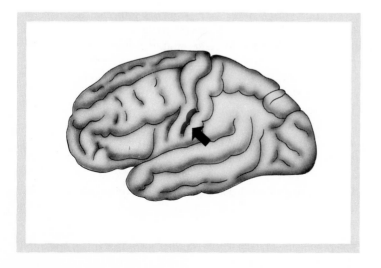

Figure 8.12 The lateral surface of the cerebral cortex showing (colored portion) approximate location of the gustatory projection area.

adrenal glands salt regulation is greatly impaired, resulting in a chronic salt deficiency. Such rats do in fact consume salt solutions with greater avidity than do normal rats (see, for example, Bare, 1949).

Somatic Sensitivity and Orientation

There are several ways of classifying the various sensory systems, none of them entirely satisfactory. For example, because the eye and the ear make it possible for an organism to gain knowledge about far distant objects, they are often called "distance receptors." But what about olfaction? In this case also the object (an odor source) may be quite distant; however, if the object is to be smelled, then "parts" of it, in the form of gaseous molecules, must make contact with the olfactory receptor. In one respect, then, the nose is a distance receptor, but in another respect olfaction is different from vision and audition.

Taste conveys information about objects, but surely not distant ones. To be tasted, an object must touch the tongue. Thus, although they are classified together as "chemical senses," according to the nature of their respective stimuli, and although they are intimately related in other ways, taste and smell are also different in an important way.

To the extent that the dimension of object-organism distance is a meaningful basis for classification, then taste would seem to belong with touch, pain, warmth, and cold. Indeed, we have already noted the closer anatomical affinity between taste and touch than between taste and smell. Despite the similarities, however, taste and the several somatic senses ordinarily are not categorized together in conventional discussions of the sensory systems. Instead, touch, pain, warmth, and cold are typically categorized together as the *somatic* or the *somesthetic senses*, along with kinesthesis, the sensory system that provides information about the location of the limbs. We will take up the somatic senses first and then very briefly discuss the *vestibular* system, which is concerned with the orientation of the head and body.

How Many Somatic Senses? As we all know, Aristotle referred to *the five senses* (and when we want to postulate some added, mysterious sensory capacity, we speak of a "sixth sense"). But in this section alone we propose to discuss six senses (touch, pain, warmth, cold, kinesthesis, and vestibular sensitivity). What happened to parsimony? Or more to the point, what is the basis for the modern convention of treating touch, pain, warmth, and cold as separate sensory systems, instead of, perhaps, as different qualities of experience within the same system?

In essence, the basis is psychophysical. The four are considered separate systems because sensitivity to their respective stimuli is distributed differently over the body surface, and therefore, presumably, because they rely on different sets of neural structures. That is, if separate maps are made of the points on an area of the skin where a person, when properly stimulated, experiences "touch," "pain," "warmth," and "cold," the maps reveal too little overlap of points for the four types of experience to be considered as arising from the same system. Thus, for example, the points that elicit "touch" sensations are not identical with those that yield an experience of "pain," or "warmth," or "cold." It is as though four separate sets of neural transmission systems were operative. We say "as though" because it is still not clear what the specific anatomical structures are that serve to differentiate the various somatic sensory systems; thus, as we mention below, there is no simple relation between the sensory experience and the type of somatic receptor structure.

The same kind of argument applies somewhat less ambiguously to kinesthesis and the vestibular sense. These are granted the status of independent sensory systems because of their quite obviously separate receptor-neural structures.

Somatic Receptor Types. Several types of somatic receptor have been identified through anatomical investigation. These types are usually further classified into three broad categories. (1) Neural fibers may be wrapped around the base of a hair; when the hair is touched, the neural fiber is activated. (2) Neural fibers may simply be embedded in the skin with no accessory structures; these are called "free nerve endings" and are typically stimulated by mechanical displacement of the skin surrounding them. (3) A variety of cellular structures are distributed throughout the body which contain, or "encapsulate," nerve endings.

Attempts to establish a one-to-one relation between receptor type and sensory function have not been successful. Instead, the relation is quite weak. Thus, movement of a hair usually elicits the sensation of "touch," but such a sensation can also be aroused where there are no hairs, as for example on the cornea of the eye. The cornea, indeed, appears to have only one type of functional somatic receptor—free nerve endings—and yet all four types of sensation can be elicited by appropriate stimulation (Weddell, 1961). In general, the type of structure (or "end organ") in which the somatic neuron is embedded seems quite unimportant (Morgan, 1965). Rather, what probably matters much more, as far as sensory experience is concerned, is the nature of the neural response to stimulation and its effects in the central nervous system.

Having only weakly justified the conventional way of classifying the somesthetic senses, we can nevertheless proceed to discuss each one briefly; though the classification scheme is somewhat arbitrary, and rests on shaky scientific grounds, it is still a useful one for the present purpose. The point to keep in mind is that this scheme is not meant to have profound theoretical significance.

The stimulus for touch, or "cutaneous" sensitivity, is light mechanical pressure on the skin, including movement of the hairs covering the body surface. When the touch stimulus is intensified it yields a sensation typically called *pressure*. Two other familiar variants of the basic cutaneous experience are *vibration* and *tickle*. These are considered variants, rather than separate systems, for the reasons alluded to above: They presumably involve the same structures as touch and are elicited by complicated patterns of simple cutaneous stimulation. Vibration is experienced when a light mechanical pressure on the skin is rapidly repeated; tickle is the result of light cutaneous stimulation applied simultaneously over two or mo.e adjacent portions of skin surface.

The problem of identifying the touch receptor has already been alluded to. The neural pathways from skin to brain involved in cutaneous sensitivity have not yet been traced; however, since touch, pain, warmth, and cold have much in common in this regard, we will defer that topic till later where we can take up the question of pathways and cortical localization for all the several somatic systems at one time.

Tactual Sensitivity and Pattern Perception. Sensitivity to tactual stimuli varies according to the area of the skin being stimulated (just as the threshold for detecting light varies with the locus of the visual target on the retina). The areas most highly sensitive to tactual stimuli are the hands and face; the back and the soles of the feet are quite insensitive. Tactual sensitivity can be assessed through any of the standard techniques for threshold measurement. The stimulus variable that enters such procedures is directly or indirectly a measure of the amount of pressure applied to the skin, as, for example, in units of grams per square millimeter. In Table 8.1, threshold values in such units are given for several areas of the body. The data in that table show

Table 8.1 Thresholds of tactual sensitivity for representative parts of the body. (Adapted from Corso, 1967, and Woodworth, 1938.)

Body Part	Threshold in Grams per Square Millimeter
Tip of tongue	2
Tip of finger	3
Back of hand	12
Abdomen	26
Back of forearm	33
Sole of foot	250

about a hundredfold variation in threshold between the most and least sensitive body parts.

Similar variation also applies to the tactual analog of visual acuity, or what is known as the two-point threshold. Here, a subject's task is to decide whether he was stimulated by a single point on his skin or by two adjacent points. The threshold is obtained by separating two stimulating points in small steps until a distance is found where stimulation by two points rather than one is reliably reported. Illustrative data of this sort are given in Table 8.2. Note, for example, that the lips are about 15 times more "acute" than the skin on the legs.

Everyday experience suggests that the tactual system is capable of responding with some accuracy to differences in the spatial pattern of stimulation. Such pattern discrimination is the basis, of course, of the Braille system, whereby blind people can "read" with their fingers. However, laboratory research does reveal certain differences between tactual and visual pattern perception. For example, in the visual recognition of form, it matters considerably how the stimulus pattern is oriented. Thus, suppose people are shown a "nonsense" form like the ones illustrated in Figure 8.13 and are then asked to pick out the one identical to it in shape among a set of alternative forms; their performance is better when the patterns are oriented vertically than when they are oriented horizontally. Whether a form is considered vertical or horizontal depends on the alignment of its widest contour, which serves as a kind of base for the form. A plausible interpretation of the superiority of the vertical orientation is that most natural visual objects, such as trees and people, as well as man-made objects such as houses, are typically seen vertically and often are bilaterally symmetrical along the vertical axis. Perhaps through some process of perceptual learning, the visual system develops general schema with which vertically oriented objects "fit" better than other objects.

By contrast, there is no typical orientation to the objects that stimulate the skin; rather, objects come in all possible orientations. Hence, for the tactual system, orientation should not be a crucial attribute of forms. Experimental evidence supports this hypothesis. When tactual forms are presented for

Table 8.2 Two-point thresholds of tactual acuity for representative parts of the body. The smaller the threshold, the greater the tactual acuity. (Adapted from Mueller, 1965.)

Body Part	Two-Point Threshold
Leg	67.5
Forearm	40.5
Forehead	22.5
Lips	4.5

recognition, their orientation does not affect the subjects' performance (Warm and Foulke, 1968). Moreover, subjects are much poorer at determining inversion of a tactual form than of a visual form (Pick, Klein, and Pick, 1966). It is of further interest to note that whereas blind subjects' (experienced in reading Braille) perform more quickly and accurately on tactual form-recognition tasks than do sighted subjects, orientation does not affect their performance (Foulke and Warm, 1967). Thus, despite their heightened reliance on and experience with tactual form, blind people do not seem to develop schema for tactual form perception in which orientation is an important attribute. Perhaps such schema must be developed very early in life or not at all, or else the difference between visual and tactual form-perception with respect to orientation is innate rather than acquired through experience.

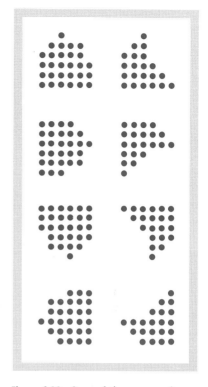

Figure 8.13 Some of the nonsense figures used to compare visual and tactual form perception. (Adapted from Warm and Foulke, 1968.)

The Hedonic Dimension of Tactual Experience. Tactual stimulation often does more than indicate the presence of physical objects in contact with the skin. Often such contact has a *hedonic* component, as in the intensely pleasurable sensations associated with stimulation of the genital organs and other erogenous tissue.

For a young child tactual stimulation is apparently quite important, especially during periods of stress. The "security blanket" is a familiar source of such comforting tactual stimulation. Moreover, laboratory research by Harry Harlow provides dramatic experimental evidence of the significance to the developing organism of "contact comfort." Indeed, Harlow has shown that for an infant monkey the adequacy of its "mother's skin," as a source of appropriate tactual stimulation, is more important than its mother's milk supply (Harlow, 1958). Thus, artificial, or surrogate, monkey mothers with soft, terry-cloth skins are preferred over similar surrogate mothers with wire-mesh skins, even if the latter are the infant's only source of milk. For the infant monkey to form a strong affectional bond to a surrogate mother, she must have, as Harlow notes, "the skin you love to touch." As it turns out, she requires other assets as well (see Chapter Fifteen for further discussion of this research), but a soft skin is indispensable.

It is somewhat ironic that pain receives so little attention in discussions of the sensory systems; traditionally, it is classified among "the minor senses." But pain is far from minor when it is being experienced. Almost half a billion dollars are spent annually on aspirin and other analgesics.

We might speculate a bit on why pain is treated so cavalierly as a topic for abstract consideration, when it obviously is of considerable importance to the individual experiencing it. For one thing, pain conveys very little information about the external world, compared, say, with vision or audition or even smell. Moreover, as a phenomenal experience, pain is really quite simple; it lacks the multidimensionality of many of the other types of sensory experience. One can distinguish among various intensities of pain and perhaps between two qualities, "bright" and "dull," but that is about all. Imagine how some intelligent organism might treat vision if the only richness in its visual experience stemmed from rather gross variation in the intensity of illumination (with no variation in color or form, and little by way of temporal patterning). In short, though very salient when it occurs, pain is also terribly uninteresting. Except perhaps for a sophisticated masochist, if there is such a person, it would be hard to conceive of an "aesthetics of pain."

Speculation aside, it is also true of pain that its physiology is still poorly understood, from the definition of the nature of the pain stimulus to the identity of the neural structures that are involved in mediating pain experience. There are certain stimuli that typically evoke pain; ambiguity about the pain stimulus comes from two sources: (1) The class of potential pain arousers seems to encompass virtually all types of stimuli to which the organism is sensitive. (2) There is considerable variation in the response to a given painful stimulus.

The Pain Stimulus. Whereas sharp objects, electric shock, or radiant heat applied to the skin in areas containing "pain receptors" characteristically elicit pain, as does damaged or distended tissue, it is also possible to arouse pain by sufficiently high-intensity stimulation of almost any sort—very bright light, loud sound, extreme heat or cold, and so on. Moreover, under certain unusual circumstances, pain is felt when there is no conventional stimulation at all, as when amputees experience pain in limbs that have been lost (so-called "phantom limbs").

The whole variety of conditions under which pain is felt, as well as the failure to localize a specific "pain center" in the brain, has led some theorists (for example, see Hebb, 1949) to hypothesize that pain is a general property of brain functioning: Pain occurs when the organization of central neural activity is disrupted. This disorganization of the pattern of electrical activity in the brain may be set off by specific stimuli (the reliable elicitors of pain), but also by either exclusively intense stimuli in any sense modality or even by the failure of normal levels of stimulation to occur (as in the amputee, whose absent fingers, for example, can no longer provide the normal level of tactual stimulation).

Variation in Response to Pain Stimuli. In general, recent theories of pain stress the importance of patterning in the neural activity taking place in different classes of neural fibers (see, for example, Melzack and Wall, 1965). Such theories also allow for the modulation of such activity by "higher" brain centers. Some sort of central control of pain seems required by certain rather dramatic phenomena. Most striking is the possibility of minimizing pain through hypnotic suggestion, to the point where surgical operations can be performed in comfort to the patient without anesthesia (see Barber, 1958). Also pertinent is the reduction in pain that can be accomplished by concurrent auditory stimulation, a finding that many dentists have used to practical advantage (see Licklider, 1961).

Perhaps even more startling than demonstrations of the relative ease with which pain can be mitigated are several well-documented instances of people who are chronically insensitive, or indifferent, to pain (see, for example, Magee, Schneider, and Rosenzweig, 1961). The case histories of such people indicate that this abnormality may have been present from birth; hence it is referred to as a congenital defect. Some, though not all of these people, have a high incidence of injuries, especially as young children; insensitivity to pain is surely a mixed blessing.

The occurrence of congenital insensitivity to pain in otherwise normal people argues for the existence of a separate pain system, or a system that at some crucial point, at least, is independent of other sensory systems. Potential inputs to this system may be unusually varied in quality (that is, it may share "stimuli" with several other sense modalities), but its output is certainly unique. It would seem likely that abnormalities in pain sensitivity are located closer to the output than the input end of the system.

The above discussion suggests that pain, like other sensory experiences, does not come in fixed, absolute amounts—that there is no simple one-to-one relation between the intensity of a pain-producing stimulus and the intensity of experienced pain. The relativity of pain is further documented by two additional types of evidence. First is the possibility of neutralizing an originally painful stimulus by pairing it repeatedly with a highly salient, pleasurable stimulus. The Russian physiologist Ivan Pavlov (whom you will meet again in the next chapter) successfully employed such a procedure with dogs—for example, immediately following a painful stimulus, such as a burn on the leg, with food. After many such pairings, the dog would salivate when the painful stimulus was presented, as it did to the food, and give no behavioral evidence of pain or even mild discomfort.

The second line of evidence that attests to the relativity of pain is the demonstration, again in dogs, that normal response to painful stimuli is dependent on certain kinds of previous experience. In particular, dogs that were reared in very restricted environments, both physical and social, turned out to be not only intellectually and socially "retarded," as had been expected, but also grossly insensitive to pain (Melzack and Scott, 1957). Similar findings of an anecdotal rather than experimental sort have been occasionally reported in newspapers and magazine stories about human children raised (by their parents) in almost total social isolation and under conditions of severe deprivation of normal physical stimulation. The implication of this type of evidence is that the normal response to pain is either learned or at least dependent on learning for its maintenance. Exactly what that experience must be is as yet unspecified.

WARMTH AND COLD

By the criterion of nonoverlapping points of sensitivity, warmth and cold are separate systems. But in terms of the kind of stimulation that gives rise to sensations of warmth and cold they clearly belong together. For the latter reason, and for the sake of convenience, we combine them here in a single section.

The Thermal Stimulus. It is, of course, the temperature of a stimulating object that the sensory systems in question responds to: an increase in temperature (from some base line, or neutral value) for warmth and a decrease for cold. Beyond that simple statement, however, lies the usual complexity that confronts us when we examine closely any sensory system.

Normal skin temperature is about 32° Centigrade. Stimulating objects will be sensed as warm or cold if they are as little as 0.1° C above or below skin temperature. However, if the skin is adapted to higher or lower temperatures, then a new thermal base line is achieved; the threshold for warmth and cold is somewhat larger under conditions of temporary adaptation than it is when the normal skin temperature serves as the base line. What is felt as warm or cold depends, then, on the adaptation level of the skin. Indeed, if the skin has been adapted to a temperature of, say, 35° C, then a 32° C stimulus will seem cold (even though ordinarily 32° C is neutral).

The same relativity prevails in the interesting case where the left hand, for example, is adapted to 35° C and the right hand to 29° C. If both are then subjected to a stimulus of 32° C, the stimulus will feel cold to the left hand and warm to the right.

Distribution of Thermal Receptors. A point-by-point mapping of the spots on the skin sensitive to either warm or cold stimuli reveals that there are many more cold than warm spots, by a ratio of about eight or ten to one.

Furthermore, the receptors for warmth and cold lie at different depths within the several layers of the skin, with cold receptors being closer to the surface. Perhaps for this reason, reaction time to cold stimuli is faster than that to warm stimuli.

As with touch and pain, thermal receptors are not evenly distributed over the various parts of the body. The greatest density of cold spots, (ranging from about 8 to 19 spots per square centimeter) is found on the lips, nose, abdomen, and chest; the palm of the hand and the front surface of the fingers have a relatively low density of cold-sensitive spots (about 3 cold spots per square centimeter), whereas the back of the hand and the fingers have an intermediate density of cold spots (about 7.5 per square centimeter). Intermediate densities of cold spots also are found on the forehead, the arms, the legs, and the back.

Several parts of the body are devoid of warm spots—the lips, the forehead, abdomen, back, and upper arm (areas that have an intermediate or high density of cold spots). The greatest density of warm spots (about 1.7 spots per square centimeter) is found on the fingers, both front and back surfaces, and parts of the face other than the lips and nose. The nose has about one warm spot per square centimeter, and the remaining body parts with any warm spots have them with a density of about half a spot or somewhat less per square centimeter.

KINESTHESIS

The kinesthetic sense enables fine control of movement of the limbs and other body parts by providing feedback about these movements as they occur. Through kinesthetic feedback the relation between planned (or intended) movements and actual movements can be assessed and any discrepancies (or errors) can be corrected or compensated for. The difference between a system with and one without such a possibility of feedback and correction is illustrated in the difference in precision between a guided missile and an ordinary artillery shell: The guided missile's path to its target is continually monitored and the missile thereby can be kept on course; once a shell is fired its path is fixed, and if it happens to be off-target, its course cannot be corrected.

Kinesthetic Events—Crucial, but Quiet. The overt behavior of animals and human beings consists solely of complex patterns of movements, effected by muscular contractions. To the extent that these movements, and the behaviors they constitute, are at all precise and skilled, they are dependent on kinesthetic feedback. If any of the senses is indispensable, it must surely be kinesthesis. At the same time, the output of the kinesthetic system is virtually without any phenomenal representation. It is a sensory system that operates almost entirely outside of awareness. Perhaps for this reason, skilled movements are difficult to teach: There is no phenomenal basis for a common language of kinesthesis whereby teacher and student can communicate. The teacher (say, of golf, or piano, or dance) can only comment on the movements ("you didn't follow through on that swing") or the products of the movements ("that B flat was too loud"), but he has little if any access to the kinesthetic events that most directly and intimately guide the intended movements.

Kinesthetic Stimuli and Receptors. The stimuli that initiate kinesthetic activity are the mechanical result of muscular interactions and of the accompanying actions that take place in the joints. Kinesthetic receptors are embedded within the muscles and joints; when stimulated by mechanical displacement (stretching, compression, and so on) they send electrical impulses coursing over the neural fibers to which they are attached.

Given the remarkable precision of movement of which organisms are capable, we ought to expect a similar degree of sensitivity in the kinesthetic system. One basis for such sensitivity has been well-documented (see Mueller, 1965, pp. 112–114). The kinesthetic receptors in the joints turn out to be finely tuned to the angle which the bones of a joint make with each other. That is, a given receptor will be stimulated maximally when the angle falls at a particular value, say 60°; it will also respond, but with decreasing vigor, to a limited range of values around 60°, say between 45° and 75°. When the angle changes, as it does of course during movement involving that joint, different sets of receptors are activated. In this way, movements within a joint are reflected in the sequential pattern of receptor activity. Should movement cease temporarily, then the static angle is signalled by those receptors maximally sensitive to that angle, and the relative positions of the bones which meet at that joint are thereby indicated.

SOMESTHETIC AND KINESTHETIC NEURAL PATHWAYS

We have put off until now discussion of the neural pathways related to the somesthetic and kinesthetic senses because of their considerable similarity. From the point of view of neural organization, the body is composed of several segments, or *dermatomes*. Neural fibers from all receptors within a dermatome are intermixed within a single nerve, which they share with motor neurons carrying impulses to the muscles in that body segment.

The sensory ("afferent") and motor ("efferent") neurons in a given spinal nerve part company just outside the spinal cord, as depicted in Figure 8.14. One branch, or *root,* of the nerve, the *dorsal root,* contains sensory neurons, the other, the *ventral root,* contains motor neurons. This functional arrangement of the two roots of each spinal nerve was discovered independently in the nineteenth century by the French physiologist François Magendie and the British physiologist David Bell; in their honor, it is referred to as the *Bell-Magendie Law.*

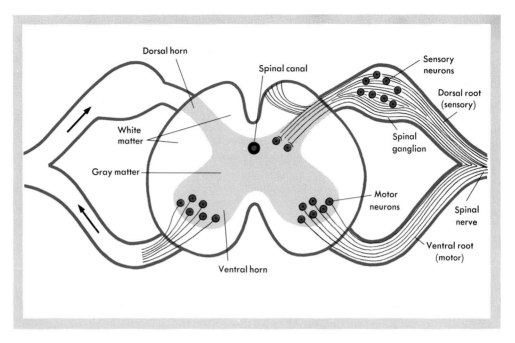

Figure 8.14 Schematic drawing of a cross section of the spinal cord, with dorsal and ventral roots.

Though they are scrambled within the nerve serving one dermatome, the neurons carrying impulses from touch, pain, temperature, and kinesthetic receptors do arrange themselves into two groups prior to their entry into the spinal cord. One group contains mainly touch and kinesthetic neurons, the other those for pain and temperature. Touch and kinesthetic neurons are, for the most part, large in diameter and heavily insulated with a fatty sheath called myelin; pain and temperature neurons are small in diameter and lightly myelinated. (The larger the diameter and the heavier the myelinization, the faster the impulses travel along the neuron.)

The cell bodies of the sensory neurons lie outside the spinal cord in a cluster, or *ganglion*. The neurons entering the cord split, sending fibers both up toward the brain and down to lower segments of the cord, where they participate in spinal reflexes. The "up fibers" from one sense modality are joined within the cord by similar fibers from other dermatomes and together they travel in *tracts*, ultimately arriving, through a series of way-stations too complex to present here, at the cerebral cortex of the brain.

To fill out this rather gross sketch of somesthetic and kinesthetic pathways, we need to provide a few additional details. For one thing, the spinal nerves we have been discussing serve only segments of the trunk and limbs. A separate set of *cranial nerves* (discussed earlier in this chapter) carries somesthetic impulses from the face and head directly to the level of the hindbrain (in the *medulla* and *pons*), where they join neurons traveling up from the spinal cord on their way to the *thalamus*, at the level of the fore-brain. When the various tracts, segregated by sensory function (touch, pain, and so on), reach the thalamus, they lose their functional organization (fibers for touch, pain, and so on are intermixed). An organization based on body parts, or a *topographical* organization once again prevails. Thus, within the thalamus, there is an area containing all fibers serving the somesthetic senses of the legs, the arms, the trunk, the face, and so on. This same type of topographical organization is characteristic of the somatic areas of the cortex.

As with the other senses, the somesthetic senses serve both a specific informational function and a general arousal function, the latter by way of collateral fibers to the *reticular formation* of the midbrain from the main somesthetic tracts that run between the medulla and pons and the thalamus. Recall that stimulation of the reticular formation has an arousing or activating effect on the cortex; sensory stimulation thus generally prepares the cortex for the reception of specific sensory information.

Finally, we might mention three additional points about the projection of somatic fibers onto the brain. (1) Kinesthetic fibers terminate in what is otherwise a motor, not a sensory portion of the cortex (the *precentral* cortex), providing an obvious opportunity for kinesthetic information to modulate impulses going from the cortex to the effector organs. (2) Pain fibers apparently terminate in the thalamus and are not projected onto the cortex (for this reason, surgical operations on the cortex can be performed without pain, providing, of course, that the tissues injured on the way to the cortex are anesthetized). (3) In general, the more sensitive a portion of the body to somesthetic stimulation, the larger is the area of the cortex devoted to that body part. For example, despite their relatively small size, the lips and the fingers have much larger areas of the cortex devoted to them than do the back or the legs.

THE VESTIBULAR SYSTEM

Like the kinesthetic system, the vestibular sense is quiet but crucial. Damage to the vestibular system results in gross impairment in locomotor activity; excessive stimulation of the vestibular system may lead to heightened arousal of the autonomic nervous system, with concomitant heart-rate acceleration, sweating, and, as in sea and air sickness, dizziness, nausea and vomiting. A person is certainly aware of the symptoms triggered by a damaged or unusually stimulated vestibular system; vestibular activity itself, however, like kinesthetic activity, is not phenomenally salient.

The function of the vestibular system is to provide information about the position of the head (and the body to which it is attached) and about the movements of the head and body through space, especially rotary or "angular" movements. Through vestibular cues alone, a person can tell with some accuracy whether his head is in the normal position, or whether the entire body is right-side-up or upside-down. Further vestibular activity signals the fact that the head is moving through space, rather than being stationary, and allows some assessment of the speed of movement (though the system is much more responsive to acceleration than it is to constant speed).

The Vestibular Receptor Organ. The vestibular receptor organ is located in the inner ear; its major elements are shown in Figure 8.15. The figure depicts a complex structure, with three "tubes," or *semicircular canals* emanating from an area containing two sac-like structures. One of the canals is oriented vertically, one horizontally, and one sagittally (that is, in a plane perpendicular to a line passing between the two ears).

The canals are filled with fluid (*endolymph*). At the base of each canal is a bulbous portion, called an *ampulla*. Within each ampulla is a smaller structure, a *crista*. The crista in turn contains at its tip a gelatinous portion, the *cupula*. When the head moves, the cupula bends, because its inertial resistance to movement is less than that of the endolymph surrounding it. As the cupula bends, *hair cells* within the crista are stimulated and electrical impulses are generated in the neural fibers appended to the hair cells. The rate of firing of these vestibular neurons depends on the extent to which the hair cells bend; the latter is a direct function of both the degree of acceleration of the head movement as well as its direction. Maximum activity occurs in that semicircular canal which is oriented most nearly the same as the direction of movement. All three canals are affected by any head movement; it is thus the pattern of neural firing in fibers from all three canals that characterizes a given head movement.

We mentioned two sac-like structures at the base of the three canals. The

Figure 8.15 Sketch of the vestibular receptor organ and its location in the head. (Adapted from Mueller, 1965.)

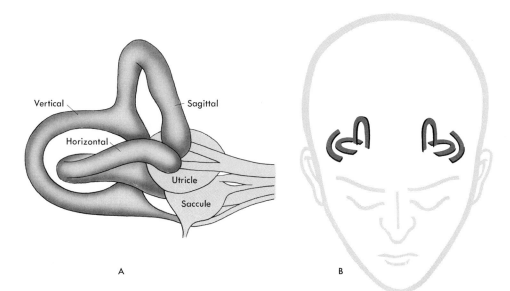

Vertical

Sagittal

Horizontal

Utricle

Saccule

A

B

fluid-filled structures, the *utricle* and *saccule,* contain the receptors that signal the static position of the head, relative to the force of gravity (though there is some uncertainty about the function of the saccule—see Mueller, 1965). The utricle is directly connected with the semicircular canals. Along the bottom of the utricle are structures called *maculae,* similar to the cristae of the semicircular canals. Rising up from the maculae are hair cells, the tips of which are covered with a gelatinous substance. Loosely imbedded in that substance are crystalline particles of calcium carbonate, heavier than the surrounding fluids, called *otoliths.* When the head is inclined, then the weight of the otoliths displaces the hair cells from their normal position. The greater the inclination of the head, the greater the displacement of the hair cells, and the greater the resulting rate of firing generated in the neurons serving this organ.

Note that the receptor cells of the utricle (and perhaps the saccule) respond to the static position of the head, whereas the receptors in the semicircular canals respond primarily to change in position. Through this combination of receptor structures, the vestibular system is able to supply the brain with information that adequately defines the orientation of the body in space. This information serves as the basis for a large number of reflexive movements that help maintain balance and normal locomotor activity. Incidentally, you might consider how the functions of the semicircular canals on the one hand and the utricle on the other might be affected under conditions of weightlessness, as during orbital flight around the Earth.

Vestibular Pathways. Neural impulses initiated in the vestibular receptor organ travel along the VIIIth cranial nerve, which vestibular neurons share with those serving the auditory system. Within the brain vestibular and auditory neurons follow separate routes. The vestibular system is represented in several brain loci. At the level of the brain stem, vestibular neurons terminate in the *cerebellum,* a hindbrain structure that is crucial for the regulation of locomotor activity (see Figure 7.21 in Chapter Seven). At the forebrain level, there is probably vestibular representation in the *thalamus* (a relay station for most of the sensory systems). In the *cerebral cortex* itself, vestibular fibers are projected onto an area that controls eye-movements; here undoubtedly is the origin of one of the characteristic effects of the rapid rotation of the body, that is, nystagmic eye-movements in the plane of rotation. Finally, there is also evidence for vestibular projection on the temporal lobe, close to the area where neurons from the auditory system are heavily concentrated.

ARE THERE OTHER SENSES?

It would be misleading to conclude this chapter without making it explicit that the sensory systems we have mentioned do not exhaust the number that are known. If we were to expand our discussion beyond the basic human sense modalities, we would certainly want to refer, for example, to the possibility that certain animals are sensitive to magnetic fields and perhaps use this sensitivity for navigational purposes. Moreover, we do not wish to imply that all the sensory systems have already been discovered, whether in human beings or in other species. It is not impossible that sensory systems are operative but as yet unknown.

What about extrasensory perception, ESP? Here we are less tentative. Our position is that ESP, as defined by those who propose it, is not a viable scientific concept: If communication occurs between organisms, or if an organism is affected by some physical event, then the medium of the communication (or the perception) must be within the realm of physics and the message must be received through the mediation of some physiologically defined structure. These hypothetical forms of physical energy may not be known in contemporary physics, and the presumed receptor structures may be still unthought of by physiologists. If, however, their existence is demanded by otherwise inexplicable behavioral data, then we will assume that they can, at least in principle, be discovered. But until those data are in hand (and the evidence for ESP is still unimpressive), why worry about hypothetical stimuli and receptors? To understand the sensory systems we know to exist is certainly challenge enough.

SUMMARY

The auditory, or *acoustic*, stimulus is described as a wave; sound occurs when an acoustic stimulus is adequate to affect the ear. The speed of sound waves is about 1100 feet per second when traveling through air—quite slow when compared to the speed of light. *Frequency* (in cycles per second) and *amplitude* (either in pressure units such as dynes per square centimeter or in units of power such as watts) are important parameters of a sound wave. A complex sound results from the mixture of simple, *sinusoidal* waves; through mathematical techniques (Fourier analysis) or physical instruments, complex sound waves can be analyzed into their sinusoidal components. The auditory receptor (loosely, the "ear") performs a similar function.

Structurally, the ear has three divisions—the *outer, middle,* and *inner* ear. The *pinna* of the outer ear helps gather sound waves, which then travel through the external *meatus* to the *tympanic* membrane (the "eardrum"). Vibrations of the eardrum stimulated by sound waves are transmitted to the middle ear through three small bones, or *ossicles*, the *malleus, incus,* and *stapes.* The *oval window* links the stapes to the main auditory structure of the inner ear, the *cochlea,* a coiled structure containing three fluid-filled canals. Separating these canals from one another are *Reissner's membrane* and the *basilar membrane.* The latter bulges when the ear is stimulated; the point of its maximum bulging is determined by the frequency of the sound wave. The bulging of the basilar membrane stimulates *hair cells* on an adjacent structure, the *organ of Corti;* stimulation of particular hair cells results in activation of particular neurons in the auditory nerve. In effect, the hair cells act like a high-fidelity microphone, reproducing in their electrical output (recorded as a *cochlear microphonic*) the parameters of the acoustic stimulus. Neural firing in the auditory nerve also matches the frequency of the acoustic stimulus, and hence is a potential basis for frequency discrimination, but only for stimuli up to about 4000 c.p.s. How that matching might occur (given the fact that any single neuron can fire no faster than about 1000 c.p.s.) is explained in the *volley theory* of Wever and Bray. To account for sensitivity to high-frequency sounds (above 4000 c.p.s.), various *place theories* have been proposed, most recently in a model of cochlear functioning developed by von Békésy. In von Békésy's model the entire burden of frequency discrimination—that is, for low- and high-frequency sounds—is carried by the pattern of bulging of the basilar membrane. In other models, the place on the basilar membrane where maximum bulging occurs is considered to be the basis for discrimination among high-frequency stimuli.

The auditory nerve, which originates in the cochlea, carries impulses to *cochlear nuclei* in the *medulla,* whence through a series of complex pathways auditory impulses travel to the *medial geniculate* body of the *thalamus* and ultimately to several areas of the cerebral cortex, chief among them the *temporal lobe.*

The *audible range* of acoustic wave frequencies for normal human beings is from about 20 to 20,000 c.p.s. Wave frequency is the major physical correlate of the psychological attribute of *pitch,* and wave amplitude largely determines the *loudness* of sounds. But wave frequency affects loudness since the ear is not uniformly sensitive to all frequencies; maximum sensitivity is for sounds in the range from 1000 to 10,000 c.p.s.

Other attributes of sounds are *timbre* (related to the pattern of *fundamental* and *harmonic* frequencies that characterize a particular kind of sound source such as a musical instrument), *chroma, volume, brightness,* and *density.*

The absolute threshold of a 1000 c.p.s. tone is about .0002 dynes per square centimeter. The loudness of sounds is usually defined in relation to that value. The *decibel scale* of loudness translates physical intensity into loudness units, but its validity is limited by the failure of Fechner's Law to apply over the full range of acoustic intensity. Stevens has proposed a *sone scale* of loudness, based on direct loudness judgments.

The lateral location of a sound source is apprehended primarily through two cues, difference between the two ears in the *intensity* of a sound and in its *time of arrival.* Interaural intensity difference is not effective for high-frequency sounds, whereas difference in arrival time is most effective for low-frequency sounds. The *elevation* of a sound source cannot be apprehended through auditory cues alone unless head movements transform elevation into lateralization. The fact that we have two ears is relevant not only for the localization of sound sources. Binaurality is pertinent to methods of enhancing the quality of recorded sounds such as of orchestral productions—that is, through *stereophonic* recording and presentation. Experiments have been done on *dichotic* listening, in which different messages are fed into the two ears. Under these special circumstances, the two ears act like separate channels, rather than in their usual integrated fashion.

The ear's remarkable sensitivity carries with it the price of vulnerability to damage of various sorts and resulting hearing deficits, up to total deafness. *Audiologists* can readily determine whether a particular hearing loss is the result of damage to the structures of the ear (*conduction* deficits) such as the eardrum, ossicles, and basilar membrane, or whether it results from neural damage. This distinction is important because at present conduction deficits can potentially be treated, but neural deafness cannot.

Smell (*olfaction*) and taste (*gustation*) are referred to as chemical senses because of the nature of the adequate stimulus for each. The two modalities are further joined in that there is considerable interaction between them—with, for example, the smell of a substance often highly affecting its taste.

The most promising of olfactory models, by Amoore, proposes a key-and-lock scheme, whereby a particular substance has a characteristic odor because of the three-dimensional shape and size of its constituent molecules. Various substances that smell alike do so because they are sufficiently similar in molecular structure to fit into the same hypothesized apertures in the olfactory receptor surface. Enough is known about the gross anatomy of the olfactory system to identify the hair cells, or *cilia*, that line the mucous membrane deep within the nasal cavity as the primary receptor structures. A neural axon extends from each hair cell to the *olfactory bulb* of the brain. A major issue in olfactory theory is to specify the minimum number of primary odors from which all complex odors can be synthesized. In Amoore's theory, seven such primaries are identified. Odor has considerable biological significance, perhaps more for lower animals than for man. For example, many animals secrete odorous substances, called *pheromones*, that serve to mark off territory, and perhaps to identify for an animal that path over which it has recently traveled. Odor also plays an important role in sexual behavior.

The taste stimulus takes the form of a dilute chemical solution of any readily ionized solution. Taste receptors are located within groups of cells called *taste buds*, distributed in the ridges covering the surface of the tongue. Each taste cell is served by a neuron that is stimulated when an appropriate chemical solution reaches the cell through openings in the taste bud. Stimulation of taste cells is a relatively slow process. Four taste primaries have been identified, sweet, sour, salty, and bitter, each associated with a particular class of chemical substances, and each mediated by taste cells concentrated on a restricted portion of the tongue. Taste receptors are not exclusively stimulated by particular substances; rather, their specificity is determined by the different patterns of neural activity that results from different types of stimulation. The neural pathway from tongue to brain is quite complex, involving three of the 12 cranial nerves. The major relay station is in the *thalamus*, where taste fibers are intermixed with those serving facial touch neurons. Taste and touch neurons travel together from the thalamus to the *somatosensory* area of the cerebral cortex. One obvious way in which taste has biological significance is suggested in experiments that show taste preference to be affected by an animal's nutritional state. For example, rats with an artificially induced salt deficiency consume salt solutions with greater avidity than normal rats.

Touch, pain, warmth, and cold are classified together as the *somatic*, or the *somesthetic* senses, in that they relate primarily to conditions of the body rather than to properties of external objects; for that reason it is appropriate to include along with them *kinesthesis*, which conveys information about the location of the limbs and other movable body parts, and the *vestibular sense*, which helps a person orient himself in space. Touch, pain, warmth, and cold are considered separate senses largely because sensitivity maps of the skin surface reveal that each is sensed by a separate receptor system. Several types of somatic receptors can be distinguished on morphological grounds, but it is doubtful that there is a close relation between receptor type and receptor function.

The adequate stimulus for touch, or *cutaneous* sensitivity, is light pressure on the skin. More intense stimulation results in sensations of *pressure*. Rapidly repeated cutaneous stimulation yields *vibration*, and *tickle* results from light cutaneous stimulation applied simultaneously at two or more adjacent points on the skin. Tactual sensitivity varies over the body surface, with the hands and face most, and the back and soles of the feet least sensitive. Tactual *acuity* is especially high on the lips and fingers. Tactual forms, like visual forms, can be apprehended, and this ability can be improved with training. Tactual and visual form perception do differ, however; for example, the orientation of a tactual form is irrelevant in form-discrimination tasks, but it is quite important in visual form-discrimination. This difference may be a function of differences in people's typical experience with tactual and visual forms, rather than the result of structural differences between the two modalities. The biological significance of tactual sensitivity goes beyond providing information about the presence, location, and form of objects; tactual stimulation also has hedonic qualities, as dramatically shown in Harlow's research on the role of contact comfort in the emotional development of monkeys.

There is considerable ambiguity about the properties of stimuli that elicit pain, as is well illustrated by people who experience severe pain in "phantom limbs." Furthermore, the response to pain can be modified by concurrent stimulation in other modalities. Moreover, some people are congenitally insensitive to pain, and it has been shown that dogs (and perhaps people) deprived of normal stimulation in infancy are markedly unresponsive to typical pain stimuli, as are dogs that have been trained to anticipate pleasurable stimulation following painful stimulation.

Warmth and cold are elicited by increases and decreases, respectively, from a base line in skin temperature. The normal base line is about 32° C but it can be changed through adapting the skin to higher or lower temperatures. There are many more "spots" on the skin surface sensitive to cold than to warmth. Cold and warm spots are unevenly distributed over the body, with the greatest density of cold spots on the lips, nose, abdomen, and chest and the greatest density of warm spots on the fingers; many parts of the body, such as the lips and forehead, are entirely devoid of warm spots.

The kinesthetic sense is crucial to skilled movements, but people ordinarily do not consciously experience kinesthetic sensations. Kinesthetic receptors are embedded in the muscles and joints and are sensitive to fine differences in limb location.

The somesthetic and kinesthetic systems have a common neural arrangement, based on the body's organization into segments, or *dermatomes*. Neural fibers from all receptors within a dermatome reach the spinal cord over the same nerve, which they share with motor neurons carrying impulses to the muscles of that dermatome. Sensory and motor fibers of a nerve separate just outside the cord, with the *dorsal root* being sensory in function and the *ventral root* motor (the Bell-Magendie Law). As they enter the cord, neurons serving touch and kinesthesis are grouped together, as are those for pain and temperature. Within the spinal cord sensory neurons travel both up toward the brain and down to lower segments of the cord. "Up" fibers from different segments, but the same modality join in *tracts* on their way to the cerebral cortex. A similar arrangement prevails for somesthetic fibers from the head which enter the central nervous system over cranial, rather than spinal nerves.

When fibers from spinal and cranial nerves reach the *thalamus* (in the *forebrain*), they are again organized *topographically* (according to body parts) rather than according to sensory function; the same is true of organization in the cerebral cortex itself. Kinesthetic fibers terminate in what is otherwise a motor, not a sensory portion of the cortex; pain fibers apparently terminate in the thalamus and are not represented in the cortex. In general, the more sensitive a portion of the body to somatic stimulation, the larger the area of the cortex devoted to that body part.

The vestibular system operates through a complex structure located in the inner ear. Three fluid-filled tubes, or *semicircular canals,* and their several internal parts supply information about the direction and velocity of head movements. A related structure, the *utricle* (and perhaps the *saccule*) conveys information about the static position of the head. In both the semicircular canals and the utricle it is movement of hair cells that initiates neural activity in the VIIIth cranial nerve that carries neural impulses to several parts of the brain, including the thalamus, the *cerebellum* (a hindbrain structure that controls bodily balance and movement) and portions of the cerebral cortex.

The large number of known sense modalities far exceeds the five specified by Aristotle and there may be additional modalities as yet unknown. It seems fruitless to be concerned with information transmission that by-passes the receptor organs (and their undiscovered counterparts) and that is carried by nonphysical media—in short, ESP—when so much remains to be learned about the conventional sense modalities themselves.

SUGGESTED READINGS

Geldard, F.A. *The human senses.* New York: Wiley, 1953.

Gibson, J.J. *The senses considered as perceptual systems.* Boston: Houghton Mifflin, 1966.

McGaugh, J.L., N.M. Weinberger, and R.E. Whalen (eds.). *Psychobiology.* San Francisco: Freeman, 1967. Chapters 32 ("The Ear" by G. von Békésy), 36 ("Taste Receptors" by E.S. Hodgson), and 37 ("The Perception of Pain" by R. Melzack).

Mueller, C.G. *Sensory psychology.* Englewood Cliffs, N. J.: Prentice-Hall, 1965.

PART THREE

Simple Forms
of Behavior Modification

C H A P T E R N I N E   The modifiability of behavior is one of its most prominent features. In this chapter we discuss two simple types of behavior modification, or learning. First, we describe instances of change in responsiveness to repeated stimulation: an increase in responsiveness, or sensitization; and a decrease, or habituation. Then, in the bulk of the chapter, we consider the modifications in reflex responses, and their theoretical implications, that can be effected by the procedure of classical conditioning, as discovered and investigated by the Russian physiologist Ivan Pavlov.

Human and animal behavior is highly modifiable. Ironically, although psychological theory recognizes this property in its marked emphasis on the learning process, a satisfactory definition of learning is hard to come by. Nevertheless, psychologists quite successfully investigate learning in animals and human beings and rarely run into conceptual difficulties for lack of a perfect definition of the process they are presumably studying. With the active researcher as our model, we will try here to get along without a formal definition of learning, though perhaps an operational one will develop as we explore the variety of instances that have been categorized as learning.

As an organizing principle in the material that follows, we will start with the simplest cases of behavior modification we can find and then move on to more complex instances. The terms "simple" and "complex" themselves are not easy to define, but obviously the former pertains to primitive levels of phylogeny and ontogeny, as well as to lack of complication in the form of the behavior (twitching a muscle is simpler than playing a violin sonata) and in the conditions necessary to effect a behavior modification.

Note that although it is behavior that psychologists observe and behavior modification on which we are presently focusing, the ultimate interest of the learning theorist lies in the unobservable processes that presumably mediate the behavior modification. Since it is awkward always to reserve one term, learning, for the observed events and another for the hypothetical processes, you may not be able to tell from the *language* employed which realm is being discussed; the context, however, should make that clear, especially if you are alert to the distinction.

Temporary Change in Responsiveness

The very simplest organisms are responsive to stimulation and also subject to changes in responsiveness as a result of exposure to stimulation; we can think of such changes as manifestations of the simplest form of learning. If an organism's responsiveness to a stimulus following repeated exposures *increases,* the process is referred to as *sensitization;* if responsiveness *decreases,* it is called *habituation.*

Sensitization. Instances of both sensitization and habituation can be found in organisms low on the phylogenetic scale. For example, the amoeba, a single-celled, very primitive organism, moves by extending *pseudopods,* as illustrated in Figure 9.1. This movement can be inhibited by intense light and also by a series of repeated lights of less intensity. The lights that come late in the series have the same effect as a single, more intense light (Mast and Pusch, 1924). Obviously, we can conclude that the repeated stimulation has increased the amoeba's responsiveness to light, though the exact protoplasmic changes that accompany this sensitization are as yet unknown.

Habituation. For an example of decreased responsiveness to a stimulus, let us go up the phylogenetic scale to the phylum Mollusca. The snail, a species of the gastropod class in phylum Mollusca, is easily aroused to movement by mechanical stimulation, but if the same stimulus is frequently repeated, the response to it gradually diminishes (see, for example, Thompson, 1917).

Habituation is quite evident in higher species, at physiological as well as behavioral levels. For example, an animal's initial reaction to a buzzer might involve a complex pattern of movements; depending on the stimulus intensity and suddenness of onset, the movements are called *startle* or merely *orientation.* In the latter case, the animal turns its head in the direction of the sound source; a dog might prick up its ears and there may be a pattern of mild

Figure 9.1 An amoeba, showing pseudopod. (Courtesy Carolina Biological Supply Company.)

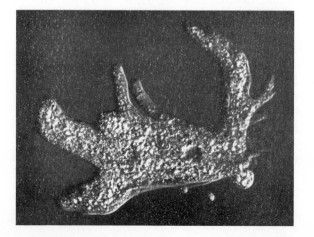

arousal in the autonomic nervous system—pupil dilatation, piloerection (a standing up of the dog's hair), an increase in respiration rate, and so on. But, again, repetition of the buzzer may ultimately neutralize its arousal potential. Of a person we might say that he had "lost interest in" the buzzer.

You might argue that habituation reflects not a central change (such as a loss in the interest value of the stimulus), but more simply some sort of fatigue in the motor, or output, end of the behavioral system. We can easily show that this is not so, at least in typical instances, simply by making a small change in the quality of the stimulus. For example, change the buzzer to a bell, and the full orientation response will be reinstated. Clearly, then, the habituation is stimulus-specific.

An especially interesting example of the specificity of habituation is given in an experiment with cats (Sharpless and Jasper, 1956). After a cat had fallen asleep, it was presented with a tone loud enough to awaken it, as evidenced by its behavior and by the electrical activity (the EEG) recorded from its brain. After the cat had gone back to sleep, the signal was again presented. Eventually, the tone no longer elicited arousal, either behavioral or electrophysiological. Habituation had occurred. But if the pitch of the tone were changed, arousal of both sorts could again be effected.

Similar findings are reported with new-born human infants. In one such experiment (Bartoshuk, 1962) the baby's heart-rate response to a tone was recorded. The response, under the conditions of the experiment, was an acceleration of heart rate; the tone was one that gradually increased in pitch over an eight-second period. Then, after the acceleration in heart rate ceased to occur, a tone was presented that decreased in pitch over its eight-second duration. To this modified signal, the heart rate again accelerated.

It is the stimulus specificity of habituation that makes the phenomenon a clear instance of learning. That is, a specifically encoded representation of the habituated stimulus must be present in the nervous system to be compared with the stimulus currently being presented. If the current stimulus and the encoded representation (often referred to as an *engram*) match, no response is forthcoming. If, however, they fail to match, the standard response to the test stimulus will occur. Clearly, the organism has been modified by the initial experience, and at a central rather than a peripheral level: The potential to respond is still present as is the sensitivity of the receptor organs. In species like cats and human beings, the central modification undoubtedly takes place in the nervous system. As we mentioned earlier, it is not so obvious what protoplasmic changes mediate habituation in primitive organisms such as amoeba.

Because of the presumed temporary nature of habituation and sensitization, some theorists are hesitant to consider them as bona fide instances of learning. Yet, in other contexts permanence is not considered an essential characteristic of learning. Indeed, much learning is of quite brief duration, as you are reminded when between phone book and telephone you forget the number you have just looked up.

Modification of Stable
Stimulus-Response Relations

Certain responses to particular stimuli are readily habituated, but many other stimulus-response relations are highly resistant to habituation, though evocation of the responses may temporarily be diminished through muscular fatigue. Pupillary constriction to intense light is one such highly stable relation; another is the knee-jerk response to a tap on the patellar tendon. Such reliable and sturdy stimulus-response relations are usually called *reflexes*.

REFLEX RESPONSES

One major distinction between a reflex and the easily habituated orienting response referred to earlier lies in the degree of specificity of the stimulus that elicits the response as well as the specificity of the response itself. The orienting response is highly diffuse, involving several muscle systems (for example, those involved in head turning, pupillary dilatation, breathing, and so on). Further, no particular, single stimulus elicits the orienting response. Instead, the response follows on a broad class of stimuli; the crucial characteristic of an effective stimulus here seems to be its novelty and general attraction-getting ability. By contrast, a reflex response is usually quite delimited (an eye blink, pupillary constriction, knee jerk, and so on), and the effective stimulus is also usually quite restricted.

Because reflex relations are so resistant to habituation and so reliable (stimulus X almost invariably will elicit response Y), most theorists assume that they are mediated by built-in neural mechanisms. A simple model of such a mechanism is that of the *reflex arc*, depicted in Figure 9.2. The arc has three components corresponding to the three elements (the stimulus, the response, and the reliable relation between them) of the behavioral reflex it is meant to model. They are (1) an afferent (sensory) neural path from receptor organ to spinal cord or brain, (2) an efferent (motor) neural path that terminates in some effector organ, such as a muscle or a gland, and (3) a synaptic connection (perhaps effected by an intermediary neural unit within the central nervous system) between the afferent and efferent paths.

Such reflex arcs are not myths. They do exist and can be anatomically traced. It turns out, however, that very few reflexes are mediated by "arcs" as simple as the model. For the most part, the neural interconnections are quite elaborate, frequently involving excitatory and inhibitory influences from several levels within the nervous system, including the cerebral cortex itself. Behaviorally, this added neural complexity means that no reflex is independent of the rest of an organism's behavior.

Furthermore, the neural complexity in which the reflex arc is embedded

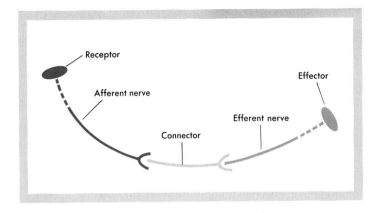

Figure 9.2 A hypothetical reflex arc.

lays open the possibility of modification that is absent in a more simply conceived reflex arc. In short, although reflex relations may be "built in," and hence exceedingly reliable, they may also be modifiable, in the sense of being subject to the long-term aftereffects of experience that we associate with the concept of learning. We have come, via this rather roundabout route, to the topic that has intensely occupied the attention of researchers and theorists in the area of learning for the past half-century—the *conditioned reflex.*

A reflex is stable, which means that a relevant stimulus will very probably elicit a specific response, but it does not necessarily mean that only that stimulus can be effective. Learning might occur, then, as an extension of the number of stimuli that can elicit a particular response. In this form of learning, the effectiveness of the original stimulus is not diminished, but other new stimuli are rendered effective that before learning were ineffective, or "neutral."

The Investigation of Conditioning

The preceding paragraph may sound as though this form of learning is merely hypothetical, but it does indeed take place and is identified by a special label—*conditioning.* The systematic investigation of conditioning was initiated by the renown Russian physiologist Ivan Pavlov (1849–1936), and much of the special terminology associated with this form of learning, as well as the theoretical structure that has been built to account for it, bears the Pavlovian stamp. Since it is likely that Pavlovian terminology will be retained, whatever the developments and refinements in conditioning models, a student of the learning process must be familiar with that special vocabulary. But before introducing the terminology, and before discussing the empirical relations with which conditioning models must cope, we will consider some biographical background on Pavlov and describe his basic experimental approach.

As mentioned, Pavlov was a physiologist. Before his discovery and pursuit of conditioning, he was noted for his research on the circulatory and digestive systems, for which he was awarded the Nobel prize in medicine and physiology in 1904. One of Pavlov's major contributions to research on the digestive system was the development of surgical techniques that allowed direct observation of the gastric secretions of the stomach and the secretions of the salivary glands in otherwise intact animals. With the proper techniques available, these secretions, which play a central role in the digestive process, could be subjected to quantitative and qualitative analysis, and it became feasible to investigate the variables that affect the gastric and salivary secretions—amount and kind of food, noxious substances, such as acid or sand placed in the mouth, and so on. Typically, Pavlov's experimental animal was a dog.

Psychic Secretions and Higher Mental Processes. In the course of such investigation, Pavlov observed that secretions could often be elicited before the food or acid was introduced into the dog's mouth. Merely presenting the substance visually, for example, was an adequate stimulus. Pavlov spoke of these responses as "psychic reflexes." His decision to embark on a thorough study of these "psychic reflexes" was significant, not only for his own career but also for the development of physiology and psychology. Although other scientists had observed the same behavior, Pavlov first saw the potential power in studying it. Moreover, he was ready to devote the energy necessary for both the empirical investigation of the behavior and the formulation of a theoretical structure to explain its many complex facets.

Figure 9.3   Ivan Pavlov. (Brown Brothers.)

As for the "power" referred to above, Pavlov saw in the behavior in question a means for finding out about the functioning of the nervous system, specifically the cerebral cortex; for it was the cortex, so Pavlov believed, that controlled the "psychic secretions." A dog could not talk, but its "higher mental processes" could be probed objectively and systematically through the "psychic secretions." Pavlov was highly skeptical of the possibility of a scientific psychology that relied on introspection and verbal reports. But with the "psychic reflex" available as an objective, quantifiable indicator of cortical functioning, he was convinced of the possibility of a scientific psychophysiology.

Whatever the scientific merits of his arguments, it happened that Pavlov's scientific objectivism meshed with the political ideology and materialistic philosophy that came to the fore in Russia during the period of the Bolshevik revolution, and his position helped shape the course of—or at least provide a scientific rationale for—many of the socioeducational developments in that country. Despite the political significance that was read into his ideas, however, Pavlov himself remained virtually untouched by the turmoil that followed the Revolution, frequently indeed expressing his disagreement with the current wielders of political power, especially as they intruded on scientific and academic affairs. He was able to pursue his scientific investigations with a marked degree of freedom from outside interference. Pavlov's biography, both personal and political, is a fascinating one; further detail can be found in the references listed at the end of this chapter. Now to look at the work itself.

THE PAVLOVIAN CONDITIONED REFLEX: BASIC TERMINOLOGY AND PROCEDURES

First, we must introduce a change in terminology. "Psychic secretions" did not last long in Pavlov's language. They were replaced by the now-familiar *conditioned reflexes*. To use the terms that were introduced earlier, the establishing of a conditioned reflex increases the probability that an initially ineffective, or neutral, stimulus will elicit a response that is normally given as a reflex to some other stimulus. In Pavlov's terminology, the reflex relations that constitute an animal's pre-experimental behavior are called *unconditioned reflexes*. These unconditioned reflexes most likely are innate, but that property is not an essential criterion. What is crucial is that the stimulus is reliably and stably followed by the response, that the relation is strong and not subject to habituation.

For a concrete example, let us examine in more detail the conditioned reflex that first attracted Pavlov's attention—the secretion of saliva when food was displayed to the dog. Although Pavlov did not intentionally establish that relation in his first dog in order to show the "psychic secretions," he found that he could readily produce it, or its analogs, through a rather simple experimental procedure, now referred to as *classical, or Pavlovian, conditioning*. Here is how it works.

Salivary Conditioning. First, by the surgical techniques Pavlov developed, the salivary duct is brought outside the dog's cheek, so that it becomes possible to count the number of drops of saliva delivered on any occasion and to do chemical analyses of their composition. The dog is then placed in the experimental apparatus, which is constructed so as to keep the animal comfortably confined and isolated from extraneous stimulation.

When the animal is adapted to the situation, the experiment proper is ready to begin. A stimulus is presented, called the *conditioned stimulus* (abbreviated CS), which is known not to elicit the response to be conditioned—salivation for this example. The CS might be a buzzer, or a light, or any stimulus that is sufficiently attractive to elicit an orienting response. The presentation of the conditioned stimulus, say a buzzer, is followed by the presentation of a stimulus that does elicit the salivary response; this latter stimulus is called an *unconditioned stimulus* (abbreviated US). For this example let the US be food powder placed in the dog's mouth. Reflex salivation to the food powder is referred to as the *unconditioned response* (UR).

The sequence of events, CS→US→UR, constitutes one conditioning trial. Remember, the intent is to modify the dog's nervous system so that salivation will eventually occur to the CS in the absence of the US. When that goal is achieved, then conditioning has taken place, and the original unconditioned response—salivation to food power—has been extended into a *conditioned response* (abbreviated CR)—in this example, salivation to a buzzer. To establish a strong conditioned response of the sort described in the present example usually requires several conditioning trials. Typically, as the number of trials increases, the vigor of the conditioned response becomes greater, as manifested, for example, by an increase in the number of drops of saliva in response to the CS.

Note that if the CS and the US are separated by only a brief time period, then it might not be possible to ascertain whether the salivation is an unconditioned response to the food powder or a conditioned response to the buzzer. For that reason, it might be necessary to omit the US on some trials during the course of the experiment. Such trials become *test trials* rather than training or conditioning trials. (They might be more than simply test trials, as we will see later when we discuss the phenomenon of *experimental extinction*.)

Pavlovian Conditioning: Basic Form or Special Case of Learning? The development of a CR can be shown graphically, as in Figure 9.4 which is derived from a real experiment. Here, the strength of the CR is plotted on the

Figure 9.4 Strength of conditioning as a function of number of reinforced stimuli applied to the skin. (Adapted from Deese and Hulse, 1967; based on an experiment by Hovland, 1937, with human subjects.)

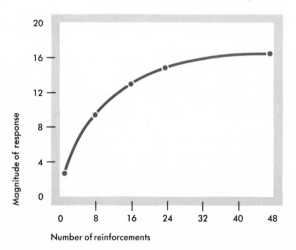

ordinate, and training trials on the abscissa. Note how the curve rises rapidly at first and then levels off. Because this general shape is typical of many different types of *learning curves,* some theorists believe that all forms of learning follow the same basic laws and that the investigation of simple forms, like Pavlovian conditioning, yields results that can be broadly generalized. Some theorists, indeed, believe that all instances of learning are special cases of Pavlovian conditioning. However, just to make matters more interesting, there are also those who consider Pavlovian conditioning a special case of another, more basic type of learning. Finally, there are a few theorists for whom conditioning and other forms of learning are distinct classes, each with its own laws. This theoretical controversy has lent considerable spice to what might otherwise be a fairly dull area of investigation, though it may leave the uninitiated with a feeling of intolerable ambiguity.

Basic Variables in Pavlovian Conditioning

The description of Pavlovian conditioning offered above was necessarily general. Omitted were any details about the specific values of the variables that determine the strength of conditioning. Although the Pavlovian design may seem simple, it nevertheless affords a host of possible variations and combinations of conditions, many of which by now have been empirically studied. It has been found that conditioning can be markedly affected, depending on which values of the several manipulable variables are employed.

TEMPORAL VARIABLES

The schematic diagram given in Figure 9.5 presents the major temporal variables that influence conditioning. In that diagram, the upper line represents the onset, duration, and termination point of the CS, while the lower lines represent some possible values of the same temporal parameters of the US; the upper line and any of the lower lines considered simultaneously reflect the relations among the temporal parameters of the CS and US—for example, how CS termination relates to US onset.

The CS-US Interval. Of all the temporal relations, the time between CS termination and US onset is probably the most important; it certainly has received a substantial amount of attention from researchers and theorists. The generalization which has emerged from this work holds that for strongest conditioning to occur there is an optimal interval between CS termination and US onset of about 500 milliseconds (one-half second). Conditioning becomes progressively weaker as that interval grows longer or shorter. In a special case called *backward conditioning,* when the interval has a negative value (that is, when the US precedes the CS), the strength

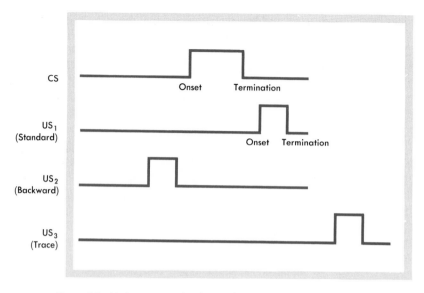

Figure 9.5 Various temporal relations between CS and US. US₁ is the standard relation; US₂ is the backward conditioning paradigm; US₃ is the paradigm of trace conditioning.

of conditioning drops abruptly; indeed, backward conditioning may be impossible to establish.

Pavlov found two other types of temporal relation between CS and US of particular interest, *trace conditioning* and *delayed conditioning*.

Trace Conditioning. In trace conditioning, the CS goes on and off, and then after a lengthy interval the US is presented. Presumably the association to be formed between the originally independent events, CS and US, is contingent on the subject's maintaining a "trace," or neural representation, of the now absent CS; this trace enters into the formation of the new neural relation between CS and US. Indeed, the ability to establish a trace-conditioned response implies the existence of some trace-maintaining neural mechanism; the term *reverberating circuit* is often used by contemporary theorists to refer to such a mechanism.

The idea is that there is in the brain some way of maintaining, for at least brief time periods, the neural activity aroused by a particular stimulus after that stimulus is withdrawn. That is, the activity initiated by a stimulus does not cease as soon as the stimulus terminates; rather, that activity continues somewhat like a series of echoes (hence the word "reverberating"), gradually declining in volume unless reinstated by the recurrence of the stimulus. Such a reverberation may even be considered a rudimentary form of learning, the nervous system being temporarily modified by the stimulating event. Indeed, the reverberating circuit may form the neural substrate of what is often called *short-term memory* or, by some psychologists, *very short-term memory*. One task for the learning theorist is to specify the conditions under which temporary traces are transformed into long-lasting modifications, as well as the conditions that prevent or interfere with that transformation. For a concrete example, what determines whether a phone number you look up will "last" long enough to allow you to dial that number accurately or whether the number will be "lost" by the time you reach the phone? What are the conditions under which a phone number becomes permanently available in memory? Questions of this sort reveal how merely separating the CS and US in time raises fundamental problems about the kinds of neural structures involved in the learning process.

If the optimal interval between CS and US is about 500 milliseconds, then trace conditioning, where the interval might be a few seconds, is very clearly difficult to establish; but it is a possibility as is an extreme form called "long-trace" conditioning, where the interval might be several minutes. To obtain long-trace conditioning, however, it is probably necessary to start with a brief interval between CS and US and then gradually extend the interval.

Despite the apparent fragility of the trace, the simultaneous occurrence of CS and US is not optimal for conditioning; obviously the neural events in the conditioning relationship involve at least one trace—that of the CS. Surely, this must have some bearing on the nature of the learning process, though what it exactly implies is not entirely obvious. Perhaps the neural activity directly evoked by a stimulus cannot enter into associations with other ongoing neural activity (as from the US), and associations might form only between traces. Or perhaps there is an optimal level of intensity of the neural activity that represents the CS; if the CS itself is quite intense, then the neural activity which it immediately evokes may be too intense, and only when the CS terminates and its weaker trace is present can conditioning be maximally attained. The foregoing are not serious hypotheses, but only examples of the kind of speculation that is aroused by considering the implications of basic conditioning data. Nevertheless, it is worth noting that Pavlov himself believed that the CS must evoke a less intense neural response than does the US if conditioning is to occur.

Delayed Conditioning. In delayed conditioning the CS begins and stays on for several seconds before the US is presented. Note that delayed conditioning differs from a trace-conditioning procedure only in that the interval between CS onset and US onset is "filled" with the CS.

What is of primary interest in delayed conditioning is that the CR, when it does develop, occurs just prior to the onset of the US. That is, the CR does not follow immediately on the presentation of the CS but is delayed (hence the label) over what may be a fairly lengthy interval. As conditioning progresses, the CR may work its way back in time toward the CS—as indeed often happens also in trace conditioning—but in any event, it does not occur right after the CS.

One interpretation of the behavior characteristic of delayed conditioning is that the CS becomes in part inhibitory. In this situation a dog appears to be simultaneously excited by the CS to make the CR and also inhibited from making the CR "too soon." Why such inhibition should develop is not entirely clear, since the experimenter does not, at least intentionally, impose it as a "requirement" on the subject; that is, the US will be presented on schedule regardless of whether or where the CR is made. (Incidentally, this noncontingent relationship between the occurrence of the CR and the presentation of the US is what distinguishes Pavlovian, or classical, conditioning from a type of conditioning referred to as instrumental, to be discussed in the next chapter.)

Invoking inhibition becomes necessary only if the CS is assumed to acquire an excitatory effect during the course of conditioning. If the CS does become excitatory, as in some sense it must if it is to arouse the CR, then the CS onset might be expected immediately to call forth the CR. The fact that the CR is delayed is what must be accounted for, and that is where inhibition enters.

Delayed conditioning raises another question. How do we explain the animal's rather precise "placement" of the CR just before the US? This behavior suggests that the dog is able to appreciate the absolute value of the delay interval. We might say that what effectively elicits the CR in this situation is *time* and that the function of the CS is to signal the onset of a time interval. The dog's self-imposed task is to estimate the end of that interval and give a CR.

Temporal Conditioning. That time can serve this role for animals is evidenced quite clearly in another of the many conditioning paradigms. In this one, there is no specific CS. Instead, the US is presented repeatedly at regular intervals—say, once every two minutes. In effect, the US marks both the end of one interval and the onset of the next. The subject, however, must "estimate" the passage of time, and in fact dogs and other animals can make CR's with considerable accuracy just prior to the onset of each US. This paradigm is called *temporal conditioning;* Pavlov reported successful temporal conditioning with intervals as long as 30 minutes. Exactly how a dog accomplishes the time estimation is not known, although there are other instances in which lower organisms have given evidence of some sort of "internal clock" (see Chapter Fifteen).

CS Intensity. The intensity of the CS is generally assumed to affect the strength of conditioning—the more intense the stimuli the more effective the conditioning. At the low end of the intensity scale, this must certainly be so, since if the CS intensity is too weak it will fall below threshold. There is some question, however, about the relation at the very high end of the intensity scale, for it may be that a stimulus can be too intense to serve as a good CS. Such a reversal in the relation at the high end might be expected from Pavlov's notion that an important difference between the CS and the US, besides time of onset, is that the latter evokes more intense neural excitation than the former. This difference in degree of neural activity determines the direction of the conditioning—that is, whether the buzzer will come to elicit salivation or whether food powder will come to elicit ear pricking and head turning. This difference in intensity must be relevant when CS and US go on and off simultaneously.

The picture is not entirely clear, however. One fascinating, but somewhat embarrassing, finding reported by Pavlov is that stimuli which evoke intense pain, such as pinching or burning the dog's skin can be used as effective conditioned stimuli. Instead of the normal reaction to these painful stimuli, the dog, through classical conditioning, can be made to salivate to them or to make some other ordinarily inappropriate response.

Within the range of intensities between the subthreshold and the excessively intense, the relation between CS intensity and strength of conditioning is, according to Pavlov's results, a direct one. However, attempts to replicate these results with human subjects have not been successful (see Kimble, 1961). The relation may be confined to dogs.

The Distinction between Learning and Performance. Another possibility is that Pavlov's results were themselves misinterpreted, for on any *test* of strength of conditioning, the test-stimulus intensity, in Pavlov's experiments, is identical with the CS intensity. It may indeed be that conditioning is not affected by the intensity of the CS, but that the strength is a direct function of test-stimulus intensity. The distinction between the strength of conditioning (a hypothetical value) and the strength of the conditioned response evoked by a test stimulus is a fundamental one in learning theories developed by American psychologists. The difference is often referred to as one between *learning* and *performance*. The point, then, is that CS intensity may not influence the strength of learning, but it may affect the vigor of performance of a learned response. Any empirical test of strength of conditioning must be so designed that these two effects are not confounded.

One way to accomplish this is to train each of a group of subjects at a different level of CS intensity and then test all groups at the same intensity level. Any difference in performance cannot be attributed to differences in intensity of the test stimulus, but might be attributed to the differences that prevailed during the training phase. But even with this sophisticated design a problem in interpretation remains; as we shall see below when we discuss the phenomenon of *stimulus generalization,* the ability of a test stimulus to evoke a CR is a function not only of its absolute intensity but also of its similarity to the CS employed during the establishment of the CR. Thus, the problem arises about which single value of test-stimulus intensity to use. One solution is to use not one, but several values of test-stimulus intensity along with the several values of CS intensity employed during conditioning. (For a technical presentation of the details of such designs, you might consult Kimble (1961) as well as the other texts listed at the end of the chapter.)

The Limits of Pavlovian Conditioning

So far we have considered the variables of time and intensity that affect the strength of conditioning. Now we want to turn to the circumstances under which conditioning is at all possible.

CONDITIONABLE RESPONSES AND STIMULI

What kinds of responses can be conditioned through classical procedures? Contemporary Russian researchers report a remarkable variety of potentially conditionable responses. Some of the more interesting responses that have been successfully conditioned in human subjects are gastro-intestinal secretions, constriction and dilatation of the blood vessels, galvanic skin response (that is, change in the electrical resistance of the skin), respiration rate, and even certain immunity reactions, which occur as unconditioned responses when toxic substances enter the blood stream (see Kimble, 1961, p. 51). These are all responses that human subjects are unaware of making.

A related question, and one that also has yielded some startling answers, has to do with the kinds of stimuli that can serve as conditioned stimuli. Aside from stimuli applied to receptors on the surface of the body—that is, *exteroceptive* stimuli (lights, sounds, odors, tactual stimuli, and the like)— several types of *interoceptive* stimuli have also been successfully used, as when the CS takes the form of stimulation of the internal organs, stimulation of which the subject is not aware. (Here, incidentally, is an instance in which subthreshold stimuli serve as effective CS's, in apparent contradiction to the earlier statement that CS intensity must be at least above threshold to be effective. It may be that different rules apply for interoceptive and exteroceptive stimuli.)

Conditioning Without Awareness. With conditioned stimuli of which the subject is unaware and responses which also occur without awareness, it may very well be possible to establish conditioning when both the CS and the CR lie outside the subject's awareness. It is perhaps this possibility that lends to the conditioned response its aura of mystery and danger. Can people indeed be trained to respond, unwittingly, to events outside their awareness? If so, can this possibility be used in the service of malevolent or even well-intentioned persons (the "mad scientists," the totalitarian government, the commercial advertiser, the loving parent, and so on) to the detriment of individual freedom? Indeed, many of our important visceral, vascular, and other subtle internal reactions may well occur as conditioned responses to stimuli with which they have been fortuitously associated; furthermore, these responses may play a part in our emotional reactions to certain social stimuli.

Emotional Conditioning. There is a well-known demonstration of what might be considered the induction of attitudinal or emotional responses through classical conditioning (Watson and Raynor, 1920). In this famous experiment, the CS and US were both well above threshold, though the paradigm might apply to situations in which either stimulus is subthreshold. The subject in the experiment was a baby, named Albert. The US was a sudden loud noise, the UR a startle response followed by crying. During the conditioning period, the occurrence of the US was preceded by presentation of a white rat as the CS. Before conditioning, the white rat only elicited an orienting response. After several pairings of CS and US, however, Albert began to show some of the same emotional, or "affective," response to the rat as he did to the loud noise.

If attitudes are diluted emotional responses—or predispositions to respond with a particular affect to a class of stimuli—then it is reasonable to assert that Albert's originally positive attitude toward white rats had been transformed, through the conditioning procedure, into a negative attitude. It is tempting indeed to wonder how many of our important attitudes are formed in this manner, though perhaps more subtly and fortuitously. Think, for example, of a young child who, upon approaching and petting a friendly-appearing dog, is nipped on the hand. A conditioned association of this sort might be formed: Dog (CS) elicits withdrawal and crying (UR). Might it not happen over time that "dog" eventually elicits only a fragment of the original CR, perhaps just a feeling of uneasiness that finds verbal expression as "I hate dogs"? From this kind of example it is easy to proceed to the more significant types of social attitudes, such as racial prejudice, that may have their genesis in some accidental pairing of stimuli.

One-Trial Conditioning. There is one feature of our example of the child bitten by the dog that may seem out of line with all our previous discussion. We have "allowed" conditioning to take place after only a single pairing of CS and US, and yet elsewhere we state that conditioning becomes increasingly strong with increasing numbers of training trials. You might question the possibility of such *one-trial* learning in the face of so many experiments that conform to the notion that acquisition of a CR is a gradual, multitrial affair. There are, however, experimental reports of one-trial conditioning, involving aversive unconditioned stimuli of great intensity such as a very powerful electric shock. After only one exposure to such a severe US, dogs form a strong avoidance response to the stimulus used as the CS. Indeed, the *conditioned avoidance response* is so well established on a single trial that it is almost impossible to eliminate from the dog's behavioral repertory through the usual procedures (to be discussed below) for extinguishing a learned response (Solomon, Kamin, and Wynne, 1953). One-trial conditioning, then, is possible under certain circumstances; there is, therefore, no reason in principle why such conditioned responses cannot be established outside the laboratory—especially in young children for whom apparently mild stimuli may actually be traumatic. For example, a toddler named Laura learned, much to the surprise of her parents, to keep her inquisitive fingers away from electrical outlets by virtue of only one occasion on which she approached an outlet and was rather moderately admonished "no-no, Laura" by her father. The "no-no" elicited an unexpectedly vigorous and virtually inconsolable crying response—and wall outlets were henceforth carefully avoided.

Not all attitudes are negative. The application of conditioning principles to the explanation of certain positive attitudes might also prove fruitful. Yet is it hard to find in the psychological literature a laboratory demonstration of positive emotional or attitudinal induction through classical conditioning that is parallel to the Watson and Raynor experiment with Albert. One series of studies that fits fairly well, however, was conducted by Gregory Razran (1938a, 1938b, 1940, 1954).

In those studies—which are more complex in design than can be briefly summarized here—college students served as experimental and control subjects. The experimental subjects were brought to the "laboratory" on several days at or after the lunch hour ostensibly to participate in a study of the way "different stimuli get connected up in one's mind and how eating effects such connections" (Razran, 1954, p. 279). The different stimuli consisted of such items as paintings, musical passages, political slogans, pictures of girls, and so on. While examining these stimuli, the experimental subjects, who were quite hungry, also ate a lunch provided by the experimenter.

The intent was to associate the stimuli with the salivary response (UR) made to the food. With that association established, Razran wanted to find out whether the various CS's would evoke the CR of salivation and, of greater interest, whether the experience would increase the subjects' positive feelings toward the stimuli. To test these expectations Razran compared the experimental subjects' behavior with that of control subjects who went through exactly the same procedures except that they had already eaten lunch before arriving at the laboratory. In a set of experiments (Razran, 1938a, 1938b, 1940), the expected effects were observed: The experimental subjects made conditioned salivary responses to the paintings and other stimuli used as CS's; furthermore their ratings of these stimuli revealed an increase in their liking for them.

Razran's experiments demonstrate the possible role of conditioning-like procedures, in a fairly naturalistic setting, that have generalized attitudinal consequences. How much of our emotional-attitudinal behaviors are built on simple conditioning experiences is, of course, an open question. That classical conditioning may play a role in the formation of these structures is certainly suggested by studies such as those of Watson and Raynor and of Razran.

We got into the preceding discussion of attitudinal-affective conditioning by asking what types of responses are conditionable. An adequate answer to that question must take into account the obvious fact of vast phylogenetic and ontogenetic differences in behavioral repertories and nervous system structure (if any). That is, possible conditioned responses for one species, at one ontogenetic level, would not necessarily overlap entirely with those for another species, or for the same species at a different level of development. Clearly, it is essential to look into the phylogenetic and ontogenetic aspects of conditioning. Two questions worth considering are: (1) How low on the phylogenetic scale can classical conditioning be demonstrated? (2) How early in his development can a human being be conditioned?

Paramecia and Planaria. In response to the first question, we can turn to the several attempts to demonstrate behavior modification in animals at the lowest end of the scale, single-celled protozoa such as *paramecium aurelia.* These animals, shown in Figure 9.6, are about 150 microns in length and about 40 microns in width, a micron being 0.001 millimeter. Though single-celled, they do have differentiated structures; for example, they move in water by means of the beating action of hair-like processes called *cilia.* In addition, they have specialized structures for the ingestion of food and the expulsion of waste material, and they appear to have a crude behavior-integrating structure, in the form of a *neural fibril,* that interconnects the cilia. The paramecium is sensitive to certain environmental conditions, such as the chemical composition of the fluid medium in which it exists; for example, it will swim into an area with a weak concentration of acid. An examination of the paramecium's behavior reveals a variety of fixed patterns, such as a tendency to "cling" to the walls and floor of the container in which it is held, especially when carbon dioxide concentration is high. Beyond these fixed patterns, the paramecium also exhibits considerable behavioral variability (see the comprehensive monograph by H.S. Jennings, 1906).

Given the rather extensive and somewhat flexible behavioral repertory, a very primitive, but nonetheless

Figure 9.6 A paramecium. (Courtesy Carolina Biological Supply Company.)

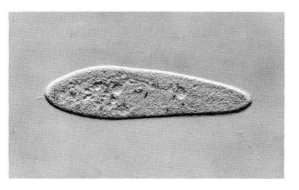

effective, integrating structure (the neural fibril), and sensitivity to at least a few external "stimuli," it is not inconceivable that the paramecium is conditionable. However, the one serious claim for the establishment of a CR in paramecium by Beatrice Gelber (1952) has not withstood the test of rational and empirical criticism (Jensen, 1957, 1959). The Gelber-Jensen controversy is sufficiently instructive concerning the specific problem of demonstrating conditioning, as well as the general problem of interpreting the results of behavioral investigations, that it deserves detailed attention here.

Gelber employed the following general procedure. A group of paramecia were placed in a dish filled with clear water. On each of several trials a platinum wire was introduced into exactly the same place in the water. On "training" trials the tip of the needle would be baited with bacteria, of the sort normally ingested by the paramecia; on test trials, which lasted three minutes, the tip was sterile. As the number of training trials increased, so did the number of paramecia found in contact with the sterile wire on the intermittent test trials. No such change was noted in control animals, for which the platinum wire had never been baited. In the language of conditioning, some aspect of the platinum wire, or of its insertion into the water, is a CS; the bacteria serve as a US that elicits the UR of approaching and adhering to the wire. The increasing number of paramecia in the vicinity of the wire on test trials can be thought of as indicative of the growth of a CR.

Gelber herself carefully reported these observations in fairly neutral terms, referring to the change in the animals' behavior, though not specifically to "learning" or "conditioning." Other writers, however, in interpreting her findings, spoke of them as evidence for learning in paramecia. It was to this interpretation that Jensen objected. On rational grounds he was skeptical of the possibility of establishing conditioning under the circumstances employed, not necessarily because learning *per se* seemed unlikely in such a primitive organism, but more simply because the "application of the concept 'approach response' to the behavior of *Paramecium aurelia* overestimates the sensory and motor capabilities of the organism" (Jensen, 1959, p. 83). But whatever the merits of the rational arguments, pro and con, the specific issue concerning the proper interpretation of Gelber's results was neatly disposed of by Jensen in a beautifully conceived set of experiments (Jensen, 1957). First, he demonstrated that repeated insertion of the baited needle created in the dish of water a localized area of heavy bacteria concentration. Second, Jensen showed that paramecia tend to remain in such an area once they have entered it. Finally, he showed that paramecia, while in an area high in bacteria concentration, exhibit a strong tendency to adhere to solid surfaces. The observations, based on carefully executed experiments, are sufficient to explain the behavior of Gelber's animals. In the spirit of parsimony, an explanation that does not require reference to such a high-level process as learning is preferable to one that does. Whether subsequent experimentation will reveal convincing evidence of learning in protozoa remains to be seen.

Not too much farther up the phylogenetic scale from protozoa is the phylum Platyhelminthes. This phylum, in which bilateral symmetry of the body makes its first appearance, contains the flatworms, planaria, on which psychologists interested in conditioning have recently focused a great deal of attention.

Planaria are tiny creatures, but considerably larger than paramecia, on the order of one-half to one inch in length. In addition to bilateral symmetry, true synaptic transmission of neural impulses appears in this phylum for the first time. Planaria are also differentiated into head and tail ends, the head end containing light-sensitive receptors and clumps of neural cells called *ganglions* that constitute primitive brains. A distinctive characteristic of planaria is their ability to regenerate complete bodies if they are cut into two or more pieces.

If a planarian is stimulated by a mild electric shock, two unconditioned responses are observed: (1) a turning of the head end and (2) a longitudinal contraction of the body. These responses apparently can be transformed into CR's through classical conditioning procedures. Thus, if the electric shock is preceded by a light, the light gradually comes to elicit the head-turning and body-contraction responses. Control experiments indicate that the behavior change exhibited by animals receiving light-shock pairs is true conditioning and not simply the result of a general increase in sensitivity to all stimuli, produced by the repeated shocks (Thompson and McConnell, 1955). Results from a typical experiment are presented in Table 9.1. Although some psychologists remain skeptical, the present consensus is that simple learning is demonstrable in planaria.

What have generated even greater interest, and further skepticism from certain critics, are experiments purporting to show two types of transfer of this learning: (1) transfer to regenerated portions of planaria that have been trained and then cut up, and (2) transfer to other planaria that have been fed the chopped-up bodies of trained planaria. Considering the current excitement over these results, especially the latter, we will briefly describe a prototypic experiment of each sort.

In one experiment (McConnell, Jacobson, and Kimble, 1959), planaria were given 50 conditioning trials per day, as decribed above, until they reached a criterion level of performance, defined as 23 CR's within 25 trials. Then each animal was cut in half, leaving a head end and a tail end, and the halves were allowed four weeks to regenerate. Following that period, retraining was instituted and the number of trials necessary to reach criterion performance was again determined.

The results are summarized in Table 9.2. Note that criterion performance was achieved much more rapidly in the retraining phase than in the original learning phase—a common finding in conventional learning experiments, referred to as "savings." Of special interest is the highly similar performance of the two groups comprised of regenerated heads and tails. The lack of difference suggests that whatever organismic changes mediate the original

Group	Type of Response	Early	Late	Difference	p
E	Turns	12.6	16.6	4.0	.01
	Contractions	1.2	5.0	3.8	.01
LC	Turns	11.7	7.6	—4.1	.01
	Contractions	0.6	2.1	1.5	N.S.
SC	Turns	5.4	4.2	—1.2	N.S.
	Contractions	0.2	0.4	0.2	N.S.

Table 9.1 Mean number of responses "early" and "late" in training for the experimental group (E) and the two sensitization control groups, light control (LC) and shock control (SC). For the E and LC groups Early and Late refer to the first and last 50 trials, respectively; for the SC group the reference is to the first and last 15 trials. N.S. means the difference was not statistically significant—that is, a difference that is likely to have occurred just by chance; p values of .01 means that the probability of the difference occurring by chance is 1 in 100: The difference is highly significant. Note that for the LC group the mean number of turns significantly declined over "training," making the significant increase for the E group even more impressive. (Adapted from McConnell, 1962.)

conditioning are diffused throughout the planarian's entire body, not localized in the head end.

To assure that the apparent savings exhibited by the regenerated animals was indeed transferred from the original learning, and not produced by

Table 9.2 Mean number of trials to criterion for the experimental (E) group and for the regeneration control (RC) and time control (TC) groups. See text for description of conditions. (Adapted from McConnell, 1962.)

Group	Original Training	Retest Head	Retest Tail
E	134	40	43.2
RC		248.6	207.8
TC	185.4	39.8	

some kind of sensitization to all stimuli attributable to the bisection or the regeneration period, a control group was included in the experiment. The control animals were given no training before being cut in half, but after regeneration, the conditioning procedure was applied. These animals required an average of more than 200 trials to reach criterion: The operation, if it had any effect, slowed down the rate of acquisition of the unconditioned response.

Another question investigated concerns the number of trials to reach criterion during the retraining phase as compared with the number that would be required by planaria that were trained, then retrained after a four-week interval had passed. Why did the regenerated animals need so many retraining trials? The performance of a control group indicated that what the regenerated animals had lost was largely attributable to the mere passage of time.

An even more dramatic experiment (see McConnell, 1962) investigated the possibility of transferring a conditioned response from one planarian to another. After a variety of unsuccessful attempts, such as injecting protoplasm from a trained planarian into an untrained one, the experimenters hit on the simple procedure of allowing untrained planaria to eat the ground-up bodies of trained planaria. Control animals were fed on the remains of other untrained planaria. Following their cannabalistic feast, the experimental and control planaria were given the usual conditioning trials, and the experimentals made about 50 per cent more CR's early in training than did the control animals.

Some hint about the mechanisms of learning and transfer in planaria is offered in an elegant experiment by Corning and John (1961), designed to test the hypothesis that the protein molecule *ribonucleic acid* (RNA) is involved in the retention of learned associations. Corning and John argued that trained planaria that are cut and allowed to regenerate in a medium containing the enzyme *ribonuclease*, which is an inhibitor of RNA, would fail to show the normal amount of transfer. This indeed was the case for the regenerated tail ends, which behaved just like untrained animals. But not so for the regenerated head ends, which exhibited considerable transfer. For them, retention of the original conditioned response seemed independent of RNA. The experimenters suggest that the learning which occurs in the head end of a planarian involves some kind of change in the neural structure itself, with no RNA involvement. The retention exhibited by normally regenerated tail ends is, however, dependent on RNA. Therefore, the learning in the tail ends must be carried, not by neural changes, but by RNA.

If RNA does play a part in the process of retention, then it might be the vehicle by which transfer of conditioning from one planarian to another is effected. On this tenuous basis, we might expect that RNA extracted from the brain of a trained animal of any species could, if properly injected, substitute for training in another member of that species. A host of experiments, using rats as subjects, has been done to test that intriguing hypothesis. Some have been supportive of the hypothesis (for example, Jacobson, Babich, Bubash, and Jacobson, 1965), but replication attempts have not been uniformly successful.

The mere demonstration of conditioning in planaria is sufficient to provide a tentative answer to the first of the two questions we asked at the beginning of this section: Conditioning can occur in animals at least as low on the phylogenetic scale as the phylum Platyhelminthes. At this level there exists a very primitive, but nevertheless true synaptic nervous system; an integrating mechanism of at least that degree of complexity may well be a prerequisite for the establishment of a conditioned response. It is interesting to note that Pavlov originally thought conditioning to be the province of the cerebral cortex; he later modified his thinking to include the simultaneous formation of conditioned responses in cortical and subcortical centers. But the evidence cited here of conditioning in planaria and other simple organisms rules out the necessity of such highly complex nervous structures as the subcortical centers in advanced animals like the dog.

Conditioning of the Human Fetus. As for the second question—the ontogenetic one—the evidence is not extensive, but it too suggests that developmentally primitive forms can be conditioned. There is no doubt about newborn human babies. Moreover, there seems to be fairly good evidence of classical conditioning of the fetus. For example, in one study (Spelt, 1948) a vibratory stimulus to the mother's abdomen served as a CS and a high-intensity noise as the US. The UR was something akin to a startle response that could be measured by sensing devices on the mother's abdomen. After as few as 15 trials, presentation of the CS alone led to the occurrence of the response. A variety of control procedures ruled out alternative explanations (except perhaps general sensitization), including the possibility that the mother rather than the fetus was being conditioned. The fetuses in this study were quite close to birth; unfortunately, there seem to be no data that would allow a conclusion about how early in fetal development such conditioning is possible.

The possibility of fetal conditioning has led some psychologists to speculate about naturally occurring patterns of stimulation that might simulate the features of a classical conditioning experiment. If such were the case, the newborn infant would not necessarily be the untutored, naive organism that it is ordinarily assumed to be. For example, it was argued by E.B. Holt (1931) that many of the presumed "unconditioned" reflex reactions are really acquired prior to birth as the result of certain contingencies that naturally prevail in the womb—that in some sense the developing organism conditions itself. Holt's position is exemplified in the following passage:

> Suppose, for instance, that owing to anatomical configurations, the random contractions of a muscle stimulate other sense-organs than those within the muscle itself. Consider a random impulse reaching the flexor muscle of a

finger. In the fetal position the fingers are often closed over the palm of the hand, and the least random flexion of a finger will cause it to press on the palm. Then (what is not random) afferent impulses ('tactile') from the two surfaces in contact (palm and finger) will be sent back to the central nervous system, where by the principle already cited (classical conditioning) they will find an outlet in the motor paths that were just now excited, that is, those of the flexor muscle of the finger in question. When this has happened a few times (as it is bound to happen) the reflex-circle will be established: and then a pressure stimulus on either palm or finger will cause the finger to flex and so to close down on the object that caused the pressure. Such is the origin of the 'grasping reflex,' which is so useful through all the later life. This reflex is regularly established before birth. (Holt, 1931, p. 38.)

Holt argues that an infant's entire reflex repertoire is established in this fashion. The fetus is indeed a *tabula rasa,* as Locke and Hobbes had proposed, but from Holt's point of view, the newborn is already a thoroughly "trained" organism.

Of course, Holt was writing in the heyday of the Pavlovian era in American psychological theorizing. He had no doubts about the ubiquity of conditioning or about the ease of its establishment. But he failed to note that the hypothetical instances he cites (a random response is made; the response has sensory aftereffects; these sensory events become attached, through conditioning, to the response) are all dependent on the possibility of backward conditioning. From what is known about conditioning in mature organisms, backward conditioning is extremely difficult, if not impossible to establish. In fairness to Holt's very radical position, however, we should also note that limitations that apply to mature organisms may not be pertinent to the developing fetus.

There is another way out for Holt's hypothesis, which can be illustrated with an example from the behavior of the young infant, rather than of the fetus. The *circular-reflex* hypothesis has been applied to the postnatal as well as the prenatal period. One classical application of the hypothesis is an attempt to account for a baby's imitation of sounds, a precursor of language development. The argument runs as follows:

The baby emits a sound—for example, "da;" he then hears that sound. The auditory stimulus "da" becomes associated with the motor impulses that controlled the vocalization. With repeated pairings of this sort, the sound "da" becomes a conditioned stimulus for saying "da." Hence, when someone says "da" to the baby, the baby will respond, with what seems an imitative response, by himself saying "da."

Note that this explanation also depends on the possibility of backward conditioning: The vocalization precedes the auditory feedback. But one slight change in the example will rescue the circular-reflex explanation. The initial vocalizations need not be monosyllabic; they may, at least sometimes, be repetitive—that is, the baby might very well say "da-da," or even longer chains of the syllables. Babies are certainly known to babble in that fashion. Now, if the infant says at least "da-da," then backward conditioning need not be invoked. The auditory stimulus from the first element precedes the vocalization of the second element, and hence is a good candidate to become a CS for that response. Concretely, baby says "da," hears "da," says "da." The temporal relations, in this case, are compatible with the conditions that are generally accepted as optimal for the establishment of a classically conditioned response. Whether in fact these conditioned responses are actually formed, before or after birth, is another question, but at least they are not as unlikely as they seem in the original formulation.

Pavlovian Conditioning: Related Phenomena

Pavlov's research went well beyond an investigation of the variables that affect the formulation of a conditioned response. His work led to the discovery and elucidation of several related phenomena; Pavlov and his followers also attempted to explain these phenomena in terms of a brain model. Not all of this material can be discussed here; what follows is a brief description of some of the better-known phenomena and their theoretical implications.

STIMULUS GENERALIZATION

It was found that once a CR has been established, the response can be elicited by stimuli that are not identical with the original CS. For example, if the CS were a tone of 1000 cycles per second, then a tone differing in frequency might also be effective as an eliciting stimulus (for convenience, let us use the abbreviation ES for eliciting stimulus). This phenomenon— the ability of a stimulus other than the original CS to serve as an ES—is referred to as *stimulus generalization.*

Not every stimulus can act as an ES in relation to a given CS. For example, with a tone as the CS, it is less likely that a light would be an effective ES than would be another tone, but such generalization across sense modalities has been reported (see Razran, 1949).

Extent of generalization is a direct function of the degree of *similarity* between CS and ES. In much of the work on stimulus generalization, the CS falls at some point on a scale of a psychological attribute (for example, brightness). The attribute in turn is usually identified with a simple physical dimension (for example, luminance). Degree of similarity is then inferred from the physical difference between CS and ES. In one of Pavlov's procedures, for example, the CS was a tactile stimulus applied to a particular point on a dog's leg; various ES's were generated by stimulating at different points on the leg. The distance between CS and ES points is interpreted as a direct indicator of the degree of similarity. There are undoubtedly dimensions for which this type of interpretation is appropriate, but many others for which it is not. But leaving aside the considerable problem of defining and measuring the similarity between two stimuli (see, for example, Dember,

1960), this conclusion seems to have gained wide acceptance among researchers and theorists in the area of conditioning. Note that the functional relation specified between similarity of stimuli and extent of stimulus generalization is a continuous one: the greater the similarity, the more the generalization. A graphic representation of this relation is shown in Figure 9.7.

Irradiation. We have called your attention to the *form* of the proposed relation between generalization and similarity because of its theoretical significance, especially in Pavlov's model. Pavlov argued that generalization occurs by virtue of some sort of spread of excitation outward in the brain from the locus of excitation associated with the CS. His term for this process of spreading was *irradiation.* As excitation irradiates from the brain locus of the CS, it falls on brain loci associated with other stimuli; these brain loci then also participate in the formation of the conditioned response. Hence, the stimuli that would normally excite these loci take on some of the functional potency of the CS. The degree of potency to elicit a CR decreases with the distance of the "irradiated" locus from the locus associated with the CS, since, as Pavlov assumed, the intensity of irradiation decreases with distance. One final assumption is needed to complete the model. The closer their associated brain loci the more similar are two stimuli. For example, the model requires that the points in the brain where tones of 1000 c.p.s. and 2000 c.p.s. are represented by electrical excitation are closer to each other than are points excited by tones of 1000 c.p.s. and, say, 5000 c.p.s.

Stimulus generalization, then, becomes in Pavlov's theory an automatic by-product of the spread of excitation and the topographic organization of the brain. Three major problems with Pavlov's model immediately arise. First, there is no direct evidence for the irradiation of excitation. Second, although the topographic assumption might make sense for certain attributes of stimuli—for example, different points along the skin of a dog's leg are probably represented with a corresponding spatial regularity in the brain—it does not seem to fit the realities of brain organization for many other attributes—for instance, visual brightness or color. Finally, there are two types of generalization for which the topographic assumption simply will not work. One of these is the generalization across modalities already referred to. The second is called

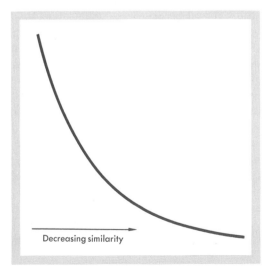

Figure 9.7 The gradient of generalization—magnitude of the CR as a function of the similarity between the conditioned stimulus (CS) and the evocation stimulus (ES).

Magnitude of CR

Decreasing similarity

Similarity between CS and ES

semantic generalization. In this latter type, the CS is a symbol, say a word, and the ES is another symbol semantically but not perceptually related to the CS. Thus, if the word "girl" is used as a CS, a CR might be given to the ES "woman." Or, if the CS is a geometric form, say a square, then an effective ES might be the word "square." The concept of irradiation by itself simply cannot cover the many documented instances of semantic, or symbolic, generalization.

Mediated Generalization. Pavlov recognized the special significance of human language and differentiated in his general theory between simple sensory events (which are carried over what he called the *first signal system*) and semantically meaningful events (which are carried over the *second signal system*). In certain theories developed by American psychologists, the same distinction is made in terms of simple, sensory generalization, or "primary" generalization, and secondary, or "mediated," generalization. In a mediated generalization the effectiveness of an ES is the product of a common response (other than the CR) which both the ES and CS elicit. Thus, if two stimuli are the word "square" as ES and the square geometric form as CS, the generalization between them is mediated by a response to which they both give rise, perhaps the lip, tongue, and mouth movements that form the vocalization "square."

Like other responses of greater magnitude, these hypothetical mediating responses might themselves give rise to certain stimuli called *response-produced stimuli*, perhaps in the form of kinesthetic feedback. If we consider these response-produced stimuli as sensory events to which the concept of primary stimulus generalization applies, we may be able to rescue the assumption of irradiation; that is, in semantic generalization and perhaps also generalization across modalities, irradiation applies, not directly to the CS and ES as sensory events, but to the mediating response-produced stimuli to which they give rise. To the extent that these response-produced stimuli are similar, generalization of the CR will be observed.

Failure of Discrimination. An alternative model, which eschews speculative neurophysiology, is based on the assumption that organisms undergoing conditioning categorize stimuli as either "the same as" or "not the same as" the CS. If, by virtue of its perceptual similarity to the CS, an ES is categorized as "the same," then a full-fledged CR is forthcoming. If the ES is categorized as "not the same," then no CR is made. This model anticipates data that would appear discrete rather than continuous. That is, only two values of CR strength are expected—full strength and zero strength. In this model, or its variants, stimulus generalization represents a *failure of discrimination*. If, under the circumstances of the experiment, a subject had been able to discriminate the ES from the CS, or perhaps simply had been inclined to do so, then he would not have made the CR. Stimulus generalization, from this alternative point of view, is the outcome of a decision-making process rather than the automatic result of irradiating neural excitation (see, for example, Lashley and Wade, 1946).

There are two major drawbacks to the all-or-none model of generalization. The most obvious is that generalization data typically do appear continuous, as in Figure 9.7. The second is that the model makes generalization virtually a cognitive function, and there is some reason to be hesitant about attributing "categorizing" to lower organisms.

As to the first problem, one could argue, by analogy with threshold measurement, that the behavior of an individual on a given trial is discrete and that the typical *generalization gradient* is an artifact of averaging data over trials and over individuals. The second problem boils down to a matter of theoretical strategy. To use the term categorization in reference to processes in lower organisms may seem to violate Morgan's canon. On the other hand, the term could be employed in a metaphorical sense: It is as though the ES were categorized as the same as or different from the CS. Even human subjects need not render a conscious judgment before the CR is allowed expression. But if the concept of categorization is too much diluted, it would certainly lose any power that it might have. The question remains open, at this point, whether the Pavlovian concept of irradiation, the joint notions of categorization and failure to discriminate, or some other alternative will ultimately prove the most valid. In the meantime, stimulus generalization remains an important behavioral fact in conditioning studies, as well as a useful concept in the application of conditioning principles to the explanation and control of more complex behavioral phenomena.

Generalization, Anxiety, and Schizophrenia. In this latter regard, an attempt has been made to account for certain aspects of schizophrenic behavior by reference to the schizophrenic's excessively broad stimulus-generalization gradient (see, for example, Mednick, 1958). From this point of view the core of the schizophrenic's problem is that because of a very high level of chronic anxiety, he responds to disparate stimuli with excessive generality; for him stimuli are equivalent that for the normal person are quite distinguishable. This mode of responding becomes especially problematic for instances of semantic generalization. Mednick's argument has met with considerable criticism—including the crucial point that, contrary to his assumption, it has not been shown convincingly that high levels of anxiety lead to broad generalization gradients. Still, his work is illustrative of the manner in which a concept developed for one, rather simple behavioral domain, might be applied to domains of much greater complexity. A similar story can be told for many of the concepts associated with classical conditioning. Indeed, in both Russia and the United States serious attempts have been made to develop psychotherapeutic techniques on conditioning principles (see, for example, Wolpe and Lazarus, 1966; Franks, 1968).

Once a CR has been made to an ES that is different from the original CS, and stimulus generalization has thus been demonstrated, how might such generalized responding be reduced, perhaps even to the degree that a CR is given only to stimuli that are psychophysically indistinguishable from the CS? The answer to that question, and to questions about the mechanism of discrimination (as it was called by Pavlov) turns out to be a special case of the answer to a more general issue. We must dispose of the general issue first; then we can return to the specific question related to discrimination.

EXTINCTION

The more general question concerns the elimination of any CR, whether it is given to a generalized ES or to the original CS. The procedural and empirical aspect of the question is: Can a well-established CR be removed from a subject's behavioral repertory, and if so, how? The theoretical aspect is: How can we best understand CR elimination, or *extinction* as it is technically labeled? These questions, of great concern to Pavlov, have retained their importance in current theories of behavior modification.

How to Get Extinction. As with many psychological phenomena that seem superficially to be rather simple, extinction, on close examination, turns out to be challenging both to the experimentalist and the theorist. One rule, however, is very well established. The way to get a subject to stop making a CR is to present the CS repeatedly and fail to follow it with the US. In Pavlov's terminology, occurrence of the US was said to *reinforce* the bond between CS and CR, and the US was referred to as the *reinforcer*, or reinforcing stimulus. In these terms, then, extinction of a CR will be effected through the nonreinforced presentations of the CS.

Typically, extinction, like the formation of a CR, proceeds gradually, as illustrated in Figure 9.8. It is as though whatever is responsible for extinction accumulates by small increments. When enough of these increments have been added together, the CR will cease to occur.

The Source of Extinction. Even at this point several significant theoretical issues begin to arise. One especially controversial question has to do with identifying the source of the extinction process. In particular, is extinction the result of the repeated, nonreinforced presentation of the CS, or of the frequent nonreinforced elicitation of the CR? (An analogous question concerning the role of the response in the formation of a conditioned response will be raised later in this chapter.)

In Pavlov's model, extinction is associated with the CS, not the CR. According to Pavlov, as a result of the repeated presentation of the CS unaccompanied by the reinforcing excitation of the US, the CS acquires an *inhibiting* property. That is, the CS does not simply lose its effectiveness in eliciting the CR, it actively inhibits the CR. Since Pavlov distinguished among several types of inhibition, this one was given a special label in his model—*internal inhibition.*

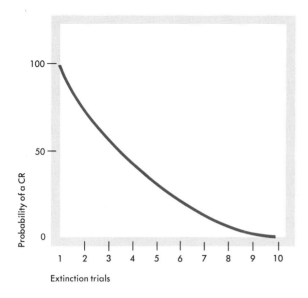

Figure 9.8 An idealized curve showing how conditioned responding declines as the number of extinction trials increases.

An alternative position is to associate inhibition with the CR itself, to argue that, when the CR is not reinforced, an inhibitory state develops which interferes with further elicitation of the CR. This position is taken in the behavior theory created by the American psychologist Clark Hull (1943). Though in many ways modeled after Pavlov's theory, Hull's version contained several departures from the original, his approach to the process of extinction being one of the most significant; another modification will become evident when we consider the role of the response in the establishment of a CR.

Pavlov postulated two varieties of internal inhibition, temporary and permanent, to accommodate the behavioral facts of the extinction process. The temporary type was revealed in a phenomenon called *spontaneous recovery:* If after a series of extinction trials adequate to inhibit the CR, an animal is given a rest period (perhaps a day), the CS will once again elicit the CR. It is as though some of the inhibition that was built up during the extinction period has dissipated; to the extent that inhibition spontaneously dissipates, it is obviously of a temporary, rather than a permanent sort.

Two additional observations shed further light on the distinction between temporary and permanent inhibition. The first is that spontaneous recovery is not complete; the full CR is not elicited by the CS, only a fraction of it. Thus, if the strength of the CR after training is, say, 12 drops of saliva, then on the first spontaneous-recovery trial after extinction, the animal might make a CR of only eight drops. There is, then, some residual, nontemporary inhibition following the rest period.

The second observation is more directly pertinent. If extinction series are repeated often enough, eventually no spontaneous recovery occurs. In short, extinction can be made permanent. Hence, there must be a form of inhibition that is also permanent.

What Happens to an Extinguished Response? The word "permanent" may be misleading. We really should say "permanent unless something active is done to make it otherwise." Through certain experimental operations, we can, in fact, reinstate conditioned responses that have ostensibly been permanently extinguished. Two procedures will be mentioned here because of their implications for the nature of both extinction and conditioning.

First, an extinguished response can be restored to full strength by rein-stituting the conditioning procedure—that is, by following the CS with the US. And what is most interesting, it takes fewer trials to bring the CR back up to its pre-extinction level than it does to form the initial conditioned response. Furthermore, if several successive conditioning-extinction cycles are employed, reconditioning becomes successively easier until it becomes possible to restore an extinguished CR after only one or two reinforced trials. Similarly, extinction becomes increasingly easier until complete extinction can be accomplished after very few nonreinforced trials.

One implication of the data obtained from the above procedure is that extinction does not wipe out the original learning that produces the CR. Rather, the original learning remains intact; the extinction procedure simply prevents the CR from being expressed in behavior. In short it seems that the CR is suppressed, not eliminated through extinction. Indeed, Pavlov believed that once a CR was established, the physiological change underlying it was permanent. Any vicissitudes in the behavioral manifestation of that change were attributable to further changes superimposed on it. A very similar view, especially in regard to the learning that occurs in early childhood, was held by Freud. He asserted that much of what appears to have been forgotten (as through some passive decay process occurring simply as a function of the passage of time) is in reality still present, but prevented from any direct behavioral expression by factors that actively suppress it.

The second Pavlovian procedure by which an extinguished CR can be rearoused—though in this case only temporarily—is known as *disinhibition.* To describe disinhibition, we must first introduce a closely related phenomenon, *external inhibition.* The term refers to the phenomenon (and the hypothetical mediating process) wherein a well-established CR is not made when the CS is accompanied by an unexpected, neutral stimulus. For example, when salivation has been conditioned to a light, if on an occasional trial a tone is presented along with the light, the conditioned salivary response will not occur. This effect will be observed so long as the extraneous stimulus continues to elicit an orienting response.

In external inhibition, an unexpected stimulus and its resulting orienting response interfere with the excitatory process associated with occurrence of a CR. Disinhibition is analogous: The unexpected stimulus interferes with the inhibitory effect of an extinguished CS. Thus, if salivation has been conditioned to a light as CS, and then through extinction the CS becomes inhibitory, presenting a tone along with the light will often lead to the occurrence of the CR. The tone temporarily inhibits the inhibiting effect of the CS, thereby allowing the CR to occur: hence, disinhibition. Again, the phenomenon suggests that the excitatory change underlying the CR has not been erased or reversed during extinction, but has instead remained intact though behaviorally inert. With the superimposed inhibition temporarily removed (by the arousal of the orienting response), the CS once again elicits the CR.

Now that we have a procedure for extinguishing a CR, we can return to the problem of discrimination—that is, how to get the subject to narrow the range of stimuli to which it responds. What is called for, obviously, is to extinguish conditioned responses that are made to stimuli other than the CS. The way to do so is to present these generalized stimuli (GS) without presenting the US.

That would be the end of the problem were it not for one interesting complication. Just as excitation generalizes, so does extinction. Thus, when a GS is presented without reinforcement, the inhibition developed with respect to that stimulus generalizes to the original CS. In extinguishing generalized responses, we run the risk of inadvertently extinguishing the response to the CS as well. As a general rule, we can overcome the problem by intermixing extinction trials on the GS and reinforced trials on the CS. Of course, introducing reinforced trials on the CS will impede extinction of responding to the GS, and extinction effects on the GS will generalize to the CS. But in the long run, the net amount of excitation associated with the CS will exceed the net amount of excitation associated with the generalized stimuli, and in this fashion the conditioned response can ultimately be restricted only to stimuli that are psychophysically equivalent to the CS.

Experimental Neurosis. Discrimination training, however, does not always proceed smoothly. Certain circumstances seem conducive to serious disruptive effects on an animal's emotional state. For example, in the course of determining the limits of a dog's ability to respond differentially to a circle and an ellipse, one of Pavlov's colleagues discovered a behavioral pattern that became known as *experimental neurosis*. The following excerpt describes these unexpected but exciting findings. Similar observations have subsequently been reported from Pavlov's laboratory as well as by other investigators.

> A projection of a luminous circle on to a screen in front of the animal was repeatedly accompanied by feeding. After the reflex had become well established a differentiation between the circle and an ellipse with a ratio of the semi-axes 2:1, of the same luminosity and the same surface area, was obtained by the usual method of contrast. A complete and constant differentiation was obtained comparatively quickly. The shape of the ellipse was now approximated by stages to that of the circle (ratios of the semi-axes of 3:2, 4:3, and so on) and the development of differentiation continued through the successive ellipses. The differentiation proceeded with some fluctuations, progressing at first more and more quickly, and then again slower, until an ellipse with ratio of semi-axes 9:8 was reached. In this case, although a considerable degree of discrimination did develop, it was far from being complete. After three weeks of work upon this differentiation not only did the discrimination fail to improve, but it became considerably worse, and

finally disappeared altogether. At the same time the whole behaviour of the animal underwent an abrupt change. The hitherto quiet dog began to squeal in its stand, kept wriggling about, tore off with its teeth the apparatus for mechanical stimulation of the skin, and bit through the tubes connecting the animal's room with the observer, a behaviour which never happened before. On being taken into the experimental room the dog now barked violently, which was also contrary to its usual custom; in short it presented all the symptoms of a condition of acute neurosis. On testing the cruder differentiations they also were found to be destroyed, even the one with the ratio of the semi-axes 2:1. (Pavlov, 1927, 290–291.)

Individual Differences. Observations of such disturbed behavior as well as evidence of marked individual differences among dogs in their behavior under less stressful, standard conditioning procedures, led Pavlov to speculate about the possible neural bases of general personality differences, not only among dogs, but among people as well. Pavlov conceived of all behavior as the outcome of a conflict between excitatory and inhibitory influences. Some individuals, Pavlov believed, were inherently highly excitable; others were readily inhibitable. In between these extremes were the normal, or balanced, individuals, who were neither excessively excitable nor inhibitable, though perhaps inclined more one way than the other.

These various types of neural response to stimulation (two extreme and two within the normal range) were associated with four different types of temperament that are reminiscent of the types described as long ago as the fourth century B.C. by the Greek physician Hippocrates—the choleric, the melancholic, the sanguine, and the phlegmatic. For example, the highly excitable nervous system gives rise to an individual who is easily conditioned, but also easily irritated and aggressive, corresponding to Hippocrates' choleric type. The melancholic type possesses a nervous system that is highly susceptible to inhibition; for such an individual, the ordinary events of daily life are inhibitory rather than exciting, leaving him depressed and pessimistic. Whatever the merits of both the behavioral typology and the manner of characterizing differences in nervous systems, it is interesting to note, as we have done in previous instances, how easy it is to jump from the routine concerns of the laboratory to the pressing issues of "real life." And there are indeed contemporary psychologists (see, for example, Eysenck and Rachman, 1965), who have pursued with some success Pavlov's notion of excitable and inhibitable nervous systems.

The Formation of a CR: Two Issues

Operationally, a CR is established through the proper sequencing of the two stimuli, the CS and the US. However, the apparent simplicity of the Pavlovian situation is not matched by a comparable simplicity in theoretical formulation. Among the many unsettled issues raised by conditioning, two are especially significant; every learning theory, including Pavlov's, has taken a stand on them. Indeed, these two issues provide a good basis on which to categorize, at least partially, the various theories of learning (see Spence, 1951).

S-S OR S-R BONDS?

The first issue concerns the nature of the bond that is presumably formed when conditioning occurs. What gets attached to what? For Pavlov, the bond was established between CS and US or, more exactly, between the brain locus excited by the CS and that excited by the US. When these two brain loci are frequently excited in proper sequence, some change occurs in the neural tissue so that eventually arousal of the CS locus is adequate to excite the brain region serving the US. With the US locus thus aroused, the UR is automatically made. In this model, then, the CS becomes a substitute for the US, and elicits the response by virtue of its acquired ability to excite the brain locus that can ordinarily be stimulated only by the US.

An alternative to Pavlov's conception is possible. Assume that the bond is formed directly between the CS and UR or, again more exactly, between the two brain loci that serve these events. When conditioning has been established, presentation of the CS directly arouses the brain locus of the UR, and the response (now called a CR because it was elicited by the CS) is made.

The two assumptions about the nature of the bond can be shown diagrammatically, as in Figure 9.9. The Pavlovian assumption, at its most abstract, is representative of those learning theories called "S-S," that is, theories which assume that the learned bond, or association, is formed between stimuli. The alternative assumption, that the association is formed between a stimulus and a response, characterizes theories labeled "S-R." Hull's is one of these. For the past several decades, one of the great challenges to learning theories has been the design of an experiment that would allow a choice between these two seemingly contradictory assumptions. Some of the relevant research is reviewed in Chapter Ten.

Figure 9.9 Two models of the hypothetical bond that is formed during conditioning. In one a direct bond is formed between the CS and the response (S-R learning); in the other a bond is formed between the CS and the US (S-S learning).

THE FUNCTION OF THE US

In Pavlov's model, the US has a clear and simple function. For conditioning to occur, the US must be presented in order for the bond to be established between it and the CS. But there are

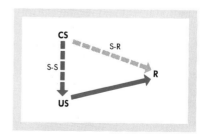

other possible functions of the US. It is, after all, more than just another stimulus, for it reliably arouses a particular response, the UR. Moreover, the US is typically important in the animal's biological adaptation. For example, salivation to food has an obvious adaptive function. Indeed, a catalog of all the effective unconditioned stimuli would show that virtually all have a high degree of adaptive significance.

But merely focusing on the biological role of the US does not necessarily divorce us from Pavlov. He, too, was certainly aware of the special property of the typical US. To create an issue of this conception we have to go a step further—as some learning theorists have done—and endow the US with *two* properties: (1) It elicits an UR; (2) it, or one of its aspects, acts to reduce the level of some biological drive. For example, food not only elicits the salivary response, but also decreases the current level of hunger. In this sense, the US plays the role of a reward in those theories of learning, such as Hull's, which insist that learned bonds are formed only if the paired elements are followed by a rewarding event. Clearly, in classical conditioning, it is unnecessary to endow the US with rewarding properties. The point of doing so is to bring Pavlovian conditioning into accord with the reward theories of learning, which have been devised to account for more complex forms of learning. Representative instances of these more complex types of learning, and some of the models offered to account for them, are the subject of the following chapter.

SUMMARY

Learning, the process whereby behavior is modified through experience, is a basic concept in most psychological theories. A very simple temporary form of learning is manifested in changing responsiveness to a repeated stimulus— *sensitization* when responsiveness increases and *habituation* when it decreases. That these changes can be central rather than peripheral is well-documented in demonstrations of the stimulus-specificity of habituation.

Habituation typically involves a decrease in a diffuse orienting response to a variety of interesting stimuli. By contrast, specific reflex responses to specific stimuli are highly stable in that the proper stimulus reliably will elicit the appropriate response. However, such reflex relations are modifiable; through procedures developed by Pavlov called *classical*, or *Pavlovian*, *conditioning* it is possible to increase the number of stimuli that can elicit a reflex response.

The classical conditioning procedure involves the presentation of a neutral stimulus (the *conditioned stimulus*, or CS) followed by a stimulus (the *unconditioned stimulus*, or the US) that reliably elicits a response (the *unconditioned response*, or UR). Conditioning is manifested when, after a number of such paired presentations of CS and US, the CS evokes the response (in which case we refer to the *conditioned response*, or CR).

Conditioning is easiest to accomplish when the US follows the CS by about half a second. *Backward conditioning*, where the US precedes the CS, is very difficult to effect. Animals can learn a *trace-conditioned* response, where a long interval occurs between the termination of the CS and the onset of the

US. *Delayed conditioning* is also possible; here, the CS is of long duration and the CR is made at the end of the CS presentation at the point where the US begins. To perform appropriately, the animal must *inhibit* the CR to the onset of the CS and make it instead when the CS terminates. Successful delayed conditioning suggests a sensitivity to the passage of time that is directly verified in *temporal conditioning*, where the CS is, in effect, a temporal interval.

In general, the more intense the CS the stronger the conditioning; however, excessively intense stimuli may not be ideal as conditioned stimuli. Moreover, it is possible that CS intensity is a relevant variable not so much in the formation of a CR as in its evocation once conditioning has occurred.

A wide variety of stimuli and responses have been employed in conditioning experiments. Especially interesting are responses and stimuli of which the subject is unaware. Such conditioning without awareness may shape a person's attitudes and emotional responses. *Affective conditioning*, with awareness, is exemplified in the well-known experiment by Watson and Raynor, in which the baby, Albert, was trained to fear a rat. Whereas conditioning usually requires several training trials, *one-trial conditioning* may be possible with highly intense aversive stimuli. Conditioning procedures have been used to increase people's positive attitudes towards such complex stimuli as paintings.

The purported demonstration of conditioning in such phylogentically primitive organisms as paramecia has been seriously questioned; however, successful conditioning has been effected in planaria, not far up the phylogenetic scale from paramecia. Planaria have also been used to explore the hypothesis that *ribonucleic acid* (RNA) is involved in the learning process. Some evidence exists for the possibility of transferring learning in planaria as well as rats, by donating RNA taken from trained animals to untrained animals. Conditioning in ontogenetically primitive organisms has also been demonstrated; newborn human infants as well as fetuses have been successfully conditioned, the latter supporting to some extent the radical hypothesis of Holt that much of the human infant's behavioral repertory is learned, not built-in, prior to birth.

Pavlov, and others since, have investigated several phenomena related to conditioning. Of special importance is *stimulus generalization,* as revealed in a CR to stimuli similar to, but not identical with, the CS; strength of the CR declines with increasing difference between the CS and the generalization stimulus (GS). Pavlov accounted for stimulus generalization by postulating *irradiation,* a spreading of brain excitation from its primary locus in the brain to adjacent loci. Other explanations have also been offered, not relying on speculative neurophysiology, that may also better account for secondary or *mediated* generalization as well as generalization across sense modalities. Generalization has been invoked as an explanatory principle for many interesting behavioral phenomena, including, for example, certain abnormalities in the behavior of schizophrenics.

Extinction refers to the weakening of a CR through presentation of the CS without a subsequent US. Extinction is in part temporary, as revealed in the phenomenon of *spontaneous recovery* (where an apparently extinguished CR returns to the behavioral repertory, though not at full strength, following a rest period after extinction); extinction can be made permanent through repeated series of extinction trials. However, the CR can be restored by reconditioning, and more rapidly so than it was first learned, suggesting that the extinction procedure suppresses (through *internal inhibition,* in Pavlov's terms) but does not wipe out the original learning. Further evidence for this hypothesis is provided in the phenomenon of *disinhibition,* where an extinguished response is temporarily restored through presenting a novel stimulus along with the CS (just as in *external inhibition* a CR is temporarily suppressed by pairing a novel stimulus with the CS).

Generalized responding can be diminished by extinguishing the CR to the GS while continuing to reinforce (through presentation of the US after the CS) responding to the CS. This process of *discrimination* training is difficult to accomplish because extinction of the GS generalizes to the CS, and reinforcement of the CS generalizes to the GS. Discrimination training may be so stressful to the subject that an *experimental neurosis* ensues.

Pavlov relied heavily on the joint concepts of excitation and inhibition. He believed that individuals differed in their characteristic degree of excitability and inhibitability, and that the relative strengths of these opposing tendencies determined an individual's personality type.

Two crucial theoretical issues raised by conditioning remain unresolved. (1) Is the learned bond formed between stimuli (the CS and the US) or between stimuli and responses (the CS and the UR)? Is it the function of the US simply to evoke the UR or is the US effective as a reinforcer because it also satisfies some biological drive, such as hunger? Stands taken on these two issues define some of the prominent learning theories developed to account for Pavlovian conditioning and for more complex forms of learning.

SUGGESTED READINGS

Huxley, A. *Brave new world.* Garden City, N.Y.: Doubleday, 1932; New York: Bantam, 1968.

Kimble, G. *Hilgard and Marquis' conditioning and learning* (2nd ed.). New York: Appleton-Century-Crofts, 1961.

Pavlov, I. *Conditioned reflexes* (trans. by G.V. Anrep). London: Oxford Univ. Press, 1927.

Wolman, B.B. *Contemporary theories and systems in psychology.* New York: Harper & Row, 1960. pp. 42–75.

Instrumental Learning:
Types and Models

C H A P T E R   T E N We continue our discussion of learning, in this chapter examining instrumental learning as it is studied in each of four experimental situations: the problem-box, the Skinner box, the maze, and the shuttlebox. Cognitive and stimulus-response interpretations of the learning process are described, along with the kinds of experiments that have been done to test them. We take up also such topics as schedules of reinforcement, the role of punishment in extinguishing learned responses, reversal and probability learning, and some theoretical issues surrounding avoidance learning.

Classical conditioning was introduced in the previous chapter as a simple form of learning. Indeed, if sensitization and habituation are discounted as authentic instances of learning, then classical conditioning is perhaps the simplest of all the types of learning that have so far been investigated. In this chapter, we will be concerned with several varieties of more complex forms of learning and with the models offered to explain them. These complex instances are known collectively as *instrumental* learning, to distinguish them from classical, or Pavlovian, conditioning.

The use of this common label, instrumental, does not imply that the same, single model exactly fits all the types to which the label applies. On the contrary, it is likely that there are enough different subtypes within the "instrumental learning" category to require more than the one, all-inclusive model that parsimony would dictate. But at this still-early stage in the development of learning theory, it is futile to speculate on the outcome of the competition among the many attractive models available. The question for the present chapter, then, is not "what is the correct model of instrumental learning?" but rather "what are the various types of instrumental learning, what do we know about them, and what models have been suggested to account for what we do know about them?" Since both research and theory on the topic of learning have been major preoccupations of modern psychology, the material in this chapter is only representative of the scientific literature on instrumental learning. More exhaustive, and perhaps exhausting, treatment can be found in the technical volumes written on this topic, as suggested at the end of the chapter.

The Nature of Instrumental Learning

Although theoretical controversy surrounds classical conditioning and instrumental learning, we can satisfactorily define the distinction between them in operational terms. Whereas in classical conditioning the occurrence of the reinforcement (the US) is not contingent on the subject's making some predetermined "correct" response (the CR), in instrumental learning the occurrence and perhaps even certain additional features of the reinforcement are dependent in part on the subject's making the response to be learned. In this sense, the subject's behavior is *instrumental* in determining certain of the events that follow it. It is not that the response-to-be-learned (R) has any necessary intrinsic relation to the reinforcement, but rather that the experimenter has so programed the situation that the outcome is different depending on whether the R is properly made or not made. The contingent relation between the R and the reinforcement is arbitrarily designated by the experimenter, but while the program is in effect, the subject has the reinforcement under his control: To produce it he need only make the R. By contrast, the subject in a classical conditioning experiment has no control over the reinforcement; its occurrence is not contingent on the CR.

An Example of Instrumental Learning. The remainder of this chapter is devoted to various instances of instrumental learning; a specific example here might make concrete the abstract considerations discussed above. Let us look at two slightly different versions of the task of training a dog to raise its left hind leg at the sound of a bell.

In one situation, an electrode is attached to the dog's paw so that an electric shock can be delivered through the electrode. The shock serves as the US; the UR is leg lifting (other diffuse responses such as barking are ignored); the CS is a bell. Training trials consist of pairings of bell and shock, until the bell elicits the leg-lifting response. This situation conforms to the classical-conditioning paradigm, in that neither occurrence nor nonoccurrence of the shock is contingent on the CR; the shock is delivered on schedule whatever the dog does.

A slight change in procedure yields the instrumental situation. We simply attach the electrode to the floor on which the dog's paw is resting. When the leg is raised, contact with the shock electrode is broken. In effect, by lifting his leg the dog can turn off the shock. The CS then can be used as a signal that shock is imminent; if the CS-US interval is sufficiently long, then the dog can avoid shock altogether. Even at worst, when CS and US go on simultaneously, the dog can shorten the duration of the shock. In either case—where shock *avoidance* is possible or where rapid *escape* from shock is possible—it is clear that the dog's response does have a bearing on the fate of the US.

In the instrumental example the US is *aversive:* The subject, if possible, will avoid or escape it. A similar analysis can be provided for unconditioned stimuli to which the subject is attracted; these are called *appetitive.* Pavlov's own favorite US, food powder, can be employed this way. A classical procedure with food powder as the US can be transformed into an instrumental procedure by making the presentation of the food powder contingent on the occurrence of the CR. That is, to obtain the food powder, the dog must first salivate.

Largely, for historical reasons, certain instrumental procedures are associated with the more general term, learning. For example, we might say "instrumental, appetitive conditioning" for the preceding illustrations but use the phrase "instrumental, appetitive learning" for the very similar procedure whereby a dog gets food by depressing a lever. But for our purposes this distinction is unnecessary, so we will use the terms conditioning and learning synonymously.

An Operational Definition. We need to make only one additional introductory remark. In shifting our attention from classical to instrumental learning, we will find it convenient to stop using the term unconditioned stimulus and substitute for it the more general term *reinforcement.* Our operational definition of instrumental learning thus becomes *a procedure in which the occurrence of the reinforcement is contingent on the occurrence of the response to be learned.* Note that reinforcement, or the reinforcing stimulus, can be either aversive or appetitive—or in less technical language, punishing or rewarding.

We are now prepared to survey the various types of instrumental learning situations, paying particular attention to their implications for models of the learning process. There are many possible ways of organizing this material; no profound implications are intended in the particular scheme used here.

The Problem-Box

THORNDIKE'S EXPERIMENT

One of the early researchers of learning in both lower animals and human beings was the psychologist Edward L. Thorndike (1874–1949). To investigate learning in cats, he developed the problem-box, which was used in this way: A hungry cat would be placed inside a box. Outside the box, but visible, would be a morsel of the cat's favorite food, say a dish of salmon. The cat's task was to learn the necessary responses to get out of the box and gain access to the food. He might, for example, be required to move a latch, placed in one wall of the box, which when properly moved allows the wall to drop and the cat to emerge. Thorndike's interest was in the cat's gradual acquisition of this particular response, a response that he selected because it was initially unlikely to occur in the cat's behavior.

The Law of Effect. From his investigation of cats' behavior in such situations, Thorndike drew a conclusion that eventually took on the status of a psychological law—the Law of Effect. In essence, Thorndike asserted that the learning, as evidenced by the decrease over a number of trials in the time required to make the correct response, comprised two aspects. First, incorrect responses were eliminated, or "stamped out." Second, the correct response was "stamped in." Through this dual process, the cat's behavior became increasingly efficient. To formalize this conception, Thorndike proposed that responses are either stamped in or out depending on their consequences, or effects. In particular, the Law of Effect states that responses leading to satisfying consequences are stamped in, whereas those that are followed by unsatisfying effects are stamped out.

As you might imagine, Thorndike's language might be offensive to those theorists who take seriously the dangers of anthropomorphism. To speak of "satisfying" and "unsatisfying" consequences for a cat is to introduce a degree of subjectivism that borders on the unscientific. What was needed was an objective, operational substitute for the two adjectives. Thorndike obliged by defining a satisfying state of affairs as one that an animal would do everything he could to achieve or enhance and would do nothing to remove or diminish; an unsatisfying state of affairs was defined operationally as one the animal would do nothing to achieve or enhance and do whatever it could to eliminate or diminish. In short, the identification of any particular event as satisfying or unsatisfying is based on the behavior it elicits from the kind of experimental subject (such as the typical cat) under investigation. Thus, it is appropriate to label salmon as satisfying for cats, because given free choice cats will approach and consume it.

In such a fashion, Thorndike was able to cope with the apparent anthropomorphism in his law. But other doubts remained. For one, was it necessary, and valid, to postulate two components to the acquisition of a response? In particular, could not a workable model be based only on the increased probability associated with successful responses, with the unsatisfying effects of incorrect responses playing a neutral rather than an actively inhibiting role? That is, it might be argued that nonreinforced responses simply fail to gain in strength and hence appear to drop out only because the reinforced responses gain sufficient strength to become dominant. Thorndike himself eventually came to accept this latter view and proposed a truncated Law of Effect, according to which the strength of a response changed only by virtue of satisfying effects; unsatisfying effects played no role in this revised law of learning.

The Truncated Law of Effect. This modification in the Law of Effect was stimulated by data obtained by Thorndike from both animal and human subjects. For example, in certain experiments with people the subject had to guess which one of several alternative verbal responses should be made to a stimulus word. If the subject chose the incorrect alternative, the experimenter said "wrong." If the subject picked the correct response, the experimenter said "right." Subjects were assigned long lists of such associations to form, with particular stimulus-response pairs repeated several times. When their performance was closely examined, it was found that the positive reinforcer ("right") did increase the probability of the subjects' repeating the immediately preceding response upon subsequent presentation of its stimulus word. However, the negative reinforcer ("wrong") appeared to have little if any effect on the subjects' choice of response the next time the stimulus word was presented.

This frequently observed disparity in the effects of positive and negative reinforcers led Thorndike to modify the original Law of Effect in the manner already specified. By virtue of his central position in American educational circles, the revision in Thorndike's theory was reflected in a changing emphasis in educational practice, from the use of punishment for eliminating incorrect responses to the use of reward for strengthening correct responses. On several subsequent occasions, a similar change in educational practice has followed on some significant and well-publicized modification in the psychological *Zeitgeist*. For example, in recent years there has been a substantial impact—in the form of "teaching machines" and "programed instruction"—from the virtually single-handed efforts of B.F. Skinner, who has translated his behavioral principles, induced largely from research on pigeons and rats, into applicable procedures. We will cover the highlights of the Skinnerian approach to learning later in this chapter.

Aside from the already noted problems associated with the Law of Effect, there is one further issue of considerable significance. Does the Law of Effect assert a necessary relation between the events following responses and their acquisition of those responses, or does it simply describe conditions under which learning is facilitated? That is, is reinforcement *necessary* for learning or does reinforcement simply make learning easier or more likely?

THE GUTHRIE AND HORTON EXPERIMENT

There is little doubt that, in situations like the problem-box experiment, reinforcement facilitates the acquisition of the "correct" response. What is at issue here is the universal necessity of reinforcement. Are there some types of learning for which reinforcement is not essential and perhaps not even important? Indeed, in at least one major theory, that of E.R. Guthrie, reinforcement does not play a central role in the learning process; its role is peripheral, almost accidental. In essence, Guthrie argues that reinforcement is usually effective because it assures that the response defined as correct is the *last* response made in the situation. Why that should matter will become evident in what follows.

Using an experimental situation much like Thorndike's, Guthrie and Horton (1946) trained cats to escape from a problem-box by moving a lever. The unique feature of their experiment was the use of a motion picture recording of the cats' behavior. When the films were analyzed frame-by-frame, so as to yield a fine description of the cats' movements, it became apparent that each cat developed a very rigid, stereotyped response pattern for moving the lever. Whatever response happened to work was the one the cat learned. One cat, for example, might learn to back into the lever; another might learn to nudge the lever with its nose.

Guthrie's interpretation of learning in the problem-box, based on the above analysis—indeed, his view of learning in general—is that learning consists of the automatic formation of stimulus-response (S-R) bonds and that such bonds are formed each time a response occurs in the presence of a stimulus. A particular response gradually becomes the dominant one in a situation by becoming associated with more and more of the stimulus elements of the total situation.

One-Trial Learning and Gradual Acquisition. Thus, in Guthrie's model, any particular S-R bond is established on one trial, simply as a function of the occurrence of the response in the presence of the stimulus. The gradualness that is typical of most learning experiments reflects the fact that the subject's environment provides more stimuli than can be apprehended on any one trial; moreover, every change in the subject's posture and orientation implies a change in the stimuli with which it is confronted. For example, the lever in the problem-box becomes a different stimulus when viewed from different positions. In order for a response to be firmly and reliably elicited, it must be associated with enough of the stimuli in the situation so that the elements present on a given trial are likely to include some that have been attached to the response. The greater the number of elements associated with the "correct" response, and the fewer with competing responses, the more dominant the correct response will be.

The Role of Reinforcement. Note that this model attributes no special properties to the kinds of stimuli referred to as reinforcements. Although the effectiveness of reinforcing stimuli cannot be denied, their role in the learning process is subject to alternative interpretations. Guthrie and those theorists who have followed his approach view reinforcement as a device for assuring that the response defined as correct is the last one to occur in the situation. In this manner, potential competing responses are prevented from becoming associated with the stimulus elements. The reinforcement in this sense protects the correct response.

The appeal of Guthrie's model lies in its utter simplicity. It avoids the necessity of postulating a special class of stimuli, reinforcements, and accounting for their special potency; it makes all learning a one-trial, all-or-none affair, thus obviating the need to explain why in some instances learning is achieved in one trial while in others the acquisition seems to be a gradual process; at the same time, the model can account for the typical learning curve, with its incremental nature.

A Test of Guthrie's Model. The Guthrian model, despite its great virtue of simplicity, has not won wide favor among learning theorists, perhaps because it is so difficult to put to an adequate empirical test. Nevertheless, there have been a few attempts to design experiments that do justice to the assumptions of the model, and the results have been favorable to Guthrie's position. One such test was conducted by Virginia Voeks (1954), using human subjects. The UR was an eyeblink, which is reflexly made to a puff of air on the cornea. In order to minimize trial-to-trial variability in the stimulus situation, Voeks was careful not only to control external stimuli but also to restrict the movements of the subjects, so as to limit fluctuations in movement-produced stimuli. Her major finding was that for virtually every subject there was an abrupt transition in conditioned responses from none to maximum frequency. The curve that plotted frequency of CR against trials thus took a step-wise form, rather than the gradual, incremental form of the typical learning curve. But, as Voeks further points out, when the data from all subjects were combined into a "group curve," the shape of that curve was of the typical sort. Her argument, then, is that when stimulus variability is minimized, and when the behavior of individual subjects rather than that of a group of subjects is examined, then the outcome is suggestive of a step-wise, all-or-none process rather than a gradual one.

The Skinner Box: Operant Conditioning

There is no compelling reason why a problem designed for an animal needs to conclude with the animal's escape from the apparatus. Indeed, Thorndike's problem-box employs two reinforcers—escape from the box and food available upon escape—thereby unnecessarily complicating the experiment. A slight modification translates the problem-box into the closely related Skinner box, which is now extensively used for investigating learning and related phenomena in animals as well as people. The apparatus is named after B.F. Skinner, whose work in this area has been especially influential, and who, as mentioned earlier, applied the principles derived from investigations of animal behavior in the Skinner box to human learning.

In addition it was Skinner who developed the now ubiquitous teaching machine and the general educational procedure known as programed instruction.

The Skinner box, in essence, consists of a chamber in which an animal is confined; within the chamber, or box, is a fairly conspicuous object that is easily manipulable by the species being used. For example, if the animal is a rat, the object to be manipulated, the *manipulandum,* might be a simple lever, which can be depressed by slight pressure from the rat's forepaws or its snout; if the subject is a pigeon (one of Skinner's favorite species for research of this sort), the manipulandum might be an illuminated disc which the pigeon "manipulates" by pecking with its beak. Illustrations of these two most frequently used versions of the Skinner box are given in Figure 10.1.

The Task. The subject's task, in general, is to operate the manipulandum, say, to press on the bar. When that operant response has been made, a reinforcement immediately becomes available to the animal—such as a small pellet of food or a sip of water. To assure immediate reinforcement, the apparatus is usually so designed that the reinforcing agent is delivered at a spot close to the manipulandum; for example, the food pellet might fall into a cup next to, or perhaps underneath, the bar. The animal can get the pellet without leaving his position by the manipulandum. This em-

Figure 10.1 Skinner boxes for use with rats and pigeons. (Courtesy B.F. Skinner.)

phasis on immediate reinforcement for the response to be learned derives from Skinner's principle (based on many years of experience in investigating the learning process) that the last response prior to reinforcement is the one that is the most effectively strengthened on any trial. Any delay in reinforcement following the correct response may inadvertently lead to the strengthening of whatever responses happened to intervene between them.

Automated Experiments. One of the major advantages of the Skinner box and its many variants is that it readily lends itself to automation. Thus, it is possible both to program what is called the *reinforcement schedule* (the basis on which reinforcements are delivered) and to record automatically the animal's responses. From its beginning as a simple, crude bit of apparatus, the Skinner box has evolved into a highly complex piece of equipment, served by sophisticated electronic components. In the modern *operant conditioning* laboratory, we might find banks of such Skinner boxes, populated by animals, hardly touched by human hands, that work for hours at a time generating reams of data.

Learning or Performance? But what kinds of data? And what do they mean? First, on close examination it turns out that the typical operant conditioning experiment reveals very little, if anything, about learning *per se,* if learning is identified with the period during which the response (for example, bar pressing) is being acquired. That may seem a strange thing to say, considering the topic of this chapter. Nevertheless it is true that in most of the research employing the Skinner box, the experimenter's interest lies not primarily in the acquisition of the operant response but rather in its expression, particularly in the rate at which the response is made (*operant level*) following acquisition and in its resistance to extinction. Indeed, procedures are often employed to accelerate the acquisition phase so that variables affecting postacquisition performance can be studied more efficiently.

For example, a technique called *shaping* is frequently used as a means of getting the animal to make the operant response; in essence, the animal is reinforced for successively closer approximations to the operant response. Thus, any response that leads the animal toward the manipulandum might initially be reinforced; once the animal is regularly approaching the manipulandum, reinforcement is reserved only for responses that bring the animal into contact with it. Finally, only the correct operant, such as an actual bar press, is reinforced.

A crucial part of the shaping technique is the use of properly timed reinforcements. To gain control over reinforcement application, an experimenter might begin an animal's training by familiarizing it with the reinforcer—say, food pellets—and getting it to consume the pellets. At the same time that the animal is "learning to eat," another kind of learning is also introduced: A distinctive stimulus—often a click—is paired with the delivery of each pellet, usually just preceding the appearance of the pellet. This contingent relation between click and food pellet is picked up by the animal, so that eventually the click itself takes on reinforcing properties. In the technical jargon of learning theory, the click becomes an acquired, or a *secondary,* reinforcer (the food pellet being a primary reinforcer). What this means operationally is that the click can serve the function of a reinforcer: Its occurrence increases the probability that the response which preceded it will be made again under similar circumstances.

For purposes of behavior shaping in the Skinner box it is not necessary to know the mechanism whereby secondary reinforcers are acquired (though that is a problem intriguing to a theorist concerned with all types of learning). In the present context, it is sufficient to be able to generate an effective secondary reinforcer. That done, it becomes quite easy to apply the reinforcer at just the right moment so as to shape the animal's behavior in the desired manner. Then, once the animal is reliably making the operant response, the primary reinforcer (here the food pellets) can take over.

With various shaping techniques contaminating the acquisition phase, it is obvious that little can be discovered about learning from the typical Skinner-box experiment. Of course, if shaping is not employed, then it is possible to study the variables that influence the acquisition of an operant. But, as mentioned, Skinner-box research is usually devoted to other problems, in particular those related to the *performance* of a learned response.

Schedules of Reinforcement. The major contribution of this now vast enterprise has been the development and assessment of various *schedules of reinforcement.* These schedules have an important influence on the animal's behavior once the operant response has been acquired.

A schedule of reinforcement is, in essence, a rule stating the basis on which reinforcements will be delivered. One such rule might be that a reinforcement will occur after each occurrence of the operant response. This was the rule that Skinner followed in his early research; with no alternative rules available, of course, the 100 per cent reinforcement schedule was being applied not as an explicit rule but as an implicit procedure that was simply taken for granted. Skinner reports (1956) that he first hit upon the possibility of other reinforcement schedules as the solution to a practical problem. He had automated his apparatus to the extent that each bar press released one food pellet from a magazine. Skinner himself manufactured the pellets through a laborious and time-consuming process. At one point the pellet supply became too low to carry to completion the experiments with rats that he was conducting; to replenish the supply would take more time than he was ready to devote. The obvious solution was to cut down on the number of reinforcements. Instead of reinforcing each response, Skinner decided to try a schedule in which a pellet was delivered at most only once a minute. Suppose a reinforcement has just occurred. The next one would not be given until the first response after one minute has elapsed. This procedure not only had the desired effect of decreasing the number of pellets used, and hence the number that had to be manufactured, but it also had an interesting effect on the rats' behavior. Rate of responding stabilized remarkably, approximating what in other scientific fields is called a *steady state*. Impressed by this regularity, Skinner embarked on an investigation of various schedules of reinforcement.

The example mentioned above is illustrative of *fixed-interval* schedules. Note that the delivery of the reinforcement is no longer solely contingent on the animal's response; it is also tied to a clock. To be at all effective, however, such a procedure can be instituted only after an animal has been trained to respond at a fairly high rate through conventional reinforcement procedures.

In a modification of the fixed-interval schedule, the passage of time remains a criterion for the delivery of reinforcements, but the time interval can vary around an average value, instead of being fixed. For example, reinforcements might occur once a minute on the average, but not necessarily exactly once a minute. Such a schedule is called a *variable-interval* schedule.

The two types of interval schedule have somewhat different behavioral effects. Although both are associated with stable response rates, the distribution of responses within the interval differs. In the fixed-interval schedule, an animal tends to "pile up" its responses toward the end of the interval. Thus, if by virtue of its level of hunger (which is the prime determinant of response rate), an animal is giving about 20 bar presses per minute, most of them will occur as a burst of activity just prior to the delivery of the reinforcement. It is as though the animal has a timing mechanism that enables it to place its responses where they are likely to do the most good. In this regard, the behavior is analogous to temporal conditioning, described in the previous chapter.

Of course, a perfectly efficient organism would make only one response per minute—the one that is required to yield the one pellet per minute that the schedule allows. But rats and pigeons cannot be perfectly efficient; they do not have clocks to rely on; and besides, bar-pressing in an otherwise empty Skinner box may be more rewarding than doing nothing at all. In any event, the pattern of responding on the fixed-interval schedule is usually as described. In Skinnerian terminology, the curve plotting response rate as a function of the passage of time has a *scalloped* shape. Figure 10.2 illustrates what is called a *cumulative-response curve* and shows the scallops that are characteristic of the fixed-interval schedule. A cumulative-response curve is generated by moving recording paper at a constant speed under a pen-writer; each time a response is made the pen moves up one unit toward the top of the recording paper. Thus, the height of the pen at any moment reflects the total number of responses that have been made up to the moment.

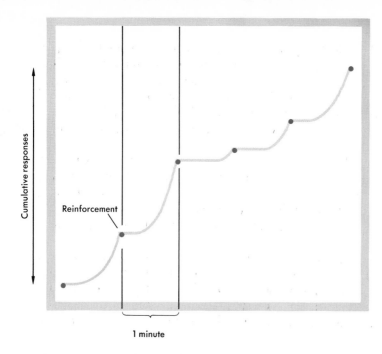

Reinforcement

1 minute

Cumulative responses

Figure 10.2 A cumulative-response curve showing the scallops typical of fixed-interval reinforcement schedules (in this case the interval is one minute).

Use of a variable-interval schedule removes the scallops, for the responses are distributed fairly evenly throughout the interval, since there are no temporal cues. If there are practical reasons for preferring this type of response distribution, then the variable-interval schedule is obviously the procedure to choose.

Analogous to fixed- and variable-interval schedules are two types wherein reinforcement is contingent on the number of operant responses; that number can either be fixed or vary around a mean value. The labels for these two types—*fixed-ratio* and *variable-ratio*—reflect the relationship of each reinforcement to a given number of responses. The schedule in which *each* response is reinforced is the special case of a 1-to-1 ratio. In a 1-to-10 schedule, a reinforcement is delivered after each block of 10 responses (either exactly 10 in a fixed-ratio schedule, or 10 on the average in a variable-ratio schedule).

Using a ratio rather than an interval schedule gives the experimenter considerable control over the quantity of the animal's responses. Whereas response rate in the interval schedule is determined largely by the animal's motivational state (the hungrier the rat, the faster the response rate), it is possible with the ratio schedule to achieve remarkably high response rates. If, for some reason, the experimenter wants to get a high regular response rate, then he should select one of the ratio procedures. In particular, the lower the ratio, the greater the response rate. Of course, as the ratio gets increasingly small, the procedure more and more resembles straightforward extinction, and the danger arises that responding will cease altogether. One way to obviate this danger is to bring the animal down to the desired ratio in very gradual steps—through a kind of postacquisition shaping procedure.

You may have noticed an analogy between the ratio schedule and a common device for enhancing the productivity of human workers. That is, the worker is paid (reinforced) not a fixed salary or by the hour, but rather an amount proportional to the number of units he has produced. With human workers the pay is typically received after some fixed time period (such as a week) rather than after a small block of "responses," as with rats and pigeons in operant conditioning experiments. But then human beings are capable, through self-administered verbal reinforcements, of providing frequent substitutes for the final tangible, though also symbolic, paycheck. Thus, after a day's work, a person can calculate how much he has earned as a result of that day's productivity. Even human beings can maintain this self-reinforcing mode only if their "faith in the system" is reliably confirmed by periodic paychecks or other equivalent rewards for their effort.

Experiments designed to compare the behaviors characteristic of various reinforcement schedules typically assign a given subject to a given schedule; in some instances, a subject may be faced *in sequence* with the various schedules, and a comparison is then made among the final, or asymptotic, performances achieved by the subject under each of the schedules. In the latter case, the subject's behavior ordinarily shifts appropriately, as he moves from one schedule to another; these behavioral transitions are often remarkably rapid, indicating considerable sensitivity to schedule differences.

Even more interesting, for what they reveal about the complexity and flexibility of the structures mediating conditioned operant responses, are those experiments that employ *multiple concurrent* schedules. As you might guess, these are experiments in which the subject is trained to operate more than one manipulandum, usually two, and each is associated with its own type of reinforcement schedule. For example, a Skinner box with two bars might be used, with one bar programed to deliver reinforcement on a fixed-interval schedule, the other on a variable-ratio schedule. This arrangement puts a considerable strain on the subject's information-processing systems, so it is quite impressive that even the lowly rat and pigeon exhibit response rates and patterns for both bars that would normally occur for each alone.

The various reinforcement schedules depart from the historically standard procedure of giving one reinforcement for each appropriate response. In general the "departures" come much closer to simulating conditions in the "real world" outside the laboratory than does the standard procedure. A 100 per cent, or continuous, reinforcement schedule is certainly highly atypical, either in the formal training procedures of a school or in the informal behavior modification of children in the home. Indeed, one of the major lessons a child must learn is to continue performing in the absence of regular reinforcements. It may be appropriate to say "good boy" to the two-year-old whenever he removes his shoes in preparation for bed-time, but something is wrong if the five-year-old requires continuous reinforcement.

The real world is also characterized by variability in other aspects of reinforcement. For example, reinforcements do not always come in standard-sized units like the precisely milled food pellets that are delivered in the Skinner box. In the jargon of psychology, *reinforcement magnitude* is typically quite variable outside the laboratory. The same is true of another important parameter called *delay of reinforcement*—that is, the time that elapses between the occurrence of a response and the delivery of the reinforcement. In general, the less regular the relation between parameters of reinforcement and occurrence of responses in laboratory experiments, the more valid will be the applications of the results of these experiments outside the laboratory.

The Partial-Reinforcement Effect: A Theoretical Dilemma. There are several learning theories derived from Thorndike's that consider reinforcement essential to the process whereby S-R bonds are formed; the most prominent and influential of these was developed by Clark Hull (1943). In Hull's theory it is assumed that the greater the number of reinforced training trials, the stronger the S-R bond, or habit, at least until the habit has reached its maximum possible strength. It is further assumed that nonreinforced trials (when the response is evoked but not followed by reinforcement) contribute to the inhibition of the learned response. Thus, a nonreinforced trial weakens in two ways the tendency to express the habit: (1) directly, by generating inhibition, and (2) indirectly, by not reinforcing the habit and thus strengthening it. Further, Hull's theory asserts that the stronger the habit, the more resistant it is to extinction. Operationally, this means that the stronger the habit, the greater the number of extinction trials necessary to extinguish the response fully.

The above considerations would lead us to expect that the introduction of nonreinforced trials into the "training period" in the formation of a habit would decrease that habit's resistance to extinction. And yet it is well established that habits which have been acquired under *partial-reinforcement* schedules are more resistant to extinction than those acquired under 100 per cent schedules. This principle holds in the Skinner box, as well as in other settings and for types of learning other than operant conditioning. Because it so obviously does not fit with expectations from Hull's highly influential theory, the partial-reinforcement effect, or PRE as it is abbreviated, has been the subject of a great deal of theoretical speculation. Among the many alternative explanations that have been offered for the PRE, the following two are given here as illustrative examples.

The Similarity between Training and Extinction Procedures. One suggestion holds that the inclusion of nonreinforced trials in the training phase leads an animal to "expect" a mixture of nonreinforced and reinforced trials. Then when nonreinforcement is first encountered in what the experimenter has defined as the extinction phase, it does not imply to the subject the end of reinforcements. And so it continues to make the response, well beyond the point where it would otherwise have stopped—that is, if it had been trained without prior experience with nonreinforced trials. This explanation, as appealing as it seems, does smack of anthropomorphism, and thus has not gained wide acceptance. Those theorists to whom it does sound right, however, have tried to salvage it by couching the explanation in terms that do not require endowing rats and pigeons with such human qualities as expectations.

One such purified version points to the greater similarity between extinction and training phases for a partially reinforced habit than for a continuously reinforced habit. In this approach, reinforcement contingencies are treated as a part of the general stimulus complex to which the responses becomes conditioned. Switching abruptly from a 100 per cent to a 0 per cent reinforcement schedule is tantamount to introducing a massive change in the stimulus situation; it is analogous to changing the CS in a classical conditioning experiment. Just as a CR is hard to evoke when the CS, or the general environment, is modified between conditioning and evocation trials, so too is an operant hard to evoke (or conversely, easy to extinguish) when the stimulus situation has been changed between training and extinction phases, as it presumably is for the subject trained under continuous reinforcement. Since the partially reinforced subject is not faced with as great a change, his response tendency does not decline as much. In this rather ingenious fashion, the PRE is made a special case of the well-established phenomenon of stimulus generalization.

This account of the PRE refers to change in the stimulus situation, but we have said nothing yet about the exact nature of the change. In fact, differences among the several suggested explanations of the PRE can in large part be attributed to differences in stimulus elements that are considered to carry the change.

In one early application of the generalization explanation (Sheffield, 1949), it was noted that an animal trained under continuous reinforcement begins each trial—especially if trials are close together in time, or massed— with the aftereffects of the previous trial present, either as actual stimuli or as active traces. For example, if food is the reinforcing agent, then the animal may still be chewing on bits of food or at least savoring its taste. For a partially reinforced animal, many trials begin devoid of these aftereffects of reinforcement. The extinction procedure, in which no trials contain reinforcement aftereffects as part of their general stimulus situation, is clearly more like the partially reinforced than the continuously reinforced training phase.

The above analysis was developed to account for the behavior of rats that learned to run down a straight runway to a goal compartment containing food, though it can readily be applied to other learning situations, including the operant conditioning procedure on which this section is focused. However, it does demand massed trials if the identification of the specific cues associated with aftereffects of reinforcement is to be taken seriously. Unfortunately for this particular interpretation, it has been shown that the PRE still obtains even if animals are allowed only one trial per day of both original training and extinction (Weinstock, 1954).

Frustration and the PRE. Another attempt to specify exactly how the similarity between extinction and training phases is mediated makes use of a pair of hypothetical concepts, the *frustration response* and the *response-produced stimuli* associated with frustration (Amsel, 1958). In essence, this account of the PRE concentrates on the aftereffects of nonreinforcement, postulating that a nonreinforced trial, embedded in an array of reinforced trials, elicits from an animal a frustration response. This hypothetical response necessarily in turn produces a set of hypothetical stimuli, frustration stimuli. These stimuli and/or their traces are present at the onset of subsequent reinforced responses. In short, the animal makes the instrumental response (bar-pressing, running down the alley, and so on) in the presence of frustration stimuli. Hence, frustration stimuli become incorporated into the S-R habit, and their presence during the extinction phase does not disrupt the making of the instrumental response.

For an animal that was continuously reinforced during training, the frustration stimuli induced by nonreinforcement in the extinction phase contribute only to increasing the dissimilarity between training and extinction trials. In addition, the frustration stimuli may very well naturally lead the animal to make overt responses that are incompatible with the instrumental response.

By analogy, imagine that you have never had any trouble in answering the questions on class tests. Then one day you are given a test in which you experience considerable difficulty on the first item, perhaps to the point of not being able to answer it. This sudden and virtually unique frustration may have two kinds of deleterious effects on your performance on the remaining items: (1) Since you have rarely, if ever, confronted a test item while experiencing the frustrating aftereffects of failing to answer a previous item, the test-taking habits you have acquired may be seriously disrupted. (2) Your responses to this novel frustrating situation may directly interfere with efficient performance on the remainder of the test; these frustration-induced responses may range from such overt acts as breaking your pencil, cursing, tearing up the test, and leaving the room (all incompatible with smooth test-taking) to covert, but still disruptive, ideational responses, such as thinking about the uncompleted item while trying to think clearly about subsequent questions, and engaging in aggressive fantasies, directed at the teacher or at yourself, that intrude on the logical, rational, controlled behavior that good test performance demands.

There is no reason to believe that any single category of stimulation can carry the entire burden of accounting for the PRE in all settings. It is only a concern for parsimony that makes the search for a one-concept account meaningful. But in the competition between parsimony and adequacy, it is obviously the latter that must prevail. Further, it remains to be seen whether explanations developed for the PRE in the behavior of "lower" animals such as rats and pigeons can be appropriately applied to human beings, as for example to gambling behavior. There is no doubt that human beings feeding coins to, and pulling the levers of, slot machines markedly resemble pigeons pecking at a key on a very-low-payoff, variable-ratio schedule. It is not so clear, however, whether the analogy, and others like it, is anything more than superficial.

EFFECTS OF PUNISHMENT
ON A CONDITIONED OPERANT RESPONSE

The conventional method for decreasing the probability of occurrence of a conditioned operant response is to omit the reinforcement. Eventually, the operant rate will return to the original, pretraining level. Just how quickly extinction proceeds is a function of many factors, and, as indicated above, especially of the reinforcement schedule. Just as it is still controversial how reinforcement works to effect learning, so it is as yet unsettled how omission of the reinforcement serves to produce extinction. Along the lines suggested by the interpretation of Abram Amsel that an extinction trial is a frustrating event which elicits a negative emotional reaction, we might speculate that failure to reinforce is moderately punishing. If so, then extinction might be accelerated by additional punishment to supplement that provided by non-reinforcement. For example, we might substitute an electric shock for the positive reinforcer and hence not only fail to reinforce but also actively punish the conditioned operant. Despite the data that led Thorndike to truncate his original Law of Effect by omitting reference to the effects of punishment, there still is reason to entertain the idea that punishment can facilitate extinction, at least under some circumstances.

Are Punishment and Nonreinforcement the Same? The psychological equivalence of punishment in the form of electric shock and nonreinforcement is supported, at least inferentially, in some fascinating research by Nathan Azrin (1967). In a series of experiments Azrin followed up an initially serendipitous observation that a rat which is shocked in an enclosed area, such as a Skinner box, will strike out in an aggressive manner against another rat or even an inanimate object. This observation was found to apply to a variety of species under a variety of circumstances. The principle that emerged from this work was that pain leads automatically to aggression if there is an object against which to direct the aggression.

Then the question arose of whether pain *per se* was the only instigator of aggressive behavior or whether other noxious events might be equally effective. In particular, would abrupt failure to reinforce a well-learned operant serve as a goad to aggressive behavior? The answer clearly was "yes." When a pigeon made the operant response and no reinforcement was forthcoming, it first pecked furiously at the manipulandum, and then turned toward another pigeon (restrained nearby for the purpose by the experimenter) and vigorously attacked it. The marked similarity between the responses to shock and other painful stimuli and to nonreinforcement suggests that nonreinforcement is psychologically a form of punishment.

There is evidence, however, that the punishment of painful stimuli such as electric shock and that of simple nonreinforcement may not have identical effects on the course of extinction. In a classic experiment, William Estes (1944) found that nonreinforced operant responses accompanied by painful electric shock serve only temporarily to *suppress* the operant response in rats, but do not contribute to the permanent extinction of the response. Apparently, if the response is to be truly extinguished, rather than merely suppressed, then the response must be made a certain number of times without reinforcement. All that punishment seems to accomplish is to postpone the occurrence of the particular number of responses that are required for permanent extinction.

There is, moreover, other evidence to suggest that excessive punishment may even strengthen the response that is to be extinguished. Rather than weakened, the response seems to become *fixated*; or perhaps the better interpretation is that the *animal* (not the habit) becomes rigid and inflexible in the face of excessive punishment and hence becomes impervious to nonreinforced trials (see Maier, 1949). It is not unlikely that a similar recalcitrance to learn is imposed by the indiscriminate use of punishment, for "habit-breaking" purposes, in the case of the human animal, especially the child.

When punishment does seem to be effective in aiding the extinction of an habitual response, it works probably not so much because it weakens the habit, but rather because it elicits responses incompatible with the habit; one or more of these new responses can then be reinforced and seriously compete with the old response. In this sense punishment works, when it does, because it provides the opportunity for new learning to take place and thus to replace the old response. But it should be remembered that recourse to the use of punishment does carry with it the dual dangers of (1) reducing, instead of increasing, the individual's plasticity, and (2) suppressing, or postponing, expression of the old response rather than eliminating the old habit which underlies the response.

INSTRUMENTAL CONDITIONING OF AUTONOMICALLY CONTROLLED OPERANT RESPONSES

Although the typical operant conditioning experiment employs an operant response under the control of the somatic nervous system (movements of limbs or other body parts effected by the striped musculature, as in barpressing, key-pecking, and the like), operant conditioning is also effective on responses controlled by the autonomic nervous system. For example, it is possible to condition a rat either to accelerate or decelerate its heart beat through appetitive reinforcement. The experimenter monitors the heart rate; when a change in the desired direction takes place, the animal is immediately reinforced. In this manner, the heart rate can be modified from its normal operant level (for the rat about 300–450 beats per minute) to one that is slightly different by about 5 per cent from normal (Trowill, 1967). Similar results have been obtained for other autonomically controlled responses, such as the galvanic skin response, intestinal contractions, salivation, and so on (see Kimmel, 1967, and Miller, 1969, for a review of this research).

Two features of the experiment by Jay Trowill are worth note. The reinforcement consisted in direct electrical stimulation of the brain, in a region known to mediate rewarding effects. Furthermore, the change in heart rate was not secondary to the conditioning of a skeletal-muscle response mediated by the somatic nervous system. That is, the animal was not learning to make some conventional operant, which had the side effect of modifying heart rate, as running might. Such behavior was precluded by paralyzing the animal with a drug, curare, which blocks the transmission of neural impulses at the myoneural junction (between the tip of the axon and the muscle) for all striped muscles, though not for the smooth muscles nor the special cardiac muscles.

The degree of change in the Trowill experiment was not impressive. But N.E. Miller and L.V. DiCara (1967) used a shaping procedure that imposed an increasingly severe criterion of responding for reinforcement to be given, and they were able to effect a change in heart rate of about 20 per cent. Further, they were able to get rats to discriminate between a period when these abnormal heart-rate responses would be rewarded (during a "time-in" period, signaled by a pattern of light and sound) and a period when the reinforcement would not be available. In Skinnerian terminology, they were able to establish in the rat a *discriminated operant,* in this case a cardiac response, just as a rat can be trained to press a bar for food only when a light is on.

It thus appears that operant conditioning is not exclusively the province of the somatic nervous system. This finding lays to rest the frequent assertion that classical conditioning and instrumental learning are distinguishable in terms of the portion of the nervous system that subserves them (for example, Skinner, 1938).

Maze Learning

One of the first devices used in the investigation of the learning process in animals was the complex maze. Willard Small, who introduced the maze into American psychology, was perhaps the first American psychologist to

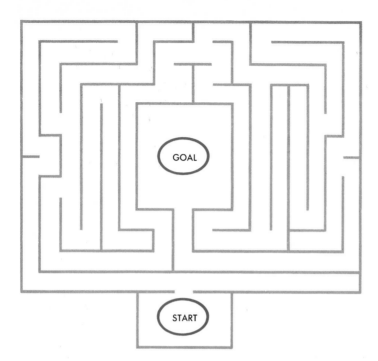

Figure 10.3 Diagram of a rat version of the Hampton Court Maze.

study maze learning in the rat. His apparatus was a miniature replica of the famous Hampton Court maze, which had been constructed out of hedges in the gardens of the Hampton Court Palace in England for the amusement and consternation of guests. The Hampton Court maze consisted of a collection of interconnected pathways, or "alleys," that offered no cues to distinguish between the correct paths and blind alleys, or "cul de sacs." With repeated trips through the maze, however, a person could gradually improve his performance, in the sense of entering fewer and fewer blind alleys. Such a gradual decline in errors obviously reflects a modification within the person that fits our conception of learning.

With that point as his rationale, Small determined to investigate learning in the domestic rat, *Rattus norvegicus,* by observing how the rat comes to find his way efficiently through a rat-sized replica of the Hampton Court maze and through similar structures. The floor plan of one of Small's mazes is shown in Figure 10.3.

Small's experimental procedure was primitive by modern standards—for example, he allowed more than one rat at a time into the maze and left the animals in the maze for long periods without observing or recording their behavior. But his general conclusion is undoubtedly valid. Rats are quite capable of learning their way about in such a complex maze (Small, 1901). Similar experiments subsequently conducted by other investigators have verified that conclusion.

Once it had been established that rats could indeed learn a complex maze, and once other more detailed information about their performance had been obtained, the major research endeavor was directed at determining the identity of the cue or cues on which an animal based its responses at the choice-points between correct and incorrect alleys. Did the rat use visual, olfactory, tactual, or kinesthetic cues, or some combination of these? One strategy that became popular was to deprive the subjects systematically of one or more of their sense modalities and note the effect of their performance. (John Watson, the founder of the Behavioristic school of psychology, took this approach when he selected the problem of the sensory control of maze learning for his doctoral dissertation.) The outcome of this line of research was the conclusion that no single sense modality is crucial for maze learning, although kinesthetic cues probably play a major role in guiding the animal through the maze.

Cognitive versus S-R Interpretations. Aside from posing an interesting empirical question, the problem of the sensory control of maze learning also took on theoretical significance. There are alternative ways of conceptualizing what happens when an animal has "learned" a maze. One approach is to assume that as the animal gains experience with the maze elements, he gradually forms an increasingly clear and valid "mental map" of the maze. With such a map available, the animal is then capable of efficient maze performance—should efficient performance actually be called for by the animal's motivational state. Thus, if a rat is hungry; if it has developed a map of the maze; and if that map contains information on the location of food—then the rat will move smoothly and with a minimum of errors from its starting point to the place where the food is located, relying on sensory cues to coordinate map and environment. This is the *cognitive* approach to the conceptualization of maze learning. The psychologist who did most to develop this approach into a formal model was Edward C. Tolman (1932).

S-R models of maze learning attempt to follow the admonition of Morgan's Canon; in particular such concepts as "maps" are deemed to be too high level for application to subhuman species. Instead of invoking maps or

Figure 10.4 A cartoonist's version of the controversy between cognitive and S-R models of learning. (Drawing by W. Steig; © 1969 The New Yorker Magazine, Inc.)

"How can I talk to you? I give you ideas, and all I get back is conditioned responses!"

analogous cognitive structures, S-R theories try to get by with reference to mechanical, automatically established habits (conceived as stimulus-response bonds) that are evoked when the proper stimuli are presented to the animal. From this point of view, sensory stimuli serve not as "cues" to guide and orient the animal, but as "goads" that elicit the conditioned responses to which they have become arbitrarily attached. An animal, in S-R models, is essentially an automaton, programed by his previous experience in the maze to make specific responses to specific stimuli.

Consider a rat approaching one of the choice-points in a complex maze. For simplicity, let us assume that the choice-point is distinguished by a particular odor. Also, let us assume that the animal has already "learned" the maze and that what we are seeing now is the behavioral manifestation of that learning at the particular choice-point in question. The cognitive animal senses the unique odor at the choice-point, treats it as a landmark, and selects the path that the map indicates is appropriate ("at the choice-point with the peculiar smell, turn left if you want to get to the place where the food is"). The S-R rat on approaching the choice-point is stimulated by the odor; that particular stimulus has been conditioned to a left-turning response, and so a left-turning response is evoked from the animal.

One appealing feature of the S-R approach is that responses are accounted for solely in terms of the interaction between S-R bonds, or habits, and stimuli (as well as the animal's motives or "drives," which are considered, however, as internal stimuli). By contrast, in the cognitive approach, the rat at the choice-point is left "buried in thought," as critics of that point of view have said. The problem, as these critics see it, is how to translate the animal's cognitions into behavioral action. One solution, though it obviously does not enchant the S-R theorist, is simply to assert, as part of the model, that given the proper cognitions, the proper responses will be forthcoming. How cognitions are turned into actions is left unspecified. Although such an approach may seem incomplete, it may also be that in order to achieve the appearance of completeness (that is, when all the links in the chain between stimulus and response are specified), S-R models have sacrificed something else; they may be bypassing, or ignoring, behavioral complexities that are just not amenable to an S-R type of analysis.

Such issues aside, attempts have been made to weigh the relative merits of the two approaches in terms of specific behavioral predictions. A few examples of prototypic experiments will indicate the nature of those attempts and the difficulty of testing theories that are not completely formulated.

TESTS OF COGNITIVE
AND S-R INTERPRETATIONS

Watson's Research. Watson himself conducted experiments that yielded apparently conflicting results. In one experiment, rats were trained in a complex maze until their performance was smooth and errorless. Then they were placed in a second maze which was an exact replica of the first except that the lengths of the alleys were decreased. Many of the animals ran right into the blank walls at the ends of the alleys, as though they were making habitual responses that were triggered by feedback from their own ongoing running responses. That is, each of these rats kept moving in a straight line until it had gone a certain distance (as "measured" by kinesthetic feedback) and then turned right or left, depending on its prior learning. When the distance between choice-points was reduced, the rats ran, or tried to run, right past them.

Such blind running would seem incompatible with the notion that the animals were basing their behavior on a match between a map of the maze and continuing assessment of where they currently were in relation to that map. This expectation would certainly be valid if the rat's assessment of its present location were made on a visual basis, or, more generally, on the basis of external rather than internal cues. However, kinesthetic maps are not excluded in principle from cognitive theories; and so what seems at first like a dramatic confirmation of an S-R interpretation of maze learning is no more than a demonstration of the dominance of kinesthetic over exteroceptive cues in maze learning. In fairness to Watson, it should be noted that, while his interpretation of the rat's learning was of the S-R variety, the experiment itself was not designed to test the model at that level, but rather to investigate the cues that triggered the habitual responses.

Evidence against the total dominance of kinesthesis in maze performance was provided in another experiment by Watson (1907). After the animals had been trained, the original maze was simply rotated 180 degrees. With maze orientation thus modified, the animals' previously efficient performance was markedly disturbed, clearly implying that other cues besides kinesthetic ones control their behavior. Whatever their exact identity, these cues must be both outside the animal and outside the maze itself.

But the kinds of experiments Watson and his followers conducted bore only indirectly on the broad theoretical issue of the nature of learning. It was left up to those taking the minority position—the cognitive approach—to devise the "crucial" experiments. The burden of proof was on those who wanted to forsake parsimony of the grounds that the simplicity of the S-R approach was inadequate to the task of explaining all forms of learning.

Latent Learning. Several attempts have been made by cognitive theorists to upset the basic assumptions of the S-R model. One experiment relates to the assumption in Hullian theory that S-R bonds are formed through the reinforcing, or rewarding, effects of the reduction in some drive like hunger. Even in Guthrie's radical S-R theory, rewards function to preserve the "correct" stimulus-response bonds. In cognitive theories like Tolman's, however, the animal can learn a great deal about its environment in the absence of specific rewards. Should a reward be available in some part of the environment and should the animal be so motivated that the reward is relevant, then it will use the map it has formed in order to obtain the rewarding object.

Tolman and Honzig (1930) conducted an experiment to test what seems a clear-cut theoretical difference. One group of hungry rats was trained in a complex maze with a food reward located in the goal box of the maze from the outset of the experiment (Group I). For a second group of hungry rats (Group II), the goal box was empty for the first several trials. Only after experience with such unrewarded trials did the rats encounter food when they entered the goal box. A third group was never rewarded.

According to the Hullian model, the first rewarded trial for Group II constitutes the first true learning trial. The group rewarded right from the beginning had the considerable advantage of having run many more training trials than the other group; this advantage should have shown up in the superior performance of the Group I animals—at least until Group II had the opportunity to catch up. But from the point of view of cognitive theory, the animals in Group II were learning a great deal about the maze (in particular, the location of the cul-de-sacs) before the introduction of the food. Once food had become available in the goal-box, the Group II rats should have traversed the maze as efficiently as the animals in Group I.

The results, as depicted in Figure 10.5, conform to the expectation from cognitive theory. Though the Group II rats were at first making more errors than the animals in Group I, that difference rapidly disappeared once the food reward had been encountered. Given some incentive to exhibit what they had been learning about the maze, the rats in Group II did indeed quickly match the performance level of the Group I subjects, despite the marked discrepancy in number of rewarded training trials.

As often happens when a model is challenged by data, supporters of the model find arguments with which to discount the data. The Tolman and Honzig experiment, which purports to demonstrate what has come to be known as *latent* learning, is no exception. For example, supporters of the S-R model point out that even during the prereward phase the Group II animals were gradually decreasing the number of errors made; they were learning, though of course not as rapidly as the rewarded animals. But if they were learning prior to the introduction of food reward, then some type of reinforcement must have been present. Perhaps the rats were mildly rewarded each time they made the "correct" response at a choice-point because by so doing they were spared the frustration experienced on entering a blind alley. But until food was present, the motivation to perform the S-R habits was still relatively weak. Once the incentive was introduced, the rats performed the habits they had been learning.

Such arguments suggest the weakness of both of the competing models. The Hullian approach is ambiguous about what constitutes an effective reward, and on occasion it makes the circular assertion that some reward must have been present in a situation since learning occurred. The cognitive model is also weak in that it fails to specify a set of conditions under which

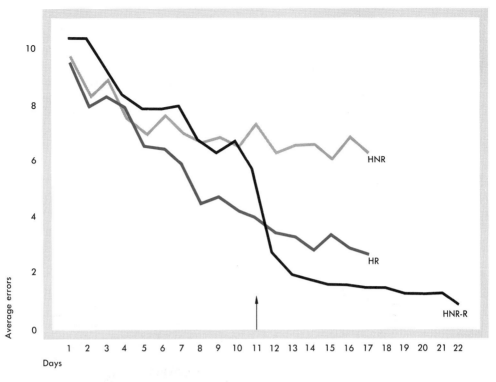

Figure 10.5 Learning curves for the animals in Tolman and Honzig's latent-learning experiment. Group HNR (hungry, nonrewarded) was not rewarded in the maze; HR was rewarded throughout the 22 days of the experiment; HNR-R was first rewarded on the eleventh day. Note how the errors for Group HNR-R abruptly decline after day 11. (Tolman and Honzik, 1930.)

maps will be formed that is unequivocally different from the conditions demanded by S-R theory. Thus, for a rat to form a cognitive map of a complex maze, it must engage in locomotor activity, in the course of which it experiences the rewards and punishments that are inherent in the process of moving around in a complex environment. How then can it be possible to claim that neither locomotor activity nor reward is essential for learning if both are inevitably associated with any empirical test of the model?

Even though a crucial test between the two approaches seems doomed to failure by virtue of ambiguities in both models, adherents of the models have not been completely deterred from trying to formulate such a test. And whether or not these experiments have actually served their intended purpose, they have provided interesting information about the learning process that ultimately will have to be assimilated into any comprehensive learning theory.

Place versus Response Learning. Another attempt to discriminate between an S-R and a cognitive approach employed a much simplified version of the traditional complex maze; in this version a single unit is abstracted out of the total, yielding the now-standard T-maze. The T-maze, or a variant such as the Y-maze, presents the animal with one choice-point and two alternative behaviors. Typically, the reinforcement is placed at the end of one of the cross-arms of the T, hidden from view and not otherwise accessible to any of the animal's senses until after a choice has been made. In order to acquire the reinforcement, the subject must guide its behavior according to the contingencies imposed by the experimenter. Learning enters as the means by which those contingencies come to affect the subject's behavior.

With respect to whether the learning is of the cognitive-map variety, the animal's task is ambiguous. Regardless of what the experimenter's definition of the task might be, the rat can learn to achieve the reinforcement in either of two ways. Suppose a piece of food is always located as indicated in the diagram in Figure 10.6. To the rat, that diagram may imply (a) "make a right-turning response when encountering the stimuli associated with the choice-point," or (b) "the food is located in the part of the room near the windows." In short, the task can be either to make a particular *response* (turning right) or to go to a particular *place*. As far as reinforcement contingencies in the T-maze are concerned, either interpretation will work. But S-R theory insists that the animal learns to make particular responses, while the cognitive approach asserts that the animal learns *about* its environment and then responds accordingly. If it were possible to devise a situation so that response learning and place learning made different demands on the subject, then a test of the two approaches might be available.

In fact, with slight modifications in the standard T-maze, it becomes possible to require a rat to learn either a particular response or a particular location. Suppose we transform the T-maze into a cross-shaped maze, as depicted in Figure 10.7. We let some trials originate at S and others at N,

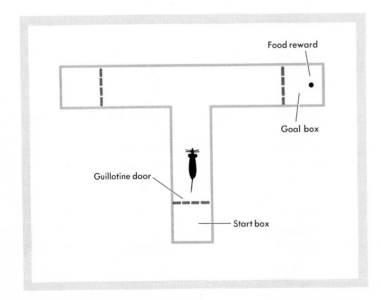

Figure 10.6 A T-maze used in learning experiments.

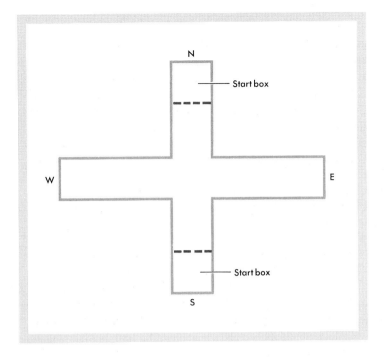

Figure 10.7 A cross-shaped maze, used to compare place and response learning.

blocking off the unused starting alley at the choice-point. For half the rats, the reinforcement is always located in, say, the W goal arm. To get to it, a rat has to turn either left or right, depending on whether the trial began at S or N. For the other half, the reinforcement is so located that the animal must make, say, a left-turning response to reach it even though this means sometimes going into the west and other times into the east goal arm (W if the subject starts from S, E if it starts from N).

If the rats are pure response learners, then they should not be able to learn at all when the locus of the reinforcement is defined geographically. If they are place learners, then they should be at a great disadvantage when the locus of reinforcement is defined in relation to a particular turning response. Hence, we seem to have developed a crucial test of the two models. What are the data?

In one of the early experiments following the above design (Tolman, Ritchie, and Kalish, 1946), place learning was found to be the easier of the two tasks. That experiment employed an *elevated maze*, which lacks the confining walls of the standard T-maze and has pathways which are raised off the ground; the rat remains in the maze simply because it would otherwise fall from a relatively great height to the floor. With the usual side walls absent, the elevated maze gives good access to external cues by which the rat can orient in space. By contrast, in the enclosed T-maze, the rat is cut off from most of such external cues. You might expect that place learning would be difficult in an enclosed T-maze, and indeed, it does lose its superiority over response learning exhibited in an elevated maze. But the notion of a cognitive map does not demand that learning be easy under all circumstances; a map can neither be formed adequately nor utilized without proper environmental support in the form of external cues. It is somewhat embarrassing to the cognitive model, however, that rats can learn on the basis of the reduced cues of the enclosed T-maze—embarrassing unless the concept of a cognitive map is broadened to include feedback from the animal's motor responses. There is nothing in principle to preclude the inclusion of cues that originate within one's own body in a cognitive structure, or "map." That clearly is what *must* happen in the learning of motor skills, such as playing the piano, ice skating, dancing, hitting a golf ball, or for the very young, crawling, walking, feeding oneself, dressing, and so on.

In short, a cognitive model of maze learning, if it is to have any generality at all, needs to incorporate cues that are response-induced. Once that has happened, what looks like "response-learning" can be considered a special case of the formation of a cognitive map, and the two competing models are seen to fuse. The merger has come about from the other direction also. In order to take account of the learning that looks like place learning, as in the Tolman, Ritchie, and Kalish experiment, S-R theory has had to broaden the concept of "a response." Whereas in a restricted model, response is identified with a specific set of muscle movements (as in making a right turn in a T-maze), it is possible to liberalize the model so as to allow for "an approach response." According to this broader conception, then, a rat can learn the response of "approaching the goal" in the presence of certain cues. Thus, place learning becomes possible within an S-R framework, though it is necessary to accept a very general definition of a response.

Learning without Overt Responses. Good controversies do not die easily, and that certainly holds for cognitive-versus-response learning. Ingenious and hopefully crucial experiments have continued to be devised well after the question seemed to have been resolved, or perhaps dissolved. Seeking an uncompromising victory over S-R theory, proponents of the cognitive approach have, for example, tried to demonstrate the occurrence of learning in the absence of any opportunity to make a relevant motor response on the part of the experimental subject. For example, in order to preclude the occurrence of any overt motor response during the acquisition phase of a learning experiment, animals have been trained while their striped muscles were completely paralyzed through use of drugs such as curare and its derivatives. These drugs, as mentioned earlier, block the transmission of neural impulses between motor nerves and striped muscles; however, they leave the organism receptive to stimulation. Under such circumstances, learning apparently can occur, as evidenced by the subjects' behavior on test trials administered after the effects of the drug have worn off (for example, Black, Carlson, and Solomon, 1962; Solomon and Turner, 1962). These experiments have typically employed a classical conditioning paradigm. However, in one such study rats were trained to avoid one arm of a

T-maze by being transported through the maze, while paralyzed, in a little trolley car and being shocked whenever the car carried them into the "wrong" goal arm (Gleitman, 1963). In this case, the animals seem to have acquired an instrumental response without having made it. But again, an interpretation that is compatible with a liberalized S-R model can be offered. You might want to try your hand at this game, so the interpretation will not be spelled out here. Keep in mind, though, both the locus of the action of the drug and the question of what constitutes a suitable definition of a response in a broadened S-R model.

OTHER USES OF THE MAZE

The use of the T-maze in studies of learning has not been confined to the controversy between S-R and cognitive-map models. Many other issues have lent themselves to investigation by means of the T-maze, a few of which we will note briefly.

Discrimination Learning. In order to maximize reinforcement, an animal must utilize a specific environmental cue in selecting the goal arm to enter. For example, one goal arm is black, and the other is white. The arbitrarily designated "correct" response might be to enter the white arm. The location (right or left position) of the black and white arms is randomly varied from trial to trial. To exhibit learning, the animal must be able to discriminate between the two cues, black and white. Therefore, learning implies successful discrimination, and performance of the learned response can be treated as an indicator of discrimination. In short, discrimination learning experiments can be thought of as psychophysical experiments, though the precision afforded by the T-maze for control of the stimuli is not very impressive; neither is the sensitivity of the response measures taken, for an animal may readily discriminate between two stimuli but fail to reveal that fact because of a deficiency in ability to learn.

Reversal Learning. Although species differences do not typically show up in simple discrimination learning, they do appear in a variant known as *reversal learning.* This procedure consists of repeatedly reversing the identity of the correct alternative after the animal has achieved a criterion level of correct performance. If the black arm is correct initially, it will be made incorrect once the animal has learned the first discrimination. After the reversed problem has been mastered, the correct alternative is again reversed, and so on. In comparative studies of reversal learning, it has been found that some species (for example, rats and pigeons) show progressive improvement in their performance with succeeding reversals, taking fewer and fewer trials to reach criterion. Other species, such as turtles, do not show this effect; for them, each reversal is like an entirely new problem (Bitterman, 1965).

Learning-to-Learn. Progressive improvement over succeeding reversal problems in the T-maze is closely analogous to what has been observed in discrimination-learning situations employing other apparatus. For example, monkeys may be presented with pairs of geometric forms or simple objects, one of which is designated as correct by the experimenter. The monkey must touch the correct alternative, or pull it toward him by a string, or shove it aside, depending on the particular apparatus employed. If his choice is correct, he is rewarded, perhaps with a raisin or a grape. As the number of such discrimination problems increases, it takes fewer and fewer trials for the animal to reach criterion (such as nine correct choices out of ten trials). In short, highly sophisticated animals can learn a discrimination problem in very few trials, indeed sometimes after only a single error. Such animals are said to exhibit *learning-to-learn* or to have formed *learning sets* (strategies for efficiently solving discrimination problems). The pioneering work on this phenomenon was done by Harry Harlow and his collaborators (see Harlow, 1949), who devised the basic apparatus used in such research, the Wisconsin General Test Apparatus. Differences among species in the facility of forming learning sets correspond pretty much to expectations based on phylogenetic position. Some representative data are shown in Figure 10.8.

Probability Learning. In the typical T-maze learning experiment, reinforcement is associated with only one of the alternatives. However, just as one can employ partial-reinforcement schedules in the Skinner box instead of 100 per cent reinforcement, so too is flexibility possible in the T-maze. In particular, an investigator might reinforce both alternatives, but with unequal probabilities. .For example, the food reward might be located 70 per cent of the time in the left arm of the maze and 30 per cent in the right arm. What effect does this kind of manipulation of reinforcement contingencies have on behavior?

For human subjects in a very similar situation—for example, being asked to guess which one of two lights will be turned on next, when one light is programed to come on more frequently than the other—the typical pattern of response is called *probability matching.* In short, subjects guess at about the same probability level as the two alternatives occur. Thus, if alternative A occurs 70 per cent of the time and B 30 per cent, subjects will guess "A" 70 per cent of the time and "B" 30 per cent.

Lower animals, such as rats, also exhibit the matching pattern under many experimental conditions. In some settings, however, a different pattern is observed in both human subjects and lower animals. The subject selects the more probable alternative on every trial. This pattern is called *maximizing,* because it assures the subject the highest possible likelihood of being correct, or of receiving the reinforcement.

Why does this latter pattern assure maximal reinforcement? Consider the case above, where A occurs 70 per cent of the time and B only 30 per

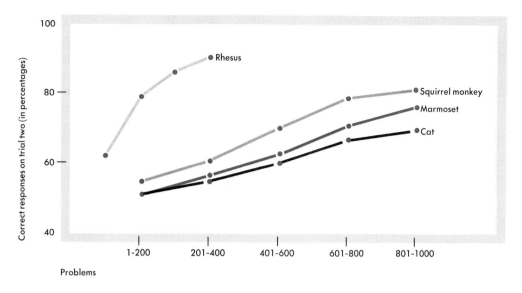

Figure 10.8 Data on learning sets for four species. Each point illustrating rhesus data represents a block of 98 problems; squirrel monkey, marmoset, and cat performances are summarized in 200-problem blocks. (Myers, Mc-Quiston, and Miles, 1962.)

cent, and where the distribution of A's and B's over trials is random. If the subject chooses A each time, he will be right on 70 per cent of his choices. How well can he do if he employs the matching "strategy"? He will choose A 70 per cent of the time and B 30 per cent of the time. But only on 70 per cent of the occasions when he selects A will A occur, on the average. Hence he will be correct on .70 × .70 of the trials, or 49 per cent of the time. Similarly, on the 30 per cent of the trials when he selects B, B will occur, on the average, 30 per cent of the time. This will add 9 per cent correct guesses. Thus, over 100 trials he will, on the average, guess correctly 49 + 9, or 58, times. That value is considerably less than the number he would get right if he guessed A each time, that is, 70.

In general, probability matching is a less effective strategy than choosing the more frequently reinforced alternative more often than the probability of its occurrence (picking the 70 per cent alternative 80 per cent of the time is better than matching; it will yield 62 reinforcements over 100 trials), and selecting the more probable alternative every time produces maximum reinforcement.

Although matching behavior is stupid on mathematical grounds, it may nevertheless reflect, at times, a more intellectual approach than maximizing. When human subjects match, they may be trying to "beat the game," to outwit the experimenter by finding a system (which unfortunately is not there) that will bring more reinforcements than the mathematical limit allowed by the logic outlined above. Subjects who choose the more probable alternative every time may appear to be maximizing, but they may instead simply be passively allowing their behavior to be shaped by the reinforcement contingencies. That is, in picking the more likely alternative they may just be blindly making the stronger of two competing habits.

So it is not clear what is implied when a lower animal, such as a rat, matches or maximizes. Hence, comparative investigations of probability learning have yielded ambiguous interpretations. It is worth reporting, however, that under conditions where rats and monkeys maximize, fish, turtles, and pigeons match. Since turtles and fish are also inferior on reversal problems (suggesting inferior intelligence, in accord with their phylogenetic position), it seems reasonable to interpret maximizing, for lower animals at least, as the more "intellectual" approach (see Bitterman, 1965). Studies of maze learning are not ordinarily directed at the problem of assessing intellectual ability; however, reversal and probability learning do suggest how relatively simple learning situations can be transformed into revealing indicators of higher-order processes.

Aversive Learning

In terms of a distinction made at the beginning of this chapter, the types of learning discussed so far have all been of the appetitive variety. A considerable amount of research has also been done on *aversive* learning, that is, learning of a response that enables the subject to avoid, or otherwise diminish or delay, an "unpleasant" stimulus.

AVOIDANCE LEARNING

The prototype of aversive learning is referred to as *avoidance learning*. In this paradigm, the subject is given the opportunity entirely to avoid the aversive stimulus; he need only make the operant response on schedule. For example, a rat is placed in a box with a grid floor through which shock can be delivered. Onset of the shock is signaled by a buzzer; to avoid the shock the rat must run to the opposite end of the box within five seconds after the buzzer starts. This type of apparatus is called the Miller-Mowrer shuttlebox, in recognition of the psychologists (Neal Miller and O. Hobart Mowrer) who developed it. A variant of the shuttlebox is an arrangement whereby the animal has to perform some instrumental response other than shuttling—for example, turning a wheel, or jumping over a barrier, or biting a tube, and so on.

Animals can learn an avoidance response, and they do so fairly quickly. Indeed, with sufficiently intense shock, dogs can acquire an avoidance response in a single trial (Solomon and Wynne, 1954), and the response is unusually resistant to extinction procedures. But not all avoidance responses are that stable. On the contrary, one of the puzzling results of some avoidance-learning experiments is the spontaneous extinction of the response. That is, after a rat has acquired the response, with no changes in the experimental procedure it stops making the avoidance response (see, for example, Coons, Anderson, and Myers, 1960; Anderson and Nakamura, 1964).

What Is the Reinforcement in Avoidance Learning? This unexpected instability in the avoidance response does have theoretical significance, as will become evident below. The major theoretical issue concerning avoidance learning has been the specification of the reinforcement. Compare *escape* with avoidance learning. In the former, the animal cannot avoid the aversive stimulus, but can terminate it rapidly by efficiently making the requisite operant response. Thus, shock comes on; the animal runs to the other end of the shuttlebox and gets away from the shock. What is the reinforcement? Surely, it is the termination of the aversive stimulus or the attendant decrease in pain. But what is the reinforcement that establishes and maintains an avoidance response? The buzzer sounds, the animal runs, and . . . then what? Physically, nothing else happens. That is, since the shock did not come on, it cannot terminate. If shock termination constitutes the reinforcement in escape learning, what event plays that role in avoidance learning?

That question has plagued learning theorists for decades, to such an extent that some of them simply avoid avoidance learning as a suitable problem on which to devote their intellectual efforts. Those that have tangled with the question have had limited success, either because their constructions tend too much toward the anthropomorphic or because they do not hold up under careful scrutiny.

Neal Miller's model (1951) exemplifies the latter case. Very briefly, the model is based on the concept of *fear*. Aversive stimuli are assumed to elicit a "fear response." This fear response becomes conditioned to the warning signal (the buzzer in our example). The reinforcement for the establishment of that habit (making the fear response to the buzzer) is shock termination, a primary reinforcer. But fear is itself aversive. When the buzzer sounds and the animal makes the operant response in time to avoid shock, the fear elicited by the buzzer can quickly dissipate since it is not maintained by shock occurrence. Thus, what follows the operant response is a rapid reduction in fear. And, as noted, since fear is aversive, fear reduction is reinforcing. Thus, the avoidance response is established and maintained through the reinforcing power of fear reduction.

So far so good. However, as long as the animal continues to make the avoidance response, it is never shocked. Under those circumstances, we would expect the fear response to extinguish, because its strength is dependent on the reinforcement provided by shock termination. With no shock onset, there can be no shock termination; hence each successful avoidance trial becomes an extinction trial as far as the fear response is concerned. If so, once the fear response is extinguished, no reinforcer is available to maintain the avoidance response. Thus, the avoidance response itself should extinguish.

The weakness of the Miller model is that it unintentionally predicts the spontaneous extinction of the avoidance response. But the apparent weakness is an asset since it turns out that avoidance responses do indeed sometimes spontaneously extinguish. Thus, the initially unsettling observation that it is difficult to maintain an avoidance response supports an unintended implication of Miller's model. The only problem remaining is to explain why some avoidance responses not only fail to extinguish spontaneously, but are virtually impossible to extinguish under any circumstances—as is the case with Richard Solomon's one-trial avoidance-learning experiments on dogs alluded to earlier. Of course, given what appear to be mutually exclusive observations about avoidance behavior (it extinguishes spontaneously; it is very difficult to extinguish), no simple model is likely to be entirely satisfactory. One way out, at least temporarily, is to segregate varieties of avoidance learning and develop models appropriate to each subtype.

PASSIVE AVOIDANCE

Within the category of avoidance learning a distinction between *active* and *passive* avoidance learning has proven useful. The former includes instances of the sort we have been discussing: An animal learns to *make* an operant response in order to avoid aversive stimulation. In passive avoidance, the animal first learns an appetitive instrumental response (such as poking its head into a hole) and then learns to inhibit that response through aversive reinforcement; the passive avoidance response, in essence, consists in "doing nothing" in the face of temptation so as not to be punished. That this distinction is functionally useful is evidenced by the fact that damage to certain portions of the brain (for one, the hippocampus) interferes with passive avoidance learning, but either facilitates active avoidance or leaves it intact (see Douglas, 1967).

SUMMARY

In *instrumental* learning, whether *appetitive* or *aversive*, the occurrence and other characteristics of reinforcement are contingent on the occurrence of the response to be learned. Instrumental learning has been studied with the use of several standard types of equipment.

The *problem-box* was used by E.L. Thorndike to investigate the acquisition by animals of a simple response, such as pushing a lever, that was followed by the animal's release from the box and its access to food. Thorndike formulated the *Law of Effect* to account for the acquisition of such responses. In one version of this law, responses that resulted in a "satisfying" state of affairs were mechanically "stamped in," and those that resulted in an "unsatisfying" state of affairs were "stamped out." The terms satisfying and unsatisfying were given operational definitions so as to obviate the criticism of anthropomorphism. The law was subsequently modified by Thorndike as a result of evidence, mainly from human subjects, that unsatisfying consequences of a response had little if any behavioral effect. The truncated law was restricted to the effects of satisfying events, or in contemporary terminology, positive reinforcers. The exact role of reinforcement in the problem-box was examined by Guthrie and Horton, who concluded that learning occurs simply as a result of the occurrence of a response in the presence of a stimulus. Reinforcement enters into the formation of stimulus-response (S-R) bonds only indirectly; it protects the learning of a particular S-R association by taking the animal out of the situation containing the S or by preventing the occurrence of responses incompatible with the R to be learned. In Guthrie's learning model, a particular S-R association is formed at full strength any time the S and the R occur together; that is, learning occurs on one trial. The gradual acquisition of a response typical of most learning experiments is viewed as an artifact of the typical variability in the stimulus situation. When special care is taken to minimize this variability, step-wise, rather than gradual, learning curves can be obtained.

A simplification of the problem-box yields the Skinner box. In this apparatus the animal or human subject must learn to make a simple response, an *operant*, usually involving manipulation of a conspicuous object, the *manipulandum*, such as a lever or a key. Occurrence of the operant is immediately followed by a reinforcement, such as a food pellet. One advantage of the Skinner box is that it is readily automated; for example, the *reinforcement schedule*, which determines the exact relation between responses and reinforcements, can be automatically programed, and an automatic record can be made of the subject's rate of responses (the *operant level*). As typically employed, the Skinner box is used more to study the variables that affect the performance of a learned response than its acquisition. To facilitate acquisition, a *shaping* procedure is usually followed whereby successively closer approximations to the desired response are reinforced, often with *secondary* reinforcers, such as the click of the mechanism that delivers the food pellets.

Various reinforcement schedules have been devised besides the 100 per cent, or continuous, reinforcement schedule originally employed by Skinner in which each correct response is reinforced. In *interval* schedules a reinforcement is delivered only after a specified time has elapsed since the previously reinforced response—*fixed* interval when the time period is constant and *variable* when the time period fluctuates around an average value. In *ratio* schedules, a reinforcement is delivered for each N response— exactly N in *fixed-ratio* schedules and about N in *variable-ratio* schedules. Each schedule yields a characteristic pattern and rate of responding. Mixed schedules have also been used in which each of two or more operants is reinforced on a different schedule. Variability in *magnitude* and *delay* of reinforcement, along with noncontinuous schedules, are typical of the world outside the laboratory, but can be studied experimentally.

A major theoretical problem is posed by the finding that responses are less easily extinguished if originally reinforced on noncontinuous, or *partial*, reinforcement schedules than if they had been continuously reinforced. Among the more interesting explanations offered for the *partial-reinforcement effect* are those relying on the concepts of stimulus generalization and frustration. The role of punishment in extinguishing a habit is ambiguous. Some data indicate that the psychological consequences of punishment and of nonreinforcement are equivalent. Other data suggest that punishment temporarily suppresses, but does not eliminate, habits. In some situations punishment may make the subject so inflexible that it prevents extinction instead of facilitating it. It is likely that punishment works best in the extinction of habits when it allows new responses to be learned that are incompatible with the response being extinguished.

Though it is the instrumental learning of such responses as limb movements that has most often been studied, it is possible to apply instrumental procedures to the learning of smooth-muscle responses mediated by the autonomic nervous system.

Maze-learning by rats has stimulated two major theoretical issues: (1) What is learned, cognitive maps or stimulus-response associations? (2) Is reinforcement necessary, or does it merely provide the occasion for the animal to exhibit what it has been learning? Experiments on *latent learning* and of *place-vs.-response* learning are supportive of a cognitive model, but the results of such studies can be interpreted within an S-R framework. The same ambiguity applies to experiments showing learning in animals paralyzed by drugs and therefore incapable of making overt limb movements during their exposure to a maze.

Simple mazes have been employed to study animals' *discrimination* abilities; though ease of learning a simple discrimination, either in the T-maze or in other kinds of apparatus, does not reflect species differences, certain variants of the discrimination problem do, such as *reversal learning, learning-to-learn,* and *probability learning.*

Subjects can learn to escape from or avoid unpleasant, or *aversive,* stimulation, as for example by running from one side of a shuttlebox to the other. The reinforcement in *escape* learning is easy to identify, but considerable controversy has arisen over the nature of the reinforcement in *avoidance* learning. One hypothesis is that avoidance learning is reinforced by a reduction in fear that follows the correct response. The fear itself is presumed to be learned, through association of an innate fear response to aversive stimuli, such as electric shock, with the stimulus that signals the impending onset of the aversive stimulus. But once an avoidance response is learned, the aversive stimulus no longer occurs, in which case the acquired fear should extinguish. If the fear extinguishes, then the subject should also stop making the avoidance response—and in some situations that does indeed happen. The type of learning in which the subject must actively respond in order to avoid aversive stimulation is distinguished from *passive avoidance,* in which a prepotent response must be inhibited if the aversive stimulation is to be avoided. That this distinction is functionally important is shown by the differential effects on active and passive avoidance of certain kinds of brain damage. Lesions in the hippocampus disrupt passive avoidance learning, but either do not affect or even may enhance active avoidance learning.

SUGGESTED READINGS

Goldstein, H., D.L. Krantz, and J.D. Rains. *Controversial issues in learning.* New York: Appleton-Century-Crofts, 1965.

Logan, F.A., and A.P. Wagner. *Reward and punishment.* Boston: Allyn & Bacon, 1965.

Mednick, S.A. *Learning.* Englewood Cliffs, N. J.: Prentice-Hall, 1964.

Reynolds, G.S. *A primer of operant conditioning.* Glenview, Ill.: Scott, Foresman, 1968.

Walker, E.L. *Conditioning and instrumental learning.* Belmont, Cal.: Brooks/Cole, 1967.

Human Learning
and Remembering

CHAPTER ELEVEN Up to this point we have been concerned with the development of general learning principles which we have supposed to be applicable to all species. It is now time to ask what we know about human learning. It is obvious that adult human beings know a great deal about the world and know how to do a staggering variety of tasks. Can the acquisition of this knowledge and skill be described in the same way we have described the learning of mazes by rats and the acquisition of salivary responses by dogs? In this chapter we will consider the attempts of psychologists to study learning in human beings, giving special attention to their attempts to cope with forgetting, a phenomenon rarely studied in animals but quite obvious to any person who has tried to learn and retain some set amount of material. We will introduce here a problem that was met first in animal learning but that grows in importance as we study human beings, the problem of what-is-learned. This question, which looks transparently simple at first, turns out to be a key issue in the contest between competing theories of learning.

A classic philosophical problem concerns the way the human organism comes to know anything about the world. As we pointed out in Chapter Four, the polar positions can be characterized very roughly as *nativism* and *empiricism*. Plato and Leibnitz are typical of the philosophers who have held that many important determinants of knowing and understanding are innate. The British associationists, led by Locke, represent those who have held that the only innate capacity is the capacity to associate and that knowledge and understanding, therefore, are acquired through experience with the world and consist of the associations resulting from that experience.

In the main, experimental psychology, and especially the psychology of learning, has been dominated by the associationist position. Most of the data on learning of any sort, human or animal, has been collected from this standpoint. Similarly, most of the efforts to develop learning theories have focused on the formation, growth, decay, and dissolution of associative bonds. As we will see in this chapter, however, there is much to be said for models that encompass more mental machinery than the formation of simple associations, and there are indications that new formulations are in the making.

A Variety of Views

Among the associationists there are two major traditions. One is that of the "learning theorists," men who elaborated *general* theories of learning from their work on animal learning. Their basic tenet has been that the principles of learning are much the same (or even identical) throughout the whole animal kingdom. From the 1930s through the 1950s theoretical work in American psychology consisted largely of the efforts of such theorists.

The second associationist tradition is that of the students of "rote learning," or memorizing, who have been concerned with the learning and retention of verbal material. Most of these investigators have been "functionalists" who have avoided widespread, general theories in favor of specific descriptive laws that apply to particular experimental settings. *Analysis* is a key word, and the favored activity is to take a particular problem, like learning a list of words, and study all the variables that affect it. The functional laws observed are then offered as the analysis of that special learning problem. Although theoretical development has been intense, theory has remained close to the data and highly specific rather than remote and general.

Among the nonassociationists there are several heterogeneous groups. Some of these, like the psychologists engaged in the study of motor skills, are essentially a-theoretical. They have developed principles of learning or training of motor skills to be sure, but they tend to study each situation with a view toward finding an acceptable solution to a practical problem. This is one of the few areas of experimental psychology where concern with individual differences is found (again because of the practical problems involved), but the studies have been descriptive and have not led to general theories of skill learning and their relation to individual abilities.

A second group of nonassociationists who *are* theoretically oriented is composed of the Gestalt psychologists. These investigators have tried to point out the complexity of human learning and the major role of "organizing factors" in determining what is learned and how it is retained. Their theory has remained vague and diffuse, however, serving more as a reminder of the complexity of mental processes in higher animals than as a comprehensive model of that complexity.

Finally, in the last decade we have witnessed the emergence of small groups of psychologists with no allegiance to any of the classic positions who are interested in "information-processing," "computer simulation of human behavior," "artificial intelligence," "competence theory," and the like. These investigators, along with the workers in mathematical learning theory, have been attempting to devise elegant and precise accounts of the behavior of subjects in a host of specific experimental situations. Their work, dependent for the most part on the modern high-speed computer, is creating a new atmosphere for the development and testing of theories. By its very thoroughness, this work is revealing inadequacies in older theories and suggesting new levels of complexity that future theories must be ready to contemplate.

While we cannot hope to do credit to the richness of all these approaches, in this chapter we will treat four major aspects. First, we will sketch the general difficulty of applying theories of animal learning to human learning. Second, we will discuss the verbal-learning tradition in some detail, both for its contribution to general psychology and for its interest to students who are concerned with governing their own learning of this sort. Next, we will briefly describe the study of motor skills in contrast with verbal learning. Finally, we will explore the movements aimed at understanding the role of organization and activity in human learning.

The Learning-Theory Approach

The approach of the learning theorist stresses the evolutionary continuity of species and rests on the faith that learning consists of the formation of associations between stimuli and responses. What counts as a stimulus and what counts as a response are obviously determined by the native equipment of the organism and will differ from one species to another. The associative principle, however, is expected to be the same.

The learning theorist argues persuasively that a scientist ought to work with the simplest organism available in order to avoid complexities involving the forms of the stimulus and the response, while at the same time working with the essential problem, the formation or dissolution of associations. Surely, he insists, it is wiser to work with a worm, a rat, a pigeon, or a dog than to attempt to tackle man, the most complicated organism that we know. In addition, we are not willing to subject human beings to the deprivations and special conditions that are essential to the study of certain problems. (For example, we may raise chimpanzees in isolation and silence to see whether they develop their system of vocal calls spontaneously, but we are not willing to run the risk of raising a human child without language for fear of permanently crippling him intellectually.)

This approach either minimizes the importance of species-specific behaviors or argues that such behaviors are special, isolated cases. Complex human behaviors are ordinarily not discussed because too many unknown factors are involved. Usually, learning theorists assert that complex behaviors can be accounted for *in principle* but that the task is too formidable in practice. A good example of this tendency is found in the work of Clark Hull (1943), who claims that language is just another case of learned behavior but that once it is learned, it makes possible "secondary generalizations" along patterns so complex that we cannot hope to understand them.

The work of E.L. Thorndike, whom we encountered in Chapter Ten, furnishes a good example of some of the difficulties faced by a learning theorist who seriously proposed extending his principles of learning to human beings. In his work with animals Thorndike found two laws to be sufficient, the Law of Effect and the Law of Exercise. According to the first, responses that lead to satisfying states of affairs will increase in probability (will be "stamped in") and responses that lead to discomforting or annoying states of affairs will decrease in probability (will be "stamped out"). The second law held that the connection of a response to a situation is increased in proportion to the number of times that it has been connected with that situation in the past.

Thorndike conscientiously tried to apply his laws to human learning in simple situations and revised his laws as he found necessary. When he rewrote his formalization to include human learning, he found that he had to include some new rules (Thorndike, 1932, 1935). The Law of Effect, as we saw, was altered to make it a Law of Reward because Thorndike found the effect of punishment to be unreliable among people. (It also became apparent that rewards tend to be more informative than punishments. For example, if a person has a choice of five responses and picks the right one, he has a great deal of information. If he makes a wrong choice and is punished, he still does not know which one of the remaining responses is correct.) The Law of Exercise was retained but was viewed as a weaker law than the Law of Effect.

Thorndike introduced a set of extra principles to attempt to account for the differences in materials or conditions that produced differences in learning in his human subjects. The most interesting of these principles was *belonging*. By *belonging* Thorndike referred to the fact that some combinations of materials were readily learned while other combinations, apparently benefiting from the same contiguities, were not learned. Suppose a subject is asked to say the appropriate number to a word, as in the following list:

Table   21

Book   6

Lamp   13   etc.

With repeated readings of the list of pairs he can learn to give the number to the word (for example, to *table* he would say *21*), but ordinarily he will not know the next word after a number (given *21* he could not give *book*). Language provides another example. If a subject tries to learn a list of sentences such as:

Mr. Thompson is our butcher. Mr. Smith is the mailman. . . .

He associates *Thompson* rather than *Smith* with *butcher* even though *butcher* and *Smith* are closer together. *Belonging,* then, refers to some ordering or structuring of relations in the materials that enter into the determination of what is learned. Clearly, this principle implies that something had gone wrong with the simple notion of the automatic association of contiguous items.

Other principles seem to be reasonable extensions of some of Thorndike's earlier notions that became more specific as human experimentation continued. These were the principles of *impressiveness* (the vividness of relevant stimuli favors learning), the closely related notion of *identifiability* (the more easily the appropriate stimulus and response can be discriminated, the more rapidly learning will proceed), *availability* (readiness to perform the response increases the rate of learning), and *polarity* (performance of an association is easier in the direction in which it was experienced during learning, that is, the order of items is important in determining what leads to what).

Thorndike's problem was prophetic of the difficulties that later general learning theorists were to encounter. His last four principles seem to be legitimate extensions that might be related to the different stimulus and response capacities of human beings and lower animals. They are clearly well within the tradition of associationism. But the introduction of "belonging" and the weakening of the Law of Exercise represent failures of the associationist point of view.

PROBLEMS IN EXTENDING THEORY

Successful demonstrations of the application of principles of learning theory are most common when the task for the human being is made very much like the task performed by the animal. Thus, we can find many studies of eyelid conditioning and shock-avoidance conditioning in people that have features in common with the conditioning studies of Pavlov and that seem to follow much the same laws. It is important to note, however, that demonstrations of human conditioning can be rendered very different from typical animal conditioning studies if the instructions are changed just a little. For example, ordinarily in a finger-withdrawal experiment, the subject is shocked on the finger after the conditioned stimulus is presented. If he is told to try very hard to keep his finger on the key, no withdrawal conditioning will be observed in a substantial proportion of the cases. The "best" instructions are usually something like, "Place your finger on the button. If it feels as if it wants to come off, just let it." Similarly, one can often "remove" a conditioned response by saying, "OK. That's all. We aren't going to shock you anymore." And one can "create" a conditioned response by saying, "When the light goes on, you will receive a severe shock." Without any training, the onset of the light will now produce marked changes in the subject's autonomic nervous system, as well as avoidance responses and the like (see for example, Cook and Harris, 1937).

As is readily apparent in these examples and elsewhere, a major problem for the learning theorist is human language. Because of it, Pavlov postulated the *second signal system* as a separate system available to human beings only. He held that the second signal system could override and control the first signal system (that is, the reflex system), and, more importantly, that it showed different characteristics in conditioning, being much more volatile and readily altered. American learning theorists, differing from Pavlov, have usually argued that language itself will eventually be understood in terms of general learning theory and that all human behavior will be explained under a single theoretical framework. (Some of the efforts to understand language in this way are treated in the next chapter.) At the present, however, no one has developed a satisfactory account of the mechanisms and the effects of language either within or without the learning theory camp, so all such claims are statements of faith or bets about the future.

Two of Hull's disciples, Neal E. Miller and John Dollard, have made ambitious attempts to show how learning theory of the Hullian sort could be used to explain many human behaviors (Miller and Dollard, 1941; Dollard and Miller, 1950). In order to simplify their work, they have used an abbreviated form of the theory, one that is reduced largely to the following chain:

Drive—Cue—Response—Reward

This is a handy pattern that permits them to discuss matters from social behavior to psychotherapy, talking about plausible accounts of behavior in terms of individual histories and situations. As is usual for human behavior, however, *drives* are almost free for the inventing, if learned motives are included; *cues* are hard to discover or are described as "complex situations"; *responses* are also complex and vary from motor movements to elaborate plans of activities; and secondary reinforcement permits almost anything to be a *reward* for someone under some condition. In short, although these extensions offer stimulating ideas about human behavior that encourage experimentation and exploration, they are largely metaphorical applications of laboratory terminology offered in the hope of building plausible explanations.

Today, B.F. Skinner is one of the few psychologists who strongly advocates applying the findings of animal research directly to people. For many years he has argued that *theories* of learning are illusory and troublesome and that they naturally lead to difficulties when one goes to the human case. He believes that simple functional generalizations, however, stay close to the data and are not beset with such problems. He has shunned theoretical concepts of any appreciable complexity, preferring to identify just a few concepts such as *stimulus, response,* and *reinforcement* only in terms of the functional relations into which they enter. Therefore, Skinner is not surprised when some particular event does not function as a stimulus or as a reinforcer or when some particular behavior does not function as a response. If one makes no general claims about such matters, one cannot make any errors. One identifies stimuli, responses, and reinforcements by the roles they play—the study of learning in a particular situation identifies the events that constitute these concepts—hence, Skinner's followers often describe their work as "the analysis of behavior."

Skinner has devoted most of his attention to studying the effect of schedules of reinforcement on the rate or probability of a response. He maintains that these lawful relationships hold just as well for human beings as for rats or pigeons, pointing to the "one-armed-bandit" or slot-machine (a variable-ratio reinforcement device) as an outstanding proof of his point.

A second reason Skinner has little trouble with the human case is that he has always held that getting the desired behavior to occur initially ("shaping the response") is a matter of artistry, emphasizing the skill and ingenuity of the experimenter. Thus, matters of instruction, hints, partial learning, use of already-learned structures, sets, and so on, afford him no embarrassment. He sees the total learning process as one which is defined by a period of shaping, (dependent on the investigator and the situation) plus a period of scheduling the occurrence of the response (dependent on his laws concerning reinforcements).

At the present time there are no major academic movements that explicitly claim to develop human learning theory on the basis of animal theory. Many of the concepts and terms from learning theory are applied loosely to both areas, but the meanings are more metaphorical than literal. The unification of all learning in a single theoretical formulation, a goal that was pursued so ardently one or two decades ago, does not seem to command much optimistic support currently.

The other branch of association psychology that tackled human learning has fared better in many ways by restricting its scope and addressing itself solely to the problems of verbal learning. It is to this branch that we now turn.

The Verbal-Learning Tradition

The verbal-learning tradition has a unique, identifiable origin. Although memory systems had been proposed from the time of Hippias of Elis, a Greek sophist (ca. 500 B.C.), it had apparently never occurred to anyone to examine learning and memory scientifically until Hermann Ebbinghaus, a young German philosopher, undertook the task in the late 1870s. Ebbinghaus, who stumbled across scientific psychology when he picked up Fechner's book on psychophysics in a second-hand bookstore in Paris, was intrigued by the notion of applying scientific method to mental events. He was then struck with the fact that no one had yet applied such methods to the "higher mental processes" and resolved at once to remedy that neglect. For the higher mental process to study he chose memory.

Ebbinghaus's conception of memory was taken directly from the British associationists. Memory, it was held, consists of associations between ideas or events. These associations are, of course, the product of experiences that are contiguous in time. To study *learning*, he only needed to give a subject a series of experiences. If he counted how many times the subject had to be exposed to the series before he could recall it completely, he would have a measure of learning difficulty. This procedure amounts to measuring learning by the amount of rehearsal it takes to reach a given criterion or level of performance. The measurement of *memory*, however, was a more thorny problem. If you learn something (say, a poem) to a given criterion level (say, one correct recitation) but the next day can recall none of it or only bits and pieces, how can an experimenter get a measure of memory? Ebbinghaus's happy insight was that he could require the subject to relearn the material on the next day and see how many rehearsals it took him to reach the same criterion he reached the day before. That is, he would measure memory by calculating how much savings there had been in re-learning.

Ebbinghaus's next problem was to find suitable material. Prose, poetry, Latin, and various other subject matters seemed too unequal in basic difficulty to use in a study that required careful measures. Ebbinghaus, therefore, developed his own materials, *nonsense syllables*. These materials, consisting of consonant-vowel-consonant combinations, could be made up readily (Ebbinghaus constructed more than 2200 of them) and had the virtue that most of them did not mean anything (for example, BIK, WUC, GAX, LUP).

Ebbinghaus solved the problem of obtaining subjects by using himself. He started an experimental program that lasted for several years, actually scheduling his life around the experiments and systematically testing himself in one set of conditions after another. Proceeding in this fashion he identified the basic issues of learning and memory for verbal materials and set forth the major functional relations bearing on such learning. His results were published in 1885 in the book *Ueber das Gedächtnis (On Memory)*.

TECHNIQUES FOR STUDYING VERBAL LEARNING

Ebbinghaus's kind of list-learning is now called *serial learning*. His technique was simple. He studied each list carefully, reading each syllable in turn to the ticking of a metronome. When he felt that he had the list in mind so that he could recite it once, he stopped that list and went on to his next task.

This technique has two disadvantages. First, it requires an experienced subject (which Ebbinghaus certainly was) who must judge when he has the list well enough in mind, and second, it furnishes little information about the details of learning. The procedure has been modified by contemporary psychologists to *serial anticipation learning.* Now material is exposed to a subject one item at a time on a fixed time schedule (usually two seconds per item). The subject reads each item and tries to anticipate the next. The list is scored correct when the subject successfully anticipates everything in it. This procedure does not require an experienced subject, gives information about the learning independent of the subject's judgment, and provides detailed information about the learning of every single item in the list. The latter information is not available at all under Ebbinghaus's method.

The most popular method for studying verbal learning today is *paired-associate anticipation learning.* Here, the subject is presented with pairs of words or other items to learn instead of lists. One member of the pair (the stimulus) is first presented alone. This is followed at some fixed interval (usually two seconds) by the other member of the pair (the response). The subject is told to try to learn to anticipate the response before it appears. Any number of pairs may be used (ordinarily six to twelve). Between trials, the order of the pairs is commonly changed, but not the words paired together. The subject is considered to have completed learning when he gives the correct response to each stimulus item as it appears before the response term is exposed.

CLASSIC FINDINGS

Ebbinghaus opened a whole new field and, despite the limitations of his method, he anticipated many of the fundamental findings. Some of his classic work is sketched below.

The Relation between the Amount of Material and Learning Time. Everyone knows that a *lot* of material is harder to learn than a *little* bit of material. But how much harder? The reason for the question is easy to see. If someone asks you to remember a digit or two for a few minutes, you find it easy. If he asks for three or four digits, that is easy too. And so it goes until your questioner asks you to remember seven or more digits. At just about this point the task gets hard. With eight to ten digits, you may need several repetitions. With 20 digits you have a long learning task in front of you. Clearly, at some point the time per digit goes up very fast. With one to seven digits, you need to hear the digits only once; then, if you are not disturbed, you can hold them in *immediate memory.* But when the material exceeds seven digits in length, your time per item increases sharply because you need to hear or see the list of numbers several times (see Miller, 1956).

Ebbinghaus learned many, many lists of different length and recorded the numbers of trials which were required to achieve one correct recitation. His findings are given in Table 11.1. Obviously, the number of trials increases very rapidly as the list is lengthened and the time required to learn increases correspondingly. For the shortest list the time per syllable is less than half a second and for the longest list it is over 20 seconds, a truly dramatic increase in the cost of adding items to the material to be learned. Subsequent work by many other investigators has confirmed these findings for many kinds of materials, including real words and digits (see Thurstone, 1930; and Carroll and Burke, 1965).

Relation between Passage of Time and Forgetting. All of us know that there is some kind of loss of memory, or forgetting, over time. A fact you knew "perfectly well" last week absolutely escapes you on the examination today, but the material you "crammed" last night may (with luck) be with you this morning. What is the relation between time and forgetting?

As we said, Ebbinghaus measured forgetting by the savings method. After learning a list of nonsense syllables, at some fixed interval later (ranging from a few minutes to a month) he would relearn it. If relearning the list took the same number of trials as were needed for the original learning, then there had obviously been no memory of it. If, on the other hand, he could recall the list with no rehearsal, then there had been complete memory. He set as his measure of savings the percentage of original trials that were saved when he tried to relearn the list. Thus, if a list took 20 trials originally and only five trials to relearn, the saving was 15 trials, or 15/20, or 75 per cent.

The Ebbinghaus curve of retention, given in Figure 11.1 was startling.

Table 11.1 Increase in learning time as list length increases. (Data from Ebbinghaus, 1885.)

Length of List in Syllables	Number of Readings to Learn	Average Time per List	Average Time per Syllable
7	1	3 sec.	.4 sec.
10	13	52	5.2
12	17	82	6.8
16	30	196	12.0
24	44	422	17.6
36	55	792	22.0

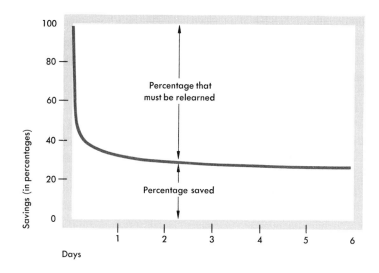

Figure 11.1 Ebbinghaus's general curve of forgetting. This shows the savings by percentages in terms of trials needed to relearn a list of nonsense syllables. (Data are from Ebbinghaus's studies of his own learning.)

Twenty minutes after he had learned a list he had a saving of only 58 per cent. After an hour the loss exceeded the saving, which had now fallen to 44 per cent. By the next day (24 hours) the saving had fallen to 34 per cent, which meant that he had to do 66 per cent of the original number of trials to relearn the list. In six days the savings measure was down to 25 per cent. In short, it appeared that learning had no sooner concluded than massive forgetting began. Forgetting was very rapid at first and then proceeded more and more slowly. In general, the retention decreased as a function of the logarithm of the time elapsed since learning.

Other workers have amply confirmed Ebbinghaus's research. E.K. Strong (1913) showed that the same kind of curve even fit the data on *recognition* of ordinary words. He presented lists of 20 common words. At specific intervals (from a few seconds to seven days) he presented the 20 words in the context of 20 other common words and asked subjects to identify which ones had been on the original list. In spite of the great differences in subjects, materials, procedures, and test techniques, the data fit a logarithmic curve very nicely, adding strength and generality to Ebbinghaus's conclusions.

Overcoming Forgetting. In the face of the formidable evidence of forgetting, it is a wonder that anything can be remembered at all. Ebbinghaus turned his attention to devices that would overcome the forgetting so dramatically evident in his work. The first focus of attack was on *degree of learning*. It is reasonable to suppose that one explanation of rapid forgetting is that the material was just barely learned. A cure for that problem would seem to be to overlearn the material, that is, to practice it well beyond the point of correct recitation, to really "get it by heart."

To study the effect of degree of learning on retention, Ebbinghaus took lists of 16 syllables and read them varying numbers of times (from eight to

64 readings). On the next day he learned the lists to **criterion** and measured the savings as compared to learning a brand-new list. The savings he found were, of course, attributed to the readings on the previous day. The results, shown in Figure 11.2, indicate a consistent and highly regular effect of the number of first-day trials. Each reading on one day brings about a saving of 1 per cent on the following day. This suggests that if Ebbinghaus read a 16-syllable list 100 times on one day, he would know it perfectly the following day; that is, he would have 100 per cent savings. Unfortunately, Ebbinghaus reported that it was impossible to read through 16 nonsense syllables 100 times without serious lapses of attention that invalidated the trials. It is clear, however, that repetition (with attention) leads to superior retention of the material later. Ebbinghaus's work has been confirmed by later work of many investigators (Luh, 1922; Krueger, 1929).

The second method of overcoming forgetting is *repeated learning*. For both nonsense syllables and for poetry, Ebbinghaus demonstrated that repeated learning had a marked effect on later relearning. Figure 11.3 shows the number of relearning trials needed each day for one of the nonsense syllable lists and for a stanza of *Don Juan*. It is readily apparent that relearning leaves material in better condition with respect to permanent memory than did the learning of the day before. It is important to understand that Ebbinghaus was not learning the material to higher criteria. He was learning it just to the point of one perfect recitation each day, exactly as he had on the first day. His 24-hour memory, however, improved markedly as the days went on. In Ebbinghaus's view the true associative connections were becoming stronger and stronger with repeated use, even though his

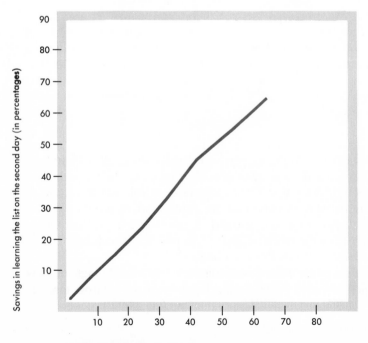

Figure 11.2 Savings on learning a list that had various numbers of readings on the preceding day. (Data are from Ebbinghaus's learning of lists of 16 nonsense syllables.)

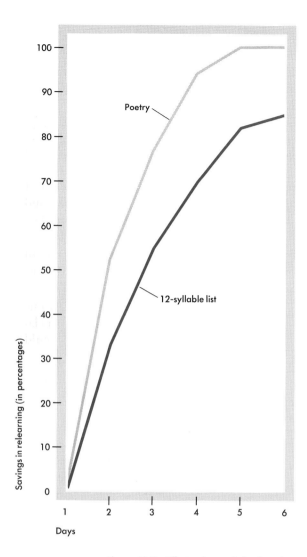

Days

Figure 11.3 Effects of repeated relearning on 24-hour recall. Each day Ebbinghaus tested himself on the same material by relearning it to one correct recitation. Each succeeding day he found that he learned the material in fewer trials. Forgetting over the 24-hour period can be radically reduced by a few days of relearning.

performance was only brought to the same point of proficiency on each occasion.

At this point you might ask whether the improvement found with relearning was the same as that found with overlearning (which was just due to more practice trials) or whether the distribution over time had something to do with the change associated with relearning. The answer is that *both* practice and distribution have an effect and that they are particularly effective in combination. Ebbinghaus studied this problem by trying to find out how many trials of distributed practice had the same effect as continuous overlearning trials. He discovered that 68 readings of a 12-syllable list made it possible for him to learn it the next day in seven trials. He then found that he could get the same effect with only 38 readings of the list *if* the 38 readings were distributed over a three-day period and the critical learning was conducted on the fourth day. Thus, both frequency of trials *and* distribution of practice were important aids to learning and effective weapons against forgetting.

A recent study by Geoffrey Keppel (1964), under very different conditions from those used by Ebbinghaus, confirms the importance of distributed practice. Keppel had his subjects learn four paired-associate lists in a row. All lists used the same stimuli but different responses, a situation that produces massive forgetting. Keppel's interest centered on the last list. One group learned it on the same day they learned the other three lists. The experimental group got three lists in one day but were given the last list over a period of days, receiving only two trials a day for four days. Recall for the last list was tested immediately after learning, after one day, and after four days. Figure 11.4 shows the great difference in recall over the retention period as a result of the distribution of practice. Such practice is obviously quite successful in overcoming forgetting.

The Nature of Memory. The results of Ebbinghaus's experiments increased his confidence in his original conceptions of memory. The learning of a list lays down traces or associations that become stronger and stronger with practice and with each relearning. *Performance* at any one instant is a function of the permanent traces plus some momentary factors. The momentary factors, of course, are dispelled with time and thus account for most of forgetting. With relearning, the permanent traces account for more and more of the performance, and, thus, there is less forgetting from day to day. The same argument, of course, applies to distributed practice.

In what is perhaps the clearest instance of theoretical work in his study of memory, Ebbinghaus chose to direct his further attention to the associations between the items in the list. He decided to test the associative doctrine by seeing how much learning transferred to related lists. He would learn one list and then 24 hours later learn a rearranged version of it. Simple associative theory predicted that the items which had been closest together would be most associated, those next closest would be the next most associated, and so on. Thus, if the initial list consisted of items 1, 2, 3, 4, 5, 6, 7, and 8, strong associations were presumed to exist between the adjacent numbered items, less strong associations between the items separated by one number (such as 1 and 3, 2 and 4), weaker associations between items further separated (such as 1 and 4, 2 and 5); distantly separated items were presumed to be relatively unconnected. In practice this meant that Ebbinghaus would learn a list and then learn a derived list made up of the same items in a new order such as 1, 3, 5, 7, 2, 4, 6, 8 (which was supposed to be closely related) or 1, 4, 7, 2, 5, 8, 3, 6 (which was supposed to be less related), or even random arrangements of the original list.

Results of the experiments are given in Table 11.2. For the most part they confirm the associative expectation. Forward associations do facilitate the

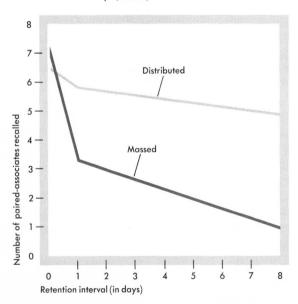

Figure 11.4 The importance of distributed practice in preventing interference from previous lists. Each group learned the list recalled here after learning three other lists. The massed group learned the fourth list on the same day as the first three lists; the distributed group learned the fourth list by means of a few trials per day. Interference from previous lists is greatly minimized under distributed practice. (Keppel, 1964.)

Relation of Second List to First	Percentage of Savings
Identical to original list	33
Derived by skipping one syllable	11
Derived by skipping two syllables	7
Derived by skipping three syllables	6
Derived by skipping seven syllables	3
Original list reversed	12
Reversed and one syllable skipped	5
Random	Less than 1

Table 11.2 Learning derived lists with various degrees of resemblance to an original list learned the day before. Sixteen-syllable lists were used. (Ebbinghaus, 1885.)

learning of a second list; the more remote the associations, the less they affect the second-list learning. There is a surprise, however; there is an appreciable saving in learning a reversed list (12 per cent), which runs counter to the associative doctrine. The explanation may be that Ebbinghaus had the whole list before him and could look back and forth, even though he tried not to. One *could* save the doctrine of sequential associates with just a little such leeway.

This part of Ebbinghaus's work has fared most poorly in the hands of later experimenters. G.E. Müller and A. Pilzecker (1900) showed, for instance, that some subjects learn lists by grouping the syllables in rhythmical patterns (dit-DAH, dit-DAH,----) and that if they tested for what was associated with a particular word from a list, they sometimes got in response another member of the rhythmical group (either forward or backward) rather than just the next member of the list. Recently there has been a considerable controversy about "what is learned" in a serial list. If it were just a chain of associations, a person could presumably transfer from the serial task to paired associates without any loss as long as he took the pairs from the serial list in order. But many investigators have found the situation to be more complicated. There is a good deal of evidence that many kinds of cues such as position in the list, rhythms, rhymes, and meaningful combinations all play a part in the learning of any particular list (Young, 1968).

Other Traditional Findings. Studies of memorization occupied much of the effort of early educational psychologists. Some of the findings are not particularly surprising from a theoretical point of view, but they supplement the Ebbinghaus tradition in useful ways. One of the most dramatic studies is readily predictable, but its lesson is sometimes forgotten. This is the work on *active versus passive learning*. Ebbinghaus kept his attention at a high level and controlled his behavior as a subject quite closely. His reading of a list was undoubtedly radically different from that of a person who casually drifts through a list while his mind wanders. In school we often find students who read material over and over but who seem to learn very little. A.I. Gates (1917) attacked this problem by asking how much time a person should spend reading and rereading material and how much he should spend in recitation (trying to recite the material to himself). The variable being investigated seems to be the difference between "passively" exposing oneself to the material to be learned and "actively" trying to produce the material. Eighth-grade students were asked to study both prose and non-sense syllables and to spend various portions of their time in recitation, ranging from no recitation time (all reading) to 80 per cent recitation time with only 20 per cent reading. Results for nonsense syllables (which were most dramatic) are given in Table 11.3. Obviously, recitation time is appreciably more valuable than reading time in securing learning and in ensuring retention. A reasonable interpretation is that recitation demands more attention and enlists more associative processes than reading. It is also probable that recitation locates the points at which the student is having difficulty and needs practice while the student who is reading does not have any clear indication of where he should be spending his time.

Research by H.F. Spitzer (1939) suggests that recitation, even without an opportunity to find out if one is correct, has a powerful effect on forgetting. His subjects (again eighth-grade students) read a 600-word article and then were tested at various intervals following the reading. The testing itself acted to retard the forgetting of the material as shown in Figure 11.5. We can suppose that the questions on the test focused the material and made relevant features salient while they were still available in memory and that

Table 11.3 Recall of nonsense syllables as a function of time division between reading and recitation. (Gates, 1917.)

Time Allocation	Percentage of Nonsense Syllables Remembered	
	Immediately	After 4 hours
All reading	35	15
⅘ reading; ⅕ recitation	50	26
⅗ reading; ⅖ recitation	54	28
⅖ reading; ⅗ recitation	57	37
⅕ reading; ⅘ recitation	74	48

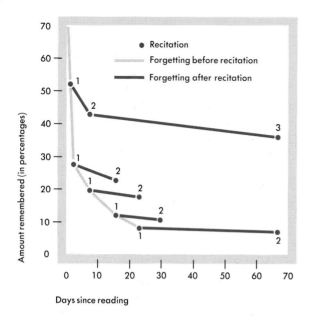

Days since reading

Figure 11.5 Retention of text material by eighth-grade students. Five different groups of students were tested at different time intervals after reading the same material. The testing itself acts to retard further forgetting. The group tested early does well on later retests but the group tested late recalls almost nothing. (Spitzer, 1939.)

this rehearsal and organization of the material played an important role in retarding the forgetting that otherwise was proceeding quite rapidly.

Another classic problem has to do with *whole-versus-part learning.* Everyone who has ever memorized a poem, a speech, or a story has some experience with this question. Is it better to start with small units, learn each one and then combine them, or is it better to try to learn the whole thing, even though progress at the beginning may be deadly slow? Most adults try some combination of these approaches, learning first one part then another and practicing the two together before going on to learn another part.

Research has been very active in this area (see R.S. Woodworth and H. Schlosberg, 1954, for examples in various kinds of tasks), but there is no reason to think that there is a single answer to this question. For one kind of material, whole learning may be helpful, because it provides efficient distributed practice for the parts. In another case, whole learning may be superior because it makes the parts "more meaningful," thus greatly assisting learning. In still another case, whole learning may be superior because the parts are not separable in a realistic sense from the total act. (Imagine, for example, trying to learn to walk a tightrope by practicing first walking a straight line, then practicing carrying a balance pole around, and so on, rather than practicing the act itself.)

On the other hand, parts may provide reasonable subgoals for the learner, and such subgoals have important effects on his continuing motivation and feelings of success. Learning parts may facilitate learning the whole when the material has natural and obvious subdivisions that are relatively independent. Or learning parts may permit concentration of effort at particularly difficult places without wasting the subject's time in rehearsing material that he has already conquered. Thus, although whole-versus-part learning was once a popular subject of inquiry, research on the topic has declined because it appears that there is no general answer. There are only particular answers depending on the material and on the subject's background, knowledge, motivation, and the like.

Memory Aids. Mnemonics have been popular since the time of the Greek orators and probably have existed since man developed language. Structural features like balanced constructions, rhythm, and rhyme undoubtedly assist a learner in acquiring material and aid him in retaining it. It is probable that early prayer, magic, and history were often coded into song, verse, and ritual to assure their retention in "proper" and "acceptable" form. Although such needs have diminished with the invention of writing, most of us find such structures helpful or effective even without our intention to learn, as when we find that we have learned a popular song or even a singing commercial to which we have been exposed.

Many aids to memory involve similes and metaphors that are easily recalled. An old rule for speakers that one of the authors once learned remains with him because of this kind of device. "A good speech is like your hand. The introduction is like your thumb, short and meaty, like the parts to come but not identical with them. The body of the speech should have three main points. Like your first three fingers, each one should be well-developed and clearly different from the others. The summary should be like your little finger, short and to the point."

Finally, many mnemonics rely on a small amount of specific learning that provides cues for the more extensive material that is to be remembered. For keeping the order of colors in the spectrum straight, the name ROY G. BIV is supposed to be helpful. You first recall the name and then attach the appropriate colors to the letters (red, orange, yellow . . .). Such memory systems must themselves be well learned if they are to be effective, otherwise both the mnemonic and the material to be remembered will be lost. The best devices take this into account and themselves have internal structures that make use of auxiliary devices. A favorite trick for keeping a list in order is to learn the series:

One is a bun.	Six is bricks.
Two is a shoe.	Seven is heaven.
Three is a tree.	Eight is a gate.
Four is a door.	Nine is a swine.
Five is a hive.	Ten is a hen.

The mnemonic is easy to learn because the counting series (which keeps the pairs in order) is familiar and because each object rhymes with the number. Then when a person wishes to "learn" a list of items (such as a shopping list) he merely imagines each item in some bizzarre relation to the appropriate object in the rhyming list. Thus, if his first item is cigarettes, he may imagine a bun stuffed with cigarettes, or cigarettes poked clear through a bun, or a person trying to smoke a cigarette through a bun. If his second item is oranges, he may imagine them rolling out of his shoe or his shoe squashing an orange. After he has gone through a list in this fashion it is easy to recover any item by reciting the correct cue. What was the first item on the list? "One is a bun. Bun goes with cigarettes."

The function of such visualization in memory "systems" is not completely understood but it is known to be helpful. Further, the more active and unusual the visualization is, the better it works. If you want to remember that *dog* and *gate* go together, picture a dog and a gate; even better, picture a dog going through a gate; best of all, picture a dog swinging wildly back and forth on a gate. Apparently such activities work because they increase resistance to interference; interference, as we shall see, is a major factor in the forgetting of word lists and word pairs (see Rohwer, Lynch, Suzuki, and Levin, 1967).

Modern Thought on Verbal Learning

As we have seen above, the functional relations explored by Ebbinghaus have fared rather well in modern experimentation. The theoretical notions have changed somewhat, however, and current work is much more concerned with a fine-grained analysis of the learning and retention processes than with the gross functions of learning and forgetting.

INTERFERENCE THEORY

A prime example of modern research is the study of the *causes of forgetting*. If material is once learned, why should it be forgotten at all? Early theory was quite compatible with the notion that memory traces simply decay with the passage of time. As more data were collected, however, it became clear that forgetting is more complicated than that, so alternative theories were developed. One strong competitor to decay theory is *interference theory*. According to this view, other activities and experiences interfere with the retention of material that has been learned. This is an active theory of forgetting whereas the decay theory, which is usually taken to be a function of time alone, is passive.

The most dramatic support for the interference theory came from studies of forgetting during periods of sleep and waking. J.G. Jenkins and K.M. Dallenbach (1924) had two subjects learn nonsense syllables in the morning and just before bed. They tested recall after various lengths of time spent either in sleep or normal waking activities. When the subjects were awake, they forgot most of the syllables very rapidly, being able to recall only 9 per cent after a lapse of eight hours. When they were asleep, however, the loss was greatly reduced. The evidence given in Figure 11.6 suggests that after the subjects were asleep, there was no further loss, as measured by a recall test on waking. An experiment by E.B. van Ormer (1932) using the savings method confirmed the difference in effect between sleep and waking, even though he had his subjects learn three lists at each sitting, a procedure which appears to have greatly increased the interference in both conditions.

Forgetting theory, then, came to the position that the activity after learn-

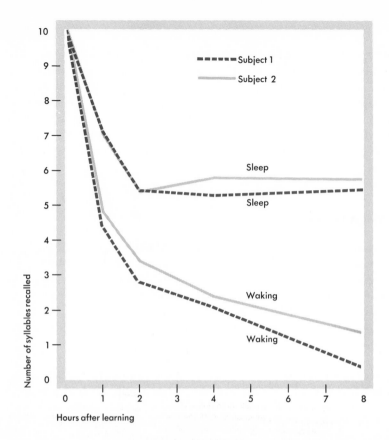

Figure 11.6 Forgetting and retroactive inhibition. The relative effects of sleep and waking activity on recall of nonsense syllables. (Jenkins and Dallenbach, 1924.)

ing is especially important. Some theorists hold that the original learning "consolidates" during this period and that activity interferes with consolidation. Others hold that new activity interferes with the old by introducing competing responses or by causing unlearning. Regardless of the alternative chosen, it became apparent that forgetting is a function not merely of the passage of time but also of what the subject does during that time.

Retroactive Interference. A simple and direct hypothesis about the nature of interference is that new responses get attached to the stimuli of the original learning task. The hypothesis is easy to test with paired-associates learning. First, the experimenter has a subject learn a list made up of pairs of nonsense syllables. This is called an *A-B list,* A standing for the syllables used as stimuli, B for the syllables used as responses. Then, the subject is required to learn a second list, an *A-C list,* with the same syllables for stimuli but *different* nonsense syllables for responses. If the subject is now asked to relearn or recall the original list, he is likely to have trouble. As each A term is given, he ought to have a strong tendency to respond with the appropriate C which he has just learned. He must restrain that response, however, and try to find the appropriate B.

In the general case the outcome is as expected. The subject cannot recall

B in the time required, and if he relearns the *A-B* list, it takes him more trials than subjects who did not have to learn an *A-C* list. The loss of the original list as a result of learning a second list is called *retroactive interference*.

How does this happen? Are the responses competing with each other, like two people trying to get through a door at the same time, with the stronger one (the more recent *C* term) winning? Or has something happened to the *B* terms during the *A-C* learning so that they are no longer available? A certain amount of the interference seems to result from competition. Many subjects actually give responses from the second list when they are trying to relearn the first list even though they "know" that it is wrong. But there doesn't seem to be enough loss from this source to account for all the difficulty in relearning the first list.

J.M. Barnes and B.J. Underwood (1959) followed an "unlearning" hypothesis. They supposed that the first-list response was not just a poor competitor but that it had been actively *unlearned* (or inhibited or suppressed) during the learning of the second list. They presented some persuasive evidence (Figure 11.7) showing that responses from the first list become increasingly unavailable as the responses to the second list are learned. They stopped their subjects at successive stages of second-list learning and had them try to recall responses from both lists. It is clear from the results that something was happening to the first-list responses as the learning of the second list went on.

A fair summary of the present state of knowledge concerning retroactive interference is this: Some forgetting is attributable to disruption from general activity (not specifically related to the learned material); some forgetting is attributable to competing or actively interfering responses that get in the way of correct responses at the time of recitation or relearning; and finally, some forgetting is due to unlearning of the original material that takes place during intervening learning of other materials.

Proactive Interference. Once the idea has been suggested, retroactive interference seems to be a reasonable and commonplace notion. It still has to be worked out in detail, but it is easy to understand and easy to imagine

Figure 11.7 The decreasing availability of the first-line responses as second-list learning proceeds. Subjects were asked to try to recall responses from both lists at various points in second-list learning. As List 2 was being increasingly better learned, List 1 was being unlearned. (Barnes and Underwood, 1959.)

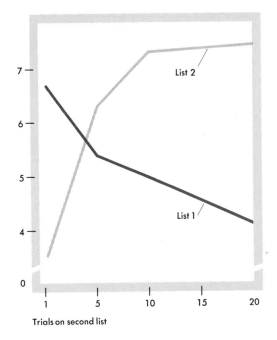

Mean number of correct responses

List 2

List 1

Trials on second list

possible mechanisms for it. Much less apparent, but perhaps even more powerful, is its logical counterpart, *proactive interference,* the effect of previous learning on the retention of material more recently learned. A little reflection, however, will convince you of the plausibility of this kind of interference. If you were to learn a new arrangement of the letters of the alphabet today, you would expect your old habits to make the new learning difficult. If you further assume that the old order is not obliterated by the new learning (which it surely would not be), you would expect it to interfere with your ability to recall the new order tomorrow.

In a very thorough paper, B.J. Underwood (1957) directed attention to the magnitude of proactive interference. He pointed out that all major studies of forgetting which showed great losses involved experienced subjects who had learned many lists of nonsense syllables. But Underwood observed that inexperienced subjects who learned only one nonsense-syllable list in their lives retained it extremely well over a long period. He studied the retention of materials as subjects learned more and more lists and found that it grew progressively worse. Even with common items like pairs of adjectives, retention for 48 hours fell off remarkably as a function of the number of adjective lists the subjects had learned earlier. Figure 11.8 shows how much more poorly subjects recall later lists than the first list.

Given these findings, it is a wonder that college students can remember anything at all. It is important to note that the research is on unorganized materials (lists and pairs) and that there is no particular reason for any list to be similar to or systematically related to any other list. Lists of the same kind tend to interfere with each other but not with lists of different materials (that is, nonsense syllables interfere with the future retention of other nonsense syllables, adjective lists with other adjective lists, and so on). This may imply that systematic learning is not only the best but perhaps the only way to master a great deal of material in any single area. At the very least, it does point to an important difference between rote learning and our commonplace observation that the more one knows in a field, the easier it is to learn still more (see also the topic of transfer of learning).

LEARNING AS A SET OF ACTIVITIES

Of course, older lists do not "act forward" on newer lists and newer lists do not "act backward" on previous lists. These terms are only our way of describing the effects on a subject's performance of sequences of activity. The more data we collect, the more we see the need for examining the activities of the learning, retaining, and remembering organism and the interactions that occur when new activities are required.

The old picture of learning and memory that was sufficient for Ebbinghaus's research no longer seems adequate. The early associative conceptions implied that the "things" to be remembered were somehow given in direct experience and that the business of learning was to provide connections

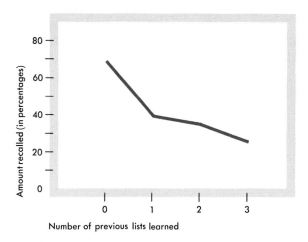

Amount recalled (in percentages)

Number of previous lists learned

Figure 11.8 Recall of lists of paired adjectives after 48 hours as a function of the number of such lists previously learned. (Underwood, 1957.)

between them. The connections were thought of as traces or bonds that were strengthened by repeated pairings of the objects in experience. Forgetting consisted of the fading of traces with time or because of interference from other traces or bonds. The picture is one of "things" tied together with silken threads that can build up through repetition to the density of ropes.

Learning is now seen as something more than a simple cumulation. The learner is an active participant who uses new and old techniques and the knowledge that he already has in order to produce a satisfactory performance. Since the active learner reconstructs and rearranges his resources and employs his skills in different ways from time to time, forgetting must be a consequence of what the organism now has to do and what it has done in the past, rather than some passive process.

As an example of differences in point of view, let us examine briefly the current conception of paired-associate learning. The classic position was that such learning consists of forming the connections or associations between the two fixed items, namely, the stimulus and its response. When that is done, the task is done. The forming of connections described the learning process and the set of connections was what had been learned.

Current views differ markedly from this account. In the first place, we have the problem of finding the units that are to be associated. If we study the subject's errors, it is clear that much of the time spent in learning paired-associate nonsense syllables is devoted to "response integration," that is, a subject must get the response knit together as a single unit before he can use it (for example, if he does not know that ZYR is all one response, he cannot give it successfully to the appropriate stimulus). Underwood and Schulz (1960) thought this activity important enough to advance a two-stage theory of paired-associate learning: Response integration and the formation of a pool of such responses formed its first stage; the second stage consisted of associating these responses to the appropriate stimuli. Much of the advantage of highly meaningful material in learning (for instance, words versus nonsense syllables) seems to occur during the first stage, for the more meaningful units are already integrated or can be integrated easily.

The unity of the "stimulus" term is a very different affair, however. Unlike the response, the stimulus need not be integrated; it only needs to be discriminated from the other stimuli involved in the task. If every stimulus is a long and complex series of letters but every one begins with a different letter, a subject only needs to attend to that fact. From that point on, he can respond on the basis of initial letters and forget the remainder of the stimulus. That subjects do exactly that has been shown by J.J. Jenkins (1964) and by L. Postman and R. Greenbloom (1967).

A loose description of the current view of what happens in paired-associate learning suggests a three-ring circus more than a straightforward automatic process. A subject begins attempting to integrate the responses he is supposed to use and attempts to form these into a "response pool" which is kept active and available. At the same time he begins studying the stimuli in an attempt to find some kind of cues that are sufficient to discriminate among them. He also hunts for aspects that will provide clues for the selection of a particular response from the pool he is forming. He may also search for interconnections between these terms and terms he already knows based on past learning of many sorts. Finally, we must suppose (if all else fails), he does some plain, ordinary rote learning.

This view, though it is scarcely neat and pretty, makes sense of many kinds of data. For example, it explains why paired associates are hard to learn when the stimuli are all similar to one another in form, sound, or meaning. It explains why responses that are unusual combinations of letters, or are unpronounceable or difficult to execute make learning very difficult. It explains why materials that might be difficult responses (like those just given) may be excellent stimuli if they have even one readily discriminable aspect. Surely, this is a more realistic model than the classic one.

WHAT IS LEARNED: TRANSFER STUDIES

Once an active picture of learning begins to emerge, it becomes possible to consider what a person is doing in a particular learning task and what he is really learning. It would seem like a simple solution to just ask the person, but, as we shall see, he often does not know and cannot tell us. One way to answer our questions is to conduct transfer studies. If a person has learned something about the activities of learning or if he has learned some specific material in a given fashion, it should be possible to demonstrate his knowledge by some appropriate transfer task.

At one extreme the studies can inquire into whether the subject has *learned to learn*. Chapter Ten reported dramatic learning-to-learn in discrimination problems for lower animals. For human beings more complex questions may be studied. Here an investigator asks if the subject has acquired a technique or skill rather than particular items of learning. The available evidence indicates that learning-to-learn is a very real and powerful form of learning. D.R. Meyer and R.C. Miles (1953) have given us an excellent example of the development of the skill of learning nonsense syllables. They had subjects study a different nonsense-syllable list every day for 20 days, giving them a fixed amount of time for study and for recall each day. As Figure 11.9 shows, there was an appreciable increase in the subjects' ability to learn nonsense syllables from the beginning to the end of training. This is an impressive instance of very general transfer.

At the other extreme, a transfer study can be conducted to reveal exactly what parts of stimuli and responses have been learned. If the stimulus in learning is fairly complicated, subjects might (knowingly or unknowingly) choose only one aspect of it to respond to. Suppose a learning task is set up so that the stimuli are colored cards with nonsense syllables on them and the responses are simply numbers. If each color is unique to a single nonsense syllable (that is, the red card always has XIJ on it), it is clear that there are at least two ways to learn the task. The subject can learn the color/number pairs or the nonsense-syllable/number pairs or both. We can find out which method the subject has used by giving him a transfer task involving just the colored cards without nonsense syllables or just the nonsense syllables on white cards. In this way we can split up the stimuli and determine how hard it is for the subject to supply the correct responses.

What happens in this kind of experiment shows the interaction of variables. When the nonsense syllables are easy to discriminate, the subject transfers readily to either nonsense syllables alone or colors alone. When the nonsense syllables are difficult to discriminate, the subject transfers very well to colors alone but shows almost no transfer to the syllables, even though he may have been reading them out loud on every trial (see Figure 11.10). This is a precise use of specific transfer to detect exactly what was learned (Underwood, Hamm, and Ekstrand, 1962; Jenkins and Bailey, 1964).

Transfer studies increase our conviction that people learn something more complex than unit-to-unit connections. Everyone is influenced by things he already knows and their relations to things that he must now learn. C.E.

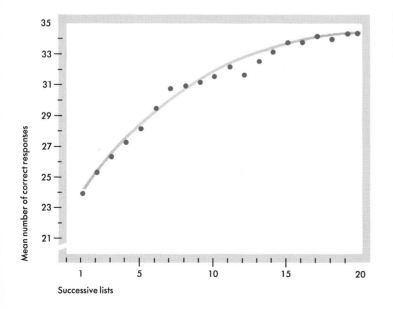

Figure 11.9 Learning-to-learn scores across 20 successive lists of nonsense syllables. (Meyer and Miles, 1953.)

Mean number of correct responses

Successive lists

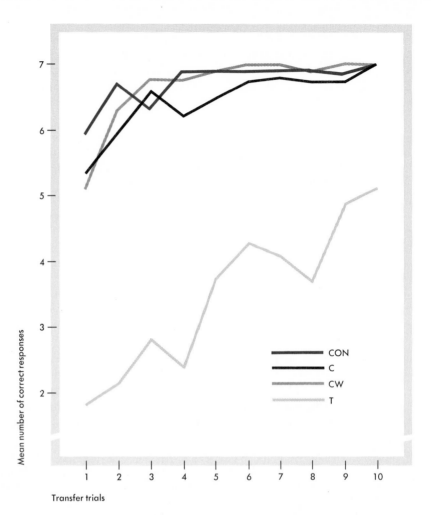

Figure 11.10 Transfer to colors and nonsense syllables after learning different nonsense syllables on colored backgrounds. The CON group is a control group that continued to get the original stimuli after a pause. The C group received only colored squares as stimuli and the CW group had names of the appropriate color as stimuli. These groups show almost complete positive transfer. The T group received only the nonsense syllables without colors and showed almost no transfer. (Bailey and Jenkins, 1964.)

Osgood (1949) proposed a set of generalizations based on the notion that all forms of similarity and dissimilarity relating old and new stimuli and old and new responses can be treated on the same dimensions. He argued that all available data could be summarized under three general rules:

1. When the responses of a second list are the same as those of the first, second-list learning will be speeded. (Positive transfer.) Memory of the

first list will be aided rather than interfered with. (Retroactive facilitation.) If the stimuli of the second list are made more and more similar to the first list, both of these effects will increase. This says: If you know A-B, C-B will be easy to learn and learning it will not have a bad effect on recalling A-B. Further, if A and C resemble one another, everything gets easier.

2. When the stimuli on the second list are the same as those of the first but the responses are different, second-list learning will be hampered. (Negative transfer.) Memory of the first list will be interfered with. (Retroactive interference.) If the responses on the second list are made more and more similar to the responses on the first list, both of these effects will decrease. This says: If you know A-B, A-C will be hard to learn and will hurt recall of A-B. But if B and C resemble one another, both these effects will be minimized.

3. When both stimuli and responses on the second list are different from the first list, learning of the second list will be somewhat hampered. (Negative transfer.) Memory for the first list will be interfered with. (Retroactive interference.) These effects are mild when the stimuli on the second list are unrelated to the first list but become increasingly disruptive as the stimuli on the second list become like those on the first list, for instance, as condition 3 approaches condition 2. This says: If you know A-B, C-D will be a little harder to learn and will slightly hurt A-B recall. But if A and C resemble one another, both these effects will be intensified.

There are many difficulties with a simple formulation such as this, but these rules capture a good part of the experimental information we have and a good deal of folk wisdom too. The first generalization implies that if you know how to do something, you can easily learn to do it in a new situation. Furthermore, doing it in a new situation will not make you forget it in the old situation. The second generalization says that it is hard to learn to do something new in a familiar situation. If you do learn such new behaviors, you will forget the old ones. The third generalization says that unrelated tasks interfere only mildly with each other, but they become more facilitating as the behaviors become more alike and more interfering as the situations become more alike.

As with all such sweeping generalizations, defects become apparent on closer examination. With these rules, the greatest weakness lies in special conditions that can easily be developed in the laboratory, though they may not be common in daily life. We may ask, for example, what happens to learning and interference when both the stimuli and the responses stay the same but the items are put into new pairings? This situation turns out to be enormously interfering, but it is not covered unambiguously by any of the Osgood rules. E. Martin (1965) considered three such special situations and showed that different rules for transfer and interference had to be developed for each of them. As an overall framework for discussion and experimentation, however, the Osgood generalizations are quite useful.

Even when subjects take the stimuli and responses that the experimenters give them and appear to learn connections between them, there is still some doubt that they are actually forming new associations. Subjects often report that they seek interconnections between the stimulus and the response through past experience and knowledge. The stimulus reminds them of a word that sounds like the response. Or the stimulus reminds them of a word that categorizes the response. Or the stimulus and the response can be put together in a meaningful sentence. Or the words are both related to a third word that can be used to bridge between them, and so on. Thus, in a study conducted by one of the authors, an "unrelated" pair of items, SUN-BAT, turned out to be extremely easy to learn. Some of the reasons given by subjects were: "SUN goes with SON and all kids play baseball, hence, to BAT." "When the SUN goes down the BATs come out of old houses." "I thought of taking a SUN-BATh." "I thought of a man watching his SON BAT." "The SUN shines in the daytime, the BATs fly at night."

J.A. Adams and W.E. Montague (1967) had subjects learn adjective pairs in an *A-B* list and then learn new pairs in an *A-C* list, and afterwards asked the subjects how they had learned each pair. Explanations offered involved the kinds of interconnections given above (called natural language mediators) for 67 per cent of the original items and for 87 per cent of the second-list items. In this case at least, by far the greatest part of this rote learning was not by rote at all.

A further interesting fact bears on the interference issue that we discussed above. The items on the original list that had been learned with natural language mediators were more resistant to interference than the items that had been learned without mediators, indicating that easy items suggest mediators or that the mediators themselves function as important aids to learning and memory.

Some investigators have attempted to study mediation experimentally by "building in" associative connections for the subjects to use in later learning. The first list may consist, for example, of *A-B* pairs. When these are well learned, a *B-C* list is given, and when it is learned, the subjects are tested on an *A-C* list. It is assumed that the subject can learn the third list through mediation by chaining (implicitly) the items from the first two lists. Thus, when a particular stimulus *A* appears on the test list, the subject thinks of the appropriate *B* response, which then acts as a stimulus and leads to the proper *C* response:

$$A \rightarrow (B \text{ as implicit response} \rightarrow B \text{ as implicit stimulus}) \rightarrow C \text{ response}$$

This is typically called "associative chaining" or mediated association.

It is easy to see that there are other arrangements to study different patterns of mediation. In order to investigate whether common responses to the same stimulus become associated, we can study the learning of A-B, A-C, and finally test on B-C. Similarly, to examine whether stimuli that have a common response become associated, we can use the pattern A-B followed by C-B and test with A-C. D.L. Horton and P.M. Kjeldergaard (1961) investigated eight different arrangements of such lists and found evidence for facilitation of final-list learning for all of them except the ones that involved purely "backward" chains. (In a backward chain the subject learns A-B and B-C and then is tested on C-A.)

Through studies of both natural and experimental mediation there is a growing awareness that current learning and future retention depend on the relation of the material being studied to the material that the subject already has learned. The more systematically related the material is, the more easily it is learned and the more it resists forgetting.

If we look at the whole sweep of research in verbal learning and forgetting, it is apparent that the emphasis is moving toward approaches which stress the role of activities of the learner. The simple notions of learning as a matter of connecting static items by associative links have given ground to notions that involve the subject as an active agent who is busy integrating responses, selecting stimuli, looking for possible relations, and exploiting old learning.

Learning Motor Skills

Motor-skill learning is not very much like either the learning studied by the animal theorists or the learning studied by those in the Ebbinghaus tradition. Research on skill learning has a quite different background, arising from the work of applied psychologists on the learning of useful specialized activities. Because the work has been specific and essentially problem-oriented, it has not given rise to much theoretical development. Rather, interest has focused on finding efficient ways of learning to type, to send and receive Morse code, to fly an airplane, to hit a target, or to operate a machine. Even without any specific theoretical concern, however, evidence has accumulated that motor-skill learning is like verbal learning in a few ways and unlike it in several others.

The typical task confronting the subject in skill learning is very different from that in verbal learning. As a result, the way we choose to score skill learning must necessarily be different. In verbal learning we ordinarily rehearse the subject in discrete trials. When the subject gets a perfect trial, the learning is considered complete. We wait a bit and have the subject try to recall what he learned, measuring memory by counting the number of items remembered correctly or counting the trials he takes to relearn. Obviously, we cannot easily adapt these procedures to a task like learning to

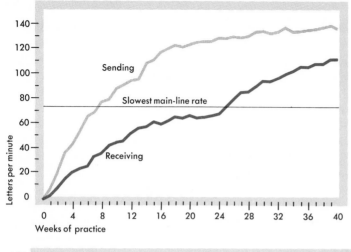

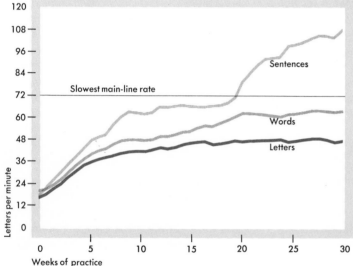

Figure 11.11 Performances of two students learning telegraphy. The top graph shows the performance of one student in sending and receiving ordinary messages. The bottom curves show the performance of the second student in receiving individual letters, words, and connected messages. (Bryan and Harter, 1897.)

ride a bicycle. What counts as a unit? When is learning complete? How shall we measure the obvious improvement that takes place after a person is able to get around without crashing to the ground, but before he accomplishes smooth, easy execution of the task? The traditional solution to this problem is to adapt our measures to permit us to describe how fast or how accurately a person can complete some performance, not just whether he can do it at all.

The classic study of skill learning is the research in telegraphy by W.L. Bryan and N. Harter (1897). These investigators studied the performance of young men apprenticed as telegraphers who were learning their jobs from the very beginning. The study is realistic and natural because the men had actually been employed on their jobs and did not know they were being studied. Records were obtained by studying their performance every week for periods up to nearly a year. Receiving of code was measured by sending faster and faster messages and determining the speed at which the subjects asked for repetition. Sending was measured by recording the number of letters that they sent per minute. Typical curves for the acquisition of this kind of skill are shown in Figure 11.11. The curves show large gains at the beginning followed by smaller and smaller gains until they level off at consistent, fast performance. Such curves of diminishing returns are called *negatively accelerated curves*.

In the earlier days of learning research there was a good deal of concern about finding *the* learning curve. This is an unrealistic demand to make, of course. There is no reason to believe that there is one curve that is typical of all learning. The curves we observe are a product of the kinds of measures we make, the skill we are studying, how good the subject is at the beginning, and a host of other variables. If we start to teach a college student to juggle four balls simultaneously and measure the number of minutes in each quarter hour that he has all four balls in the air, the learning curve will be *positively accelerated* (a hypothetical curve is given in Figure 11.12). The curve will stay at some very low value for a long time, then there will be little gains and, finally, very large gains as he eventually masters the task. By necessity, however, the curve will eventually level off as the student reaches the measurement limit. After all, there is no way he can score more than 15 on our task. Thus, the curve must change at some point from positively accelerated to negatively accelerated.

Notice that, although the learning curve is not moving up at the beginning and end of the example, this does not mean that learning is not taking place. It means that we are not measuring the changes that may be happening. This is the *learning–performance* problem that we have met before. We must always remember that it is performance that we measure and that learning is always inferred.

If we return to the example of the Bryan and Harter telegraphy study and look at the receiving rates for various kinds of materials, we see an important characteristic of much of skill learning. The performance measured in the complex task is an organization of skill into smooth sequences

Figure 11.12 Hypothetical curve of learning for juggling. The curve would be positively accelerated at the beginning (increasing gains) and then negatively accelerated as the subject reached the limit of scoring.

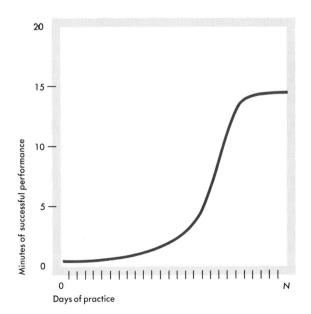

Minutes of successful performance

Days of practice

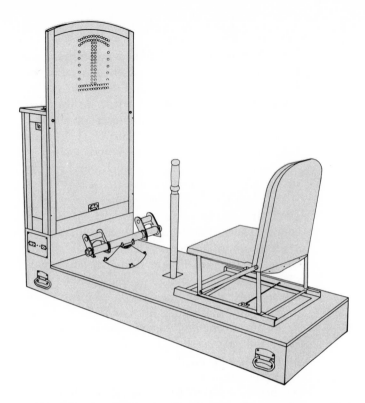

Figure 11.13 The Complex Coordinator shown above requires a subject to match the light patterns appearing on the display in front of him by moving the stick and pedal controls. As soon as the patterns are matched, another display is presented. The chart (p. 413) shows the abilities that contribute to performance at different stages of practice. The importance of each skill is shown by the area associated with it at each stage. Notice especially the increase of factors specific to this task. (From Fleishman, 1957, and Fleishman and Hempel, 1954.)

of larger and larger portions of behavior. From the very beginning the student knows *how* to do his task and he knows *what* to do. His problem is to get the details of his behavior so automatic that his attention can be directed to sequencing his behavior at the highest level possible. The three receiving curves shown in the lower figure illustrate this exactly. The rate of receiving individual letters does not increase appreciably past the middle of the training period but the rate of receiving words continues to increase. Then, about the time the rate for individual words levels off, the rate for connected discourse climbs dramatically. Thus, while the rate for the smallest elements shows no additional improvement, the over-all rate keeps increasing as the operator learns to make use of relations that hold for higher levels of organization (words and sentences). Telegraphy shows us a hierarchy of skill wherein each level exploits the levels below it and adds its own special characteristics to facilitate performance.

In modern motor-skills research a great deal of attention has been given

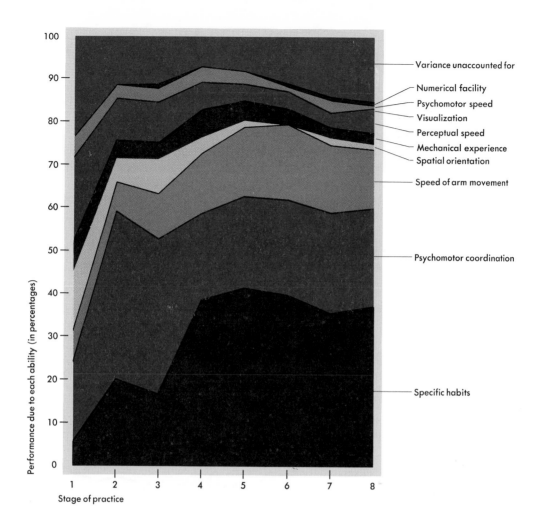

to more complex coordinations such as those involved in flying and driving. Studies of such skills have furnished evidence that the nature of the task itself changes as the learning proceeds. Edwin Fleischman has been a leader in the factor analysis of complex coordination tasks in the laboratory. In this procedure, each man is tested for his various skills prior to learning. Then by looking at the pattern of the correlations of the particular skill measures with the performance on the coordination task, the investigators infer which factors play an important role in the performance at each stage of learning. Figure 11.13 shows the outcome of one such study. It is apparent that different skills are employed at different stages. *Spatial relations* and *visualization* both play an appreciable role in the performance at the beginning of training, yet both drop out almost completely as practice increases. More and more of the variation is attributed to the specific skill being trained as if it were a unique synthesis of the subjects' original abilities.

Skill learning furnishes many striking examples of one of the features of learning we encountered under verbal learning, namely, the effect of distributed practice. Figure 11.14 shows the effect of massed practice as opposed to distributed practice on a pursuit-rotor test, in which the task is to keep a stylus on a moving dot. One group was given trials with rest periods interspersed and the other group was given one trial right after another. It is clear that distributed practice led to much higher performance. Inspection of the figure shows a group that got a rest period only once. The increase in the score on the next trial is remarkable. These results suggest that, for this task, massed practice is actively harmful to performance rather than that distributed practice is especially helpful. In this example it appears that the *learning* going on is about the same in all the groups but that massed practice has a bad effect on *performance* through fatigue, boredom, or interference. When rest is introduced, performance leaps up but then declines as massed trials are resumed.

A fascinating problem intimately involved with the study of motor skills

Figure 11.14 Effects of massed and distributed practice in pursuit-rotor learning. The task consists of keeping a stylus on a moving dot. One group had short rest periods between trials (distributed practice); the other two groups received one trial after another, but of these, the rest group was given a five-minute rest after the fifth trial and showed remarkable improvement in performance until fatigue set in again. (Adapted from Kimble and Garmezy, 1968; unpublished data by Marsha H. Graves.)

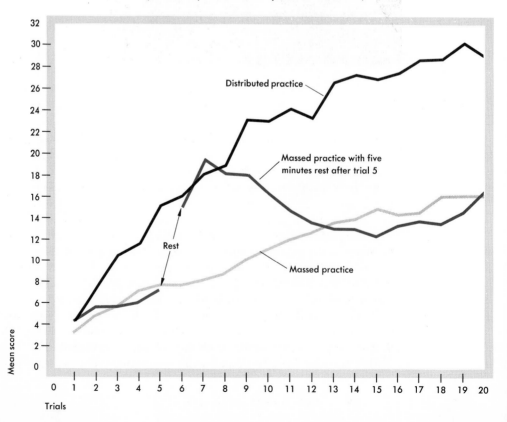

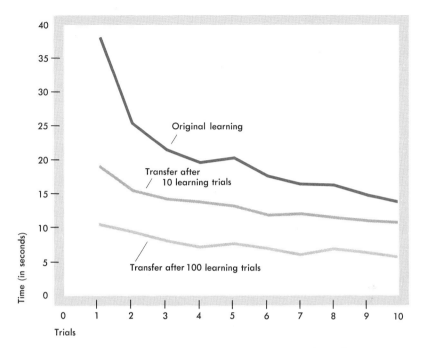

Figure 11.15 Transfer of training in mirror drawing. Subjects learn to trace a star seen in a mirror. After original learning they are tested on opposite hand or foot. (After Cook, 1933.)

is the specification of what is learned. We commonly avoid this problem by using gross descriptions like "learning to ride a bicycle," "learning to type," or "learning to drive a car." We should not be deceived that these phrases mean we understand what is learned or that we have an analysis of it when we have a learning curve. As before, we should ask questions about what is learned by attempting transfer tasks. When we do so, some of the findings are surprising.

One of the early transfer problems investigated by psychologists was the transfer of skill from one hand to the other. In general, when a person has learned to do a task with one hand, he shows marked facilitation in the performance of the task with the other. Figure 11.15 shows the result of learning to trace a star (viewed only in a mirror) with one hand and then with the other. It is clear that there is a great deal of transfer; it is not just a question of the right hand being trained in making certain responses.

More extensive studies find the greatest transfer from one side of the body to the other side with the same member (hand to hand, foot to foot), next most from hand to foot and vice versa on the same side, and, finally, least transfer for diagonally opposite members (right hand to left foot) (Cooke, 1934). Intensive studies on the hands show that best transfer from hand to hand occurs for movements in laterally opposite directions. If the right hand goes clockwise, transfer is greatest to a task where the left hand goes counter-clockwise (Milisen and Van Riper, 1939). It seems wise to conclude that much motor learning is of a very general sort and does not consist of specific muscle responses. Thus, a person can give evidence of his learning with various portions of his anatomy and with various kinds of movements. Most of the learning is *not* specific to given movements or particular musculatures, though we often find some complementary muscle groups and some aspects of task relationships (like bilateral symmetry) that are favored.

A final characteristic of motor learning must be mentioned. As you probably expect if you have been reflecting on your own history, most motor skills show little loss over time. Just as you do not forget how to ride a bicycle even if you have not ridden for a few years, people do not forget their complex motor coordinations over such a span. Pursuit-rotor, coordination, and tracking tasks have been examined over periods of time up to two years from original learning and have usually shown little loss in speed and accuracy (see, for example, Fleishman and Parker, 1962). This finding may be attributable to the great overlearning that such skills are usually given or it may be a characteristic of the very general nature of the learning.

Although this sample of research on the learning of motor skills is fragmentary, it does illustrate several important features of the area. First, it reminds us that the measurement of learning is always an indirect affair. In verbal learning and animal learning it is perhaps too easy for us to think of performance as a "natural" measure of learning, but in motor skills the problem of measurement is always fresh before us. Second, it shows in several ways that complex behaviors are complicated assemblies of other behaviors in combinations that may change with time and degree of expertness. Third, it stresses the difficult problem of "what is learned" when we find that a behavior does not consist of just particular movements by the same muscles but may readily transfer to different sets of muscles or wholly different parts of the body. Finally, specific findings of motor-skills research, like the excellence of bilateral transfer and the importance of bilateral symmetry of movement, compel us to recognize that important components of learning and performance are biologically determined.

Other Approaches to Memory

The excursion into motor skills has perhaps readied you for the other types of approaches to learning and memory. The strict associationist tradition has long suffered from its readiness to confer reality on the things remembered. The process of learning and memory often appears to consist of making a copy of some object, event, or experience and storing it "somewhere," whence it is automatically retrieved when a particular stimulus calls for it. Given our philosophical background, this notion of learning as a storage operation and remembering as a relocation of stored objects is difficult to avoid. It is, however, an unconvincing model at best.

Ulric Neisser (1967) in his book *Cognitive Psychology* calls this conception of memory the "Reappearance Hypothesis," since it supposes that old copies of things are made to reappear in the mind's eye. He points out that although many psychologists, including the famous William James, have fought against this idea as an impossible model of mental activity, it still persists. Clearly this kind of model of memory is of no use at all in explaining motor skills where we cannot even imagine what "items" would be stored or how their reappearance could explain the complex adaptation of old skills to ever new and changing current situations. The more one looks at the learning and remembering of complex activities, the more one rejects the reappearance hypothesis.

MEMORY AS RECONSTRUCTION

Imagine that you are hearing a story that you want to tell to a friend at a later date. You pay close attention and "try to remember" it. Some time later you encounter the friend and tell him the story. What is it that you have remembered? Is it common experience that we do not recall the particular words in which a story was originally told (which is why so many people "ruin" jokes that depend on particular phrases or exact wording). We may not even recollect who told the story or when. We remember, rather, the "sense" of the story, or its "outline," or its point. On the occasion of retelling, we "generate" an instance of the story or create it in a new, specific form. It is as if a set of directions for the story is remembered and then the story is built around that set. The process looks like *abstraction, coding, decoding,* and *elaboration* rather than simple storage. Because of these many steps, rather interesting effects can be shown in the matter of memory distortion. Two instances will illustrate such experiments.

Sir Frederic Bartlett (1932) conducted extensive investigations of creative reconstruction in the service of memory. His typical experiment was to present an odd stimulus (a strange story, say, or an unusual picture) to a subject and then ask him to reproduce it at some later date. As a shortened version of this experiment, he sometimes had one student tell a story to another, the second tell it to a third, and so on. Both of these procedures show the effect of constructive errors. When something is vague or unrelated to the main theme of the story (as the listener perceives it), the material gets dropped or changed. In one of Bartlett's stories (borrowed from an Indian legend), two young Indians go down to the river to hunt seals and then have some odd adventures. In the retelling of the story, the circumstance usually became a trip down to the river to fish, a much more likely and reasonable event for Bartlett's students.

A classic experiment by L. Carmichael, H.P. Hogan, and A.A. Walter

(1932) attempted to examine the coding aspect of memory by giving subjects memory "aids" that suggested particular codings which might produce systematic changes in the recall of the original materials. Figure 11.16 gives the set of visual materials that they presented to their subjects for recall, and it shows the different words or phrases that were provided to the subjects as the visual forms were presented, "The next figure resembles. . . ." As expected, students who got the biasing names for the stimuli tended to draw the figures at recall in ways that reflected the bias. Some marked examples are given in Figure 11.16. The outcome is compatible with the hypothesis that the visual material was recoded for storage in a fashion that depended on the label. This experimentation includes, of course, the possibility that perhaps the label itself was stored and the figure was generated from the label when needed.

Experiments like the two just given have been available for many years. Modern psychology has not been much moved, however, since no theory of learning and remembering has appeared along with them. Objections without countertheory remain only demonstrations that something is missing. They do not in themselves furnish a new view.

Reproduced figures	Word list I	Stimulus figures	Word list II	Reproduced figures
	Curtains in a window		Diamond in a rectangle	
	Bottle		Stirrup	
	Crescent moon		Letter "C"	
	Beehive		Hat	
	Eyeglasses		Dumbbells	
	Seven		Four	
	Ship's wheel		Sun	
	Hourglass		Table	
	Kidney bean		Canoe	
	Pine tree		Trowel	
	Gun		Broom	
	Two		Eight	

Figure 11.16 Extreme examples of distortion of figures given to subjects with the "memory aids" shown. Twenty-six per cent of the pictures drawn by subjects were major distortions and an average of 73 per cent of the distorted figures were in the expected direction. The different stimuli and cues varied greatly in their power to evoke changes. The seventh figure produced few changes under either cue; the eighth and tenth figures were very consistently changed. (Carmichael, Hogan, and Walter, 1932.)

Since the 1920s the Gestalt psychologists have hammered away at behaviorism and associationism in both the realm of perception and the realm of memory. A whole set of arguments is found in Wolfgang Köhler's *Gestalt Psychology* (1947). With reference to learning and memory, the Gestalt position is that the importance of organization has been totally neglected. When you learn a tune, for example, you are scarcely likely to have learned the key it was in and, therefore, as you recall it you may not use the original notes at all. What is learned is the set of relations, the organization, the pattern. "Association," says Köhler, "is the aftereffect of organization."

Gestalt psychologists have attacked many of the flaws of the associationist position, arguing that it is not reasonable to think of elements and their arbitrary connections as the essence of learning. They point out that items in a list are likely to behave as a new whole. Even though a person can recite an entire list, he may not be able to say what follows some designated item when asked for just that information. H. von Restorff, who explored many aspects of the organization of rote materials, showed that when an item in the middle of the list was made to stand out somehow (being printed in red ink or being a number in a list of letters), the organization of the list changed and the middle items became easy to learn instead of being the most difficult, as is usually the case. She also showed that such "odd items" in paired-associate lists are retained better than items of the common material (von Restorff, 1933).

The Gestalt psychologists pointed to the "belonging" principle of Thorndike as evidence for organizational factors. They made much of the fact that "intention to learn" is an important variable and that learning does not proceed by automatic associations when a person is merely exposed to material. They also made much of the Zeigarnik effect, which we discussed in Chapter Two, the tendency to remember uncompleted tasks as opposed to completed ones. Undoubtedly, some of the attention that psychologists in verbal learning have given to "activities" of their subjects has been in response to objections of the Gestalt psychologists to simple association theory.

The major difficulty with the Gestalt position is that it furnishes no strong countertheory for learning. Instead, the advocates of Gestalt have suggested that their dynamic model of perception could be extended to cover memory as well. Their emphasis, therefore, is on organization and progressive change of what is being remembered. They hypothesize that the "memory trace" is subject to the same kinds of unifying forces that act on perception. Thus, they predict that remembered items will steadily change toward "good form." If so, three processes will take place: *regularization* (the form should become more symmetrical and more regular), *sharpening* (irregular features that did not disappear should be accentuated), and *normalization* (the form should be identified with some familiar object).

In criticism, we can say that these principles do not yield unambiguous predictions. If a circle with an irregularity is remembered as a circle, that is compatible with regularization and normalization. If it is remembered as being more distorted, that is evidence for sharpening. Although there is good evidence that symmetry increases in the reproduction of remembered figures, the evidence is not convincing for the other process. Identification with a common object is often found (as in the Carmichael, Hogan, and Walter experiment above), and sometimes there is evidence for sharpening, but usually it is not possible to show that these phenomena increase over time the way they are supposed to. Often it is not possible to tell whether the distortion takes place in initial perception or in memory.

Another major problem of the Gestalt view is that we often do not know how to apply these rules to materials that are not spatial forms. True, we can talk metaphorically about auditory form and make intuitive judgments of regularization, sharpening, and normalization of rhythm, melody, and the like, but we are likely to have increasing difficulty when we talk about memory of successive lists of materials, stories, or motor tasks. Most disappointing is the failure of the Gestalt psychologists to give us a new model of memory. Their proposal is, in essence, still a copy theory, even though the copy is expected to be a "bad one" in systematic ways. The "memory trace" is still floating around in the subject's head even though it is supposed to be undergoing change.

MEMORY AS CONSTRUCTION

The Gestalt experiments do make us aware of the thin barrier between perception and memory and make us admit that we do not always know how to divide the two. If we have an active theory of perception, an active theory of learning, and an active theory of memory, it is not at all clear that perception, learning, and memory can be separated. Nevertheless, we may be able to make some advances.

If perception can be a construction and memory is a construction, it may be that memory does not store a set of objects or their copies but rather consists of activating the set of rules that were used in constructing the original perception. For a crude illustration of this notion, we can draw on the experiments of G. Katona (1940). In one experiment he asked subjects to memorize the following strings of numbers:

$$2 \quad 9 \quad 3 \quad 3 \quad 3 \quad 6 \quad 4 \quad 0 \quad 4 \quad 3 \quad 4 \quad 7$$
$$5 \quad 8 \quad 1 \quad 2 \quad 1 \quad 5 \quad 1 \quad 9 \quad 2 \quad 2 \quad 2 \quad 6$$

One group was given three minutes to "discover the principle involved" and the other group spent three minutes memorizing the numbers in rhythmic triplets. On an immediate test about a third of each group made perfect reproductions of all of the digits. After three weeks, however, about a quarter of the first group made perfect reproductions and *none* of the second group made perfect reproductions. What is the difference? Those students who discovered the principle were no longer looking at arbitrary strings of digits. They saw, instead, a series beginning in the lower left-hand corner with a single digit (5) and adding three and four alternately to produce the numbers. Old learning (addition) combined with new learning (the rules of this particular organization) to enable these students to produce the series on demand. Notice too that the series now is no longer a string of isolated digits, like 5,8,1,2,1,5,1,9, but, it is rather, 5, 8, 12, 15, 19, and so on. It is clear that the principle effectively reorganized the stimulus and the structure of what was to be generated on recall.

Most experiments of this sort are impressionistic demonstration experiments. We do not have clear notions about what kinds of generating rules and elements of construction will prove to be most useful. Perception and memory will probably turn out to be intimately interrelated, but since the study of perception is still the scene of rapid development, it is too early to know what the elements and rules of memory look like, even assuming that the constructive hypotheses are true.

CURRENT DEVELOPMENTS

A survey of new experimentation in the field of learning and memory leads us to believe that we can expect more and more analysis of processes but that the kinds of processes analyzed will be quite different from those examined in the old tradition. A new group of researchers has developed who claim as their major interest "information-processing." They are interested in all kinds of gathering, interpreting, storing, and retrieving of information. Their models are drawn currently from the work of the computer scientists and their theories are frequently tested through computer programs which they hope will simulate the behavior of human beings who are perceiving, learning, and remembering. Work of these investigators will be treated in Chapter Thirteen on cognition.

Another young movement of impressive development is that of the mathematical learning theorists. Beginning with the work of W.K. Estes in 1950, there has been a mushrooming development of precise mathematical theories for specific problems in learning. Despite common use of the terms, there is no general mathematical learning theory as such; there is, rather, a way to approach problems and try to formulate specific solutions in the clear uncompromising language of mathematics. Thus, such a theory must not just predict that a learning curve will rise; it must describe the curve with a mathematical function. The hope of the investigators is that through rigorous descriptive work they will be led to better and better psychological models, with specific mathematical expressions given to the important psychological variables. Such work will clearly increase in the future and should be helpful in bringing more clarity to the critical issues in human learning and memory (see E.R. Hilgard and G.H. Bower, 1966, for a simple introduction to the area).

Nativism and Empiricism

We began this chapter with the classic problem of knowing about the world and the perennial issue in philosophy and psychology of nativism versus empiricism. Can we now add anything to the discussion?

The fate of the study of human learning and memory seems to be a steady drift toward nativism from a point far out on the empiricist side. When learning entered the laboratory, investigators held the secure belief that all that had to be studied was the formation of associations and their decay over time. In the ensuing 90 years of research, association theory has encountered one limitation after another and many doubts have crept into the belief system of modern investigators. In the first place, there is the increased evidence that there are many species-specific behaviors and that these play an important role in many kinds of learning. Second, many kinds of learning show unaccounted "weak spots" where learning occurs easily or not at all without any reason thought of by the classical associationists. Third, learning tasks of almost any degree of complexity show organizational phenomena that are difficult to account for by orthodox theory. Fourth, learning is conceptualized in more complicated ways and is being analyzed into more and more activities. It shows, consequently, less of the automatic quality that was thought to characterize the formation of associations. Fifth, motor-skill learning seems quite unlike the sort of learning the associationists had in mind. It seems different from verbal learning in important ways in addition to showing a clear biologically determined preference for certain kinds of transfer. Sixth, constructive and reconstructive theories of learning seem to be gaining some support though they still lack an embracing theory. Overall, it appears that nativism is gaining ground after centuries of neglect, and it is to be hoped that some new models of learning and memory are on the horizon.

SUMMARY

Learning theory was largely developed through animal studies. Attempts to apply such theory to human beings have not been markedly successful. Human behavior often seems too complicated to yield to simple analysis, though plausible accounts of human learning can be constructed. One difficulty in such constructions is that most of the terms applied are used metaphorically rather than being strictly defined. A special problem arises in cases in which organizing principles seem to be involved. Thorndike tried to apply his Laws of Effect and Exercise to human beings and found that he needed modifications. He had to add new principles of *impressiveness, identifiability, availability,* and *polarity.* Most importantly, he had to invent a new kind of principle, *belonging*, which recognized that the materials being learned had a structure of some sort that influenced what was learned. A form of behavior that has been particularly hard to deal with is language, which not only shows phenomena like belonging, but also seems to have the capability of altering many other behaviors through directions and instruction.

B.F. Skinner holds that theories of learning are too incomplete to be useful. He believes that the functional findings concerning reinforcement and the control of behavior can be applied to the human case, however, when we know what behaviors we want to control.

A direct attack on human learning and forgetting is found in the verbal learning tradition which began with Ebbinghaus's careful work on memory. Ebbinghaus invented the *nonsense syllable* to provide a neutral material for his studies. He learned lists of these materials (*serial learning*) and his successors use an *anticipation* version of such learning as well as *paired-associates* learning. Ebbinghaus showed that the time to learn an item depends on the length of the list it is in, varying from about half a second for an item in a short list to 22 seconds for an item in a list of 36 syllables. He discovered that most forgetting occurs immediately after learning and that the losses are very great. He found that overlearning reduced the amount of forgetting in direct proportion to the amount of extra trials and that repeated learning (*distributed practice*) results in less forgetting than the same number of trials at one session (*massed practice*). Ebbinghaus thought of memory as a set of links between adjacent items in the lists. He showed that *related lists*, taking every other item in a list he just learned, were easier to learn than random orders of the same words.

Verbal-learning studies typically show that *active learning* is better than *passive learning*, that time spent in recitation leads to less forgetting than time spent in just reading the material. Similarly, testing on material seems to help the subject recall it later. *Part-versus-whole learning* seems to vary with the material and the person learning. Sometimes part is better than whole and sometimes the reverse. Memory aids (*mnemonics*) seem to be helpful in keeping things in the right order and reducing interference if the mnemonic itself is well learned.

Modern verbal-learning studies stress the role of *interference* in disturbing what has been learned rather than simple forgetting. Materials are better remembered if subjects sleep after learning rather than engaging in normal waking activities. Interference from new material learned after the original learning is called *retroactive interference*. New learning affects old material through *competition* and actual *unlearning* of the older material. Interference from something learned before the items of interest is called *proactive interference*. Here old learning interferes with the material more recently acquired. Underwood has shown that this kind of interference is very important and that the retention of laboratory learning is a function of how many lists the subject has learned before. Learning is now viewed as more complex than it was formerly. The subject is seen as actively working on the task, selecting aspects of the stimulus to respond to, integrating the response items, finding relations between stimuli and responses through concepts and items of knowledge he already knows.

Transfer studies are useful in helping to specify what is learned. Very general *learning to learn* seems to take place though it is not well understood. Many studies show that a specific learning task may involve other items than the apparent stimulus and response. Transfer studies also show that systematic relations between old and new learning have consistent effects on the memory of the old and the learning of the new. In general, when the responses stay the same from one task to another, the learning is facilitated. When the stimuli stay the same and the responses are different, the learning is hindered. When successive lists bear particular relations to each other, such as *A-B, B-C, A-C,* we find evidence for *mediated associations* in the last list. Presumably the subjects put together the first two lists in a constructive fashion to generate the responses needed on the last list: $A \rightarrow (B) \rightarrow C$.

The learning of *motor skills* presents different problems in measurement since we are usually not only interested in what the subject knows how to do but also how well he can do it. Studies of typewriting, telegraphy, coordination, and the like have been typical topics of study. Ordinarily, learning curves are *negatively accelerated*, showing large gains at the outset and smaller and smaller gains as the subjects become proficient. Evidence is often found for *hierarchies of skills* as proficiencies in executing small units are combined in larger and larger units, such as letters into words and words into sentences. As skill learning goes on, the nature of the performance may change and different skills may be involved to different extents at various stages of learning. In the motor-skills area the importance of distributed practice can be shown easily, and it is typically found that there is very little forgetting of skills. In this area, too, the distinction between *learning* and *performance* is obviously important.

Nonassociative approaches to memory stress the active nature of memory as opposed to the "reappearance hypothesis." They typically postulate some sort of *coding process* which is then *decoded* and *elaborated;* that is, the thing remembered is *constructed* rather than merely *recalled.* The Gestaltists tried to describe remembering as they do perception, with emphasis on organization and structure. The automatic nature of associative learning is challenged and stress is put on organization of the "memory trace," which is supposed to be subjected to *regularization, sharpening,* and *normalization.* Gestalt experiments show that organization and principle learnings are retained after specific rote learnings have been forgotten. No thorough theory of learning and forgetting has emerged, however. Interest in complex, constructive models of remembering has also recently become evident in the work of the information-processing theorists.

Association theory, which has been the groundwork for almost all theories of learning, has become more and more complex of late. Attempts are being made to deal with organizational factors and particular processes involved in learning. In addition, the conviction that all learning is automatic and associative has been progressively weakening. There is renewed interest in active theories, some of which suppose innate mechanisms.

SUPPLEMENTARY READINGS

Bartlett, F.C. *Remembering: a study in experimental and social psychology.* London: Cambridge Univ. 1932.

Johnson, D.M. *The psychology of thought and judgment.* New York: Harper & Row, 1955.

Jung, J. *Verbal learning.* New York: Holt, Rinehart & Winston, 1968.

Katona, G. *Organizing and memorizing.* New York: Columbia Univ. Press, 1940.

Neisser, U. *Cognitive psychology.* New York: Appleton-Century-Crofts, 1967.

PART FOUR

Language

C H A P T E R   T W E L V E   Now that we know something about human learning in its general senses, we turn our attention to one of man's greatest learned activities, language. This marvelous and subtle behavior is the most accessible of the higher mental processes and affords an important subject of study not only for its own sake but also for the understanding it may contribute to the less accessible aspects of experience and behavior that are hidden in words like thought, meaning, and problem-solving. Four different views of language will be considered here and the strengths and weaknesses of each model will be examined. In addition, we will ask how language is said to be acquired under each view and to what extent it accounts for individual differences in language behaviors. The models discussed here have their parallels in the models of learning we have just studied and are forerunners of the different models of thinking that we will examine later.

Over the entire period for which we have any record of man's thoughts and speculations, we have both hints and direct evidence that he has been interested in language. By analogy with primitive peoples who are studied today, prehistoric man is believed to have been superstitiously concerned with language for purposes of religion and magic and to have been impressed with the imagined power of names, prayers, and chants. The first known grammar is a highly sophisticated work on Sanskrit, written over 2000 years ago. And there is evidence that the early Greek philosophers from the time of Heraclitus (535–475 B.C.) dealt with such questions as whether words really embody the nature of things and whether the structure of language reflects the structure of the world. Early debates focused on whether language is fixed or arbitrary (whether *chair* could be called *table* or *great* could be called *small*). The Greeks identified parts of speech, syntactic constructions, and inflectional categories (such as word endings), though they failed to solve some of the deeper problems of multiple meanings of words and the separation of formal systems from natural systems. Many of the problems they struggled with, however, such as the relation of thought and language, are still very lively problems today.

In the eighteenth and nineteenth centuries, philosophers of the Western world devoted a great deal of thought to language and language processes as they attempted to develop a picture of man and his thought. Particularly influential in the history of psychology was the work of the British associationists whom we have encountered in earlier chapters. These philosophers presented the workings of the mind as a succession of images or words. Which of these two (images or words) was most popular seemed to depend on which point was being illustrated. When a succession of ideas or a stream of consciousness was itself the subject matter, words were the favorite choice of illustrative material since the association of words appeared to be so clear. Sometimes, the units of language were identified with the units of thought as if the two were inseparable. Thus, we find Hobbes saying:

> The cause of the coherence . . . of one conception to another, is their first coherence . . . at that time when they are produced by sense: as for example, from St. Andrew the mind runneth to St. Peter, because their names are read together; from St. Peter to a stone, for the same cause; from stone to foundation, because we see them together; and for the same cause from foundation to church and from church to people and from people to tumult; and according to this example, the mind may run from almost anything to anything. (Hobbes, 1651.)

The whole-hearted identification of thought with language has often obscured the study of both. Noam Chomsky, a linguist, comments on seventeenth- and eighteenth-century linguistics:

> Another reason for the failure of particular grammars . . . to attempt a precise statement of regular processes of sentence formation and sentence interpretation lay in the widely held belief that there is a "natural order of thoughts" that is mirrored by the order of words. Hence, the rules of sentence formation do not really belong to grammar but to some other subject in which the "order of thoughts" is studied. . . . The same view appears in many forms and variants. . . . Diderot concludes that French is unique among languages in the degree to which the order of words corresponds to the natural order of thoughts and ideas. (Chomsky, 1965.)

Needless to say, French was Diderot's native language.

B.F. Skinner, the psychologist, makes a similar complaint from the psychological point of view in criticizing ideas and meanings:

> . . . An utterance was felt to be explained by setting forth the ideas which it expressed. If the speaker had a different idea, he would have

uttered different words or words in a different arrangement. If his utterance was unusual, it was because of the novelty or originality of his ideas. If it seemed empty, he must have lacked ideas or have been unable to put them into words. . . . All properties of verbal behavior seem to be thus accounted for. . . .

It is the function of an explanatory fiction to allay curiosity and to bring inquiry to an end. The doctrine of ideas has had this effect by appearing to assign important problems of verbal behavior to a psychology of ideas. The problems have then seemed to pass beyond the range of the techniques of the student of language, or to have become too obscure to make further study profitable. (Skinner, 1957.)

A Variety of Language Models

To develop a psychology of language, one must have some notions about what language is. In this area, perhaps more clearly than any other, the critical interaction of the nature of the subject matter and the nature of psychology is plain. Language can be taken in a variety of ways and the way a person takes it largely determines the kind of psychology he develops. Conversely, if he is wedded to a particular kind of psychology, it will determine what he thinks language is.

The science of linguistics came into great intellectual prominence (as philology and historical linguistics) shortly before the birth of psychology as an independent discipline. Because the only language family that had been extensively studied was Indo-European, massive sets of common features of that family seemed to be the "constants" of language. The early psychologists, therefore, had a picture of language as a system that preserved important and powerful internal relationships even though it changed gradually over time. Wilhelm Wundt, for example, felt that language preserved some important aspects of the functioning of the human mind, aspects that could be captured by studying the systematic nature of language and that might not be available to the investigator in any other way.

With the study of the languages of the American Indians, however, the supposed "universal" nature of Indo-European languages was ripped to shreds. Languages were discovered that appeared to be radically different from the kinds previously known, and the pendulum of scientific thought began to swing in the other direction: Perhaps it is possible for a language to take any form whatsoever; perhaps all languages are completely arbitrary and *any* set of conventions or rules can be employed. New hypotheses arose from "new world" linguists who proposed that language determined the nature of the mind rather than vice versa.

It is not hard to see that the older point of view is readily compatible with a psychology that stresses the innate nature of the mind and of thought and that the second view is compatible with a psychology that stresses the role of environment and the plastic nature of the mind. Thus, psychology of language is another area contested by nativism and empiricism.

In a much more specific sense a man's analysis of language determines the kind of psychology he writes for it. Since language is a system with many levels of analysis, units of analysis can be chosen in many different ways. Most of the work that experimental psychologists have done with language can be represented under four models:

> language as words
> language as strings of words or word classes
> language as utterances
> language as a structural system

We will look at each of these models and see what its particular virtues are. Our questions will be concerned with what we can learn from each model and where it is appropriate. We will also ask what each says about the acquisition of language and about individual differences in language function.

Model I: Language as Words

One obvious fact about language is that it is made up of words. The ancients seem to have thought so since many systems of writing have been based on some sort of characterization for every word (sign writing, pictograms, ideograms, and so on) long before the alphabetic system based on a small number of sounds was developed. For a variety of reasons, word-based systems of writing are hard to learn and difficult to use, and, with a few notable exceptions such as Chinese, they have been replaced by the more efficient alphabetic systems. Yet their widespread existence confirms the "wordiness" of language. Every child seems to discover that "things" have names and goes through a period in which "What-is-it?" is a constant question and a name (a word) is the standard response. We currently recognize the status of words by marking them with blank spaces on either side when we write them and we find it difficult to read material in which this convention has not been followed:

> Removingspacessometimesdeletescuesthatareusedbyreaders.
> Fal ses pac eso fte ncr eat edi ffi cul tie sfo rth ere ade r.

For these and other reasons, the word has been a frequent candidate for the unit of analysis of language.

Granted that words are important, what can we do with them? For one thing we can count them. And doing so leads to a number of interesting findings.

A little reflection convinces us that words are not very evenly distributed in frequency of usage. Some words like *a, is, I, like,* and *and* are used very commonly, and others such as *castigate, invariant, reticule,* and *noxious* are rarely used. Perhaps surprisingly, it turns out that there are many, many words that are rare and only a few words that are highly used. G.K. Zipf studied the frequency of usage and the number of different words involved and found a relationship now known as Zipf's Law. In its simplest form, the law states that the frequency of usage of a word times its rank order equals a constant ($f \times r = C$). If we count the words in a text and find that the most frequent word (the word with rank 1) occurs 5000 times, we expect the next most frequent word (rank 2) to occur 2500 times, the third most frequent word to occur 1666 times, and so on down to the five-thousandth word, which should occur only once in the text. Examples of counts are given in Figure 12.1. Zipf (1949) interprets this distribution as a result of the tension between speakers and listeners (or writers and readers) as each tries to follow a "law of least effort." Presumably the speaker tries to do as little work as possible. Ideally, he would say a single word and the listener would know just what he wanted. This would put a huge burden on the listener, however. In the listener's ideal world the speaker does all the work, making everything clear by making every utterance completely different from every other. Real language, says Zipf, is a compromise. The speaker does some of the work and uses different words on occasion while the listener does some of the work by trying to interpret the same words when they mean different things.

Although the meaning of Zipf's Law has been widely debated (and in fact only holds for certain sizes of samples), there is consensus that word frequency *is* systematically distributed. Furthermore, there are a number of interesting properties that vary in an orderly fashion with frequency. Zipf showed, for example, that frequent words tend to be short while infrequent words tend to be long. There is some evidence that we shorten, abbreviate, or change long words as we find frequent need for them: *gasoline* becomes *gas; television* becomes *TV; North Atlantic Treaty Organization* becomes *NATO;* and *psychology laboratory* becomes *psych lab.* In general the correlation between word frequency and word length in a sample taken evenly from each frequency range is about —.75.

As you would expect, there is a positive relationship between the frequency of usage of a word and the number of meanings that are given for that spelling in a dictionary. Words such as *like, take,* and *set* are usually found high in any word count and, of course, they have many meanings listed in a typical dictionary. It can be argued, of course, that it is not correct to count every occurrence of a particular string of letters (such as

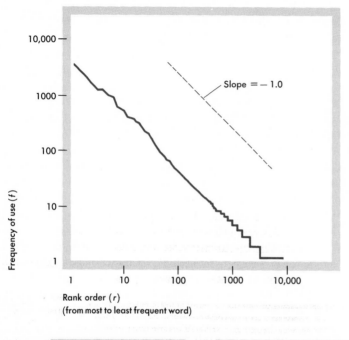

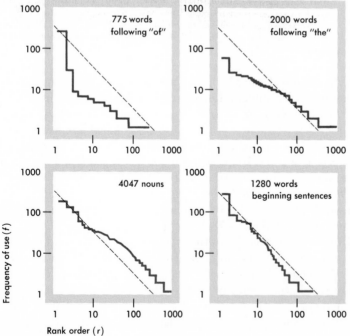

Figure 12.1 The top figure shows the standard curve for English words. The frequency of occurrence of different words (in logarithms) appearing in American newspapers is plotted against the rank of the words (also in logarithms) when they are ordered with respect to frequency. (Miller, 1951; data from Zipf, 1935.) The bottom group shows the standard curves for specially selected words. Few different words can follow "of" but many different words can follow "the." Context affects the curve. Logarithm of frequency is plotted against logarithm of rank as above. (Miller, 1951; data from Yule, 1944.)

s-e-t) as an instance of "the same word," since in fact it may be just an instance of another word that is pronounced in the same way. The *set* in *set the table* is not the same word as the *set* in *set of tennis, mathematical set,* or even *set the box here.* Counts that do not recognize the distinction between words of different meanings are, of course, much easier to make than counts that do try to keep meanings separate. The word count most used by psychologists is the count by E.L. Thorndike and I. Lorge (1944) which usually pools all meanings. When an isolated word is presented to a subject, there is no way to know how he is going to take it so we might as well pool all the frequencies that go with that set of letters if we are looking for frequency-of-usage laws. As a matter of fact, this procedure works quite well for many purposes, as will be shown below. Interestingly, the finer analysis of word meanings and frequencies only serves to illustrate further the mysteries of language and the Chinese box nature of it. If we break down the frequency count according to the frequencies for each separate meaning of a word, it again turns out that some meanings are much more commonly used than others and that the frequencies of usage distribute over the separate meanings in general accordance with Zipf's Law.

AN ILLUSTRATION

An interesting series of experiments on perception some years ago led to the establishment of many relationships between word frequency and perceptual ease. It began with a series of studies which was supposed to show that a person's values and interests influence what he sees or hears in a difficult perceptual situation. L. Postman, J.S. Bruner, and E. McGinnies (1948) selected students for having certain interests, and demonstrated that they were quite good in perceiving words that were related to those interests. In subsequent studies of this effect (Solomon and Howes, 1951), however, it was shown that the perception of words exposed only briefly was a function of the frequency of usage of the words as counted in the Thorndike-Lorge tables. Later work demonstrated that the frequency effect could be created in the laboratory by showing subjects nonsense words different numbers of times (having them read the words and spell them from one to 25 times) and then testing them for recognition at high-speed exposures. In these cases, as in the natural-language experiments, the more frequent the word, the more readily it was perceived. Figure 12.2 gives an example of this relationship. Other investigators showed that this is also true for the auditory perception of words in the presence of noise or of different words heard simultaneously in the two ears. In the former case, as the noise increases, low-frequency words become harder to hear. In the latter case, high-frequency words are correctly reported and low-frequency words are not.

Some investigators claimed that these were true perceptual effects but others argued that the effects were due to people's tendency to respond with highly frequent words no matter what was presented to the eye or ear. I.

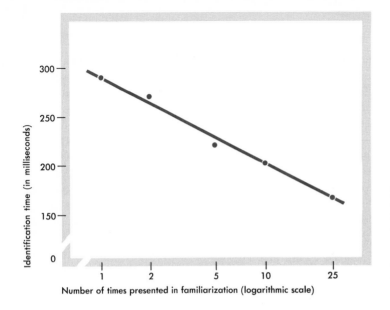

Figure 12.2 Recognition time as a function of word frequency. After being made familiar with nonsense words different numbers of times, subjects are tested for visual threshold for these words. The more familiar they are with the word, the faster they can identify it. (King-Ellison and Jenkins, 1954.)

Goldiamond and W. Hawkins (1958) conducted a "perception" experiment in which on some trials no real stimulus was presented. They showed that subjects really do guess highly frequent words when they have no perceptual information to go on.

Over the course of these and related experiments, three different effects were discovered. First, it appears that people with a given interest do see and hear more readily the words connected with that field of interest. Second, the more contact that a person has with a natural or artificial word, the more readily he will see or hear it. This may account for the first finding: People who are interested in an area are more likely to have greater exposure to everything associated with the area. Third, in the absence of any other cues, people show a response bias or guessing bias that is a function of the frequency of the items in the material with which they think they are dealing. This finding could, in principle, account for the second finding, but in fact a full consideration of all the experimental facts suggests that there is both response bias and a perceptual readiness, or predisposition, involved in the relationship of general frequency and perception.

A good deal of research indicates that word frequency is a good index of how effectively a person can process a given word in a whole variety of psychological tasks ranging from memorizing through perceiving. As one index of the importance of frequency, experimental psychologists now seldom run a study involving single words in which they do not control or manipulate this variable no matter what primary effect they may be studying.

If you think that language consists of words, how it is acquired presents no formidable problem. You merely have to show how a child learns individual words. This achievement can be viewed in two ways: As the motor skill involved in saying words and as the process of attaching the words to meanings. The traditional analysis of this problem rests on a straightforward combination of instrumental learning and classical conditioning.

According to this view, a child begins to acquire language by making noises almost at random, using the full range of sounds possible in the human vocal tract. When he makes sounds similar to those actually used in the language of his family, he receives reinforcement from his parents, who are eager to hear him talk and can be counted on to hear him say words and praise him if there is any excuse at all ("Listen, dear, he said, 'Da-Da'."); he also receives secondary reinforcement, accruing to the noises themselves, as he approximates the sounds made by the people who provide him with primary reinforcement in the form of food, comforts, and so on. Thus, the parents shape vocal behavior by their reinforcing activities, and the child shapes himself as the noises become closer to those of the language, and, hence, more secondarily reinforcing. In this fashion, it is supposed, the child learns to make the sounds and sound sequences that are important in the language and to drop out the foreign and unusual sounds that he made at an early age.

Although this analysis provides a partial account of the imitation of language and the way the child acquires the necessary skills to talk, it is clear that this procedure does not provide the sounds and sound sequences with meaning. The traditional view of meaning focuses on labeling objects in the environment (referential meaning). Knowledge of labels is explained by appealing to classical conditioning. The child learns behavior that is appropriate to objects in the world. He learns to hold and suck on a bottle, to recognize and fondle a doll, to hold, squeeze, grasp, and throw a ball, and so on. To borrow a famous paradigm used by Floyd Allport (1924), when a doll is presented to a child, it serves as the unconditioned stimulus for all the relevant responses to the object doll. If at the same time, the parent says *doll*, the word will play the role of the conditioned stimulus and, as a result of classical conditioning, the word *doll* will be associated with the responses appropriate to the object doll. Also, if the child has learned to imitate (or if there is a circular auditory-oral reflex as Allport hypothesized), he will say some approximation of *doll* on hearing the word spoken and thus, again by simple association, will learn to label objects correctly. Therefore, simple conditioning with a few assists from instrumental conditioning accounts for both the development of the ability to *understand* language (words are associated with objects and with appropriate responses) and the ability to *use* language correctly (objects elicit the right words); see Figure 12.3.

The only other kind of meaning that is considered is "emotional meaning," which is similarly attributed to the conditioning model. Words, or the objects they represent, are experienced under pleasant or unpleasant conditions, and the responses to the conditions are associated with the words and objects by classical conditioning. Thus, if a child's mother does not like moths and he is around her when she is frightened by one, it is likely that he will be in an emotional state of distress because his mother is disturbed; further, this distress will become associated with the sight of the moth and the words she speaks, "Look out for the moth!" "Oh! There's a moth!" The child thus will develop the same fears and biases as his parents and will associate the same emotional responses with many people and institutions. (For a good example, consider the strong correspondence between the political preferences of parents and children.)

The further development of language is easy to chart once it has started.

Figure 12.3 Allport's model of word acquisition. In Stage 1, the child learns vocal control through the circular reflex. In Stage 2, he imitates the sound when it is made by someone else. In Stage 3 the object (to which the child already has responses) is present when the name is spoken which elicits the vocal response from the child. In Stage 4 the sight of the doll now evokes the vocal response as a result of the prior steps of conditioning. (Allport, 1924.)

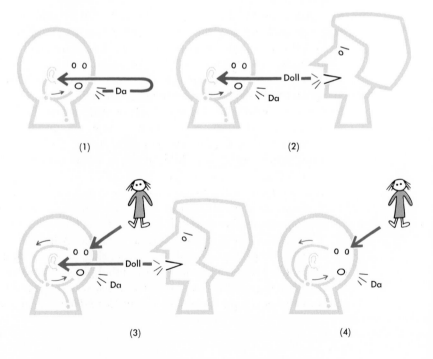

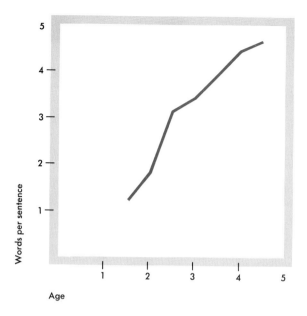

Figure 12.4 Increase in sentence length with age. (After McCarthy, 1946.)

Dorothea McCarthy has summarized a great deal of the data on language growth in a review of children's language published in 1946. For example, the number of words the child knows shows steady growth—indeed this is true virtually throughout the life span. The number of words per sentence increases over the early years (see Figure 12.4) and stabilizes at about adolescence. Comparable figures are available for the number of words spoken per day, the average length of written sentences, the number and proportion of simple sentences used, the number and proportion of complex sentences used, and other verbal categories.

For this view of language, questions of growth are mainly solved by charting number of units at each age level. Growth is merely the expected result of the automatic action of the learning processes and, once the growth has been simply described, the task is pretty much over. This model has been especially important in calling attention to the vocabulary limitations of children and to the importance of word frequency. In both these respects the impact of the model on education has been considerable. It has been the custom, ever since Thorndike's early work on word counts, to devise reading materials for school children on the basis of data on frequency of usage and restrictions of vocabulary size. Thus, a typical grade school reader is carefully crafted to introduce new words at some given rate and in order of frequency of usage so that the children will learn the most useful materials as rapidly as possible. Similarly, the number of words per sentence is carefully controlled and increases steadily over the training years. Recently it has been the fashion to commission talented writers to create original stories with the limited vocabulary of high-frequency words. Although such productions seem more enjoyable than the routine offerings, no evaluation of the educational effectiveness of this material is available.

INDIVIDUAL DIFFERENCES

From the point of view of the word model of language, there are rather naturally two major aspects of individual differences in language: The words a person knows and the rates at which he acquires and uses them. In both respects the model has pointed to important psychological variables.

The words that an individual knows constitute his vocabulary. However, most of us "know" more words (that is, recognize more words) than we use in our own speech, so it is customary to talk of a passive (recognition) vocabulary and an active vocabulary. It is also plain that we use different words when we speak and when we write, so we can further divide the active vocabulary into speaking and writing categories. Further reflection will convince us, though, that these vocabularies can be still further subdivided: We all use words in talking to our friends that we do not use in church or in the presence of our maiden aunts, and we use words with professional colleagues that we do not use in general social exchange. Special "languages" may grow up without limit in relation to hobbies, crafts, trades, professions, neighborhood groups, political organizations, and religious, economic, or fraternal associations. We surely expect word counts of law books to be different from word counts of medical books or novels, and we expect all of those to be different from common speech.

The existence of multiple vocabularies has two consequences. We expect, on the one hand, that the behavior of an individual will change in relevant ways as he moves from one kind of setting to another. On the other hand, we expect that the vocabularies he knows will reflect and be indicative of the situations in which he uses language. In general, vocabulary varies with intelligence and, as we will see in another chapter, is the single best predictor of academic or scholastic ability. The size of a specific vocabulary tends to be related to the degree that one knows and understands the specific field. For example, a test of psychological vocabulary would correlate very highly with any other kind of examination for evaluating your knowledge of this course. The facts about perception as a function of word frequency suggest that we could move one step further and use the perception test itself as a measure of a person's degree of interest in and exposure to a particular field. Unfortunately, such measures are not specific or precise enough to be trustworthy in vocational selection and would, of course, be more time-consuming and expensive than a regular vocabulary test.

When we look at vocabulary and compare it with other ways in which people differ, we find many interesting relationships. There is, for example, a large sex difference in both vocabulary and rate of word production. In every culture studied, girls talk earlier than boys and at any given age they surpass boys in degree of linguistic sophistication (longer sentences, bigger vocabularies, and so on). It is also true that girls typically excel in the rate of word association; that is, if boys and girls are asked to say as many words as they can think of or to write down all the words that some word makes them think of in one minute, girls will typically outproduce the boys. In specific subjects like mechanics or science, however, the boys may do better than the girls.

The relationship of vocabulary to age is more remarkable than it seems at first blush. Most of the abilities and skills of human beings reach a peak fairly early in life and then go into slow decline. Abilities closely tied to specific physical systems, as are hearing and vision, are the first to falter, followed by general motor skills. There is a peak in the effectiveness of performance in almost any task, and these peaks tend to be passed by the early forties at the latest. But mastery of vocabulary keeps increasing (at least in the academically active populations for which data are available) on up into the sixties. Word knowledge appears to be a cumulative matter that goes on almost as long as one lives. Further, barring brain damage which produces specific language loss, vocabulary is singularly resistant to attrition; vocabulary tests can be used as estimates of peak general intelligence after other kinds of tests requiring performances in other modes (such as design, puzzles, speed, memory) show serious impairment.

Since the relations of vocabulary and fluency with other variables, such as socio-economic level, occupation, and race, parallel the data on intelligence, these matters will be found in Chapter Fourteen on intelligence.

Model II: Language as Strings of Words

The study of language as words is both interesting and rewarding, but most of us must feel somewhat uncomfortable about stopping with that kind of simple conception. The second thing that "everybody knows" about language is that the words are combined in sequences and that the exact pattern of the sequences is often critical. *Brutus killed Caesar* has radically different meaning from *Caesar killed Brutus. The little girl rode on a horse* is a clear and unambiguous sentence in English, but an alphabetical assembly of the same words is just a list—*a, girl, horse, little, on, rode, the.* Ordering by word length is no help—*a, on, the, girl, rode, horse, little*—and inverting the original order is just nonsense—*Horse a on rode girl little the.* Clearly, what a collection of words means may depend on the ordering of the words, as in the first example, and whether a string of words has any meaning whatsoever may depend on the ordering, as in the second example. In general, if you take a sentence of ten words or so and put them in all possible orders (there are 3,628,800 possible orders for ten words), only a handful will make English sentences and even they may not say anything reasonable. A collection of words must be ordered properly to form an instance of language.

A psychologist approaches this problem in two different ways: He may take the tack that human beings learn the probabilities with which words follow one another and then string the words together in common, high-probability arrangements, or he may hold that words are learned as members of classes and that certain sequences of classes form permissible sentences. Both of these approaches attempt to cope with the general problem of sequence, both are readily related to general psychological traditions, and both produce interesting insights into language phenomena. In addition, the approaches are ultimately compatible and can be employed in a joint model, which we could call the probabilistic linking of classes.

A measure of the interconnectedness of language is our readiness to supply missing parts of any string of language. If we see a sentence with a word deleted or a word with a letter missing, we can scarcely avoid thinking of some acceptable filler. And the chances are that what we think of will be something like the original item that was replaced by the blank. The examples below are illustrative:

> The _____ is playing in the yard.
> dictio___ary

In the first case, you are likely to supply a word that names an animate being, probably a human word (*dog, squirrel, boy, girl, child*). The second case is so constrained that there is only one letter that makes a successful substitute. In both cases, as you can see with a little experimentation, it is possible to tighten or loosen the constraints on the substitutions by manipulating the context. In general, as a first rule, the more context there is, the narrower the choice. With only one letter

> i__

there are several possibilities for successful completion (*t, s, d, f, n*) but a long series may only have one possible letter substitution (in English). The second rule is that the fewer the members of the class, the more the choice is restrained. Thus, it is usually no trick to fill in the missing vowels in a series of words such as:

> Th__ b__x __s __n th__ t__bl__.

But it is usually very difficult to fill in the consonants in a series such as:

> __ __e __o__ i__ o__ __ __e __a__ __e

even though you have nearly the same number of letters and spaces given (and the sequences are, in fact, complementary parts of the same sentence). We can summarize both these rules this way: Elements that are highly variable (whether they are classes of letters, words, or other units) carry a lot of information, and elements that can vary only a little bit carry little information. If you have a letter sequence starting with *q . . .*, the blank can be filled in without further examination. In English the next letter following *q* always must be *u*. Thus, the blank is easy to guess and the actual presence of *u* conveys very little information. The sequence *s__p* has only four possibilities (*sap, sip, sop, sup*); the sequence *sa__* has at least nine possible endings (*sac, sad, sag, sam, sap, sat, saw, sax, say*); and the sequence *__ap* has at least ten beginnings (*cap, gap, jap, lap, map, nap, pap, rap, sap, tap,* and possibly *bap, yap,* and *zap*). Thus, we would say that the first letter in this sequence has a lot of information because it does most to help us to choose among many alternatives, the last letter has the next most information, and the middle letter, the vowel, has the least information because it only helps us choose among the smallest number of alternatives.

This use of the term "information" is a little unusual but it plays an important role in the notion of the amount of information conveyed by any unit of language and in the development of a statistical measure of communication and uncertainty called *information theory.* We will not go into the measurement of information here; but it is an important idea for communication specialists and has practical and theoretical implications.

For our purposes here, you should note that information in this sense is related to the phenomena of word frequency that we encountered under the first model of language. The more likely a particular word is to occur, the less information it contains. The less it contains, the easier it ought to be to identify when it is flashed on a screen, spoken in noise, and so on. Under the present model, however, we also take account of the sequence effects and try to determine how likely a given unit is in the presence of other units, not just alone. This suggests that we should be able to run the same kinds of experiments with words in sequence as we ran with words all alone. If we have a sequence that clearly calls for one particular word, then it should be easy to see or hear it in that place. If we have a sequence where just any word could go, it should be harder to see or hear the particular word that happens to be there.

Let us consider first how we find the likelihood of a word in context. This is a very different matter from just counting words. Suppose the text we are counting has only 1000 different word types; we only need 1000 categories or lines on which to tally. Then we would just count the occurrences that we find. But if we are going to count the number of times each word follows each other word, we would need 1000 times 1000 categories; and if we were interested in the sequence of the two preceding words, we would need 1000 $\times$ 1000 $\times$ 1000, and so on. Needless to say, such word counts are not common. We can approximate such sequences rather than counting them. Suppose we just go to the dictionary and take words randomly. This would be a sample of words unweighted by frequency or by context. This is called a *zero-order of approximation* to English. Then, suppose that we take the first word on each page of a collection of novels. This would be weighted by the frequency of usage of words but would include no effects of immediate context. This is called a *first-order approximation* of English. (We might also approximate this measure by asking many different people to give us the first word they think of.) Beyond this point we might give subjects one-word contexts and ask them to supply "the next word." This would be a *second-order approximation.* Then we could give subjects two-word, three-word, four-word contexts, and so on and in each case ask them to supply the next word. We would take these as representatives of third-order, fourth-order, fifth-order approximation of English. Such materials do, indeed, look more and more as if they approximate English, as the adjacent examples indicate.

Approximation to English

Zero order—taken from dictionary randomly

. . . provinciality Herat store sense Bursa energy high-priced ralliform talon watchband dialing boyant unceremoniously . . .

First order—taken from popular books

. . . until this do grows he destiny the but the his same needs and profession in one before those there . . .

Second order—constructed by having the preceding word

. . . have to take a part of their house is to make that here is nothing is close to twenty-two three blind man and then he . . .

Third order—constructed by having two preceding words

. . . several more people than ever before he went to the cupboard is empty of milk and cream are good boys and girls go to the class is . . .

Sixth order—constructed by having five preceding words

. . . Almost anyone can see that there is something beyond this world he knew there was sometimes something funny about the boy caught in the school was a teacher of children expected that they would come to our house every time that you looked you could see that he wanted to go . . .

Given such materials, we can easily perform experiments that show the effects of context on psychological performance. In one of the first of these studies, G.A. Miller, G.A. Hiese, and W. Lichten (1951), required subjects to listen to words pronounced over earphones in the presence of "white noise" (noise made up of all frequencies from very low to very high, sounding mostly like a low-pitched hiss). Subjects were tested with the noise at levels varying from silent to the point where the words were drowned out completely. The results are given in Figure 12.5. Single words drawn from a limited list (like the numbers one through nine) were easy to identify when the subjects knew that those were the only possible choices. Unfamiliar nonsense words were hard to hear correctly even under relatively good conditions. Words in a familiar context (a good approximation to English) were easier to hear correctly than the words alone or the words in unusual contexts (low approximations to English).

These same general phenomena turn up in many contexts. J. Deese (1961) found that the amount of material a subject could recall after hearing it just

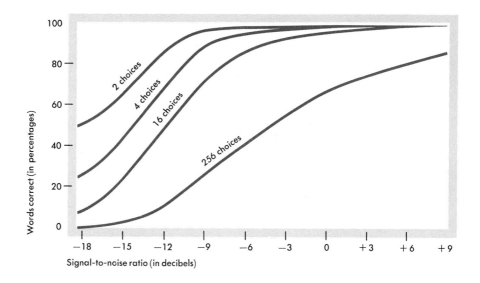

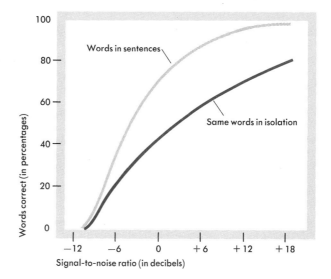

Figure 12.5 Identification of words heard in noise. Identification scores are plotted as a function of the amount of noise present. Minus numbers mean more noise than signal; positive numbers mean more signal than noise. Top shows that subjects can distinguish between a small number of words even in a great deal of noise. When the number of alternatives increases, the signal must be much stronger than the voice. Bottom demonstrates that a fixed set of words is more easily heard in sentence contexts than when they are presented alone. When there are few alternatives the words are easily heard. (From Miller, Heise, and Lichten, 1951.)

once increased systematically as the material increased in its approximation to English. Easy-reading material in general contains high-frequency sequences and can be read easily under conditions of mutilation and illumination in which hard material (with low-frequency sequences) can be read only very slowly and haltingly.

Evidence such as this furnishes powerful support for the contention that context is important in the perception and processing of language materials. It is now easy to capture this dependency statistically and to describe the amount of "information" in given material and to give a precise measure of the redundancy (predictability) of the piece of language under consideration. It does not, of course, explain why language is redundant or how it is redundant, it only describes what is known.

When you consider these phenomena of sequential dependency, it is easy to suppose that language learning must just be a matter of learning probabilities. A child learns what-follows-what just as surely and in the same fashion as he learns what-means-what. In general, the argument is that a person learns and produces probabilistic strings under particular sets of complex stimulus circumstances. Notice that this "simple" explanation places an enormous burden on the capacity of the subject to learn associations and their probabilities extending over many words and linked to many slightly varying external situations. The notion that these thousands of thousands of thousands of combinations are learned is troublesome to say the least. We will return to it again later.

A VARIATION OF THE MODEL

A differing view is that the context effects in language are due to meaningful relations between terms and objects in the world and that the sequential dependencies in language reflect facts about the world rather than some unique facts about the language sequences themselves. Thus, although a sequence like *The purple cows on the roof are eating pancakes* would be good English, no one would ever guess the key words in the sequence on a completion test because the world has never presented us with this sight. This point of view says that associations between words are the important psychological outcome of both verbal and nonverbal experience. The structure of language in large part develops from the associations as well as the other way around. For example, adherents of this position would argue that there is a strong tendency to complete *Boys and* _____ . . . with the word *girls* because boys and girls often are seen together, have many features in common (young, animate, human, small), engage in many of the same activities, and so on. As a result of all of these variables, the sequence occurs frequently in the language. All that the language provides is a series of slots or frames in which members of such classes can appear. Thus we can say:

                    Boys and girls are noisy.
                    Boys and men are noisy.
                    Boys and dogs are noisy.

but we don't say

                    Boys and very are noisy.
                    Boys and run are noisy.

The task for those with this point of view is to show that words do get
related in the proper classes and that these kinds of classes are meaningful
and will explain the contextual effects seen above. Then, if it can be shown
that there is some fixed number of permissible sequences that make up
sentences, the variety in sentences can be accounted for by running different
terms and their associates (the class members) through the frames and
generating hundreds of thousands of sentences. (This notion is close to what
linguists call an "item-and-arrangement" grammar.)

Word Association. A natural place to start is with the notion of word association itself. This technique was invented by Sir Francis Galton a hundred
years ago. As a technique it follows quite naturally from the thinking of the
British associationists. But, whereas the philosophers drew their examples
from *supposed* streams of words and images, Galton actually observed
word-to-word (or idea-to-idea) relations. He wrote a set of single words on
slips of paper and put them away until he had forgotten their specific
content. Then he exposed the words one at a time over the edge of a book.
He would peek at a word and then sit back and write down the first two
things it made him think of. In a similar fashion, he let himself associate
words to objects he saw as he walked along the Mall in London and then
tried to recall his associations and write them down when he got home.
After he had collected a great deal of data on himself, he summarized his
research with the following observations:

> . . . I found the experiments to be extremely trying and irksome and . . .
> it required much resolution to go through with them . . . Nevertheless
> the results well repaid the trouble. They gave me an interesting and un-
> expected view of the number of operations of the mind, and of the obscure
> depths at which they took place, of which I had been little conscious before.
> The general impression they have left upon me is likely that which many of
> us have experienced when the basement of our house happens to be under
> thorough sanitary repairs, and we realize for the first time the complex
> system of drains and gas and water pipes, flues, bell-wires and so forth,
> upon which our comfort depends, but which are usually hidden out of sight
> and with whose existence, so long as they acted well, we had never troubled
> ourselves. . . .
> It would be very instructive to print the actual records at length, made
> by many experiments, if the records could be clubbed together and thrown
> into statistical form; but it would be too absurd to print one's own singly.

They lay bare the foundations of man's thoughts with curious distinctness, and exhibit his mental anatomy with more vividness and truth than he would probably care to publish to the world. (Galton, 1883.)

Experimental psychologists rapidly adapted the word-association experiment to their laboratories and discovered, as Galton had suspected, that some associations were quite common and were given rapidly while others were rare and were given only after a considerable delay. The law expressing this relationship between frequency and speed of association is called *Marbe's Law*, after one of the early investigators. The law states that the speed of an association is a function of its commonness or frequency of occurrence. A modern rendering of these data is given in Figure 12.6.

Clinicians became interested in associations and especially the extent to which one's associations differed from "normal." C.G. Jung (1918) developed the notion of a "complex" (an interlocking structure of associations) and used the association test to detect such complexes. For this work, extensive word-association norms were required, and in the United States, G.H. Kent and A.J. Rosanoff (1910) tested 1000 heterogeneously selected people with a set of 100 words for the first large-scale set of normative data. Such work has been continued for both clinical and experimental reasons, and as a result norms are presently available for groups ranging

Figure 12.6 The relation between speed and commonness of association. Each point represents the median log reaction time of all responses with a given degree of commonness. Very popular responses are given very rapidly; rare responses typically take a lot of time. (From Schlosberg and Heineman, 1950.)

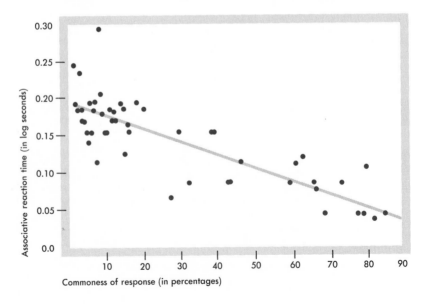

from preschool children through adults. Examples from a recent normative collection for college students are given in Table 12.1.

Experimental Findings. Word-association data reveal many findings that related to those already discussed. Marbe's Law is like a frequency-of-usage law: the more frequent, the more readily employed. The distribution of word-association responses in general follows Zipf's Law, the most

Table 12.1 Example of word-association norms. (Data for college students, Palermo and Jenkins, 1964.)

Stimulus Word: TABLE				Stimulus Word: TROUBLE			
Response	Frequency			Response	Frequency		
	500 Men	500 Women	Total		500 Men	500 Women	Total
Chair	325	366	691	Bad	50	57	107
Food	35	24	59	Police	34	19	53
Desk	17	16	33	Danger	24	18	42
Top	20	10	30	Fear	19	15	34
Cloth	16	13	29	Sorrow	10	24	34
Eat	15	8	23	Fight	20	8	28
Leg	9	2	11	Worry	7	20	27
Lamp	4	4	8	Anger	12	13	25
Dish	2	6	8	Shooter	17	6	23
Legs	4	3	7	Problem	6	14	20
Wood	2	5	7	Hard	10	9	19
Kitchen	4	2	6	Help	11	6	17
Fork	0	5	5	Mad	7	9	16
Spoon	4	1	5	Anxiety	7	7	14
Salt	3	1	4	Problems	6	8	14
Dishes	0	4	4	Pain	4	9	13
Brown	2	2	4	Bob	5	6	11
Dinner	2	2	4	Sat	1	9	10
Flat	3	0	3	Jail	4	6	10
Plate	0	3	3	Peace	5	4	9
Set	1	2	3	Easy	6	3	9
Table cloth	1	2	3	Maker	8	0	8
Cards	2	0	2	Double	7	1	8
Round	2	0	2	School	4	4	8
Tennis	1	1	2	Money	8	0	8
etc.				etc.			

popular response to a stimulus word has a very high frequency, the next most popular falls off rapidly, the next less rapidly, and so on; most cases exhibit something very much like the "rank $\times$ frequency = constant" relationship.

Other phenomena fit nicely into place as well. If words from strong word-association pairs (like *table-chair, dark-light, eagle-bird*) are mixed up in a list and read to subjects for immediate recall, the words tend to come in pair-wise order. Even though *table* may be the third word on the list and *chair* the twelfth, people are very likely to recall them in immediate succession when they try to remember the list. This suggests that one way that memory is organized is in associative clumps or networks (Cofer, 1965).

It has also been discovered that associated words "prime" each other in a variety of ways. For example, in the perception of words in context, the identification of a word that is flashed for a few hundredths of a second is greatly improved if the subject has just seen an associated word. The subject is shown one word with a long exposure (so that he "will know where to look") and then the other word is briefly flashed at the same place. If *table* is shown before the word *chair* is flashed, *chair* will be identified in about 60 per cent of the time that it takes to identify it when it follows some unrelated word (O'Neil, 1953).

It is also possible to show that there is strong "generalization" between associates (sometimes called "semantic generalization"). Thus, if a person learns to press a lever to the word *chair*, he is likely on test trials to press to the word *table* as well (Mink, 1957). If he is conditioned to salivate to one of these words (by eating candy or pretzels while it is being exposed on a screen before him), it is possible on test trials to detect excess salivation in response to words that are associated (Razran, 1949). If he has been shocked in the presence of one of these words, he is likely to show a conditioned galvanic skin response when confronted with the associated word (Branca, 1957). If he learns to give one of these words as a response to a particular stimulus on a learning task, it is easy to learn a new task that involves giving the associate to the same stimulus and hard to learn a task that requires giving the associate to another stimulus (Jenkins, Foss, and Odom, 1965).

There is now convincing evidence that these effects apply not only to direct associates but also, though more weakly, to chains of associates. For example, W.A. Russell and L. Storms (1955) showed that a string of associates could be employed to effect transfer. They developed chains of the following sort: As a stimulus in free association, *soldier* elicits (among other responses) the word *sailor; sailor* as a stimulus elicits the word *navy. Navy*, however, is not directly elicited by *soldier;* they are connected only by the mediating word *sailor.* Thus, we can think of a chain of words *soldier-sailor-navy.* If we have a subject learn a list of pairs in which *soldier* is the correct response to, say, DAX, we can see if he will show positive transfer when we have him learn another list that contains the pair DAX-

navy. The expectation is that when he learns the second list, DAX will elicit *soldier* (subvocally, as a result of learning the first list); *soldier* will elicit *sailor* (inferred from word-association norms); *sailor* will elicit *navy* (inferred from association norms); the subject will identify *navy* as the correct response and say it aloud. The experimentation by Russell and Storms showed that this kind of positive transfer is obtained. Further studies (McGehee and Schulz, 1960) demonstrated that this transfer does not depend on some vague "similarity" between the end terms (here, *soldier* and *navy*) because the transfer only works in the predicted direction; it does not work backward (from DAX-*navy* to DAX-*soldier*) in the absence of backward associations.

Language and Associations. Since association seems to be so strong and so thoroughly involved in the processes that are related to language activity, it would be simple to assume that linguistic behavior is merely some modification or resultant of associative behavior. The grammatical study of word associations is helpful in examining this assumption. The most popular associations to high-frequency words are typically of the same grammatical class as the stimulus word (*table-chair, dark-light, large-small, sick-well, running-jumping, happy-sad, quickly-slowly*). Further down in the list of responses, however, we usually find "continuation" responses such as *table-cloth* (continuing the word), *dark-night* and *large-house* (continuing a noun construction), *running-home* (continuing a verb construction), and *quickly-run* (which seems to supply the earlier part of the verb construction). The implication is that associations do two kinds of work: They knit together words that are very much like one another in grammatical class and in meaning, and they serve to link one class to another. Perhaps all of grammar is to be found in association, direct or mediated.

This idea offers a great deal of comfort to the psychological analyst of language since it relates language to association and association is clearly part of the long tradition of empirical psychology. In fact, however, the task is only begun at this point since he must now account for the source of associations and then show how they work in the production and understanding of language. This has been somewhat more difficult.

In the traditional view, word associations arise from experience. One very important part of experience is hearing and learning to say language sequences. (Note that the discussion here applies equally well to the general case of sequential dependencies and hence both to associations and to the probabilistic chain analysis described earlier.) Early word associations, then, ought to be associations from a word to the next most likely word in a sequence. Thus, if a child often hears a sequence of words A-B-C-D-E-F-. . ., each link in the sequence eventually ought to elicit the next one. That this is at least partially so is evident in our associations to single letters and numbers where we tend to give the next in the customary order (the most common letter response to A is B; the most common response to *one* is *two*, even for adults). Studies of children's associations show far more sequential responses than among adults and an increase in the rate of "same class" responses with increasing age.

But how do the associations change to yield the adult response patterns, which are, as we have seen, heavily loaded with words from the same classes rather than subsequent classes? This theoretical difficulty was overcome by postulating *mediated association,* which hypothesizes that any two things that are associated with a third thing will become associated with each other. This approach suggested that different words occurring in the same sequences might become associated through their network of associations to other items. For example, there might be a common sequence *A-B-C-X* and another *A-B-C-Y.* The general argument is that these sequences are learned individually and, after they are well-learned, the presentation of *A-B-C* . . . brings to mind *both X and Y,* and thus *X and Y* become associates *even though they have never occurred explicitly together.* This is a very important notion for association theory and is invoked to explain why words that are related in meaning (and hence likely to occur in the same contexts) and of the same grammatical class (and hence occurring at the same place in sentences) come to be associated with each other very closely. It is obvious that opposites, for example, are frequently highly associated. According to the above argument, this is virtually inevitable since they apply to the same situations and are of the same part of speech.

In the last chapter we pointed out that there was abundant evidence for mediated learning and that learning different responses to the same stimulus (*A-B, A-C*) made it easy to learn a connection between the two responses (*B-C*). The most convincing study, however, was performed by D. McNeill (1963) who had subjects learn "sentences" containing nonsense words. The "sentences" were structured so that one sentence might contain a sequence ....X..........Y...., where X and Y were nonsense terms, and another sentence would contain ....X..........Z...., where Z was another nonsense word. After subjects had been given various amounts of training on these sentences, they were given association tests on the nonsense words. For those subjects who were just beginning to learn the sequences, the usual response to X was either Y or Z and the most usual response to Y or Z was any other nonsense word. As subjects learned the sentences thoroughly, however, association between the Y and Z terms began to appear and rapidly grew to high strength. This, of course, is exactly what would be predicted by the association-through-mediation hypothesis.

ACQUISITION

The account of acquisition of language here is easy to imagine. It begins exactly like the single-word model sketched before. Next it stresses the permissible sequences and the learning of many such overlapping sequences. Then, it suggests that the words in the overlapping sequences begin to be related to one another in classes as well as chained in sequence. Thus, if a child has many strings like:

> There's kitty.
> There's bear.
> Where kitty?
> Where bear?

and if he learns a new sequence like *Fix kitty*, we can expect him under "appropriate" circumstances to say *Fix bear*.

It should be noted that this view is not restricted to associations in classes resulting only from language. On occasion we can appeal to the association of objects, pictures, and events as additional reasons for the association of the words that describe these objects, pictures, and events. Attention has been given to mediating ideas in part because they seem to explain so dramatically how previously unassociated materials can become associated without any direct pairing. Mediation, therefore, seems to account for novel but appropriate behavior (see Jenkins and Palermo, 1964).

The treatment of the development of the sequences of classes that are permissible has unfortunately been slighted. It is normally assumed that this sequencing consists of some sort of chain of items or classes of items and that it is a simple matter to show that chains of behavior can be learned. This is true—but only for chains made up of specific items, not chains of abstract classes. It is easy to demonstrate that a rat can build up a behavior sequence consisting of pulling a chain, getting a marble, rolling it across the cage, pushing it up a ramp, and dropping it in a hole. Such demonstrations are common and usually are constructed by beginning at the goal and working backward (the marble is lodged on the edge of the hole and the rat is rewarded for any movement toward it, then for any movement that knocks it in, then for moving it a quarter inch so it falls in the hole, and so on). It is *not* easy to show how these behaviors and all their variants can be assembled in other chains for other purposes. Further, there is no evidence that language sequences are built up in this fashion (back to front) even for particular sequences.

In general, the sequence part of the problem has been left to the linguists with the general assumption that the linguists would come up with some list of sequences that would be "basic" and that these would serve as targets for the psychologist's work when he got around to that part of the research. At present, however, fewer and fewer linguists hold the faith that a small number of patterns exist and that people learn these frames or sequences of classes and then make new sentences by substituting in the frames the members of the classes that current stimuli evoke from them.

Experiments with Children. Direct support for the "item-and-arrangement" point of view in language learning is minimal because the theory of acquisition has not been sufficiently spelled out. The best evidence is McNeill's experiment cited above. Support for *some sort* of contextual learning is available in several experiments, however. H. Werner and E. Kaplan (1950) studied the manner in which a nonsense term developed its meaning through verbal contexts. They presented children with sets of sentences containing nonsense terms and asked each child to find the meaning of the artificial word. For example, a child might get this series of sentences:

1. A CORPLUM may be used for support.
2. CORPLUMS may be used to close off an open space.
3. A CORPLUM may be long or short, thick or thin, strong or weak.
4. A wet CORPLUM does not burn.
5. You can make a CORPLUM smooth with sandpaper.
6. The painter used a CORPLUM to mix his paints.
(Correct translation: CORPLUM = stick or piece of wood.)

After each sentence, the child was asked what the word meant. The results showed, of course, many more correct solutions for older children (13 years old) than for younger children (9 years old). The major error of younger children was a tendency to take the general meaning of the sentences and say it was the meaning of the word (A CORPLUM is something that doesn't burn) and to assimilate new meanings as more sentences were added (A CORPLUM is wet and smooth if you rub it with sandpaper). These "meanings" appear to be largely sequential verbal associations. Such errors drop off markedly after age 10. The second major kind of error consisted of giving the artificial word a wide, diffuse meaning which was privately determined by the child and did not reflect sentence associations. (For instance, for the sentence, "The way is clear if there are no ASHDERS" one child responded: "The way is clear if there are no parts of a radio that don't fit in right [together]." For this child ASHDER referred to a radio-repair situation.) These errors disappear more slowly than the first kind. The older child, however, seeks and finds a relatively precise, grammatically appropriate substitute for the artificial word.

In an interrelated series of studies, R.W. Brown and J. Berko found that even younger children are quite sensitive to grammatical cues and that they use them appropriately for both language and nonlanguage behavior. Berko (1958) showed that four- and five-year-old children know how to apply inflectional endings (plurals and verb tenses) to completely new words. She gave a child a card with a nonsense animal on it and said, "Here is a wug; now [going to next card] there are two of them; there are two _____." If the child supplied *wugs,* he was credited with knowing how to detect a noun and knowing how to make the appropriate noun plurals. Similarly, she displayed a card with a man in action on it saying, "This is a man who knows how to wug; he wugs every day; yesterday he _____." Her results indicated that four- and five-year-old children had mastered the commoner forms of inflectional endings in English.

Brown (1957) tested children with cards picturing, for example, actions on substances in odd containers. Then he would say, "There is *some latt* in this picture," or "There is *a latt* in this picture," or "There is *latting* in this picture," thus giving grammatical cues for a mass noun (like milk, sand, or dirt), a count noun (usually objects with fixed contours), or a verb. He found that preschool children readily made use of these cues to detect the appropriate substances, objects, and actions.

Finally Brown and Berko (1960) tested the hypothesis that free-association responses were related to grammatical sensitivity or grammatical awareness. They worked with children in the first, second, and third grades and with college students. Each subject was given a word-association test with stimuli drawn from six different parts of speech and a sentence-meaning test. The sentence test consisted of presenting a card with a picture of a person or an animal on it and saying, "Do you know what a wug is? This is a picture of a little girl thinking about a wug. Can you make up what that might mean?" This presentation identifies *wug* as a count noun. For *wug* as a mass noun, there would be sentences like, "This is a cat thinking about some wug." When *wug* was to be an intransitive verb the experimenter said, "Do you know what it means to wug? This is a picture of a little boy who wants to wug." With a transitive verb, he said, "This is a woman who wants to wug something." When it was an adverb, the sentence was about a boy doing something *wuggily*. The child's "translation" was recorded and checked for the part of speech he assigned to the nonsense word (for example, in the original sentence the child might say, "The little girl is thinking about a doll," which would be a correct part-of-speech assignment).

Both the free-association test and the sentence translations were scored for responses that were in the same part of speech as the stimulus word. The results showed that the younger children gave more sequential associations on the word-association test and more sentence translations that were simply contextual associations. The older children and the college students tended to give word associations that were the same part of speech as the stimulus word and gave more precise, equivalent meanings for the nonsense words. Brown and Berko concluded that a child does increasingly order his vocabulary into the syntactic classes called parts of speech and that he improves markedly in his ability to use part of speech cues as indicators of meaning. Thus, an intimate relationship is apparent between association processes and the acquisition of syntax.

INDIVIDUAL DIFFERENCES

Extensive studies of individual differences in word-to-word relations are easy to find, but almost none of them is directed at understanding language. There is a vast literature dealing with the uses of word associations in clinical work, in lie detection, and in tests of interest, sex differences, introversion, conformity, maladjustment, emotionality, and endless other topics. For the most part, these matters are aside from our current concern.

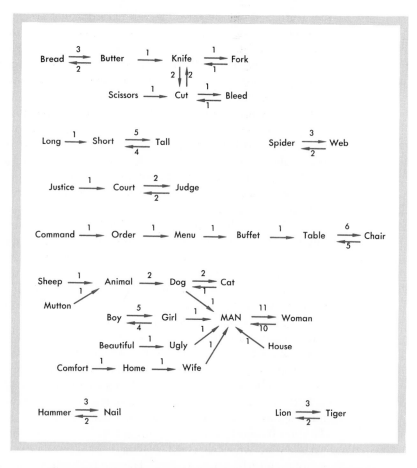

Figure 12.7 Network of word associations obtained from a subject who typically gives popular responses. Each arrow indicates a stimulus-response connection. The numbers indicate the number of times the same association was repeated in the testing. Her associations were highly similar one month later. (Peterson and Jenkins, 1957.)

For insights into the functioning of language, it would be of interest to report experiments concerning the individual associative habits of subjects and their relation to linguistic behavior and experimental tasks. Unfortunately, little of this kind of work has been done, though two subjects were studied almost daily for a three-month period in an attempt to discover leads concerning the relation of associative habits to a variety of other behaviors (Peterson and Jenkins, 1957). One subject was selected because she was "super high" in giving common responses to the Kent-Rosanoff word-association test and the other subject was selected because he was "super low," making almost entirely uncommon responses. The picture presented by these two deviate subjects (though not supported by a more extensive investigation over the middle ranges of the test) is a fascinating one.

The high-scoring subject was a composite of "the average person." Her behavior in the experiments and in writing tasks was easily forecast. She reliably showed all the phenomena described in the experiments in this section (associative clustering in recall, perceptual facilitation, transfer, and so on) and performed in identical fashion when the same tasks were repeated at a later date. Her associations were highly predictable and stable from one time to another. She had little curiosity about the experiments and seemed completely unaware of their purpose. Her essays were stereotyped and unoriginal. When every fifth word was deleted and other students were asked to fill in the missing words, they were highly successful, supplying 69 per cent of the missing words correctly.

A graph of the associative matrix for this girl is shown in Figure 12.7. You can see that everything is arranged in neat little packages of related items. When this mapping operation was repeated a month later, her associations were almost exactly the same.

The low-scoring subject, on the other hand, was a picture of nonconformity. His college grades varied from one extreme to the other. He had been in 14 different schools before coming to college. He showed highly variable behavior on the experiments and his associative patterns changed radically from one day to the next. When he was given experimental material that showed associative bonds at work (like the recall task), he was more likely to utilize the normative high-strength connections than his own responses of a few days or a few weeks previously. His verbal behavior was highly unpredictable and unstable. He was interested in the experiments at the beginning of the summer, but by the end he resented them and tried to get out of the program. His essays were off-beat and unusual. When students were asked to fill in the missing words after every fifth word had been deleted, they were far less successful than they had been with the high-scorer's essay, getting only about 46 per cent correct. A graph of part of his associative matrix is shown in Figure 12.8. It makes a vast interrelated sprawl, with a few key words that connect everything together. When he was retested a month later, the pattern was an entirely different sprawl and some of the "key words" failed to appear at all.

It is tempting on the basis of these case studies to leap to conclusions stressing conformity-creativity, order-disorder, and other such polarities, but such conclusions are unjustified. Subsequent work has suggested that these "personality traits" are not well-measured by an association test. In fact, it is not clear that any simple dimensions are tapped by the general association test. In the last ten years it has become evident that most people can shift their scores toward the popular response end if they want to or if they are instructed to do so and, of course, no one has ever doubted that people can give unusual responses if they choose to do so. The point is that most people have good "norms" for their fellow men readily available and that they

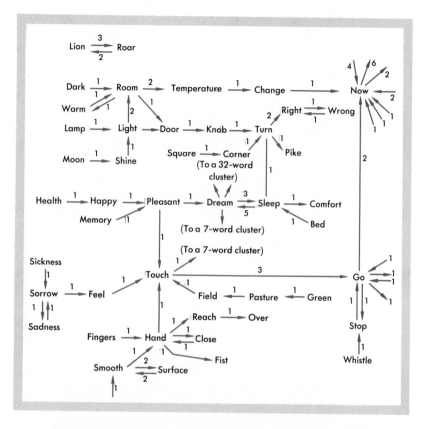

Figure 12.8 Network of word associations obtained from a subject who typically gives unpopular responses. This is only a part of the graph; the interconnections are too numerous to represent here. Almost none of these associations were obtained on retesting one month later. (Peterson and Jenkins, 1957.)

"know" how to act like "most people." The more appropriate conclusion to draw from the case study, then, is that the popular responses are related to the stable and predictable aspects of language. It may be that the association test is a poor indicator of specific personality traits within the normal range precisely because it is such a powerful indicator of general language habits available to everyone.

Wilson Taylor, who pioneered in the study of the deletion technique (usually called the "Cloze Technique" from its presumed relation to the Gestalt principle of closure), used it mainly to measure the difficulty of reading materials. In essence, his thinking was that the more blanks an average reader can fill in, the more "readable" the material is. This approach makes excellent sense under the kinds of theory represented in Model II.

Taylor extended this thinking to show how to use this device for individual measurement in technical schools. He took passages of the technical texts, deleted words randomly, and used the resulting text as a test for entering students. A student could draw on his previous knowledge of the field as well as his general intelligence to figure out the words that were supposed to fill the blanks; that is, the deleted passages formed a combined intelligence-and-information test. The Cloze test turned out to be an excellent predictor of success in the technical schools. This work of Taylor's demonstrates the effectiveness of the measurement of language habits in assessing an individual's competence in a particular field.

Model III: Language as Utterance

The orientations toward language given above have appealed to simple notions related to what we all know about language, namely, that it is composed of words and that it has important ordering properties. But a different approach is possible and has been recommended by Skinner in his book *Verbal Behavior* (1957). Skinner argues that we should approach language just as any other behavior and ask what the functional units are, rather than assume that they are immediately given in our prior conception of the behavior. His contention is that language is of special interest merely in that it happens to be behavior which is reinforced only by other human beings; it does not produce any reinforcement or serve any obvious biological function apart from its effect on someone else.

The questions for Skinner, then, are concerned with the functional stimuli for verbal utterances, the functional classes of the responses made by the speaker, and the reinforcements that are applied to increase the probability of given classes of behaviors in the presence of given stimuli. Skinner firmly asserts that behavior is at all times a result of past history and current circumstances and that the task of the psychologist is to make clear how these variables control the behavior. The ultimate test for Skinner is the prediction and control of functional units of behavior, not the accounting for behavior as it happens to be described by someone else (such as a linguist). He suggests that psychologists keep in mind "specific engineering tasks" involving language, such as teaching, doing therapy, and writing articles, to make sure that they are considering the kinds of processes and relationships which are truly productive, that is, those that will help us achieve these goals effectively.

In Skinner's scheme, verbal behavior is divided into two great classes, *mands* and *tacts*. Mands function to obtain some specific reinforcement for the speaker and are under the general control of his states of deprivation or needs. Examples are: *Please pass the salt. Water! Got any cigarettes? Can I have something to eat?* (The word relates to com*mand* and de*mand*.) Tacts say something about the state of the world. Examples are: *It's raining out-*

side. Here comes the postman. There's bread in the cupboard. (The word comes from con*tact,* suggesting contact with the world.)

Obviously mands work for the speaker and are successful to the extent that they bring about the desired reward. Thus, mands are shaped like any other instrumental act and are maintained in strength by reinforcement. When a mand stops working in a given situation, it will be extinguished. (A child will "fuss" to get its mother's attention as long as she provides it in response to that behavior. If she stops, the child eventually stops too.)

It is more difficult to see how tacts work since they are not in any obvious sense to the speaker's advantage. They do, however, provide the listener with some information which he may want or need. Skinner argues that the listener gives the speaker *generalized reinforcement* for telling him things about the world. The listener cannot always use food or any other single reward as a reinforcer because he may need the information when the speaker is not hungry. Thus, a generalized reinforcer like praise, smiling, or thanks is substituted. This substitute is presumably a secondary reinforcer. Because of its wide generality and intermittent association with primary reinforcement, it does not wear out its reinforcing properties.

To these two major categories of verbal behavior, Skinner adds a number of useful minor categories. *Echoic* responses are those that echo or copy language just heard. Reinforcing particular cases of copying produces a general disposition to imitate. This obviously is an important asset in the acquisition of new items of language behavior. *Textual* responses involve reading, aloud or silently; they are important skills to acquire and powerful mechanisms for governing subsequent behavior both verbal and otherwise. *Intraverbal* responses are associations between verbal items. All of the word-association behaviors we studied above are included by Skinner as raw material on which a person can work in the process of composing new utterances. In addition, he regards almost all academic knowledge as a process of building up appropriate sets of intraverbal responses. Finally, as a special class of intraverbals, Skinner discusses *autoclitics* or, more simply, statements about one's own statements. For example, a person may say, *I guess . . ., I think . . ., I'm sure . . .,* to indicate the degree of strength of whatever statement follows the phrase.

One of the great virtues of Skinner's approach is that it keeps the investigator focused on the task that language is supposed to be doing. His view calls attention especially to the role of the audience in creating a stimulus situation controlling language and in providing reinforcements that further shape language behavior. In a particular interaction the variables might be analyzed as shown on page 459.

It is noteworthy that many of the phenomena that Skinner has referred to have important roles in maintaining our behaviors. There is undoubtedly a very strong need on the part of a speaker to get some acknowledgement from his audience that his behavior is being effective. If you try to remain

Person A

(Being without cigarettes; wanting to smoke; seeing *B*; knowing that *B* is a smoker and a fellow student)

How about a cigarette?

(Note that this is a mand. Other members of this verbal response class that are likely to occur to the same stimuli are:

May I have a cigarette?
Do you have a cigarette to spare?
Got any smokes?
Can I bum a weed?
etc.)

Person B

(Familiar with the verbal stimulus, recognizes *A* as fellow student and perhaps as a previous source of reinforcements.)

Sure.

(Offers cigarette.)

(Accepts cigarette, a reinforcement for his mand)

Thanks.

(Reinforces *B* with generalized reinforcer for his behavior.)

You're welcome.

(Reinforces the reinforcement.)

passive and unmoving when a friend is speaking to you, your friend will talk louder and louder, move around and ask questions (*Isn't that so? O.K.? Right?*) in an attempt to elicit a response. If you maintain silence, the ultimate result is likely to be anger or even more demanding questions (*What's wrong with you anyway?*).

ACQUISITION

Obviously in the Skinnerian view, reinforcement plays a key role in the development of language; this model is not concerned with problems such as the development of classes and sequences other than to point out that every time a speaker makes a better approximation to the language of his community, the likelihood and speed of reinforcement increase. Therefore, the general assumption is that an individual's language behavior approaches the normative language automatically and that it is idle to speculate on the particular machinery involved, just as it is idle to speculate on the particular musculature involved when a rat presses a lever in a Skinner box. The only things that count are the conditions which set the contingencies for reinforcement. If the Skinner box is set up appropriately, an experimenter can put a rat in it and come back in a few hours with the near certainty that the rat will be pressing the bar at a prescribed rate. If you object that he cannot predict whether the rat will be pressing with his left or right paw, his answer will be that you didn't ask him to control that behavior. If you want him to control that, he can do so in exactly the same way with a little more elaborate machinery. But, he will argue, the principles are exactly the same. Nothing new is added or subtracted, only the conditions have been altered appropriately. As for language, he will not attempt to tell you in detail how all of language is acquired, but if you are interested in some functional aspect of it, he will show you how to control it.

Most of the experimentation that has been done within this framework has been oriented toward two problems: showing that generalized reinforcers work (obviously crucial to the model) and showing that various instances of verbal behavior can be increased and decreased in frequency as a result of reinforcement. Many experiments have tackled both problems at once. Such experiments on reinforcement have generally taken the following form: The subjects are given a verbal task, such as saying words, making sentences, or choosing phrases. The experimenter monitors their work until he establishes a base rate for the behavior in which he is interested (for example, using the first-person pronouns *I* and *we*). Then the experimenter begins reinforcing the subject by saying *good* or *umm-hmm* (generalized reinforcers) when the subject says a sentence with *I* or *we* in it. Usually during this period, the rate of the response increases over the base line value. Finally, the experimenter stops reinforcing the behavior and the rate usually drops. Examples are given in Figure 12.9.

These experiments have been criticized on the grounds that many subjects "know" what is going on and are

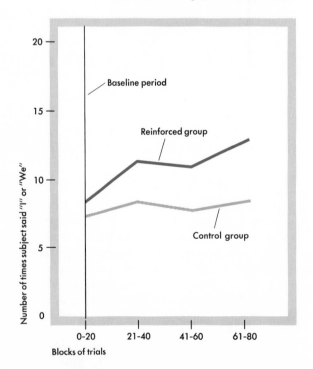

Figure 12.9 Effect of the social reinforcer "good." Subjects were hospitalized mental patients. The task was making sentences. In the reinforced group the experimenter said "good" if the sentence used "I" or "We." In the control group the experimenter said nothing. (After Taffel, 1955.)

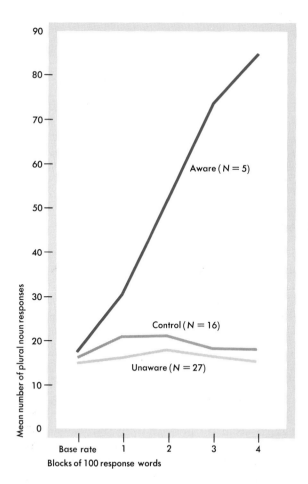

Figure 12.10 The role of awareness in the effectiveness of verbal reinforcement. Subjects were requested to say words. When they said a plural noun the experimenter gave them a verbal reinforcement ("good"). Subjects who were aware of what was going on showed increases in the giving of plural nouns. Other subjects who were not aware showed no change in rate and looked just like the control group. (DeNike and Spielberger, 1963.)

trying to do what the experimenter wants them to do. There is an extensive literature on the question of whether the subject's "awareness" is important in this kind of manipulation of his behavior. In the course of the controversy, it turned out that "awareness" was very poorly defined and that many investigators had very different ideas about what they meant by it: Awareness that the experimenter was saying something? Awareness of the function of what he was saying? Awareness of what conditions were involved in determining when the experimenter said it? Awareness of the connection between the experimenter's "reinforcer" and the subject's behavior? Awareness of the purpose of the experiment?

It has now been demonstrated that the subject's awareness of the conditions of the experiment is an important factor in determining whether he will show appropriate reinforcement effects. L.D. DeNike and C.D. Spielberger (1963), for instance, divided their subjects on the "awareness" variable with the results shown in Figure 12.10. Finally, it is also clear that the subject's desire for the reinforcer, his hypotheses about the experiment, and his intentions about his actions enter into the experiment in systematic ways (see Dulany, 1968). As you might suspect, some subjects are "aware" but decide that they want to keep the experimenter quiet (*I didn't like his saying "good" all the time*), while some subjects for other diverse reasons decide that they are not going to "play the game." A summary of this series of experiments is that reinforcement (with awareness and with intention to cooperate) can make significant changes in human behavior, but that it cannot be viewed in a simple fashion as a force that has automatic effects on behavior without regard to the state of other variables.

No appreciable work has been done on individual differences except with respect to the verbal-reinforcement issue. It is clear that the more impressive and "statusful" the experimenter is, the more effective his reinforcements are. The more the subject is aware of the contingencies and wants the reinforcers, the more effect they have on his verbal behavior.

Model IV: Language as a Rule System

In the final orientation to be described here, the argument (as with Skinner) is that simple notions about language being made up of words and orderings are a poor base for a psychology of language. There is sharp disagreement with Skinner, however, over what to do about it. Whereas Skinner goes into laboratory psychology in a search for methods of prediction and control, adherents of this position go into modern linguistics in search of a more adequate description of the nature and structure of language. As a result of their findings, they argue that association psychology is not adequate to account for the demonstrable complexity of language behavior (Chomsky, 1957, 1959). This movement toward a linguistic conception of language is recent, and as yet it is not well integrated into the psychological framework. However, the work of the linguists seems to provide fresh suggestions for the psychologists to consider and strong arguments that the psychological devices of the associationists are not enough to explain language behavior.

According to this view, language is infinitely variable; that is, there is no limit to the possible length and variety of sentences in English. This means that the assumptions of the earlier models are incorrect. In respect to the view of language as words, this model asserts that a sentence is more than a word heap. Extending the argument, it flatly denies the assumption of the second model that some fixed number of sentence frames is sufficient to describe the sentences of a language. It is argued instead that what is learned is not words or particular sentence orders but rather *productive rules* that enable the speaker to produce the infinite variety of sentences that he says and to understand the infinite variety of sentences that he hears.

The argument here has great generality for psychology. It applies over all areas in which complex behaviors and skills are involved. In its simplest form, it is easy to see and appreciate. Consider the skill of multiplication. We do not try to teach grade school students the products of all numbers multiplied by all other numbers. We break the task into a series of steps that require only a small amount of sheer memory work (namely the multiplication tables—the products of all combinations of pairs of numbers from 0 through 9) and the acquisition of a set of rules about what to do when we get more than single digits to multiply. Most of us have learned these procedures so well that we have forgotten the extensive rules that we mastered.

> Place the two numbers one above the other so that the right-hand digits are directly above each other. Start with the furthest right digit in the lower figure. From the multiplication table get the product of this digit with the right-hand-most digit of the upper row. If the product is a single digit, write it in the first available row beneath the lower digit in the same column as the lower digit. If the product is two digits, write the right-hand member of the two-digit number in the place described and carry the left-hand digit . . . etc., etc.

The virtue of this abstract approach (as opposed to learning all the products of all the possible numbers) is that the rule system will generate a product for any set of numbers that a person has the patience to work through. The rules are recursive; they can be applied again and again until the problem is complete. With the complete memorization procedure, on the other hand, it would take most of a lifetime to achieve learning to even a reasonable level (say, all the digit pairs up to 1000×1000), and one would always face the hazard of running into a problem for which one had never learned the answer. Our whole educational system has elected to learn a *computing technique* rather than to memorize the items of information that would be required in the superlarge multiplication table.

Although this example may seem far-fetched since no one in this age would suggest the method of memorizing all possible number pairs, there is a sense in which psychologists' proposals about language learning have been similar to this memorization procedure. A strong pressure is now felt toward a rule-based explanation of language. It is not supposed, of course, that the rules for language are learned as single particular grammatical rules or that people even know that they "know" the rules. It *is* supposed that language is "computed" rather than "stored" and that this is what accounts for our tremendous capacity to utter novel but appropriate sentences and to understand new sentences when we hear them.

The attempt to specify the nature of the rules of language is instructive with respect to the kinds of models that psychologists have tried to employ. On the one end, as we have seen, language has been treated as a set of words. This approach implies unitary meanings that just add together within the sentence. At the other extreme we have the sentence (or some larger utterance) as a unit which is to be understood as a single whole. Both of these approaches attempt to discover and settle on the right level of analysis, the right unit size, and so on. But the rules of language as the linguist sees them do not argue for any single level or single kind of unit. The rules of language are, instead, sets of nested and interlocking rules showing how the various levels interact in the complete structure of language.

We cannot compress a course in linguistics into a few pages, but we can indicate the direction that linguistic analysis takes. Traditionally, three major areas are recognized in linguistics: semantics (meanings), syntax (grammar), and phonology (sounds). A linguistic utterance can be spelled out in terms of *phonemes* (the sound categories that count in the language) or in terms of *morphemes* (the roots of words and the inflections that can be applied to them) or in terms of *phrases* (the constituents of the sentence organization) or in terms of *sentence type* (declarative, interrogative, and so on) or in other ways.

At each level of analysis, the utterance can be divided into identifiable and classifiable segments; that is, we can say "this segment is like that segment." For example, at the level of meaningful sound units we can talk about "the phoneme /p/." We can say that the /p/ in *pa* is like the /p/ in *pea* and both of them are like the /p/ in *pooh*. This level is called the *phonemic* level. It is important to note that the segments that we are calling /p/ may have quite different acoustical properties. Experiments with synthetic speech show that the physical noise that we hear as the /p/ sound at the beginning of *pea* does not sound like /p/ when it is put in front of the vowel sound *ah*. In fact, that combination is heard as *ka*. The constancy that we hear as a single type of speech sound may have a highly variable acoustic base. Further, psychologically and linguistically, we treat these speech sounds as if they were the same at the beginning, middle, and end of words (*pat, apt, tap*), as if they were separable and interchangeable. Physically they are vastly different acoustic signals. The important point is that there is an abstract level of linguistic analysis at which these *are* identical elements, even though our instruments tell us that there is a physical level at which they are not.

Above the phonemic level we encounter the meaningful sequences called *morphemes*. The problem of specifying meaningful units that are represented in strings of phonemes is not a simple matter. For a string like *boy* we may want to talk about a referent and try to establish a relationship between this string and some class of items in the world. But for a string like *maybe* it is not reasonable to talk about a referent at all. Other strings like *if* and *to* (as in *he has to go*) frustrate any simple analysis.

Above the morphemic level, there are collections of *syntactic units* (phrases, clauses) which have new unities of their own; that is, they stand in certain specifiable relationships to one another that are not indicated either by their sounds or by their meanings. Thus we can say that *the girl* and *a man* are similar in a fashion that does not depend on overlapping in sound or being both human and animate, but rather on the fact that they can both be subjects or objects of certain kinds of sentences or can take given roles in noun, prepositional, or other phrases. In short, at some level of abstraction these segments of sentences are instances of "the same thing."

Beyond this level, we can see that the two segments *The boy hit the ball* and *The dressmaker cut out the pattern* are similar to each other in some fashion (active sentences) that neither sentence shares with *The machine was assembled by the man* (a passive sentence). And we also know that the first two sentences can be changed to make them like the third (*The ball was hit by the boy*) and vice versa (*The man assembled the machine*). Thus we can recognize the abstract property of sentence form and that we know ways to convert sentences from one form to another.

This kind of analysis can be extended in either direction. On the one extreme, the units of sound can be regarded as being composed of bundles of distinctive features (voicing, nasality, and so on), and on the other extreme, whole sets of sentences can be systematically interrelated. At this point all we need to establish, however, is that verbal utterances can be divided into segments and that these segments can be regarded as being relevant at different abstract levels. The problem in giving a complete description of language lies in specifying what the levels are, what rules apply at each level, and how the levels and rules interrelate.

Relations among Levels. It is obvious that the levels of language are not independent of one another, yet it is important to note that they are not completely dependent either.

When we spell out a text in the phonemic alphabet, there are special constraints on what combinations can appear at the beginning, middle, or end of a word (for example, no English word starts with /ft/ but this combination can occur in the middle or end of a word). If we did not consider both levels of analysis (morphemic and phonemic) at the same time, we would miss these constraints, or having seen certain statistical regularities, we would fail to see their source. The higher levels are not usually specifically represented in the lower levels. For example, the semantic similarity of *man* and *boy* is not reflected at all in the phonemic level. In general, higher levels constrain and modify events at lower levels in indirect ways. Aside from these specific constraints, however, the lower levels may vary freely according to their own rules. What this combination of dependence and independence means for the psychologist is that attempts to limit the analysis of language to any particular level will encounter phenomena which *cannot* be explained because they are dependent on the ways the levels are related.

As a different example of this limitation, let us try for a moment to construct a sentence-generating machine that tries to build sentences out of words as single units. Imagine a machine that has an initial state (no part of the sentence has been made) and a final state (the sentence is finished). Between these two states the machine has a finite number of intermediate states. This simply means that the machine can be part way through a sentence and confronted with a finite set of choices. When it makes a choice, it finds itself in a new state, usually confronting another set of choices. Once started, the machine proceeds from state to state until it comes to the final one. We can think of the operation of this machine as a network (see Figure 12.11), with each choice represented by a line and each state by a square. As the state of the machine changes, we can think of it as moving from square to square, printing out the word that is on the line it chooses. (Statisticians call such a procedure a Markov process.)

The simplest model would consist of a machine that moved directly from the initial state to the final state and produced a whole sentence each time. Such a machine would have a different pathway for every possible sentence. But that would mean that the machine would have to store all the sentences of English as items in a list, and we have already decided that this approach is impossible. The most convenient model for the psychologist's point of view would be the one described in the probabilistic model above that prints out a single word, then chooses the next word, then the next, and so on, so that the machine would only need to store the probabilities of one word following another. At first blush this looks as though it is on the right track. The trouble is that such a machine produces mostly non-English sentences. This is just the second-order approximation to language that we described above. But if we restrict the machine in certain very severe ways, we can make it give only English sentences. The example in Figure 12.11 will make an indefinitely large number of sentences without making mistakes (A *young boy ran home. A very young boy ran home. A very very young boy* . . . etc.).

Figure 12.11 A Markov process for sentences. Any path through the network will produce an English sentence. Notice that the terms in parentheses cannot be inserted as simple additions to the network.

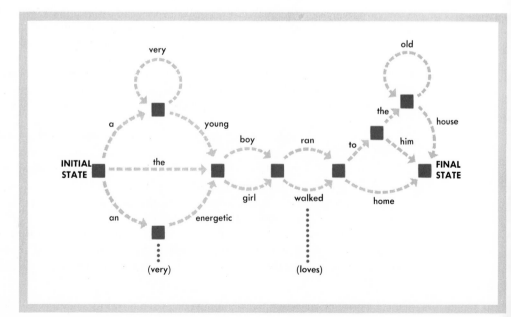

There are many problems with this device, however. Notice that it does not make these particular words generally available. It only makes them available in this specific context. Notice too that it does not let you say, *A very energetic boy* . . . because it has modified the article to *an,* as it must be before a word like *energetic* which begins with a vowel. Thus, although it potentially generates a large number of sentences, the machine is still very limited.

The property that finally breaks down the usefulness of this attack is that it is always limited by being "path dependent." The machine should move from one state to the next state and then find the next move independently of the past moves. This is obviously possible in the particular diagram, which is already a restricted set of paths. If we try to do more work utilizing this network, we can see how really limited it is. We cannot, for instance, make an addition that will permit the sentence, *The girl loves home.* Such a path from *girl* to *home* would also make possible non-English, as in *The girl loves to the old house,* or *The boy loves to him.* It is clear that the particular paths we have chosen have sharp limits that emerge as soon as we try to get the device to do something more for us.

Another way to see the limits of these finite-state models is to try to employ conjunctions such as *and.* If we try to sketch the path for a sequence like *the boy and the girl* it is clear that the path has to include a determination of the noun and the conjunction before it branches to other nouns. We do not want to get a sequence like *the boy and running,* but we will want sequences like *playing and running,* so we must have *and* appear in at least two diagrams, one where the path is limited to nouns and one where it is limited to verb forms. It is apparent that we cannot just take anything that follows *and* and permit it to occur regardless of what preceded it.

But sometimes we do want a sequence like *the boy and running.* Consider: *John is playing with the boy and running through the meadows* or *She saw the boy and, running down the street, she saw his brother.* And, what is worse, we cannot even interchange these two sentences. It does not make a sentence to say, *John is playing with the boy and running down the street she saw his brother* or *She saw the boy and running through the meadows.* If we study the permissible examples, we may decide that the first consists of the fusion of two separate sentences (*John is playing with the boy. John is running through the meadows*) whereas the second may be either of two sets of three sentences. The point is that the use of *and* here depends on a path that has enough of the previous material to guarantee a complete sentence before the use of *and* but that would still permit a specified sentence fragment to follow it. In general, then, the machine must have a single path that corresponds to the longest sentence a speaker will want to coordinate with some other sentence and at the same time it will have to have paths short enough to coordinate any appropriate pair of words that might stand in the "proper" relation to one another. This amounts to demanding an infinite number of paths. But that is exactly what we are trying to avoid.

The dilemmas posed by the problems of the "correct" length of path over which to compute probabilities force us to consider whether it is possible to define the paths and states of such a device in any way that will be generally useful. The answer seems to be that we either list all possible sentences as states (that same old unacceptable solution), settle for an error-filled model as the best one possible right now, or abandon the attempt and decide that the general class of models is inappropriate for language so we must try something else.

Many Levels and Rules. The approach of the linguist is not that of the psychologist, but the linguist's work can describe what the psychologist has to explain. The linguist tells us, for example, that a sentence can be adequately described by giving a list of the rules that would have to be used to generate that sentence if it were produced by a special grammatical machine. In overview, the machine would generate an underlying structure by special rules, called phrase-structure rules, would alter that structure by certain formally specified transformational rules to produce a terminal structure, and then would spell out the terminal string with the proper phonemic rules. Linguists do not assert that this is what a speaker does or that a hearer "unpacks" a sentence by reversing the process in some way. All they assert is that this much machinery is needed to specify what a sentence is and to describe it. If that is so, the argument goes, then the psychological account must be at least as complex, for it must explain as much in the way of segmentation and rule structure.

This argument has sometimes been scorned as leading to absurdities: Explaining how a dog can catch a ball would involve showing that the dog knows how to compute differential equations. The notion occasions merriment on the side of the animal trainers who know that one trains and rewards a dog for the act of ball-catching, one does not try to teach him mathematics. But the argument is met with solemn agreement by the new theorists who say that real understanding of the dog's ability to catch a ball entails precisely such an account because it is exactly what physics tells us the skill requires. It appears that different ends are sought and the antagonists have different goals in mind. "Explanation" to the first group consists of a procedure for getting the animal to perform the act. "Explanation" for the second group consists of understanding how the animal can do the act at all.

ILLUSTRATIVE RESEARCH

Research in the area of grammatical rules is not very well developed but a few instances will serve to indicate directions being pursued.

Some investigators have been working with the perceptual and learning phenomena that may be related to the surface structure of sentences. As mentioned above, it is part of linguistic analysis to specify the segmentation of a given sentence so that it can be represented by a *tree* or by parentheses. The sentence *The plumber dropped the pipe* is depicted in Figure 12.12. The sentence has a major division between the constituents *the plumber* and *dropped the pipe*. The last part itself has two parts, *dropped* and *the pipe*. It is argued that a listener must make such an analysis in order to understand the sentence. If this is so, then it is reasonable for the psychologist to look for some perceptual divisions where the linguistic bracketings occur.

J.A. Fodor and T.G. Bever (1965) set out to investigate this problem by means of a perceptual-displacement effect. If an external noise, like a click, is introduced in a sentence, it is very hard for a person to indicate the point

Figure 12.12 Partial description of a simple sentence.

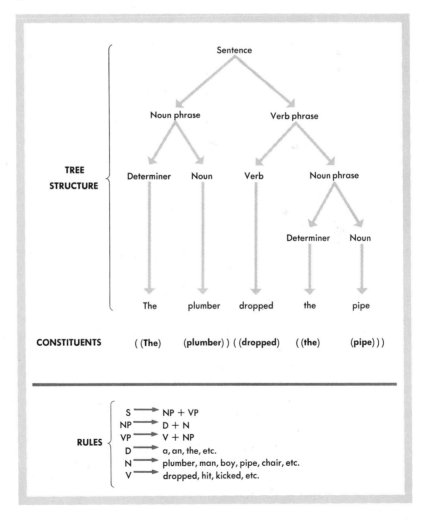

of its occurrence (Ladefoged and Broadbent, 1960). In general, people seem to "hear" the click earlier than it actually occurs. Fodor and Bever reasoned that when the click occurs while a subject is processing a perceptual unit, he "displaces" it. Thus, if you knew where the subject thought the click occurred, you would have some evidence that this was one edge of his perceptual unit. If the perceptual units of speech are the syntactic units, as we might suppose, the subjects should hear the clicks as displaced to the syntactic boundaries, regardless of when they really occur. In the sentence in Figure 12.12 we can predict that a click occurring at the same time as *plumber* will be heard as coming after the word and a click occurring at the same time as *dropped* will be heard as coming before the word. Because *plumber* is part of the larger unit of the noun phrase and *dropped* is part of the larger unit of the verb phrase, any clicks in the vicinity should "migrate" to the major syntactic boundary between these two words. In general, the experimental results confirmed the hypothesis. The majority of the clicks heard wrongly were moved toward the syntactic break or actually into the break.

You might argue that there is a real pause between these constituents and that the perceptual finding is an effect of the pause rather than the grammatical grouping. However, acoustic instruments show that a physical pause is not usually observed at such a point (even if you think you hear one). Of course, one may eliminate a bias due to pauses by using tape recordings of ambiguous constructions like the following sentences:

> His *hope of marrying Anna was unrealistic.*
> In her *hope of marrying Anna was unrealistic.*

The first sentence has a grammatical break between *Anna* and *was;* the second sentence has such a break between *marrying* and *Anna.* If the hypothesis of perceptual structuring is correct, a click sounded over the word *Anna* should be heard in the first case as *following* the word *Anna,* and in the second as *preceding* the word *Anna* even though the italicized sections of the sentences are exactly the same tape recordings spliced onto the other words of the sentences. Again the prediction was confirmd. In each sentence type, the majority of clicks were heard as displaced in the predicted direction.

N.F. Johnson (1965) has used learning experiments in a different kind of demonstration of the psychological reality of linguistic units. His task required subjects to learn complete sentences as responses to a set of numbers. When Johnson noted the places where the subjects broke off in a sentence that they did not fully know or places where they made a mistake, he found that these errors piled up at the major grammatical boundaries. To use our example sentence again, a profile of transitional errors would show a peak between the words *plumber* and *dropped.* Thus, it appears people code and process sentences in the units the linguists have marked for us.

G.A. Miller suggested in 1962 that it would be fruitful to look at behavior involving the transformation of sentences into various related forms. His argument can be paraphrased in this fashion. A simple declarative sentence like *The plumber dropped the pipe* is clearly related to the passive sentence *The pipe was dropped by the plumber*. In the same way, *The plumber didn't drop the pipe* is related to *The pipe wasn't dropped by the plumber*. If we look at these sentences in another way, we can see that the two active versions (*The plumber dropped the pipe. The plumber didn't drop the pipe*) have the same relationship to each other as do the two passives (*The pipe was dropped by the plumber. The pipe wasn't dropped by the plumber.*) These relationships appear to represent the same linguistic variables—the application of passive and negative transformations to some underlying sequence. Now we can ask the behavioral question, that is, whether they represent the same psychological variables. There are a variety of ways of working with this kind of problem. Miller began with a matching task, giving a list of simple declaratives and having the subjects find the appropriate passives in a list as quickly as possible. Then he had subjects match negatives to passives, then declaratives to negatives, and so on, until all possible comparisons had been made. He found that the times required to go from active to passive forms (and vice versa) were about equal and that the times to go from affirmative forms to negative forms were about equal. Importantly, he found that if a person had to make both changes at once (such as going from active to passive *and* from affirmative to negative), the time required was about equal to the sum of the other two times. This result hints at a stepwise addition of transformations that would be one possible model of language processing.

Other studies of language behavior by Miller and his students led to the hypothesis that sentences being memorized are stored in some kind of kernel form with a set of tags for the linguistic transformations to be applied. Thus, if in storage (memory) a person forgets or loses a tag, the hypothesis would be that he would be likely to recall a simpler sentence than the one he is trying to remember. Some evidence tends to support this view (Mehler, 1963), but it is hard to separate this kind of effect from other kinds of response bias and from scoring peculiarities.

C.E. Clifton and P.B. Odom (1966) studied eight kinds of sentences and a variety of tasks (rating similarity of sentences to each other; recalling sentences; and recognizing sentences). They found a common relational structure for the sentences for all of these tasks. The model of the structure is shown in Figure 12.13. In general, it made a great difference if the sentences compared were affirmative or negative and it made a lot of difference if they were active or passive and if they were interrogative or declarative. But there were strong interactions. Within the questions, it made little difference whether the sentences were affirmative or negative (*Was the pipe dropped by the plumber?* and *Wasn't the pipe dropped by the plumber?* seem very much the same). The result corresponds closely to the linguistic analysis of transformations, which holds that negative questions are not "true" negative transformations but just optional forms of regular questions.

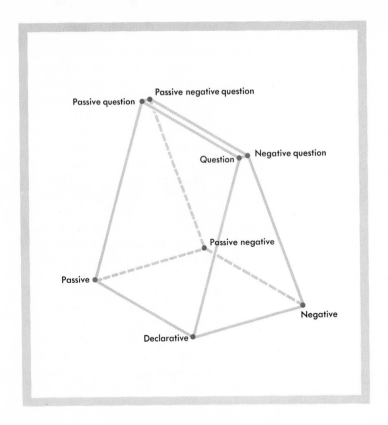

Figure 12.13 Prism representing phrase-structure relationships among sentences. (After Clifton and Odom, 1966.)

The fact that essentially the same pattern emerged from these different psychological tasks (similarity, memory, and recognition) is very encouraging as an indication of regularities of behavior with respect to the linguistic variables.

Other investigators have worked on sentence-comprehension time. P.B. Gough (1965), for one, showed subjects a picture of some action, such as a girl hitting a boy, then gave them a sentence about it to which they were to respond "true" or "false." The sentences might be declarative (*The girl is hitting the boy*), passive (*The boy is being hit by the girl*), negative (*The boy is not hitting the girl*), and negative-passive (*The girl is not being hit by the boy*) in both true and false forms. His findings, given in Table 12.2 are typical of those of other investigators of this problem. In general, active forms are answered more rapidly than passive forms, affirmative forms are answered more rapidly than negative forms, and "true" answers are given more rapidly than "false" answers. The grammatical differences are consonant with the notion that the simple declarative sentence is the simplest to process and that additional transformations take longer to interpret.

	Affirmative		Negative	
	True	False	True	False
Active	.92	1.06	1.30	1.28
Passive	1.01	1.20	1.35	1.36

Table 12.2 Mean verification time (in seconds) as a function of sentence-type and truth value. (Data from Gough, 1965.)

ACQUISITION

Little is known about the acquisition of the rules of language. Given the rate at which language is acquired and the flexibility of a child in his awesome ability to learn any human language readily, it is conjectured that the child has some powerful innate mechanisms that determine his choice of behavioral rules when he is exposed to language. There is little evidence that a child is carefully tutored or "shaped," as psychologists have sometimes hypothesized. Indeed, D. McNeill (1966) presents an example (taken from a tape recording of an actual exchange) that humorously taunts the whole notion:

> Child: Nobody don't like me.
> Mother: No, say "nobody likes me."
> Child: Nobody don't like me.
> "
> "
> "
> (eight repetitions of this dialog)
> "
> "
> "
> Mother: No, now listen carefully; say *"nobody likes me."*
> Child: Oh! Nobody don't likes me.

What *is* apparent and well-documented is that a child is very systematic in his approach to language. He may move from one system to another, testing, changing, testing, trying again, or he may choose one system and progressively differentiate it into finer and finer portions, but the evidence that he is doing something systematic is overwhelming. The kind of thinking presented in the examples under the mediation explanation (pp. 449–453) can be appealed to here. More broadly, however, there is evidence that the child is struggling with a system for producing and comprehending language at every stage and in very complex ways.

There seems to be agreement from several sources that the first "grammars" of children are "pivot-open" grammars as described by M.D.S. Braine (1963), W. Miller and S. Ervin (1964), and R.W. Brown and C. Frazer (1964). A child seems to develop two classes of words—*pivots* (P), which are widely applied to many situations and objects (examples are words like *fix, where, that, here, see*), and an *open* (O) class of things, events, and actions that the pivots may be applied to. Membership in the open class expands rapidly (hence the name) while the pivots seem to be a limited set. For a given child, utterances may consist of P + O, O alone, or O + O. If a new word comes into his lexicon, he may readily use it with several P class members. It is not known whether this is a necessary stage for the development of a child's language or even if every child goes through some such stage. In either event, the complexity of a child's language grows rapidly and a variety of complex language behaviors are observed that we are not sure how to describe, much less account for.

An interesting example of sweeping change is provided by Susan Ervin's (1964) longitudinal study of the language development of a few children. She got tape recordings on a weekly basis and tested the children frequently. In these records Ervin found a rather startling demonstration of the child's systematic approach to language: The first verbs that children ordinarily acquire tend to be irregular verbs. They usually learn these correctly in several tenses, for example, *take-took, run-ran, come-came*. When the regular verbs begin to appear, the child almost immediately regularizes the irregular verbs. Even though he had them right and practiced them many times, he now begins to produce errors (which, we must note, he has neither heard nor been reinforced for). Now we find *take-taked, run-runned, come-comed*, and so on. Clearly, in this case the language system the child is developing overcomes the concrete examples and the practice. Later, the child has to relearn the irregularity he once knew.

Other researchers who have looked at language acquisition of older children see evidence of systematic development in the more complicated levels of syntax. Ursula Bellugi (1967), for example, has conducted a very careful study of the development of negation in three children who were studied longitudinally over a major part of their language development. She found good evidence for "stages" of development in their abilities to employ the full range of negations in English. The stages can be roughly characterized as follows:

> Period A: Children attach a negative element to a sentence nucleus.
>   No a flag, No the sun shining, No go back.
> Period B: The negative element is now positioned internally in the sentence and has several forms like *no, not, don't, can't*.

I don't see top to that, He can't go, Don't want me pull it? Why not he take bath? Why we didn't?

Period C: Auxiliary verbs appear along with their transformational rules; number and tense agreement are problems to be worked out.

Mommy, they not wet, The sun is not too bright, It's not big enough, That not go in here, I don't like some, You don't want some supper, Why I can't put them on?

Later periods are much less clear; in Bellugi's view they have to do with problems of special rules in English, since the children seem to have mastered the fundamentals of negation. Persistent problems concern certain verb forms which are irregular or permit optional treatment of the negative. For example, *I think he isn't going* and the form *I don't think he's going*. The children construct the first form but not the second. A second problem has to do with indefinite terms (*some, none, any, somebody, nobody, anybody*); here, the children fail to recognize restrictions on the amount of negation permitted (*I can't do nothing with no string, You're not gonna have no friends, Nobody won't recognize us.*). A third problem has to do with tag sentences that are usually appended to sentences to ask negative questions. Presumably the difficulty here pivots on the rules of agreement that govern such tags. Children's errors suggest that they have the general form but not quite the right rules; *You are a poor lady, weren't you? You 'posed to cut out the lines, don't you? I have a lot of Ursula's toys, don't we?*

Through these developments, Bellugi sees the constant organization and reorganization of the child's rule structures, each change making some constructions possible but creating errors in other places where the rules are not sufficient. A new mastery in one area (such as auxiliary verbs) creates new problems in another area (where and how to create a negative with auxiliaries). Mastering the declarative-negative still leaves the problem of the question-negative to be solved, and the errors in word order show the child struggling with the two sets of transformations at the same time, with only partial success.

The important thing about studies like Bellugi's is that they show consistent parallels from one child to another. This consistency argues that there is a ground plan for the development of rule structures for us to study. It may even suggest that there is a universal plan that transcends the particular language being learned. That suggestion is not supportable at the present time, but there are hints in the study of Russian and Japanese children that there may be impressive constancies when we know how to analyze them (see Slobin, 1966).

To date, the current study of the psychology of language seems to be producing interesting fresh examinations of language acquisition by suggesting that "what-is-learned" is a quite different thing from what the proponents of simpler models of language ever considered. Psychologists are now thinking about new mechanisms to explain complex learnings.

The approach to language as a rule system has little to say about individual differences for two reasons: first, because the approach is relatively new, and second, because the approach is directed toward the understanding of the basic mechanisms of language which must be nearly universal rather than differentially distributed. However, we can ask a general question about where individual differences can fit into such an approach. The answer is twofold. First, there are undoubtedly differences in the rate of language development and the extent of some aspects of it (such as vocabulary), even though all normal human beings do learn language. Bellugi's work, mentioned above, furnishes an example. One of her children was through the third stage in the use of negatives at 26 months of age whereas others were still in the first stage up through 30 months. Second, it seems reasonable to suppose that there may be some capacity limits to language mechanisms—for example, limits on the number of applications of some of the rules that the new view of language deals with. An illustration is afforded by a phenomenon called center embedding, which can be explained as follows. English syntax permits us to say several things in a sentence at one time and gives us several devices for it. We might say either of the following:

> This is the rat that stole the cheese.
> This is the cheese that the rat stole.

These forms are about equally intelligible, but if we continue in this fashion, one form rapidly becomes more difficult:

> This is the cat that killed the rat that stole the cheese.
> This is the cheese that the rat that the cat killed, stole.

Still worse:

> This is the dog that worried the cat that killed the rat
> that stole the cheese.
> This is the cheese that the rat that the cat that the dog
> worried, killed, stole.

The first form is called right branching. In effect it disposes of each subject in turn and goes on to explain the next. The second form is called center embedding. To find out what happened to a particular subject, we must hold on all the way through the sentence and then sort out all the verbs in inverse order to the subjects. Almost everybody readily understands a single center embedding and almost no one notices it. But with two or three center embeddings, the comprehensibility of the sentence seems to disappear. Research work by W. Stolz (1966) suggests that there are large individual differences in the ability of subjects to process such sentences correctly, as if specific memory capacities, or place-keeping skills, vary widely.

SUMMARY

Psychologists have concentrated on four approaches to language, viewing it as words, strings of words, utterances, or as a structural system.

Language as words has led to studies of word counts. Zipf's Law states that the rank of a word times its frequency is a constant ($r \times f = c$). Some of his subsidiary findings are: Frequent words tend to be short; rare words tend to be long. Frequent words have more meanings than infrequent words. Highly frequent words are more readily seen and are more readily heard in noise than infrequent words. They are also easier to learn and remember.

This view holds that language is learned by conditioning responses to objects to the presence of appropriate words as stimuli. Sometimes a circular reflex is invoked and it is held that the child echoes a word on hearing it and so learns when to say it. Emotional words acquire their feeling tone by being experienced in situations in which the emotions are activated by events or other people.

People differ widely in word knowledge or vocabulary. In those who are associated with schools or verbal professions, vocabulary increases throughout the life span (unlike almost all other traits). Generally, women are more verbal than men at all age levels in all societies.

Language as strings of words or classes focuses attention on word order. Demonstrations reveal that a context of words or letters exercises powerful constraints on what you can choose to fill in a blank. Generally, the more things that would be possible, the higher the *information* any particular word or letter is said to convey. Consonants carry more information than vowels; unlikely words carry more information than common or expected words. A context in which a word is expected or common makes it easy to see or hear the word if it does occur. The more probable it is, the easier it is to perceive it.

A complementary view holds that language is structured by events in the world and that our associations to words reflect our experience with the world. Thus, word associations are seen as basic in language. Word associations have been studied for over 100 years and are used in both laboratory and clinical studies. Associated words are easy to learn, tend to be recalled together, are easy to see or hear in each other's presence, and mediate the transfer of verbal learning and conditioned responses. Even chains of associates (*A-B-C*) are known to influence learning and transfer. It is assumed that word associations arise partly through experience with the world and partly through experience with language itself. Children give associations that are sequential in language usage, but as they grow older they shift to associations that can fill the same linguistic position in a sentence. Mediated learning can be used to explain this shift and then associations can be used to explain further mediated learning. Children acquire general meanings for words from both situations and sentences. As they grow older, they learn to use grammatical cues to know what to look for in the environment when they hear a new term. Maturity in grammatical use mirrors increasing maturity in type of word association.

Language viewed as utterances is the recommendation of B.F. Skinner. He holds that the two major classes of language behavior are *mands* and *tacts;* the first consists of utterances calculated to earn reinforcements for the speaker, the second consists of information statements that presumably reinforce listeners. Language behavior is considered as a special case of operant conditioning or instrumental learning in which reinforcement depends on other people. Understanding such behavior is viewed as accounting for its occurrence in terms of the past history and present circumstances of the speaker.

Acquisition of language is seen as a process of shaping behavior by reinforcements. Of special importance are generalized reinforcers, such as social approval, smiling, and thanks, that do not depend on specific needs of the hearer for their effects. It appears that awareness and other variables such as attitudes and intentions play important roles in determining the effectiveness of such reinforcers.

Language as a rule system is a relatively new view that borrows its description of language from the linguist. This approach to language stresses its rule-governed nature and tries to relate psychological effects to units of analysis and types of rules isolated by current linguistic efforts. Simple models of language production are discarded in favor of more complex hierarchical models. Experimental research has concerned itself with showing that linguistic units do function as psychological units in perception and memory, and that sentences are systematically related to each other in terms of similarity, recall, and recognition as grammatical transformations suggest they might be.

Studies of the development of language in children show the rapid growth of systematic behavior, as if the child were mastering a set of rules for producing more and more complex sentences. Little effect of deliberate tuition has been found but systematic sequences of stages of language behavior seem to be revealed by careful study of children's utterances.

SUGGESTED READINGS

Brown, R. *Words and things.* New York: Macmillan (Free Press), 1958.

Carroll, J.B. *Language and thought.* Englewood Cliffs, N.J.: Prentice-Hall, 1964.

Cherry, C. *On human communication.* Cambridge, Mass.: M.I.T. Press, 1957.

Chomsky, N. Review of Skinner's "Verbal Behavior." *Language*, 1959, 35, 26–58.

Lenneberg, E.H. *New directions in the study of language.* Cambridge, Mass.: M.I.T. Press, 1964.

Miller, G.A. *Language and communication.* New York: McGraw-Hill, 1951.

Thinking

C H A P T E R   T H I R T E E N   All of us would like real knowledge about thinking. This activity seems so important, so powerful, and so characteristic of man that it should unlock the nature of humanity. But by now you are prepared for frustration. If the psychologist cannot handle learning in a consistent way and fails to decide on a single model for such specialized activity as language, it is a foregone conclusion that the treatment of thinking is going to be even more difficult. In this chapter we will look at three models of thinking. They are variations of positions that you have already studied so you will recognize them as old friends. For each model we will give an instance of a classical experiment that will help you characterize the position and will make clear its typical claims. You will see that what a theory can account for is influential in determining what kinds of experiments its supporters conduct. These differences between the theories rarely come into direct conflict because the theories are seen as relevant to different sorts of situations. A general theory applicable to all kinds of thinking has not yet appeared, though there are some suggestions about what such a theory might be like.

Of all the traditional topics in psychology, *thinking* is probably the most common focus of dispute. Although psychologists have often disparaged colleagues' concern with psychophysics on the one extreme or clinical psychology on the other, they have rarely held that the pursuits are impossible or illegitimate. But the study of *thinking*, still trailing misty streamers of the mind and the soul, has frequently received both criticisms. Its investigation has been held to be impossible, its substance to be beyond the scope of science, and at times its very existence has been denied. In one historical period, the study of *thinking* may be as respectable as the study of sensation, but in another, it may be classed with spiritualism and extrasensory perception as beneath the notice of "respectable" scientists.

Some philosophers, most notably Kant, held that the dimensions and patterns of thought are given *a priori* in the nature of man. Others held that thought, like action, develops in commerce with the events of the world. Of late, Jean Piaget has argued (as we will see in Chapter Fourteen on intelligence) that both views are partly correct, that a child brings certain concepts to the world and that maturation and experience lead to a progressive complication, coordination, and extension of the powers of thought and analysis.

Caught in the midst of both conceptual and methodological battles, the study of thinking reflects in its history the difficulties involved in the study of all of the higher mental processes. These processes are not available for study in any direct way but are always inferred from observations of complex relations between the particular situation of the organism and the particular response he makes. If we could get along with just specifying individual stimuli and individual responses and straightforward laws that connect them, we would have no need to postulate the higher mental processes. Problems arise when we are confronted with behavior that is not explained by a known stimulus-response connection but rather seems to imply some connecting series of events or processes within the organism. The knowledge that these "events" and "processes" are implicit and invisible may not cheer us in our analysis of thinking, but it does not excuse us from the task if our goal is the complete understanding of human psychology.

Roots of Current Positions

Wilhelm Wundt held that thinking could not be studied experimentally. He felt, however, that one could gain some understanding of thought by examining the products of society. As we saw in Chapter Twelve, he believed that the study of language was particularly important and argued that generalized thought processes were revealed through the development and change of languages. Since experimental psychology concerned itself with elements of consciousness and the connections between those elements, it was clear that without identifying the elements of thinking (which he thought was impossible), there could be no experimental psychology of thought.

After Ebbinghaus brought memory into the laboratory, researchers began to get more venturesome and tried to include *thinking* in their studies. Psychologists at the University of Würzburg, however, reported that they obtained little data about thinking when they examined it by traditional introspective techniques. Their subjects (who were other highly trained psychologists) tried to tell them about the contents of their consciousness, but the experimenters could find no clue to what took place during the mental operation itself. In judging weights, describing feelings, or giving word associations, the subjects reported images and sensations, but none of them were closely involved with the acts of thinking that presumably were required by the tasks. In many cases, the Würzburgers noted, the images and sensations *followed* the acts in which they were supposed to be involved! As far as the subjects could report, answers to problems set by the experimenter just appeared in consciousness without intervening states of consciousness. If a subject was asked to give the opposite of a word like *father,* the response word *mother* simply came to mind. There was nothing in consciousness to report during the brief interval between hearing the stimulus word and uttering the response word. It was as if the subject had done all the thinking before he even knew what the stimulus word was. The Würzburg psychologists argued that psychology needed to turn its attention to "sets," "attitudes," and "determining tendencies." They believed that a psychology of thought needed not only elements but functions of some sort. But the problems of doing experiments on "functions" and "mental acts" defeated them in the end. They called attention to thoughts without images, but they never succeeded in sustaining a new school of experimentation on the elusive thoughts themselves.

The Gestalt psychologists in their turn argued that neither sensory content nor an operation on sensory elements (such as attending and perceiving) provides the right analysis for higher mental processes. What is experienced is *form* in itself, independent of its elementary sensations. Thus, one perceives a circle directly whether it is made up of dots, dashes, or X's, and one perceives a melody directly as form over time without regard to the particular notes involved. Similarly, in a problem-solving situation, a person might directly apprehend relations or he might have "insight" into a particular problem without having particular experience with individual stimuli. The laws that we mentioned in Chapter Eleven in discussing dynamic models of remembering may be regarded as general (and vague) descriptions that also have importance in the Gestalt approach to thinking.

A markedly different approach to mental activity grew up in the psychological clinic. Sigmund Freud was especially important in stressing the extent to which complex mental processes are unconsciously motivated and controlled. He believed that reasoning, thinking, and dreaming are all similar in nature though differing in the degree of "control" exercised by the situation and by the person himself. Freud also directed attention to the symbolic functions of the higher mental processes through which a clock might stand for a woman, a rifle for a man, and a complex event for a person-to-person relationship.

American psychology contributed only narrowly to research on higher mental processes. The advent of Behaviorism constrained the research in two ways. On the one hand, radical behaviorism declared thinking to be "out of bounds" to respectable academic psychologists as a nonscientific pursuit. On the other hand, thinking was explained away as being merely covert responding—normal, ordinary muscular behavior going on at such a reduced level as to be invisible or nearly so. Watson said that more elaborate thinking was just subvocal speech and speech was just muscle movement. He went on to obscure that pronouncement by saying that *any* muscle movement might come to "stand for" any speech utterance with which it had occurred through conditioning. Although this approach stimulated some interesting work in the measurement of muscle movements and a real attempt to clarify implicit responding, in the main it produced little work in the way of cognitive experiments.

An exciting new view of thinking, and of behavior generally, has recently developed outside the mainstream of theoretical psychology. This development, which we will call the *information-processing approach*, has grown up around the programing of the digital computer. It owes its existence to the invention of the computer and to the related development of appropriate mathematics, languages, and programs.

It is common knowledge that thinkers are often inspired by the technology of their times. Descartes thought that men could be viewed as machines (like the clockwork devices with which he was acquainted) except when the soul intervened in its mysterious manner. Thorndike and Watson were impressed with the telephone switchboard and found it a ready analog for their associationism or connectionism. Self-governing machines, like Watt's steam engine that controlled its own speed or the lowly thermostat that controls its own temperature, led to servomechanistic and homeostatic views in biology and psychology. So, too, the computer, with the obvious ability to accept various information, digest and transform it, and act in complex ways with regard to it, furnishes a tempting model to the theorist of the current day.

The computer, of course, is neutral with respect to any theory. It does exactly what it is told to do. What can be done, however, is to take a very complex theory about a task or a problem and program the theory so that the machine behaves exactly the way an organism would behave if this theory held for it. Thus, the computer *simulates* an organism behaving in any situation that the investigator wishes to specify. The investigator must specify exactly what information the computer can accept from the world, when and how it accepts it, what the computer does with the information, what behaviors the computer can perform, what the relation is between the states of information and the behaviors selected, and so on. One of the great virtues of the computer is that it demands every step to be specified exactly; a theorist cannot slide off a difficult problem by appealing to common sense or suggesting that "everybody knows" what happens at some point. The computer, of course, does not know anything and its common sense cannot be appealed to; it can only proceed on specific directions.

Once a program has been prepared, a researcher can compare the "behavior" of the computer with that of a real organism that faces the same problems. To the extent that the computer does the same things the organism does, the computer program is a theory of the behavior. Most psychologists are now agreed that one criterion of understanding or explaining a piece of behavior is the ability to create a computer program that adequately simulates that behavior.

In experimental psychology today, there are three active points of view about thinking: the associative approach, the wholistic approach, and the approach through information-processing. Before developing these models of thinking, we will first illustrate some of the phenomena that lead to the postulation of "thinking" in the first place.

Evidence for Higher Mental Processes

The presence of "something more" beyond simple stimulus-response connections is most readily detected in puzzles and problem-solving situations. If the tasks are easy, the whole process may appear automatic. "Give me the name of an animal that starts with B." Almost before the question is asked, the answer is ready. The subject blurts out *bear* (or *buffalo, bull, badger, bison,* or the like). It is not easy to say what has happened but the problem is solved. Somehow the subject comes up with the answer even if he has never been asked that question before. We can slow the process down by asking a harder question, "Give me the name of an animal that starts with V." Now the subject has no ready reply. He seems to be searching in a variety of ways. He does funny things with his mouth. He stares into space. He looks about the room. After some time he may come up with an answer. What he has done in the interval presumably is some kind of thinking.

A memory expert stands on the stage accepting words as they are shouted out from the audience. He now recites them (perhaps a list of several hundred) forward, backward, every third one, and so on. The repetition we might call memory, but the rearrangement and reclassification must be some aspect of thinking.

A student is given six matches and told to make four identical equilateral triangles out of some arrangement of the matches. He mumbles, fiddles with the matches, crosses them, screws up his face, stares at the table, says it can't be done, and then, suddenly, he puts the matches into the one correct three-dimensional arrangement that solves the problem and produces the desired triangles. Clearly, this is thinking too.

A physicist *generates* a new equation for a particular task; a student *calculates* the answer to an arithmetic problem; an inventor *designs* a new gear that will do something special for him; a little boy *figures out* a way to get to the cookie jar; a girl *plans* to drop her notebook just before she passes the football hero; an old man rocks in the sun and *dreams* of his youth. All these are instances of thinking and all of them pose problems for the psychologist.

The Associative View of Thinking

The oldest theory of cognition is that thinking consists of running off associations both overtly and covertly in the search for solutions to problems or in response to other motivating forces. Somewhat surprisingly, adherents to this broadly stated view include both the traditional associationists and the dynamic psychologists such as the psychoanalysts. Although these two groups disagree markedly about the wellsprings of behavior and place very different emphases on motivating variables, they are alike in accepting an associative basis for thought and other cognitive activities such as dreams, fantasy, literature, and artistic creation. They also differ with respect to the sources of symbolization (the dynamic psychologists stress the innate nature of many symbols), and with respect to the degree of automatic functioning of associations. But they are similar in accepting associative chains and networks to map the structural mechanisms supposedly involved in thought.

The associationist holds that mental events are responses to some form of stimulation. The mental events are linked together as a result of experience. The thought of one item serves as a stimulus to elicit another item, that item in turn leads to another, and that to still another, and so on. Thought thus moves in linear fashion along chains of associations. In literature we speak of the *stream of consciousness* to describe writing with such characteristics.

Aristotle said that experience produced associations through *contiguity* of events, *similarity* of events, or *contrast* of events. Later philosophers either added new refinements or tried to reduce the number of notions that the theory required, but they held to the general form of the theory. The British associationists of association down to one: contiguity. They argued , and any other particular class of association could be contiguity when it was needed.

Modern associationism introduced a little more biology and a great deal more observation into the picture but kept the fundamentals essentially the same. Pavlov was clearly in the camp of the associationists with his laws of conditioning. He provided support for their arguments by showing that new associations could be created merely by the contiguity of a signal and the stimulus that triggered the reflex. The American learning theorists added more underpinning by demonstrating the importance of the contiguity of responses to their rewards and punishments. Thus, contiguity of stimuli and reactions to them as well as contiguity of acts and their consequences could be viewed as part of the associative scheme. The next task was to broaden the application of these simple mechanisms in order to explain behaviors that appeared to reflect *knowledge* of the world and *planning* to take advantage of that knowledge. The association psychologist had faith that by elaborating his simple principle of contiguity, he could account for all thinking, problem-solving, and invention.

A typical representation of the association approach to problem-solving is E.L. Thorndike's classic experiment with the cat in the puzzle box. As you will recall from Chapter Ten, the boxes demanded rather unusual behavior (for a cat), such as pulling a string or stepping on a pedal to be released. The cats, of course, had no way to know what was required either in advance or in the situation itself because the mechanism was not visible to them even if they could have understood it. Thorndike (1911) reported that cats try to squeeze out through any opening, claw and bite at the bars and the wire, thrust their paws out the slats, and in general struggle vigorously. Each cat escapes accidentally in the course of this behavior. The next time in the box it may concentrate its efforts more around the part of the box where it was the last time when it escaped. Over many trials, inappropriate responses (biting and clawing randomly) drop out and only the necessary response remains.

This view of problem-solving contains two important elements. First, it is assumed that the animal has a repertoire of responses available in the situation. In more formal terms it has a set of habits that are already related to the stimuli that are present. This is called a *habit-family hierarchy*. The cat runs these habits off in some order depending on how strong they are. When some response is successful, the second principle comes into play: the Law of Effect. The last responses before the escape are assumed to be strengthened and the others are either weakened (partially extinguished) or at least are not strengthened. Thus, over many trials, the cat comes to select the best response and escapes readily when it is returned to the situation.

This is the general associative picture of thinking or problem-solving. The subject makes responses determined by his past experience, no matter how remote. When one of these works or brings him closer to solution of his problem, it is strengthened relative to other responses. Thus, behavior changes to cope with the new situation and new behavior patterns result.

You may very well object that thinking does not at all resemble the cat's behavior in the puzzle box. Your notion of a man thinking does not entail his running here and there, trying first this thing and then that. But the associationist is not disturbed. The next step in his explanation is designed to answer this kind of objection. He now adds the assumption that human beings and, perhaps, other highly developed animals, can respond *covertly*, that is, without the response being obvious to the casual observer. Yet the response may be strong enough to furnish new stimuli to the organism. The commonplace example is subvocal speech. All of us know that we can "talk to ourselves" without the outside world being aware of it. And we all know that such speech may furnish cues for what we do next; that is, we may "suggest" courses of action to ourselves, "hit upon" an idea, "think" of an appropriate thing to say or do, and so on. Similarly, you may look at a puzzle and find yourself responding to it imperceptibly, imagining that you are trying a certain move or jiggling this piece in that place. This imagining and trying may be accomplished by muscle movements on a very reduced scale. These little movements may serve as stimuli to lead you to the normal consequences of such movements. If the outcome associated with your implicit movement is the one desired, the problem is solved. You "go ahead" and perform the act, thus solving the problem. If the associated outcome does not appear to solve the problem, you do not perform the act but make some further response, either to the new stimulus you have given yourself or to the original stimuli of the problem, making other responses now that the first one is weaker.

The clearest evidence for trial-and-error behavior in human beings is probably seen with difficult mechanical puzzles such as *the-heart-and-the-bow* puzzle in Figure 13.1. Many people try to figure out the puzzle by making implicit responses and testing the presumed consequences. If they have had previous experience with this class of puzzle, they may succeed after a little time. If they fail, however, they must resort to overt, random movements of the pieces. Typically, they will finally stumble on a solution, not even knowing, perhaps, how they succeeded. Over the next few trials, they concentrate their efforts more and more in the correct location and with the right movements until the solution is rapid and the subject can even explain how the problem is solved.

The view of thinking as implicit trial and error working through a variety of implicit responses and their implicit stimuli was developed by the learning theorists in elaborate detail. Clark Hull published a series of papers in the 1930s that deals with these intervening responses and their production of stimuli, showing how they might account for knowledge, purpose, and the goal-directed quality of behavior. Two of his colleagues, Neal Miller and John Dollard (1941), expanded this general approach to account for social learning and imitation in human beings. An example of a hypothetical account is given in Figure 13.2.

Because behaviorism made so strong a case for observation and "hard" data, many experimenters were quite uncomfortable with the extensive use that theorists were making of unseen responses. The growth of such theorizing was thus responsible for many attempts to see if the assumed implicit

Figure 13.1 A mechanical puzzle, the heart and bow, used to study trial-and-error problem-solving. The problem is to separate the heart from the bow. The first trial usually takes a long time and the subject may not even know how he solved it. Then with further trials he concentrates on the part of the bow with the diamond shape and on the tongue portion of the heart. After a few trials the subject can verbalize that he is running the tongue of the heart through the loop and out around the end of the diamond. His solution time then falls to a few seconds, though at the beginning it might have been five or ten minutes. (Ruger, 1910.)

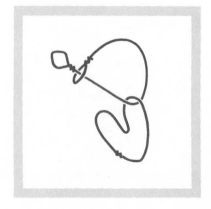

Figure 13.2 Social learning using implicit responses. (A) The word "No" is followed by scolding or punishment; subsequently "No" stops the child's activity and produces escape behavior. (B) The child learns that pulling on the drapes is followed by the stimulus "No." (C) The child approaches the drapes. The stimulus of the drapes elicits in the child the associated response "No" (learned in B). "No" is now a stimulus the child has given himself. In response (as he learned in A), he turns away from the drapes.

responses could be detected by special instruments. A number of studies were conducted to see if the minimal muscle movements could be found in the right places and at the right times to account for thinking in the way that had been hypothesized.

The most famous of these studies were those of E. Jacobson (1932) and L.W. Max (1935, 1937). Jacobson taught his subjects to relax as completely as possible. In this resting state he measured the tiny electric currents present in their muscles. Following this, he suggested some mental activity to his subjects such as, "Imagine that you are lifting a heavy suitcase in your right hand." He then observed the electrical activity of the muscles of the right arm as compared to the left arm. He discovered that appropriate muscular activity frequently accompanied the suggested mental activity and ceased when the subjects were told to stop thinking and relax again. Similarly, he found that the muscles around the eye became active when the subjects were told to think of visual images of various sorts.

Max took the case further by measuring the muscle activity in the forearms of deaf mutes when they were given problems to solve. (His subjects normally used finger spelling and sign language.) He found that significant muscular activity accompanied reports of problem-solving, imagining, and thinking about conversations. In addition, he studied his subjects while they slept and found evidence that such forearm activity was closely associated with dreaming in the deaf subjects, though not normal subjects.

In spite of the encouraging nature of these research efforts, the peripheral theory of thought that led investigators to search for covert responding as the locus and source of thought has declined in interest and importance. Much ambiguity has been found in the studies. Perhaps a subject who *visualizes* himself lifting a suitcase cannot be expected to show muscle potentials in the arm; perhaps he should show them around the eye. The subject who imagines himself speaking may show activity of the vocal chords, lips, and tongue; but what if he imagines that he is hearing his own voice? In other words, it is not clear that there could really be negative evidence for the theory. Further, no one has been able to show that muscular activity is *necessary* to thinking and few psychologists now hold that the peripheral muscle system must be involved in any measurable way in thinking. At present, it is thought likely that muscle movements may accompany thinking when it is especially effortful, but muscle movement is rarely held to be essential to thinking.

The more general question is whether the conceptualization of implicit responding and implicit stimulation is a reasonable way to describe thinking. This question can be asked without commiting oneself to the additional question of whether the response and the stimulus are central or peripheral in nature. It amounts to asking whether the general scheme is adequate to account for the phenomena we observe when we study thinking. We will ask this question immediately below.

Like any other group, the associationists have chosen certain preferred problems in the area of thinking. They have dealt chiefly with concept-formation, problem-solving, meaning, and originality. In each of these areas we shall see that they have had some success although the conceptions employed appear to be severely limited.

Concept-formation has been a favorite topic for the associative theorists for many years. A concept is not taken to be an idea or an abstraction, however. It is usually defined in terms of classification of objects or symbols into arbitrary groupings. The simplest instance of concept-formation occurs when all the stimuli to be classified together share some stimulus element. The subject's task is to discover the critical element so that he may respond correctly not only to all of the specific stimuli he is being trained on, but also to new examples of the concept when they are presented in test trials.

The classic example is Hull's study (1920) using Chinese characters as stimuli. As the examples in Figure 13.3 indicate, the subjects had to learn to give a particular nonsense syllable to a set of characters. Chinese characters contain certain elements called *radicals*; unknown to the subject, a par-

Figure 13.3 Six of the Chinese radicals used by Hull in a concept-formation experiment, with their assigned nonsense names and some characters containing each radical. (Hull, 1920.)

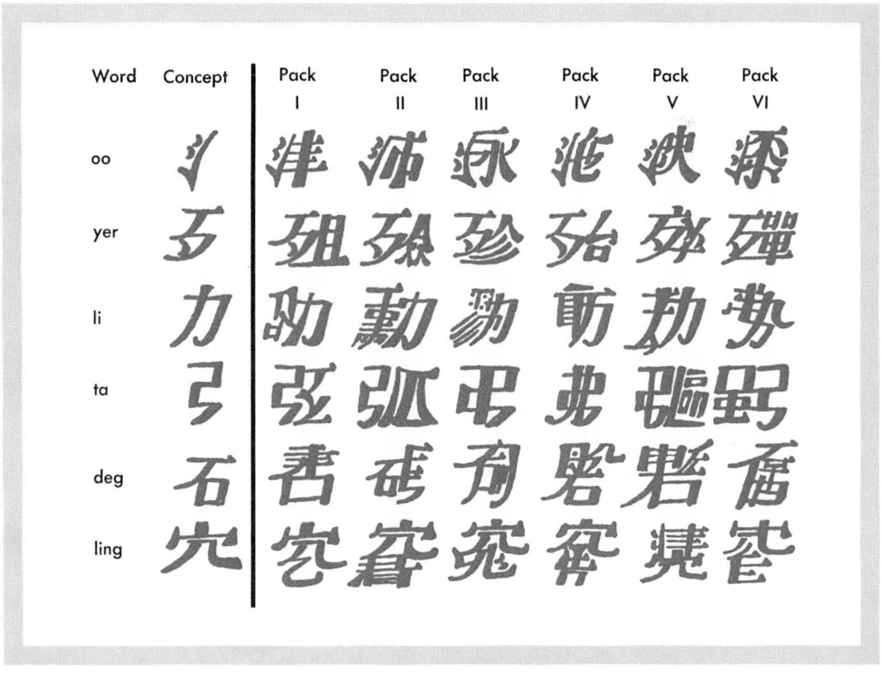

ticular radical appeared in every complex character that was called by a particular name. The subjects learned one list of stimuli and responses involving 12 different names, then a second list using the same names, then a third list and so on until six lists had been learned. The extent to which subjects could guess correct responses and showed positive transfer from list to list were measures of their concept learning. The subjects gained increasing mastery of the concepts (that is, they began responding to the common element) as they learned more lists and were able to guess which of the nonsense syllables went with the new characters for more than half the items when they first saw the sixth list.

The explanation by the association theorist is that the particular radical involved in each concept became a discriminated stimulus for the particular verbal response just as a red light becomes a discriminative stimulus for bar-pressing (as we saw in our discussion of instrumental learning). Thus, a nonsense-syllable term becomes the name for a particular stimulus configuration even if the subject cannot describe in detail the particular radical to which he is responding. No awareness or insight is required. Simple learning procedures that bring the common element of the stimulus into contiguity with the proper response are believed to be sufficient to achieve automatic association.

The formation of such concepts in animals has been shown with stimuli involving colors, forms, and designs. A convenient form of experiment with human beings involves the use of card-sorting. Such tasks may be readily arranged to be as complex as one likes. Classes of stimuli may include number, color, form, design, texture, borders, and so on, and the concepts may involve any of these stimuli singly or in combination. The subject's task is ordinarily to discover some correct class in the midst of all the variation or to find the rules that relate particular stimuli in the correct combinations.

A second kind of concept-formation seems to involve somewhat more complex thinking. Typically, subjects are given pictures of familiar objects and asked to sort them into the correct classes. The experimenter usually tells a subject whether his sorting of each picture is right or wrong. Correct sorting may be based on how the objects are used, the function they perform, the names they are called, and the like. In this kind of task there is often no observable physical aspect that is shared; for example, all the pictured objects in one class may be known to taste bitter, or they may all be used to move dirt, or they may all have names that start with the same letter. In this case, without earlier experience with the objects (having tasted them, or used them, or known their names), it would be difficult to learn to respond correctly to the original stimuli, and transfer to new instances when they appeared in the test trials would be impossible.

The learning of these concepts more clearly belongs in the realm of thinking. It also fits nicely with the notion of implicit responses serving as stimuli. Presumably, a subject makes a variety of implicit responses to each item until he finds the response that belongs to all members of that particular class. This process is easily represented in associations. A stimulus appears and the subject makes many responses to it that have been associated with the stimulus in past experience. He makes a particular overt response such as putting the card in a particular place or calling it a particular name. This response then attaches to all of the associations that he made covertly (through mere contiguity). When the next instance of the class comes up, only a few of the implicit responses will overlap with those of the first stimulus and so these responses will begin to get stronger as implicit responses than other nonoverlapping implicit responses. Finally, since only the correct implicit response is consistently present with the correct label or sorting response, it will come to be the strongest of all the implicit responses. In turn, its connection to the naming or sorting responses will be strongest and it will therefore mediate the correct concept-identification response.

It is easy to see how rapidly this process converges on a few possible implicit responses. If you are told that *sugar* belongs in Class I, you do not know whether the class will consist of white objects, granular substances, solubles, things that taste sweet, objects found in kitchens, or what. If you then learn that *syrup* and *lollipops* belong in Class I you are almost immediately down to one reasonable possibility, and when *ice cream* appears, you sort it as Class I as well.

A third kind of concept that has been studied is more difficult to describe and to handle theoretically. The constancy that is central to the concept is neither in the particular stimulus objects nor in the implicit responses that one has learned to make to the particular objects. Usually such a concept concerns *relations* between stimuli or some aspects of the stimuli. A common example is found in the *oddity problem*. Subjects can learn to respond to the odd item in a set of items where the only defining property of the correct stimulus is that it is different from the other stimuli that appear with it. For example, a circle might be an instance of a correct stimulus if it appears with a set of rectangles but on the very next trial the same circle might be an incorrect stimulus if it appeared with many curved forms and a single rectangle. (The rectangle would be correct in this case, of course.) Other simple relational tasks are: choosing the middle-sized object out of any number of objects presented, always choosing the smallest object, choosing the object that most resembles the object on the far left, and so on. Complex relations might involve deciding whether a string of words is a sentence or whether an equation balances.

The important thing to notice in all such cases is that there is no particular physical property of the correct object that identifies it; it is, rather, identified by a set of rules or relations. One way that association theorists have tried to deal with these phenomena is by saying that the subject is responding verbally to the whole set of stimuli and then picking the item that he calls *the odd one* or *the middle-sized one* and so on. The trouble with this solution (which, in fact, is often descriptive of the situation) is that we have now only moved the problem back one step. What is the stimulus that controls the verbal response? We may let the response do the work for us in solving the concept problem, but now we cannot say what determines the verbal response. The problem of relations as stimuli is still a stumbling block for simple associationism (see Jenkins, 1966).

Associationists have tended to devise problems that fit in sensibly with their systems of explanation. Problems devised by other investigators sometimes seem too vague and messy to put into the explanatory system. A typical problem of the associationists is to present a set of elements and have the subject try to create proper items out of them (for example, presenting a set of letters and having subjects make words out of them). Then the investigators measure the speed of solution or the number of solutions as a function of the number of associative relations between elements (the letters) or the associations around the solutions (the words). The more richly the letters are connected and the more the words are related, the more solutions are expected.

When the problems get complicated, association theorists commonly rely on verbal processes (either overt or covert) to mediate the subject's progress from one stage of the solution to another. In the most ambitious attempt to use verbal processes in a complex experiment (Judson, Cofer, and Gelfand, 1956), the investigators took a classic problem (devised by Maier, 1931) and attempted to give their subjects indirect help in problem-solution through verbal chains that were learned independently before the test situation. The problem was the Maier Two-String Problem (see Figure 13.4).

Figure 13.4 The two-string reasoning problem. The subject's task is to tie the two strings together.

The situation consists of a room with two strings suspended from the ceiling, hanging down too far apart to be grasped at the same time. The subject's task is to tie the strings together. There is miscellaneous equipment in the room that the subject can use. Common solutions are holding one string and fishing for the other with a stick, and anchoring one string to a chair while getting the other. The most creative solution is supposed to be the *pendulum solution,* which consists of tying a small object to one string and setting it to swinging like a pendulum. The subject can just walk over and take the other string, wait for the first string to swing over to him, and then tie the strings together.

Two weeks before the problem situation was to be given, the investigators taught a set of word lists to their subjects as part of their regular laboratory classes. Some of the word lists were just controls, but one of them contained the words *rope, swing,* and *pendulum* in succession. The group that was trained on this list achieved more pendulum solutions of the two-string problem when all the groups were tested later. The explanation, of course, is that the sight of the strings as stimuli aroused the related word *rope* as an implicit response and that the earlier training on the word list led from *rope* to *swing* and *pendulum,* thus suggesting that particular solution. The experimenters performed a repetition of the study to be sure that the outcome was not accidental, but other investigators have had difficulty getting the same results (Maltzman, Belloni, and Fishbein, 1964). The experiment is, however, an excellent example of the associative approach to problem-solving.

MEANING

The association theorist looks at meaning in a way that is consistent with his other views. The meaning of an object, a picture, or a word is just the responses (overt and covert) that you make to that stimulus. Stimuli that elicit many responses are called *more meaningful* and those that elicit few responses are *less meaningful.* To say that a stimulus is meaningful does not tell *what* it means, only that it has many potential responses. As we have seen earlier, highly meaningful stimuli are readily learned and easily recalled.

In the associative tradition, what a stimulus means to you depends on the particular responses that you make to it. Thus, if an investigator knew all the responses that you could make to a word, he would have a precise index of its meaning to you. The request to collect such data is, however, an unreasonable one. It would take a very long time to exhaust the responses that you could make to a word (such as *mother* or *sweetheart* or your own name). In addition, you might start responding to your own responses as stimuli, or the nature of your responses might be changed by little changes in the presentation of the word, the situation, the audience present, and so on. One way to minimize these problems is a rating scale called the *Semantic Differential* developed by C.E. Osgood, G.J. Suci, and P. Tannenbaum

(1957). These investigators asked people to rate words on a number of bipolar scales such as *good------bad; thick------thin; hot------cold,* and the like. By statistical analysis they found that the ratings of nouns tended to fall along three major dimensions:

Dimension	Key Scale
Evaluation:	Good ------------Bad
Potency:	Strong------------Weak
Activity:	Active------------Passive

They concluded, however, that these dimensions do not serve to show the denotative meaning of a term (that is, they do not tell *what* the word means), but they do serve to tell about connotative meaning (that is, how someone feels about the word). Thus, *lady* and *white rose buds* may be rated very much alike on the *Semantic Differential* (both *very good, somewhat weak,* and *passive*) and *doctor* and *God* might be alike (*very good, very strong,* and *very active*), but this similarity does not indicate that *lady* and *white rose buds* mean the same thing or that *God* and *doctor* are synonyms.

ORIGINALITY AND CREATIVITY

Several investigators have tried to deal with the elusive notions of originality and creativity within the associative framework (see Mednick, 1962, and Maltzman, 1960). The usual approach is to argue that individuals who have many responses to stimuli are original and that those who have just a few are not.

The term *creativity* can be reserved for a person whose ideas happen to match a social need or whose originality is appropriate to the situation in which he finds himself. Although some work has been done on this conception of originality and creativity, there is little of value to report. No one has made very great use of these ideas, though it has been demonstrated that tests for the number and the diversity of a person's word associations can be built. It remains to be shown that such tests are related to what we would be willing to term serious creative activities.

The Wholistic Approach

The view most often contrasted with the association tradition is that of the Gestalt psychologists. This school of thought, which grew from diverse branches of older psychologies, was initially concerned mostly with perceptual phenomena. The Gestalt psychologists were different from more conventional students of perception in arguing that form was directly perceived rather than put together out of elementary sensations. This view was characterized in many ways but perhaps most often tagged with the slogan, "The whole is greater than the sum of its parts."

Although many Gestalt theorists were concerned with the problem of thought, the classic Gestalt work on thinking was achieved as a result of an accident. Wolfgang Köhler, who had been working on perceptual problems from a Gestalt view, was making a visit to the British island of Tenerife when World War I was declared. As an enemy alien he was interned on the island but given permission to conduct what scientific work he could. He devoted his attention to a colony of chimpanzees for the next few years and the resulting work, published as *The Mentality of Apes* (1925), provided the psychological world with a refreshingly new view of the animal mind.

Köhler tried to use natural problem situations in which an animal could clearly see the goal and all the elements of the problem. For example, he would suspend a piece of food from the top of the ape's enclosure or put it on the ground outside the bars of the cage and see how the hungry chimpanzee coped with the problem of getting to the food or getting the food to him. Sometimes the materials available in the cage were such that the food could be knocked down or pulled into reach. Sometimes the apes had to discover that they could reach the food by going around obstacles or by climbing sticks or boxes that could be pulled into appropriate positions. In contrast to Thorndike's puzzle box, the elements of the problem were all available and the problems were somewhat like those that one could suppose that chimpanzees might have to solve in the natural state. The results of Köhler's experiments were impressively different from those obtained by the associationists.

The simplest kind of problem Köhler used was the *detour* problem. An animal was placed on one side of a short fence and the food was placed a little way back from the fence on the other side. Chimpanzees and dogs solved this problem readily, immediately going around the end of the fence to the food. Chickens, on the other hand, rushed headlong into the fence and then ran back and forth directly opposite the food but seemed to be unable to execute the detour. On a more complicated problem, an animal would be placed in a cage and the food placed outside the cage attached to a string that ran up to the bars. Dogs failed this test but chimpanzees solved it at first glance. On still more complicated problems, the chimpanzees lacked immediate solutions, but random behavior was still not much in evidence. In one series, Köhler placed food outside the bars (out of reach) and put a stick in the cage. The account of Neuva, a four-year-old female, is especially revealing:

> . . . between lamentations and entreaties, some time passes, until—about seven minutes after the fruit has been exhibited to her—she suddenly casts a look at the stick, ceases her moaning, seizes the stick, stretches it out of the cage, and succeeds, though somewhat clumsily, in drawing the bananas within arm's length. Moreover, Neuva at once puts the end of her stick

behind and beyond the objective. [That is, she did not just touch or push the food randomly. She used a stick as a rake the very first time.]

Later Köhler repeated this experiment with the same animal without a stick. He reports:

> She at once tried to pull it towards her with rags lying in her cage, with straws and finally with her tin drinking bowl which stood in front of the bars, or to beat it towards her—using the rags—and sometimes successfully. (Köhler, 1925.)

One ape, Sultan, not only solved these kinds of problems but also discovered that the sticks, which were bamboo, could be joined together to make a longer stick. On several occasions, he made use of this construction technique to solve reaching problems. Sultan, who appears to have been something of a chimpanzee genius, also led in the solution of the problems that required the use of boxes to reach food suspended from the top of the enclosure. He not only used single boxes to stand on and leap from but also stacked boxes to achieve extra height as if he were building a stairway.

Where Thorndike's cats had showed slow acquisition over many trials of the behaviors that served to release them from their cages, Köhler's apes showed sudden insightful solutions to their problems of obtaining food. Where Thorndike's cats had engaged in furious activity described as trial-and-error learning, Köhler's apes wandered about complaining or sat and contemplated the problem situation until they understood it. Where Thorndike's cats used only their native equipment to solve their dilemmas, Köhler's apes piled up boxes as stairways, used sticks to pull in food, and put two sticks together to make longer sticks when these were needed. The result of Köhler's work was a more complicated picture of animal behavior and a different approach to thinking and problem-solving in the human being.

Köhler viewed the problem situation as a field under a state of tension. The situation (the motive, the goal, and the possible paths to the goal) was thought of as dynamic and capable of reorganization when it was correctly perceived. Thus, when an animal "sees" a path to the goal, he is credited with insight. He is expected to go ahead and execute the behavior to reach the goal in the desired manner. The Gestalt psychologists, following Köhler's lead, stress the reorganization of the field, the sudden character of the solution following a preparation period in which the elements are grasped, and the lack of dependence of the solution on explicit training in that solution; that is, they stress the novelty of the solution.

The kind of situation described by the Gestalt psychologists sounds much more like the stories in the autobiographical literature about discovery and invention than the situations chosen by the associationists where a particular solution exists and must be selected out of a set of possible things the organism can do. For human creativity, the specifics of the problem are not ordinarily known, that is, the problem does not have a simple definite shape and there is no guarantee that a solution exists. In most such instances, the solution may be grasped as a new organization of the problem, and the details of the solution or even the choice of particular modes of solution are often worked out after the major breakthrough in organization.

Examples from the work of mathematicians and physicists often look like the Gestalt psychologists' examples, only at a much higher and more complicated level. Here is a famous account from the mathematician Henri Poincaré from a lecture at the Société de Psychologie:

> For fifteen days I strove to prove that there could not be any functions like those I have since called Fuchsian functions. I was then very ignorant; every day I seated myself at my work table, stayed an hour or two, tried a great number of combinations and reached no results. One evening, contrary to my custom, I drank black coffee and could not sleep. Ideas rose in crowds; I felt them collide until pairs interlocked, so to speak, making a stable combination. By the next morning I had established the existence of a class of Fuchsian functions, those which come from the hypergeometric series; I had only to write out the results, which took but a few hours.
>
> Just at this time I left Caen, where I was then living, to go on a geological excursion under the auspices of the school of mines. The changes of travel made me forget my mathematical work. Having reached Coutances, we entered an omnibus to go some place or other. At the moment when I put my foot on the step the idea came to me, without anything in my former thoughts seeming to have paved the way for it, that the transformations I had used to define the Fuchsian functions were identical with those of non-Euclidean geometry. I did not verify the idea; I should not have had time, as, upon taking my seat in the omnibus, I went on with a conversation already commenced, but I felt a perfect certainty. On my return to Caen, for conscience' sake I verified the result at my leisure.
>
> Then I turned my attention to the study of some arithmetic questions apparently without much success and without a suspicion of any connection with my preceding researches. Disgusted with my failure, I went to spend a few days at the seaside, and thought of something else. One morning, walking on the bluff, the idea came to me, with just the same characteristics of brevity, suddenness and immediate certainty, that the arithmetic transformations of indeterminate ternary quadratic forms were identical with those of non-Euclidean geometry.
>
> Returned to Caen, I meditated on this result and deduced the consequences. . . . I made a systematic attack upon them and carried all the outworks, one after another. There was one however that still held out, whose fall would involve that of the whole place. But all my efforts only served at first the better to show me the difficulty, which indeed was something. All this work was perfectly conscious.
>
> Thereupon I left for Mont-Valerien, where I was to go through my military service; so I was very differently occupied. One day, going along the street, the solution of the difficulty which had stopped me suddenly appeared to me. I did not try to go deep into it immediately, and only after my service did I again take up the question. I had all the elements and had only to arrange them and put them together. So I wrote out my final memoir at a single stroke and without difficulty. (H. Poincaré, 1908.)

Surely this experience (which is reported over and over again by mathematicians) is an excellent example of the Gestalt point of view. The general direction toward the goal is present. The elements needed for the solution are well in hand and have been explicitly reviewed. The solution bursts on the mathematician with suddenness, reorganizing the entire field in a clear and definitive way. The notion of the solution and the conviction that it is correct precedes the working out of details.

Even by non-Gestalt psychologists, there has long been agreement that really novel solutions to problems follow some sort of stepwise sequence though it does not fit in any easy way into particular psychological theories. The general stages are:

1. *Seeing the problem* and getting it stated in some preliminary form. (Note well that the form of the question may change and that its change may itself be an important aspect of problem-solution.)

2. *Getting the facts.* Assembling the data or rules or devices that might be useful in solving the problem.

3. *Incubating the problem and the facts.* Doing something else when stumped in ordinary procedures. Waiting for something unusual to suggest itself or to be suggested by circumstances or unconscious processes.

4. *Seeing the solution.* Having the inspiration. Sometimes this amounts to recasting the problem so that it falls in the class of problems that one knows how to solve.

5. *Testing the solution.* Verifying the notion by working out the procedures in detail.

Although these are very general stages, they do seem to describe many creative events, such as Archimedes's discovery of the hydrostatic scales (remember *Eureka?*), Gutenberg's invention of the printing press, Kekule's dream that led to the postulation of benzene rings, and Köhler's apes finding their way to a solution of the food problem.

The difficulty with such a formulation is that it is both nonspecific and full of mystery (though it may, in fact, be true). To say that discovery may follow incubation is not to explain discovery nor does it allow one to predict a discovery, because the inspiration may not follow, no matter how long one incubates. Further, some inspirations fail of verification. Many of the brilliant ideas of the night before seem futile and stupid when put to the test the following day, yet they seem to have all of the certainty and clarity of correctness when they first occur, just as if they were sound and truly insightful.

The general difficulty with the Gestalt approach has been much the same. The metaphors for thought and problem-solution have been taken from the perceptual area that gave birth to the theoretical position. To talk about reorganizing the whole perceptual field of, say, a problem in mathematics is not very useful as a scientific view any more than is Poincaré's metaphor of "colliding crowds of ideas." While we may feel that we have an intuitive account that is revealing and satisfying, it does not take us any further in a scientific understanding of creation and problem-solving.

As an aside, we should probably say that there is no reason to expect a *complete* account of invention or discovery. If such an account were possible, we could presumably write "procedures for having a brilliant idea" or something of the sort. Perhaps it would be more reasonable for us to attempt reconstructions that simply try to account for what did happen in a particular case in appropriate terms that show how the requirements of the situation were met and what psychological processes seemed to be involved.

Some efforts have been made, though they have not been systematic, to relate the associationist and the Gestalt forms of explanation. H.G. Birch (1945) conducted an interesting experiment which showed that insight does not operate effectively in an experiential vacuum. He took six young chimpanzees who had been carefully studied all their lives. Five of them were known to have had no opportunity to play with or use sticks for reaching. These animals were given a variation of the typical Köhler stick problem. In this case, the food was arranged so that pulling a T-shaped hoe would bring it directly to the bars. In spite of the simplicity of the situation (well within the capacity of even a young chimpanzee), only four of the animals succeeded in obtaining the food in a 30-minute period and only the one with experience solved it properly. Following this task, the animals were given sticks to play with in their cages for a three-day period. After this play experience, the animals were again given the test situation. On this occasion, *all* of the animals solved the problem by the direct method in less than half a minute. This strongly supports the role of past experience in insight.

It should be noted that both schools score points in the Birch experiment. The associationists substantiate their claim that prior experience is involved, and the Gestalt psychologists demonstrate that the animal does not merely repeat reinforced actions but can reorient to the situation in the light of his experience and solve the problems with sudden insight.

K. Duncker (1945) presented verbal problems to subjects and carefully recorded their thoughts (which they were instructed to recite) as they struggled to solve them. Much of his material suggests that both associative processes and directional, general field forces played a role in the subjects' thinking. Typical problems he used were:

1. When a steel ball falls on a steel plate, the impact flattens the ball. It bounds up again because the elastic forces make it regain its former shape. How could you show that the ball was actually flattened?
2. Why are all six-place numbers of the repetitive form *abc abc* divisible by the number 13? (For example: 123,123 or 762,762 or 935,935.)

Such problems take a good deal of thinking about if one has never tried them before. In the first case, visualization is helpful and some notions of physical recording are also useful. (One might, for example, smoke the steel surface with soot and obtain a record of the shape and size of the impact.) In the second case, one must come to the realization that all such numbers are multiples of the number 1,001 and that 1,001 is divisible by 13, hence all such numbers must be divisible by 13.

Duncker's protocols show his subjects trying various lines of attack and gaining insight (sometimes successfully and sometimes unsuccessfully) to general approaches, finding places to concentrate effort and particular solutions. He began to think in terms of a hierarchy of insights from very vague gropings to precise articulated solutions. He also saw that in all of the problems, it was an advantage to remain flexible and ready to try new approaches, to accept new directions, and the like.

Duncker also drew attention to an aspect of problem-solving that he called *functional fixedness*. Once an object is seen in one role it is difficult for a subject to think of it in another role. In one of his problems, the subject was to make a pendulum. Available to him were a string with a lead weight on the end of it and a nail but no hammer. Only 50 per cent of his subjects thought to use the pendulum weight as a hammer. When the problem was presented with the weight and the cord lying separately on the table and the weight was not designated as a pendulum weight, all of the subjects used it as a hammer on their way to the solution of the problem. One problem in achieving effective solutions, then, is to keep an open mind about the role and properties of the materials available to you.

A different kind of fixedness has been shown in a famous series of experiments on the "water jar" problem by A.S. Luchins (1942). In this series, three containers are available and a subject has to find a way to measure out a particular amount of water. Table 13.1 shows the jars given the subject and the amount he is to measure out. (Of course, the problems are verbal and the subject does not actually measure the water, he merely recites how it could be measured out.)

In the first problem, the subject reports that he fills A and then pours B full three times, leaving the right amount in A. From the second problem to the sixth problem, one pattern of actions will solve all the problems: Fill the largest container (which is always B) and pour off the amounts needed to fill A once and C twice. The amount left in B is then the desired amount. Although the seventh problem can be solved in the same manner, you can see that there is a shorter method: Fill A and pour out the amount needed to fill C. This method will also solve the remaining problems, while the original formula fails to solve the ninth problem. Nevertheless, almost all subjects from grade school to college persist in trying to use the formula that worked for problems 2–6 if they have been exposed to those trials. Controls who go directly from the first to the seventh problem do not. This persistence in a reinforced pattern when a simpler procedure is available has been called functional fixedness and has been used as a measure of "rigidity."

This series reflects again the mixture of Gestalt and association principles that seem to be involved in any complex problem. Clearly, the subjects are

Task	Jars Provided (Quarts)			Amount Desired (Quarts)
	A	B	C	
1	29	3	—	20
2	21	127	3	100
3	14	163	25	99
4	18	43	10	5
5	9	42	6	21
6	20	59	4	31
7	23	49	3	20
8	15	39	3	18
9	28	76	3	25
10	18	48	4	22
11	14	36	8	6

Table 13.1   The Luchins water-jar problem.

behaving in a "habitual" way; that is, they are behaving as if particular responses have been reinforced and they are simple habit-strength machines. On the other hand, we must notice that the "response" here is a *rule* and that it is this abstract rule that has become fixed, not a particular set of words that the subject says or movements that he makes. Clearly, there is some aspect of truth in both approaches.

MEANING AND CONCEPTS

Most of the work of Gestalt psychologists on thinking has concentrated on problem-solving, and there has not been any attempt to specify a simple theory of meaning and concept-formation that we can compare with the theories advanced by the association theorists. As you should suspect by this point, the Gestalt view stresses the total context in which the concepts are to be formed and the framework, both linguistic and situational, in which a new word is encountered. An elaboration of meaning or concept-formation thus involves the elaboration of all of the rest of Gestalt theory, a task that we will not pursue here.

Very generally, a few principles can be mentioned. Concepts and meanings are not formed by simple automatic processes even though they may at times be simple and uncomplicated. They are, instead, a product of an organism's view of, and interaction with, the situation. Thus, for a young child a word is likely to have a concrete meaning and be bound to particular instances because this is the nature of his world. For an older child or adult, a word may have multiple meanings and may enter into metaphors freely as it is applied to one aspect and then another of the complex perception that the older person has of the world. Thus, we experimentally find that little children have simple, material meanings for words like *hard* and *cold* and that they think these words cannot be applied to people or, if they are applied to people, that they have literal meanings. The older child realizes that such words can be used to apply to people and that they have reasonable meanings. The still older child or adult recognizes that the words are "the same word" whether applied to people or objects and relates the meaning of the word in its metaphorical use to the more literal meaning (see Asch and Nerlove, 1960).

Words and concepts cannot simply be assigned meaning by simple contiguities. They assimilate (take to themselves) the meanings that the situation already has for the subject. If the situation is well understood and its parts are clearly related in a good organization, appropriate word meanings and concepts can be applied and learned correctly. But if the situation is incompletely understood and the parts poorly differentiated and interrelated, the terms used may simply be related to the gross situation or to almost any isolated aspect that the organism does apprehend. Thus, in the Gestalt theories, there is great emphasis on the developmental stage of the organism and on his perception of the situation rather than on laws that relate sets of physical stimulus variables to sets of physical response variables.

Thinking as the Processing of Information

The newest approach to the understanding of thinking is both brash and attractive. It is brash in that it threatens the older theories by challenging them to submit to the severest possible test: stating the theory precisely enough to run it on a computer without outside help. Spokesmen for the information-processing point of view believe that traditional theories are mostly vague words and empty sentences filled in with common sense and unspoken assumptions that enable a theorist (who has common sense and makes the hidden assumptions) to make a few special predictions here and there. They argue that none of the current theories can be made explicit enough to act as a program for a digital computer and make it do what the organism is supposed to do. In this respect, they are unquestionably correct.

The new approach is attractive in that it appeals to the interest that most of us have in building machines or robots that actually work. If one is successful in this kind of theory-building, he can show it off by having a computer actually run off the behavior that he is concerned with. This is surely the strongest way to show that one has a theory that works, whether it is the best theory or not.

A note about the use of computers in this fashion is in order. When computers came on the scene during World War II, they were used chiefly for carrying out detailed, tiresome, and monumental calculations. Their advantages were speed, endurance, and immunity to boredom. As more (and more powerful) computers became available and more thought was given to their capacities, they were set to more varied tasks. They began to keep books, make payrolls, keep tabs on factory production, monitor manufacturing processes, and run an air-defense network. A major change in thinking about computers was the realization that they could be thought of as general symbol manipulators, not just number machines. Whereas they had begun as brute-force calculators, they were now seen to be capable of any kind of symbolic communication that anyone cared to specify. Thus, computers moved on to decision-making, strategies, games, and even some kinds of language translations.

Playing games with computers may not seem like serious scientific work, and, indeed, many times this activity may be inspired by the spirit of play or scientific recreation. But to use a computer in this way means that you have supplied it with enough appropriate instructions that it can behave like another player. Thus, if you can program a computer to play checkers, you have by that very fact made the computer a model of a checker player in at least some important respects.

What can you learn from a model you just invented to do a particular job? The answer is: It depends. If you just want a machine to play games with, you may give it special properties that ordinary players do not possess. You might, for example, give the computer a perfect memory and let it re-member every move of every game that it played. Given enough games and some clever ways of using the information, it should get to play a pretty good game of checkers. But such a procedure would have some disadvan-tages. It would be very expensive in memory units and the machine might be reduced to helplessness by a bad player who made moves that the computer had not seen before. Finally, of course, this is not the way we suppose that people play checkers.

If you model your computer-player with a more limited and temporary memory, you will have to put more emphasis on general rules of play and strategy. The chances immediately increase that your model and its be-havior will be more like human players and their behavior. At some point you might be willing to say that you had developed a machine that not only played checkers but played it the way real players do. Such a statement would be equivalent to saying that your program for the computer was a theory of the human checker player.

The approach developed here is very closely related to the final view of language that we encountered in the last chapter. What it says, in essence, is that behavior is "computed" by rules and procedures rather than simply being called out of a huge storehouse of stimulus-response connections or chains of such connections. The example of how one multiplies large numbers is again appropriate. In the language of the information-processing theorists, each of us has a general program for calculating such numbers. The program directs us to specific items of information ("Take the two right-most digits"), calls for certain subroutines ("Consult memory for the product of 4 times 3"), stores intermediate calculations ("Write down the 2 in the space immediately below the 3 and 'carry' the 1"), shifts to new subroutines ("If there are no further numbers, begin adding the columns created in intermediate memory"), and stops the program when it is completed ("If there are no further numbers to add, print out the answer").

Such a consciously learned routine is an instance of the information-processing approach that all of us know how to do. The theorist is ready to argue that, even when we do not know we are doing information-processing, our behavior is "computed" in a similar fashion. His approach to behavior is to describe it as a program of some sort with complicated subroutines being called and dismissed under appropriate conditions.

G.A. Miller, E. Galanter, and K.H. Pribram (1960) tried to show the applicability of such general conceptions over a wide range of behaviors. They included plans for activities ranging from hammering a nail (see Figure 13.5) to creating a sentence. Although such procedures can be roughly outlined and although it is plausible to consider a program as a psychological theory of the action, it is also clear that alternative programs can be devised that can accomplish exactly the same thing. Thus, there may be many possible theories of a complex behavior (perhaps even an infinite number). The problem, therefore, is not merely to find a way that the task could be done but also to narrow down the possible theories by requiring that they do this and other activities in the same way that human beings do them. This last requirement means that we are going to ask a lot of a program before we are willing to accept it as a candidate for a psychological model. We want it to have the same units of behavior, the same internal organizations, the

Figure 13.5 The hierarchical plan for hammering nails. (From Miller, Galanter and Pribram, 1960.)

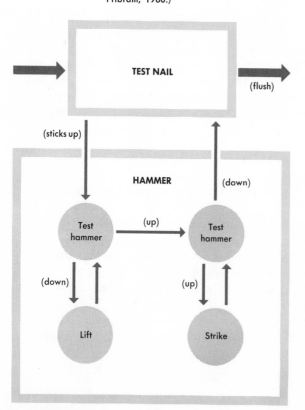

same tendencies to errors, and the same time delays that people show when they try to accomplish the tasks. We will further want the machine's program to change and develop with experience the same way that humans do; that is, we will want it to learn, show transfer phenomena (both positive and negative), recognize new cases of old problems, and so on.

Now these are very formidable demands indeed. It takes a long time to develop a reasonable program for a complex bit of behavior and enormous amounts of time to see if the program can cope adequately with the additional requirements. As a result, there are very few instances of the kind of theory that we are talking about here, although we may expect many more in the near future as more and more gifted people turn to this new area of theory-building.

It is hard to give an example of information-processing research that is as representative as the puzzle box is of the association theorist's approach and the insight problems are of the Gestalt approach. The classic problem is not really an experiment at all in the usual sense, it is a "thought experiment" designed by one of the great computer theorists, A.M. Turing. In response to the question, "Can machines really think?" he suggested that a test situation was possible (in principle) to decide the question. He said we might put a person in one room, a computer in another, and ourselves in a third. Our room would be connected to the other rooms by teletype, but we would not know which room was which. Our task in this game would be to decide which of our communicators was a real person and which a machine. We could ask any questions we liked; the person would try to let us know that he was the real person and the machine would try to convince us that it was a person too.

You may suppose that this game would be too simple to be instructive, but it might not be. The person could say, "I am the real person; don't believe anything it says," but the computer could be programed to say that too. We might give our sources long arithmetical problems to work and choose as the person the one that made mistakes, but a clever programer might have arranged for the machine memory to be limited and let it make errors too. We might pose problems about common experiences such as, "What large black bird is commonly used by poets as a symbol of death?"—knowing that every American school child is familiar with Poe's *The Raven.* But we would not be sure that every school child had got the symbolism straight nor would a careful programer have left out such a common piece of knowledge from the "education" of his computer. The chief problem here would be whether the program recognized what item of information was being called for. This question would resolve itself into an indexing problem and a language-interpretation problem which the programer could attack. We can go on in this fashion. For each kind of question we can think of, we should try to think of a way the machine could be programed to provide a human-sounding, though not necessarily correct, answer. If we can always think of a way to generate an answer that will deceive the game player at least part of the time, then we must concede the ability to think to the programed computer. In addition, we will have provided at least some candidates for theories of how people think by the programs that we have prepared.

Even though Turing's task is stimulating and thought-provoking, it is far beyond our abilities at the present time since it involves the simultaneous programing of *all* human intellectual abilities and knowledge, including language, education, a plausible personal history, and a reasonable personality. Obviously, that is far too ambitious. We can start, however, by seeing if we can get a computer to solve some simple problem in the same way a person does (with the same errors and the same lines of attack). If we succeed at that, the next interesting question is whether the same program can solve other, similar problems the same way humans do. To the extent that the program still works when we change from one problem to another, it is an even more powerful theory of problem-solving. If new problems require radically new programs, we can conclude that our program-theories are so specific as to be useless, or we can conclude that psychology needs to separate problems into types before it even sets out to build theories about problem-solving. In either case, we will have a much more precise notion of how strong our theories are than we would have if we did not try out these approaches.

An example of this kind of research can be found in programs developed (Simon and Kotovsky, 1963) to solve letter-series completion-problems such as those used on intelligence tests. Customarily, a person is presented with a string of letters of some arbitrary length and asked to fill in the next letter or two. Examples might be:

A C E G I K M _____

G M H M I M J M _____

P X A X O Y B Y N Z _____

It is easy to see that these problems can be quite complicated and difficult, and many college students have trouble solving the hard ones. A program for such a task must have access to the necessary knowledge as part of the memory store of the machine. The machine must recognize letters as being different from one another and yet know that a given letter is the same when it is repeated. The memory must include the alphabet in both forward and reverse order and the notions of "coming before" and "coming after." The program then has to attempt to develop a pattern description of the sequence presented to it in terms of its alphabets and their successions and must try to develop cycles (repetitions in some systematic form) that could produce the description. It then has to predict on the basis of the pattern by extending it to the next case.

The business of developing the right description is, of course, the difficult part of the program. In the simplest case, the computer could be instructed to look for the next letter in the alphabet; if it finds it, it could be instructed to look for the next letter after that at the same interval away. If that yields nothing, the program might search the backward alphabet, then the alphabet for the second or third next items, and so on. At some point, failing in this, the program can look for repetitions of elements broken at fixed intervals (AAAZZZMMMO_ _) and so on. Obviously, there is no real limit to the number of relations or their dimensionality that could be included, because human beings might under some circumstances detect them. (For example, a rule might deal with the sound of the letters, in which case the program would have to have this auditory information coded in its memory and some directions about when to include this kind of relation in its search routine.)

The investigators developed several variations of this model with increasing degrees of complexity in terms of the descriptions that the programs could establish. The weakest programs did about as well as the poorest high school and college students trying to solve the problems and the strongest programs did about as well as the best students who were examined. Both the students and the programs ranked the problems in about the same order of difficulty (which was generally in terms of increasing demands on the memory load).

The most dramatic accomplishment to date is the *tour de force* attempted by A. Newell, J.C. Shaw, and H.A. Simon (1958), who tried to build a program that would prove theorems in symbolic logic, an undertaking far more difficult than you might at first suppose. Because proofs look mathematical, it is easy to think that a program to prove theorems is just like a program to multiply or perform some other complicated arithmetic. There is a very great difference, however, between arithmetical procedures and proofs, and it is important to understand the nature of the difference.

There are two general ways of finding solutions to problems. These are called *algorithms* and *heuristics*. An algorithm is a guaranteed path to the solution of a problem; a heuristic is merely a helpful strategy or technique for attacking a problem. It may work sometimes but it cannot be guaranteed to work on every problem. Let us take a simple example. Suppose we have a game in which a friend may put a checker on the checker board somewhere and our task is to guess which square it is in. An *algorithm* for the solution of this problem is to start guessing at one corner and guess each square in the first row, then each square in the second, then each in the third, and so on. This procedure must eventually locate the checker or tell us that there is no checker on the board. In most games each guess would cost us some price and the algorithm would turn out to be a very expensive way to find the checker, especially if our friend understood what strategy we were following. We would probably want to develop some less certain method that might get us to a solution faster. For example, we might have observed in past games that people often put the checker just outside the center squares on the board but almost never against the edge. Our best bet then would be to guess the circle of squares around the middle; and if we guess more than half the squares on the board without finding the checker, we might want to shift our bet to the bet that there is no checker on the board at all. This procedure is much more uncertain than the first, but it has the chance for an early win and offers occasional spectacular hits.

Many mathematical tasks (like multiplication of numbers) have algorithms but some (like making proofs) do not. For the latter case we often develop heuristics that may help us to see the solution but obviously are not guaranteed to do so. Interviewing mathematics students shows that they employ many useful tricks to help them find proofs. For example, students often take the theorem to be proved and work backward from it, attempting to see if they can get it in a simpler form that they might know something about. If the student has already proved some theorems, he will try to get the theorem that he is trying to prove written in the same symbols that he has used before, in the hope that he can use some of the theorems he has been successful with. If the theorem involves different terms on the two sides of an equation, the student often tries to write all the terms on one side in the same symbols that have been used on the other side in the hope that he will find an identity. In addition, almost all students come to realize that after they have given some fixed amount of time to any approach, they should go on to another problem or try another approach because their odds of solving the problem by the particular technique being employed are decreasing.

Newell, Shaw, and Simon decided to build many of these strategies and rules of thumb and good advice into their program and then give the program a series of problems that students are sometimes asked to prove. In this set of experiments, the Logic Theorist program worked as expected. It proved a set of theorems presented in the classic work on symbolic logic, *Principia Mathematica*, with a fair degree of success (73 per cent correct proofs within an arbitrary time limit). Newell, Shaw, and Simon felt that the program demonstrated many human characteristics and provided a milestone in the simulation of productive thought. As they pointed out, the program (1) was capable of solving problems (that is, it really did prove theorems), (2) it used past theorems to help in proving further theorems just as real logicians do, (3) it showed both preparatory and directional set, (4) it kept trial and error within reasonable bounds but still made use of them, (5) it classified expressions in symbolic logic in simple ways, and (6) it made use of a hierarchy of problems and subproblems, reducing more complicated problems to simpler ones and trying to solve them first.

The information-processing theorists do not have a wealth of examples to give us, but they are currently providing a vigorous stimulus to theory and they are making a strong and important claim. Their claim is that human behavior is to be described in terms of abstract concepts and processes rather than by input-output connections or chains of such connections. When a rule says, "Take a number," it is using an abstraction. A "number" is not a particular stimulus or response; it is the name of a class of some sort. When a rule says "Search" or "Add" or "Store" or "Take the next item," it is referring to operations that can be applied to many items of abstract classes, sometimes even in different ways in varying contexts. The notions of hierarchies of routines and subroutines implies classes and operations that themselves involve other classes and operations before one gets down to observable behaviors.

You should also notice that these machine descriptions do not mean that behavior is either mysterious or that it is "simply mechanical." The descriptions are indifferent to our concerns with such emotional terms. These descriptions do imply, however, that psychologists have a more difficult task than the associationists believed. The problem of getting from behavior to machine descriptions may be very hard indeed. Can you imagine sitting looking at the input to a computer and at its output some moments later and trying to guess what its programing is like? For a program of even a little complexity such as a standard statistical program, it would be impossible unless you already knew the statistics, could guess how the results were being ordered, knew how the input was grouped, and so on. A.M. Turing was so impressed with this problem that he built a little demonstration program (with only 1000 memory units) that transformed numbers. The machine accepted any sixteen-digit number and almost immediately output another sixteen-digit number by applying some fixed set of rules (known only to Turing). For a given input the output was always the same, that is, the behavior of the machine was determined and completely reliable. But Turing challenged anyone to learn from looking at a record of inputs and outputs how the program worked or what it would do to a new input number that had not yet been studied. This does not mean that Turing had invented some mysterious kind of rule. It just means that there are so many possibilities as to what Turing might have done in preparing the program that there is no way to determine, among the vast set of possible rules and their combinations, the particular set selected by Turing. He might, for example, have taken the first three digits, cubed them, taken the three middle most digits from that number and entered them in spaces 9, 5, and 16 in the output digit, then taken the next four input digits, squared the first, subtracted the second from it, divided that number by the third, added the fourth and distributed the last four digits of that result in spaces 15, 3, 7, 12, and so on until he had produced the 16 digits he needed.

Reflecting on this example may be discouraging. If we cannot unlock the secrets of Turing's 16 digits readily, how can we hope to understand something as complicated as a human being? There is no guaranteed answer, of course. We may never fully understand human behavior. We can take encouragement, however, from our faith that the human system is not arbitrary or capricious (as Turing's rules might be). We can gain insight into the nature of human machines by studying the world in which we evolved, by studying related animals, and by asking questions of people who are engaged in various behaviors. Finally, we have the great advantage of being human beings ourselves, which gives us insights into the structure of the inputs and outputs and valuable cues about the nature of the internal processing. These advantages should help us to formulate good ideas for theories that can be subjected to careful study.

As an aside, it must be mentioned that the use of computers has nothing to do with their similarity (or lack of similarity) to the nervous system of man. Occasionally, exaggerated claims are made by someone who is carried away with the analogy between nerve cells and on-off relays, between the nervous system and the networks of intercommunication of the computer, and the like. There are two things you should note here. First, this is not at all what we are interested in. As far as we are concerned, the computer could be mechanical (as Charles Babbage first conceived of such machines over a century ago) or hydraulic, or it could even consist of hordes of little people running to and fro carrying messages. The only relevant point is that the digital computer is an all-purpose machine that can carry out instructions. It is the set of instructions and their consequences in which we are interested, not the actual physical workings of the machine.

The second matter worth noting concerning the brain-computer analogy is that the similarity in circuitry is superficial; there are many ways in which men and machines are very different. For example, the brains of living organisms are complex enough and redundant enough that they will operate with a good deal of precision even after parts of the system are damaged or destroyed. Most machines are much more fragile. Second, most computing machines are precisely designed with very specific networks of interconnections. Brains, although they do have great tracts and courses of fibers running from one location to another, appear to be almost randomly interconnected in many local areas. Third, computers ordinarily work on a serial processing system; that is, one thing is done, then another, then another, and so on. Brains, however, seem to process many things at once or, more technically, they engage in parallel processing. Fourth, machines are ordinarily either digital (operating on one or zero "bits" of information) or analog (operating on varying voltages) while the brain seems to be a complex mixture of both kinds of systems. Fifth, whereas we know what the internal language of the machine is like, we do not at present know what the coding units are for mental functions; that is, we do not know the machine language of the brain.

SUMMARY

The psychologist turns to the study of thinking when he is faced with behaviors that are not easily related to particular stimuli in a straightforward way. Such complex relations call for the postulation of some sort of inferred internal processing, whether it is "covert responding," "perceptual reorganization," or "information-processing." These terms characterize the three views of thinking that are of current importance: the associationist, the Gestalt, and the information-processing view.

Associationism stresses *trial and error*, either implicit or explicit. Thorndike's cats solving the puzzle box represent a classic example. The subject runs through his *habit-family hierarchy* (all the responses that he has to this stimulus complex), until he finds a response that moves him toward reinforcement. Successful responses are rewarded and therefore increase in strength. Unsuccessful responses are extinguished. The result of these two processes is more and more rapid solution of the problem and the development of smooth patterns of behavior. Behaviorists looked for evidence for *implicit responding* and found that appropriate muscles are indeed active during thinking and dreaming. But in spite of this evidence, few psychologists today regard muscle movements as necessary to thought. *Concept-formation* has been a favored research topic of the associationists. They have studied the growth of concepts that *share a particular stimulus* attribute (all red objects, all square objects) and the growth of concepts that depend on *sharing a particular response* (things that are named alike or are used in the same way). Finally, concepts that depend on relations between stimuli have been studied but, although their acquisition is apparent, the theory has some trouble explaining how this happens. *Problem-solving* is treated as a chaining of elementary stimuli and responses to form an implicit route from some cue to the problem-solution. *Meaning*, on the other hand, is treated as the set of responses that a person can make to the stimulus presented (usually a word). This conception of meaning is much like the notion of habit-family hierarchy, and one might just say that the meaning of a word is the habit-family hierarchy aroused by the word. It has been shown that *connotative meaning* (how you feel about a word) can be measured by rating the word on the dimensions of evaluation, potency, and activity on the *Semantic Differential*. Finally, some investigators have attempted to relate the richness and unusualness of the habit-family hierarchy to the notions of *originality* and *creativity* of individuals.

The *Gestalt*, or *wholistic*, approach stresses *perceptual reorganization* and emphasizes *dynamic* qualities of the problem field. The classic examples are the experiments of Köhler on chimpanzees in *detour puzzles* and complicated food-retrieval problems. These differ from the associationists' problems by presenting the animal with all the information and material needed for the solution of the difficulty. The animals frequently showed sudden and complete solutions to many problems and demonstrated insight rather than trial and error. The Gestalt approach sounds much more like the experiences reported by scientists and mathematicians about solving problems. Such accounts can be divided into stages: *seeing the problem, getting the facts, incubating the problem, seeing the solution,* and *testing the solution.* Such a formulation, while interesting and revealing, is not particularly helpful in understanding the nature of thought. Gestalt psychologists have studied *set* and *direction* in problem solution and several studies of *functional fixedness* and *rigidity* have shown that subjects carry over successful forms of solutions to new tasks even though there may be better and more successful ways for their performance. Gestalt *theories of meaning* stress the interaction of the subject with the world and point out that meanings at first may be concrete, becoming more general and metaphorical as a child grows older and has more experience. This does not imply that words are originally attached to things but rather that they are related to particular situations as the situations are construed by the subject. The stress, as usual in the Gestalt approach, is on the organism's view of the world rather than on contingencies actually occurring in the world.

Information-processing draws its inspiration from the computer. The essential notion is that theories of cognitive behavior in human beings must be complex and precise, preferably of such a form that they may serve as *programs* for machines that then can act out the behaviors and "run" the theories. The most famous experiment is a "thought experiment" designed by Turing in answer to the question of whether machines could think. He proposed trying to have a machine simulate a human being. If that was successful, he said, it would constitute evidence that machines could think. Work in the simulation of human behavior has made precise some rather fuzzy thinking about how people go about solving problems. To make a successful computer program, all of the fine details must be spelled out and all of the assumptions must be made explicit. Programs that solve letter-sequence tasks, like those found on intelligence tests, and programs that prove theorems indicate that the approach is promising and powerful. Clever techniques that may find a solution to a problem (*heuristics*) and powerful techniques guaranteed to solve certain problems (*algorithms*) can be programed in combinations that resemble human procedures on similar problems. Careful consideration of information-processing suggests that the psychologist's task in trying to understand thinking may be very hard. It is clear, however, that powerful tests of the adequacy of any theory of thinking are now available, and the information-processing group will insist on rigorous theories of the sort we have neglected somewhat in the past.

SUGGESTED READINGS

Bernstein, J. *The analytical engine.* New York: Random House, 1963.
Johnson, D.M. *The psychology of thought and judgment.* New York: Harper & Row, 1955.
Koestler, A. *The act of creation.* New York: Macmillan, 1964.
Newman, J. *The world of mathematics,* vol. 4. New York: Simon and Schuster, 1956.
Voss, J.F. *Approaches to thought.* Columbus, Ohio: Merrill, 1969.
Wertheimer, M. *Productive thinking* (2nd ed.). New York: Harper & Row, 1959.

Intelligence

C H A P T E R   F O U R T E E N   In this chapter we will turn for a time from the study of processes to the question of individual evaluation, because intelligence is one area in which the technical aspect has far outstripped the theoretical aspect. A pressing need for intelligence measurement existed and a technology grew up to meet the need without ever solving the formidable theoretical questions involved. We will trace a little of the history of intelligence measurement to see how this was possible. Along the way, we will mention the traditional models of intellect. Questions concerning the sources and determiners of intelligence are still vigorously debated. We will outline the issues and sketch in the facts as they appear to us today. Finally, we will turn to efforts to study intelligence from two radically different theoretical viewpoints and try to indicate the new directions that psychology is taking in attempting to understand the nature of intellect.

Intelligence: Its Measurement and Analysis

The traits most prized by ancient man were probably strength and agility, which were, after all, crucial to daily survival. Ranking close behind these traits, however, must have been keenness of hearing, vision, and smell, which would have played an important role in his decisions about where, when, and how to apply his physical skills. Following these sensitivities must have been the "mental" factors involved in decisions and actions—cleverness of ideas, inventiveness, judgment, memory of earlier events, and the like.

In our first records of man's reflections on man, we find a recognition of individual variation in physique, sensitivity, and intellect as well as the accompanying notion of specialization. The caste system (as an ideal) is a plan for specialization of activities based on assumed differences between groups. In a related vein, Plato, writing in *The Republic,* discussed three classes of people and characterized their traits. There are, he said, workers (farmers and artisans) whose task is to provide the material goods of life and whose "virtues" are *obedience* and *temperance.* Next there are warriors, who defend the state against attack. These are expected to excel in *energy* and *courage.* Finally, there are the philosopher-kings, who must possess *wisdom.* Plato argued that man's nature is analogous to the stratification of the state. At the base there are appetites that must be controlled and restrained. Above that level is energy, or "spirit." Finally, at the peak comes the mind, the site of wisdom; this is the ruling faculty that must coordinate and govern the lower levels.

Such catalogs of specialization, abilities, and "virtues" are of little use as scientific constructs, but they do indicate an awareness of differences of function and a sensitivity to different patterns of skills and abilities. Plato even proposed the selection of children for their role in life at an early age and a rigid program of education to ensure that they became what they were supposed to be.

In spite of such philosophical concerns, a science of the mental faculties was not to develop for many centuries. Before its emergence, three events had to take place. First, there had to arise a psychology of individuals as opposed to a psychology of classes and castes or a psychology that aimed at completely "general laws." Second, there had to be some reason to believe that the mind could be measured so that investigators would attempt to develop methods of measurement. Third, there had to be sufficient support in the development of mathematical and statistical tools for describing, relating, and interpreting measurements when they were made. These prerequisites were not simultaneously met until late in the nineteenth century, 2200 years after Plato.

The first requirement, concern with individuals, was met with the birth of political and social philosophies that respected the individual for himself, rather than for his class, his wealth, or his beliefs. This concern was further strengthened by the development in biology of the theory of evolution, which put dramatic emphasis on the role of individual variability as the key to survival and the evolution of species. The second requirement, belief that the mind can be measured, was met with the development of scientific laboratory psychology in Germany and with the undoubted success of psychophysical measurement, as we have seen in earlier chapters. The third requirement, mathematical and statistical tools, was met by statisticians who devised formulas for purposes as diverse as computing gambling odds and describing the biological characteristics of a population. These mathematicians made it possible to understand entire distributions of data with a few measurements and to characterize relations among sets of distributions. Such statistical advances were of great importance to all of the sciences, of course, but they were crucial in transforming the social sciences from speculative philosophies to quantitative disciplines.

Measuring Intelligence

No mental trait has been the subject of more concern than *intelligence*. It was recognized very early that men differ in intellectual capacity and that some men are capable of enormous mental accomplishments far beyond the grasp of ordinary people. The towering achievements of such men as Galileo, Newton, Descartes, Leibnitz, and Gauss demand recognition of their intellectual superiority. But even in the classroom of an ordinary school, a teacher is likely to be impressed by the differences between students in capability and in progress in difficult subject matter. It is natural, then, that many early efforts were made toward the evaluation of intelligence.

ELEMENTS OF INTELLIGENCE

The first attempts at the scientific measurement of the intellect took their lead from the analytic spirit of nineteenth-century psychology. The argument was a simple one. Clearly, superior intelligence is made up of an assembly of superior mental elements. Therefore, one should measure each element that enters into the performances called intelligent and then just combine these measurements for the over-all measure of intelligence.

The most famous study of elements was initiated by a Dutch physiologist, F.C. Donders, in 1862. He argued this way: Take the time involved in a simple reaction and the time involved after some complication is added; the difference in the time taken by the two reactions is a measure of the psychological process involved in the complication. For example, let us take a *reflex* as the simplest reaction since it is involuntary and wholly automatic. If we now take the time of an *automatic action* involving that reflex (a response practiced so long that it occurs automatically when the occasion is right) and subtract the time taken by the reflex action, we have a measure of the time taken by the *voluntary* component of an action. If we go on to a simple instructed reaction time ("Let up on the key as soon as you see the light") and subtract the automatic action time, we have a measure of the time it takes to perceive the light. We can proceed in this fashion to add many stimuli, responses, associative reactions, judgments, and so on in order to make the appropriate subtractions and find the time taken for cognition, choice, association, or judgment. "Mental chronometry," as this approach was termed, was very popular for about 30 years.

This persuasive idea is revived from time to time in different contexts. It surely *is* reasonable, but, unfortunately, it has never proven to be true. Furthermore, it seems to be untrue in several ways. First (and most importantly for the formulation), psychological functions cannot be thought of as a chain of elementary functions laid end to end, each one taking up just so much time. Different tasks *replace* each other rather than just adding on to each other. And even when two psychological functions are involved, they may run off simultaneously rather than successively. Second, there appears to be no general value that describes a person's discrimination time, choice time, and so on when he moves to different kinds of materials or is given different sets of choices. That is, there is no mental entity—such as pure discrimination, perception, or choice—to measure independently of particular situations. Finally, even if there were such assemblies of elements at low levels, there is no reason to think that they relate to the higher mental functions.

Sir Francis Galton, who was convinced that all sorts of physical and mental abilities should be measured and studied, argued that intelligence is a complex ability of some sort that could only be evaluated by systematic sampling techniques, or "sinking shafts at critical points." He seems to have had in mind the notion that there is some level of general intellectual ability which characterizes any man and that, if one makes measures with just the right tasks, including intellectual complexity, one begins to locate that level for the individual. But in spite of his interest and his general theory, Galton never succeeded in advancing the cause of measuring intelligence. However, he provided much of the statistical thinking and some of the measurement concepts that were later required.

COMPLEX FUNCTIONS AS INTELLIGENCE

The man to whom history gives the credit for designing the first functional intelligence test was an energetic French psychologist, Alfred Binet. It is not a matter of chance or accident that this honor falls to him. Binet spent many years in the search for effective indicators of intelligence. He tried everything from head size and palmistry on the one hand to reaction-time and discrimination judgments on the other. He was driven by his insatiable curiosity, his burning energy, and his very real concern for the diagnosis and classification of feeble-minded or retarded children. He was impressed early in his career with the poor and unreliable methods used for deciding the fate of children suspected of being feeble-minded and the equally poor means of evaluating their progress under one course of education or another. He realized that a radical change was needed and that some kind of *objective* assessment was necessary. His early papers on intelligence were attacks on the laxness of the medical professions with regard to classification and pleas for more objective reporting of what a child actually did or did not do. Binet reported investigations of children of very high and very low intellectual skills, including the "lightning calculators" who could perform amazing feats of computation and "idiot-savants" who possessed some great skill in art or mathematics or memory even though they were of subnormal intelligence in everyday affairs.

Binet finally chose to view intelligence as the faculty of "judgment, otherwise called good sense, practical sense, initiative, the faculty of adapting one's self to circumstances. To judge well, to comprehend well, to reason well, these are the essential activities of intelligence." How judgment is to be measured is still another question, of course. Binet answered this question by choosing a series of "little puzzles" and problems that confronted his subject with simple everyday exercises of judgment. Can a child recognize the difference between a square of chocolate and a square of wood? If so, he is more intelligent than if he cannot. Can he repeat a string of digits spoken to him? If so, he is brighter than if he cannot. Can he tell how two common objects are different? Can he put five weights in order from light to heavy? Can he define common words by function? Can he complete a sentence? In this fashion Binet and his young colleague, Theodore Simon, prepared a test of 29 items that they recommended to the Minister of Public Instruction of Paris as tests of intelligence. Their proposal was to give the little puzzles to normal school children and to compare the performance of classmates to see if they had similar ability or if they were more like the children in the class above or the class below. They would then see which children were advanced and which held back in school and would compare them with regard to their test results. In addition, they would find which ones were esteemed bright and which dull by their teachers and compare their test results.

The *tests* were presented to the field in 1905 and met with reasonable acceptance. In practical affairs, they immediately proved to be valuable. Both in the clinic and in the laboratory, however, psychologists were generally indifferent. In 1908 Binet and Simon presented a measuring *scale* for intelligence. Here they gave evidence of still more insight, for they had created many new tests, rearranged them, and grouped them by appropriate "normal" age. With this scale it was now possible to talk about the *mental age* of a particular child and to describe with precision how many years advanced or retarded he was in intellect. Today we know that this was a major advance in psychometric thought, but at the time even those psychologists who had accepted the *tests* thought that the *scale* was out of the question. It is difficult to imagine now the radical innovation in psychological thought that the scale represented or the extent of the criticism that was directed at such testing from all sources. H.H. Goddard, one of the first Americans to appreciate the work of Binet, wrote in the introduction to *The Development of Intelligence in Children* by Alfred Binet and Theodore Simon:

> Probably no critic of the scale during the past six years has reacted against it more positively than did I at first reading. It seemed impossible to grade intelligence that way. . . . The article was laid aside for some weeks. One day while using the old tests, whose inadequacy was great, . . . I decided to give it a fair trial. . . . Our use of the scale was a surprise and a gratification. It met our needs. A classification of the children based on the scale agreed with the Institution experience. (Binet and Simon, 1916.)

What in fact did Binet do and what kind of model guided his actions? From a consideration of these questions, we can see how his model matured and how he used his evolving notions of psychometrics to establish the scale of intelligence.

In the beginning, Binet was guided in a very general sense by the procedure of Galileo. He knew that there were gross indications of intelligence by which he (and others) could separate people into extreme groups even if they could not adequately discriminate among those in the average run. By trying out new puzzles on obviously very bright or very dull individuals, Binet got a first crude approximation of the usefulness of any particular task. Clearly, if a measure or procedure did not at least separate these extremes, it could not be useful in more refined discriminations. In this way, he was using a crude test of separation of extremes to determine whether a measure was worth following up, just as Galileo used a crude measure (his pulse) to estimate whether another event (the swinging chandelier) was regular. And just as the pendulum principle was used to build accurate timepieces, Binet hoped to use the measures that passed through his first screening to build a more precise instrument that could then be used to collect new information about intelligence.

The gross screening techniques that Binet employed enabled him to discard anatomical measures, such as head size and forehead height, as indicators of intelligence. Further, these procedures were sufficient to lead him to reject the analytic-synthetic approach of measuring the atomic elements of intellect and then combining them. He finally concluded that intelligence has to be measured by tasks that directly involve intelligence. In effect, he decided that a complex trait has to be measured by complex tasks that are actual samples of the functioning of the trait in question.

It is not immediately obvious that this conclusion helps an investigator if he lacks a general definition of a trait that will spell out appropriate items for a test of it. As we have seen, Binet defined intelligence as "judgment," but what he actually did was to select tasks by a whole set of criteria that provided an effective screen for irrelevant items. *First,* Binet himself had to believe that an item related to everyday common sense. If he felt it did not, he rejected it immediately. *Second,* the item had to be a part of daily life. Success in chess playing might be evidence for intelligence, but since not everyone has a chance to learn to play chess, it is a poor test of intelligence. A person may fail simply because he does not know the game. Common language tasks, making change, detecting absurdities, pointing to and naming common objects, and following directions, however, are all good candidates for items because everyone is acquainted with them. *Third,* and most important, each item had to separate bright from dull children. Binet knew that many items which might pass his subjective criteria would not measure intelligence. He was wary, for example, of tests of memory, for he knew many retarded children with normal or even exceptional memories. He wrote:

> . . . one would be tempted to give it (memory) a very conspicuous part in an examination of intelligence. But memory is distinct from and independent of judgment. One may have good sense and lack memory. The reverse is also common. Just at the present time we are observing a backward girl who is developing before our astonished eyes a memory much greater than our own. We have measured that memory and we are not deceived regarding it. Nevertheless that girl presents a most beautifully classic type of imbecility. (Binet and Simon, 1916.)

Finally, the item had to be practicable and easy to administer. Binet knew that children are distractible and that their performances are likely to be affected by fatigue, inattention, shyness, and nervousness. He appreciated the importance of a friendly relation with the child as well as the necessity of avoiding giving hints or cues to responses.

Thus, Binet's procedure for selecting items was a series of successive screens or filters, some objective and some subjective, that pitted each item against a variety of criteria. Failure to pass any stage resulted in the rejection of the proposed item. There was no assurance, of course, that items selected in this fashion would work together efficiently, but it was almost certain that if an item failed these tests its chances of success were very poor.

Binet put his set of puzzles together and tried them out on extreme groups and on people he knew intimately. Satisfied that they were promising, he took them to the school system for further refinement. With the school as a proving ground, he tried to build up a body of data that would justify these measures as true measures of intelligence. In the school situation, Binet used two different indexes of intelligence. First, he reasoned that intelligence must increase with age in children. The older the child, *all other things being equal,* the more intelligent the child should be. It is commonly observed that older children are capable of more difficult intellectual tasks than younger children in mathematics, language, and problem-solving. The first requirement, then, was that the tests should detect a gross change with increasing age, that they should be correctly performed by increasingly higher percentages of children at increasing age levels.

Binet's second crude measure was success in school. Everyone agrees that school presents a child with a highly complex intellectual task. To be successful in school must indicate, at least in part, high intelligence. Conversely, failure in school must be due, at least in part, to low intelligence. On the average, then, Binet thought, children who are successful in school ought to perform better on the tests than children who are unsuccessful in school.

Binet and Simon put their tests up against these criteria and were reassured. Their 29 tests were successfully arranged in order of difficulty from simple psychomotor tests (following an object with one's eyes and grasping it) to difficult verbal tests (defining abstract vocabulary items). The older the children tested, the higher the scores. When "successful" children (candidates for rapid advancement in school) were compared with "unsuccessful" children (candidates for being held over in grade or being sent to special schools), large differences appeared, on the average. The investigators concluded that they had built the first objective, practical instrument for the measurement of intelligence.

But Binet did not stop his research. He realized that he had found a new route to the measurement of the individual, going "from the individual to the general in order to come back to the individual." The first "tests" yielded an ordering of individuals, but Binet was eager to find a measure that would tell him more exactly the difference between two performances on his puzzles. He recognized that he had only an ordinal scale and that it had disadvantages. Every item was not equal to every other item nor did problems differ in difficulty by some common amount. His scale was like a rubber yardstick, stretched in some places and compressed in others, the ordering of the inches was correct but the distances at the different places were not commensurable. Binet wanted to advance to an interval scale in which the interval would have some known psychological meaning. As he plotted his data for each item against the ages of the students, he saw the possibility of using the average performance of each age group as a standard. Rather than just assign a mean score on the test to each age group, however, he decided to make the maximum use of his information by assigning an age level *to each item*. This difference is an interesting one and reflects in a revealing way on the selection of items.

Figure 14.1 shows how items can differ in two respects, *difficulty* and *discrimination*. The item-difficulty index for Binet was the age group in which 50 to 75 per cent of the children pass the item. Each item then has a particular age level associated with it. Discrimination was gauged by the percentage passing from age to age. When results are graphed, a steep line means that most children of younger ages fail the item and almost all of the children of higher ages pass the item. Such an item is sharply discriminating of the age change in intelligence and offers precise information on a child's intellectual level. On the other hand, a line with a flat slope means many children below the age level of the item pass it and many children above the level fail it. Such an item offers less information about where a child stands in mental age even though it would pass the usual criteria; that is, success on the item increases with increasing age and the item probably would separate extreme groups.

Binet saw that a good test would consist of items of high discrimination at each difficulty, or age, level in about equal numbers. This distribution would permit an investigator to gauge mental ability throughout the age

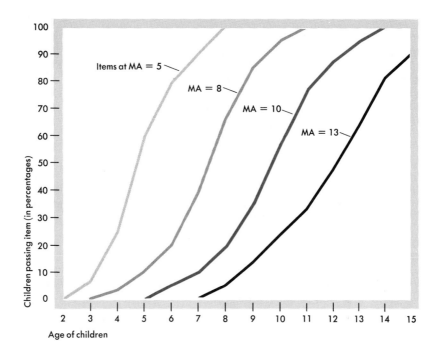

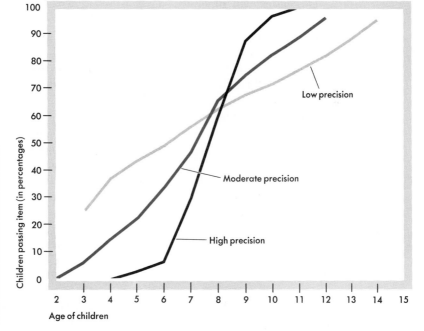

Figure 14.1 Items differing in mental age—index of difficulty (above). Items differing in precision—index of discrimination (below). Lower left, Alfred Binet. (Culver Pictures, Inc.)

range and would let him give an accurate statement of the mental ability of the child in terms that could be understood by others. Thus, he could say that a given child has the mental ability of an eight-year-old, thereby providing a reasonable characterization of what the child could or could not do. In addition, in considering the chronological age of the child, the investigator could say with precision how much the child was accelerated or retarded in mental development.

W. Stern, a German psychologist, later proposed that mental acceleration and retardation ought to be expressed as a proportion of the child's chronological age; that is, he argued that a two-year acceleration or retardation for a child of four was as important as a four-year retardation or acceleration for a child of eight. Binet's work fit this conception perfectly and provided the raw material, a value for mental age. Psychologists could now talk about a child's *intelligence quotient,* or IQ, as the ratio of *mental age,* MA, to *chronological age,* CA. To avoid fractions or decimals, we ordinarily multiply this ratio by 100 as in the following formula:

$$IQ = \frac{MA}{CA} \times 100$$

This index will obviously have an average value of 100 for every age group because of the way both MA and IQ are determined. It provides a quick statement of the *relative brightness* of an individual independent of his absolute level. Thus, two children might have a mental age of six years, but one might be only four years old and the other might be eight years old. Although they have the same absolute level of ability, one of them is bright (the four-year-old) with an IQ of 150 and one of them is dull (the eight-year-old) with an IQ of 75.

Because it was relatively easy to understand, *mental age* was accepted as an important unit of measurement in the popularization of intelligence tests. Similarly, the IQ was given wide publicity as the index of relative brightness. Although these measures were of great important in the beginning of intelligence testing, they have specific limitations as psychometric tools and they have been replaced by standard scores for most applications of intelligence tests.

Even though Binet's ideas met with initial resistance, the immense practical importance of his work eventually won the day. The Binet test was translated into many languages and put to work in schools and institutions all over the world. The notion that intelligence could be measured was firmly established, and one result was waves of research on the correlates of intelligence and on the changes in the measures under different conditions. There were also hosts of conferences on the definition of intelligence and on the "real" nature of intelligence, but in the main the research work went on without much attention to the problems of definitions or the disputes about the nature of what was being measured. Binet had built an instrument for which there was enormous construct validity. He said his test measured intelligence, and virtually every time someone tried it on a task widely assumed to have some relation to intelligence, the test showed that the relation was there. It not only did the things it was built to do, separating the extreme groups and predicting success in school, but it did things that it had not been designed for, such as ranking the occupations in a reasonable fashion with respect to the degree of intellect demanded, picking successful candidates for technical training, and identifying bright but uneducated children.

Models of Intelligence

In our account of the attempt to measure intelligence, we have so far considered two models. The first was Donders's sequential-processing model, which was compatible with the notion of measuring elements of complex behavior and then summing them. We have called it analytic-synthetic in terms of measurement, but in terms of theory it might be called a sequential-components model.

The second model was Binet's. This was a general intelligence model which held that complex behaviors involving judgment are measures of the general trait. This model fits a psychometric scheme of sampling complex behaviors of many sorts and evaluating each task by the characteristics of the people passing and failing it rather than the task's overt or superficial content. Binet's work was compatible with the notions of Galton concerning intelligence and with the general biases of the leading investigators of intelligence in the early part of the century.

The third model of intelligence was that of Charles Spearman, an Englishman on whom the mantle of Galton descended. Spearman was a talented, statistically oriented psychologist who turned his critical eye in on the tests themselves instead of out toward their correlates as Binet had done. Binet was concerned above all with validity; Spearman had as his first concern internal consistency and reliability. As early as 1904, Spearman published a theory and supporting data which suggested that any test of intelligence has a specific content that is independent of intelligence itself. As the theory evolved, it postulated a general intelligence (g) that was involved to some extent in most tasks. Each task that qualified as an intelligence test measured partly g and partly task-specific factors (s_1 for task 1, s_2 for task 2, etc.). For example, in a heterogeneous test battery you might have: discrimination of shades of gray which would involve some g for the abstract ability to discriminate and a specific factor (s_1) for the visual aspects of the task; an addition test which involves g and a specific factor for the particular arithmetic skills (s_2); matching columns of names and numbers which involves

g plus specific clerical-perceptual skills (s_3), and so on. The job of the investigator is to find tasks high in g and low in s. Averaging over many tests with different s factors should suppress specifics and leave a fair measure of general intelligence (Spearman, 1927).

Spearman's work gradually merged with other views that had been growing in the United States. The earliest was that of Edward L. Thorndike who felt that the appearance of generality in intelligence was simply a function of the overlap of specific neural connections that were involved in the infinite series of possible mental acts. What appeared to be general intelligence was not a particular faculty but rather an index of the number and extent of neural connections which a person could form and had formed in ways that were useful when he came to deal with the test. In effect, Thorndike's *connectionism* substituted number of connections for general capacity and in the end was not very easy to distinguish from it.

As psychologists became more sophisticated and more conscious of the apparent conflict between the views of Binet and Spearman, they began asking how they could justify adding scores together on group tests (such as the Army Alpha devised to select and classify troops in the First World War). Carl Brigham (1930) argued that it was like adding together peaches, apples, horses, and cows. It was true that a number was the result, but there was no assurance that the number really stood for anything. Brigham and T.L. Kelley (1928) began to view intelligence as being made up of loosely linked "group factors." The linkage (the fact that they always had positive intercorrelations with other group factors) was the source of the appearance of general intelligence. The group factors themselves seemed to involve reasonable divisions of intellectual behavior—quantitative, verbal, spatial, perceptual and so on. At the same time, Spearman began broadening his notions about specific types of intelligence and recognized that specific factors could become group factors if he included several tests of related sorts. Thus, the picture began to emerge of a general intelligence that is a core of overlapping abilities with group factors that vary around the level of the general intelligence.

During the 1930s Louis and Thelma Thurstone (1941) made the case for *independent* group factors. They argued that intelligence could be properly divided into *primary mental abilities* that are relatively independent. What was wanted, they argued, was not a gross measure of general ability but rather a set of measures that would give a good analytic picture of the underlying types of intelligence which were only poorly described by some over-all score. The general score was weak, they said, because it gave no further diagnostic information to indicate which components contributed to the score.

Hot debates took place concerning the theory of intelligence and equally hot debates surrounded the development of the statistical techniques required to give order to the many test scores involved. Although these techniques were somewhat esoteric and frightfully laborious, they were all essentially correlational, and the burning question was always to determine "what went with what." As usual, assumptions varied and the results reflected them. After the debates died down and tempers cooled, it became apparent that there are several ways to view intelligence and that an investigator might want different models for different kinds of work.

The oldest model is the simple *general intelligence model*. The problem here is to determine a general level, like finding the level of a water table in an area where neither the subterranean structure nor the surface varies radically. You sample at a variety of points and come to a general conclusion. (Figure 14.2 may help you to a graphic understanding of the differences between the models.)

The second model makes room for *specific intelligence factors* involved in particular tests and makes a determined effort to evaluate these carefully so that they can be removed from the estimate of general intelligence. Closely related to the first model, this model is an attempt to refine the measurement.

According to the *specific-connections model*, one must measure the results of collections of specific elements across a never-ending set of tasks. The running average of these task levels, then, creates the appearance of general intelligence though that entity was not specifically recognized.

The *group-factor* theorists can be represented by a limited number of factors, all standing on the same basis of nonspecific intelligence. Different theorists disagree about the amount of generalized intelligence they need to invoke. *Primary mental abilities* are presented here as if there were no general component at all.

The *hierarchical approach* now tries to incorporate some features of all the views and argues that the best representation of intellect provides for general intelligence, group factors, specific intelligences, and finally, the detailed skills and task factors involved in each individual task. Such a model has been advocated by C.L. Burt (1949).

Since there are data to support all these views, how can we choose among them? If you think of the intelligence test as a practical device, the answer is simple: Do not try to unravel the Gordian knot, simply cut it with the validity coefficients. Ask what each approach does in relation to your problem. Now things will begin to sort themselves out. If your problem is a general selection or classification problem applied to a widely heterogeneous population, such as all fifth-grade children in a large city or a draft sample in the army, the general intelligence approach is both adequate and appropriate. The range of scores on every test will be very great and the scores on the various types of tests (arithmetic, verbal, spatial, and so on) will all be highly correlated. Anyone of these tests will do the work of the others and a mixture of them (as on the Army General Classification Test) is highly effective and probably slightly better than any particular form of test since it permits specifics to balance out somewhat.

If, on the other hand, you are in charge of selecting the best candidate for graduate school or the best bet for executive training from a group of su-

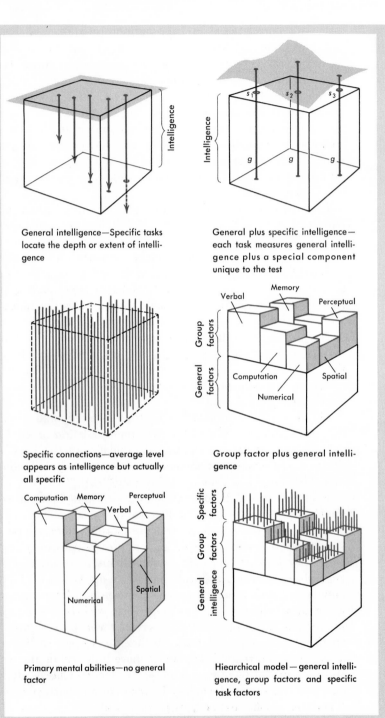

General intelligence—Specific tasks locate the depth or extent of intelligence

General plus specific intelligence—each task measures general intelligence plus a special component unique to the test

Specific connections—average level appears as intelligence but actually all specific

Group factor plus general intelligence

Primary mental abilities—no general factor

Hiearchical model—general intelligence, group factors and specific task factors

Figure 14.2 Models of theories of intelligence.

perior college graduates, an intelligence test of the usual sort is going to be useless. All of your candidates will have fairly high scores and there will be little difference between them. (After all, they have all been screened for four years by a complex device, called college, which is supposed to discriminate on the basis of intellect.) Now, if you know some other ability needed in the task you are trying to predict such as verbal fluency, perceptual acuity, or mathematical abilities, you will surely want to evaluate it because the candidates are much more likely to vary on that dimension than they are on general intelligence. Similarly, you might want to turn to nonintellectual factors such as motivation or work habits, which are likely to determine success or failure once everyone is equated on intelligence.

These two reasonable decisions reflect not only the practical but also the theoretical way to look at models of intelligence. All of these models are incorporated in the hierarchical model and all belong to one great class of *simple additive models*. Which variant of the models you want to look at or which level of the hierarchy you want to study depends on your particular reasons for being concerned with intelligence at all. Arguments about the "true" nature of intelligence have, fortunately, gone out of style and there is widespread realization that the measurement of intelligence can be accomplished under any of these views as long as the investigator varies his instruments as he shifts to new populations and new problems.

The Relation of Intelligence Test Scores to Other Variables

Given a way to measure intelligence, what can we say about the thing that is being measured? In fact, a network of relationships can now be built up around this construct, a network that tells us more and more about the nature of the construct that we are measuring. In effect, we expect to lift ourselves by our bootstraps into more knowledge.

Two historical developments need to be noted. First, Binet's model provided a general method, and other psychologists built tests, selected items, and validated their tests on much the same criteria as did Binet. In the United States, Lewis Terman at Stanford University followed this route in the development of the 1916 Stanford-Binet Test. This became the standard individually administered test in the country. It was revised by Terman and Maud Merrill in 1937 and again in 1960. In the minds of most Americans it is *the* IQ test. Second, group testing appeared. Binet would have surely disapproved since he felt that the clinical observations of the child made during testing were of critical importance. But when the United States entered the First World War, a group of psychologists (including Terman and his student, A.S. Otis) developed a group test, the Army Alpha, which could be given as a paper-and-pencil test to many people at once. During the war, 1,700,000 soldiers were tested, classified, and assigned, and the worth of group testing was firmly established. In addition, valuable normative data were developed and many relations of the intelligence test to social class, occupation, place of residence, race, schooling, educational level, and other variables were determined in a simple descriptive manner. Group testing made possible an enormous expansion of the testing movement and greatly speeded the collection of data.

One of the first areas of study was the relationship of intelligence to age. In the development of the tests, of course, items had been selected to show an increase in the proportion of children passing with increasing age. But beyond the mid-teens it proved to be difficult to find such items. After repeated attacks on the problem with large pools of items similar to those that worked so well at earlier ages, investigators finally concluded that intelligence leveled off at some point in early maturity and that the average person did not show further growth with increasing age. This was a radical notion that was much misunderstood and bitterly resisted. Newspapers and magazines accused psychologists of fostering the myth of the "child mind" and attacked the testers vigorously every time an advertiser brought out a silly ad or a publisher promoted a pulp magazine. Columnists freely criticized psychologists for doing idiotic work or took the work as proof of what the columnists had known all along, that the mass of the people were stupid. In fact, of course, both of these reactions were misguided.

Two important methodological findings emerged from the study of age and intelligence measures. First, it was discovered that an item capable of functioning as an intelligence item at one age level might not remain so at another level. For example, a performance test works very adequately for children under ten years of age; that is, the percentage of those passing increases with age and it correlates with school achievement. But at age ten or so, performance tests begin to lose this capacity. The speed at which the task can be performed levels off so there is no further increase with age and the variables that determine which children are best on the task seem to have more to do with maturing motor skills than with intellect. Figure 14.3 shows a comparison of two kinds of tests with increasing age which makes this limitation clear.

This phenomenon is also found at the other end of the age scale. The performance of older persons declines on different kinds of tests at different rates. In general, performances on *speed* tests (tests with tight time limits) are likely to show a decline almost without regard to the content of the test as age increases beyond 30. On the other hand, on *power* tests (which permit the subject to take all the time he wants) scores may continue to increase for many years. With some tasks, such as those depending on vocabulary, the scores may increase throughout the entire life span, especially if a person is in a verbal occupation such as writing or teaching.

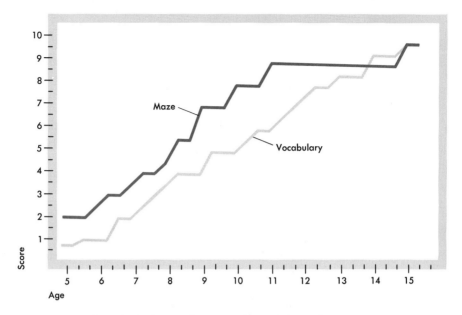

Figure 14.3 Age trends on two subtests of the Wechsler intelligence scale for children. Notice that the performance test reaches asymptote about 11 years of age. (Wechsler, 1950.)

Cross-Sectional Studies. The second interesting methodological finding was related to how age studies were done. In the early studies, the testing was, of course, performed on *cross-sections* at various ages. That is, the testers located samples of children, teenagers, and adults wherever they could find them. This approach created two problems.

First, the samples that were used were differentially selective. You can easily get a sample of normal school children that is a good representation of the population, but it becomes harder and harder to get representative samples as children leave school and take up various occupations. Some people are too busy to be tested, some do not want to bother, some are afraid to be tested, some are hidden away by their relatives or put in institutions, some die, some drift out of the normal reach of society "on the road" or in skid row. There is no easy way to find out whether the sample at succeeding years is representative of its age group as in the early years.

The second problem is that even if a person were sure that he had a good sample at every particular year, the samples differ in more ways than age alone. All of the variables that are changing in our society over time are changing as we move across the age groups in the study. Thus, because the average amount of education is increasing in the United States, a representative sample of 50-year-olds will have had many fewer years of schooling than a representative sample of 25-year-olds. Few of us realize how massive such changes have been in our population, but even a simple survey shows huge differences among age groups in theatre attendance, books and magazines read, recreation, size of town lived in, availability of radio and television, church-going, nutrition and diet, life expectancy, and even such variables as height and weight (see Kuhlen, 1940). Given all these differences, it is difficult to assign any particular differences found on intelligence tests to age alone. The differences might just as well be attributed to any or all of the other factors.

The typical cross-sectional study shows a rapid growth in intelligence and a slow decline beginning in the 20s and continuing down till death. Figure 14.4 shows such a study. Another finding of the cross-sectional studies is that the time of onset of the decline is related to the brightness of the individual. In general, the brighter individuals in the cross section show more rapid growth in intelligence for a longer time and a much-delayed decline. Such individuals are usually employed in "intellectual" occupations and gain higher educations than the rest of the distribution, so it is not clear whether the difference is attributable to superior endowment or to educational training and practice.

Longitudinal Studies. As the problems of the cross-sectional study became clearer, psychologists became less confident about interpreting the cross-sectional data and turned to tedious, expensive *longitudinal studies,* which attempt to correct the shortcoming of the cross-sectional study by drawing a sample of individuals at some particular age and then measuring them year after year. This method avoids the problems of changes in representa-

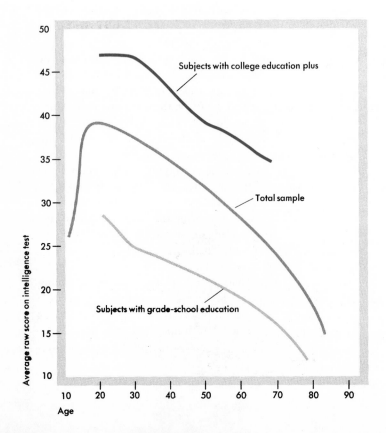

Figure 14.4 Intelligence test score as a function of age and level of education. Average score on the test is about 29; standard deviation is about 10. Test is a speed test. (After Miles and Miles, 1932.)

Subjects with college education plus

Total sample

Subjects with grade-school education

Average raw score on intelligence test

Age

tiveness with successive samples. Whatever bias the sample has is consistent from year to year and cannot contribute to the differences to be attributed to age. It also avoids attributing effects of cultural differences to age differences, since the cultural conditions are constant for the members of the group as they proceed from age to age.

The longitudinal method is not perfect, however. It produces new problems because of repeated testing. That is, the testing itself may induce changes as the members of the sample become skilled test-takers or there may be learning and memory effects carrying over from one testing to the next. The problem of equivalent tests becomes acute in any attempt to compare progress from childhood through adulthood, and it is hard to know what counts as a comparable measurement. In addition, it is difficult to keep a sample of individuals intact as time goes on. After even a year or two, it will not be possible to locate all the members of the initial sample. Inevitably, the losses from the sample will be highly selective, rather than random; the brighter ones will appear in more records and be easier to trace; the ones who cannot pay bills will skip town; those who achieve fame or notoriety will be easily located while the undistinguished may disappear, and so on.

The most famous case of a longitudinal study is Terman's study of gifted children. Between 1911 and 1924, Terman and his associates located 1000 gifted children in the California schools. Their hope was to draw a sample that was representative of children with IQ's above 140 (that is, about two-and-one-half standard deviations above the mean, the top one-half of one per cent of the population). Terman was interested in determining the characteristics of these children at the time (obtaining immediate descriptive data concerning their interests, personality, achievements, home and school activities) and in following them later to see whether they fulfilled their early promise or sank into mediocrity as some writers had predicted. As the study went on, Terman was forced to invent new measuring instruments since the children "ran out the top" of the early measures. When they began to marry he devised studies of marital happiness, and when they chose occupations he struggled with the issues of measuring vocational interest and job satisfaction. Then, of course, the gifted children had children and they in turn became subjects for study and their careers came similarly under scrutiny. Now the original gifted children are approaching retirement and studies of their adaptation to retirement are of special interest. To date five volumes have appeared in the Genetic Studies of Genius, published by Terman's group. Four of them have been devoted to these particular subjects (see Terman and Oden, 1959).

With respect to the change of intelligence with age, the results of the longitudinal study contradict the cross-sectional studies. The children selected by Terman, bright as they were, did not show a decline in intelligence with increasing age. Indeed, they seemed to get brighter and brighter with the passing years. It is not easy to evaluate all of the data since people were lost to the sample through illness, war, and simple disappearance, but the success of the group is amazingly clear. They collected every sort of intellectual honor one can imagine and contributed far more than their share to the intellectual and cultural life of the nation.

Although Terman's study contains very valuable information, it does not, of course, tell us about the course of intellectual development in the more nearly average person. In the late 1940s, W.A. Owens, Jr. (1953) at Iowa State University discovered a batch of Army Alpha examinations that had been given to psychology classes at Iowa State in 1919. He immediately sensed the opportunity this cache provided and started a follow-up study. He located 127 men of the original sample and retested them on exactly the same instrument after a lapse of 31 years. To his surprise he found that there was no decline in the average score on any subtest of the Army Alpha (even though it is a speed test) and on several subtests there were appreciable increases in scores. The tests showing improvement at the older age level were those involving verbal skills and routine operations (information, comprehension, arithmetic, and memory span for digits).

David Campbell (1965) did a similar follow-up on university students who had been tested and counseled at the University of Minnesota in the mid-thirties. Retesting them after 25 years, he found that they exceeded the scores they had made on the entrance tests as college freshmen. He also noted that they did a little less well than today's freshmen when they were tested with the current admissions test. Thus, Campbell's study seems to catch the essential difference between the longitudinal and cross-sectional studies. The same sample of subjects at age 45 (approximately) appear brighter than they themselves were when they were 20 (the longitudinal comparison), but at the same time they seem less bright than today's 20-year-olds (a cross-sectional comparison).

Berkeley Growth Study. The most ambitious attempt so far to sum up the changes in intelligence with age is that of Nancy Bayley (1955) with the data from the Berkeley Growth Study. It is important to know whether intelligence is relatively stable and to what extent it can be predicted from data early in life. Hundreds of studies show that intelligence is stable for short periods (say from year to year) in school children with test-retest reliabilities in the .80s and .90s. But such short-run stability does not necessarily argue for long-term stability or for long-term predictability. One of the first findings of the Berkeley Growth Study was that *infant* test scores, based largely on such capacities as motor development, attention to stimulation, and vocalization, are useless in the prediction of future intelligence test scores. After many attempts to build such scales, it seems fair to conclude that, except for obviously pathological cases, there is no reason to think that test data gathered earlier than two years of age has any appreciable validity in predicting later intelligence. After two years of age the tests begin to measure something which correlates a little with later test scores. Finally, after age five or six, the tests seem to be measuring the traditional general intelligence and permit reliable classification of children in at least broad categories such as average, dull, and bright.

Many problems of measurement arise because some tests are only appropriate at particular ages and must be replaced at other ages. In addition, some tests give only "pass-fail" results while others yield numerical scores. Comparing tests at different ages and combining scores of different sorts of tests can be very difficult. Bayley has tried to solve these problems by use of a scale which she calls the *16-D score*. She developed this score essentially by putting the test results of the children at age 16 into standard scores. Then she worked with test performance at adjacent ages (15 or 17) and put those in terms of 16-year-old equivalents. In this fashion she worked up and down in age one year at a time setting the tasks equivalent to each other in terms of the special scores based on the 16-year-old performance. Although this kind of scaling requires many assumptions, it is a convenient way to get a common set of numbers that will permit us to talk about changes from one year to the next and will let us compare a particular child's standing at one time to his standing at another.

Bayley's general growth curve is given in Figure 14.5. Although it is hypothetical in many ways, it probably furnishes a fair summary of the present common view of the growth of intelligence. It pictures that growth as being very rapid from two to ten years of age, then gradually slowing down into the mid-teens, and becoming still slower in the late teens. Several aspects of the curve should be noted. One is that growth does not stop short at some point. Indeed, Bayley's data suggest that intelligence is still increasing (although very slowly) at age 25 Another is that the dispersion in intelligence increases with increasing age. The difference between a bright and a dull eight-year-old is less than the difference between a bright and a dull 16-year-old. That is, bright children gain at a faster rate than

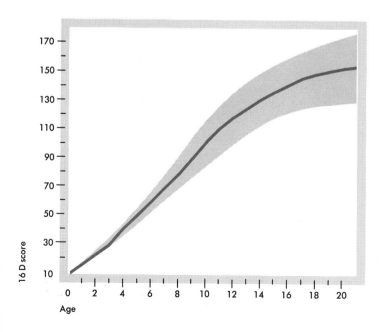

Figure 14.5 Curves of means (heavy line) and standard deviation of intelligence (indicated by shading) by 16D units, up to age 21. (Bayley, 1955.)

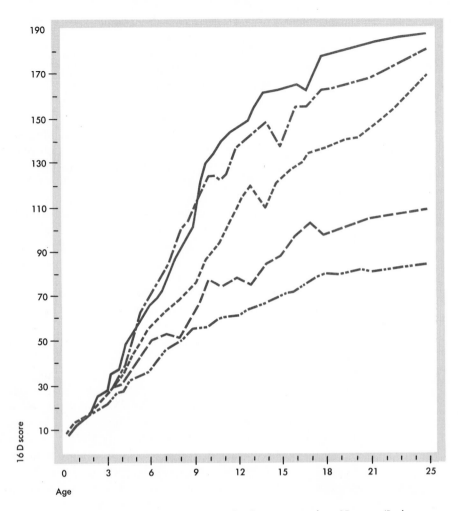

Figure 14.6 Growth curves for five boys, one month to 25 years. (Bayley, 1955.)

dull children and go on gaining longer. The individual data from many other studies seem to confirm this finding, as do the individual curves from the Berkeley study in Figure 14.6. A study of the individual curves shows that, while there is a lot of variability, there is also marked consistency. In general, bright children remain bright and dull children remain dull, though there may be many individual exceptions.

S E X

One popular subject for debate has always been whether men are brighter than women. A glance at history, a quick turning of the pages of *Who's Who*, a systematic search through *American Men of Science* (just note the title), all confirm that men achieve more than women in virtually every field of intellectual endeavor. It is also true, however, that a tour of state institutions for the retarded or the mentally ill will turn up more men than women. Proponents can choose their weapons as they like and prove either side of the argument. Which is correct?

Fortunately or unfortunately, as the case may be, psychologists do not have a simple answer to this apparently simple question. In the standardization of the usual intelligence test, items favoring either boys or girls are ordinarily discarded on the grounds that they reflect particular experiences. Obviously, if the test items are confined to those dealing with dolls, dresses, food, and families, there is likely to be a bias in favor of girls. If, on the other hand, items are restricted to machinery, sports, science, and weapons, there will be a bias in favor of boys. Acting on the belief that items should be unbiased, test-makers commit themselves to developing a test that will not show differences between the sexes—even if they exist.

Some facts are clear. In elementary school girls make much better grades than boys, apparently because they are more docile and more likely to please the teachers. The differences between the sexes are ordinarily reduced, however, if, instead of relying on the teacher's evaluation, one looks at achievement tests that are objectively scored. With increasing age, boys' grades catch up with those of girls for several reasons. For one, it is usually easier for a boy than for a girl to leave school; boys who are doing badly in school do tend to leave, thus raising the average achievement level of the boys by withdrawing a low score from the distribution. Second, the social variable is minimized as the boys become more socialized and the tasks for which they are graded depend less on docility and obedience. Third, in at least several studies, there is evidence that the girls fall behind in the rate of mental growth. In Terman's sample of gifted children, for example, the ratio of boys to girls was about like the population ratio in grade school (116 boys to 100 girls), but in high school it turned overwhelmingly to boys (212 boys to 100 girls). In a study carried out at Fels Institute (Sontag, Baker, and Nelson, 1958), careful attention was given to the question of which children in a longitudinal study changed most in IQ and why. When the data were grouped by gains and losses, it was clear that the gainers were predominantly male and the losers were predominantly female. The personality data suggested that the children who showed gains were more independent and aggressive and those who showed losses were passive and dependent.

Whether these findings reflect some deep characteristics of the growth rates and innate abilities of girls and boys or whether they reflect only cultural pressures to conform to certain patterns is not yet known. Surely women have been limited in their achievements far below their intellectual capabilities by cultural customs that have barred them from schooling, occupations, professions, and activities where high achievements are possible.

On the other hand, what about the surplus of boys in institutions? Does this show that boys are really inferior to girls or that the distribution of intelligence among males is more variable? The hypothesis of greater variability is tempting for it would at one stroke explain the greater number of both intellectually superior and intellectually inferior males. Unfortunately, there is no real support for this view. In careful examinations of very complete population studies of sex differences (for instance, Scottish surveys that took *every child* in the country born on February 1, May 1, August 1, and November 1 in 1926 and tested them at age 12), no differences were found in either average intelligence or in variability.

The difference seems to rest on cultural practice again. A study of the children who are committed to institutions for the feeble-minded (Hollingworth, 1922) showed that boys are admitted earlier than girls but that the girls who are admitted are much more retarded than the average of boys. This pattern suggests that it is easier for a mentally retarded girl to make some kind of place for herself in the world than it is for a boy who is expected to hold a job and make a living.

When we turn to specific components of abilities of men and women, we find clear patterns of differences which are in the main what our culture leads us to believe. Some of them are incorporated in cultures the world around. For example, it is widely believed that women talk a lot. It is no surprise, then, to find that women excel men in verbal fluency, age at which they first talk, and number of words per sentence at any given age. It should be noted, however, that women do not have larger vocabularies than men. Boys in turn are better at solving arithmetic and science problems and have a better grasp of spatial relations. Girls are better at motor tasks involving fine coordinations, whereas boys are better at tasks requiring strength. Girls excel in immediate memory and in rote memory generally. They are also vastly superior to boys and men in clerical ability (speed and accuracy of perception). Many other differences can be identified. Some appear to be products of specific features of our culture or educational system and some appear to be genetically based, appearing, indeed, as early as we can measure them and persisting throughout life.

The important question to ask seems to be not whether men are smarter than women or vice versa but whether there are interesting patterns of differences between men and women that can help us understand the effects of cultural influences and the degree to which traits may be modified. In addition, of course, such differences may be of use to us in applications of psychology for counseling and placement.

RACE AND CLASS DIFFERENCES

There have been hundreds of studies of race and class differences in the United States. There are four reasons for this abundance. First, dramatically large variations in measured intelligence have been discovered in large survey studies, for example, in the data from the testing of soldiers during the First World War. Psychologists interested in understanding the nature of intelligence and what determines it have been attracted to an examination of these observed differences in race and class grouping. Second, American psychologists, sociologists, political scientists, and historians have traditionally been interested in problems of assimilation of diverse national, ethnic, and racial groups into the melting-pot culture and have turned to psychometric studies and social-status surveys. Third, practical concerns have stimulated studies of the most effective ways to assign individuals to roles in the community, particular sequences in the educational system, and jobs in the armed services. Finally, some investigators have conducted studies designed to "prove" that some political point of view was right or wrong, especially with respect to issues of equality and inequality, which weigh heavily in the American tradition.

We can save ourselves some difficulty later if we agree now that psychological variation (as long as it is nonpathological) is not a criterion for *political* judgments of equality or inequality. We do not use a man's height, metabolism, or ability to broadjump as a political criterion, nor do we get upset by the objective study of these variables. The same provisions must extend to the study of psychological variables. What action one decides to take with respect to psychological differences depends on the interpretation and understanding of the facts that can be collected. Such decisions call for judicious thought, study, and experimentation, not for action impelled by emotion and unanalyzed beliefs. The nonpsychological examples just mentioned may be valuable as models. We know that systematic height differences exist between groups and that height within any one group may be largely determined genetically. We also know, however, that a radical change of diet may change the average height of an entire generation (making it either taller, as in Japan following World War II, or shorter, as in Germany in the period immediately following World War I). Similarly, we know that we can manipulate metabolism, sometimes from pathological to normal, but we also know that there are inner controls which dictate how much change we can effect. Finally, in broadjumping we know that training and proper nutrition are important. But we also know that, even if everyone receives proper food and training, there will still be very large differences among individuals in their ability to broadjump.

Facts and Interpretations. Descriptive facts about occupations, educational levels, nationality groups, social classes, and racial groups in the United States are not hard to find. In the usual general-purpose intelligence test, consistent differences are found between groups classified on these various dimensions (see Figure 14.7). It is obvious, of course, that we need to know many other things to interpret these data. For example, no one should attribute the nationality differences found in the early part of the twentieth century in the United States to the population of the nation from which the

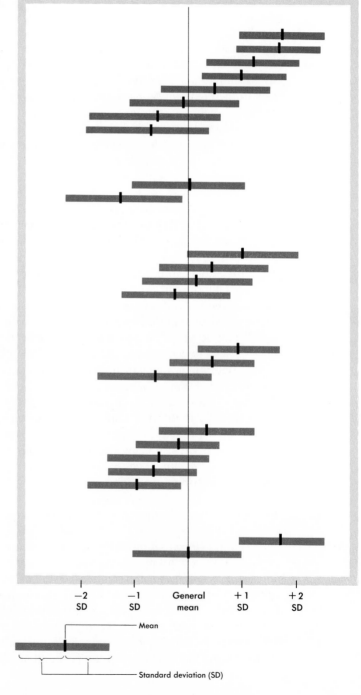

OCCUPATIONS

Accountants
Engineers
Bookkeepers
Clerk-typists
Sales clerks
Painters
Farm hands
Teamsters

"RACIAL" GROUPS

White
Negro

SOCIOECONOMIC CLASS
Children of:

Professionals
Clerical-skilled
Semi-skilled
Laborers

EDUCATION
Adults who completed:

Some college
Twelfth grade
Sixth grade

IMMIGRANTS TO U.S. (early 1900s)

English
Swedish
Irish
Greek
Italian

ARMY RANKS (WW I)

Officers
Enlisted men, draftees

−2
SD

−1
SD

General
mean

+1
SD

+2
SD

Mean

KEY

Standard deviation (SD)

Figure 14.7 Samples of group differences in intelligence.

immigrants came. The differences among nationality groups in the United States appear to reflect most directly the reasons for migration. Many immigrants from southeastern Europe came as cheap labor. Many immigrants from northwestern Europe were changing countries for political or religious reasons. We should not be surprised to find that such groups are very different.

An example helps make this point clear. R.N. Franzblau (1935) studied teenage girls in communities of Danes and of Italians in the United States and other girls in Copenhagen and Rome. She used a nonverbal intelligence test. Although she found that the American Danes scored higher than American Italians, she found no differences in the European groups in their home cities. The variation was attributable to the very high scoring of the American Danes since the American Italians were equal to both the Copenhagen and Rome samples. The U.S. Danes may have represented a very selective sample or they may have managed to settle into an exceptionally favorable environment. It is clear that we are *not* entitled to conclude that northwestern Europeans are brighter than southeastern Europeans.

We can raise parallel questions concerning differences in schooling shown in Figure 14.7. Are we to interpret these findings as indicating that bright people go to school longer or that going to school longer makes them brighter? Surely we want to give ourselves a chance to choose both of these options. Given two children who differ substantially in intelligence at age five, it is a good bet that the brighter one will go farther in school (and in the long run will arrive in a higher-status job). But given two children at age five of equal brightness, it must also be a good bet that the one who pursues schooling farther will get a higher score on a general intelligence test at age 25. Correlational studies cannot settle the interpretation. It is easy to design experimental studies of this kind of problem, but no one is willing (for good reasons) to put them to the test. All we would need to do is select pairs of children who are comparable in the characteristics we are interested in and then randomly choose one child of each pair for extensive schooling and the other for restricted schooling. Naturally, we do not want to conduct this kind of study. If, on the other hand, we compare children who have continued in school with those who have not and match them *after the fact*, there is no assurance that the matching means anything. Obviously, the children must have differed in some important way so that one went on and one did not, and that variable (or set of variables) may be responsible for any difference we find in test scores later. Torsten Husén (1951) investigated this problem in follow-up studies in Sweden. After making reasonable adjustments and admitting that there can be no rigorous solution to the problem of causal analysis in these kinds of studies, he estimated that, relative to primary school (through sixth grade), senior secondary schooling through grade 12 was worth about 7 to 10 IQ points. Junior secondary schooling (through grade 10) was worth about 5 to 7 IQ points. In both cases part of the difference is attributable to *losses* in the IQ of children who stop schooling. Although such studies are far short of proof, they suggest that the continued stimulation of school is an important factor in intelligence-test scores.

Occupational differences may at first appear to be forced outcomes of the relation between intelligence and schooling and the requirement of various occupations. Since many occupations are closed to persons without college degrees or specialized training, members of the occupation are automatically screened for intelligence. The argument cuts both ways, however, since it can be argued that these occupations developed their standards from experience and that the standards reflect valid cutoff points that really work. For example, the military service has from time to time been greatly pressed to develop technicians and experts in many highly technical capacities. Here, where it is to the advantage of the service to use the lowest standards compatible with successful completion of the course of training, we still find occupational hierarchies and intelligence requirements for admissions because these criteria do the job effectively. The median scores for various Air Force Technical Specialties are given in Table 14.1. They reflect differential intelligence levels resulting from experience with trainees and specialists during the development of the specialty.

Special Problems. Social-class and racial differences are hot issues in today's political and scientific discussions. Almost everyone has strong opinions, but few have struggled to understand the facts about race and class differences in intelligence. These facts are not by any means easy to gather nor do they speak unambiguously when they are gathered. There are three major sources of confusion in the area. First, "race" and "class" are difficult terms to apply with any degree of precision. Some anthropologists argue that mankind is not really separated into races and other anthropologists argue that there are as many as ten reasonably good racial groupings. Social class as a category is as bad or worse. Few people believe that social classes are clearly separated in the United States. But almost everyone believes that relatively different levels can be established (which vary as the indexes used vary) and that some gross general effect is shown by comparing groups that are well separated on many criteria. To further complicate the problem, the terms "race" and "class" are inconsistently defined and applied. Though race, for example, is supposed to be a biological concept, it is clear that what is ordinarily under study is not biological categories but, rather, groups that are classified as races on the basis of a variety of superficial physical and social criteria.

The second major problem after the definition problem concerns measurement. If two groups are noticeably different, can the same test be applied to both the groups? This is a delicate and difficult problem for which no thoroughly adequate solution exists. Suppose someone asks you to take the Bushman's General Ability Examination (which we have just made up for the occasion). The test consists of photographs, mostly of hard, rocky

Examples of Specialties	N	AGCT Score
Weather forecaster	726	137
Weather observer	4,516	126
Bombsight mechanic	1,764	124
Aerial photographer	657	120
Tabulating machine operator	400	119
Photographer	501	115
Photo lab technician	6,496	115
Machinist	2,898	110
Airplane & engine mechanic	103,542	110
Supply clerk	10,431	106
Electrician	2,462	104
Mess sergeant	5,467	102
Sheet metal worker	287	102
Construction foreman	1,525	102
Auto mechanic	5,491	95
Baker	3,348	94
Military policeman	5,755	94
Tractor driver	1,118	91
Cook	36,279	90
Messenger	1,783	89
Hospital orderly	4,748	86
Barber	341	84
Orderly	2,675	80
Laborer	12,304	75

Table 14.1 Army general classification test results for Air Force specialists. (Harrell, 1946, pp. 341–349.)

ground, and your task is to say what kind of animal or creature passed this spot, which way he was going, and how long ago it was. You later learn that this test has high validity as a measure of the intelligence of Bushman adults and that you have scored at the idiot or imbecile level. You surely would protest that this was not a fair examination, that you had no experience with these kinds of materials, that you did not even know the names of the possible animals, and so on. In precisely the same way the case can be made against the use of tests standardized on white, urban, middle-class children for the measurement of intelligence for individuals in any other group. However, it could be argued that the Bushman test is *valid* even for you because it would predict pretty well the likelihood of your survival *if* you were suddenly dropped alone into the Bushman environment. The point, of course, is that intelligent behavior is dependent on many kinds of knowledge, skill, and experience and that we cannot measure intelligence in any direct way apart from the influence of these items. Thus, we must ask what is being measured when a test is applied to any new group and we need to discover in each new case what the test scores can be used for.

The third major problem goes beyond the definition of the group and the validity of the scores. It has to do with why the scores are the way they are. Even if we know that two groups are different and that the test scores predict the same things for the two groups, we still need to understand why the differences exist. This leads us to the slippery old questions of heredity and environment, nature and nurture. Most group comparisons involve groups that are different in many, many ways at once. The groups are likely to differ in biological constitution, social class, culture, language, amount of schooling, type of schooling, family income, aspirations, motivations, job opportunities, quality of nutrition, attitudes toward authority, and so on without limit. To which sets of variables are the differences to be ascribed?

These three problems suggest that we psychologists should be more specific and less ambitious in our work on race and class differences. If theoretical clarity is not possible, we should ask the applied questions to which we need answers in the clearest and most effective ways possible. The ordinary applied question is not directed at race or class *per se*, but at some particular group or groups that we can identify for social or educational purposes. We must not permit ourselves to think that we have a racial or class sample that will permit us to generalize our findings to other groups with the same race or class labels. A sample of black children in a Minneapolis kindergarten is more like a sample of white children in Minneapolis that it is like a sample of black children in Charleston, South Carolina (see Brown, 1944). The grounds of comparability are more likely to rest in background and experience than they are in skin color or racial label.

The above considerations also suggest that for each group that the tests measure we must re-establish the same functions. Although this sounds obvious, it is more often forgotten than not. A good instance of correct procedure is found in partial validation of the Army performance test used in World War II. Many illiterates were drafted. It was to the Army's advantage to teach them to read and write. The performance test was evaluated on its ability to predict which men could be taught to read and which could not. The tests worked equally well in the white and Negro groups, though they rejected many more Negroes than whites. Thus, it was fair to conclude that the tests measured the same kind of thing in the two groups. Critics, however, often point out that most schools (even Army schools) are biased in the same way the tests are and that the common bias creates the correlation between them. There is no convincing evidence that this is so, nor does this charge suggest what should be done if it were indeed true.

One way out of the problem of constantly evaluating tests for each situation and each population would seem to be the development of tests that do not depend on any particular learning or experience. Several investigators have tried to devise "culture free" or "culture fair" intelligence tests. Such tests avoid language and generally employ materials that are new to all persons being tested, often taking the form of spatial analogies. These tests may reduce the specific training that shows up on the test score but, of course, one may still talk about the general advantage enjoyed by subjects raised in a culture that widely employs geometrical designs and figures and one in which there is little such experience. In addition, such a test must still be shown to function as an intelligence test for each group in which it is to be applied, and that requirement often is not met.

Race and Class. In the United States, clearly there are large race and class differences on standard intelligence tests. For example, Negroes in the cities and rural areas test lower than whites in those areas (see Figure 14.8). But we do not know whether this difference is to be attributed to the race, the class, the local schools, or the 1000 other variables that go along with the race, class, and environment. Many studies have attempted to control factors to some extent by making special comparisons. It is now well known, as Table 14.2 shows, that northern blacks score higher than southern blacks and that northern whites score higher than southern whites. Thus, although

Figure 14.8 IQ distribution of Negro children in five southwestern states compared with Terman-Merrill normative sample. (Kennedy, Van de Riet, and White, 1963.)

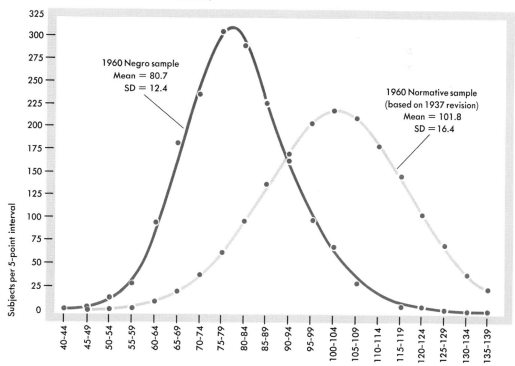

IQ interval

		Skin Color	
		Black	White
Northern	Mean	12.0	14.1
	SD	2.4	2.6
Southern	Mean	9.8	12.7
	SD	1.8	2.4

Table 14.2 Scores on the combined scale (scores from the Army Alpha and Army Beta Tests) for northern and southern black and white recruits in World War I. Northern states are Illinois, New York, Ohio, and Pennsylvania. Southern states are Arkansas, Georgia, Kentucky, and Mississippi. Notice that northern Negroes score about as well as southern Whites and that their mean is a full standard deviation above the mean of the southern Negro. (From Alper and Boring, 1944.)

whites score higher than blacks in the same location, at least part of the variation in intelligence is attributable to regional variation, probably in education and economic opportunities.

One study (Bruce, 1940) compared whites and blacks in very low economic circumstances in southern Virginia. Here, where socio-economic status was controlled by going to the bottom, so to speak, the black-white difference was still found, with the whites running 14 to 17 IQ points higher. A study in Canada (Tanser, 1939) attempted to look at the other end of the scale, comparing Negroes and whites in a relatively stable, middle-range environment with little racial bias. Here the whites scored about 15 to 19 IQ points above the blacks. In a small Northern city a careful matching of 71 black and white children (matching on age, sex, grade, education, residential area, and father's occupation) yielded only 6 IQ points difference (McQueen and Browning, 1960). It could be argued, of course, that in this case so much was controlled that neither sample was representative of anything so much as the other sample.

The last study, a fairly extreme one, should cause us to stop and examine this whole line of research. Surely when we have controlled on enough variables related to intelligence, we will be able to select samples that will prove to be similar to each other on intelligence. In the most radical form, all that this sort of study says is that there are some people in the two distributions who are alike and that if we are clever, we can develop indirect means of finding them. At the other extreme, in the "no control" kind of study, we can show that if we take two groups who are different with respect to virtually all the variables that we know to be related to intelligence, they will be vastly different on intelligence too. Small wonder.

Rather than impale ourselves on either horn of this dilemma, it is probably better to seek a point of view and a general attitude toward the major problems that will do justice to what we now know but still allow us to assimilate new evidence as it appears and as conditions change to permit more adequate studies. In a book on precisely this problem, *Social Class, Race and Psychological Development*, the introductory chapter by I.I. Gottesman (1968) presents a thoughtful and balanced position, based largely on theoretical considerations, which is consistent with the present data but open to new findings. Gottesman, a behavioral geneticist, stresses the point that we observe only *phenotypes* (surface manifestations) and that we are attempting to draw conclusions about *genotypes* (basic genetic characteristics). Given the radically different environments that surround racial groups in the United States, he argues that the task of inference is simply impossible. His best judgment at this point is that environmental deprivation is a major source of the phenotypic differences in intelligence that we observe between racial groups. He feels that the drop in IQ with increasing age that typically has been found in studies of Negro children suggests strongly that the scores are a cumulative effect of exposure to inadequate environments. Results of enrichment and special training of young children of all races will be especially interesting to watch as they bear on this viewpoint.

With respect to social-class differences *within* a particular racial group, however, a different situation may prevail. If the society is truly open and has a decent educational system, genetic selection may well be taking place with respect to intelligence to produce the observed differences. If class is not fixed by birth, individuals may ascend to higher classes or descend to lower classes depending on their skills, abilities, and efforts. Cyril Burt (1959) has pointed out that the criteria of class probably change as nations mature and social groups evolve. At first, physical strength may be most important, then blood relationship, then property or wealth, and finally mental efficiency. If we have a society in which one of the important determiners of class is mental status, then it follows that we have a selective system that will sort people out on those abilities. The fact that class differences persist from one generation to the next indicates that mobility is at work maintaining the differences by letting bright people from the lower classes work upward and dull people from the upper classes drift downward. If mobility is denied, then a paradoxical outcome ensues; the classes will become more alike in intelligence because the bright lower-class members remain in the lower level and the dull upper-class members remain in the upper level. What might appear to be an attempt to enhance class differences would thus actually diminish them. Conversely, if the society were perfectly open and if there were only one criterion for class membership, say intelligence, the difference in intellectual level of the classes would be greatly increased. Our present system seems like a compromise of some sort between these extremes.

Over-all, then, it seems to be wise to take the position that where we find great differences in environment, as in the race question, we will be cautious about making inferences to genetic differences. Where we find minimal differences in environment but major differences in social mobility, we will suspect differences in genetic endowment. Neither position is more than a reasonable base for research. It is always possible, on the one hand, that genetic differences are instrumental in creating environmental differences, and on the other hand, that what appear to be minor differences in environment (such as emotional climate of the home) produce sizable differences in intellect and social movement. Evidence on the first alternative is hard to accumulate in the human case but evidence on the second alternative is sometimes available through accidental experiments of nature. It is to these experiments on manipulating environments that we must now turn.

HEREDITY AND ENVIRONMENT

Fierce debates have raged in psychology and sociology concerning the extent to which intelligence is determined by heredity and environment. An all-or-none question is spurious, of course. Many, many factors, both genetic and experiential, contribute to a complex trait such as intelligence, and these variables certainly interact in complicated ways. As a result, we cannot talk about the absolute value of a particular kind of experience or training, rather we must talk about the value of such training for a child of given talents with a given background at a given time in his development. Studies of imprinting in animals (referred to in Chapter Fifteen) make clear that the effect of an experience may be dramatic if it occurs at a particular time in the life of the organism. We know that in particular species such experiences can determine the choice of "mother object," the kind of food preferred, the choice of a mate, and so on.

We do not know much about the effects of specific experiences on human beings. Early studies of intelligence dealt heavily with "good" and "poor" environments and with "good" and "poor" heredities without specific knowledge of what constituted them. The studies are useful only in showing the usual variations to be expected as heredity and environment (used as broad nonspecific terms) vary.

In general, bright children are found in bright families and dull children are found in dull families. Several classic studies have traced family lines of brilliant families like the Edwards in England (replete with men of status and achievement) or the Jukeses in the United States (full of criminals and morons). These studies, however, do not permit us to separate the effects of the variables involved; they only serve to convince us that the most likely bet on any family tree is "more of the same."

The average correlation between members of the same family with respect to intelligence is +.50, between parents and children and between the children themselves. There is not usually any greater correlation between the mother and the children than between the father and the children. With more remote degrees of relationship (uncles, aunts, grandparents), the correlation decreases, as Figure 14.9 indicates. This evidence is not only compatible with the notion that intelligence is a direct function of degree of genetic relationship, but it is also a reflection of the likelihood that the people concerned see each other often, grow up in similar circumstances, etc.

A dramatic exception to the usual pattern is provided by identical (monozygotic) twins. Since such individuals have the same heredity, they would be expected to be far more similar than other siblings. The usual finding is that identical twins correlate very highly (+.87 to +.92) in scores on intelligence tests. Nonidentical, or fraternal (dizygotic), twins, who share some of the similarities of identical twins without being genetically closer than ordinary siblings, intercorrelate in intellectual measures more highly than siblings (+.52 to +.70) but less highly than identical twins. These data are subject to conflicting interpretations. Some argue that the results are virtually direct evidence for the dominance of heredity in determining intelligence. Others point out that identical twins are treated more alike than any other related individuals while fraternal twins may be treated very differently (especially if one is a boy and the other a girl). Thus, they say, the results reflect the great environmental similarity of identical twins compared to the heterogeneous circumstances of less closely related children.

Some light is shed on the question by studies of children with identical heredities who have different environments (that is, identical twins who are raised apart) and children who have unrelated heredities but are raised in the same homes (that is, adopted or foster children compared with biological children of the parents). Although this literature is complicated and some of the studies very tangled, a few generalizations are well substantiated.

Figure 14.9 Degree of genetic overlap and approximate correlation with respect to intelligence.

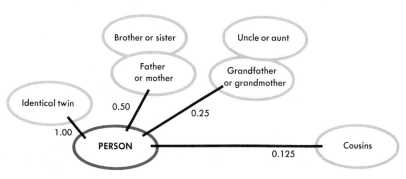

Children raised in "good" homes on the average will make higher intelligence-test scores than children raised in mediocre homes. Of course, adoption agencies do not normally permit placements into really poor families so the data do not usually include the real span of possible home environments. Comparing the adopted children in the better homes with those in the poorer homes within the adoption range usually shows an average difference of 5 or 6 IQ points. These data agree with the evidence on identical twins raised apart—the average difference in favor of the twin in the better environment is 6 IQ points. If you selected people at random you would expect them to differ in IQ by about 15 points on the average. Thus, the influence of environment in these studies is about one-third of the ordinary difference that you expect to find between people.

Large differences in environment produce sizable effects on intelligence-test scores while small differences produce little. Not surprisingly, the amount of intellectual difference is a function of the difference in the circumstances. In a study of identical twins (Newman, Freeman, and Holzinger, 1937), the largest difference within a pair was 24 IQ points. These were twin girls, separated at 18 months of age; one was reared in poor backwoods country and given only two years of schooling, the other was reared in a prosperous town and received a college degree; between them there was a difference of 14 years of schooling. Over-all, in this twin study there was a correlation of +.79 between estimated educational advantages and the IQ difference between the twins. The correlation is almost wholly attributable to cases where the educational differences were very substantial, from three to 15 years of formal education.

Relative ability levels persist, though absolute levels may change with consistent changes in environment. This generalization sums up two rather different kinds of data. First, the identical twins reared apart (sometimes under radically different conditions as we noted above) still showed a high correlation with each other (+.77) in intelligence-test scores. Thus, if one twin were markedly above or below average, his pair member was likely to be similarly above or below average in spite of any difference in environment. Second, studies of adopted children show that they tend to have much the same relative status in intelligence as their true mothers and fathers even though they are growing up in foster homes.

These data on relative status should not conceal the fact that sometimes the absolute level of intelligence of the foster children is quite different from what we would have predicted if they had been raised by their true parents. This effect showed up dramatically in a long-term follow-up study (Skodak and Skeels, 1949). The children in this study were all placed at six months of age or younger in solid middle-class homes or better. A number of the *true* mothers were tested at the time they gave up their babies. They scored poorly, with an average IQ of 86. When their children were tested at age 13, they scored an average IQ of 106, far above what one would have predicted from their mother's scores. (Although data from the true fathers are not available, the investigators believed that they were not much different in intellect from the mothers.) The high scores of the adopted children, then, are to be attributed to the quality of the foster homes in which they were placed. It is interesting, however, that the children's scores did not correlate appreciably with the education or occupation of the *foster* parents. Surprisingly, the children's scores correlated to almost the usual extent with their *true* mother's test scores (+.44)—even though the children had never lived with them. Thus, this study shows both aspects of the generalization: first, a major shift in the absolute level of intelligence that the children would have been predicted to develop, presumably due to the stimulation of the environment, and, second, an hereditary determination of the relative standing of each child in the adopted group as a function of his biological mother's abilities.

The outcome is a reasonable one. If a person has innate capacities for intellectual tasks, he needs a stimulating and rich environment to develop them. If a person is confronted with a particularly rich environment, he has to have the proper capacities to utilize it to the fullest extent. The brightest man of today, placed in an isolated primitive society as an infant, would surely fail to make a contribution to modern science or thought. Conversely, a moron, given all the advantages our civilization and technology can provide, will surely likewise fail.

The Nature of Intelligence

So far we have summarized the most general psychometric concept of intelligence. It is time that we moved from this general level and returned to the hoary old question: What is intelligence? You will recall that early investigators hoped that intelligence could be synthesized from experimentally isolated elements. If so, by that very operation we would have known what we had synthesized. But the experimental attack proved fruitless. Binet's great contribution was to by-pass what-is-it and capture how-much. But, as we have seen, the study of the correlates of intelligence does not necessarily increase our understanding of its nature.

There are two general approaches that can be taken to the analysis of intelligence, one psychometric, one experimental. We can characterize these two approaches by considering the work of two outstanding investigators, J.P. Guilford and Jean Piaget.

PSYCHOMETRIC ANALYSIS

Guilford's approach is the logical extension of the work in factor analysis discussed earlier. As more and more factors were turned up in educational, industrial, and military research, Guilford saw the need to organize and systematize psychological knowledge concerning intellectual factors. Feeling that he could see a systematic structure emerging, he organized the data in three categories: *operations, contents,* and *products.* This amounts to a program to evaluate the kinds of behaviors people perform (operations) on different materials (contents) to produce different outcomes (products). In his scheme, the operations are broken down into five classes (cognition, memory, divergent thinking, convergent thinking, and evaluation). These operations are applied to four kinds of contents, or materials (figural, symbolic, semantic, and behavioral). And six kinds of outcomes can be produced (units, classes, relations, systems, transformations, and implications). Every combination of operations, contents, and products is considered as a possible factor of intellect. In this fashion Guilford organized his search for 120 factors (5 × 4 × 6), as Figure 14.10 indicates. This approach has two characteristics that set it apart from previous work. First, it does not require (or even suppose) that the factors be completely independent; their descriptive ability rather than their uniqueness or independence is stressed. Second, the scheme helps suggest the kinds of materials and procedures that will fill in missing cells. An additional advantage of this systematic program is that it provides materials and check points for integrating new work with previous work.

Guilford's continuing task is to develop tests that will identify each cell in the theoretical structure and then to show through statistical techniques

Figure 14.10   A cubical model of the structure of intellect. (Guilford, 1960.)

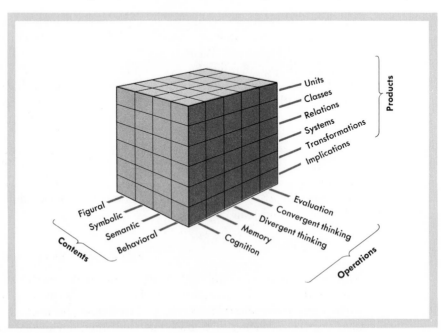

that he does indeed have tests that are consistently related as the theory proposes. We can illustrate his work by studying the top front row of the solid. Tests that will fill the top front row must employ the operation of cognition, that is, they will have to do with knowing and recognizing. In addition, they must be tasks that require that the person being tested produce units of some sort for his answers. Finally (as we move across the row), they will involve the four different kinds of contents, figural (having to do with real figures), symbolic (letters, digits or other signs), semantic (linguistic meanings and ideas), and behavioral (having to do with social situations).

For the first cell (cognizing figural units), Guilford suggests tests which require the subject to recognize familiar visual objects in outline when they are partially obscured, or to recognize melodies and sounds in noise, or to identify kinesthetic forms. If the three different sense modalities all intercorrelate highly, he will call the resulting tests one factor. If not, he is prepared to recognize that he might have multiple factors in the figural column.

For the second cell (cognizing symbolic units), he suggests tests like the following:

Put vowels in the blanks to make real words:
P__W__R
M__RV__L
C__RT__N
Rearrange letters to make words:
R A C I D
T V O E S
K L C C O

For the third cell (cognizing semantic units), Guilford recommends a vocabulary test such as:

Gravity means _____
Circus means _____
Virtue means _____

Materials for the behavioral column are not well worked out but presumably a test in the fourth cell would involve recognizing or recalling some unit of social behavior (perhaps identifying a friendly gesture or a kind attitude).

In just this fashion Guilford proposes to fill out the entire solid with tests which measure all combinations of operations, contents and products. More than three-quarters of the cells have now been filled with at least some representative tests.

Special interest has been directed toward Guilford's *divergent* and *convergent* thinking. The first is concerned with the search for a variety of ideas or solutions and has been thought of as closely associated with creativity and originality while the second is concerned with focusing in on the best or most appropriate solution to a problem. Divergent thinking stresses flexibility and fluency; convergent thinking is supposed to deal with producing a particular well-defined response under specific directions.

Guilford's plan and its execution is well anchored in the American psychometric tradition. He has rationally defined his task and is building up measures block by block in a systematic way so that he will be able to make rational and extensive measures on men; then he can look for external correlates. The approach still is formative and cannot yet be evaluated. You should note, however, that he does not propose to discover how the mental machinery works or how it developed in the organism. For an attack on those problems we must turn to another tradition and to a very different methodology.

EXPERIMENTAL-DEVELOPMENTAL ANALYSIS

Jean Piaget has been Director of Studies of the Institut Jean-Jacques Rousseau in Geneva for almost 50 years. During this period he has worked persistently on the problem of the development of knowing and knowledge, the cognitive life of the child. As a young man he worked briefly at the Binet-Simon Institute in Paris but found that he was more interested in the errors children made than in the development of norms. His search for the source of children's errors led him to a lifetime of research on the mind of the child.

Although Piaget's early work relied heavily on "clinical" interviews, he came to depend on a combined clinical-observational-experimental technique. His main subjects were his three children, who are probably the most carefully studied children in the world. Piaget and his wife kept careful notes on their spontaneous behaviors in natural situations and supplemented these with care, devising probing little experiments to investigate Piaget's hypotheses and furnish data that would be more precise and interpretable than the uncontrolled natural situation or the child's verbalizations alone.

Piaget's early work on language, thought, and moral judgment received recognition and attention all over the world. It did not have a lasting influence in the United States, however. Since the work was based largely on verbal behavior, it was judged too impressionistic and mentalistic for the "hard-nosed" learning theorists of the 1930s and 1940s. By the 1950s, however, American psychology was beginning to change, and in the 1960s Piaget's work again became the focus of attention of child psychologists and educational psychologists everywhere. Piaget's work itself changed, matured, and deepened over all these years, of course, though the trail of his thought is rather difficult to follow through more than 26 books and 150 journal articles. In addition, his writing is obscure and his terminology unfamiliar. His work often needs a good deal of interpretation before it be-

Figure 14.11 Jean Piaget. (The New York Times.)

comes clear to most readers. It is not possible here to do justice to Piaget's position, of course, but we can sketch in its salient differences from a traditional simple model.

The most elementary representation of intelligence is probably connectionism, which holds that people differ in intelligence in the number of connections that they can form or use at any one time and in the particular connections that they have already formed. This view is readily compatible with an elementary stimulus-response psychology and requires a minimum of mental machinery. Notice that it is generally passive (experiences happen to the organism), that it has no "operations" or 'rules," that there are no levels or stages, that development is a matter of maturation (getting more potential connections) and cumulation (adding particular bonds or habits), and that it is readily amenable to linear additive statistics.

Piaget's view is opposed to connectionism in virtually every respect. Its most salient features are *stages* of mental development, in which quite different phenomena and operations appear, and *active interactions* of the child with his environment, which are essential (along with maturation) in determining his progress from one stage to the next. As with motor development, the order of the stages and their nature does not change appreciably from one child to the next, though the rate of progress may be very different. The major stages of the development of intelligence are outlined below along with some of their characteristic features.

1. *Sensorimotor Intelligence.* (Birth to one and one-half years.)

This stage is characterized by perceptual activity and the formation of simple habits and schemas. A child presumably begins with no internal representation of the world. His work in this stage consists of acquiring the perceptual constancies, developing the notion of "objectness," discovering the simple motor ways of contacting and dealing with objects (touching, grasping, following), and finally cultivating imagery. These may sound like strange activities, but examples will make some aspects of them clear.

A very young child seems to have no notion of object constancy. When an object is present, he may try to contact it, manipulate it, and so on. But if the object is put behind a screen, he acts as if it ceases to exist. Out of sight really means out of mind. When he is a little older, however, he will persist in his efforts to get to the object. He will look behind the screen, move covers, and so forth. He now seems to have the idea that the object has an existence apart from his perception of it; it endures. At the same time we can show another change. At first, if an experimenter puts his hand behind a screen holding a black cube and pulls it out holding a red ball, a child shows no particular reaction. But when he has achieved the idea of object existence, he shows great surprise when this sleight-of-hand takes place. He laughs, looks for the first object, checks the screen, and shows delight or puzzlement.

During this period a child discovers important means of manipulating himself and the world. He learns how to keep interesting objects in view. He learns how to move toward and away from objects. He finds new ways of bringing material into his grasp and new ways to get where things are. As his conceptions change, the changes lead him to new behaviors which in turn lead him to new conceptions. Representations of the world and results of actions on the world become integrated into coherent schemas. The child differentiates between himself and not-himself and, by the end of the stage, has representations of the world (images) at his command.

2. *Preoperational Thought, Representational Thinking.* (One and one-half to four or five years.)

Intellectual development during this period is mainly concerned with interiorizing actions, that is, developing representations for things that one can do. This is also the period in which a child acquires control over the language system. The emphasis throughout these years is on the emergence and refinement of symbolic function. An important indicator of this period is the appearance of symbolic play. An object is used as a symbol of something else. A stone is a truck, a stick is a car, a rag is a bed. The child pretends and symbolizes the pretended world.

A child passes from static images to images signifying actions that he can imitate internally. Piaget believes that the first signifiers are private symbols and that their existence makes possible the development of language rather than vice versa. Once language is acquired, of course, it can be put to use as a symbolic system in its own right, but intellectual development does not wait on language; language waits on it. This is another example of complex change and interaction. Symbolic representations develop and make possible the development of language which in turn makes even more complex symbolism attainable.

During this period, thought is not suddenly freed from constraints, however. It seems to be limited in characteristic ways. A child appears to be unable to take the position of another person. He cannot tell you what a landscape in front of him would look like if he were at some other point.

He cannot stand off and review his own thought processes; he thinks but is left with the results of his thinking without awareness of the path he has followed. His thoughts and his perceptions are *centered*, by which Piaget means that they are captured by one outstanding feature of an object and fail to take into account more than one aspect at a time. The child is therefore likely to be a victim of his immediate perceptions. He has difficulty following transformations of objects to which he is attending when one salient feature or another grasps his attention from one state to another. Although it is hard to find a single way to typify this period, it is best known for the famous *conservation experiments*.

Suppose that we want to test for conservation of amount. We take two identical glasses and fill them (or have the child fill them) until both he and we agree that there is the same amount in the two glasses. His judgment can be determined in a number of ways ("If I drank this one and you drank that one, would I have just as much in my tummy as you would have?" "If I gave you this glass and you gave me that glass, would we each have just as much?" "If you drank this one and then that one would it take you just as many swallows?"). Then, when equality is established, the experimenter pours the contents of one of the glasses into a wider glass and asks if the amounts are still equal. Children at this stage now unanimously report that the amounts are *unequal*. If the liquid is poured back in the first glass, they will study the glasses and report that now they are equal again. Repetition of the cycle does not change the child's responses and, typically, he cannot be argued out of his position. Although this may seem unintelligible, a little thought will convince you that you cannot bring the child face-to-face with the apparent contradiction. If he has no notion of the conservation of amount, *there is no contradiction* for him when the amount changes and changes back without any liquid being taken away or added. From the child's limited point of view, that is simply a fact about the world and as good as any other fact.

3. *Preoperational Thought, Intuitional Thinking.* (Five to seven years.)

During this period a child becomes more and more aware of multiple aspects of the objects of his attention. He focuses much more readily on the tasks put to him and begins to take account of more than one variable at a time. Conservation of amount appears and then becomes unshakably established to the point that the child does not even look at the transformed material, he "knows" that it has to be the same. Conservation of quantity, number, and weight begin to appear. And with these there appears the first glimmering of the notion of the reversability of certain operations. The child in short moves farther and farther from a perception-dependent view of the world to a construction of reality which includes more and more dimensions of objects and events at the same time. The child still fails to have a firm, reliable construction, however, and may not be able to justify or hold his insights under changing conditions. Hence, the term *intuitional* is used to imply the unsystematized nature of this period.

4. *Concrete Operations.* (Seven to eleven years.)

In this stage, cognitive actions are organized into operational systems. The child now establishes consistent ways of dealing with the world. He can take the percepts of the moment and organize them into a systematic view of the world that preserves the constant properties and predicts correlated changes when events are altered. By the end of the period the conservations of amount, quantity, number, weight, and volume are established and rationalized. The child now regards questions about conservation as silly and is amazed that anyone could doubt them. He can now order objects properly on any dimension specified (height, weight, color) and deal with information about order to place an item in a series. He can classify on many dimensions simultaneously ("Sort out all the small, blue circles with an X in the middle"). In general, the child develops the ability to perform the operations and to deal with the classification problems before he can successfully report verbally on what he is doing. After he has performed the task, he can give the principle that he used or the method that was employed. But the ability to solve such problems at the concrete level does not mean that they can be solved at the abstract verbal level. Thus, a child may be able to order any series of sizes, weights, or amounts, but still not be able to solve such a problem presented in verbal form ("Edith is taller than Susan. Edith is shorter than Ann. Which one is the shortest?").

5. *Formal Operations.* (Twelve years to adult.)

This stage consists of the relearning, systematizing, and generalizing at the formal level the operations that were learned at the concrete level. The child becomes more and more free of the specific concrete objects. Thus, his operations are at once more general and abstract and at the same time more free of distractions of particular aspects of stimulus objects that are irrelevant to the operations involved. These formal representations can then be joined with other formal operations in more completely integrated systems of formal operations.

One great power of formal operations is that they are not limited to what is present, or even what has been present sometimes, but can be extended to anything that might be potentially present. We can imagine systematically all possible combinations, all possible sortings, all possible outcomes. We can imagine circumstances, deduce outcomes, and examine evidence to see if the premises are compatible with what is then observed. In short, we are at a level where scientific thinking is possible.

FUNCTIONS

Throughout development on all levels and in every stage we find adaptive functions that play an important role in the emergence of later stages. Piaget proposes that a child pursues an *equilibrium model.* At each stage, experiences impinge on him. He "reaches out" to contact the experience. He tries to *assimilate* it, that is, to understand it, to incorporate it in his structure of knowledge. In the assimilation attempt he must *accommodate,* that is, he must change in some way as he copes with the experience. Assimilation and accommodation together constitute *adaptation,* the total process in which the child affects the world and the world in turn affects him. Successive adaptations result in changing cognitive structures and the advancement to successive levels of mental functioning.

Although this account is largely metaphorical, it hints at the processes at work. It argues that engagement of the environment in active fashion is necessary to the progress of cognitive development. It suggests that there are sequences of experience that may have beneficial effects in accelerating (or at least assuring the normality of) mental development. With the growing concern of American psychologists for the problems of cultural and intellectual deprivation and increasing attention to early schooling experiences, Piaget's formulation is stimulating much experimental work. No one else has furnished such powerful demonstrations of the intellectual and conceptual characteristics of children and no one else has furnished anything like the description of cognitive development that he has given us.

Rather surprisingly, Piaget's formulations have not been embraced by the psychometrists. It would seem reasonable to develop a set of psychometric devices for careful appraisal of stages and evaluation of the child's development, but such an exploitation of the theory has not yet taken place. The gulf between psychometric models and experimental models is deep and resists bridging.

SUMMARY

The measurement of intelligence, which presented an unsolvable problem a century ago, is now commonplace. Early attempts to measure intelligence by measuring the component mental processes and summing them, as Donders recommended, failed. These experimental attempts were replaced by the clinical-psychometric approach developed by Binet. Using school children as subjects, Binet and Simon showed that intelligence could be measured by little puzzles which demanded judgment. An intelligence scale based on *mental age* was developed. Items were selected for *difficulty* (age level) and *discrimination* (steepness of slope). Relative brightness was measured by the ratio of mental age to chronological age, called the *Intelligence Quotient* ($IQ = MA/CA \times 100$). Validity was established by the correlation of test scores with school success, achievement in Army training programs, and such methods.

Psychometric modeling of intelligence became popular. From Binet's simple general intelligence theory, a host of other models emerged. Spearman advocated a general intelligence (g) and specific components (s) due to particular tests. Thorndike's model stressed the number of connections available to the person. Group factors were emphasized in the United States (Brigham, Kelley, Thurstone), and finally a hierarchical model emerged (Burt). What model one uses depends largely on the task in hand. Heterogeneous groups can be best measured with general intelligence tests, whereas selected groups require more specialized measurement.

A great fund of data has been accumulated on intelligence test scores and their relations to other variables. Studies of test scores and age show different effects depending on whether the studies are *cross-sectional* or *longitudinal*. *Cross-sectional* studies show large decreases in intelligence test scores with increasing age after maturity. *Longitudinal* studies show continuing small gains through the mature years. All studies agree that intelligence develops rapidly up to the mid-teens or so. Early testings (before age two) have little ability to predict later scores. Scores are relatively consistent for school-age children, however.

Differences between men and women with respect to intelligence and special skills are much like what cultural stereotypes would predict. Women excel in verbal and clerical tasks, men excel in mathematical and scientific pursuits. Mixed social, biological, and cultural variables such as race and socioeconomic class are associated with large differences in average intelligence-test scores. Obviously, it is difficult to draw conclusions about the source and nature of the differences. It seems likely that interactions of innate abilities and circumstances are the rule and that interpretations of data must be cautious. Similarly, the general questions concerning heredity and environment are not simple to answer. Gross measures of the general effect of good environments versus mediocre environments give the former an advantage of 5 to 6 IQ points on the average. Group variability does not decrease, however, and relative rank in one's group seems to be consistently related to one's parents' intelligence when immediate environment is more or less equalized.

There are two current proposals concerning the nature of intelligence. Guilford makes a psychometric analysis into operations, contents, and products, attempting to categorize adult intelligence by functions, inputs, and outputs. A radically different proposal is that of Piaget, who offers a conception of mental development consisting of stages that blend into one another in sequence as maturation and adaptation change the structure of the child's mind. *Sensorimotor intelligence* gives way to *representational thinking*, which in turn shades into *intuitional thinking*. These are followed by the mastery of *concrete operations*, performed on objects in the world, and this stage is succeeded by the stage of *formal operations*.

SUGGESTED READINGS

Anastasi, A. *Differential psychology* (3rd ed.). New York: Macmillan, 1958.
Brown, R. *Social psychology.* Chapter 5, The development of intelligence. New York: Macmillan (The Free Press), 1965.
Flavell, J.H. *The developmental psychology of Jean Piaget.* Princeton: Van Nostrand, 1963.
Miller, G.A. *Psychology: the science of mental life,* Chapters 18 and 19. New York: Harper & Row, 1962.
Tyler, L.E. *The psychology of human differences* (3rd ed.). New York: Appleton-Century-Crofts, 1965.

Arousal and Affect

CHAPTER FIFTEEN   Casual observation of the behavior of human infants and adults reveals major fluctuations in level of activity, or arousal, ranging from deep sleep through alert, excited wakefulness. Adequate description and understanding of behavior require reference to arousal level as well as to the qualitative emotional or affective states that impart psychological meaning to physiological arousal. We take up the topic of arousal in this chapter, beginning with the issues of sleep and dreaming. Other fluctuations in physiological systems that have a daily, or circadian, period are discussed along with brief fluctuations in arousal and their behavioral effects. We also consider the physiological effects of chronic, intense arousal, or stress. Finally, several issues related to the topic of emotions are discussed, such as culturally imposed evaluation of various forms of emotional expression and its impact on emotional development, models of emotional development, empirical studies of the effects of early experience on later emotion, and attempts to measure specific emotions through physiological and behavioral indicators.

A human baby spends much of his time sleeping, but when awake, he displays several types of behavior. One is crying; another is eating (and related biologically crucial functions); still another, though not so demanding on the parents, is exploratory activity. This latter behavior may be accompanied by vocalizations and other responses, such as smiling and laughing, which are interpreted as indicators that the baby is "happy" or mildly excited.

Even casual observation of a human baby leaves no doubt that a complete description of its behavior must include the two major conditions, sleep and wakefulness, as well as different degrees of these conditions. Current terminology refers to *level of arousal*, and arousal is usually treated as a continuum, with deep sleep at one pole and frenzied excitement (or some equivalent, though perhaps more austere and scientific-sounding term) at the other. Moreover, in the waking condition (though perhaps also indirectly measureable during sleep) certain behavior patterns are readily apparent such as crying and "gurgling," frowning and smiling, thrashing about wildly and moving in a modulated, controlled manner. These characteristic, highly stereotyped patterns we categorize as emotions, or affects; and we usually have no trouble in further differentiating within this category between "negative" and "positive" affects. Furthermore, emotions involve at least three distinct domains: (a) overt actions, such as crying; (b) covert phenomenal states, such as the misery that we impute to the crying baby; (c) physiological concomitants, such as changes in blood pressure and heart rate, adrenalin discharge, and so on.

Certain behavior patterns readily apparent in the waking state seem to demand the postulation of *drives* or *motives*. These patterns are characterized by persistence and vigor, by an exclusive focusing of behavior on certain stimuli, such as the bottle or a mobile, over extended periods of time.

What holds for a baby also applies to individuals of all ages. That is, a comprehensive psychology must deal not only with such categories as sensation, perception, learning, memory, thinking, problem-solving, and so on, but also must handle phenomena associated with arousal, affect, and motivation. We consider arousal and affect in this chapter and motivation in the next.

Arousal

THE SLEEP-WAKEFULNESS CYCLE

The periodic fluctuation between sleeping and waking is far more rapid in infants than in older children and adults; the latter typically do all their sleeping in a single nocturnal block varying in duration from six to ten hours. One question that the shift in pattern raises is whether nocturnal sleeping is intrinsic to the adult nervous system or is acquired under cultural pressure.

Acquisition of Sleep Patterns. Under the constraints of job requirements people do learn to sleep during the day. For this reversal to be successful, however, it helps considerably to simulate nighttime conditions of darkness and quiet. Apparently, then, the typical relation between clocktime and sleeping is an artifact of the environmental conditions that ordinarily prevail during the "nighttime" hours of the clock. In that sense, there is probably no necessary relation between when people sleep and the day-night cycle. Lower animals can also reverse their typical cycle with a reversal of environmental conditions. For example, rats usually sleep during the day and are active at night. However, in a laboratory, they will sleep at night if their living area is illuminated at night and kept relatively dark during the day.

On the basis of his extensive pioneering research into the nature of sleep, the physiologist Nathaniel Kleitman (1939) concluded that there are really two kinds of wakefulness. One, "wakefulness of necessity," is intrinsically controlled by subcortical brain centers. The other, "wakefulness of choice," is superimposed on the intrinsic sleep-wakefulness cycle and is cortically controlled. Thus, the sleep-wakefulness cycle, like other complex behavior patterns, is the product of intrinsic and acquired factors. We will pursue this idea again in a later discussion of other cyclic fluctuations that have about a 24-hour period, the "circadian rhythms."

What is Sleep? Behaviorally, sleep is characterized by a marked reduction in gross motor activity as well as a decrease in responsiveness to stimulation. It is only within recent years that a refined and comprehensive description has become available of the physiological concomitants of sleep. The main features of sleep, physiologically defined, are given below, beginning with some remarks about the brain.

Rhythmic electrical activity can be recorded from various portions of the brain, usually through the skull, with the aid of elaborate electronic equipment. The record is known as the electroencephalogram, or EEG. This brain activity probably represents the integration of very small fluctuations in electrical potential, or voltage, occurring in large groups of single neural cells. These integrated potential changes are themselves quite small in amplitude, on the order of microvolts (millionths of a volt), which is why their measurement requires highly complex and sensitive equipment. In any event, the EEG records obtained from the brain fall into a limited number of patterns that are characteristic of a person's state of arousal. In general, the lower the arousal level, the more regular, or synchronized, the EEG waves are; recordings typical of an alert, but inactive person show waves that are predominantly "fast" (with short cycles) and low in voltage (about 50 microvolts); as arousal level declines toward sleep, the predominant wave pattern has a relatively slower (larger) cycle and higher amplitude. The common record obtained from a person who is awake, but mentally inactive, usually with closed eyes, is called the *alpha* rhythm; it has a periodicity of about ten cycles per second (c.p.s.) and a relatively low amplitude. If the person is visually stimulated, or even perhaps actively engaged in mental activity, though otherwise quiet, the alpha wave may be *blocked;* it disappears from the record. At the other extreme of arousal, deep sleep, we see slow waves (one or two c.p.s.) of high amplitude, called *delta* waves. Thus, one major physiological concomitant of sleep is the presence, in the EEG, of the high-voltage, low-frequency waves.

Stages of Sleep. Sleep is not a homogeneous state, at least physiologically. Various stages of sleep can be defined according to certain physiological indexes, among them the EEG. In terms of the EEG, the following scheme has been offered by William Dement, one of the most innovative and productive of a growing group of sleep researchers (see Dement, 1965). Dement identifies four stages of sleep. Stage 1 occurs just as a person falls asleep; the EEG record contains a mixture of slow and fast waves, all of low amplitude. In Stage 2 "sleep spindles" make their appearance; these are bursts of regular waves of about 12-14 c.p.s., occurring in a background of low-amplitude activity. Sleep spindles are also evident in Stage 3, in addition to a moderate amount of low-frequency (one-two c.p.s.), high-voltage waves. Finally, in Stage 4, there is continuous activity of the low-frequency (one c.p.s.), high-amplitude type. See Figure 15.1 for an example

Figure 15.1 Examples of the recorded tracings of EEG stages of sleep for the same subject over a period of a single night. The recording paper was moving under the pens at one-third the standard speed, so the waves are somewhat pushed together, but only one-third as much paper is needed during the night, a considerable saving in eight hours of continuous recording. The top line shows the 10-per-second alpha waves characteristic of the "Awake" EEG; mean amplitude, for comparison with the sleep patterns, is about 50 microvolts. Stage 1 shows a mixture of low-voltage, irregular, relatively fast waves. The sample of Stage 2 shows the characteristic waxing-waning bursts of regular waves (*sleep spindles*) lasting one to two seconds. The frequency of the spindle waves is about 12 to 14 per second. A moderate amount of high-voltage, slow activity is seen in the Stage 3 tracing. Stage 4 is characterized by continuous, high-voltage, slow activity. The frequency is about one per second. (Courtesy William C. Dement, 1965.)

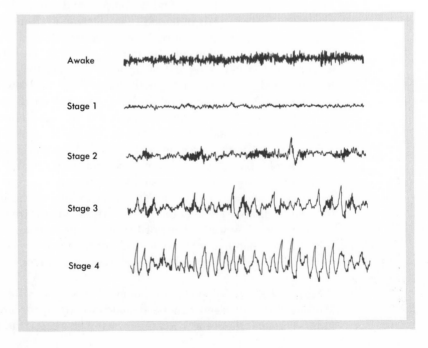

of EEG records from each of these stages. During sleep, a person passes cyclically through these stages; having reached Stage 4, he may then return, passing through 3 and 2, to Stage 1. In the course of a night's sleep, Stage 1 EEG activity recurs frequently.

Stage 1 sleep that occurs after its first appearance in the EEG for a night is called "terminal" Stage 1 sleep. Dement has singled out terminal Stage 1 sleep for special consideration, since it is characterized by a set of physiological events that make it quite distinct from the other three stages. The most significant of these events is the occurrence of *rapid eye movements;* these are conjugate movements, in that both eyes move together, just as they do during the waking phase when a person shifts fixation from one place to another. Indeed, if you saw only his eyeballs as they move during terminal Stage 1 sleep, it would seem as though the person were awake and actively scanning an interesting scene. Of course, during sleep the eyelids are closed; eye movements are recorded through electrodes, located near the eyes, which pick up the small voltage changes that are generated by movements of the eyeballs.

REM Sleep. Rapid eye movements (REM) are found only during terminal Stage 1 sleep. They occupy from 15 to 40 per cent of each Stage 1 phase, the exact percentage being characteristic of the individual sleeper. Dement distinguishes between REM periods and all non-REM periods, or NREM. The first REM period usually occurs about 90 minutes after the onset of sleep.

The observation of eye movements during sleep and the hypothesis that they were related to dreaming had been made three-quarters of a century ago (Ladd, 1892), but it was Kleitman and his colleagues (see Aserinsky and Kleitman, 1953) who first systematically tested the hypothesis that when a person's eyeballs are moving during sleep, he is, in effect, looking at the various visual components of his dream.

Before examining the question of whether the rapid eye movements recorded during terminal Stage 1 sleep do indeed indicate the occurrence of dreaming, we might first list some of the other physiological concomitants of the REM period. The following are increased or accelerated during REM sleep: respiration rate, heart rate, blood pressure, cortical blood flow—all suggesting increased arousal or attention and supporting the idea that something psychologically interesting is happening during the REM period.

The REM and NREM periods are also distinguishable on other grounds. A REM period is preceded and followed by high levels of gross bodily activity; during the REM period itself there is very little gross movement but a considerable amount of finger movement. In addition, spontaneous activity of single neural cells, especially in the visual cortex, is high during REM sleep. This last finding was obtained from cats, which like other animals show very much the same physiological patterns during sleep as human beings.

Dement concludes that with one exception REM sleep resembles the waking state—despite the tremendous amount of activity of the central nervous system going on during REM sleep, bodily manifestations of this high degree of arousal are absent. There is, apparently, an inhibition of gross motor activity, as well perhaps as an inhibition of the receptor systems.

The indirect evidence thus points to the REM period as one in which a great deal is happening, though covertly. Is all this activity related to dreaming? To summarize a considerable amount of research, the answer pretty conclusively is "yes." When people are awakened during a REM period, over 80 per cent of the time they report dreaming. During NREM periods, there are very few if any reports of dreaming, although there are reports of some fragmentary thinking (Foulkes, 1966). Indeed, Dement argues that "all phases of sleep are associated with some kind of subjective experience or mental activity . . . conscious mental activity does not cease at any time during sleep" (Dement, 1965, p. 192). But true dreaming does seem pretty much confined to the REM period.

DREAMING

The identification of the physiologically defined REM period with the psychological phenomenon of dreaming has revolutionized the investigation of dreaming. The topic has long been of interest to psychology, largely by virtue of the significance of the dream in psychoanalytic theory and practice. In conventional attempts to record dreams, a major weakness has been the necessity of relying on patients' or subjects' recall of the dream content over long periods of time; in addition, the several dreams that people have in one night are easily fused with one another, making it virtually impossible to segregate the content of a specific dream. Freud made the most of this weakness by simply asserting that "the dream" is whatever the patient reports. For purposes of psychoanalytic therapy that may be an entirely acceptable decision. For purposes of controlled, scientific research, however, it would seem desirable to obtain a record of the dream as closely as possible to its occurrence, and with minimal interference from subsequent dreams.

The procedure of awakening the person when the EEG and eye-movement recordings indicate a REM period and asking him to report any dreams that he has just been having would seem a natural solution to the problem of getting an accurate dream record. That procedure has been employed, over the past few years, with considerable success by several investigators. Some of the results of that endeavor are summarized below.

Dream Duration and Content. One of several questions they have tackled concerns the way properties of the REM records relate to characteristics of the dreams that are reported on awakening from REM sleep. Dreamers' estimates of the durations of their dreams agree closely with the length of the recorded REM period during which the dream was presumably occurring. This relation further supports the proposal that the REM record is an objective indicator of dreaming—and the tempting corollary that one can study dreaming by measuring REM.

An additional, more subtle source of support for this position is the relation between dream content and type and extent of REM records. Thus, in dreams containing a great deal of physical action, there is more associated REM activity than in dreams with more peaceful content. Furthermore, it is often possible to associate particular types of eye movements with dream content. If the action in the dream takes place predominantly in the vertical dimension, then vertical eye movements are prevalent in the REM record. For example, an unusually large amount of vertical eye movements were recorded during a period when a dreamer, on being awakened, reported that the main imagery of the dream involved watching leaflets dropping from a blimp. In a controlled investigation (Roffwarg, Dement, Muzio, and Fisher, 1962), it was found that trained judges could with considerable accuracy "predict" the type of physical activity in dream content, in the sense implied above, from an examination of the REM records.

In general, then, the relation between REM and dreaming is a strong one. The use of a REM record as a substitute for a reported dream, as is done in many of the studies referred to below, certainly seems justified at this point.

Who Dreams? People vary considerably in their reports of dreaming, especially when those reports are delayed until the next day. Some people insist that they never dream. However, to judge from REM records, everyone dreams. Indeed, self-styled "nondreamers" show about as much REM sleep as other people, and if awakened immediately after a REM period, they do report dreams, though less frequently (about 46 per cent) than the average for a large group of normal subjects (about 83 per cent). It seems highly likely that the "nondreamers" are good forgetters of their dreams.

How Much Dreaming? Individual differences here are fairly large, as well as differences due to the age of a subject. According to ontogenetic data (Roffwarg, Muzio, and Dement, 1966), for the typical college-age subject in dream studies, about 21 per cent of total sleep time is occupied with dreaming, as evidenced by the REM record. Newborns (one–fifteen days old) show both the greatest amount (about eight hours) and highest percentage of REM sleep (about 50 per cent of total sleep time). Both absolute and relative amounts of REM decline with age, though adolescents and young adults show a slightly higher percentage of REM sleep than do children in the age range five–thirteen years. In the elderly, dreaming drops off to its lowest level, both in terms of absolute amount of dream-time per night (slightly less than one hour) and percentage of total sleep devoted to dreaming (about 14.5 per cent).

Dreams occur cyclically throughout the night, along with terminal Stage 1 sleep. Dement estimates that in a typical night's sleep, there are about 10 to 20 distinct dreams. He believes that what otherwise might be lengthy, continuous dreams are broken up into separate, briefer dreams through the intervention of gross body movements.

Do Dreams Have a Function? Freud argued that dreams serve a significant biological function, in that they protect sleep by providing a safe outlet for repressed impulses. From this point of view, the sleep-preserving function of dreams is central, and their provision of a means for safely expressing forbidden impulses is secondary in importance. But one could argue, within a Freudian framework, that dreams are crucial in their own right; that whatever their biological role in protecting sleep might be, dreams are necessary for the maintenance of psychological balance.

It is now possible to assess the significance of dreaming, independent of sleeping, by taking advantage of the clear distinction between REM and NREM sleep, and by applying the awakening technique. That is, if a researcher wanted to minimize dreaming, it would only be necessary to awaken the person every time eye movements began to appear during Stage 1 sleep. Of course, doing so would also deprive the person of a certain amount of sleep, and perhaps be irritating as well. As a control for these latter factors, he could awaken people from NREM sleep and then compare the effects of "dream deprivation" with an equal amount of nondreaming sleep deprivation.

Such experiments have in fact been performed. As summarized by Dement, the results conclusively reveal the special significance of REM sleep. In one study, people who were allowed on five consecutive nights only a minimal amount of REM sleep, and hence presumably little dreaming, became progressively more irritable and anxious during the daytime; they complained of tiredness and inability to concentrate. Individual subjects gave other specific indications of considerable emotional upset. For example, six out of eight male subjects "developed raveneous appetites and showed significant weight gain during dream deprivation" (Dement, 1965, p. 241). When these same people were subjected to comparable deprivation of NREM sleep, none of these symptoms of emotional upset became evident.

It would seem, then, that it is not sleep *per se* which is crucial to emotional and biological well-being, as Freud has assumed, but the opportunity to dream afforded during REM sleep. A further bit of dramatic evidence adds weight to the hypothesis that people *need* to dream, just as they need to eat. When a person is deprived of food for a time, he tends to make up for the deficits by excessive eating once food is made available again. A similar behavior pattern obtains in dream-deprivation experiments: Following each night of being awakened from REM sleep, subjects showed an increase in the number of REM periods the next night. After the awakening procedure was discontinued, REM sleep on the next several nights was markedly greater than normal. Again, this effect was not observed when subjects were awakened from NREM sleep.

In this same context, the question has been raised about characteristics of good and poor sleepers. The latter complain about not being able to fall asleep rapidly, awakening frequently during the night, not getting enough sleep, and not feeling rested and refreshed in the morning. When a group of poor sleepers, so defined, was compared with a normal control group on several physiological indexes, taken both during sleep and the waking state, the poor sleepers were found, among many other differences, to be markedly low in amount of REM sleep (Monroe, 1967). In general, the poor sleepers seemed to be functioning at a much higher level of arousal than the control subjects. But since the study was correlational in design, it is not possible to assign a causal direction to the interesting relationships obtained. One question in particular stands unresolved: Is it the lack of normal amounts of REM sleep that makes these people tense, or is it their chronic anxiety that prevents them from settling down to a normal sleeping pattern with the normal amount of REM sleep? Or both? Perhaps excess tension, anxiety, or arousal (or whatever it is that exactly describes the self-styled poor sleepers) disrupts the normal sleep pattern, and a by-product of that disruption is a failure to enjoy an adequate amount of REM sleep, which in turn increases irritability, tension, and so on.

The psychologist who conducted the above study also points out an interesting practical implication of his results. He notes that various sleep-inducing drugs to which poor sleepers often resort may have various effects on the total sleep pattern. Some, for example, may not induce enough REM sleep. Such drugs might thus exacerbate the problem, rather than alleviate it. The ideal drug, in terms of present knowledge, would induce the normal sleep pattern, thus allowing the normal amount of REM sleep.

Experiments on "dream deprivation" in animals reveal results similar to those obtained from people. For example, lesions in a certain portion of the brain stem (the *nucleus pontis caudalis*) of cats eliminate REM sleep. Cats so affected exhibit many symptoms of severe emotional disturbance (Jouvet, 1962). In some cats the effects of the lesion were temporary, and REM sleep returned after several days. These cats exhibited normal waking behavior following restoration of REM sleep; however, the remaining cats, in which the effects of the lesion were not reversible, all died, as Dement reports, "in a state that seemed to resemble acute manic delerium" (Dement, 1965, p. 242).

Interpretation of "dream" research on animals is, of course, fraught with difficulty, since there is no direct way of establishing a relation between REM sleep and dreaming. Indirect methods might be developed. For example, monkeys might be trained to make an operant response, such as flexing their fingers, whenever they are presented with "dreamlike" visual images on a screen. It is possible for such operants to be elicited during sleep. Hence, if a sleeping monkey is experiencing the same kind of hallucinatory visual images that characterize human dreams, they might "report" this by making the operant response.

Raising the question of whether animals actually dream during REM sleep suggests another way of looking at dream-deprivation experiments on human beings. It may be that dreams *per se* are not necessary but are simply concomitants of REM sleep; some other event, perhaps biochemical, associated with REM sleep may be what a person is deprived of when repeatedly awakened. The "deprivation" may take the form of the accumulation in the brain of an excess of some noxious metabolic product; the behavioral effects of REM sleep deprivation may thus not be manifestations of a need to dream, and the compensatory increase in amount of REM sleep following deprivation may similarly not serve directly to make up for lost dream time. In short, it is still not clear, from the evidence available, whether dreaming does have the function of helping to maintain emotional equilibrium. But considering the dramatic breakthroughs that have occurred in research on sleeping and dreaming only in the past few years, it seems likely that the ambiguity still remaining will shortly be resolved.

CIRCADIAN RHYTHMS

In addition to the obvious periodic fluctuation in sleep and wakefulness that we have been discussing, living organisms, from plants through human beings, exhibit regular cyclic variation in many physiological functions. One of the striking features of these cyclic functions is their period of approximately 24 hours. Such cycles, or rhythms, are called *circadian,* from the Latin *circa,* "about," and *dies,* "day." There are other cyclic functions with longer periods that seem to be related to basic astronomical or climatological regularities. The circadian rhythms have been of especial interest to physiologists, who are primarily concerned with short-term variations in the processes which they investigate. For example, it has been found that body temperature varies in a 24-hour period, reaching a maximum in the evening and a minimum early in the morning. Indeed, the physiologist Jurgen Aschoff (1965) asserts that all physiological processes can be described in terms of circadian rhythms.

Internal Clocks. By virtue of the close correspondence between the period of these rhythmic fluctuations and the clock-length of the day, the notion has arisen that there is an "internal clock," perhaps an adaptive mechanism developed through the process of evolution. But as with the sleep-wakefulness cycle, we can ask whether such an hypothetical internal clock has any intrinsic properties or whether it is entirely synchronized with—or in Aschoff's term "entrained" by—such cyclic external events as the light-dark cycle, regular daily fluctuations in temperature, and so on, as well as by such artificial time markers, or *Zeitgebers,* as clocks and watches. What happens to the internal clock in the absence of *Zeitgebers?*

To answer a similar question about the sleep-wakefulness cycle, Kleitman (1939) located subjects in Mammoth Cave, cutting them off from external stimulation and thereby enabling him to impose whatever external conditions he wanted on his subjects, such as the length of an artificially imposed light-dark cycle. A similar technique has more recently been employed by Aschoff. With *Zeitgebers* eliminated, the internal clock is capable of maintaining a reliable periodicity, though somewhat different from the normal 24-hour cycle. From continual physiological records, as of body temperature and urine, as well as from behavioral indexes of arousal and activity, Aschoff reports his own "free-running" clock to have a period of about 25.9 hours. This value stabilized after only a few days had been spent in isolation, during which time the internal clock apparently became disengaged from its dependence on the 24-hour period of external clocks. Thus, the internal clock, when entrained by *Zeitgebers*, takes on the 24-hour periodicity that characterizes the Earth's rotation; this value of the period is temporarily maintained, through some sort of inertia, even when the person is isolated; but then an intrinsic rhythm is manifested, which is circadian, but not necessarily of exactly 24 hours' duration. In this regard, Aschoff reports that one subject, after 18 days in isolation, was waking from sleep at 8:00 P.M.

Multiple Clocks. Under normal conditions, when the internal clock is supported by external regularities with 24-hour periods, measures of various physiological functions, including general activity level, are characterized by a single period of about 24 hours, though they may attain maxima and minima at different times within that period. Under artificial conditions, with no *Zeitgebers*, these functions may become dissociated; they not only get out of phase with one another, but each may also have its own period. This desynchronization suggests the existence of multiple internal clocks, perhaps one for each physiological subsystem, which are kept in synchrony only when the whole system is entrained by the same set of external events. An alternative hypothesis, the one favored by Aschoff, is that the asynchrony under conditions of isolation is a temporary matter, reflecting differences in the time it takes for each subsystem to break free from the 24-hour period. Aschoff speculates that with enough time for adjustment to the artificial conditions, the subsystems would eventually become synchronized, in conformity with the demands of the internal, free-running clock.

There are some intriguing psychological implications of physiological circadian rhythms. For example, certain behavioral functions might be most efficiently carried out during particular phases of the physiological processes. In the extreme this is obvious; one would not choose to run a footrace while asleep. But to take a less evident example, it might be that problem-solving is most effective when body temperature is at its normal peak. If so, and if a person has freedom to apportion activities, would it then not make sense to assign problem-solving tasks, to oneself or to others, according to measures of body temperature? Or perhaps creativity is best when body temperature is low. Perhaps other psychological functions are independent of body temperature but closely related to the phase of some other physiological measure. Finally, it may be that there are fairly large individual differences in the times when the upper and lower limits of significant physiological indicators are reached. In that case, it would be useful to determine these for each person, and tailor his activities to fit his individual rhythmic profile.

SOME PROBLEMS
IN MEASURING AROUSAL LEVEL

Considering the amount of successful effort recently devoted to the physiological investigation of arousal, it is not surprising that psychologists concerned with motivation and emotion have turned to the concept of arousal, or "activation," for help in solving their theoretical problems. For some theorists, level of arousal has been virtually equated with emotion. For others, arousal has taken over half the task typically assigned to motivation concepts; that is, level of arousal serves to account for the *intensive* aspect of behavior (why is X behaving so vigorously?), leaving the directional aspect of behavior (why is X engaging in behavior A rather than B?) to be accounted for in motivational terms.

Those who have relied on arousal for these purposes tend to assume that the level of arousal is measurable on a single dimension, or continuum. Furthermore, they tend to locate the low end point of the presumed continuum at "sleep" and the other somewhere within the wakefulness phase, perhaps identifying it with periods of peak emotional activity.

Variation in Arousal During Sleep. We have already encountered some problems with this type of approach. First, sleep is not homogeneous, being differentiated into at least two important phases, REM and NREM. Certainly, within the REM phase a great deal goes on physiologically as well as psychologically. A person who awakens from a nightmare with pounding heart and covered with perspiration has not just been in a condition of "low arousal." Indeed, there is some reason to believe that sudden death during sleep, due to cardiac malfunction, may sometimes be attributed to excessive arousal associated with dreaming. In any event, to locate the low point on the arousal continuum indiscriminately at "sleep" is not a useful procedure.

Variations among Physiological Subsystems. Second, in circadian rhythms there are regular peaks and low points in many, perhaps all, physiological processes. Although fluctuations in these processes are normally in phase with one another, the maxima and minima do not necessarily occur at the same times. But since that is so, which process, if any, best represents arousal level? Might it not be more profitable to think of several types of arousal, associated with different physiological subsystems, each perhaps related to some, but not all, types of psychological activity? That is, to repeat an earlier example, perhaps effective problem-solving is best when body temperature reaches its normal diurnal peak, whereas creativity may be best when body temperature is minimal; or indeed perhaps creativity is unrelated to body temperature, following instead the fluctuations in some other subsystem. In short, wakefulness, like sleep, exhibits various types of arousal. So to refer to a single arousal continuum may not be the most fruitful approach. A better, though much more tedious strategy to follow at present might simply be to determine empirically those patterns of activity in physiological subsystems that relate to significant psychological processes, without prejudging the issue on the basis of a premature, and oversimplified generalization about arousal level and behavioral performance.

Interactions between Arousal and Behavior. Finally, we can note a third barrier to any simple assertions about arousal level as an independent variable: Arousal level is not static. Superimposed on the regular circadian rhythms are changes in level of arousal induced by ongoing behavioral events, so that what may at one moment be independent variable (arousal level) becomes at the next moment dependent variable. Thus, a moderate level of arousal may facilitate certain behaviors that may in turn have consequences which either increase or decrease arousal level.

For example, with a moderate arousal level, you may choose, among many alternative behaviors, to read a novel; but the ideas triggered by the novel may have physiological consequences (for instance, an increase in sexual excitement) that in turn lead to increased arousal. Similarly, starting at a moderate level of arousal, you may be forced to choose between watching TV or doing homework. The latter may, however, demand a somewhat higher level of arousal than momentarily prevails; so the TV is turned on, and by virtue of what is available to watch, your arousal level may be sufficiently lowered that you end up falling asleep.

Between arousal and behavior there is such a continual interaction that it becomes virtually impossible to predict from knowledge of a person's arousal level at one time, where he will be later either in terms of behavior or arousal level. Empirical attempts to relate level of arousal as an independent variable to other behavioral variables will undoubtedly require examining lengthy samples of both physiological and behavioral events; this will undoubtedly complicate the researcher's already difficult task.

MOMENTARY AROUSAL FLUCTUATIONS AND BEHAVIOR

Despite the great difficulty in obtaining valid and stable physiological measures of arousal, some empirical relations with psychological processes have been established. In one series of experiments (Lacey and Lacey, 1958) the investigators found two types of people who were differentiated by their patterns of short-term fluctuation in arousal level. These two types emerged under relaxed conditions during which various measures of autonomic activity, such as heart rate, were continually recorded. The records from some subjects were quite even, reflecting the quiet, unchanging circumstances in the experimental room; other subjects, however, showed a fairly high rate of bursts of spontaneous physiological activity, as though their arousal level were repeatedly going up and down. The former subjects were called *stabile,* the latter *labile.* On subsequent retesting, this labeling turned out to be quite reliable, although correlations between measures from different autonomic subsystems (such as heart rate and skin resistance) were surprisingly low.

Correlates of Autonomic Stability and Lability. When people can be categorized in this fashion, what is the meaning of the distinctions? To get at meaning, we must search for other ways in which the types differ. Are there any interesting behavioral correlates of autonomic stability and lability? On the basis of highly involved speculation, the Laceys argued that the lability of the autonomic nervous system, as reflected for example in spontaneous accelerations of heart rate, would have direct impact on the central nervous system centers that control and modulate motor activity. In particular, they predicted that people categorized as autonomic labiles would be "impulsive" in motor activity, in the sense that they would have difficulty in withholding an incorrect motor response.

In a test of this prediction, they presented subjects who had been categorized labile or stabile with a row of seven lights. The subjects were instructed to release a key whenever the center light was illuminated, but not to respond when any of the peripheral lights came on. The emphasis for the subjects was on speed of reaction—even though the experimenters were primarily concerned with the number of erroneous responses made by the two kinds of subjects. It was expected that labiles would make more responses to the peripheral lights than would the stabiles. The results conformed to prediction, as illustrated in Figure 15.2. A second finding from this experiment was that labiles had faster reaction times than stabiles, though that difference does not account for the greater number of errors made by the labiles.

In subsequent research on the relation between indexes of autonomic reactivity (and presumably arousal, or "activation" level), John Lacey (1959) has pursued the hypothesis that the autonomic nervous system plays a "gating" role for the central nervous system. In particular, he speculates that a period of accelerated heart rate places a person in a state of decreased sensitivity to external stimulation; in such a state, the person can efficiently perform purely "mental" operations undistracted by external events. By contrast, when efficient performance requires vigilant alertness to external stimulation, then cardiac deceleration is called for, and typically occurs.

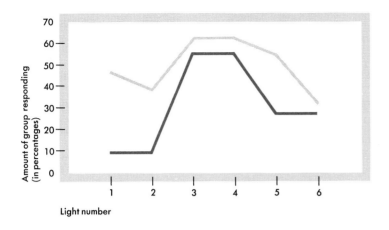

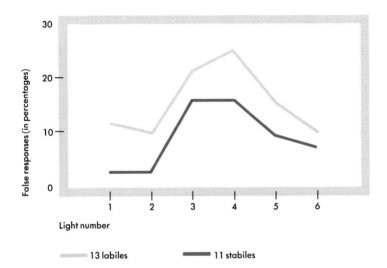

Figure 15.2 Stabiles are less prone to make errors (impulsive responses) in a stimulus-generalization experiment (see text) than are labiles. Peripheral light positions are indicated by numbers. Light 1 is the most extreme left light, and so on to light 6, the light on the extreme right of the visual field. Each light was presented four times to each subject. The ordinate of the top graph shows percentages of each subgroup responding at least once to the indicated peripheral light. The ordinate of the bottom graph shows the percentage of all trials (subjects times trials) in which errors were made. (Adapted from Lacey and Lacey, 1958.)

This speculation is based on results of experiments in which cardiac activity was measured while people were subjected to the two types of task (internally organized or externally controlled).

REACTIONS TO STRESS:
THE GENERAL ADAPTATION SYNDROME

We have noted so far the existence of periodic fluctuations in arousal level on a circadian cycle as well as momentary shifts in arousal as indexed by spontaneous bursts of autonomic activity. The arousal levels in question fall within what we might think of as the "normal range." Researchers have paid considerable attention, in addition, to levels of arousal that fall outside the normal bounds, particularly at the high end. What happens when excessively high levels of arousal are induced, when, to use the terminology frequently employed in this context, the individual is subjected to conditions of *stress*?

One approach to this question is to concentrate on the physiological consequences of stressors that are themselves essentially physiological in nature. The pioneering research of this type has been carried out by Hans Selyé, a Canadian physician. Out of his empirical research, Selyé (1956) has evolved a descriptive model of successive stages in an organism's response to chronic, excessive stress. He refers to the total reaction to stress as the *General Adaptation Syndrome*. In crude outline, the syndrome comprises the following three consecutive stages.

1. *The alarm reaction.* The initial behavioral reaction to sudden, intense stress may be immobilization, or "freezing," accompanied physiologically by a reduction in normal levels of autonomic function. But this phase is soon replaced by one in which the body's physiological defenses against the stressor begin to get mobilized; in general, the sympathetic branch of the autonomic nervous system becomes dominant, with a resulting rise in heart rate and blood pressure; sweating increases; pupils dilate; breathing becomes more labored and less regular.

Another response to stress is an increase in the hormonal output of the adrenal gland. One part of that gland, the adrenal *medulla*, which is activated by the sympathetic nervous system, secretes two types of hormones into the blood, *epinephrine* and *norepinephrine*. These two hormones, in general, have effects on the various organ systems that add to those induced by sympathetic activity itself. Another portion of the adrenal gland, the adrenal *cortex*, is stimulated to unusually high levels of activity in the second of the three stages described by Selyé.

2. *The resistance stage.* With prolonged, intense stress, the system moves into a state of chronic, high-level activation, the resistance stage. It is in this stage that the adrenal cortex becomes heavily involved. Hormonal output of the adrenal cortex is itself stimulated by a hormone originating in the pituitary gland, ACTH (an abbreviation for adreno-cortico-trophic-hormone, that is, a hormone that is "attracted to" the adrenal cortex). Under stimulation by ACTH, the adrenal cortex secretes a large number of hormones; these are variously involved in promoting metabolic processes and serve to facilitate the abnormally high energy expenditure demanded by chronic stress. During the resistance stage the adrenal gland actually increases in size, just as a muscle does with exercise. Enlarged adrenals are thus an indicator that an organism has undergone considerable stress.

3. *The stage of exhaustion.* The supranormal activation of the autonomic nervous system and the ductless glands, such as the pituitary and the adrenal, cannot be maintained indefinitely. The emergency measures demanded by stress, as they occur during the resistance stage, imply their own ultimate failure, in what Selyé calls the exhaustion stage. In a sense, the

defensive system, by being pushed for too long beyond its normal level of functioning, destroys its own continued usefulness. Eventually the system is so depleted that it becomes incapable of responding normally even to moderate stress. Thus, after removal of the original stressor the system may not be able to return to its normal status; severe psychosomatic disorders may result and often the exhaustion stage is a prelude to premature death. For a crude analogy, think of the unwanted consequences that may result from an army's shelling its own troops in order to destroy an infiltrating enemy force.

Psychological Stress. Selyé's concern is primarily with physiological reactions to stressors that are physiologically defined, such as starvation, excess heat or cold, and so on. These variables are of interest to psychology as well; however, a psychologist is likely to go beyond physiological stressors, as independent variables, and beyond physiological reactions, as dependent variables, in his attempt to understand the full range of events implied in the phrase "reactions to stress." The psychologist is well aware (as, of course, is the physiologist) of the profound implications, physiological and behavioral, of events that physically are innocuous but which, symbolically, are fraught with meaning. Consider, for example, the healthy, well-fed, physically comfortable college student, with pounding heart, sweaty palms, dilated pupils, irregular breathing and thinking disorganized—about to give his first ten-minute talk in Speech 101.

In short, to restrict ourselves to a discussion of arousal and its vicissitudes, as though it were a purely physiological category, would omit much that is fascinating in human life. We have come to the point where it is necessary to inject psychological meaning into the events under discussion—to move from "arousal" to "emotion."

Affect

The adult human being experiences in his lifetime a myriad of different affects, or emotions, both within himself and in others. Names abound for identifying slight nuances in the various affects, as well as for quantitative distinctions. Indeed, the dictionary contains many more descriptive labels than psychology so far has had any use for, in very much the same way that the number of color names far exceeds the needs of the theorist of color vision.

NEGATIVE AND POSITIVE AFFECTS

One crude categorization distinguishes between *negative* and *positive* affects. These labels carry an evaluative connotation, whether intended or not, implying that negative affects are in some sense "bad" and positive ones are "good." In the negative category fall such emotions as fear, anxiety, anger, boredom, depression, rage, disgust, and so on; the positive affects include happiness, love, joy, contentment, and so on. Although it would be easy to get agreement on categorizing any particular emotion, it is not at all clear why this division has won such universal acceptance among psychologists. What is the rationale for segregating the emotions in this way?

The Evaluation of Affective Behavior. Here we can only guess, but it is likely that one basis for the positive-negative distinction is how psychological theorists, *as people*, themselves emotionally respond to, and evaluate, affective behavior in themselves and in others, as well as how they react to the conditions that presumably evoked the affective behavior in question. These responses in turn are probably in large part culturally defined.

In Western culture, and perhaps universally, fear is evaluated negatively. It is an emotion to be avoided in oneself and to be deplored in other people who are positively evaluated (family, loved ones, friends, colleagues, and so on); of course, fear in those one despises can be a source of pleasure. Fear connotes weakness, helplessness, loss of control; but the ideal person, the male especially in Western culture, is strong, effective, competent to cope adaptively with realistic threats, and not easily aroused by events that only superficially are dangerous.

The typical parent is embarrassed and perhaps angered by a child who is afraid of the dark, who is too scared to dive into a swimming pool, who is apprehensive about going to kindergarten, who is reluctant to meet unfamiliar people, and so on. An adolescent's peers are ruthless in their response to signs that he is "chicken." Fear is perhaps better tolerated among adults, but only if it is realistic, and especially if that fear is kept from dominating a person's behavior—that is, if he can function well in spite of the debilitating effects of fear. Bravery—facing danger adaptively despite one's fear—is indeed one of the highest virtues in Western mythology; to "disintegrate," or run away in the face of threat, is surely considered one of the lowest vices.

A similar evaluation applies to the other so-called negative affects, though perhaps with more variation among subcultures. For example, intense anger is generally an intolerable emotion. However, there are circumstances under which it may be highly valued, at least up to the point where the angry person does not lose control and dissipate the impact of his anger. And in certain subcultures the chronically angry person may be most highly respected, because in the face of injustice and hypocrisy, anger is considered the only honest emotion.

A psychologist labels affects positive because of a similar combination of individual experience and cultural values; as a person, he attaches a positive evaluation to such affects as love and joy, so he classifies them as "good," just as fear and anger are "bad."

The Modulation of Affective Expression. We start evaluating the affective behavior of a child early. It is the rare parent who does not respond intensely to an infant's expression of emotion. Crying and thrashing are about the only way the infant can express distress. And, in general, the more serious the infant's needs, the more vigorous his affective response. Thus, this behavior pattern has obvious survival value, as does the typical parental reaction to it. Indeed, it is quite possible that both the infant's affective behavior and the parental reaction to it are unlearned, evolved adaptations.

How, in fact, do parents respond to their infant's outbursts? There are, of course, considerable differences among parents and even within the same parent from moment to moment and over time. But we can safely call attention to two broad classes of response. The typical parent will try to restore the baby's equilibrium and, depending on sophistication, skill, emotional stability, and so on, will do so quickly and efficiently. The parent may wake from a sound sleep when the baby cries, run over hypotheses about the cause of the baby's discomfort (hunger, colic, illness, soiled diaper, and so on), and then try the obvious things that are likely to work: offering a bottle, holding him, changing the diaper, checking for fever, and so on.

Also included in the parental reaction is a second class of responses, themselves emotional, ranging from mild annoyance to anger and even sometimes uncontrolled fury. However intense the parent's love for the baby, affective outbursts are far from pleasant, on several grounds. Altruistically, it is distressing to be made aware of what, to infer from behavioral signs, must be considerable misery in a loved one, especially a helpless, dependent baby. Selfishly, parents have other things they want to do, such as sleep, besides caring for their infants. The baby's cry is a demand that is hard to deny, and as such is often resented, in much the same way that a middle-of-the-night phone call might be.

At still a different level, if the parent is unsuccessful in finding and removing the cause of the baby's emotional outburst, and the crying continues unabated, the inevitable result is frustration, mingled with feelings of incompetence and perhaps anxiety that the problem is beyond solution. Under these conditions, the sturdiest parent may experience and express intense anger and hostility directed at the baby. At this point, even an emotionally stable parent may curse at the child, replace him roughly in the crib, and stalk out of the room. There may even arise fantasies of getting rid of the baby. At this same point, an emotionally unstable parent may very well beat the infant, inflicting serious bodily harm, or perhaps try to muffle the unbearable crying with a pillow and so suffocate the baby—acting out the normal parent's fantasies. Finally, in response to his own emotional reaction to the baby's expression of affect, the typical parent is also likely to feel ashamed and guilty, a further reason to devalue the baby's emotional behavior.

In short, despite its adaptive significance, which on rational grounds affords it a positive evaluation, the baby's expression of distress also gets a negative evaluation from the parent. And that negative evaluation is communicated to the baby. A young child, by kindergarten age if not earlier, is well aware that to please his parents and other adults he should refrain from all but the most necessary emotional outbursts (of the sort we label "negative"). Some children learn this lesson so well that they use crying fits and tantrums to punish their parents. But the typical child is embarrassed by his tears and prefers to hide them.

The affects we call "positive" in general get the opposite treatment. A contented, happy, affectionate child evokes a similar response in his parents. It is pleasant to see one's child in good spirits and not at all demanding on one's intellectual or emotional resources. Even here, however, some pressure toward modulation of affect begins to be imposed as the child gets older. The reasons are obscure, but it is not unusual for parents to insist that children tone down their shrieks of delight, at least in public, not be so openly affectionate, to restrain their exuberant play. Thus, even the positive affects are brought under some control, perhaps only in the interest of transforming the child's behavior into a pattern that is considered "mature."

EMOTION AS A PSYCHOLOGICAL CONCEPT

Disrupting and Mobilizing Effects. There has been a great deal of controversy concerning the nature of emotion and its role in psychological theory. Some theorists have attended to the disruptive consequences of affect on other behaviors; a frequently used example here is "stage fright," whereby what would otherwise be a smoothly executed performance of a complex behavioral sequence, such as playing a piano concerto, is impaired by the performer's anxiety concerning audience evaluation of his talent.

Other theorists, while recognizing the potentially disintegrative effects of strong emotion, have noted that a certain amount of emotional response is helpful in mobilizing one's energies in the face of a difficult task. Thus, a pianist who has no concern whatsoever about the audience and its evaluation of him might not be sufficiently aroused to perform at the top of his skill and vigor. Similarly, athletes frequently develop techniques of self-arousal in order to achieve a peak of energy mobilization, such as "talking themselves" into hating their opponents. Coaches, of course, often attempt the same thing, with their pregame and half-time pep talks.

It is, then, fairly easy to find examples of both disruptive and facilitative effects of emotion on behavior. Clearly, "emotions" are not a homogeneous set of events, with simple, direct effects on all other behaviors. A given emotion, say anger, may facilitate performance of one kind of task (throwing the discus) but disrupt the performance of another (performing a neurosurgical operation). Similarly, emotion at one level of intensity may be facilitating, but at another level it may be disruptive. For certain people, at least, a moderate degree of anxiety facilitates their performance on academic examinations, though intense anxiety may be a precursor of failure.

Emotions as Incentives. A further complication is implicit in our previous remarks about how the various affects are evaluated. That is, whatever their role while active, emotions also serve in the regulation of behavior as *incentives*, or anticipated goal "objects." Just as an animal might learn to perform an operant response for food reinforcement or to avoid shock, so too will people regulate their behavior in order to minimize certain emotional states and maximize others.

It is not clear whether emotional states are intrinsically positive or negative; be that as it may, once they have become so evaluated, through the process we have sketched above, then they can act like any other goal objects. Thus, a young child might learn a variety of behavioral devices for avoiding situations in which he is likely to exhibit some negative affect, in part perhaps to avoid the experience itself, but also in large measure to avoid the social consequences. For example, if playing with "rough boys" is likely to lead to tears, then that activity is carefully avoided.

It is interesting, in view of the emphasis in our culture on modulation of affect, to note the spread among adolescents and young adults of behaviors directed at magnifying their emotional experience, particularly through the use of certain drugs, such as LSD, or other agents, that exaggerate rather than diminish the variety and intensity of emotional experiences. Do these behaviors contradict our hypothesis of a culturally imposed negative evaluation on affective expression? Not necessarily. We could say, of course, that the hippie is a cultural outsider; that the process of socialization of affect simply has not taken in his case, though it works well for most.

An alternative interpretation is also available, one that would seem to have more general applicability. After all, though affective expression may be devalued, it is not taboo. Indeed, our society provides for the emotional reactions of its members, and not simply in the sense of sanctioning naturally occurring affective expression under the proper circumstances, such as at funerals and weddings. Beyond that, cultural institutions have developed for eliciting emotional reactions: The radio and TV soap opera is prototypical. A spectator is supposed to be depressed by modern drama, to be elated by musical comedy, to be terrified by a horror movie, to express hostility and anger at a boxing match, to be scared on a roller coaster. Laughing, crying, shrieking—the whole range of affects and affective expression—are not only allowed; they are actively encouraged, *but on cue and in their place*. You can scream and yell all you want Saturday afternoon in the football stadium (at least if everyone else near you is doing so), but you won't get away with it the next morning at breakfast in the cafeteria. You can weep over Willie Loman as you watch *Death of a Salesman* on TV or in the theater, but don't cry when you get a failing grade on your term paper.

You can scream in terror, or mock terror, on the roller coaster, but don't try it before your first piano recital.

The hippie culture may simply allow for affective experimentation that is otherwise prohibited. Interestingly enough, it is the positive affects that this culture encourages. There are probably rather large differences among subgroups in our culture in the extent to which the display of emotion is allowed or encouraged. In this way, a person's affective style may be determined broadly by his subgroup memberships, grouping based, for example, on ethnic background, sex, and even occupation.

EMOTIONAL DEVELOPMENT

In the manner sketched above, the expression of affect becomes acculturated. Along with this modulation in intensity of emotional expression, as a child develops, the range of emotional experiences is greatly expanded from the few primitive types present in infancy. Exactly how many and which emotions are present has been the subject of some controversy.

Watson's View. The Behaviorist John Watson, for example, held that the infant's emotional repertory is probably limited to three distinct types: (a) fear, (b) rage, and (c) love. The typical events that produce each of these affects are, respectively, (a) loud noise or loss of support, (b) bodily restraint, and (c) stroking or tickling of the skin (especially of the erogeneous zones), gentle rocking, and patting. While expressing some doubts about the complete accuracy of his conclusion, which was based on considerable observation of and experimentation on babies, Watson believed that the three basic emotions "form the nucleus out of which all future emotional reactions arise" (Watson, 1927, p. 49). Emotional development, for Watson, proceeds through the conditioning of these emotional reactions (considered as unconditioned responses) to various arbitrary conditioned stimuli, as in Watson and Raynor's classical experiments with the baby Albert.

Hebb's View. Others have attempted to catalog the basic emotional responses and their precipitating conditions. D.O. Hebb, for example, studied emotional behavior in young chimpanzees. Fear was certainly prominent, but the conditions for its occurrence were more general than the two (loud noise, loss of bodily support) specified by Watson. Following are some of the fear-inducing items that Hebb found: "a carrot of an unusual shape, a biscuit with a worm on it, . . . a sculptured head or a death mask of a chimpanzee . . ." (Hebb, 1958, p. 15).

It would seem reasonable to characterize these all as instances of the violation of some strong expectation, or to use slightly different terms, as the imposition on the animal of excessive uncertainty. Watson's two basic conditions are easy to fit into such a scheme. His failure to observe other effective fear inducers in the babies he observed may reflect their cognitive immaturity, as compared with Hebb's chimpanzees. If expectations are to be violated, they must first exist.

The point of view exemplified by Hebb's analysis of fear provides a more flexible approach to emotional development than does the Watsonian conditioning model. In particular, Hebb's approach locates emotions within a general theoretical framework that includes perceptual and cognitive processes along with learning. Emotional development, then, is not simply the outcome of arbitrary, conditioned associations (which may indeed take place), but part of the total psychological development of the individual. Thus, as a child's perceptual and cognitive structures increase in complexity, there will be a corresponding increase in the number and kinds of events that become capable of eliciting an emotional response. Stimuli that are emotionally inert at one point in the child's development may be quite potent at a later point, not because of a fortuitous pairing of those stimuli with some unconditioned affect-arousing stimulus, but because of changes in the way the child perceives and categorizes them.

The Smiling Response and Stranger Anxiety. A neat illustration of that idea is provided by the infant's response to other people. At a fairly young age, usually around three months, a baby responds with a characteristic smile when stimulated by a moving face or a facsimile of a face (Spitz and Wolf, 1946). This smiling response shares the properties of certain reflexive behaviors exhibited by lower animals in the presence of specific stimulus patterns, called by ethologists "sign stimuli." Whether the smiling response, at this age, is indicative of any positive affect is a moot point, though it certainly elicits considerable positive affect in the person behind the smile-inducing face. In any event, the young infant's response to other people is quite indiscriminate. Parent and stranger are treated alike.

A profound change occurs sometime after the child is six months old, usually around the age of eight months. Familiar and strange faces now get different responses; a frequent reaction to the sudden appearance of a strange face is an outburst of crying and other behaviors indicative of extreme fear or anxiety. Although "stranger anxiety" is often an embarrassment to the parents (the stranger may be a visiting grandparent), it is the normal reaction, and its absence might rather be a source of concern.

The occurrence of stranger anxiety is part of a larger developmental pattern, including what must be a newly developed ability on the part of the baby to discriminate, perceptually, between the highly familiar features of the parent and the similar but unfamiliar features of other people. Note that the baby does not react with anxiety to all *objects* besides the parent; the response is specific to other *people*, suggesting something like the following as the basic elicitor of the reaction: "the approaching object is my mama —no, it looks like her, but it's a little different—I want mama, not this other thing that reminds me of her—what's happened to my mama?"

It is interesting, in the above regard, that stranger anxiety is a transient phenomenon. By the time the baby is about a year old, he has sufficiently matured so that the disappointment, anger, and anxiety attendant on the appearance of a strange person do not occur. By then, strangers are perceived sufficiently differently from parents and other familiar figures that they are not improperly categorized at first. The baby may not like strangers, but they are no longer sources of primitive anxiety.

Labeling and the Differentiation of Affects. In Watson's analysis of emotional development, he emphasized the question of how emotional responses come to be elicited by originally neutral stimuli. Development in that sense implies an increase in the number of emotionally relevant stimuli. But that is only part of the problem, and a small part. The adult's emotional repertory differs from the child's not only in the range of effective stimuli but also in the range of emotional responses available. Watson's fear, rage, and love certainly do not cover the number and variety of affects exhibited by the adult. A basic problem, then, is to explain the process whereby the myriad of emotions experienced by the adult become differentiated out of the initial, limited infantile matrix. We can only speculate here, since sound empirical evidence is lacking. However, it seems likely that labeling, under parental tutelage, significantly helps a child to discriminate among subtly different affective experiences.

For example, consider the following two situations. (1) A young girl, who tends to be rather shy and easily upset, is getting ready to visit at a friend's house, on the other side of town. (2) That same girl is about to go to Sunday school, where she is to participate, reluctantly, in a play. In both circumstances she experiences considerable excitement and behaves accordingly, yet it is difficult to note any differences in her behavior in the two situations. But her mother, who by now understands her well, assumes that the former situation elicits a mixture of a little apprehension and a lot of pleasurable anticipation, while the latter evokes largely apprehension mixed with only a small amount of pleasurable anticipation.

To aid her child in identifying her own emotional nuances, she provides labels. In the former case, she may pick up and reinforce a phrase the child herself may have used in similar circumstances: The mother asks, "Do you have that excited feeling in your chest?" In the latter case, she may say something like, "I guess you're scared about the play, but it probably will turn out to be fun." With the aid of such labeling, the child becomes aware of the existence of a variety of similar but still distinguishable affects within her, and starts to search for differences that she might otherwise have glossed over.

In the meantime, the girl's baby brother can also be learning about affects through labels. For a long time, when he was refused something he wanted, he would simply burst into tears and cry inconsolably for several minutes, much as he might if he were physically injured and in great pain. But surely, being refused to be allowed to play with a sharp knife must elicit a somewhat different emotional experience from being cut by that knife—even though the overt behaviors seem much the same in each instance. It becomes clear to the boy's mother that the affect aroused by the refusal is akin to anger; gradually, with cues provided by her the little boy learns to say through his tears, "Mommy, I'm mad at you." Eventually, the words will suffice and the emotional reaction will no longer be necessary. Thus the labeling actually serves two functions: (1) It helps in the differentiation among similar affects, and (2) it provides a restrained substitute for a primitive, uncontrolled, affective outburst.

Labeling, under the tutelage of a sensitive observer, is probably a potent factor in the development of a validly differentiated affective repertory. But labeling can also work in the opposite direction. That is, useful distinctions among affects can be blurred by improper labeling, just as one might prevent a child from learning that there are dogs and cats by calling them all "doggies" well beyond the age when the child is ready to make the discrimination.

It may also be possible to do violence to a child's emotional development, in the sense in which we have been using that phrase, by improper labeling of the affects expressed by the people around him. Thus, suppose a mother is frequently angry at her child and exhibits that anger in facial expression, tone of voice, and other gestures; but suppose that the mother simultaneously denies being angry, perhaps out of a feeling of guilt at being so easily upset, and insists instead that she "just has a headache." This distortion of emotional reality, through improper labeling, must have some adverse impact on the child's own developing affective repertory.

SOME EMPIRICAL RESEARCH
ON EMOTIONAL DEVELOPMENT

Not everything that can be said about emotional development is anecdotal and speculative. Some interesting empirical research has been done, though seldom on people. Whether the results of that research can be generalized to human beings is, at this point, an open question. We refer below to three lines of research, which are both interesting in their own right and hold promise of some generality: (a) effects of early stress on later emotionality; (b) imprinting; and (c) the impact of early social and affectional relations on later behavior.

Early Stress. There is considerable variation among adults in the level of emotionality exhibited under stress or even under relatively innocuous circumstances. Some people are chronically anxious, for example, while others are unusually relaxed. Such differences are often extreme enough to be of clinical significance. In searching for the etiology of intense, chronic anxiety, personality theorists have entertained the hypothesis that adult anxiety has its origin in emotionally traumatic events experienced very early in life.

Freud, for example, suggested that the prototype of adult anxiety was the reaction of the neonate to the "birth trauma," by which he meant the abrupt change from the quiescence of the intrauterine environment to the flooding of stimulation experienced during and after birth.

Pursuing the line of reasoning which attributes differences in adult anxiety to differences in early experiences, we might argue that individuals who are subjected to early emotional stress will be more anxious, or "emotional," in later life than individuals whose early experience is not abnormally stressful. Furthermore, it would seem that if special care were taken to shield an infant from stress, then his level of later emotionality should be unusually low. Attempts to investigate the validity of these hypotheses with human beings have been meager, for obvious practical and ethical reasons. But a great deal of work has been done on this problem with other species, especially rats.

One question that immediately arises is how early is "early"? If postnatal trauma is effective, how about stress applied prenatally? In one experiment (Thompson, 1957) designed to investigate that question, female rats were first placed in a shuttle-box avoidance-conditioning situation, where a buzzer signaled impending shock. The rats learned to avoid shock by responding to the buzzer. It was assumed that the buzzer had acquired fear-inducing potency as a result of the training.

The female rats were then impregnated, and half were subjected to further avoidance trials. These animals were not shocked during pregnancy, since they reliably responded to the buzzer; thus, any later influence of this treatment on their offspring could not be attributed to a direct effect of shock on the fetuses. If there were emotional consequences of the treatment it presumably would be mediated by the fear induced in the pregnant rats by the buzzer.

Two groups of subjects were available when the pups were delivered (the gestation period for rats is about 21 days): an experimental group (E) consisting of rats whose mothers had been frightened during gestation, and a control group (C), whose mothers had earlier gone through avoidance conditioning, but not during pregnancy.

The animals in the E and C groups were further subdivided. Half the pups in each group were nursed by their own mothers, and half were given to foster mothers from the opposite group. This procedure was instituted to control for any possible emotional effects of the rats' postnatal experiences. Even though the prenatal treatment might prove ineffective, the groups might behave differently because the rats reared by mothers that had undergone the extra buzzer trials during pregnancy would be more emotional than rats reared by the mothers that had received the control treatment. As it turned out, this control was unnecessary, since no effects were found that could be attributed to postnatal conditions.

The E and C groups did differ, however. On several behavioral measures the E rats appeared more fearful than the C rats, both when they were tested between 30 and 40 days of age and again 100 days later. For example, when placed in a strange environment, the E rats were the less active, presumably because they were more inhibited from exploring by virtue of their higher anxiety level. Similarly, the E rats were more hesitant to leave their home cages when the cage door was left open and were slower to eat in a strange place.

Apparently, then, subjecting pregnant females to emotional stress can influence the later emotional responsiveness of their offspring. Concerning the mechanism, Thompson suggested an endocrine basis for the transfer of stress effects from mother to fetus, though the exact details of the process have not been worked out. However, it is not hard to imagine how the mother's hormone output might influence the development of the fetus's own endocrine glands, especially the adrenals, thereby providing a structural basis for the later functional difference between E and C animals.

Further experiments lend credence to these speculations. For example, pregnant rats were injected with either epinephrine, norepinephrine, or a neutral saline solution once a day during the second week of gestation; an additional control group was given no injections at all. Their offspring were later tested for fearfulness and learning ability. In general, the mothers that had been injected with either epinephrine or norepinephrine produced the more fearful offspring (Young, 1963, 1964), with the effect tending to decrease as the offspring got older.

Emotional effects of early postnatal manipulations have also been investigated, with some surprising results. This research is sufficiently extensive so that only a brief sampling can be provided here.

One question considered was whether a positive emotional experience early in life helps protect an individual against later stress. To test this idea, an experiment with rats (Bernstein, 1957) employed three degrees of "gentling." One group of rats was given 10 minutes a day of gentle handling between the age of weaning (about 21 days) and 59 days. A second group received the same treatment, but only between 50 and 59 days of age. The third group was left alone. When the three groups were tested, beginning at age 60 days, on a T-maze learning task, they scored in the order given on efficiency of learning. On a test of exploratory behavior, the first group exceeded the other two. The first group was also significantly heavier by the age of 46 days than the group that had received no gentling.

Along with Bernstein's work, several similar studies have compared handled (and thus presumably "gentled") and nonhandled rats on a variety of behavioral and physiological measures. In one type of experiment (Weininger, 1953) it was found that rats handled early in life survived total deprivation of food and water longer than nonhandled control rats; the average difference in survival time was about 54 hours. In a similar study (Levine and Otis, 1958) the experimenters found that handling was more effective before weaning than after weaning. And in a more elaborate experiment than his first effort, Weininger (1956) noted that handled rats, as compared with nonhandled ones, (a) showed less marked systemic reactions (such as less stomach bleeding, less cardiac damage, smaller adrenal glands) to severe stress at maturity, (b) grew heavier and longer, though they ate no more than controls (presumably their metabolism was more efficient), and (c) were more active and venturesome in an unfamiliar environment.

Why should early handling decrease later susceptibility to stress? The original hypothesis was that handling (petting, stroking, and so on) constitutes a form of positive emotional experience of the sort that, in human beings, could counteract later emotional and physical stress. We might argue, in a somewhat different vein, that the nonhandled animals, without the gentling influence of the warm, protective human hand, must face early stress unprotected—that they are more susceptible to stress later in life simply because they have already begun to be worn down. Indeed, we might even hypothesize that, to rat pups, being held in a huge, strange human hand is itself *mildly stressful;* that the handled rats, rather than being gentled are being given doses of stress small enough to cope with, and thereby are immunized against the debilitating effects of later stress. By contrast, the nonhandled rats meet later stress unprepared by prior experience.

According to the results of a series of experiments by Seymour Levine and his colleagues (see Levine, 1960), the latter interpretation is probably correct. For example, rats that have been handled in infancy do not differ from rats that have been handled and also given mild electric shock, but both groups are superior to nontreated controls. Apparently, then, mild stress in infancy leads to the most successful emotional development; too little stress or too much both have deleterious effects.

In the Thompson experiment on prenatal effects on later fearfulness, the cross-fostering procedure turned out not to have been necessary since the experience of the mother rearing a pup was not relevant to its later behavior. However, the mothers were not subjected to stress after the pups were born, and the prenatal fear-induction may have left no general aftereffects on the mothers. We can still ask whether the mother's emotional state during rearing affects the emotional behavior of her offspring. That question, combined with a continued concern for prenatal conditions, inspired an experiment (Denenberg, 1963) in which the emotional state of the mother was systematically manipulated both pre- and postnatally.

Rather than attempt to induce fear in pregnant rats, as Thompson had done, Denenberg selected two groups of females on the basis of his assessment of their chronic level of fearfulness, one group high in fearfulness and the other low. Animals within these groups were mated, and their offspring were assigned to foster mothers, also classified as high or low in fearfulness. Combining pre- and postnatal fearfulness of the mothers in this way yielded four groups of offspring, as indicated in Table 15.1. Shown in the table is the average activity score earned by animals in each of the groups when tested at 50 days of age. Note that a high activity score indicates low fear-

Mother's Fearfulness		Activity Score on Open-Field Test
Biological	Foster	
High	High	61
High	Low	88
Low	High	96
Low	Low	106

Table 15.1   Fearfulness of rats at 50 days of age as a function of the fearfulness of their biological and foster mothers. The higher the activity score the less the fearfulness. (Adapted from Denenberg, 1963.)

fulness. The data reveal both pre- and postnatal effects: The most fearful offspring came from highly emotional biological mothers and were reared by highly emotional foster mothers; the least emotional offspring were the product of biological mothers and foster mothers low in fearfulness. Offspring from the mixed conditions—one "mother" high, the other low—emerged as intermediate in fearfulness.

In subsequent research (Denenberg and Rosenberg, 1967) it was shown that fearfulness induced in offspring by emotional mothers carries over to the next generation. That is, when the female offspring of emotional mothers are mated and have litters, these animals are found to be more emotional than the offspring of mothers that had been reared by mothers low in fearfulness. Of course, the time scale here is very much compressed, compared to the number of years separating a human grandmother from her grandchildren, but it is still tempting to draw implications from the rat experiments about the possibility of transmitting anxiety over several generations of human beings.

Early Bonds of Affection: Imprinting. The interaction between mother and child is given considerable weight in virtually all approaches to emotional development, especially the "attachment" of the infant to the mother.

Ethologists have long been interested in one manifestation of a strong infant-mother attachment that is easily observed in nature, especially among fowl. It is common to see a string of baby ducks swimming along right behind the mother duck, and indeed following close by wherever she goes on water or land. Similar instances of *following behavior* can be observed in many species of birds and some mammals.

The biological utility of a young animal's sticking close to its mother is obvious, so it is tempting to speculate that the behavior has a simple genetic basis. Perhaps the newborn bird has a built-in image of "mother" and matches that image with an external object; "mother" in this case might be a generalized image appropriate to any adult female of the species.

This kind of romantic hypothesis was quickly discarded when it was shown (Spalding, 1873) that birds can be induced to accept, as the object to be followed, virtually any salient stimulus, provided it is the first such stimulus to which they are exposed after hatching. A bouncing ball, a wooden decoy, indeed even a human being can assume the role of "mother" if introduced to the newly hatched bird under the proper circumstances. The specific attachment, then, is clearly not innate but acquired—although this is not to say that a proclivity for forming such attachments is not built in.

A formal model to account for the facts of following behavior, as they were then known, was prosed by the ethologist Konrad Lorenz (1937). He called the process *imprinting*. Lorenz argued that imprinting has certain characteristics that make it different from ordinary associative learning of the conditioned-response variety. Two such characteristics seem especially noteworthy. Imprinting, Lorenz claimed, can occur only during a limited *critical period*, early in the infant's life, and once the attachment is formed, it is permanent (lasting throughout the bird's life) and irreversible (not transferable to another object). By contrast, according to Lorenz, ordinary learning can occur just about any time, and learned relations can be broken or transformed.

Recently, attempts have been made to formulate competing models of imprinting. Howard Moltz (1960) considered following behavior an operant response, which is maintained through the anxiety-reducing effect of the "imprinted" object. That particular object has special anxiety-reducing potency, according to Moltz, because it was present and prominent during the brief period in the bird's life shortly after hatching when its anxiety level is abnormally low. Moltz claims that whatever stimulus is present and sufficiently salient (for the then quite insensitive bird) will be associated, through classical conditioning, with the set of responses that constitute a low-anxiety state. Later, when the bird's anxiety level is high, the presence of the imprinted object will elicit these low-anxiety responses, thereby neutralizing the anxiety-provoking effects of other stimuli.

Moltz provides some experimental evidence in support of his model. For example, the amount of following behavior increases when an animal is tested under circumstances that arouse anxiety and decreases when it is tested under low-anxiety conditions. Moreover, an adult, nonimprinted bird can be successfully imprinted (contrary to the notion of a critical period) under the influence of a tranquillizing drug, meprobamate, which presumably restores the unusually low state of anxiety characteristic of the period just after hatching.

In its most general terms, Moltz's model is applicable to other instances in which infants become strongly attached to certain objects, whether inanimate or animate (including their mothers). For example, the well-known attachment of babies and young children to a particular blanket or stuffed animal, illustrated so aptly by Linus in the comic strip "Peanuts," may develop through a process similar to the one postulated by Moltz for following behavior. The "security blanket" is certainly a potent anxiety-reducer. And it may very well be that a child's strong attachment to his mother is at least partly based on the same mechanism.

Figure 15.3 The world's best-known security blanket. ("Peanuts," by C. Schulz © United Feature Syndicate, 1968.)

Early Affectional Bonds: What Makes a Monkey Mother? In the large primate laboratory maintained at the University of Wisconsin under the direction of Harry Harlow, the practice for a time was followed of raising infant monkeys within sight and sound of, but not in direct bodily contact with, other monkeys, including their own mothers. The infants raised under these conditions appeared to develop normally, but when they reached adolescence, certain behavioral abnormalities became evident. Especially prominent was their complete sexual inadequacy.

Partly as a result of that serendipitous finding, but largely out of a long-standing interest in general theoretical issues concerning motivational and emotional development, Harlow instituted a program of research designed to assess the minimal rearing requirements for normal primate behavior. The most striking aspect of this research is a comparison of the effectiveness of two types of substitute, or surrogate, inanimate monkey mothers. One type, called the "wire mother," was constructed of uncovered wire mesh; the other type, the "cloth mother," was essentially identical to the first, except that it was covered with soft terry cloth (Figure 15.4, page 593). Several experimental variations concerned access to one or both types of mother, which mother was the source of milk, and so on. In general, as a large number of different behavioral tests indicated with no ambiguity, the cloth mother was by far the more effective surrogate, even if the wire mother supplied the infant's milk. Moreover, the infant monkeys apparently developed little, if any, affection for the wire mothers, but a strong bond was formed to the cloth mothers, very much like that of monkeys reared by their real mothers.

One major conclusion drawn by Harlow was that reduction of the hunger drive by real or surrogate mothers is trivial in the formation of bonds of affection compared with the effectiveness of a comfortable "skin," or what he calls *contact comfort*. To dramatize this conclusion, in a major address given before the American Psychological Association in 1958, Harlow composed the following verses:

THE HIPPOPOTAMUS

This is the skin some babies feel
Replete with hippo love appeal.
Each contact, cuddle, push, and shove
Elicits tons of baby love.

THE SNAKE

To baby vipers, scaly skin
Engenders love 'twixt kith and kin.
Each animal by God is blessed
With kind of skin it loves the best.

THE RHINOCEROS

The rhino's skin is thick and tough,
And yet this skin is soft enough
That baby rhinos always sense,
A love enormous and intense.

THE ELEPHANT

Though mother may be short on arms,
Her skin is full of warmth and charms.
And mother's touch on baby's skin
Endears the heart that beats within.

THE CROCODILE

Here is the skin they love to touch.
It isn't soft and there isn't much,
But its contact comfort will beguile
Love from the infant crocodile.

(Harlow, 1958, pp. 677–678.)

But in singing the praises of the cloth mother, Harlow overstated the case. For once again, when the infants reared on the surrogates without access to other monkeys reached adolescence, they revealed the same inadequacy as those that had earlier been raised in isolation. Regardless of the type of surrogate mother available during infancy, the monkeys, male and female, were woefully incompetent as sexual partners. Furthermore, when some of the females were finally successfully impregnated, they turned out to be totally irresponsible mothers.

In a series of follow-up studies, Harlow has sought to determine the factors involved in the development of normal sexual and maternal patterns. The conclusion now seems to be that the crucial variable is early access to peers. For example, monkeys raised with cloth mothers and given only 20 minutes each day in a special play room with other young monkeys reveal normal sexual and social behavior; by contrast, infants raised by their own, real mothers are quite retarded socially if denied some contact with peers.

Figure 15.4 Two types of surrogate monkey mothers used in Harlow's research. (Photo by Sponholz for the University of Wisconsin Primate Laboratory.)

Thus, the bond of affection between an infant monkey and its mother is mediated by the mother's ability to offer "contact comfort." But for the development of normal social and sexual effectiveness, even a good mother is not enough. For this, early interaction with peers is apparently essential (Harlow, 1962). In any event, it is clear that the emotional development of a monkey is at the mercy of its early encounters with both a source of contact comfort and with whatever is provided by peers. If these variables are so important to the monkey, they must be even more so for the developing human being. Although experimental data on this problem are entirely lacking, there is some clinical evidence to support the significance of mothering for the emotional well-being of the child (Spitz, 1945). Infants raised in institutions under conditions of severe restriction in physical stimulation and with very limited contact with foster mothers show extreme retardation in emotional development. What weight to assign to the inadequate mothering is, unfortunately, impossible to determine. Indeed, it may be that for the human child, both the inanimate and animate elements in its environment are crucial to normal emotional development—though a competent human mother might be a source of both. That is, she would herself provide the human equivalent of "contact comfort," and in addition would assure adequate stimulation from the physical environment as well as opportunity for appropriate interactions with peers. An incompetent mother might fail in one or more of these activities.

Because a baby has such a limited emotional repertory, it is usually fairly easy to identify whatever affective state he happens to be exhibiting. The observer's task is simplified too by his knowledge of the environmental conditions surrounding the baby, the events immediately preceding the emotional response, and something about the typical reaction of babies in general, and this one in particular, to events of that sort. Furthermore, a baby does not modulate its affective expression; there is nothing subtle about its emotional behavior.

As an individual matures, such aids gradually lose their effectiveness. As the emotional repertory expands, the variables operative in the person's life are multitudinous, complex, and often not even observable, so that the contextual cues which facilitate identifying emotion in the infant are much less useful for the adult. Often the same event will arouse more than one affective response—that is, "mixed emotions" within the same person as well as different responses in different people; for example, some people react to hostility with anger, but others respond with depression. The adult, moreover, has learned to suppress his affective expression, to keep his fears and anxieties and even his positive emotions to himself; the affective life of an adult proceeds in large part behind a bland and noncommittal exterior appearance. At least in the United States, and in similar cultures, the name of the game is "cool." For reasons such as these, it is not at all easy to tell from casual observation whether a given person is experiencing intense emotion, and it is especially difficult to assess the nature of that affect.

Psychologists have been challenged by the problem of identifying affect in adults. A great deal of research has been devoted to determining the behavioral and physiological indicators of emotion; this work is sampled in the remaining pages of this chapter. We have organized the potential indicators of emotion into three classes: (1) physiological patterns; (2) facial expression and gestural response; (3) verbalization.

Physiological Patterns. We know already that emotion implies general activation of the autonomic nervous system. But are there specific physiological patterns associated with particular affects? Can fear and anger, for example, be distinguished through characteristic patterns of autonomic response?

For a time it was believed not, but recent work has been more promising. We mentioned earlier that under stress the adrenal gland discharges *epinephrine* and *norepinephrine*. These two hormones serve to increase blood pressure; epinephrine accomplishes this by affecting the heart, while norepinephrine acts on the blood vessels, constricting them and thereby indirectly raising blood pressure. It turns out (Ax, 1953) that experimental subjects respond to anger-inducing events with an increased output of norepinephrine, while fear arousal is accompanied by an increase in secretion of epinephrine. On the basis of these results, it would seem possible to infer "anger" or "fear" in an aroused person by assessing the relative amounts of those two hormones in his bloodstream.

An indirect, but simpler approach also seems feasible (Funkenstein, 1955). If a person's blood pressure is unusually high, it is possible to tell whether epinephrine or norepinephrine is responsible for the rise by injecting the drug mecholyl, which is a stimulant of parasympathetic activity. Mecholyl lowers blood pressure, but only for a brief time if the high blood pressure is induced by norepinephrine and for a much longer time if by epinephrine. Thus, by observing the reaction of the person's blood pressure to mecholyl, we can infer whether he is angry or fearful. There might be easier ways, such as asking him, but that is beside the point. What does matter is the promise of establishing physiological assay methods that may ultimately enable us to bypass or supplement the sometimes unreliable alternative ways of identifying affective states. Some of these other potential indicators are discussed below.

Facial Expression and Gestural Response. In lower animals, stereotyped movements of the facial musculature and of other parts of the body are reliable indicators of specific affective states. For example, a dog with his tail between his hind legs is probably experiencing the canine equivalent of fear. Other dogs certainly respond as though that tail position bore such an implication; for example, chow dogs that are trained as fighters will less readily attack another chow with its tail up, curled over its back, than one with its tail down (Kuo, 1967). Facial configuration in dogs also has signal value for other dogs, such as the snarling expression achieved when the lips are pulled back, exposing the teeth. Similar stereotyped facial and gestural patterns are evident in other species; they are aroused by specific stimulus conditions and in turn are responded to by other animals of like kind in a manner that is consistent with an anthropomorphic interpretation of their emotional meaning. Some examples are shown in Figure 15.5.

Human infants also reveal stereotyped facial expressions and bodily movements under specific conditions. There is little difficulty in distinguishing by facial expression alone a happy from an unhappy baby. Fine nuances of emotional experience may not be so easily distinguished on this basis, however, and we usually have to know the precipitating event to know whether the expression illustrated in Figure 15.6 is fear or anger.

The ambiguity of facial expression increases markedly with age. Experimentation on this question is sparse, but what data there are suggest that facial expression alone, as given, say, in still photographs, is a useful but not

Figure 15.5 Facial expressions of a dog and a chimpanzee. (Left: H. Armstrong Roberts; right: Courtesy of the American Museum of Natural History.)

an entirely reliable or valid indicator of emotional experience (Schlosberg, 1952).

Darwin (1872) asserted that there are universal emotional expressions in man, and he argued that these are vestiges of what were, in the course of evolution, functional responses. For example, the human sneer, which expresses contempt, Darwin claimed had its precurser in the snarling expression of an animal threatening to attack. But along with built-in expressions,

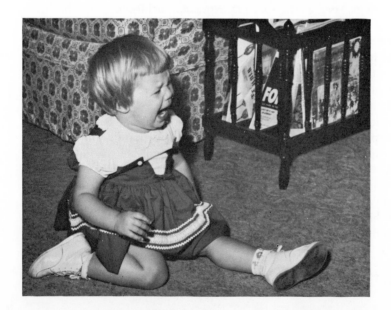

Figure 15.6 A little girl showing "fear" and/or "anger." (Bloom from Monkmeyer.)

there are considerable cultural differences in the facial expression of affect. A frequently cited example is the expression accompanying surprise; in Western culture, the eyebrows are lifted, whereas the Chinese stick out their tongues. The existence of these cultural differences is enough to suggest that some aspects of emotional expression are acquired rather than innate. This probably accounts for some of the difficulty in utilizing facial expression for identifying emotional states; undoubtedly, there are not only cultural differences, but also, within a culture, differences associated with subgroup, class, and even family membership, as well as patterns that are idiosyncratic to the individual.

If there is ambiguity in the emotional meaning of facial expression and other bodily gestures (for example, wringing the hands, characteristic of anxiety; tapping the foot, expressive of boredom; and so on) there will be differences in individual ability to "read" accurately the expressive behaviors of others. This ability is a considerable asset to people in certain occupations, such as salesmen, and crucial for practitioners of some professions, such as psychiatry. Part of the training of these people might include an attempt to sharpen their utilization of subtle emotional cues; but for such training to be effective, considerable research still needs to be done to establish the validity of particular cues for particular groups of "clients."

Verbalization. A rich source of affective cues is potentially available in a person's verbal responses, both in content and form. As for content, two types of affective indicator are available. The first is what we might call the direct, *introspective* indicator; the second is an indirect, *expressive* indicator.

The direct indicator involves asking a person to report on his present emotional state or on how he typically feels and behaves under particular circumstances, for instance, when taking an examination. Thus, to assess his level of anxiety about exams, we might give him a list of statements referring to emotional symptoms, or behavioral consequences of emotional states, that are likely to be associated with taking tests, and ask him whether each, in turn, applies to him. Examples of such statements are: "Whenever I take an important test, my heart beats much faster than usual." "Worrying about exams prevents me from doing my best when I prepare for them." "While taking difficult tests, I often have trouble thinking clearly."

The person's responses to such statements are taken essentially at face value; if he says that he is anxious about exams, either in his own words or in answer to a questionnaire, he is considered to be anxious about exams. Just how anxious he is, however, may be a relative matter—that is, relative to the response of other people with whom it is legitimate to compare him. The problem of measurement in this context is no different from the general problem of psychological measurement discussed in Chapter Three. A common solution to measuring anxiety, whether test anxiety or anxiety in general, is to make *anxiety scales*, comprising several items, standardized on large populations, checked for reliability and validity, and so on (see, for example, Mandler and Sarason, 1952; Alpert and Haber, 1960).

The same approach can be applied to affects other than anxiety, although in recent years psychologists seem to have been preoccupied with that particular emotion, perhaps reflecting a general cultural concern. A major drawback to the indiscriminate use of such scales is their dependence on accurate introspection and honest reporting.

An alternative approach to assessing affect from verbal responses is to treat the responses as indirect, expressive indicators. The verbalizations are not necessarily taken at face value but are transformed into indicators by "putting them through" a scoring system, based on a theoretical and/or an empirical rationale. For example, theory might assert that a person who claims no anxiety symptoms while taking an exam is really a highly anxious person. Hence, the interpretation of his response demands transforming it from its face value to its theoretically implied meaning: "no," on this item, means "yes."

To take another example, it may turn out empirically, but for no established theoretical reason, that people who are known to be depressed are likely to endorse the statement, "My father was a good provider," while people who are not depressed are likely to say "no" to that item. A depression scale might be composed from a set of such items that would allow good discrimination between depressed and nondepressed people, and perhaps even a quantitative assessment of degree of depression. And note that it is irrelevant whether father was or was not a good provider.

Instruments for measuring affect through the use of such items are known as *structured* tests. Attempts have been made to develop *unstructured* tests for the same purpose. The latter require a subject to use his own words (other than just answer "yes" or "no"); the protocols they yield have much richer content than those from structured tests, but they also are more difficult to analyze.

The prototype of the unstructured test is the thematic apperception test (TAT), in which a subject is shown a set of pictures and asked to make up a story about each one. Such instruments are used in a clinical setting to assess a variety of functions—cognitive, emotional, motivational, and so on—in order to form a description of the individual personality. But their use can also be restricted, especially for research purposes, to measuring one or more affects. For example, in an unpublished study by Cynthia Dember, a scoring system for measuring depression in children's TAT stories was developed, and then validated by showing that children who had recently lost a parent had higher depression scores than control subjects. Examples of a typical story told by a bereaved and a control subject are given below. Can you spot depressive indicators in the bereaved child's story?

I think the boy wants to be a fiddler when he grows up and he's poor and he doesn't have enough money to get a fiddle till he's big enough to get a job—and he's about 10 years old, I'd say, and he wants—his father probably died and they don't have enough money to buy a fiddle for him and the reason why he probably wants to do it is because his father and grandfather used to play a fiddle. He probably lives in a house that don't have any lights and is in the country. I can't think of anything.

Well . . . the only trouble I can't figure out what that is. The teacher passed out some paper and the boy's trying to think what to draw and he finally decided to draw a fiddle and he started drawing a fiddle and he found he could draw a fiddle pretty good and he kept on drawing and he found he could be a pretty good artist and he was known as one of the best artists in the world. [How does he feel?] Pretty proud of hisself.

A second type of unstructured test for measuring affective states is one in which subjects are simply asked to talk for five minutes about some significant event in their lives. This "verbal sample" is then scored, by an explicit content-analysis procedure, to yield measures of several affects, including anxiety, hostility directed outward, hostility turned against oneself, and so on (Gottshalk and Gleser, 1969).

Finally, some attention has been devoted to the nonlexical, or paralinguistic, features of verbalization which are indicative of affect. Everyone assumes that he can infer meaning from the "tone of voice" of a speaker, and there is probably considerable validity to that assumption. But to turn it into an exact indicator of particular affective states is still a problem requiring painstaking research.

One promising paralinguistic indicator of affect that has been investigated is the frequency of events that interrupt the smooth flow of speech. George Mahl has developed a set of *speech-disturbance* categories, including "ah," stuttering, repetition, omission of parts of words, slips of the tongue, and so on. These can be applied to a speech sample taken during clinical interviews, from the telling of TAT stories, and so on. Mahl (1963) has further devised a *speech-disturbance ratio* computed as the ratio of the sum of occurrences of all the disturbance categories except "ah" to the total number of words spoken. This ratio is reported by Mahl to vary directly with short-term variation in a subject's anxiety level, as independently assessed. Why "ah" fails to work, he does not say. What is clear, though, is that the kind of refined analysis of paralinguistic events exemplified in Mahl's work, in conjunction with content-analysis methods that are both theoretically and empirically based, should ultimately yield methods for assessing affect that are powerful and applicable to a wide variety of situations in which speech is a natural component. In that sense, the unstructured "tests" designed to provide samples of expressive behavior seem more promising as instruments for determining quality and intensity of affect than the structured tests that so far have been the more popular, at least with research psychologists.

SUMMARY

A major dimension along which behavior varies is that of level of *arousal*. Heightened arousal is often accompanied by particular behavior patterns, such as crying, and characteristic phenomenal states (fear, anger, misery, and so on), as well as typical changes in physiological indexes (blood pressure, heart rate, and so on). We call such collections of overt behaviors, covert feelings, and physiological changes *emotions*, or *affects*.

The most obvious instance of fluctuation in arousal level is the sleep-wakefulness cycle. Development of the typical adult sleep pattern is to some extent learned, as evidenced by the relative ease with which people and animals can shift their sleep pattern under environmental pressure.

Changes in electrical activity in the brain, as recorded in the electro-encephalogram (EEG), is a prominent accompaniment of the marked decrease in motor activity and responsiveness to stimuli that are characteristic of sleep. "Brain waves" during sleep are relatively slow and of high amplitude. Within sleep, four distinct stages can be identified. Of special interest is *terminal stage 1 sleep*, during which rapid eye movements (REM) occur. During REM sleep the central nervous system is highly active, but the motor expression of this activity is inhibited. People awakened right after REM sleep report just having dreamed, and do so with a much higher frequency than when awakened from non-REM sleep; fragmentary thoughts, however, occur throughout sleep.

The evidence is strong that REM sleep is indicative of dreaming. By this criterion, everyone dreams, including self-styled "nondreamers," who do, however, dream less frequently than others. People of college age dream during about 21 per cent of the time they are asleep; newborns exhibit REM sleep, and presumably dreaming, during 50 per cent of the time they are asleep; dream time percentage is lowest (about 14.5) for the elderly.

Depriving people of REM sleep has effects that are consistent with the Freudian hypothesis that dreams are necessary for psychological equilibrium; however, it may be some physiological or biochemical concomitant of REM sleep, rather than dreaming *per se*, that is responsible for the effects of REM sleep deprivation.

Other physiological functions besides sleep have a daily period. These *circadian rhythms* suggest the operation of *internal clocks*. Certain behaviors may best be performed at specific levels of activation of specific physiological subsystems.

Despite the difficulty in measuring arousal level at a given moment, research has been done relating differences among individuals in such behavioral variables as impulsiveness to differences in the *stability* or *lability* of spontaneous activity of their autonomic nervous systems.

Chronically high levels of arousal, instigated by stressful physiological agents, may lead to a sequence of physiological reactions termed the *General Adaptation Syndrome*, consisting of (a) an *alarm reaction*, (b) a *resistance* stage, and (c) a stage of *exhaustion*, in which severe bodily disorders and sometimes death may occur.

Within the broad category of emotions, a major distinction is often made between *positive* and *negative* ones, based in large part on cultural evaluation; indeed, uncontrolled emotional expression of either sort is negatively valued in many cultures. Children are trained to modulate affective expression, or to channel it in culturally acceptable ways. The incentive value of different types and degrees of emotional expression varies considerably between cultures and among subgroups within a culture.

In the behaviorist model of emotional development, the infant starts with three basic response patterns—fear, rage, and love—each with a very limited set of instigating conditions. Development proceeds by adding effective stimuli to the set through classical conditioning. Recent analyses view emotional development as a complex process closely linked to perception and cognition and dependent in part on the *verbal labeling* of subtly different affective states.

One line of empirical research on the effects of early experience on emotional development has shown that fearfulness in mature rats can be increased by both pre- and postnatal maternal fear. However, moderate stress in infancy has the opposite effect, leaving rats both less fearful as adults and less susceptible to the damaging bodily effects of severe physiological stress.

In another line of research, the following by newly hatched birds of their mothers, or other salient objects, has been investigated. One model of the *following response* postulates a special type of learning called *imprinting;* in another model following is treated as an instrumental response serving to reduce anxiety.

The bond of affection between infant and mother monkey has been the subject of a third line of research. This work has revealed the great importance of the *contact comfort* that a mother (real or artificial) provides for her infant and the equally crucial role that an infant monkey's peers play in social and sexual development.

Attempts to measure emotion through physiological indexes and expressive behaviors have met with some success. Measures based on verbal responses also seem promising, particularly those indirect measures based on both the content of verbal responses and on their *paralinguistic* accompaniments.

SUGGESTED READINGS

Candland, D. *Emotion: bodily change.* Princeton: Van Nostrand, 1962.

Plutchick, R. *The emotions: facts, theories, and a new model.* New York: Random House, 1962.

Reinberg, A. and J. Ghata. *Biological rhythms.* New York: Walker and Co., 1964.

Sluckin, W. *Imprinting and early learning.* Chicago: Aldine, 1965.

Webb, W.B. *Sleep: an experimental approach.* New York: Macmillan, 1968.

Motivation

C H A P T E R   S I X T E E N   Use of the concept of motivation entered academic psychology largely through the influence of Hull's learning theory and the dynamic theory of Freud. The Hullian and Freudian approaches to motivation share a reliance on the homeostatic concept developed to account for the action of automatic bodily mechanisms that are operative under conditions of physiological imbalance, or need. Hunger is one such need; its behavioral and physiological correlates are treated in some detail in this chapter. Limitations on the generality of the concept of homeostasis for theories of motivation are pointed out and the arguments for a "new look" in motivation, as well as the details of a representative model, are presented.

The Concept of Motivation

CHARACTERISTICS
OF MOTIVATED BEHAVIOR

Motivation, like other concepts employed in psychological theory, is an abstraction. We do not observe motivation, only behavior. Motivation is inferred from certain aspects of behavior, and it is invoked to help account for certain others. Very generally, the following seem to demand a concept of motivation:

1. *Variability in response to a fixed stimulus.* Certain behaviors (such as eating), called consummatory acts, occur frequently and periodically. They constitute a significant portion of an organism's total behavioral repertory, and they occur, not haphazardly, but cyclically. As a corollary, the organism will at one time evince great and persistent "interest" in something (such as

food), but at other times will treat it with apparent indifference. Such fluctuation in response to a stimulus is paralleled by variability among similar individuals in response to the same stimulus.

2. *Variation among objects in attractiveness.* Certain objects have considerably more attractive value, or "valence," than most other objects. This attractiveness may be exerted only periodically—indeed, the times when an individual evinces little interest in them usually closely follow bouts of heightened interest—but when it functions, it has compelling potency. We call such objects *goal objects*, or *incentives*.

3. *The reward value of goal objects.* The same things that serve as goal objects, in the sense of exerting control over an organism's free-ranging movements, also have the peculiar property of being effective reinforcers for establishing learned responses; that is, they are not only good incentives ("attention getters") but good rewards. This characteristic of being able to effect learning is the conventional operational criterion for determining whether some object or event is, indeed, to be classified as a reward (Miller, 1951).

Observations of the three types mentioned above are frequently summarized by reference to the *directionality* of behavior—that is, out of all his possible responses an individual engages in a select few of them. Motivation, as a concept in psychological theory, has the role of accounting for the selectivity, or directionality, of behavior.

How, for example, can we account for an individual's obvious interest in food at one time and his indifference to it at another? Surely, because at one time he is hungry and at the other he is not. Why does person A put so much effort into his course work, while B spends his time playing bridge? Perhaps their motives are different. Perhaps A is strongly motivated to academic achievement, while B is highly motivated to be with other people under congenial circumstances. To put it differently, perhaps for A a good grade average is a powerful goal object, whereas for B the presence of other people is. Clearly, motives and the goal objects that satisfy them are interdependent. To identify a potent goal object is to imply a strong motive; conversely, to assert the presence of a strong motive is to set limits on the kinds of objects that will act as incentives or rewards.

Directionality of behavior need not be confined to overt responses; it can also apply to sequences of ideas. If we had some way of knowing the direction of A's thoughts and fantasies, we could very well ask, why that chain of ideas, at that time, rather than some other? In his theory, Donald Hebb (1949) assigns motivational relevance as much to the direction that thoughts take as he does to the choices an animal makes in traversing a maze. A similar position is taken by psychoanalysts, who assume that the content of ideational activity, including fantasies, daydreams, and night dreams reveals (to the trained observer) a person's dominant drives and impulses. This assumption is, of course, behind the use of free association in psychoanalytic therapy and the use of projective tests, such as the Thematic Apperception Test (TAT), in diagnosis and personality research.

4. *Emotional Response to Deprivation.* A fourth class of observations that seem to demand a concept of motivation arises when an individual is deprived of access to goal objects. For example, if an animal is not allowed to eat for an unnaturally long period, certain striking behavioral changes occur. The animal's level of activity increases; it may become less docile; in general, it exhibits signs (such as vocalization) of increasing arousal and negative affect.

In human beings, the emotional impact of deprivation is more directly evident. A baby kept waiting beyond the usual time for its next feeding first becomes irritable, then "fussy," and eventually he cries inconsolably. Older children and even adults behave similarly—for example, an adult who is on a severe diet, especially in the first few days, or a person who has given up smoking. The emotional consequences of such deprivation, whether imposed or self-initiated, are quite obvious, to the trained and even to the casual observer.

MOTIVATION IN PSYCHOLOGICAL SYSTEMS

In light of the above, it is puzzling that the importance of the motivation concept has fluctuated considerably in the history of psychology. The systematic psychologies that began to be formulated in the beginning of the present century focused mainly on perceptual and cognitive processes. Thus, the system of Structuralism, originated by Wilhelm Wundt (1832–1920) and developed by Edward B. Titchener (1867–1927), was concerned chiefly with an analysis of conscious experience into its elementary components and with the laws by which these components are synthesized. The major systematic opposition to Structuralism, Gestalt theory, quarreled with the Structuralists' methodology (introspective analysis of experience into its elementary components), but agreed that experience was the proper subject matter for a scientific psychology.

Two other systems arose in reaction to Structuralism. One, Functionalism (see, for example, Angell, 1907), retained an interest in conscious experience but was concerned less with analyzing it than in discovering what the function of experience was in the organism's adaptation to its environment. The other, Behaviorism, rejected experience as appropriate subject matter for scientific investigation and insisted on a stimulus-response analysis of behavior (see, for example, Watson, 1913). Both Functionalism and Be-
.orism, for somewhat different reasons, emphasized *learning*, at the ex-
se of other processes.

Motivation and Learning. A concern about learning does not necessarily imply a corresponding interest in motivation as we might assume from contemporary learning theory. Watson's learning model, for example, was essentially the same as Pavlov's, in that both relied entirely on the temporal contiguity of the elements to be associated to carry the burden of association formation. A similar position, you may recall, was maintained by Guthrie. In none of these models does reward play a central role; similarly, the motivational state of the subject is assigned no special importance, except that of enhancing the vigor and probability of occurrence of the response to be learned. Thus, as Pavlov recognized, presenting food to a dog that was not hungry elicited little salivation. But hunger, *per se*, did not enter into the process of association formation. In a similar vein, Guthrie acknowledged the role of reward by interpreting it as an effective means of "protecting" the response to be learned; motivational states, such as hunger, were also only peripherally relevant, insofar as they affected the occurrence of the response and as sources of stimulation; that is, motivational states together with external stimuli constitute the total stimulus complex of the S-R bond.

With the development of Hull's learning theory (1943), the significance of motivational variables (including both internal states, such as hunger, and related rewards, such as food) became firmly established within academic, experimentally oriented psychology. The Hullian approach to motivation, as we indicated in Chapter Four, was derived largely from the work of the eminent physiologist Walter Cannon (1871–1945), particularly the central concept of *homeostasis*.

Motivation in Freudian Psychology. The emerging prominence of motivation in psychological theory was fostered by a second development, which had been for a long time on the periphery of academic psychology—the "dynamic" psychiatry of Freud, with its emphasis on the motivational (albeit unconscious) determinants of behavior. Despite the obvious dissimilarities between Hullian and Freudian theory, and between the training, experience, style, and domains of discourse of the two theorists, their conceptions of motivation, at heart, have much in common. That common core will be one theme running through the present chapter. A second theme is provided by the growing reaction against the homeostatic approach to motivation and the resulting formulation of fresh models for a "new look in motivation" (Dember, 1965).

The Homeostatic Model of Motivation

The homeostatic motivational model takes as its prototypical example the *biological drives* of hunger, thirst, and sex. Presumably, all these drives share a set of basic properties and so can be discussed as a general class despite their many dissimilarities. In essence, the homeostatic model is built on the following simple propositions. These are specifically abstracted from Hull's (1943) presentation, but they apply broadly to a larger class of motivational models.

1. There are certain vital physiological conditions, such as the level of blood-sugar concentration and the level of water balance in the cells.

2. For each such vital physiological condition, an optimal value, or range of values, can be defined.

3. When a vital physiological condition departs significantly from its optimal value, then certain mechanisms become operative to help restore the system to its optimal level. For example, if blood-sugar level is low, the pancreas gland is activated and it in turn functions so as to release sugar stored in the liver.

These mechanisms function much like the thermostat attached to a furnace or an air-conditioning unit. If the optimal temperature is arbitrarily defined as 72° Fahrenheit, and if the temperature of the air surrounding the thermostat falls below 72°, then certain changes within that mechanism activate a switch. As long as the switch is in the "on" position, the furnace runs and the air is heated. When room temperature reaches 72°, the switch moves to the "off" position, and the furnace shuts down.

The analogy between the body mechanisms and the thermostat is carried by two shared properties: (1) They are automatically activated by a departure from a present optimal value, or by "error"; (2) the events that they in turn activate reduce the amount of error. In this sense, these mechanisms operate on a principle of *negative feedback*. Thus, the remarkable homeostatic (that is, "self-stabilizing") devices of the body that Cannon investigated are instances of the more general class of servomechanisms, or automatic, error-reducing devices.

4. The departures from optimum, or "errors," define what is meant by *needs;* needs, therefore, are concepts that pertain to physiological theory, but they also have psychological counterparts called *drives.*

5. In complex organisms like mammals, the drive-reducing devices can (at least to delimit spheres of academic interest) be partitioned into two subsets: (a) the relatively simple, automatic, physiological *homeostats* and (b) *behavioral patterns,* involving effector organs such as the limbs, the mouth, and so on, which are of primary interest to the psychologist. These behavioral patterns are not nearly so orderly as the homeostats or, rather, they cover a wide range from the orderly—that is, stereotyped—to the variable and irregular. For instance, at the highly orderly end of the range are reflexive responses, such as the sucking reflex that can be elicited in a baby by stimulating the area around his mouth; at the other extreme are the fussing, crying, and diffuse thrashing about of a baby that has gone too long without food.

6. Each organism has a repertory of behavioral responses to drive states.

Some of these responses are common to many, if not all, types of drive; these are the general, diffuse shifts in activity that distinguish the satiated from the driven organism. *The thoroughly satiated organism is assumed to be behaviorally quiescent; the introduction of a drive state is a necessary and sufficient condition for transforming a behaviorally inactive into a behaviorally active organism.* It is this key proposition that unites the otherwise quite disparate Freudian and Hullian theories; it is in reaction to this proposition that the "new look" in motivation has been formulated.

Along with the generalized arousal that accompanies any drive state, each drive has unique properties. In Hullian terminology, *drive level*, or D, refers to the arousal or activation function common to all drives, while drive stimulus, or S_D, refers to the discriminative properties of the various drives. Thus, hunger and thirst may both raise general activation level, but the two drives are also distinctive. Phenomenally, hunger is associated with sensations localized in the stomach region, whereas thirst is associated with dryness in the mouth and throat. Moreover, the two drives can be shown to be distinctive on purely behavioral grounds. For example, rats can be trained to turn left in a T-maze when hungry and right when thirsty (Hull, 1933; Amsel, 1949). Untrained behavioral differences of a more subtle nature have also been observed. For example, rats are more variable in their movements in an unfamiliar environment under a strong hunger drive than they are under intense thirst (Petrinovitch and Bolles, 1954).

Of course, the most obvious indicator of the uniqueness of each drive is consummatory activity. Given access to dry food and water, a thirsty rat will drink; a hungry rat may eat and drink, since eating dry food is thirst-inducing, but its major preoccupation will undoubtedly be with the food.

To some extent, ability to identify one's own drives must be learned. A young child often needs to be reminded to take a drink of water, for example, when a parent infers, from the child's irritability and from the fact that he has had nothing to drink for several hours, that he must be thirsty. Similarly, children being toilet-trained frequently have difficulty in deciding whether they are uncomfortable because of a need to defecate or to urinate, and indeed they sometimes even seem not to be aware of their own discomfort.

On the other hand, there is evidence of a remarkable degree of discrimination among the multitude of incentives relevant to a general drive system. For example, in a classic study, infants were offered a range of foods, cafeteria style, over extended periods of time. These infants over the long term made a nutritionally balanced selection, so that special needs, such as for vitamins, were met in the course of satisfying the general need for food (Davis, 1928). Similar selectivity has been observed in lower animals. For example, rats will choose foods enriched with a particular vitamin of which they have been deprived (Scott and Verney, 1949), although a distinctive flavor may have to be associated with the vitamin-rich alternative.

7. Objects that are initially inert, in the sense of having neither drive-

inducing nor drive-reducing value, can acquire either value through a simple process of conditioning. Any stimulus that precedes a drive increase will take on drive properties; as such it has become a *secondary, or acquired drive*. And any stimulus that accompanies drive-reduction takes on drive-reducing or rewarding properties; as such, it becomes a *secondary,* or *acquired* reward.

8. The entire set of motivationally relevant events comprises the primary and secondary drives and rewards.

The general homeostatic model sketched above has taken several different specific forms. It certainly does not appear in the behavior theory of Hull in the same detail as in the psychoanalytic theory of Freud. And even within the Hullian camp, deviations and revisions have emerged in response to both empirical data and rational criticism. Nevertheless, the homeostatic model has been an important contender in psychology's attempt to understand behavior. Before cataloging the sources of dissatisfaction with this model, we might look closer at hunger, which has so often served in academic psychology as the prototypical primary drive. After all, not all research on motivation is devoted to settling issues of model selection; indeed, much of the work done on the topic of motivation has had the modest aim of providing empirical answers to specific questions of both a behavioral and physiological nature. Implications of the empirical data for broad theoretical problems have typically been uncovered after the data were available; only in a few instances have experiments been designed with the self-conscious intent of putting the classical homeostatic model to a test.

Hunger

BEHAVIORAL CORRELATES OF HUNGER

The conventional operation for inducing the hypothetical hunger state is to deprive an organism of food. There are two popular variants of this procedure:

1. A subject is offered food only during a brief period, say for a half-hour; the subject can eat as much as desired, but then will have no further access to food until a specified amount of time has elapsed; the degree of hunger is assumed to vary directly with the length of that time. For rats, a period of 18 to 24 hours is typically used to establish a "high" level of hunger. For human beings, skipping one or two meals is usually considered adequate.

2. Feeding is normal, except in quantity. The amount of food is less than usual so that the organism's weight declines and stabilizes at some lower value, say 80 per cent of normal weight. Presumably, the lower the per-

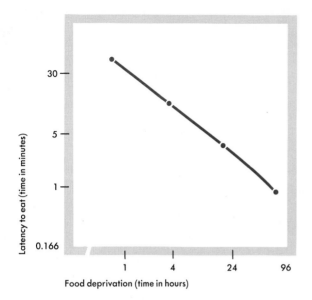

Figure 16.1 Latency to eat as a function of deprivation time. Both coordinates are on logarithmic scales. (Bolles, 1967.)

centage the hungrier the animal. These two operations may lead to somewhat different behavioral consequences, but for our purposes, we can speak simply of food deprivation, ignoring operational distinctions, and then ask in general what the consequences of deprivation are.

Food Consumption, Activity Level, and Performance of Learned Responses. The following statements summarize the major behavioral consequences of food deprivation, as revealed largely by the psychologist's favorite laboratory subject, the rat.

1. The greater the deprivation, the sooner will an animal start eating after having been offered food. This relation is shown graphically in Figure 16.1.

2. As deprivation increases, general activity level increases, at least until the animal becomes too weak to move. Activity level, in such research, is measured in a variety of ways, frequently by counting the number of revolutions the animal makes in an "activity wheel."

3. As deprivation increases, measures of the intensity or vigor of the performance of learned responses increase. The hungrier a rat, the faster it will run down a straight alley (Figure 16.2) it has been trained to traverse for food reinforcement. Similarly, hungry animals make operant responses, such as bar presses, or a classically conditioned response such as salivation (Zener and McCurdy, 1939), at a higher rate than less hungry animals.

4. In complex learning, such as discrimination learning, increasing deprivation does not always lead to improved performance. Instead, a very hungry rat may make more errors than a moderately hungry one, especially during early acquisition trials. In general, for complex or difficult tasks, the optimal level of hunger (or of any drive) is not the maximal level but a level of intermediate value. This relation has been formalized as the *Yerkes-Dodson Law.*

In general, excessive concern with the rewards for one's performance may interfere with, rather than facilitate that performance. This is especially so when the performance involves a complex set of discriminations or an intricate set of responses and when "good performance" is defined in terms of quality, precision, and integration instead of simply in terms of intensity or vigor. Thus, very high levels of motivation may serve well in

Figure 16.2 A rat on a straight runway about to enter the goal box. (Brown Brothers.)

running the hundred-yard dash but may wreak havoc with the playing of a piano concerto.

Acquisition of Learned Responses. The above statements apply mainly to performance. What of the relation between hunger level (or drive level in general) and acquisition of a learned response? According to Hull, the level of hunger during acquisition of a response reinforced by food does not affect either the rate of learning or the strength of the S-R bond. Once a habit is acquired, however, hunger level interacts with habit strength to determine the potential for making the learned response. Hunger level is considered a "performance" variable rather than a learning, or "acquisition," variable.

One design for investigating the role of hunger level in acquisition involves shifting that level, up or down, and comparing the performance of shifted subjects with that of subjects that have been run continually at the same high or low drive level. The results of such experiments tend to support Hull's hypothesis, in that postshift performance essentially matches performance under comparable steady levels of drive. If, for example, high drive level assured high learning strength, then animals shifted from high to low should perform better than animals run only at low drive level. That they do not, documents the independence of drive level and strength of learning.

Incentive Value. Analogous statements can be made about the value of the food incentive offered the animal. We might define incentive value in several different ways, all of which seem intuitively compatible with the notion that some incentives are more potent than others. In general, two types of manipulation are available: (1) those involving the quality of the incentive—that is, the extent to which the subject prefers it over other incentives in equal quantity (for instance, for monkeys raisins would be a higher-quality incentive than sunflower seeds, whereas the reverse would hold for rats); (2) those involving amount or quantity (four grams of lab chow have greater incentive value than two; two sunflower seeds have greater value than one).

In Hull's theory, incentive magnitude (either qualitative or quantitative) affects the final, or *asymptotic*, value of habit strength. That is, given enough rewarded trials for habit strength to reach its maximum possible value, that maximum is a direct function of the magnitude of the incentive employed.

There is controversy, even among learning theorists of Hullian persuasion, about the exact role of incentives in learning, and indeed about what constitutes the habit that is being acquired (see, for example, Logan, 1960; Logan and Wagner, 1967). In this regard, the role Hull assigned to incentive magnitude is only one of several possible ways of interpreting the available data—for example, running speed in a straight alley does increase directly with incentive magnitude. In Hull's theory, it is the value of habit strength that is affected by incentive magnitude, and running speed is an indicator of habit strength. Logan, however, takes the interesting position that, during training, an animal is learning the incentive value of the reinforcing agent and also is learning *to run at a particular speed* appropriate to the value of the incentive. For Logan, running speed is not an indicator of the strength of the running habit; running at a particular speed *is* one of the habits that is acquired. A rat learns, in effect, to run slowly or speedily, depending on what response speed is maximally rewarded.

In conventional experiments, the more quickly an animal reaches the goal, the sooner it obtains the reinforcement. Further, it is generally true that delay of reinforcement acts like a decrease in incentive magnitude—that is, the longer the delay, the less the incentive value. Thus, in the typical straight-alley situation, fast running is more powerfully reinforced than slow running, and we would expect the "fast-running response" to be selected from the animal's response repertory on the basis of differential reinforcement. That, according to Logan, is the rationale for the observation which Hull takes for granted—that running speed will increase as learning strength increases.

Logan's analysis has led to a novel procedure, one that the Hullian model would be highly unlikely to suggest. If running speed, or running at a particular speed, is a learnable response, it should be possible to reverse the usual relation and *train animals to run slowly*. All that is necessary, according to Logan's model, is to make reinforcement contingent upon the animal's running slowly.

This kind of novel procedure has been followed in several studies (for example, Bower, 1959). Suppose that under conditions of immediate reinforcement, rats run a straight alley in about four seconds. We now require the rats to take, say, six seconds to traverse the alley in order to be reinforced immediately on entering the goal compartment. If they run too fast (less than six seconds), then reinforcement is delayed. Under such rules—which are a marked departure from the standard situation wherein running speed and incentive value are positively correlated—the rats do learn to "run slowly." Typically, they gradually approximate a running time that is just a little longer than the criterion time, as illustrated in Figure 16.3.

Why the quotes around "run slowly"? Because if we look at the rats rather than at the clocks that are recording the time between onset and termination of a trial, it is apparent that they are not literally running slowly. What the rats do instead is to find ways of filling up time; each animal develops its own particular set of responses that help it achieve the criterion running time, for example, running rapidly down the alley to the entrance of the goal compartment and then turning around and running back to the start box.

In short, although we might think of the running response as a skilled act that normally is performed at high speed but can be done in "slow motion" if required, the rats do not actually behave that way. They do not run slowly, as one might play a piece on the piano slowly. But they are responsive to the reinforcement contingencies and will learn to delay entry into the goal box, if that is the criterion for receiving the preferred incentive.

The Crespi Effect. Statements about incentive value are usually made in terms of physical properties (two pellets are better than one) and therefore by implication in absolute terms; however, incentive value even for rats is a relative matter. Thus, for an animal that has been receiving four pellets of food per trial, an abrupt shift to two pellets will depress its

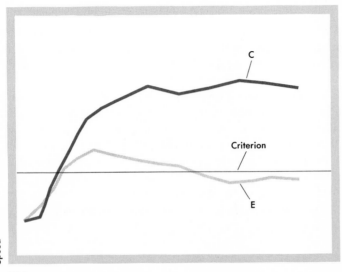

Figure 16.3 When animals (Group E) are rewarded only if they run more slowly than a criterion speed, they gradually learn to do so. Control animals (Group C) are rewarded in the standard manner: The faster they run the more quickly they get the reward. (Adapted from Logan, 1960.)

C

Criterion

E

Speed

Trials

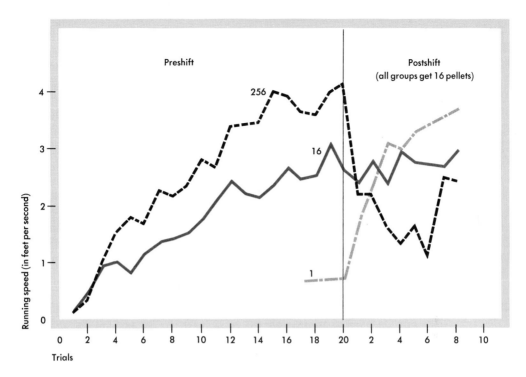

Figure 16.4 The Crespi effect. For the first 19 trials different groups were given 1, 16, or 256 pellets of food (acquisition data for the 1-pellet group are not presented); from trial 20 on, all subjects were given 16 pellets. (Adapted by Bolles, 1967, from data by Crespi, 1942.)

behavior below the level of animals that have continually had a two-pellet reward. Similarly, an upward shift in incentive magnitude will raise performance above that of rats accustomed to the higher level of reward. As shown in Figure 16.4, when incentives are shifted performance over- or undershoots the level of behavior associated with comparable fixed values of incentive magnitude. This result is known as the *Crespi effect,* for the psychologist who first reported it.

Even behavioristically oriented psychologists account for the Crespi effect in perceptual terminology. Reference is often made to contrast effects, as in brightness perception, or to the concept of adaptation level in explanations of the relative nature of incentive magnitude (see, for example, Logan and Wagner, 1967). Once again, with the kind of reinterpretation of what constitutes a response that Logan's theory provides and the transformation of incentive magnitude from an absolute, physically defined term to one that is partially relativistic, a strict S-R approach even to the simple problem of rats running in a straight alley appears to be no longer tenable. And learning, motivation, and perception are becoming more closely integrated than they have been for many decades under the dominant influence of a behavioristic psychology.

The relative nature of incentive magnitude is, of course, not surprising to those who have had experience with the problem of motivating human performance. What constitutes an adequate salary, for example, is partly determined by the salaries being received by other people. Thus, a professor earning $20,000 a year might feel inadequately compensated when he hears of peers receiving $30,000 at a different institution. Or a 10 per cent salary increase may seem highly satisfactory if one's colleagues have received only 5 per cent increases.

In a similar vein, to return to the topic of hunger and food, the attractiveness of particular food incentives fluctuates with experience. Imagine, for example, being served filet mignon for dinner every night for several weeks or even several days. Under the circumstances a shift to hot dogs would undoubtedly be welcome. That is, one can become satiated, perhaps "bored" with a highly preferred incentive if it is repeatedly offered. Especially so when the incentive serves as more than a simple hunger-reducer—when its function is to satisfy appetite, not just to fill an empty stomach.

The Autonomy of Incentives. Must a drive be present in order for an incentive to be effective? Consider hunger and food incentives. Surely, as hunger increases, the attractiveness of food increases, even up to the point where ordinarily aversive foods become not only palatable but even enjoyable. On the other hand, the relation between hunger level and the incentive value of food is not so strong that hunger is a necessary condition for eating. If it were, there might be many fewer obese people than there are, and the market for low-calorie foods would be nil. It is quite clear, from everyday observation if not from controlled research, that people need not be hungry in order to eat.

We might argue that eating in the absence of hunger satisfies some motive other than hunger. A good deal of such behavior is socially motivated. We eat at parties and banquets because others are eating, or to have something appropriate to do, or to be a good guest. Many people are virtually trained by their parents to eat beyond need in the sense that eating more of mother's food than one needs is an act of love or good faith on the part of the child.

But there is also pleasure in eating when not hungry that closely mimics the good feeling that accompanies hunger-motivated eating. Some items of food and drink are simply pleasurable in their own right. Moreover, certain foods seem to create appetite where there was none before. Thus, the first mouthful of salted peanuts or of potato chips often produces a real desire for more. That is, contact with certain incentives is under some circumstances a drive-inducing experience. In that respect, incentives have a certain degree of autonomy; their potency is partially independent of drive states, and indeed they can often serve to arouse drive in an otherwise undeprived, satiated individual.

In human beings, at least, symbolic representations of incentives can also be powerful drive-inducers. This effect is especially obvious in young children, for whom words can serve very effectively to arouse strong drives. Parents must be careful with young children not to mention objects that they should not have at the moment. For a two-year-old to hear the words "ice cream" is tantamount to his truly needing ice cream; and, as parents soon discover, once a need has been aroused in a young child, there is no waiting and no acceptable substitution of other objects. To cope with this problem, parents often resort to all sorts of circumlocutions (or to spelling, talking in a language the child does not understand, and so on).

The techniques of advertising, of course, are built partly on this very fact. It is possible, even in adults, to generate desire for objects, in the absence of any genuine need for them, by careful presentation of visual images and linguistic symbols. Advertising does more than that, but at its base lies the partial autonomy of incentives.

PHYSIOLOGICAL MECHANISMS

One can be impressed with the many behavioral regularities associated with hunger without being concerned with their mediating physiological mechanisms. How, to put it loosely, needs get transformed into drives is a question that psychologists do not have to face. But for some researchers that issue has proven compelling, and we can profitably discuss at this point the kinds of evidence that are accumulating on the physiological basis of hunger. Again we will take hunger as prototypical and let this discussion suggest the form, if not the details, of similar treatments of other biological drives.

The investigation of physiological mechanisms in hunger motivation can be broken down into several questions. Thus, we can ask, about eating in general, what conditions initiate (or are concomitant with the initiation of) eating and what conditions are involved in its termination. By "conditions" we mean both peripheral (biochemical, hormonal, and so on) states and central neural activities. With regard to central nervous system mechanisms, we can separate questions about the location of possible hunger "centers" from questions about details of neural functioning. And having probed the various aspects of the problems of starting and stopping eating, we can turn to specific hungers—that is, appetites—and ask about the mechanisms, peripheral and central, that regulate the selection of specific foods for specific needs, as happens, for example, when animals suffering calcium deficiency show a preference for calcium-rich foods.

Stomach Contractions. If you were to ask a person where he feels hungry, he would probably indicate his stomach. In accord with this common experience, the hypothesis has long been entertained that sensory feedback from contractions of the stomach, when it is relatively empty of food, is the prime source of the hunger cue. This hypothesis was investigated experimentally by Cannon and Washburn (1912), who correlated subjective reports of hunger with the occurrence of stomach contractions. (The contractions were measured by having a subject swallow a deflated balloon and then inflating it within the stomach. Gastric contractions squeezed the balloon; the squeezing was picked up as a change in the air pressure inside the balloon and recorded on a kymograph. A sample record is shown in Figure 16.5.) The occurrence of contractions tended to be correlated with subjective reports of hunger.

This neat and simple result has been subjected to criticism on several grounds, however. It has been suggested, for example, that the balloon technique induces stomach contractions that do not occur naturally; when contractions are recorded electrically, without the introduction of objects into the otherwise empty stomach, they are found to occur very infrequently. Furthermore, people whose stomachs have been removed for medical reasons report normal feelings of hunger. When similar operations have been performed on animals for experimental purposes, the only marked change in eating behavior has been an understandable increase in the frequency of food intake. In short, whatever the hunger cues may be, they do not necessarily include sensory feedback from stomach contractions as was originally believed.

But that is not to rule out the stomach entirely as a factor in hunger. In particular, the amount of food present in the stomach seems to be involved in the *cessation* of eating. For instance, there are sugar solutions that are equally palatable but that differ markedly in osmotic pressure. Rats will drink these substances with equal vigor at first; however, after a few minutes their drinking rate will decrease more rapidly for those solutions that are high in osmotic pressure than for those that are low (Young, 1957). Similarly, if rats' stomachs are preloaded with substances differing in osmotic pressure as well as in other properties, when the animals are offered sugar solutions to drink, the amount of inhibition of drinking that is attributable to the preloading relates only to the osmotic pressure of the substances introduced into the stomach prior to the test.

It is interesting that although cessation or inhibition of eating is controlled by quantitative factors, such as osmotic pressure, eating can begin quite independently of such factors. Recall that in the studies by Young mentioned above, the solutions were of equal preference. Response to

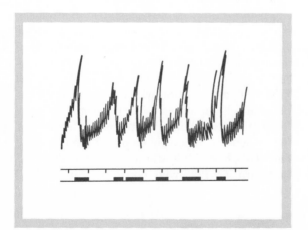

Figure 16.5 The top record represents intragastric pressure (the small oscillations due to respiration, the large to contractions of the stomach); the middle record is time in minutes (10 minutes); the bottom record is the subject's report of hunger pangs. (Adapted from Cannon and Washburn, 1912.)

them was initially the same; the difference in response, related to osmotic pressure, appeared only several minutes after the onset of the consummatory response. It is evident that the cues for starting to eat are not simply the converse of those for stopping.

Oral Factors. Experiments suggest that the initiation of eating is partly under the control of mechanisms associated with the mouth. The mouth is where preferences based on taste or palatability are established. In addition, there is evidence of the significance of the mouth in the cessation of eating. In one experiment (Berkun, Kessen, and Miller, 1952), rats were preloaded with milk either through direct injection into the stomach or through normal eating. A subsequent test revealed that the rats that had received their milk normally drank less additional milk than did the others. This difference might imply that the inhibition of eating is under both oral and gastric control. That is, an animal can reach the same level of hunger satisfaction either by having less food pass into the stomach through the mouth or by having more food placed directly into the stomach.

The exact nature of the oral component is not entirely clear, however. Are we dealing with an appetite, which can partially be satisfied through stimulation of taste receptors, or does the act of eating itself—the consummatory response—contribute to satisfaction of the hunger drive? These two variables have not been isolated experimentally. An anecdote here may be instructive, however. A young girl was with her father close to dinner time. They were driving home through heavy traffic; progress was slow and both were hungry and irritable. The young girl, normally quite voluble, was talking incessantly, almost compulsively. Finally, the father was provoked to interrupt and ask why she was talking so much, and with so little point. "Well," said the child, "I'm very hungry and when I'm hungry I feel better if I can keep moving my mouth." The father, of course, was put in his place, but he also came away convinced that mouth movements *per se* do indeed play some role in alleviating hunger.

One question raised about the role of the mouth concerns animals' preference for foods containing nutritional elements of which they have been deprived. Does such a preference reflect a lowered sensory threshold, which enables an animal to detect the presence of the needed element in very low concentration? A rat with its adrenal glands removed cannot retain enough salt and so develops salt deficiency. Such rats show a marked increase in their preference for salty solutions, even for solutions of very low concentration. Are these rats more sensitive to the presence of salt? The evidence, both behavioral and electrophysiological, suggests not. Apparently, detection thresholds—at least for salt—are not decreased in a deprived subject; the preferential response seems rather to be mediated by a change in what the animal finds palatable. That is, the effect is directly on preference *per se*, not on sensitivity. Needed substances "taste" better than those same substances when there is no deficiency. Unfortunately, it remains quite unclear what, physiologically, a shift in palatability means. It seems likely, however, that this shift is a central, rather than a peripheral one.

Blood Chemistry. We noted earlier, in describing homeostatic mechanisms, that one of the effects of food deprivation is a lowering of blood-sugar level; this "error" acts as a signal for the initiation of homeostatic devices for raising the level of blood sugar to its optimal value, as through the release of glycogen from the liver. It would seem reasonable that a drop in blood-sugar level would also serve as a peripheral cue for overt behavioral acts, such as eating or searching for food, that would help to reduce the state of deprivation and supplement on a long-term basis the relatively short-lived effectiveness of the internal, homeostatic mechanism. We say "short-lived" because neither animal nor man forever feeds on his stored supplies of bodily fuel. However, the experimental evidence indicates that blood-sugar level is not a significant hunger cue (see Morgan, 1965). For example, in one study (Scott, Scott, and Luckhardt, 1938) no relation was found in human subjects between level of blood sugar and degree of reported hunger.

The search for some chemical transmitter of information to the brain that "a state of food need exists" has continued. A major goad to that search is the finding that hunger-motivated behavior proceeds normally after all neural connections have been severed between the stomach and the central nervous system. The only remaining candidate is some substance or substances carried in the bloodstream. But if not blood sugar, what? At one time it was proposed that there might be a "hunger hormone" secreted by the stomach and carried in the bloodstream (see Morgan and Stellar, 1950), but this hypothesis appears to have fallen into disfavor. Recent interest has shifted from peripheral to central neural mechanisms, and the issue of peripheral factors is still largely unsettled.

The Hypothalamus. Like the several sensory systems, which are controlled in specific places within the brain, the biological drives such as hunger and thirst are also regulated in brain centers that can be located with considerable precision. The structure that has been identified as the prime center is the *hypothalamus;* the position of this small but crucial structure is shown in Figure 16.6.

It has been known for quite some time that destruction of a portion of the hypothalamus (the *ventromedial portion*) is followed by a marked increase in an animal's consumption of food and resulting obesity. The total set of concomitants of this damage is called *hyperphagia* (meaning, as you might have guessed, overeating). A rat suffering from the hyperphagic syndrome is pictured in Figure 16.7.

An animal's excess eating proceeds only to some upper limit of obesity, and then the amount eaten returns to about normal levels; the animal's weight, however, remains well above normal. Experiments have shown that

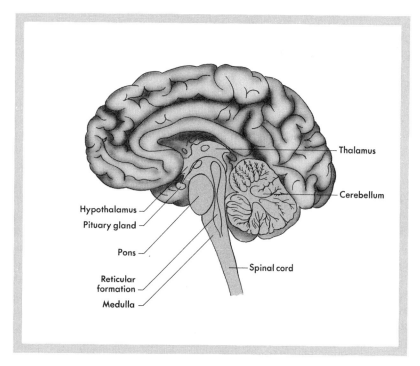

Figure 16.6 The location of the hypothalamus, which regulates hunger, thirst, and other biological drives.

the obesity is indeed a direct result of the hyperphagia, rather than an indirect result of some metabolic insufficiency. Thus, the obesity occurs only if the animal is allowed to eat as much food as it can. If restricted to a normal amount of food, the rat does not become obese.

It would seem that hyperphagia implies an abnormally high level of hunger drive. That is not so, however, at least in any simple sense, for the overeating takes place only if food is readily obtainable. By contrast with normal animals, hyperphagic rats will consume less food if they have to work for it, or if some other barrier, such as shock, is put between them and food, or if the food is made less palatable, as by mixing in with it some bitter-tasting quinine (Miller, Bailey, and Stevenson, 1950; Teitelbaum,

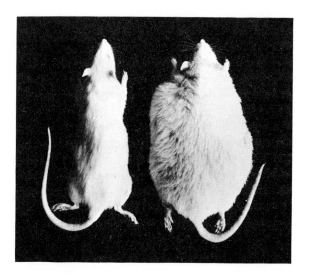

Figure 16.7 Hypothalamic obese female rat (right) compared with its normal control. (Teitelbaum, 1964).

1955, 1957). One conclusion from several lines of research is that the hyperphagic animal is obese, not because of an increase in drive level *per se,* but because it continues to eat good-tasting food long after a normal rat would have stopped eating. How this comes about is the subject of further speculation. One hypothesis that seems tenable is that, by virtue of the damage to ventromedial hypothalamus, the animal becomes less sensitive than normal to some substance released by cells in other areas when an adequate amount of food has been consumed. That is, the signal to inhibit eating comes from elsewhere in the hypothalamus and is ordinarily picked up by cells in the ventromedial hypothalamus.

A second syndrome is also associated with damage to the hypothalamus. If lesions are made in the *lateral* region of the hypothalamus, the animal becomes *aphagic* (a "non-eater"). Clearly, the lateral hypothalamus is involved in the initiation of eating, just as the ventromedial region regulates the cessation of eating. Various experiments suggest that aphagia, like hyperphagia, is related not to drive level *per se,* but to palatability. Normally acceptable food becomes, for the aphagic, aversive. Among rats that survive the operation (being kept alive by tube feeding into the stomach), there remains an aversion to all but the most highly preferred foods. In this respect the aphagic rat is similar to the human *anorexic,* who cannot eat adequate amounts of food because most foods, for psychopathological reasons, are as offensive to him as certain items are, for cultural reasons, to normal people (such as pork to an orthodox Jew).

Eating, then, is controlled by at least two brain areas, one (the ventromedial region of the hypothalamus) containing an inhibitory, or "Stop," mechanism, the other (the lateral region of the hypothalamus) a facilitating, or "Start," mechanism. Both seem to work through an effect on the palatability of food.

So far we have referred only to research in which the experimental intervention involves damage to the hypothalamic centers. A great deal of work has also been done in which these centers are left intact and stimulated, either electrically or by minute amounts of chemicals. For example, if the lateral hypothalamus is electrically stimulated, an animal that is not hungry will begin to eat if food is available (Smith, 1956).

Finally, we want to remind you of the work originated by Olds and Milner (1954) that was described in Chapter Two. Recall that animals will perform an operant response that is followed by a brief pulse of electrical stimulation to certain areas of the brain. It turns out that the hypothalamus is one of the structures that is a very effective locus for "rewarding" self-stimulation. Furthermore, the impact of the electrical stimulation interacts with the drive state of the animal. For example, with electrodes in the lateral hypothalamus, self-stimulation is decreased if the animal has just eaten (Hoebel and Teitelbaum, 1962). In general, considerable evidence points to the intimate relation between drive states and the effectiveness of electrical self-stimulation of the brain. This is exactly what we might expect if the brain areas associated with self-stimulation serve as central projection areas for peripheral, rewarding stimulation, and if incentive value is partly dependent on drive level.

Dissatisfactions with the Homeostatic Model

Our extensive, yet abbreviated discussion of hunger as a prototypical biological drive certainly reveals the considerable power inherent in a motivational model based on homeostatic principles. By following this approach, it is possible to go a long way in accounting for much of animal behavior and certain aspects of human behavior. However, a point is reached where the explanatory effectiveness of the homeostatic model begins to wane. There are many who believe that the classic view needs to be modified, or at least supplemented, so that a more comprehensive motivational model can be created. These critics of the old view do not deny the very obvious importance of biological drives; what they do object to is the overgeneralization whereby these drives reveal the attributes of all motives. The dissatisfaction in academic psychology with the classical, homeostatic model was paralleled in psychoanalytic theory; Freud's insistence that quiescence is the optimal state (from the organism's point of view) and that all ego development proceeds under the domination of primitive biological urges and out of the conflicts surrounding them are two assumptions against which recent analytic theorists have rebelled.

THE RELATION BETWEEN NEEDS AND DRIVES

One of the virtues that Hull saw in his motivational model was its objective, operational nature. With it, physiological needs can be given objective definition, and the operations for creating and eliminating them can be specified. For example, physiologically, hunger can be virtually equated with food deprivation; psychologically, or behaviorally, hunger is a concomitant of the physiological need state. The objectivity of the latter thus accrues to the former, through a kind of "innocence by association." A second, and for Hull perhaps more salient, virtue of the tie between need and drive is that it places the behavioral model within a broader, Darwinian framework.

Is There a Drive for Every Need? But in the search for objectivity and for good theoretical company, Hull may have imposed overly restrictive limits on his general model. Thus, we can ask whether Hull's approach demands that every need have a drive associated with it and vice versa. In short, do needs and drives exist in a one-to-one relation?

At one time it was useful for the sake of argument to pose examples of needs for which there are no apparent concomitant drives. For example, the need for oxygen is not manifested in a corresponding "oxygen drive." The struggling for air that typically occurs in oxygen deprivation is a response, not to oxygen lack, but to an excess of carbon dioxide. In the absence of excessive carbon dioxide, people deprived of oxygen do not appear to be "driven," and yet the need for oxygen requires faster satisfaction than any of the biological needs. Other similar examples of needs without corresponding drives could be mentioned here. But the point is clear without listing them: Not every need gives rise to a drive. The relation is not one-to-one.

Is There a Need for Every Drive? What about the other half of the relation? That is, can we find a need to accompany each drive? Here is where the critics of the Hullian approach have concentrated their efforts. After all, we should not expect perfection in a biological system, even one that has survived the tests of evolution. The existence of needs without associated drives is not embarrassing to psychological theory; it simply reflects a failure of evolutionary forces to mold entirely the biological substrate of behavior.

However, it is crucial to the approach followed by Hull (used here to exemplify a larger group of theorists) that each drive be tied to some physiological need. Thus, to identify drives for which that relation does not hold is to cast doubt on the classical, homeostatic model. And similarly, since drives and rewards are complementary in that model, to find rewards that bear no relation to physiological needs, or that do not lead to need-reduction, is to expose a weakness of the model.

A series of learning experiments was performed (Sheffield and Roby, 1950; Sheffield, Roby, and Campbell, 1954) in which the reinforcing agent did not in fact satisfy any apparent physiological need. The reinforcing agent was a saccharine solution, which presumably has no food value despite its sweet taste. Yet a variety of behavioral measures revealed that the saccharine solution was a powerful incentive and an effective reinforcer for instrumental learning. Some question has since been raised about the physiological inertness of saccharine. But in the meantime, under the prodding of critics like Sheffield, the Hullian position was modified by one of its leading proponents, Neal Miller.

The Strong-Stimulus Model of Drive. On the grounds that the need-drive relation is unnecessarily restrictive and leaves the general S-R reinforcement theory vulnerable to attack on essentially trivial grounds, Miller (see Dollard and Miller, 1950) proposed a model in which the central motivational construct is *drive*, but drive no longer tied to physiological need. Drive, for Miller, is defined as any *strong stimulus*. Reward, or reinforcement, is equated, not with need-reduction, but with drive-reduction.

This liberalized definition of drive still allows for the relevance of needs, in the sense that many needs do indeed lead to strong stimulation. But in

Miller's revision of the Hullian approach any stimulus, if sufficiently intense, can serve as a drive: The strong stimulation may, but does not have to, come from physiological need states. So long as stimuli are related to physically measurable events, as they are assumed to be in a strict S-R theory, then Miller's definition of drive retains the objectivity characteristic of Hull's. If anything was lost, it was the flavor of Darwinism, which had so appealed to Hull. Even there, however, if we view intense stimuli as potentially harmful, then their relevance for survival becomes apparent. In short, Miller's liberalization of the drive concept was purchased at little, if any, expense.

Drive-Reduction or Drive-Induction? But does it work any better than its Hullian predecessor? The critics of the general homeostatic approach remain dissatisfied. Again, Fred Sheffield and colleagues (Sheffield, Wulff, and Backer, 1951) attempted to show experimentally the inadequacy of the homeostatic model, whether need- or drive-based. Specifically, they designed an experiment in which learning would be manifested, not simply in the absence of need-reduction or drive-reduction, as in the saccharine experiments, but, more dramatically, under reinforcement conditions that could be interpreted as drive-inducing. Male rats were run in a standard learning situation for sexual reinforcement; however, the "reinforcement" consisted in allowing copulation but preventing ejaculation. If we may anthropomorphize here, it is likely that the experience in the goal box served to increase the rats' sexual drive; there was, at least, no opportunity for the reduction in drive that follows normal sexual activity. Nevertheless, the rats showed clear evidence of learning, as for example, by increasing their running speed over trials.

The impact of this experiment depends, of course, on how we interpret the events. Is interrupted copulation indeed a failure of drive-reduction for the rat? If the case of the critics rested on that one experiment, it would not be a very strong one. But additional evidence from other sources suggests that the basic premise of the homeostatic model is untenable, the premise being that all motivation is simply a function of intensity of stimulation that falls above a critical value and that all rewards act by reducing intensity of stimulation to a level below that critical value. As we wend our way through the ensuing tangle of anecdote, experimentation, and interpretation, we will see ultimately that the issue finally resolves into the appropriateness of picking out *intensity of stimulation per se* as the crucial characteristic of motivationally relevant events.

THE NATURE OF INCENTIVES

Increase in Stimulation as Reinforcement. It is rather easy to think of events and objects that appear to have incentive and/or reward value even though (perhaps because) they involve increases in stimulation. The Sheffield sex and saccharine studies provide two such examples. There is a host of analogous experiments in which rats are trained to make an operant response, such as bar-pressing, by using either an increase or a decrease in illumination as the reinforcing event (for example, Roberts, Marx, and Collier, 1958). Monkeys behave similarly (Moon and Lodahl, 1956). Rats will learn a T-maze discrimination problem in which the reinforcement is provided by a large goal box partitioned into several compartments which the rat can traverse; the nonreinforced alternative leads to an empty goal box (Montgomery and Segall, 1955). Rats will learn to run down a straight alley if some aspect of the goal box is repeatedly changed between trials (Chapman and Levy, 1957). Monkeys will solve discrimination problems for the opportunity to peek through a window at such objects as a toy railroad train (Butler, 1953). The several dozen such experiments that have been reported all indicate the existence of a class of reinforcers that do not reduce stimulation intensity; on the contrary, their effectiveness seems correlated with their ability to increase stimulation.

At the beginning of this chapter we referred to three criteria for identifying an object or event as an incentive. Potency as a reinforcer was one. The kinds of objects and events in the experiments mentioned above meet that test. What about the other two? (1) Do they attract the organism and induce "consummatory" activity? (2) Does their prolonged absence generate negative affect?

The Attraction-Value of Stimulation. The question of attraction is implicitly answered in the evidence on reinforcing power. That is, an animal may learn an instrumental response as a means of removing a barrier between it and the incentive; the end result of the learning is to make the incentive more available. This scarcely differs from merely having to make the proper orienting response or moving directly to reach the incentive. Thus, the fact that an animal will learn to run fast down an alley to get to a food-containing goal box virtually implies that it will move toward that food, touch it, sniff it, probably eat it in the absence of any instrumental contingency. Similarly, if change in illumination is an effective reinforcer for a bar-pressing response, it probably will also be found to attract an animal's attention, as evidenced by simple head-turning or approach responses. It should therefore not come as a surprise to learn that the class of events under question does attract attention. A few examples of confirmatory, experimental evidence should suffice to make the point.

In one experiment (Dember, 1956), rats were placed in the starting alley of a T-maze and allowed to wander up to the choice-point area. The two goal arms were blocked off with glass partitions; the rats could look into the goal arms, but not enter them. One goal arm was white and the other black. After several minutes, the rats were removed from the maze, and one of the goal arms was changed, from black to white or white to black. With the glass partitions removed, the rats were given the opportunity to enter one of the goal arms. A significant proportion entered the arm that had been changed in brightness, though on the choice trial both arms were either black or white. On the reasonable assumption that the changed arm was a source of greater "stimulation" than the unchanged alternative, we can conclude that the animals were attracted by an increase in stimulation. This result has been replicated by other experimenters (Fowler, 1958; Walk, 1960; Woods and Jennings, 1959) and extended to other species, such as ferrets (Hughes, 1965).

Moving up the phylogenetic scale to human beings, recall the experiments by Robert Fantz which were mentioned in Chapter Six. His general procedure involved placing pairs of visual stimuli above human infants, who were lying comfortably on their backs, and he found that the infants had reliable preferences for certain of the visual stimuli, as evidenced by the amount of time they spent gazing at each of the stimuli in a pair. Some of the stimuli employed by Fantz are shown in Figure 16.8, with an indication of the rank order of preferences. Similar research has since been conducted in other laboratories (for example, see Brennan, Ames, and Moore, 1966).

However we may choose to characterize the basis for the infants' stimulus preferences—whether related to intensity or some other property of stimulation—it is clear that these stimuli do exert considerable control over the infants' direction of fixation. To try to relate these stimuli to conventional biological drives, or even to suggest that they have acquired reward value, would be to do violence to the process of scientific interpretation. Furthermore, it is quite evident that looking fixedly at a particularly attractive visual stimulus does not serve to reduce the level of stimulation; the way to do that is to close the eyes.

The extensive experimental evidence on the attracting power of drive-irrelevant stimuli can readily be supplemented by anecdotal material from many familiar sources. For example, much of the gimmickry in TV advertising makes use of the various ways of organizing and presenting stimuli that are likely to capture a few moments of the audience's attention. One simple device is to increase the volume of the sound that accompanies the visual display. Another is to utilize unexpected or incongruous elements, such as many of the detergent ads are so infamous for. The problem with the latter—aesthetic considerations aside—is that individual ads lose their effectiveness on repetition (the particular incongruity having lost its impact through habituation).

Even without an endless list of examples, experimental or anecdotal, it should be apparent that need- or drive-related objects are not the only ones that can exert control over the direction of behavior. There is another vast, perhaps infinite, set of stimuli that share this property. The one difference

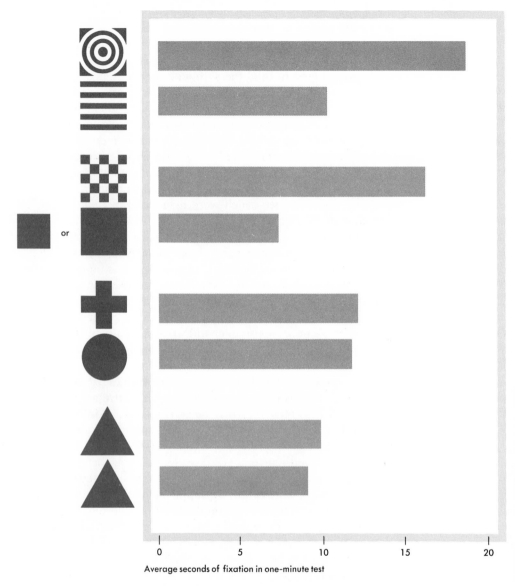

0   5   10   15   20

Average seconds of fixation in one-minute test

Figure 16.8 Infants' reactions to various pairs of patterns (left) presented together. (The small and large plain squares were used alternately.) The more complex pairs received the most attention, and within each of these pairs differential interest was based on pattern differences. These results are for 22 infants in 10 weekly tests. (Adapted from Fantz, 1961.)

between the two sets is that drive-relevant objects, such as food, in general retain their effectiveness despite repetition, whereas the others have, individually, only short-lived potency. However, even that distinction should be qualified. On the one hand, even the most attractive food loses value with excessive repetition; on the other hand, although it is true that a person adapts quickly to particular attention-attracting events, it is a simple matter to find effective substitutes.

Indeed, attention is always directed somewhere during waking hours and perhaps even during sleep. The proportion of time during which attention (to use that term in its broadest sense to include overt behavioral acts, from orienting responses to locomotor and manipulative sequences, as well as covert acts of thinking, problem-solving, fantasy, dreaming, and so on) is directed toward drive-relevant objects is probably quite small. Of course, in people at least, any given object has multiple facets, some drive-relevant and some not; to the average male a mini-skirted girl is simultaneously a sexual object and (until the novelty wears off) an interesting visual stimulus by virtue of the configuration of her clothing, especially in relation to conventions of style and taste that form the observer's expectancies.

In short, it would seem that segregating attractive objects into drive-relevant and drive-irrelevant categories, though possible, is not likely to prove fruitful. An alternative that may yield greater theoretical profit would be to search for a single scheme into which all stimuli could be fit. One such scheme has been proposed and will be presented in some detail after we have disposed of the remaining property of drive-related stimuli—that is, the negative affect experienced in their prolonged absence.

Deprivation of Stimulation. When people have suffered chronic food deprivation, profound emotional effects accompany the expected physical deterioration. Similar emotional responses occur with extended deprivation of other biological needs, such as water, an appropriate sexual partner, and so on. Negative affect, then, is a likely concomitant of a high drive state and can indicate that some important biological need is going unsatisfied.

Once again, however, this property is shared by drive-irrelevant stimuli. If a person is prevented from experiencing adequate stimulation, he exhibits much the same negative affect as the person deprived of drive-relevant goal objects. Moreover, the intensity of the affective response as well as its quality is related to the severity of the stimulus deprivation. Thus, a mild degree of boredom and irritability might accompany lengthy inescapable exposure to monotonous stimulation, for example, an uninformative, dully presented lecture or an overly familiar piece of music.

Imagine a person confined in a situation in which essentially all sources of stimulation are cut off. A polio victim lying in an iron lung might fit this description. Certain occupations frequently subject people to prolonged monotonous conditions, such as cross-country truck drivers, who are almost immobilized for long periods of time and who have very little stimulus variety, especially on modern superhighways. Think also of a prisoner in solitary confinement, shut off from normal channels of stimulation, reading matter, radio, views of the outside world, and indeed other people.

Anecdotal evidence indicates that under such conditions people do experience a variety of negative affects, along with other symptoms, such as cognitive disorganization and even hallucinations. By simulating extreme *sensory deprivation* in the laboratory, psychologists and psychiatrists have been able to study in detail what happens to people under such conditions. The experimental data substantiate the anecdotal reports.

In a now-classic study (Bexton, Heron, and Scott, 1954), college students were recruited to serve as paid subjects in an experiment which, as described in advance, must have seemed attractive. To earn his $20 a day all a subject had to do was to lie in a comfortable bed, in a quiet isolated room, with translucent goggles over his eyes and cardboard cuffs over his hands and forearms. His bodily needs were to be taken care of; otherwise he was to remain in bed. At specified times he might also be asked to perform simple, cognitive tasks; at times also he could hear recorded material over a loudspeaker. He was free to terminate his participation on request but was urged to remain for as long as the experimenters needed him.

The reactions of subjects can be described in affective, perceptual, and cognitive terms, as well as by the theoretically neutral but easily interpretable measure of duration of participation in the experiment. For our purposes, the relevant effect was the considerable emotional impact of sensory deprivation. Many subjects dropped out early because they found the experience unbearable. In part this reaction was associated with the unexpected occurrence of hallucinations, an effect usually confined to psychotics or people under the influence of hallucinogenic drugs.

Since this experiment, other researchers have conducted a host of additional studies of sensory deprivation, exploring in finer detail the specific independent variables that are operative (for instance, whether the social isolation of the subjects is significant) and the exact nature of the behavioral effect (for example, whether hallucinations spontaneously occur or are suggested to the subjects by the experimenter). It is sufficient here to remark that, as the experimental as well as the anecdotal evidence very clearly substantiates, the response to inadequate stimulation is like the response to inadequate supplies of drive-relevant commodities. To speak of "food for thought" apparently is much more than to utter a trite metaphor. The brain needs input just as the stomach needs nutriment. How to translate that basic idea into a formal model is a problem that has begun to intrigue many motivational theorists.

The "New Look" in Motivation

INTENSITY OR INFORMATION-VALUE?

If the "old look" in motivation stressed biological drives, or more generally the intensive aspect of stimulation, the new look attends to the *informative* aspect. That point is only implicit in the preceding section, where reference to stimulation was kept intentionally vague, in the interests of separating data from their interpretation. Thus, the fact that people become emotionally upset when deprived of stimulation contradicts the notion that minimal stimulation is the desired goal state, but it is otherwise theoretically neutral. In particular, such evidence might be interpreted to mean that the classic identification of stimulus intensity as *the relevant* variable for motivation is still correct; to set things straight we need only reverse the classic assumption about which end of the intensity continuum is the "good end." Perhaps organisms seek to maintain or increase rather than to decrease intensity of stimulation.

An Ideal Level of Stimulus Intensity above Zero. But the latter interpretation is patently untenable if it is meant to have universal application, for it seems to violate all that we know about the reaction of organisms to excessive stimulation, whether from internal sources, like hunger pangs, or external sources, such as electric shock. Yet both tendencies exist. Under some conditions a decrease in stimulus intensity is preferred, while under others the goal is an increase in intensity of stimulation. It is quite clear that we could define for any set of circumstances some ideal level of stimulation; departures from that ideal level can take place in either direction; the level can be restored by reversing the direction.

So far so good. You may have noted however, that we have not yet broken free of the homeostatic model. All we have accomplished is to shift the optimal level of stimulus intensity from zero to some larger value and, as a corollary, to allow departures from that value in either direction to serve as cues for whatever action might move the system back toward its optimal level.

Actually, the critics of the old look in motivation have no quarrel with the homeostatic model *per se*. Rather, certain unessential embellishments on the model are the source of dissatisfaction, specifically (1) building a motivational structure on the base of the biological drives, and (2) limiting departures from the ideal to increases in stimulus intensity. Neither of these is an intrinsic feature of a general homeostatic model and neither is general enough to warrant retaining.

There are two additional properties of the "old look" that have been subjected to criticism. These are probably not so obvious as the first two. One, which has already been alluded to, is the identification of stimulus intensity as the significant variable. The second relates to what might be called in the old approach its *static* character.

The Inadequacy of Intensity. First, what is wrong with attributing central importance to stimulus intensity? In brief, to confine our thinking to intensity is to ignore an aspect of stimulation that is much more pervasive and much more significant, especially the higher we go in the phylogenetic and ontogenetic scales—the information-bearing property of stimulation. Stimuli in linguistic or symbolic form are especially obvious cases of contrasting the intensive and informative aspects of stimulation.

Consider, for example, the psychological significance of exchanging the first and third letters in the word DOG. It would be difficult to argue that stimulus intensity is the least bit relevant to the relative impact of the two words. In a similar vein, you can take a set of musical tones and place them in a virtually unlimited number of patterns, some of which would be pleasant to hear while others would be neutral or unpleasant. The same can be said of pictorial elements: With intensity held constant, by varying the spatial arrangement of elements you can generate pictures that cover the whole range from uninteresting to esthetically pleasing. In a most simplified form, that is what characterizes the alternatives in the experiment with rats mentioned a few pages back; they were exposed to a black arm and a white arm, and then given a choice between, say, two black arms. On the choice trial, the two alternatives were identical in intensity, but one was still preferred—the one that had been changed between exposure and choice.

Another experiment with rats (Dember, Earl, and Paradise, 1957) is also revealing of the difference between intensity and information as they bear on the incentive value of stimuli. A piece of apparatus called the figure-8 maze allowed rats access to either of two intersecting circular pathways; the rats could move freely within and between the two alternatives. External stimulation was restricted so that any preference exhibited by the rats was attributable to the properties of the two paths. The only effective difference between the paths was the patterns lining their walls: One path was decorated with black and white vertical stripes, the other was lined with horizontal stripes. In terms of total black and white stimulation the two paths were equivalent. It was assumed, however, that the vertical stripes provided the richer source of changing stimulation for the rat moving around in the pathway. That is, although the two paths did not differ in intensity of stimulation, they did differ in pattern, and in such a manner that one bore the greater degree of stimulus change, which can be considered as the primitive base of the informational property of stimulation.

The different visual patterns did influence the amount of time the rats spent in the two pathways. Each subject was tested for about 45 minutes a day on each of two days. On the first day, 11 of the 17 subjects showed a strong preference for the vertical alternative and two a weak preference; 12 of those 13 animals retained that preference on the second day. Of the remaining four rats, three showed a preference for the horizontal stripes on the first day; one rat apportioned its time almost equally between the two paths. On the second day, all preferred the vertically striped pathway.

In a second experiment, similar in design to the first, the horizontally striped path was pitted against either an alternative of plain white or plain black. Each rat was put in the maze for one hour a day over a five-day period. The pattern of responses was similar to that in the first experiment, and even a little neater. In general, by the end of the experiment all 16 rats reliably preferred the horizontal stripes, which in this experiment was the alternative offering the greater amount of stimulus change.

Preference for Change and Changes in Preference. Two points are important to note about the above study. First, the informational aspect of the stimuli was shown to be motivationally relevant. Second, the rats' preferences were not fixed; rather they changed over time. However, and this point will be detailed below, the changes in preference were unidirectional: If a change occurred, it was highly likely to be from the lesser amount of stimulus change to the greater. This second feature of the data relates to our earlier remark about criticisms of the static character of the old approach. There is ample reason to reject any motivational model, even one that recognizes the significance of the informational aspect of stimulation, which fails to make provision for change to occur in the incentive value of a stimulus, or set of stimuli, as the responding organism itself changes. In particular, it should be expected that systematic changes will take place in the level of information which is maximally attractive. To offer a concrete example, the type of music that appeals to the uninitiated listener is quite different from what the sophisticated listener takes greatest pleasure in. Similar changes in preference can be noted in many other stimulus domains, from the purely esthetic, such as art and architecture, to the more nearly intellectual, as in poetry, drama, fiction, and so on.

THE DEMBER-EARL MODEL

To indicate the kind of formal structure that is emerging from the body of anecdotal and experimental material sampled above, we sketch here the basic terms and assumptions of one such model, offered first by W. Dember and R. Earl (1957) and expounded in rigorous detail by Earl (1961). The essential features of this model have found their way, sometimes only implicitly, in the theorizing of others whose ideas take very similar form.

Stimulus Complexity. The model specifies the information value of stimulation as *the* motivationally relevant variable. To preclude potential misinterpretation of the term information value, a synonym, *complexity* value, is substituted. Every stimulus is said to have a complexity value on each of its many attributes, such as color, form, tonal quality, texture, smell, and so on. Although complexity value arises from the physical properties of a stimulus (for example, a homogeneous gray patch is likely to be evaluated as less complex than a black-and-white pattern), it is itself a *psychological* variable, to be assessed properly by psychological measurement. In some appropriate way, we have to "ask" the subject how complex a particular stimulus is. Sometimes, the experimenter substitutes his own assessment for that of the subject (as was done in the experiment with rats in the figure-8 maze), but that is always a compromise with the theoretically purest procedure.

Individual Complexity. The model assumes that individuals as well as stimuli have complexity values. Thus, at any moment in time, each person can be assigned, in principle, a complexity value for each attribute of each stimulus. These values are not static; they change, perhaps with maturation, but most importantly as a function of the person's experience with stimulation of varying degrees of complexity. When change occurs in the complexity value associated with an individual, that change always brings the person to a higher level of complexity. Note that in certain circumstances, as for example when a person is under great emotional stress, temporary regression in complexity level may occur. But permanent changes in complexity level are always upward.

The Ideal. It is the relation between an individual's complexity level and that of the stimuli with which he is faced that determines their incentive value for him. The theory assumes that the individual's own level of complexity, called his *ideal,* defines the complexity level of the stimuli he most prefers. Suppose a person encounters a set of stimuli that fall on either side of his ideal; if the degree of preference were then plotted against stimulus complexity, the resulting curve would have the inverted V-shaped form illustrated in Figure 16.9. Since we can conceive of some stimuli less complex than the simplest person and some that are more complex than the most complex individual, the curve in Figure 16.9 expresses the general relation between stimulus complexity and preference.

The model does not specify any particular operations for measuring preference or complexity. These are problems to be dealt with in elaborations of the model and in its application to various stimulus and behavioral domains.

Figure 16.9 The hypothetical relation between stimulus complexity and stimulus preference.

Pacers. One measure of preference used with both animal and human subjects is the amount of time freely spent with the alternative stimuli. That is the measure used in the study employing the figure-8 maze mentioned earlier. A similar measure was also used by Earl (1957) in an experiment with children who were offered puzzles to work on as long as they wished to do so. In that study, one finding was translated into a general principle and given the status of an additional assumption of the model: An individual

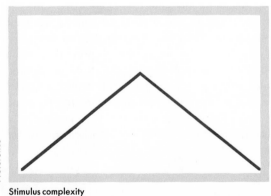

Preference

Stimulus complexity

will spend the greatest amount of time with stimuli that are within a small range of complexity values just above the value of his ideal. These hyperattractive stimuli—those that are a little more complex than the person is—are called *pacers* and are given a special function in the model. Pacers help to raise a person's complexity level; that is, as a result of those processes that occur while the individual is actively and ultimately successfully engaged in viewing, organizing, making sense of, solving, in general *coping with* pacers, he himself eventually takes on their complexity value. This is the dynamic principle of the model.

Note that because they serve to bring the person up to their level, particular pacers eventually do themselves out of jobs, for once he has reached their level, a person begins to lose interest in the former pacers. At the same time, of course, he is then prepared to tackle stimuli of even higher complexity. Whether there are limits to the level of complexity that a person can achieve is an empirical question. However, even if it should turn out that growth of this sort is limited by the person's innate neural structure, the theory holds out the consolation that progression up the complexity ladder occurs independently for different types of stimuli. Thus, growth in music may leave a person unchanged with respect to poetry, for example. As a result, a person may have nowhere to go on the one dimension (a condition, according to the theory, which is conducive to massive ennui) but room for considerable additional development on the other.

Tests of the Model. Numerous tests of the model have generally confirmed it. A wide variety of stimulus materials, has been employed including visual figures (see, for example, Dorfman and McKenna, 1966; Munsinger and Kessen, 1964; Vitz, 1966a), musical passages (Vitz, 1966b), and in one study, poems (Kammann, 1966). This last experiment is a good one with which to illustrate the methodological problems of measuring complexity.

A poem is, in absolute terms, a highly complex object, and its complexity arises from many sources, some structural (meter, rhyme scheme, and so on) and some semantic (the meanings of the words and combinations of words). How might we obtain a measure of the relative complexity of a poem—as compared with other poems—so that complexity of a poem can be related to preference? How can we assess differences in individual complexity with respect to poetry so that the relation between a person's ideal and his personal preferences can be determined? According to the model, the more complex the person, the more complex the poems that he would most prefer.

Richard Kammann hit on a solution to both problems, whereby relative complexity of poems and relative complexity of persons could be determined from the same set of behaviors. The procedure employed by Kammann is the Cloze technique, which involves deleting every nth word from a passage; these fragmented items are then presented to subjects whose task is to guess what word belongs in each blank space. In Kammann's study, the items were a set of 15 poems. As used in conjunction with the Cloze technique, each poem was presented with every fourth word omitted. An example of one of these fragmented poems is given in Figure 16.10.

It seems intuitively valid to assume that the fewer the blanks that can be accurately filled, the more complex the material. If the missing elements of the passage are highly predictable, then they carry very little information; were they actually present, as they are in the intact poem, they would not be surprising to the reader. A totally intact poem, then, comprised of highly redundant (that is, expected) elements is likely to be a very simple object, in contrast to a poem whose elements are not readily predictable. Thus, Kammann argued that poems getting high Cloze scores (with many of the blanks filled in correctly) are less complex than those getting low Cloze scores.

From the point of view of the subjects, those who succeed in making many correct guesses are considered to be more complex than those who correctly fill in only a small number of blanks. Hence, each subject who performs the Cloze task can be assigned a relative complexity score by counting the number of blanks he filled in correctly in all the fragmented poems. In addition, each poem gets a relative complexity score from the number of correct responses made to it by all subjects. Thus, from the subjects' responses on the Cloze task, measures of complexity of both poem and person can be obtained.

Some time after the subjects performed the Cloze task, they were given the intact poems to read and evaluate according to several criteria. For example, they were asked to put the poems in rank order according to their "goodness." In addition, they were asked to pick those poems which they would most, and least, like to memorize, to hear discussed by an expert, to debate with a friend, and so on.

The results showed a high positive correlation between individual complexity and complexity of each person's preferred poem. Furthermore, as expected from the model, poems of intermediate complexity were given the highest ratings of "goodness," and were also the ones that subjects said they would most like to memorize. However, in response to the question, "Which would you like to debate with a friend?" subjects tended to choose either the simplest or the most complex poems. This latter finding points up an important distinction within the model —that is, the difference between goal objects and objects that serve as means

Figure 16.10 One of Kammann's (1964) mutilated poems. How many blanks can you fill in correctly? The missing words can be found in the footnote on page 638.

What's ——of death, from ——who never will ——?
Think you the ——that fashioned you ——clay,
The thumb ——set the hollow ——that way
In ——full throat and ——the long eye
——roundly from the ——; will let lie
——forgotten, under foot ——day
Your unimpeachable ——,and so slay
——work he most ——been remembered by?

——tell you this: ——of dust to ——
Goes down, whatever ——ashes may return
——its essential self ——its own season,
——such as yours ——not to be lost,
——, cast in bronze ——his very urn,
——known him Master, ——for what good ——

to other goals. The predictions of the model refer to objects that function solely as goals. Thus, we can evaluate a poem as an object for pure enjoyment. But if that poem is going to serve as a vehicle for achieving some other goal (for example, the esteem of one's peers or one's teachers), than it may be evaluated on some other basis. When objects serve as means rather than as goals, predictions concerning them no longer fall in the province of the model under discussion. This point is emphasized here because it is very easy to miss the theoretically crucial distinction between objects as goals and objects as means and hence to misapply the model and to test its implications under inappropriate conditions.

The Place of the Biological Drives. What room is there in the "new look" for the biological drives? After all, to be disenchanted with hunger as the paradigm of all motivational processes is not to deny that hunger exists.

Two obvious solutions come to mind, one easy and the other difficult. The easy solution would be simply to establish two categories of motivational events, one for the biological drives and whatever acquired drives and rewards may have originated within that category and the second for the information-seeking motive (we can call it "curiosity" for convenience) that is emphasized in the "new look." The more difficult solution would be to find some way of integrating the biological drives and curiosity into a single category. Whether the latter is feasible is an open question; its appeal lies partly in the intellectual challenge it offers and partly in its conformity to the scientific canon of parsimony. To think of organisms operating on the basis of two motivational systems, each with its own rules, is to violate an ideal that most theorists cherish. Nevertheless, the easy solution may turn out also to be the more valid one.

How might the biological drives be incorporated into the framework of those models that assert the primacy of information-seeking? A suggestion has been offered which, if developed, may point the way to an eventual solution. We might, the argument runs, think of drive stimuli in the same way that the model considers external stimulation:

> Hunger, for example, can be considered as a source of intense, persistent, little-changing, and very familiar stimulation; as such it is dealt with by the animal in the same manner as any other monotonous stimulation. (Fowler, Blond, and Dember, 1959, p. 613.)

The way a person deals with external stimuli that are either too simple or too complex is to break off contact with them and to seek to establish contact with stimuli closer to the ideal level of complexity. To get rid of hunger stimuli, which an individual carries about with him wherever he goes, it is not possible simply to "turn away" (although hunger and other biological drives can diminish remarkably when one is engrossed in some fascinating activity). Eventually, he must eat. The act of eating is obviously the way to get rid of unpleasant hunger stimuli. In addition, eating can be a source of rewarding stimulation if the meal is "interesting." Thus, there is little difference in principle between the events associated with the hunger drive and those characteristic of the motive underlying the information-seeking and "consumption" that is central to the new look.

How far we can push the above argument remains to be seen. In the meantime there is good reason to believe that, with no basic inconsistency in the properties of the two categories of motives, a unified motivational theory might very well emerge from the present incomplete and tentative formulation.

Complexity, Coping, and Competence. Our discussion so far has emphasized the nature of *goal objects*, focusing on their complexity in relation to personal complexity as the significant variable. It would be improper to stop here without attempting to discover why the complexity of objects should be the potent variable that it seems to be. In the course of that endeavor we will also be in a position to show the relation between the complexity model and those very similar approaches, within the "new look," that stress the motivational significance of the subject's *responses*.

The human child is a good place to begin. We have already remarked on an infant's graded responsiveness to stimuli of various degrees of complexity. We were concerned with the kinds of objects that attract the infant's attention; the bodily movements that occur were treated as indicators of the attentive process and were otherwise of no special interest. In other instances, however, the crucial events seem to be the movements themselves, and the objects may be of only limited significance.

For example, watch a six- or seven-month old child pulling himself up to a standing position at the rail of his crib. You need no theoretical sophistication to be struck by the tremendous amount of effort he expends in achieving the upright position, as well as the considerable positive affect that accompanies the successful accomplishment of that act. The child's glee is expressed vocally with laughter or what might be called "crowing" and gesturally with huge smiles and excited jumping or dancing movements. Clearly, the source of all that joy is not in the tactual contact with the bed rail or even in the visual stimulation made possible by the upright position; there are plenty of interesting things to look at lying down. In this case, and others like it, the central event is the act itself: The baby must have a strong urge to pull itself up, and it is the successful fulfillment of that urge which triggers the affective response.

We see the same pattern in later stages of development. When the right time comes, somewhere around a year, the child exhibits a virtually compulsive urge to walk. His first steps are greeted with equal pleasure by himself and his parents. Not irrelevantly, this activity persists despite the frequent falls and injuries that accompany his learning to walk.

At about this same time the baby begins to assert his autonomy in the issue of feeding. Previously, he was content to let his mother feed him; but now, much to the mother's annoyance, he starts grabbing the spoon and trying to take over from her the task of filling and guiding the spoon to his mouth. These initial attempts are usually quite inept; more food is spilled than taken. Surely, the efficient procedure would be to allow the mother to go on as in the past. But unless the baby's attempts at self-feeding are heavily suppressed, this essay into autonomy continues, until eventually the baby develops the coordination to do the job skillfully. At that point, it is interesting to note, the baby is no longer reluctant to let his mother feed him once in a while as a treat for her, if not for the baby.

Each new developmental challenge is met in this way, whether it be dressing and undressing, toileting, getting in and out of the car, opening doors, climbing stairs, and so on. The baby whose strivings for autonomy have not been squelched turns into the young child who "needs" to cross the street by himself, who needs to learn to ride a bike, roller skate, jump rope, swim, and, later, to do arithmetic problems, to read, to build, to dance, to sing—in short, *to use his motoric and intellectual equipment to the limits of their capacity.* However this "fact of life" is eventually translated into theoretical language, it must be recognized as being indicative of a potent motivational process.

Acknowledgment of the primacy of this *striving to function*—to *cope* with the environment by employing one's own resources—has been made within several theoretical frameworks. The so-called "ego psychologists" of the psychoanalytic school (see, for example, Hartmann, 1951) speak of the "primary autonomy of ego functions" or "conflict-free functions of the ego" in recognition of the initial independence of these functions from other primitive drives and conflicts. Of course, being supreme realists, the psychoanalytic theorists also know that the independence of these ego functions may readily be destroyed, so that, for example, the pure gratification of walking or self-feeding becomes mixed with a concern for pleasing others; that is, to use our earlier language, what was initially a "goal object" becomes in part a means to another goal.

What then is the magic of complexity? Why the particular potency of pacers? We might think of pacers, as the term implies, as challenges to an individual's competence. Just as a mechanical rabbit entices racing dogs to perform at the limit of their physical ability, so do certain stimuli demand the heightened operation of a person's information-processing capacities. Stimuli of optimal complexity thus call into play the perceptual and cognitive functions; they induce the system to act at its best and that, after all, is what the system is there to do. Furthermore, there seems to be a built-in requirement that the systems not only operate, but that they do so, if possible, in such a way as to be self-modifying, that is, to "work" themselves into ever-increasing levels of competence. Development of both motoric and cognitive skills reflects this principle.

Intrinsic and Extrinsic Motives. This "need to develop" is *intrinsically* motivated; superimposed on it is a set of *extrinsic* motives. We have already noted how learning to walk is gratifying both in its own right and as a source of positive affect by virtue of its impact on others, especially parents. These extrinsic gratifications can be very potent; at times the need to *appear* competent may interfere with the smooth development of genuine competence. Indeed, it is quite possible for extrinsic motives to conflict with, or even supplant, the intrinsic core. For example, some mothers are threatened by their infants' strivings for autonomy and actively inhibit their expression, usually on grounds of "neatness" in self-feeding and "safety" in locomotor activities. Even if mother approves of acts of autonomy, conflict may still be engendered if the infant is ambivalent in his feeling toward her: "If she's for it, I mustn't be too enthusiastic about it." And, it should be added, it is the rare child whose affection for his parents is not tinged with some ambivalence.

In various ways, then, it is almost inevitable that the intrinsic motivational core is intermixed with a variety of extrinsic motives. And this is not necessarily bad. A productive scientist, for example, may have to have a blend of curiosity and ambition (or "achievement" or "affiliation" motivation). The trick is not to let the extrinsic motives gain the upper hand. Imagine, if you can, Einstein creating the theory of relativity on contract with the Department of Defense. On the other hand, try to imagine a medical researcher discovering a polio vaccine with no concern for the welfare of people or no desire for fame, recognition, or power.

Thus, to accept the central core of intrinsic motivation is not to deny the significance of extrinsic motives. It would be an unwise school teacher, for example, who expected her students to learn to read solely for the sake of learning to read; if she denied them the supplementary gratifications derived from her expressions of approval, from opportunities to "show off" their new skills, and so on, she would be doing justice neither to her students nor to the complexity of human motivation.

NOTE—missing words (in order) for Figure 16.10: this, you, die, wrist, in, that, just, your, lidded, so, forehead, broken, some, body, the, had, I, whatever, dust, of, to, in, loveliness, will, but, upon, make, and, reason.

SUMMARY

The concept of motivation is invoked to account for certain general properties of behavior. Among these are the cyclical consummatory interactions between an organism and specific classes of objects (such as food), the marked variation among individuals in their attentiveness to the same stimuli, and the variability among objects in attention-getting potency. Those objects that can elicit strong and sustained interest are called *goal objects,* or *incentives.* Goal objects can further be identified by their ability to effect learning. In general, the complementary concepts of motives and goal objects serve, in psychological theory, to explain the directionality of behavior, broadly defined to include covert thoughts as well as overt behavioral acts. An additional property of goal objects is that their prolonged absence leads to heightened arousal and intense negative affect.

The concept of motivation was not important in the psychological systems of Structuralism or Gestalt theory, and was relatively unimportant in Functionalism and early Behaviorism. Its present significance in theoretical psychology is largely the joint responsibility of the behavior theory of Hull and the dynamic psychology of Freud. Despite major differences, both models follow a *homeostatic* approach, in which automatic physiological and behavioral mechanisms operate to maintain or restore physiological balance.

In the particular motivational model developed by Hull, departures from optimal physiological states are defined as needs; the psychological counterparts of needs are *primary drives*. When drives are absent, the organism is inactive. Activity level increases and specific responses occur as specific drives are aroused. *Secondary drives* can be acquired through repeatedly presenting a neutral stimulus just prior to a drive increase; *secondary rewards* are acquired through presenting a neutral stimulus just prior to a reduction in drive. Primary and secondary drives and rewards constitute the total set of motivationally relevant events.

Hunger is one of the so-called primary drives. Operationally, hunger is produced by food-deprivation. The following are concomitants of an increase in food-deprivation level: (1) a decrease in the time to start eating when offered food; (2) an increase in general activity level; (3) an increase in the vigor with which learned responses are performed; (4) a decrease in the efficiency of performance of complex discriminations or skilled acts (if drive level is excessively high). Strength of learning *per se* may not be affected by drive level during training.

In Hull's theory it is postulated that strength of learning is affected by the incentive value of the rewarding objects, as evidenced by increased running speed with increasing incentive value. This is a controversial assumption, however. In Logan's modification of Hull's theory, a particular running speed itself is considered to be what the animal learns. Ordinarily, it is fast running that is rewarded, but animals can be trained to "run slowly" if slow running is what achieves the best rewards.

The effectiveness of a particular reward depends not only on its absolute value but also on the individual's experience with other reward values; that is, rewarding stimuli are subject to contrast effects just as are other stimuli. The *Crespi effect* reflects this relativity in reward value: A reward of given magnitude is more effective if it follows rewards of lesser magnitude than if it follows rewards of the same magnitude. To some extent the effectiveness of an incentive is independent of the individual's drive level; that is, incentives are partly autonomous. Indeed, some incentives, such as salted peanuts, can arouse a drive in the absence of the usual deprivation conditions.

Research on the physiology of hunger has focused on both peripheral and central mechanisms. Among peripheral factors that play some role in hunger are stomach contractions (which, however, are not essential for hunger to occur). The stomach is probably concerned with regulating the cessation of eating, whereas taste primarily determines the initiation and vigor of eating. Attempts to specify a chemical transmitter in the blood of the information that food is needed have not been successful.

The control of eating in the central nervous system is localized in the *hypothalamus*. Damage to the *ventromedial* portion of the hypothalamus leads to *hyperphagia* (overeating) and a resulting obesity; damage to the lateral hypothalamus leads to *aphagia* (undereating). Hyperphagia seems not to involve a change in hunger *per se*, but rather a failure of some mechanism to inhibit the eating of highly palatable food when. nutritional needs have been met. Aphagia probably results from normally palatable foods' losing their attractiveness. Through electrical stimulation of the hypothalamus it is possible to initiate eating in a satiated animal.

As useful as it has been, the homeostatic model of motivation has not gone unchallenged. Critics of the model point to many exceptions to its assumption of a one-to-one correspondence between needs and drives. A modification of the model, in which drive is the central concept, has been proposed by Miller, with drives defined as any strong stimuli, whether need-related or not. In that model a reduction in drive is the essence of reinforcement. But Sheffield argues that drive increase can be reinforcing; there is considerable evidence that animals and people are attracted to, and rewarded by, increases in stimulation. Moreover, if the prevailing level of stimulation is too low, as in *sensory-deprivation* experiments, people respond with the same kind of negative affect that they exhibit when severely deprived of such conventional drive-reducing objects as food. Of course, excessively intense stimulation is aversive. Clearly, there must be some optimal level of stimulation that is neither too low nor too high.

But reference to stimulus intensity may not capture the essence of all those objects and events that can act as incentives and reinforcers. An aspect of stimulation that seems more generally applicable is that of its *information value*, or its *complexity*. In one of the several "new look" models of motivation, the Dember-Earl model, complexity plays a central role. It is the relation between the complexity value of stimuli and that of the individual himself (the *ideal* level of complexity) that determines his response to them; stimuli closest to the ideal will be preferred. Stimuli that lie just above the ideal level, called *pacers*, are those that the person will devote special attention to; out of his encounters with pacers the person's own ideal will increase in value and his preferences will change accordingly. The importance of stimulus complexity is probably a function of the opportunity that complex stimulation provides for a person to utilize to their fullest his intellectual and motoric resources.

SUGGESTED READINGS

Cofer, C.N., and M.H. Appley. *Motivation: theory and research*. New York: Wiley, 1964.

Haber, R.N. *Current research in motivation*. New York: Holt, Rinehart & Winston, 1966. See especially articles by F.D. Sheffield (pp. 98–111), D.O. Hebb (pp. 267–278), and J. McV. Hunt (pp. 355–370).

Harlow, H.F. Mice, monkeys, men, and motives. *Psychological Review*, 1953, 60, 23–32.

Hull, C.L. *Principles of behavior*. New York: Appleton-Century-Crofts, 1943, pp. 57–67.

White, R. Motivation reconsidered: the concept of competence. In *Functions of varied experience* (edited by D.W. Fiske and S.R. Maddi). Homewood, Ill.: Dorsey, 1961, Chapter 10.

Conflict, Control, and Psychopathology

CHAPTER SEVENTEEN Though all behavior is the resultant of conflicting tendencies, certain types of conflict are sufficiently serious to have marked behavioral and emotional impact. We examine in this chapter several types of intrapersonal conflict, from those that have been experimentally studied in lower animals to those severe, unconscious conflicts that are considered in psychoanalytic theory to be the basis of psychopathology. In discussing the latter variety, we examine in some detail the major mechanisms of defense that serve as unconscious controls against the direct expression of unacceptable unconscious impulses and ideas.

All organized behavior emerges from conflict, whether conceived in Pavlovian terms as between the excitatory and inhibitory tendencies that any stimulus arouses, or whether conceived in theoretically neutral terms as between the opposing tendencies to act and not to act. Indeed, the very notion of organization in behavior implies that at any given moment certain responses have been selected from a myriad of possible alternatives. The fact that you are reading these words implies that there are many other acts, both cognitive and motor, in which you are not engaging. One of our tasks as authors is to assure your selection of this act.

Ordinarily, people are not aware of the multitude of conflicting tendencies with which they are constantly beset. The acts that constitute "everyday living" proceed relatively smoothly, with little of the hesitancy, vacillation, and doubt that accompany obvious instances of severe conflict. Even intense conflict may go unnoticed by a person himself, though it may be readily apparent to observers.

We have already uncovered in these opening remarks two interesting dimensions of conflict: (1) its severity as evidenced in overt behavior and (2) the extent to which it enters awareness. This chapter will be concerned with those instances of conflict strong enough to have significant behavioral impact. Of particular interest are those that people are unaware of despite their powerful behavioral effects; these are the unconscious conflicts to which psychoanalytic theory attributes much of psychopathology. In examining these conflicts we will necessarily consider the controls and defensive maneuvers postulated to account for their being "unconscious." In this latter regard we will lean heavily on Freudian conceptions.

Conflict implies incompatible elements. In this chapter we will be concerned with elements that are associated with a single individual, with *intrapsychic* conflict, or *inner* conflict, as it is often called; this type is distinguished from interindividual and intergroup conflict (that is, conflict between individuals, as when a husband and wife disagree about which television program to watch, or between groups, as when Democrats and Republicans vie for the voters' loyalty or when nations go to war). Conflict between individuals or groups does of course have intrapsychic ramifications; the husband may not only want his own way, but also be apprehensive about arousing his wife's antagonism, and surely some of the individuals in a nation at war may have doubts about the nation's aggressive actions. Thus, to the extent that interindividual or intergroup conflict has internal representation it falls within the scope of the present chapter; otherwise, it becomes the province of social psychology, a branch of psychology which we will touch on in the next chapter.

Intrapsychic Conflict

Even within the category of intrapsychic conflict, several varieties of situation can be distinguished: (1) where an object has both positive and negative incentive value; (2) where motives or goal objects are incompatible; (3) where "ideas" are incompatible; and (4) where there is a clash between impulses and controls.

CONFLICTING INCENTIVE VALUES

A given object or event can be purely positive or purely negative in its incentive value. Food, for a hungry rat, is positive, electric shock negative. However, food can be simultaneously positive and negative. Thus, if the rat is both hungry and thirsty, dry food will satisfy the hunger but also exacerbate the thirst. A highly preferred food can be adulterated—for example, by the addition of bitter-tasting quinine—so that it is both attractive and aversive. Hungry rats will reveal the conflict by their hesitancy in eating the adulterated food, if they do indeed continue to eat it. Another way of adding negative valence to an initially positively valued object, such as food, is to associate the object with punishment. For example, cats might be trained to obtain food from a cup and then on one occasion, when they are about to mouth the food, a strong blast of air is directed at their snouts.

Examples of objects with both positive and negative valence to human beings are not hard to find. For instance, ambivalence typifies the relation between parent and child. For the child, the parents are simultaneously his major sources of gratification and the most frequent agents of punishment and frustration; as a consequence, they are both loved and hated. Inanimate objects too are often regarded ambivalently. A new car, for instance, can be an object of desire but also of concern, insofar as it is a potential drain on financial resources.

A Graphic Model of Approach-Avoidance Conflict. To translate incentive value into behavioral tendencies, objects with ambivalent incentive value elicit incompatible responses. Very generally, they elicit both *approach* and *avoidance* responses. One wants to move toward them, either literally or figuratively, and also move away from them. Except in fantasy, the incompatible tendencies cannot be granted simultaneous expression. That, of course, is what we mean by conflict, or at least what is interesting about conflict. What does happen, behaviorally, when two incompatible tendencies are aroused?

To help come to conceptual grips with conflicts of the sort described, as well as some of those yet to be discussed, theorists have created models of conflict. Perhaps the best known of these models was developed by Neal Miller (1944); it is cast in a behavioristic mold, and as such makes use, where necessary, of the already existing concepts of the Hullian system. It is a model that also lends itself easily to graphic representation, as will become apparent below.

The approach-avoidance conflict is represented, in Miller's scheme, by the graph shown in Figure 17.1. The ordinate (y axis) of the graph refers to the strength of either the approach or the avoidance tendency. Along the abscissa (x axis) are plotted values of the individual's "distance" from the goal. The zero value on the abscissa is where the individual and the goal object meet. Note that although distance ordinarily means spatial separa-

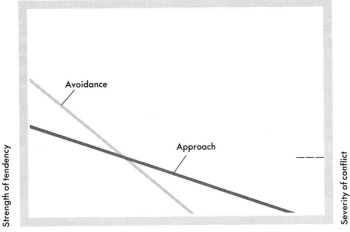

Figure 17.1 Graphic model of an approach-avoidance conflict.

tion, it can also refer to temporal separation, as when a person is awaiting a future event such as marriage, graduation, a vacation, and so on.

The graph comprises two curves, one for the approach, the other for the avoidance tendency. These curves are drawn with a slope greater than zero; that is, they are not parallel to the abscissa; rather, as distance from the goal decreases, the strength of both tendencies increases, with maximal strength achieved when the goal is reached. The exact shape of the curves is not crucial for the present discussion, so long as distance and strength of tendency are monotonically related. The slope of the curves is meant to capture the psychological notion that the closer a person (or animal) is to a desired object the more desirable it becomes, and if it is also aversive, the more aversive it becomes.

In addition to the experimental evidence that supports the form of the curves (Brown, 1942; 1948), there is also theoretical justification for assuming that the slopes as drawn are accurate. The closer a subject gets to an incentive, positive or negative, the more similar the total setting is to the one that prevails when the goal is actually present. Imagine a hungry rat running down an alley for the nth time toward a piece of food. From a great distance there are very few cues to arouse anticipatory responses, such as chewing movements, salivation, and so on; however, as the rat approaches the goal box there is usually an increase in the number of cues that can elicit anticipatory goal responses—or to put it slightly differently, the greater is the similarity between the rat's present location and the goal area. Modern learning theories give anticipatory goal responses a function equivalent to drive itself. That is, arousal of the anticipatory goal response is tantamount to increasing drive level; both show up behaviorally as an increase in running speed.

A similar argument holds for aversive goal objects. The farther away they are, in space or time, the less effectively can they arouse "fear" or "hostility" or whatever the relevant anticipatory response is to the negative incentive. Indeed, the analysis runs, the relation between distance and avoidance tendency is even stronger for negative incentives than for positive ones. Thus, a rat carries around with it a potent source of cues—its hunger—for the arousal of the anticipatory eating response; external stimuli support the internal cues, but are not necessary for the occurrence of the anticipatory goal response. By contrast, the animal's fear of the goal object (let us say it has been shocked in the goal box) is contingent on whatever cues are available for eliciting the anticipatory fear response; there are no internal fear-arousing stimuli analogous to hunger cues. The negative incentive, and stimuli similar to it, carry the entire burden. Hence, the arousal of the negative tendency should be more abrupt than the arousal of the positive tendency; graphically, the curve representing the negative tendency should have a steeper slope than the corresponding curve for the positive tendency.

Our reference to the growing *similarity* of the cues in the animal's present location to those of the goal area might have suggested to you the concept of *stimulus generalization.* The preceding argument might in fact have been phrased in terms of that concept; that is, distance from the goal reflects the similarity of present cues to goal-box cues; the greater the similarity, the greater the response conditioned to the goal-box cues, according to the principle of stimulus generalization. Our more extended analysis lays out in detail what is implicit in the preceding statement.

The Significance of the Crossing Point. The approach and avoidance curves are not only different in slope, they also cross each other somewhere between possible locations of the subject and the goal object. This last property reflects the occurrence of *behavioral vacillation,* or *behavioral arrest.* If the avoidance tendency were weaker than the approach tendency throughout the entire range of distances so that the curves did not cross before the goal was reached, then the net tendency to approach the goal might be weakened, but the approach response would still prevail. We might still speak of conflict in this case, but the behavior would lack a property that is observed in the behavior that occurs when conflicting tendencies reach equal value (at the point where the curves cross). It is then that we see overt signs of conflict. The animal cannot approach closer to the goal; neither can it run away. It may do both in rapid alternation, now moving tentatively forward, now retreating. In effect, the animal is arrested at the point where the two curves cross, and that is the quality of behavior that the model is designed to capture.

Another way of describing the approach-avoidance conflict is to borrow from physical systems the concept of a *stable equilibrium.* Imagine, for example, a saucer-shaped container with a ball placed on one wall of the saucer. The ball will roll down the wall and then continue for a way up the opposite wall; but then it will stop and roll back down, and so on, until eventually it comes to rest at the lowest point in the saucer. At that point all the forces acting on it are equal; it is in equilibrium. It can be moved out of its temporary equilibrium state by application of a force in one direction, but if left alone the ball will again return to the same resting point.

A major difference between the physical situation and behavior is that the forces acting on the ball are external to it and fixed in value. A subject placed in an approach-avoidance conflict, however, is not simply a passive object, following the dictates of fixed, external forces. External stimuli are important, but they are not the sole determinants of the "tendencies" out of which the behavior emerges. Those tendencies are a joint product of external and internal events, and the latter especially are not static. For example, if the approach tendency is mediated by hunger, its strength will fluctuate as hunger level changes. Thus, in order to get the subject "off" the equilibrium point, it may not be necessary to prod it from the outside, as we might give the ball in the saucer a shove. Despite this big difference, however, the physical analogy is useful for comparing approach-avoidance with other types of conflict, as we do below.

The Resolution of Approach-Avoidance Conflicts. But first, what else does the model tell us about conflict? How, for example, might an approach-avoidance conflict be reduced? Again, consider the hungry rat attracted to, but afraid of, a goal box containing food. One potential way of resolving the resulting conflict would be to do something that would move the crossing point of the two curves far enough to the left (see Figure 17.1) that it no longer fell between the subject and the goal. That shift could be accomplished either by lowering the over-all level of the avoidance gradient or by raising the level of the approach gradient. The former would require some sort of extinction procedure for reducing the rat's acquired fear of the goal box. The alternative of raising the level of the approach tendency might be accomplished by increasing the animal's hunger drive; another would be to raise the incentive value of the food, but this method demands getting the animal and the new incentive together—which the conflict precludes. So let us try to push the crossing-point to the left by making the rat hungrier. If, indeed, we do succeed in raising the approach tendency to a sufficiently high level, the conflict should be resolved, as depicted in Figure 17.2. But what are the consequences if the approach tendency is not raised far enough to shift the crossing-point past the goal? What if we create instead the situation shown in Figure 17.3?

In terms of the graphs, shifting the crossing-point to the left, by increasing the level of the approach gradient, necessarily raises the *height* of the crossing-point. Whether that has any behavioral implications is left unclear in the model. We could speculate, however, that the relative height of the crossing-point reflects "severity of conflict." Thus, when two relatively weak tendencies cross, a relatively weak conflict results; as the strength of the tendencies increases so too does the intensity of the resulting conflict. With respect to the occurrence of vacillation or behavioral arrest, severity of conflict may be irrelevant. However, the emotional concomitants of conflict may still vary with the levels of the two tendencies and hence with the height of the crossing-point. For example, you may want a piece of cake for

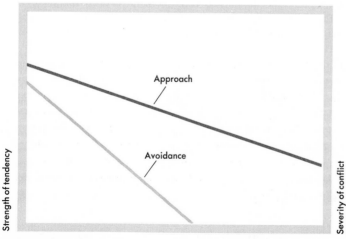

Figure 17.2 Graphic model of competing approach-avoidance tendencies where the conflict has been resolved by raising the height of the approach curve so that it does not intersect the avoidance curve.

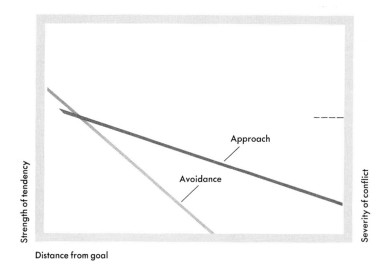

Strength of tendency

Distance from goal

Approach

Avoidance

Severity of conflict

Figure 17.3 The height of the approach curve has been raised over that in Figure 17.1, but not enough to keep the approach and avoidance curves from intersecting; the outcome is not a resolution of the conflict but an increase in severity of the conflict (compare the heights of the crossing points here and in Figure 17.1).

dessert but also be apprehensive about calories. These two tendencies may interact to generate a genuine conflict, but its emotional concomitants would be mild compared with those aroused by the conflict in a soldier who is about to kill his first enemy.

Should the above argument prove valid, then it would follow that attempts to resolve conflicts of the approach-avoidance type, either through raising the motivation underlying the approach tendency or through increasing the positive incentive value of the goal, are not to be made lightly. If the attempt fails, the individual caught up in the conflict will suffer even greater emotional stress than originally. This phenomenon may explain the anxiety often observed in persons in the early stages of psychotherapy. En route to the resolution of some of their inner conflicts they may be forced to undergo increasingly severe conflict. Once the feared goal is attainable (an appropriate marriage partner, the ability to act aggressively, or what have you), then its negative aspects can be extinguished or at least reduced to realistic levels. But the price of ultimate reduction in conflict may be a prolonged period of increase in its severity.

CONFLICTING MOTIVES AND/OR INCENTIVES

In an approach-avoidance conflict, there is one object with both positive and negative valence. Conflict may also be induced by two or more incentives that demand incompatible responses. Just as you cannot simultaneously move toward and away from a single object (unless you happen to be on a circular path), so too you cannot approach two objects at the same time if they are spatially separated.

Approach-Approach Conflicts. We can identify, then, a class of conflict known as approach-approach. The classic, if inadequate, example is the jackass that starved to death between two bales of hay. As we shall see, however, a pure approach-approach conflict is not likely to result in permanent behavioral arrest.

Graphically, we can represent an approach-approach conflict as in Figure 17.4. Each curve in the graph stands for the tendency to approach one of the goals. At the point of intersection the two tendencies are equal, and that is where a true behavioral conflict can be said to arise. Anywhere else along the abscissa one of the tendencies is stronger than the other, so that the net effect is an approach response.

An approach-approach conflict is clearly a case of a highly *unstable* equilibrium. Once the individual moves off the crossing-point the conflict is resolved. Indeed, the approach response becomes increasingly vigorous as the individual moves farther from the crossing-point. Contrast this with the approach-avoidance conflict, where the subject is increasingly impelled back to the crossing-point the farther away from it he is. All that is necessary to resolve an approach-approach conflict is to move the individual momentarily off the crossing-point. This can result simply from a small fluctuation in the relative evaluation of the two goal objects or, more concretely, simply by a slight physical displacement of the individual or one of the goal objects. That is why the example of the starving jackass is a poor one.

According to the above analysis, a pure approach-approach conflict would be characterized by behavioral arrest but a minimum of vacillation. And since there is only one point where behavioral arrest can occur, the probability of observing a true approach-approach conflict is very low. We often do, however, see people stuck in what looks like an approach-approach conflict, for instance, a woman who cannot choose between two suitors or a professor who has great difficulty in choosing between two job offers. Such conflicts are frequent. To the extent that vacillation occurs they do not fit the simple approach-approach paradigm.

Figure 17.4 Graphic model of an approach-approach conflict. Once off the crossing point the individual can move freely to one of the two goals (A or B).

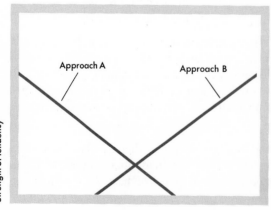

Double Approach-Avoidance Conflicts. To handle such cases, we invoke a third class of conflict, the *double approach-avoidance* conflict. Here, each goal object has negative as well as positive valence, as shown graphically in Figure 17.5. These circumstances produce stable equilibrium, and resolution of the conflict requires drastic modification in the values of the four tendencies.

The major difference we find between a single and a double approach-avoidance conflict is that in the latter the individual is likely to swing, or *oscillate*, violently between the two

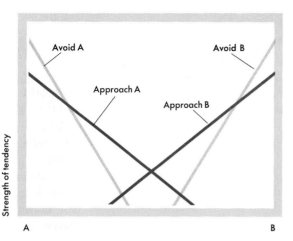

Figure 17.5 Graphic model of a double approach-avoidance conflict.

points where a negative and a positive tendency cross.

Consider the woman who is being courted by two suitors. Each is proposing marriage, but she cannot make up her mind which to accept. Both men are very attractive to her. Her inability to make a choice, however, indicates that each man also has negative qualities—that the situation can be described as a double approach-avoidance conflict. The woman might favor one of her suitors for a while, spend a great deal of time with him, and come close to saying "yes." And then abruptly, as she gets close enough to the "goal" to be repelled by that suitor's negative features, she may refuse to see him and begin exclusively to date his rival.

Of course, the above example presupposes that the men in the case remain passive and their incentive values, positive and negative, remain fixed. But the example is nevertheless not too far-fetched and should at least serve to illustrate what a double approach-avoidance conflict might be.

Avoidance-Avoidance Conflicts. There is a fourth class of conflict which resembles the approach-avoidance and double approach-avoidance types in having stable equilibrium, the *avoidance-avoidance* conflict, depicted in Figure 17.6. In this type, the individual is pushed away by one negative incentive, but as a consequence encounters and is repelled by a second negative incentive, much like a ping-pong ball being batted back and forth across the net. There is, however, an important difference between the avoidance-avoidance conflict and the two other types that are characterized by stable equilibrium. Note that both the approach-avoidance and the double approach-avoidance conflicts have built into them a source of attraction for the individual, which keeps him in the situation, that is, the positive value of the goal or goals. In the avoidance-avoidance case, there is no such attractive force. What then keeps the individual from leaving the situation entirely? Clearly, for an avoidance-avoidance conflict to be operative, the individual must be confined spa-

Figure 17.6 Graphic model of an avoidance-avoidance conflict.

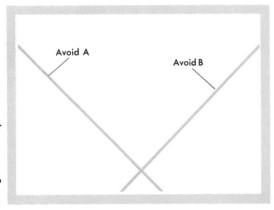

tially so that his movements can take place only "on a line" between the two negative incentives. Should he get off that line, the two negative tendencies would combine to propel him away from them and out of the conflict situation. Squeezed on both sides he might very well "pop up into the air."

Obviously, then, additional factors must be present before two negative incentives can combine to create a lasting conflict. Those factors take the form of barriers, whether physical or psychological, or both, that keep the individual constrained within the field. For example, for a college student caught between two negative incentives, studying for a difficult examination and failing the course, both alternatives have high negative valence. What makes this a true conflict is the presence of additional forces which keep him from simply "dropping out"—perhaps parental pressure, fear of the draft, or a genuine desire to get an education. An avoidance-avoidance conflict can be resolved in either of two ways: (1) One of the negative incentives must be reduced to a tolerable level, either objectively or through some sort of subjective re-evaluation, or (2) the barriers to leaving the situation must be removed.

CONFLICTING COGNITIONS

In the two categories of conflict discussed so far—the one involving positive and negative valence of a single goal object, the other multiple motives and goal objects—the individual is confronted with responses that are physically incompatible.

In other situations, conflict may entail, not incompatible, *overt* responses, but covert elements—that is, ideas or attitudes, or generally, *cognitions*—which do not demand overt behaviors. Conflict of this sort can be quite potent, however, and have behavioral consequences.

The Theory of Cognitive Dissonance. Several models have been proposed to deal with the problem of conflicting, or unbalanced, cognitions (see, for example, Brown, 1962; Rosenberg and Hovland, 1960). One of these, the *theory of cognitive dissonance,* has proven especially fruitful, though controversial, and will serve here as the vehicle for introducing this type of material. The theory was originally formulated by Leon Festinger (1957) and has since been developed and extended by him and others (see, for example, Brehm and Cohen, 1962; Brehm, 1962; Lawrence and Festinger, 1962).

A favorite illustration of the genesis and consequences of cognitive dissonance is the heavy smoker who has been exposed to the argument that smoking may contribute to a variety of diseases, including cancer, and to premature death. Wherein lies the conflict? The person has these two basic cognitions: (1) "I am a heavy smoker of cigarettes." (2) "Cigarette smoking is deleterious to my health." These two elements are part of a general cognitive framework that also includes the important idea: "I act in my own self-interest," or "I am a rational person." Given the assumption that his behavior is rational, how does the person reconcile the other two cognitions? It makes no sense to engage in an act that he knows is not in the best interest of his own health.

The theory of cognitive dissonance asserts that the presence of incompatible cognitions is tension-inducing; as with any tension, a person will seek ways of reducing it. How might the dissonance-induced tension of the heavy smoker be decreased? Several possible solutions are available. For example, he could stop smoking. However, a powerful habit is hard to break just in order to relieve one source of tension, since the habitual behavior itself is undoubtedly providing considerable gratification.

Other alternatives, requiring few, if any, changes in overt behavior, involve changes in cognition. He could convince himself that the evidence linking smoking and ill health is imperfect—as was indeed pointed out in Chapter Two. The data are still primarily correlational and therefore subject to more than one interpretation. In minimizing dissonance through discrediting the evidence, he could also seek information that would help rationalize the continuation of smoking, for example, assertions that smoking is a way of relaxing and thereby conducive to mental if not physical health. While vigilantly seeking out information that supports the behavior, he might also be careful to avoid dissonance-inducing information.

Or, he could accept the evidence, but detract from its significance by calling to mind all the other ways in which one can fall ill or lose one's life. Considered as just one small element in a large collection of dangerous, everyday events—such as driving a car, crossing a street, breathing polluted air, indeed leaving one's house at night—the particular importance of smoking begins to pale. It turns out, incidentally, that the preferred mode of dissonance-reduction in this context is to minimize the danger to *oneself*, while accepting the dangers of smoking to people in general (Pervin and Yatko, 1965).

Quite clearly, dissonance-inducing cognitions can have wide-ranging effects, overt and covert. It happens that the theory was developed as a means of accounting for certain social-psychological phenomena, and probably for that reason research on dissonance theory has been largely the province of social psychologists. But the theory itself has considerable generality. Some examples of experiments conducted to test predictions from dissonance theory are sketched below; they have been selected to illustrate the wide variety of its applications.

When Prophecy Fails. One of the situations which first intrigued Festinger, and motivated development of the theory, is suggested by the title of a popular book written in 1956 by Festinger, Riecken, and Schachter, "When Prophecy Fails." The book concerns a religious sect that grew up around a woman who claimed to receive messages from "above." Chief among the messages was one which prophesied the end of the world on a particular date. True believers would be saved, however, if they appeared at a certain location whence they would be whisked away in a flying saucer. Many members of the group accepted the prophecy, sold their belongings, and showed up at the appointed time and place. But the saucer never came, and the world went right on as before.

What would be the state of one of the faithful, who has divested himself of his property and stood in the cold of a Chicago winter for several hours, without external compulsion, and all for naught. With that much of a stake in an action, it would be a great blow to self-esteem simply to admit to having been, at best, foolish. There are, however, other alternatives; the one taken by the group seems to be fairly typical of such situations. Whereas, prior to the day on which the prophecy failed, the group made very little effort to get publicity or to win converts, once the dissonance-inducing event had occurred there was a considerable increase in proselyting activity. Newspaper reporters were called in and given interviews, and in general the members of the group who had not defected (some had) were more than ever convinced of the truth of their revelation. In brief, the failure of the prophecy enhanced belief and resulted in the attempt to gain additional support for the belief by bringing in new members. Finally, the failure of the prophecy itself was explained away as a test of the members' faith, and a new date was set for the end of the world. Needless to say, the second prophecy also failed. What happened then need not be discussed here; it is neatly told by Festinger and his co-authors, who had observed the proceedings of the group, having passed themselves off as believers.

For our purposes, and Festinger's, the crucial point is the way in which dissonance was reduced through a renewal of faith and especially through attempts at getting social support for what by themselves are highly untenable ideas. By surrounding oneself with people who hold to the same ideas it is possible to mitigate the otherwise potent dissonance-inducing effects of those ideas. In this sense, other people serve as sources of information, and when their beliefs coincide with one's own, they provide a welcome milieu in which to be immersed. It is very likely that many groups identified with "kooky" positions serve this function for their members. No wonder that many social psychologists, who are interested in the nature of groups and in the interactions between individuals and groups, find the dissonance concept so appealing.

Induction of Dissonance through Initiation Ceremonies. Many groups put new members through some sort of initiation ceremony. This is particularly true of religious groups; the initiation may occur as early as the first week after birth, as in the Jewish rite of circumcision, or at one or more points during childhood and adolescence, as with confirmation or the Bar Mitzvah. Fraternal and service organizations have their own forms of initiation rituals. Very often the neophyte is put through considerable embarrassment, and frequently the experience is physically painful, as in the hazing in many college fraternities or the basic training of military organizations. What is the function of these ceremonies, especially those that are punitive? And why is it that a person who is severely paddled, or deposited naked late at night on a lonely road far from home, or made to undergo some humiliating and degrading experience does not end up hating those who inflicted the punishment on him? Some, of course, do. But the typical result of initiation ceremonies is to generate a great deal of loyalty toward the group, if not toward the tormentors themselves.

Again, dissonance theory provides a convincing answer. The cognitive elements in conflict are these: "I, who am (1) a *rational, self-respecting person,* have (2) with virtually *no coercion* allowed myself to be subjected to a very (3) *unpleasant experience* so that I might (4) be granted membership in this *group*." But why, of his own "free will," would a sensible person submit to punishment? Membership in the group, the goal of that instrumental act, must be of considerable value. Hence, the more extreme the punishment the more valuable must be the group. The dissonance generated by the initiation ceremony is thus reduced by enhancing the perceived value of group membership. Clearly, then, one function of the initiation ceremony is to create in the members of the group a strong attachment to it. This function may not be known to the participants—the initiation ceremony may just be an unquestioned part of the group's tradition—and it may not be the only function served by the initiation procedure (which may indeed satisfy certain sadistic needs of the group members). Nevertheless, dissonance-induction, with the resulting increase in the value of the group, would seem to be a major reason for the survival of such procedures.

Several experiments have been done to test the prediction from dissonance theory that the greater the negative valence associated with an instrumental act *freely* engaged in, the greater will be the perceived value of the goal. Note that we are not asserting the trivial, that the greater the perceived value of the goal, the more "punishment" the person will accept in order to achieve the goal. The increase in the goal's perceived value follows the act; it does not precede the act. In the words of proponents of dissonance theory, it is a theory about postdecisional conflict, not predecisional conflict.

In one direct test (Aronson and Mills, 1959) of the dissonance account of the initiation ceremony, female college students, who had volunteered to participate in a "group discussion," were first engaged in an embarrassing interview by the experimenter, centering on sexual matters. They then listened to what they thought was a group discussion; in fact they heard a tape recording of a discussion. The material on the tapes was designed to be quite dull, and yet when the girls who had undergone the "initiation" procedure were asked to rate the discussion, they gave it more positive evaluations than did control subjects who had not undergone the embarrassing interview.

In such experiments the theory demands a minimum of perceived coercion on the part of the subjects. If they felt that their participation in a distasteful or difficult situation was forced on them, then an alternate route to dissonance-reduction would be opened; that is, they could justify their suffering on the grounds that they had no choice. There would be no need, in that case, to modify their evaluation of the task or of the goal of whatever their instrumental activity happened to be.

Forced Compliance. Coercion can take several forms. One is to offer a person an extrinsic reward, such as money, for his performance. If he is paid a substantial sum to do something unpleasant, dissonance will not be induced, or if it is, it will quickly be dissipated by reference to the large reward he received for participating.

Experiments on the effects of *forced compliance* have yielded mixed results. One set of studies takes off on a procedure in which subjects are asked, with minimal coercion to comply, to write an essay in which they make as strong a case as they can for a position on some issue which is the opposite of their own position, that is, a *counterattitudinal* essay. For example, if the issue is capital punishment, those who are opposed to capital punishment write in its favor, while those who support it write against it. The expectation, and it is borne out by the results (Cohen, Brehm, and Fleming, 1958), is that writing such an essay will move a person away from his original position, toward that upheld in the essay. You might see an analogy between this procedure and the use of false confessions in the attempted conversion of prisoners of war.

It would seem to be a straightforward prediction from dissonance theory that the effectiveness of this manipulation would be greatly diminished if subjects felt compelled to comply with the request to write or speak in a manner inconsistent with their own attitudes or beliefs. In particular, subjects given a large monetary reward for such utterances should show less change in attitude than those given a small reward. Yet this prediction seems to run counter to reinforcement theory, which holds that a large reward more effectively stamps in preceding behavior than a small reward.

In one of the early tests of the dissonance-theory prediction (Festinger and Carlsmith, 1959), the experimenter asked subjects in what was a very dull experiment to tell the next person waiting to serve that the experiment was quite interesting. The "waiting subject" was actually a confederate of the experimenters. The true subjects were induced to lie to him by being told that the assistant who was hired to mislead the waiting subjects had failed to show up; since the assistant was paid for the job, the subject would get the same pay, if he could be called on for future assignments. It was found that those subjects given $1 to carry out the instructions (to tell a "fellow student" that the dull experiment was interesting and exciting) showed a greater positive change in their evaluation of the experiment than did those paid $20 to tell the same lie.

A flurry of criticism followed the Festinger and Carlsmith study. For example, it was argued that $20 was so large an amount for so simple a task that it must have aroused the subjects' suspicions and induced effects unrelated to dissonance theory. To counter this argument, Arthur Cohen (1962) performed a similar experiment, using the essay writing procedure and smaller incentives ($.50, $1.00, $5.00, and $10.00), and found the predicted inverse relation between magnitude of reward and amount of attitude change. In this study, the subjects were Yale students and they were asked, in their own rooms, to write essays in support of the New Haven police. The less they were paid the more favorable they became in their attitude toward their perennial enemy.

Some subsequent experiments have yielded just the opposite result (for example, Rosenberg, 1965; Janis and Gilmore, 1965; Elms and Janis, 1965), while some have partly replicated the original findings (for example, Nuttin, 1966). Close examination of these many experiments reveals some obvious procedural differences, which may have contributed to the disparate results. In one attempt to tease out the relevant procedural differences (Carlsmith, Collins, and Helmreich, 1966), the experimenters found that they could replicate the original result (greater change through lesser reward) if the subject's behavior was overt and occurred in a face-to-face encounter with a fellow student who trusted him. However, if the subjects wrote out their counterattitudinal statements to be read only by the experimenter, then the opposite effect was found—the greater the reward, the greater the change in attitude. These results are illustrated in Figure 17.7. Note that three incentive values were used, $.50, $1.00, and $5.00.

Carlsmith, Collins, and Helmreich ask why their essay experiment produced the direct relation between attitude change and amount of incentive, contrary to the results of the very similar experiment by Cohen (1962). Although they offer no definitive answer, they do point out that in both conditions the subjects receiving the $5.00 reward felt "in a better mood" than the other subjects; this mood effect might very well have generalized to cover the perceived "interestingness" of the experiment. If so, it would work opposite to the dissonance-related effect in the face-to-face condition, suggesting that the dissonance-induced effect was even greater than it appears to be.

Although we are obviously dealing with complex and somewhat slippery situations, it is clear that dissonance (by that or any other name) is a potent variable. To illustrate further the broad applicability of the concept, we

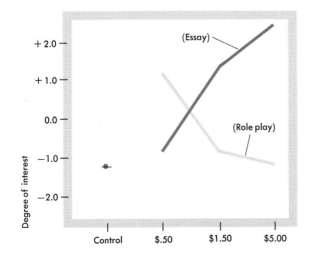

Figure 17.7 Evaluation of an intrinsically dull task by subjects who were either paid various amounts to write that it was interesting (Essay) or to say so to a fellow student (Role play). (From Carlsmith, Collins, and Helmreich, 1966.)

mention one further experiment, this one by M. L. Brehm, K. W. Back, and M. D. Bogdenoff (1964). Subjects who were deprived of food and felt very hungry agreed with minimal coercion to continue going without food for several additional hours. These subjects were contrasted with a group given a very strong pitch to prolong their food-deprivation experience. The expectation from dissonance theory was that more dissonance would be created in the former than the latter group.

How might the dissonance ("I am very hungry and have just agreed to go without food for an additional period of time") be resolved? The subjects can re-evaluate the degree of their hunger. Perhaps they are really not so hungry as they thought they were and a few more hours without food will not be hard to take. And that apparently is what happens. Hunger level declines following their commitment to continue the deprivation—when that commitment is given under conditions of minimal justification. The most exciting result of this study is that the presumed decrease in hunger was manifested not only phenomenally but also *physiologically*. Blood samples were taken from the subjects at various times and amounts in the blood of free fatty acid (which varies directly with hunger level) were assessed; in the low-coercion group, the amount of free fatty acid declined following the subjects' commitment to extend the deprivation period. Thus, added to the types of cognitive reorganization that are induced by cognitive dissonance there is a direct effect on a physiological process. (An impressive set of similar experiments has been reported by Philip Zimbardo, 1969.)

CONFLICTING IMPULSES AND CONTROLS

There are many things people want to do, at least momentarily, but do not do. The presence of an "impulse" without a corresponding overt act suggests the operation of some sort of conflict. For example, a student may be impelled to cheat on an examination by copying his neighbor's answer to a problem, but he does not. Or, to repeat an example used in an earlier chapter, a mother may have the impulse to smother her crying baby, but, usually, she does not do so. We could relegate these examples to the category of conflicting motives ("I want to do X and I want to do Y, but X and Y are incompatible"), but there is something about them which suggests special consideration.

We are dealing here with what might be called a conflict between impulse and control. For many theorists, controls are more than additional impulses, although an exact specification of the distinction is not easy to come by. Everyday language, however, readily accommodates the distinction. Consider the connotative difference between these two assertions: (1) "I do not want to steal money from the blind man," and (2) "I should not steal money from the blind man." The first statement has a casual aura about it; it conveys no more intensity of conviction than the statement "I do not want any dessert" or "I do not want to take a bath today." Perhaps tomorrow "I" will want dessert, and perhaps under other circumstances "I" will want to steal from the blind man. But when "I do not want to" is replaced by "I should not," what then? The latter phrase conveys an aura of depth of feeling, intensity of conviction, and reliability. It would be extremely unlikely that tomorrow would bring a change of mind: "I should steal money from the blind man."

What seems to be involved here, then, is a degree of firmness that is missing from the usual run of impulses or motives. Of course, even those controls that constitute *conscience* can be overcome by sufficiently strong impulses. A man whose children are starving may, indeed, steal the money from the blind man in order to buy bread for his children (though here perhaps we have introduced a case of one control taking precedence over another: "I should not let my children suffer" is more potent than "I should not steal, especially from one so helpless as a blind man").

Guilt and Violation of Controls. When violations of this type of control occur, they reveal in still another way the special nature of these controls. Typically, such violations are followed by a unique emotional response, *guilt*. If one motive wins out over another (you eat the dessert so that you will not displease the hostess), no guilt is aroused. You may be a little angry at the hostess for insisting that you share her cake, or at yourself for so easily succumbing to social pressure when you really did not want to eat the dessert, but you would feel no guilt. You might even engage in some cognitive reorganization, as dissonance theory would expect, and end up deciding that the cake was exceptionally good and that you actually were still hungry, without knowing it. But violate a moral proscription and watch the consequences. There may be some hostility directed at yourself, your children, society, even at the blind man, but if you steal his money, you will also feel guilty. The anticipation of guilt is a powerful deterrent.

The controls that enter into conflict with impulses are thus sufficiently different from impulses themselves to warrant special mention in this section of the chapter. Their nature, their origin, and their impact on a person's total functioning are issues of such considerable importance, however, that they deserve more than passing mention. Indeed, it is generally accepted that much of human psychopathology stems from conflicts of the present sort, rather than from the relatively trivial conflicts around incompatible goals or inconsistent cognitions with which we have so far been concerned. The next section of this chapter, then, is devoted to a more elaborate treatment of what we have been calling conflict between impulses and controls and of the potential psychopathological consequences of such conflicts. As mentioned at the outset of this chapter, the orientation of what follows is psychoanalytic, although we will attempt to remain as close as possible to empirical observations. A more theoretical presentation of these and related issues is reserved for the next chapter.

UNCONSCIOUS ELEMENTS IN CONFLICT

We have proceeded through our entire discussion of affect, motivation, and conflict without referring explicitly to an assumption which lies at the heart of the psychoanalytic view of these processes. This is the assumption that people are unaware of many fantasies, ideas, impulses, controls, and conflicts. These psychological events are known only by inference. In Freudian terminology, these inferred events reside in a "part" of the mind called the unconscious, though Freud's topography should not be taken literally. To speak of *the unconscious*, as Freud does, is to use a convenient fiction; one would not go looking for the unconscious with an electrode or a microscope. Nevertheless, to be safe we will avoid reference to the unconscious since it is so easy to slip into the error of endowing that fiction with tangible reality. Allusion to "unconscious events" should not pose the same danger.

According to psychoanalytic theory, there are unconscious impulses that, if uninhibited, would be expressed in behavior. These unconscious impulses are potent and troublesome—troublesome because there are equally potent unconscious barriers to their translation into overt behavior. In short, a continual conflict is being waged within the individual among combatants he knows about, if at all, only by hearsay—that is, through what psychoanalytic thinkers have to say about them.

One of the difficulties, incidentally, in presenting the notion of an unconscious wish or impulse or fantasy is that convincing, concrete illustration is virtually precluded; much of what we write about you can check against your own experience or against some figure provided in the text. But if we write of an unconscious impulse, the wish to "X," where is the "X" in your experience to check our example against? If "X" is well chosen you will not be aware of its presence within yourself. You may well be skeptical and resistant from here on out; but we will go on anyway, since the ideas being presented have had a great impact not only on psychological theory but also on modern drama, literature, and art. And they may even be valid.

PSYCHOANALYTIC MODELS

As we noted in Chapter Four, psychoanalytic theory is a composite of three interrelated models. The development of personality is accounted for in the *genetic* model. The classification of processes into levels of awareness (conscious, preconscious, unconscious) is made within the *topographic* model. In the *structural* model three major "institutions" of the mental apparatus are postulated. Unconscious impulses are "contained" within the *id*. The prohibitions against expression of these impulses "reside" in the *superego*, a sort of "unconscious conscience." Finally, the ego consists of the various sensory, cognitive, and motoric functions (the functions on which academic psychology has primarily focused) that mediate among the demands of id, superego, and external reality. To use a political analogy the ego corresponds to the executive branch of government, the id loosely to the legislative branch (which issues orders—that is, laws—for the executive to put into effect), and the superego to the Supreme Court, which oversees the appropriateness of proposed demands and their execution.

The ego, though largely conscious, also has its unconscious components. According to the theory, the ego includes the *defense mechanisms*, but these functions operate outside of awareness.

Types of Unconscious Conflict. As for conflict, it occurs among three classes of unconscious elements: (1) id impulses, which demand immediate and total gratification, (2) superego demands, which are rigid and uncompromising in prohibiting the vast majority of id impulses, and (3) the unconscious defense mechanisms of the ego, which not only keep the id impulses unconscious so that they do not overwhelm the conscious ego, but also provide some means of safe expression in disguised or indirect fashion.

The "controls" to which we have repeatedly referred consist of both the unconscious proscriptions of the superego and the unconscious defense mechanism of the ego. It is the effective operation of these controls that, according to the theory, assures the healthy functioning of the individual. Ineffective operation of the controls can arise either from insufficient development or from excessively severe application.

DEFENSE MECHANISMS

Lists of defense mechanisms vary from author to author. The basic identification of the major defenses was made by Freud, though even his system of classifying and weighing the importance of specific mechanisms fluctuated during the development of his thinking. His daughter, Anna Freud, has provided a statement of the topic from an orthodox psychoanalytic point of view in her book *The Ego and the Mechanisms of Defenses.* What follows is based on her presentation.

Repression. If any one defense mechanism is accorded special importance by all theorists, it is surely the mechanism that Freud called *repression.* This is the device whereby unacceptable, taboo impulses and ideas are prevented from entering a person's awareness. Repression having occurred, then the other mechanisms can also come into play. Repression is thus central to the total defensive structure.

The function of repression is to keep unconscious any ideas or impulses that would, if allowed to enter awareness, flood the ego with anxiety and thereby render it ineffectual. These ideas might either (1) originate within and be intrinsic to the id (the unacceptable impulses and fantasies we have alluded to but not yet identified) or (2) stem from specific traumatic events that were so painful that they cannot be allowed to continue as conscious memories. The latter type was once conscious but has been pushed into unconsciousness and maintained there through the operation of the repression mechanism. But what makes events "traumatic" and therefore worthy of repression? The theory asserts that no conscious event would in itself sufficiently provoke anxiety so as to require repressing if it were not in some way related to already existing unconscious conflicts. It is because the event has the potential for arousing repressed ideas that it is "traumatic."

Clearly, we need an example here. Dramatic instances of repressed traumatic experience have been found in soldiers who, having engaged in violent combat, with great loss of life on both sides, suffer amnesia for the period covering this highly frightening episode. They simply do not and cannot recall their participation in the traumatic event. The amnesia itself is a major symptom of the experience, and it may be accompanied by additional, related symptoms, which perhaps render such a soldier incapable of further duty. Without these additional symptoms (perhaps the soldier cannot get out of bed, or cannot hold and fire a rifle, or cannot see clearly), we might argue that his memory of the traumatic event had simply been obliterated or erased, as it might be through application of an electric current or a scalpel to just the right part of his brain. What is evident, however, is that despite his inability to remember the episode, its effects are still being felt, as manifested by his other pathological behaviors. The theory would argue that the memory of the traumatic event has not been "erased" but repressed. By implication, therefore, the event is still represented in the psychic apparatus, but has been stripped of its conscious aspect and is being maintained in that condition through active inhibition by the repression mechanism. This argument might be further bolstered by the demonstration that under hypnosis or under the influence of certain drugs, such as sodium amytol, the "forgotten" events can be remembered.

As to the question of why that particular combat episode had to be repressed for that particular soldier, the theory would insist—a convincing demonstration would require reference to all the facts of a real, rather than a hypothetical, case history—that the soldier reacted as he did because, for example, the wounding, maiming, and killing he witnessed and took part in touched unconscious aggressive and destructive impulses within him. These impulses might relate to hostility directed at other people and also toward himself (the "death wish," or Thanatos proposed by Freud to help account for the horrors of World War I). Thus, to begin to become aware in oneself of such unacceptable impulses as the wish to destroy others and perhaps even oneself under the prodding of battlefield experience is to call up one's most powerful defensive maneuvers. The episode must be repressed if it is not to set off a train of uncontrollable ideas and fantasies that would overwhelm the ego and render it incapable of functioning.

Total amnesia for recent events, no matter how traumatic, is probably quite rare. However, partial forgetting or distortion of significant features of affect-laden episodes is undoubtedly a rather frequent occurrence. Witnesses of crimes or accidents, for example, are notoriously unreliable reporters. And recall how often people have come away from a heated discussion with entirely different versions of what was said by whom.

Along with these lapses or distortions in memory, people often fail to perceive certain obvious features of an object or scene that are presumably threatening to the tenuous balance of their inner conflicts. Two little girls, for example, overheard their mother chuckling over the picture of a doll in a toy catalog. They asked what was funny and were shown the picture. Both girls, thoroughly sophisticated for their age about sex, through verbal explanation and through casual exposure to their baby brother, studied the picture of the doll and expressed considerable puzzlement about their mother's reaction to it. When asked what was different about the doll, the girls looked again and finally volunteered, somewhat hesitantly as though not really satisfied with their own answer, that it had long hair. "Is it a boy or a girl?" asked their mother. Taking another look, they answered, "A girl, because it has long hair." What they apparently did not see was that the doll had male genitals, a novelty of such magnitude that it should have immediately captured their attention.

One major consequence of repression, only indirectly alluded to so far, is the sensory or motor impairments that are the symptoms of *hysteria*. It was, indeed, the hysterical symptoms of many of his *neurotic* patients that set Freud off on his theoretical adventure. He saw patients with anesthesias, for example, or with paralyses for which no physical etiology could be traced. Freud came to understand that these somatic symptoms were the manifestation of partially repressed impulses, often aroused by highly charged events in the early life of his patients. For example, in the book by Breuer and Freud, *Studies in Hysteria,* the case of Elizabeth R. is reported. Freud was able to trace her prominent symptom, pain in the thigh and some difficulty in walking, to a series of episodes involving her father, her sick sister, and her brother-in-law with whom she was unconsciously in love. According to Freud, her unconscious erotic fantasies—which engendered unconscious guilt—were severely repressed and replaced by the somatic symptoms, which were both punitive and symbolically expressive of particular aspects of the events associated with her case.

In the sense that hysterical symptoms of a somatic variety provide an opportunity, albeit disguised, for the partial expression of repressed ideas, they might be thought of as contributing to the total defensive structure. On the other hand, we might view the symptoms simply as the outcome of inadequate defensive maneuvers. In any event, when hysterical symptoms appear, they usually do so in the context of a defensive structure based largely on repression. It is of further interest that the hysterical person very often presents a remarkable degree of unconcern about, or indifference to, his symptoms, a further example, perhaps, of repression serving to neutralize those elements of conflict that have "slipped past" the repression barrier.

Many attempts have been made to demonstrate perceptual effects of the mechanism of repression under controlled laboratory conditions. Two types of possible effect are suggested by the theory. One is the type illustrated above, whereby elements of a stimulus complex are not perceived or are distorted; these failures to detect, recognize, or clearly perceive potentially threatening stimuli are referred to as *perceptual defense*. But such a defense implies another operation, for if a person is successfully to prevent certain items from entering awareness, he must be especially sensitive to them, so that they cannot elude the defensive system. This operation is called *perceptual vigilance*.

Thus, to the exasperation of people who like to think in simpler terms, the theory makes the seemingly paradoxical prediction that threatening stimuli will be both easier and harder to perceive. Of course, a complete prediction would specify under what conditions either vigilance or defense would prevail. Unfortunately, the theory is not sufficiently well developed for that essential degree of precision. In much of the research done on this problem, the issue has been ignored, and in some the experimenter's persuasiveness has substituted for clear-cut deductive rigor.

A good example of an attempt to demonstrate perceptual effects of repression is provided in one of the first experiments done on this problem that was both methodologically sound and sophisticated in its application of the psychoanalytic concept of defense (Blum, 1954). Blum argued that if threatening stimuli were presented in very brief exposures and if the subject's task only minimally engaged the rational, discriminating, problem-solving functions of the ego, then those stimuli would elicit perceptual vigilance. However, if exposure duration were increased to a value near the recognition threshold of the stimuli and if the subject's task demanded a high level of ego functioning, then threatening stimuli should arouse the defensive maneuvers that would keep them from awareness. Thus, vigilance is expected when interaction of the stimuli and the conscious portions of the ego is minimal and defense is expected when the contact between stimuli and ego is great enough to initiate the anxiety that signals danger to the ego.

Blum's experiment was run in two parts. In the first part, where vigilance was predicted, a set of four pictures was presented at a brief exposure duration; the subjects were asked simply to indicate which picture "stood out the most." The pictures were arranged in a cross, with one at the top of a rectangular background surface, one at the bottom, one left and one right, and the subject's response was to say "top," "bottom," "left," or "right." The pictures themselves were taken from a personality test developed by Blum—the Blacky Test, in which the characters are the dog "Blacky" and his canine family. Each picture in the Blacky Test was devised to tap some area presumed to be sensitive to conflict (for people, of course). For example, in one scene Blacky is depicted licking his genitals; in another he is about to have his tail cut off (designed to arouse anxiety about castration, which according to the psychoanalytic genetic model is of great concern to preschool children and leaves a residue in the adult). Blum picked one such picture likely to be unconsciously threatening to male subjects and a different one for females. He predicted that these pictures would be selected as "standing out the most" at greater than chance frequency under the vigilance-inducing conditions. That result was obtained when the data were analyzed for male and female subjects separately.

In the second part of the experiment, in which perceptual defense was predicted, the exposure duration was increased, and the active participation of the ego was sought by introducing a problem-solving task. That is, the subject was shown the threatening picture alone, for a long time, and then was asked to locate it when flashed on the screen along with three others. To further engage unconscious defensive processes, Blum had each person look at the threatening picture between the two experiments and recall a situation in his own experience of which it reminded him. In the second experiment, as predicted, the threatening picture was correctly located less frequently than a comparable, but less threatening picture.

In suggesting that hypervigilance for id-related material is to be expected along with defensive action to keep it from conscious awareness, we attributed the vigilance to the defensive structure itself. To defend against the enemy you must be constantly on the lookout for him. However, vigilance has another source, and that is within the id itself. As mentioned, the id impulses are continually "striving" for expression, preferably directly, but if thwarted, then indirectly. Psychoanalytic theory assumes that the id seeks out external events that promise to provide disguised and therefore effective routes for the partial expression of id impulses. Thus, not only the defensive structure of the ego but also the id is vigilant for id-related stimulation, especially if it comes in disguised, distorted, hidden, innocent-looking form. The id is assumed to make use of such stimuli for its own purposes. This notion is quite clearly presented in Freud's theory of dreams, where it is asserted that the content of dreams is composed of fragments of trivial events of the preceding day called *day-residues*. These events are trivial, however, only in the sense that their relation to id impulses and fantasies is not apparent to the dreamer's ego; that is, they look innocuous and they are on the surface, but at a deeper level they are id-relevant and therefore provide a vehicle for the expression of id impulses.

Attempts to test this general conception experimentally have taken several forms. Typically, they fall under the rubric of "subliminal stimulation." In such research, stimuli that go undetected, or unnoticed, or unrecognized by a subject are shown nevertheless to have some impact on his behavior.

In one set of experiments, originating with the work of a psychiatrist, Charles Fisher (for example, Fisher, 1954; Fisher and Paul, 1959), complex scenes were presented to subjects fast enough to preclude clear recognition of the items in the pictures. Following that procedure, the subjects were asked to return to the laboratory the next day and to report whatever dreams they had during the intervening night; they were also to draw pictures of any salient images in their dreams. Comparison of the dream images with the pictures convinced the experimenter, at least, that elements of the scenes had been incorporated into the dreams in many instances, as illustrated in Figure 17.8.

Figure 17.8 The upper picture was presented tachistoscopically. The two lower pictures are drawings made by subjects to illustrate dreams they had on the night following their exposure to the picture. (Courtesy C. Fisher, 1954.)

Figure 17.9 Left to right, the neutral, "happy," and "unhappy" faces used in the experiment by Fox (1959).

Why should those particular fragmentary percepts have taken precedence over all the other possible day residues as material from which to compose the dream images? The answer is offered that the relationship between subjects and experimenter was highly charged emotionally for the subjects and was therefore a likely point for unconscious impulses to focus on. Furthermore, the dreams were reported in the same experimental setting where the stimuli were first presented; thus, it is likely that those dreams, out of the many which occur in a night, are the ones to have been recalled. The paradigm developed by Fisher has been elaborated to include better controls and more objective behavioral measures (see, for example, Shevrin and Luborsky, 1958, 1961). And the same hypothesis has been tested under somewhat different circumstances, with generally favorable results. In one type of study (Klein, Spence, Holt, and Gourevitch, 1958), emotion-laden visual stimuli, such as drawings of genitalia, were briefly presented and then masked by subsequent stimuli. Subjects' immediate responses to the masking stimuli revealed an effect of the masked, and presumably undetected, first stimuli.

In a very similar type of research (Fox, 1959), the response to a drawing of a face was influenced by subliminal lines superimposed on the face that gave it—when the lines were visible—either a happy or an unhappy appearance, as shown in Figure 17.9. The subliminality of the lines was carefully documented by proper psychophysical procedures.

Each subject (male college students were used) was tested in three conditions. In one, designed to elicit the ego's problem-solving function, the subject was given the task of selecting from a lengthy list those ten adjectives which characterized the face that was just presented. In a second, he was asked to tell what kind of a person this face might belong to; this second condition entailed a greater degree of freedom and looseness of ego functioning than the first one. The third condition was designed to encourage maximal freedom of ego functioning, so as to minimize defensiveness and thereby allow expression of any unconscious ideas triggered by the subliminal stimuli; in this third condition the subject was to report any images that came to mind, whether they were related to the face or not.

The prediction was that the effects of the subliminal stimuli would be behaviorally revealed in direct relation to the subject's freedom from the constraint of a logical, problem-solving approach; that is, the closer the experimental condition to that of the dream, the more likely that the subliminal stimuli would get into the system and then "get out" again in a form that a well-trained, sensitive judge could pick up.

Under each condition each subject saw four "happy" and four "unhappy" faces, randomly intermixed, as well as one face with no subliminal lines. Each stimulus was presented for 15 seconds, and then the response was given. As one precaution, the experimenter did not know which face the subject was seeing on any trial. Similarly, when it came time to judge the subjects' responses the raters did not know which subliminal faces had been presented.

An elaborate scoring system was devised. The judges' task for the free-description and imagery conditions was to put each subject's protocols in rank order in terms of the degree of happiness or "euphoria," expressed. If there was no subliminal effect, these rankings would be unrelated to the type of face presented. If, on the other hand, there was an effect, and the judges picked it up with perfect accuracy, then the four happy faces would have been assigned ranks 1–4, the neutral face rank 5, and the four unhappy faces rank 5–9. From a comparison of the obtained ranks with chance expectation it was determined that a significant effect of the subliminal stimuli had occurred in both the "free" conditions, but not in the least-dreamlike, adjective-selection condition (which was scored in a somewhat different, but appropriate way).

The Fox experiment has been replicated, with some additional features, by Joel Allison (1963) with remarkably similar results. These studies, along with many others too numerous to cite here, show both the tentative validity of some of the psychoanalytic conceptions, and more importantly perhaps, their accessibility to careful experimental investigation.

Denial. Through the mechanism of denial certain aspects of reality are either not accepted or are transformed into their opposites (reality may refer both to external events and to inner feelings and impulses). Denial is considered by many theorists to be the most primitive of defenses, ontogentically as well as structurally. It is a characteristic defense of the young child, who has not yet developed a superego (which is assumed to occur at about age four or five) and for whom accurate and consistent testing of reality is not yet a firmly established principle of ego functioning. The child, moreover, is encouraged to engage in denial by adults, who act, for example as though the pain from an injury can be ameliorated by a kiss. When a child cries, parents often assert firmly that there is nothing to cry about (what they mean is that nothing happened that would make an adult cry). These attempts at restoring equilibrium through denial are often quite successful, but they leave the child with a defense that is bound ultimately to be inadequate, since reality cannot always be so readily turned off.

As the child matures, and reality obtrudes, more sophisticated defenses develop, including repression and the other mechanisms to be described below. In some adults, however, denial remains a potent defense. For them, "every cloud has a silver lining." Evil, pain, ugliness, tragedy are ignored or turned into virtues. Others, falling back on denial as a temporary expedient, may use it to supplement more mature defenses. There are people who eagerly seek out activities that are, realistically, dangerous (mountain-climbing, automobile-racing) but who deny both the danger and their fear; some such people may indeed be excessively afraid of the very dangers they court but through the mechanism of denial they are enabled to engage in what is called "counterphobic" behavior. Denial is also a prominent defense of *psychopaths,* who are very adept at rationalizing their criminal, immoral, antisocial behavior.

To the extent that all defense mechanisms distort the inner reality of unconscious impulses and affects, then denial is universally present, though in a form that is neither so blatant nor so obvious as in the young child. Its use by adults as a major defense, in the form of "massive denial," suggests a degree of pathology that is found in psychotics, who are characterized by a lack of contact with reality. For example, a woman who will not accept the fact of the death of her child and continues to act as though the child is present is engaging in massive denial of psychotic proportions.

Reaction Formation. Another of the many defense mechanisms listed by psychoanalytic writers is *reaction formation;* this mechanism reflects the psychoanalytic assertion that phenotypic opposites are often genotypically identical. It also easily lends itself to abuse by amateur analysts, who can point out with great glee that the socially commendable behavior of others is really an indication of the nastiness of their underlying impulses. Reference to reaction formation is certainly the preferred put-down of the self-righteous.

In essence, reaction formation is invoked to account for behaviors that seem to stem from a given motive but are instead aroused, though unconsciously, by just the opposite motive. For example, there are people who are excessively neat; any signs of disorder, disarray, or dirt elicit compulsive attempts to get things neat and clean. Of course, there is nothing unhealthy about organization and cleanliness, but it can be carried to such extremes that it interferes with the satisfaction of more important motives. Imagine a roommate or spouse who is continually busy picking up your clothing, putting your desk in order, straightening pictures on the wall, emptying ashtrays while they are still in use—in short making any kind of relaxed and pleasant living arrangement virtually impossible. It is this kind of compulsive neatness with which we are concerned.

What does such extreme behavior suggest? It might be interpreted as reflecting a strong, unconscious need to be messy. But for reasons that the genetic model ascribes to conflicts involved in toilet training, the impulse to be messy and the enjoyment of dirt are not acceptable and must be repressed. Further to protect the ego against the anxiety elicited by hints of their continued presence, the defense of reaction formation is brought into play. "Me, messy? Why I'm a bug for cleanliness!"

Once the logic of reaction formation becomes clear, it is fun to play with it by applying it to other situations. Is the pacifist defending himself against unconscious aggressive impulses? Is the prohibitionist fighting an urge to drink alcohol? Are the "citizens for clean literature" a little too much interested in pornography, struggling against unacceptable tendencies to voyeurism and exhibitionism? What about the policeman—is he a latent criminal? Does the political reformer unconsciously revel in the corruption and dishonesty he is trying to stamp out? Is the Don Juan type expressing an unconscious terror of women?

Of course, it would be folly to make such blanket allegations about whole categories of people. In particular instances, however, with adequate data, an interpretation in terms of reaction formation might be valid. It becomes especially pertinent when the defensive maneuvers partially or temporarily break down, and the compulsively clean woman, for example, is discovered to have a corner reserved somewhere for mess, or, when, as in *Rain,* the minister who preaches against adultery allows himself to be seduced by the harlot.

Another point needs to be made here. Although it is of theoretical interest that phenotype may indicate the opposite genotype, what matters about real people living real lives is not their motives but their actions. It does not matter to society whether a policeman has unconscious impulses to engage in criminal acts; what does matter is that he perform his job in an acceptable manner. And if pornography should be suppressed, it does not matter—unless the campaign is thereby jeopardized—whether the leaders of the movement to eliminate pornography are, unconsciously, no purer than the rest of us. His motives and defenses may, of course, be of great importance for an individual and his life style. If because of his reliance on the reaction-formation defense he is forced into behaviors that interfere with the expression of his other legitimate needs and talents, then he might attain a better personal adjustment by adopting a less restrictive defense.

Reaction formation and denial are obviously quite similar. Indeed, in reaction formation denial is implicit—that is, denial of the counter impulse, as in "I do not have a hostile feeling in me." Reaction formation takes the denial one step further: "Not only is there no hate in me, but by my actions you can see that I love everyone." In this regard, we might wonder at the seething hostility that may lie beneath the surface of the hippie love cult.

Projection. The supplements to repression are brought into play presumably because repression by itself is not thoroughly effective in keeping unconscious the anxiety-provoking material emanating from the id. Suppose a certain amount of hostility is able to invade the ego, leading not to awareness of the raw impulse, but rather to a vague feeling that "there is hostility in the air." But where might it originate? Certainly, it cannot be coming from within oneself; hence, one must be in the presence of hostile people.

To impute, unconsciously, one's own unconscious impulses to others is the essence of *projection*. In one sense projection is a more rational defense than others, since the chances are very good that other people are indeed hostile or have other unacceptable impulses. Of course, projection remains irrational in that the existence of one's own unconscious wishes is denied. Furthermore, by imputing to others all of the hostility, for example, that is "in the air" a person exaggerates the degree of hostility actually present in other people. They may be hostile, but not nearly so much as he unconsciously assumes them to be. Thus, excessive or extreme use of projection renders the person incapable of objectively reading other people. Those whose business or profession requires a great deal of interaction with others are especially vulnerable to the disruptive effects of projection.

Fortunately for psychologists, something useful can be salvaged from the mechanism of projection, for it does provide a promising means of assessing a person's unconscious motives and fantasies. All that is necessary is to let projection operate on a neutral, ambiguous object, say a picture containing the figure of a man. Suppose subjects are asked to make up a story about the picture. Since the man in the picture is a good object on which to project one's own impulses, the stories are likely to contain references to the man's behavior and his motives that are centered on the motives of the story writer. A trained judge then can infer from the characteristically different stories differences in the strength and salience of the writers' unconscious motives. A frequently used clinical instrument for personality evaluation, the Thematic Apperception Test (TAT), uses peoples' stories about pictures from which to make inferences about their unconscious motives. Other psychological instruments have also been devised on the basis of the same logic as the TAT. The ultimate validity of these devices for getting at repressed material is still a subject for careful empirical investigation. In the meantime, many of those who must make day-to-day clinical judgments find such instruments highly useful; certainly, if you accept the theoretical background from which projective tests have emerged, the rationale for their use is very compelling.

Furthermore, if stories told on demand to an ambiguous picture reveal through projection repressed material, then in principle virtually anything a person creates might serve the same purpose. Thus, the projection hypothesis would suggest interpreting the works of poets, playwrights, novelists, artists, and so on, in the same manner that one might approach material from a standard projective test. Analyzing the artist from his products is a popular sport, and one perhaps with some basis. Artists, however, are also craftsmen; their products are not just spontaneous creations, but rather are carefully molded, modulated, and shaped to conform not only to inner, unconscious demands, but also to precise, highly intellectualized rules and criteria. To interpret a novel solely as a personal revelation would be like evaluating a TAT story that a subject has been allowed to take home for a week to edit, revise, and perhaps modify according to criticism from his family and friends.

Projection is a common defense and, within bounds, rather innocuous. Indeed, as has been pointed out (Schafer, 1954, p. 280), through projection a person can gain insight into the needs and feelings of others. But it can also lead to serious distortions in interpersonal relations. Beyond that, projection carried to extreme blends into the very serious pathology known as *paranoia*. The paranoid is one who is continually suspicious of others, who expects people to be out to get him in one way or another, who interprets the most innocent and friendly of gestures as ominous and threatening. When a paranoid style is combined with a psychotic break with reality, the *paranoid schizophrenic* appears, a person with elaborate delusional systems designed to give structure and meaning to erupting unconscious material.

Isolation and Intellectualization. Certain individuals, as a supplementary defense to keep anxiety under control, strip emerging unconscious material of its normal emotional accompaniments. The content of ideas is thus isolated from their emotional significance and these neutralized ideas can enter awareness in relative safety. As Roy Schafer puts it:

> . . . ideas may become conscious that would otherwise be subjectively intolerable and strictly tabooed. Such ideas may involve death wishes against loved ones, suicidal fantasy, physically sadistic fights, and the like. As the isolator experiences it, these ideas "pop into mind for no reason at all," or, if he is a psychologically sophisticated intellectualizer, he may speculate that he is "probably" angry and that it is "probably" for this or that reason, but he will have no subjective experience of anger and no conviction as to what he is angry about. (Schafer, 1954, p. 337.)

The reference to the "intellectualizer" points to one variant of the general defense of isolation whereby a highly logical, rational, unemotional approach is taken indiscriminately to all ideational content; when the intellect is used in this defensive manner, it precludes appropriate emotional response in contexts where affect and feeling are called for. In its less rigid and uncompromising form an intellectual approach is, of course, highly prized in our culture. Intellectualization even as a defensive maneuver may have its personally adaptive and socially useful consequences (it may yield a mathematical theory or a beautiful psychodiagnosis), but these benefits come at a price, as do the products of all defenses.

Through the defense of intellectualization, it becomes possible not just to entertain, but even to ruminate obsessively on, otherwise inadmissable ideas. Indeed, a person can build a professional career on this basis. An anatomist, for example, might express strong voyeuristic and perhaps sadistic tendencies through meticulous dissections and logically sound schemes of classification of parts of animal and human bodies. A sex researcher can count "outlets" and put them into the cells of contingency tables, or record with polygraph and oscilloscope the electronic equivalents of physiological changes during sexual intercourse—all in a dry, objective manner, devoid of any apparent personal response to his subjects or his subject matter.

The personal danger of the defense of isolation is that it may so permeate one's general life style that any affective response, even in a setting devoid of threat, is eliminated. Thus, a heavy investment in intellectualization may destroy normal sources of gratification. It certainly can yield a person who is lacking in the warmth and spontaneity that ordinarily are expected of friends and family members.

Indeed, a vicious circle may be generated, whereby reliance on isolation in one area interferes with previously successful areas of personal relationships; this in turn opens up new problem areas into which the defensive troops of isolation and intellectualization can rush. What may have begun as a means of dealing with, say, aggression spreads to virtually all social situations. In this sense, the word isolation has two applications: the isolation of ideation from affect, and the resulting isolation of the person from other people for whom affect is the currency of a meaningful relationship.

Sublimation. As we have seen, the various defense mechanisms accomplish their ends at a price, and the general assessment of these mechanisms tends to be negative. Certain defense mechanisms may have positive outcomes, however, if not for the person himself then at least for society. Effective police are needed, and as we have noted it does not matter what the nature of their unconscious impulses might be so long as they do their job well. Society finds use for the intellectualizer and his products, for the hypermasculine athlete (who may be struggling against passive, dependent strivings), and so on. Thus, even those defenses which in the extreme are conducive to psychopathology have their positive by-products, or "fall-out."

Beyond that, psychoanalytic theory contends that civilization itself is the product of the containment of id impulses. The psychic energy associated with the primitive drives (called *libido*) must somehow be released, while the taboo ideational content is being repressed or otherwise defended against. What happens to all that bottled-up energy? It is channeled into the constructive, adaptive activities of the ego.

This rerouting of libidinal energy into socially useful and personally rewarding behaviors is referred to as *sublimation.* And in the sense that sublimation is a generalized device for contending with the energetic aspect of repressed impulses, it certainly can be viewed as one of the defense mechanisms, although to do so may rob it of its very special significance. Be that as it may, it would be hard to quarrel with the argument that civilized living (as bad, alas, as it may be) would surely be impossible if the primitive impulses of the id were allowed continual, uninhibited expression. Even those who are ready to endow the ego with considerable autonomy (as discussed in the previous chapter), who for example do not equate curiosity with sublimated voyeurism, would probably still accept sublimation as a potent determinant of behavior, though perhaps assigning it somewhat less weight than in orthodox Freudian theory.

Choice of Defenses. By now you may have begun to wonder what determines the particular defense mechanism or mechanisms "selected" for emphasis by a given person. Why does one person rely heavily on reaction formation while another typically employs isolation? Why for some people are their defenses adequate but not excessive, while others either lack a sturdy defensive system or are overburdened with defensive maneuvers? A partial, theoretical answer to such questions is contained in the genetic model, which describes the several stages of "psychosexual" development. Each stage is characterized by a focus of libidinal energy on a particular bodily function; for example in the *oral* stage, in the first year of life, the mouth is the locus of gratification. In addition to this property, each stage has a characteristic mode of defense. If, for reasons explained in the genetic model, the development of an individual's personality is arrested, or *fixated*, in one of these stages, then his choice of dominant defense will probably be the one typical of that stage.

Fixation is assumed to occur at a particular stage of development if gratification of libidinal impulses is either excessive or inadequate during that stage. Thus, fixation in the oral stage might result either from too much pleasure in sucking and related sources of gratification or from frustration of the infant's strong oral needs. Fixation can take place in any of the succeeding developmental stages (anal, phallic, and so on). Further details of the psychoanalytic model of development are given in the next chapter.

For further explanation of differences in dominant defenses we can turn to familial and social influences. It is conceivable, for example, that parents encourage the use of a particular type of defense and discourage other types just as most parents seem to encourage denial in their very young children. Some parents may impose their own defensive style on their children, or when they see their own defenses budding in their children they may vigorously oppose them. Children may simply assimilate their parents' defensive styles through the process of identification, just as they pick up attitudes, manner of speech and body usage, values, and so on. There may, indeed, be defensive styles associated with subcultures, so that parental influence is reinforced by the social group in which the child grows up. Does Jewish culture, for example, bias its members toward intellectualization? Do Negroes employ denial? Are Catholics simple repressors, and Protestants prone to reaction formation? Do lower-class children acquire one defensive style and middle-class children another?

Clearly, what is needed here is a great deal of empirical information. A start on this considerable task has been made, as in the work reported in *Inner Conflict and Defense* by Daniel Miller, Guy Swanson, and their collaborators. That book describes some preliminary research on effects of child-rearing practices and social class on defensive and expressive style and on the formation of conscience and morality.

DEFENSE MECHANISMS, SUPEREGO, AND PSYCHOPATHOLOGY

Specific pathological consequences of rigid and severe defense mechanisms have already been mentioned. For example, reliance on repression as a major defense is often accompanied by hysterical symptoms; excessive projective tendencies can merge into paranoia; reaction formation and isolation are often associated with obsessive-compulsive neurosis, in which certain ideas dominate thinking and highly ritualized, repetitive behaviors (such as hand-washing) dominate overt action.

Excessively Rigid Defenses. To speak at a more general level, a heavy investment of psychic energy in the defense mechanisms, whatever their form, is likely to lead to psychopathology. The energy devoted to maintaining the defenses is not available for conscious ego functions. The hysterical neurotic, for example, is often listless and lacking in vigor. Further, the defensive barrier not only protects the conscious ego from invasion by anxiety-evoking material, but it also prevents the conscious ego from having access to unconscious and preconscious ideas. The latter effect may seem at first glance to be no different from the former; that is, conscious and unconscious events are segregated from each other, as East and West Berlin are separated by the Wall. But there is a difference. It is of equal importance to the East German government that East Berliners be prevented from emigrating (or "defecting," depending on your point of view) to the West as it is to limit the entry of West Germans into the East. However, to keep the id from intruding on the ego is not the same as preventing controlled access of the ego to unconscious and preconscious material. In short, as some analytically oriented theorists assume, access to such material is essential to creativity in particular and effective ego functioning in general. If the potential resources of the unconscious and preconscious levels are made unavailable to the ego through rigid and powerful defenses, then the ego is severely impoverished.

A phrase often employed in this regard is *regression in the service of the ego* (see, for example, Schafer, 1958), the notion being that there are occasions when it would be advantageous for the ego to give up temporarily and in a well-regulated fashion its typical, rational mode of functioning and to go back, or "regress," to a more primitive mode, where the demands of logic and reality are suspended. In the technical jargon of psychoanalytic theory, the *secondary process* mode is temporarily put aside while the *primary process* mode of thinking is allowed to dominate. But to engage in this kind of adaptive, problem-solving regression, a person must have both flexible defenses and a sturdy ego. To the extent that the defensive structure precludes this form of regression, the ego is cut off from its chief source of material for creative, innovative, unusual solutions to its most important problems.

Excessively Weak Defense. But what if defenses are weak? From all that we have said so far, the result of inadequate defenses would be a flooding of the ego with the contents and affects of the id, and a substitution of primary process modes of thought for the rational mode of the well-defended ego. In effect, the result would be *psychosis*, a severe type of pathology involving a break with external reality and with the constraints of logic. The several forms of psychotic pathology need not concern us here for they are principally of clinical interest. The point is, however, that serious psychopathology is likely if the defensive structure is inadequate.

Weak and Demanding Superegos. Finally, we might comment on another source of psychopathology. The proscriptions of the superego to a large extent determine what impulses are unacceptable to the ego and what actions are taboo. An overly strict superego will predispose a person to excessive feelings of guilt, often leading to depression, self-punishment, and a generally constricted behavioral repertory. On the other hand, inadequate development of the superego adversely affects both the type of defenses that are formed and the kinds of behavior engaged in. In particular, if superego demands are weak, then id impulses would have freer reign than normally, and antisocial behavior (cruelty, murder, destructiveness, rape, and so on) could emerge when the external restraints on such behavior are removed. Thus, although conscience, at both conscious and unconscious levels, would prevent the normal person from engaging in immoral or criminal behavior, even in the absence of any external observer or any possibility of apprehension and punishment, only external sanctions restrain the person without adequate inner controls. What we have sketched here is part of the picture of the *psychopathic* personality.

The origin of adequate superego controls lies, according to psychoanalytic theory, in the process of *identification*. It is through this process that parental standards and values, conscious and unconscious, are internalized and taken over as an intrinsic part of the developing personality. Normally, the process of identification is accelerated around the age of four or five years.

The theory asserts that identification occurs as a generalized means of resolving the young child's competition with the same-sex parent for the affection of the parent of the opposite sex. This competition, summed up in the *Oedipus complex* (named after the figure in Greek mythology who in-advertently killed his father and married his mother), poses a crucial developmental crisis for the young child. For the boy a major component of the crisis is his anxiety about castration at the hands of his powerful opponent. As a means of salvaging his threatened masculinity, without entirely giving up his incestuous fantasies, the young boy identifies with his father and gets his sexual gratification vicariously. It is at this point that the young boy announces that when he grows up, he wants to be a fireman, or an airplane pilot, or a daddy, and shows increased interest in clearly masculine types of play.

A similar, though less intense and less clearly defined sequence pertains to the young girl *vis-à-vis* her mother. One source of the difference between the patterns for girls and boys is that a girl is not threatened with castration; indeed, she may believe that she has already lost the penis she once possessed. With nothing more to lose, she can afford less anxiety when faced with her mother's fantasized (though sometimes realistic) jealous anger. Eventually, she does give up fantasies, often openly expressed, of marrying her father, and like the boy identifies with her antagonist. In the course of this identification she incorporates her mother's morality. But since a girl has less motivation to do so than a boy does in resolving his Oedipal crisis, her identification with her mother is not so firmly based, and her superego is accordingly less severe than is the boy's. (See Hall, 1964, for a "modest confirmation" of this hypothesis.)

Whether the details of this formulation are entirely valid or not, the behavioral observations on which they are based (observations both of adult patients in therapy and of normal and mentally ill children) are hard to deny (see, for example, Lindzey, 1967). Moreover, this account of superego formation suggests some interesting predictions. One very clear prediction is that superego formation would be impaired in a boy if his father is absent and therefore unavailable both as a threat and as a model for identification. A similar impairment would be expected in a boy with a weak, passive father who does not pose sufficiently strong competition for the mother's affections. In general, any loosening of the conventional family structure and conventional parental authority, as when a father plays the role of buddy to his son or mother and daughter are "pals," is likely to result in a poorly developed superego. It is interesting to note, in this regard, that there seems to be a marked increase in recent years in the frequency of psychopathic persons relative to neurotics, an increase that is attributable perhaps to greater parental permissiveness and a general loosening of the old-fashioned family ties that, when they went wrong, generated a stream of neurotic patients for Freud and his disciples.

The psychopath, who lacks a normal superego, may have a primitive type of morality of the "eye-for-an-eye" variety. It is this archaic moral style—concrete, absolutist, and uncomplex—that prevails in the pre-Oedipal child and that is gradually transformed into a more subtle, mature conscience following resolution of the Oedipal conflict. The psychopath also is not entirely devoid of defense mechanisms. As already mentioned, he relies heavily on denial, as when accounting for his antisocial acts ("Everybody does that sort of thing; I was just unlucky to get caught"). But the psychopath, who is fixated developmentally at the pre-Oedipal level, experiences little if any anxiety; instead of repressing his primitive impulses he acts them out behaviorally, in a thoroughly egotistical, infantile (technically, *narcissistic*) manner. He can be charming, polite, smooth, ingratiating, and disarming to his victims (who sometimes are judges or parole boards), but he is essentially incapable of a genuine, warm relationship with another human being.

Given any choice, society would undoubtedly be better off with a generation of neurotics than a generation of psychopaths. There is some indication that child-rearing practices, at least as suggested in the ladies' magazines and the child-care books, are returning to a style more conducive to production of the former than of the latter type of psychopathology. We might hope that eventually the pendulum of child-rearing fads would come to rest at some optimal point, instead of fluctuating wildly from one extreme to another.

SUMMARY

All behavior is to some extent the product of conflict, if only that between excitatory and inhibitory tendencies; it is with conflict severe enough to have significant behavioral impact that this chapter is concerned, and more particularly those conflicts that are *intrapsychic*, rather than between people or groups. We can distinguish among four types of intrapsychic conflict, where: (1) an object has both positive and negative incentive value; (2) motives or goal objects are incompatible; (3) ideas are incompatible; (4) impulses and controls clash.

An object that is simultaneously positive and negative elicits an *approach-avoidance* conflict. As conceptualized in a model developed by Neal Miller, such conflicts can be graphically represented as two intersecting lines; both lines stand for behavioral tendencies that increase as the subject gets nearer to the ambivalent object; the line representing the avoidance tendency is assumed to have a steeper slope than the one for the approach tendency. The point of maximal conflict occurs where the two lines intersect; there, *behavioral vacillation*, or *arrest*, is noted. Because the subject in such a conflict is caught at this point, the conflict is analogous to the physical condition of *stable equilibrium*. Attempts to resolve an approach-avoidance conflict by raising the approach tendency may result in increasing the severity of the conflict so long as the approach and avoidance tendencies still intersect at a point between the subject and the goal.

An *approach-approach* conflict occurs when two positive incentives are so located that they elicit incompatible responses—so that moving toward one requires moving away from the other. Such conflicts are easy to resolve; it is only necessary for the subject to move, or be moved, off the point of intersection, toward one of the two attractive objects; then the nearer object will be the more attractive. Approach-approach conflicts are analogous to physical systems in *unstable equilibrium*. Any conflict that looks like the approach-approach type, but that is characterized by prolonged vacillation, is most likely an instance of a *double approach-avoidance* conflict, one where each alternative is simultaneously positive and negative.

In *avoidance-avoidance* conflicts, the subject is repelled by each of two negative incentives, and the situation is so structured that to avoid one he must approach the other. For such conflicts to persist there must be barriers, physical or psychological, that prevent the subject from simply leaving the situation.

Several models have been proposed to deal with instances of conflicting cognitions. One of these, the *theory of cognitive dissonance,* has been especially fruitful in generating experimental research, and that research has taken a wide variety of forms, ranging from investigation of simulated initiation ceremonies to experiments on the effects of cognitive dissonance on the physiological concomitants of hunger.

It is around conflicts between impulses and controls that serious psychopathology is likely to arise, especially when both the impulses and the controls are unavailable to consciousness. Such *unconscious conflicts* have been emphasized in psychoanalytic theory. The *defense mechanisms* are unconscious devices of the *ego* that control the expression of the unconscious impulses, fantasies, and memories (unconscious "ideas," for simplicity) that "reside" in the *id.* Through the central defense mechanism of *repression* unconscious ideas are prevented from directly entering awareness and thereby flooding the ego with anxiety. The concept of repression is based on clinical observations, but it has suggested some interesting experimental research, such as that on perceptual *vigilance* and *defense* and on *subliminal stimulation.* Other defense mechanisms are *denial,* relied on heavily by people who engage in *counterphobic* activities and by *psychopaths; reaction formation,* whereby impulses are expressed through behaviors that are the opposite of what the impulse demands—for example, excessive cleanliness when the impulse is to be messy; *projection,* whereby one's own unacceptable impulses are imputed to others—at times in the extreme manner of the *paranoid; isolation* and *intellectualization,* whereby ideas are stripped of their normal accompanying affects, or where normally related ideas are segregated from each other; and *sublimation,* whereby the "psychic" energy associated with repressed material is given an outlet in socially useful behavior.

A person's "choice" of dominant defenses is considered, in psychoanalytic theory, to be determined by the developmental, or *psychosexual,* stage in which he is *fixated.* Each stage is assumed to have a characteristic defensive style. It is also quite likely that defensive style is acquired directly through parental and cultural influences.

In general, excessively severe and rigid defenses prevent the ego from having that controlled access to unconscious ideas (or *primary process* modes of thinking) that is conducive to creativity, as conceptualized in the phrase, *regression in the service of the ego.* But defenses that are inadequately developed leave the ego vulnerable to invading unconscious ideas and modes of thinking, with the resulting danger of a *psychotic* break with reality and with logical and rational (*secondary* process) modes of thinking. Finally, psychopathology may also be the outcome of either an excessively severe *superego* (the "unconscious conscience") or an inadequately developed superego, the former leading to a general constriction and inflexibility in behavior, the latter, in the extreme to *psychopathic* behavior. Superego development is considered in psychoanalytic theory to be a by-product of the *Oedipal* conflict—the struggle between the preschool-aged child and same-sex parent for the affections of the parent of opposite sex. The severity of that conflict and how it is resolved determines the extent to which the child identifies with his parents and incorporates their conscious and unconscious moral standards.

SUGGESTED READINGS

Brown, R. Models of attitude change. In R. Brown, E. Galanter, E.H. Hess, and G. Mandler. *New directions in psychology.* New York: Holt, Rinehart & Winston, 1962.

Festinger, L., H. Riecken, and S. Schachter. *When prophecy fails.* Minneapolis: Univ. of Minnesota Press, 1956.

Freud, S. *A general introduction to psychoanalysis.* New York: Liveright Publishing Corp., 1920. Reprinted in paperback by Permabooks, 1953; Washington Square Press, 1960.

Kubie, L.S. *Neurotic distortion of the creative process.* Lawrence, Kansas: Univ. of Kansas Press, 1958.

Munroe, Ruth. *Schools of psychoanalytic thought.* New York: Holt, Rinehart & Winston (Dryden), 1955. Chapters 5 and 6.

The Person and the Group

C H A P T E R   E I G H T E E N The various psychological processes can be studied in isolation, but the task of psychology is incomplete until adequate theories of the whole person are developed. Such personality theories ideally would apply to individuals, but would be stated with enough generality to be amenable to empirical testing. One strategy in developing such theories is to identify personality types and the factors that produce them. We consider in this chapter some of the major influences on the development of personality types, from demographic variables, such as a person's ordinal position in the family, sex, and "culture," to the kinds of childhood conflicts that Freud described in his genetic model. Finally, we examine one broad type of research that has occupied social psychologists—the influence of groups of people on an individual's current behavior.

Personality Theory

Imagine a totally naive observer approaching Earth from outer space. From a great distance the Earth looks like a simple, uniform, undifferentiated ball. As he gets increasingly closer, the gross physical landmarks that distinguish Earth from other planets will begin to become apparent; oceans and continents will take form; the uniform terrain of the land masses will begin to take on texture, with mountain ranges and large rivers becoming figural. The visitor finally gets close enough so that individual objects come into view, first large ones like houses, then cars, people, small animals, and so on. Of course, the naive observer may not employ a classificatory scheme similar to ours, so that the fine discriminations which we make may elude him at first.

If he starts to classify objects, chances are good that for a very long time his classification will be quite crude; only after he develops considerable familiarity with the planet will he segregate into different categories objects that seem very different to us. Broad classes of the sort we take for granted will probably emerge first, such as animate vs. inanimate. Within the class of animate objects, further differentiations might eventually be made. But surely for a very long time all primates will be classed together. And it is reasonable to expect that when the category that coincides with our notion of human beings finally is isolated, all human beings will seem to "look alike."

From our vantage point, as members of the class of human beings, the observer's failure to note obvious differences among people would be ludicrous and even infuriating. These differences are too blatant, and so numerous that it would seem an act of either stupidity or sheer obstinacy not to be struck by them. Indeed, we probably would not be satisfied with our visitor's good will and good sense until he was not only ready to admit differences among people, but also to testify that *each human being was unique.*

GENERAL PRINCIPLES AND SPECIFIC INDIVIDUALS

The observer's initial failure to segregate human beings into their own class and his recalcitrance in further subdividing them to match our own highly refined differentiations would not necessarily be simply errors on his part. People are very much more like chimpanzees or even rats than they are like trees or rocks. Failure to note that similarity is no less deplorable than ignoring the very minor differences among people. A case can be made, then, for very crude as well as for exceedingly refined categorization of human beings, ranging from "all people are essentially alike" on the one extreme to "each person is unique" on the other.

Psychologists are faced with the same task as our visitor from outer space. And they have historically reacted with the same range of responses. For many purposes in psychology, as we have seen throughout this text, people are treated as so many equivalent replications of each other, just as a biologist might work with flatworms or as a chemist might take repeated scoops of some substance from a container until he had filled enough test tubes. What the theorist and researcher are after is general principles or laws that apply uniformly to all people, whatever their superficial idiosyncracies. Weber's Law was not meant just for Germans nor Freud's defense mechanisms only for Viennese.

But to search for universals is not to imply that all people are exactly alike. All people may employ defense mechanisms, but some, as we have already emphasized, rely heavily on repression while others may turn to reaction formation, or denial, or intellectualization. All people must run the gauntlet of the psychosexual stages of development (or some equivalent developmental sequence), but some do so relatively smoothly, while others get fixated, some in the oral stage, some in the anal, and so on. In the same vein, Weber's Law may hold (remember, $\Delta I = kI$) for all, but for some subjects in psychophysical experiments, k may equal .1, for others .09, and so forth.

In short, within the constraints of universally effective variables and generally applicable laws, there is room for individual variation even to the point of individual uniqueness. The two ends of the continuum, thus, are not mutually exclusive. People can be essentially alike, while individuals can be considered as different from each other as there is need, in psychological theory or practice, to do so. Indeed, one could not meaningfully assert that A and B are different if they did not share a set of common attributes. Person A may be more intelligent than B, and in that respect be very different from him, but to say so implies the existence of a common dimension on which they are to be compared. Think how small the intellectual difference between genius and moron becomes when they are both compared with a paramecium.

Grouping Individuals into Types. The problem of the psychologist who cares about individuals is that a science of individuals is not possible; at the same time, to be applied, universal principles must be tailored to specific individuals. Some compromise is needed between the chaos of concern with individuals and the futility of the general case. One such compromise is to work with classes of people, who for certain purposes can be treated as equivalent, even though it is understood that there are many ways in which they differ from one another. These classes can take many forms. Psychologists speak, for example, of *personality types;* these are categories composed of people who share certain broad, behavioral tendencies dominant enough to override consideration of minor differences. One of the tasks of the personality theorist has been to devise such typologies, and the personality researcher (who may also be the theorist) assesses the usefulness of competing typologies.

The Task of Synthesis. In more general terms, the personality theorist assumes the difficult burden of *synthesis*—of reconstituting persons from the processes and variables sorted out from behavior by his analytically oriented colleagues. Fortunately, the task of synthesis can be approached in a somewhat piecemeal fashion; it does not need to be done all at once. The strategy of searching for *types* permits such a partial attack on synthesis.

PERSONALITY THEORY AND SOCIAL PSYCHOLOGY

Psychologists, like other people, have a way of dividing their labors according to traditional labels. There are the theorists and the researchers; the academics and the clinicians; the Skinnerians and the Pavlovians; those who count eye-blinks and those who measure the galvanic skin response; the rat psychologists and the generalists; the psychophysiologists and the physiological psychologists; the personality theorists and the social psychologists; and on and on. These labels suggest emphases or focuses of attention, but they do not imply mutually exclusive activities or goals.

Traditionally, the personality theorist has had his eye on the individual, while the social psychologist has focused on groups of individuals; the two, however, might at times find themselves doing virtually the same research. For example, a personality researcher might conduct an experiment on the relation between the strength of affiliation needs and susceptibility to pressures for conformity from a group of peers. Shift the emphasis a little, and a social psychologist might design the identical experiment, viewing it as a study of the efficacy of peer group pressure to conform on people with differing degrees of affiliation need.

We can, of course, find differences among those efforts that aim at understanding personality and those that emphasize group influence and group processes. To that extent it is meaningful to refer to both personality theory and social-psychological theory as being interrelated but distinct attempts to tackle the formidable task of synthesis. The effort at synthesis in social psychology goes beyond reconstituting the person from his components; it also seeks to put him back into the social context from which he was torn by the experimentalist and the personality researcher. Social psychology insists that in the complete integration the whole person is understood in the social setting in which he typically is found. Beyond that, in certain of its developments social psychology would take the group itself as the unit of investigation, studying, for example, the process of communication in different kinds of group structure. At some point in its shift in focus from people to groups, social psychology merges with sociology.

The boundaries between personality theory and social psychology are diffuse, but the typical concerns of each are apparent. In this chapter we will look primarily at some of the products of the personality theorist and researcher, who view the group largely as a source of influence on personality development. Towards the end of the chapter we will also examine some representative efforts of what is more purely social psychology.

Demographic Variables in Personality Formation

It is possible to make a great number of valid assertions about a person without ever having seen him or his behavior. All we need to have is information about his position in each of several demographic categories, obvious ones such as sex, age, economic status, race, nationality or ethnic affiliation, religion, and less obvious ones such as his order of birth in his family. Given such information it would be possible to make successful predictions about his behavior in a wide range of situations. Just as it is valid to speak of a typically human mode of behaving, so too is it justified to expect similar behavior in first-born male adults who are economically well off and have been raised in a large city on the East coast of the United States by white, Anglo-Saxon Protestant parents. Change any of these demographic indicators and you might expect some differences in behavior.

What is also quite evident, however, is that within such demographically homogeneous groups of people as we have defined above, there is still room for as much behavioral variability as we have the patience to track down. The demographic factors, as potent as they are, do not by any means shape personality so that it is beyond the reach of other, more subtle variables. And, of course, these demographic variables are relevant at all only insofar as they indicate the kinds of interactions and direct influences most likely to have been experienced by a person during his development. His parents' religion is relevant, for example, to the extent that it actually affects the way in which they and other significant figures, within and outside the family, interact with him. For example, if the parents by virtue of their religious sentiments are strict and moralistic, then this should have some bearing on the child's superego development. If by virtue of ethnic differences in values and life styles, the parents care a great deal about achievement and success, there should be some impact on the way they deal with their children on issues of autonomy, striving, working hard, delaying gratification, and so on. Thus, parents from one ethnic background might encourage and reward their child's innate tendencies to do things for himself, while parents from a different background might be indifferent to, or even suppress such precursors of autonomy and achievement. If first-born children are treated differently from their later-born siblings, the difference might show up (as it does, in fact—see below) in personality differences related to birth order. If because of membership in a minority racial group that is suppressed, deprived, demeaned, and in general accorded low status and opportunity, a person is raised in a setting permeated by feelings of inadequacy and futility, expectation of failure, frustration, hostility, shame, mistrust, and so on, it is not surprising to find residues of this atmosphere in his later personality characteristics.

It is clear, then, how the several demographic factors enumerated might be influential in shaping a "typical personality." How they actually work, separately and in combination, is a problem for empirical research. A great deal of such research has already been done, much more than can be accommodated in these pages, and yet also much less than is needed to yield comprehensive, unambiguous conclusions. Our strategy here will be, as it has been throughout the text, to give some representative examples of this kind of research.

BIRTH ORDER

The significance of ordinal position of birth as a determinant of personality was suggested by, among others, Alfred Adler (1870–1937), a disciple of, and later defector from, the Freudian school. It is only in recent years, however, that extensive empirical data have been collected to show some of the ways in which birth order manifests its effects. The recent work takes its impetus from a pioneering investigation by Stanley Schachter (1959). In what began as a social-psychological study, Schachter found, serendipitously, that female college-age subjects who were first-born or only children preferred to await a feared event (painful electric shock) in the company of others, while later-born subjects were indifferent about whether they waited alone or with others. This finding has been replicated by Schachter as well as by other investigators.

Affiliation Motivation. Schachter ascribed the striking difference between "firsts and onlies" and "later-borns" to motivation. He argued that first-borns and onlies (to be called first-borns henceforth, for simplicity) have a stronger need to affiliate than do later-borns, and that this motivational difference is manifested especially under conditions of stress. Attempts to test this hypothesis have been numerous, and although the results of the many published studies on the problem are not entirely consistent, their general direction conforms with Schachter's interpretation.

For example, first-borns are more susceptible to social influence than are later-borns (Ehrlich, 1958; Staples and Walters, 1961). Schachter's own subsequent research has turned up such findings as a reported difference in effectiveness of fighter pilots as a function of birth order; first-borns are inferior to later-borns in this role presumably because of increased anxiety attributable to the enforced solitary condition during periods of great stress. Schachter has uncovered other behavioral differences of this sort that one would expect from the first-borns' purported strong need to affiliate. Somewhat more direct evidence (if you accept the validity of the Thematic Apperception Test as a means of tapping motivational strength) comes from studies (Dember, 1964b; Staples and Walters, 1961) in which TAT stories written by first-borns yielded a higher score on a measure of affiliation need (see Atkinson, Heynes, and Veroff, 1954) than did stories of later-borns.

What does the opportunity to be with others do for the anxious first and onlies? The answer, in part, seems to be that it enables a person to evaluate and get social support for his anxiety. This finding is highlighted in Schachter's report that the choice of being with others, instead of waiting alone, is taken only when those others are understood to be "in the same boat" as the subject. Moreover, just being placed in a room with other subjects turns out to be anxiety-reducing for first-borns, though not for later-borns; this reduction occurs even when the subjects are not allowed to communicate with one another.

Apparently, first-borns find the sheer presence of others reassuring, beyond the opportunity it affords for comparing notes verbally (Wrightsman, 1960). It should be noted, however, that the waiting period in the Wrightsman experiment was quite brief, about five minutes. What would the course of anxiety be if first-borns were confined for a long time with other people and prevented from speaking? It would also be of interest to find out what kinds of nonverbal communication might take place during the brief waiting period. People can reassure each other without uttering a word, through eye-contacts, smiles, and so on. But whatever it is that other people provide, it is clear that first-borns make better use of it than do later-borns.

Anxiety versus Fear. It has been argued that there are some emotional states that might be resistant to this kind of social support. Although fear of an impending electric shock may be better coped with in the company of others, there is little reason for anyone to suppress expression of this fear. However, certain kinds of affect, of the sort that triggers the powerful defense mechanisms, are less readily exposed, either to others or to the scrutiny of one's own ego. Therefore, if we could arouse this kind of affect in experimental subjects, even first-borns ought to prefer to remain alone rather than to seek social support.

In an elaborately designed experiment to test this hypothesis, Irving Sarnoff and Philip Zimbardo (1961) employed two set-ups, one, like Schachter's, that was intended to induce fear of physical pain from electric shock, the other to induce anxiety about infantile oral impulses and their gratification. As a means of arousing anxiety, the experimenter led the subjects, male college students, to expect that they would have to suck on a variety of objects, such as baby bottles, pacifiers, lollipops, and so on. The general outcome was that the subjects who were made anxious about oral conflicts were far less eager for affiliation (specifically, waiting with others) than the subjects who experienced fear of painful electric shock, an emotion that is not likely to be repressed or to be hidden from others. Thus, contrary to a conclusion drawn by Schachter, the tendency of first-borns to affiliate is not manifested under all conditions of intense emotional arousal. It matters what that emotion is.

Other Correlates of Birth Order. To return to birth order as a demographic variable in personality research, we might note its relevance to other behavioral contexts besides affiliation. In an extensive investigation of the relative academic performance of first- and later-borns, William Altus (1966) followed up several previously reported statistical studies showing first-borns to be proportionately overrepresented among eminent scholars and scientists. This bias may simply reflect the first-born's greater opportunity—as, for example, through cultural tradition, economic factors, and so on—to obtain the education on which success is built or it may indicate intrinsic cognitive and motivational differences.

Are first-borns more "intelligent" than their later-born siblings? Altus has analyzed data on over 1600 finalists in the National Merit Scholarship competition. Their performance on the scholarship exam placed them at the very top (99.5 percentile) of the general high school population in academic aptitude (which is not identical with intelligence, of course, but in this case must overlap considerably with intelligence as conventionally measured). First-borns were found to be considerably overrepresented in this very special group, although birth-order effects did not show up in the larger group from which the finalists were selected. Altus also reports results of a verbal intelligence test given to undergraduates at the University of California. A small, but statistically significant effect of birth order was found, again favoring the first-borns.

The first-born's greater aptitude (intelligence?), at the high end of the range, shows up indirectly in figures on college admissions. First-borns are overrepresented in the more selective colleges and increasingly so as stringency of selection criteria increase. This bias may to some extent account for the greater eminence of first-born people mentioned earlier.

As for motivation, aside from their greater affiliation tendency already noted, first-borns also seem to be stronger in achievement motivation, as measured by a TAT instrument. Indeed, it may very well be the case that first-borns are generally more extreme on virtually any attribute, motivational or cognitive, that is sensitive to the kinds of interactions which take place between child and parents in the early years. If being extreme is adaptive, as it is for verbal intelligence in our culture, then the first-born comes out ahead. However, it is not necessarily adaptive to be extremely dependent on others in times of mild stress. Thus, the first-born's strong affiliative tendency may interfere with his establishing mutually satisfying relations with peers. In this regard, it is interesting to note that first-born college boys are not as popular with their fraternity brothers as are later-borns (Schachter, 1964). This discovery parallels an earlier finding that those high in affiliation need, as measured by the TAT, are rated by classmates less favorably than are those who score low on this measure (Shipley and Veroff, 1952). The strong affiliative tendency of first-borns may lead to behaviors which others view as overly demanding. In this same vein, but even more importantly, first-borns are probably overrepresented in the population of psychiatric patients (for example, Tuckman and Regan, 1967). Again, by virtue of what is undoubtedly an especially intense parent-child relation, when the parental influence is an unhealthy one, it is likely to be exaggerated in the first-born, who bears the brunt of the parental pathology.

Birth Order and Parent-Child Interaction. Speculation about the difference in parent-child interactions for first- and later-borns has taken many forms. Several hypotheses have been suggested, all of which may indeed be valid. For example, it is highly likely that a mother is less skilled with her first child than she is with subsequent children; she makes her mistakes on him. In addition, the first child is the only one to have the exclusive attention of his parents for a considerable period of time. Later children must share the parents with the first-born (who probably continues to get more than his fair portion of the parents' concern, and certainly does so if he is an only child). Thus, it is likely that the first-born has more verbal interchange with his parents than do later-born children, an experience that might account for the first-born's heightened verbal aptitude. In general, the parents of first-borns tend to be more overprotective, but also more demanding than they are with their later children, who are likely to be handled with less anxiety, and in a more relaxed, *laissez-faire* manner. In short, there seem to be adequate reasons, in the quality and intensity of the parent-child relationship, to account for the motivational and cognitive differences that have been reported between first- and later-borns. Whether in addition more subtle, congenital variables are operating, such as maternal prenatal anxiety or even more purely physical conditions, is a question as yet unexplored. The research showing prenatal effects on the emotionality of rats is certainly suggestive of a possible, analogous phenomenon in human beings; and it would seem likely that mothers are especially anxious both before and after the birth of their first child.

SEX

It would be uneconomical to catalog here all the ways in which a person's biological sex influences behavior, not only sexual behavior itself, but also the full range of behaviors that constitute personality. Two topics might be worth pursuing, however. One has to do with personality differences perhaps not obviously related to sex. The second concerns the origin of sex-linked behavioral differences; specifically, to what extent are so-called masculine and feminine traits biological in origin and to what extent are they shaped by socio-cultural influences? Pursuit of this second subject is beset by many of the same methodological snares that frustrate a satisfactory solution to the "nature-nurture" problem, but at least some partial answers are becoming available.

Achievement Motivation. Personality differences related to the sex of subjects are reported incidentally in a large proportion of studies on personality in which such a comparison was made (Carlson and Carlson, 1960). One especially interesting type of difference can be illustrated by the work of David McClelland and his collaborators on achievement motivation.

The main burden of this work was to develop a measure of individual differences in strength of achievement motivation. The source of this measure was TAT stories written in response to a special set of pictures like the one shown in Figure 18.1, chosen to be mildly suggestive of achievement themes. The basic strategy was to induce in a group of heterogeneous subjects a strong, if temporary, concern about achievement; their stories would then be compared with those of subjects handled neutrally. Whatever differences appeared in the stories between the two conditions (achievement-induction and neutral) would presumably distinguish between people who differed chronically in level of need for achievement (or need achievement, "nAch," in the jargon of this enterprise).

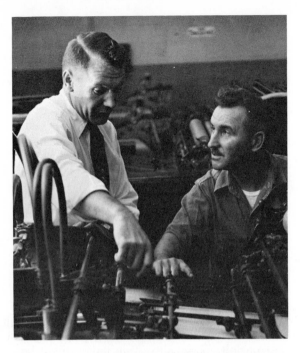

Figure 18.1 The kind of picture used for eliciting TAT stories for measuring achievement motivation. (Standard Oil Co., N.J.)

The achievement-arousing manipulation in these experiments involved an elaborate deception; in essence, a distinguished-looking professor appeared before a college class and announced that he was conducting tests on behalf of a government agency to find out how intelligent and effective the students were at X University. A series of problems were then given to the students, followed by the TAT. In the neutral condition, the instructions omitted any reference to the importance of good performance; the experimenter simply presented himself as a graduate student doing a preliminary evaluation of some new tests he was developing; in general, the impression conveyed was that the students were just helping out and that no one was interested in their performance *per se*.

Such instructional differences were effective, for they yielded the expected group differences. The manipulated students wrote stories that were more permeated with achievement imagery than were those of the students in the control group. From that basis, a refined scoring system was developed that could be applied to individuals as a means of assessing the strength of their need for achievement (for further details, see McClelland, Atkinson, Clark, and Lowell, 1953; Atkinson, 1958).

The initial research was done at a male college. Several subsequent attempts were made to use the nAch measure on female students, with disappointing results. For example, whereas for men a measure of nAch enabled an investigator to predict some achievement-related performance, the relation between nAch and performance for women subjects was negligible. The reasons for this sex difference are not entirely clear, but one lead is provided by some studies which indicate that the basic procedure for inducing achievement motivation, as employed in the developmental research, does not take for women students. That is, the group difference produced by the different "instructions" given the male subjects did not appear with female subjects. Why not? Because even under neutral conditions the female subjects were about as aroused to achievement as they could be. Apparently, female college students are walking around with a chronically high level of achievement motivation that leaves little room for experimental manipulation. Why this should be so is not at all clear, especially in view of the myth that college women are primarily concerned with hunting for a suitable mate.

Psychological Differentiation. Another line of investigation that has proven quite fruitful in recent years is the work of Herman Witkin and his colleagues on the trait originally called *field-dependence, field-independence,* and now referred to as *psychological differentiation* (Witkin, Dyk, Faterson, Goodenough, and Karp, 1962). The concept of field-dependence, field-independence was developed to account for the marked differences in responses to a simple perceptual task. Subjects were shown a luminous rod, in a dark room, and asked to set the rod so that it was aligned with some imagined vertical reference (like the flag pole outside the lab building or a surveyor's plumb line). The rod was located within a luminous square frame and both frame and rod could be rotated independently. In some conditions the frame might be tilted several degrees off vertical and the rod might also be set off vertical, either in the same direction as the frame or in the opposite direction (see Figure 18.2).

Some subjects adjusted the rod so that instead of being aligned with the vertical it was set parallel to the off-vertical sides of the frame. Other subjects made very accurate adjustments of the rod in spite of the potential error-inducing influence of the frame. With no other cues to guide them, the accurate subjects were presumably utilizing bodily cues to the true vertical; the highly inaccurate subjects were apparently unable to segregate the two sets of visual cues (the rod and the frame) and adjust the rod to conform to the information about the vertical given by their kinesthetic and vestibular sensory systems. On the basis of this particular testing situation, it was not possible to interpret unambiguously the difference between the two extreme groups, but subsequent research revealed that a general trait seemed to be operating: Some people have difficulty separating a perceptual element from the field in which it is embedded, while others can make this separation with ease, and many people fall between these two extreme groups. Those who have difficulty were designated as *field-dependent,* while those who could easily segregate figure from background were called *field-independent.*

The generality of this trait is revealed by the high correlation between

Figure 18.2 Examples of the kinds of stimulus situations facing subjects in the rod-and-frame test. The subject's task is to set the rod vertical; to do so accurately he must ignore the orientation of the tilted frame. The greater the deviation of his settings from true vertical, the more field-dependent is the subject.

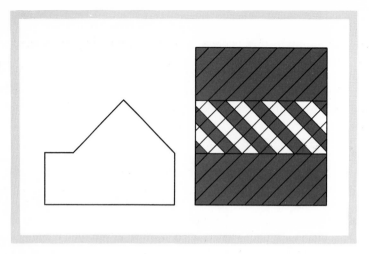

Figure 18.3 Example of an embedded figure. People who have difficulty in locating the simple figure within the more complex one tend to be field-dependent, as measured by the rod-and-frame test.

performance on the rod-and-frame test and performance on such tasks as finding a simple geometrical figure which is embedded in a more complex figure, as illustrated in Figure 18.3. Those who are field-dependent, as measured by the rod-and-frame test, take longer to find the hidden figure than do those who are field-independent.

One of the early findings of the Witkin group was a sex difference in this trait; females are in general more field-dependent than males, especially after the onset of puberty. Of course, there is considerable overlap in performance between males and females, so that many females are field-independent and many males are field-dependent. A developmental pattern was also observed; in general, field-independence increased with age, as shown in Figure 18.4. Indeed, age and sex interacted in the manner indicated in the figure.

This developmental trend toward greater field-independence is suggestive of a general principle of psychological development proposed by Heinz Werner (1948)—the *orthogenetic principle*. Werner asserts that psychological development proceeds through increasing differentiation along with increasingly complex hierarchical organization. The mature personality is capable of making refined distinctions in the perceptual, cognitive, and affective spheres; along with this increase in degree of differentiation, the more mature system is also better and more complexly organized than is the less well-developed, or "primitive," system.

Taking his cue from Werner's principle, Witkin hypothesized that the relative degree of field-independence reflected the level of general psychological differentiation. Thus, field-independence would be a perceptual manifestation of a generalized personality trait, or style of mental functioning, characterized by a high degree of differentiation. If so, those classified as field-dependent on the basis of their scores on the rod-and-frame test or the embedded-figure test should show up in many other ways as relatively primitive, or undifferentiated.

A highly differentiated person should display his developmental maturity not only in regard to external objects but also to himself, in particular to his body. Thus, a field-independent person should have a more articulated body image than the field-dependent person. In order to find out about a person's body image psychologists often have him draw pictures of himself and other people. The "draw-a-person test" is sometimes employed with children as an indication of intelligence, and it has also been used for picking up signs of psychopathology. The issue here is simply to judge the figures drawn by children, or adults, in terms of the degree of articulation displayed, to obtain a "sophistication of body concept" score that can then be related to the standard measures of field-dependence, -independence. Witkin describes the scoring system and the basic finding as follows:

> Three areas of the drawings are considered in making ratings: form level, identity or role and sex differentiation, and level of detailing. . . . In the drawings of field-dependent children, we find very little detail and unrealistic representation of proportioning and of body parts. Sexual charac-

Figure 18.4 Field-dependence as a function of age and sex. For the meaning of "deviation," see the legend for Figure 18.2. Data points are from different subjects at the several ages studied—that is, the data are "cross-sectional." Similar results are obtained from "longitudinal" studies—where the same persons are tested repeatedly as they get older. (Witkin, Goodenough, and Karp, 1967.)

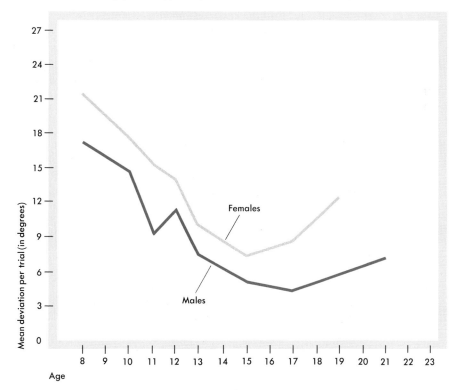

teristics are shown minimally or not at all, so that in some pairs of drawings (the child is asked to draw both a man and a woman) it is difficult to tell which is male and which is female. In most cases, there is no attempt at role representation (is this male figure a cowboy, baseball player, a policeman, and so on?). On the other hand, in the drawings of children whose perceptual performance is at the field-independent extreme we find the body drawn in realistic proportion. Parts of the body are presented in some detail and fairly realistically. There is clear representation of sex and sex differences. Aside from indication of sex through body characteristics, the sex of the figure is also indicated by such externals as clothing. We also find attempts at role representation, suggesting a sense of the uses to which the body may be put. (Witkin, 1965, p. 320.)

Some of the indexes of poor body articulation overlap with those used to assess intelligence through figure-drawings. Witkin points out that the sophistication-of-body-concept score does correlate with IQ, but the relation is carried entirely by those subtests of the standard Wechsler intelligence test which resemble the perceptual measures of field-dependence, -independence, for example, the block design and picture-completion tests. The body-image score does not correlate with other subtests, such as vocabulary, information, and comprehension.

The Witkin group have also related their perceptual measures of differentiation to behaviors that are of direct interest to clinical psychologists and psychotherapists. For example, it would be expected that the choice of defense mechanisms would be influenced by degree of differentiation. If so, the relatively undifferentiated person should prefer the more primitive defenses such as denial and repression, while the highly differentiated should employ the more "mature" defenses, such as isolation and intellectualization. Just as in his perceptual style the field-independent person segregates one part from another or elements from their backgrounds, so too in his defensive style he should be biased toward breaking up separable elements, such as ideas and affects. In one study designed to test this hypothesis (Bertini, 1961), it was found that the use of isolation as a defense was indeed associated with field-independence. Still further concomitants of degree of differentiation were found in studies of dreaming. That field-dependent persons rely heavily on repression is revealed in their proclivity for forgetting dreams or reporting dreams less frequently than people in general have dreams.

Finally, Witkin has extended the differentiation hypothesis into psychopathology. The extremely field-dependent person has a poorly articulated body image, and a poor sense of identity, a basically dependent and passive style of relating to people and coping with problems, and a set of primitive defense mechanisms, such as denial and simple repression. What kind of mental illness would afflict such a person?

One of the first types of psychopathology to be empirically related to field-dependence was alcoholism. Clearly alcoholism is markedly oral; without excessive interpretation, it is fairly easy to see the alcoholic's reliance on "the bottle," or drinking, as manifestations of the infantile attachment to the mother's breast, with all its passive-dependent connotations. This obviously oral aspect of the alcoholic's behavior together with his helplessness and passivity are suggestive of the same immature developmental level that characterizes the highly field-dependent person. We might expect alcoholics, then, to be higher in field-dependence scores than appropriate control subjects. This result has been obtained in a number of studies (see Witkin, 1965, for pertinent references). Thus, a likely route for psychopathological disintegration for the field-dependent person is the one leading to Skid Road. Why some field-dependent people turn to alcoholism when they break down, rather than to some other pathology, is an unanswered question.

A person who overeats to the point of obesity also obviously has oral problems and might be expected to be drawn from the ranks of the field-dependent. This expectation has been empirically confirmed (Pardes and Karp, 1965), as has a similar prediction about ulcer patients (Gordon, 1953).

In the highly field-independent person, psychopathology when it appears is likely to take a form consistent with the more "mature" defenses, such as projection and isolation. Thus, it fits Witkin's scheme to find that paranoid schizophrenics tend to be field-independent as compared with undifferentiated schizophrenics (Janucci, 1964; Powell, 1964). Field-independence also characterizes the obsessive-compulsive type, whose defenses tend to be isolation and intellectualization (Zukmann, 1957).

To taste in greater detail the flavor of Witkin's thinking, we might again quote from his fascinating article, "Psychological Differentiation and Forms of Pathology:"

> A final illustration may be found in patients in whom paranoid reactions are central in the symptom picture. In this patient group, an articulated cognitive style is frequently found. Projection, a characteristic defense of the paranoid, is quite specialized, in comparison to such generalized tension-reducing techniques as eating and drinking. The paranoid projects his own system of ideas upon the world, and does so in a highly selective fashion—particular people, particular situations may be especially implicated. Such selectivity requires that experience of the world be articulated. In this connection, the paranoid is noted for his detailed, articulated system of ideas. As an attempt at preservation of the self, projection contrasts with the alcoholic's preferred way of dealing with stress, which in extreme cases results in the dissolution of the self in drink. The use of projection as a device for self-preservation, however bizarre, presupposes a self that has achieved some degree of differentiation. (Witkin, 1965, p. 326.)

The Origin of Sex Differences. We have certainly come a long way from asking people to adjust a rod so that it is aligned with the vertical. And the issue of sex as a determinant of personality traits may have been lost in the shuffle. We might return to that topic by inquiring about the origin of sex differences. Why, for example, are females as a group more field-dependent than males? More generally, are such differences in personality traits to be attributed to the purely physical concomitants of biological sex, or are these behavioral differences only accidentally linked to sex through cultural influences and child-rearing practices? This is indeed a big question; we can only try to suggest an answer.

First, the very great influence of culture on sex-typed behavior, or *sex-role* as it is often called, is virtually a truism and needs little documentation. Perhaps the most striking demonstration of sex-role flexibility in response to cultural demands is provided in the classical anthropological investigation of Margaret Mead (1935). Mead described three primitive tribes in New Guinea. One, the Arapesh, had sex-role norms for both males and females that were very much like those that modern Western culture prescribes only for females. But not too far away on the same island were the Tchambuli; in this tribe, sex roles were "reversed"—the females were dominant in the running of the affairs of the tribe and were the aggressive heads of their families; the males were passive, compliant, esthetically sensitive, and so on. Finally, in the Mundugumor tribe both males and females were caricatures of the Western concept of masculine aggressiveness.

The existence of these three patterns of sex roles indicates, in an extreme fashion, the great range of possibilities that are available for sex-role definition. But why were Mead's observations so startling? Why are there so few cultures that depart so markedly from the Western stereotype? Perhaps the Mead study simply shows how powerful cultural influence can be in spite of built-in sex differences.

To hypothesize such innate differences is, however, much easier than to demonstrate them unequivocally. Cultural influences directed at sex-role formation are brought to bear virtually from the moment of birth. Boy and girl babies are dressed differently. There are differences in the way their births are announced to others. Undoubtedly, boy and girl babies are handled differently, though documentation is not easy to come by. Certainly when boy babies are old enough for it, they receive rougher treatment than do girls, especially from their fathers. In a myriad of ways the culture bears down on the developing youngster to shape his or her sex-role identity so that whatever innate differences unrelated to sex might be present are thoroughly masked.

Nevertheless, there are subtle indications of such innate differences. Girls, for example, are quicker than boys to develop linguistic skills, though there is nothing obvious in the cultural norms that would dictate such a difference. Even more interesting is the finding (Cameron, Livson, and Bayley, 1967) that it is possible to predict later intelligence test scores from measures of early vocalization—*for girls but not for boys*. These measures concern the earliest age at which a particular type of vocalization was noted, as for example when the baby first vocally expressed "eagerness" or "displeasure" or said "da-da" or used two words. Since these primitive linguistic predictors of later intellectual differences are displayed during the second six months of life, it is difficult to see how even the most subtle cultural influences could have been brought into play.

Unfortunately, clear-cut experimental evidence on culture-free sex differences in human beings is simply not available. We could turn to data showing sex differences in the behavior of lower animals, but their pertinence to the present issue is only marginal. It would be interesting, for example, to find out if female monkeys are more field-dependent than male monkeys, but the results of such an investigation would at best be suggestive. At this point we can only surmise that there must be behaviorally relevant neurophysiological and biochemical concomitants of biological sex differences and be content with the assertion that these differences can either be magnified or suppressed by the potent cultural influences with which the developing child is constantly being bombarded.

CULTURE

Demographic variables such as "culture," class, socio-economic status, religion, and so on are important attributes of the person's milieu; only after the early years, during which his personality is presumably fairly well fixed, do these variables become identified as his own properties. The present religion or class status of an adult is probably much less relevant to his personality than what they imply about his upbringing. To say that X is a lower-middle-class, white Irish-Catholic may be to say something about his values, beliefs, and interests; but more importantly it means that he was probably raised as a child in a lower-middle- (or lower-) class, white, Irish-Catholic family and neighborhood. It is not that these broadly "cultural" variables stop operating entirely in adulthood, but rather that their major and most durable effects have taken hold in the early years of life. What happens to a person after the first half dozen years or so, short of profoundly moving events, does more to refine and modulate the basic features of his personality than to structure them—at least according to most contemporary theories of personality development.

We have indicated how "culture" can determine, subtly and grossly, the nature of sex-role identification (boys can be aggressive, girls should be sweet; boys should play with trucks and guns, but not with dolls; boys should be good in arithmetic, but girls do not have to be; girls should care about art and music and dancing, boys about athletics and science; and so on . . .); now we can ask in general about the medium of cultural impact. Clearly, the mediating link between culture and personality development is provided by the parents, especially if the significant years are the very early ones.

Potency of Parental Influence. Whether for masculine and feminine roles, type of preferred defense, strength of superego, level of differentiation, motives and values, or what have you, parental influence is obviously the dominant factor, as all that we know about the learning process as studied in the laboratory would indicate. Parents have the edge over other potential sources of influence for molding the young infant's innate proclivities, talents, and temperament into a mature personality; parents have the advantage of *primacy, duration,* and *intensity* of contact, and the opportunity for very close *monitoring* of the child's behavior; hence they can administer rewards and punishments with careful selectivity. And through an as yet little-understood relationship called *identification,* the parents serve as the developing child's primary *models* on which to build his own self-concept, both consciously and unconsciously.

In summary, though we cannot verify it experimentally, it is quite apparent that demographic variables have their major impact on personality development through the mediation of the parents (or parent-surrogates). Cultural influence independent of parental behavior awaits the child's liberation from the home, formally in his encounters with such official culture-bearing agents as teachers and clergy, and informally through his widening array of friends and their parents. In addition, a newly significant source of acculturation, even while a child is still a "captive" of his parents, is the mass media, especially television. Television may indeed have an homogenizing effect on the children who come under its influence. Parents differ from each other, and each set of parents differs from every other set of parents. But, at least as a physically definable event, a TV message is the same for all viewers. It is thus conceivable that the present great diversity within "American character" or "Russian character" will gradually be replaced by a much more restricted typology, perhaps approximating that of the small, simple, primitive cultures that anthropologists like Mead were able to describe with such facility.

National Character. Is it possible to capture the style of an entire nation with a few pertinent attributes? Is the model American extroverted, friendly, aggressive, ambitious, and is he systematically different from the typical Russian, or Japanese, or Frenchman? If that question makes any sense at all given extensive intranational heterogeneity, how might we try to assess national character? Until recently that task has been taken up mainly by historians and to some extent by anthropologists, while psychologists occupied themselves with less formidable assignments, such as trying to formulate what might meaningfully be said about a single person. In the past few years, however, psychologists have also been attempting to apply their special expertise to this fascinating topic. One in particular, David McClelland (1961), has tried to assess the dominant motives of various nations through an extension of the TAT technique, which you will recall was developed for application to individuals. McClelland argues that the myths, folklore, and other artistic productions of a nation may reveal something about the motivations and values of that nation just as these are partially revealed in the fantasies of a single person. Moreover, the motivational norms of a nation at a given time might be expected to have their major impact later in the behavior of the children who are being exposed to them.

If you could accurately assess the dominant motives implicit in a set of current documents, you might be able to make predictions about the motivational status of the nation's populace 25 or 50 years hence. And from motivational structure, you might then proceed to make specific behavioral predictions. Of course, to wait a generation before being able to test one's predictions is probably more delay in gratification than even the sturdiest ego could bear; but there is the alternative of going backward in history and correlating inferences from content analysis of documents from year X with relevant behavioral indexes taken at year $X + Y$. The latter strategy has been followed by McClelland with encouraging results.

For example, he obtained measures of the strength of achievement motivation by a content analysis of the elementary reading textbooks used by school children in 1925; he did so for several nations for which both the books and certain economic indexes were available, such as increase in gross national product from 1925 to 1950. His argument was that differences in national level of need achievement will be reflected later in relative dominance of achievement-oriented behavior. Given adequate natural resources, those nations whose members have especially high achievement strivings are likely to be among those that show above-average economic progress, since the latter, at least in its early stages, is in large part dependent on the sheer hard work and future-orientation that characterize those with a high need for achievement. The results in general confirmed the prediction: Those nations that in 1925 offered their children textbooks saturated in achievement themes showed the greatest economic gains from 1925 to 1950.

Others have followed up McClelland's lead, branching out into other motives and other behaviors. For example, Stanley Rudin (1968) has shown how variation among nations in certain types of psychopathology are predictable from an assessment, through content analysis of children's readers, of the relative amounts of achievement and power motives. Rudin's position is that high need achievement, for example, is both a blessing and an affliction. The price of competition and success may be hypertension (high blood pressure) or ulcers. Life in a society with high power norms may induce in a person feelings of being manipulated and exploited, which in the extreme may generate certain psychosomatic illnesses and other behavior pathologies.

Following McClelland's procedure, Rudin obtained achievement and power scores for each of 17 westernized countries in 1925 and related these scores to death rates from what he classed as psychogenic disorders in 1950. These disorders, on which good statistical data are available, were murder, suicide, ulcers, hypertension without heart disease, and cirrhosis of the liver (an indicator of alcoholism). It turns out that the five measures fall into two meaningful clusters, in terms of intercorrelation. Ulcers and hypertension go together, while murder, suicide, and cirrhosis of the liver form the other cluster. Rudin finds inhibition and repression underlying the ulcers-hypertension pair and sees "aggressiveness and acting out of impulses" in the other cluster. On the basis of that interpretation each nation was assigned an "aggressiveness" value (the sum of scores in the three-item cluster) and an inhibition value (scores on ulcers plus hypertension).

As expected, the need-achievement measure, obtained from content analysis of children's books used in 1925, successfully predicted the death rate in 1950 from the inhibition-and-repression cluster, but not from the aggressiveness cluster. On the other hand, the 1950 death rate from the aggressiveness cluster was predictable from the 1925 measure of power motivation, but not from that of achievement motivation!

Rudin argues further that the dominant motive in a particular national or cultural group changes over time; for example, the level of achievement motivation in this country started to rise around 1840, then accelerated until it reached a peak, according to content-analysis data, around 1890, and has been gradually declining ever since. One factor in this change may be the psychopathological consequences of an overemphasis on achievement alluded to above. In addition a point may be reached where, for economic reasons, achievement striving no longer pays off as it did in the "good old days"; instead, power-motivated behaviors may become the only effective routes to success; these in turn lead to the "aggressive-acting out" kinds of pathologies described by Rudin, with a consequent retreat to an emphasis on affiliation and social concern. This shifting motivational pattern, which has some obvious economic and political implications, is illustrated for the United States in Figure 18.5. Similar patterns have been obtained for other countries such as Russia and England, and Rudin makes a good case for the relevance of these patterns for the explanation of already observed as well as predicted economic and political trends in the interrelations of these countries. For example, he points out that the Russian achievement-motivation curve surpassed that of the United States in about 1954, while the United States passed Russia in power motivation about ten years later. Should these trends continue, we might predict that by about 1980 Russian economic progress will exceed that of the United States, while this country in turn will take on some of the power-motivated characteristics that we presently deplore in totalitarian countries.

There are, of course, many loose ends in these provocative studies of McClelland, Rudin, and others. How, for example, is one to consider the materials from which the motivational assessments were made? Are they merely indicators of general cultural norms, or do they also help to shape the motivational structure of the children who are exposed to them? Or both? Do school-age children pick up the subtle messages of the texts which they read, or are they already so well structured by school age that these materials do little more than elaborate on an already stabilized motivational system? What of the many other motives, conscious as well as unconscious, and the types of defenses and controls that must be operating in the populace of a nation? After all, achievement, power, and affiliation do not exhaust the list of pertinent personality variables. Finally, to what extent can knowledge of likely trends in "national character" help to modify those

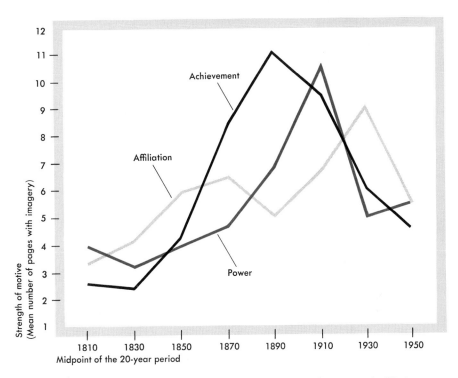

Figure 18.5 Trends in the strength of achievement, power, and affiliation motives for the United States from 1810 to 1950. Motive strength is inferred from content analysis of children's readers. Note how achievement reached its peak in 1890, power 20 years later, and affiliation 20 years after that. (Adapted from Rudin, 1965.)

trends? Questions such as these are among the many that might come to mind in connection with this kind of work. They attest, however, not to its weakness but to its fruitfulness—one of the important criteria, as you will recall, of good theory.

Models of Personality Development

To the extent that demographic variables do affect personality, it is legitimate to base personality typologies on them. We might, for example, speak of a "masculine personality" type, a typical "first-born," a "middle class, white, urban, adult Protestant American," and so on. This way of categorizing people is limited, however, as even a superficial comparison of that middle class, etc. American with his middle-class, etc. next-door neighbor will reveal. Because of such limitations there have been numerous attempts by personality theorists to develop typologies that cut across demographic variables, that have a more profound and enduring theoretical basis, and that have implications for what may be more significant aspects of the person's behavior. One major theoretical attempt of this sort originated in the genetic model of classical psychoanalytic theory.

PSYCHOSEXUAL DEVELOPMENT

AND CHARACTER FORMATION

The genetic model postulates a sequence of stages through which the developing personality passes. Each stage is characterized by typical conflicts that the young child must face and master if he is to move on to increasingly mature levels of development.

Developmental Stages. Freud's original model has been greatly elaborated, both by him and his followers, but we need only present here a simplified and highly abridged version. Three "psychosexual" stages precede the Oedipus conflict, the precipitating event in superego formation and sex-role identification. The first of these is the *oral stage,* when the child experiences problems related to passivity and dependence associated with nursing and oral gratification. The second is the *anal stage,* when the focus of conflict is toilet training and the general problems of giving and withholding, of cleanliness and order. The third is the *phallic stage,* when gratifications and fears related to the child's developing sexuality are focal and when his intrusiveness and assertiveness run into social restraints. These stages, called *psychosexual* to highlight their broadly sexual, or *libidinal,* nature, provide the basis for the formation of certain pervasive behavioral styles, referred to as *character* in analytic theory. Thus, analysts may speak of an oral, anal, or phallic character in reference to a person whose behavior is markedly permeated by elements that can be traced back to one of the three early psychosexual stages.

Fixation in a Psychosexual Stage. All people have traces of these early conflicts in their behavior, but some are noteworthy for the extent to which their behavior is dominated by oral, anal, or phallic features. Why some people proceed through these stages with relative ease—and leave them behind—while others seem to be perpetually plagued by certain infantile conflicts is a question of great importance to psychoanalytic theory. The answer, as suggested in the previous chapter, is that it is possible to become *fixated* in a particular psychosexual stage for either of two reasons. Either a person receives excessive gratification in a particular stage (in learning-theory terminology, the reinforcements for behaviors appropriate to the stage are too numerous and too potent to allow for easy extinction) or else the amount of gratification is insufficient. In the latter case, the developing child cannot move on to more mature levels because he has not "finished" with earlier ones.

The major responsibility for assuring an appropriate degree of gratification lies with the parents. It is conceivable, of course, that some children have, for reasons of physiological makeup, unusually demanding needs in certain areas, needs which even the best parent cannot satisfy; it is also possible that what would for most be a normal amount of gratification is for some children excessively gratifying, so that the well-intentioned parent cannot avoid being overly indulgent. When fixation results from parental error, it is often quite likely that the stage in question is problematic for the parent; a mother who has oral problems herself is a good candidate for the ranks of those mothers who cannot provide appropriate oral gratification for their children.

The oral stage is usually considered to have two phases. The first is a passive, receptive phase, associated with sucking; the second is an active, aggressive stage, related to biting. Fixation in one or the other of these phases might be expected to yield a particular subtype of the oral character. Thus, a person fixated in the first phase would behave in an essentially passive manner, expecting others to minister to his needs and being disappointed and demanding when they do not; for such a person, "the world owes him a living." By his passivity and overdependence, however, he is likely to alienate people, especially those close to him, who are never really able to satisfy his insatiable infantile demands. At his best, the oral character may be optimistic and cheerful, but unrealistically so. Like the year-old infant that he mimics, he is self-centered and narcissistic, and certainly is not in a position to be giving or helpful to other people: Others give and he takes.

Fixation in the second, or oral-aggressive, phase yields a character type that is marked by a kind of "biting," destructive style. Such a person may be especially adept at hostile verbal interchanges in which humor and wit substitute for genuine communication. The aggressive verbalization may be almost literally "spit out," as an infant might reject unwanted or unsatisfying foods. Often envy and excessive ambition permeate his relationships with others; people are to be used for what they can provide, but not gracefully or gratefully. The oral-aggressive person may take care of his needs in a more active manner than does the oral-passive individual, but neither is capable of mutual relationships with others.

The anal character is described as being orderly, parsimonious, and obstinate. These three attributes may be assets in a scientist, but when they are excessive and compulsive as in the anal character, they are decided liabilities. The anal character is extreme both in the degree to which he expresses these attributes and in the range of areas which they pervade. His orderliness goes beyond keeping a neat desk, or an accurate checkbook, or careful business records, and so on. Everything must be neat and clean—including *your* desk and *your* checkbook. The anal character, by virtue of unresolved conflicts over whether to withhold or give up his feces (in the right place and the right time) may have problems about retaining or letting go of objects, as in the case of the miser, like Scrooge in Dickens's *Christmas Carol* or the character Tchichikov in Gogol's *Dead Souls*. The operating symbolic equation may be, for example, that money equals feces. The anal character may be equally retentive of ideas, keeping his thoughts to himself, being suspicious of others' motives (what are they trying to get from him?), and in general behaving in a highly constricted manner. Finally, still reverberating from his early struggles with his parents for control over his own bodily functions, he may also be extremely stubborn, holding on to his point of view the way he tried as a child of two or three to hold on to his feces.

The phallic character is described as intrusive, aggressive, and domineering, again not entirely negative traits so long as they are modulated. But in a man with an infantile fixation on his genitals as a symbol of his power and as a source of narcissistic gratification, these traits are excessive in intensity and generality. This type of person may use his body as an instrument for expressing his conflicts, like certain athletes (think of a fullback crashing through the hole opened in the opposing line). Or we may see the phallic character weaving in and out of traffic in his sports car or his "hot rod," revealing his potency through the sleek and powerful machine he controls. Presumably what motivates this behavior is an unresolved conflict about the value and adequacy of his genitals, as well as their security. The phallic stage, as mentioned, precedes the period of the Oedipal conflict, during which castration anxiety becomes dominant. Precursors of this anxiety over loss of the mark of masculinity may be concerns, in the phallic stage, about whether the phallus is good or bad, adequate or inadequate (especially in comparison with father's). The behavior of the phallic character probably reflects this uncertainty. It undoubtedly does in the phallic woman, whose caricature of a masculine style betrays her childish feelings of loss and betrayal upon her discovery of her supposedly missing parts. The phallic woman is a "match for any man."

The character types sketched above are based on a combination of clinical observation and theoretical expectation. They do represent behavioral extremes, so statistically these categories take care of only an inconsequential fraction of the general population. However, instead of thinking of these character types as being isolated in separate, small, self-contained units, think of broad ranges of types, at the extremes of which fall the rigidly, pervasively, and purely oral, anal, or phallic characters. Other people, who have more or less successfully emerged from the infantile crises and stages, may have in varying degrees and varying combinations elements of these traits. It is meaningful to ask to what extent a person exhibits oral, anal, or phallic tendencies, under what circumstances, with what degree of compulsiveness, and so on. Thus, these character types, even if they are complete fictions, do serve to alert the personality theorist and the clinical practitioner to important behavioral trends that might otherwise go unnoticed or unconceptualized.

Biology or Society? One of the features of the classical typology we have been discussing is the way it ties psychological style to basic bodily functions and drives. Freud always stressed the biological nature of man. But many of Freud's critics found his emphasis on the biological substrate of personality development excessive and misdirected. For such critics what is psychologically crucial in the psychosexual stages is not the biological drives, but the interpersonal relations that surround the socialization of these drives. Thus, what matters in the oral stage is not the exact amount of libidinal gratification achieved, but the tone of the relation between child and parent. Is the mother nurturant, but not overly possessive? Are the infant's legitimate demands met realistically and consistently? In the anal stage, again the issue is not so much quantity of gratification, as the spirit of the joint effort by parent and child to help the child conform to societal demands of personal hygiene and bodily control. Is the parent firm, but not threatening? Is the child allowed to emerge from this stressful period feeling competent and autonomous, or is he so shamed for his failures that his self image is one of inadequacy and doubt? Can he feel free to be messy when it is appropriate (as when finger painting or playing in mud) and neat and orderly when that is called for?

Freud's critics see such issues as central and relevant to the psychosexual stages as they relate to personality development. Whether the critics are fair to Freud in arguing that he favored biological concepts over the more pertinent psychosocial ones is a moot point; it is clear that Freud recognized the interpersonal aspects of the situations he described, but his emphasis on their biological underpinning may have been overdone.

ERIKSON'S DEVELOPMENTAL MODEL

There are theorists who have tried to "socialize" Freud's genetic model. Chief among these is Erik Erikson (1950), who has translated the Freudian psychosexual stages into basic psychosocial conflicts.

Trust or Mistrust. Thus, for Erikson, in the oral stage a person develops a deep and pervasive sense of *trust* or *mistrust* of other people. Freud's oral passive character lacks basic trust; if he could trust others, he would not need to be continually reassured of their willingness and ability to care for him. A person with a firm sense of trust can turn to others when he needs their help, but he can also leave them alone when he does not. Trust develops, presumably, out of a parent-child relationship colored by affection and nurturance, one whereby the child's needs are gratified but not overindulged. But, as Erikson argues, it is not the quantity of gratification that matters so much as the manner in which it is given and withheld.

> . . . the amount of trust derived from earliest infantile experience does not seem to depend on absolute quantities of food or demonstrations of love,

but rather on the quality of the maternal relationship. Mothers, I think, create a sense of trust in their children by that kind of administration which in its quality combines sensitive care of the baby's individual needs and a firm sense of personal trustworthiness within the trusted framework of their cultural life style. This forms the basis in the child for a sense of identity which will later combine a sense of being "all right," of being oneself, and of becoming what other people trust one will become. (Erikson, 1950, p. 221.)

Autonomy versus Shame and Doubt. In Erikson's counterpart of the Freudian anal stage, the primary conflict is between a sense of *autonomy* and feelings of *shame* and *doubt.* Erikson expands the areas that presumably give rise to this conflict from the narrow emphasis in analytic theory on toilet training to include other endeavors on the part of the child to develop his motor and muscular apparatus and thereby emerge as a relatively self-sufficient individual. Thus, the development of a sense of autonomy would depend on successful mastery of the many basic skills that help free the child from helpless dependence on parents and other adults. Autonomy is threatened if the child's efforts towards mastery are belittled or frustrated, and if his legitimate mistakes are made the occasion for derision or punishment. It should also be noted that to be able to strive for autonomy the child needs a well-established sense of trust; if he has not been successful in coping with the problems of the "oral" stage, he will be handicapped in his later efforts at self-sufficiency. The child who trusts his parents can, for example, accept their faith that he will be able to do those things, such as controlling his bladder and bowels, which he is struggling to master. At the same time, the parents must provide reassurance that the child's developing autonomy will not get out of bounds.

Initiative versus Guilt. Erikson's correlate of the phallic stage finds the child beginning to develop a sense of *initiative;* not only can he now act independently, he can also set his own goals. Autonomy is joined by a new feeling of competitiveness, directed not so much at siblings as at the wielders of the greatest power in the family, the parents.

In utilizing his newly developing locomotor and intellectual abilities, the phallic child is busy exploring and exploiting his own body and also the world around him. The young boy delights in climbing, in getting into things, in building elaborate structures and towers with his blocks, in playing with cars and trucks, and so on. At one level, he is appropriately assuming a masculine identity. At the level of fantasy, however, his impulses to compete with and even replace his father may be both exciting and frightening; he may experience an unrealistic feeling of guilt over the things he would like to do and as a result overly modulate the things he can and should do as a boy who someday will be a father. The conflict in this stage, then, is between *initiative* and *guilt.*

The outcome of this general conflict between initiative and guilt is determined by the resolution of the Oedipal conflict that becomes the focus of parent-child interaction as the phallic stage unfolds. If the child's strivings for power and position are too severely beaten down, the result is a loss of initiative, a generalized, and perhaps also a specific sexual, impotence that precludes development through later stages of adult identity and adult competence. On the other hand, as we have already mentioned in the previous chapter, inadequate superego formation, resulting from lack of opportunity to face and solve this basic conflict, can be equally destructive. A mature personality requires a mature superego.

In psychoanalytic theory, psychosexual development does not cease with the resolution of the Oedipal conflict. Freud postulates a *latency* period, during which sexuality is relatively dormant. During this phase—which coincides with the elementary-school years—intellectual pursuits and the world outside the family come to the fore. The psychosexual volcano erupts again, however, with the onset of puberty. At this point Freud's developmental model begins to get vague; somehow or other, if the adolescent makes it through this troubled period, in which many of the pre-Oedipal and Oedipal conflicts are raised and solved anew, he ends up as a more or less healthy adult, whose sexuality is genuinely *genital,* rather than phallic, and who is ready to create the children who will start the cycle again.

Erikson's model, by contrast, does not trail off with the latency period as does Freud's. He carries the person into maturity and old age with a degree of articulation that goes well beyond what is found in the Orthodox, psychoanalytic approach. In all, eight stages are defined, the three already mentioned (trust-mistrust; autonomy-shame, doubt; initiative-guilt) plus the five briefly sketched below.

Industry versus Inferiority. The latency period brings forth a conflict between *industry* and *inferiority.* During this stage the child moves out of the family and begins his apprenticeship as a member of society. He learns to work and to enjoy work, to produce, and to be attentive and diligent. His brain is the chief organ of pleasure and accomplishment. However, should the community not be prepared to facilitate his development, should the school stifle rather than encourage his industry, should his family not allow him to "leave home," then joy in work may turn into a feeling of inferiority and unworthiness that will pursue him through later developmental stages. In this latter regard, think especially of the shock to a child whose progress through developmental stages under family control has been adequate and who is suddenly confronted with social institutions, such as schools, that treat him at the outset as an inferior being. That such a shock is probable for Negro children has finally been acknowledged. But it awaits any child who is confronted with institutions which are insensitive to the crucial role they play in shaping the identity of latency-age children. Feelings of inferiority and pleasure in work and productivity are incompatible.

Identity versus Role Diffusion. The next developmental stage begins with puberty and is characterized by the polarity *identity* versus *role diffusion.* In essence, the main problem of the adolescent is to discover who he is, as a person in general, and more specifically as a young man or young woman with a future that bears some continuity with the past, and a fairly clear path toward attainment of adult goals and roles, marriage, family, and career.

Unfortunately, many a middle-aged adolescent has never gotten beyond this stage. He still does not know who he is and continues to quiet his doubts by identifying with the heroes of his youth (witness the otherwise unbelievable popularity of such spectator sports as professional football) or by seeking out casual alliances with extramarital sexual partners.

Intimacy versus Isolation. With identity formation safely on its way, it is then possible to enter into the next stage, where the goal is *intimacy* and the failure to achieve that goal is *isolation.* It is in this stage that mutually satisfying sexual relations between loving, trusting, heterosexual partners becomes possible—sexual relations that are free of pregenital, self-centered, obsessive, and sadistic components. Mature sexuality thus assured, its absence can be tolerated when necessary, and it becomes possible also to engage fully in other pursuits, recreational and especially occupational. Finally, the achievement of intimacy can allow sexuality to lead to its biological purpose, procreation.

Generativity versus Stagnation. The having and caring for children is prototypical of a broader concern with using one's resources in a creative and helpful fashion. This concern lies at the heart of Erikson's seventh stage, one in which *generativity* and *stagnation* are the polar alternatives. The intimacy that characterizes success in the preceding stage is not the culmination of the developmental sequence, nor can it forever feed on itself. A continued, mutually satisfying marital relation eventually requires that energies be turned toward the nurturance of the children who are the products of that relation and toward the creation of increasingly valuable inanimate products of one's occupational efforts. The alternative to generativity is the boredom and ennui that exclusive absorption in oneself, or one's spouse, is bound to induce.

Ego Integration or Despair. But the same is ultimately true of generativity itself. Just as a child's development demands his moving out of the family into society, so too does the continued development of the adult— not a literal moving out of the family, but rather a turning of attention from the nurturance of his children to a concern for mankind in general and a perspective on life that enables acceptance of his past and the imminence of death. In this eighth developmental stage *ego integration* is pitted against *despair.*

Personality types based on developmental models, whether Freud's, Erikson's, or some other theorist's, are potentially very rich insofar as what happens in a given stage is at least partly independent of what occurred in preceding stages. Imagine, for example, that you could discriminate reliably seven positions on a scale measuring the outcome of the first stage, trust-mistrust. Passed through the filter of that stage, seven different personality types emerge. Suppose that a similar screening is done at the second stage, initiative-shame, doubt, and that again seven degrees of "success" can be discriminated. If a person's position on this second scale is independent of his position on the first scale, then there are 49 (7^2) potential types at the end of stage two. Such an analysis carried through all eight stages would generate 7^8 personality types. Of course, it should be expected that the stages are not entirely independent, so that a realistic estimate of the number of personality types based on the eight stages would be less than 7^8, but it would still be considerable. Adding sex as a second dimension immediately doubles the number of personality types. Putting the profile based on stages together with sex, socioeconomic status, nationality, religion, birth order, and so on, as well as those aspects of such variables as defensive preferences, superego controls, and ego differentiation, which are independent of the stages profile, will obviously generate a huge number of types, more indeed than there probably ever would be need for. One major task for the personality theorist, then, is to find superordinate categories with which to reduce this diversity to manageable proportions. The search for such categories will require a great deal of patience and perseverance, both on the part of the searchers and of those who are awaiting the searchers' success.

Behavior in Groups

Up to now, we have stressed "the group" as a potent source of influence on personality development. Now we will briefly consider some of the work, done largely by social psychologists, on the effect of groups on the behavior of an individual with a developed personality. It is the transient behavior of the individual that is of interest here, not any enduring effects of the group experience (as in the two-person group of conventional psychotherapy or in multi-person group therapy and its many variants).

GROUP INFLUENCE
ON INDIVIDUAL JUDGMENTS

There are two classical experiments on the influence of the group on the judgments of individuals in it. The first is a study by Muzafer Sherif (1947) on the way in which members of a group tend to converge in their responses to an ambiguous stimulus—that is, a situation in which no "correct" response can be defined. The second is an investigation by Solomon Asch (1956) of the shaping of individual judgments by group influence so that they violated obvious "objective" reality.

The Sherif Study. In the Sherif study, subjects were shown a dimly illuminated, fixed spot of light in a dark room. Under proper conditions most people come to see the stationary light move. This kind of apparent movement of a fixed light is called the *autokinetic effect.* The degree of the autokinetic effect varies from one person to another, so that although everyone may see movement, for some the amount of movement is small but for others it is large.

Sherif measured the extent of movement typical for each of several subjects when tested alone. Then he brought groups of three subjects together. Suppose one person usually saw the light move only a small extent, while two others experienced a typically large autokinetic effect. The three subjects would be asked to announce their judgments about the extent of movement to the experimenter, and thereby also to one another. It was found that the range of judgments gradually narrowed, until all three subjects would give similar responses. The informal group norm tended to be intermediate among the initial individual values. In such a situation, where reality is subjective, people modify their behavior so as to minimize their differences from others in their group, even without explicit pressures to conform to some group standard.

The Sherif experiment provides an excellent opportunity to study factors that might affect the degree of self-induced conformity. One factor is likely to be the perceived nature of the other group members. Suppose, for example, that there are only two people in a group, one a stooge of the experimenter's and the other a true subject. The ability of the stooge's announced judgments to affect those of the subject might be expected to vary as a function of his perceived status. What if the subject were a prejudiced white student and the stooge a black. So long as there was no reason for him to consider the Negro especially expert in judging the extent of movement of a small spot of light, we would expect the prejudiced student to show less conformity to the stooge's position than to that of a neutral influence source. Moreover, for some people the status of others is especially significant; these status-oriented people, who show up as "dogmatic" or "close-minded" on a scale developed by Milton Rokeach (1960), would be especially sensitive to the perceived status of a stooge. It turns out that, as contrasted with "open-minded" people, they do indeed markedly change their judgments in a Sherif-type situation, both *toward* those of a high-status stooge (a "college-professor") and *away* from those of the same stooge introduced as a high-school student (Vidulich and Kaiman, 1961).

The Asch Experiments. In the second of the classic studies of group influence, the task was again perceptual, but much less ambiguous than the one facing Sherif's subjects. In this case subjects were asked to judge the length of lines. Specifically, each subject was seated among a group of stooges. The experimenter explained that each of them had to match a standard line with one of a set of three comparison lines. The seating was arranged so that the true subject was always the next to last to report his judgment, the reports of course being made publicly.

The task was quite an easy one, for one of the variable lines was always a good objective match for the standard and the two alternatives were clearly different from it. On the first several trials all subjects' reports agreed. Then, some of the subjects announced judgments that were "wrong"; they picked a line that was shorter than the standard. And they did this again on the next trial. A conflict was generated within the true subject: His eyes told him one thing, his ears another. What should he do?

In a typical experiment of this sort, about one-third of the reports conform with the group consensus, and hence run counter to what the subject would say if alone. Some subjects conformed on virtually every trial, some were reliably resistant to the group pressure, but most subjects sometimes gave in and sometimes did not. Physiological measures taken on such conflict trials indicate a high degree of arousal on those occasions when subjects resisted group pressure (Bodgonoff, Klein, Estes, Shaw, and Back, 1961).

The Asch procedure is relatively inefficient for data collection, since only one true subject is run at a time. A major innovation in procedure was to automate the situation so that large numbers of subjects could be run simultaneously. Each subject was put in a booth by himself and told that he would be part of a group; communication among group members would occur via an intercom system. The subject never saw these other members; indeed, they existed only as voices on a tape recording, giving a pattern of responses that was precisely programed to suit the needs of the experiment. Under these somwhat artificial conditions the conformity effect still prevailed (Crutchfield, 1955).

Other modifications in the basic Asch method include varying the nature of the stimulus materials and the type of judgments required. The conformity effect operates, for example, not only on a variety of perceptual judgments (about which people may have firm positions, based on faith in their perceptual apparatus, but which are otherwise affectively neutral) but also on statements of opinion heavily laden with affect. Under group pressure, subjects can be made to endorse statements of opinion that they would vehemently reject under other circumstances.

Of course, not everyone yields to group consensus, either in the Asch experiment or in "real-life" situations to which it is analogous. The "hung jury" is a good case in point, for one person may hold out against the strenuous efforts of 11 of his peers to get him to change his mind. Who are the nonconformers, and under what circumstances are conformity pressures maximally and minimally effective on such people? With such questions we turn from pure social psychology to the interaction of personality and social-psychological variables.

One obvious hypothesis, in light of our previous discussion of birth order, is that first-borns and onlies might be more susceptible to group pressures than later-borns. Experimental tests of this hypothesis have generally confirmed it, at least for male subjects (see, for example, Sampson, 1967). In general, people who are highly susceptible to Asch-type conformity pressure are relatively low in intelligence, self-confidence, self-reliance, and originality, and have strong authoritarian tendencies (Crutchfield, 1955).

It is interesting to note that many of these experiments were done during a period when college students were being derided for their conforming tendencies. The militant nonconformity of the present generation of college students suggests that they might, in general, be less conforming in the experimental laboratory than were their recent predecessors.

OBEDIENCE TO THE EXPERIMENTER

Although the word "group" usually connotes a large number of people, the two-person group has been studied with increasing vigor over the past few years by social psychologists. One variant of the two-person group is a pair consisting of a subject and an experimenter. To what extent can the experimenter intentionally influence the behavior of the subject? We have already noted in Chapter Two how experimenters can sometimes *unintentionally* bias their subjects' responses.

Subjects are typically polite and compliant. When an experimenter asks them to be seated, they usually sit down. And they rarely protest when asked to provide information about themselves, sometimes of an intimate nature, or to engage in difficult or boring tasks, or to undergo a certain amount of pain, and so on. Just how far can people be pushed? Can a forceful experimenter, for example, induce subjects to engage in essentially antisocial acts in the interests of science or out of simple politeness to a respected authority figure? And if people are readily manipulable by an experimenter with little power over their daily lives, what does this imply for their malleability at the hands of a potent leader?

The Milgram Experiments. A convincing demonstration of subjects' compliance with an experimenter's pressures to engage in rather extreme acts of apparent cruelty to another person was reported by Stanley Milgram (1963). Milgram's subjects were 40 males, ranging in age from 20 to 50; they were all local citizens responding to a newspaper advertisement, rather than the usual college students. Each subject was met by the experimenter (a rather stern-looking high school teacher in a gray lab coat, hired by Milgram to play the role) and another person, who presumably was also a subject. That other person, a 47-year-old, mild-mannered gentleman, was actually a paid stooge. The subject and the stooge drew lots to see who would serve as "teacher" and who "learner" in a learning experiment. The stooge always came out as the learner. He retired to a booth where he was strapped into a chair, making it clear that he could not get out until released.

The experiment was described as an attempt to find out the effects of strong shock on learning and memory. It was the teacher's task to get the learner to learn perfectly a list of paired-associates. Each time an error was made, the teacher was to administer an electric shock to the learner; each shock was to be "15 volts" higher than the previous one, starting with a value of 15 volts and going up to 450 volts. Of course, the stooge was never really shocked.

Responding in a prearranged manner, the learner kept making enough errors so that—if the subject followed orders—the shock level would reach points on the teacher's console labeled "Very Strong Shock," "Intense Shock," "Extreme Intensity Shock," "Danger: Severe Shock." The central issue here was at what point the subject would refuse to comply with the experimenter's insistent demands to continue shocking the learner.

To increase the authenticity of the deception, and to heighten the pressure against compliance, the learner began pounding on the wall when the shock level reached 300 volts, and he also stopped signaling his responses to the learning task. The teacher was instructed to treat failure to respond as an error, and to proceed with the learning trials. There was more pounding from the stooge at 315 volts and then silence thereafter. Reluctance on the part of the subject to continue was met by increasingly firm instructions from the experimenter to keep on with his job. However, after the fourth prod the subject was allowed to stop.

No subject refused to participate at a shock level of less than 300 volts. Five subjects quit at that point, another nine refused to proceed somewhere between 300 and 375 volts (where the label on the console read "Danger: Severe Shock"). And 26 of the 40 subjects complied with the experimenter's demands right up to the maximum shock value of 450 volts.

The remarkable, and frightening, message of this study and those like it is that people will comply with demands, despite their own strong reservations about what they are doing, for no other apparent reason than that an authority-figure tells them they must. It should be made clear that the subjects who were obedient to the experiment up to the maximum voltage were often seriously disturbed by what they were doing. One such subject was described by an observer as follows:

> I observed a mature and initially poised businessman enter the laboratory smiling and confident. Within 20 minutes he was reduced to a twitching, stuttering wreck, who was rapidly approaching a point of nervous collapse. At one point he pushed his fist into his forehead and muttered: "Oh God, let's stop it." And yet he continued to respond to every word of the experimenter, and obeyed to the end. (Milgram, 1963, p. 377.)

Other subjects, equally agitated, did have the strength to disobey. One who quit in defiance of the experimenter's pressure said:

I think he's trying to communicate, he's knocking. . . . Well it's not fair to shock the guy . . . these are terrific volts. I don't think this is very humane . . . Oh, I can't go on with this; no, this isn't right. It's a hell of an experiment. The guy is suffering in there. No, I don't want to go on. This is crazy.

The question that immediately comes to mind is why some people resist while others comply. There was no attempt in Milgram's experiment to determine the different personality characteristics of the two groups. In subsequent research, a somewhat different issue was investigated. That is, to what extent noncompliance can be socially facilitated. If, for example, the subject is pressed by the experimenter to continue but sees other subjects refusing to go on, will he be in a better position himself to disobey? The available evidence suggests that disobedience of this sort can be socially facilitated (Milgram, 1965). In this case, a peer group can influence a person not to conform to the demands of an authority figure, just as in the Asch situation conformity is induced. Although conformity has negative connotations, it becomes apparent when the Asch and Milgram situations are compared that conformity in itself cannot be judged either good or bad until we know the specific behaviors that constitute the expression of the conformity.

In some absolute sense, however, it may be appalling to discover how compliant people are in the face of attempts at influence by authority figures as well as peer groups. Much of social psychology seems to be devoted to demonstrating the generality of that fact, in the areas of attitude change, propaganda, crowd phenomena, small-group interactions, leader-follower relations, and so on. Personality theorists and researchers might well try to discover ways of regulating personality development or modifying personality through therapy so that socially responsible independence is fostered. In this regard, the ideal person is one who can remain an effective member of a group without losing his individuality to it.

DECISION-MAKING AND PROBLEM-SOLVING

Not all small-group research has been devoted to studying subtle or blatant attempts at influence. We might mention here two further lines of investigation that have proven fruitful.

Group Decision-Making. A host of studies has demonstrated that people who are allowed to come to a decision after free and open group discussion are much more likely to remain committed to that decision than if it were handed down to them "from above." The potency of group decision-making probably results from several factors. For example, it is likely that in the process of freely discussing a complex issue, most of the pros and cons will have been raised and dealt with; thus, it is unlikely that people will later change their minds as a consequence of suddenly thinking up, or being exposed to, contrary information. Not so when decisions are imposed, without the opportunity to air all the arguments. Second, in the course of group discussion, participants are likely to announce their positions publicly; having done this, they are less likely subsequently to adopt a different position. Added to this factor of public commitment is the sheer amount of effort and time devoted to arriving at a decision; both of these factors, from the perspective of dissonance theory, operate so as to enhance the value of the decision. Finally, chances are good that the members of a natural group (a university faculty, a fraternity, a union, residents of a housing project, and so on) are for the most part positively disposed to one another. And considerable research has shown that if A likes B, and B favors X, then A will strive also to favor X. By this same token, if a group is hostile to the person imposing a decision, then their hostility is likely to transfer to the decision itself, even if it is a meritorious one: "If that SOB is for it, it can't be good."

Group Problem-Solving. An offshoot of work on group decision-making is the recent use of groups for purposes of solving problems. Many organizations, for example, utilize what has been called "brainstorming" to help in the search for high-quality solutions to their problems. Here the notion is that people working together on a problem so facilitate one another's thinking that the group product is likely to be better than the best of the solutions arrived at by the same people working in isolation. Why such an hypothesis might prove valid is fairly easy to see. An individual often gets into ruts in his thinking; but if he is exposed to other people, they will not put up with it ("You've said that several times already; let's try a different approach"), and what they say may help him to initiate new lines of thought.

It is also possible, however, to imagine ways in which group problem-solving might be inferior to solitary efforts. A strong, dominating group member might inhibit innovative thoughts in the other group members, or so lead them down the wrong path to problem solution that they cannot consider alternative routes that might readily have been tried otherwise. Moreover, groups have a way of striving for consensus and so may prematurely accept solutions that seem good, but that are not as good as they might have been. Finally, there are probably many people who simply think better in solitude; the group situation interferes with, rather than facilitates, their best efforts.

We might speculate further that the efficacy of the method will turn out to be a function of the kind of problem to be solved as well as of the composition of the group. Should the group members be homogeneous in sex, personality type, and so on, or is there some ideal mixture? Is there an optimal group size for various kinds of problems? Should the group have a leader? Questions such as these have not been ignored by those who study group processes, but solid answers are not yet available. This is one of the numerous problems in psychology where the cliché "further research is necessary" is clearly pertinent.

SUMMARY

The personality theorist assumes the task of understanding the whole person by synthesizing the elements that have been analyzed out of behavior in the work of those who focus on smaller units. Moreover, the personality theorist is faced with the problem of making statements about individuals that are sufficiently general to be testable through the methods of scientific psychology. The social psychologist goes a step further and attempts to put the individual person into the context of the group in which much of his behavior occurs.

A common strategy of personality theorists is to deal with *types* of individuals who share certain important features, or *traits*. The question for research then becomes one of identifying the conditions that yield the various personality types. One set of significant personality-shaping conditions we have characterized as *demographic*. Included are such obvious variables as the person's ordinal position in the family and the person's sex, both of which have been extensively investigated.

In general, those people who are first-born or only children have stronger affiliative tendencies, especially under stress, than later-born individuals. They are also more likely to have successful academic careers, and probably are more competent verbally. Indeed, it may be that first-borns and onlies are more extreme on many attributes, including those that are defined as pathological. These differences probably reflect both greater intensity of the parent-child relationship, for firsts and onlies, and greater parental anxiety and ineptitude.

Sex differences in personality are easily demonstrable. For example, experimental procedures that arouse achievement motivation in men are ineffective in women college students, possibly because the women chronically have a high level of achievement motivation. Women are more *field-dependent* than men, and in general do not score as high as men on measures of *psychological differentiation*, an attribute that is manifested over a wide range of behavior, from ability to segregate a visual figure from its background to defensive style and type of psychopathology. Sex differences are clearly influenced by culturally defined behaviors, and styles of behavior, appropriate to each sex—that is, by *sex-role* expectations. It is also likely, but not easy to document with experimental evidence, that there are innate differences between the sexes.

Cultural norms, as transmitted initially by parents and later by institutions, have a considerable influence on personality development, to the extent that there is some validity in speaking of *national character*. Attempts to assess the dominant motives in a society have made use of content analysis of children's readers and textbooks, as well as other documents; relations have been found between measures of national motives (such as achievement and power) as of 1925 and indexes of economic growth and psychopathology in 1950.

There have been attempts to create models of personality development that transcend demographic variables. The most ambitious of these is the Freudian genetic model, with its developmental stages, each tied to a specific bodily zone. Developmental *fixation* in a given stage, through inadequate or excessive gratification, produces a particular *character* type—thus, *oral, anal,* and *phallic* characters. Freud's emphasis on the biological basis of "psycho-sexual development" has been criticized and alternative approaches have been offered, stressing the quality of the social interactions that take place during the early years. Erikson's model postulates eight stages (reaching into maturity and old age), each characterized by a central conflict (trust vs. mistrust, autonomy vs. shame and doubt, initiative vs. guilt, industry vs. inferiority, identity vs. role diffusion, intimacy vs. isolation, generativity vs. stagnation, ego integration vs. despair).

Experimental investigation of a person's behavior in groups has taken many forms. A major concern in such research is the effect of group norms and pressures to conform on individual judgments. In a classic study, Sherif showed how group norms influence individuals' judgments of the extent to which a stationary light seemed to move (the *autokinetic effect*). Another line of research was initiated by Asch; again individuals' judgments were shown to be affected by the publicly announced judgments of others. Both intrapersonal and environmental factors have been identified that determine the extent to which socially *conforming* behavior occurs. A person's obedience to the demands of an experimenter (to engage in apparently severely punitive behavior to others) is still another type of recent social-psychological research. Finally, the relative efficacy of group, as compared with solitary, problem-solving has been investigated. In all of these investigations, the effort is made to simulate in the laboratory the kinds of social situations that people might encounter in their everyday affairs.

SUGGESTED READINGS

Brown, R. *Social psychology.* New York: Macmillan (Free Press), 1965.

Erikson, E.H. *Childhood and society* (2nd ed.). New York, Norton, 1963.

Fraiberg, Selma. *The magic years.* New York: Scribners, 1959.

Sarason, I.G. *Contemporary research in personality.* Princeton: Van Nostrand, 1962.

White, R. *Lives in progress* (2nd ed.). New York: Holt, Rinehart & Winston, 1966.

Conclusion

Psychological Knowledge and Its Use

Now that you have completed your examination of psychology at the introductory level, it is fair to ask what good it is. This question brings us back to the topics that we illustrated in the introduction when we were trying to show you some examples of the application of knowledge about psychology. You should now see the relevance of the illustrations and be able to answer some of the questions that were raised there.

The usefulness of what you have learned here can be reviewed under a few simple headings. These can serve to remind you of the areas you have studied and at the same time furnish a framework for the things that psychologists are doing as they go about their business of being psychologists.

The Nature of Science

You have some notions about science now that are probably different from the ideas with which you began the book. We have treated science as a matter of mapping, modeling, and theory-building. Extending scientific thought is a matter of trying to find even more effective representations of the phenomena in which we are interested, if we take "more effective" to mean that the predictions are more accurate, the descriptions are more appropriate, the theories are more readily tested, the formal structures are more elegant, and the over-all theory is both as simple and as powerful as possible.

We have argued that science is almost always interested in *genotypes* rather than in *phenotypes;* that is, it is interested in underlying variables rather than particular behaviors or particular experiences. Throughout, we have strongly preferred abstract representations as opposed to descriptions of the surface appearance of things.

You now know more about the many possible beginnings of research studies. In addition, you can appreciate the different kinds of conclusions

717

that can be drawn from various kinds of studies, particularly the important difference between correlational and experimental studies. In the second chapter we told you about research in a vacuum, so-to-speak, giving examples from one psychological area or another, but the examples could not hope to capture the interplay of experiment, theory, applications, contradictions, and further experimentation that you now have seen in many areas. You know that science does not proceed in straight lines, simply assembling strings of information, but, rather, that it follows tortuous paths, trying one notion then another as it seeks to find a way ahead.

Now that you are sophisticated in these matters in psychology, it is fitting to remind you that the pitfalls discussed in the second chapter (the experimenter effect, the Hawthorne effect, the placebo effect, and the like) are not the exclusive property of the psychologist. They are very real hazards to research in all behavioral, social, and educational fields. What you have learned can be critically applied to all other kinds of social science research that you encounter—from market research to industrial engineering. In fact, you should probably look all the more closely for these phenomena in the applied areas because financial motives enter into such research and sometimes make the researcher or his employer blind to defects in techniques.

Your appreciation of the nature of experimentation has doubtless grown since the early chapters. Above all, you know now that an experiment is done for a particular purpose at a particular time in a particular theoretical network. You know that "controls" are not just a simple matter of studying some subjects without an experimental treatment. Controls that are appropriate for a given experiment at one stage in the development of a science may not be at all adequate at another stage. The function of control groups is to control for likely alternative hypotheses. Because alternative hypotheses change with the growth of knowledge and the growth of experimental technology, control operations too must change in sometimes radical ways.

To see how much you have learned about science and methodology, return to the first two chapters and skim them again. You will find that they are much more easily understood at this point in your development. You will also see new ideas in these chapters that reflect the changes in your background information during the progress of the book.

Measurement

One of the tasks that psychologists are called on to perform in many settings is measurement. The relation between one's logic and one's measures was stressed in Chapter Three. It is clear that the psychologist faces some of the most formidable measurement tasks that we know. He may be asked to develop a scale to measure the status of mental patients in order to provide information on whether their behavior in the ward is getting better or worse. If a new therapy is tried in a hospital (even if it is as "unpsychological" as a new operation for ulcers), the psychologist is likely to be asked to help in the design of the research and to advise concerning the nature of the behavioral measures to be employed. When a school system invests in expensive equipment, such as teaching machines, closed-circuit television, or on-line computers, administrators will ask psychologists to design tests, observation schedules, and rating scales to see if the new devices are producing the changes they are supposed to effect.

In all of these matters, the psychologist draws on both his theory of the behavior involved and his knowledge of measurement. In the clinic, the school and the laboratory, he must try to build measures of high reliability and validity. If he does a good job and if his theory is close to being adequate, he frequently develops an instrument or set of instruments that enables him to predict to some extent who will profit from a given therapy, who will succeed in a given school sequence, or who will perform well on a particular kind of task.

The most broadly used psychological measures today are probably the college entrance examinations. In just a few hours these tests attempt to appraise enough behaviors of just the right sort to permit prediction of academic achievement over a period of several years. This startling feat is generally so well done that we take it for granted. In fact, we are likely to show considerable irritation if the prediction goes far wrong. Yet this entire technology was created in just the last half century. It succeeds even though we do not have effective measures of many other important aspects of college life, such as a person's motives and emotions. Although there may not be much drama in such work and although many people resent the "mass-testing" approach, the social and personal importance of good psychometric information and prediction is very great.

One of the best-known everyday applications of psychology is personnel work. The personnel man (who may not be a psychologist himself) ordinarily makes use of psychological information of many types, ranging from simple "good-bad" ratings to very complex personality inventories. The recommendations that he must make concerning hiring, training, transfer, discharge, and promotion are all based on small amounts of data. Only rarely in modern business does the personnel man know the employees well on a face-to-face basis. Usually he relies on indirect evidence such as test scores, reports, and ratings when he is called on to make judgments. Concern with measurement and with careful assessment of relations between measures to assure their reliability and validity is a daily part of his job.

Applied Experimental Psychology

Though most of this book is devoted to experimental psychology, it is hard for most laymen to think of any application of the findings of experimentalists to any problems that "count." Experimentalists themselves are eager to argue that experimental psychology is under no obligation to be useful. It is enough, they say, that it is a basic science and that it is devoted to increasing knowledge of living organisms and their behavior. Science does not have to justify itself by showing that it is "good for something."

Without presenting it as a justification, we must point out, however, that the findings of laboratory psychology have proved useful in a variety of ways. Furthermore, the techniques developed in the laboratory have found application over a highly varied set of practical problems. These activities have been called *applied experimental psychology* and *human engineering*.

As man designs more and more complicated machines for his use and tries to work in more and more complicated environments, he must face the possibility that the machines and environments may make unreasonable demands on the human being involved. The first airplane can be put together in such a way that it takes a skilled acrobat to fly it; but when we want airplanes for mass production and we expect thousands of people to qualify to fly them, we must make sure that the displays and controls make this possible. After some point of development, it is no longer economical, or even possible, to find personnel who fit the job requirement: We must tailor the job requirements to human beings.

The most obvious uses of information concerning the nature of the human being in interaction with nonhuman machines have been those of the armed forces. Given complex machines such as airplanes, submarines, tanks, defense networks, space ships, and the like, the problems become dramatically clear and the need for solutions becomes urgent.

During and following World War II, there was a vigorous rush to the research literature and to the research laboratory to provide information needed to solve design problems such as these:

> Designing controls so they can be identified and operated by touch alone, even through gloves.
> Designing display panels so that one man can monitor a great deal of information.
> Selecting the right kind and size of instruments so that they can be read with the desired accuracy.
> Choosing the color, size, and form of the indicator on a detection device (such as radar or sonar) so that detection remains accurate over a long period of time.
> Conducting studies of vigilance, that is, finding how alert a person can be in the course of a two-, four-, or six-hour watch.

Experimental psychology was called on to help solve these problems in two major ways. First, much of the required information already existed but needed to be collected and interpreted for designers. This task called for searching the literature and writing catalogs of data that summarized the relevant information on vision, hearing, reaction times, fatigue, work arrangement, and the like. These summaries could be given directly to engineers who had to construct displays, controls, and work environments.

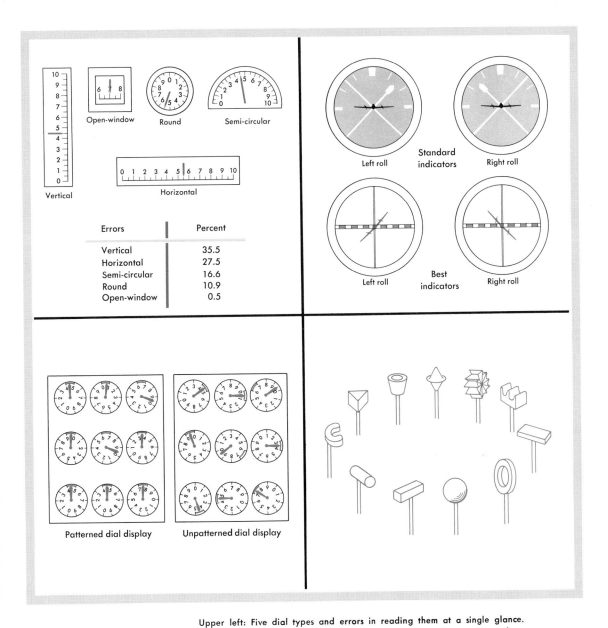

Upper left: Five dial types and errors in reading them at a single glance. (Sleight, 1948.) Upper right: Indicators showing the rolling position of an airplane. In standard indicators the horizon moves as it would appear from the cockpit. In the better indicators the horizon is fixed and the plane displayed at a tilt as it would appear to a fixed observer behind the plane (an outside-in display). (Loucks, 1947.) Lower left: Patterned and unpatterned dial displays. Patterning permits the reader to see at a glance which dials are in the normal operating range. (Chapanis, Garner, and Morgan, 1949.) Lower right: A set of knob shapes judged as best in Air Force and Navy studies. These shapes were least likely to be confused with one another and can be identified by touch even through gloves. (Jenkins, 1947.)

Second, the methods of discovering and representing information that had been developed in the laboratory were put to work finding new information needed about man's capacities in new, hitherto unimagined settings. Thus, both the findings and the methods of experimental psychology were applied in ways that seemed remarkably distant from the laboratory settings of colleges and universities where the science was born.

Because of the utility of such basic research, many nonacademic institutions have been finding ways to support experimental psychologists doing "pure" research on fundamental problems. One of the best-known of these is the Bell Telephone Laboratories, where psychologists in the last few years have done original pioneering research on psychological scaling, visual masking, visual illusions, synthetic speech, short-term memory, learning from textual material, and learning of miniature linguistic systems.

Learning and Training

Psychology has had a long history of interaction with education, and theories of psychology have inevitably had their repercussions in the halls of learning. In recent years the emphasis in educational psychology has moved toward treating the learning situation as an explicit instance of operant or instrumental learning. Following the lead of the learning theorists, educational psychologists have been led to think about the contiguities of cues, responses, and rewards that are available in the school situation.

B.F. Skinner has started what amounts to a national movement in education with his notions of programed learning and the accompanying excitement about teaching machines. The teaching-machine fad is fast disappearing as people have discovered that no matter what machine they have, it is just a gadget; it is the program that counts. Programed instruction is founded on a few basic principles: The objectives of the teaching must be carefully and exactly spelled out in behavioral detail. The route to those objectives should be divided into steps as small as possible. The program should be arranged to elicit correct responses from the learner as frequently as possible. The subject should spend his time actively responding. Correct responses should be reinforced immediately.

Results of this effort are apparent everywhere, but they are somewhat mixed. Books have turned out to be more popular than machines for presenting the program. Like ordinary books and ordinary instructors, some programs are good and some are bad. Research on the principles of programing has also been mixed. Some studies show that it does not make much difference whether a student actually makes the responses or not. Some studies do not find bad effects for delaying the "reinforcement" (which is usually just knowing the right answer). There is active debate about whether there should be one path to the objectives or whether there should be branching programs that let people follow different paths to the same goal when they have different kinds of problems or come from different backgrounds.

The controversy seems to be fruitful. No one can deny that it is a good thing to take a careful look at the objectives of any course of instruction. No one doubts that it is helpful to think about the different ways in which the objectives might be achieved. The more one thinks about this in detail, the more he is likely to be able to teach and write adequately for students regardless of the particular format he uses. The argument about single-track programs and branching programs stresses the need for research into individual differences and their relation to subject matter. Finally, the more one thinks about programing at all, the more one is impressed with the fact that we do not understand how a body of knowledge ought to be taught because we do not fully understand how it is learned.

One thing became clear very early. A psychologist is not a substitute for a subject-matter specialist. If you ask the psychologist how to write a program, he can tell you. If you ask him what should be taught first and what should be taught second, he is forced to inquire of the person who knows the field and has experience teaching it. We do not know enough about the structure of subject matters or enough about the way structures are learned to let us say much more at this point.

Currently, interest in *computer-assisted instruction* is very high. This should not be thought of as merely an expensive, big, programed book but rather as a new kind of flexible teaching device that makes many innovations possible. The most dramatic example of "real" computer-assisted instruction is to have a computer simulate the characteristics of a new airplane. The pilot trainee then sits down in front of a control and instrument console and "flies" the "plane." If he makes a mistake, the computer informs him that he has just (theoretically) destroyed a $20,000,000 airplane. Would he like to try again and not make that mistake? This realistic and economical training would simply not be possible without a computer.

Many firms and universities are now working on ways to use the computer's capacities in instruction. A computer can govern many display units at once. It can give instruction, helpful hints, and commands, each depending on what the learner does. It can keep records of where the student is in a course, what he is doing, and how well he has done in the past. It can test him and evaluate both him and the program that instructed him. The computer can simulate a chemistry lab ("You have just blown up the laboratory. Would you like to try again and this time not make *that* mistake?") It can compute for the scholar and let him see the results of his experiments rapidly so that in a day he may gain the experience of several months of actual work. This development, too, makes us aware of the limits of our knowledge by raising many questions about the optimal way to employ resources or to regulate experiences to achieve a desired end.

Another application of instrumental-learning theory is leading to more effective social control in classrooms. Aside from the questions involved in teaching a subject matter, there is the general problem of regulating the activities of the pupils, keeping their attention, keeping them at work on a problem, getting them to "behave" in their interactions with each other, and the like. In these matters, the ingenious application of the techniques of reinforcement theorists has shown remarkable increases in classroom control. Psychologists observing the classroom as a laboratory have charted the level of several behaviors and then manipulated the reinforcement contingencies to change the pattern. In many classrooms the teacher pays attention to the children who are disruptive, destructive, or noisy. She may well never pay attention to them when they "act nice." Under this system, the children, rather naturally, choose attention over neglect and get "paid off" by an upset teacher. By systematically rewarding "studying behavior" and "learning behavior," the teacher can modify the social situation and achieve a group that is ready to learn instead of being ready to erupt.

Counseling and Therapy

The most popular image of a psychologist is that of someone who is going to help you raise your children, adjust your ailing marriage, or cure your neurosis. This image is scarcely differentiated from that of the psychiatrist, though the training and background of the two fields are very different. The psychiatrist with his medical background is much more likely to be oriented toward neurological disorders and toward therapy that involves medication or physical treatment of various sorts. The psychologist, on the other hand, is likely to play a more important role in diagnosis and assessment and to conduct portions of treatment that require specialized information about the world or learning new responses to it.

The counseling psychologist may not do any therapy at all. He may be a specialist who knows a great deal about job markets, training, interests, and abilities and who helps people find the fields in which they will be happiest and most adequate. Some counselors are specially trained to work with people who are handicapped or crippled or require special aids in the course of their rehabilitation. Such counseling has grown rapidly in the last decade and has assumed more and more importance.

Counselors who are concerned with personality problems and clinical psychologists who work with neurotics and psychotics may have a very different role to play and a very different orientation to the field. Many of these specialists are members of teams (at hospitals, clinics, schools, churches) and work with psychiatrists and social workers to effect changes in a patient's life situation and behavior. Most of them have a broad background in psychology plus a specialized knowledge in some approach to therapy or diagnosis and perform valued services to the community. An example of this kind of cooperation is a cleft palate team, which is likely to include a surgeon, an orthodontist, a speech therapist, a psychologist, and a social worker. A family therapy team may consist of a psychiatrist, a psychologist, a social worker, and a family counselor.

Other psychologists in these areas commit large amounts of time to research rather than service. They use the tools of the experimentalist and the tools of the theorist to study and understand the nature of mental disturbance and the nature of therapy. Among these psychologists we find the men who are experimenting with "behavior-modification therapy," applying the techniques of operant conditioning to changing the behavior and the mental life of the patients. Similarly, we find the "conditioning therapists" who have been attempting the same kind of modification via Pavlovian conditioning techniques. Dramatic results have been achieved by both schools of therapists, and interest has increased in these technologies for changing the behavior of the patient.

In addition, there are a variety of clinical specialties, such as psychopharmacology, which devotes its energies to ascertaining the effects of drugs on behavior. In the last 20 years, chemical agents have become very important in controlling and modifying behavior. We now have many varieties of tranquilizers, antidepressants, stimulants, and the like. In addition, of course, there is much interest (both social and theoretical) in the effects of certain drugs that seem to have marked psychological effects, the addictive drugs (morphine, heroin, cocaine) and the nonaddictive drugs (marijuana, LSD, and other hallucinogenic chemicals). These researchers have been developing techniques that serve to identify properties of new drugs by seeing how they affect animal behaviors, and they have gone on to develop complicated studies of habitual users (for example, chimpanzee morphine addicts) and the consequences of drug modification and withdrawal.

Social Psychology

Many psychologists have been drawn in recent years to the study of the organization and functioning of groups ranging in size from large organizations to two-person groups. Such research has implications for other areas of psychology since it appears, for example, that people often evaluate themselves and form impressions of their own personalities from the way other people respond to them. In addition, of course, this research has important implications for organizations of all sorts, from business institutions to revolutionary groups.

Social research in psychology has moved toward an experimental base in the last 20 years and is less concerned with the general study of social institutions, which has become (perhaps more properly) the domain of the sociologist. The experimental work has, in turn, led to more emphasis on studying the factors that lead to changes in goals, attitudes, and behaviors of individuals as a response to activities and events involving the group or social structure.

Techniques of social influence and group characteristics determining the amount of change have been of great interest to these investigators, and research on individual goals and behaviors in the group situation have often yielded findings that differ from the "obvious" results that we commonly assume. It is apparent, for example, that people do not work chiefly for money (as economists used to believe) and that important social controls are exercised over work productivity and other behaviors that are of interest to the relevant group.

Military organizations have studied the characteristics of successful air crews and submarine crews as well as other groups that live in close proximity and are concerned with the accomplishment of specific achievements. In this as well as in industrial work, applied social psychology has interacted with personnel psychology to study ways in which particular people and groups affect each other.

Academic and Research Psychologists

Finally, there are many psychologists, pursuing some of the puzzling problems we sketched earlier, who are still far removed from the level of applied problems. These men and women are interested in problems that may have great impact on all our lives and our activities if they are successful, as we believe that they eventually must be. These psychologists are interested in extending our knowledge to include all forms of behavior and experience. They want to know how the total mental apparatus of the human being works. They want to know how the sensory systems bring the world to us. They want to know how knowledge is represented in the brain and how the world is represented in the nervous system so that perception and practical knowledge are possible. They want to know the relation between thought and language.

These psychologists are trying to see how children acquire the notions of volume, quantity, and even the notion of "objectness" itself. They want to know how a child can learn a language from bits and pieces of inputs. They want to know the limits of modifiability of the human apparatus and the extent to which change is possible at every age. They want to understand the riddle of psychological development in the interaction with the world and spell out in detail how the human machine begins, changes, and ends.

These are questions for basic research. But answers to these questions could change the world and its people in remarkable ways.

GLOSSARY

REFERENCES

CREDITS

Glossary

We have not found it easy to shift from the role of psychologist to that of glossarist, but our students insist that it is useful to have some definitions of terms handy. To make the explanations more useful we have followed the brief definitions with a page reference—usually the first occasion of the use of the term and most of the time a place where the term is used in informative contexts.

absolute threshold The level of a physical stimulus at which it can just be detected reliably. [75]

accommodation In physiology, a change in the shape of the lens of the eye that enables the focusing of objects at varying distances from the eye. [155]

accommodation In Piaget's system, the change in the child as he tries to cope with experience. [557]

achromatic Without hue. [196]

acoustic Having to do with sounds. [263]

acoustic reflex An automatic contraction of the stapedius muscle to moderately intense sounds; it attenuates the effective intensity of sounds, thereby protecting the cochlea from being damaged, as it might be by excessively intense stimulation. [264]

active avoidance learning A learning task in which the subject must make a prescribed response in order to avoid an aversive stimulus. See **passive avoidance learning.** [376]

active learning Learning procedures that stress recitation and performance as opposed to simple reading of materials. [396]

actuarial Pertaining to the empirically established probabilities relating events to one another, without regard to the theoretical basis for the relation; probabilistic. [48]

algorithm A method of attacking a problem which is assured of success. Contrasted with **heuristic.** [507]

all-or-none law If a neural impulse ("spike") occurs at all, it occurs at maximal amplitude for that neuron; the magnitude of the impulse is independent of the intensity of the impulse-instigating stimulus. [164]

alpha rhythm A low-amplitude wave pattern found in the EEG during periods of relaxed alertness. Has a frequency of about ten cycles per second. See **electroencephalogram.** [563]

amnesia The inability to recall events in one's past, sometimes including one's own identity. [660]

analog computer A computer that operates on continuous signals of varying voltages. Contrasted with **digital computer.** [510]

anal stage In the genetic model of psychoanalytic theory, the stage of development in which libidinal interest and conflicts center on excretory functions and toilet training. See **genetic model; libido.** [700]

anechoic chamber An enclosure the walls of which are especially absorbing of sounds; without echoes. [80]

anisocoria A pathological condition in which the pupils of the two eyes are of unequal diameter. [151]

anomaloscope An instrument for distinguishing among various types of color-deficient individuals, especially **deuteranopes** and **protanopes**. [198]

anorexia Pathological aversion to food. [620]

anosmic Insensitive to odors. [277]

anthropomorphize The attribution of human-like psychological processes to animals. [128]

anticipation learning A form of rote-learning procedure in which the subject tries to give the next item in the list during each trial. Affords a running account of the subject's progress. [389]

aphagia Extreme undereating. See **hyperphagia**. [620]

approximation to English Procedures that yield materials that are more and more constrained to resemble English as one goes from zero-order (random selection) up to orders that depend on long sentence-like sequences. [441]

Army Alpha The intelligence test used by the U.S. Army in the First World War. The first effective group test of intelligence. [527]

association, laws of See **laws of association**.

associationism The philosophical view that what-is-learned consists of associations between ideas where ideas are determined by experiences in the world. See **empiricist**. [382]

audiogram A graphic plot of the threshold for acoustic stimulation as a function of the frequency of the stimulus. [265]

autoclitics Verbal behavior about one's own verbal behavior indicating its strength, accuracy, certainty, etc. [458]

autokinetic effect The apparent movement of a physically stationary spot of light viewed in a dark room. [708]

automatic action A well-practiced response that occurs "automatically" when its appropriate stimulus is presented. [515]

autonomic nervous system That part of the nervous system that regulates organs controlled by smooth muscles. It is composed of two branches, the **sympathetic** and the **parasympathetic**. [150]

axon A neural fiber that transmits electrical impulses away from the cell body of a neuron. See **dendrite**; **neuron**. [163]

backward conditioning A procedure in which the US precedes the CS. See **classical conditioning**. [317]

behavioral arrest Immobility resulting from severe conflict. [645]

behavioral vacillation Repeated cycles of movement toward and then away from a goal, characteristic of approach-avoidance conflicts. [645]

behaviorism A system of psychology which asserts that overt, observable behavior is the only proper subject matter of a scientific psychology. [113]

bel; decibel A bel is a unit of auditory intensity relative to the auditory threshold; a decibel is one tenth of a bel. The decibel scale is often used as a scale of auditory loudness, though its validity for that purpose is questionable. See **sone scale**. [272]

Bell-Magendie law The principle that the dorsal root of a spinal nerve is sensory and the ventral root is motor in function. [296]

belonging A principle invoked by Thorndike to describe the effects of relations on what was learned. [384]

binocular disparity The difference between the images projected onto the retinas of the two eyes by a solid object; the major binocular depth cue. [253]

blind spot That part of the visual field in which stimuli cannot be seen because their images are projected onto the optic disc—a part of the retina devoid of receptor cells. See **optic disc**. [161]

Bloch's law The inverse, linear relation between the duration of a visual target and its threshold. [192]

boot-strapping Lifting one's self by the bootstraps. In science, using a crude measure or procedure to derive a better one. [65]

cardiovascular Pertaining to the heart and blood vessels. [150]

centile rank A measure of relative position in a group indicating what percentage of the norm group had poorer performance than the individual being measured. [93]

central nervous system Neural cells located within the spinal cord and brain. [296]

central tendency A measure—such as the **mean, median,** or **mode**—that characterizes the center of a distribution of scores. [89]

CFF (critical flicker frequency) That frequency at which a light that is going rapidly on and off appears to be steadily on. [209]

chronological age Age in years. [522]

CIE chromaticity diagram A three-dimension model that reflects the main principles of additive color mixture. [197]

circadian rhythm A cyclically occurring event with a period of about 24 hours. [570]

classical (Pavlovian) conditioning A procedure for effecting learning in which a "neutral" stimulus (the conditioned stimulus, CS) is repeatedly paired with a stimulus (the unconditioned stimulus, US) that reliably elicits a particular response (the unconditioned response, UR). After a sufficient number of such pairings (conditioning trials), the conditioned stimulus takes on the ability of the unconditioned stimulus to elicit the response (now the conditioned response, CR). [315]

Cloze technique A procedure in which words are deleted from verbal passages and subjects are required to identify the missing words. [633]

cochlear microphonic Electrical activity recorded from the cochlea of the ear that closely matches the frequency and amplitude of the acoustic stimulus. [266]

coefficient of correlation See **correlation coefficient**. [97]

cognition The process of knowing, perceiving, and recognizing; most generally, thinking. [484]

cognitive dissonance A drive-like state resulting from the simultaneous presence of cognitions that are mutually incompatible. [650]

complementary colors Two hues that yield an achromatic additive mixture. [196]

computer program A set of directions telling a computer with great explicitness exactly what to do. [504]

computer simulation Programing a computer to "behave" in exactly the way specified by a theory. More generally, programing a computer to do something an organism does. [482]

concept A general representation of a class of objects, events, or relations. May depend on common attributes, responses, or structures. [489]

concrete operations The fourth stage advanced by Piaget in his theory of development. Characterized by consistent cognitive ways of dealing with the world. Child can order and classify on several dimensions at once. Seven to eleven years. [556]

connectionism The theory that the major activity of the central nervous system is simply to connect stimuli and responses. Intelligence is viewed as a function of number and availability of connections. [524]

conservation The knowledge that pouring liquid into different-sized containers does not change the amount, deforming clay does not diminish it, spreading out a line of checkers does not increase the number, etc. [555]

constancies Manifestations of the tendency for the perceived properties of objects (such as their shape, color, and brightness) to remain stable despite marked changes in the retinal images cast by the objects. [258]

constriction With regard to the pupil of the eye, a decrease in its diameter; in general, contraction or shrinking. [148]

construct validity The extent to which a particular instrument measures some abstract trait or concept that can only indirectly be verified. [102]

content validity The extent to which a particular instrument samples the content it is supposed to measure. [102]

contextual learning The assimilation of meaning to a new item from the surrounding context. [452]

convergent thinking Thinking directed at a solution to a particular well-defined problem. [552]

correlation coefficient A measure of the degree of relationship between two variables. Varies from -1.00 to $+1.00$. Zero means no relationship. Positive values mean the variables increase or decrease together. Negative values mean one increases as the other decreases. [97]

covert responses Responses too reduced to be observable; implicit responses. [483]

Crespi effect When the magnitude of reinforcement is abruptly increased or decreased to particular levels, performance of a learned response over- or under-shoots that characteristic of a fixed reinforcement magnitude at those levels. [613]

criterion validity The extent to which a particular instrument predicts achievement or status on some criterion. [102]

cross-sectional studies Studies in which samples are drawn at each age or experience level and compared with each other. Noncomparability of samples is a crucial issue. [529]

culture-free test A test supposed to be independent of particular language and cultural biases. [543]

cytoplasm The protoplasmic material surrounding the nucleus of a cell. [163]

day-residues Apparently trivial (but unconsciously important) events of the day that appear as elements in dreams. [663]

decibel See **bel**. [67]

defense mechanism An unconscious device within the ego for dealing with unconscious conflicts and resultant anxiety. See **ego; structural model**. [659]

delayed conditioning A procedure in which a CS of long duration is employed and the onset of the US occurs at the end of the CS presentation. See **classical conditioning**. [319]

delta waves A high-amplitude, low-frequency wave pattern, found in the EEG during periods of low arousal and sleep. [563]

demographic Pertaining to characteristics of populations; used loosely to refer to such characteristics as sex, age, social class, ethnic background, and so on. [682]

dendrite A neural fiber that transmits electrical impulses toward the cell body of a neuron. See **axon; neuron**. [163]

denial Refusal to acknowledge the existence of, or reality of, highly threatening events, either external or internal; a primitive defense mechanism. [666]

derived lists Learning materials arranged so that subsequent lists are systematically related to original lists by taking every other item in order, every third item, every fourth item, etc. [394]

detour problem A problem in which the subject has to learn to take a roundabout route to a goal instead of trying to approach it correctly. [495]

deuteranope A dichromat with a red-green deficiency, possibly because of insensitivity to blue-green light. See **protanope.** [198]

dichotic stimulation Presentation to the two ears of different auditory stimuli. [276]

dichromat A color-defective individual whose full range of color experience can be produced by the mixture of two (rather than the normal three) primary colors. [198]

diffraction The spreading of light waves as they pass over the edge of an object. [147]

digital computer A computer that operates on two-valued signals, typically $+1$ and 0. Contrasted with **analog computer.** [502]

dilatation (dilation) With regard to the pupil of the eye, an increase in its diameter; in general, enlargement. [150]

dioptric power The ability of a lens to bend, or refract, light. [207]

discriminated operant An instrumentally learned response that is reinforced only if made in the presence of a particular stimulus. [363]

discrimination In the context of conditioning, the learned inhibition of a generalized response to a stimulus that is similar to the CS. See **stimulus generalization.** [339]

disinhibition The temporary restoration of an extinguished response that is manifested when the CS is accompanied by a novel stimulus. See **classical conditioning; external inhibition.** [338]

dispersion A measure such as the **range** or **standard deviation** that shows the spread of scores in a distribution. [91]

distributed learning Spreading learning trials over time instead of doing all learning at once. Aids retention. [393]

divergent thinking Thinking that is concerned with a variety of ideas; novel, creative, imaginative thinking. [547]

dizygotic twins Fraternal twins. [547]

DNA (deoxyribose nucleic acid) A complex nucleoprotein implicated in the coding of genetic information. See **RNA.** [129]

echoic response Saying something that one has just heard; copying; echoing. [458]

EEG (electroencephalogram) A recording of the electrical activity of the brain. [563]

effect, law of See **law of effect.**

ego In the structural model of psychoanalytic theory, the largely conscious, but partly unconscious "mental institution" that is responsible for perceptual, cognitive, and motoric functions. See **structural model.** [659]

electromagnetic radiation Waves emitted as a result of interactions at the atomic level, ranging in frequency from about 10^{24} to 10^0 (or 1) cycles per second. [143]

electron micrograph A photograph of an object "viewed" through an electron microscope. [156]

Emmert's law The principle that the perceived size of an image on the retina varies directly with the perceived distance of the object that presumably is projecting the image. [257]

emotional meaning Connotative meaning as opposed to denotative meaning. Meaning suggested by a term or symbol beyond its explicit or referential meaning. [436]

empiricist One who attributes the behavior of mature individuals, especially behavioral differences among individuals, to the specific experiences they have had in the course of their development, rather than to their genetic endowment. See **nativist.** [109]

engram A hypothetical change in the nervous system that is the physiological counterpart of learning. [311]

epinephrine; norepinephrine Hormones secreted by the medulla of the adrenal gland, having a generally arousing function; sometimes called adrenalin and noradrenalin. [587]

epistemology That branch of philosophy concerned with the acquisition and validity of people's knowledge about the world. [112]

equilibrium model Piaget's conception that the child interacts with the world and through assimilation and accommodation adapts to it. [557]

ethology That branch of zoology concerned with the behavior of animals, especially as it occurs in the animals' natural habitats. [128]

evoked potential A very small change in voltage recorded from the cerebral cortex of the brain following stimulation of one of the sense modalities. [211]

experimental neurosis Symptoms of emotional disturbance that sometimes follow an animal's confrontation with a difficult discrimination task. [339]

experimenter effect (Rosenthal effect) The effect on subjects' behavior attributable to the experimenter's expectations about how the subjects should perform. [56]

external inhibition The temporary suppression of a conditioned response that is manifested when the CS is accompanied by a novel stimulus. See **classical conditioning; disinhibition.** [338]

extinction The elimination of a learned response, accomplished by repeated elicitation of the response without a reinforcing stimulus. [336]

false negative report A report that a signal or event was not present when in fact a signal was actually presented. [80]

false positive report A report that a signal or event was present when no signal was actually presented. [80]

Ferry-Porter law The relation between the apparent brightness of a flickering light (with a frequency greater than the CFF) and the duration and intensity of the "on" portion of the light-dark cycle. [209]

field dependence/independence A personality trait characterized by relative ability or inability to separate perceptual elements from the context in which they are embedded. [219]

figural aftereffect A change in the apparent shape or location of a visual figure following inspection of another figure. [241]

fixation In psychoanalytic theory, failure of psychosexual development to proceed normally from one stage to the next. In the context of the topic of vision, fixation refers to the point in space at which the eyes are directed. In the context of animal behavior, fixation refers to an animal's inability to reject an incorrect stimulus (or extinguish an incorrect response) in favor of a correct one. [672]

fixed-interval schedule A reinforcement schedule in which a reinforcement is delivered after every response that follows a specified time period since the previous reinforcement. See **variable interval schedule.** [355]

fixed-ratio schedule A reinforcement schedule in which a reinforcement is delivered after every n responses. See **variable ratio schedule.** [356]

formal operations Piaget's final stage of development (12 years to adult). Consists of systematizing and generalizing at the formal level the knowledge of the world achieved at the level of **concrete operations.** [556]

Fourier analysis A mathematical procedure for finding the simple sinusoidal components of a complex wave form. [264]

fraternal twins Twins developed from two different eggs. Their genetic relation is the same as that between ordinary children in the same family. [547]

frequency of usage A count of how often a particular event occurs in some block of time or sequence of behavior, most commonly how often a particular word occurs in a text. [430]

functional fixedness Thinking of an

object in only one way, which prevents a subject from seeing how the object could be used in another way to solve a problem. [500]

functionalism A system of psychology which emphasizes the adaptive significance of conscious experience. [113]

g See **general intelligence.** [523]

ganglion A cluster of neural cell bodies outside the central nervous system. [297]

ganzfeld A visual field devoid of visible contours or texture; a homogeneous field. [202]

GAS (general adaptation syndrome) A pattern of physiological responses to extreme stress. [575]

general intelligence A trait postulated to account for the positive relation found between many different kinds of tests of abilities and achievement. Nonspecific intelligence. [523]

generalized reinforcement A form of secondary reinforcement that is not specifically related to any single need state. Examples are praise, smiling, thanks, etc. [458]

genetic model That part of psychoanalytic theory concerned with personality development. [658]

genotype The underlying structure of objects or events inferred from their phenotypic properties. See **phenotype.** [23]

Gestalt A configuration, or pattern. Also, a system of psychology that emphasizes the significance of patterns. [224]

grammar A systematic description of the elements, relations, and structures of a language. [427]

group factors Psychological factors postulated to account for interrelations of groups of tests; typically numerical, clerical, verbal, spatial, etc. [524]

GSR (galvanic skin response) A change in the electrical conductivity of the skin, often used as an index of emotional arousal. [322]

habit-family hierarchy Habits related to a given stimulus situation varying in degree of strength. Theory says the strongest occurs, then the next, etc. [485]

habituation An outcome of repeated stimulation whereby a particular response temporarily becomes harder than usual to elicit. See **sensitization.** [310]

Hawthorne effect The effect on subjects' performance attributable to their knowledge that they are serving as experimental subjects or being treated in a special manner. [52]

hedonic Pertaining to the dimension of pleasantness-unpleasantness. [291]

heuristic A shortcut way to solve a problem which may or may not work. Contrasted with **algorithm.** [507]

hierarchical model of intelligence The view that intelligence is hierarchically structured with general intelligence, group factors, specific factors, and, finally, specific information in an interdependent system. [525]

hierarchy of skill A task that displays several levels of organization or structure. Performance curves often show interesting evidence of such structure. [412]

homeostasis The process of self-regulation in physiological systems. [605]

hyperopia Farsightedness; deficient acuity for close objects. [204]

hyperphagia Excessive eating. See **aphagia.** [618]

hypomania Excited, agitated, euphoric, optimistic beyond the normal level but not wildly out of control. [10]

hysteria A form of neurosis, often accompanied by somatic symptoms, such as paralysis or anesthesia of body parts, presumably resulting from the excessive application of repression. [661]

id That "mental institution" in the structural model of psychoanalytic theory which serves as the repository of unconscious ideas and impulses. See **structural model.** [658]

identical twins Twins developed from the same fertilized egg and, thus, having identical heredities. [547]

identification In the genetic model of psychoanalytic theory, the incorporation by the developing child of the parents' conscious and unconscious personality characteristics. [674]

idiot-savant A person with marked skill or talent in some specific activity (art, carving, calculation, etc.) although his general intellectual level is low. [516]

immediate memory The recall of material presented only once; memory without repeated trials or practice. [389]

implicit responses Responses of such small magnitude as to be unobservable; covert responses. [488]

imprinting A hypothetical process, akin to learning, whereby animals of certain species, especially fowl, become "emotionally attached" to whatever stimulus they are first exposed to shortly after hatching or birth; the attachment is manifested by the animal's persistent following after the imprinted object (often its own mother). [589]

Indo-European languages A family of languages including most of those spoken in Europe and southwestern Asia. [429]

inflectional endings In English the element of a word indicating plural and possessive in nouns (houses, house's) and number and tense of verbs (walk, walks, walked). [452]

information The measure of how much uncertainty is reduced by a stimulus. If there are many alternative events, the occurrence of a particular one carries a great deal of information. If only one thing can happen, its occurrence carries almost no information. [441]

insight The label given to sudden complete solution of a problem; connotes understanding. [496]

instrumental learning A procedure in which the occurrence of reinforcement is contingent on the occurrence of the response to be learned. [346]

intellectualization A form of the defense mechanism of isolation in which events or ideas are stripped of their normal emotional concomitants and treated in a coldly intellectual manner. [670]

intelligence A trait postulated to underlie abilities to make judgments, solve problems, succeed in academic activities, etc. Many models have been developed describing how these abilities relate to each other. [515]

interference theory In human learning the theory that forgetting is due to interference from other materials learned earlier (**proactive interference**) or from materials learned later (**retroactive interference**). [399]

internal clock A hypothetical physiological mechanism that regulates the cyclic variations recorded from many physiological systems. See **circadian rhythm.** [570]

internal inhibition A hypothetical process postulated by Pavlov to account for extinction. See **extinction.** [336]

interval scale Numbers arranged to order a variable in such a way that equal changes in the variable are represented by equal differences in the numbers. See **ordinal** and **ratio scales.** [70]

intraverbal responses Verbal responses that are related to other verbal responses; word associations; facts known through verbal chains: "Columbus—1492." [458]

intuitional thinking Characteristic of Piaget's third developmental stage. The child learns to take many things into account at the same time. He shows conservation phenomena. Five to seven years. [555]

IQ (intelligence quotient) Mental age as a proportion of chronological age. $IQ = 100 \times \frac{MA}{CA}$. An index of relative brightness. [522]

irradiation A hypothetical neurophysiological process postulated by Pavlov to account for stimulus generalization. See **stimulus generalization**. [333]

irregular verbs Verbs that take idiosyncratic modification rather than regular endings to show change of tense: run-ran, take-took, etc. [474]

isolation A defense mechanism in which ideas, or ideas and emotions, are kept separate from one another when they would normally be integrated or associated. See **defense mechanism; intellectualization**. [670]

item difficulty A measure of how hard or easy an item is. In intelligence testing one may use the age at which 50–70 per cent of children pass the item. [520]

item discrimination A measure of how sharply an item distinguishes between high and low scorers, or people possessing more or less of the trait being measured. [520]

jnd (just noticeable difference) The smallest difference between two stimuli that can be detected reliably. [75]

Landolt ring A figure in the shape of a C, or a ring with a small gap, used in the laboratory assessment of visual acuity. [204]

latency stage In the genetic model of psychoanalytic theory, the stage of development, beginning about age five, in which "sexuality" is relatively quiescent and intellectual functions and peer relations are paramount. [705]

law of effect The principle that responses which are immediately followed by reinforcement will be learned. [348]

laws of association Classic treatment of knowing and thinking which held that associations arose from three sources: similarity, contrast, and contiguity in space or time. [484]

learning curve A record of performance over trials from which learning may be inferred. [411]

learning-to-learn (learning sets) The observation that subjects become increasingly proficient at discrimination-learning tasks the more such tasks they have been given. [374]

libido In psychoanalytic theory, "psychic energy." [671]

lightning calculator A person who can perform amazing feats of computation in his head in very little time. [516]

longitudinal studies Studies in which a sample is chosen and then followed as age and experience increase. Problems involve keeping track of the numbers of the sample and keeping the tests comparable. [530]

luminosity The effective brightness of light, with intensity constant—a result of the varying sensitivity of the visual system to different wavelengths of light. [194]

Mach bands Visual contours that appear where there is no corresponding physical discontinuity in light intensity. [221]

magnitude estimation A psychophysical technique in which the subject assigns a set of numbers to stimuli so that appropriate ratios are maintained between pairs of sensations and pairs of numbers. [77]

mand A verbal utterance under the control of the state of deprivation of the speaker. A basic form of verbal behavior in Skinner's system. [457]

Marbe's law The generalization that the latency of a response in word association increases as the popularity or commonness of the response decreases. [446]

massed practice Bunching learning trials close together without rest periods. Adversely affects performance and sometimes retention. [393]

mean The arithmetic average; the balance point; the sum of all scores divided by the number of scores. [90]

meaningfulness The measurement of the number of responses a subject can make to a stimulus in some unit of time. Indexes ease of learning. [493]

median The middle score; half the scores or values lie above it, half lie below. [90]

mediated association Association between two items via another item. Thus, if A is associated with B and B is associated to C, A is mediately associated with C. [408]

memory trace A hypothetical entity supposed to be what-is-remembered. Gestalt psychologists hold that the trace undergoes systematic change and reorganization. [419]

mental age A term applied to both items and scores on intelligence tests. For an item, the age level is that age at which 50–70 per cent of children pass the item. For an individual it is the age group of children who would pass the same items he has passed. [517]

mental chronometry Attempt to measure mental functions by subtracting simpler tasks from more complex ones. [515]

mnemonics Memory aids or systems for learning materials. [398]

mode The most frequent score in a distribution; the class with the greatest number of entries. [90]

monochromator An instrument for producing light of a very narrow wavelength band. [146]

monozygotic twins Identical twins. [547]

Morgan's canon The admonishment, in the interest of scientific parsimony, not to attribute to animals of one phylogenetic level psychological processes that are appropriate to animals of higher levels. [128]

morpheme A word or part of a word that conveys meaning. *Man* is a morpheme; *manly* is two morphemes and *manliness* is three morphemes. [464]

mosaic hypothesis The postulation of a simple one-to-one correspondence between perceptual experience and physical stimulation; the basic weakness, according to Gestalt theorists, in the system of Structuralism. See **Structuralism; Gestalt.** [224]

movement parallax The difference in the rate of motion over the retinal surface of images projected by objects at different distances from a moving observer. [250]

myelin sheath The fatty, or lipid, substance that surrounds the axons of some neurons. The greater the degree of myelinization, the greater the speed of transmission of neural impulses. [164]

myoneural junction The meeting point between neural axons and muscle fibers. [363]

myopia Nearsightedness; deficient acuity for distant objects. [207]

narcissistic Self-centered, egotistical, gratification-oriented; characteristic of the infant and of persons whose personalities retain infantile features, such as psychopaths. [676]

nativist One who attributes the behavior of mature individuals, especially behavioral differences among individuals, to their genetic endowment, rather than to the specific experiences they have had in the course of their development. See **empiricist.** [108]

negative acceleration A value that changes by smaller and smaller steps as a function of time or trials. In learning curves, a curve of diminishing returns. [411]

nerve A bundle of neural fibers (neurons) outside the central nervous system. [150]

neurohumor A chemical substance emitted at the tips of neural fibers that participates in transmission of impulses across the synaptic junction. See **synapse.** [169]

neuron A cell specialized for the transmission of electrical impulses; the structural unit of the nervous system. [158]

neurosis A type of psychopathology

in which a person's effectiveness is severely limited either by somatic symptoms, as in hysteria, or by cognitive and behavioral inflexibility, presumably the result of overly rigid or overly developed defense mechanisms. See **hysteria; defense mechanism; psychopathology.** [661]

noise Background of stimulation in which signal is embedded; unwanted signals. [81]

nonsense syllable Combinations of consonant-vowel-consonant making a syllable-like cluster. Used to control for familiarity of material in learning studies. [388]

normal distribution The symmetrical, bell-shaped distribution used in statistics and in trait measurement. Commonly assumed as a base for standard scores. [87]

norm group The group with which an individual is being compared, usually to interpret the results of a psychological test. [95]

nucleus That portion of a cell containing genetic material. Also, a group of cell bodies within the central nervous system. See **ganglion.** [174]

nystagmic eye movements (tremors) Low-amplitude, high-frequency involuntary movements of the eye. [148]

oddity problem A problem in which the solution lies in choosing the stimulus item which is unlike the others. If two circles and one square are presented, the square is correct. [491]

Oedipus complex In psychoanalytic theory, the conflicts resulting from the young boy's competition with his father for his mother's attention and affection. [675]

ogive A curve that is loosely described as S-shaped. [183]

ontogenetic (genetic) Pertaining to development within the members of a species. See **phylogenetic.** [134]

operant level The rate at which a response is emitted prior to the introduction of a reinforcement schedule. [353]

optic disc That part of the retina where the optic nerve exits from the eye, consequently a part with no receptor cells. See **blind spot.** [161]

oral stage In the genetic model of psychoanalytic theory, the stage of development in which libidinal interest and conflicts center on the mouth—on sucking, eating, biting, and so on. See **genetic model; libido.** [700]

order effect An effect on behavior attributable to the specific sequence of experimental conditions to which subjects are exposed. [59]

ordinal scale Numbers arranged to correspond to the increase or decrease in the variable being measured. A set of ranks. Contrast with **interval** and **ratio scales.** [70]

orthogenetic principle The generalization that the psychological development of individuals is characterized by increasing differentiation among the subparts of their personalities and by increasingly complex organizational structures among those parts. [690]

osmotic pressure A difference in the concentration of fluids on either side of a semipermeable membrane. [616]

overlearning Reciting or rehearsing material past the point of getting it all correct. [391]

paired-associate learning A form of rote-learning experiment in which the subject learns stimulus-response pairs. To a particular stimulus he learns to give a particular response. [389]

paranoia Pathological suspiciousness of others' motives, especially as they relate to oneself. [670]

paranoid schizophrenia A type of schizophrenia in which paranoid tendencies predominate. [670]

parasympathetic system The branch of the autonomic nervous system that serves primarily to modulate or dampen activity in the organs controlled by the autonomic system. See **autonomic nervous system.** [150]

part learning Learning by dividing the materials into subsections or units, then combining at the end. [397]

passive avoidance learning A learning task in which the subject must refrain from making a prepotent response in order to avoid an aversive stimulus. See **active avoidance learning**. [378]

percentile See **centile rank**. [93]

perceptual defense Failure to recognize stimuli that are threatening because of their relation to unconscious conflicts. See **perceptual vigilance**. [662]

perceptual displacement Perceiving an event as having occurred at some other time or place than its actual occurrence, usually as a consequence of the structure of its context. [469]

perceptual vigilance Heightened sensitivity to stimuli that are threatening because of their relation to unconscious conflicts. See **perceptual defense**. [662]

performance Recordable, overt behavior. What the organism actually does. The data base for inferences about knowledge, experience, learning, etc. [414]

personal equation The correction of an observation for the observer's time error (from astronomy). [66]

phallic stage In the genetic model of psychoanalytic theory, the stage of development in which libidinal interest and conflicts center on the sexual organs. See **genetic model; libido**. [700]

phantom limb Term applied to sensory experiences seeming to arise in a limb, or part of a limb, that has been amputated. [292]

phenotype Observable properties of objects or events which allow them to be classified. See **genotype**. [23]

pheromone A chemical substance secreted by members of certain species that functions as a trail marker or as an indicator of the limits of an animal's territory. [282]

philology The study of written records and texts, now, generally, linguistics. [429]

phi phenomenon The apparent movement that occurs when two or more visual figures are successively illuminated. [244]

phoneme A class of related sounds that can be regarded as a single sound in transcribing or recording an utterance in a language; roughly an alphabetic character. [464]

phonology The study of the system of speech sounds within and across languages. [464]

photopic Pertaining to visual functioning under conditions of relatively high-intensity illumination. See **scotopic**. [193]

phrase In grammar, a group of words that can function as a constituent or element in grammatical structure. [464]

phrenology A system developed by Franz Joseph Gall for identifying types of people by examining their physical features, especially the configuration of "bumps" on their skulls. [117]

phylogenetic Pertaining to the scale of evolutionary development. See **ontogenetic**. [134]

pivot-open grammar A grammar with two classes of words: the pivots, a short list of words that operate on other words, and the open class, a long list of items to which new cases may be readily added. [474]

placebo effect The effect of a treatment on physiological or behavioral reactions that is attributable to the recipient's expectation of how the treatment is supposed to affect him. [54]

positive acceleration A value that changes by larger and larger steps as a function of time or trials. In learning curves, a curve of increasing returns. [411]

power law The principle that sensation increases as some power of the physical stimulus. $S = aI^K$ where

S is sensation, I is intensity of the physical stimulus and a and K are empirically derived constants. [77]

PRE (partial-reinforcement effect) The greater resistance to extinction of responses learned on a schedule with a reinforcement ratio less than 1.00 than of responses learned on a schedule with a ratio of 1.00. See **fixed-ratio schedule; extinction.** [358]

presbyopia Deficient visual acuity in old age, attributable to loss of flexibility of the tissues of the lens, resulting in decreased ability to accommodate. See **accommodation.** [207]

primary drives The behaviorally activating concomitants of physiological need states; in some motivational models, the innate motives on which all others are based. See **secondary drives.** [608]

primary mental abilities Major components of intelligence. Group factors posited by the Thurstones as a result of factor analyses. [524]

primary-process thinking In psychoanalytic theory, thinking that is permeated by unconscious material or characterized by a disregard for logic and reality. See **secondary-process thinking.** [674]

primary rewards Substances or events that abruptly reduce the level of primary drives; in some learning models, the innate rewards on which all others are based. See **secondary rewards.** [608]

proactive interference Interference with recently learned materials as a result of earlier learning by the subject. [401]

probability matching In a discrimination task where each stimulus alternative has a finite probability of being correct, the tendency of subjects to respond to each stimulus with a probability that approximates the probability that the stimulus is correct. [374]

projection A defense mechanism in which one's unacceptable impulses are kept unconscious by attributing them to others and denying them in oneself. See **defense mechanism.** [669]

projective test A test designed so as to enhance the likelihood that the test-taker's motives and conflicts, and his style of dealing with them, will be revealed in his responses. [56]

protanope A dichromat with a red-green deficiency due to a relative insensitivity to red light. See **deuteranope.** [198]

protocol A record of behavior from which scientific data may be extracted. [25]

psychoanalytic theory The complex personality theory developed by Sigmund Freud and his disciples which emphasizes unconscious ideas, motives, and conflicts and which stresses the biological-sexual basis of personality development. [658]

psychometric Having to do with psychological measurement. [549]

psychopath One who is not deterred from committing immoral or antisocial acts by the anxiety that normally accompanies such behavior; attributable, according to a psychoanalytic interpretation, primarily to an inadequately developed superego. [667]

psychopathology Mental illness; severe emotional disturbance; abnormal or antisocial behavior. [122]

psychophysics The study of the quantitative relation between changes in physical stimulation and changes in sensory experience. [65]

psychosexual development In the genetic model of psychoanalytic theory, movement from one developmental stage (oral, anal, and so on) to the next. See **genetic model.** [700]

psychosis Severe psychopathology, characterized by a break with external reality, presumably because the ego is flooded with unconscious material as a result of inadequately functioning defense mechanisms. [674]

Purkinje shift The increase in the brightness of light of the shorter wavelengths relative to longer wavelength light, as illumination level shifts from photopic to scotopic values. [194]

range The distance from the lowest score to the highest score in a distribution. [92]

ratio scale An interval scale beginning with a true zero point. Only on such a scale are ratios meaningful. See **interval** and **ordinal scales.** [73]

raw scores Numbers originally assigned to performance; usually uninterpretable without further data. [93]

reaction formation A defense mechanism whereby a person keeps unacceptable impulses unconscious by engaging in behavior that would ordinarily be motivated by impulses just the opposite of those that are repressed. See **defense mechanism.** [667]

reappearance hypothesis The notion that copies of images are stored in memory and that remembering consists of making these copies reappear. [417]

reconstruction The notion that memory consists of an abstraction and coding process and that recall involves decoding and elaboration. [417]

reductionism The point of view that explanation of events at one level (for example, psychological) is best accomplished by reference to processes at a "lower" or more basic level (for example, physiological). [135]

redundancy The extent to which stimuli are predictable and repetitious. The converse of independent and unpredictable. [444]

referential meaning Meaning having to do with the relation of a term or symbol to an object; label, name. [435]

refraction The bending of light waves. [146]

refractory phase The period following the occurrence of a neural impulse when the neuron's threshold is higher than normal. [167]

reinforcement schedule A rule specifying the occasions on which reinforcements will be delivered. [354]

reliability The extent to which a test or other instrument measures consistently and accurately. Two kinds are discriminated: stability over time and internal consistency. [101]

REM sleep A stage of sleep in which rapid eye movements are recorded and during which dreaming is most likely to occur. [565]

repeated learning Relearning material previously learned back to the point of mastery. Reduces forgetting subsequently. [392]

representational thinking Characteristic of the second stage in Piaget's system. The child develops representations for things that one can do. One-and-a-half to four years. [554]

repression The basic defense mechanism, whereby unacceptable memories, fantasies, and impulses are rendered or kept unconscious. See **defense mechanism.** [659]

response integration Unitizing or knitting together a complex response to be learned. A necessary prerequisite to the associative (hook up) stage. [403]

retinal densitometer An instrument for measuring the amount of photosensitive pigment in the retina of a living organism. [160]

retinal receptive field A small area on the retina which, when stimulated, gives rise to electrical activity in a single neuron in the visual neural system. [171]

retroactive interference Interference with (forgetting or inhibition of) earlier learned materials by more recent learning. [400]

reversal learning A discrimination-learning procedure in which the roles of the "correct" and "incorrect" stimuli are switched after the subject has reached a criterion performance level. [373]

rhodopsin The photosensitive pigment found in the rod cells of the retina of the eye. [158]

Ricco's law The inverse linear relation between the area of a visual target and its threshold. [191]

rigidity The characteristic of continuing to perform a task in a stereotyped fashion even after better methods become possible. [500]

RNA (ribose nucleic acid) A complex nucleoprotein synthesized by DNA, and involved in the synthesis of other protein molecules; hypothesized by some to be implicated in memory storage. See **DNA.** [129]

rote learning Learning verbatim; learning "by heart"; sometimes, learning without understanding. [382]

saccadic eye movement (saccade) An abrupt, automatic movement of the eye that serves to return the eye to its original point of fixation following a "drift" away from fixation. [152]

Sanskrit The classical Old Indic literary language, described in detail by the linguist Pānini in the fourth century B.C. [427]

savings The measure of retention (or forgetting) by relearning the original material and computing the proportion of original trials required. [390]

scattergram A way of displaying the relation between two variables by plotting on a graph. [98]

schizophrenia A form of extreme psychopathology, characterized by inadequate contact with reality, severe thought disorders, and inappropriate affect. [670]

scotopic Pertaining to visual functioning under conditions of relatively low intensity illumination. See **photopic.** [193]

secondary drives Drives acquired through the contiguity of previously neutral stimuli and primary drives. See **primary drives.** [607]

secondary-process thinking In psychoanalytic theory, thinking that is relatively free of unconscious material and that is characterized by a strict regard for logic and reality. See **primary-process thinking.** [674]

secondary rewards Rewards acquired through the contiguity of previously neutral stimuli and primary rewards (or the abrupt reduction in the level of primary drives). See **primary rewards.** [608]

second signal system The language system; the system unique to human beings which could override the reflex system, according to Pavlov. [386]

Semantic Differential A rating-scale approach to connotative meaning. Each concept is rated on a series of bipolar scales like *good-bad*. [493]

semantic generalization Transfer of a response from one word to which it was initially learned to another word that is meaningfully related to the first stimulus. [448]

semantics The study of the relation of signs and symbols to what they mean or denote. [464]

sensitization An outcome of repeated stimulation whereby a particular response temporarily becomes easier than usual to elicit. See **habituation.** [310]

sensorimotor intelligence The first stage in Piaget's system. A child acquires object constancies and representations of the world. Birth to one-and-one-half years. [553]

serendipity The experience of finding one thing while looking for another. [42]

serial learning A form of experiment in rote learning in which a list of items is learned in a fixed order. [388]

shaping A procedure whereby reinforcements are delivered for responses that more and more closely approximate the response ultimately to be learned. [353]

signal-detection theory A technique of psychophysics that permits estimates of the detectability of the signal and the bias of the observer. [79]

simultaneous contrast The effect on brightness or color produced by presenting in close proximity, and at the same time, complementary visual stimuli. [201]

Snellen chart A series of letters varying in size, used for the clinical assessment of nearsightedness. [203]

somatic nervous system That part of the nervous system that regulates effector organs controlled by striped muscles and that transmits neural activity originating in the several receptor organs. [152]

sone scale A scale of auditory loudness based on direct loudness judgments. [273]

specific factors Reliable component of a test score specific to the test itself, that is, not correlating with other tests. [523]

spectral Pertaining to the visible band of wavelengths within the range of electromagnetic radiation. [196]

spike potential The large amplitude change in electrical potential that constitutes the "neural impulse"; the magnitude of the spike follows the all-or-none law. [167]

spontaneous recovery The reoccurrence of an extinguished response following a rest period between extinction and retesting, and with no retraining. [337]

stabilized retinal image An image that remains fixed in location on the retina, despite the occurrence of nystagmic eye movements. Typically, such stabilized images rapidly disappear. [153]

stages of development Periods in the development of a child when his mental operations can be characterized in a particular way and certain phenomena can be observed. The sequence of stages is supposed to be constant though the rate of progressing through them may differ. [553]

standard deviation A measure of dispersion. The square root of the average squared deviations from the mean. With the mean it defines a normal curve. [92]

standard score A relative score that indicates an individual's relation to the norm in terms of the number of standard deviations by which he deviates from the mean. [93]

stereogram One of the stimulus patterns employed in a stereoscope. [255]

stereoscope An instrument for presenting one visual stimulus to the right eye and a different stimulus to the left eye; used in the laboratory for investigating the perception of depth. [255]

stimulus generalization The elicitation of a learned response by a stimulus similar to, but not identical with, the CS. See **classical conditioning.** [332]

Structuralism A system of psychology that emphasizes experience as the proper subject matter of psychology and analysis of experience into its elementary components as the proper psychological methodology. [224]

structural model That part of psychoanalytic theory concerned with the three mental "institutions," or functions—**ego, id,** and **superego.** [31]

structured test A test that permits the selection of only particular given response alternatives. [85]

sublimation The application of libidinal energy to socially productive behaviors. See **libido.** [671]

subliminal stimulation Stimulation that falls below some psychophysical threshold but that still has a measurable behavioral effect. [663]

superego The "unconscious conscience," one of the mental institutions in the structural model of psychoanalytic theory. See **structural model.** [658]

surface structure In linguistics, the constituents (phrases, clauses, etc.)

into which the actual sentence can be divided or parsed. [469]

sympathetic system The branch of the autonomic nervous system that serves primarily to arouse, or increase activity in the organs controlled by the autonomic system. [150]

synapse The junction of two or more neurons. [165]

synesthesia The induction of experiences characteristic of one sense modality by stimulation of another modality. [240]

syntactic boundary The edges of constituents of sentences. [470]

syntax The arrangement of words as elements in a sentence showing their interrelationships and dependencies; sentence structure. [464]

tabula rasa In reference to the mental content of a newborn, the empiricist notion that the mind is initially a "blank tablet" to be inscribed upon by experience. [112]

tact A verbal utterance under the control of events in the world rather than specific needs of the speaker. A basic form of verbal behavior in Skinner's system. [458]

temporal conditioning A procedure in which the CS is the passage of a particular period of time. See **classical conditioning.** [320]

textual response Reading; saying what one sees written. [458]

thinking The name for a collection of higher mental processes that are inferred in connection with situations involving puzzles, problem-solving, reasoning, imagination, and the processing of information. [479]

timbre An attribute of auditory tones, independent of pitch and loudness, that is characteristic of the instrument producing the sound waves. [269]

topographical model That part of psychoanalytic theory concerned with different levels of consciousness (conscious, preconscious, unconscious). [31]

trace conditioning A procedure in which the CS terminates a considerable time before the onset of the US. See **classical conditioning.** [318]

tract A bundle of neural fibers within the central nervous system, analogous to a nerve. [297]

trait A characteristic of personality; an observable dimension along which people may be measured. [84]

transfer studies Studies that ask about the effect of one activity (typically a learning task) on another activity (typically another learning task). If the first facilitates the second, the transfer is called positive. If the first interferes with the second, the transfer is called negative. [404]

trial and error Trying first one thing and then another until success is achieved or the problem abandoned. [485]

trichromat A person with normal color vision. [198]

tritanope A dichromat with a blue-yellow deficiency. [198]

unlearning The hypothesis that subsequent learning interferes with earlier learning by making the earlier material unavailable or dissolving the earlier associations. [401]

unstructured test A test that allows responses to vary widely so as to be revealing of personality. [85]

validity The extent to which a test or other instrument is a measure of what it is supposed to measure. Three kinds are discriminated: content, criterion, and construct validity. [102]

variable-interval schedule A reinforcement schedule in which a reinforcement is delivered after every response that follows a time period, variable around a fixed mean value, since the previous reinforcement. See **fixed-interval schedule.** [355]

variable-ratio schedule A reinforcement schedule in which a reinforcement is delivered after every *n* responses on the average. See **fixed-ratio schedule**. [356]

veridical In close correspondence with the outcome of "objective," or physical, measurement. [250]

visual cliff An apparatus for investigating depth perception, so constructed that one part of it appears deeper than another, even though the two parts are of the same physical depth. [252]

vocabulary The words used by a person (active vocabulary) or the words understood by a person (passive vocabulary). [438]

vocal tract The entire assembly of the organs of speech. [435]

von Restorff effect The tendency of nontypical items to "stand out" in a learning list and thus to be more easily learned. [419]

Weber-Fechner law As a physical stimulus increases logarithmically, the associated sensation increases arithmetically. [65]

Weber fraction ($\triangle I/I$) The ratio of the threshold increment to the base-line intensity. [182]

white noise Noise often used in experimentation consisting of a flat spectrum of energy at all frequency levels. [442]

whole learning Learning the entire set of materials as a unit rather than by parts. [397]

word association A technique for eliciting responses to single words. A word is presented and the subject is directed to respond with the first word it makes him think of. [445]

word-association norms Tables of the frequency of occurrence of various responses to stimulus words for particular populations such as school children, college students, neurotics, etc. [446]

Zeigarnik effect Better recall of uncompleted than completed tasks. [41]

Zeitgeber An event, external to the body, that is indicative of the passage of a particular period of time and that helps to maintain the periodicity of certain physiological functions. See **circadian rhythm**. [571]

Zipf's law The observation that the frequency of usage of a word in a text times its rank order equals a constant ($f \times r = C$). [431]

References

Adams, J.A., and W.E. Montague. Retroactive inhibition and natural language mediation. *Journal of Verbal Learning and Verbal Behavior,* 1967, *6,* 528–535. [408]

Allison, J. Cognitive structure and receptivity to low intensity stimulation. *Journal of Abnormal and Social Psychology,* 1963, *67,* 132–138. [666]

Allport, F.H. *Social Psychology,* Boston: Hougton Mifflin, 1924. [435]

Allport, G.W. *Becoming.* New Haven: Yale Univ. Press, 1955. [114, 139]

—— and H.W. Odbert. Traitnames, a psycholexical study. *Psychological Monographs,* 1936, *47,* No. 1. [69]

Alper, T.G., and E.G. Boring. Intelligence-test scores of Northern and Southern white and Negro recruits in 1918. *Journal of Abnormal and Social Psychology,* 1944, *39,* 471–474. [544]

Alpert, R., and R.N. Haber. Anxiety in academic achievement situations. *Journal of Abnormal and Social Psychology,* 1960, *61,* 207–215. [597]

Altman, J. *Organic foundations of animal behavior.* New York: Holt, Rinehart & Winston, 1966. [164, 297]

Altus, W.D. Birth order and its sequellae. *Science,* 1966, *151,* 44–49. [685]

Amoore, J.E. Stereochemical theory of olfaction. *Nature,* 1963, *199,* 912. [278]

——, J.W. Johnston, Jr., and M. Rubin. The stereochemical theory of odor. *Scientific American,* 1964, *210,* 42–49. [279–281]

Amos, J.R., F.L. Brown, and O.G. Mink. *Statistical concepts: a basic program.* New York: Harper & Row, 1965. [106]

Amsel, A. Selective association and the anticipatory goal response mechanism as explanatory concepts in learning theory. *Journal of Experimental Psychology,* 1949, *39,* 785–799. [607]

—— The role of frustrative nonreward in noncontinuous reward situations. *Psychological Bulletin,* 1958, *55,* 102–119. [360]

Anastasi, Anne. *Differential psychology* (3rd ed.). New York: Macmillan, 1958. [558]

Anderson, N.H., and C.Y. Nakamura. Avoidance decrement in avoidance conditioning. *Journal of Comparative and Physiological Psychology,* 1964, *57,* 196–204. [377]

Angell, J.R. The province of functional psychology. *Psychological Review,* 1907, *14,* 61–91. [604]

Army Air Forces, Staff, Psychological Section. Psychological activities in the training command. *Psychological Bulletin,* 1945, *42,* 37–54. [96]

Aronson, E., and J. Mills. The effects of severity of initiation on liking for a group. *Journal of Abnormal and Social Psychology,* 1959, *59,* 177–181. [653]

Asch, S.E. *Social psychology.* Englewood Cliffs, N. J.: Prentice-Hall, 1952. [37]

—— Studies of independence and conformity. A minority of one against a unanimous majority. *Psychological Monographs,* 1956, *70,* No. 9. [708]

—— and H. Nerlove. The development of double function terms in children. In *Perspectives in psychological theory* (edited by B. Kaplan and S. Wapner). New York: International Universities Press, 1960. [502]

Aschoff, J. Circadian rhythms in man. *Science,* 1965, *148,* 1427–1432. [570]

Aserinsky, E., and N. Kleitman. Regularly occurring periods of eye motility and concomitant phenomena during sleep. *Science,* 1953, *118,* 273–274. [565]

Atkinson, J.W. *Motives in fantasy, action, and society.* Princeton: Van Nostrand, 1958. [27, 688]

——, R.W. Heyns, and J. Veroff. The effect of experimental arousal of the affiliation motive on thematic apperception. *Journal of Abnormal and Social Psychology,* 1954, *49,* 405–410. [684]

Ax, A.F. The physiological differentiation between fear and anger in humans. *Psychoso-*

matic Medicine, 1953, *15*, 433–442. [594]

Azrin, N. Pain and aggression. *Psychology Today*, 1967, *1*, 27–33. [361]

Bachrach, A.J. *Psychological research: an Introduction.* New York: Random House, 1962. [62]

Bakan, D. The mystery-mastery complex in contemporary psychology. *American Psychologist*, 1965, *20*, 186–191. [62]

Barber, T.X. The concept of "hypnosis." *Journal of Psychology*, 1958, *45*, 115–131. [293]

Bare, J.K. The specific hunger for sodium chloride in normal and adrenalectomized white rats. *Journal of Comparative and Physiological Psychology*, 1949, *42*, 242–253. [287]

Barnes, J.M., and B.J. Underwood. "Fate" of first-list associations in transfer theory. *Journal of Experimental Psychology*, 1959, *58*, 97–105. [401]

Bartlett, F.C. *Remembering: a study in experimental and social psychology.* Cambridge, England: Cambridge Univ. Press, 1932. [417, 424]

Bartley, S.H., and T.M. Nelson. A further study of pulse-to-cycle fraction and critical flicker frequency. *Journal of the Optical Society of America*, 1961, *51*, 41–45. [210]

Bartoshuk, A.K. Human neonatal cardiac acceleration to sound: habituation. *Perceptual and Motor Skills*, 1962, *15*, 15–27. [311]

Barzun, J. *Science: the glorious entertainment.* New York: Harper & Row, 1964. [37]

Bayley, Nancy. On the growth of intelligence. *American Psychologist*, 1955, *10*, 805–818. [532]

Beck, L.H., and W.R. Miles. Some theoretical and experimental relationships between infrared absorption and olfaction. *Science*, 1947, *106*, 511. [278]

Békésy, G. von. Similarities between hearing and skin sensa-

tions. *Psychological Review*, 1959, *66*, 1–22. [265, 268]

——— *Sensory inhibition.* Princeton: Princeton Univ. Press, 1967. [268]

Bellugi, U. The acquisition of the system of negation in children's speech. Unpublished doctoral dissertation, Harvard Univ., 1967. [474]

Berko, J. The child's learning of English morphology. *Word*, 1958, *14*, 150–177. [452]

Berkun, M.M., Marian L. Kessen, and N.E. Miller. Hunger-reducing effects of food by stomach fistula versus food by mouth measured by a consummatory response. *Journal of Comparative and Physiological Psychology*, 1952, *45*, 550–554. [617]

Bernstein, J. *The analytical engine.* New York: Random House, 1963. [512]

Bernstein, L. The effects of variation in handling upon learning and retention. *Journal of Comparative and Physiological Psychology*, 1957, *50*, 162–167. [587]

Bertine, M. Il tratto difensivo dell' isolamento nella sua determinazione dinamica e strutturale. *Contributi dell' Istituto di Psicologica*, 1961, Serie XXV. [692]

Bexton, W.H., W. Heron, and T.H. Scott. Effects of decreased variation in the sensory environment. *Canadian Journal of Psychology*, 1954, *8*, 70–76. [628]

Binet, A., and T. Simon. *The development of intelligence in children* (trans. by E.S. Kite). Vineland, N.J.: Publication of the Training School, No. 11, 1916. [517, 519]

Birch, H.G. The relation of previous experience to insightful problem-solving. *Journal of Comparative Psychology*, 1945, *38*, 367–383. [499]

Bitterman, M.E. The evolution of intelligence. *Scientific American*, 1965, *212*, 92–100. [373, 376]

Black, A.H., N.J. Carlson, and R.L. Solomon. Exploratory

studies of the conditioning of autonomic responses in curarized dogs. *Psychological Monographs*, 1962, *76*, No. 29. [372]

Blackwell, H.R. *Psychophysical thresholds: experimental studies of methods of measurement.* Ann Arbor: Univ. of Michigan Press (Engineering Research Bulletin No. 36), 1953. [189]

Blum, G.S. An experimental re union of psychoanalytic theory with perceptual vigilance and defense. *Journal of Abnormal and Social Psychology*, 1954, *49*, 94–98. [662]

Bogdonoff, M.D., R. F. Klein, E.H. Estes, Jr., D.M. Shaw, and K.W. Back. The modifying effect of conforming behavior upon lipid responses accompanying CNS arousal. *Clinical Research*, 1961, *9*, 135. [709]

Bolles, R.C. *Theory of motivation.* New York: Harper & Row, 1967. [609]

Boring, E.G. *A history of experimental psychology.* New York: Appleton-Century-Crofts, 1950. [139]

Bower, G.H. Correlated delay of reinforcement. Unpublished doctoral dissertation, Yale Univ., 1959. [611]

Braine, M.D.S. On learning the grammatical order of words. *Psychological Review*, 1963, *70*, 323–348. [474]

Branca, A.A. Semantic generalization at the level of the conditioning experiment. *American Journal of Psychology*, 1957, *70*, 541–549. [448]

Brehm, J.W. Motivational effects of cognitive dissonance. In *Nebraska symposium on motivation* (edited by M.R. Jones). Lincoln, Nebr.: Univ. of Nebraska Press, 1962, 51–76. [650]

——— and A.R. Cohen. *Explorations in cognitive dissonance.* New York: Wiley, 1962. [650]

Brehm, Mary L., K.W. Back, and M.D. Bogdonoff. A physiological effect of cognitive dissonance under stress and deprivation. *Journal of Abnormal and Social Psychology*, 1964, *69*, 303–310. [656]

Brennan, W.M., Elinor W. Ames, and R.W. Moore. Age differences in infants' attention to patterns of different complexities. *Science*, 1966, *151*, 354–356. [625]

Breuer, J., and S. Freud. *Studies in hysteria*. London: Hogarth Press, 1955 (first published, 1895). [661]

Brigham, C.C. Intelligence tests of immigrant groups. *Psychological Review*, 1930, *37*, 158–165. [524]

Brill, M. Parameters of odor-trail avoidance in the rat. Unpublished doctoral dissertation, Univ. of Cincinnati, 1967. [283]

Brindley, G.S. Afterimages. *Scientific American*, 1963, *209*, 84–93. [201]

Broadbent, D.E. The role of auditory localization in attention and memory span. *Journal of Experimental Psychology*, 1954, *47*, 191–196. [276]

——— A mechanical model for human attention and immediate memory. *Psychological Review*, 1957, *64*, 205–215. [37]

Brown, F. An experimental and critical study of the intelligence of Negro and white kindergarten children. *Journal of Genetic Psychology*, 1944, *65*, 161–175. [542]

Brown, J.S. The generalization of approach responses as a function of stimulus intensity and strength of motivation. *Journal of Comparative Psychology*, 1942, *33*, 209–226. [644]

——— Gradients of approach and avoidance responses and their relation to level of motivation. *Journal of Comparative and Physiological Psychology*, 1948, *41*, 450–465. [644]

Brown, P.K., and G. Wald. Visual pigments in single rods and cones of the human retina. *Science*, 1964, *144*, 45–52. [197]

Brown, R.W. Linguistic determinism and the part of speech. *Journal of Abnormal and Social Psychology*, 1957, *55*, 1–5. [452]

——— *Words and things*. New York: Macmillan (The Free Press), 1958. [478]

——— Models of attitude change. In *New directions in psychology*. New York: Holt, Rinehart & Winston, 1962, 1–85. [37, 650, 678]

——— *Social psychology*. New York: Macmillan (The Free Press), 1965. [558, 716]

——— and J. Berko. Word association and the acquisition of grammar. *Child Development*, 1960, *31*, 1–14. [453]

——— and C. Fraser. The acquisition of syntax. In *The acquisition of language* (edited by U. Bellugi and R.W. Brown). Monographs of the Society for Research in Child Development. Lafayette, Ind.: Child Development Publications, 1964, 43–79. [474]

Bruce, M. Factors affecting intelligence test performance of whites and Negroes in the rural south. *Archives of Psychology*, 1940, *36*, No. 252. [544]

Bryan, W.L., and N. Harter. Studies in the physiology and psychology of telegraphic language. *Psychological Review*, 1897, *4*, 27–53. [410]

Bryden, M.P. Order of report in dichotic listening. *Canadian Journal of Psychology*, 1962, *16*, 291–299. [276]

Burt, C.L. The structure of the mind: a review of the results of factor analysis. *British Journal of Educational Psychology*, 1949, *19*, 100–111, 176–199. [525]

——— Class differences in general intelligence: III. *British Journal of Statistical Psychology*, 1959, *12*, 15–53. [545]

Bush, R.R., and F. Mosteller. *Stochastic models for learning*. New York: Wiley, 1955. [21]

Butler, R.A. Discrimination learning by rhesus monkeys to visual-exploration motivation. *Journal of Comparative and Physiological Psychology*, 1953, *46*, 95–98. [624]

Cameron, J., N. Livson, and Nancy Bayley. Infant vocalizations and their relationship to mature intelligence. *Science*, 1967, *157*, 331–333. [694]

Campbell, D.P. A cross-sectional and longitudinal study of scholastic abilities over twenty-five years. *Journal of Counseling Psychology*, 1965, *12*, 55–61. [532]

Candland, D. *Emotion: bodily change*. Princeton: Van Nostrand, 1962. [601]

Cannon, W.B., and A.L. Washburn. An explanation of hunger. *American Journal of Physiology*, 1912, *29*, 441–454. [615–616]

Carlsmith, J.M., B.E. Collins, and R.L. Helmreich. Studies in forced compliance: I. The effect of pressure for compliance on attitude change produced by face-to-face role-playing and anonymous essay writing. *Journal of Personality and Social Psychology*, 1966, *4*, 1–13. [655]

Carlson, E.R., and Rae Carlson. Male and female subjects in personality research. *Journal of Abnormal and Social Psychology*, 1960, *61*, 482–483. [687]

Carmichael, L., H.P. Hogan, and A.A. Walter. An experimental study of the effect of language on the reproduction of visually perceived form. *Journal of Experimental Psychology*, 1932, *15*, 73–86. [417]

Carroll, J.B. *Language and thought*. Englewood Cliffs, N.J.: Prentice-Hall, 1964. [478]

——— and M.L. Burke. Parameters of paired-associate verbal learning: length of list, meaningfulness, rate of presentation and ability. *Journal of Experimental Psychology,* 1965, *69,* 543–533. [390]

Chalke, F.C.R., and J. Ertl. Evoked potentials and intelligence. *Life Sciences,* 1965, *4,* 1319–1322. [212]

Chapanis, A. Men, machines, and models. *American Psychologist,* 1961, *16,* 113–131. [37]

———, W.R. Garner, and C.T. Morgan. *Applied experimental psychology.* New York: Wiley, 1949. [722]

Chapman, R.M., and N. Levy. Hunger drive and reinforcing effect of novel stimuli. *Journal of Comparative and Physiological Psychology,* 1957, *50,* 233–238. [624]

Cherry, C. *On human communication.* Cambridge, Mass.: M.I.T. Press, 1957. [478]

Chomsky, N. *Syntactic structures.* The Hague, the Netherlands: Mouton, 1957. [462]

——— A review of *Verbal behavior* by B.F. Skinner. *Language,* 1959, *35,* 26–58. [462, 478]

——— *Aspects of the theory of syntax.* Cambridge, Mass.: M.I.T. Press, 1965. [428]

Clifton, C., Jr., and Penelope Odom. Similarity relations among certain English sentence constructions. *Psychological Monographs,* 1966, *80,* No. 613. [471]

Cofer, C.N. On some factors in the organizational characteristics of free recall. *American Psychologist,* 1965, *20,* 261–272. [448]

——— and M.H. Appley. *Motivation: theory and research.* New York: Wiley, 1964. [640]

Cohen, A.R. An experiment on small rewards for discrepant compliance and attitude change. In *Explorations in cognitive dissonance* (edited by J.W. Brehm and A.R. Cohen). New York: Wiley, 1962, 73–78. [655]

———, J.W. Brehm, and W.H. Fleming. Attitude change and justification for compliance. *Journal of Abnormal and Social Psychology,* 1958, *56,* 276–278. [654]

Cohen, W. Color perception in the chromatic *Ganzfeld. American Journal of Psychology,* 1958, *71,* 390–394. [202]

Cook, S.W., and R.E. Harris. The verbal conditioning of the galvanic skin reflex. *Journal of Experimental Psychology,* 1937, *21,* 202–210. [386]

Cook, T.W. Studies in cross education: II. Further experiments in mirror tracing the star-shaped maze. *Journal of Experimental Psychology,* 1933, *16,* 679–700. [415]

——— Studies in cross education: III. Kinaesthetic learning of an irregular pattern. *Journal of Experimental Psychology,* 1934, *17,* 749–762. [415]

Coons, E.A., N.H. Anderson, and A.K. Myers. Disappearance of avoidance responding during continued training. *Journal of Comparative and Physiological Psychology,* 1960, *53,* 290–292. [377]

Corning, W.C., and E.R. John. Effect of ribonuclease on retention of conditioned response in regenerated planarians. *Science,* 1961, *134,* 1363–1365. [329]

Corso, J.F. *The experimental psychology of sensory behavior.* New York: Holt, Rinehart & Winston, 1967. [271, 289]

Crespi, L.P. Quantitative variation of incentive and performance in the white rat. *American Journal of Psychology,* 1942, *55,* 467–517. [613]

Crosby, Elizabeth C., Tryphena Humphrey, and E.W. Lauer. *Correlative anatomy of the nervous system.* New York: Macmillan, 1962. [164]

Crutchfield, R.S. Conformity and character. *American Psychologist,* 1955, *10,* 191–198. [709]

Darwin, C. *The expression of the emotions in man and animals.* London: Murray, 1872. [596]

Davis, C.M. Self-selection of diet by newly weaned infants. *American Journal of Diseases of Children,* 1928, *36,* 651–679. [607]

Deese, J. From the isolated unit to connected discourse. In *Verbal learning and verbal behavior* (edited by C.N. Cofer). New York: McGraw-Hill, 1961. [442]

——— and S.H. Hulse. *The psychology of learning.* New York: McGraw-Hill, 1967. [316]

Dember, W.N. Response by the rat to environmental change. *Journal of Comparative and Physiological Psychology,* 1956, *49,* 93–95. [624]

——— *The psychology of perception.* New York: Holt, Rinehart & Winston, 1960. [239, 332]

——— *Visual perception: the nineteenth century.* New York: Wiley, 1964a. [261]

——— Birth order and need affiliation. *Journal of Abnormal and Social Psychology,* 1964b, *68,* 555–557. [684]

——— The new look in motivation. *American Scientist,* 1965, *53,* 409–427. [605]

——— and R.W. Earl. Analysis of exploratory, manipulatory, and curiosity behaviors. *Psychological Review,* 1957, *64,* 91–96. [631]

———, R.W. Earl, and N. Paradise. Response by rats to differential stimulus complexity. *Journal of Comparative and Physiological Psychology,* 1957, *50,* 514–518. [630]

Dement, W.C. An essay on dreams: the role of physiology in understanding their nature. In *New directions in Psychology II.* New York: Holt, Rinehart & Winston, 1965, *135,* 257. [564, 566, 568–569]

Denenberg, V.H. Early experience and emotional development. *Scientific American,* 1963, *208,* 138–146. [588–589]

—— and K.M. Rosenberg. Nongenetic transmission of information. *Nature,* 1967, *216,* 549–550. [589]

DeNike, L.D., and C.D. Spielberger. Induced mediating states in verbal conditioning. *Journal of Verbal Learning and Verbal Behavior,* 1963, *1,* 339–345. [461]

Detwiler, S.R. Some biological aspects of vision. *Sigma Xi Quarterly,* 1941, *29,* 112–129. [149]

DeValois, R.L. Color vision mechanisms in the monkey. *Journal of General Physiology,* 1960, *43,* Part 2, 115–128. [174]

—— and I. Abramov. Color vision. In *Annual review of psychology,* 1966, *17,* 337–362. [201]

Dollard, J., and N.E. Miller. *Personality and psychotherapy: an analysis in terms of learning, thinking and culture.* New York: McGraw-Hill, 1950. [386, 622]

Dorfman, D.D., and Helen McKenna. Pattern preference as a function of pattern uncertainty. *Canadian Journal of Psychology,* 1966, *20,* 143–153. [633]

Douglas, R.J. Cues for spontaneous alternation. *Journal of Comparative and Physiological Psychology,* 1966, *62,* 171–183. [283]

—— The hippocampus and behavior. *Psychological Bulletin,* 1967, *67,* 416–442. [378]

Dulany, D.E. Awareness, rules and propositional control: a confrontation with S-R behavior theory. In *Verbal behavior and general behavior theory* (edited by T.R. Dixon and D.L. Horton). Englewood Cliffs, N.J.: Prentice-Hall, 1968, 340–387. [461]

Duncker, K. on problem-solving. *Psychological Monographs,* 1945, *58,* No. 270. [499]

Earl, R.W. Problem-solving and motor skill behaviors under conditions of free-choice. Unpublished doctoral dissertation, Univ. of Michigan, 1957. [631, 632]

—— *A theory of stimulus selection.* Fullerton, Calif.: Hughes Ground Systems, 1961. [631]

Ebbinghaus, H. *Ueber das Gedachtnis,* 1885 (translated by H.A. Ruger and C.E. Bussenius). New York: Teachers College, 1913. Reissued as paperback, New York: Dover, 1964. [388]

Ehrlich, Danuta. Determinants of verbal commonality and influencibility. Unpublished doctoral dissertation, Univ. of Minnesota, 1958. [684]

Elms, A., and I. Janis. Counternorm attitudes induced by consonant versus dissonant conditions of role-playing. *Journal of Experimental Research in Personality,* 1965, *1,* 50–60. [655]

Erikson, E.H. *Childhood and society.* New York: W.W. Norton, 1950. [703]

Ervin, Susan. Imitation and structural change in children's language. In *New direction in the study of language* (edited by E. Lenneberg). Cambridge, Mass.: M.I.T. Press, 1964, 163–189. [474]

Estes, W.K. An experimental study of punishment. *Psychological Monographs,* 1944, *57,* No. 263. [362]

—— Toward a statistical theory of learning. *Psychological Review,* 1950, *57,* 94–107. [421]

—— The statistical approach to learning theory. In *A study of a science,* Volume 2 (edited by S. Koch). New York: McGraw-Hill, 1958. [21]

—— Learning theory and the new "mental chemistry." *Psychological Review,* 1960, *67,* 207–223. [21]

Eysenck, H.J., and S. Rachman. *The causes and cures of neurosis.* San Diego: Robert R. Knapp, 1965. [340]

Fantz, R. The origin of form perception. *Scientific American,* 1961, *204,* 66–72. [201, 215, 626]

——, J.M. Ordy, and M.S. Udelf. Maturation of pattern vision in infants during the first six months. *Journal of Comparative and Physiological Psychology,* 1962, *55,* 907–917. [205, 206]

Feigenbaum, E.A., and J. Feldman (eds.). *Computers and thought.* New York: McGraw-Hill, 1963. [8]

Fender, D., and B. Julesz. Extension of Panum's fusional area in binocularly stabilized vision. *Journal of the Optical Society of America,* 1967, *57,* 819–830. [256]

Festinger, L. *A theory of cognitive dissonance.* Stanford, Calif.: Stanford Univ. Press, 1957. [650]

—— and J.M. Carlsmith. Cognitive consequences of forced compliance. *Journal of Abnormal and Social Psychology,* 1959, *58,* 203–210. [654]

——, H.W. Riecken, Jr., and S. Schachter. *When prophecy fails.* Minneapolis: Univ. of Minnesota Press, 1956. [651, 678]

Fisher, C. Dreams and perception. *Journal of the American Psychoanalytic Association,* 1954, *2,* 389–445. [664]

—— and I.H. Paul. The effect of subliminal visual stimulation on images and dreams: a validation study. *Journal of the American Psychoanalytic Association,* 1959, *7,* 35–83. [664]

Flavell, J.H. *The developmental psychology of Jean Piaget.* Princeton: Van Nostrand, 1963. [559]

Fleishman, E.A. A comparative study of aptitude patterns in unskilled and skilled psychomotor performances. *Journal of Applied Psychology,* 1957, *41,* 263–272. [412]

—— and W.E. Hempel. Changes in factor structure of a complex psychomotor test as a function of practice. *Psychometrika.* 1954, *19*, 239–252. [412]

———— and J.F. Parker, Jr. Factors in the retention and relearning of perceptual-motor skill. *Journal of Experimental Psychology,* 1962, *64*, 215–226. [416]

Fodor, J.A., and T.G. Bever. The psychological reality of linguistic segments. *Journal of Verbal Learning and Verbal Behavior,* 1965, *4,* 414–420. [469]

Foulke, E., and J.S. Warm. Effects of complexity and redundancy on the tactual recognition of metric figures. *Perceptual and Motor Skills,* 1967, *25*, 177–187. [291]

Foulkes, D. *The psychology of sleep.* New York: Scribner's, 1966. [566]

Fowler, H. Response to environmental change: a positive replication. *Psychological Reports,* 1958, *4,* 506. [625]

————, Joyce Blond, and W.N. Dember. Alternation behavior and learning: the influence of reinforcement magnitude, number, and contingency. *Journal of Comparative and Physiological Psychology,* 1959, *52,* 609–614. [635]

Fox, Cynthia. Modification of perceptual and associative response by subthreshold stimuli. Unpublished doctoral dissertation, Yale Univ., 1959. [665]

Fraiberg, Selma. *The magic years.* New York: Scribner's, 1959. [715]

Franks, C. (ed.). *Assessment and status of the behavior therapies and associated developments.* New York: McGraw-Hill, 1968. [335]

Franzblau, R.N. Race differences in mental and physical traits: studied in different environments. *Archives of Psychology,* No. 177, 1935. [539]

Freud, Anna. *The ego and the mechanisms of defense.* New York: International Universities Press, 1946. [659]

Freud, S. *A general introduction to psychoanalysis.* New York: Liveright Publishing Corp., 1920. Reprinted in paperback by Doubleday (Perma Books), 1953. [139, 678]

———— *New introductory lectures on psychoanalysis.* New York: Norton, 1965. [37]

Funkenstein, D.H. The physiology of fear and anger. *Scientific American,* 1955, *192,* 74–81. [595]

Galanter, E. Contemporary psychophysics. In *New directions in psychology.* New York: Holt, Rinehart & Winston, 1962. [215]

Galton, F. *Inquiries into human faculty and its development.* London: Macmillan, 1883. [445]

Gates, A.I. Recitation as a factor in memorizing. *Archives of Psychology,* 1917, No. 40. [396]

Gelber, Beatrice. Investigation of the behavior of *Paramecium aurelia:* I. Modification of behavior after training with reinforcement. *Journal of Comparative and Physiological Psychology,* 1952, *45,* 58–65. [326]

Geldard, F.A. *The human senses.* New York: Wiley, 1953. [305]

Gibson, Eleanor, and R.D. Walk. The "visual cliff." *Scientific American,* 1960, *202,* 64–71. [253]

Gibson, J.J. Adaptation, after-effect, and contrast in the perception of curved lines. *Journal of Experimental Psychology,* 1933, *16,* 1–31. [241]

———— *The perception of the visual world.* Boston: Houghton Mifflin, 1950. [249, 254]

———— *The senses considered as perceptual systems.* Boston: Houghton Mifflin, 1966. [252, 305]

Gleitman, H. Place-learning. *Scientific American,* 1963, *209,* 116–122. [373]

Goldiamond, I., and W.F. Hawkins. Vexierversuch: the log relationship between word-frequency and recognition obtained in the absence of stimulus words. *Journal of Experimental Psychology,* 1958, *56,* 457–463. [434]

Goldstein, H., D.L. Krantz, and J.D. Rains (eds.). *Controversial issues in learning.* New York: Appleton-Century-Crofts, 1965. [380]

Gordon, B. An experimental study of dependence-independence in a social and a laboratory setting. Unpublished doctoral dissertation, Univ. of Southern California, 1953. [693]

Gottesman, I.I. Biogenetics of race and class. In *Social class, race and psychological development* (edited by M. Deutch, I. Katz, and A.R. Jensen). New York: Holt, Rinehart & Winston, 1968, 11–51. [545]

Gottschalk, L.A., and Goldine C. Gleser. *The measurement of psychological states through the content analysis of verbal behavior.* Berkeley: Univ. of California Press, 1969. [599]

Gough, P.B. Grammatical transformations and speed of understanding. *Journal of Verbal Learning and Verbal Behavior,* 1965, *4, 107–111.* [472]

Graham, C.H., R.H. Brown, and F.A. Mote. The relation of size of stimulus and intensity in the human eye. *Journal of Experimental Psychology,* 1939, *24,* 555–573. [190]

Granit, R. *Sensory mechanisms of the retina.* London: Oxford Univ. Press, 1947. [171]

Green, D.M., and J.A. Swets. *Signal detection theory and psychophysics.* New York: Wiley, 1966. [188]

Gregory, R.L. *Eye and brain.* New York: McGraw-Hill, 1966. [215]

Guilford, J.P. Three faces of intellect. *American Psychologist,* 1959, *14,* 469–479. [550]

Guthrie, E.R., and G.P. Horton. *Cats in a puzzle box.* New York: Holt, Rinehart & Winston, 1946. [350]

Haber, R.N. *Current research in motivation.* New York: Holt, Rinehart & Winston, 1966. [640]

Hall, C. A modest confirmation of Freud's theory of a distinction between the superego of men and women. *Journal of Abnormal and Social Psychology,* 1964, 69, 440–441. [675]

Harlow, H.F. The nature of love. *American Psychologist,* 1958, 13, 673–685. [291, 592]

——— The heterosexual affectional system in monkeys. *American Psychologist,* 1962, 17, 1–9. [593]

——— The formation of learning sets. *Psychological Review,* 1949, 56, 51–65. [374]

——— Mice, monkeys, men and motives. *Psychological Review,* 1953, 60, 23–32. [640]

Harrell, T.W. Army General Classification Test results for Air Force Specialists. *Educational and Psychological Measurement,* 1946, 6, 341–349. [541]

——— and M.S. Harrell. Army General Classification Test scores for civilian occupations. *Educational and Psychological Measurement,* 1945, 5, 229–239. [538]

Hartline, H.K., and C.H. Graham. Nerve impulses from single receptors in the eye. *Journal of Cellular Comparative Physiology,* 1932, 1, 277–295. [77]

Hartmann, H. Ego psychology and the problem of adaptation. In *Organization and pathology of thought* (edited by D. Rapaport). New York: Columbia Univ. Press, 1951, 362–396. [637]

Hays, W.L. *Basic statistics,* Belmont, California: Brooks Cole, 1967. [106]

Hebb, D.O. *The organization of behavior.* New York: Wiley, 1949. [223, 292, 603]

——— *A textbook of psychology.* Philadelphia: Saunders, 1958. [582]

Hecht, S. Vision II. The nature of the photoreceptor process. In *Handbook of general experimental psychology* (edited by C. Murchison). Worcester, Mass.: Clark Univ. Press, 1934, 704–828. [159]

Helmholtz, H. von. *Sensations of tone.* 1st German edition, 1862; 6th English edition, New York: Peter Smith, 1948. [267, 271]

Hess, E.H. Attitude and pupil size. *Scientific American,* 1965, 212, 46–54. [150]

Hilgard, E.R., and G.H. Bower, *Theories of learning.* New York: Appleton-Century-Crofts, 1966. [422]

Hobbes, T. *Leviathan,* 1651. Reprinted, New York: Dutton, 1950. [428]

Hochberg, J.E. *Perception.* Englewood Cliffs, N.J.: Prentice-Hall, 1964. [178, 261]

Hoebel, R.G., and P. Teitelbaum. Hypothalamic control of feeding and self-stimulation. *Science,* 1962, 135, 375–377. [620]

Hollingworth, L.S. Differential action upon the sexes of forces which tend to segregate the feebleminded. *Journal of Abnormal Psychology,* 1922, 17, 35–37. [536]

Holt, E.B. *Animal drive and the learning process.* New York: Holt, Rinehart & Winston, 1931. [330]

Horton, D.L., and P.M. Kjeldergaard. An experimental analysis of associative factors in mediated generalization. *Psychological Monographs,* 1961, 75, No. 515. [409]

Hovland, C.I. The generalization of conditioned responses: IV. The effects of varying amounts of reinforcement upon the degree of generalization of conditioned responses. *Journal of Experimental Psychology,* 1937, 21, 261–276. [316]

Hubel, D.H. The visual cortex of the brain. *Scientific American,* 1963, 209, 54–62. [178]

——— and T.N. Wiesel. Receptive fields, binocular interaction and functional architecture in the cat's visual cortex. *Journal of Physiology,* 1962, 160, 106–154. [171]

Huff, D. *How to lie with statistics.* New York: Norton, 1954. [106]

Hughes, R.N. Spontaneous alternation and response to stimulus change in the ferret. *Journal of Comparative and Physiological Psychology,* 1965, 60, 149–150. [625]

Hull, C.L. Quantitative aspects of the evolution of concepts: an experimental study. *Psychological Monographs,* 1920, No. 28. [489]

——— Differential habituation to internal stimuli in the albino rat. *Journal of Comparative Psychology,* 1933, 16, 255–273. [607]

——— *Principles of behavior.* New York: Appleton-Century-Crofts, 1943. [21, 139, 337, 384, 605–606, 640]

Hurvich, L.M., and Dorothea Jameson. An opponent-process theory of color vision. *Psychological Review,* 1957, 64, 384–404. [194]

——— and ——— *The perception of brightness and darkness.* Boston: Allyn & Bacon, 1966. [215]

Husen, T. The influence of schooling in IQ. *Theoria,* 1951, 17, 61–88. [539]

Huxley, A. *Brave new world.* Garden City, N.Y.: Doubleday, 1932; New York: Bantam, 1968. [344]

Ittelson, W.H., and F.P. Kilpatrick. Experiments in perception. *Scientific American,* 1951, 185, 50–55. [247]

Jacobson, A.L., F.R. Babich, Suzanne Bubash, and Carolyn Goren. Maze preferences in naive rats produced by injection of ribonucleic acid from trained rats. *Psychonomic Science,* 1966, 4, 3–4. [129]

———, ———, ———, and Ann Jacobson. Differential approach tendencies produced by injections of RNA from trained rats. *Science,* 1965, 150, 636–637. [330]

Jacobson, E. Electrophysiology of mental activities. *American Journal of Psychology*, 1932, *44*, 677–694. [488]

James, W. *Principles of psychology*. New York: Holt, 1890. [205]

Janis, I., and J.B. Gilmore. The influence of incentive conditions on the success of role playing in modifying attitudes. *Journal of Personality and Social Psychology*, 1965, *1*, 17–27. [655]

Janucci, Gloria I. Size constancy in schizophrenia: a study of subgroup differences. Unpublished doctoral dissertation, Rutgers State Univ., 1964. [693]

Jenkins, J.G., and K.M. Dallenbach. Obliviscence during sleep and waking. *American Journal of Psychology*, 1924, *35*, 605–612. [399]

Jenkins, J.J. Stimulus "fractionation" in paired-associate learning. *Psychologial Reports*, 1963, *13*, 409–410. [404]

—— Meaningfulness and concepts: concepts and meaningfulness. In *Analyses of concept learning* (edited by H.J. Klausmeier and C.W. Harris). New York: Academic Press, 1966, 65–79. [492]

—— and V.B. Bailey. Cue selection and mediated transfer in paired-associate learning. *Journal of Experimental Psychology*, 1964, *67*, 101–102. [405]

——, D.J. Foss, and P. Odom. Associative mediation in paired-associate learning with multiple controls. *Journal of Verbal Learning and Verbal Behavior*, 1965, 141–147. [448]

—— and D.S. Palermo. Mediation processes and the acquisition of linguistic structure. In *The acquisition of language* (edited by U. Bellugi and R.W. Brown). Monographs of the Society for Research in Child Development, Lafayette, Ind.: Child De-

velopment Publications, 1964, 141–169. [451]

Jenkins, W.O. The tactual discrimination of shapes for coding aircraft-type controls. In *Psychological research on equipment design* (edited by P.M. Fitts). U.S. Government Printing Office 1947, 199–205. [722]

Jennings, H.S. *Behavior of the lower organisms*. New York: Columbia Univ. Press, 1906. [325]

Jensen, D.D. Experiments on learning in paramecium. *Science*, 1957, *125*, 191–192. [326]

—— A theory of the behavior of *Paramecium aurelia* and behavioral effects of feeding, fission, and ultraviolet microbeam irradiation. *Behavior*, 1959, *15*, 82–122. [326]

Johnson, N.F. Linguistic models and functional units of language behavior. In *Directions in psycholinguistics* (edited by S. Rosenberg). New York: Macmillan, 1965, 29–65. [470]

Johnson, D.M. *The psychology of thought and judgment*. New York: Harper & Row, 1955. [424, 512]

Jouvet, M. Recherches sur les structures nerveuses et les mécanismes responsables de differentes phases du sommeil physiologique. *Archives of Italian Biology*, 1962, *100*, 125–206. [569]

Judd, D.B. Basic correlates of the visual stimulus. In *Handbook of experimental psychology* (edited by S.S. Stevens). New York: Wiley, 1951, 811–867. [199]

Judson, A.J., C.N. Cofer, and S. Gelfand. Reasoning as an associative process: II. "Direction" in problem solving as a function of prior reinforcement of relevant responses. *Psychological Reports*, 1956, *2*, 501–507. [492]

Julesz, B. Binocular depth perception without familiarity cues. *Science*, 1964, *145*, 356–362. [256]

Jung, C.G. *Studies in word association* (translated by M.D. Eder). London: William Heinemann, 1918. [446]

Jung, J. *Verbal learning*. New York: Holt, Rinehart & Winston, 1968. [424]

Kammann, R. Cognitive complexity and preferences in poetry. Unpublished doctoral dissertation, Univ. of Cincinnati, 1964. [634]

—— Verbal complexity and preferences in poetry. *Journal of Verbal Learning and Verbal Behavior*, 1966, *5*, 536–540. [633]

Katona, G. *Organizing and memorizing*. New York: Columbia Univ. Press, 1940. [420, 424]

Kaufman, L., and I. Rock. The moon illusion. *Scientific American*, 1962, *207*, 120–130. [257, 261]

Kelley, T.L. *Crossroads in the mind of man*. Stanford, Calif.: Stanford Univ. Press, 1928. [524]

Kennedy, W.A., V. Van de Riet, and J.C. White. A normative sample of intelligence and achievement of Negro elementary school children in the southeastern United States. *Monographs of the Society for Research in Child Development*, 1963, *28*, No. 6. [543]

Kent, G.H., and A.J. Rosanoff. A study of association in insanity. *American Journal of Insanity*, 1910, *67*, 37–96, 317–390. [446]

Keppel, G. Facilitation in short- and long-term retention of paired associates following distributed practice in learning. *Journal of Verbal Learning and Verbal Behavior*, 1964, *3*, 91–111. [393]

Kimble, G.A. *Hilgard and Marquis' conditioning and learning* (2nd Ed.). New York: Appleton - Century - Crofts, 1961. [321–322, 344]

—— and N. Garmezy. *Principles of general psychology*. New York: Ronald Press, 1968. [414]

Kimmel, H.D. Instrumental conditioning of autonomically mediated behavior. *Psychological Bulletin*, 1967, *67*, 337–345. [363]

Kimura, K., and L.M. Biedler. Microelectrode study of taste bud of the rat. *American Journal of Physiology*, 1956, 187–610. [285]

King-Ellison, P., and J.J. Jenkins. Visual duration threshold as a function of word frequency. *American Journal of Psychology*, 1954, 67, 700–703. [434]

Klein, G.S., D.P. Spence, R.R. Holt, and Susannah Gourevitch. Cognition without awareness: subliminal influences upon conscious thought. *Journal of Abnormal and Social Psychology*, 1958, 57, 255–266. [665]

Kleitman, N. *Sleep and wakefulness*. Chicago: Univ. of Chicago Press, 1939. [563, 571]

Kline, M. *Mathematics in western culture*. New York: Oxford, 1953. [64]

Koestler, A. *Insight and outlook*. Lincoln: Univ. of Nebraska Press, 1949. [230]

—— *The act of creation*. New York: Macmillan, 1964. [512]

Koffka, K. *Principles of Gestalt psychology*. New York: Harcourt, Brace & World, 1935. [231]

Köhler, W. *The mentality of apes*. New York: Harcourt, Brace & World, 1925. [495]

—— *Gestalt psychology*. New York: Liveright, 1947. Reprinted in paperback, New York: New American Library (Mentor), 1959. [225, 261, 419]

—— and H. Wallach. Figural after-effects: an investigation of visual processes. *Proceedings of the American Philosophical Society*, 1944, 88, 269–357. [241]

Kolers, P. The illusion of movement. *Scientific American*, 1964, 211, 98–106. [244]

Krech, D., and A.D. Calvin.

Levels of perceptual organization and cognition. *Journal of Abnormal and Social Psychology*, 1953, 48, 394–400. [227]

Kristofferson, A.B. Foveal intensity discrimination as a function of area and shape. Unpublished doctoral dissertation, Univ. of Michigan, 1954. [190, 191]

Krueger, W.C.F. The effect of overlearning on retention. *Journal of Experimental Psychology*, 1929, *12*, 71–78. [392]

Kubie, L.S. *Neurotic distortion of the creative process*. Lawrence, Kansas: Univ. of Kansas Press, 1958. [678]

Kuhlen, R.G. Social change: a neglected factor in psychological studies of the life span. *School and Society*, 1940, *50*, 14–16. [530]

Kuo, Z. *The dynamics of behavior development*. New York: Random House, 1967. [595]

Lacey, J.I. Psychophysiological approaches to the evaluation of psychotherapeutic process and outcome. In *Research in psychotherapy* (edited by E.A. Rubinstein and M.B. Parloff). Washington, D.C.: National Publishing Co., 1959. [574]

—— and Beatrice C. Lacey. The relationship of resting autonomic activity to motor impulsivity. *The brain and human behavior*, 1958, *36*, 144–209. [573, 575]

Ladd, G. Contributions to the psychology of visual dreams. *Mind*, 1892, *1*, 299–304. [565]

Ladefoged, P., and D.E. Broadbent. Perception of sequence in auditory events. *Quarterly Journal of Experimental Psychology*, 1960, *12*, 162–170. [470]

Lashley, K.S., and M. Wade. The Pavlovian theory of generalization. *Psychological Review*, 1946, 53, 72–87. [335]

Lawrence, D.H., and L. Fes-

tinger. *Deterrents and reinforcement*. Stanford, Calif.: Stanford Univ. Press, 1962. [650]

LeMagnen, J. Les phenomènes olfacto-sexuels chez le rat blanc. *Archives des Sciences Physiologiques*, 1952, 6, 295–331. [283]

Lenneberg, E. *New direction in the study of language*. Cambridge, Mass.: M.I.T. Press, 1964. [478]

Levine, M., and G. Spivack. Rate of reversal of the Necker Cube in diffuse brain injury. *Journal of Clinical Psychology*, 1962, *18*, 122–124. [220]

Levine, S. Stimulation in infancy. *Scientific American*, 1960, *202*, 80–86. [588]

—— and L. Otis. The effects of handling before and after weaning on the resistance of albino rats to later deprivation. *Canadian Journal of Psychology*, 1958, *12*, 103–108. [587]

Licklider, J.C.R. Basic correlates of the auditory stimulus. In *Handbook of experimental psychology* (edited by S.S. Stevens). New York: Wiley, 1951, 985–1039. [271, 273]

—— On psychophysiological models. In *Sensory communication* (edited by W.A. Rosenblith). New York: Wiley, 1961, 49–72. [293]

Lindzey. G. Some remarks concerning incest, the incest taboo, and psychoanalytic theory. *American Psychologist*, 1967, *22*, 1051–1059. [675]

Logan, F.A. *Incentive*. New Haven: Yale Univ. Press, 1960. [611–612]

—— and A.R. Wagner. *Reward and punishment*. Boston: Allyn & Bacon, 1965. [380, 611, 613]

London, I.D. Research on sensory interaction in the Soviet Union. *Psychological Bulletin*, 1954, *51*, 531–568. [239, 241]

Lorenz, K. The companion in the bird's world. *Auk*, 1937, *54*, 245–273. [590]

——— *King Solomon's ring.* New York: Thomas Y. Crowell, 1952. [139]

Loucks, R.B. An experimental evaluation of the interpretability of various types of aircraft attitude indicators. In *Psychological research on equipment design* (edited by P.M. Fitts). U.S. Government Printing Office, 1947, 111–135. [722]

Luchins, A.S. Mechanization in problem-solving. *Psychological Monographs,* 1942, *54,* No. 248. [500]

Luh, C.W. The conditions of retention. *Psychological Monographs,* 1922, *31,* No. 142. [392]

Magee, K.R., S.F. Schneider, and N. Rosenzweig. Congenital indifference to pain. *Journal of Nervous and Mental Disease,* 1961, *132,* 249–259. [293]

Mahl, G.F. The lexical and linguistic levels in the expression of the emotions. In *Expression of the emotions in man* (edited by P.H. Knapp). New York: International Universities Press, 1963, 77–105. [599]

Maier, N.R.F. Reasoning in humans: II. The solution of a problem and its appearance in consciousness. *Journal of Comparative Psychology,* 1931, *12,* 181–194. [492]

——— *Frustration: the study of behavior without a goal.* New York: McGraw-Hill, 1949. [362]

Maltzman, I. On the training of originality. *Psychological Review,* 1960, *67,* 229–242. [494]

———, M. Belloni, and M. Fishbein. Experimental studies of associative variables in originality. *Psychological Monographs,* 1964, *78,* No. 3. [493]

Mandler, G.S., and S.G. Sarason. A study of anxiety and learning. *Journal of Abnormal and Social Psychology,* 1952, *47,* 166–173. [597]

Martin, E. Transfer of verbal paired associates. *Psychological Review,* 1965, *72,* 327–343. [407]

Mast, S.O., and L.C. Pusch. Modification of response in amoeba. *Biological Bulletin,* 1924, *46,* 55–59. [310]

Matthews, B.H.C. The response of a muscle spindle during active contraction of a muscle. *Journal of Physiology,* 1931, *72,* 153–174. [76]

Max, L.W. An experimental study of the motor theory of consciousness: III. Action-current response in deaf-mutes during sleep, sensory stimulation and dreams. *Journal of Comparative Psychology,* 1935, *19,* 469–486. [488]

——— An experimental study of the motor theory of consciousness: IV. Action-current responses in the deaf during awakening, kinaesthetic imagery and abstract thinking. *Journal of Comparative Psychology,* 1937, *24,* 301–344. [488]

McCarthy, D. Language development in children. In *Manual of child psychology* (edited by L. Carmichael). New York: Wiley, 1946, 476–581. [437]

McClelland, D.C. *The achieving society.* Princeton: Van Nostrand, 1961. [696]

———, J.W. Atkinson, R.A. Clark, and E.L. Lowell. *The achievement motive.* New York: Appleton-Century-Crofts, 1953. [688]

McConnell, J.V. Memory transfer via cannibalism in planaria. *Journal of Neuropsychiatry,* 1962, *3,* 1–42. [328, 329]

———, A.L. Jacobson, and D.P. Kimble. The effects of regeneration upon retention of a conditioned response in the planarian. *Journal of Comparative and Physiological Psychology,* 1959, *52,* 1–5. [327]

McGaugh, J.L., N.M. Weinberger, and R.E. Whalen (eds.). *Psychobiology.* San Francisco: Freeman, 1967. [305]

McGehee, N.E., and R. Schulz. Mediation in paired-associate learning. *Journal of Experimental Psychology,* 1961, *62,* 565–570. [449]

McNeill, D. The origin of associations within the same grammatical class. *Journal of Verbal Learning and Verbal Behavior,* 1963, *2,* 346–351. [450]

——— Developmental psycholinguistics. In *The genesis of language* (edited by F. Smith and G.A. Miller). Cambridge, Mass.: M.I.T. Press, 1966, 15–84. [473]

McQueen, R., and C. Browning. The intelligence and educational achievement of a matched sample of white and Negro students. *School and Society,* 1960, *88,* 327–329. [544]

Mead, Margaret. *Sex and temperament in three primitive societies.* New York: Morrow, 1935. [694]

Medina, R.F. Frontal lobe damage and flicker fusion frequency. *Archives of Neurology and Psychiatry,* 1957, *77,* 108–110. [211]

Mednick, S.A. A learning theory approach to research on schizophrenia. *Psychological Bulletin,* 1958, *55,* 316–327. [335]

——— The associative basis of the creative process. *Psychological Review,* 1962, *69,* 220–232. [494]

——— *Learning.* Englewood Cliffs, N.J.: Prentice-Hall, 1964. [380]

Mehler, J. Some effects of grammatical transformations on the recall of English sentences. *Journal of Verbal Learning and Verbal Behavior,* 1963, *2,* 346–351. [471]

Melzack, R., and T.H. Scott. The effects of early experience on the response to pain. *Journal of Comparative and Physiological Psychology,* 1957, *50,* 155–161. [294]

———— and P.D. Wall. Pain mechanisms: a new theory. *Science*, 1965. *150*, 971–979. [293]

Meyer, D.R., and R.C. Miles. Intralist-interlist relations in verbal learning. *Journal of Experimental Psychology*, 1953, *45*, 109–115. [404]

Meyers, W.J., M.D. McQuiston, and R.C. Miles. Delayed-response and learning-set performance of cats. *Journal of Comparative and Physiological Psychology*, 1962, *55*, 515–517. [375]

Miles, C.C., and W.B. Miles. The correlation of intelligence scores and chronological age from early to late maturity. *American Journal of Psychology*, 1932, *44*, 44–78. [530]

Milgram, S. Behavioral study of obedience. *Journal of Abnormal and Social Psychology*, 1963, 67, 371–378. [710–711]

———— Liberating effects of group pressure. *Journal of Personality and Social Psychology*, 1965, *1*, 123–134. [712]

Milisen, R., and C. Van Riper. Differential transfer of training in a rotary activity. *Journal of Experimental Psychology*, 1939, *24*, 640–646. [416]

Miller, D.R., and G.E. Swanson. *Inner conflict and defense.* New York: Holt, Rinehart & Winston, 1960. [673]

Miller, G.A. The magic number seven, plus or minus two: some limits on our capacity for processing information. *Psychological Review*, 1956, 63, 81–97. [398]

———— *Language and communication.* New York: McGraw-Hill, 1951. [432, 478]

———— *Psychology: the science of mental life.* New York: Harper & Row, 1962. [559]

———— Some psychological studies of grammar. *American Psychologist*, 1962, *17*, 748–762. [470]

———— *Mathematics and psychology.* New York: Wiley, 1964. [37]

———— , E. Galanter, and K.N. Pribram. *Plans and the structure of behavior.* New York: Holt, Rinehart & Winston, 1960. [37, 504]

———— , G.A. Heise, and W. Lichten. The intelligibility of speech as a function of the context of the test materials. *Journal of Experimental Psychology*, 1951, *41*, 329–335. [442]

Miller, N.E. Experimental studies of conflict. In *Personality and the behavior disorders* (edited by J. McV. Hunt). New York: Ronald Press, 1944, 431–465. [643]

———— Learnable drives and rewards. In *Handbook of experimental psychology* (edited by S.S. Stevens). New York: Wiley, 1951, 435–472. [377, 603]

———— Learning of visceral and glandular responses. *Science*, 1969, *163*, 434–445. [363]

———— , C.J. Bailey, and J.A.F. Stevenson. Decreased "hunger" but increased food intake resulting from hypothalamic lesions. *Science*, 1950, *112*, 256–259. [619]

———— and L. Di Cara. Instrumental learning of heart-rate changes in curarized rats: shaping and specificity to discriminative stimulus. *Journal of Comparative and Physiological Psychology*, 1967, *63*, 12–19. [363]

———— and J. Dollard. *Social learning and imitation.* New Haven: Yale Univ. Press, 1941. [386, 486]

Miller, W., and Susan Ervin. The development of grammar in child language. In *The acquisition of language* (edited by U. Bellugi and R.W. Brown). Monographs of the Society for Research in Child Development. Lafayette, Ind.: Child Delevopment Publications, 1964, 9–34. [474]

Mink, W.D. Semantic generalization as related to word association. Unpublished doctoral dissertation, Univ. of Minnesota, 1957. [448]

Moltz, H. Imprinting: empirical basis and theoretical significance. *Psychological Bulletin*, 1960, *57*, 291–314. [590]

Monroe, L.J. Psychological and physiological differences between good and poor sleepers. *Journal of Abnormal Psychology*, 1967, *72*, 255–264. [569]

Montgomery, K.C., and M. Segall. Discrimination learning based upon the exploratory drive. *Journal of Comparative and Physiological Psychology*, 1955, *48*, 225–228. [624]

Moon, L.E., and T.M. Lodahl. The reinforcing effect of changes in illumination of lever-pressing in the monkey. *American Journal of Psychology*, 1956, *64*, 288–290. [624]

Morgan, C.T. *Physiological psychology* (3rd edition). New York: McGraw-Hill, 1965. [169, 178, 280, 286, 288, 618]

———— and E. Stellar. *Physiological psychology* (2nd edition). New York: McGraw-Hill, 1950. [618]

Mueller, C.G. *Sensory psychology.* Englewood Cliffs, N.J.: Prentice-Hall, 1965. [290, 296, 299–300, 305]

Müller, G.E. *Darstellung und Erklärung der verscheidenen Typen der Farbenblindheit.* Gottingen: Vandeneck and Ruprecht, 1924. [199]

———— and A. Pilzecker. Experimentelle Beitrage zur Lehre vom Gedachtniss. *Zeitschrift für Psychologie*, Ergbd., 1900, *1*, 1–288. [395]

Munroe, Ruth. *Schools of psycholanalytic thought.* New York: Holt, Rinehart & Winston (Dryden), 1955. [678]

Munsinger, H., and W. Kessen. Uncertainty, structure, and preference. *Psychological Monographs*, 1964, 78, No. 9. [633]

Neisser, U. *Cognitive psychology.* New York: Appleton-Century-Crofts, 1967. [417, 424]

Newell, A., J.C. Shaw, and H.A. Simon. Elements of a theory of human problem-solving. *Psychological Review*, 1958, 65, 151–166. [507]

Newman, H.H., F.N. Freeman, and K.J. Holzinger. *Twins: a study of heredity and environment*. Chicago: Univ. of Chicago Press, 1937. [548]

Newman, J. *The world of mathematics*, vol. 4. New York: Simon and Schuster, 1956. [512]

Nuttin, J.M., Jr. Attitude change after rewarded dissonant and consonant forced compliance. *International Journal of Psychology*, 1966, 1, 39–57. [655]

Olds, J. Physiological mechanisms of reward. In *Nebraska symposium on motivation* (edited by M.R. Jones). Lincoln, Nebr.: University of Nebraska Press, 1955. [43–44]

———— and P. Milner. Positive reinforcement produced by electrical stimulation of septal area and other regions of rat brain. *Journal of Comparative and Physiological Psychology*, 1954, 47, 419–427. [620]

O'Neil, W.M. The effect of verbal association on tachistoscopic recognition. *Australian Journal of Psychology*, 1953, 5, 42–45. [448]

Orne, M. On the social psychology of the psychological experiment: with particular reference to demand characteristics and their implications. *American Psychologist*, 1962, 17, 776–783. [62]

Osgood, C.E. The similarity paradox in human learning: a resolution. *Psychological Review*, 1949, 56, 132–143. [406]

———— and A.W. Heyer, Jr. A new interpretation of figural after-effects. *Psychological Review*, 1952, 59, 98–118. [242]

————, G.J. Suci, and P.H. Tannenbaum. *The measurement of meaning*. Urbana: Univ. of Illinois Press, 1957. [493]

Owens, W.A., Jr. Age and mental abilities: a longitudinal study. *Genetic Psychology Monographs*. 1953, 48, 3–54. [532]

Palen, G.F. Focusing cues in the visual cliff behavior of day-old chicks. *Journal of Comparative and Physiological Psychology*, 1965, 59, 452–454. [252]

Palermo, D.S., and J.J. Jenkins. *Word association norms—grade school through college*. Minneapolis, Minn.: Univ. of Minnesota Press, 1964. [447]

Pardes, H., and S.A. Karp. Field dependence in obese women. *Psychosomatic Medicine*, 1965, 27, 238–244. [693]

Pavlov, I.P. *Conditioned reflexes* (translated by G.V. Anrep). London: Oxford Univ. Press, 1927. [339, 340, 344]

Pervin, L.A., and R.J. Yatko. Cigarette smoking and alternative methods of reducing dissonance. *Journal of Personality and Social Psychology*. 1965, 2, 30–36. [651]

Peterson, M.S., and J.J. Jenkins. Word association phenomena at the individual level. Technical Report No. 16. *Studies of the Role of Language in Behavior*. ONR contract N 8-ONR-66216, Minneapolis, Minn.: Univ. of Minnesota, 1957. [454]

Petrinovich, L., and R. Bolles. Deprivation states and behavioral attributes. *Journal of Comparative and Physiological Psychology*, 1954, 47, 450–453. [607]

Pfaffman, C. De gustibus. *American Psychologist*, 1965, 20, 21–33. [285]

Pfungst, O. *Clever Hans* (edited by R. Rosenthal). New York: Holt, Rinehart & Winston, 1965. [62]

Pick, H.L., Jr., R.E. Klein, and Anne D. Pick. Visual and tactual identification of form orientation. *Journal of Experimental Child Psychology*, 1966, 4, 391–397. [291]

Plutchick, R. *The emotions: facts, theories, and a new model*. New York: Random House, 1962. [601]

Postman, L., J.S. Bruner, and E. McGinnies. Personal values as selective factors in perception. *Journal of Abnormal and Social Psychology*, 1948, 43, 142–154. [433]

———— and Greenblom, R. Conditions of cue selection in the acquisition of paired-associate lists. *Journal of Experimental Psychology*, 1967, 73, 91–100. [404]

Powell, B.J. A study of the perceptual field approach of normal subjects and schizophrenic patients under conditions of an oversize stimulus. Unpublished doctoral dissertation, Washington Univ., 1964. [693]

Ratliff, F. *Mach bands: quantitative studies on neural networks in the retina*. San Francisco: Holden-Day, 1965. [222, 223]

———— and H.K. Hartline. The response of *Limulus* optic nerve fibers to patterns of illumination on the receptor mosaic. *Journal of General Physiology*, 1959, 42, 1241–1255. [170]

Razran, G. Music, art, and the conditioned response. *Psychological Bulletin*, 1938, 35, 532. [324]

———— Conditioning away social bias by the luncheon technique. *Psychological Bulletin*, 1938b, 35, 693. [324]

———— Conditioned response changes in rating and appraising socio-political slogans. *Psychological Bulletin*, 1940, 37, 481. [324]

———— Stimulus generalization of conditioned responses. *Psychological Bulletin*, 1949, 46, 337–365. [332]

———— Semantic and phonetographic generalization of salivary conditioning to verbal stimuli. *Journal of Experimental Psychology*, 1949, 39, 642–652. [448]

———— The conditioned evocation of attitudes. *Journal of Experimental Psychology,* 1954, *48,* 278–282. [324]

Reinberg, A., and J. Ghata. *Biological rhythms.* New York: Walker and Co., 1964. [601]

Révész, G. Experiments on animal space perception. *Proceedings of VIIth International Congress of Psychology,* 1924, 29–56. [238]

Reynolds, G.S. *A primer of operant conditioning.* Glenview, Ill.: Scott, Foresman, 1968. [380]

Riggs, L.A. Light as a stimulus for vision. In *Vision and visual perception* (edited by C.H. Graham). New York: Wiley, 1965, 1–38. [178]

———, F. Ratliff, J.C. Cornsweet, and T.N. Cornsweet. The disappearance of steadily fixated visual test objects. *Journal of the Optical Society of America,* 1953, *43,* 495–501. [154]

Rivers, W.H.R. Introduction and vision. In *Reports of the Cambridge anthropological expedition to the Torres Straits* (edited by A.C. Haddon). Cambridge, England: The University Press, 1901. [234]

——— Observations on the senses of the Todas. *British Journal of Psychology,* 1905, *1,* 321–396. [234]

Roberts, C.L., M.H. Marx, and G. Collier. Light onset and light offset as reinforcers for the albino rat. *Journal of Comparative and Physiological Psychology,* 1958, *51,* 575–579. [624]

Roffwarg, H.P., W.C. Dement, J.N. Muzio, and C. Fisher. Dream imagery: relationship to rapid eye movements of sleep. *Archives of General Psychiatry,* 1962, *7,* 235–258. [567]

———, J.N. Muzio, and W.C. Dement. Ontogenetic development of the human sleep-dream cycle. *Science,* 1966, *152,* 604–619. [567]

Rohwer, W.D., Jr., S. Lynch, N. Suzuki, and J.R. Levin.

Verbal and pictorial facilitation of paired-associate learning. *Journal of Experimental Child Psychology,* 1967, *5,* 294–302. [399]

Rokeach, M. *The open and closed mind.* New York: Basic Books, 1960. [708]

Romanes, G.J. *Animal intelligence* (2nd ed.). London: Kegan Paul, 1882. [127]

Rosenberg, M.J. When dissonance fails: on eliminating evaluation apprehension from attitude measurement. *Journal of Personality and Social Psychology,* 1965, *1,* 28–42. [62, 655]

——— and C.I. Hovland (eds.). *Attitude organization and change.* New Haven: Yale Univ. Press, 1960. [650]

Rosenthal, R. On the social psychology of the psychological experiment. *American Scientist,* 1963, *51,* 268–283. [62]

——— *Experimenter effects in behavioral research.* New York: Appleton-Century-Crofts, 1966. [58]

——— and Lenore Jacobson. Teachers' expectancies: determinants of pupils' IQ gains. *Psychological Reports,* 1966, *19,* 115–118. [58]

Rudin, S.A. The psychology of nations. *Discovery,* 1965, *26,* 22–28. [699]

——— National motives predict psychogenic death rates 25 years later. *Science,* 1968, *160,* 901–903. [697]

Ruger, H. The psychology of efficiency. *Archives of Psychology,* 1910, No. 15 [486]

Rushton, W.A.H., and F.W. Campbell. Measurement of rhodopsin in the living human eye. *Nature,* 1954, *174,* 1096–1097. [160]

Russell, W.A., and L. Storms. Implicit verbal chaining in paired associate learning. *Journal of Experimental Psychology,* 1955, *49,* 267–293. [448]

Sampson, E. Birth order and conformity. *Journal of Personality and Social Psychol-*

ogy, 1967, *5,* 398–407. [710]

Sarason, I.G. *Contemporary research in personality.* Princeton: Van Nostrand, 1962. [715]

Sarnoff, I., and P.G. Zimbardo. Anxiety, fear, and social affiliation. *Journal of Abnormal and Social Psychology,* 1961, *62,* 356–363. [685]

Schachter, S. *The psychology of affiliation.* Stanford, Calif.: Stanford Univ. Press, 1959. [684]

——— Birth order and sociometric choice. *Journal of Abnormal and Social Psychology,* 1964, *68,* 453–456. [686]

Schafer, R. *Psychoanalytic interpretation in Rorschach testing.* New York: Grune & Stratton, 1954. [670]

——— Regression in the service of the ego: the relevance of a psychoanalytic concept for personality assessment. In *Assessment of human motives* (edited by G. Lindzey). New York: Holt, Rinehart & Winston, 1958, 119–148. [673]

Schlosberg. H. The description of facial expressions in terms of two dimensions. *Journal of Experimental Psychology,* 1952, *44,* 229–277. [596]

——— and C. Heineman. The relationship between two measures of response strength. *Journal of Experimental Psychology,* 1950, *40,* 235–247. [446]

Schwartz, M. Physiological psychology: or can a science over 95 afford to be "grubo"? *Psychological Bulletin,* 1967, *67,* 228–230. [139]

Scott, E.M., and Ethel L. Verney. Self-selection of diet: IX. The appetite for thiamine. *Journal of Nutrition,* 1940, *37,* 81–91. [607]

Scott, J.P. *Animal behavior.* Chicago: Univ. of Chicago Press, 1958. [139]

Scott, W.W., C.C. Scott, and A.B. Luckhardt. Observations on the blood sugar level before, during, and after hunger periods in humans. *American*

Journal of Physiology, 1938, 123, 243–247. [618]

Seashore, H.G. Methods of expressing test scores. Psychological Corporation Test Service Bulletin, No. 48, 1955. [94]

Segall, M.H., D.T. Campbell, and M.J. Herskovits. The influence of culture on visual perception. Indianapolis: Bobbs-Merrill, 1966. [233–235]

Selyé, H. The stress of life. New York: McGraw-Hill, 1956. [576]

Shapiro, A.K. A contribution to a history of the placebo effect. Behavioral Science, 1960, 5, 109–135. [62]

Sharpless, S., and H. Jasper. Habituation of the arousal reaction. Brain, 1956, 79, 655–680. [311]

Sheffield, F.D., and T.B. Roby. Reward value of a non-nutritive sweet taste. Journal of Comparative and Physiological Psychology, 1950, 43, 471–481. [622]

——, ——, and B.A. Campbell. Drive reduction versus consummatory behavior as determinants of reinforcement. Journal of Comparative and Physiological Psychology, 1954, 47, 349–354. [622]

——, J.J. Wulff, and R. Backer. Reward value of copulation without sex drive reduction. Journal of Comparative and Physiological Psychology, 1951, 44, 3–8. [623]

Sheffield, Virginia F. Extinction as a function of partial reinforcement and distribution of practice. Journal of Experimental Psychology, 1949, 39, 511–526. [359]

Sherif, M. Group influences upon the formation of norms and attitudes. In Readings in social psychology (edited by T.M. Newcomb and E.L. Hartley). New York: Holt, Rinehart & Winston, 1947. [707]

Sherrick, M.F., and W.N. Dember. Trial-two goal arm alternation to direction of movement in trial-one straight alley. Psychonomic Science, 1966, 6, 317–318. [283]

Shevrin, H., and L. Luborsky. The measurement of preconscious perception in dreams and images: an investigation of the Poetzl phenomenon. Journal of Abnormal and Social Psychology, 1958, 56, 285–294. [665]

—— and ——. The rebus technique: a method for studying primary process transformations of briefly exposed pictures. Journal of Nervous and Mental Disease, 1961, 133, 479–488. [665]

Shipley, T.E., and J. Veroff. A projective measure of need for affiliation. Journal of Experimental Psychology, 1952, 43, 349–356. [686]

Silverstein, A. The "grubo" psychology: or can a science over 95 be happy without reductionism? Psychological Bulletin, 1966, 66, 207–211. [139]

Simon, H.A., and K. Kotovsky. Human acquisition of concepts for sequential patterns. Psychological Review, 1963, 70, 534–546. [506]

Skinner, B.F. The behavior of organisms. New York: Appleton-Century-Crofts, 1938. [363]

—— Science and human behavior. New York: Macmillan, 1953. [386]

—— A case history in scientific method. American Psychologist, 1956, 11, 221–233. [45, 62, 354]

—— Verbal behavior. New York: Appleton-Century-Crofts, 1957. [429, 457–462]

Skodak, M., and H.M. Skeels. A final follow-up study of one hundred adopted children. Journal of Genetic Psychology, 1949, 75, 85–125. [548]

Sleight, R.B. The effect of instrument dial shape on legibility. Journal of Applied Psychology, 1948, 32, 170–188. [722]

Slobin, D.I. The acquisition of Russian as a native language. In The genesis of language (edited by F. Smith and G.A. Miller) Cambridge, Mass.: M.I.T. Press, 1966, 129–148. [475]

Sluckin, W. Imprinting and early learning. Chicago: Aldine, 1965. [601]

Small, W.S. Experimental study of the mental processes of the rat. II. American Journal of Psychology, 1901, 12, 206–239. [364]

Smith, O.A. Stimulation of lateral and medial hypothalamus and food intake in the rat. Anatomical Record, 1956, 124, 363–364. [620]

Solomon, R.L., and D.H. Howes. Word frequency, personal values and visual duration thresholds. Psychological Review, 1951, 58, 256–270. [433]

——, L.J. Kamin, and L.C. Wynne. Traumatic avoidance learning: the outcomes of several extinction procedures with dogs. Journal of Abnormal and Social Psychology, 1953, 48, 291–302. [324]

—— and Lucille H. Turner. Discriminative classical conditioning in dogs paralyzed by curare can later control discriminative avoidance responses in the normal state. Psychological Review, 1962, 69, 202–219. [372]

—— and L.C. Wynne. Traumatic avoidance learning: the principles of anxiety conservation and partial irreversibility. Psychological Review, 1954, 61, 353–385. [376]

Sontag, L.W., C.T. Baker, V.L. Nelson. Mental growth and personality development: a longitudinal study. Monograph of the Society for Research in Child Development, 1958, 23, 1–85. [535]

Spaulding, D.A. Instinct, with original observations on young animals. Macmillan's Magazine, 1873, 27, 282–293. Reprinted in British Journal of Animal Behavior, 1954, 2, 2–11. [590]

Spearman, C. *The abilities of man.* London: Macmillan, 1927. [524]

Spelt, D.K. The conditioning of the human fetus in utero. *Journal of Experimental Psychology,* 1948, 38, 338–346. [330]

Spence, K.W. Theoretical interpretations of learning. In *Handbook of experimental psychology* (edited by S.S. Stevens). New York: Wiley, 1951, 690–729. [341]

Spitz, H.H. Field theory in mental deficiency. In *Handbook of mental deficiency* (edited by N.R. Ellis). New York: McGraw-Hill, 1963, 11–40. [243]

Spitz, R.A. Hospitalism: an inquiry into the genesis of psychiatric conditions in early childhood. Part I. *Psychoanalytic Study of the Child,* 1945, 1, 53–74. [593]

——— and Katherine M. Wolf. The smiling response: a contribution to the ontogenesis of social relations. *Genetic Psychology Monographs,* 1946, 34, 57–125. [583]

Spitzer, H.F. Studies in retention. *Journal of Educational Psychology,* 1939, 30, 641–656. [396]

Staples, F.R., and R.H. Walters. Anxiety, birth order, and susceptibility to social influence. *Journal of Abnormal and Social Psychology,* 1961, 62, 716–719. [684]

Stevens, S.S. The attributes of tones. *Proceedings of the National Academy of Sciences,* 1934, 20, 457–459. [271]

——— A scale for the measurement of a psychological magnitude: loudness. *Psychological Review,* 1936, 43, 405–416. [77]

——— On the psychophysical law. *Psychological Review,* 1957, 64, 153–181. [77–78]

Stolz, W. Self-imbedding that experiments that I have done involved will be discussed. Address at Human Learning

Center, Univ. of Minn. 1966. [477]

Strong, E.K., Jr. The effect of the time-interval upon recognitive memory. *Psychological Review,* 1913, 20, 339–372. [391]

Swets, J.A. (ed.). *Signal detection and recognition by human observers.* New York: Wiley, 1964. [188]

———, W.P. Tanner, Jr., and T.G. Birdsall. Decision processes in perception. *Psychological Review,* 1961, 68, 301–340. [80]

Taffel, C. Anxiety and the conditioning of verbal behavior. *Journal of Abnormal and Social Psychology,* 1955, 51, 496–501. [460]

Tanser, H.A. *The settlement of Negroes in Kent County, Ontario.* Chatham, Ontario: Shephard Publication Co., 1939. [544]

Taylor, W. "Cloze procedure": a new tool for measuring readability. *Journalism Quarterly,* 1953, 30, 415–433. [456]

Teevan, R.C., and R.C. Birney (eds.). *Color vision.* Princeton: Van Nostrand, 1961. [215]

Teitelbaum, P. Sensory control of hypothalamic hyperphagia. *Journal of Comparative and Physiological Psychology,* 1955, 48, 156–163. [620]

——— Random and food-directed activity in hyperphagic and normal rats. *Journal of Comparative and Physiological Psychology,* 1957, 50, 486–490. [620]

——— *Physiological psychology.* Englewood Cliffs, N.J.: Prentice-Hall, 1964. [223, 620]

Terman, L.M., and M.A. Merrill. *Revised Stanford-Binet intelligence scale: third edition.* Boston: Houghton Mifflin, 1960. [527]

——— and ———. *Measuring intelligence.* Boston: Houghton-Mifflin. 1937. [527]

——— and M. Oden. The gifted group at mid-life. Stan-

ford, Calif.: Stanford Univ. Press, 1959. [531]

Thomas, G.J. Equal-volume judgments of tones. *American Journal of Psychology,* 1949, 62, 182–201. [272]

Thompson, Elizabeth L. An analysis of the learning process in the snail, *Physagyrina Say. Behavior Monographs,* 1917, 3, No. 3, 1–97 [310]

Thompson, R., and J.V. McConnell. Classical conditioning in the planarian, *Dugesia doroto cephala. Journal of Comparative and Physiological Psychology,* 1955, 48, 65–68. [327]

Thompson, W.R. Influence of prenatal maternal anxiety on emotionality in young rats. *Science,* 1957, 125, 698–699. [586]

Thorndike, E.L. *Animal intelligence.* New York: Macmillan, 1911. [485]

——— *The fundamentals of learning.* New York: Teachers College, 1932. [384]

——— *The psychology of wants, interest and attitudes.* New York: Appleton-Century-Crofts, 1935. [384]

——— and I. Lorge. *The teachers' word book of 30,000 words.* New York: Teachers College, 1944. [433]

Thurstone, L.L. The learning function. *Journal of General Psychology,* 1930, 3, 469–493. [398]

Thurstone, T.G. Primary mental abilities of children. *Educational and Psychological Measurement,* 1941, 1, 105–116. [524]

Tinbergen, N. *The herring gull's world.* Garden City, N.Y.: Doubleday (Anchor Books), 1967. [139]

Tolman, E.C. *Purposive behavior in animals and men.* New York: Appleton-Century-Crofts, 1932. [365]

——— and C.H. Honzik. Introduction and removal of reward, and maze performance in rats. *Univ. of California Publications in Psychology,* 1930, 4, 257–275. [368–369]

———, B.F. Ritchie, and D. Kalish. Studies in spatial learning. II. Place learning versus response learning. *Journal of Experimental Psychology*, 1946, *36*, 221–229. [371–372]

Trowill, J. Instrumental conditioning of the heart rate in the curarized rat. *Journal of Comparative and Physiological Psychology*, 1967, *63*, 7–11. [363]

Tuckman, J., and R.A. Regan. Ordinal position and behavior problems in children. *Journal of Health and Social Behavior*, 1967, *8*, 32–39. [686]

Tyler, Leona E. *Tests and measurements*. Englewood Cliffs, N.J.: Prentice-Hall, 1963. [106]

——— *The psychology of human differences* (3rd edition). New York: Appleton-Century-Crofts, 1965. [559]

Underwood, B.J. Interference and forgetting. *Psychological Review*, 1957, *64*, 49–60. [401]

———, M. Hamm, and B.R. Ekstrand. Cue selection in paired-associate learning. *Journal of Experimental Psychology*, 1962, *64*, 405–409. [405]

——— and R.W. Schulz. *Meaningfulness and verbal learning*, New York: Lippincott, 1960. [403]

Van Ormer, E.B. Retention after intervals of sleep and waking. *Archives of Psychology*, 1932, No. 137. [399]

Vernon, M.D. *The psychology of perception*. Baltimore: Penguin, 1962. [261]

Vidulich, R.N., and I.P. Kaiman. The effects of information source status and dogmatism upon conformity behavior. *Journal of Abnormal and Social Psychology*, 1961, *63*, 639–642. [708]

Vitz, P.O. Prefernce for different amounts of visual complexity. *Behavior Science*, 1966a, *11*, 105–114. [633]

——— Affect as a function of stimulus variation. *Journal of Experimental Psychology*, 1966b, *71*, 74–79. [633]

Voeks, Virginia W. Acquisition of S-R connections: a test of Hull's and Guthrie's theories. *Journal of Experimental Psychology*, 1954, *47*, 137–147. [351]

Von Restorff, H. Uber die Wirkung Von Bereichsbildungen in Spurenfeld. (In W. Köhler and H. Von Restorff, Analyse Von Vorgangen in Spurenfeld.) *Psychologische Forschung*, 1933, *18*, 299–342. [419]

Voss, J.F. *Approaches to thought*. Columbus, Ohio: Merrill, 1969. [512]

Wald, G. On the mechanism of the visual threshold and visual adaptation. *Science*, 1954, *119*, 887–895. [160]

Walk, R.D. Response of dark- and light-reared rats to stimulus change. *Journal of Comparative and Physiological Psychology*, 1960, *53*, 609–611. [625]

——— and Eleanor J. Gibson. A comparative and analytical study of visual depth perception. *Psychological Monographs*, 1961, *75*, No. 519. [252]

Walker, E.L. *Conditioning and instrumental learning*. Belmont, Calif.: Brooks/Cole, 1967. [380]

——— and J.W. Atkinson. The expression of fear-related motivation in thematic apperception as a function of proximity to an atomic explosion. In *Motives in fantasy, action, and society* (edited by J.W. Atkinson). Princeton: Van Nostrand, 1958. [28]

Warm, J.S., and Foulke, E. Effects of orientation and redundancy on tactual perception of form. *Perceptual and Motor Skills*, 1968, *27*, 83–89. [291]

Watson, J.B. Kinaesthetic and organic sensations: their role in the reactions of the white rat to the maze. *Psychological Monographs*, 1907, *8*, No. 33. [367]

——— Psychology as a behaviorist views it. *Psychological Review*, 1913, *20*, 158–177. [604]

——— Experimental studies on the growth of the emotions. In *Psychologies of 1925* (edited by C. Murchison). Worcester, Mass.: Clark Univ. Press, 1927, 37–57. [582]

——— and Rosalie Raynor. Conditioned emotional reactions. *Journal of Experimental Psychology*, 1920, *3*, 1–4. [323]

Webb, W.B. *Sleep: an experimental approach*. New York: Macmillan, 1968. [601]

Wechsler, D. Intellectual development and psychological maturity. *Child Development*, 1950, *21*, 45–50. [529]

Weddell, G. Receptors for somatic sensation. In *Brain and behavior*, Volume I (edited by Mary Brazier). Washington, D.C.: American Institute of Biological Sciences, 1961, *13*, 48. [288]

Weininger, O. Mortality of albino rats under stress as a function of early handling. *Canadian Journal of Psychology*, 1953, *7*, 111–114. [587]

——— The effects of early experience on behavior and growth characteristics. *Journal of Comparative and Physiological Psychology*, 1956, *49*, 1–9. [587]

Weinstock, S. Resistance to extinction of a running response following partial reinforcement under widely spaced trials. *Journal of Comparative and Physiological Psychology*, 1954, *47*, 318–323. [360]

Werner, H. *Comparative psychology of mental development*. Chicago: Follett, 1948. [241, 690]

——— and E. Kaplan. Development of word meaning through verbal context: an experimental study. *Journal of Psychology*, 1950, *29*, 251–257. [452]

Wertheimer, M. *Productive*

thinking (2nd ed.). New York: Harper & Row, 1959. [512]

Wever, E.G. *Theory of hearing.* New York: Wiley, 1949. [270]

—— and C.W. Bray. The perception of low tones and the resonance volley theory. *Journal of Psychology,* 1937, *3,* 101–114. [267]

Wheatstone, C. Contributions to the physiology of vision— Part the first. On some remarkable, and hitherto unobserved, phenomena of binocular vision. *Philosophical Transactions,* Royal Society of London, 1838, *128,* 371–394. [255]

White, R. Motivation reconsidered: the concept of competence. In *Functions of varied experience* (edited by D.W. Fiske and S.R. Maddi). Homewood, Ill.: Dorsey, 1961, 278–325. [640]

—— *Lives in progress* (2nd ed.). New York: Holt, Rinehart & Winston, 1966. [716]

Witkin, H.A. The perception of the upright. *Scientific American,* 1959, *200,* 50–56. [218]

—— Psychological differentiation and forms of pathology. *Journal of Abnormal Psychology,* 1965, *70,* 317–336. [692–693]

——, Ruth B. Dyk, Hanna Faterson, D.R. Goodenough, and S.A. Karp. *Psychological differentiation.* New York: Wiley, 1962. [218, 689]

——, D.R. Goodenough, and S.A. Karp. Stability of cognitive style from childhood to young adulthood. *Journal*

of Personality and Social Psychology, 1967, *7,* 291–300. [691]

Wolman, B.B. *Contemporary theories and systems in psychology.* New York: Harper & Row, 1960. [344]

Wolpe, J., and A.A. Lazarus. *Behavior therapy techniques.* Oxford: Pergamon Press, 1966. [335]

Woods, P.J., and Sallie Jennings. Response to environmental change: a further confirmation. *Psychological Reports,* 1959, *5,* 560. [625]

Woodworth, R.S. *Experimental psychology,* New York: Holt, Rinehart & Winston, 1938. [289]

—— and H. Schlosberg. *Experimental psychology* (rev. ed.). New York: Holt, Rinehart & Winston, 1954. [397]

Wright, W.D. A re-determination of the trichromatic coefficients of spectral colours. *Transactions of the Optical Society* (London), 1928–29, *30,* 141–164. [196]

Wrightsman, L.S., Jr. Effects of waiting with others on changes in level of felt anxiety. *Journal of Abnormal and Social Psychology,* 1960, *61,* 216–222. [684]

Yerkes, R.M. (ed.). Psychological examining in the United States Army. *Memories of the National Academy of Science,* 1921, *15.* [538]

Young, P.T. Psychologic factors regulating the feeding process. *American Journal of Clinical Nutrition.* 1957, *5,* 154–161. [616]

Young, R.D. Effect of prenatal

maternal injection of epinephrine on postnatal offspring behavior. *Journal of Comparative and Physiological Psychology,* 1963, *56,* 929–932. [587]

—— Effect of prenatal drugs and neonatal stimulation on later behavior. *Journal of Comparative and Physiological Psychology,* 1964, *58,* 309–311. [587]

Young, R.K. Serial learning. In *Verbal behavior and general behavior theory* (edited by T.R. Dixon and D. L. Horton). Englewood Cliffs, N.J.: Prentice-Hall, 1968, 122–148. [395]

Yule, G.U. *The statistical study of literary vocabulary.* London: Cambridge, 1944. [432]

Zener, K., and H.G. McCurdy. Analysis of motivational factors in conditioned behavior: I. The differential effect of changes in hunger upon conditioned, unconditioned, and spontaneous salivary secretion. *Journal of Psychology,* 1939, *8,* 321–350 [610]

Zimbardo, P.G. *The cognitive control of motivation.* Glenview, Ill.: Scott-Foresman, 1969. [656]

Zipf, G.K. *The psycho-biology of language.* Boston: Houghton Mifflin, 1935. [432]

—— *Human behavior and the principle of least effort.* Cambridge, Mass.: Addison-Wesley, 1949. [431]

Zuckmann, L. Hysteric compulsive factors in perceptual organization. Unpublished doctoral dissertation, New School for Social Research, 1957. [693]

Credits

FIGURES AND TABLES

Chapter One. 1.1 Hull, C.L. *Principles of behavior.* New York: Appleton-Century-Crofts, 1943. [21] **Table 1.1** Walker, E.L., and J.W. Atkinson. The expression of fear-related motivation in thematic apperception as a function of proximity to an atomic explosion. In *Motives in fantasy, action, and society* (edited by J.W. Atkinson). Princeton: © 1958, by Litton Educational Publishing, Inc., by permission of Van Nostrand Company. [28]

Chapter Three. 3.4 Stevens, S.S. On the psychophysical law. *Psychological Review,* 1957, *64,* 153–181. [78] 3.10 Courtesy Psychological Corporation, Test Service Bulletin No. 48. [94] 3.11 Staff, Psychological Section, Fort Worth, Texas, Psychological activities in the training commands, Army Air Forces. Psychological Bulletin, 1945. Copyright © (1945) by the American Psychological Association, and reproduced by permission. [96]

Chapter Five. 5.6 Riggs, L.A., F. Ratliff, J.C. Cornsweet, and T.N. Cornsweet. The disappearance of steadily fixated visual test objects. *Journal of the Optical Society of America,* 1953, *43,* 495–501. [154]

Chapter Six. 6.11 Fantz, R. The origin of form perception. *Scientific American,* 1961, *204,* 66–72. Copyright © (1961) by Scientific American, Inc. All rights reserved. [205] **6.12** Fantz, R., J.M. Ordy, and M.S. Udelf. Maturation of pattern vision in infants during the first six months. *Journal of Comparative and Physiological Psychology,* 1962, *55,* 907–917. Copyright © (1962) by the American Psychological Association, and reproduced by permission. [206]

Chapter Seven. 7.1 Witkin, H.A. The perception of the upright. *Scientific American,* 1959, *200,* 50–56. Copyright © (1959) by Scientific American, Inc. All rights reserved. [218] 7.6 Teitelbaum, P. *Physiological psychology.* Englewood Cliffs, N.J.: Prentice-Hall, 1964. [223] 7.7 Ratliff, F. *Mach bands: quantitative studies on neural networks in the retina.* San Francisco: Holden-Day, 1965. Courtesy the author. [223] **7.26, 7.27, 7.31** Gibson, J.J. *The perception of the visual world.* Boston: Houghton Mifflin, 1950. [249, 254] 7.32 Julesz, B. Binocular depth perception without familiarity cues. *Science,* 1964, *145,* 356–362. Courtesy the author. [256]

Chapter Eight. 8.4 Wever, E.G. *Theory of hearing.* New York: Wiley, 1949. [270] **8.6** Licklider, J.C.R. Basic correlates of the auditory stimulus. In *Handbook of experimental psychology* (edited by S.S. Stevens). New York: Wiley, 1951, 985–1039. [273] **8.7, 8.8, 8.9** Amoore, J.E., J.W. Johnston, Jr., and M. Rubin. The stereochemical theory of odor. *Scientific American,* 1964, *210,* 42–49. Copyright © (1964) by Scientific American, Inc. All rights reserved. [279–281] **Table 8.1** Corso, J.F. *The experimental psychology of sensory behavior.* New York: Holt, Rinehart & Winston, 1967. [289] **Table 8.2** Mueller, C.G. *Sensory psychology.* Englewood Cliffs, N.J.: Prentice-Hall, 1965. [290] **8.13** Warm, J.S., and Foulke, E. Effects of orientation and redundancy on tactual perception of form. *Perceptual and Motor Skills,* 1968, *27,* 83–89. Reprinted by permission of author and publisher. [291]

Chapter Nine. 9.4 Deese, J., and S.H. Hulse. *The psychology of learning.* New York: McGraw-Hill, 1967. [316] **Tables 9.1 and 9.2** McConnell, J.V. Memory transfer via cannibalism in planaria. *Journal of Neuropsychiatry,* 1962, *3,* 1–42. [328]

Chapter Ten. 10.5 Tolman, E.C., and C.H. Honzik. Introduction and removal of reward, and maze performance in rats. *Univ. of California Publications in Psychology,* 1930, *4,* 257–275. Reprinted by permission of the Regents of the University of

California. [369] **10.8** Meyers, W.J., M.D. McQuiston, and R.C. Miles. Delayed-response and learning-set performance of cats. *Journal of Comparative and Physiological Psychology,* 1962, *55,* 515–517. Copyright © (1962) by the American Psychological Association, and reproduced by permission. [375]

Chapter Eleven. **11.4** Keppel, G. Facilitation in short- and long-term retention of paired associates following distributed practice in learning. *Journal of Verbal Learning and Verbal Behavior,* 1964, *3,* 91–111. Copyright © (1964) by Academic Press, Inc. [393] **11.5** Spitzer, H.F. Studies in retention. *Journal of Educational Psychology,* 1939, *30,* 641–656. [396] **11.7** Barnes, J.M., and B.J. Underwood. "Fate" of first-list associations in transfer theory. *Journal of Experimental Psychology,* 1959, *58,* 97–105. Copyright © (1959) by the American Psychological Association, and reproduced by permission. [401] **11.8** Underwood, B.J. Interference and forgetting. *Psychological Review,* 1957, *64,* 49–60. Copyright © (1957) by the American Psychological Association, and reproduced by permission. [401] **11.9** Meyer, D.R., and R.C. Miles. Intralist-interlist relations in verbal learning. *Journal of Experimental Psychology,* 1953, *45,* 109–115. Copyright © (1953) by the American Psychological Association, and reproduced by permission. [404] **11.13** Fleishman, E.A. A comparative study of aptitude patterns in unskilled and skilled psychomotor performances. *Journal of Applied Psychology,* 1957, *41,* 263–272. Copyright © (1957) by the American Psychological Association, and reproduced by permission. Fleishman, E.A., and W.E. Hempel. Changes in factor structure of a complex psychomotor test as a function of practice. *Psychometrika.* 1954, *19,* 239–252. [412] **11.14** Kim-

ble, G.A., and N. Garmezy. *Principles of general psychology.* New York: Ronald Press, © 1968. [414]

Chapter Twelve. **12.1** Miller, G.A. *Language and communication.* New York: McGraw-Hill, 1951. Zipf, G.K. *The psycho-biology of language.* Boston: Houghton Mifflin, 1935. Yule, G.U. *The statistical study of literary vocabulary.* London: Cambridge, 1944. [432] **12.5** Miller, G.A., G.A. Heise, and W. Lichten. The intelligibility of speech as a function of the context of the test materials. *Journal of Experimental Psychology,* 1951, *41,* 329–335. Copyright © (1951) by the American Psychological Association, and reproduced by permission. [443] **12.6** Schlosberg, H., and C. Heineman. The relationship between two measures of response strength. *Journal of Experimental Psychology,* 1950, *40,* 235–247. Copyright © (1950) by the American Psychological Association, and reproduced by permission. [446] **12.10** DeNike, L.D., and C.D. Spielberger. Induced mediating states in verbal conditioning. *Journal of Verbal Learning and Verbal Behavior,* 1963, *1,* 339–345. Copyright © (1963) by Academic Press, Inc. [461] **12.13** Clifton, C., Jr., and Penelope Odom. Similarity relations among certain English sentence constructions. *Psychological Monographs,* 1966, *80,* No. 613. Copyright © (1966) by the American Psychological Association, and reproduced by permission. [472] **Table 12.2** Gough, P.B. Grammatical transformations and speed of understanding. *Journal of Verbal Learning and Verbal Behavior,* 1965, *4,* 107–111. Copyright © (1965) by Academic Press, Inc. [472]

Chapter Thirteen. **13.5** Miller, G.A., E. Galanter, and K.N. Pribram. *Plans and the structure of behavior.* New York: Holt,

Rinehart & Winston, 1960. [504]

Chapter Fourteen. **14.1** Harrell, T.W. Army General Classification Test results for Air Force Specialists. *Educational and Psychological Measurement,* 1946, *6,* 341–349. [541] **14.3** Wechsler, D. Intellectual development and psychological maturity. *Child Development,* 1950, *21,* 45–50. Copyright © (1950) by The Society for Research in Child Development, Inc. [529] **14.4** Miles, C.C., and W.B. Miles. The correlation of intelligence scores and chronological age from early to late maturity. *American Journal of Psychology,* 1932, *44,* 44–78. By permission of University of Illinois Press. [530] **14.5, 14.6** Bayley, Nancy. On the growth of intelligence. *American Psychologist,* 1955, *10,* 805–818. Copyright © (1955) by the American Psychological Association, and reproduced by permission. [533–534] **14.8** Kennedy, W.A., V. Van de Riet, and J.C. White. A normative sample of intelligence and achievement of Negro elementary school children in the southeastern United States. *Monographs of the Society for Research in Child Development,* 1963, *28,* No. 6. Copyright © (1963) by the Society for Research in Child Development, Inc. [543] **Table 14.2** Alper, T.G., and E.G. Boring. Intelligence-test scores of Northern and Southern white and Negro recruits in 1918. *Journal of Abnormal and Social Psychology,* 1944, *39,* 471–474. Copyright © (1944) by the American Psychological Association, and reproduced by permission. [544] **14.10** Guilford, J.P. Three faces of intellect. *American Psychologist,* 1959, *14,* 469–479. Copyright © (1959) by the American Psychological Association, and reproduced by permission. [550]

Chapter Fifteen. **15.1** Dement, W.C. An essay on

dreams: the role of physiology in understanding their nature. In *New directions in Psychology II.* New York: Holt, Rinehart & Winston, 1965, *135,* 257. Courtesy the author. [564] **15.2** Lacey, J.I., and Beatrice C. Lacey. The relationship of resting autonomic activity to motor impulsivity. *The Brain and Human Behavior,* 1958, *36,* 144–209. [575] **Table 15.1** Denenberg, V.H. Early experience and emotional development. *Scientific American,* 1963, *208,* 138–146. Courtesy the author. Copyright © (1963) by Scientific American, Inc. All rights reserved. [589]

Chapter Sixteen. 16.1 Bolles, R.C. The readiness to eat and drink: the effect of deprivation conditions. *Journal of Comparative and Physiological Psychology,* 1962, *55,* 230–234. Copyright © (1962) by the American Psychological Association, and reproduced by permission. [609] **16.3** Logan, F.A. *Incentive.* New Haven: Yale Univ. Press, 1960. [612] **16.4** Bolles, R.C. *Theory of motivation.* New York: Harper & Row, 1967. From Crespi, L.P. Quantitative variation of incentive and performance in the white rat. *American Journal of Psychology,* 1942, *55,* 467–517. [613] **16.7** Teitelbaum, P. Appetite. *Proceedings of American Philosophical Society,* 1964, *108,* 464–472. [619] **16.8** Fantz, R. The origin of form perception.

Scientific American, 1961, *204,* 66–72. Copyright © (1963) by Scientific American, Inc. All rights reserved. [626]

Chapter Seventeen. 17.7 Carlsmith, J.M., B.E. Collins, and R.L. Helmreich. Studies in forced compliance: I. The effect of pressure for compliance on attitude change produced by face-to-face role-playing and anonymous essay writing. *Journal of Personality and Social Psychology,* 1966, *4,* 1–13. Copyright © (1966) by the American Psychological Association, and reproduced by permission. [655] **17.8** Fisher, C. Dreams and perception. *Journal of the American Psychoanalytic Association,* 1954, *2,* 389–445. Courtesy International Universities Press, Inc. [664]

Chapter Eighteen. 18.4 Witkin, H.A., D.R. Goodenough, and S.A. Karp. Stability of cognitive style from childhood to young adulthood. *Journal of Personality and Social Psychology,* 1967, *7,* 291–300. Copyright © (1967) by the American Psychological Association, and reproduced by permission. [691] **18.5** Rudin, S.A. The psychology of nations. *Discovery,* 1965, *26,* 22–28. By courtesy of *Science Journal* (incorporating *Discovery*), London. [699]

Conclusion (lower left). Chapanis, A., W.R. Garner, and C.T. Morgan, *Applied experi-*

mental psychology. New York: Wiley, 1949. [722]

QUOTATIONS

Olds, J. Physiological mechanisms of reward. In *Nebraska symposium on motivation* (edited by M.R. Jones). Lincoln, Nebr.: University of Nebraska Press, 1955. [43–44]

Kline, M. *Mathematics in western culture.* New York: Oxford, 1953. [64]

Allport, G.W. *Becoming.* New Haven: Yale Univ. Press, 1955. [114]

Köhler, W. *Gestalt psychology.* New York: Liveright, 1947. [225]

Pavlov, I.P. *Conditioned reflexes* (translated by G.V. Anrep). London: Oxford Univ. Press, 1927. By permission of Clarendon Press, Oxford. [339–340]

Harlow, H.F. The nature of love. *American Psychologist,* 1958, *13,* 673–685. Copyright © (1958) by the American Psychological Association, and reproduced by permission. [592]

Schafer, R. *Psychoanalytic interpretation in Rorschach testing.* New York: Grune & Stratton, 1954. [670]

Witkin, H.A. Psychological differentiation and forms of pathology. *Journal of Abnormal Psychology,* 1965, *70,* 317–336. Copyright © (1965) by the American Psychological Association, and reproduced by permission. [691–692, 693]

INDEXES

Name Index

Coons, E., 377
Corning, W., 329
Cornsweet, J., 154
Cornsweet, T., 154
Corso, J., 271, 289
Crespi, L., 316, 612
Crosby, E., 164
Crutchfield, R., 709, 710
Dallenbach, K., 399–400
Darwin, C., 126–128, 130, 134, 596
Davis, C., 607
Deese, J., 316, 442
Delgado, J., 4
Dember, C., 598
Dember, W., 239, 261, 283, 332, 605, 624, 630–631
Dement, W., 564–569
Denenberg, V., 588–589
Denike, L., 461
Detwiler, S., 141
DeValois, R., 174, 201
DiCara, L., 363
Dickens, C., 702
Dollard, J., 386, 486–487, 622
Donders, F., 515
Dorfman, D., 633
Douglas, R., 283, 378
Dulany, D., 461
Duncker, K., 499–500
Dyk, R., 218, 689
Earl, R., 630–632
Ebbinghaus, H., 387–396
Ehrlich, D., 684
Einstein, A., 21
Ekstrand, B., 405
Elms, A., 655
Erikson, E., 703
Ertl, J., 212
Ervin, S., 474
Estes, E., 709
Estes, W., 21, 362, 421
Eysenck, H., 340
Fantz, R., 201, 205–206, 215, 223, 625–626
Faterson, H., 218, 689
Fechner, G., 65, 74–76, 180
Feigenbaum, E., 8
Feldman, J., 8
Fender, D., 256
Festinger, L., 650–652, 654, 678
Fishbein, M., 493
Fisher, C., 567, 664
Flavell, J., 559
Fleishman, E., 412–413, 416
Fleming, W., 654
Fodor, J., 469
Foss, D., 448
Foulke, E., 291
Foulkes, D., 566

Fowler, H., 625, **635**
Fox, C., 665–666
Fraiberg, S., 715
Franks, C., 335
Franzblau, R., 539
Fraser, C., 474
Freeman, F., 548
Freud, A., 659
Freud, S., 31–32, 37, 42, 122–125, 130, 137, 139, 230, 338, 568, 605, 607–608, 621, 658–659, 661, 663, 675, 678, 680, 700, 703–705
Funkenstein, D., 595
Galanter, E., 37, 215, 504
Galileo, G., 4–65
Gall, F., 117–119
Galton, F., 97, 445, 516
Garmezy, N., 414
Garner, W., 624, 722
Gates, A., 396
Gauss, K., 87
Gelber, B., 326
Geldard, F., 305
Gelfand, S., 492
Ghata, J., 601
Gibson, E., 252–253
Gibson, J., 241, 248–249, 252, 254, 305
Gilmore, J., 655
Gleitman, H., 373
Gleser, G., 599
Goddard, H., 517
Gogol, N., 702
Goldiamond, I., 434
Goldstein, H., 380
Goodenough, D., 218, 689, 691
Gordon, B., 693
Goren, C., 129
Gottesman, I., 545
Gottschalk, L., 599
Gough, P., 472
Gourevitch, S., 665
Graham, C., 77, 190
Granit, R., 171
Graves, M., 414
Green, D., 188
Greenblom, R., 404
Gregory, R., 215
Guilford, J., 549–552
Guthrie, E., 349–351, 367, 605
Haber, R., 597, 640
Hall, C., 675
Hamm, M., 405
Harlow, H., 135, 291, 374, 591–593, 640
Harrell, M., 538
Harrell, T., 538, 541
Harris, R., 386
Harter, N., 410

Hartline, H., 77, 170–171
Hartmann, H., 637
Hawkins, W., 434
Hays, W., 106
Hebb, D., 223, 243, 582–583, 603
Hecht, S., 159
Heineman, C., 446
Heise, G., 442–443
Helmholtz, H., 115–117, 194, 199, 201–202, 246, 267, 271
Helmreich, R., 655
Hempel, W., 412
Hering, E., 194
Heron, W., 628
Herskovits, M., 233–235
Hess, E., 150–151
Heyer, A., 242
Heyns, R., 684
Hilgard, E., 422
Hippocrates, 340
Hobbes, T., 331, 428
Hochberg, J., 178, 261
Hoebel, B., 620
Hogan, H., 417–418
Hollingworth, L., 536
Holt, E., 330–331
Holt, R., 665
Holzinger, K., 548
Honzik, C., 368–369
Horton, D., 409
Horton, G., 350
Hovland, C., 316, 650
Howes, D., 433
Hubel, D., 171, 178
Huff, D., 106
Hughes, R., 625
Hull, C., 21–22, 30–31, 33, 120–121, 137, 139, 337, 341, 384, 489, 605–608, 610, 621–623, 640, 643
Hulse, S., 316
Hurvich, L., 194, 199–202, 215
Husen, T., 539
Huxley, A., 344
Ittelson, W., 247
Jacobson, A., 129, 327, 330
Jacobson, E., 488
Jacobson, L., 58
James, W., 205
Jameson, D., 194, 199–202
Janis, I., 655
Janucci, G., 693
Jasper, H., 311
Jenkins, J.G., 399–400
Jenkins, J.J., 404–405, 434, 447–448, 451, 454, 456, 492
Jenkins, W., 722
Jennings, H., 325
Jennings, S., 625

Paradise, N., 630
Pardes, H., 693
Parker, J., 416
Paul, I., 664
Pavlov, I., 2–3, 137, 293, 313–
315, 318, 320, 330–342, 347,
605, 641
Pervin, L., 651
Peterson, M., 454–456
Petrinovich, L., 607
Pfaffman, C., 285
Pfungst, O., 56, 62
Piaget, J., 238, 552–557
Pick, A., 291
Pick, H., 291
Pilzecker, A., 395
Plato, 109–111, 381, 513
Plutchick, R., 601
Poincaré, H., 497
Postman, L., 404, 433
Powell, B., 693
Pribram, K., 37, 504
Pusch, L., 310
Rachman, S., 340
Rains, J., 380
Ratliff, F., 154, 170–171, 222–
223
Raynor, R., 323–325
Razran, G., 324–325, 332, 448
Regan, R., 686
Reinberg, A., 601
Révész, G., 238
Reynolds, G., 380
Riecken, H., 651, 678
Riggs, L., 154, 178
Ritchie, B., 371–372
Rivers, W., 234
Roberts, C., 624
Roberts, W., 4
Roby, T., 622
Rock, I., 257, 261
Roffwarg, H., 567
Rohwer, W., 399
Rokeach, M., 708
Romanes, G., 127
Rosanoff, A., 446
Rosenberg, K., 589
Rosenberg, M., 62, 650, 655
Rosenthal, R., 56–58, 62
Rosenzweig, N., 293
Rudin, S., 697–699
Ruger, H., 486
Rushton, W., 160
Russell, W., 448
Sampson, E., 710
Samuel, A., 8
Sarason, I., 716
Sarason, S., 597
Sarnoff, I., 685

Schachter, S., 651, 678, 684–
686
Schafer, R., 670, 673
Schlosberg, H., 397, 446, 596
Schneider, S., 293
Schulz, R., 403, 449
Schwartz, M., 139, 212
Scott, C., 618
Scott, E., 607
Scott, J., 139
Scott, T., 294, 628
Scott, W., 618
Seashore, H., 94
Segall, M., 233–235, 237, 624
Selyé, H., 576–577, 596
Senden, M. von, 222
Senter, R., 272
Shapiro, A., 62
Sharpless, S., 311
Shaw, D., 709
Shaw, J., 507–508
Sheffield, F., 622–624
Sheffield, V., 359
Sherrick, M., 283
Sherif, M., 707–708
Shevrin, H., 665
Shipley, T., 686
Silverstein, A., 139
Simon, H., 506–508
Simon, T., 516–523
Skeels, H., 548
Skinner, B., 45–46, 62, 349,
351–355, 363, 386–387, 428–
429, 457–462
Skodak, M., 548
Sleight, R., 722
Slobin, D., 475
Sluckin, W., 601
Small, W., 363–364
Smith, O., 620
Solomon, R., 324, 372, 376, 433
Sontag, L., 535
Spaulding, D., 590
Spearman, C., 523–524
Spelt, D., 330
Spence, D., 665
Spence, K., 341
Spielberger, C., 461
Spitz, H., 243
Spitz, R., 583, 593
Spitzer, H., 396–397
Spivack, G., 220
Staples, F., 684
Steig, W., 365
Stellar, E., 618
Stevens, S., 77–79, 271, 273
Stevenson, J., 619
Stolz, W., 477
Storms, L., 448
Strong, E., 391

Stumpf, C., 56
Suci, G., 493
Suzuki, N., 399
Swanson, G., 673
Swets, J., 80, 188
Taffel, C., 460
Tannenbaum, P., 493
Tanner, W., 80, 188
Tanser, H., 544
Taylor, W., 456
Teevan, R., 215
Teitelbaum, P., 223, 620
Terman, L., 527, 531–532
Thomas, G., 272
Thompson, E., 310
Thompson, R., 327
Thompson, W., 586–588
Thorndike, E., 347–350, 358,
361, 384–385, 433, 485, 524
Thurstone, L., 390, 398, 524
Thurstone, T., 524
Tinbergen, N., 129, 139
Titchener, E., 604
Tolman, E., 365, 368–372
Trowill, J., 363
Tryon, R., 58
Tuckman, J., 686
Turing, A., 505, 509–510
Turner, L., 372
Tyler, L., 106, 559
Udelf, M., 205–206
Underwood, B., 401–403, 405
Van de Riet, V., 543
Van Ormer, E., 399
Van Riper, C., 416
Verney, E., 607
Vernon, M., 261
Veroff, J., 684, 686
Vidulich, R., 708
Vitz, P., 633
Voeks, V., 351
Von Restorff, H., 419
Voss, J., 512
Wade, M., 335
Wagner, A., 380, 611, 613
Wald, G., 160, 197, 199, 280
Walk, R., 252–253, 625
Walker, E., 28, 380
Wall, P., 293
Wallach, H., 241–242
Walter, A., 417–418
Walters, R., 684
Warm, J., 291
Washburn, A., 615–616
Watson, J., 323–325, 365–367,
582–584, 604–605
Webb, W., 601
Weber, E., 65, 180
Wechsler, D., 529
Weddell, G., 288

Subject Index

Absolute pitch, 271
Absolute threshold, 75, 83
Accommodation, 114, 155
Achievement motivation:
　and birth order, 686
　measurement of, 688
　national differences in, 697–699
　sex differences in, 687–689
Acoustic reflex, 264–265
Acquired drive, 608
Acquired reward, 608
Acquisition of language:
　as rule system, 473–475
　as strings of words, 450–453
　as utterance, 459–461
　as words, 435–437
Active versus passive learning, 395–396
ACTH, 576
Adopted children, intelligence of, 547–549
Adrenal gland:
　and reactions to stress, 576, 594–595
　in salt regulation, 287
Aerial perspective, 250–251
Affect (see Emotion)
Affiliation motivation:
　and birth order, 684–685
　national differences in, 698–699
Age:
　and critical flicker frequency, 211
　and dreaming, 567
　and intelligence, 528–534
　and psychological differentiation, 690–691
Alarm reaction, 576
Alcoholism, 692–693
Algorithms, 507–508
All-or-none law, 164–165

Allport's model of word acquisition, 436
Alpha rhythm, 563
Ampulla, 299
Anal stage, 700–702, 704
Anisocoria, 151
Anomaloscope, 198
Anorexia, 620
Anosmia, 277
Anthropomorphism, 128
Anxiety, 597–599
Aphagia, 620
Apparent movement, 244–245
Applied experimental psychology, 719–721
Approach-approach conflict:
　definition of, 647–648
　graphic model of, 648
　as unstable equilibrium, 648
Approach-avoidance conflict:
　definition of, 642–643
　graphic model of, 643–647
　resolution of, 646–647
　as stable equilibrium, 645
　and stimulus generalization, 645
Approximations to English, 441–444
Army Alpha test, 527
Arousal:
　and EEG, 563
　and emotion, 561–562
　fluctuations in, 573–575
　measurement of, 572–573
　as psychological process, 132
　and pupillary response, 150–151
　and sleep-wakefulness cycle, 562–565, 572
Association psychology:
　in human learning, 381–409
　versus cognitive learning, 416–418

Association psychology (Cont.):
　versus Gestalt view of learning, 419–421
　view of thinking, 484–494
Attention, 624–627
Attitude change:
　through cognitive dissonance 654–656
　through conditioning, 324
Audiogram, 265
Audiology, 277
Audition (see Hearing)
Autistic child, 10–11
Autokinetic effect, 708
Autonomic nervous system:
　lability and stability in, 574–575
　parasympathetic branch of, 150
　and pupillary response, 150
　sympathetic branch of, 150
Average, statistical, 90–91
Aversive learning, 376–378
Avoidance-avoidance conflict, 649–650
Avoidance learning:
　active, 376–378
　one-trial, 323–324
　passive, 378
Awareness, in verbal-reinforcement experiments, 460–461

Backward conditioning:
　and circular-reflex hypothesis, 331–332
　definition of, 317–318
Basilar membrane, 265–268
Behavior control, 4, 6, 723–724
Behaviorism, 604
Bel, 273
Bell-Magendie law, 296

Electromagnetic radiation, 143–144

Elevated maze, 371–372

Embedded figures, 218–219, 690

Emmert's law, 257

Emotion:
conditioning of, 322–324
evaluation of, 577–580
as incentive, 581
indicators of, 594–599
modulation of, 579–580
as psychological concept, 580–582
and stimulus deprivation, 627–628

Emotional development:
Hebb's model of, 582–583
in institutionalized infants, 593–594
and maternal fearfulness, 588–589
in monkeys, 591–593
prenatal influences on, 586–587
research on, 585–594
role of verbal labeling in, 584–585
Watson's model of, 582

Emotional expression:
in facial responses, 595–597
through gesture, 597
through verbalization, 597–599

Empiricism, 108–114, 381, 422

Endolymph, 299

Epinephrine, 576, 587, 594–595

Epistemology, 112

Equilibrium model, 557

Erikson, E., 703

Ethology, 128–129

Evoked potential, 211–212

Evolution, 126–128

Experimental extinction (see Extinction)

Experimental neurosis, 339–340

Experimenter effect, 55–59

Explanation, and model-building, 24

External inhibition, 338

Extinction:
incremental nature of, 336–337
models of, 336–337
procedure for obtaining, 336
and spontaneous recovery, 337

Extrasensory perception, 301

Eye:
and camera, 148

Eye (Cont.):
cornea, 151, 154
fovea, 152, 155
lens, 148, 154–155
movements, 148, 152–154
pupil, 148–151
retina, 148, 155–162

Eye-movements, 148, 152–154, 174

False negative decisions, 80–84, 187–188

False positive decisions, 80–84, 187–188

Fear:
in avoidance learning, 377
physiological indicators of, 594–595
and postnatal stress, 587–589
and prenatal stress, 586–587

Fechner's law, 273

Ferry-Porter law, 209

Field dependence, 219, 689

Field effects, 225, 233, 237

Field independence, 219, 689

Figural aftereffects:
definition of, 241–242
individual differences in, 242–243
and intelligence, 243
Köhler-Wallach model of, 242

Figural identity, 223

Figural unity, 223

Figure-ground reversal, 220

Figure-ground segregation, 216–217, 222–224

Filters, 147

First-language learning (see Acquisition of language)

First signal system, 334

Fixation:
and defense mechanisms, 672
in psychosexual development, 700–701
and punishment, 362

Flicker, 208–211

Focusing, 154–155

Food deprivation:
and general activity, 609
and latency to eat, 609
and learning, 610–612
and performance, 610

Food selection, 607, 615, 617–618

Forced-choice indicator, 187–189

Forebrain, 285

Forgetting:
and active learning, 395–396
and organization, 420–421

Forgetting (Cont.):
and overlearning, 391–392
and repeated learning, 392–394
and skill, 416
and time, 390–391

Formal operations, 556

Foster children, 547–549

Fourier analysis, 264

Fovea, 152, 155

Frequency polygon, 89

Freud, S., 122–125

Frustration, 360–361

Functional fixedness, 500–501

Functionalism, 604

Fundamental frequency, 270–271

Galileo, 64–65

Gall, F., 117–119

Ganzfeld, 202

General adaptation syndrome, 575–577

General reinforcement, 458–461

Generative rules, 462–477

Genetic differences in intelligence, 545–549

Genetic model, 658

Geniculo-striate bundle, 174–175

Genotype, 22–24

Geometric illusions:
in chickens, 238
cross-cultural differences in, 232–235
examples of, 231–238
ontogenetic development of, 237–238
role of learning in, 231–235, 237–238

Geometric optics, 147–148

Gestalt theory, 137, 224–226, 233, 243, 243–244, 419–421, 494–502, 604

Gifted children, 531–532, 535

Goal object, 603, 637

Good continuation, 228–229

Grammars, 464–468, 474–475

Grammatical experiments, 451–453, 468–477

Group influence, 707–711

Growth curves of intelligence, 532–534

Guilford's structure of intellect, 549–552

Guilt, 657

Gustation (see Taste)

Habit-family hierarchy:
in learning, 121

Habit-family hierarchy (*Cont.*):
in problem-solving, 485
Habituation, 310–311
Hair cells:
in cochlea, 266
in nasal cavity, 280
in vestibular system, 299
Hallucinations, 628
Harmonics, 270–271
Hawthorne effect, 52–53
Hearing:
absolute threshold of, 272
binaural effects in, 275–277
deficits in, 277
neural mechanisms in, 268–269
receptor for, 264–268
stimulus for, 262–264
Helmholtz H., 115–117
Heredity and environment:
in intelligence, 546–549
in philosophy, 108–114
Hering's illusion, 235
Heuristics, 507–508
Hierarchy of skill, 412
Hindbrain, 285–297
Hippocampus, 378
Histogram, 89
Homeostasis, 120–121
Homeostatic model:
dissatisfactions with, 621–628
propositions of, 605–608
Hull's motivational model, 120–121, 621–623
Human engineering, 5, 719–721
Human learning:
associationist approach to, 383–387
cognitive approach to, 416–422
Gestalt approach to, 419–421
motor skills in, 409–416
of verbal material, 387–409 ·
Humor, 230–231
Hunger:
behavioral correlates of, 608–615
and blood chemistry, 618
and cognitive dissonance, 656
and the hypothalamus, 618–621
oral factors in, 617–618
physiological mechanism in 615–621
and stomach contractions, 615–617
Hyperopia, 204–207
Hyperphagia, 618–620

Hypothalamus, 618–621
Hypothesis-testing, 39, 43, 46–47
Hysteria, 661–662

Id, 658–659, 663
Identification, 674–675, 696
Illusions (*see* Geometric illusions)
Imageless thought, 480–481
Implicit responses, 485–489
Imprinting, 589–591
Incentive:
autonomy of, 614–615
change in, 612–613
definition of, 603
and learning, 610–614
nature of, 623–628
relativity of, 614
Incus, 264
Independent variable, 50, 53
Indicator response, 187–189
Individual differences:
in CFF, 211
in classical conditioning, 340
in evoked potential, 211–212
in figural aftereffects, 242–243
in figure reversal, 220–221
in frequency of dreaming, 567
in language, 437–439, 453–457, 462, 476–477
origins of, 108–109
in perceptual organization, 227–228
in reaction time, 66
Induction, 34
Information:
and complexity, 631
in language, 440–444
processing of, 131–132
as thinking, 502–510
reception of, 131
and stimulus intensity, 628–630
Inhibition:
in auditory-frequency discrimination, 268
in delayed conditioning, 320
in experimental extinction, 336–337
external, 338
internal, 336
in neural functioning, 170–172, 200
and temperament, 340
Innate hierarchy, 121
Insight, 495–501

Instrumental learning:
of autonomic responses, 362–363
and classical conditioning, 320
definition of, 345–347
reinforcement in, 350–351
Intellectualization, 670–671, 692
Intelligence:
and age, 528–534
and birth order, 685–686
and body image, 692
and CFF, 211
and conformity, 709
and early vocalization, 694
and evolved potential, 211–212
and figural aftereffects, 243
Guilford's model of, 549–552
heredity and environment in, 546–549
measurement of, 515–523
models of, 523–527, 549–552
and perceptual organization, 227–228
Piaget's model of, 552–557
race and class determinants of, 536–546
in twins, 547–549
Intelligence quotient (IQ), 522–523
Interference in learning:
proactive, 401–402
retroactive, 400–401
theory of, 399–402
Internal clock:
in circadian rhythms, 570–572
in temporal conditioning, 320
Internal environment, 119
Internal inhibition, 336
Interposition, 249–250
Interval scales, 70–73
Intrinsic motivation, 638
Introspectionism, 224
Irradiation, 333–334
Isolation, 670–671, 692–693
Item-and-arrangement grammars, 445, 451
Item difficulty, 520–521
Item discrimination, 520–521

Just noticeable difference (jnd), 75

Kelvin scale, 73
Kinesthesis:
and fine-movement control, 295–296
in maze learning, 365–367

Problem-solving (*Cont.*):
by computer, 505–508
Gestalt view of, 495–501
in groups, 713
stages in, 494
Productive rules, 462–463
Programed learning, 349, 721–724
Programs as theories, 502–508
Projection, 669–670, 693
Projective test, 56
Protanope, 198–199
Protective coloration, 227–228
Protocols, 25–28
Proximity, 226–227
Psychiatry, 122–125
Psychic reflexes, 314–315
Psycho-active drugs, 169
Psychoanalytic theory:
and character formation, 700–703
and defense mechanisms, 659–672
models in, 658–659
and motivational models, 605
and psychopathology, 673–676
and the roots of psychology, 122–125
Psycholinguistics (*see* Language)
Psychological differentiation:
and age, 690–691
and body image, 691–692
and defense mechanisms, 692
and dreaming, 692
measurement of, 689–690
and psychopathology, 692–693
Psychological research:
ambiguity in, 48–52
control in, 50–52
dependent and independent variables in, 50
design of, 47–61
Psychology:
developmental approach to, 134–135
historical roots:
in biology, 126–129
in philosophy, 108–114
in physiology, 114–121
in psychiatry, 122–125
multiple strategies of, 130–137
physiological approach to, 135–136
process approach to, 131–134
as scientific discipline, 15–19

Psychopath, 667, 674–676
Psychopathology:
and birth order, 686
and defense mechanisms, 124
and national character, 697–698
Psychophysical methods, 65–66, 74–77, 84, 180–189
Psychosexual development:
Erikson's model of, 703
Freudian model of, 700–703
Psychosis, 674
Punishment, 361–362
Pupil:
and arousal, 150–151
constriction of, 148–149
dilatation of, 150–151
and illumination control, 148–150
innervation of, 150
Purkinje shift, 193

Quantification (*see* Measurement)

Race:
and intelligence, 536–546
problem of defining, 540
Rank order, 70
Range, 92
Rapid eye movements:
description of, 565
and dreaming, 565–570
Ratio scales, 73
Reaction formation, 667–668
Reaction time, 66, 116
Reading machines, 7
Reappearance hypothesis, 417
Recitation, 396–397
Reconstruction as memory, 417–418
Reductionism, 135–136
Reflex arc, 312–313
Refraction, 146
Refractory phase, 167
Regression, 673–674
Reinforcement:
in instrumental learning, 347, 350–351
primary, 354
schedules of, 353–358
secondary, 354
Reissner's membrane, 265
Reliability of measurement, 101–102:
in relation to validity, 104
Repeated learning, 392–394
Replication, 45–46
Repression:
as basic defense mechanism,

Repression (*Cont.*):
659–662
and hysteria, 661
laboratory research on, 662–666
and memory, 660–661
and perceptual defense, 662–663
and perceptual vigilance, 662–663
in psychoanalytic theory, 123–125
and psychological differentiation, 692
Research:
correlational versus experimental, 47–49
origins of, 39–47
Resonance theory, 267
Response-produced stimuli, 334
Response to change, 170, 624–625, 630
Reticular activating system, 43–44, 239–240, 268–269, 298
Retina:
and camera film, 148
structure of, 155–162
Retinal densitometer, 160
Retinal disparity, 253–257
Retinal receptive fields, 171, 192
Retroactive interference, 400–401
Reverberating circuit, 318
Reversal learning, 373
Reversible figures, 219–220
Reward:
in classical conditioning, 342
as drive-reduction, 121
through electrical stimulation of brain, 43–44
Rhodopsin, 157–158
Ricco's law, 190
Rigidity, 500–501
RNA, 129:
and memory transfer, 329–330
and neural structure, 163
Rod-and-frame test, 219, 689–690
Rods, 155–161
Romanes, G., 127–128
Rule-governed behavior, 462–477, 503–508

Saccades, 152
Saccharine, 622
Saccule, 300
Salivary conditioning:
in dogs, 315–316

Salivary conditioning (*Cont.*):
in humans, 324
Satiation, 242
Saturation, 195–196
Scales of measurement:
interval, 70–73
nominal, 69
ordinal, 70
ratio, 73
Scattergram, 98–99
Schedules of reinforcement, 353–358
Schizophrenia:
and perceptual functioning, 240
and psychological differentiation, 693
and stimulus generalization, 335
Science, 15–17
Scores:
centile, 93
raw, 93
standard, 93–95
Scotopic vision, 193
Secondary drive, 608
Secondary process thinking, 674
Secondary reward, 608
Second signal system, 334, 386
Security blanket, 291, 591
Selyé's model of stress, 576–577
Semantic differential, 493–494
Semantic generalization, 334
Semicircular canals, 299
Sensitization, 310
Sensorimotor intelligence, 553–554
Sentence transformations, 470–473
Sequential behavior, 450–451
Serendipity, 42–45
Serial anticipation learning, 389
Sex differences:
in achievement motivation, 687–689
in intelligence, 534–536
in language development, 694
origins of, 693–695
in psychological differentiation, 688
in psychological research, 687
in skills, 536
Sex role, 694–695
Sexual selection, 126
Shading, 250–251
Shape constancy, 258–259
Shaping, 353–354
Short-term memory, 318–319
Shuttlebox, 376

Signal-detection theory, 79–84, 181, 188
Sign stimuli, 583
Similarity:
and the partial-reinforcement effect, 358–360
in perceptual organization, 227
and stimulus generalization, 332–333
Simulation, 482–483
Simultaneous contrast, 201–202
Size perception, 257–259
Size-weight illusion, 237
Skewed distributions, 90–91
Skill learning, 409–416
Skinner, B:
principles of operant conditioning, 351–357
model of language, 457–462
Sleep:
acquisition of patterns in, 562–563
disturbance in, 569
nature of, 563
periodicity in, 562
stages of, 563–566
Smell:
and alternation behavior, 283
models of, 278–279
primary qualities in, 281–282
receptor mechanisms for, 279–280
stimulus for, 277–279
and taste, 277, 286
Smiling response, 583
Snellen chart, 203, 207
Solitary nucleus, 285
Solitary tract, 285
Social class:
and defense mechanisms, 672–673
and intelligence, 536–540
problem of defining, 540
Somatic senses:
neural mechanisms in, 296–298
problem of classifying, 287–289
receptor mechanisms for, 288–289
Somesthetic senses (*see* Somatic senses)
Sone scale, 273
Sound localization, 273–275
Sound waves:
basic parameters of, 263
Fourier analysis of, 264
mixture of, 263–264
physical basis of, 263

Sound waves (*Cont.*):
speed of, 263
Spatial summation of excitation, 190–192
Species:
learning differences among, 374–376
origin of, 126
Specific nerve energies, 115, 166–167
Speech center, 119
Speech-disturbance ratio, 599
Speech perception, 7
Spike potential, 165, 167
Spinal nerve, 296
Spontaneous alternation, 283
Spontaneous recovery, 337
Stability:
of intelligence, 532–534
of test scores, 101
Stabilized retinal image, 153–154
Stage fright, 580
Stages:
of intellectual development, 553–557
in problem-solving, 494
psychosexual, 700–707
Standard deviation, 92
Standard score, 93–95
Stanford-Binet test, 527
Stapedius muscle, 264
Stapes, 264
Statistics, 89–101
Stereochemical model of smell, 278–279
Stereogram, 255–256
Stereophonic stimulation, 275–276
Stereopsis (*see* Depth perception)
Stereoscope, 255
Stimulus deprivation, 627–628
Stimulus generalization:
and autonomic reactivity, 574–575
and conflict, 645
gradient of, 333, 335
and irradiation of excitation, 333–334
models of, 333–335
and the partial-reinforcement effect, 358–360
and schizophrenia, 335
and similarity, 321, 332–333
Stomach contractions, 615–617
Stranger anxiety, 583–584
Stress:
in emotional development, 585–589

Stress (*Cont.*):
and the general adaptation syndrome, 576–577
Striate cortex, 174–175
Stroboscopic movement, 244–245
Stroop test, 61
Structuralism:
and the concept of motivation, 604
Gestalt criticism of, 224–225
Structural model, 658–659
Structured tests, 85, 598
Structure of intellect (*see* Models of intelligence)
Subjective colors, 203
Sublimation, 671–672
Subliminal perception, 125, 663–666
Superego:
definition of, 658–659
and psychopathology, 674–676
Superior colliculus, 173–174
Symbolic functions, 554
Synapse, 165–169
Synesthesia, 240–241
Syntax (*see* Grammar)

Tacts, 457–459
Target:
duration:
and CFF, 210–211
and detection, 192
locus:
and acuity, 155–159
and CFF, 209
and detection, 156–159
shape, 191–192
size:
and CFF, 209
and detection, 190–191
wavelength, 192–194
Taste:
neural basis of, 285–286
preferences and need state, 286–287
primary qualities in, 284
receptor mechanism for, 284–285
and smell, 277, 286
stimulus for, 277, 284
and touch, 286
Taste buds, 284
Teaching, 721–724
Telegraph learning, 410–412
Temperament, 340
Temperature scales, 71–72
Temporal conditioning, 320
Temporal lobe, 269, 300

Tensor tympani, 264
Test-retest reliability, 101–102
Texture density, 248–249
Thalamus, 268, 285, 298, 300
Thematic Apperception Test, 598–599, 669–670, 696
Theory:
and data, 34–35
criteria for evaluating, 32–34
and scientific models, 30–32
Thermal sensitivity, 294–295
Thinking, 479–512:
associative view of, 484–494
Gestalt view of, 494–502
history of, 480–483
information-processing in, 502–510
Thorndike, E., 347–349, 384, 433
Thorndike-Lorge word count, 433
Threshold:
classical model of, 184–187
definition of, 186–187
methods for measuring, 180–189
visual detection, 189–194
Tickle, 289
Timbre, 270
Tonality (*see* Chroma), 271
Topographic model, 658
Touch:
absolute threshold in, 289
hedonic property of, 291–292
pattern discrimination in, 290–291
receptor mechanism for, 289
stimulus for, 289
and taste, 286
two-point threshold in, 290
Trace conditioning, 318–319
Trait measurement, 84–89
Transactionalists, 247
Transfer of training:
mediation in, 408–409
in motor skills, 414–416
Osgood's model of, 406–407
through RNA, 329–330
in verbal learning, 404–409
Trichromat, 198
Tritanope, 198–199
True negative and true positive decisions, 82–84
Turing's thought experiment, 505
Two-string problem 492–493
Tympanic membrane (*see* Eardrum)

Ulcers:
and national character, 697–698
and psychological differentiation, 693
Unconditional reflex, 315–316
Unconditioned stimulus:
definition of, 316
function of, 341–347
Unconscious conflict, 658–659
Unconscious impulses:
defenses against, 659–673
definition of, 658
in psychoanalytic theory, 123–125
Unstructured tests, 85, 598
Utricle, 300

Vacillation, 645
Validity:
construct, 103–104
content, 103
criterion, 103
relation of to reliability, 104
for different groups, 540–542
test, 102–104
Variance of scores, 92:
of predicted scores, 100
Ventriloquism, 275
Verbal learning, 387–399:
findings on, 389–399
interference theory and, 399–402
as set of activities, 402–404
techniques for studying, 388–389
transfer of, 404–407
what-is-learned in, 408–409
Verbal reinforcement, 460–461
Vertical-horizontal illusion, 234–235, 237
Vestibular system:
damage to, 298
function of, 298–299
neural mechanisms in, 300
receptor mechanisms in, 299–300
in spontaneous alternation, 283
Vibration sensation, 289
Visible spectrum 144–145
Visual acuity:
defects in, 207–208
measurement of, 203–207
Visual cliff, 252–253
Vocabulary growth, 437–439
Volley theory of hearing, 267
Volume of sounds, 271–272

Warmth (*see* Thermal sensitivity)